Brian Charles MacDermot, Editor

THE CATHOLIC QUESTION
IN IRELAND AND ENGLAND 1798–1822

The Catholic Question in Ireland & England
1798*1822
The Papers of Denys Scully

BRIAN MacDERMOT

EDITOR

IRISH ACADEMIC PRESS

This book was typeset at
The Spartan Press Ltd, Lymington, Hants.
for Irish Academic Press Ltd,
Kill Lane, Blackrock, Co. Dublin

BRITISH LIBRARY CATALOGUING IN PUBLICATION DATA

Scully, Denys, *1773-1830*
The Catholic question in Ireland and
England 1792-1822: the papers of Denys
Scully.
1. Ireland. Political events, 1792-1822
I. Title   II. MacDermot, Brian Charles
941.507
ISBN 0-7165-2423-6

Printed in Great Britain by
Billing & Sons Ltd, Worcester

Contents

Acknowledgements

My thanks are above all due to Denys Scully's great-grandson, Mr Michael Scully, whose generous support has made the preparation and publication of this work possible.

I am scarcely less indebted to Professor Maurice O'Connell, for his guidance and encouragement, and to Betty O'Connell, his wife, who not only rendered every kind of editorial assistance but typed out the greater part of the manuscripts.

For their permission to publish the documents from the sources listed at the end of this volume I am grateful to the Trustees of the National Library of Ireland; the Board of Trinity College Dublin; His Grace the Most Reverend Dr Desmond Connell, Archbishop of Dublin; Father Fergus O'Donoghue SJ of the Jesuit central province archive; Father Kieran Hanley SJ, Rector of Clongowes Wood College; the British Library Board; the Department of Palaeography and Diplomatic of Durham University; the Keeper of the Public Records at Kew; the Kent Archives Office; Lord Congleton; Sir Robert Throckmorton; and (for the Huddleston Papers) Major A. C. Eyre.

Particular thanks are due to Mr Brian McKenna and his staff at the National Library of Ireland; Miss Mary Purcell and Mr David Sheehy at the Dublin Diocesan Archives; the Librarian of Trinity College, Dublin; Miss Elizabeth Poyser at the Westminster Diocesan Archives; Mr J. M. Fewster of Durham University; Mr Alexander Hunter, Librarian to the Marquis of Bute; the staffs at the County Record Offices at Cambridge and Warwick; Lord Congleton; and Lord Clifford of Chudleigh. For their kindness in drawing my attention to documents that I might otherwise have missed I am grateful to Mr Thomas Power, Dr Gerard O'Brien and Father Feargus O'Fearghail of St Kieran's College, who also supplied me with much useful information about Kilkenny. Father Roland Burke Savage and Father Fergus O'Donoghue procured for me documents from the Clongowes Wood and Jesuit archives. A special mention is due to Mr Roy Donovan for his help with photocopying facilities. Among many others who have helped in various ways I owe acknowledgments to Mrs W. Bonaparte Wyse; Father Philip Caraman SJ; Dr K. P. Ferguson of the Military History Society of

Ireland; Dr Richard Fitzgerald MB; Mr William Fraher; the Earl of Granard; Sister Gregory of the Bar Convent, York; Lieutenant-Colonel R. P. Lidwill DSO; Mr H. Montgomery Hyde; Anthony and Patrick McCan; my son M. B. MacDermot MA, B. Phil.; Mrs Norma McDermott of the County Library at Thurles; Sister Margaret Helen of New Hall Convent; Revd Bernard Massey of St Mary's College, Oscott; Dr S. C. O'Mahony of the Mid-West Archives, Limerick; Mr Trevor Parkhill of the Public Record Office of Northern Ireland; Mr John Martin Robinson, Librarian to the Duke of Norfolk; Prince Sforza Ruspoli; Monsignor Daniel Shanahan; Mr William Sweetman MA; and Mr Walter Williams, Grand Secretary of the Grand Orange Lodge of Ireland.

Abbreviations

Add.MSS	Additional Manuscripts in the British Library (formerly British Museum)
BL	British Library
Burke LG	Burke's *Landed Gentry*
LGI	*Landed Gentry of Ireland*
PB	*Peerage and Baronetage*
DC	*Dublin Chronicle*
DS	Denys Scully
DDA	Dublin Diocesan Archives
DEP	*Dublin Evening Post*
DNB	*Dictionary of National Biography*
EH	*Evening Herald*
FJ	*Freeman's Journal*
HO	Home Office
NLI	National Library of Ireland

Note

Frequently referred to sources are cited by short titles in the text; for further details see Select Bibliography

Introduction[1]

Denys Scully was born on 4 May 1773, the seventh child and second son of James Scully, a prospering grazier of County Tipperary, whose wife was Catherine Lyons of Croom House, near Limerick, and who settled at Kilfeacle near Golden in 1780. All that is known of his early years is that he was educated at the Kilkenny Academy (now St Kieran's College), where he figured prominently in the prize lists of 1785 and 1786. In 1791 his father signed an agreement apprenticing him to the Dublin merchant house of Roche, but if he ever started on a commercial career he abandoned it when the Relief Act of 1792 opened the Irish bar to Catholics. He was admitted to the Middle Temple on 25 October 1793 and on 27 June of the following year he entered Trinity College, Cambridge, as a pensioner. A Common Place Book which he then opened records his having been told (by a future Vice-Chancellor) that he was the first Catholic remembered to have been at the university; and it lists among his college contemporaries two of his future correspondents, the Parnell brothers, as well as a future Tipperary supporter, the Earl of Lismore. In the Hilary term of 1794 he was called to the Irish bar, but he seems to have returned to London for further studies and not to have begun to practise until two years later. He joined the Leinster circuit, which included his own home county, and regularly attended the Assizes, but he never made a mark as an advocate and seems to have settled into the role of a consultant on property matters, with a special interest in the penal laws that affected them.

Scully may have missed the 1798 rebellion, but by the end of August of that year he was settled in Suffolk Street and probably already a member of the Lawyers Corps. While the correspondence of the next two years shows him consorting in the Moira House circle with vehement opponents of the proposal for a legislative union with Great Britain it is probable that like the rest of his family he accepted the measure in the expectation that it would soon be followed by Catholic emancipation. In November 1801 he married the thirty-four year old Mary Huddleston of Sawston Hall near Cambridge, where he may have gone to Mass when he was at the university. Although now impoverished, her old Catholic family could boast of Plantagenet blood and they were neighbours of the third Earl of Hardwicke, the new Lord

Lieutenant of Ireland: after they settled at 34 Baggot Street Mary Scully was called on by Lady Hardwicke and Denys was eligible to attend viceregal levees. When in 1803, at the time of the renewal of the war with France, he made his first venture into public life, with an offer in the name of his father to raise a regiment and a pamphlet of his own urging his countrymen not to side with the French, he was to outward appearance a "Castle Catholic", working in conjunction with the pensioned Theobald McKenna.

Already by 1804 Scully was credited by O'Connell with "a long and minute attention" to the Catholic question, but his active career in the cause began on 27 October of that year when he attended the second of a series of meetings organised by a Dublin businessman, James Ryan, the outcome of which was a petition (drafted by Scully) that was taken to London by a deputation (of which he was a member) and after its rejection by Pitt in an interview on 12 March 1805 entrusted to the parliamentary opposition. Abundant material in the Home Office archives, the Hardwicke Papers and Scully's own records not only testify to the importance of his role but show that much of it took the form of a secret intrigue with the Chief Secretary, Sir Evan Nepean, conducted behind the backs both of the Lord Lieutenant and the leader of the deputation, Lord Fingall. His correspondence with the Marquis of Sligo in the present volume is suggestive of a second intrigue in a vain attempt to extract a declaration from Pitt that would make it unnecessary to go to the opposition. Although for Scully, who had placed all his hopes in Pitt, the mission was a failure, he had been able to argue his case with the Prime Minister personally, had had Charles Fox for an hour and a half with him in his lodgings and had met most of the leading friends of the cause, among them Charles Butler, who made him a member of his Cisalpine Club. Because of their relevance to his future conduct a few points illustrating his thinking at this time deserve attention. At the meeting of 27 October he observed that delegation was prohibited under the law of the land and those present could not claim to call themselves representatives of the Catholics of Ireland, or even of Dublin.[2] When a question arose as to whether the merchants of Dublin should be admitted to the committee he pointed out that all the merchants of the kingdom had as good a pretension as those of Dublin and that the landed interest was perhaps to be considered before either of them.[3] In reply to an enquiry from Dr Milner when he was in London he explained in a now missing letter that the petition did not touch on the Irish clergy, in accordance with the wishes of the clergy themselves.[4] While in London he made a first essay in management of the press, an introduction from one of his brothers-in-law having provided an opportunity of inserting a few paragraphs in the *Morning Post*.

Ryan's meetings had not been advertised in the newspapers and were attended only by small numbers of "respectable" Catholics, of whom fewer than a hundred signed the petition. With the publicity following the rejection of the petition by Pitt and the debates in parliament, new and more aggressive adherents rallied to the cause, meetings in private houses were condemned, aggregate meetings became the font of authority and John Keogh came to the fore at the head of a popular party of Dublin Catholics. To these changed circumstances Scully had yet to adapt himself and until well into 1810 he remained either in the background or on the sidelines. In April 1806 his wife died and the departure of the Hardwickes in the same month lost him his contact with Dublin Castle. In September the death of Fox, on whom he had called in September 1805 and again in February, severed his most important link with Westminster. In 1807 he appears to have collaborated behind the scenes with Lord Ponsonby who was attempting to avert a petition that might lead to the fall of the Ministry of All the Talents. Throughout this period he must have been occupied in compiling material for his work on the penal laws. In February 1808 he came before the public with an abortive project for a Catholic Society modelled on the Cisalpine Club but having as its object the raising of funds. On the foundation of the English Catholic Board in June Charles Butler, aiming at improved collaboration with the Irish Catholics, began to write to him on a more regular basis. His second marriage, on 8 September, with the twenty-five year old Catherine Eyre of Sheffield Park, brought with it the first of thirty-nine letters from Dr John Milner, who appears to have arranged the match. In the meantime he had organised a Catholic committee in his own county of Tipperary which, with similar committees in the other counties, he envisaged as linking up in some as yet unspecified relationship with the General Committee in Dublin.

Having settled down with his new wife at 2 Merrion Square (where they remained until they moved to No. 13 in 1815), Scully joined the General Committee again in May 1809 and was a member of the various sub-committees that prepared the petition for 1810, but the sources are silent as to any part played by him in the events leading up to the break with the English Catholics over their Fifth Resolution of 1 February 1810, seen by many on the Irish side as a pledge to accept some form of crown veto. When Scully did intervene it was with conciliatory resolutions from his Tipperary Catholics on 31 March, which included one putting forward a proposal for the domestic nomination of Bishops that was taken up by Grattan in the 1810 debate. However, while he continued to use his Tipperary platform, a fortuitous event encouraged a return to a more central role at a time when John Keogh's dominance was approaching its end. Lord Grenville having declined to present the Irish Catholic petition himself, a replacement had to be found and at the end of February the choice fell on the Earl of Donoughmore, who lived near Clonmel and had known Scully's father ever since the Scully interest had helped him to carry Tipperary for the Union in 1799. While Scully saw in Lord Donoughmore a spokesman for his own views, Lord Donoughmore was glad to make use of Scully in his dealings with the Catholic Committee, often conducted through his brother Francis Hely-Hutchinson, who lived in Dublin.

Since Scully had voiced his apprehensions about the Convention Act in 1804 the Irish administration had tacitly tolerated a General Committee speaking in the name of the Catholics of Ireland and had turned a blind eye to annual elections held by the Dublin parishes. He had now come round to the view that so long as meetings were held only for the purpose of petitioning the last clause of the Act, upholding the subject's right to petition, overrode the other provisions forbidding delegation. In the autumn of 1810 plans were laid for an enlargement of the General Committee and a year later, in defiance of a circular to magistrates in February and a formal proclamation of 30 July, there came into ephemeral existence an assembly that was quickly dubbed "Catholic Convention" and was seen by Wellesley-Pole, the Chief Secretary, as an Irish parliament because of there being ten delegates from each county and five from each Dublin parish. What part Scully played in the development of the scheme is not recorded but he was the leader most closely involved in its execution — from his speech of 31 July which prevailed on the Catholics to ignore the proclamation to the seeming triumph of 23 November when Dr Sheridan, the first arrested delegate, was acquitted by the jury, and the ultimate failure when the Attorney-General succeeded in procuring the conviction of a second delegate on 29 January 1812. The elections as they proceeded county by county, the arrests and the counter-proceedings taken by some of the arrested delegates against the Chief Justice who had signed the warrant were all prominently reported in the press and produced a state of excitement which culminated in a big dinner given by the Catholics on 19 December as a demonstration against the administration. On the same day Hugh Fitzpatrick brought out the first part of the *Statement of the Penal Laws*: although published anonymously it was soon generally known to be by Scully and, matching as it did the mood of the moment, it won for him an acclaim that continued into 1813 with the prosecution of Fitzpatrick for a libel in a footnote of the second part, which appeared in June 1812.

After the acquittal of Dr Sheridan on 23 November William Parnell tried to induce Scully to make peace with the administration and to that end persuaded Lord Holland to take the initiative in writing to him. That Scully was not altogether averse to an accommodation can be inferred from the fact that Parnell showed the Attorney-General a letter of his (now missing), but at the end of the year he was feeling intransigent enough to sound Dr Milner on the possibility of getting the Irish clergy to discourage recruiting. The same spirit of militancy was carried forward into 1812. Acting on a hint from Henry Parnell, who had now begun to report to him from Westminster, he got the Tipperary Catholics on 20 March and the Dublin aggregate meeting of 18 June to resolve that Catholic freeholders should withhold their votes in parliamentary elections not only, as in the past, from candidates who opposed emancipation but also from any who supported a hostile government. If he did not propose, he certainly drafted the "witchery resolutions" of 18 June, deploring the baneful influence of Lady Hertford on the Prince Regent. In the same month he attacked the Irish administration by getting William Tighe to raise in the House of Commons the case of a pardon granted to an Orangeman who had murdered a Catholic, and in July Earl Grey at his request questioned the propriety of the manner in which an information had been laid by the Attorney-General against his publisher. In the general elections of the autumn he waged a vigorous campaign in County Tipperary to ward off the attack of a government candidate on the two sitting members, and accepted a fee of five hundred guineas for saving a seat which, according to F. W. Conway, he hoped one day to occupy himself.

In the meantime the Catholic cause had won its first success in parliament. In anticipation of their possible return to power after 17 February when the restrictions imposed on the Prince of Wales' regency were due to expire, the opposition had brought on debates on the state of Ireland in which the conduct of the Irish administration in 1811 had come up for criticism and Scully's *Penal Laws* had been attacked by the Chief Secretary; although the Prince in the event had retained his existing minister in power, negotiations for the formation of an alternative administration had brought the Catholic issue into the foreground; a petition from Irish Protestants had shown an unprecedented degree of support for Catholic claims; and on 23 April the division on the Irish Catholic petition, drafted this year by Scully, had been good enough to warrant hopes of future success. On 6 May George Canning had given notice of a motion, which he successfully carried on 22 June, calling upon the Regent to take the Catholic question into consideration during the parliamentary recess with a view to ascertaining what securities might be needed to safeguard the established Church. Because this seemed to open the door to a veto it was not relished by all and Scully had already been obliged to amend a passage in his petition which was felt by some members of the Board in Dublin to echo the Fifth Resolution of the English Catholics: nevertheless at the end of May, in a letter to Henry Parnell which was shown to Canning, he seems to have given the latter an assurance of his support.

With the dissolution of parliament Canning's motion lapsed, but the momentum was not lost, for Grattan had already asked Charles Butler to draft an emancipation bill for him and had thus set in train the sequence of events that culminated on 24 May 1813 when a bill, after getting a second reading, was killed in the committee stage upon the Speaker carrying by four votes an amendment offering everything except seats in parliament. Grattan took only a few close friends into his confidence and the Irish Catholic Board were not consulted at all. Scully, however, had seen Butler's draft and hearing from Butler at the end of January that he had had an interview with Lord Castlereagh and promised to show him his bill he broke off his correspondence with him, evidently fearing to be seen as conniving in an unauthorised approach to the government. To Grattan's success in getting leave to introduce a bill he made a modest contribution in a notably speedy operation. Sir Henry Parnell (as he had now become) having asked in a letter of 1 March for some conciliatory message from Dublin, notice of a resolution given at the Board was published in the *Dublin Evening Post* in time for it to be read out before the division on 9 March. In April Scully was hopeful enough of a favourable outcome to have in readiness a proposal for the recruitment by his father and other leading Catholics of a corps of five thousand Emancipation Guards. In the same month he must have become aware that Grattan's bill was to be accompanied by clauses proposed by Canning, for he was drawn by Lord Donoughmore into an obscure discussion with the Archbishop of Dublin, but at this stage he would still have been under the impression that the bill was the comprehensive one drafted by Butler. When he discovered that Butler's bill had been superseded by a short one confined to a repeal of the test oaths, and received the full text of the Canning clauses (setting up boards of commissioners to inspect correspondence with Rome and issue certificates of loyalty) his attitude changed. After a meeting of the Board on 1 May he sent a list of objections to be communicated to the drafting committee by Parnell and Lord Donoughmore, constituting in the words of the latter "a general reprobation of the whole measure". While awaiting the outcome the Board maintained an official silence, but Scully and O'Connell kept in close touch with the Bishops who, on 25 May, before the news of the Speaker's amendment reached Dublin, publicly declared that the Canning clauses in their existing shape could not have their concurrence.

The disappointment of the high hopes raised by the initial success of Grattan's bill was aggravated by the circumstances in which it had been lost. There was a feeling that if Dr Milner had not intervened with a fly-leaf circulated to members of parliament the Speaker might not have won his narrow majority and the bill might have emerged from the committee stage in a more acceptable form, and some resented the presumption of the Irish Bishops. In England the Catholic Board closed ranks in disowning Dr Milner. In Ireland the Board split. O'Connell and Scully with some difficulty carried a motion thanking the Bishops, but many of the class of "respectable" Catholics ceased to attend, some dropping out altogether (one of them being Scully's collaborator P. B. Hussey), others reappearing later as a group of seceders. For Scully personally the affair, which he regarded as "an unfortunate blunder throughout", marked the end of his connexion with the English Catholic Board, and a beginning of a break with Lord Donoughmore, who had refused unlike Parnell to pass on his criticisms of the bill on the ground that "they would have been scouted out of House".

In a speech to an aggregate meeting on 29 June Scully, taking an optimistic view, argued that repeated petitioning and the recent debate had narrowed the issue to a single point: whether or not, as in the case of two merchants who trusted each other, a formal security was really necessary. In less conciliatory language, however, and in contrast with what seems to have been his view at the time he maintained that if the Catholics had been more importunate in 1806 the influence that had enabled Fox to abolish the slave trade in Africa must have given him power to abolish the slave trade in Ireland. The militancy which this outburst reflects had been enflamed since the latter part of 1812 by the reaction of nervous Protestants to Canning's motion, which he saw as a renewal of persecution; by the circulation of a big anti-Catholic petition which was presented at the bar of the House of Commons on 23 February 1813; and by the prosecution of his publisher. On 6 February he had tried to make a political issue of Hugh Fitzpatrick's trial by intervening in it with an offer to reveal the name of the author of the *Penal Laws* if the Attorney-General would consent to try the work as a whole. Now on 4 August, eight days after O'Connell had made a political event of the trial for libel of John Magee, Scully drafted the Kilkenny resolutions which Robert Peel, the Chief Secretary, saw as insinuating that the judge had been partial, the jury corrupt and the prosecutor venal. As the government learnt of the existence of a draft of the resolutions in his handwriting he remained for many months in danger of being prosecuted for them.

The Kilkenny resolutions were Scully's last gesture of defiance. A report of the end of April 1815 about a refusal on his part to send up to the chair a sample resolution of thanks in his own handwriting[5] suggests that fears for his own safety induced a spirit of caution, but he was under pressure from his friend William Parnell to drop a quarrel in which the government had won the upper hand and much of which was a personal vendetta against the Duke of Richmond as the Lord Lieutenant appointed by the first "No Popery" administration. The departure of the Duke at the end of August offered an opportunity for an accommodation and on 4 October Darcy Mahon, a Protestant friend claiming to speak on Scully's behalf, told Peel that the Catholics were disposed to be on friendly terms with the new Lord Lieutenant, Lord Whitworth, who, it was suggested, might begin his administration with an act of favour, the release of Fitzpatrick and Magee. This overture having been ignored Scully would seem to have been contemplating another peace feeler in June 1814, when however a pro-clamation dissolving the Board pre-empted it.

In the spring of 1814 two major events coincided. The near success of Grattan's bill had induced the English Catholics, through the Vicar

Apostolic of the London District, to seek a ruling from Rome on the attitude to be adopted if another bill on the same lines were introduced, and on 26 April the reply reached London in a document known as the Quarantotti Rescript, which, with minor reservations, allowed Catholics to accept a bill like Grattan's. On 27 April the cessation of hostilities was announced in parliament: the Pope was released from French custody and returned to Rome on 29 May. On 2 May Dr Milner set off for Rome, where he was joined by Dr Murray from Dublin, and on 25 June he secured the virtual revocation of the Rescript. On 26 April 1815 a new ruling was substituted for it: the so-called Genoese Letter which denied the crown a veto over episcopal appointments once canonically made but allowed the prior submission of lists from which obnoxious names might be expunged. In the meantime Lord Castlereagh and Cardinal Consalvi were at the Congress of Vienna together and suspected by some of plotting to settle the Catholic question between them. In August 1815 the Catholic Association, which had replaced the abolished Board, followed the example of the Prelates in sending a remonstrance to Rome in the care of Reverend Richard Hayes OFM, who was also instructed to press for the domestic nomination of Bishops. Scully made a modest contribution towards Father Hayes' expenses but seems to have otherwise held aloof, probably for the reason he gave on 9 February 1815 when he opposed a motion by O'Connell to send a deputation to Dr Murray to ask about his recent visit to Rome: Catholics looking for their civil rights, he said, had nothing to do with Bishops or the court of Rome, or any other court.

Two new developments of 1815 show O'Connell and Scully taking the reins into their own hands. At the end of 1813 they had tried in vain to persuade Grattan to take the Catholic body into consultation over the petition for the next year and in 1814 Grattan, finding parliament preoccupied with the winding up of matters arising from the end of the war, had on his own responsibility refrained from tabling a motion. At an aggregate meeting of 24 January 1814, when an attempt by O'Connell to reunite the Catholic body collapsed with Lord Fingall walking out upon a resolution for unqualified emancipation being put, only an appeal from George Lidwill thwarted a motion to put the 1815 petition in new hands. When Grattan returned an unsatisfactory reply to a new invitation, however, Scully declared that "it was high time to send this teazing correspondence" and on 23 February the adjourned aggregate meeting resolved to place the petition in the hands of a member who would have it debated in the current session. On 26 April Sir Henry Parnell (as he had now become) accepted the charge, adding (according to a press report) "that to suggestions or instructions he had no sort of objection". This was followed on 26 June by the appearance of a new newspaper, the *Dublin Chronicle*, under the editorship of Eneas McDonnell: according to R. L. Sheil it was established by O'Connell and Scully, both of whom, but especially the latter, contributed their money and their talents to its support.

As over seventy letters in the present volume show, the suggestions and instructions that Sir Henry Parnell received came from Scully, who in return received reports on the situation at Westminster and recommendations on how to react to it. While the correspondence gives an insight into the difficulties of winning a parliamentary majority against the hostility or indifference of the government, the positive results of the experiment were meagre. In 1815 Parnell, having the field to himself, was not only able to carry his motion on the petition to a not unsatisfactory division, but managed to bring before the House the text of the Irish Catholics' own bill, published in Dublin on 19 May, by recasting it in the form of ten resolutions. In 1816, when the seceders drew up a petition of their own which they entrusted to Grattan, he was only able to get a hearing by seconding a motion proposed by the latter, as the Commons would not tolerate two debates on the same subject; an attempt to introduce his resolutions again had to be dropped; and an address to the Prince Regent, which was intended to bring the issue directly before the cabinet, was ignored. He complained to Scully that his efforts to win parliamentary support were being frustrated by the unfair attacks of the *Dublin Chronicle* on Grattan and the seceders, which were resented by their friends in parliament; and Lord Donough-more, who presented the seceders' as well as the Association's petition, complained in the House of Lords of the paper's slander against himself, the work, he said, of a few individuals who had set themselves up as the directors of the whole Catholic feeling of Ireland: he suspected Scully of being the author of them. In December 1816 an aggregate meeting in Dublin made a gesture towards the seceders by adopting for 1817 the text of Scully's petition of 1812, the last to be presented before the Catholic body split, but the main debate was on a motion by Grattan who re-introduced the seceders' 1816 petition. There were no petitions in 1818; and in 1819, when the House cut short another motion introduced by Grattan, Parnell was given no petition to present.

While Sir Henry Parnell constantly displayed an optimism that was belied by the results, he was already in 1815 asking Scully whether the Catholic body would accept anything short of complete emancipation and continued in the following two years to discuss the possibility of concessions on what he called subordinate subjects. A pronouncement in the *Dublin Chronicle* of 3 January 1816, perhaps inserted by Scully himself, said that unqualified emancipation did not mean total emancipation, and that any concessions that were not qualified would be accepted "as an instalment of the great national debt". Actually to ask for such concessions was another matter, but from Parnell's letters and a letter from Edward Hay to Lord Donoughmore of 6 June 1817 it can be inferred that Scully came very close to doing so.

James Scully of Kilfeacle died on 11 February 1816 leaving Denys and his younger brother James as executors of his will. On 27 November following, his widow, instigated thereto by her youngest son, Jeremiah, challenged its provisions by filing a bill in Chancery. On 8 December 1821 the Lord Chancellor gave judgement for the plaintiffs and the executors appealed to the House of Lords. The case was heard in May 1825, with O'Connell as counsel for the appellants, and lost in June when the decision of the Irish court of Chancery was upheld. Writing in 1828 R. L. Sheil said that this lawsuit, coming at the height of Scully's political influence, "ingrossed all his mind [and] and induced him to retire in a great measure from public life". The tapering off of Scully's correspondence, the closure of the *Dublin Chronicle* and the failure to petition in 1818 confirm this opinion. While the continuation of his correspondence with Sir Henry Parnell and Dr Milner shows that he still took an interest in the Catholic question, he appears to have played no part in the manoeuvres which gave W. C. Plunket charge of the Catholic petition after the death of Grattan in 1820, in Plunket's bill of 1821, or in the visit of King George IV to Ireland during August of the same year (at which time Scully entertained Dr Milner in Dublin and introduced him to O'Connell). In 1824, when he was fully retired after being incapacitated by a stroke, he made a last but anonymous foray into public life with a pamphlet entitled *A Letter to Daniel O'Connell Esq . . . by a Munster Farmer*. It was a detailed critique of the resolutions passed by the aggregate meeting which adopted the petition of that year, but remains worth reading for the insight it gives into the difference between the old and the new dispensations. If, argued Scully, the Union and its consequences, absentee landlordism, rack-renting, tithes and the over-large temporalities of the established Church were to be made subjects of complaint, O'Connell and his friends should have constituted themselves into an association for redeeming the wrongs of Ireland: the only proper object of a Catholic petition, in Scully's eyes, was to seek redress for grievances which afflicted Catholics specifically as Catholics — by and large this was the view that had prevailed since Scully drafted the petition of 1805.

In the spring of 1823 Scully went on circuit as usual and was back in Dublin at the end of April. On or about 26 May he fell from his horse in what appears to have been a fit of apoplexy and lost the use of his writing hand. After a temporary improvement he set off for the summer Assizes but did not complete the circuit and never went on one again. His five sons and three daughters were at this time aged between six and fourteen: although he was able to provide handsomely for all of them as well as his widow the loss of earnings at the bar, the expenses of the lawsuit and debts incurred on new investments in property may well have left him short of cash, and in November he started pressing O'Connell for repayment of a loan of £2000 he had made to him in 1815. Of his last years nothing is known except that he continued to engage in business dealings and divided his time between Dublin and Kilfeacle. He made a will on 3 August 1830. After being seized by another apoplectic fit while visiting a neighbour he died at Kilfeacle on 25 October and was buried in the family plot on the Rock of Cashel, where a tomb was subsequently built for him out of stone ordered from Italy.

In physical appearance Scully was in his later years "low, squat and clumsy" (Thomas Wyse in 1829); like Napoleon "when the latter grew round and stout" (R. L. Sheil in 1828); "perfectly square, being fully as broad as he is long" (O'Connell in 1823). The nickname of Bulstag of Bull-stag given him by the *Milesian Magazine* in 1812 may reflect the stocky bearing implied in O'Connell's "great brute of brutes" in 1830. He was probably already corpulent as a young man, for on 16 January 1800 Lady Granard wrote to her brother that "our fat friend" would be sending him the recent Catholic resolutions.[6] In social accomplishment the polish that might have been expected from an habitué of Moira House had evidently worn off a bit by 1823 when O'Connell remarked that his manners were not in his favour. In everyday life he wore an expression that was described according to taste as a smile, a grin or a sneer. According to Sheil it was impossible to detect his sensations in his features, only the quivering of a hand indicating the influence of emotion. In utterance, says Sheil, he was remarkably slow and deliberate, his cadences monotonous, his sentences ending in an unpleasing see-saw of the voice. In 1806 he was described by his friend Robert Marshall as having strong Catholic feelings and being attentive to his religious duties, for which he was much respected by Bishops and clergy,[7] and all the signs are that he remained a good practising Catholic. W. H. Curran, writing in 1823, speaks of his having a stock of "mortuary anecdotes" about Orangemen who sent for priests at the point of death, but his many friendships with Protestants show that he was no bigot and he was worldly enough in 1810 to follow "the laws of society" by issuing a challenge to a duel. A few surviving letters of 1830 show him as a landlord employing agents who resorted to the usual methods of collecting unpaid rent, but a letter of 1824 indicates that he disapproved of the rackrenting practised by some of his main tenants. In his political conduct he acquired a reputation for deviousness: too wary to commit himself (F. W. Conway in 1812) and too cunning to be implicated (an informer[8] in 1815); deep and designing, with a desire to do mischief and escape the consequences (Robert Peel in 1813); a Jesuit knowing no arms but the stiletto and "that little Jewish conspirator who puts others foward to satisfy his own malignity" (Lord Donoughmore[9] in 1814 and 1815); hating the direct line and preferring to come to the most obvious consequences by a circuit (Thomas Wyse in 1829).

If O'Connell was better known to the wider public closer observers saw Scully as at least on a par with him and some of them, including informers reporting to Dublin Castle, regarded him as the one who pulled the strings.

In the retrospect of 1829 O'Connell[10] saw him only as "a principal but underhand agent in Catholic affairs", but in 1828 R. L. Sheil wrote of his "ascendancy in the councils of the Catholic Committee" at a time when O'Connell's influence was not as great as it subsequently became, and in 1829 Thomas Wyse made the extravagant claim that "no man was less ostensibly before the Catholic public, yet no man more thoroughly governed it". In cases where power is alleged to be wielded by secret means the truth is necessarily elusive, but while there is enough evidence to make it plain that Scully's supposed dominance was restricted to a sphere of his own choosing and not absolute even in that, the new course taken by the movement when it regained its momentum after his retirement tends to confirm Sheil's judgement. An apostrophe to O'Connell in his 1824 pamphlet hints that Scully himself felt he had occupied a position from which he had been displaced: "At different periods other men seemed almost to outshine your brightness, but they have all passed away. . . ."

Scully seems to have used his letters from important people not only for his own information but to impress others. Luke Plunkett in 1810 spoke of his "almost telegraphic facility of communication" with Charles Butler and in May 1813 the *Milesian Magazine* scoffed at Counsellor Bull-stag from Tipperary

> Who pulled out all his letters
> That he got from all his betters
> Such as Prime Ministers, Bailiffs and Setters
> And one of his letters was from Charlie Fox
> And two of them were from Watty Cox.

To the extent that he had not already done so as he went along, he probably tidied his correspondence up in the years of his retirement, a few letters from his steward and rent collectors escaping destruction because they were received in the last months of his life. He seems, however, to have left them in bundles, in their covers, arranged on no consistent principle. If he kept letter books for his outward correspondence they are now missing. After his death the collection, together with the papers of his father and grandfather, would have remained at Kilfeacle until the death of his widow in 1843 and then have passed to Vincent James Scully of Mantlehill, whose elder brother had been murdered in 1842. Towards the end of the century Scully's grandson, another Vincent, gave each bundle a Roman numeral and each letter within it an arabic number, following which he compiled a catalogue entitled Rough Analysis.[11] In 1907 he sent thirty-three bundles, together with the notebooks recording the 1805 deputation to London and the diaries of Scully's father and elder brother, to Revd Dr William Hunt, the new President of the Royal Historical Society in London. On 20 February 1908 Dr Hunt, in an inaugural address to the Society, which was printed in its

Journal, gave a full and lively account of the deputation to Pitt, but gave no indication that he had looked at any of the remainder apart from Scully's letters to his second wife. The selection was returned to Ireland and no further attempt seems to have been made to arouse interest in it. By the time Vincent Scully died in 1927 his elder son had emigrated to Canada and the collection passed into the custody of the second son, Lieutenant-Colonel Marcus Scully, who lived in England. In a letter of 4 February 1938 to Father Dowling at St Kieran's College, Marcus Scully mentioned that the papers had recently been put in order by his sister, Manuella, a nun at Streatham: it was perhaps she who arranged the correspondence in the alphabetical order, by writers' names, in which it now stands. After his death in 1941 they remained in the possession of his widow, the divorced wife of Captain Bernard de Lérisson Cazenove, who kept them in the Essex home of her younger Cazenove son. In 1968 she supplied Professor Maurice O'Connell with photocopies of the O'Connell letters which he published in his *Correspondence of Daniel O'Connell*: the originals, evidently not returned to the file, have since then been missing. In 1980 her grandson and granddaughter, with whom the collection was then stored, agreed that it should be returned to Ireland and with the consent of Denys Scully's senior surviving grandson, the late Vincent Scully of Montreal, it was deposited with the National Library of Ireland in October 1983.

B. C. MacDermot, March 1988.

[1]Sources will be cited only for such statements as are not covered by the text and its accompanying notes.
[2]HO 100/99 f.163.
[3]HO 100/123 f.124.
[4]Diary 13.3.1805.
[5]Peel Papers, Add. MSS. 40,201 f.11.
[6]Loudoun Papers A 188.
[7]Richmond Papers MS. 60, f.264.
[8]Peel Papers, Add. MSS. 40,201, f.115.
[9]DDA 390/1, XI, 22, 29.
[10]*Correspondence*, IV, 1545.
[11]MS. 27,565.

Editorial Note

As almost all the letters to and from Denys Scully in the National Library of Ireland are arranged in alphabetical order and fully catalogued in Special List A7 under the two heads of MS 27,485 and MS 27,506 specific source references are given for only those items from the Scully Papers that bear other MS numbers.

The great majority of Charles Butler's letters are, in whole or in part, in the hands of one or other of his clerks. Except in a few cases where it is otherwise indicated the remainder of the collection consists of holographs.

In the headings the spelling of the place-names follows that of the covers which accompany most of the letters. In the date-line all dates have been standardised. In the text as well as in the headings, abbreviations such as Mr., Dr., etc have been modernised by the omission of full points. While salutations have been retained closings have been omitted except in a small number of cases.

Sparing use has been made of *sic*: proper names are sometimes silently corrected in the notes or index.

In the Biographical Notes of Appendix D members of the peerage are entered under their titles and wives under their married names unless they are first mentioned in the text under their maiden names.

Letters and other papers
1798–1822

1   *From his brother Roger Scully[1] to No. 8 Paul's Grove Place, Strand, London*

Kilfeacle [Co. Tipperary] 26 December 1793

Dear Denis,

I rec'd your very affectionate & excellent favor, w'ch was only charged single. The Probability you mention of your having *now* a Prospect of being called to the Bar in two years arises, perhaps, from an Advertisement inserted in the *Dublin Evening Post*[2] from the Society of King's Inns, w'ch you might have seen; however lest it might have escaped your notice, I now enclose it for your Perusal. Nevertheless my Father desires me let you know that he wd *considerably* prefer paying an additional *200* Guineas for the third Year, to your overhastening your studies & running a risque of injuring both your Health & your future legal knowledge. *If possible*, by any means do not exceed the *200* Guineas per Annum. If that sum is not sufficient for your yearly expences, I request you'll mention it in your next, & I will endeavor to supply the Deficiency without my Father's knowledge, as he supposes he has done miracles by granting such an Allowance. Let me know if there will be a Deficiency & if so, how much it will be & I'll endeavor to remit it you soon as possible. Observe my Father never yet gave but a *tacit* Consent to the *200* Guineas per Annum, however tho' he may grumble a little at such an Yearly Expence, still I do not think it would be a measure that wd by any means make him violent. With respect to Thady,[3] I cannot well determine how he is inclined, however my Father is determined to pursue the Plan you recommend for him, & he will be accordingly sent to Dublin immediately after the Holidays, where he'll enter the College as Pensioner & will remain there, according to the present Plan for two Years.

I am glad you are getting well of the Pain in your Chest. Take a good deal of the Air & you'll be completely rid of it. It was rather unfortunate you was [*sic*] not at home when the Lord Mayor [4] returned your Visit. He wd have been a choice Acquaintance. Nich: Maher's Children are more trouble to you, than he and they are worth. How does his Son John promise? Dick Sause is now in Dublin with his father. D.S. will be *positively* married this or next Week.[5] He gets *£1000* now & *£1000* payable in three years. A letter from [?] T.N. this day mentions nothing new, but that A: Grehan[6] has returned to Dublin in a very bad State of Health, so much so, as that a Consultation of Physicians despaired of his recovery. My Uncle Ned,[7] who is now much better, has been ordered to Bath immediately after Christmas, & from thence to Buxton. How soon he'll set out, I know not. My Mother wishes to know, whether you've got your new Shirts. Believe me, Dear Den, your ever affectionate Roger Scully James.[8]

[*Source*: Scully Papers]

[1]Born 1772, died 7 March 1797 after a fall from a horse.
[2]Of 24 December 1793. It announced that students enrolled in the King's Inns or in any English Inn before the Michaelmas term of 1793 could be called to the bar after a prescribed number of terms and by keeping at the King's Inns the entire term in which they applied to be called. Scully had been admitted to the King's Inns in the Trinity term of 1793 and graduated from there in the Trinity term of 1796. He was admitted to the Middle Temple on 25 October 1793.
[3]William Timothy Scully, a younger brother. In the event he was admitted to Trinity College Dublin in 1797 from Mr Clarke's School, which was at Cashel.
[4]Paul Le Mesurier, Lord Mayor from 9 November 1793.
[5]Richard Sause, Scully's brother-in-law: his wife had died in 1788 and he was about to marry Jane Duffy.
[6]Probably Andrew Grehan, 9 Lower Ormond Quay, second son of the brewer Thady Grehan.
[7]Edmund Scully of Cashel.
[8]Roger Scully's younger brother Edmund also added James or Jas. to his signature, presumably to distinguish himself from other Scullys with the same first name.

2   *From his Common Place Book*

To a lady, who appeared unexpectedly on the esplanade in a yellow veil, contrary to her custom.
Written at Weymouth in May, 1794, at her lover's request.

My gentle maid, Ah, why conceal
That mild angelic face,
Or under sullen yellow veil
That fatal batt'ry place?

. . . .

When time shall chill youth's sportive heat
And visit beauty's gloss,
Ev'n there a lovely fair you'll meet
In W......... R...[1]

Written for J. Mortimer,[2] by D.S.   [*Source*: Scully Papers.]

[1]Evidently Williamina Ross, eldest daughter of William Ross of Sandwick in Scotland. In 1800 she married Hon. Richard Fitzgerald King, 5th son of the 2nd Earl of Kingston and brother of Hon. Margaret King, wife of the 2nd Earl of Mount Cashell.
[2]Unidentified. There were Mortimers at the Kilkenny Academy where Scully was at school.

3   *Advice from Lord Clonmell*[1]

November 1796

I shall be always happy to see you; and shall take particular pleasure in affording you every notice and encouragement, and in doing you every service when you come to practise. Your coming to the bar will be a matter of course. If you attend to your business diligently and with application you must certainly make some money by it, especially as the country grows richer; and indeed it will be the case whether the country becomes richer or poorer — the law must thrive in either case. As to special pleading and conveyancing, if you have fixed your mind upon them and are resolved to go to the toil, I would recommend your doing so, but if you have not finally determined and will deliberately take advice I will give you my opinion as you ask for it. Let me see, how old are you? (answered) —— a pause of some time —— Sir, I never knew any man come to the bar so young as you are, who ever afterwards did any good in it, excepting two, and those had singular luck; you have plenty of time, you could come at the age of 25[2] to the bar with that superior store of practical & theoretical knowledge, that would bear down competition and put you at once in a leading situation. You could spend two years in those offices with infinite profit. This however is provisionally that your father will give his acquiescence, and that he can assist you conveniently to himself. If he is willing to make you a good allowance, and will not make too great difficulties in the expence, I would by all means advise you to adopt that course. Were it the case of a man struggling with pecuniary difficulties and so encumbered with a very large family as to be unable to afford this assistance to his son, it were another question; but in this case, if I may hazard a conjecture, your father is able to afford you a genteel support and an allowance suitable to this undertaking, without impoverishing himself or injuring his family — and from his known property and character of good sense, I should incline to believe that he will not refuse his assent.[3] To you also I would observe that it requires determined resolution and firmness to go thro' those offices with due advantage; it is a matter of toil and labour and strict application. You were bred at Cambridge and tho' the course of education in the sciences taught there must have divided your time and attention, yet it was highly useful and advantageous.[4]

In England they commonly come to the Bar at a later age than here; they are better grounded in principles; they devote more time to business and are more laborious in their profession. A lawyer in London has none but professional habits; he does not vie with mere gentlemen or keep company with them; he scarcely ever sees the face of one of them; he is merely the man of business. By study in their offices you can intimately observe them and their method of transacting business; you cannot fail of imitating in some measure their example, of acquiring their habits and attaining an insight into practice — Here a man after 3 years in London, half amusing and half instructing himself between elegant literature, poetry, the classics & Belles Lettres, comes to the bar unacquainted with practice; he is frightened at the first brief he gets; afterwards, during his first years, which are years of leisure, he gets into knots & clubs of barristers & young men, who pass their evenings not unpleasantly, (I will add, not very improvingly) over a bottle and gay conversation, now and then regaled by a good song; from this way of life he rarely emerges. These are the men that overstock & croud the profession — I see acres of their wigs daily before me in court; but talents, good conduct, good sense and assiduity never fail to attain eminence and distinction.

You have many and numerous connections; and belonging to a particular class or party you have advantages and disadvantages; many, many advantages. You come to the bar under such circumstances, that much will depend upon your first actions; and it would be advantageous and creditable if you were enabled at the assizes to acquit yourself with superior skill & signal ability. Special pleading is not so much cultivated as it ought to be, and always has been a sure means of bringing a man into notice & lasting employment. Conveyancing also, wills and marriage settlements form a very useful & principal part of practice; it is an honourable branch, and, to you especially, would be lucrative also. I know the value of those branches. In your county I first set out in life, and saw the utility & necessity of them. Finally, I would, all things considered, strenuously advise & recommend the measure. I would have you, when in England, attend Westminster Hall now and then and go the summer circuit — But, as I said before, the whole will depend upon your father's sentiments & situation in money affairs and upon his willingness or reluctance to give you the necessary assistance in the pursuit of the plan I recommend.[5]   [*Source*: Scully Papers MS 27,505.]

[1]The heading reads: "Lord Clonmell to me, in November 1796, present Richard Sause in Harcourt Street". John Scott (1739–1798), 1st Earl of Clonmell, lived in Harcourt Street and was at this time Chief Justice of the King's Bench. Sir Jonah Barrington remarks that "he made a point of discovering every young man likely to succeed in public life, and took the earliest possible moment of being so civil as to ensure a friend, if not a partisan" (*Personal Sketches of his life and times* (London, 1827–32), p. 317.
[2]When Scully was admitted to Trinity College, Cambridge, on 27 June 1794 his age was recorded as nineteen, and the licence for his first marriage in November 1801 gave it as twenty-six — both figures implying that he was born in 1775. His father recorded in his journal however that he was born on Tuesday, 4 May 1773, making his age twenty-three at the date of this interview and twenty-five after the two years of further study recommended by Lord Clonmell.

[3]Lord Clonmell would have known James Scully well at least by repute, being not only a Tipperary man himself but closely connected with the Scullys' neighbours, the Mathews of Thomastown.

[4]Scully's Common-Place Book shows that he studied some Plato, Sophocles, Euripides and Tacitus; mathematics; some science; logic; and a book of the New Testament. It mentions no history, law or modern literature.

[5]There is evidence in the Common Place Book suggesting that Scully followed Lord Clonmell's advice: from August 1796 to March 1798 he was buying books from London booksellers; and an entry of 1818 implies that it was in 1798 that he started practice at the Irish bar.

4   *From his Common Place Book*

March 1798

Heraldry.

The arms of the Scully family are not to be found (tho' fully searched by me on 31 May 97) in the Herald's Office in London, but are recorded in the Ulster King of Arms Office in Dublin — In the former there are several Schoolys & Scholys, but the name which approaches nearest, is that of Richard Scoly Esq. of Goberhall in Yorkshire, Gentleman waiter in ordinary to Queen Elizabeth — For which see Guillim's Heraldry also. There are also families of the name of Scoly or Scholy at or near Radnorth in Yorkshire. [Accompanying sketch illustrates the arms] *Crest*: a sheaf of wheat circled with a ducal wreath. *Arms*: Blue on a band azure three hurtes. [The whole entry down to this point was crossed out]

Since I wrote this article, I have learned to condemn the foppery of heralds and the nonsense of genealogy — I perceive that I had been, in common with others, under the dominion of a ridiculous vanity in this instance, but every body becomes, or ought to become, wiser by experience, time & learning, the great purifiers of the mind from errors.

[*Source*: Scully Papers]

5   *From the dowager Countess of Moira, Baroness Hastings*

Moira House, Dublin, Thursday 23 August 1798

On Tuesday the 21st a Box was carefully left at my house by the guard of the coach, but my servants never inquired from whom it came, when opened it was full of the finest looking peaches[1] ever seen, and they were quickly found to answer in taste, to their appearance. I had by chance several persons with me, they had a curiosity to learn whence such remarkable fine fruit came, but of that point I had not a single guess, till I recd, Sr, your very obliging letter (dated the 18th) on Wednesday the 22^d — this is the first day consequently in my power to acknowledge that letter — & to return my very best thanks for your very kind attention, of which I wish to express myself most fully sensible — Cousin Joe[2] who since the guards of yeomen prowess, have been discontinued, has fewer disastrous adventures to relate; when he heard who was the donor of the luxury, he was sharing in, he burst forth into eulogies upon the Lawyer Corps[3] — Lord Gormanston being returned to the country he has no *kindred* inducements to run those hazards you have heard him so often detail beneath this roof in our dining hours, & of the hair-breadth "scapes" from sentinels ignorant of his senatorial rights he has also no longer cause to complain — the vigilance of an individual of that class (one of the Buckinghamshire Militia) was lately a matter that might have proved of fatal consequence — this man a sentry at the Park upon Lord Cornwallis coming out of his house after supper, fired off his piece at him — Lord Cornwallis went up to him thinking the piece had gone off by accident, & asked him if he was hurt, by that accident: No said the man I was firing at you, & seized his Excellency prisoner, who calling to his people they immediately ran out — The sentinel said he had not answered his challenge, the Marquis said he had never challenged him, on which the man said he had challenged as was ordered, by striking thrice his cartridge pouch, which it seems was a method of challenging in the Duke of Marlborough's wars but wherefore adopted unknown to the commanding military personage in the kingdom, & his Excellency left ignorant of it, not easily to be explained; the matter for a few hours made a talk, but was speedily hushed into silence[4] — The report of the Secret Committee[5] I learn, proves that Lord Camden's administration was the wisest, the best & the most fortunate of all possible governments, & that everything done in it, was equally just, right and successful — & that it also unfolds an Irish Executive Directory consisting of Mr Arthur O'Connor, Counsellor Emmet & Doctor McNevin to have existed in Ireland — This report however is not yet printed, & what one hears in conversation is not to be absolutely depended upon, for there appears as much difference in the hearing, as in the eye sight among those who repeat what they have seen or heard — the rational and cool belief here is, that rebellion is extinguished, & that the benevolent wishes of his Excellency, & the noble & prudent conduct of Genl. Dundas Genl. Moore, & the Marquis of Huntley,[6] will restore perfect peace & tranquillity in the former rebellious counties; yet others affirm that a rebel force is still, to great numbers, on foot — & there are not only compliments, but much impatient censure against his Excellency for not permitting country squires vested with a brief military authority to tyrannize, to exercise that tyranny as they think proper & follow the example of the Tipperary Mr Fitzgerald.[7]

Lady Mountcashel has been brought to bed a few days ago of a son[8] & is perfectly well — Mr Preston Mr Murphy & Miss Forde[9] desire your acceptance of their best comp[ts.] & I remain, Mr Scully,

> much obliged & faithful
> humble servt.
> E. Moira Hastings etc, etc.

[P.S.] Lord Moira[10] is on a grouse shooting party in Yorkshire — I hope that you found all your family well on your arrival amongst them.

> [*Source*: Scully Papers]

[1]Probably grown at Kilfeacle by his father, in whose diary (MS 27, 579) there are several entries showing he was proud of his peaches.
[2]Unidentified.
[3]In 1803 Scully was serving in the Lawyers Corps of Yeomanry (see No. 54) and the implication here is that he was already enlisted in it. The day after this letter the corps was called out on news being received of the French landing in Killala Bay (*The Times* 31 August 1798).
[4]A note in the *Correspondence of Charles, first Marquis of Cornwallis* (London, 1859), III, p. 121, says that the incident took place on 11 August.
[5]On 21 August Lord Castlereagh had given the Irish House of Commons a summary of the findings of the Secret Committee which had been investigating into the origins of the rebellion and had recently been taking evidence from the three leaders of the United Irishmen mentioned by Lady Moira (*FJ*, 30 August 1798).
[6]Ralph Dundas (d. 1814); John Moore (d. Corunna 1809); George Gordon, later 5th Duke of Gordon.
[7]Thomas Judkin Fitzgerald.
[8]Edward George, born on 18 August.
[9]Revd John Murphy. Mr Preston and Miss Forde remain unidentified.
[10]Her son, the 2nd Earl, later Marquis of Hastings.

6   *From Lady Moira to Kilfeacle, Cashel*

> Moira House, 4 September [17]98

I acknowledge again my obligations to Mr Scully for some very fine fruit and nuts of the finest filbert kind I ever saw, & request him to accept my very best thanks for the donation — I am fallen again beneath the controul of martial law, & tho' I return from my visit at ten o'clock (having past a couple of hours with Lady Mount Cashell in her confinement,) yet I have usually my privilege to insist upon as I pass the four courts guard, I find that the Attorney & Lawyers Corps are blended now to perform that duty — You possibly hear more of our French visitants[1] than we do here — It was unfortunate that they gained the first advantage, owing to the incapacity of General Lake, to cope with his adversary; General Hombert or Humbert who commands the French is not a man whom I recollect being mentioned amongst the French generals — The yeomanry (who were from various places) all ran off, on the first shot that was fired — The French indeed inspired a panic in the whole military, & there were other corps who were light-footed also, but several are very falsely charged as whole bodies running when only some individuals of them had weak nerves; Lord Ormond behaved with all the valorous gallantry of his antient race & tho' some of his people retreated too soon others stood out to the very last; Lord Granard's Regt. was ordered to proceed to Castlebar by forced marches the last of 30 miles he reached Castlebar at eleven o'clock at night, at half hour after two on Monday 27th the troops were ordered to their arms, on which they rested till 6 o'clock, when they were attacked by the French who instead of coming by Foxford came over mountain roads supposed to be impassible & brought with them two pieces of heavy cannon — The fight lasted above an hour Ld. Granard escaped unhurt, but had two of his officers killed, & three wounded & taken prisoners, the officers are released upon their parole[2] — General Hombert keeps strict discipline & had five of the Irish who had joined him executed for some enormity that they had been guilty of, & would not permit Castlebar to be plundered & burnt, on which acct, it is said that the few who had joined the French army immediately left it. A person who goes by the name of Pistol Blake[3] had brought in 400 to the enemy, he sent word to Lord Cornwallis that he wd surrender himself & them, & take advantage of the proclamation & amnesty, Lord Cornwallis informed him that he might surrender but it must be on fresh terms, for that the proclamation & amnesty did not extend to those who had joined the king's enemies — But in Dublin it is reported that very few have joined them — Lord Cornwallis has 12,000 men 49 pieces of heavy artillery & two miles length of carriages with flying artillery, ammunition & military stores — he accompanies the army, shares with the soldiers in their fare goes to no gentleman's house rests when they do at the meanest inn on straw & attends to the care of the private soldier if he is ill or meets with an accident — In short he is a source of wonder by comparing him to former commanders in chief, & every one looks up to his worth as well as his exertions with a confidence of success.

Mr Preston, Mr Murphy, & Miss Forde all join in their best compts to you.

[P.S.] Lord Moira is gone to London, but was well by letters I got by this morning's packet. [*Source*: Scully Papers]

[1]The French expedition under General Joseph Amable Humbert had landed in Killala Bay, Co. Mayo, on 23 August.

[2]See H. A. Richey: *A short history of the Royal Longford Militia 1793–1893* (Dublin 1894); and Richard Hayes: *The Last invasion of Ireland*, Dublin 1937. The Longford Militia, stationed at Ennis, Co. Clare, had marched 80 miles in three days. At the Castlebar engagement they were in reserve, to the left and behind the Kilkenny

Militia commanded by the 18th Earl of Ormond. When the French charged both regiments fled. Lord Granard rallied enough of his men to fight a rearguard action as they withdrew into Castlebar, where they held the bridge for half an hour. Fifty-three of the Longfords who fell into the hands of the French enrolled in the Irish force serving with them and most of them were hanged when caught after the battle of Ballinamuck.

[3]George Blake, of Garracloon. His offer of surrender was made on 31 August and reported in the press on 3 September (*The Times*, 9 September 1798 — which adds that he was called Pistol because of his "querulous courage"). He was hanged after the battle of Ballinamuck.

7   *From Lady Moira to Suffolk Street*

Castle Forbes, Longford, 30 November 1798

S[r.]

   Your obliging & very amusing letter I found upon my table this morning upon quitting my bed, for at so uncomfortable an hour as twelve at night did the post arrive, when I was in my first sleep. We chatted over all particulars contained therein & the contents of our other letters at our family breakfast where I make one; & I was set down to write when visitants from ten miles distance were announced; they were agreeable people, one of whom, an authoress of merit,[1] I had not met with for twelve years past, they did not leave us 'till it was time to prepare for dinner; & it is after that meal that I hurry off these few lines of thanks to Mr Scully whilst my young friends under the guidance of Miss Forde are practising the song replete with humour, & which we should not have seen, but from the kind attention of a friend — And I do suppose that not any newspaper will venture to admit it becoming a paragraph of intelligence in their communications — Since I came down I have begun the perusal of Lord Orford's works,[2] but have not yet got further than his poetry & his horrid tragedy, all in my thinking bad — Yet to quote some of his rhyming texts respecting liberty would in Ireland hurry one off to "durance vile" — I was much interested to see Mr Tone's Life, you were so good as to send me the first part, the part which contains an attack upon Doctor Drenan[3] I did not get, nor any of the papers I expected to receive by Mr J. Atkinson's[4] orders. Lord Strangford was so good to send me the day's Journal of the 29th — Doctor Drenan is a very pleasing poet, to mention his poetical talents in the most moderate term of praise — & is a very sensible man — As for his success as a fashionable practiser in the medical line having an independent tho' small property, I have heard that he was indifferent to having much practice, therefore I am surprised he should be mortified with being charged as not being a noted personage in his profession. I conclude that the Union will prove a reduction of all the privileges that have been granted to Ireland, particularly those for which Mr Grattan got his premium; & that the late attacks upon that once popular character were to try in what estimation he was as yet held by the people; & Ministry perceive that his oratory & influence would be now bestowed upon the deaf adder "charmed he ever so wisely".[5] I must hasten to conclude, that I may not lose the first opportunity of forwarding the enclosed,[6] the which I hope, either in your travels to yr Christmas party in the country or in yr return from thence to Dublin, may induce you to visit this place; yr old friends will be made happy by yr yielding to the request, & that you will acquire an increase of friends here, what I think can be assured to Mr Scully by his etc.   [*Source*: Scully Papers]

[1]Possibly Maria Edgeworth from Edgeworthstown, Co. Longford.

[2]Better known as Horace Walpole: he had succeeded his nephew in 1791 as the 4th Earl of Orford. Following his death in 1797 a collected edition of his works had been published early in 1798. The horrid tragedy was no doubt *The Castle of Otranto*.

[3]Theobald Wolfe Tone after being captured in a French warship had arrived in Dublin on 8 November and died on 19 November. The *Life* to which Lady Moira refers was published in instalments in *Faulkner's Dublin Journal* under the heading of "Biographical Sketches". The issue that Lady Moira had seen was that of 27 November which contained a letter from William Drennan denying that he was an unpractising physician of Newry and insisting that he earned enough to enjoy an honest and honourable independence (text in *Drennan Letters* No. 729), The part that she had not read referred to "an unpractising physician of Newry" who had been amongst the foremost of the Northern Reformers and "neglected and disappointed in his professional hopes, he was now ready for any desperate undertaking".

[4]John Atkinson, of Atkinson and Woodward, who were the Dublin agents of the Longford Militia (Wilson's *Dublin Directory*, 1802). A letter of 6 August 1804 from Lady Granard in the Loudoun Papers implies that the firm were also Lord Moira's personal agents.

[5]Grattan's name was erased from the list of Privy Councillors on 6 October (*The Times*, 10.10.98). He was at that time regarded by most of the Irish loyalists as largely responsible for the rebellion. (For an account of the campaign against him see Lecky, *History*, Vol. V Ch. XI.).

[6]A letter from Lord Granard dated 1 December inviting Scully to visit Castle Forbes, where he would get good shooting and a warm welcome.

8   *From Lady Moira to Suffolk Street*

Castle Forbes, Longford, Saturday 15 December 1798

I shall only trouble Mr Scully with a few lines, as we expect the pleasure of meeting him here so soon. In antient days the liver was esteemed the residence of cares & sorrows, modern times have transferred them to the heart. In my frame I always experience their effects upon the former, as productive of bodily sufferings, perhaps from its having been many years in a diseaseful state — The bile flowed in its acrimonious as well as gloomy current on receiving the intelligence of our loss in poor Miss Bushe.[1] I know from others with whom she had long been in habits of friendship that she was worthy & valuable, as to intrinsic merits — In my later acquaintance I found her a most pleasant agreeable associate, calculated to act a capital part in cheerful social intercourse, & estimated her as an acquisition to any circle of society during the short period I had to exist — Consequently, disappointment & regret are what I selfishly feel for her early death. Yet whoever has had a length of days will agree that those are happy who have speedily run their race thro' this rugged world; where happiness is precarious & where if not actual misfortune strikes, continual ills must occur to those of honour & upright mind by suffering for others; & reflecting that they are subject every instant to some possible calamity — A kind unfinished letter intended for me found in her writing box pained and yet indulged me, since to be remembered to the latest period with kindness by a person one has liked & esteemed is gratifying. To the agitation of my mind I impute the indisposition I have encountered & which would not have allowed me to write more than these lines this day; tho' I feel to have thrown off the attack this evening. The post boy's horse having fallen dead upon the road our letters, which should have come in late last night, did not reach us till past three o'clock in the afternoon this day. The gentlemen were reading with expressions of much approbation a pamphlet that has the following Shakespearian motto: "The king drinks Hamlet to thy better breath; & throws a Union in thy cup"[2] — they were full of praises respecting it, I have not yet had leisure to read it — But as we shall so soon be able to talk over pamphlets & occurences, I shall only add Ld & Lady G[ranard]'s & Miss Fordes best compts & assure Mr Scully how sincerely I am his etc.

[P.S.] Many thanks for the inclosure.

My chaise shall be in Longford to convey you to Castle Forbes on Wednesday which is the day you mark to favour us with your company.

[*Source*: Scully Papers]

[1]She died suddenly in Upper Mount Street (*Dublin Magazine*, January 1799). Unidentified.

[2]A misquotation from *Hamlet*, V, ii. The pamphlet was *An address to the people of Ireland against an Union: in which a pamphlet entitled Arguments For and Against the Measure is considered . . .* by a Friend to Ireland. It is a reply to the anonymously published pamphlet by Edward Cooke and is attributed in the National Library of Ireland catalogue to Robert Orr.

9   *From Revd John Murphy to Kilfeacle*

Castle Forbes, 7 January 1799

My dear Sir,

Inclination no less than the request of Lady G[ranard] induces me to trouble you with a few lines by this night's post — 'twas her intention to have written, and inclosed the papers relative to which she had spoken to you; but a violent complaint in Lord G.'s eyes, attended with a considerable degree of inflammation, calls so loudly for that attention which even to strangers she is so ready to devote, that however you may regret the disappointment, I am sure you will esteem her for the cause of it. With regard to the papers, she will send them by Mr Hardy, who proposes leaving this place in a few days, for the purpose of attending the meeting of Parliament, and who will take an opportunity of giving them to you upon your return to Dublin.

As to news, we have heard none, or at least of moment, since you left us — the robbery of the Longford mail and consequent loss of our letters have left us totally in the dark as to what has been lately done in other parts of the kingdom relative to the intended union. Longford and Westmeath have followed the example of Dublin, and sent requisitions to their respective Sheriffs to request they will immediately convene the counties for the purpose of entering into some resolutions, and instructing their representatives relative to the measure — I trust that upon this occasion the gentlemen will act with spirit and unanimity — You have doubtless heard of Mr Grattan's return to Ireland — We have received a private letter which mentions it, and which likewise states that supported by the interest of Ld. Fitzwilliam he will be returned for the county of Wicklow[1] instead of Mr Hume;[2] who, if my information is correct, resigns in his favour. Should this hereafter happen otherwise you will recollect I give it you as a report only, but at the same as a report not totally devoid of foundation.

I should consider myself undeserving of your friendship was I to conclude this letter without acquainting you with the general and I may add sincere regret of this family on account of the shortness of your visit. Your departure spread an universal gloom, and the individual regrets expressed by Lady Moira, Lord and Lady Granard and their dear children were highly flattering to a person so interested in your welfare as I am. As to your friend Miss Ford she has not yet recovered her cheerfulness. She you know piques herself on her penetration; and the sentiment of esteem which your conduct so justly merits, was so gratifying to her, that she has availed herself of every opportunity of encouraging that regret which collectively and individually the whole family has expressed on account of your very hasty departure. When you go to Moore Park, I beg you will have the goodness to present my most affectionate remembrances to Ld. and Ly. M[ountcashell].

[P.S.] By this post I send the sonnet on the year 98 to Moore Park — Ly. M. will give you a copy of it.   [*Source*: Scully Papers]

[1]The *Freeman's Journal* of 5 January had reported the arrival of Grattan in Ireland on 1 January and his attendance at a Wicklow county meeting on 4 January. It reported on the 10th that the electors of Wicklow had resolved in favour of someone "not even suspected of being intimate with the traitors of this kingdom."

[2]William Hoare Hume, of Humewood Co. Wicklow, who had replaced his father, William Hume, in the Co. Wicklow seat when the latter was shot by a party of rebels in October 1798. Represented the county in the imperial parliament until his death in 1815.

10   *From Revd John Murphy to Suffolk Street*

Sunday morning [?20 January 1799]

My dear Sir,

I thank you for your promised favor, mentioned in Lady Granard's letter, which her Ladyship desires I will acknowledge, and which she will take an opportunity of answering by post — the memoire relative to O'Berne[1] I have not yet finished, but will be able to send it you in a few days — Lady G. thanks you for your care of the Moore Park letters, and Miss Ford and your Castle Forbes friends join in assurances of remembrance and esteem.

[P.S.] Extreme haste obliges me to conclude this soon — Have the goodness to present the inclosed to our friend at Milltown,[2] with my sincere regard to her, and the whole family.

Miss E.[3] was so good to say I should have a copy of the memoire — As I shall make a much longer stay here than I expected, beg of her to let you have it, and send it by Ld.G or some other safe opportunity.

[*Source*: Scully Papers]

[1]Dr Thomas Lewis O'Beirne, who had just returned from a visit to England to take up his appointment as Bishop of Meath. The memoir referred to seems to have been a draft (see No. 25).

[2]The following letter makes it clear that the reference is to Casino, the home of the parents of Robert Emmet, at that time a country house between Milltown and Dundrum.

[3]Maryanne Emmet.

11   *From Lady Moira*

Castle Forbes, Sunday, 20 January 1799

Dear Sr.

A thousand thanks for your obliging letter, which I sh'd have before
acknowledged had I not been apprehensive of its missing you at Kilfeacle &
Moore Park. At this place we know not what is passing but by vague reports
alternately contradicting one another — If you are so good to send me any
real intelligence make it into a packet with some trifling publication & send it
to Moira House to be delivered there to Mr Hart to be forwarded as a parcel
by the stage. I expect that Lord G[ranard] will be divested of his
employment & regt. for having signed the requisitions for assembling the
freeholders of the counties of Westmeath & Longford.[1] But he is a person
with whom honor & conscience precede every other consideration. — Lady
G[ranard], Miss Forde, Mr Murphy, Lord Forbes & all the young people
unite in best remembrances to you — & I assure you that Francis and
Hastings most gratefully recollect your notice of them. Lord Granard & Mr
Hardy will tell you every trifling occurence that has past since you left, very
trifles indeed they have only been that have taken place.

[*Source*: Scully Papers]

[1] At the Westmeath meeting on 14 January resolutions were adopted, but not
unanimously, disapproving of the Union (*FJ*, 17 January 1799). No report of the
Longford meeting has been found.

12   *From Revd John Murphy to Suffolk Street*

Castle Forbes, 22 January 1799

I have received, my dear Sir, and read with much satisfaction your very
kind letter of Saturday, and while I acknowledge it and the inclosures with
which you were so good to favor me I beg you to accept my thanks for
gratifying your Castle friends with the very interesting news of Dublin, by
desiring Lady G[ranard] to open my letters during my absence — it
happened most fortunately that your directions to that effect were written in
the cover, for I had not at that time returned from Westmeath where I had
been for a few days on a hunting party — You have in some measure,
'though not entirely, done away my anxiety for our mutual friends at
Milltown — the confinement of Mrs E,[1] however voluntary, cannot in my
mind be totally devoid of danger — I shall be much surprised if this
momentous day has passed in perfect tranquillity, or even without consider-

able commotion; and should that insurrection which I think the infamous measure now depending so imperiously calls for from a people not yet totally enslaved, should take place while she is still in their power, I cannot even for a moment encourage the hope that the villainous agents of the still more vile administration would not sacrifice to their resentment, or rather to their revenge, even the unoffending relatives of the men who possessed the virtue and the courage to attempt the emancipation of their countrymen — Not only I, but I may add *we*, (for the inhabitants of this mansion are equally anxious,) will be miserable till we hear the events of this momentous night.[2] I beseech you will therefore ease our apprehensions for our friends, and by the return of post make us acquainted with their fate — How admirable was the conduct of A.C.[3] to the valorous thief-catcher! I enjoyed it from my heart, and have to lament that his associates and himself have not more frequently met such treatment.

Inclosed I take the liberty of sending you a letter which I am sure you will have much pleasure in delivering to Miss E. and with it I trust you will have the goodness to say everything from me that a most sincere esteem and the highest admiration of her talents can dictate to you — I rely entirely on you to assure that whole family how truly grateful I feel for their goodness to me, and how mortified I am at the delay which has prevented my calling on them before this time. You will perceive by the letter which I inclose[4] that I have heard from Moore Park. Lady M[ountcashell] speaks as [you] would wish, and in a manner which, as your friend, has gratified me most exceptionally — She was extremely sorry you could not make a longer stay, but has hopes of seeing you there at some other time.

[P.S.] I have many apologies to make for numerous mistakes, but really your friend Miss F[ord] has so tormented me while writing that I knew but little of my subject. [*Source*: Scully Papers]

[1]Jane Patten, wife of Thomas Addis Emmet, who had been in gaol with the other leaders of the United Irishmen since May, 1798. She was confined with him because, having secured permission to visit him at Newgate, she gained entry and refused to leave. She was later allowed to follow him to Kilmainham, where he now was. Bribing the gaoler's wife, she made one sortie to visit a sick child at Casino but otherwise remained with her husband until he was deported to Port George on 20 March 1799 (Thomas Addis Emmet MD, *Memoirs of Thomas Addis and Robert Emmet*, New York, 1915).

[2]The opening of the Irish Parliament, when the measure of a legislative union was expected to be announced in the King's Speech.

[3]Unidentified. "Thief-catcher" was probably, like "thief-taker", slang for a police officer.

[4]Apparently a letter from Lady Mount Cashell to Miss Emmet (see No. 13).

13   *From Revd John Murphy to Suffolk Street*

Castle Forbes, 23 January 1799

My dear Sir,

I have many apologies to offer for my neglect relative to Miss E[mmet]'s letter — 'twas my intention to have forwarded it and I had it upon the table for the purpose of inclosing it in my last; but, to be candid, I was really so much worried by two or three ladies who sat by me, and who from the moment I took up my pen insisted that I wanted to compose a letter full of "prettyisms" (if I may be allowed the expression) that I not only neglected what I should have considered most material (the forwarding Lady M[ountcashell]'s letter) but also, I fear, trespassed upon your goodness by expecting you should wade through what at the moment of sealing it, I was totally ignorant of — tho' little better circumstanced tonight, I will be more particular with regard to my inclosure, and rely solely on you to obtain my pardon from my interesting and invaluable friend, Miss E.

Our letters from Dublin by this morning's post afford but little hope that our "virtuous representatives" will oppose the legislative union with England, so contrary and opposite to the wishes of the Irish people — are we then to become in the true and literal sense "West Britons"? or will not rather the indignant spirit of our common countrymen rise in opposition to a system which threatens not only to render themselves despicable in the eyes of Europe, but also to engulf posterity and their country in that *charibdis* whence they never can hope an escape. Much as I have been interested in those scenes which have of late occupied our attention, I candidly acknowledge that the present complexion of affairs is so much more gloomy than anything I have hitherto witnessed, that my heart sinks at the prospect and I shall fear if we are mean enough quietly to submit to this projected union, that the liberty of Ireland is lost for ever. I beseech you therefore to take the trouble not only of acquainting me with what has passed upon the subject, but also to give me an opinion which I really look up to (you will not consider it flattery when I say I mean your own) upon this interesting subject — An express this moment from Dublin — Good God! and is it possible we have lost the question by a single voice?[1] What has become of Wm. Moore?[2] Had he been in his place as he should have been, on what high ground would this poor country have stood — Never again could the measure have been proposed, never again would any man have presumed to sink the independence of Ireland in an union with a country which she ever has had reason to detest. You must forgive my concluding this hastily — I have no one consolation at this moment, but in the hope however faint, that we have still the spirit to assert our liberties — God bless you — I beg to be most affectionately remembered to my friends.

[P.S.] Lady G[ranard] has insisted upon my opening this to assure you that nothing but the very agitated state of her mind should have prevented her writing to you before this time — if you have any pity do we beseech you send us details of all you hear and see.   [*Source*: Scully Papers]

[1]The reference is to the defeat by 106 to 105 votes of an amendment to the address moved by the opposition, asserting the right of Ireland to an independent legislature as settled in 1782 (*FJ*, 24 January 1799).
[2]For the explanation of his absence see No. 14.

14   *From Lady Moira to Suffolk Street*

Castle Forbes, 26 January 1799

By the best of all possible young curates, as he is denominated by all Mr Scully's young friends beneath this roof, I convey these lines to thank him for his obliging letter & the pamphlet. As Mr Davison[1] was going to town I prefered sending it by him rather than by the posts, for I would not choose to be thought to doubt by Lees & Co.[2] Yet notwithstanding the *hitherto* appearance of success, I apprehend that the business is but commenced, & that many a trick will be played the consequences of which cannot be foreseen. Out of 300 members only 214 have appeared on this momentous occasion.[3] What are become of the other 86? Is it from apathy or intention that they have kept away? If from the former cause, as well as from the latter, a majority may certainly still be purchased from amidst these absentees by Government. The plan believe me is not given up; if asserted it is only to put the opposition to it off their guard — It was shameful the Bishops (in the mass) voting as they did,[4] persons without a shilling of landed property in the kingdom, holding all they possessed in honorable trust for their successors — equal was the shameful procedure of such English Irish peers who are merely titular Your Lordships, without any property in this kingdom. — We have not any intelligence here but what comes from Dublin, that of insurrections & rebels being again on foot so near to us as Athlone, certainly not true or we shd. have learnt it from a place within twenty miles of this place — Upon Lord Granard's return I intend setting out for Dublin (when there is a tolerable moon for travelling) & I think you will not quit Ireland till you see what is the issue of the present pursuit of Administration — Lord Cornwallis I conclude will go immediately, & his successor undertake in some new method the same game — & I should think a dissolution of Parlt. not improbable — I am anxious to learn how Mr George Moore does, after that anxiety he must have so tediously endured & which is not yet come to its termination — & I fear that measures of lenity will be exchanged for harsh proceedings[5] — I grieve that the mob are grown active, it being an unfortunate circumstance, for the point in debate, & for the national welfare at this juncture — Lady Granard & Miss

Forde desire to be most particularly remembered with their best comp —
Lady Elizabeth sends many thanks for the ribbon[6] & joins with Lord Forbes,
her sister Adelaide, Francis & Hastings in very cordial remembrances — I
agree with you perfectly respecting the opinion you have given of the
pamphlet. I was much mortified at Mr Wm. Moore's delay, had he been
arrived the first day the numbers wd have been even & the Speaker wd have
had the casting voice; the ill wind that blew the vessel he was in to off the Isle
of Man blew good for the Castle, tho' bad for the Speaker, whose triumph
could he have thus given his wished for decision on the first motion must
have been complete — Our friend Lady M — will regret this disappointment
as much as I do. Her Ladyship will be gratified by Ld. M's conduct in the
House of Lords.[7]

I am persuaded that you will stay to behold the issue of a contest so
material to your native land, & that from the arrogance & folly of the
schemers that it will be pursued I am convinced, and therefore I am sure that
if it pleases God that I shd live to return to town I shall have the pleasure of
seeing you in Dublin.   [*Source*: Scully Papers]

[1]Probably Revd Francis Davidson, Curate of Moyglare in the diocese of Meath;
Rector of Clanrickard 1813.
[2]John Lees was Secretary of the Post Office.
[3]In the night of 24 January the opposition in the Irish House of Commons had
succeeded in deleting from an amendment to the Address a paragraph referring to
the proposed legislative union. The voting had been 109 for and 104 against, making
with the Speaker a total of 214 (*FJ* 26 January 1799).
[4]On the motion for the Address to the King of 22 January only the Bishop of Down
and Connor had voted against the Union (*Journal of the Irish House of Lords* p. 193).
[5]He was probably anxious about his elder brother, Counsellor John Moore, who was
in solitary confinement awaiting trial for having accepted office under the French
invaders as President of the Provisional Administration of Connaught (*The Times*,
27 September 1798, 30 October 1798, 19 November 1798; Hayes: *The last invasion of
Ireland*). He died at Waterford 6 December 1799.
[6]By the first week in December ribbons were beginning to be worn in Dublin: they
were of Garter blue inscribed in silver with the words "British Connection. Irish
Independence. No Union" (*The Times* 14 & 16 December 1798).
[7]The Earl of Mount Cashell had been one of twelve peers who voted against the
Union in the debate on the Address (*Journal* p. 193).

15   *From Revd John Murphy*

                                    Castle Forbes, 29 January [1799]
My dear Sir,
I have just now received by the stage your kind letter of Sunday for
which I beg you to accept my most sincere thanks — the information

however which it contained relative to my last inclosure for Miss E[mmet] has excited a degree of surprise as well as indignation which cannot well subside while there remains a hope or probability of exposing and punishing the person who could be guilty of an act so very mean and base as prying into the secrets and correspondence of families — Lord F[orbes] was so good as to seal the letter in which he also folded my inclosure, and Ly G[ranard] sent it by the stage under cover to Hart at M[oira] H[ouse] — so that if you will take the trouble to request of Miss E. to let me have this unfortunate letter again, we shall find it no very difficult matter to detect the person who could be guilty of so very infamous an act. Lady M[oira] will also write to enquire which of the servants left it at your lodging, so that there can be no doubt of our fixing it upon the right person, and I am sure you will agree with me that it is a duty incumbent on us all to detect him and as far as in us lies prevent his practising such acts in future — I am more mortified at it than I can well tell you, having been advised to keep the letter in my possession 'till my return to town; but, being positive, I thought no accident could happen from forwarding it by the stage — I know 'tis unnecessary to press what you can do toward easing my mind about it — I will therefore say no more at present upon the subject.

You seem to be of opinion that Govt. will be so very imprudent as to attempt once more at least the carrying of a measure so decidedly contrary to the sentiments of the people and the opinion of Parliament as the union — probably it may be so, but after reading the debate of Thursday as reported in the *D[ublin] E[vening] P[ost]*[1] I am so sanguine as to think they will not bring the question forward very suddenly, tho' in this belief I have the presumption to differ not only from you but from the greater number of my friends here — a short time at any rate will do away that suspence which the independence of our country naturally causes in a true Irish heart.

When you visit Milltown[2] I intreat you will have the goodness to be very particular in saying everything from me which the highest respect and esteem on my part can dictate to you.

[P.S.] Many thanks for my ribbons.   [*Source*: Scully Papers]

[1]Of 24 January.
[2]Where the Emmets lived.

16   *From the Countess of Granard*

[Castle Forbes] 29 January 1799

Dear Sir,

I feel very censurable in not having sooner acknowledged your most obliging attention in writing to me, but the truth is my anxious mind has been so devoted to the national question that I was incapable of thinking of any thing else — Your ribbons[1] are admirable, Ponsy[2] completely taken in but suspects Hardy for being the friend who sent him his — & you pass unsuspected. I got two from my nephew[3] before I received yours, & clearer sighted than Ponsy — grasped immediately by whom they originated with, more from the neat cleverness of the device than from the motto — I have not been faithless as to the promised memoir, which I promised you, but some very curious facts having been hinted to me, to embellish it with, I wait only to authenticate them, & add them to the notes already written for you and then I shall transfer the office of an episcopal biographer to a much abler pen than mine, & I flatter myself with perseverance that we may repay some of our country's wrongs to that learned prelate[4] whose irritable pride & low born self sufficiency makes him open to every attack which lowers his dignity.

I am very triumphant & very happy at the turn things have taken but by no means satisfied. I have seen enough of the world to know that nothing is so injurious to a cause as the calm which succeeds a victory, if not followed up with spirit. — There were many absentees may be brought forward & many tricks played, & they either should vote an exclusion to the question of union, by a penalty on whosoever should dare to propose it, or vote short money bills, otherwise the Parliament will be dissolved & union carried. All this circle join in best compts. to you, & will all rejoice whenever they can have the pleasure of again seeing you here. I hear there is a pamphlet called the Philosopher[5] which is admirable, tho' suppressed by the hand of power. Would you get it for me, perhaps your friends at Milltown[6] could put you in the line of doing so. Have the goodness when you have leisure to recollect your county of Longford friends by a few lines & believe me, dear Sir,

Your very much obliged Humble servt.

[P.S.] Murphy is in a fidget about his letter.[7] I think Lady M[ount] C[ashell] who is very careless did not seal down the wafer well.

If you get the pamphlet don't trust it to post or any thing particular — a sealed parcel left at M[oira] House for me will always come safe.

[*Source*: Scully Papers]

[1]See No. 14 n.6.
[2]Probably Revd Ponsonby Gouldsbury, Lord Forbes' tutor (see No. 30).
[3]Probably the Earl of Mount Cashell whose mother was Lady Granard's half-sister.
[4]Dr T. L. O'Beirne. The memoir is referred to again in No. 25.
[5]*A demonstration of the necessity of a legislative union of Great Britain and Ireland, involving the refutation of every argument that has been or can be urged against that measure*, by a Philosopher, College Green, 1799. Drennan (*Letters* No. 744 of 15 January 1799) identifies the author as Robert Holmes (who married Maryanne Emmet in the autumn). Ostensibly on the theme that the union was inevitable, it

represented it as the death of the country and the authorities, who stopped the sale, may have seen a covert call to rebellion in the exhortation, printed in capital letters, "Let no country submit to be a province which has strength to be a nation".
[6]Where the Emmets lived.
[7]See No. 15.

17   *From Joanna Scully to Lr. Suffolk Street, Dublin*

Kilfeacle [Co. Tipperary] 30 January 1799

My dear Den's,

I received your affectionate Letter of the 26 and thank you for all the intelligence it contained, which here I assure you is a great treat. I am very glad that the Union was rejected, as I was afraid if it was agreed on that you would go live to England.[1] My Unkle Ned[2] is very unwell this week past with the Gout; Mrs J. Murphy[3] has got a young Daughter. The Jail of Mitchelstown was broke open by the Rebels friday night last. The Co. Clare is now perfectly quiet. Jam's[4] sent his last Letter to you by Alleyn[5] the attorney. He mentioned to you that he would send it by Ware[6] but my Father preferred the former. Let me know your opinion of Mrs S. Roches[7] & her Sister. Mrs M[8] is allarming these here every Letter that she is dangerously ill & that the Physicians order her to Buxton if she does not recover immediately. What she is at is to try if my Father will take her but I think she will be disappointed for I don't think he will go this year there. I think it must [be] very fatigueing to you & I am afraid injurious to your health sitting up so late at the Debates. My Father answered Mr Ledwills[9] Letter. We had Nick Maher & his son Vall here for 2 days. Vall returns to Dublin with the Father.

I remain my dear Den's your attached sister Joanna Scully.

[P.S.] We have received the Books perfectly safe & my Father is highly pleased with your bargain & only regrets that he had not them those years past. They are really most valuable Books in a House. [*Source*: Scully Papers]

[1]William Drennan wrote to his sister on 28 October 1798: "The prospect of the Union and, as the young lawyers say, the consequent ruin of their professional prospects in this country, lead them all to declare they will leave it. . . ." (*Letters* No. 724).
[2]Edmund Scully of Cashel.
[3]Her 1st cousin Mary Canny, who married a John Murphy on 21 July 1796.
[4]Her brother James Scully.
[5]Samuel Alleyn, of Goldenville, who was married to a daughter of William Scully of Tipperary and was on friendly terms with the Scullys of Kilfeacle. He was an attorney who practised in Main Street, Tipperary, and 7 Castle Street, Dublin.
[6]Possibly Bartholomew Ware, an attorney of 64 Stephen's Green, Dublin.
[7]Unidentified — perhaps the wife of the Stephen Roche mentioned in No. 479B.
[8]Her sister Anne, wife of Thomas Mahon.
[9]Probably one of the Lidwills of Dromard.

18   *From Lady Moira to Suffolk Street*

Castle Forbes, 6 February 1799

[No salutation]

I defered writing till William's return, as being a more certain conveyance.
He returns to his duty with what I esteem langor & apathy. He will act
honorably whether or *no* that his heart & soul is in the pursuit, & I think Mr
George Ponsonby will not let him loiter, as that orator has the tye of
connection to empower him to watch & urge[1] — Those who have interest or
connections in the county of Cork are at least lukewarm — The ignorance of
all that has past respecting the Irish debates in England prevents my entering
upon that subject — Perhaps before William goes some intelligence may
arrive — My opinion is that the union will be attempted with redoubled force
& obstinacy, & when I consider how easily people are terrified in this
kingdom, how inconstant is the multitude, & how depraved the bulk of
mankind, I am apt to fear that those who nobly have taken the advanced case
will not be supported. I have been told that the bulk of the Roman Catholics
have acted a weak part divested of the credit of calm independence, that
they have substituted for it servile adulation — & that this conduct has
resulted from secret promises, not to be divulged. Private letters say that Mr
Pitt in his speech was bitter against the Roman Catholics, & repeatedly
asserted that he would not grant them any thing[2] — Lord Camden[3] came
over for that purpose, Mr Pelham[4] avouched it in the Irish House, the
present Secretary bred a rigid Presbyterian[5] from early prejudice & from
subjection to the projects of the English Minister, will not be less intolerant
than the late Viceroy & his English dictator — to the Roman Catholics is
attributed in England the late rebellion, stained with every cruelty &
atrocity that human fancy can invent, & the hundreds of Protestants shut up
in their church for their religion & burnt to death, is credited like the Gospel
— I did not particularly learn the words of Mr Pitt in his speech concerning
the Roman Catholics, nor can I conceive perfectly why it was omitted in the
Courier[6] — I have indeed been informed that Mr Pitt's popularity was never
at so great a heighth [*sic*], from his having overcome the horrid rebellion of
the papists, who intended to murder all the Protestants — With such a
current belief, false as it is, do you think any concessions will be made to the
Roman Catholics? And according to the insidiousness of the Secretary & his
employers, is any dependence to be placed upon secret promises for the
future? — That the Roman Catholics shd. be silent & quiet may be prudent
& proper — But that they should be brought to sign a request for the union
wd. be giving themselves a death blow whichever party prevailed — One
party wd. recollect the surrender of rights which once yielded to their

adversaries they wd. have no right to claim; & the other wd. state their self renunciation as a power to do what they pleased with them. — The ribbon you inclosed was most admirable both as to the design & device — I received one before I recd yrs, such was the pleasing reception it gained, & the haste to distribute it — I intend to have a painting taken of it by one of my protegés when I come to town, to have the remembrance of the idea preserved for posterity — With some additions an excellent caricature might be made of it — The Secretary beating Time (Time represented in his artist figure) to which might be added many other alluding figures & written devices — Our weather is unpleasant, excessive cold, & frost, & snow, the latter threatening to increase.

Lord Granard is at Clonhugh,[7] he will leave before the 11th if it is necessary for him to attend the House — Lady Granard & Miss Forde request their best compts. Your young friends talk of you perpetually, & as you wd. like, for in the affectionate sincerity of early youth there is something that is particularly engaging — They all desire to be particularly remembered to you. Mr Murphy is with Lord Granard, Mr Goldsbury attendant on Lord Forbes lost in guesses his most prevalent one resting on the quiet passive Mr Hardy, who cannot exert himself on any point but political speaking. — As Mr Moore does not go till his attendance on the 11th[8] I inclose this to town — I shall trouble you, Sr., with a small packet for England to my dear Charlotte,[9] it is not of any bulk — You will therefore hear from me in the course of next week as I fear I shall not see you before you quit Ireland.

[P.S.] Mr Moore not going as I expected I inclose this to Dublin.

[*Source*: Scully Papers]

[1]William Moore's name does not appear on either side of the division list of 25 January (*Hibernian Journal*, 28 January 1799). His eldest son voted for the Union and (according to W. P. Burke, *History of Clonmel*, p. 321) was rewarded with a postermastership.

[2]In moving resolutions for the Union on 31 January Pitt made it clear that the admission of Catholics to power even after the Union depended on their conduct and temper (*Parliamentary History*, XXXIV, 254). Lord Holland, in his *Memoirs of the Whig Party*, (London, 1852–54) p. 139 says that opponents of the Union reprinted and circulated the speech and quotes Lord Lansdowne as remarking that "there's a great deal of gout" in it.

[3]The 2nd Earl, Lord Lieutenant 1794–8.

[4]Thomas Pelham (later 2nd Earl of Chichester), Irish Secretary 1795–8.

[5]Although Viscount Castlereagh had been educated as a member of the established church his father was a Calvinist (H. Montgomery Hyde, *The Rise of Castlereagh*, 1933, p. 37).

[6]The *Freeman's Journal*, which published a summary on 5 February, did not publish the full text until the 9th.

[7]Near Mullingar, where he had a lodge.

[8]A matter affecting his constituency was to be raised. On 11 February Jonah Barrington alleged that the military had intervened to deter discussion on the Union, particularly at Clonmel. If Moore intended to speak he did not get the opportunity as the Speaker ruled that there was no case before the House (*Dublin Journal*, 12 February 1799).

[9]Her daughter, Lady Charlotte Rawdon.

19   *From Lady Granard to Suffolk Street*

[Castle Forbes], 7 February 1799

Dr. Sir,

As the post is quicker than another opportunity, I write merely to say that I received the two novels[1] you sent me perfectly safe, & am infinitely pleased & gratified by their perusal. If you can get copies of them do get two more, for a friend of mine in England who loves foolish books as well as I do — & keep them 'till you hear again from me which shall be very soon. All your friends here join in a thousand compts. & good wishes to you.

[*Source*: Scully Papers]

[1]See postscript of the following letter.

20   *From Lady Granard to Suffolk Street*

8 February [1799]

[No salutation]

Many many thanks for your letter & pamphlets — they are incomparable, that to Lord Castlereagh[1] will gall them ten times more than the other, because it will suit all comprehensions, & be understood by vulgar as well as enlightened minds — *The Philosopher*[2] might be circulated with great safety — how few country squires are there who would understand a page of it? none within my neighbourhood I will venture to vouch, it is admirably written but the simpler stile of O'Connor's will have more weight with the multitude — & every man capable of distinguishing right from wrong will be shocked at the statement he makes of the treatment he has received — When men or ministers deviate from integrity, the next step is to have recourse to every vicious subterfuge to hide what they dare not justify. I shudder & recoil from the times we live in when such things could happen. — I burned your letter, because in these days I make it a point of honor to trust nothing to chance when my friends are so kind as to communicate their opinions to me, therefore whenever you do write rely on that attention & I will expect the same from you —

If you go to England, Willy (Mr Moore) will ask you to carry a letter for me, & if you can get duplicates of those pamphlets you will do me the greatest favor if you will carry them to my brother[3] for me — the notes you wrote in those I got are an admirable illustration to draw their attention to the main points — Lord G. begs his best compts. & will intreat you if you make but a short stay in London, to bring him over a hat which Lord Moira's own man Clarke has for him — this is treating you as a friend to give you this trouble without ceremony & allow me to give you a caution, if my married sister[4] should be at my brother's, when you call there, do not speak on politics before her, as you would before my younger, for she differs in opinion from her family — I am sorry you have given up your Hamburgh excursion[5] because it would have been very pleasant but I trust a quiet summer will enable you to resume it. If you should not go, if you could get me the pamphlets Willy Moore may be safely trusted with them, as he is impressed with proper caution & will send them by some safe conveyance — We are much obliged by your promise of visiting us, which we shall most selfishly remind you of, when you have leisure. All your friends here join in best compts.

[P.S.] I wrote you a few lines by post to acknowledge the receipt of the pamphlets by post, stiling them novels.   [*Source*: Scully Papers]

[1]Arthur O'Connor's pamphlet *A letter to Lord Castlereagh* had appeared in Dublin on 30 January. It accused the Chief Secretary of having violated the government's compact of 29 July 1798 with the leaders of the United Irishmen. O'Connor, who had been in Kilmainham Gaol, was transferred on 7 February to the harsher conditions of Newgate (*The Times* 9 February 1799).
[2]See No. 16 n.5.
[3]The 2nd Earl of Moira.
[4]Her elder sister Anne, wife of the 1st Earl of Aylesbury, who was Treasurer of the Queen's Household and owned a borough which returned members supporting the administration (Aspinall: *Later Correspondence of George III*, No. 2583).
[5]No more is heard of the proposed excursion.

21   *From Lady Moira to Suffolk Street*

Castle Forbes, Saturday 9 February [1799]

Lady Moira finds that she has made a grievous blunder respecting Mr Scully's going to England, supposing that the twentieth not the twelfth was the day, & has but just found out her mistake — However, she thinks that Mr Scully will stay a day or two till the weather is settled, & by the Longford coach on the twelfth at noon a small parcel will be at Moira House which Lady Moira will request him to carry for her to Lady Charlotte — Mr William Moore is hastening off for his Parliament on Monday & Lady M. has only time to transmit her best remembrances & those of all the family beneath this roof to Mr Scully.   [*Source*: Scully Papers]

22   *From Lady Moira to Southern Bar, Waterford*

Castle Forbes, 23 March 1799

Dr. Sr.

I had the pleasure last night of getting your letter from Dublin, by a person coming down to this house — & it afforded me much pleasure to find that you were safely arrived — & we likewise congratulate with you on your successful prosecution.[1] I have been tormented with repeated inflamations in my eyes & am at this time tormented with one of these attacks — but I would not omit a single post acknowledging your letter. I recd. a letter from Mrs Moore, & as she was so obliging to offer to make further [genealogical] inquiries I troubled her again with a request. . . . I am extremely obliged to you for acquiring the Verstigan.[2] When I consider however that I am on the threshold as it were to quit my tenement of clay, I feel how ridiculous it is for me to be amused with antiquarian researches — & yet such is the singular propensity of some minds to this favourite pursuit, that tho' admitted to be fruitless & unavailing nothing but death can extinguish ideas that might almost be pronounced innate.

As to Story's narrative[3] it is one proof out of many what the representations of history are — Yet from that exaggerated acct. — a statement may be made of the numbers who fell in those wars, & what have fallen victims in the present rebellion — and many other conjectures can be made from it — Of the falsity of the relations given there is very recent testimony, in a spurious letter (for such it must be) of Genl. Nugent to Genl. Lake printed in the military magazine[4] respecting the battle of Ballynahinch — which is pourtrayed in colours superior to a victory of the great Frederic over his opponents, if it does not create him the stated hero therein equal to Julius Caesar. & not only relates what is contrary to the bulletins of the day but likewise asserts impossibilities: the surrounding of a wood by a Col. Stewart[5] on one side, which was bounded & secured by the river on the other, is one instance; the wood extends at least three quarters of an English mile, & the river in the summer months may be passed dry-shod in many places, in the others not ancle deep; he took from the rebels 8 guns, the wretches had two small iron ship guns, which they could not fire; it appears by the acct. that they fled carrying off their dead, tho' cars, provisions, a great quantity of ammunition (which they had not) was left behind. A note is added to this acct. replete with many more lies, that that acct. would have been published in the Dublin Gazette but that the mail by which it was sent to Genl. Lake was robbed. I shall investigate that assertion — as I think I have letters from the north of the same date which arrived safe — You will receive from Dublin later public news than I can transmit — I expect to be in Dublin soon, to pass a few weeks there, & then return to Lady Granard as I conclude that Lord G. must rejoin his regt. I am detained at present by an old person lying in their death-bed at Moira-House. We have some patriarchal customs in our family, the poor woman is mother to upper servants of mine & Lady Granard, & she resided with me to pass the remnant of her days in quiet & indolence. My servant Hart & Lady G's woman are gone to attend her dying moments (being her son-in-law & daughter). When the melancholy scene is concluded & Hart is returned to attend me on my journey I shall directly set off for Dublin & shall meet you there, possibly by the time you reach it — Lord & Lady Granard, Lord Forbes & all the young people send you not mere compts but a thousand friendly remembrances. Miss Forde & Mr Murphy unite in best compts.   [*Source*: Scully Papers]

[1]Scully was on the Leinster Circuit and the Assizes of Waterford had begun on 11 March. The prosecution has not been identified.

[2]Richard Verstegan alias Rowlands (under which name he is entered in the *DNB*) was an antiquary who set up a printing business in Antwerp and assumed his grandfather's name. Scully's Common Place Book shows that the work he bought for Lady Moira was his *Restitution of Decayed Intelligence in Antiquities*, first published in 1605, at Antwerp. It is a history of the origins of the English people, with chapters also on the Anglo-Saxon language, philology and etymology.

[3]George Walter Story, author of *An Impartial History of the War in Ireland*, 1691–3, on which Scully comments in his Common Place Book: "This is a scarce and interesting work, written by a Dutchman, who had attached himself to the service of [King] William — He writes with tolerable fairness, & much humanity — generally free from the prejudice and party spirit of the day, and affording abundant room to an impartial reader to collect the real facts and events of the wars in Ireland from 1689 to 1691".

[4]The report has not been found. Lady Moira was familiar with the topography as the battle was fought on the Moira lands.

[5]Lieutenant-Colonel Charles William Stewart, commanding the 5th Regiment of Dragoons (disbanded for indiscipline 12 January 1799); half-brother of Viscount Castlereagh and later 3rd Marquis of Londonderry.

23   *From Revd John Murphy to Suffolk Street*

Castle Forbes, Sunday [14 April 1799]

[No salutation]

It is with much pleasure I avail myself of a wish expressed by Lady Moira, that I should apologise to you for the length of time she has suffered to elapse without any acknowledgment of your last kind letter and Inclosure — this I have the more readily undertaken as it gives me an opportunity of renewing

a correspondence the interruption of which I have not ceased to regret —
Lady Moira has for some weeks had a feverish cold attended with a very
considerable inflammation in her eyes — the hope of a favourable change in
the weather, which she hoped would be equally favourable to her health,
induced her to postpone from day to day the answering your letter thro' the
medium of a second person; but as she feels so very particularly obliged both
to you and your genealogical friend,[1] for your kind attentions, she could not
longer defer the acknowledgment of a favor which she hopes her health will
permit her to thank you for in a few days — If not inconvenient she also begs
you will mention to your friend, Mrs Moore, how uneasy she has felt under
an indisposition, which has deprived her of the satisfaction she derived from
the receipt of her very kind letter — to this I have to intreat you will add my
best compliments. — Mrs Moore is a lady for whom I feel the highest
respect, as well from your representation of her character, as from
possessing an indescribeable something in her manner and appearance,
which, however I may admire, I have so very rarely met with.

Would it not be in your power to come down here for a few days? Ly.
G[ranard] desires I will say how happy it will make her that she might have
an opportunity of personally thanking you for her book — You will
doubtless call at Milltown as frequently as your business will permit —
however often it may be, I beg you will always assure them of my best wishes
— Mr Patten[2] has a pamphlet for me — have the goodness to ask it of him,
and send it to me — if left sealed up with Mrs Walsh at M[oira] H[ouse] she
can forward it by the first person coming down — I have not one word of
news to send you — this part of the country is perfectly tranquil — how long
it will continue so 'tis impossible to say — at present there is no appearance
whatever of commotion — but this may be the deceitful calm which presages
the tempest — Adieu —   [*Source*: Scully Papers]

[1]Probably the Mr Colpitts mentioned by Lady Moira at the end of No. 31.
[2]John Patten, brother of Thomas Addis Emmet's wife.

24   *From Lady Moira to Suffolk Street*

Castle Forbes, 19 April 1799
[No salutation]
I desired Mr M[urphy] to write a few lines mentioning that indisposition
had prevented me from being able to acknowledge yr obliging letter & the
very kind communications of your ingenious friend.[1] How I envy you such an
acquaintance & to covet such an instructor I do believe is not a breach of the
commandments. The different pursuits of the human mind are wonderfully
singular, there is not any research into antiquity however apparently

uninteresting & dry that I do not prefer to any other pursuit of inquiry; tho' I never met with a person that had the slightest inclination for such an occupation, or could yield me further assistance than the naming of certain books which contained information on the points. As for genealogical knowledge, it is so combined with the development of historical facts, that I am convinced it is absolutely requisite to the ascertaining of the latter as far as they may be ascertained. — Tho' I am rather inclined to agree with Lord Orford (the famous Sr Robert Walpole) who being in his old age & retirement asked by his son (the late Lord Orford[2]) whether he should to divert him read to him some history, he answered Oh no; my son, for I know them to be all lies — The repeated attacks of inflammation & subsequent weakness in my eyes has not only been troublesome in the debarring me from writing, & vexatious in preventing my acknowledgment of obliging attentions, but has impressed me with the gloomy reflection, that even diminished eye-sight in the decline of life is a heavier calamity than in youthful days. — *That* independence which results from the employment of the mind, by reading & writing, is in everyone's power who can feel the value of self-occupation — and the infirmity & weight of years is heavily increased by being incapacitated to benefit from such a soother of time — I have resolved to have recourse to the metallic tractors[3] of which I have heard much from England affirmed by persons not credulous and was recommended to purchase them (& have done so) from a Mr Langworthy,[4] who was recommended to Lady Charlotte by a person who knows his family. Langworthy is by profession a surgeon & well spoken of in that profession. The other vendor of these modern sorceries or witchcraft is said not to be endowed with genuine skill therein. I forget his name, but he advertises — Verstigan & Story[5] reached this place late last night — the former a most delightful acquisition to me — the latter Lady Granard wished for, as it is much mentioned by various writers, some as a collection of truths, others as a compilation of lies. But there is not infrequently curious matter to be extracted from the extremes of lying — I conclude at the period in which it was written there was not any answer to it published.

There is much to say about the times, if weak eyes did not feel that the subject was too extensive for a sheet of paper to contain — & also doubt show[s] it to be too subtil for prudence to dwell upon — The proceedings in Parliament respecting Sheriff Fitzgerald must be termed scandalous, as they will throw into a strange appearance to other nations the presiding governors & Parliament of this kingdom[6] — the Chancellor's attack upon the Roman Catholics[7] extraordinary — Lord Granard, Lord Forbes & a party of gentlemen have been for now a week past at Clonhugh in Westmeath — I have been prevented coming to Dublin for some time past by a person who lies upon her death-bed in my house — I never shun mortality nor quit my house on that account, but I do not seek funereal scenes — What becomes of you? Another visit to Castle Forbes, when embellished with the appearance of summer, is as fully expected as wished for — But as to the destiny of Lord Granard, where or when he is to go from home, or whether he will be permitted to stay with his family, is not known — He will not be one of those who offer to carry his regiment out of the kingdom, thinking it very unfair to the individuals, men ballotted for on terms of public faith, who compass it; either to deceive them to yield compliance, or give his own consent.[8] — There have certainly been great victories, & the French have hitherto always as rapidly declined in their conquests after a defeat or two as they have risen in their successes — may it now be so.

[P.S.] May I intreat you to make my excuses to Mrs Moore for having as yet left her last obliging letter unacknowledged, which the complaint in my eyes has occasioned. [Source: Scully Papers]

[1]Probably Colpitts (see No. 31).

[2]Horace Walpole.

[3]Two short pieces of metal, which were alternately drawn or stroked over the affected part. They were invented by an American, Elisha Perkins (1741–1799), whose son opened an office in Leicester Square, London, in 1795. In 1800 Dr John Haygarth of Bath (in *DNB*) read a paper on *The imagination as a cause and a cure of disorders in the body*, claiming he had effected as many cures with tractors of painted wood, but this did not stop the foundation of a Perkinean Institute in London in 1803 (*Dictionary of American Biography*).

[4]According to Haygarth the agent for England. Probably the surgeon William S. Langworthy. The agent in Dublin seems to have been a Mr Porter, who advertised in *Saunder's News Letter* of 10 April 1799.

[5]See No. 22.

[6]On 14th March 1799 Thomas Judkin Fitzgerald had been convicted by a Clonmel jury on a charge of battery and assault inflicted on Bernard Wright during the rebellion. On 6 April Lord Mathew had presented a petition from him to be indemnified for acts done by him as High Sheriff of Tipperary, and had also asked for an investigation by the House of Commons itself to consider evidence that might endanger Fitzgerald's sources if given in open court. Strong opposition having been voiced to the intervention of the legislature in an individual case it had been announced on 16 April that a bill would be brought in extending the provisions of the existing Indemnity Act. This was passed on 22 April and the verdict of the Clonmel jury set aside (Howell, *State Trials*, XVII, 766–819).

[7]In a speech of 15 April on the grant to Maynooth College (*FJ* 16 April 1799).

[8]Under the Militia Act of 1793 (33 Geo. III Ch. XXII) recruits engaged to serve in Ireland.

25   *From Lady Granard to Suffolk Street*

Castle Forbes, 2 June 1799

Dear Sir,

I have to acknowledge your most obliging letter & inclosures — which I received safe & will return by Mr Verschoyle[1] who goes up in two or three days — the letter is admirably written & will assist our biographical friend — I will transmit you all anecdotes & you shall revise & compile them, for though our friend may be equal to collecting facts for memoirs, their [sic] talents are very inadequate to arranging them — One grand fact has come to my knowledge which is that the person in question was refused ordination for your church, from episcopal disapprobation of his morality tho' afterwards received into ours.[2] The letter to Lady M. contains a question I cannot answer without an enquiry from a person I expect to see in Westmeath, but as it is merely domestic business that delay makes no difference. The post office have been cruel to us about letters, very few written by either to each other reach their destination — I hope if they read this, that library researches, and domestic annals, will not meet their high & potent disapprobation.

My mother is better & we all go to Clonhugh Lodge in the county of Westmeath for about three weeks tomorrow, our post town is Mullingar & an every day post — I wish we had any chance of seeing you there, it would give all your friends great pleasure & a daily mail coach is not inconvenient, you could come & go without delay — do think of it. All the circle of your friends here join in best compts. to you — A thousand thanks for the book which I am greatly obliged to you for, those sort of old books throw much more light on historical facts than newer works, — & from men's own boasts, written in the fury of party — when that party has subsided by time, one can fairly judge of their misconduct, for what they took pride in, in later ages covers them with [word missing].   [*Source*: Scully Papers]

[1]John Verschoyle, rent collector for the Moira Dublin estates.
[2]The reference is to Dr T. L. O'Beirne, Bishop of Meath, who had been refused admission to the Irish College in Paris for failing to bring back from his parish priest a certificate of having frequented the sacraments regularly. "There is not an ounce of priest's flesh on this young man's bones" said the President of the College, "he *may* turn out a good layman, but he would certainly be a *bad priest*". (Anthony Cogan, *Diocese of Meath*, II, (Dublin, 1867) pp. 185–7.)

26   *From Lady Granard to Suffolk Street*

Clonhugh Lodge, 7 June 1799

[No salutation]

Have the goodness to inclose the inclosed to Moore Park[1] — Murphy rejoices us truly by saying we shall see you here, it will give us all sincere pleasure — but my satisfaction is damped by telling you that in common with our other guests you must consent to sleep at a house across the lawn for this cottage admits not of a bed for a friend. You will have a large party to walk with you after supper if you can put up with that inconvenience & a sincere welcome from all your friends at Clonhugh Lodge.   [*Source*: Scully Papers]

[1]Near Kilworth, Co. Cork, seat of the Earl of Mount Cashell.

27   *From Lady Moira to Suffolk Street*

Clonhugh Lodge [Mullingar], 9 June 1799

[No salutation]

I am at length arrived at this place — Mr M.[1] & his family came into our neighbourhood two or three days after our arrival & gave us the pleasure of informing us that you would indulge us with a visit here — Fastidious personages who have a rigid attention to their ease loudly complain of the situation, as trespassing on lazy indulgence — For my part, I am as indolent as most created beings; but I am not insensible to inconveniences & difficulties when I see that the ordering of them sensibly adds to the satisfaction of others. This place is an idol of Lord Granard's & he apprehended that I might be a prevention to his having his family about him, because coming hither wd. be an objection to me. To walk three or four times a day a hundred yards, from the cabin where we breakfast, dine & pass the evening, to my bed chamber in an adjoining thatched dwelling, I find no hardship in — Last night I had a moon light walk thither, it was a novelty and I am amusing myself with the future prospect of one at the full moon — Poor Mr Hardy looks upon midnight walks as distressing, I consequently feel myself not the most indolent person in the circle of my acquaintance. I certainly prefer the old ruins of Castle Forbes to this cottage habitation, but allow it to be a beautiful place for prospect. Yesterday was the first appearance of summer, this day the weather is divine & the lake[2] is superb from reflecting the sun in all its glory. If you reconcile yourself to walking home at night — I think that you will not require much exertion on that occasion — for I found no hardship in it even during a mild rain — &

depending on your curiosity to see this dwelling & our manner of living here, I shall defer till we meet all our chat, & much discourse respecting your ingenious friend, for whom I shall have some memorandums of inquiry that I shall intreat you to present to him — Will you be so good to present the inclosed to Mrs Moore to whom I have long been indebted for thanks — I have not time to write all my preventions from the not having before offered them, but when we meet you shall hear them & probably acknowledge them as excuses which may be admitted as just apologies — Lord & Lady G. & some of your younger friends all unite in respective remembrances, the rest of yr. acquaintances are gone out walking or boating — I know that in ten days the term ends, when Ld & Lady G. expect to learn that you will inform them of the day you intend to pay your visit here — & I hope it will be soon.

[*Source*: Scully Papers]

[1] Probably Revd John Murphy.
[2] Lough Owel.

28   *From Revd John Murphy to Suffolk Street*

Clonhugh Lodge, 17 June 1799

My dear Sir,

I was yesterday equally surprised and pleased by the account, mentioned in your letter to Lady Moira, of your late confinement — surprised as it was the first intimation of your illness, and pleased by the report of your recovery — Anxious however as I am to congratulate you on the happy termination of so very dangerous a disorder, another reason almost equally urgent induces me to lose not the first opportunity of writing — It is the anxiety so visible in the countenance of your friend Lady G[ranard], evidently caused by the workings of her mind from her desire to see you here, and her fears for her children — the measles is a disorder of which she entertains the most terrifying apprehensions, and as it has already been fatal in her family, no time, at least in the common acceptance of the term, is sufficient to wipe away her fears — Her children have yet to encounter it, and she dreads its introduction more than the most dangerous fever — Knowing this to be so, I feel that you would not consider me as having acted by you as a friend if I was not to request of you to defer your visit (of which we are all equally anxious) to the end of the circuit, rather than to make it in the beginning — It can make but a trifling difference as you propose travelling in your gig, and the impression of danger will be completely removed from Lady G.'s mind by time and travel. It is unnecessary to add that I write this totally of myself, as even the hinting an intention of it would make Lady Granard still more miserable — you will therefore have the goodness not to mention what has determined you to alter your plan, in any letter written to her Ladyship or

Lady Moira, as I would not for any consideration they should suppose I had interfered. When able to visit Milltown I trust you will have the goodness to offer my best wishes to my friends there,[1] as also to Mr, Mrs and Miss Moore,[2] and to believe me your very truly assured friend.

P.S. Since the death of his sister[3] Ld. F[orbes] has such a dread of the measles that he constantly expresses a conviction that it will be fatal to him, should he ever take it. [*Source*: Scully Papers]

[1]The Emmets.
[2]Edward Moore, his mother and his sister Anne.
[3]Selina Frances (1788–91).

29 *From Lady Moira to Suffolk Street*

Clonhugh Lodge, Mullingar, 22 June 1799

I should have acknowledged Mr Scully's first letter before this had it not been for an attack of the inflammation in my eyes, a complaint the which for a few years past I have been frequently a tedious sufferer from — I have got rid of the disorder for the present, by the aid of leeches, with bleeding them, I always receive transient relief, but my eyesight continues weak for some time after the attack — We were made happy expecting your promised visit, when your second letter arrived; yet I had my doubts whether you would not be called home directly by your friends, to take precautions as early as possible against the consequences of the dreadful malady you were just recovered from[1] — I term it dreadful as I have known its fatal & unexpected termination in a few hours after recovering from it was announced by medical attendants — Besides laying the foundation of disorders as dangerous as itself, a twelvemonth must elapse before those who have been attacked by it can hold themselves secure. At a ball I gave several years ago Lady Cecilia Lenox, sister to Lady Louisa Connolly & the Duke of Richmond, was suddenly struck whilst dancing. She went home & got through the complaint apparently not severely, & mixed in the world as usual, a slight difficulty of breathing then took place, but so trifling as not to be regarded, till a galloping consumption in a very few weeks laid her in the grave.[2] A similar instance of its latent baleful effects I know respecting a young man from a slight cold taken a few weeks after, & an acquaintance of mine, only by changing her bed too soon after she was recovered so far as not only to take the air but also to visit in the morning, lingered three months & died — These are but a few of the instances which have come within my knowledge & which has caused me to think that every precaution should be taken to prevent these treacherous & deadly consequences which result from that malignant disorder, which from sharp sorrow & sudden affliction I have imbibed a terror of — & I venture to request that you will be attentive to the remonstrances of your relations when you get into the country, & for three or four months to take care not to use excessive exercise, to shun the night air & catching cold — Everything seems perfectly peaceable & quiet in this County Westmeath & the neighbouring one of Longford, & I have the same good accts. elsewhere — the counties I have named have been fortunate as to the military governors who have presided over them —General Moore & General Barnet[3] have long acted in a manner to do credit to their characters. With the latter named general I am highly pleased — being possessed of the most liberal sentiments & proof against all insinuations of the Orange Party to act with intolerance respecting religious opinions — The union will undoubtedly take place, but upon what terms not yet known, tho' vague report deals out two members for each county, & it is added some compensation for boroughs but of what kind not divulged. Victories over the French & Spanish fleets may be looked upon as certainties — & the expedition to restore the Stadtholder[4] cannot but succeed from the French troops being withdrawn & the bulk of the people anxious for the restoration of the Prince of Orange — Suwarrow (or as the Russians pronounce the w thus placed) Subroff,[5] is a religious enthusiast, who never yet lost a battle; & his devout fervor may be a match for atheistical fury. . . .

Lord & Lady Granard request their best compts. to you & regrets not to see you, but as Ld Granard soon joins his regt. for a short time we shall not be long at this place — & when you return to town they hope Castle Forbes will be taken in your way. Lord Forbes, Francis & Hastings, Miss Forde, Lady Elizabeth & Lady Adelaide do not forget you & are anxious to see you again, & all but Lord Forbes, who is partial to this place & wd to show his favorite residence, very desirous to show you the Old Castle in its summer beauty. This letter goes to the post by the messenger who brings out letters from thence, therefore if there is any public news we have not yet learnt it — Mr Murphy who is here requests his best remembrances — It seems as if he wd. soon be settled as tutor in Lord M[ount] C[ashell]'s family to the two young boys — but it is not yet talked of even amongst our own circle publickly. The letters inclosed to you were on that subject & reached safely their destination, he was stopt of a curacy it was thought by a letter in his favor having been inspected.   [*Source*: Scully Papers]

[1]Measles (see No. 28).
[2]Lady Cecilia Lennox died in Paris in 1769. Lady Louisa Augusta Lennox, who married Thomas Conolly of Castletown in 1758, died in 1821. They were sisters of the 3rd Duke of Richmond.
[3]John Moore; and Charles Barnet, Brigadier General on the Irish staff 1798–1801.
[4]William V the Stadtholder was exiled in England. The expedition to restore him

began on 13 August and ended in disaster, the Dutch not stirring a finger to help (J. S. Watson, *Reign of George III*, p. 379).
[5]Count Alexander Suvarov, in command of a combined Russian and Austrian army, had been scoring spectacular successes against the French in northern Italy.

30   *From Lady Moira to Kilfeacle, readdressed to*
                    Mr Varley's, 3 Oldham Street, Manchester[1]

Castle Forbes, 1 September 1799

I have many apologies to make to Mr Scully for having so long delayed acknowledging his obliging letter; but I have been an invalid beneath the pressure of an irritating & at the same time a languid bilious complaint — & having just thrown off that — am now again attacked with that inflammation in my eyes, which is frequent in the return of its attempts to molest me, tho' its violence is kept [? in check] by bleeding with leeches & the outward application of laudanum, yet it is equally dispiriting as well as painful to write with such a complaint — & it has prevented my arranging some queries which I wished to have had conveyed thro' you to your ingenious friend,[2] on points of genealogical matter — I expect to be now very soon in Dublin, to prepare for the reception of all this family to pass the winter with me — Your friend Francis strongly urges me to stay till his birthday is passed, saying Grandmother there will be no amusement, no fun unless you stay — When one is closely advancing to three score & ten there is some flattery conveyed in the idea of being able to amuse the young personages of ones grand children.

You will have seen or heard that Mr Murphy is gone to be tutor to Lord Mount Cashell's little boys. Mr Gouldsbury who is an old friend of the family is Latin preceptor to Lord Forbes, who goes to his English academy in a couple of months, when Francis will next spring go under his tuition for Latin & Greek — & French being so necessary a language to acquire a French emigrant Abbé has been got from England, merely to teach the French language to the young people — He was recommended by the Bishop of St Pol de Leon, & conveyed by a passport from the Duke of Portland. An [sic] hitherto the Abbé Jannen[3] seems to have been created for his situation, to instruct young persons, they all being extremely fond of him — Francis you know is very penetrating & he gives a high character of his French instructor — Of all what your religious persuasion is now doing I say nothing — I hope, more than expect, it will be to your future advantage — You know well that I am liberal both in religious & political matters — & look only on what is passing as a passenger embarked on board a vessel, with various others, all guided in their course by those whom chance has decided that we are to be navigated by, the infallibility of the Capt. & Master or the skill of the mariners are opinions at least of doubt[4] — The unfortunate Chouans[5] are certainly up again in great numbers — What is to ensue from the secret expedition,[6] a matter of great expectation & at present of much anxiety.

Lord Granard is at Ennis with his reg't. Lady Granard, Miss Forde, Lady Elizabeth & Lady Adelaide, & Francis & Hastings unite, the former in their compts. & the latter in their youthful remembrances. In a few weeks I hope that we shall all meet in Dublin.   [*Source*: Scully Papers]

[1]Bancks' *Manchester and Salford Directory* for 1800 shows a Richard Varley, fustian manufacturer. On 10 March Lady Moira wrote to her son that Scully was paying a visit to Manchester, the purpose of which he did not reveal as he was under some sort of secrecy. She guessed that he had gone on some business between Dublin and Manchester merchants in view of the probable consequences of a Union (Loudoun Papers, A 204).

[2]Probably the Mr Colpitts of the next letter.

[3]Probably Jean François Jehannin, who died in 1816 a curé in the St Malo diocese (D. A. Bellenger, *The French exiled clergy in Britain*, Downside Abbey 1986.)

[4]Bishop Percy of Dromore wrote to his wife on 14 May 1798: "the old lady openly professes the most violent enmity to all religion and has banished all bishops from her house except my good brother of Limerick" (BL Add. MSS. 32, 335).

[5]The insurgents of the Vendée in France who had held out against the revolutionary regime in Paris. The 2nd Lord Moira had commanded an abortive expedition to help them in 1793 (*DNB*).

[6]Probably Lord William Bentinck's mission to Marshal Suvarov in northern Italy, of which Sir Henry Clinton was a member (*DNB*). There had been a rumour in February that Lord Moira was to go as second-in-command to Suvarov (Loudoun Papers A 188).

31   *From Lady Moira to 3 Oldham Street, Manchester*

Castle Forbes, 13 September 1799

I have just received Mr Scully's obliging letter from England. When my health & eyes permitted I wrote to Kilfeacle, the which letter it does not appear you have received[1] — Lord Granard had been called upon to join his Regt. in consequence of their being to be inspected by the general commanding over the district in which they were stationed. This brought us hither & I waited till his Lordship's return, expecting it in a week or ten days, for to begin my journey to Dublin — But he is detained to hold a *civil* court martial, this & General Nugent's proclamation[2] in terms of martial law forbidding the inhabitants of the north be out of their houses before sunrise or be out of them after sunset, & to post lists upon their doors of the names of the inhabitants & the guests they might have therein, with the weekly trials & executions in the county of Wicklow & its neighbourhood by the Orange party, might induce you to think that there were troubles existing in Ireland, yet all agree that it never was in a more perfectly quiet state, & the linen manufacture in the north is so flourishing that from the demand for linen it now sells three times higher than the former accustomed price it bore.

I see that your father & all your friends have signed addresses for the union[3] — It seems to me singular to approve of a measure before your religious persuasion know what you are to get by it. If you are put upon the footing with the Roman Catholics in England you will [be] worse off than you are at present, & as a land tax must take place you will have a double tax to pay for yr. religion[4] — Can you forget that when England got possession of Canada, the outcry that was raised by the people now in rule, at leaving the Canadians in possession of the creed they were found with & the endeavors to excite a religious crusade, to establish religious reformation? Do you recollect the insurrection excited by some trifling indulgences to the English Roman Catholics? Do you suppose that these people who have seen London set on fire in fourteen places from the incitement of one illiberal enthusiast,[5] will hazard now they are ministers to produce similar scenes, by actually favoring the Roman Catholics under English acts of Parliament? — Ireland has made speedy advances in its welfare since America has made itself independent — Its own Parliament must as that increases favor the majority of the nation, but the Roman Catholics when united to England will not be the majority of the British Empire — Sound policy prompts your persuasion therefore to keep yourselves as a political majority. Your bishops are promised £500 pr annum & your priests one hundred,[6] you must pay this bribe to them, and it is a strange inducement to sell your own consequence upon such terms. As to the union, I am not a partisan, for or against it, I am too indolent to take a share in any political pursuit — I estimate Irish Parlts. as cheaply as any mortal can — But the present pursuit of bribing underhand the sale of them, & robbing a consequential minority little inferior to the majority not only of their very antient rights but a portion of real property, is a scandalous procedure in my opinion — Yet as it is an occurence that is to take place I look at it as I do at the numerous disgraces, of nations & people, which degrade the termination of this century. — Why your people should pay court to what was never intended for their benefit, which cannot do credit to their understanding, any more than be serviceable to their interests, nor can give any high idea of their regard for the property held by others, seems at least puzzling. — The Roman Catholic bishop of this diocese[7] assembled his congregation at Longford & in a meeting in the which reigned a contest wherein much vulgar abuse even prevailed, the address was produced & Lady G — was waited upon by the Bp. to desire her to write to Ld G. to present it — Lady G — hearing that it was contrary to the opinion of the majority of his people answered that she was certain that Ld G. wd. not present it & his Lordship since has given that answer — & a counter-address is going to appear, stating therein that persons names who were not present were set down, & some who were averse to the measure[8] — What these last persons assert is reasonable — They desire first to learn what advantages they are to get by the change; & to know how they are to be assured to them — & surely that line would have been a most rational one to have been taken by the chief bulk of a nation.

My eyes tho' they are free at present from inflammation are so greatly weakened that my writing becomes very illegible, which you must excuse. In Dublin I hope soon to talk with you, & if you visit Donington where they will expect you (from my letter to my dear Charlotte) we shall have an additional subject to discourse upon[9] — Lady Granard wrote to your brother as directed respecting the sheep, as Lord Granard was absent — She requests that you will accept her thanks upon that subject & her best compts. Forbes, my grand-daughters & yr. two little friends & Miss Forde unite in many cordial remembrances & compts. L & Lady G. & all the young people will follow me soon to Dublin (& if it pleases God that we live) I hope to pass the winter surrounded with that part of my family — In our Moira House society we look forward to having you, Sr, of our party, as when I was last in town — & if nothing unforeseen occurs you will find me settled beneath my own roof, from which I have been long a wanderer, nine months at my age is a serious period of time.

[P.S.] My health & eyesight have been so indifferent that I could not get arranged the questions for Mr Colpitts,[10] & I have not the few materials (I have now in my possession) for such matters of statement with me, tho' I thought I had brought them.

[*Source*: Scully Papers]

[1]Her previous letter reached Scully on the 16th and he replied to both letters on 30 September.

[2]Not found. Its terms would have been those authorised by the Insurrection Act of 1796 for counties proclaimed under the Act (see Lecky, *History*, III p. 451).

[3]She is referring to a requisition dated 3 August 1799 in which supporters of the Union in Co. Tipperary called upon the High Sheriff, Francis Hely Hutchinson, to convene a meeting to take the sense of the people. This, with its long list of signatories, was published in the *DEP* of 20 August 1799. Among the Normanton Papers at Winchester there is a copy of the requisition on which the (Protestant) Archbishop of Cashel has put a "p" against the names of all the papists. Scully's father, as a magistrate, comes high up on the list, second to Thomas Lalor among the Catholics. Not all James Scully's friends signed. His neighbours, the Mathews of Thomastown, led the opposition, and his son-in-law Richard Sause appears in a Tipperary list of January 1800 as an opponent. The Lord Lieutenant was particularly pleased with the Tipperary result: "the accession of Tipperary to those counties before declared, gives us the entire province of Munster; and its weight will be the more authoritative, as it is an inland county, and not decided by commercial prospects" (Cornwallis to Portland 13 August 1799 in *Memoirs and Correspondence*

of Viscount Castlereagh, London, 1848–9). On 6 June 1810 Lord Donoughmore, who as Governor of the county had headed the list of signatories, claimed that the first favourable turn in the question of the Union after its first rejection was marked by the Tipperary address, "carried as it was greatly by the means of Catholic support". He added that the Catholics had looked forward to emancipation as the certain consequence of the Union (*Hansard*, XVII, 435).

[4]Lady Moira's information was out of date: the double land tax imposed on the English Catholics was repealed after the relief act of 1791 (Charles Butler, *Historical Memoirs*, V, p. 48).

[5]A reference to the Gordon Riots of 1780 which followed upon Lord George Gordon's petition for the repeal of the Catholic relief act of 1778.

[6]The proposals in contemplation allotted £500 to the Archbishops. Bishops were to get £300, Vicars General £150–100 and parish priests £50–30 (HO 100/99).

[7]John Cruise, Bishop of Ardagh and Clonmacnoise 1788–1812.

[8]A correspondent claimed in the *Dublin Evening Post* of 1 September that not more than a hundred attended the meeting, on 31 August, of whom the majority were clergy; that strongly opposed resolutions in favour of the Union were carried only by clerical influence; and that the names of many persons were subscribed without their knowledge.

[9]Donington, in Leicestershire, formerly the seat of the Earls of Huntingdon, had been inherited by the 2nd Earl of Moira from his uncle, and his sister, Lady Charlotte Rawdon, was keeping house for him. Scully's Common Place Book shows that he was there on 17 October 1799.

[10]Unidentified.

32   *From his Common Place Book*

7 November 1799

Conversation.

The polished taste of Louis the fourteenth's court refined the selection of French phrases for conversation to a purity unknown in any language since the brilliant days of Athenian glory. This delicacy has purged and defecated conversation from every phrase & word, tending to shock the senses or to excite the least disgust in the mind of the most fastidious hearer.

Our English language soon participated of this improvement — Addison & Bolingbroke set the example, which now enjoys an universal influence thro' the care of Hume, Robertson, Blair, Junius, together with the parliamentary & pulpit orators. Yet it required much difficulty to surmount the barbarisms of the last century. The clergy of all persuasions had indulged in such filthy coarseness of language, the comedians had written with such broad licentiousness, the hypocritical Puritans of the Commonwealth had stuck with such pertinacity to the most exceptionable & vulgar phrases of the Bible, and the profligate favourites of the restored family had strayed so far into the opposite extreme, in fine, our language was so choaked by the noxious & offensive weeds which grew from its parent soil, the German language, that it is really surprising how successfully it has been cultivated to its present state of refinement — Yet no modern language is now more pure in phraseology, or more capable of imparting the gentlest and softest emotions, the most exquisite and exalted sensations, to a cultivated mind.

No language possesses more powers of kindling the flame of virtue without the blaze of enthusiasm, or of calling forth the noblest efforts of courage and generosity without the rough agitations of inward struggle & violence.

No language can inspire higher pleasure with less of the dross of sensuality; and this I deem the test of literary purity.

Yet in this kingdom (Ireland) I have the misfortune frequently to hear phrases of a nature, which have been long rejected even by the lower class in the sister kingdom; and I observed with pain, that they often proceed from that sex and that class of life, where they are least to be apprehended & in whom they are consequently most unbecoming.

I have often heard Irish ladies (who possessed rank or birth, or fortune, or education, or some or all of those advantages together) express themselves in words which would shock an ear of common delicacy in England, such as the following, "stinking", "dirty", "nasty", "fat woman", "the fellow's carcase", "swim in blood", "rotten", "to spit" — with fifty other phrases (nauseous to collect) which are in England confined to the drunkard, debaucher, or the butcher & scavenger — Yet it is a fact that they possess as much native innocence of mind, genuine modesty, & rather more prudery, than the English women — And I impute the use of those coarse phrases (which are inconceivably grating to the ear from a female voice) to the ignorance of mothers in a few instances, but more generally to their shameful neglect of cultivating the style of conversation and many other useful attainments — Nothing is more easy for a mother than to provide for her daughter some such nomenclature as the following, and to impress such general maxims as will enable her to discriminate between subjects fit to be conversed upon, and others which should only be glanced at indirectly.

The English language is so copious that synonims are easily acquired & may be applied somewhat thus:

"stinking" by the words "fetid", "rancid" or "offensive", "dirty" "nasty" by "soiled", "neglected" or "careless", "fat" by "large", "embonpoint" or "corpulent", "rotten" by "putrid", "carious" or "decayed"

and so of all the other phrases.

Those who have not attended to this subject can form no adequate conception of the difference which a choice of language makes between women, otherwise equal in all respects — The learned and unlearned feel it alike, and its influence is as sudden, & always more durable, than that of beauty — Purity of style often purifies the sentiments: they are generally supposed to be closely connected, & that woman wields an irresistible weapon, whose conversation always presents the picture of a mind innocent & untainted.

Love is rarely founded on youth, beauty or (what are termed) accomplishments: it consists in an idea, which seizes the lover's mind, of the excellence or perfection of the object: it therefore rests wholly on opinion or fancy. This opinion can never originate in, or be supported by, the *actions* of a woman, on account of the very limited sphere of female action; her soul and character have no opportunity of being displayed in action; they therefore appear only in *conversation*; and she, who has neglected to cultivate this science and to acquire the means of rendering justice to her own merit, is cut off from the first & finest source of female pleasure and instruction.

D.S. 7 November 1799

[*Source*: Scully Papers]

33   *From Lady Moira*

Moira House, 9 November 1799

Lady Moira is obliged to request Mr Scully's assistance in an excuse to Major Huddleston[1] for not being able to have the pleasure of his company to dinner to-morrow — The truth is she has not any apparatus in her kitchen for dressing a single dish of meat — Three weeks ago all things were ordered & appointed; the overseer of the work, a builder, who is paid weekly to oversee, & get in the necessary articles & workmen, gave notice that they were in the house on Tuesday last, & wd. be up in one day; Lady Moira therefore thought herself perfectly secure in naming the Sunday following — & behold it is now decided that it cannot be finished till Monday night — Lady Moira therefore must postpone the pleasure of Mr Scully & Major Huddleston's company 'till Wednesday, as she durst not trust to the promise of Monday — The times, & thence the absconding of wretches, who are employed as painters & journeymen from fear of Botany Bay etc, renders disappointments in workmen's labor very frequent; Lady Moira must express how much she is vexed — It is but this instant that she is told, that it cannot be finished till Monday.

[*Source*: Huddleston Papers C3/M32]

[1]Major Richard Huddleston, who was stationed in Dublin with the Cambridgeshire Militia.

34   *From Lady Moira to Kilfeacle*

Moira House, Dublin, 1 September 1800

It gave me a sincere pleasure to receive a letter from Mr Scully tho' I was rather disappointed that I was not to have the satisfaction of seeing you before you went to England. I was desirous to transmit by you a letter to Major Huddlestone, whose letter arriving to me by the same post with that which announced the sudden and unexpected death of a beloved son I was incapable of a recollection of any other circumstance. . . . He fell young, a martyr to fatigue and climate[1] — Military warfare, & the vain & delusive prospects of fame consequently have no influence on my mind, & very recent scenes have shown to me that mankind selected from the lower classes, & called into action, surpass every ravenous beast in savage ferocity — & the military species of the human race are little less to me than objects of extreme disgust.

Mr George Moore has published a second edition of his work with an appendix,[2] he certainly writes incomparably well, tho' he does not convince me. Part of the Kings coronation oath is as follows. . . . It seems fortunate that "authority" according to the Shakespeare[3] phrase "has a medicine in itself to skim vice o the top" for else the breach of oath coming from a person unlicenced by authority [would] be deemed something similar to a perjured conduct — As for those who bought in, or were placed in boroughs, voluntarily & purposely to break their oaths made to the respective corporations, swearing in Parliament to maintain the constitution, what can that be termed but gross & wilful perjury?

Lady G[ranard] and I have had the pleasure of seeing Mrs Moore[4] several times, & lately carried her down to Lady Mount Cashells near Bray; we both agree as to liking her extremely & in thinking her a most agreeable woman — I asked her concerning Major Huddlestone's marriage with a Miss Siliard, a beautiful woman with sixteen thousand pounds to her fortune — I had been informed that they were actually married — She did not think it was so — & since I have heard that the beauty was married to a Mr Jernaghan, son of a baronet, but that there was another sister of the same fortune tho' not so handsome, & it might be he that was married to her[5] — I wonder that he is not married, if he chose to enter that state, for he is very handsome and very amiable. It is said that he proposed for Lord Kenmare's eldest daughter, that Ld K. was for the match, & that Miss Browne declined the offer, contrary to her friend's wish — I said that it was impossible that she shd refuse him.[6] Lord Kenmare is undoubtedly to be a Marquis, to the great delight of her Ladyship. It is owing to the acquiescent deportment of the bulk of the Roman Catholics respecting the union that the rank is bestowed upon him. How little was known, if that be the case, of his Lordship's little interest with those of his profession of faith — I leave my dear Selina to answer respecting the sheep, we expect Lord Granard every day, who has imbibed all the spirit of farming prevalent in England. A report was prevalent that the Duke of Bedford[7] was coming over to the Ballinasloe Fair — A second was built upon that, that every Irish beauty had sent down & engaged lodgings there — I heard from Donington last post, Lord Moira not yet returned from his grousing expedition, my dear Charlotte & Forbes both well.

I think you will not go to England this year as you must be back in Nov & your Irish pursuits will take you some time & the autumn weather from the past heat be probably very bad & rainy. A thousand thanks for your obliging intention respecting the peaches. You were so bountiful in your last donation that it demands only to be triennial. All walled fruit has failed this summer which is owing it is said to the wet season of the preceding year — I beg my best compts. to your father, & leave to Lady Granard's pen all the essential arrangements of business. . . .   [*Source*: Scully Papers]

[1]George Rawdon (1761–25 March 1800) had been taken a prisoner at Saratoga when he was sixteen and had later undermined his health by residence in the West Indies.
[2]The first edition of his *Observations on the Union* . . . had come out in 1799. It was now republished as "a new edition with an appendix suggested by the late debate in the Irish Parliament, and the resolutions of certain bodies of the city of Dublin". Its main argument was that the Union would emancipate the Catholics from party government, whereas little benefit would descend to the great body of the people from emancipation. Its relevance to the coronation oath is not apparent.
[3]*Measure for Measure* I.ii.
[4]Anne, widow of James Moore of Mount Browne.
[5]Edward Sulyard of Haughley Park in Suffolk had died in October 1799 leaving three daughters as co-heiresses. The eldest, Sophia, married John Cary of Hampstead in 1799; the youngest, Frances Henrietta, married Sir George William Jerningham (later Lord Stafford) on 26 December 1799; Lucy married Sir Hugh Smythe of Acton Burnell in 1803.
[6]Charlotte Browne was the daughter of Lord Kenmare's first wife, Charlotte Dillon, whose sister, Lady Jerningham, told Jane Huddleston in May that her niece had £10,000 and suggested her as a match for Richard (Huddleston Papers C3/HD76). However, her heart was already given to George Gould, whom she married in 1802.
[7]The 5th Duke, elder brother of the future Lord Lieutenant.

35   *From Lady Granard to Kilfeacle*

Moira House, 6 September 1800

Dear Sir,

I waited for Lord Granard's arrival to return you my thanks for your very obliging offer about the book, at the same time, that I might give you his answer about the sheep. The book I have already got from Cork, thro' Lord Strangford, but am equally obliged to you for recollecting my wishes for it — My Lord desires his best compts. to your father, & requests he will send the sheep to Castle Forbes, where the man who conducts them shall be paid his trouble & all expenses, (not in the manner which the Cloghan innkeeper paid him last time which I always reflect upon with vexation) & he also intreats Mr Scully will have the goodness either to draw on him for their price or let him know where he shall pay it to his order. Should it be inconvenient to send the sheep the whole way to Castle Forbes my Lord will send a man to meet them at any place Mr Scully shall appoint.[1]

We begin, at last, to think of leaving town & shall be extremely happy to have the pleasure of seeing you at Castle Forbes should leisure or inclination allow you to gratify us. I flatter myself my mother will not long remain after me, & that I shall only leave her to prepare for her reception. My Lord unites with me in best compts, [*Source*: Scully Papers]

[1]James Scully's stockbook (MS.27, 480) shows that in August 1800 he had about 2200 sheep. He began improving his stock in 1792, when he sent his son Roger to Dishley in Leicestershire, where he bought two two year old rams from Robert Bakewell (MS.279, 579). Sir John Bernard Burke's introduction to the Scully pedigree book quotes a saying there was for excellence in anything: "They are like the Scullys' sheep, they speak for themselves".

36 *From Lord Granard to Kilfeacle*

Moira House, 11 September 1800

Dear Sir,

I am extremely obliged to Mr Scully[1] relative to the ewes, I will write this night to my steward to send a careful man for them, as I expect every day the arrival of two very fine rams from Leicestershire, I shall wish them as soon together as I conveniently can. — The money shall be lodged as he directs & every care taken of the ewes to do them justice. — I hope we shall have the pleasure of seeing you at Castle Forbes where we shall be established the middle of next month, & any time that is agreeable to you after that, we shall be extremely happy to have the pleasure of receiving you. — Give my compliments to Mr Scully & say I wish he would make Clonhugh Lodge his way to Ballinasloe, it will be very little out of his way & I shall be there at that time & happy to see him. — Lady Moira & Lady Granard join with me in best compliments to him and you. [*Source*: Scully Papers]

[1]Denys Scully's father, James Scully.

37 *From Lady Moira*

28 February [1801]

Lady Moira sends Mr Scully the English frank for Major Huddlestone; she intended to have got it for Monday, & to have inclosed in it also some lines of her own, but there was a mistake, & the date is for this day, when she cannot possibly write, having letters that must go by this post. Mr Scully will therefore excuse to Major Huddlestone her delay of a few posts — till the hurry of curiosity is abated — Lord Moira already expects the pleasure of seeing the Major, Lady Moira has fully stated to him their antient kindred[1] — His Majesty very ill, his pulse remains still 140, that fever heat not long to be sustained by human nature — such is this day's melancholy intelligence.

[*Source*: Scully Papers]

[1]See No. 44 n.3.

38   *To Major Richard Huddleston, Sawston, Cambridge*

Dublin, 5 March 1801

Dear Major,

Your letter of the 10th February gave me much pleasure, and I believe that these rumours have now died away.

As to that part of my former letter, which you wish to have explained, I am sorry on every account that I am not at present in a situation to comply with that wish & my own inclinations — that passage escaped from my pen, whilst I meant to express my persuasion that I have done no more in your behalf, than you would on a similar occasion do in mine. When I can say more to any person on the subject (which may be shortly or not at all) I will say it to you & remind you of the assurance you gave me. You will then see, that my present reserve is perfectly consistent with my high opinion of you & my confidence in your friendship, and founded upon considerations which may entitle me to your approbation & to a continuance of that friendship.[1]

Lady Moira desires me to apologise to you for her past silence. She will shortly do so particularly by Letter — her health has not been good, and her mind has been much occupied by those political events, which are so rapidly succeeding each other and which may prove interesting to some of her family.[2] She has had a letter lately from Lord Moira, in which he desires very particularly to make your acquaintance & wishes to see you in London.

She therefore requests that, when you go to Town, you will call at St James's place — & he will be happy to see you. This arrangement is somewhat different from that which we laid down at Sawston, but I suppose that it is conformable to military Etiquette. She says, that you may possibly not meet him at home the first time, as he is much employed, but that circumstance will prove no obstacle to the establishment of an acquaintance and friendship between you, if you have your address.

Mrs M. is well. She says that it is not likely that the Ladies will accompany Mr O'C to England.[3] I do not know whether I can go to London this Spring as I intended. I am now going for a fortnight to my father's, about 80 miles hence, and on my return here I shall be able finally to decide upon that subject, and also upon some others connected with it, in which I am much interested.

As you are at or near the source of public intelligence, I can offer nothing to you from this distance but conjectures and surmises resembling those at your side of the water, which would become old before this letter can reach you.

With respect to the internal state of this part of the United Kingdom, it is as tranquil and peaceable as it has been in the most quiet part of the last Century.

The Scarcity of provisions is severe, but probably less so than in Britain — we are accustomed to a more moderate diet, and to more habitual privations of comfort, & therefore the pressure of famine, were it equally heavy here (which I believe it is not by any means) would be less sensibly felt than by a people who have been bred and supported on the fullest scale of nourishment, and, if they have not always had abundance, yet have never before experienced want — the Scarcity is, at all events, only a temporary Evil. — Our Agriculture is advancing rapidly, and the country people have generally acquired habits of industry and sobriety, which a[re] the surest pledge of internal peace & improvement. [1 word missing] our Capital retains its pleasures, notwithstanding the Union. Some of our overgrown nobility & a very few of the Gentry are gone to London. In truth we are not concerned for their departure — few of them were useful or estimable public or private characters, and the gaudy splendour of their style of living, their pernicious habits, & the scandal of their example only served to provoke public discontent and to exhibit to us the vanity & worthlessness of those who draw immense sums from the country, who enjoy all public emoluments & who, to secure that monopoly, would depress the rest of the country, & would involve all things in confusion and ruin rather than consent to the Emancipation of the Catholics. You will probably meet some persons of this stamp in London — and they will pretend to speak very confidently of this country. At Lord Moira's you will not meet them, for they dread him. I hope to hear from you shortly and I beg you will present my best regards to your father & mother and family. Your sisters are probably in London, & will, I hope, accept my best respects. Believe me to be, with much regard,

Very sincerely yours,
D. Scully

[P.S.] Is your friend Lord H.[4] to be our Viceroy, as report says [?]

I did not expect to see Col. Y.[5] appointed to be Secretary at War.

[*Source*: Huddleston Papers C3/S3]

---

[1]He is hinting at his father's opposition to his contemplated marriage with Richard's sister Mary.

[2]Pitt's announcement early in February that he intended to resign on the Catholic

question and support a new administration under Addington had been followed by a recurrence of the king's illness. For a few days his life had been in danger and it was not until 14 March that he was fit enough to transfer the seals to Addington (Aspinall: *Later Correspondence of George III*, III, p. xx). If the Prince of Wales had been appointed Regent his great friend Lord Moira might have been invited to join a new administration.

[3]Mr O'C is Valentine O'Connor senior, whose deceased wife was a sister-in-law of Mrs Moore. One of the ladies would have been his daughter, Maria O'Connor; the other probably Mrs Moore's daughter Anne.

[4]Philip Yorke, 3rd Earl of Hardwicke, whose appointment as Lord Lieutenant was officially announced on 17 March but who was not sworn in until 25 May as a successor had to be found for Lord Cornwallis in his role as Commander-in-chief (Aspinall, *op. cit.* No. 2369 n.1). He was well known to the Huddlestons, not only because his seat at Wimpole was near to Sawston but because Richard and Edward Huddleston had served under him in the Cambridgeshire Militia since the regiment was first formed in 1793 (Huddleston Papers C2/H4).

[5]Charles Yorke, Lord Hardwicke's half-brother, who had been appointed Secretary at War on 20 February.

39   *From Lady Moira*

2 July 1801

[No salutation]

I am sorry to learn that you have been indisposed, & tho' I have been almost intirely occupied by nursing attendance upon my daughter — I missed the pleasure of your calling upon me & supposed that you were gone out of town. Lord Granard is gone for about a fortnight to Clonhugh Lodge & Castle Forbes — My dear Selina is as well as can be expected but it is yet too early a period to have my heart quite at ease. Will you dine with [us] on Sunday if not otherwise engaged? — There is a Gazette of news — which I find is much exaggerated in the newspapers. Its authenticity & extent are very similar to bulletins I once viewed — I wd. send you the Cambridge paper[1] but Mr Berwick has it, & will not bring it back till Saturday.

[P.S.] A secret expedition is going out under the command of Clinton, God knows where, for its destination is a political mystery.[2]

[*Source*: Scully Papers]

[1]Probably the *Cambridge Chronicle* of 20 June, containing an announcement that Lady Hardwicke would be leaving in a few days for Dublin.

[2]Lieutenant Colonel William Henry Clinton, whose appointment to command an expedition to Madeira had been approved by the King on 23 June (Aspinall, *Later Correspondence of George III* No. 2454).

40   *From Lady Moira*

[4 July 1801]

Mr Berwick carried off the Cambridge papers, he has promised to return them to me, & perhaps I shall get them tomorrow — when as you have not made any excuse I shall hope to see you at dinner to eat roast beef in a family party. I am in all the hurry of writing to England on business, therefore excuse these abrupt lines.   [*Source*: Scully Papers]

41   *From Lady Moira*

[? July 1801]

Sir,

I am much concerned to find that you are arrived indisposed — as I hoped that you wd. have met Lord Mount Cashell here tomorrow at dinner. My family have all left me, Miss Forde is alone with me to make a resident stay — I have myself got a slight cold by my visit to Lady Mount Cashell, who has not yet got abroad, but I hope in a few days that you will meet his Lordship & her beneath this dwelling — By letters I have just got from Donington Lord Moira is not yet returned to Donington from attending Parlt. — At Castle Forbes they are all well.   [*Source*: Scully Papers]

42   *From Lady Moira to Kilfeacle re-addressed to Youghal*

Moira House, Dublin, 29 August 1801

I received safely Mr Scully's fine & excellent present of peaches which came in a state of perfection as if just gathered; & must request you to present my very best thanks & compliments to your father for that very agreeable donation — & Lord & Lady Granard being returned we have been daily feasting thereon.

The successes of Mahomet[1] was celebrated in London with firing of cannon & ringing of bells, & much rejoicing; here we did not pay such Musselman-like joyous tribute — & many are still remaining puzzled why the intelligence was so long retarded & fear that some drawback accompanies the news, as it did not raise the stocks, as success of any kind in war is usually accustomed to do — How different are the scenes presented in different ages! When St Lewis died in Africa of the plague he was warring against the Mahommedans, our now dear friends & allies — I should expect that this eastern disappointment of a favorite plan of Buonaparte's may be productive of troubles to him — as he has a strong party against him in France & the arrival of discontented generals & their troops will possibly add to their strength, besides that military glory by which he arose becoming clouded the caprice of the French nation, added to the general prejudice of human nature to be caught by the success of occurences & never weighing the instability of fortune's favor, will decrease his influence & undermine his power, & it is not the interest of any other nation to support him against any other party or usurper — & I think his duration in power & even his existence very precarious. Lord Nelson & Bronte it is thought is gone to attack the Dutch, his late failure will add to his natural rashness, which has been formerly successful to him, & he will either acquire a splendid victory or be annihilated, & a short period will produce that determination.[2]

Mr Todd Jones has written a letter to Sr Richd. Musgrave & so far printed it that he has sent several printed copies of it to several persons here — He did not send one to me but I have been shown one of them in print — My old friend Jones (whom I have known from his infancy) generally writes most admirable letters on private subjects; but I never saw any of his resentful publications that were not (in my poor opinion) faulty or deficient; & as I objected to the attack he made upon the Roman Catholics respecting pecuniary matters, and thought his newspaper justification of himself wrongly timed & ill-stated, it prevented his sending to me I suppose his attack upon Sr Richd. I asked (before I saw it) from a person of yr. acquaintance, if he had kept sight of civility thro' his course of expressed resentment, & was answered as to keeping sight of civility that there was not a word thro' the whole that could appear to have lost sight of what never once appeared in it — It is very virulent, & conveys not the keen edge of the razor of satire, it is an oister knife that hacks & hews, & he has lost an opportunity, from an injudicious manner & coarse terms, of doing credit to himself & the cause of humanity. Even in a challenge (which it certainly imports) a short & nervous censure, & a statement founded upon due information, would have been more desirable for himself & the cause that he espouses — But Sr Richd. will not fight, he has apologised to several persons in full terms when called upon. How far the composition is actionable in the eyes of you lawyers, I am an incompetent judge.[3]

Lord & Lady Mount Cashell have been three days in Dublin, they dine with me (the last time whilst they stay) this day & sail for England tomorrow, wind & weather permitting. It was a great pleasure to me to see them; I called upon her yesterday, the first time I have walked up any stairs but my own since her Francis[4] confined her to her room by his birth, having totally given up all intercourse with the world exept beneath my own roof. Lord & Lady G[ranard] & their eight children still with me. Ld Granard a capital farmer & his sheep doing admirably well. — & Lord Rancliffe (who is a ward of Lord Moira's) accompanied Lord Forbes to Ireland — The young men return soon to England, Lady G. will stay with me, I hope, till she has inoculated the little Ferdinand (her last child) not in the new fashion, of the vaccine inoculation, but in the old practice of inoculation, not liking to run the chance of imparting cow diseases.

I cannot procure a frank, that privilege being over with my friend,[5] therefore not to make this a double letter I must hasten to conclude — Requesting my best remembrances to your father & the rest of your family, & desiring you to accept of Ld & Lady G.'s compts. & most affect. remembrances to you from your young friends I remain etc.

[*Source*: Scully Papers]

[1]News of the "reduction of the castle and city of Cairo by his Majesty's and the Ottoman army" was confirmed in London on 15 August (*The Courier*).

[2]In the night of 15–16 August Nelson had been repulsed when he attempted to capture or destroy a flotilla in Boulogne harbour assembled for an invasion of England. He did not go on to attack the Dutch (*DNB*).

[3]In his *Memoirs of the different rebellions in Ireland*, 1801, Vol. I p. 114, Sir Richard Musgrave had accused William Todd Jones, along with other Protestant barristers "of abilities, but desperate circumstances, and totally destitute of all religious principle", of having been hired by the Catholic Committee. Todd Jones replied to this in a printed letter dated 30 January 1801, which he had circulated in Dublin: this was the letter that Lady Moira had not received. The affair ended in a duel which took place at Rathfarnham Grounds in May 1802 (Particulars are given in Todd Jones' leaflet: *Authentic Detail of an Affair of Honour*, 1802).

[4]Born on 28 October 1800; died young.

[5]Unidentified.

43   *To Ferdinand Huddleston*

London, 24 November 1801

I shall not suffer Judgements[1] to be enter'd up on either of the Warrants of Attorney of this date executed by Mr Huddleston, until a fully sufficient time shall have elapsed, after a demand & refusal to satisfy them by a good security upon land.

The practice of annexing Warrants to Bonds is universal in Ireland & never deemed in the least rigorous — &, I can assure Mr H. that I am most heartily willing to wave them upon my part if my father will sign the marriage settlement without requiring judgements & it is my intention in shewing these warrants to him to manifest on the [part] of Mr H.'s family a willingness to perform every engagement, & justify the high opinion which my father has conceived of the integrity of Mr H.'s character.[2]

[*Source*: Huddleston Papers C3/S4]

[1]A judgement was a certificate of an assignment of chattels etc. made by a court,

evidently required by Scully's father in this case because no land had been offered as security for the dowry of Mary Huddleston, whom Scully was to marry in two days' time.

[2]For some particulars of the marriage settlement see Nos. 46 and 48.

44   *From Lady Moira to 7 Thayer Street, London*

Moira House, Dublin, 13 December 1801

I am certain that Mr Scully has attributed my delay of not congratulating him as a friend, on his becoming by marriage[1] my kinsman, to my having been detained by some cause which impeded me in the performance of my inclination to have instantly acknowledged his obliging letter — & tho' I & my young people have been preserved from the dreadful fever which has been fatal to several of our acquaintances, & from amongst our relatives has carried off one of the late Lord Moira's grand-daughters,[2] yet we have shared the general epidemic attack of severe colds, & mine (as lately accustomed to do in that complaint with me) was attended with weakness & inflammation in my eyes; & at my time of life sight is if possible a greater object of estimation than even in youth, since at that late period it is the sole resource to employ whereby an independent mind is enabled to wile [sic] away by the command of amusing occupations the days of life — & however trifling such occupations may be, they equally liberate the proud & the indolent person from seeking or soliciting the alms of amusement from others — Be assured Sir that I take the first opportunity in my power to present my best compts. by you to Mrs Scully & to assure her that I purpose to myself much pleasure in seeing her in this kingdom, where I conclude however that she will favor us but with transient visits till the character this country has lately received, & which doubtless has been impressed upon the mind of Mrs Scully's friends, shall be removed by her own judgment, & her conviction that it is possible to live very safely & comfortably in Ireland, in the which kingdom I have now resided nearly fifty years, & I believe the south a much more agreeable place of residence than the north wherein I resided.

I have been engaged in recalling to my memory connections & subsequent circumstances respecting Mrs Scully's family & mine own[3]. . . .

I conclude that you have seen Sir Watkins W. Wynnes letter in the *Courier*[4] (he may have got some person to write that letter for him) — & in England it may gain credence — but in the north the antient Britons were termed the infernals & Wynne's Lambs in derision, & their conduct notorious,[5] besides after what has been known to have been acted upon the living, what has been done to the dead is very inconsequential — Lord & Lady Granard, Elizabeth & Adelaide & the little Caroline are at present all at Donington Park, Forbes & Lord Rancliffe (a ward of Ld Moira's) was over with us, & returned to England with Lord & Lady G — whom I expect to return the latter end of this month as Lord Moira will then return to town. He has been in London but returns to the country to receive Monsieur[6] & his suite who are to pass a few days with them. Francis, Hastings, Angoulême[7] & Ferdinand have remained with me, & as I dine with the three elder ones at an early hour I do not see as much company as I otherwise shd. do — Even our dining hour prevents me receiving late morning guests, who are amazed to find me at dinner before four o'clock, but I like to have my little people as much with me as possible, holding them as a sacred charge not only due to myself but also to others — I have not ventured out of my house for some time, the last time when the duty of attentive condolence obliged me to go & leave my cards with Mr Henry & Lady Emily on the death of his sister,[8] I went & left my tickets with Mrs Moore but have not seen her since — Indeed the weather has been dreadful, & also till I had got proper mourning & the funeral was over it was the decorum to be denied to visitants, & I found my people very indiscriminate, as to not permitting the entrance of some I might have seen, but I did not learn Mrs Moore's name amongst that list.

I know little of what is going on in Ireland. I shd. like to learn what that act of amnesty[9] meant, at Wicklow this assizes one Michael McDaniel was sworn against & stood his trial for harbouring a rebel & false traitor, one Andrew Thompson. Mr McNally[10] his counsel argued that as there was no record of high treason or judgment of outlawry for that crime by act of attainder, the indictment could not be supported for that Thompson was shot dead without any form of trial whatever, civil or military — It appears that Michael McDaniel was not however acquitted in consequence of Mr McNally's argument, but the trial put off & the prisoner bailed.

Lord & Lady Mount Cashell I have not heard further of than from Calais, where Lady Mt.C. was much amused with such sudden change of scenes & the numberless interrogations they experienced from the sea shore [word missing] they were admitted into that town.[11]

Francis & Hastings request to be very particularly remembered to you — The Abbé [Jannen] remained with me and them — He is the worthiest of all human beings and a striking proof that without natural or acquired sense, without genius, talents or information, it is possible to be estimable, worthy & in some degree useful in the course of our existence.

[P.S.] I request my best compts. to Major Huddleston. You will perceive by my writing how weak my eyes are, & the relief I always find from bleeding with leeches on my temples which immediately removes the inflammation, this very severe weather, is what I am forbid to practise whilst the severity of it continues.   [Source: Scully Papers]

[1]Henry Huddleston wrote to his father on 26 November 1801: "My sister was married this morning both by priest and parson. I gave her away. . . . She is certainly

deserving of a good husband and I think Scully will prove such" (Huddleston Papers CD/HD 42).

[2]Mentioned below as the sister of Mr Henry.

[3]The 1st Earl of Huntingdon, from whom Lady Moira was descended, married Elizabeth Huddleston, daughter of Sir W. Huddleston and Isabella Montague, a niece of Warwick the Kingmaker. Particulars of the Huddlestons' Plantagent descent are given by Burke, *History of the Commoners*, 1838.

[4]*The Courier* of 1 December 1801 published a letter written by Sir Watkin William Wynn as Lieutenant Colonel of the Antient British Fencible Cavalry refuting a statement on page 212 of J. Gordon's *History of the Rebellion in the year 1798* alleging that the Antient Britons had committed atrocities on the body of Father Michael Murphy after the battle of Arklow.

[5]In the disarming of Ulster in 1797 (see Lecky, *History*, IV, p. 40).

[6]The exiled pretender to the French throne, to which he was restored in 1814 as Louis XVIII.

[7]Born 10 July 1796; so named because his godfather was the Duke of Angoulême, who ascended the French throne in 1824 as Charles X.

[8]John Joseph Henry, a grandson of the 1st Earl of Moira by his first wife, had on 13 March 1801 married Lady Emily Fitzgerald, daughter of the 2nd Duke of Leinster.

[9]The Act of General Amnesty and Oblivion passed on 17 July 1798 (Lecky, *History*, V, p. 18).

[10]Leonard McNally (1752–1820), called to the Irish bar 1776 (see *DNB*).

[11]Although the peace treaty had not yet been signed the Mount Cashells had crossed to Calais on 29 November and had been thoroughly searched for contraband (E. C. McAleer, *The Sensitive Plant*).

45   *From Major Richard Huddleston*

[16] January 1802

[Copy[1]]

Dear Scully,

I am sorry to write to you upon a subject upon which there is any difference of opinion between us — it is that of the warrants of attorney[2] of which I had heard nothing till I went to Sawston a few days before Christmas — I am extremely hurt that they should ever have been thought of; the opinion of all those with whom I have taken occasion to converse upon the nature of such instruments being but one, namely that they are highly disgraceful to those from whom they are required and that they are so only from persons of bad principle, likely to fail or otherwise not responsible — when I interested myself in the affair which has taken place this month I did it from regard for you and my sister far from thinking to bring a stigma upon my family — I am well assured you were as far from suspecting any tendency in these judgements to do so — you are convinced of my father's honor & of mine — the allowance he has agreed to make, tho' a larger one than it would be in his power to make the rest of his children as well as any other engagements of his whether with regard to paying the interest or principle, in case it should fall to me to execute them will be religiously observed by me — it was from seeing a letter from my brother a day or two ago that the warrants were not [yet] entered up and were of no force till [they] are that I trouble you with this. I earnestly wish some other security may be thought of & these totally given up. I am confident from what I have said they will be, I shall anxiously await your answer upon this head.

P.S. It gave me great pleasure to hear you & my sister were safely arrived in Dublin.[3]   [*Source*: Huddleston Papers C3/HD80]

[1]Taken from the text which Major Huddleston wrote out in full for his sister Jane in a letter dated 18 January. He tells her that it was sent two days before and that he sees nothing in it to give offence.

[2]i.e. the judgements mentioned in No. 43.

[3]She and Denys went on to Kilfeacle, where they arrived on 24 January. Her father-in-law noted in his diary: "she seems a mild modest woman". A letter in the Huddleston Papers from Ferdinand Huddleston to James Scully speaks of his daughter's having been received with the greatest politeness and attention and adds that "by every intelligence from Ireland . . . your son and her are quite happy in one another." After a second visit to Kilfeacle Mary wrote to her mother on 3 May saying that "the old gentleman" had made her a present of horses, that she had every reason to believe that she found great favour at Kilfeacle and that they were sorry at her going.

46   *To Major Huddleston, Cambridgeshire Militia, Yarmouth*

Dublin, 11 February 1802

Dear Major,

The best answer I can give to your letter about the Judgments[1] will be a plain narrative of the whole transaction, tho' I did not expect to hear of it from you, as you gave it up & left town when it was broken off, and we had not afterwards the pleasure of seeing you either upon the occasion of our marriage or of our visit at your house.

Two or three days after you & your brother left London for Sawston, the latter wrote to me that Mr Huddleston would pay your sister's fortune according to your former letter by giving £1,000 *down*, & £50 a year until the second £1,000 should be paid. I wrote to my father accordingly. When I afterwards went to Sawston, Mr H. told me, in the only conversation we had upon the subject, that he could *not* pay the £1,000 down, as he should want money for enclosing, but he would pay the £100 a year. I made no observation as the enclosure was to be so beneficial an application of the sum to the family, and I hoped to reconcile my father to this second departure from what he understood. Afterwards I received my father's consent to adhere to his first arrangement, notwithstanding the difficulty which, as you know, had broken it off, but upon *express condition* that your family should perform at least their last engagement — this I communicated to Henry & your family — & the affair was resumed.

[Scully goes on to observe that Henry Huddleston, after proposing bonds to secure the £2000 instead of judgments, which he regarded as disgracing the family, had expressed himself satisfied when Scully, after a visit to Sawston, had reported Ferdinand Huddleston's willing acquiescence. Nevertheless, out of respect for Henry's feelings, he had left London without entering judgments.[2] And now, with the business unfinished and his father not having yet signed the marriage settlement, had come this letter from Richard, who had to all appearances declined further interference and left all arrangements to his father and brother. Although it is term time Scully is writing this long reply as he feels Richard will form a just opinion when he knows the facts of the case and because he wishes to nip in the bud any misunderstanding between himself and the Huddleston family. He goes on to explain the nature of judgments, which are the universal security of property in Ireland].

After all, I can only do with those warrants (as your family must have seen all along) what my father shall direct. I shall see him, I hope, in two or three weeks; then and *not till then*, shall I know more of the matter than I did when leaving London.

It is my wish that this letter should not only be favoured with your full attention but also be shewn to those of your family who are concerned in the subject, as I collect from the tone of your letter, that an erroneous judgment of me in many respects may possibly have been formed. Your sister is well and desires her love to you.   [*Source*: Huddleston Papers C3/S4]

[1]No. 45.
[2]On 3 January 1802 Henry Huddleston wrote to his father: "Scully and I agreed that one judgment should be entered up, however he has left it where it was . . . he is a good fellow, I am very well convinced, and has a regard for us which is more than some people seem to have who have at least as much reason to be attached to the family" (Huddleston Papers C2/HD46).

47   *Mary Scully to Mrs Huddleston, Sawston Hall,*
                  Saffron Walden, Essex

                          [Dublin] [postmarked. 29 April 1802]
Dear Mama,
    . . . . My sojourn at Kilfeacle was of very great service to me. I am grown fatter and feel much stronger. Since these few days I have begun the cold sea Bath which I find agrees extremely well with me and the Baths if they were

nearer would be very convenient. I wish Jane could come to me. I shall be ready to receive her in two months time and any time after that and make her I hope very comfortable, for we have bought a house which we enter the middle of June. A sea voyage is an excellent thing for a bilious person; if she could come immediately I could accomodate her tho' not so pleasantly for herself equally agreeable for me to receive her. Our house is a two roomed one like the London ones — the apartments a very good size. I think the smallest drawingroom the size of Mr Bell's[1] largest room and the other something larger. I mention Mr Bell's because all who go to London have seen it. It is charmingly situated as to air at the upper end of Baggot Street (R'd knows that part of the town I imagine), has a very pretty garden with Coach house, stable etc. We have the two parlours and two Drawing rooms ready furnished, the drawing rooms very handsomely but the parlours in some respects not so. We give for it £1200 fine and £70 a year Irish money, which if I count right is £1,100 English and something better than £64 a year. When I left Kilfeacle the Old Gent made me a present to buy horses. We have not done so yet and shall not until we get our own stable for them. I hire when I want them. I have every reason to think that I found great favour at Kilfeacle. They both spoke to me in the kindest manner when I was coming away and seemed very sorry at our going. They pressed exceedingly come again this summer and I have since had a very obliging letter from Mrs S. repeating the invitation. Mr S. is going to set up a bank at Tipperary which will most likely be no small addition to his riches.[2]

There is to be a grand Ball and supper at the Castle to night to celebrate the peace[3] to which all are invited that have been presented. I mean to go as they say it is very well worth seeing. I know several Ladies that will be there and I consider it as a kind of Publick meeting. Tell R'd I saw Miss Dunsany Plunket[4] last night for the second time. It was at Mr O'Connor's.[5] She is staying with Ly Fingal. She looks altogether pretty and has a very good figure and pleasing manner, upon the whole I like his taste as to her but I do not hear she has money. Mrs Sherlock[6] enquired after him as she generally does. R'd means to remain I imagine in the celibate if he loses Miss O'C.[7] It is I think his own fault. I gave him warning that if he lets a few months longer pass away it is possible she may have other offers and hearing nothing of him will keep herself no longer as Mr Barington[8] said in pickle for him. There was a Gentleman Denys put off seeing more of her about a year ago that admired her much, on R'd's account. It is not impossible that he might think of her again, not that I ever heard he had any further thought of her, but it is possible. R'd will think I teaze him about this business but this is the last time I will give him any exhortation on the subject. My love to him and all. I received Betsey's and Fanny's[9] letters and will answer them. They were both much fuller of information and much more interesting to me than mine can be to them as I am in a strange land. Believe me my Dear Mama ever most truly your affectionate d'r M.S.

[P.S.] I hope the Enclosure goes on agreeably. My Duty to my Father. Am very happy to hear he is so well, hope you are so now. I know the beginning of Spring does not suit you. Denys desires to be kindly remembered to all.

[*Source*: Huddleston Papers C1/MH76]

[1]Henry Bell, of Gray's Inn, under whom Henry Huddleston had studied conveyancing in 1790.
[2]Established in partnership with his third son, James Scully: it appeared in a list of registered banks published by the *Dublin Evening Post* on 14 August 1804.
[3]The Peace of Amiens, signed on 27 March.
[4]So described to distinguish her from other Plunkets. Lord Dunsany's eldest daughter Margaret married Lord Lowth in 1808; his youngest, Anne, married Philip Roche of Limerick at Cheltenham in August 1803.
[5]Valentine O'Connor senior.
[6]Probably Jane, daughter of Alexander Mansfield of Ballymultina, Co. Waterford, wife of Thomas Sherlock of Killaspy.
[7]Maria O'Connor.
[8]Possibly Jonah Barrington, but the name might also be read as Berington.
[9]Her first cousins, Elizabeth and Frances Huddleston.

48   *To Mrs Huddleston from her daughter Mary Scully to*
            Sawston Hall, Saffron Walden, Essex

Dublin, 12 June [1802] Saturday

Dear Mama,

I was very happy to receive your kind letter tho' some of it contains rather a bad account of your own and R'd's Health. I wish you were as near a bathing place as I am. I remember that always did you good. I wish R'd may find benefit from his tour; he should not hurry himself too much. I believe the bathing agrees with me as they tell me I look better than I did. I shall be better still when the weather mends. At present it is very cold and changeable. Jane I find is very gay, more so I think than normal. She will be with you no doubt at the commencement.[1] We are much taken up at this moment with Mrs Siddons and I believe Denys & myself are the only persons in Dublin that have not yet seen her perform. I mean to see her next week. Last Sunday I dined in company with her which is accounted here a very enviable piece of good fortune. She is an extreme well behaved woman and handsomer off than on the stage.[2]

My Father would greatly oblige me if he would write himself to old Mr Scully saying that he is satisfied with the terms upon which he consents to sign the settlements which are that I should have but £300 a year jointure out of the estate and the other £100 Denys to settle upon me out of my own fortune.[3] Harry's writing will not do in this case and as to forcing him to sign them as they are it is only doing me mischief instead of good; I hope I shall never be in the way of receiving a jointure but if I am I shall have the £400 per annum just the same as Denys has the power of disposing as he will of my Fortune the old Gentleman having nothing to do with it. I wish the writings to be signed soon as besides any thing that might happen to the old Gent, he is going to set up a Bank which will involve his property.

Frank[4] came to town on Tuesday last. He is now entirely out of the service and upon half pay which is £90 a year.

I would have my Father give Mr S. Sen'r a hint of the confidence he placed in his honour & property.

We are to enter our house on Wednesday next. I wish I had the least chance of seeing you and my Father in it at any time. I should be *toute glorieuse* as the French say. . . .

I have not seen the Hardwickes very lately but dined at the Phoenix Park in a private way since they left the Castle. Lord H. said many fine things of R[ichar]d. Denys was very near going to the last Levee. His dress was all prepared etc. but he was prevented by his law business. I suppose you will be very much smoked this summer by burning the land — it is a pleasant smell however that brings in money. You have had it the two last summers without the profit. I would send this by Frank but it is uncertain what time he will leave Dublin and the post is more to be depended upon.

Mrs Siddons has been the occasion of several duels being fought here from quarrels at the Play house. I am glad Denys is so sober and domestic or I should often be in fear about him for a little thing produces a challenge here to the no small amusement of all friends and acquaintances. . . .

[*Source*: Huddleston Papers C1/MH77]

[1]The degree giving ceremony at Cambridge University, which was also a great social occasion.

[2]The dinner was at Moira House, as shown by the invitation which Scully kept. On this has been added in another hand an Italian saying: *Aspettare e non venire/Star in letto e non dormire* (to wait and not to come/To lie in bed and not sleep). Written on the cover in what appears to be the same hand are the words "Mrs Siddons Mr Park Street".

[3]That her father did write is shown by a reply from James Scully in the Huddleston Papers (C2/S6) promising to sign the settlement. On the cover of the present letter Ferdinand Huddleston copied out another letter in which he declines an invitation from James Scully to visit Ireland, on grounds of expense and age.

[4]Her cousin, Captain Francis Huddleston, who was put on half pay on 12 June 1802 (*Army List*), following the signature of the peace treaty.

49   *From Lady Granard to Bagot Street*

M[oira] House, Wednesday[1]

Lady Granard's compts. to Mr Scully & returns him a thousand thanks for his most obliging attention — Lord Southwell goes with Lord Forbes, in the kindest manner; Coll. Southwell,[2] Lady Granard herself wrote to, & sent it to Castle Hamilton by a messenger but got no answer, they said he was then absent — this was a fortnight ago — but will get Lord G. to call on him tomorrow & is infinitely indebted to Mr Scully for his kind hint.

[*Source*: Scully Papers]

[1]Scully, evidently relying on memory, wrote "1802" on the cover, but it is tempting to link this letter with one that Lady Moira wrote to her son on 15 May 1803 telling him that Colonel Southwell was about to write to him about raising a regiment (Loudoun Papers A 208). The Lord Lieutenant told Colonel Southwell on 20 August 1803 that there was no immediate opportunity of employing him in a military situation (Hardwicke Papers, Add.MSS. 35, 741, f.325).
[2]Robert Henry Southwell (1745–1817), of Castlehamilton, Co. Cavan, was a Lieutenant-Colonel in the 8th Dragoons and uncle of the 3rd Viscount Southwell.

50   *From Lady Moira*

Castle Forbes, 15 February 1803

I am much obliged to Mr Scully for his kind attention, by his imparting to my spirit of curiosity a share of that information respecting antient times which by occupying with its gossip much of my former time has prevented my gossipping propensities from molesting the peace & quiet of my neighbours.

In respect to the Irish barony of Hastings . . . after the death of Henry the 8th's father in law (though he left other children than the scaffolded ones) I cannot find how it went. At length Sr John Davies became Attorney General in Ireland. . . . Whatever his abilities might be, of which I am not capable of the appreciating (only I dare to say that I think his poetry wretched), I have not a high opinion of his moral rectitude from the immense riches he did acquire in Ireland. . . . He returned from Ireland an Hibernian nabob & purchased for his only daughter (Lucy Davies) a husband in my great-grandfather, then Ld Hastings, afterwards Ferdinand Earl of Huntingdon. . . . Much was expected from this union . . . but these destined flattering prospects were speedily obliterated, Sir John Davies scarcely surviving the nuptial feast. . . . Whether the Irish manor of Hastings was a grant from the crown to Sir John Davies or a purchase I know not — scites[1] of religious houses & chapels & advowsons (of which the living of Orney[2] was one) were undoubtedly grants from the crown. But from some flaw in the settlement, after the death of Lord Huntingdon & his eldest son (my grandfather being a younger son), she [Lucy] sold all her father's property which (excepting money) was totally acquired & purchased in Ireland — & my family possesses not a shilling of Irish pillage. . . .

Of all compilations the justification of a conduct is the most difficult, especially when it includes the conduct of others therein. . . . But this is a topic, as it must be diffuse, that we will talk over if we ever meet again. My advanced time of life & that daily increase of debility, mental & corporeal, that I sustain causes me to hold existence as a very precarious possession. . . . This lassitude of mind, & the weakness in my sight, contracts the power of my corresponding to a very narrow circle, & seldom permits my writing. The severe and continued frost we long had in this centre of the kingdom oppressed me much, as I always find myself indisposed in frosty weather. If I ever return, my purpose is no more to quit my own roof; I take my last leave of the habitation of my beloved daughter & my most kind son-in-law who to me has behaved with the affectionate attention of a son on my return from hence — But still a stronger seclusion from the world than I have even hitherto practiced I think becomes suitable to my years — I have sent up Hart to have my house repaired from the injuries it has recd. from storms & the floods, & to have some painting done — so that if I am not to inhabit it, it may receive comfortably Lord & Lady Granard when they come to Dublin. If I return I must amuse myself with doing such trifles to improve it as my finances permit me to spend — & I have replanted my torn-up trees, as if I had the prospect of having them flourish & shade my walks in the remaining course of those days I may have to come.

There is a variety of reports respecting the government of Ireland, not any I should imagine well founded. Surely the present governor conducts himself in a manner to satisfy the ministry, as well as the people he presides over — they certainly both are, Lord & Lady Hardwicke, most amiable, excellent, worthy people; & a Viceroy Stork & his mate not a desirable exchange — Amongst the various ones named as their successors by vague report I know not any from character who would be near as eligible as they are.

I do not know where Lady Mount Cashell now resides; I heard (but from mere report) that all the children (except the one she is nursing) are left under the care & direction of Mr Egan[3] at Nismes or Avignon[4] — a point which I own surprises me — I know that you have a better opinion of Mr Egan than I have — that he is vulgar & absurd are rested ideas in my mind, which I have received from those who are perfectly well calculated to appreciate characters — A mere trifle has impressed on me an opinion of his conceited airs — Upon his going from London to Paris, a person accustomed to travel said it would be requisite that he should take a French courier from one metropolis to the other. He answered that *he* shd. not *do that*, lest the children shd. acquire a bad accent of the French language in their travelling

— This to me appeared a touch of "the insolence of office" — two of the boys cd. scarcely speak their own language, & the third in a weeks travelling cd. hardly attain words from an outrider with whom he cd. not converse five minutes in the day, & who was to quit them on his arrival. It was that petty air of ruling consequence that only folly could suggest — Lady M.C. will be vexed at Genl. Morrison's removal from command.[5] He offended the English ministry so highly by his false representations that he was also to be struck off the staff. He went to England to endeavor to avert that disgrace, I know not how it has succeeded — I will request you to remember me most particularly & kindly to Mrs Moore. I recd. a very polite & agreeable letter from her in answer to a note I left for her at her house before I quitted town. My lassitude & the weakness in my sight prevented my thanking her & from hence nothing amusing there is able to be transmitted.

The renewing the ballot for the militia I hope will not yield any interesting matter — In the last business of that kind Ld Granard's life was twice attempted — & he is now engaged in a similar pursuit, but with no present prospect of disturbance.[6]

I request my very best compts. & affect. remembrances to Mrs Scully. You will perceive by my writing how much my eyes are still affected by weakness, but I was anxious to assure Mr Scully how truly I felt myself obliged to him for his various communications & that we regretted that you & Mrs Scully did not take Castle Forbes in yr. return from Tipperary — Ld Granard is become a great farmer & besides his fine bull called Donington cd. have shown to you an ass from one of the African islands, which they inform me is a noble animal & a great curiosity from its stature — In respect to myself, I acknowledge that I am not the least a judge of the merits of quadrupeds.

My boys, as I style the three youngest, remember you with great gratitude, & are all I cd. wish them to be, regretting much the good Abbé,[7] who has not been yet re-instated or provided for — Lrd Forbes is a charming youth, created to be an eldest son & elder brother — He is going abroad immediately. My grand-daughters all well — L & Lady G., my grandsons & their sisters & Miss Ford all unite in their best compts. to you & Mrs Scully.

[*Source*: Scully Papers]

[1] An old spelling of "sites" — cf. *Hansard*, XXVII, 931.
[2] Not listed in the *Townland Index* — perhaps a misspelling of Urney in Co. Tyrone.
[3] Egan, travelling later with the three elder boys, had joined the Mount Cashells in Paris in the early summer of 1802 (Catherine Wilmot, *An Irish Peer on the Continent*, London, 1923). Lady Moira's comment on his manners suggests that he was John Egan, son of Sylvester Egan, a Dublin druggist, aged about nineteen when he took his B.A. in 1797. At the visitation of Trinity College in April 1798 he confessed to being a United Irishman and was described by an eyewitness of the scene as "a low vulgar wretch" (Journal of William Blacker in Constantia Maxwell, *History of Trinity College, Dublin*).

[4]The Mount Cashells had left Paris for Italy on 15 September 1802. En route they bought a house at Nîmes, where they left the children with their tutor and governess. On the renewal of the war Egan was put in prison and the children were sent to Geneva (McAleer, *The Sensitive Plant*.)

[5]Major General Edward Morrison was a brother-in-law of Lady Mount Cashell, having married her younger sister Caroline in 1800.

[6]The militia had been disembodied on 12 May 1802 but in November 1802 Lord Granard had received circular instructions to prepare for embodying it again. H. A. Richey, *Royal Longford Militia* is silent about attempts on his life.

[7]Jannen (see No. 30).

51   *From Mary Scully to Mrs Huddleston, Sawston*

[?March 1803]

Dear Mama,

I think this is the best time to write to you now that you and my Father are quite alone tho' I do not promise much entertainment. I had Jane's[1] letter and have given notice that R'd[2] means to visit this Country during the summer. I think he will be then able himself to judge how far he is likely to succeed with the Lady in question[3] much better than I can. All I know is that we shall be extremely glad to see him. I hope he will come before July or the beginning of August, for I have promised Mrs Scully to go with her to a watering place[4] in July, which I could put off however, in case that is the only time he can come. At all events I could manage some how or other if I have but timely notice. I hope Ned[5] will accompany him. I wish Jane could have been with me this Winter as we have had a great deal of gaiety in Dublin and many Balls and concerts at the Castle which are in that kind of Vice Regal stile that is worth seeing and would suit Jane's taste. Ld H. told me some time since that Ld Royston[6] was gone into the Cam: Militia and that he should write to R'd to recommend him to his tuition.[7] I think the Daughters improve all three of them as to Beauty (the little one will do so in time I hope). They are all extremely well behaved and much liked. Mr James Scully, Denys's next B'r is with us at present for a few days. I think it probable we may have the Old Gentleman again soon. He thinks of coming to Town for advice about a hurt he got some time since in his toe which has been extremely bad tho' now better.[8] Our Chancellor's expected to bring a Wife over with him very shortly. They say here that he has sold his estates in England and means to purchase here. No doubt that he is building at his country seat about 4 miles from here and making great improvements.[9] I hope you and my Father have not had the Influenza. My Aunt tells me it is at Sawston. Many have been laid up here with it. Mr S. has had it, and all the servants, but I have escaped. Lady Moira is expected in Town in a short time. I hope she will be here when R'd comes. I think our friend Prince Ruspoli[10] is come off with great honour, he is an excellent man. Miss Betsy Plunket[11] that R'd used to drink tea with, is at last married to Capt. Williams. When some old Lady dies she and her uncle will come into a very good fortune. As to Frank[12] I think you need not have any scruple about what you said of him. He is bad enough I fear to merit [paper torn] have heard nothing of him lately.

[Paper torn. ? I am   ] a little hurried as I am to have company at Dinner today indeed if I had not I have very little to add. If you see Ned tell him Mr & Mrs Stoddart[13] that he recommended to me here, seemed very well pleased with the attention I paid them, and I thought them very pleasant good people.

With Duty to my Father I remain Dr Mama ever your affectionate dutiful d'r, M. Scully
[P.S.] Denys joins me in all [that is] kind.

[*Source*: Huddleston Papers C1/MH75]

[1]Her sister.
[2]Her brother Richard.
[3]Maria O'Connor.
[4]The Scullys of Kilfeacle usually went to Castleconnell, on the Shannon above Limerick, a then fashionable resort.
[5]Her brother Edward.
[6]Lord Hardwicke's eldest son, Philip, Viscount Royston.
[7]Richard Huddleston was Major of the Cambridgeshire Militia. Letters in the Huddleston Papers show that Lord Hardwicke, as Colonel, corresponded with him about regimental matters.
[8]An entry in James Scully's diary for 12 March 1803 shows that he had his sore toe then. It was still sore on 29 March.
[9]The Chancellor, Lord Redesdale, married a sister of Spencer Perceval on 6 June 1803. A letter he wrote to his future brother-in-law on 27 November 1802 indicates that he was living in a cottage at Kilmacud (near Stillorgan, Co. Dublin) while work on a house was proceeding. He called it Ardrinn (Perceval Papers, Add. MSS. 49, 188 f.79). When Dr Milner visited it in 1807 he found it being used as a Catholic boarding school (*Letters from Ireland*, p. 39). It is now called St Michael's.
[10]Fra Bartolomeo Ruspoli (1754–1836), a younger brother of the 3rd (Papal) Prince, was a Balí of the Order of Malta. He came to England in 1802 on a passport obtained for him by Monsignor Erskine and was there when the Pope appointed him Grand Master of the Order on 16 September 1802. He was apparently reluctant to accept the post for it was reported in *The Times* of 11 February 1803 that a second brief had been sent to him urging his acceptance. On 7 March *The Times* reported that the Pope had appointed someone else. Mary Scully's approval of his conduct may have been influenced by the political context. Under one of the articles of the Peace of Amiens the British undertook to evacuate Malta when various arrangements had been made, one of which was that the Order would take over the government when a

Grand Master was appointed (W. M. Brady, *Anglo-Roman Papers*, Paisley, 1890, p. 149; William Hardman, *History of Malta . . . 1798–1815*, 1909, pp. 449, 461, 462).
[11]Unidentified.
[12]Her first cousin, Francis Huddleston.
[13]Stephen Stoddart was a Lieutenant in the Enniskillens during Edward Huddleston's brief tenure of a cornetcy in that regiment (*Army List* 1800).

52   *To Ferdinand Huddleston, Sawston Hall, Saffron Walden, Essex*

Bagot Street, Dublin, 21 June 1803

My dear Sir,

    . . . . In the course of this summer I mean to visit England with Mary. . . . And as it becomes necessary for me to provide for expences and payments to be made there to the amount of £500, I beg you will allow me to reckon upon your assistance as far as that sum — in which case I shall be well content to wait until next year for the remainder of the first Bond of £1000 which has been due since May 1802[1]. . . . The want of money here is daily encreasing, owing to the War, & to the immense sums spent by our Landlords in foreign countries — and one effect is, amongst others, that the Exchange, or loss by taking it over to England, has risen to £17 in every £100. And that exclusively of the Interest and Commission to be paid on borrowing it here, which exceed £10 more in the £100. . . .   [*Source*: Huddleston Papers C2/S1]

[1]See No. 46.

53   *To the Earl of Hardwicke, Lord Lieutenant of Ireland*

Bagot Street, Tuesday, noon 26 July [1803]

My Lord,

    I have the honour of enclosing to your Excellency my father's proposal for raising a regiment in the county of Tipperary, somewhat altered in words but not in substance from that contained in the letter.[1] My brothers, tho' not bred to the army, might prove good officers, especially the younger of them; and they have had a good deal of cavalry service in 1798.

    If the proposal shall be accepted with the condition that the service of the regiment shall extend to Europe generally, as your Excellency was pleased to suggest, I believe that the men would enlist for that extent of service, if they could rely upon being commanded by one of my brothers.

    It would afford my father sincere gratification to have an opportunity, in this or any other manner, of testifying his personal attachment to your Excellency & his sense of the benefits derived to this country from your administration.

I wrote to him to send me accounts, from time to time, of the state & disposition of the people in that part of Ireland, & I shall take the liberty of transmitting to your Excellency such of those accounts as shall appear to deserve your attention.[2]   [*Source*: Hardwicke Papers Add. MSS. 35, 741 f.20.]

[Enclosure]

[Draft]
    The proposal of James Scully in the county of Tipperary.
    Willing to support his Excellency's government of this country to the utmost of his power, Mr Scully hereby offers to raise forthwith in the County of Tipperary for his Majesty's service any complmt. of men not exceeding 500 upon the same terms and to serve in the same countries, as are prescribed by the late Act of Parlt. for raising the Royal Army of Reserve in Ireland.[3]
    As he reckons much upon the attachment of individuals to himself and his family in raising these men, he begs to suggest that the execution of the plan would be facilitated by the appointment of one of his sons to the command of the Regiment or Corps to be raised. And (as his eldest son is serving in the Lawyers Corps in Dublin) he offers his second or third son[4] for the situation —they are respectively 26 & 24 years & are active energetic & loyal.
    But as he does not propose to himself or his family any pecuniary advantage from this undertaking, he will cheerfully acquiesce in any modification of this proposal that Govt shall point out by placing an officer of experience at the head of the corps, or immediately under his son, as may be thought expedient.
    Should this proposal not be accepted, he intreats his Excellency to accept the offer of his & his family's best services influence and exertions in the south of Ireld. to be employed in such a manner as his Excellency shall deem conducive to the safety of this country.[5]   [*Source*: Callanan Papers]

[1]The enclosure is missing from the Hardwicke Papers but can be supplied from a draft/copy in the Callanan Papers.
[2]No such reports have been found among Lord Hardwicke's papers.
[3]Entitled "An act to enable his Majesty more effectively to provide for the defence and security of the realm" (Geo. III 43 Ch. 55 section II). It had received the royal assent on 11 June 1803.
[4]James and Edmund Scully.
[5]"This truly spirited offer" was reported in the *DEP* of 30 July. It was duly entered in Lord Hardwicke's Applications Book (Add. MSS.35,785) but the space for the answer given was not filled in. It was not included among some two hundred offers to raise or serve in regiments transmitted by the Castle to the Home Office from June to the middle of August (HO 100/111). According to an obituary on James Scully in the *Dublin Chronicle* of 8 March 1816 it was politely declined along with a similar offer from Lord Melville.

54   *To the Earl of Hardwicke, Lord Lieutenant of Ireland*

Bagot Street, Thursday morning, 28 July [1803]

My Lord,

I had the honour of transmitting my father's proposal on Tuesday evening to your Excellency, thro' a person who happened to be going to the Castle & undertook to deliver it to your Excellency. It was my intention to take it myself, but the unexpected call on my corps that afternoon detained me on guard.[1]

If by any accident it may not have found its way to your Excellency's hands, I should be happy to be informed of it, & in that case shall immediately replace the paper which I have sent by a copy.

[*Source*: Hardwicke Papers Add. MSS.35, 741 f.44]

[1]After the Emmet rising on 23 July the Lawyers Corps with the rest of the Dublin yeomanry had been placed on permanent duty. Whoever took Scully's letter would appear to have conveyed also a short message from him which is recorded in the Lord Lieutenant's Applications Book (see No. 53 n.5): "On coming to town on Saturday he [Scully] took shelter in a cabin from a shower of rain two miles on the other side of Naas. The women told him they hoped he would escape as something should happen in Dublin & throughout the country. He observed there was not a single labourer in the fields between Naas and Dublin".

55   *To Mrs Bostock*

8 August 1803

[Extract][1]

since my last to you we have continued in a state of profound quiet & we have every prospect of continuing so & I was happy to learn to day from Ld Hardwicke & Doctr. Lindsay[2] that government make very light of the late attempt[3] which was endead very despicable tho' very gasconading the little of contrivance that was in it has been all disclosed — I have inclosed three copies for yourself & our frinds of our letters upon the late Catholick address[4] we conceived it to be unwise unwelcome to Government & servile because it proposes to forego our Emancipation which we understand that the English Catholicks lately solicited for. Ld Fingal Sir I. Beleu[5] & a couple of bishops hoped to be considered as our sole pilots & to lead us to approve of this counter address to that of the English Catholicks who very handsomely solicited our cooperation but where refused by these our pilots.[6]   [*Source*: Huddleston Papers C3/B19]

[1]From a copy which Mrs Bostock wrote out for her nephew Richard Huddleston on 15 August: it was no doubt read aloud as she took it down in her own idiosyncratic spelling and punctuation.
[2]Dr Charles Dalrymple Lindsay DD
[3]The Emmet rising of 23 July, which in *A Catholic's Advice to his brethren* (see No. 56) Scully dismissed as not exceeding in numbers that of rioters at a country fair; and which his father described as "a rising of the lower orders of the people . . . a wicked plot against our present government" (diary, 2 August 1803).
[4]The pamphlet, of which Scully kept four copies among his papers (MS.27, 507), was entitled: *The address of the Irish Catholics to the Lord Lieutenant, with answer, and two letters by Theobald McKenna and Denys Scully*. It criticised an address presented to the Lord Lieutenant on 4 August by a deputation consisting of Lord Fingall, two Archbishops and other prominent Catholics because in condemning the rising it had assured the government that however ardent their wish might be to participate in the full benefits of the constitution they could never seek such participation other than through the unbiassed determination of the legislature.
[5]Sir E. Bellew.
[6]Plowden (*History*, I, p. 165) says that he himself put forward the draft of an address to a score of English and Irish Catholics who happened to be in Lord Kenmare's house in London, and it was agreed that it should be shown to the Home Secretary for approval. The latter, however, returned it with so many alterations that it was decided not to present the address at all.

56   *From John Purcell*[1]

August 15 [1803]

Dear Sir,

I have read with particular pleasure your very interesting and valuable Address.[2] Nothing can be better calculated to open the Eyes of our deluded Countrymen. At this eventful Moment the happiest effects may be expected from a Performance so judicious and well timed; which merits, and must receive, the Applause of every true friend to Ireland. [*Source*: Scully Papers]

[1]John Purcell MD (1744–1806), of Kilkenny and Dublin — a leading medical practitioner of Dublin, one of whose patients was Lady Moira. His son assumed the surname of Fitzgerald and was father of Edward Fitzgerald, translator of the *Rubaiyat*. He signed the 1805 petition, giving his address as Sackville Street.
[2]*An Irish Catholic's Advice to his brethren, how to estimate their present situation and repel French invasion, civil wars and slavery*, the first edition of which had just been published by Hugh Fitzpatrick. It evoked a number of replies through which it received considerable publicity, including an attack in the autumn number of the *Anti-Jacobin Review*. In 1804 Scully brought out a second edition, with a long introduction replying to criticisms: this was reviewed by the *Gentleman's Magazine* of October 1804. The pamphlet did not please the extremists on either side. On the one hand, it showed Scully as a "Castle Catholic", for he spoke approvingly of

Cornwallis, Castlereagh, Hardwicke and Redesdale, excusing their shortcomings on the pleas that all governments are liable to make mistakes. On the other, Protestant critics asked what his advice would have been if the French were not the blackguards he made them out to be; took exception to his calling King William a Dutch invader; and protested at his putting the massacre of Catholics in hot blood at Ballinamuck on an equal footing with the murder of Protestant prisoners on Wexford bridge. The *Anti-Jacobin* sneered at his parentage: "It is a singular coincidence that Mr Scully's grandfather and Napoleon's were both butchers". On reading this passage Henry Huddleston wrote to his father asking "why will people who have such vulnerable points dare others to the field?". There is no evidence, however, that Scully's grandfather was a butcher, though his great-uncle was.

57   *From Theobald McKenna to Clonmel*

27 August [18]03

Dear Scully,

I have had my eye on the circulation of yr work[1] & I have the pleasure to tell you that it has circulated well & widely and laid ample grounds for yr reputation. It was indeed admirably timed and executed with spirit.

The arrest of Emmet[2] makes a good deal of sensation, nothing transpires as to the evidence agt. him, I fear it is not strong altho I have not a doubt that he was the French agent and the contriver of the whole business. I have been sworn one of the Alfridian duennaries[3] to preserve the peace of my parish[4] & I have notified to Mrs Moore & her fair neighbours not to keep disorderly houses. God bless you.

[P.S.] Grace[5] reprinted my Fogarty[6] but he omitted some strokes calculated to mark the characteristic circumlocution of the Irish.

I don't believe I have praised you enough for a young author but upon my word I think highly of your performance.   [*Source*: Scully Papers]

[1]*An Irish Catholic's Advice* (see No. 56 n.2).
[2]Robert Emmet had been arrested on 25 August. He was examined by the Privy Council on 30 August, tried on 19 September and executed the following day.
[3]A made-up word, probably reflecting King Alfred's reputation as the founder of a nunnery.
[4]Although at this season McKenna was writing to the Castle from his little farm at Grove Lodge, Stillorgan, his Dublin address was Great Denmark Street. Both Temple Street, where Mrs Moore seems to have lived with her son Edward Moore, and Dominick Street, where her O'Connor relations resided, were in the same area.
[5]Perhaps Richard Grace, later in business at 3 Mary Street, as a bookseller and stationer, but more probably George Grace who had recently founded the *Clonmel Herald*: he was a barrister and seeking favour from the Irish administration (*The Irish Booklover*, XVII, No. 2, 1929).

[6]On 26 August McKenna had sent to Marsden in the Castle "some honest sentiments in native form" together with his revision of them and on 3 September he said in the postscript to another letter "Pray read Paddy Fogarty" (Official Papers 524 153/82). As no trace of the pamphlet has been found it may be surmised that the Castle advised against its publication.

58   *To Ferdinand Huddleston, Sawston Hall, Saffron Walden, Essex*

7 Thayer Street, Manchester Square, London[1] 17 September 1803
My dear Sir,
   I had the pleasure of receiving your letter in Ireland & should be unwilling to put you to the inconvenience of paying the whole £1,000 at once, as £500 will be sufficient for my occasions at present. I brought no money from Dublin, on account of the Exchange being 20 per Cent against me at present, and therefore am obliged to request your assistance (until I can have the pleasure of seeing you next month) as far as £150 or £200 for which you can perhaps send me, by Post, a draft on London. The rest can lie over until the 10th of next month, until which time I shall be detained in Town by some business.
   We came here yesterday, & had the pleasure of conveying Miss Jane from Lord Shrewsbury's.[2] She, and your other friends here, are well. Mrs Bostock has been in indifferent health, but appears now to be pretty well. Mary is a little fatigued by the length of her journey. She joins in best regards to you, Mrs Huddleston, & the family.   [*Source*: Huddleston Papers C2/S7]

[1]The address of his wife's aunt, Mrs Bostock.
[2]The 15th Earl. A letter of 25 May 1805 from Jane Huddleston to her mother speaks of seeing Lady Shrewsbury almost every day.

59   *To Ferdinand Huddleston from London, 13 October 1803*

   Acknowledges the receipt on 20 September of £150 paid by Lefevre & Co on 20 September and the remaining £350 paid yesterday by Henry Huddleston. The £50 due on 5 October to Mrs Bostock remains unpaid. His wife, Mary Scully, is suffering from a colic accompanied by fever, and from the consequences of a strain received two months ago when jumping from a low wall. She is gaining ground but slowly. In other respects she had previously enjoyed uniform good health, beyond what could be expected from the delicacy of her frame and constitution.

[*Source*: Huddleston Papers C2/S2]

60   *Petition on printed form to an Orange Lodge*[1]

November 1803

The Petition of Denis Scully Esq *to the Worshipful Master and Brethren of*
O L No. 216[2]

    humbly sheweth,

    That your petitioner . . . solicits the honor of being admitted a member of
the lowest order which he will esteem as the highest honor that cou'd be
confered on him. . . .

We the undernamed Brethren of O L No. 0 *do recommend to* the above
named Denis Scully to take it into consideration if he had not better apply to
the Hon[le.] Society of Crops[3] as his sentiments and opinions seem to agree
more with theirs than with loyal subjects.[4]   [*Source*: Scully Papers]

[1]The words in italics are printed in the original, which is a standard form of
application for membership.
[2]One of six lodges in the Stewartstown District of County Tyrone (information
kindly supplied by the Grand Secretary of the Grand Orange Lodge of Ireland).
[3]According to Edward Hay (*History of the insurrection of the county of Wexford*,
Dublin, 1803, p. 57): "any person having their hair cut short and therefore called a
croppy, by which appellation the soldiery designated an United Irishman".
[4]In his *Advice* (see No. 56 n.2) Scully had said some hard words about Orangemen,
who would not have liked King William being called "a Dutch invader".

61   *From Charles Butler*

Lincolns Inn, 2 May 1804

Dear Sir,

    I felt myself much obliged by your sending me your pamphlet,[1] which I
have read with great pleasure. I have desired the bearer to leave with you, a
little work[2] which I request your acceptance.[3]   [*Source*: Scully Papers]

[1]Probably the second edition of *An Irish Catholic's Advice to his brethren*, a copy of
which, along with two other pamphlets, is to be seen in a bound volume in the
Bodleian Library marked with Charles Butler's name.
[2]Scully's Common Place Book shows that on 9 May he received from Charles Butler
as a present *Horae Juridicae Subsecivae — Notes respecting the geography,*
chronology and literary history of the principal codes and original documents of the
Grecian, Roman, Feudal and Canon Law.
[3]This letter, written by a clerk, is addressed in what seems to be Butler's own hand to
"Counsellor Skully".

62   *From Edmund Scully to Baggot Street, Dublin*

Kilfeacle [Co. Tipperary] 21 July 1804

My dear Denys,

I think proper to send by James O'Reilly[1] of Tipp'y a Copy of the entire Proceedings of the Court of Enquiry with my Defence,[2] as I have got no answer from Ld Conyngham as yet I fear he has forwarded them to Dublin. If so I hope you'll do what you can for me. Ld Mathew's Interest will also be in my favor.[3] Had you but known the party & underhand actions during the entire proceedings I am sure 'twould give you a dislike to this Country which should now be free from prejudices & Orange principles. They have got the Monaghan Militia here who are all declared Orangemen & support Sir Tho's Fitzgerald[4] & his party. They are to march in a few days for the Curragh. I am happy to tell you Sir Tho's Fitzgerald has got a complete beating in the Mendoza Line from Jerry.[5] As he intends writing the particulars to you by tomorrow's post I shall say no more but that Jerry has come off with high honor, his Conduct is much approved of, by my father & every liberal minded Man in this Country. Tho' Sir Tho's got every provocation to send him a message he preferred lodging informations.

I have every reason to think my match with Miss O'Brien will very soon take place. I hope you'll keep it entirely secret for a few Days. I am very much interested about the Court of Enquiry and I hope you'll if possible not allow those damned Orangemen to triumph should the proceedings go to Dublin. As to the opinion of the Court I understand it is what every Catholic who knew the members supposed they'd deliver, a most partial one & decidedly against me & my Men. Yet government I hope are more liberal.

I expect you'll as often as convenient should anything occur in Dublin write to me.

Believe me your most affect'e Brother Edm'd Scully James

[P.S.] Please to give my best Regards to Mrs Scully   [*Source*: Scully Papers]

[1]Unidentified.

[2]It is probable that Scully submitted the papers to the Lord Lieutenant, for Hardwicke wrote to the Military Secretary at the Castle on 23 July (Add. MSS.35, 777) saying that he had read the proceedings with great attention. From his comments it appears that the incident occurred on 1 July and that the main charge against Edmund Scully was that he had failed to exert his influence as an officer and neighbour over two of his men who had torn a lily from a Protestant's buttonhole. He had then behaved in a violent and intemperate manner when the two men were arrested, and in the presence of two witnesses had made some assertion (unspecified) to Lord Conyngham (the General). Hardwicke suggested to the Military Secretary that no steps should be taken until it appeared whether Scully

was disposed to make an apology. Edmund would seem to have complied, for in writing to the Home Secretary on 11 November 1804 (Add. MSS.35,709) Hardwicke mentioned having done a service to Denys Scully's brother by putting an end to a quarrel.

[3]Hardwicke's letter of 23 July shows that Edmund was an officer in the militia regiment known as Lord Mathew's Legion.

[4]He had been created a baronet in 1801.

[5]Jerry or Jeremiah was the youngest of the Scully brothers. Daniel Mendoza (in *DNB*) was a well known pugilist of the time. If Jerry wrote the letter referred to, it has not survived and the nature of the quarrel remains unknown.

63   *From Jeremiah Scully to 34 Bagott Street, Dublin*

Tipperary, 4 September 1804

Dear Denys,

I had a letter from James[1] yesterday, from Castleconnell where he and the rest of the family have been this week past. They are all well. My father is recovering. He desires I would remit to you the enclosed draft for £62.10.–, of which £37.10.– is for William,[2] the remaining £25.– together with £40– you owe my father, he would thank you to give Nancy.[3] James settled his difference with King: Penefather[4] about the horse. *My father gives Penefather 50 Guineas, so that he has the horse for 50 Guineas.* I would thank you to acknowledge the receipt of this, as the Bill is at short sight.

I remain your affectionate Brother, Jerem'h Scully.

P.S. I hope Mrs S. is well.   [*Source*: Scully Papers]

[1]His brother.
[2]The brother who was a doctor in Devon.
[3]His sister Anne Mahon.
[4]Kingsmill Pennefather (d. 1819), son of Richard Pennefather of New Park.

64   *From his mother Catherine Scully to 34 Baggott Street, Dublin*

Kilfeacle [Co. Tipperary] 1 October 1804

My Dr Den's,

I was very happy to find by your letter to James yesterday that you were well and it gave us very great pleasure to hear from Linny Keating[1] that Mrs Scully is wonderfully recover'd. I hope she still continues to ride out every day. The bearer goes for the carraige[2] and I am extreamly oblig'd by all the trouble you had about it. I never got the Lucan water that Mic Dwyer[3] promised to send me. It was only last Saturday that I got a letter from him

leting me know it was at Munstereeven. I may as well and better get it from Dublin as from thence six dozen I expect'd perhaps it cou'd be pack'd into the carraige which wou'd save me the trouble of sending so far for it. My coachman expects that Mr Collier[4] will not forget him as he is very carefull of his carraige for which he said he wou'd give him a couple of guineas. I shall expect a little varnish from him for the Boot. Your Father received great benefit by Castle Connel — he is now able to ride and is quiet free from pain (thank god). Mun[5] only stay'd a week there — he did not seem to injoy the place — he came home and remain'd here ontill the morning we were expect'd home and then went to Tramore where he still remains. He wrote to his Father this day on the former subject. Marraige the Army or a seperate settlement to none of which your Father wou'd consent but for him to come home and mind his business as usual which I fear he will not consent to. God help him he is very badly advised. He has no complaint but that he cou'd not live here by any means without a seperate establishment. It is a great pity that he is led away in such a manner for he has no vice and he has a good heart and ontill now I thought he had a good head. James left us this morning for the races of Limerick and from thence to the fair of Balinaslo. Your Father and Joanna[6] unite in love to you and Mrs Scully and compliments to Miss Hudleston[7] with My D'r Den's — your loving and affect'e Mother, Catherine Scully
[P.S.] Will you tell Mic Dwyer to let me know the expence of the Lucan water. Your Father does not go to Balinaslo.   [*Source*: Scully Papers]

[1]Her daughter Lucinda (Lucy), wife of Leonard Keating of Garranlea.
[2]The numerous misspellings in this and other letters reflect Mrs Scully's weakness in orthography.
[3]Probably Michael Dwyer of Fox Dwyer and Co., Batchelor's Walk, Dublin, mentioned in No. 409.
[4]The *Dublin Directory* shows two coachmakers of this name: Charles Collier of 12 Coles's Lane and William Collier & Sons of 14 Kevan St.
[5]Her son Edmund.
[6]Her unmarried daughter.
[7]Jane Huddleston.

65   *From Mr Dugald Campbell[1] for the Lord Lieutenant*
                      to Bagot Street

                                      Dublin Castle, 2 October 1804
Sir,
     I am directed by the Lord Lieutenant to acknowledge your letter of the 30th ultimo, enclosing a memorial from a person of the name of Edmund

Scully, and to inform you that His Excellency will cause immediate enquiry to be made into the circumstances of his case, of which you shall receive further and he hopes early information.[2]   [*Source*: Scully Papers]

[1]Described in the Dublin Directory as Private Secretary to the Lord Lieutenant and Gentleman-at-large in his household.
[2]Possibly in connexion with the proceedings against him referred to in No. 62.

66   *From Sir E. Nepean to 34 Bagot Street, Dublin*

                    Chief Secretary's Office, Dublin Castle, 5 October 1804
Mr Taylor[1] by direction of Sir Evan Nepean, acquaints Mr Scully that in consequence of the removal of the Books and Papers from the House of Lords,[2] it has not been possible as yet to arrange them, but when they are put in order, his application for Lord Mount Cashel[3] will be attended to. Mr Scully will be pleased to mention what particular volumes of the Statutes are due to his Lordship.   [*Source*: Scully Papers]

[1]The *Dublin Directory* of 1804 lists two clerks in the Chief Secretary's Office called Taylor — William and Thomas.
[2]The Irish House of Lords.
[3]Still in Italy. See No. 50 n.4.

67   *From Michael Hughes[1] to 34 Baggot Street, Dublin*

                    Georges Quay [Dublin] 11 October 1804
Copy
Mr M. Hughes
Sir,
    We will give the Roman Catholic Parish Estate by the proper authorised persons Three Hundred Pounds for a renewal of our present leases in stocking lane[2] for their entire term provided it also includes the right & possession of the Gateway under our now holding in said stocking lane for the like term and request your taking the proper steps to lay this *our final* offer before the persons who are authorised to agree thereto as soon as possible.

                                        John & Pat Boylan[3]
                                        Grafton Street 10 October [1804]
Sir,
    As a Trustee to the Townsend street Chapel Estate you will please to

attend at a meeting on sunday next in said Chapel between one & two o'Clock for the purpose of taking the above proposal into consideration.

[*Source*: Scully Papers]

[1]Of Georges Quay. One of the representatives of St Andrew's Parish on the committee of Dublin Catholics in 1806 (see No. 146); also recorded in 1806 and 1811 as a member of the General Committee.
[2]Off Townsend Street.
[3]Unidentified.

68   *From Lord Fingall to Baggot Street, Dublin*

Saturday morn. [?3 November 1804][1]

Private

My dear Sir,

   I came late yesterday and had not time to call on you. You rendered so much service to the Cath. cause at our last Meeting — you will I hope attend to day. I am convinced prudence and delay, would bring abt. unanimity, which, if possible shd not be sacrificed.   [*Source*: Scully Papers]

[1]The cover is endorsed by Scully "October 1804", but a report from Sir Evan Nepean to the Home Office shows that the meeting of 27 October was the first attended by Lord Fingall and explains what Scully's service was. Arguing that a communication should first be established with Pitt he secured a week's adjournment to 3 November and it is this adjourned meeting which Lord Fingall hopes he will attend. Its outcome was reported by Nepean on 4 November. Scully, he said, had forcefully opposed petitioning and had referred to the Convention Act of 1793, "an act prepared by Lord Clare for the express purpose of preventing Catholic meetings"; in a discussion on the admission of Dublin merchants to the committee he had argued that all the merchants of the kingdom had equal pretensions, while the landed interest was perhaps to be considered before either of them. To give time for differences to be resolved the meeting was further adjourned to 17 November (HO 100/123, ff.114, 134).

69   *From his mother Catherine Scully to Baggott Street, Dublin*

Kilfeacle [Co. Tipperary] 3 November 1804

My Dr Den's,

   I wou'd have reply'd to your affectonate letter before now but wait'd to know the result of Joanna's match with Mr Sadleir.[1] It was agreed on the day before yesterday but is not to take place ontill your Father returns from Cork to which place he went this day and I belive will not return for three weeks ontill he will finish his cattle. I find Joanna was more partial to Sadleir as being near home than to Harney[2] tho the later has much a larger fortune and that for ever. I had a letter from William yesterday. He mentions that he has sent his wife[3] and child home to Dublin to her Mother who imposed on his youth in geting them illegally married when he was not eighteen years of age and not capable of knowing what he was about. Your Father thinks it is all a scheam of his to get an addition from him to his income. I hope it is no more for as he did not part her at a much earlier period than now I don't think it wou'd look well in the eyes of God or the world to do so now. Your Father forgot to leave me Mr Collier's account that I may inclose it to you. He before gave you his receipt in full for the new carraige. The additional charges he makes in cushin and long reins we did not order or want as we drive from the saddle. The spring curtains and carpet were possitively left in the old carraige for which he ought to allow. I have not yet got the Lucan water nor do I belive ever shall. I shall be very much oblig'd to you to send me a few dozen of it by a Cashill Carrman to be left at William Murphy's. It was of infinite service to me when I drank it in Dublin and for a short time after while I had it. I beg to know whether Mrs Scully still continues to ride out. I am told she is geting fat fair and strong, which I assure you gave me pleasure. With best wish's to her and Miss Hudleston, I remain My Dr Den's, your loving and affect'e Mother, Catherine Scully

[*Source*: Scully Papers]

[1]Clement Sadleir of Shronehill.
[2]Charles Harney (also spelt Hartney).
[3]Anna Sophia Roe, daughter of a widow and without a fortune, for marrying whom William had incurred his father's wrath.

70   *From his father James Scully to Bagot Street*

Cork, 13 November 1804

Dr Dens.

I recd. yr. favr. My friends & I are of oppinn. that Mr Pitt is the proper person if to be [one word illegible]. If Mr Foster[1] wd. undertake it he is now a popular & (I am told) more liberl. man. Some other Irishman should be prefered to any man in opposition — I wd advise not to let this business go through any man sharp agst. governmt.[2] The noblemen & gentlemen that will meet in Dublin are best judges of the business.   [*Source*: Scully Papers]

[1]Presumably John Foster, formerly Speaker of the Irish House of Commons and now Chancellor of the Exchequer for Ireland.
[2]James Ryan and his friends had from the beginning determined that if Pitt refused to sponsor the Catholic petition they would hand it over to the opposition, not wanting to embarrass Pitt but realising that they would do so (Nepean to King 24 October

1804: HO 100/123, f.104). Denys Scully's behaviour throughout shows that he had grave misgivings about resorting to this alternative.

71   *From James Ryan to Baggott Street, Dublin*

Friday Evening, 23 November 1804

Dear Sir,

   You are requested to meet the Gentlemen who were appointed to prepare an application on behalf of the Roman Catholics of Ireland for the repeal of the Laws still in force against their Body at Lord Fingall's House in Gt. Denmark Street on Sunday next at One O'Clock.[1]   [*Source*: Scully Papers]

[1]The meeting called for Sunday 25 November was that of a select committee appointed by the third General Meeting of the Catholic body on 17 November to prepare an application for the total repeal of the penal laws and report to the next general meeting on 2 December. In the interval there had been two developments. On 20 November the Lord Lieutenant, on instructions from the Home Secretary, had informed Lord Fingall of Pitt's decision to oppose a petition (HO 100/123, f.182). On 17 November, however, Sir Evan Nepean, without informing the Lord Lieutenant, had sent direct to Pitt the minutes of the meeting of 17 November as provided by Robert Marshall, thus allowing the Catholics to believe that the decision was not final (see No. 83 n.1).

72   *To the Earl of Hardwicke, Lord Lieutenant of Ireland*

Bagot Street, 4 December 1804

My Lord,

   Your Excellency was pleased upon my father's application through me in July last, to recommend a Mr Walter Scully[1] of Tipperary to His Highness the Duke of York for a commission in the army and it was signified to me, through your Excellency's Secretary, that His R. Highness had accordingly placed him upon his list. This gentleman informs me that he has anxiously watched the Gazette since that time without seeing his name included amongst the numerous military appointments which have appeared and he intreats me to lay his situation again before your Excellency. Possibly the list may have been very numerous or some other difficulty or cause of delay may exist, of which he is not aware — I hope not to be deemed importunate in complying with his desire. I merely do so having been the medium of the application in the first instance — not presuming however to suggest a single observation upon it.   [*Source*: Hardwicke Papers, Add. MSS.35, 754, f.38]

[1]A second cousin of Scully's, an ensign in the Tipperary militia. The application is entered in Lord Hardwicke's Applications Book (Add. MSS. 35, 785) under 22 May

1804 and the answer given was "will recommend him". It was not until 9 March, when he was in London with the delegation to Pitt, that Scully was informed of this, by Sir Evan Nepean. Walter Scully was commissioned as an ensign in the 89th Foot on 12 April 1805.

73   *From Daniel O'Connell/19 December 1804/*

He has been thinking about sending someone to London on the business of the petition[1] and offers to go himself, even during term, expenses to be paid out of a fund to which he also would contribute.

> [*Source*: O'Connell: *Correspondence* I, No. 137, taken from the now missing original in the Scully Papers]

[1]See No. 71 n.1. At the second meeting of the select committee on 2 December Randal McDonnell, seconded by John Keogh, had proposed that the committee should content themselves for the present with a mere statement of grievances but Scully had argued in strong language for a petition and it had been unanimously agreed to recommend one to both Houses of parliament. A subcommittee of five, which included Scully and O'Connell, had been appointed to draft it. On 16 December the draft had been unanimously approved by the General Meeting, which then adjourned to 2 February, leaving the management of the petition in the hands of the drafting subcommittee augmented by four new members, who were to have the power to summon an augmented select committee of thirty-one members. Reporting to the Home Secretary on 16 December Lord Hardwicke said that the petition was in very temperate language and that "it is no part of their plan to aggrandise the bishops of their own communion" (Hardwicke Papers, Add. MSS.35, 754, f.167).

74   *From Daniel'O Connell, Tralee, to Baggot Street,*
21 December 1804

He now thinks there will be no difficulty in finding persons to undertake part of the business of the petition, in which case Scully will not mention his name, but he is willing to sacrifice earnings at the bar if it is necessary. In any event he would fain persuade Scully to share the burden, as his long and minute attention to the Catholic question peculiarly qualifies him. He is convinced the business cannot be well done without Scully's assistance.

> [*Source*: O'Connell, *Correspondence*, I, No. 138, taken from the now missing original in the Scully Papers]

75   *From his mother Catherine Scully to Baggot Street, Dublin*

Kilfeacle [Co. Tipperary] 29 December 1804

My Dr Den's,

I am extreamly concern'd to find by your last affect'te letter that poor Mrs Scully continues to be so ill. Your Father saw your Uncle Jerry[1] in Cashill this day and was sorry to hear from him that she look'd mighty delicate. May the great God restore her to her health. As the fine weather will now soon approch I hope it will serve her. Indeed the present very cold frosty weather is very unfavourable to her but when it grows mild and that she will be fit to travel don't loose time in taking her to England as that climate must agree with her much better than this. We have Mr Harney and his Brother here since last Sunday. He seems to be a steady proper gentleman like young man. I wish you cou'd see him. I suppose your Father wrote you formerly every thing about him and property and settlement which I belive cannot be finish'd without your assistance. I beg you'll let me hear often how Mrs Scully is going on. This family unite in love to you and her wishing you both many happy years. Compliments to Miss Hudleston. I remain My Dr Den's, your loving and affect'te Mother Catherine Scully.

[P.S.] Many thanks for the trouble you had about the Lucan water. I desir'd a Tip'y carrman call for it.   [*Source*: Scully Papers]

[1]Jeremiah Scully, of Silverfort.

76   *From Mr [James] FitzGerald*[1]

12 January 1805

Mr FitzGerald will consider himself highly obliged by Mr Scully's informing him of the result of this day's meeting.[2]   [*Source*: Scully Papers]

[1]Identified by Scully on the cover as "late Prime Sergeant". Parliament was due to open on 15 January and as MP for Ennis he no doubt wished to get the latest news of the petition, which he supported when it was debated in the division on 14 May 1805.
[2]There is no record of this meeting, which would have been one of the select committee entrusted with the petition.

77   *From Randal MacDonnell to 34 Baggot Street, Dublin*

Allen's Court, Mulinahack [Co. Dublin] 16 January [1805]

Dear Sir,

I have seen Lord Fingall this evening, & he has fix'd to be at my House to-morrow at one O'Clock, when I hope it will be convenient to you to come; I regretted very much the disappointm't wch his not arriving in Town in time this day occationed [*sic*] to you.[1]   [*Source*: Scully Papers]

[1]In a letter of 17 January Alexander Marsden, Undersecretary at the Castle, told the Lord Lieutenant that he was paying attention to R. MacDonnell because of his influence on the Catholic body, and flattering his vanity. Three days earlier MacDonnell had offered him a copy of the petition, which he said had already been given to Nepean. He had replied that he did not want to see it, as he entirely disapproved of its being brought forward, and urged MacDonnell to add his weight to Lord Fingall, showing him a letter from Lord Cornwallis received two days ago, which he had also communicated to Lord Fingall. In consequence, Marsden continued, Lord Fingall had called on him that day, the 17th, and asked what the reaction would be if the Catholics, instead of petitioning, presented the Lord Lieutenant with a statement of their case: they would not expect an answer other than that it had been transmitted to London. Marsden replied that on the understanding the idea was Lord Fingall's own it would be given due consideration (HO 100/128, f.11).

78   *From Joanna Scully to Bagot Street, Dublin*

Kilfeacle [Co. Tipperary] 19 January 1805

My Dear Denys,

I had the pleasure of receiving your affectionate Letter for which I am much oblig'd. As I know that you are interested to know my future destiny, which has been this day finally agreed upon, the money matters I do not know any thing about but I have no dread but my Father looked sharp to them. The only favor I have now to request of you is that you will indulge me with seeing you here before I take a new Name. As to poor Mrs Scully I sincerely regret she is not equal to coming so far & if she was I should indeed be very forgetful of her kindness & attention to me at all times if I would not be happy to see her also. I will thank you to present her with my love & best wishes for her happiness. I mentioned to my Mother your kind offer of taking the trouble to assist at the writings for which I am much oblig'd. I hope you will like your intended Brother.[1] He seems a sensible steady very well tempered man. At least he is a great cheat from his countenance if he proves otherwise. I remain my dear Denys your ever affectionate sister
          Joanna Scully   [*Source*: Scully Papers]

[1]Charles Harney (Hartney). An entry in James Scully's diary on the same day reads: "Mr Harney and I signed an agreement of marriage this day between his son Chas. and my daughter Joana — to her I give £3500 fortune".

79   *From James Ryan to Baggott Street, Dublin*

22 January 1805

Dear Sir,

You are requested to attend Lord Fingall's House in Gt. Denmark Street on Sunday the 27th Inst. at one o'clock.[1]

[1]See No. 81 n.1.

80   *From Ed Moore to Bagot Street, Dublin*

Temple Street [Dublin] 24 January 1805

Dr Sir,

I can let Lord Fingal have a copy of the Petition tomorrow night or Saturday morning.

If you think it would be advisable to put the marginal notes annexed to it, be so good as to send me your Copy again & it shall be done, the person who made my Copy omitted them.

I think the two Notes viz, pointing out the words of the Oath, & the preamble of the Irish Act relieving the Chs. [Catholics] should not be admitted.[1]

My Mother[2] & I beg our best respects to Mrs Scully.

[*Source*: Scully Papers]

[1]There are no marginal notes in the surviving manuscript petition to the House of Lords, but the printed text published by Keating, Brown & Co. was accompanied by explanatory footnotes, one of which referred to the oath and another to the preamble of the Irish Act of 1778.

[2]The Mrs Moore frequently mentioned in Lady Moira's letters.

81   *From James Ryan to Baggot Street, Dublin*

Thursday 31 January 1805

Mr James Ryan requests Mr Scully will attend at Lord Fingall's tomorrow at half past 3 o'Clock to take into consideration a proposal Mr MacDonnell means to submit to the meeting.[1]   [*Source*: Scully Papers]

[1]At the meeting of 27 January (see No. 79) Randal MacDonnell had proposed that the petition should be laid aside and some other method adopted, such as communicating through the Irish government or sending one or two gentlemen over to communicate with Pitt. The idea had not received much support and it had been

decided to hold another meeting which would recommend a course to the General Committee on 2 February (Hardwicke to the Home Secretary 28 January 1805: HO 100/128, f.29). On the 28th Hardwicke had received authority (ibid.) to transmit a representation of Catholic claims and MacDonnell's proposal may have taken this new factor into account. No record has been found of the meeting of 31 January.

82   *From his mother Catherine Scully to Bagott Street, Dublin*

Kilfeacle [Co. Tipperary] 9 February 1805

My Dr Den's,

I have been in expectation those some posts past of geting a letter from you as I am very anxious to know how Mrs Scully is or whether she is geting better which I hope is the case. Our post boy was robbed last night which I suppose deprived me of the pleasure of hearing from you this day.

You are in possession of all about Mr Harney's business[1] and hope it meets your approbation and that you'll come to the wedding. The papers are not come here yet. Of course there is no day yet fix'd but as the time is now but short before Lent it will soon take place so that the sooner you can come the more agreeable to us. Your Father, Joanna and the boys unite in love to you and Mrs Scully (who I most sincerely wish cou'd make one of our party) with My Dr Den's your loving and affect'te Mother Catherine Scully.

[P.S.] I pray my compliments to Miss Huddleston   [*Source*: Scully Papers]

[1]See No. 78.

83   *From James Ryan to Baggot Street, Dublin*

Thursday Evening [?14 February 1805]

Dear Sir,

I request you will meet a few Gentlemen at Sir Thomas French's in Dominick Street tomorrow morning at 10 o'Clock for the purpose of taking into consideration the proposal w[hic]h will be submitted to the Com[mittee at Lord Fingall's at halfpast 3 o'Clock.[1]   [*Source*: Scully Papers]

[1]Apart from the meeting of 1 February, which took place at Lord Fingall's house, the only Friday meeting on record is that of 15 February when the select committee met to prepare the agenda for the general meeting on the following day. What transpired at Sir Thomas French's house is unknown. For the meeting at Lord Fingall's in the afternoon there is a partial account by William Bellew which Lord Hardwicke transmitted to the Home Office on 6 May 1805 (Hardwicke Papers: Add. MSS.35, 705, f.272). According to this Scully contradicted Lord Fingall when he asserted that ministers would oppose the petition, and denied that the Home Secretary's letter to the Lord Lieutenant (see No. 71 n.1) was any authority to the contrary. He argued

that although Pitt did not want to appear to promote a discussion he would not be sorry to have it pressed on him. Writing to the Irish Lord Chancellor on 11 March (Add. MSS.35, 777) Lord Hardwicke observed: "I have also understood, what was by no means unnatural when people are disposed to catch at anything, that Scully's connection with a Cambridgeshire family and acquaintance with me from that circumstance gave a greater degree of weight to what he alleged in reference to Mr Pitt's real sentiments". When he saw Lord Hardwicke on 19 February Scully denied questioning the authenticity of the Home Secretary's letter but said that the idea of making an application to Pitt himself had been strengthened by the Chief Secretary's having asked for a copy of the petition, it was supposed at Pitt's express desire (HO 100/128, f.67).

84   *From his father James Scully to Bagot Street*

Kilfeacle, 16 February 1805

Dr Dens.

I recd. both your letters [a paragraph on the marriage settlement of his daughter Joanna]. . . . As to the Catholick petitn. yr. country must have a good opinion of you to rank you among the noblemen & gentlmn. mentioned to hand it.[1] I would advise yr. going, as I am sure you wont [?] disappoint them. . . .   [*Source*: Scully Papers]

[1]See No. 85 n.2.

85   *From Lord Fingall*

Gt. Denmark Street [Dublin] 17 February 1805

Dear Sir,

It was merely in consequence of Sir Ed. Bellew's wish that we should meet, that I troubled you to call here. I fear he intends to be off the journey to London,[1] & have been endeavouring to prevail on Ld Southwell as he is invited to form part of the deputation. I wish he would accept *the trust*.[2] I am sorry I was dressing for the Levee when you were here and by that means had not the pleasure of seeing you.   [*Source*: Scully Papers]

[1]In the event Sir Edward Bellew went to London.
[2]The General Meeting of the previous day had not only nominated five deputies (Lord Fingall, Sir Thomas French, Sir Edward Bellew, Denys Scully and James Ryan) but also provided for other peers "acceding" to the deputation, Lords Gormanston and Southwell being mentioned as present at the meeting. Lord Southwell accepted the trust and went to London.

86   *From R. MacDonnell to 34 Baggot Street, Dublin*

Allen's Court [Mulinahack, Co. Dublin] 22 February [1805]

Dear Sir,

Some of your Co-Delegates have promised to dine with me on Monday, & I hope all will; that we may have an oppoy. of conversing on the subject of yr important mission — this I wish'd to state to you this day, & to request the pleasure of yr Compy on that day but I was not fortunate enough to meet you at home.   [*Source*: Scully Papers]

87   *From Dominick Rice to Baggot Street, Dublin*

24 February 1805

Dear Sir,

I called yesterday at Mr Ryan's to sign the petition but was informed that there was not one there. I have to request you will put my name to it[1] & beg you will take charge of three bottles of Usquebagh[2] for a particular friend who is in yr Govt. Wishing you a pleasant voyage & safe return. I remain, Dear Sir, yr affte & obt. servt.   [*Source*: Scully Papers]

[1]His name appears in both petitions, in which he is described as "barrister, Dawson Street".
[2]The Irish and Scotch Gaelic word from which whisky is derived. Scully's diary of his visit to London makes no mention of these bottles.

88   *From George Ponsonby*

26 February 1805

Dear Sir,

I inclose you the letters[1] & heartily wish you a good voyage & a successful embassy.   [*Source*: Scully Papers]

[1]Scully's Diary shows that the introductions were to George Ponsonby's nephew, John Ponsonby, who succeeded his father as the 2nd Baron Ponsonby in 1806; Charles Grey, whose wife was the latter's sister; and Charles James Fox. Scully landed at Holyhead on 27 February and reached London on 2 March.

89   *From William Fletcher*

[c. 26 February 1805]

Dear Scully,
   Enclosed you have the letter[1] which I have left open and you will be good
enough to seal.

[1]An introduction to Denis Bowes Daly (Diary, 9 March 1805).

90   *From Sir Evan Nepean to No. 7 Thayer Street,*
                              Manchester Square, London

Admiralty, Sunday ½ past Two [3 March 1805]

Dear Sir,
   I have this moment returned to the Admiralty[1] and found your Card on
my table. I am sorry that I should not have been in the way when you did me
the favour of calling.
   I am just going to Fulham to dinner, and if you will do me the honor to be
there at six, you will stand a chance of meeting some of your Irish friends[2]
and be sure of a hearty welcome.
[P.S.] My House is on the Banks of the Thames within half a mile of
Parson's Green.   [*Source*: Scully Papers]

[1]In September 1804 he had accepted a seat on the Admiralty Board while still Chief
Secretary, thus in Lord Hardwicke's opinion (Add. MSS.35, 706) belittling his Irish
post.
[2]Probably the other members of the deputation. Scully received the invitation too
late to accept it. His diary records that he spent the night of 8 March with Nepean at
Fulham and visited him again there on 17 March.

91   *From Sir Evan Nepean to No. 7 Thayer Street,*
                              Manchester Square

Admiralty, Monday 4 March [1805]

Dear Sir,
   I did not receive your letter until my return to town today at an hour too
late to admit of a note reaching you before one o'Clock. If I have not the
pleasure of seeing you in the course of the day, I shall take the liberty of
paying my respects to you on my way to town tomorrow morning at half past
ten when I shall call in Thayer Street.   [*Source*: Scully Papers]

92   *From Lord Fingall to No. 7 Thayer Street,*
                Manchester Square, London[1]

3 George Street, Hanover Square [London]
Monday morning [4 March 1805]

Dear Sir,

Owing to disapointments in Post Horses in two or three different places
we did not arrive till past 8 o'Clock last night.[2] I am this morning settling
myself in my Lodging, which, is not exactly in the neighborhood I wished,
but fully convenient to every thing. Will you be so good as to come to
breakfast at ten to-morrow, and if you wd have the goodness to mention to
Mr Ryan that I should be much obliged to him to let me have the pleasure of
his company also, I would send to him but do not know where to address
him.   [*Source*: Scully Papers]

[1]Where Scully was staying with his wife's aunt, Mrs Bostock, until he moved into
lodgings in Great Ryder Street on the 4th (Diary).
[2]Lord Fingall and his brother Colonel William Plunkett had sailed for Holyhead in
the same packet as Scully (Diary).

93   *From Colonel J. McMahon*

Cha[rle]s Street [London]
½ past 10, Monday morng. [4 March 1805]

My dear Sir,

Nothing but an unexpected call on particular business when it was too late
to prevent your coming here, should induce me to go out when I expected
the pleasure of seeing you which I must now regret to defer until tomorrow
or Wednesday whichever is most convenient to you.[1]   [*Source*: Scully Papers]

[1]Scully records in his diary that he left his address and asked McMahon to make the
next appointment. McMahon called on him on the 7th and they had three other
meetings.

94   *From Charles Butler to Thayer Street [London]*

Lincolns Inn, 5 March 1805

Dear Sir,

Mrs Butler desires me to mention to you, that she has some music on
thursday, and that she shall be very happy to be favored with your company.

I suppose you have seen the paragraph in the *Morning Post* of yesterday, which has so favorable an appearance to the Roman Catholics.[1] I had heard that the King was more favorable to them than he had been, but as I did not hear it from any authority, I paid no attention to the report, particularly as I know Lord Moira mentioned to a friend of mine that the proceedings of the Irish Catholics were kept an entire secret from his Majesty. I hope you will turn in your mind your publication of the petition with an introduction, as I am sure some information is much wanted to the public of this Country.

[*Source*: Scully Papers]

[1]An entry in Scully's diary of the delegation shows that he himself wrote it, after being introduced by Henry Huddleston to a Catholic attorney called Green who was one of the proprietors of the *Morning Post*. It hinted that Pitt had been heard to approve the language of the petition and regarded it as a happy omen that the deputies were personally respected by both ministry and opposition.

95   *From the Marquis of Sligo to 7 Jermyn Street,[1] London*

Grafton Street [London]
Wednesday, 6 February [*recte* March 1805]
    Lord Sligo presents his compliments to Mr Scully & being too ill to converse freely with him this day on some points of general & deep interest, he will be much obliged if he will be so kind to call tomorrow at Twelve o'Clock. Ld Sligo being confined to the house takes the liberty of giving Mr Scully this trouble which he hopes he will be so kind to excuse.[2]

[*Source*: Scully Papers]

[1]Scully's lodgings were at 7 Great Rider Street, off Jermyn Street.
[2]When Scully called again on the 7th he found the family at breakfast and was unable to talk on the Catholic question, but he called again on the 8th. Lord Sligo wrote to the Lord Lieutenant on the 6th: "Our Irish Ambassadors are arrived, and from some probably false intelligence they have had from Sir Evan Nepean, they expect that something will be conceded, if not all. Scully has been here this moment with credentials from Marshall, there were persons at the time with me but he left a note with my porter that he would call tomorrow and communicate with me. I shall cultivate these dispositions in any of them in the hope of contributing to the publick good by keeping them at least from the advice of those that have different intentions" (Hardwicke Papers: Add. MSS.35, 757, f.35).

96   *From Henry Grattan to c/o Sir Thomas French Bart,*[1]
7 Great Rider Street, London

Bray, 6 March 1805

Dear Sir,

When I had the pleasure of seeing you last you mentioned some particulars regarding the actual state of the Catholics under the present laws. Would it be too troublesome to let me have in writing that statement as soon as you could conveniently. I have one in mind but perhaps not accurate.[2]

[*Source*: Scully Papers]

[1]A member of the deputation, who however did not reach London until the night of 15 March.

[2]Scully noted on the cover that he received this letter on 15 March and answered it on 31 March — when he was back in Dublin. In the meantime the negotiations that had been proceeding through Fox for the return of Grattan to Parliament had resulted in his election for Malton (*DNB*; Fox to Grattan 13 March 1805 in Grattan, *Life and Times*, V, p. 254.

97   *From Charles Addis to Great Ryder Street, St James's, London*

13 New Boswell Court, Lincolns Inn, 9 March 1805

Sir,

In consequence of the Letter of my Friend Mr Huddleston to you of yesterday, I called on you this morning at ten o'clock, and will take the liberty of repeating my visit in the course of today or to'morrow; the object of which I will state to you. Thinking it extremely probable that the Catholic Deputation from Ireland may find it necessary to employ some one in copying confidential letters or correspondence or in taking minutes of any proceedings or Resolutions that may be adopted, I beg leave to say that I should be happy to fill such situation. I have the honor to possess the confidence and be employed, in this country, as the Solicitor for the Earl of Kenmare and Lord Trimlestown and should any person be wanted to fill the situation I have alluded to, but which, I confess, I cannot exactly define, I could rely on their Lordships recommendations in my favour. I beg leave to add that I have recently formed a Partnership with Mr Norris,[1] a gentleman well known to Mr Huddleston, and connected with some of the most respectable Catholic Families in this country.[2]   [*Source*: Scully Papers]

[1]Thomas Norris of 12 King's Road, Bedford Row. He was a subscriber to the English Catholic Board.

[2]His offer of services was accepted (see No. 178).

98   *From John Joseph Dillon to 3 Great George Street*
                        or 7 Great Ryder Street

L[incoln's] I[nn] 11 March 1805

Dear Sir,

Some of the points on which I touched yesterday are of such importance
that I cannot forbear troubling you with a few lines on the subject.

If the Catholics of Ireland have determined with themselves, under
particular circumstances not to press the restoration of their rights in the
present moment, I should suppose they are anxious to obtain the best terms
for their forbearance; and they are certainly entitled to material concessions
from Mr Pitt.

These concessions I think should be the full enjoyment of the benefits to
which they are already entitled, and pledges to that effect: also the exertion
of ministerial influence in suppressing the scurrility and invective which are
so frequently issued against the Catholics by persons dependent upon and in
the pay of government.

The first point which is of the greatest importance involves very material
considerations. It relates principally to the construction of the respective test
acts, and by want of attention in this particular our Irish act of 1793 became
almost a new penal law.[1] From similar inadvertence the Catholics of this
country have nearly fallen into a most serious error in an address which was
in contemplation to have presented upon the renewal of the war to the
throne,[2] that which I was the means of preventing by an amendment which
was proposed by me, and adopted after a very painful and unpleasant
discussion on my part, which I shall never forget. The manner in which some
of the English Catholics received my exertions to save them from introducing into a public address an incorrect statement of the law, made
considerable impression on my mind, and determined me almost never to
volunteer my services on a future occasion.

By an attention to the rules of sound construction it will appear, that the
Catholics of both countries are actually entitled to more advantages under
the existing system than is generally imagined, and I am sure you will agree
with me in thinking no pains should be spared on our part, to procure the
adoption of a liberal construction by the government — a more favourable
opportunity has never occurred. Should the deputation be able to negotiate
this point in all its branches, the Catholic body will owe them very great
obligations; and if our exclusion is to be continued (and which I fear is the
case) our sufferings may be in some measure alleviated.

[P.S.] May I request you to communicate this letter to the members of the
deputation.[3]   [*Source*: Callanan Papers]

[1]The point at issue is explained by Scully in his Diary. Dillon told him that some years earlier the Attorney and Solicitor-General of the time had replied in the negative when asked for their opinion as to whether the King could without injury to the Test Laws appoint Catholics to offices of which by law they were capable. Dillon had suggested that the deputation should ask Pitt to direct a revision of that opinion by the present Law Officers.

[2]The address drafted by Francis Plowden (see No. 55 n.6).

[3]Scully read the letter to the deputation on 11 March. It was thought better to defer the matter for the present lest it should seem as if they were soliciting a partial concession (as opposed to complete emancipation).

99   *From Charles J. Fox to 7 Great Rider Street [London]*

Arlington Street [London] Wednesday Night, 13 March 1805

Dear Sir,

I wish to know by one line whether you & the other Gentlemen expect to find me *alone* tomorrow or whether, you would wish to find with me other respectable Persons favourers of the Cause. In this last case I shall desire Mr Grey & Mr Windham to be present, Ld Fitzwilliam & Ld Grenville are out of town.[1]

[P.S.] It is perfectly indifferent to me which way you answer my question.

[*Source*: Scully Papers]

[1]On the morning of 12 March the deputation had been received by Pitt who had told them that he would oppose the petition. In the afternoon Fox had called on Scully to learn the result of the meeting and had suggested the names of various persons who might handle the petition if the deputation preferred not to give it to Fox himself. At noon on the 13th the deputation had met and decided to ask Lord Grenville and Fox to introduce the petition, and Scully had been asked to make an appointment for the next day with Fox. The latter, who had been out when Scully called, had come to Scully's lodgings in the afternoon and had found Lord Kenmare there with him. An appointment had been made for 12.30 the next day. Scully, who recorded all this in his Diary, received the present letter when he returned home that night and replied that he saw no reason why Windham and Grey should not be present.

100   *From Jeremiah Scully to 7 Thayer Street,*
Manchester Square, London

Kilfeacle [Co. Tipperary] 16 March 1805

Sir,

I have the honor of your fav'r of the 13th inst. For it and the trouble you have taken for my information, I return you my most sincere thanks. What money I have or I may count on to purchase is mostly due of others, and for fear I may be disappointed, I won't go far in debt at present. Gortnagap[1] I will give twenty three years purchase for, by giving me the year's rent, due of said lands the 1st of May next and on my son's return will send you a Bill on Dublin for the amount. This is 3 years over its value. Your answer at y'r leisure, will oblige Sir,

Your etc. etc.

James Scully

The above is a copy of my father's letter to Councellor [sic] Burrowes.[2] My father has expected a letter from you these few days past in answer to one he wrote to you.[3] Our post from Clonmel to Cashell was robbed on Thursday last which might have a letter from you.

I am your very affectionate Brother,

Jerem'h Scully   [Source: Scully Papers]

[1]In the parish of Tullaroan, Co. Kilkenny. The transaction was probably completed as the property was later in Denys Scully's possession (see No. 637).
[2]Peter Burrowes was in London and Scully records in his diary meeting him on the 25th.
[3]The diary records that Scully wrote to his father on 9 March.

101   *From Lord Sligo*

Grafton Street [London] Sunday [17 March 1805]

Confidential

Dear Sir,

I am most happy to hope things will be arranged according to our wishes, & am satisfied with you that a right understanding is all that is wanting for a very desireable arrangement — that much is due to your good sense & moderation from the publick. I have fixed with *Mr H*[1] to receive you tomorrow at ten o'Clock, in course you will call upon him at *that hour* punctually.   [Source: Scully Papers]

[1]William Huskisson, at this time an Undersecretary in Pitt's administration. His letter to Lord Sligo is with the Scully Papers. Scully records in his diary that the interview lasted an hour and a half; that Huskisson thought Pitt might be willing to express to the House of Commons his opinion in favour of the principle of a measure of relief, confining his objection merely to the point of time; and that, if Pitt so authorised, Huskisson would write Scully a note that day to the effect that "understanding from Lord Sligo . . . that we had conceived Mr Pitt to have declared himself bound to oppose our petition, not only in principle but in every other manner, he was willing to take an opportunity of correcting that misconception in another interview". No such invitation materialised. Shortly after noon the deputation met the opposition leaders, who undertook to present the petition.

102   *From General W. Dalrymple[1] to 46 or 47 Great Ryder Street,*
          St James's, London addressed to J. Scully

Chelsea, 17 March 1805

Sir,

In obedience to your wishes signified to me by Mr Marshall I lost no time in writing to the Earl of Egremont.[2] Yesterday I received his answer. He will be in Town immediately and very happy in the honor of your acquaintance and though a Stranger to your person is well acquainted with your reputation. I will give you early intimation of his arrival and be very happy in bringing you together.[3]   [*Source*: Scully Papers]

[1] A brother of the 5th Earl of Stair, now retired as Lieutenant-Governor of Chelsea Hospital. Formerly Colonel of the 47th Foot; in command at Belfast in 1795 and at Cork in 1796 when the French fleet appeared in Bantry Bay.
[2] Sir George O'Brien Wyndham (1751–1837), 3rd Earl of Egremont.
[3] There is no mention in Scully's diary of a meeting having taken place.

103   *From Daniel O'Connell, Dublin, to London,*
              19 March 1805

Not a single despatch has been received from Scully[1] and the Committee which met this day would have been deficient in information but for a letter from Lord Kenmare. Scully may be assured that the interpretation given by the delegates to the phrase *most eligible*[2] meets with the approbation of all except Bellew[3] and if the persons with whom the petition now is should wish to have it unfettered with any restrictions he may count on the certainty of their being taken away by the unanimous vote of a general meeting.[4] Not even the repeal of the obnoxious code could give more satisfaction to the public mind than the turn affairs have now taken. Pitt's rejection of the measure has created a sentiment of contempt for him that is finely contrasted by Irish enthusiasm for the Prince and his friends. Should further signatures be necessary they can be provided in the greatest abundance and of the best sort.   [*Source*: O'Connell; *Correspondence*, I, No. 140, taken from the now missing original in the Scully Papers.]

[1] Scully noted in his diary of the delegation (MS.27, 514) that he replied to this letter just before leaving London. Otherwise there is no record of his having written to any member of the committee but Randal MacDonnell (see No. 104).
[2] The instructions to the delegation given in Scully's diary laid down that if Pitt declined introducing the petition they should procure its introduction by such other member as should seem most eligible. On 13 March the delegation had decided, in

the absence of any neutral member of sufficient standing, to approach the opposition.
[3]William Bellew who, says Scully in his diary, wrote to Lord Fingall and Sir E. Bellew disapproving of going to the opposition.
[4]See No. 104 n.1.

104　　　　　　*From R. MacDonnell to No. 7 Thayer Street,*
　　　　　　　　　　Manchester Square, London

　　　　　　　　　　　　　　　　　　　Dublin, 20 March 1805
My Dear Sir,

I have just read the letter you favd me with of the 14th inst & thank you for the detailed & satisfactory information it convey'd, relative to the object of your delegation. Mr O'Connell shall see it this night, and the Committee with[ou]t delay. We had a meeting yesterday for the purpose of knowing the information each of us might have rec'd, of wch there was dispersed & imperfect reports; before your letter I had only recd J. Ryan's communication to me of the 12th inst after yr interview with Mr Pitt; but a most satisfactory letter from Lord Kenmare to Mr Rice supplied the want of information each of us noticed. Your intentions & determinations, as convey'd in Lord Kenmare's letter met our fullest approbation wch, I am sure, will be still more confirmed by your letter. The Mail of the 16th is arrived, & I infer we had not rec'd direct information, sanctioned by all the delegates, untill after an interview with Lord Grenville, who was not to be in London, I see by your letter, untill that day.[1] I am glad we shall so soon see you here, as your profession requires you to go Circuit, & as our Question is to be postponed, untill you can return to London, wch I think will still be necessary. Your suggestion of application to Irish Members of Parliament,[2] will be attended to, as well as any thing else wch the delegation will recommend; and I hope we will all, finally, succeed, in the objects we have in view for the good of our Country, & of those of our Religion, by perseverance & unanimity; always seeing the force & importance of the latter as it struck me from the beginning.

I hope this letter will reach you in London, as I wish you should receive this expression of my acknowledgement for your letter — & I request you will present my best compts to each of my friends, your Coleagues;

　　　　　　　　　　　　　　　　　[*Source*: Scully Papers]

[1]At noon on 16 March Lords Fingall and Kenmare had an interview with the opposition leaders (Lord Grenville, Fox and Grey) who told them that they did not like the way in which the deputies' instructions were worded. The difficulty seems to have been that these obliged the deputies to offer the petition to them on the same terms as to Pitt: that if Pitt felt precluded from supporting the measure they would

not press for its immediate adoption. The opposition leaders may have felt that this prevented them from tabling a motion on the petition or that if they did so the Irish Catholics might not as a body back them up. When the deputies met again in the afternoon and on the following day there was a conflict of opinion, which ended with a majority vote in favour of empowering the opposition leaders to introduce the petition in whatever manner they deemed most eligible, Lords Fingall and Southwell being with Scully himself in the minority (MS.27, 514 (i); Scully's Diary).

[2]Of the 100 Irish members 44 voted against the petition on 14 May, and 29 for. Their names are given in the *DEP* of 23 May 1805.

105   *From Ed Moore to 7 Thayer Street, Manchester Square, London*

Dublin, 21 March 1805

My Dear Sir,

At a meeting of the Catholic Committee this day,[1] your letter of the 14th Inst. to Mr MacDonnell was read; the proceedings of the delegates as therein detail'd gave considerable satisfaction; as you expressly desired that your letter should be considered merely a confidential communication & not in any manner official, the committee did not take any proceedings in consequence; they have appointed to meet again on Saturday next in expectation of having further communication by that time & then to propose such plans as the intelligence they receive may suggest — such as applying to the different County Members etc conceiving that the business is now in that state to require the close attention of the Committee & frequent communication with the deputation, they have come to the determination of meeting constantly & if necessary from day to day & have appointed me to act as Secretary; their proceedings will be regulated by the advice they receive from the Delegates, in whom they place the highest confidence, concurring entirely in the steps that have been taken — from the reception you have met with in England, the friends to the cause here are much more sanguine in their hopes of the benefit to be derived from the petition, than before you left this. Mr Pitt's refusal was expected, his reception of you & manner of refusing the petition, more satisfactory than was expected.

As anything further takes place I shall advise you

[P.S.] Mr French brother to the member for Roscommon[2] called on me this day to enquire when [our ?] petition was likely to be brought on. He authorises me to inform you that it is his brother's intention to go over for the express purpose of supporting it.   [*Source*: Scully Papers]

[1]No report of this meeting appears to have survived.

[2]Arthur French of Frenchpark (1764–1820) sat for Roscommon county 1783–1820. He voted in favour of the Catholic petition on 14 May. He had four brothers.

106   *From Lord Fingall to 7 Great Rider Street, London*

Friday, 22 March 1805

Dear Sir,

   If not inconvenient you will much oblige me by calling here tomorrow any time before twelve. I was at your door with Lord Kenmare today. You will find breakfast at ten — the Colonel's[1] good coffee.[2]   [*Source*: Scully Papers]

[1]His brother, Colonel William Plunkett, of the Austrian service.
[2]Scully entered in his diary on 23 March that Lord Grenville having asked for a written statement of the penal laws still in force Lord Fingall had asked him to draw it up and he had agreed.

106A   *To Edward Hay Esq., Portland Hotel [London]*

[? 24] March 1805

   Mr Hay will please to accept from Mr S[cully] one of the first copies of the Catholic petition that has been struck off — He should have had a MS copy sooner, if it had been consistent with the confidence imposed upon the deputies.

   Lest any advantage should be taken of its having been printed before being presented it is intended to be kept from circulation [until Tues]day or Wednesday and therefore Mr S. [about three words missing] take care that no copy [words missing] until then, lest it should get into [words missing] hands.[1]   [*Source*: Dublin Diocesan Archives 390/1, XXI, (3)]

[1]Scully's Diary shows that he handed the petitions to Coghlan [*sic*], Browne and Keating for printing on 18 March; and that he left his card on Hay at the Portland Hotel on Sunday 24 March. The petitions were presented by Lord Grenville in the House of Lords and C. J. Fox in the Commons on Monday 25 March.

107   *From Sir Evan Nepean to Great Ryder Street, London*

Broom House, 25 March 1805

My dear Sir,

   I did not receive your letter, dated Friday night, till yesterday.

   Although I am nearly recovered of my late illness, yet I have still the Gout in one of my feet and I much fear that I shall not be in a situation to go to town before the day you have fixed upon for your departure. I hope however that I shall have an opportunity of taking you by the hand before you go —

perhaps, if you are not otherwise engaged, you will eat your mutton here tomorrow at five.[1]   [*Source*: Scully Papers]

[1]Scully's diary shows that he had written to enquire about his health and that he was unable to accept the invitation.

108   *From George Keating*[1]

37 Duke Street, Gro. Square. [London] 25 March 1805

Sir,

It is of the greatest importance that we should know whether the *Petition* will be presented in both houses this day, or not. This information we ought to be in possession of in the course of the Evening, as in the event of its having been presented we should at an early hour tomorrow morning commence the publication by leaving copies in the principal booksellers' shops. An early publication will be the only means of stifling catchpenny copies from being printed: for those who would lose no time in a speculation of that kind will drop the idea when they see in their own shops the Petition ready for sale almost as soon as it appeared in Parliament.

As it may not be in your power at present to say that it will positively be presented in both houses this day I shall be happy to wait (if I could obtain means of admission) at the *houses*, where no doubt you or some of your friends will be able to let me know as soon as the presentation has taken place. It is true that the *public papers* will inform us tomorrow but they often do not appear till at a very late hour. I shall take the liberty to wait upon you again this day.[2]   [*Source*: Scully Papers]

[1]Of Keating, Brown and Keating, Catholic Library and Printing Office, 38 Duke Street, Grosvenor Square.
[2]Scully's diary records that Keating called on him at one o'clock. The petitions were presented in both Houses on the same day. The original of the one presented in the Lords by Lord Grenville survives in that House's archives. Scully saw Fox present the other in the Commons a little after four, giving notice for a motion on it on 9 May. Pitt, according to Scully, said nothing but by his looks and nods evinced great pleasure at the distance of the day named. The motion was later postponed to 14 May.

109   *From Jeremiah Scully to 34 Bagot Street, Dublin*

Kilfeacle [Co. Tipperary] 2 April 1805

Dear Denys,

I was favoured with your affectionate letter on Saturday last, and would have replied to it sooner but I understood my father intended writing.

Joannah's[1] nuptials with Charles Harney are not so near taking place as we all expected. There are produced by him some objections to the articles stiled "Objections on the part of Mr Harney" (the old Gentleman). These are drawn up by a Mr Westrop and Mr Harney, father to the Bachelor. Mr Westrop is a neighbour of Harneys — a young man just retired from the Co. Limerick Militia.[2] I am confident if you saw those objections you would be much amused at the idea of their setting their opinion in competition with that of the Lawyers who drew them up. The objections are highly disagreeable to my father. One of them is a reduction of £30 a year on the jointure of Johannah.

Part of this country remains in a state of Disturbance, namely, from here to Caher, from thence to Clonmel, from there to Carrick and to Waterford proceeding from the cause my father mentioned in his last letter.

As you have not seen young Harney, I hope a description of him will not be disagreeable to you. He is about 28 years of age, corpulent, and rather inactive; he has not the smallest taste for business of any kind, nor can I say what his favourite amusement is; he is a very good-humoured man; he does not seem to be well informed, but is very good natured and good tempered. His father you saw in Dublin, a very positive old man.[3]

I conclude with best regards for Mrs S.

Your most affectionate Brother
Jerem'h Scully

[Source: Scully Papers]

[1]His sister.

[2]Probably Captain J. B. Westropp, a field officer of the Irish Militia.

[3]Harney was sometimes anglicised as Hartney (E. MacLysaght, *A Guide to the surnames of Ireland*, Dublin, 1964). A John Hartney who signed the petition to the House of Lords immediately after Scully, giving his address as Somerville instead of the more usual Summerville, was probably the young man's father.

110   *From his mother Catherine Scully to Baggot Street, Dublin*

Kilfeacle [Co. Tipperary] 3 April 1805

My Dr Den's,

We are extreamly happy to find by your very affect'te letters this day that you are arrived at home safe and well and found Mrs Scully pretty well which is a very good sign at this season of the year and as the fine weather is now advancing I hope she will continue to mend and grow strong so as to enable her to go with you to England the next time you go. I am sure you must be greatly fataguied in body and mind after your journey but as you have a prospect of success in the business you went about and that it will be of so very much for the publick good I know it will reconcile you to it. Your Father says he has nothing to write at present but expects to meet you at Clonmell assizes from whence I hope to see you here and then you can be at Joann's marraige. At present there are some obstacles start'd by old Mr Harney but I hope they will be removed. Indeed the business is a long time on foot and I doubt whether it will be finally settled ontill you come. We had an account yesterday that your Aunt Lyons[1] of Limerick died. James and Mun[2] went there this day. Your Father, Joanna, Mary Sause[3] and the boys, unite in love to you and Mrs Scully with My Dr Den's, your loving and affect'te Mother Catherine Scully.   [*Source*: Scully Papers]

[1]Probably the widow of James Lyons (1729–1788), the elder of Catherine Scully's two brothers (Burke *LGI* 1912: Lyons of Croom).
[2]Her sons James and Edmund Scully.
[3]Her grand-daughter, daughter of Richard Sause by his first wife, Catherine Scully.

111   *From Mary Scully to Mrs Huddleston, Sawston Hall,*
             Saffron Walden, Essex

[April 1805]

Dear Mama,

I should have answered your kind letter sooner, but I do not like to write without a frank as I have nothing to say of any consequence, and besides I know you hear of me, as Fanny[1] is continually writing on all sides. I hope some time in the summer that I shall have the pleasure of seeing you, as I mean certainly to go to England this Summer. Mr [S] set out last Monday[2] on circuit so that he was at home just a week. I hope you continue to recover y'r health, and that you make it y'r principal study to do so. The Enclosure business as you say has taken a great deal of money, but if it answers it cannot be called expensive. I fear Mr S. will not have the same to say of his journey to London as Cath: Deputy; nothing but honour gained there, I assure you if my F'r wants money he is only like the rest of [the] world. I suppose Jane is preparing for London where I wish her much pleasure. L'y Hardwicke, L'y Marg't and two Elder young ladies sailed last week in order to be present at the grand fête at Windsor[3] and to shew themselves. The Girls are not indeed any great matter in point of Beauty but they are really amiable and well behaved and very interesting. I was invited to dine at the Castle while Mr S. was in England but I did not go. Indeed I thought L'y H. had not been over civil lately. We have however exchanged visits since and are on good terms. L'y Marg't was particularly polite in calling again when according to Etiquette there was no obligation. My health I hope is mending, but I am weak & languid, I believe partly owing to my drink consisting only of water. They think I have some inward swelling which I should be very careful not to enflame.

Fanny is well. I wish my health had allowed me to carry her about more into company. It would have been a pleasure to me as well as to her. She, however, does not shew much regret. Indeed she is altogether very companiable [sic], and well calculated for a visitor, or to live with any person not very unreasonable. I beg my Duty to my Father and love to Jane whose letter I shall not forget to answer but I have so little to say that if in the mean time she likes to write to me I shall be very glad. My Father I hope is quite well as I hear nothing to the contrary.

Believe Dear Mama your ever affectionate & dutiful D'r

M. Scully

[*Source*: Huddleston Papers C1/MH78]

[1]Her cousin, Frances Huddleston.
[2]8 April, Scully having arrived back from London on 30 March.
[3]For the installation on St George's Day, 23 April, of the new Knights of the Garter. Lord Hardwicke was one of them but not being able to attend was represented by a proxy (*Morning Chronicle*, 24 April 1805). On 16 April he received the insignia from the hands of Lord Cathcart at Dublin Castle and on St George's Day he gave a magnificent entertainment himself at St Patrick's Hall (*DEP*, 18 April 1805).

112   *From Major Thomas FitzGerald to c/o Ambroses, Waterford*

Snowhaven [Co. Kilkenny] 13 April [1805]

Major FitzGerald presents his Compts. to Mr Scully, wishes him success in the cause[1] he has undertaken, & earnestly recommends to his attention the utility of petitioning the county, city, & borough representatives throughout Ireland. Major FitzGerald requests Mr Scully will give the enclosed letter to Mr Pendergast[2] whom he will meet at the Clonmell assizes immediately on his arrival in that town which will much oblige him as the subject is of some importance.   [*Source*: Scully Papers]

[1]Probably to bring pressure to bear in the constituencies on the Irish members of Parliament.
[2]Unidentified.

113   *From Edmund Scully to Clonmell*

Kilfeacle [Co. Tipperary] 15 April 1805

Dear Denys,

I have relied so much on your affection and friendship for me at all times, that I have always disclosed my sentiments to you, with as much freedom &

Candour as possible, when such difficulties occurred as I thought required y'r kind interference. I much fear, I have been too often troublesome to you in this Respect, but I must now require an additional favor, to the many already conferred, as I am confident your interest, will be very much in my favour.

My father, on whose account I must say I have often had much uneasiness, seems at length determined to act a most unnatural part towards me, and such as I must venture to say my Conduct never merited, as I wish you should be well acquainted with the particular Circumstances of our Difference, I must trouble you with a longer letter than I otherwise should wish. You recollect when I first fixed my affections on Miss O'B.,[1] I took the liberty thro' you of consulting my father's inclinations, which I then found so averse to my Desires, that I was determined to proceed no further. I accordingly gave up to the Will of a Father, an object, I thought no Consideration whatever should induce me to. I must tell you I first stated my father's aversion to Miss O'B. and had her full consent to act the part I did. When I afterwards thought of Miss N.[2] his objections to her were still greater, as soon as she was married he thought proper to mention thro' a friend to me, that if I acted an affectionate & dutiful part to him, till James would be married, that he would then fully agree to allow me to marry Miss O'B. or any other girl I thought proper. With this declaration I was fully satisfied, till we were at Castle Connell, when James was kind enough to ask my father's permission to allow me to go to Nenagh for a Day to see Miss O'B. This he refused in the most absolute manner, and said tho' he did once promise his Consent 'twas merely that time may alter my affections, and concluded by saying if I proceeded further, he would act to me as he had done to William[3] and abused her & her family in such a manner as I feel ashamed to mention. This conduct from a father appeared to me so cruel, that I could not possibly endure it. I then went to Tramore till I thought time may make him comply with what, he once gave me the strongest assurances of. I remained there a fortnight, when I heard from Wm. Murphy saying my father had promised his full approbation to my match, and had pledged himself in such a manner as no longer to leave the least share of doubt. I returned home immediately, and I must say my father rec'd me most affect'y. He told me shortly after as we rode to Newport fair, the purport of what Wm. M. wrote to me, and said he never had the least objection to Miss O'B. but her being a Widow's Daughter. Still she may make me as good a Wife and as happy, as a girl of a larger fortune. He assured me that he had my welfare as much at heart as any other Child and that I should have his entire approbation to alter my Condition at the time appointed. He assured me of this again in some time after, in presence of my Mother and further that no consideration should ever make him alter in the least the promises he made. Those declarations so many and various rise my hopes to the highest pitch of success — but having got an invitation about 6 weeks since to spend some time at Mr Hartney's at Summerville[4] and my father having agreed to let me go there, I thought it but right to get his leave to pay Miss O'B. a visit who was then at D. Canny's[5] at the opposite side of the Shannon. This request to pay my respects to a girl I had so strong assurances of being one day my wife, I thought but only reasonable, but I am concerned to say he refused it as absolutely as before, and said since, he did not care whom I chose to marry, that he w'd never allow me but £500 a year, and that only during Life. He declared he would immediately alter his Will and make me repent my Conduct hereafter. This declaration tho so very much to my disadvantage does not affect me near so much as he may suppose, or as his extraordinary behaviour in his breach of so solemn a promise as he so often made. I am conscious of my own innocence. He can charge me with nothing but a partiality for a girl I am convinced would make me a happy Wife, and whose merits claim my warmest affection. This partiality I shall always retain for her as long as she remains unmarried but I will not think of marrying her without sufficient means and my father's consent. The former is in my father's power as well as the latter, and when a girl is unobjectionable unless the want of £1000 or £1500 extraordinary, I think to indulge me would not be very unreasonable. I only ask what he always consented to give me as a marriage Settlement. He need never advance it if he thinks I don't merit it. I must tell you I have two principal Reasons for being anxious for this change. I know my temper is warmer than the rest of my Brothers, and I am well aware of the many oddities of old people, and how often they violently fret on the most trifling subjects, a difference may one day arise between my father and me, I may be too warm and express myself in a manner I should not wish, and which may be attended with very serious disadvantage to me. It is to guard against this breach, that I now desire what I consider would be to our mutual interest. My Debts which I am sorry to say are encreasing every day is the other cause tho I am fortunate enough to have most generous friends in the money way. Yet I am fully sensible of the great Compliment I am under to them, knowing the little security I have to offer for any sum I may require. My Father may think I am as well off as any of my Brothers in that respect, but I only account for myself and say it is impossible (from my Expences) to live clear of Debts on £60 a year. I think I manage as economical as any other person in my line but 'twould hurt my pride and feelings very much, to ask any extraordinary sum from my nearest friend when my father is so very well able to advance it, but I shall never ask but what he is inclined to give from himself. I am confident if I was once independent and had but a reasonable annuity I should never again trouble a friend. These with the very high opinion I have of Miss O'B.'s qualities are, be assured, my only reasons for desiring y'r kind interference for me at present. My father and I are on the coolest terms those 6 weeks and I should wish to continue so while the matter remains as at present. I trust (as I am sure my father will mention the matter to you) y'r exertions in my favour will be such as I at all times experienced from you and you'll advise him to some measure which may establish that harmony between us, which it is my highest ambition to secure & maintain, as there is nothing ever makes me more unhappy than to have given him the least cause of a moment's uneasiness. If he does not consent to my marriage I shall not think of it while he objects. I wish to satisfy him but I must say I will never abate the regards I have for Miss O'B. while there are any prospects of success. If he is determined to cut me off as he says I should wish to get part of what he ever intends for me that I may by industry & attention endeavour to add to it. My exertions tho poor were never wanting to assist him but I plainly see if they were ever so great and for ever so many years he may in the End do what he now purposes. I hope you'll keep the Contents of this Letter perfectly secret. I feel very much for the trouble I give you reading this long letter but hope you'll [help?] me and believe me with the greatest regard

Your ever affect'e Brother
Edm'd Scully Jam's

P.S. I have applied to McCormack[6] at the Sessions of Cashell respecting y'r certificate. He could not give it at that time as there were not 2 Magistrates present but promised W'm Murphy he'd send it from Nenagh. He since wrote to him that he would hand it to you in person at the Assizes of Clonmell.   [*Source*: Scully Papers]

[1]Mary Anne O'Brien.
[2]Unidentified.
[3]His brother William Timothy Scully, disowned by his father because of his marriage to a girl without a fortune.
[4]Or Somerville (see No. 109 n.3).
[5]Probably a first cousin: his mother's sister, Mary Lyons, married John Canny of Ballycasey, Co. Clare, in 1768.
[6]Unidentified.

114   *From R. MacDonnell to Post Office, Kilkenny*[1]

Dublin, 20 April 1805

My Dear Sir,
    I thank you for the letter you favd me with from Clonmell, and am gratified at the favorable acct it conveys of support to our Petition. The zeal of R. C. Gentn for our common cause, & their Int[eres]t in the respective Commtees will, I hope, ensure us a respectable number of Irish votes at the discussion on the 10th May, it not being considered advisable to apply for any postponement of it. The Delegates have this day rec'd the

thanks & approbation of their Constituents,[2] & been reappointed; with the addition of yr humble Servt, who intends to set out for London on Wednesday. I hope I shall soon have the pleasure of seeing you there & that you will be so good as to apprise me, at my Brother's,[3] where you will be lodged.[4]

I have shewn your letter to Mr Fitzgerald of Snow Haven as you desire.

[*Source*: Scully Papers]

[1]Where he was for the Assizes, which ended on 24 April with the return of the judges to Dublin (*DEP*, 25 April 1805).

[2]He is referring to a meeting of the General Committee which took place that day under the chairmanship of Thomas Fitzgerald of Snowhaven: there is a copy of the minutes and resolutions among the Dropmore Papers (Add. MSS.59, 255). There being no likelihood of Pitt's objection as to the expediency of presenting the petition at the present time being removed, the meeting approved of the decision taken authorising Grenville and Fox to act. The deputies were reappointed to direct and assist in the management of the petition, with the addition of the Earls of Shrewsbury and Kenmare, Lord Trimleston and Mr R. MacDonnell.

[3]Probably the merchant of Lime Street Square in the City of London, with whom Scully dined on 14 March (Diary).

[4]If Scully had any intention of returning to London he did not carry it out.

115   *From Colonel J. McMahon to Bagot Street, Dublin*

London, 2 May 1805

Private

My Dear Sir,

I am infinitely obliged by your Letter which affords a very comprehensive view of the state in which the Catholic Business at present stands but I am sorry to assure you, which I do in the utmost candour, that I hourly perceive such a rising opposition in this country to that Question, that I begin to be alarmed for its immediate discussion. The popular Applause which has attended the proceedings on the *Tenth* Report[1] in the Discoveries which have been made against Lord Melville & others, has so alarmed Mr Pitt, & his Colleagues, that they are certainly trying to raise the vulgar hue and cry every where against Catholic Emancipation, by a system of placarding thro' all the Cities & Towns "No Popery" etc., thus, hoping to extinguish the just resentments which at this time so peculiarly prevails against the Administration in the Public mind, & to endeavour to ride home upon the Catholic Question.[2] When you seriously reflect upon the Disposition of the three Estates of the Legislature, you must be sensible that the Majority in the H. of Commons will *at this time* be adverse.

In the Lords, there can be no Chance, & we will not proceed further. I could, under all those circumstances wish from my heart, it could have so happened that a *future time* had been thought of *in proper* time, for I am satisfied the wise policy would have been to *wait Events*.[3]

[*Source*: Scully Papers]

[1]Of a commission appointed in 1802 to enquire into alleged frauds and irregularities in the Naval Department. Published on 13 February 1805, it drew attention to improper conduct on the part of Lord Melville, a close friend of Pitt, whose authority was shaken. A motion for his impeachment was carried on 25 June (*DNB*).
[2]This view was taken by the opposition. On 13 April Thomas Grenville had written to Lord Grenville suggesting that Pitt's only chance would be to divert public attention to the Catholic question and thus strengthen himself with the King (*Dropmore Papers*, VII).
[3]As MacMahon acted as private secretary to the Prince of Wales the advice he gives here would have been understood by Scully as reflecting the attitude of His Royal Highness.

116   *To [the Marquis of Sligo]*

Dublin, 5 May 1805

[Draft/copy][1]
My Lord,

I deferred troubling your Lordship since my return with any communication until I should have made personal enquiry into such particulars, as you would probably desire most to ascertain.

These enquiries have been made principally in the southern counties and also Wexford & Kilkenny — and your Lordship will be pleased to know, what I have no hesitation in affirming upon the authority of [one word — paper torn] & striking evidence, that there does not exist in those districts any system of hostility to the Government or any appearance whatsoever of disloyalty or traitorous combinations. There were, indeed, in one district outrages and murders perpetrated by two or three small knots of banditti of the lowest description, who are abhorred by their neighbours. This was in and near that mountainous tract, which separates the counties of Tipperary and Waterford, but especially in the latter county. But the causes and objects of these crimes were limited to a few new tenants, valuations of farms and inclosing of mountain common — Previous to the Assizes of Waterford much alarm had been sounded. Few of the gentry hold intercourse with the lower ranks, and few of the latter speak English. When one or two outrages had occurred, the gentry were panic struck — they did not take the trouble of probing or checking the evil but generally abandoned their posts. Their fears appear now to have subsided. The whole extent and nature of the danger were thoroughly explored at the Assizes with the calmness and steadiness which belong to our criminal jurisprudence — and the result proves that very little danger existed, and that a good police and moderate exercise of the civil power would suffice for the emergency. The report of the judges who went that circuit, Lord Avonmore & Baron George,[2] is highly favourable, I am told, and agrees very much with the opinion which I had the honour of expressing to your Lordship already upon the subject.

In the other parts of Ireland there is, I believe, profound tranquillity — the people are occupied in the pursuits of industry & are attached to the Establishment in proportion as they acquire an interest in the soil or in its produce. Here only (in Dublin) does any agitation appear: but fortunately it is very little, not to be dreaded & must soon disappear. It arose thus — Your Lordship may have heard of one Giffard,[3] the proprietor of a newspaper called *The Dublin Journal*. He is a person excessively detested by the people here owing to a certain fury & virulence, with which he speaks & writes of the R. Catholics, especially Dr Troy & the Bishops, who are in truth very loyal men and respected by their flocks. I understand that he was taken from a Charity School (the Blue Coat) and set up formerly as an apothecary. He got into the Corporation, & by haranguing and otherwise, got places in the Revenue, and the patronage of the violent party men. He was turned out of the Dublin militia, 3 or 4 years ago, by his Colonel, Sankey,[4] & brother officers. He has since had numerous scrapes and quarrels, and perhaps more personal enemies than any man in Ireland. I have myself heard some of the highest of our judges speak with horror of some acts of his, and a great majority, I think, of the Protestants consider his support & manner of giving it as disgraceful to their body by its bigotry, injurious to the public quiet by its intemperance, and oppressive to the public at large by being converted to his own private emolument. For it was a gainful trade to him, and literally *ira quaestuosa*.[5] From the Government proclamations & patronage to his paper, he is supposed to have derived an income of nearly £2000 for several years past, exclusive of £800 a year in the Revenue. This was his situation, but, fortunately for the public satisfaction, his temper has caused his expulsion from it. For, whilst all was quiet in Dublin, and the Catholic subject, hitherto harmless, was likely to pass off calmly and to the general benefit, this Giffard (tho' warned to the contrary by Government), sets upon the Catholics, collectively & individually, and libels them in his paper, supposed to be the Government paper. This was beginning to produce the worst effects. But his evil genius did not permit him to stop there. For he brought forward (tho' again warned) a series of motions in the Dublin Common Council against the Catholics, with the view of giving the example [and] setting the other towns in Ireland at work, & of printing all the proceedings in his paper. This he prefaced by a violent, inflammatory and frantic harangue. The resolutions passed in a meeting of 60 or 70, composed mostly of illiterate & halfbroken tradesmen — but they are certainly contrary to the sense of the Protestant body, even in Dublin.[6]

Next morning he was dismissed from his places,[7] as a disturber of the public peace, and as the agitator of a subject the most delicate and dangerous to be obtruded in such a manner. Never, that I recollect, did so trifling an occurence produce such general satisfaction; nor has any thing happened, since the Union, so happily calculated to attach the people to the Government, and to convince them that they are regarded with an eye of good nature and protection. Already, throughout the different provinces, as I hear, as well as in the capital, has a great joy been diffused upon the occasion, not loud or exulting, but calm and durable, and promising the happiest effects. Giffard, despairing of any countenance or support here after flying in the face of his benefactors, has sailed for England to complain, as he says, to the throne. Thus Lord H[ardwicke] and G[iffard] are committed. Give me leave, my Lord, to hope that our Government at the other side are too wise and too firm not to ratify Lord Hardwicke's act, and take advantage of this little occurrence to gladden the hearts of this people, & procure a cheap defence of our properties and country by winning the affections of its inhabitants. If Lord Hardwicke's act be ratified & his system maintained, you have nothing to fear for the peace of this country.

[*Source*: Callanan Papers]

[1]Brackets and alternative wording suggest that the draft went off in a revised form, but there were no changes of substance and the original text is followed here.

[2]Barry Yelverton (1736–1805), Chief Baron of the Exchequer from 1783, 1st Baron Avonmore 1795; and Denis George, 2nd Baron of the Exchequer.

[3]John Giffard was well known to Lord Sligo, who had written to the Castle on 8 March urging that the *Dublin Journal*'s abuse of the Catholics should be stopped (State Paper Office: OP, 1025/10).

[4]On 23 May 1798 Giffard, excited by the death of his son, had engaged in reprisals against the town of Kildare and struck Lieutenant-Colonel H. Gore Sankey, commander of his regiment, the Dublin Militia. On 9 January 1801 a court martial suspended him for twelve months (Plowden, *History* I, p. 60).

[5]"Lucrative anger". Scully may have been thinking of the lucrative libel Cobbett was accused of in 1804 (Howell, *State Trials* XXIX, 33).

[6]On 26 April Giffard had carried a motion that the Catholic petition would subvert the constitution, that after the horrors of the last ten years the time was unfavourable and that a counter-petition should be presented (Plowden, II p.41).

[7]Giffard's main post was at the Customs. Lord Hardwicke explained to the Home Secretary on 11 May that he was afraid of the Catholics, who had hitherto met privately, calling a public meeting: to treat the two parties differently would have an immediate effect on Catholics of every description; on the militia, of whom three quarters were Catholics; and on the yeomanry, where the two religions were mixed (Hardwicke Papers, Add.MSS.35, 710).

117   *From Lord Sligo to Baggott Street, Dublin*

London, 10 May 1805

Dear Sir,

Your favor of the 6th[1] reached me this moment & I can in no ways shew how highly acceptable it was to me than by replying to it from the Chair on which I received it.

Your representation as to the State of Ireland is highly gratifying to me & agrees most perfectly with all which I have in publick advanced upon its subject. *Locallity* or rather local ignorance is all [the] refutation my arguments have met with & as on this very day[2] we shall probably have a repetition of lies of bloody murders & rebellions I am most happy to have got your letter to justify me in the denial of them. I have not been out of my house twice this month but I am pretty well now & shall attend with my Friends in the house of Peers this day, tho I fear I am too weak to stand long enough to give my reasons for supporting a measure that has all my mind with it & that many years of consideration confirm me in the view I have of it with more decision & confidence than I should be otherways disposed to give to any opinion of mine own more lightly taken up. The Objects that you wish for I have no doubt you will have — I mean kind & Civil treatment & a dispassionate discussion of the subject, indeed with some solitary exceptions I am very sure of it. The temperate conduct of the Catholick body, the leaving of the question wholly to the Wisdom of Parliament without promoting tumultous meetings or disturbing the peace & industry of Ireland fully entitle them to that measure of acknowledgement even from those whose minds are furthest from a concession of their objects. It gives credit & confidence to those who are inclined to the measure & will certainly fully justify their characters not only with those who oppose them but also with the publick. According to my calculation there will be nine of the Representative Peers for the measure & seven exclusive of the four Spiritual Lords against it. The Majority against it however will be very considerable in both houses of Parliament. The publick mind here is certainly against it & I am much mistaken or those in whose hands it is placed would be glad to get rid of it. There are many I know of them that will not support it. Tho I always wished the measure should not be hurried into discussion especially under so many unfavorable circumstances as could only belong to the moment, I did not foresee half of the mischief which I fear will attend it & against which there is now no possible remedy.

That Mr Pitt's heart is lost to it there can be no doubt & he was I know a sincere Friend to the measure. The Irish Members, who in support of that cause for years embroiled themselves with their political friends, totally disregarded here,[3] not entrusted with the conduct of that which belonging exclusively to their own Country it was their particular duty to have brought forward & not even thought worthy of being called into the consultations upon the subject cannot but feel themselves ill treated, & who have been gained to it [?:] The Leaders of the Opposition who in proportion as they look to power wish to get rid of that which would embarrass them in office, & in the success of which, they would neither make private friends nor rise in popularity in this Country where alone it would be useful to their Interests. Depend on it these were great & lamentable mistakes & what I am very sorry to add, *depend* on it that between these & other causes you will never see the Catholick question pass in this Country. And I am equally clear that nothing but mismanagement could have prevented its success probably with the general good will of all the people of Great Britain.

With respect to Lord Hardwick's conduct in Ireland, I hope it will be rightly understood & properly estimated. Giffard is come over here & loud in his complaints. I have not the least fears however that such an indignity will be put on the Lord Lieutenant as that of restoring him to office. That appears to me to be quite [out] of question & would create a very great & very justifiable clamor if even thought of.

Lord Fingal & Mr McDonel[4] were so good to call upon me yesterday. The Town seems very full of Irish Members. Should any thing very material occur in this business depend on it you shall hear it from me.

[*Source*: Scully Papers]

[1]No. 116.
[2]He is referring to the debate on the Irish Catholic petition that Lord Grenville was going to open the same day in the House of Lords. If he attended at all he did not vote — Plowden, (*History* II, p. 157) says that he was taken suddenly ill.
[3]Scully recorded in his diary on 14 March that Lord Sligo had suggested his own brother, the Hon. Denis Browne, as someone who might bring the petition in if Pitt agreed. In his very full minutes of the deputies' meeting of the previous day, however, there is no indication that the desirability of entrusting the petition to an Irish member was even mooted.
[4]Randal MacDonnell (see No. 114).

118   *From Lord Sligo to Baggott Street, Dublin*

London, 15 May 1805

Dear Sir,

Since my last letter to you the fate of the Catholick petition has been decided.[1] It is unnecessary for me to repeat all or any thing that pass'd upon it which you may collect from the reports of the debates in the news papers,[2] but the opinion of this nation is at this time *unequivocably* against the measure, & I shall never cease to lament that it was so prematurely brought forward as to blast the fair prospects which a few years would have realised, & which will not in this century in my judgement recur again. The Opposition acted in it as I expected they would do, wanting it only as a means for disturbing the government & condescending to seek it tho in the teeth of what they call their *Whig principles*. So soon as they got hold of another weapon[3] they wished for nothing but to get rid of the Catholicks & I am told & I verily believe they would have thrown it up had they found any decent excuse for it, but as it was *one half* of them voted against it in the house of Lords & the measure was left to be supported chiefly by its Irish Friends, (Ld Hutchinson the ablest & warmest of them), who had not been entrusted by the Deputies nor even called into their consultations on the subject, tho any one of them was more interested in the question than all the Opposition put together. I don't know how very sensible men could have been so ill advised or why they should have given strength to all the calumnies issued against themselves by first treading on their own Country-men, their tried and approved friends, friends to them when they had neither interest nor power & when their Cause had no other supporters. Ld Hardwick has now become the object of attack; his conduct by the Catholicks entitles him to their eternal gratitude, forsake him now & you will never have a friend again.

The object now of every good man will be to keep the kingdom quiet & submit as loyal subjects ought to do to the wisdom of their Parliament, bound to consider the *general* good & to decide as will best promote it, sacrificing the interests even of many to what they conceive best for the community. Mr Grattan did himself great honor. His speech was most eloquent & impressive & fully supported the high name he had acquired in the Parliament of Ireland. I shall be glad to hear that all goes on well in Ireland, where I shall soon hope to see [sic].   [*Source*: Scully Papers]

[1]Lord Grenville's motion to go into committee on the petition had been defeated by 178 to 49 votes in the House of Lords on 13 May, and Fox's similar motion in the House of Commons lost by 336 to 124 votes at 4.30 a.m. on 15 May (*Hansard* IV, 843, 1060).
[2]In the *Dublin Evening Post* of 14, 16, 18 and 20 May.
[3]The impeachment of Lord Melville (see No. 115 n.1).

119   *From Edmund Scully to Baggot Street, Dublin*

                    Kilfeacle [Co. Tipperary] 20 May 1805
Dear Denys,
    I take the liberty of troubling you on a subject which I entirely submit to your better Consideration.

You recollect the unpleasant difference which occurred last July in Tipperary.[1] It originated entirely from the Orange Badges worn by a few prejudiced people in that Town on the 1st July but afterwards forbidden by Ld Cunningham[2] on the 12th *another* memorable day.[3] It is to prevent any distinction of this kind I should wish, I think the most effectual step would be to memorial Gen'l Meyrick,[4] and I am certain from his Liberality, and the efforts of some neighbouring Magistrates & Gentlemen, it may be prevented. I could easily get the signatures of some respectable magistrates stating the necessity of putting a stop to such distinctions. As I know no person more capable of drawing up a proper & respectful address to Gen'l M'k I hope you'll have no objection to do what will tend so materially to the peace of this Country. You could if you find necessary, hint that Ld Cunningham did it last year from a similar memorial, the danger to be apprehended from such distinctions where there is so large an armed force as the Legion[5] immediately near the town and that those Lillies & Ribbons are only worn by the poorest and most insignificant Class in Tipp'y more to inflame the ignorant lower order than thro any the least motives of Loyalty. I have only hinted those to you but you are the most competent judge of the best framed Memorial. You'll be good enough to answer this when convenient to you. Believe me with best regards for Mrs Scully, your ever affectionate Brother Edm'd Scully J's.   [*Source*: Scully Papers]

[1]See No. 62.
[2]*Recte* Conyngham.
[3]Under the old style Julian calendar the Boyne was fought on 1 July 1690, Aughrim on 12 July 1691. The former is now commemorated on 12 July, its new style date in the Gregorian calendar, but at the time of this letter the two battles seem generally to have been commemorated separately on their old style dates (see Lecky, *History* III, p. 427; Plowden, *History* III, pp. 149, 763; and below No. 363 n.11).
[4]Major General Thomas Meyrick, Lieutenant Colonel of the 21st Foot.
[5]Mathew's Legion — the Tipperary militia regiment, commanded by General Montagu Mathew, in which Edmund Scully was serving.

120   *From C. Hely Hutchinson to Baggot Street, Dublin*

London, 29 May 1805

My Dear Sir,
    Many thanks for your kind letter of the 22nd which I have just now received. I can assure you with great truth that I never discharged any public duty with more gratification, or anxiety, than I did that of protecting your name from the wicked and unfounded aspersions attempted to be cast upon it, and I can add that I should have been truly ashamed of myself had I suffered such imputations to pass unnoticed, and unrefuted. I was unfortun-

ate in the lateness of the hour, by which I was deprived of as patient a
hearing as I could have wished, but I put off speaking to the last moment in
the hope of thereby having it in my power to repel such other calumnies, as
might be uttered during the Debate — besides, I apprehend, that few, if
any of the regular reporters were at that moment in the Gallery, the
consequence was that from the manner in which some of the public papers
stated the interruption I experienced, it admitted of a doubt whether this
might not have arisen from a disapprobation, on the part of the House, of
the passages quoted, whereas I can assure you that the impression was
directly the other way,[1] and I had the gratification to feel that the base
malignancy of the Dr[2] had not succeeded in the abominable & wicked
attempt to deprive you of your good name, and station in society. From a
mistake, part of what I said as to you & your family, has been attributed to
my friend Dillon who however I know has a very sincere regard for you,
and joins cordially with me in reprobating the conduct of the learned, but
unpolished, Doctor, who has but too truly verified the saying that, "the
Tongue is a fire, a world of iniquity"! This libeller however of private
worth, and National Character, is too profligately consistent, not to be, of
every honest man in the Community, the detestation and contempt. In the
indisputed possession of these his well earned rewards, let you & I my dear
Sir, leave him.[3]

[P.S.] I am only a Newspaper Colonel!   [*Source*: Scully Papers]

[1]Because of the lateness of the hour the last stages of the debate had been
inadequately reported. In its summary of H. A. Dillon's speech *Hansard* does not
mention Scully at all, and "Colonel" Hely Hutchinson is represented as reading
some extracts from Scully's pamphlet "which were so ill received by the House that
we could not collect their tenour" (*Hansard* IV, 1030, 1039).

[2]Dr Patrick Duigenan, whose speech had been reported in the *Dublin Evening Post*
of 18 May. Much of it was an attack on Scully's pamphlet (see No. 56 n.2), the
whole tenor of which, he claimed, was to excite the Romish populace to the most
furious acts of insurrection, the advice to resist Bonaparte being merely an artifice
to protect the author from legal punishment.

[3]The *Dublin Evening Post* of 21 May had published fuller summaries of Dillon's
and Hely Hutchinson's speeches sticking up for Scully. The latter, having read
several extracts from the pamphlet, went on: "I can confirm that it had a highly
beneficial and extensive influence among the Catholics at that critical juncture. It
was approved of, I understand, by the Government, and very particularly commended, if I am not misinformed, by his Majesty's Prime Minister". Here the report
inserted in brackets: "Mr Pitt nodded assent".

121   *From Mary Scully to Mrs Huddleston, Sawston Hall,*
Saffron Walden, Essex

Bagot Street [Dublin] 1 June [1805]

Dear Mama,

. . . I have had a new Physician called in about a week ago. Both agreed I must go for a few days into the country before I should be strong enough to take any medicine. I have accordingly followed their advice and went for a few days to an Inn at Bray, ten miles from here in the County of Wicklow and I hope I am something better for the excursion. Mr S. talks of going elsewhere in a few days. He values no expence he thinks can be of service to me, and indeed I cost him no small sums in the way of Drs etc. and I fear they have done me more harm than good. The advising me to leave off wine & beer has, I am now convinced been very injurious to my constitution.

Jane mistook very much when she informed you that I meant to spend my time while I was in England at Hamstead [*sic*],[1] I only meant to go there for a fortnight or three weeks with my Aunt (a scheme I do not now totally give up), but it will make no difference with regard to my stay at Sawston which you may depend upon I shall make as long as possible. My Mother in Law is in Town at present, but not staying here. She is with her D'r[2] who is lying in. We expect the Old Gentleman very soon for a short time. I hope I shall be better before he comes, as I should wish to have a little Dinner company to amuse him.

I am sorry not to be able to get a Frank for this, but I would not delay writing while you & my F'r are alone, tho' my letter indeed is not entertaining. You will however excuse that as it really is a fatigue to me to write on. I should give my F'r some Irish Politics. He will however see by the papers what is passing and indeed sometimes what is not passing as they take great liberties with us in the English papers. I hope my F'r is well, with Duty to him believe me Dear Mama most truly your affectionate D'r M. Scully
[P.S.] Mr S. & Fanny[3] join in best remembrance.

[*Source*: Huddleston Papers C1/MH81]

[1]Possibly to stay with her friend Sophia Sulyard, since 1799 the wife of John Carey of Hampstead, whom Scully had met in London in March.
[2]Probably Anne, wife of Thomas Mahon, who lost a son in 1808 aged about three.
[3]Frances Huddleston.

122   *From Hugh Fitzpatrick*

Capel Street [Dublin] Wednesday morn. [5 June 1805]

Dr. Sir,

I send herewith the first copy of the *Catholicophobia*[1] that could be procured; the author is not without some apprehensions that there are parts of it which might possibly subject him to *legal* cognizance — in your perusal of it therefore, you will please to hold that circumstance in your recollection — and have the kindness to favour us with your opinion — as soon as convenient.

[*Source*: Scully Papers]

[1]*Antidote to cure the Catholicophobia and Iernephobia* by Julius Vindex, printed for the author (Dublin, 1804). Vindex is identified as Denis Taaffe in the NLI catalogue. Scully's Common Place Book shows that he bought the work 8 June.

123   *From Edmund Scully to Baggot Street, Dublin*

Kilfeacle [Co. Tipperary] 7 June 1805

Dear Denys,

I had the pleasure this day of your affect'e letter and feel much obliged for your exertions as to the Memorial,[1] and am certain every liberal minded Man in this Country will be equally indebted as nothing can so effectually do away prejudices and unite all parties.

I am much concerned Mrs Scully continues yet so indisposed but hope the fineness of the weather & exercise may soon restore her. My father desires me say he misunderstood the purport of your letter to him. He desires you'll not answer some Bill, till he sees you, which will be next Wednesday at Dinner in Dublin. He encloses you two Bills to y'r order Amt. £400 one for £100 & one for £60.5/– for Kanning & Pennefeather[2] which he requests you may pay & take receipts for.

My father had a letter from my Mother this Morn'g. He purposes leaving this on Monday Morn'g. Will Heffernan of Derk & Heff Considine[3] slept here last night on their way to Dublin. Any commands you may have at any time in this quarter I shall most willingly execute.

Believe me with best regards to Mrs Scully, my Mother, Nancy etc. your ever affect'e Brother,

E. Scully James.   [*Source*: Scully Papers]

[1]See No. 119.
[2]Not identified.
[3]Heffernan Considine, nephew of Will Heffernan of Derk, Pallasgreen, Co. Limerick.

124   *From Edmund Scully to Baggot Street, Dublin*

Kilfeacle [Co. Tipperary] 10 June 1805

Dear Denys,

I wrote to you a few days since enclosing 4 Bills which I suppose you received in due course. I have now to mention that my father and I have at length come to a final agreement respecting Miss O'B[rien] about a fortnight since.[1] I thought it better to make an offer to him of giving up all future pretensions of choosing her as a Wife tho' at the same time I told him my affections could never be altered while she remained unmarried. He was kind enough to promise what he never did before, that I should have his full approbation to marry her either when James[2] would be married or next Sept'r two years, which he says is the longest time he would allow for James to choose a Wife. I was fully satisfied particularly as he promised he would not curtail in the least any fortune he ever intended for me. I take the liberty of troubling you at present lest he or my Mother may renew the subject in Dublin and I am convinced, if so, you will act towards me with the same affection I have always experienced. Be assured I feel the greatest delicacy in writing this Letter as Mrs S. is in so poor a state of health but I am sure you will excuse me on a matter I am so deeply interested [in] and on which I consider so much depends on your exertions. I should be very glad to hear from you when at leisure how Mrs Scully is in her health.

Believe me with best Regards for her etc.

Your ever affect'e Brother, Edm'd Scully James   [*Source*: Scully Papers]

[1]See No. 113.
[2]His brother, James Scully.

125   *From Dr J. T. Troy, Archbishop of Dublin, to Bagot Street*

Thursday, 13 June 1805

My dear Sir,

I have availed myself of the enclosed draught of a letter to Sir J. C. Hippisley, which I forwarded by last night's packet.[1]

As I am on my step to the country, I return the draught[2] with thanks. I made some alterations in it in my letter to Sir John. The Prelates Trustees of Maynooth College are to meet there on the 26th instant. They will consider the expediency of writing to Ld Grenville & Mr Fox, and the manner of addressing each. I hope to see you in the course of next week.

[*Source*: Scully Papers]

[1]The letter, dated 12 June, was printed, as Appendix I, in Sir J. Hippisley's *The*

Substance of Additional Observations intended to have been delivered in the House of Commons in the debate on the Petition of the Roman Catholics of Ireland on the 13th and 14th May, 1805 (London, 1806). It is a reply to the speech of the Bishop of St Asaph in the House of Lords on 10 May 1805, the text of which seems to have been sent to Dr Troy by Sir J. Hippisley.

[2]The draft, by Scully, is among the Callanan Papers. Dr Troy made numerous alterations in the wording and inserted twelve paragraphs of his own dealing with the distinction between the "power of order" and the "power of jurisdiction" belonging to the ecclesiastical authorities.

126   *From Dr J. T. Troy, Archbishop of Dublin, to Baggot Street*

Annfield, 21 June 1805

My dear Sir,

I send you the rough draughts of my late letters to Sir J. C. Hippisley,[1] which please to leave at Fitzpatricks on Monday next, when I intend going to town, & hope to see you. Lest I should not have this pleasure, be so good like wise to leave Dr Duigenan's speech, which I sent to you yesterday, and your draught of letter to Lord Grenville[2] at the same place on Monday. I must leave Dublin on Tuesday. The Prelates Trustees of Maynooth College to meet there on Wednesday.   [*Source*: Scully Papers]

[1]See No. 125 n.1 for his letter of 12 June. A letter of 15 June was also printed by Hippisley as Appendix III to his *Observations*. It is a detailed commentary on Dr Duigenan's speech on the Irish Catholic petition (see No. 120 n.2).

[2]Dr Troy's letter, dated 5 July, is reproduced in *Dropmore Papers* VII. It thanks Lord Grenville for his support, defines the position of the Irish Bishops in regard to the established church and affirms the compatibility of the Roman Catholic religion with loyalty to the crown. Scully's draft has not been found.

127   *From Henry Augustus Dillon to Bagot Street, Dublin*

York Street, Portman Square [London] 24 June 1805

My dear Sir,

You must by this time have received my book.[1] I take the liberty of requesting you to correct in page 5 some errors of the press — instead of *proscription* read "Ireland had a circumscribed Parliament a circumscribed trade and a proscribed people" — on page 13 read for *impregnated* with the same spirit, *animated* with the same spirit.

In page 29 after the words "it cannot be too often referred to & too much dwelt upon" — insert the words — "so that it is evident King James the second was not expelled merely for an attempt to change the religion of the country but because he had violated by his own authority the laws of the land".

I hope this letter may come in time as these alterations and corrections are necessary. You will have the goodness to send me a copy when it is out and you will observe that I have written this evidently for the north and to be circulated among the protestants as much as possible. You will have the goodness to get one hundred copies to be placed to my account and sent to the members of government, the Lord Mayor and aldermen, common council etc. and the principal persons of the bar. Written from the author the freedom of whose part will not be relished by bigots or High Churchmen or Priests but that is my view of the subject and the grounds as a protestant upon which I ever advocate your cause[2] — if we do not make an union of all the people we do nothing — and point out all the errors of our system. I do not write for popularity but to do good.

My father[3] approves much and wishes this to be sent to all parts of Ireland. I again request you will get one thousand copies dispersed thro' the north.

Pray let me hear of its success.   [*Source*: Scully Papers]

[1]His pamphlet *A Letter to the Noblemen and Gentlemen who composed the deputation of the Catholics of Ireland* had been published by Budd in London and another edition was now being printed by Hugh Fitzpatrick in Dublin.
[2]Plowden says in his *History* I, p. 271 that Dillon was intending to move for a repeal of the penal laws so far as they affected Catholics entering the army or navy but on hearing that Pitt was coming into power again abandoned the motion, in the expectation that Pitt would bring in emancipation.
[3]Charles, 12th Viscount Dillon (1745–1813), who had conformed to the established church in 1767.

128   *From Henry Augustus Dillon to Bagot Street, Dublin*

London, 2 July 1805

My dear Sir,

On my return from Oxford I found your very kind and flattering letter for which I am much obliged. Pray have you received another letter marked with some corrections.[1] I shall be much obliged to you to correct these errors. It has already gone thro' one edition here and it has had greater success than I could possibly conceive. The arguments about King William and the Protestant church have had the best effects and are approved of by many Protestants — even in the university — the great object is the north of Ireland. Pray let it go down there. I wrote it with that view. I have sent you the little squibb[2] which I beg you will not aver is mine as I wrote it merely for amusement and tho' printed is not to be made Public. You may show it to some private friends. Pray tell me what Mr

Curran[3] thinks of it. I have the best authority for the Hibernian[?] part —
which is the chief merit.

[*Source*: Scully Papers]

[1]No. 127.
[2]Not found.
[3]John Philpot Curran.

129   *From Edmund Scully to Baggot Street, Dublin*

Kilfeacle [Co. Tipperary] 12 July 1805

Dear Denys,

I take this opportunity thro' Mr Griffith[1] of mentioning to you the
pleasure several Gentlemen experienced in this Country from the orders
issued in this District to prevent any marks of Distinction from being worn
either the 1st or 12th Inst.[2] The opposite party & the Monaghan militia made
every preparation but were entirely disappointed. Major Crawford[3] (my
friend) was sent by the Gen'l[4] to Tipp'y and was very active in taking them
from some who put them up. They were indeed a good deal incensed but did
no great mischief in consequence. They only tore & abused the Caps of a few
Women who wore green Ribbons on that Day. In my opinion it will be
attended with the very best Consequences, tho a few insignificant Individuals may be disappointed yet all parties will by degrees be reconciled when
those badges are not used. Ld Hardwicke deserves every merit for his
Liberality and it is a satisfaction to every Liberal minded man, tho the
Catholics remain still deprived of privileges they have every right to enjoy,
to see so good & sensible a Man at the head of our Govern't. I cannot express
what a degree of pleasure has been diffused amongst almost every Class in
this Country by the extinction of those cursed marks and tho' I have kept it a
profound secret from every person but a few of this family the Country have
every right to be much indebted to you. A good many suspect this family
have been the cause of this great Reformation. We have taken no trouble to
convince them to the contrary. I believe we shall go to Castleconnell in about
a Week.

I should be very glad to hear from you how Mrs Scully is. We heard some
time since you & she purposed going to England. If so I hope the journey
may serve her.

Believe me with very best regards for Mrs Scully
Your ever affect'e Brother
E. Scully Jam's.   [*Source*: Scully Papers]

[1]Unidentified.
[2]See Nos. 119 and 123.

[3]Probably Robert Crawford, late of the Royal Irish Artillery, a Major in the North Cork Militia.
[4]Lord Conyngham.

130   *From Dr J. T. Troy, Archbishop of Dublin, to Bagot Street*

North King Street, Monday, 4 o'clock p.m. [15 July 1805]

My dear Sir,

At my return from the country about an hour ago, I found your note of Saturday last on my table. If you will please to meet me tomorrow at Fitzpatricks at eleven o'clock, I shall with pleasure hand you the copy of the letter to Ld G[renville] for your perusal.[1] I appoint this early hour as I am to return to the country about twelve o'clock. My action etc was tried last Thursday. A verdict in my favour. £50 damages and cost of suit. The trial [one word missing] to be printed.[2]   [*Source*: Scully Papers]

[1]See DDA 29/9 (49) for two drafts in Dr Troy's hand.
[2]See Howell, *State Trials* XXIX. Dr Troy had taken a libel action against the editor of the *Anti-Jacobin Review* which in its summer number of 1803 had accused him of knowing in advance of the Emmet rising but failing to warn the government. When he was in London in March Scully had called on Dr Troy's attorneys. The case was heard on 11 July.

131   *To Ferdinand Huddleston, Sawston Hall,*
Saffron Walden, Essex

Dublin, 19 July 1805

My dear Sir,

[Because of extra charges and increased expenses of an establishment coming together he hopes that Mr Huddleston can accommodate him by adding to the payment he made two years ago[1] a sum of £300, which Messrs Abraham Robarts & Co. bankers, London, would receive for his account].

Mary has been very indifferent during the Spring, but within these few days appears better — and we begin to think of preparing for our intended journey to England. The Physicians give strong hopes, that the change of scene and air will tend considerably to the re-establishment of her health — and to avoid fatigue she will make very easy stages.[2] We much regret the company of Miss F. Huddleston[3] who is gone to Harrowgate with our neighbours the Marshalls[4] and Mary was unwilling to detain her from an excursion which promises so much pleasure.

I shall be happy to hear that you & the family of Sawston are well, and that Mrs Huddleston derives benefit from the Sea Baths.

With affect[ionat]e regards to all (in which Mary desires to join).[5]

[*Source*: Huddleston Papers C2/S3]

[1]See No. 59.
[2]In a letter of 21 August Jane Huddleston told her brother Richard that Scully was deceiving himself, talking of travelling to England when his wife could barely go as far as Lucan. The Caldwells had found her in such a dangerous state that they had written to inform her (Huddleston Papers C3/HR88).
[3]Frances (Fanny) Huddleston, a first cousin of his wife.
[4]Mr and Mrs Robert Marshall, who lived in Baggot Street. Jane Huddleston wrote to her mother on 1 August: "Fanny is at Harrowgate by this time. In one of her letters she says Mr Marshall talks of coming to Cambridge. I intend to write to ask them to come to Sawston. I cannot, indeed, well do otherwise, he is a great friend of the Scullys & is one of the most amiable men I ever knew . . ." (ibid., C1/MH58).
[5]This letter was franked by George Ponsonby.

132   *From his brother James Scully Jr.*

Kilfeacle, 21 July [1805]

Dear Denis,

My father desires me say he wrote to you on the 13th inst. to conclude the purchase you mentioned to him, as he has not since heard from you he feared the letter miscarried. My mother Joana and Mon[1] are at Castle-connell my father goes there on Wednesday — Joana's match with Sadleir is finally agreed on, it takes place immediately on her return[2] — I hope Mrs S. is getting better health.

Yrs ever affectly
James Scully Jr.

[*Source*: Scully Papers]

[1]His brother Edmund.
[2]His sister Joanna Scully married Clement Sadleir on 19 September 1805.

133   *From Lord Fingall to Baggot Street, Dublin*

26 July 1805

Dear Sir,

After the best consideration I have been able to give the Subject you mentioned to me I really believe it is most prudent not to attempt it. We are both equally inclined to serve the person & the cause and the more I think on the business the stronger the impression on my mind that none of the good consequences we wish would follow from adopting the measure we were talking of.[1]   [*Source*: Scully Papers]

[1]No clue to the subject of this letter has been found.

134   *From Ferdinand Huddleston*

[Draft/copy][1]   [c. 27 July 1805]
My Dr. Sir,

I can sincerely assure [you] y'r l'r[1] has caused me great uneasiness [and] concern as it is entirely out of my power at present to advance the Money. It wo[ul]d make me happy to do it as I am quite conscious of the great attention you pay to my Dear Mary in her infirm state of health. I was lately disappointed of £640 wch was to have gone towds. the Inclosure wch has already cost me above £1,800. Besides wch My Tenants are much behindhand in their Rents and I am oblig'd to give them time as they have Expended large sums of money in Cattle and improving their farms wch I have no doubt will answer in time both to them & the Landlord. However I shall do my best Endeavours to procure best part of the £300 by Michaelmas or thereabouts.

Am glad to hear that Mary is rather better and it will give me great pleasure to see y'u both at old Sawston where I hope you will make y'r stay as long as you can. Mrs Hud'n has been gone ab't 3 weeks to South End w'ch is about 60 miles from hence. We have had two l'rs from her with good acc'ts of her health improving. I expect her home ab't the End of the month.

My Sons by their last l'rs are all well as likewise Jane who keeps house during her Mother's absence.   [*Source*: Huddleston Papers C2/S3]

[1]Written at the end and on the cover of No. 131, to which it is a reply.

135   *From Henry Augustus Dillon to Bagot Street, Dublin*

York Street [London] 21 August 1805
My dear Sir,

I am on the point of setting out for Vienna[1] — which prevents me from visiting Ireland. I shall however I trust have time to receive a letter from you — pray inform me what success my letter[2] has had and if you have circulated it generally — it has gone thro' a second edition here.

I congratulate you upon the glorious victory in the Co. of Down over one of the [space left blank by Dillon] to his country that ever lived — it shews real independence in the electors. I see you were prevented from illuminating[3] — pray tell me how that was and what has been the general reaction.

[P.S.] Pray tell me where the pamphlet has been circulated. I shall send you under cover a second edition corrected tomorrow.[*Source*: Scully Papers]

[1] It is unlikely that he went. Napoleon started his march to the Danube on 20 August.

[2] His pamphlet (see No. 127 n.1).

[3] On his appointment to the War Office on 10 July Lord Castlereagh had stood for re-election in Co. Down. On 13 August he had conceded defeat, at the hand of Colonel John Meade who was supported by the Downshire interest, and on news of this reaching Dublin his enemies had made plans to illuminate the city. It was reported in *The Times* of 21 August that the Mayor of Dublin had forbidden the illuminations.

136   *From Jeremiah Scully to Bagot Street, Dublin*

Tipperary, 2 September 1805

Dear Denys,

At foot you have our order, at sight, for the amount of the notes left to me. Mun[1] appeared at Breakfast, and my father received him much better than I could expect. They did not come to any explanation, my father did not even hint on his conduct, peace is once more restored but I fear it will not be permanent. From what you heard my mother say last night, you may suppose she will not remain tranquil.[2]

In reply, I would thank you to let me know how Mrs S. is. With the sincerest wishes for her health, I remain your very affectionate Brother — Jerem'h Scully

N.B. Your mare was put into a field by herself and your Bridle and saddle put in a safe place. [Lower part of letter cut off]   [*Source*: Scully Papers]

[1] His brother Edmund Scully.
[2] For the last reconciliation see No. 124.

137   *To Ferdinand Huddleston, Sawston Hall,*
Saffron Walden, Essex

Thayer Street, London, 17 September 1805

Dear Sir,

I had the pleasure of receiving your letter[1] in Ireland some time ago. I have accordingly made arrangements respecting the three hundred pounds. As my stay here will necessarily be very short you will much oblige me by naming the place where I am to receive that sum — and the sooner, the more convenient to me just now. Mrs Scully & I have reached town only this morning — & I am happy to say that the journey appears to have agreed well with her. With kind remembrances to your good family.

[*Source*: Huddleston Papers C2/S4]

[1]No. 134.

138   *To Ferdinand Huddleston from Thayer Street, London,*
23 September 1805

Formally acknowledges the receipt of £500 paid in September and October 1803 and a further £300 just received, making £800 in part payment of the bond payable to him on 24 May 1802, as well as of the interest due on this and the other Bond for £1000 up to 5 April last which has been paid to his account with Mrs Bostock.[1] Although she bore her journey well his wife has been attacked by the past three days with severe colic and spasms. He doubts whether she can soon leave town but he hopes for an improvement under Dr Baillie's care.[2]

[*Source*: Huddleston Papers C2/S8]

[1]Although Scully kept an account with Mrs Bostock, who made small payments on his behalf in London, the obscure references to the matter in the Huddleston Papers suggest that he took over the responsibility of paying an annuity of £100 due to her from the Huddleston estate.
[2]When he was in London in March 1805 Scully had consulted Dr Matthew Baillie about his wife's health.

139   *From Charles J. Fox to 7 Thayer Street,*
Manchester Square, [London]

St Anne's Hill [Chertsey, Surrey] Sunday 29 September 1805

Dear Sir,

I have this day received yours of the 27th and shall be very happy to see you any morning that you can conveniently call. Wednesday will be rather *less* convenient to me than any other day. As my small house is like to be pretty full, I am sorry that I can not propose to you to spend the day here.[1]

[*Source*: Scully Papers]

[1]No information about this meeting has been found.

140   *From his mother Catherine Scully to Baggot Street, Dublin*

Kilfeacle [Co. Tipperary] 12 October 1805

My Dr Den's,

I hope this will meet you returned safe and well and that you left Mrs Scully pretty well. It made me happy to hear that the journey agreed with her and I hope she may continue to mend now that she has got to her native air. It ought to be a great relife to your mind to have her with her own frinds.

You promis'd us that you wou'd come and spend your spare time here when you'd return from England and I hope soon to see you. I wish Nancy wou'd come with you. I wrote to her to that purpose as her Father wish'd it.[1] We are now quiet alone since Joanna[2] left us. Your Father, Mun[3] and Uncle Jerry[4] went to Cork this day. They are to return next Friday (please God). He is very well pleas'd with his bargins at Balinaslo and the beef promises to be in great demand this season. I belive that James's business with Miss W.[5] is almost conclud'd on. I have no more to add at present as I expect to see you very soon here.

I remain my Dr. Den's, your loving and affect'te Mother Catherine Scully

[*Source*: Scully Papers]

[1]Her daughter Anne, wife of Thomas Mahon.
[2]Her daughter, who had married Clement Sadleir on 19 September 1805.
[3]Her son Edmund.
[4]Jeremiah Scully, of Silverfort.
[5]Margaret Wyse, of the Manor of St John, Waterford, whom her son James married on 17 January 1806.

141   *From Charles J. Fox to 97 Wimpole Street, London*

Arlington Street [London] 5 February [1806]

Dear Sir,

Nothing but a hurry of business beyond all belief and unexampled even on an occasion like the present could have prevented my sending to you this week.[1]

I will write to Lord Shrewsbury and whether I shall see him alone or with Lord Trimleston and you I leave entirely to his Lordship.

[*Source*: Scully Papers]

[1]Fox had just assumed office as Foreign Secretary in the new Whig administration, popularly known as the Ministry of All the Talents. A list of its principal members was published in *The Times* on 1 February 1806.

142   *To Charles James Fox*

Wimpole Street [London] 5 February [1806]

Copy

Dear Sir,

The letter, with which you have honoured me, shall be communicated to Lord Shrewsbury, in whose hands that subject remains.

Had I been aware, that the events, which occasion your hurry and gratify the friends of the Country were so near at hand or even approaching, I should not have consented to write last week.

I greatly fear that it appeared to you unreasonable & therefore feel it proper to avow my ignorance candidly, rather than be thought capable of an impertinence towards you, which is far remote from my nature.

[*Source*: Scully Papers]

143   *From Lord Shrewsbury to 97 Wimpole Street, London*

6 February 1806

Sir,

I yesterday recd a letter from Mr Fox appointing 4 O'Clock on Saturday next for an interview. I have reason to think you received one to the same purport. I think you, & Lord Trimlestone (if agreable) had best meet in Stan[hop]e Str[eet][1] at 3 o'Clock on the above mentioned day.[2]

[*Source*: Scully Papers]

[1]Lord Shrewsbury's town house.

[2]*The Times* of 6 March published an account of the interview taken from a Dublin newspaper of 28 February. Fox, it said, recommended the deferment of a petition, adding that while no measure of relief was under immediate consideration the Catholics could be assured of a just and equitable spirit in the new executive; that existing laws in their favour would be faithfully executed, especially for the army; that the tone of public officials would be more liberal; and that justice would be administered without distinction of sect or party. Lord Shrewsbury and Mr Scully thanked him for the explicitness of his declaration but said they could not presume to anticipate the determination of the Catholic body. The report makes no mention of Lord Trimleston.

144   *Heads of discussion*[1]

[?8 February 1806]

[On one side]
1st. Article of war, as to going to church — Ld Fingall's letter to Dr Milner.[2]
  2. The Marr Act — in Engld only —[3]
  3. The Regist[4]
  4. Ecclesiast. property, schools, property etc.[5]
[On the other side]
  1. Stop the Police Bill, and if possible take the patronage out of the corporation crew.[6]
  2. Don't repeat the Habeas Corpus Suspension act,[7] as you don't now want it.
  3. Purify the Post Office Department, and remove all the leading officers.
  4. Let the Catholic clergy alone — it is only a political quackery.[8]
  5. Let the Poor-laws system alone — and all other *new* schemes — amend the present and it will suffice.
  6. Call for an account of the £50,000 granted in 1803 to the First Fruits Commrs.[9]
  7. Take off the revenue visits on passengers, & equalise the coins, measures etc.[10]
  8. Purge the commissions of the Peace.
  9. Change the Yeomanry system.
 10. Qy? — as to the opinions given by the Atty. and Solicitor General on the Test laws in or before 1800 — to be revised now.[11]

[*Source*: Scully Papers MS.27, 518]

[1]Jotted down on either side of a folded notice for a Cisalpine Club dinner to be held on 11 February and, as there were no speeches at the dinners of the club, probably meant for the interview with Fox on 8 February (see No. 143).
[2]The letter has not been found. The articles of war were those of the annual mutiny act and included among other disciplinary matters regulations about church attendance.
[3]Roman Catholic priests in England were not allowed to celebrate marriages even between two Catholics — Dr Milner had complained about this in his pamphlet of 1805: *A short view of the arguments against the Catholic petition.*
[4]No explanation has come to light.
[5]Under the existing penal laws Catholic churches and schools could not be endowed, a matter much to Scully's heart — see No. 197.
[6]Probably the corporation of Dublin. The Police Bill has not been identified.
[7]It was permitted to expire on 7 March, when state prisoners were released (Plowden, *History* II, p. 280).

[8]Possibly a reference to what became known as the Veto — see No. 535 n.2. for Lord Stanhope's saying he first heard of the Veto from Fox.

[9]A bill had been passed in 1803 to encourage the building of glebe houses for the Protestant clergy and the £50,000 was a sum that had accumulated in the hands of the Irish First Fruits Commissioners (Redesdale to Perceval, 17 May 1803). A copy of an obscure letter of 30 April 1806 from Lord Redesdale to an Archbishop (probably of Armagh) about an interview with the new Chief Secretary, William Elliot, suggests that some heed was paid to Scully's representations, whatever they were: "I mentioned also to Mr Elliot Mr Scully's conduct with respect to the church to which your Grace alludes, and I suggested the propriety of a parliamentary commission to set out glebes, old churchyards etc" (Calendar of Redesdale Papers).

[10]Scully's hopes echo the recommendations of the parliamentary committee "on the circulating paper, specie and current coin of Ireland" (*Reports* 1803–4 (86) IV 261).

[11]See No. 98 n.1.

145   *From R. MacDonnell to Baggot Street, Dublin*

Allen court, [Mulinahack, Co. Dublin] 6 March 1806

Dear Sir,

I regret very much that we had not the advantage of your Council & opinion at our meeting on tuesday,[1] from your not getting the summons in time; in sending them about I am sure Mr E. Moore was as prompt as he could be, after he got the list of the Committee on Monday at 3 o'clock. Whatever errors may have been committed by any of us, I think, & I hope you will join me in thinking so; that it is better for us to take up Matters as they are, & endeavour to act right in future than to dwell on the past. I wish this spirit may prevail at the meeting wch is to take place on Saturday at 11 o'Clock at D'Arcys, N. Earl Street, & to have your Cooperation there.[2]

[*Source*: Scully Papers]

[1]On the accession to power of the Ministry of All the Talents James Ryan had written to Fox asking for his advice on the course that the Catholics ought to pursue and in another letter had solicited for himself a lucrative government appointment in Dublin. Fox had replied to both points in the same letter (text in Plowden, *History* II, p. 305). On the advice of Randal MacDonnell, with whom he had served his articles, Ryan had invited about eighty Catholics to meet at his house on 1 March: uninvited guests had swelled the number to a hundred. Ryan had then read out those parts of Fox's letter advising against a petition. Taking exception to Ryan's having assumed the character of an agent of the Irish Catholics, some twenty people had walked out. From a list of names provided by MacDonnell the meeting had then chosen a committee which was to meet in MacDonnell's house of Tuesday 4 March: this was the meeting that Scully missed. It resolved that petitioning would be inexpedient and that an address should be presented to the Duke of Bedford, the new Lord Lieutenant (Plowden, II, p. 308).

[2]This meeting, a public one, was adjourned to 13 March, the full contents of Fox's letter having become generally known. Resolutions were then passed forbidding meetings in private houses and censuring the meeting in James Ryan's house as having been brought about by private invitation and partial selection (Plowden, II, p. 316).

146   *From James Walsh, Junr.*[1] *to Baggott Street, Dublin*

Dame Street [Dublin] 30 March 1806

Sir,

I am directed to acquaint you that at a General Meeting of the Roman Catholic Inhabitants of St Andrew's Parish held yesterday in their Chapel Townsend St you were chosen along with the following Gentlemen viz. Ambrose Moore,[2] Michael Hughes[3] & James Conolly[4] Esqrs to Represent them in the General Committee of the Catholics of Dublin.[5]

Your appointment is to continue for one year unless the trust shall be sooner taken away by the Voice of your Electors.   [*Source*: Scully Papers]

[1]Possibly of James Walsh & Son, Breeches Makers, 35 Dame Street.
[2]Of York Street, when he signed the 1805 petition. He was in the chair at the Catholic meeting of 13 January 1800 which passed resolutions against the Union.
[3]Of Georges Quay (see No. 67 n.1).
[4]Of South King Street.
[5]A committee of thirty-six members, four from each parish, had been elected to prepare an address to the new Lord Lieutenant, the Duke of Bedford, who had arrived in Dublin on 28 March, but the organisers had other ends in view which were revealed at a meeting on 3 April. The committee were to have the task of "further superintending" the concerns of the Catholic body on behalf of the Dublin Catholics, but an association was also to be formed comprising "the full respectability of the Catholic body" (Plowden, *History* II, p. 328). For Scully's opinion of their meetings see No. 154.

147   *From Thomas FitzGerald, Jun., to Bar Mess, Clonmell*

[Waterford c. 31 March 1806]

My Dear Sir,

Agreeable to promise I have barely to inform you, that the only Question discussed & carried at our 1st meeting on Saturday last[1] was the appointment of a Committee composed of the five following Gentlemen: Messrs T. Wyse, R. O'Shee, Rt Revd Dr Power, J. Ryan, T. Hearn MD[2] & your Humble servant for the purpose of keeping up a Communication throu'out our County & with Others when necessary. Will you then let me know whether RC gentlemen of your County will point out some medium of correspondence that we may have the benefit of interchanging & knowing each other's sentiments & whenever necessary of acting similarly.

N.B. *This to yourself* only.   [*Source*: Scully Papers]

[1]The Assizes were due to start at Waterford on 26 March and at Clonmel on 31 March (*DEP*, 17 March 1806). The meeting would therefore have been on 29 March, after Scully had left for Clonmel.

[2]Thomas Wyse of the Manor of St John; Richard Power O'Shee (c. 1763–1827) of Gardenmorris; Dr John Power, Bishop of Waterford; Jeremiah Ryan, wine merchant of Bayley's New Street; Thomas Hearn MD, of George's Street.

148   *From Thomas FitzGerald, Jun. to Bar Mess, Clonmell*

[Waterford c. 1 April 1806]

My Dear Friend,

I wrote you a few hasty lines with respect to our meeting on Saturday but omitted I believe our Resolutions, viz., 1st that a Committee be appointed to be held in Waterford, to communicate with the Gentlemen of the County, City & Vicinity upon any event that may occur relating to the General Interests of the RC body which shall be considered of sufficient Importance to require their being called together. 2nd, that the following Gentlemen do compose such Committee: Rt Revd Doctor Power, Thomas Wyse, J. Ryan, Secretary, [T] Hearn MD, Thos. FitzGerald.

And with respect to a little private business, it's my intention to cross the channel in about a week hence and well knowing your general & intimate acquaintance with most of the English RC of distinction may I request the favor of one or two introductory letters.

And now to return to the charge, would a congratulatory address to the Duke of Bedford from us *here*,[1] think you, be followed up *elsewhere*? I mean by your friends in Clonmeil or is it likely that there will be comtee. formed? I will not take up your time longer than to assure you that joined by the family of this house I remain with esteem. . . .   [*Source*: Scully Papers]

[1]In May an address congratulating the Duke of Bedford on his taking office as Lord Lieutenant was presented by Thomas Wyse, Thomas Hearn and Richard O'Shee (*DEP*, 13 May 1806).

149   *From M[argaret, Countess of Mount Cashell]*[1]
              to Bagot Street

Munich, 27 July [1806]

[No salutation]

A proof of the recollection of a sincerely esteemed friend is always acceptable but particularly so in the days of adversity; you may judge therefore how much pleasure it gave me to see your handwriting once more. I had heard of your misfortune[2] with true regret, but letters of condolence I consider as impertinent and therefore I refrained from writing — Your apologies for entering on the subjects mentioned in that before me were perfectly unnecessary, as I could never have mistaken the excellence of your motives; but in truth the good sense and really useful advice contained in your letter are almost sufficient to have rendered it acceptable had it come from a mere acquaintance, and add to the high opinion I have long entertained of your head and heart. I am particularly struck with the sound judgement exhibited in your letter as I have received several equally well intended on the same subject. Part of your advice I have already anticipated in two letters to Lady M[oira] which I hope she may receive. To Mrs M[oore] I had mentioned my state of health some time ago but not in such a detailed manner as to Lady M. by whose letter I find that matter as well as many others has been much misrepresented. As I think it most probable our good old friend will tell you what I have said on the subject of my health I shall not write you a history of that but only mention that the complaints which have determined me to pass another winter abroad are on my lungs and that I really believe that were I to spend the next cold season in any northern climate I should not be alive the summer after — Last summer Lord M[ount Cashell] took the 3 boys to England[3] (to my great satisfaction for I fear'd they would be ruined by neglect) for the purpose of placing them somewhere for their education, in which I have reason to believe he has been very successful. He remained in London afterwards till spring when he expected me & the rest of the family, intending I believe to settle himself at Moore Park again. I did not inform him of my intention to return to a southern climate till a short time before I sent the children[4] to England; for in fact I did not determine on it till after a fit of illness which I had a few weeks before they set out — I had several reasons for sending them over — I thought the education of the girls required it; I wished them to acquire the habits, manners & even prejudices of the country where they are to live and I also thought Lord M. might complain with some reason if I took them to a country where he could not go[5] — as to my poor dear Richard who is a fine manly fellow I was sure Lord M. would not refuse my request to place him at the same school for little boys where Edward has been so well taken care of & as he had the ague several times at Rome I thought it better not to bring him to any climate where that complaint is common, as is the case in most of these warm countries; but everything has been done contrary to my wish, the girls are by this time at Moore Park where they can have no masters & my fine boy is to remain among maid servants — but the truth is Lord M. never considered education as a matter of any importance and my children have never had the most trifling advantage of this sort for which my heart has not previously bled. About a week after the children left Dresden I set out for

Carlsbad where I stayed a few days & then proceeded to Eger & Ratisbon. At this last town I waited for letters and there to my great astonishment I received one from Lord M. ordering me to return to England immediately to sign articles of separation & to give up my youngest child[6] to him, threatening in case of non-compliance to stop my remittances & to find means of taking the child by force. This was accompanied by one from my eldest brother[7] remonstrating on the folly of my pretending to be ill (which Lord M. told him I did) for the purpose of having an excuse to remain on the continent and advising me as a friend to go home instantly as Lord M. was very determined in his plans. I have since had letters from my mother[8] & other persons, not seeming to suppose my illness feigned, but making so light of it as to think I was to fly to England without a moments delay. You & Lady M. are the only persons who appear to suppose that I can know my own affairs and as to my life, these other good folks seem to think it a matter of no consequence — The truth is Lord M. (who you are not new to learn is a very weak man) has fallen into the hands of false friends who have taught him to believe that his character will rise on the ruins of mine. Whether he really intends to shut my own doors against me & separate me from my children I know not, but nothing shall prevent me from endeavouring to be of use to them for whose sake I have endured more than any one has notion of, in the way of petty tyranny and trifling opposition — In one thing alone have I succeeded for their advantage and that is in giving them good constitutions, which I am well convinced they owe to my good care during the first four or five years of their lives — and I will now tell you in perfect confidence that I am resolved not to be prevented from doing the same by my dear little Elizabeth and that nothing shall force me to relinquish the performance of this duty but death; I therefore ask you as a lawyer as well as a friend whether Lord M. can take her from me by force (that is whether the law would authorise such a step) at her age, and whether I have only dreamt that a mother can keep her child with her in spite of the father till seven years old?[9] I am convinced you will not betray me and therefore I will confess to you that if I can recover my health again in sufficient strength to go through a disagreeable business of the sort, my intention is to go to Ireland in the spring & arrange my affairs myself (without applying to any third person) concealing the child untill I have settled every thing and ascertained how I am to be situated — I have suffered so much on the subject of money matters that I will never again settle myself in Lord M.'s house without knowing accurately what I am to depend on in this way as neither my health nor spirits are now strong enough to endure the eternal teasing I used to go through; and if I am to be separated from my family I shall arrange the matter myself — I have very few real friends and false ones are more dangerous than enemies — I hope soon to be in French territories (either Italy or France I am not sure which) and suppose it will not be in the power of anyone to molest me there — In perfect solitude and tranquillity I hope to recover my health — I shall seek no society — I am quite sick of knaves & fools and feel every hour more strongly the consolations of literature, the only resource that never fails — In this respect I have acquired new sources of amusement though I cannot say my last acquisition (the German) affords me much satisfaction — I am quite tired of cant & mock sentiments with which their writings are replete — but to return to the subject of your letter, I have never mentioned to Mrs Moore the reports or disagreements that subsist as she has not touched on them in her letters but I have sent my letters to Lady M. through her as I suspect I have several false friends in that house and that my letters might be suppressed — there is also a sort of good natured foolish friend which I dread much and of which I fear I have some who may attempt loudly to vindicate me — a friend of this sort is worse than a clever enemy.

I forgot to mention that I answered the threatening letters immediately but have not heard whether my answers were received or what effect they produced — I shall soon write to you again as I feel the most thorough confidence in your integrity not to betray me & in your friendship & good sense for giving the best advice. I am glad to hear that Ireland is a better place to live in than formerly & am satisfied to know of gradual improvements which are the most likely to be permanent. I was shocked at hearing of that unfortunate Lady C.[10] (though I know but little of her) and am surprised that the people about her did not continue to direct her conduct as she is so very young and uncommonly silly & childish — Mrs Plunkett was the only one of that family that I liked, but I saw very little of her at Rome as there was such a set of people in the house[11] — I think her sensible & amiable & am sure she must feel this misfortune very much —Pray write to me & direct as usual — I hope you saw my children — my heart aches when I think of them — I am happy however that the three eldest boys are saved out of the five and hope my precious Richard will be safe till I can go home — The girls I fear will suffer in their education but they have a very good hearted woman with them — Believe me ever with the most true & unalterable esteem yours very sincerely

M

[P.S.] I had forgot to say that if a separation takes place between me & Lord M. it will be by his desire as I should endure much for the sake of our children and indeed have done so for some years.

[PP.S.] I have been long in your debt for a lottery ticket — pray tell me how much — I fear it is my fate to draw blanks in every way.

[*Source*: Callanan Papers]

[1]For an example of a letter signed "M" see McAleer, *The Sensitive Plant*, p. 180.

[2]Scully's wife died at her aunt's house in London on 17 April 1806. She had just expired when he arrived to join her. (Huddleston Papers C1/MH61).

[3]It is not known whether the three boys, Stephen, Robert and Edward, travelled with their parents from Rome or were picked up by them at Geneva (see No. 50 n.4).

[4]Helena Eleanor, Jane Eliza and Richard, aged respectively 11, 9 and 4.

[5]Because of the state of war he would, as a man, have been imprisoned on setting foot on French ruled territory.

[6]Elizabeth, born in Rome in 1804.

[7]George, 3rd Earl of Kingston.

[8]Caroline Fitzgerald, wife of the 2nd Earl of Kingston.

[9]There is no evidence that Scully replied.

[10]Eliza Georgiana Morgan, wife of Valentine Brown Lawless, 2nd Baron Cloncurry, who married her in Rome on 16 April 1803 when she was not yet eighteen. Soon after their return to the family seat of Lyons, Hazelhatch, Co. Kildare she had been seduced by Sir John Bennet Piers and when they had been found in a locked room together on 6 April 1806 Lord Cloncurry had started proceedings against Piers. The case was heard before Chief Justice Downes on 19 February 1807, when the Earl of Mount Cashell and the Hon. William Moore testified to the harmony that existed between Lord Cloncurry and his wife while they were in Rome (*DEP*, 21 February 1807; Lord Cloncurry, *Personal Recollections*).

[11]Charlotte Louisa Lawless, sister of Lord Cloncurry, married (at about the same time as her brother) Edward Wadding Plunkett, a Lieutenant Colonel in the Coldstream Guards, from 1821 4th Baron Dunsany. The two couples set up house together in the Palazzo Accaioili and were joined by Lord Cloncurry's two unmarried sisters. The Mount Cashells lived near them and however withdrawn Lady Mount Cashell herself may have been her husband told the court at the trial that he saw the Cloncurrys continually.

150   *From Thomas FitzGerald to Baggot Street, Dublin*

[Postmarked Cappaquin, 6 February 1807]

My Dear Friend,

From the intimations made from Dublin relative to our Petition[1] and from the advertisement of Lord Fingall,[2] I judge you will be looked to as the most conspicuous Roman Catholick in the County Tipperary to collect the sentiments of the R[oma]n C[atholic]ks of that County. We are ready in Waterford to act in unison with those of our brethren throughout this Green Island but we rather aspire to this than to taking a lead for a general sentiment is alone likely to effect our compleat emancipation. Let me request your sentiments & opinion on the propriety of our application once more to Parliament.

P.S. I shall be in Kilkenny in the course of a few days. Pray direct there.

[*Source*: Scully Papers]

[1]On the initiative of John Keogh a series of meetings of the Dublin Catholics had begun on 7 January. When the nobility and gentry held aloof they had gone ahead on their own. A deputation had waited on the Chief Secretary, who undertook to transmit to London their enquiry as to the intentions of the government towards the Catholics. Then, on 24 January, a committee had been appointed to draw up a petition, and the secretary instructed to convene the absent noblemen and gentlemen for a meeting on 7 February (see Plowden, *History* II, p. 243, whose account is confirmed by the Lord Lieutenant's despatch of 11 February to Earl Spencer: HO 100/141 f.170).

[2]The advertisement called for a meeting on 9 February "to take an important subject into consideration" (*DEP*, 3 February 1807). The Lord Lieutenant informed Earl Spencer that Lord Fingall had decided on this step immediately after seeing the Chief Secretary to enquire what action the government intended to take, and that he did so because he and those who acted with him preferred not to be separated from the rest of the Catholic body (*Dropmore Papers* IX).

151   *From Charles Butler to Dublin*

Lincolns Inn, 18 February 1807

Dear Sir,

I am happy to see the Resolutions of the Roman Catholics,[1] as I am acquainted with your talents & your zeal in the cause; I need not say my services in this, or in any other respect, are always at your command.

I observe you call yourselves Irish Catholics.[2] In the Declaration contained in the act passed for our relief in the year 1791, we are made to declare that we profess the Roman Catholic Religion. Since that time we have always called ourselves, in our public papers, English Roman Catholics.

I am afraid the grand obstacle, from the particular feelings of a great Person,[3] upon the subject, is far from being lessened. A multitude of anecdotes, some of which I know to be true, shew this is more violent than ever; and most people seem to think that it is as much as their places are worth, for ministers to attempt to force the measure.

I shall send over to you in a few days a book,[4] of which I request your acceptance.

Perhaps you would do well either to have an accredited agent in this Country, or to let it be known, that you have none; as I hear of many persons taking an active part in your business, who, I believe, have no directions from you to do it, & who therefore with the best intentions, may do you a good deal of mischief. If any thing particular happens, I shall be very much obliged to you to let me know it.

P.S. Do you think it certain a Petition will be presented.

[*Source*: Scully Papers]

[1]With his friends, Lord Fingall attended the meeting of 7 February called by the Dublin Catholics (see No. 150 n.1) and was voted into the chair. The meeting then resolved to join itself with the meeting called by Lord Fingall for 9 February (HO 100/141 f.166). This combined meeting resolved "That this is a fit and proper time to present a petition to the Imperial Parliament for the complete Emancipation of the Catholics of Ireland." The Committee of 21 chosen by the Dublin Catholics (see No. 150 n.1) was reappointed to form with the peers and 21 country gentlemen chosen by the peers a committee to prepare a petition and report. A report of the meeting was published in the *DEP* of 12 February. In a despatch of 11 February (HO 100/141, f.174) the Lord Lieutenant noted that the immediate publication of their proceedings was a mark of renewed confidence among the Catholics.

[2]They did not call themselves "Irish Catholics" but "Catholics of Ireland", the description having been chosen according to the Lord Lieutenant (ibid. f.166) to distinguish the consolidated meeting from that of the Catholics of Dublin. Butler's point, however, was the absence of the word "Roman". The petitioners of 1805, following the English precedent, had called themselves "Roman Catholics of Ireland". In the preface to his *Penal Laws* Scully observes that it was not until 1793 (33 Geo. 3 Chap. 21) that Catholics in Ireland attained the title of "Papists, or persons professing the Popish or Roman Catholic religion" — up to 1792 they had been described merely as "Papists", "Popish People" etc.

[3]The King.

[4]Probably the second edition of his *Horae Biblicae* originally published in 1799.

152   *From Thomas FitzGerald to Baggot Street, Dublin*

[Postmarked Kilkenny, 20 February 1807]

My Dear Scully,

Many, many thanks for your very kind communications. Did I for a moment think my going to Dublin of the minutest service to that cause you have ever ably supported I would go but being as it now is in the hands of able & I think honest men I shall with pleasure take instructions from you and those forming that happy and *unanimous* (let it be) coalition at Lord Fingall's *presidency*.[1] My very humble opinion, backed by many men much my superiors in reflection is that all County meetings are now unnecessary, that in Kilkenny and in Waterford we are now or when *instructed* ready to sign the Petition, that we leave it to you to commission in each county & to nominate men of respectability to obtain the signatures alone of men of estated and commercial consequence or supposing as in '95 delegates empowered to sign for each County.[2] These and other measures I do conclude have not escaped your attention.

I think Mr Keogh has been very *animated*.[3] This I do also think, the County Dublin Grand Jury will allow I know not how they can brook so full a statement of what I am told as facts[4] I feel myself greatly indebted for your recollections of my Father[5] etc. I hear from all quarters he is stout as the old oak. I have not been at Snowhaven these 3 or 4 months. How is your inventor? Does he rally still round him at Kilfeacle the opposers of slavery & Bagwell.[6] I shall hasten to assure you I await with impatience your next letter. [*Source*: Scully Papers]

[1]See No. 151 n.1.

[2]Seemingly a reference to the Catholic Convention of 1793, in which case the date given is a slip.

[3]He was probably thinking of the meeting of 9 February at which John Keogh asked: "If Ministers now called on your Lordship and on the gentlemen present . . . could you give your government the assurance, that you could bring the population of Ireland to oppose the enemy? Could you bring your own tenantry into the field to fight for a constitution that rejected them? Could you bring your own servants? . . . But if we are now relieved we shall have time to convince our population" (*DEP*, 12 February 1807).

[4]Keogh may have said more than was reported in the press. His speech was widely regarded as inflammatory and Fitzgerald seems to mean that he had made himself liable to indictment by a Grand Jury.

[5]Thomas Fitzgerald, of Snowhaven, Co. Kilkenny (post town Waterford).

[6]The slavery was probably that of the Catholics — in parliament John Bagwell was an opponent of negro slavery (*Hansard* VI, 1021).

153　　　　*From Lord Ponsonby[1] to Clonmell, Co. Tipperary*

Dublin, 2 April 1807

My Dear Sir,

I have been detained here from day to day by a variety of circumstances[2] until it has become necessary to attend the House of Lords. I must be there on the 8th, & I sail tomorrow.[3] You must see from the late events[4] that I made but too just an estimate of the King's power. Many people imagine he will be now defeated; I should also be of that opinion, if I judged alone from the appearance of things, or from what *ought to* be the conduct of men; but I have seen too much of the power of selfish feelings to entertain much hope that [a] giver of good things should be in want of a sufficient number of supporters. However the late ministers certainly have a very great majority in the H. of Commons, much greater, I am informed, than that they produced (93) on Mr Banks's motion[5] and I believe they are not apprehensive of any defection, on the contrary they say that they have *not one unwilling supporter*. Plunkett (the Atty General)[6] has resigned, Bushe (Solr. Genl.)[7] is to do the same, Lord Donoughmore,[8] & Maurice FitzGerald also.[9] I consider this as a good omen. I received, lately, a letter from Lord Howick who presses very earnestly the necessity for absolute quiet for the moment.[10] I have taken all possible pains with the Catholick Gentlemen to induce them to withdraw the Petition, & for the present to rest upon their arms. I am convinced it is the best policy, as affording the best chance of keeping the people of England in a favorable disposition toward those men who are by inclination, principle & interest devoted to the cause of equal rights. I can not see in what way, (under existing circumstances) any other mode of conduct could produce beneficial effects & I see much mischief which might arise from the calumnies which would immediately be built upon any exhibition of warmth on the part of the Catholicks. I am fully convinced that the difficulty in which the King is now placed is the consequence of Catholick moderation. He had, (whatever else may be pretended) *given his consent* to the measures proposed (Army & Navy) imagining the *Petition* would afford him an opportunity of destroying his Ministers but finding (you know how good his intelligence is) the Petition would not be pressed,[11] he was obliged to beat back & seize as well as he could the opportunity which had so nearly escaped him, of assigning conscience etc. as the cause of his conduct towards an administration he hated, but which certainly possessed a great deal of the respect of the Country & which was therefore, too strong for him unless he could call the bigotry of the people to his aid. Our friends by dextrous conduct, yielding apparently to his alledged scruples of conscience have deprived him, in a very great degree, of his expected force, & by making their stand upon a strong constitutional principle have enlisted on their side, all those who have any real regard for the english constitution, or love of the principles of liberty. Taking a fair view of the whole question I think one must say that the contest now is whether the King shall be an Absolute or limited Monarch & I confess I feel a great deal of alarm about the issue of the contest. Should the Court be victorious we must maturely consider what should be the conduct of us Irishmen, & I shall be much obliged to you to let me hear from you on that subject. Should our friends triumph, it is to be considered how much the Catholicks will desire should be done for them, or more correctly how much it may be possible for them to force the King to grant always bearing in mind that this particular question affords him the *means* of obtaining assistance which no other measure can afford, & therefore that his Ministers must always be comparatively weak upon it. I believe we shall have no occasion to consider this last mentioned state of things.

Pray present my compts to Mr Scully, your Father, & tell him I regret being deprived for the present of the opportunity of becoming known to him & that I hope the summer will renew that opportunity which I have now lost.

My direction is No. 31 Curzon Street, London.

[P.S.] I write in a great hurry & you can easily supply any want of correction which may be in my letter.   [*Source*: Scully Papers]

[1]Lord Ponsonby, who had succeeded his father as 2nd Baron on 5 November 1806, needed to make visits to Ireland to deal with his Irish estate and it was suggested to him by his brother-in-law, Lord Howick (later Earl Grey), that he should use his personal influence to hold the Irish Catholics back from petitioning. In an unpublished letter among the Dropmore papers (Add. MSS.59, 256) Lord Grenville confirmed the understanding. In the Earl Grey Papers there is an exchange of correspondence between Ponsonby and Howick discussing in considerable detail the steps that might be taken to win over the extremists, particularly John Keogh. Ponsonby does not however reveal who his contacts were and Scully's name does not appear.

[2]See the end of the letter. The delay had evidently prevented him from accepting an invitation to stay at Kilfeacle.

[3]*The House of Lords Journal* shows that he was not present on 8 April but attended on 12 April for the first reading of Henry Bankes' Offices in Reversion bill.

[4]The events leading to the downfall of the Grenville administration, beginning on 2 March when the King was shown a despatch to the Lord Lieutenant about new clauses in the Mutiny Bill which would have opened to Catholics all commissions in the armed forces, and ending on 18 March when the Cabinet, after offering to withdraw the measure, refused to give the King an undertaking that they would never introduce a measure of Catholic relief (*Dropmore Papers* IX).

[5]It was not on Bankes' but on a similar motion by Henry Martin that the government were defeated by 93 votes on 25 March (*Hansard* IX, 219).

[6]William Conyngham Plunket did not owe his appointment to the outgoing administration but nevertheless resigned (*DEP*, 2 April 1807).

[7]Charles Kendal Bushe, who also owed his office to the previous administration, remained in office until 1822.

[8]He was invited by Sir Arthur Wellesley, the new Chief Secretary, to support the King's government in its critical situation but, as he informed the Bishop of Cork on 20 April, felt called upon as a steady supporter of the Catholics to resign his situation as Joint Postmaster General for Ireland (Donoughmore Papers, D/41 ff.16, 18).

[9]The Knight of Kerry—he resigned his situation as one of the Lords of the Treasury for Ireland (*DEP*, 11 April 1807).

[10]The exchange of correspondence in the Earl Grey Papers between Ponsonby and Howick ends on 26 March 1807.

[11]On 28 February Lord Ponsonby had sent Howick a list of the Catholic Committee on which he had marked only eight members likely to be hostile to dropping the petition: it was reasonable to suppose that the King would have access to the same sort of information.

154   *To Charles Butler*

Bagot Street, Dublin, 20 April 1807

[Copy][1]

Dear Sir,

As you expressed in your letter[2] to me a strong desire to be informed when any thing particular should occur in our Catholic affairs here, I believe you would wish to know the result of the final meeting of Saturday last.[3] The object of it was to consider the propriety of suspending the progress of the Petition for the present.

You probably know that the late proceedings originated with Mr Keough[4] & a few others of his connection, and were conducted in direct opposition to the advice and warnings of our best Parliamentary friends. Mr Grattan[5] & Mr Ponsonby,[6] our Chancellor, deprecated them earnestly, and in fact, Mr Keough's motion for petitioning had been carried at an aggregate meeting of Dublin Catholics,[7] yet it w'd be more correct to say it was not opposed, than that it was assented to or approved — for Catholic meetings, from a dread of disunion, will often tacitly sanction what a majority may tacitly disapprove. Such was really the case in February last. But the country gentlemen and landed interest, who are as intelligent as they are opulent, not feeling much respect for the origin of this movement, and perceiving that a perseverance in it at that moment should be unavailing, must certainly be embarrassing, & perhaps ruinous to their friends in power, have since strongly discountenanced those proceedings — they refused to sign the Petition, and in some parts of the South were inclined at the late Assizes to frame and publish Resolutions condemning all Mr Keough's speeches and their tendancy [sic] and what they deem the presumption of the local meetings of Dublin.

These symptoms encreasing staggered the most zealous here — for the country gentlemen being strongly attached to the Ponsonby family resented the indecorous imputations, which the Dublin speeches, very unjustly as I believe, cast upon the Chancellor's sincerity towards the Catholics[8] — and they were disposed to express this resentment in an unqualified manner. Mr Keough therefore thought it best to turn round & endeavour to get out of the scrape as well and as soon as he could. The country gentlemen pressed that the entire proceedings should be rescinded. The Dublin people, who had been hurried onwards, became irresolute, as traders generally are. A few were inclined to preserve –/–[9] their consistency & to persevere. More were eager to be extricated from the business. At length it was fixed that a resolution should be proposed declaring "that the Petition do remain in the hands of Ld Fingall, subject to the future disposal of the Catholic body". This was accordingly proposed last Saturday to the meeting, consisting of about 400 persons, one hundred of whom were persons of considerable landed or monied property or of one of the learned professions, and it was settled that Mr Keough having urged on the former business, should now undertake the task of proposing this pause. This he did in a long speech which it was remarked was an answer to his own speeches of February last on the other side of the question. He was placed in a very humiliating situation indeed but you will see the proceedings in the papers. A great majority being already predisposed to suspend all proceedings, and indeed to condemn the past, the motion was easily carried — and some other less important motions were proposed by others & agreed to.

It seems agreed, that no further aggregate meetings shall be held at least this year — and indeed we feel that the late ones have been prejudicial in a high degree, perhaps not so much by their resolutions, as by the publicity attending them, and by the circulation of hasty declamations delivered at them, for which the whole Catholic body are made responsible, altho' they are certainly in many respects not adapted [sic] or approved of by us.

Mr Keough would have been very roughly handled on Saturday last by all parties; but a feeling of compassion for his embarrassment and of regard for the general interest & character of the body (which would still be further injured by the appearance of disunion or acrimony) restrained the expression of the sentiments generally entertained upon his conduct. He will find it very difficult hereafter to bring even the Dublin Catholics into a like predicament in opposition to the advice of their Parliamentary friends.

Whilst I regret what has past, I feel some little satisfaction however in a feeling that I did not assist in those proceedings — but dissuaded in private as far as my other avocations permitted me the leisure, from embarking in such a pursuit at so impolitic a season.[10]

Now that our Friends are out of office, and we can no longer do them the like mischief, it may be a very different consideration. I mean how far it may be proper to petition early in next session and I should very much wish to be favoured with your opinion upon this subject. In the meantime much may be done out of doors, & I hope to induce those of our body here, who are most capable of cooperating, to form some general plans for meeting the existing obstacles, & procuring a gradual and total removal of them.

[*Source*: Throckmorton Papers]

[1]Transmitting this and a copy of a letter from Theobald McKenna on 25 April Butler told Sir J. Throckmorton to give preference to McKenna where the two differed.
[2]No. 151.
[3]Held in the Exhibition Room, William Street, on 18 April, Lord Fingall in the chair, "to take into consideration the line of conduct which it would be expedient to pursue in consequence of the change which had taken place in his Majesty's Councils". Letters from Grattan were read expressing the opinion of himself and the late Ministers on the inexpediency of urging the petition. John Keogh carried a motion that the petition should be consigned to the Earl of Fingall subject to the future disposal of the Catholic body and the Committee then dissolved itself (*DEP*, 25 April 1807).
[4]Scully's own spelling of John Keogh's name. See No. 150 n.1 for the origin of the proceedings.
[5]Lord Ponsonby's correspondence with Lord Howick in the Earl Grey Papers shows that Grattan, who was believed to have influence on Keogh's mind, had been under great pressure just before the fall of the Grenville ministry to be more explicit about refusing to present a petiton.

[6]George Ponsonby, as Chancellor, had been present at two of the meetings between the Chief Secretary, Elliot, and the five deputies of the Dublin Catholics (see No. 150 n.1) and Elliot's letter of 18 January to Lord Grenville (*Dropmore Papers* IX) refers to his having seen Keogh. In a letter of 26 February to Lord Howick, Lord Ponsonby suggested that the violence of Keogh's speeches resulted from his realisation that his interview with the Chancellor had excited suspicions in the popular mind as to his fidelity to the cause.

[7]On 24 January 1807 (see No. 150 n.1).

[8]The complaints against George Ponsonby are recorded in a pamphlet advertised by Hugh Fitzpatrick in the *Dublin Evening Post* of 2 May 1807: *A vindication of the conduct of the Irish Catholics*, by "a Protestant barrister" — identified in the British Library Catalogue as Thomas Wallace.

[9]A gap filling sign which in the original would have appeared at the end of the line but was slavishly copied by Butler's clerk.

[10]Scully was not a member either of the 21 Dublin Catholics chosen on 24 January or the group of 21 country gentlemen selected to join them on 9 February. His private dissuasion may have been carried out in collaboration with Lord Ponsonby (see No. 153 n.1).

155   *From Charles Butler to Bagot Street, Dublin*

Lincolns Inn, 21 May 1807

Dear Sir,

I was very much obliged by your last letter. I think all we can do at present is to see the temper of the new parliament, & to act accordingly. I conjecture the new ministers will gain much by the English members in the election.[1] The cry of "no popery" has certainly been serviceable to them.

As soon as it was perceived that it was actively circulated, & made a great impression, the Roman Catholics in London, thought it was necessary to do something to counteract it. After some conferences it was thought that the best thing which could be done was to print the oath taken by us, and the two oaths taken by you, with the opinions of the foreign universities on the questions submitted to them by Mr Pitt's direction, with some paragraphs generally expressing our indignation at the clamour excited against us & our reason for expecting a contrary treatment.

With this view, an Address has been prepared. As it has been inserted in several of the news papers, I do not send it to you.[2]

After much consultation it seemed generally to be desired that there should not be a meeting of the Roman Catholics, & that a copy of the proposed Address should be sent to Roman Catholics of consideration in London & its neighborhood. The only reason for not circulating it generally among the Catholics through out England, was, that *time* did not permit it. It was accordingly circulated, & then signed by some of the leading Roman

Catholics in London. Five thousand of them have been printed, & generally distributed. Three or four Roman Catholics seem averse to the measure but by all the others, it appears to me to be warmly approved. As far as I can perceive, it has given offence to no one, & it has produced a good effect upon many.

There is some notion of our presenting an Address to Lord Grenville, thanking him for his conduct in our regard, but the measure is not yet determined upon. If I should hear any thing which I should think worth communicating I will certainly inform you of it.   [*Source*: Scully Papers]

[1] Parliament had been dissolved on 29 April and elections were to take place at the end of May and early June. When parliament reassembled on 25 July the Duke of Portland's "No Popery" administration carried the debate on the address by 350 to 155 votes. In Co. Tipperary Scully was one of two counsel employed by Montagu Mathew, who on his re-election was presented with a gold cup worth a thousand guineas by the Tipperary Catholics (*DEP*, 2, 4 and 16 June).
[2] It appeared in *The Times* of 20 May and the *Dublin Evening Post* of 25 May 1807, signed by the Vicar Apostolic for the London district and fifty-nine prominent Catholics, including Butler himself. It reproduced the oaths and declarations of 1791 (for the English Catholics) and of 1773 and 1793 (for the Irish); and the replies of foreign universities regarding the Pope's dispensing power as obtained by the English Catholic Committee in 1788 at the instance of Pitt.

156   *From Thomas C. Parsons*[1]

2 July 1807

Dear Sir,

I return you the Book[2] you were so kind as to lend me & wish a judicious hand wd. draw from it that kind of Justice I was speaking to you of; to which should be added a short acct. of the political coalescence of the two sects. They once sat together in Parlt.[3] without discord or danger & that too when they were less liberal & enlightened than at present. Why not again! A temperate & fair statement of these circumstances cd. at no time do any injury & may at any time do some good.

[P.S.] I thought this wd have covered the Book.   [*Source*: Scully Papers]

[1] Thomas Cleare Parsons (b. 1768), 4th son of Sir William Parsons, King's County; Trinity College Dublin; Lincoln's Inn; called to the Irish bar 1792.
[2] Perhaps an early draft of Scully's own *Penal Laws*.
[3] In Chapter II of his *Penal Laws* Scully observes that Catholics were members of parliament in Ireland until 1692.

157   *From Lord Ponsonby to 11 Upper Titchfield Street,*[1]
Marylebone, London

31 Curzon Street [London] Sunday Night, 11 August 1807

My Dear Sir,

I am just arrived in Town to stay a few days & am doubtful if it will be in my power to pay my respects to you tomorrow being a good deal engaged and I shall be obliged to you to let me know when I shall be likely to find you, if what I apprehend should be the case.[2]   [*Source*: Scully Papers]

[1]Where his first wife's aunt, Mrs Bostock, now lived. James Traill reported to the Home Office from Dublin Castle on 3 September 1807: "I understand that some Catholic gentlemen who have frequently written on the Catholick question are now gone to London to write on the subject. Scully and McKenna are the only names I have heard, but it is said that there are others. Whether they mean to write in the public papers or to publish pamphlets I know not" (HO 100/142, f.142).
[2]No explanation of Lord Ponsonby's apprehension has been found.

158   *From Lady Moira to 11 Upper Titchfield Street, London*

Moira House, 17 September 1807

[No salutation]

A few hasty lines written with a hand which is on the brink of the grave, & extends now its anxiety for to exist past the 25th of the month to entitle me to a quarters payment of my annuities — My sincerely beloved friend got safe over in a passage of nine hours[1] — It is impossible to express what I feel concerning her, & I have no friend to whom in speaking of her I can relieve my mind, & I cannot bear to mention her to her enemies, or maligners — The Cloncurry family[2] are the spreaders of much malice respecting her — But I am grieved to learn (by an indirect method of information) that Mr Tighe,[3] once Ld M[ount] C[ashell]'s friend & favorite till he assumed & professed a jealousy of him, is a man of insignificance in every mental quality, & of a vanity to make a parade of being the cause of such a disagreement — which her most worthless family has taken pains & pleasure to foment & publish with most exaggerated falsehood — I fear that the character I have had of Mr T. is too just — Often her frank & generous disposition misleads her & she suspects no one, as I have perceived in her being a dupe to servants who have practised towards her the most glaring duplicity — I wish to know if that man is in England, in case that he was I think it a requisite duty to me to write to her on that subject. I find that he is the son of that Mr Tighe mentioned in Dermody's *Life*[4] — I do not know the branches of the family descendants of the gentleman whom Swift in his *Legion Club* styles Dick Fitz-Baker thro' being the occupation of his father[5] — It is also unfortunate that the bulk of the middle class of the people held the family in that style of execration, from the horrid & atrocious murder that his father & brother were guilty of, who tho' injured acted like the basest of assassins in their revenge on a sleeping wretch, so that any falsehood is credited, with the remark of what could be expected from any of them? & the judgement that awaits them is not yet but will come[6] — It is obvious to me that Ld M.C.['s] intention is a divorce — I am convinced of her uprightness & real purity of mind — but her minor errors as to judgement I cannot close my eyes upon. My sort of family connection[7] allowed me not to interfere unasked, & never was I asked or consulted as to any measure until the return to Dublin — With much difficulty I have written this & desiring you to accept my sincere thanks for yielding to my solicitations[8] respecting my friend I remain etc.

[P.S.] I cd. not get an amanuensis or wd. not have sent you this scrawl.

[*Source*: Scully Papers]

[1]On her departure from Ireland. A letter of 9 August from Lady Moira to Lord Moira refers to Lady Mount Cashell's arrival in Dublin, where she resided in a hotel, not being able to dine with the family because of her strict regime: "Her attachment to me is from the liking of me, notwithstanding the difference of age, and her tribute of the mind is most flattering" (Loudoun Papers, A 208).

[2]Lord Cloncurry and his sisters had been both in Paris and Rome at the same time as the Mount Cashells (Cloncurry, *Personal Recollections* p. 185).

[3]George William Tighe.

[4]Edward Tighe, whose brief encounter with Dermody c. 1792 is described in James Grant Raymond's *Life of Thomas Dermody 1775–1802*, the dedication of which, to Lord Moira, is dated January 1806.

[5]Richard or "Little Dick" Tighe (1678–1736 — see *DNB*), from whom George William Tighe was descended, incurred the malevolence of Swift, who gave him a place among his other bugbears in his *Legion Club*, a satiric poem published c. 1736. He called him Fitzbaker because his father had supplied wheat to Cromwell's army.

[6]See the postscript to No. 365, where William Tighe refers to a malicious libel against him and his relations published by the *Dublin Evening Post* — this may have been Lady Moira's source. She implies that the culprits were still living, but Edward Tighe was dead and George William had no brother.

[7]Lady Mount Cashell's husband was a grandson of the 1st Earl of Moira (Lady Moira's deceased husband) by his first wife; her brother, Lord Kingston, was married to a grand-daughter of the 1st Earl.

[8]Probably in the marital affairs of the Mount Cashells: in 1812 he was involved in negotiating a deed of separation (see No. 382).

159   *From Lord Ponsonby to 11 Upper Tichfield Street, London*

Alnwick[1] [Northumberland] 25 September 1807

My Dear Sir,

I have just received your letter on my return here. The Paper you enquire for Lady Fanny[2] brought with her by mistake to London where it now is locked up. I shall be in Town in the course of a fortnight or three weeks which will be soon enough I hope to deliver it to you with my own hands & which will also save you a long letter from me in answer to yours from Dublin the subject of which has been constantly in my mind ever since and to which I could not (till very lately) have given a satisfactory answer. I have now made up my mind that it is advisable to Petition this session but I have reason to think that our English friends are of a contrary opinion. I will not enter at present into a statement of my reasons for the opinion I hold; probably they are all familiar to you and those of our friends seem to me to be purely *english* reasons. I will explain myself fully when we meet. In the meantime, if you have leisure to write to me here I shall be very much pleased to hear from you some of your opinions as to the present state of our Country. I shall be in Dublin early in November.   [*Source*: Scully Papers]

[1]The Post town for Howick, seat of his brother-in-law, Charles Grey, Viscount Howick, who became the 2nd Earl Grey on 26 November 1807.
[2]His wife, Elizabeth Frances Bussy (1786–1866), 7th daughter of the 4th Earl of Jersey.

160   *From Lord Ponsonby to Bagot Street, Dublin*

Holt,[1] 14 November 1807

My Dear Sir,

I saw Curran in London & found him disposed to take any steps which may be requisite.[2] A good Irishman. — He said he shd see you. I did not tell him we had had any communication. What is Ld Fingal about? I hear he is taken great notice of by the *present* Govt. The D. of Devonshire has not given me an answer on the subject of the *Declaration etc*.[3] of which I spoke to you; of course the business is for the present at a stand. We have still two months.[4] In my opinion this Ministry must fall soon & I am therefore the more anxious for the Catholicks to speak out boldly & unanimously, that the *fears* of our friends may be overpowered by *greater* fear which may prevent them from pursuing *Half Measures*.

The difficulties which are gathering around us so fast & threatening our destruction[5] appear to me to afford us a chance of safety. You will understand me.

Could you procure for me a tolerably correct statement of the value of the Corn exported from Ireland & what proportion of it is sent to England. Also of the Pork & Butter? Be below the mark rather than above it.[6]

I am apprehensive we shall meet with difficulties from some of the Catholick Body.[7] What do you say?

I suspect the Prince is quite gone[8] — there are no terms to be kept with the Court. I hope your work is in forwardness.[9]

Pray write to me when you have leisure & let me know how things are going on. Direct to London.

There is some reason to believe our Ministers have made some attempts to negotiate with France either with a view to Peace or to deceive the people of this country into the belief that peace is not to be had. I believe they have failed & that there are terrible times coming for them as well as for the state.

[*Source*: Scully Papers]

[1]The cover is stamped Holt and it was probably therefore the Norfolk postal town of that name. He may have been visiting William Windham at Felbrigg.

[2]Curran had arrived from Cheltenham at the end of September (*Morning Chronicle*, 2 October 1807). The context suggests that he may have offered his help in organising Protestant declarations.

[3]The 5th Duke (1748–1811), who owned large estates in counties Cork and Waterford, may have been approached to support a Protestant declaration in favour of the Catholics similar to the Tipperary one published in the *Dublin Evening Post* of 9 January 1808.

[4]Before the opening of the next session of parliament on 21 January 1808.

[5]Since the Treaty of Tilsit in July England had been left alone in the field against Napoleon, with Portugal as the only remaining point of access to the continent. On 13 November the *Times* had published news of the Portuguese closing their ports to British ships; and a long account of the abortive storming of Buenos Aires had followed on the 14th, together with reports of more vigorous action by the Dutch against British commerce.

[6]Why Lord Ponsonby required the information has not transpired.

[7]Probably as to whether there should be another petition and if there were whether it should be pressed or allowed simply to lie on the table in parliament.

[8]Complaining that the Talents ministry had never consulted him the Prince had announced in a letter to Lord Moira dated 30 March 1807 that he would cease to be a party man and retire from taking any active line (Aspinall, *Correspondence of George Prince of Wales* VI, 2373).

[9]Probably his work on the penal laws, the first part of which was published at the end of 1811 as the *Statement of the Penal Laws*.

161   *From Nicholas Mahon to Kilfeacle, Cashel, Co. Tipperary*

Dublin, 12 January 1808

My dear Sir,

Our Catholic public meeting is to take place on the 19th Inst. on w'ch day I hope the approach of term will give us the advantage of your presence.[1] All our leading folks even Mr Keogh himself, as I understand, are warm for the Petition but after the transactions of last Year I cannot help haveing doubts of the sincerity of some. I do not know any thing that in my opinion would forward the measure so much or fix the desicion of those that waver more than a County meeting. Yours after the resolutions just published by the Protestant Noblemen and Gentlemen[2] wou'd appear of all others to be the most fitt and proper for the purpose. If the shortness of time wou'd permit I believe you will think with me that nothing cou'd more awaken a proper spirit than such a measure. Even a partial meeting of the neighbourhood of Tipperary wou'd have the best consequence.[3] All this I submit to your better judgment and if convenient would be glad you wou'd favor me with your sentiments.[4] I request you will present my best wishes and regard to all our good friends at Kilfeacle and believe me Dear Sir, Your aff[illegible]

Nich Mahon   [*Source*: Scully Papers]

[1]At a meeting of some thirty Catholics held at Fitzpatrick's in Capel Street on 5 January there had been differences of opinion as to whether a petition should be presented at all and if presented whether it should be pressed. It was not attended by Scully "the barrister and author" and other prominent Catholics (HO 100/147, f.13). It had nevertheless been agreed to present a petition and a meeting had been called for 19 January to consider its form and mode of presentation (*DEP*, 7 January 1808). Scully does not appear to have attended this meeting either. After an acrimonious debate a motion for transmitting a petition without delay was carried, but agreement could not be reached as to whether a delegation should accompany Lord Fingall to London with it (*DEP*, 23 January 1808).
[2]Stating that they felt no repugnance whatever to giving Catholics an equal and full share in the constitution (*DEP*, 9 January 1808).
[3]On 10 March a Tipperary meeting, "on behalf of upward of 10,000 Catholics possessing freehold lands or considerable chattels", asked the county's members in parliament to present a petition (*DEP*, 15 March 1808). A letter of 31 March from Montagu Mathew to the Catholic Archbishop of Cashel asked that signatures should be sent to Mr Scully in Tipperary (Calendar of Bray Papers).

162   *Speech to the Kilkenny Academy[1] Society [26 January 1808]*

A considerable interval having elapsed since the formation of the Society Scully recalls that it was founded because some of its students, holding in grateful recollection the benefits they derived from the Academy, wished to meet once or twice a year to commemorate in festivity and good humour the days of their boyish acquaintance.[2] The Academy was the first seminary of learning which the 18th century permitted to the Catholics of Ireland. The American war and "the returning expansion of the Protestant mind" led in 1782 to the re-opening of Catholic seminaries[3] and public spirited Catholics cast their eyes round for learned men duly qualified to profit by the opportunity. These were found in the Revd Dr James Lanigan and Dr John Dunn.[4] It was well known how quickly complete success followed upon the undertaking and no other academy ever possessed a stronger claim on the gratitude of its members. "It is not to be wondered at, if from such a nursery of youth there issue forth at various periods, much of virtue, much of learning, much of active and cultivated talent. Perhaps it is not too much for me to say at this day, 25 years from the foundation of the Academy,[5] that is has spread its benefits with its pupils into every considerable state in Christendom, nay into every climate, every service, naval, military or civil, and into every honourable profession. . . ."

[*Source*: Scully Papers MS.27, 519]

[1]Since 1814 called St Kieran's College. The prize lists show that Scully was there in 1785 (when he came first in Greek, Latin and French) and in 1786 (when he was first in Greek and Latin) (see Revd P. Birch: *St Kieran's College, Kilkenny*, Dublin, 1951). On 21 May 1786 he was awarded a certificate by the Mercantile Academy, North Strand, Dublin, for "answering most remarkably well" in arithmetic (Scully Papers: MS.27, 482). He may have sat for an external examination.

[2]In a notebook (MS.27, 513) Scully recorded the first three dinners of the society, of which he was President. On 6 December 1804, at Atwell's, College Green, the eleven members present resolved that they "should be at liberty to introduce such gentlemen (educated at the Academy) as they think proper". On 14 May 1805 only eight members came and it was resolved that "every member be at liberty to introduce one Catholic gentleman, who shall previously have been introduced to a member of the committee". As a result six visitors attended on 26 November 1805 in addition to eleven members. Although he had space to spare Scully did not record any further meetings. All told, fifteen members attended the dinners: D. Scully, J. Bergin, Dr Breen, Edward Fitzgerald, Redmond Byrne, James Byrne, another Byrne, John Burke, John Comerford, Thomas Hearns, John Brennan, James Barron, Barn. Scott, Capt Thomas Byrne and John Moore.

[3]Dr John Dunne (c. 1745–1789) was Bishop of Ossory from 1787 until his death, when he was succeeded by Dr James Lanigan.

[4]The Act of 21 & 22 Geo. III Ch. 62 passed by the Irish parliament allowed Catholic schoolmasters to teach on taking the oath of allegiance and obtaining a licence from the local Bishop of the established church. For the abrogation of the second requirement by an act of 1792 see No. 479B.

[5]A notice in the *Dublin Evening Post* of 9 January 1808 convened the dinner for 26 January, at Morrison's in Dawson Street and it would have been the opening of the first term of the Academy on 13 January 1783 that was commemorated.

163   *Resolution of Catholic Gentlemen for the formation*
of a Society

[Copy][1]   Dublin, 13 February 1808

At a meeting of Catholic gentlemen at Fitzpatrick's in Capel Street, held pursuant to general notice & request,[2]

Resolved unanimously:

That it will be highly beneficial to the interests of the Catholics, that some of them should from time to time meet together, in order to watch over and improve any opportunities, that may offer, for procuring or promoting Legislative Relief from the laws affecting their body,

but without the most distant pretension, on the part of such Catholics, of assuming to themselves any degree of power or authority whatsoever, much less of expressing the sense of any other Catholics — :

We the undersigned do approve of a Society to be formed founded upon the above Resolution.[3]

[There follows a list of 49 signatories,[4] headed by Lord Fingall and including the titular Archbishop of Dublin, John T. Troy, to whose name is added the proviso: "with a saving against any attempt to regulate Church Discipline without the concurrence and approbation of the Catholic Prelates"]

[*Alternative draft*]

We, the undersigned Roman Catholics, do adopt the following Resolutions.

1. That it would be highly beneficial [as above]
2. That we will accordingly meet together for the purposes aforesaid on the first and third Tuesdays in every month throughout the year (September & October excepted) at noon, in such convenient place as may be agreed upon.
3. That the officers of the Society be one President, 2 Vice Presidents, a Treasurer & a Secretary to be annually elected by ballot on the first Tuesday in May.
4. That towards defraying the expenses of the Society a fixed annual fund be provided — and, for that purpose, each member shall annually subscribe a sum of 5 guineas for the current year, to be paid into the Treasurer's hands. and shall also pay on his entrance a sum of 3 guineas.
5. That as soon as 50 Catholics shall have subscribed to the said fund, the said 50 Caths. (or as many of them as can conveniently attend) shall hold a special meeting for the purpose of considering & framing such further special regulations as may appear necessary —

and that, after such a number has so subscribed, all other persons desiring to be admitted shall be subject to a Ballot, wherein one black bead in seven shall exclude the candidate — Notice in writing of such Ballot, & of the mover's, seconder's & candidate's names shall be posted up in the Society-Room 4 weeks before the day of ballot.[5]

[*Source*: Scully Papers 27, 522–3]

[1]There are two loose foolscap sheets, both in Scully's hand. The one with signatures was dated by him, the other bears no date.

[2]There is a reference to this meeting in a letter written by Mark Lynch to Charles Butler, who quoted the following extract from it in his letter of 8 February 1808 to Sir John Throckmorton (Throckmorton Papers, folder 11): "There is now forming an association to superintend our affairs. Lord Fingal is at the head of it, and it will communicate with the several principal Catholics in the interior of Ireland — the nature of it and the immediate object I will communicate to you very shortly as I mean to attend the next meeting."

[3]Except that it omits the words "much less with any intention of interference in spiritual concerns" the resolution follows almost word for word one defining the purpose of the Cisalpine Club in London, adopted on 8 April 1794. Scully, who had been elected a member of this club in 1805, had a reprint of this among his papers, on which the relevant passage is sidelined (MS.27, 503).

[4]Among the signatories there are six Scullys and another six connected with Scullys by marriage. The great majority are country gentlemen and there are no representatives of the popular party who followed John Keogh.

[5]In a postscript to a letter of 11 June 1808 Butler told Sir John Throckmorton (folder 9): "I have just met Mr Skully. He has shown me a resolution of about 30 Roman Catholics of Ireland to unite for the purpose of obtaining their Emancipation. It is signed by Lord Fingal & by Archbishop Troy for himself and the other Irish prelates, saving the rights of the clergy, that the laity should not interfere in matters of faith or discipline. He says that the spirit of the Catholics is very high — the people everywhere completely favourable to them. That a subscription of *10000 a year* might be easily raised. I [2 words illegible] him, if it were proper to put my name down to the resolution, I suppose you will have no objection to doing the same . . .".

164   *From Revd John Murphy*

Thursday, 25 February [?1808[1]]

Dear Sir,

Lady Moira, who, altho' now something better, has been extremely ill, requests you will have the goodness to call upon her about three o'clock tomorrow, as she very much wishes to speak to you on material business.[2] My hand is so very cold that I can with difficulty write intelligibly — you will however excuse me and believe me, Dear Sir, your very truly assured etc etc.

[*Source*: Scully Papers]

[1]25 February fell on a Thursday in 1802 and 1808. The latter year is the more likely

one as Lady Moira was in a weak condition during the last months of her life and a letter which she wrote on 10 February 1808 to congratulate Lord Moira on the birth of his son (Loudoun Papers A 208) is both short and shakily written. Murphy was still living at Moira House, for when the young Lord Glentworth eloped with Miss Edwards in May 1808 it was reported in the press that he had illegally married them there. An official denial was issued by the Court of Chancery (*DEP*, 21 May 1808).
[2]Possibly the protection of her daughters' rights alluded to in No. 166.

165   *From Lady Moira*

Moira House, 27 February 1808

[In the hand of an amanuensis[1]]

Lady Moira's compliments to Mr Scully — When she fixed with him for dining on Sunday with Lord & Lady Granard and her family, she was not aware of his Lordship's being engaged particularly on that day — she therefore begs the pleasure of his company on Tuesday to dinner, when she will account from his Lordship's previous engagement and other particulars for the delay — and she requests this favor for Tuesday or any other subsequent day he may name as his friend and kinswoman, the niece of the Marquis of Montague, brother to Richard Nevil, Earl of Warwick, surnamed the Kingmaker.[2]   [*Source*: Scully Papers]

[1]This and the following letter are signed "E Moira Hastings Hungerford", Hastings and Hungerford being two of the titles which she had inherited from her brother.
[2]For the relationship between the Hastings and Huddleston families which made Scully a kinsman through his deceased wife see No. 44 n.3.

166   *From Lady Moira*

Moira House, Dublin, 2 March 1808, St David's Day

My friend, you are sensible what true esteem & perfect regard I have felt for you from the first commencement of our acquaintance; & how anxious I was that you shd. be connected with me, in your matrimonial connections, with a family I revered from their antient & most respectable former union with my ancestors; & those that Miss Huddlestone formerly stood in. Her ancestors & mine as brothers acquired *from* actual usurpapation to their lawful sovereigns of whom they [one word illegible] deprived. We might have expected more than one reward from crowns & sovereigns at that day but the favor of princes & their gratitude [one word illegible] showed itself.[1]
— But I rely upon you, from friendship & as a religious personage, that you will support whatever rights & claims my daughters may have, which paper will show to you, & that it was intended to divest them thro' [three words

illegible]. I hope to get your word for this promise which I know from a sense of honor & religion will be sacred — & that you will support my daughters rights of inheritance as fixed by Lord Huntingdons deed of 1789.[2] I having protested against any cession [two lines unintelligible] by ignorance of the deed of Lord Huntingdon of 1789 of which [insertion illegible] I never heard [one word illegible] till 1108 [? 1808] — & never having had by message or letter [one word illegible] Mr Hill the conveyancer or Mr Adam[3] the [one or two words illegible] communication to permit them to arrosge those powers they had arrogated to themselves & disavowing all & every [?] trick of such like underhand transactions — & [one word illegible] those friends of Lord Loudoun[4] as I have already solemnly protested against them, & I do expect from you as from a friend I respect & esteem to take the charge of the rights of my three beloved daughters, & advise & assist them how to claim them.[5] As to [one word illegible] for that expence the legacy left me by a grateful peasant shall be appointed to discharge it — & this [three words illegible] gratefully to soothe my dying hours, & if you will but soothe with a promise to be the friend of my daughters I shall dye in peace for your honor & religion will not permit you to deceive me — & this written with my dying hand wd. impress this request with [one word illegible] effort of an anxious & attached desire that a heart can possibly feel to the person [one word illegible] as Mr Scully is, must esteem herself his faithfully attached friend & kinswoman,

                    E. Moira Hastings Hungerford etc. etc. etc
mark the dying hand [one or two words: ? I plead] by it[6]

                                        [*Source*: Scully Papers]

[1]For the Hastings-Huddleston connexion see No. 44 n.3.
[2]1789 was the date of the death of the 10th Earl of Huntingdon, Lady Moira's brother. The deed referred to may have accompanied the will or have been the will itself. Under the terms of this will Lord Huntingdon's property, which included Donington, went to Lord Moira (Lady Moira's son) for life and remainder to his sons, with reversion to Lady Moira — see Mr Adam's letter of 21 October 1813 to Lady Granard (Loudoun Papers, A.166). A letter of 1 September 1807 from Lady Moira to her son (ibid., A.208) shows that she was aware of having a potential claim on Donington (Lord Moira having as yet no son).
[3]William Adam, whose letter to Lady Granard implies that he was Lord Moira's lawyer.
[4]James, 5th Earl of Loudoun, father of Flora, Countess of Loudoun, who married the 2nd Earl of Moira on 12 April 1804.
[5]Although she speaks here of her three daughters Lady Moira left the residue of her estate to two of them — Lady Granard and Lady Charlotte Rawdon, who were named as executors. A long letter from Lady Granard to Lord Moira dated 23 April 1808 (Loudoun Papers, A 189) says that the will "adverts painfully to the disposal of her supposed rights in failure of you and your sons". Lady Granard goes on: "long since, upon her application to Lord Manners [the Lord Chancellor], Lord Granard in

person, to sanction my act, carried my letter to Lord Manners, disclaiming in my own name and those of my sisters, the possibility of acquiescing in any measure contrary to your interests & pledging ourselves to renunciation if such occurred".

[6]Lady Moira died on 11 April 1808, at Moira House. On 21 April her remains were removed to Castle Forbes to be interred in the Granard vault (*DEP*, 28 April 1808). A warm obituary appeared in the *Hibernian Magazine* (reproduced in the *Annual Register* for 1808).

167   *From Henry Parnell to Bagot Street, Dublin*

London, 19 May 1808

Dear Sir,

I feel very much obliged to you for your letter of the 10th & its enclosure.[1] It has however come too late to enable me to make any use of the intelligence it gives me in the house of Commons, but I have taken steps for getting the substance of it into the public papers.

I shall on all occasions be very happy to receive information from you on Irish affairs; nothing can contribute so much to enable me or any other member to be of service to your claims as a full acquaintance with any fact connected with them, I am frequently at a loss to obtain information for want of knowing some person resident here who is well acquainted with the concerns of the Catholics; & had you any friend here to whom I might apply, I shall be much obliged to you if you will give me a letter of introduction to him.

The No Popery party have commenced their operations by posting up placards, & distributing hand bills containing the usual calumnies against the Catholic body.[2] This practice can alone be rendered ineffectual by having recourse to the same means of influencing the public opinion, & I hope that some subscription will immediately be set on foot to provide funds for publishing other placards & hand bills, & advertising the Declaration of 1792[3] in all the English Country & London Newspapers.

The custom here is for any public body that has an object to carry in parliament to prepare the public for giving their application a good reception, by expending immense sums in advertising statements favourable to their cause in the public papers, & by sending to each member of Parliament concise descriptions of their claims. I think the Catholics too much, if not entirely, neglect this opportunity of advancing their interests, & surely the expenditure of 5 or 10,000 in endeavouring to remove the prejudices of the English public would at this time be well applied. My own opinion is that all that now remains to be done to secure the measure of emancipation, is to remove these prejudices, for if the English people can be brought to understand the question, neither this or any other administration, or any king will be able to resist the necessary effects of repeated petitions to parliament.   [*Source*: Scully Papers]

[1]Missing: the subject has not been identified.
[2]The occasion of the campaign was the Irish Catholic petition. When Grattan introduced this for the first time on 12 April (then temporarily withdrawing it because of an informality in the signatures) Dr Douglass, Vicar Apostolic of the London district, noted in his diary: "Handbills inflaming the people against the prayer of this petition are again distributed about the town . . ." (Westminster Diocesan Archives).
[3]A declaration of 1774 which was republished in 1792 to repel accusations made in the Irish parliament that the tenets of the Catholics were inimical to good order and government (Henry Parnell, *History of the Penal Laws*).

168   *From Montagu Mathew to Baggot Street, Dublin*

London, 20 May 1808

My dear Sir,

I had the Pleasure of Receiving yours a day or two ago & am extremely glad to find by it that my Humble Effort in Parliament[1] has met with the approbation of my friends in Ireland & I Beg to return you my thanks for your Congratulations on my Military Promotion.[2]

Mr Grattan presents his Petition from Dublin this day[3] & I shall present that of the Co. Tipperary on Monday.[4]   [*Source*: Scully Papers]

[1]He had spoken on 5 May in support of the Maynooth grant and on 11 May against the "scandalous appointment" of Dr Duigenan to the Privy Council of Ireland (*Hansard* XI, 122, 153).
[2]He had been promoted to Major General on 25 April (*Army List*).
[3]He so calls it only because it was laid open for signature in Dublin. After presenting it on 23 May Grattan moved to go into committee on 25 May but was defeated 281 to 178 votes. On 27 May Lord Grenville's similar motion in the House of Lords was defeated 181 to 74 votes. It was what was said in these debates that sparked off the Veto controversy — Grattan, George Ponsonby and Lord Grenville announcing that the Irish Catholics were ready to concede a negative veto, and Ponsonby specifically citing Dr Milner as his authority (*Hansard* XI, 489, 549–638, 643–695).
[4]He presented it after Grattan's on 23 May.

169   *From Charles Butler*[1]

Lincolns Inn, 16 June 1808

Dear Sir,

Our printed paper will shew you that we have established a Board, for attending to the Roman Catholic concerns, so far as regards that very important article, The Press.[2] The strange abuse made of it against us, rendered it necessary, that we should exert ourselves to turn it, in some degree, in our favor. Tho' it be a powerful, it is a very delicate instrument, and requires management. We have hitherto had little acquaintance with it, but I think we have now made some arrangements which are likely to be very useful to us, and I trust we hourly make some progress in public opinion. I believe the Irish Press is universally favorable to the Irish Roman Catholics, but the English Press is far otherwise, and we shall be extremely happy that our labours shall prove useful in disposing it in your favour. Our Board may also become serviceable to the common Cause in other respects; particularly as it may prove, what we have long wanted, a point of Union to the English Catholics themselves; and a point of union between the Irish Catholics and them.[3]

I wish much to establish a regular co-operation between your body and ours. The time is momentous, and every hour that we do not make some exertion is a loss to us, and a reproach to us. That the public mind is considerably changed in our favour, admits of no doubt, and it is even said that in the most important of all quarters, we have made considerable advances. I am perfectly satisfied that we shall gain our cause, if we are not wanting to ourselves: and I think we shall be wanting to ourselves, if we do not unite and co-operate. Our friends in Parliament have done their part. One of our exertions has been to procure an exact report of their speeches; we have completely succeeded in it, and it is now in the Press. I speak from my own knowledge when I say that never were any persons more slandered than our Friends have been when they have been charged with lukewarmness in our cause when they were in power. Lord Holland sent to me, and intimated a wish, that for a few months or rather a few weeks, your application might be suspended: and he said that if it were made at that time,[4] it might turn them out of Office: but he distinctly and roundly said, that if it came on, he would vote for it and support it with all his might. To my certain knowledge the same language was held by Lord Grey and others. No conduct could be manlier. They persist in it; and I know it to be their opinion that we should exert ourselves to the very utmost. Now no exertion can be so useful to us, as establishing a co-operation between you and us. Perhaps you will establish in Ireland a Board similar to ours; and direct a correspondence between the Secretaries. But, as opportunities offer, any member of either Board may write to one or other of the Secretaries, communicating or requiring any information he wishes, or suggesting any measures which appear to him adviseable. When persons are thoroughly well disposed to one another, thoroughly understand one another, and are thoroughly agreed in their object, a very loose bond of union suffices.

Permit me now to suggest a measure which some of our friends here, think would be of incalculable service to you. It is that you should *Poll all Ireland as well Protestant as Catholic and Men and Women*. I conceive it should be in the form of a Petition; with three columns; the first for the Catholics and the second for the Protestants who sign the Petition, and the third for the Protestants, if any who refuse to sign it. The last should be annexed to it, but so as to be taken off if adviseable when the petition is presented, and thenceforth preserved separately. It should contain the names of the Protestants to whom it is presented, and who refuse to sign it, and those names may be written by the person who circulates the Petition with a particular account of their answers, when the application to them is made. I think it scarcely admits of doubt, that if such a petition is presented it must and will be followed by immediate and complete Emancipation. But the sooner it is done the better.

Another measure I beg leave to recommend is to have two Bills immediately prepared for removing all your disabilities. The first effecting it by one general and unqualified enactment, the second effecting it by several enactments. We did this in 1791,[5] and found the good effects of it. The reason for doing it in two Bills is that if they consent to the general enactment you will have a bill for that purpose ready. If (what I trust and believe will not be the case), they insist on some particular restraints being continued, you may use the necessary parts of the second Bill. But if the measure of two Bills should be adopted, I recommend the second Bill, should be kept quite private, as I would not have [it] generally known, that it is considered even to be possible that any thing short of a general unlimited and unqualified Emancipation should be acquiesced in.

I have only to make you an unreserved tender of my services to be employed by you in any manner you think proper. From London I shall not move, and I mean to give myself up to the Roman Catholic business, at least till the fate of the application of next year is determined.[6] Mr Jerningham the Secretary of our Board is a most promising young Gentleman of high birth and of great talents, activity and exertion. I must repeat my decided conviction, that we must succeed, if we are not wanting to ourselves. The Cappadocians[7] are damned to everlasting fame for having refused Liberty, when it was offered to them. We shall deserve the same remembrance in history, if we continue degraded for want of exertion. [*Source*: Scully Papers]

[1]Sent to Scully's lodgings in London (see No. 173).
[2]Members of the Catholic nobility and gentry had met on 23 May to consider the propriety of "engaging certain reporters and newspapers to give a faithful account of what passes in the two Houses of Parliament, and a correct statement of the speeches of the members on the petition of the Irish Catholics, the debate upon which is to come on soon in both Houses" (Ward, *Eve of Catholic Emancipation* I, p. 99).
[3]Resolutions passed at the meeting had also provided for subscriptions to a fund "for the general benefit and advantage of the body". In sending out the printed paper

referred to by Butler the Secretary, Edward Jerningham, expressed a hope that the subscription might lead to an association, "It being obvious . . . that unless some point of union be established, the Catholics of England can neither cooperate if necessary with their brethren in Ireland, nor do justice to their own interest at home" (*ibid.*).

[4]Early in 1807 (see No. 153 n.1).

[5]When an act for the relief of the English Catholics was passed, introduced by John Freeman Mitford, later Lord Redesdale, in the House of Commons and Lord Moira in the House of Lords (Ward, *Dawn of the Catholic Revival*, I, p. 263).

[6]Until the English Board decided whether or not to petition in 1809.

[7]Combined from Pope: *Essay on Man*, IV, 294 ("See Cromwell damned to everlasting fame") and Justin's *Epitome*, 38, referring to an event of 95 BC.

170   *From Charles Butler to Dublin*

Lincoln's Inn, 20 June 1808

Dear Sir,

You will already have received from me a very long letter[1] and I now again trouble you.

You see in the papers a debate on the charter of the Bank of Ireland.[2] We understand, that, on some late occasion, a case was laid before Mr Burston, Mr Ponsonby and another Lawyer, on the right of the admission of Catholics to the Directorship; that Mr Burston thought they had a right, and Mr Ponsonby and the other Lawyer were of a different opinion. Sir Arthur Pigot mentioned the fact to me, and I suppose it is well known in Ireland. Sir Arthur Pigot agrees in opinion with Mr Burston and has brought Mr Ponsonby over to him.[3] This he mentioned to Mr Perceval with the grounds of his opinion, and Mr Perceval was very much struck with the observations. In consequence of this circumstance he introduced the rider which you have seen in the papers.[4] Now would it not be proper to have a new case prepared and stated for the opinion of these two gentlemen and two others.[5]

The point of law is unquestionably with you, and any thing which provoke[s] discussion is favorable to us.

I remember Mr Lynch was refused admission into the spiritual court by Dr Duigenan.[6] Should you not engage him to agitate the question [?] The information that his Majesty's prejudices begin to thaw still gains ground.

[*Source*: Scully Papers]

[1]No. 169.

[2]On John Foster's motion of 27 May that "the Governor and Company of the Bank of Ireland be continued as a Corporation till the 1st January 1837" (*Hansard* XI, 701).

[3]In 1795 the Bank of Ireland expressed a willingness to accept a few Catholics on their board, but being doubtful as to the construction of the 1793 relief act they

sought the opinion of three eminent lawyers: Beresford Burston, A. Wolfe (the Attorney-General) and George Ponsonby. Burston construed the act liberally but Wolfe and Ponsonby put a strict construction on it, in a sense unfavourable to the Catholics. The directors accepted the opinion of the majority (Scully, *Penal Laws* Ch. X).

[4]Speaking on a motion by Sir John Newport on 30 May Spencer Perceval, Chancellor of the Exchequer, said that while he saw no utility in altering the existing law he had no objection to entering a declaratory clause for the future, giving the legislature a power of intervention in favour of the Catholics (*Hansard* XI, 717).

[5]On 16 June Lord Grenville proposed that the opinion of judges should be taken but was defeated 96 to 83 votes (ibid. 808).

[6]A cutting from the *Dublin Journal* which Butler sent to Sir John Throckmorton on 12 December 1805 (Throckmorton Papers) identifies him as Martin French Lynch, who had been admitted to the Inner Temple in 1785 and become a Doctor of Law at Trinity College, Dublin, but as a Catholic could not be called to the Irish bar until 1792. He signed the 1805 petition giving his address as Mountjoy Square. Scully refers to the case in Ch. IV of his *Penal Laws*, where he observed that the spiritual courts, although commonly called Ecclesiastical Offices, were invested with extensive jurisdiction in temporal matters, such as wills, marriages and tithes.

171   *From Lord Shrewsbury to Bagot Street, Dublin*

Chester, 28 June 1808

Dear Sir,

It is my intention to hear prayers tomorrow morning[1] at Holywell[2] & if I am time enough for the Packet to embark in the evening, consequently I have some expectation of being at Dublin on thursday morning instead of friday which I believe I fixed upon when I had the pleasure of seeing you at Alton.[3]   [*Source*: Scully Papers]

[1]The feast of Sts Peter and Paul.
[2]In Flint, Wales, on the road to Holyhead.
[3]Alton Towers in Staffordshire, half way between Derby and Stoke-on-Trent — one of the seats of the Earls of Shrewsbury.

172   *To Miss Catherine Eyre, Farm, Sheffield*[1]

Bagot Street, Dublin, Sunday 3 July 1808

I left your very agreeable society, Miss Eyre, with that favourable impression of your amiable disposition as to hope you will pardon the liberty I take in addressing you. I feel an earnest interest in the decision you will come to upon the subject, which I was permitted to mention to you, and very naturally am solicitous to receive from your pen what I could not then presume to obtain from your lips. The shortness of our acquaintance certainly did not allow of our being thoroughly known to each other — and few, situated as we are, can be so before marriage — but I can on my part say with strict truth, that your personal & mental charms, unaffected manners, & general sweetness of character have really inspired me with the warmest regard & esteem for you, & indeed with every prepossession becoming a person, who solicits, as I do, the honour & happiness of your hand. I am therefore perfectly sincere in saying, that, if your answer shall be favourable to me, you shall find me ever affectionate & attached, happy in pleasing you, and desirous to meet all your wishes. I am incapable of underrating a kindness, on account of its being conferred without much suspense or delay — and, in this instance, I should feel myself the more obliged in honour & gratitude to justify any confidence you may repose in me, and influenced by a real & fixed affection, not less than by duty & principle, to make you every return in my power, whilst I live. If I were to say more now, you might think me abusing this liberty and be disinclined to its being repeated by your most devoted & faithful servant

Denys Scully   [*Source*: Scully Papers]

[1]The Farm, in Sheffield Park, part of the estates of the Duke of Norfolk, was an H-shaped building, of two storeys over a cellar, with four or five bedrooms. It was incorporated in 1857 in a reconstructed larger building, which was later sold to the Midland Railway Company and demolished in 1967 (from information kindly supplied by the Librarian to the Duke of Norfolk). It is not clear when it became the residence of the Duke's agent. The 1797 Sheffield directory gives Vincent Eyre's address as 17 Far Gate.

173   *From Charles Butler to Dublin*

Lincolns Inn, 4 July 1808

Dear Sir,

I took the liberty of addressing you a long letter, which was left at your lodgings, and on enquiry afterwards, was said to be sent to you. I hope that letter and a short letter[1] I afterwards sent you, have reached you.

I shall be much obliged to you to favor me with a line informing me what you are doing. The Spanish News,[2] highly acceptable to us on other accounts, is so far unfavorable to us as it takes off from that alarm in the minds of ministers which is the greatest circumstance in our favour. This is an additional reason for present exertions. There is some reason to think there is a division in the cabinet.   [*Source*: Scully Papers]

[1]Nos. 169 and 170.
[2]*The Times* of 2 July had published official confirmation of a rising against the French in southern Spain. On 4 July Butler observed to Sir John Throckmorton that the

Spanish news was an additional reason for exertion: "I have written to Skully to inform me what they are doing" (Throckmorton Papers, folder 9).

174   *To Charles Butler*

Dublin, 12 July 1808

[Copy]

Dear Sir,

I have had the honour of receiving your three letters,[1] after some delay, occasioned by the mis-spelling of my name in the superscriptions.

Your views of the Catholic interests and of measures now fit to be adopted appear to be most just and luminous — and had we a central association or other organ of general sentiment I have no doubt they would be acceded to and acted upon, but as yet we have not made the expected progress in framing preliminary arrangements.

Your English association, appearing exclusively English, has thrown a languor upon the efforts making here, since you in London are now considered here as having undertaken the entire burthen — this I did apprehend, as I already mentioned freely to you and some other gentlemen of the Cisalpine.[2] But there is yet a greater impediment — it is now the feeling of an immense portion of the Catholic body comprising much of our talent and intelligence, and a considerable share of property, that all further application to England, its Government or Parliament, are nugatory and ineffectual — And, tho' they are sanguine in pursuit of their liberties they expect nothing from Parliament, or from that quarter. Such is the consequence of the No Popery cry. All this class of course discountenance plans such as you and I approve of, and even reject the very principle upon which these plans rest. I find other impediments, but they are only temporary.

As yet therefore the Catholics here act only individually, but they are not idle — they are occupied according to their respective situations in life, and successfully occupied in augmenting the mass of Catholic property, industry, intelligence & consequent weight and influence with their Protestant countrymen. I perfectly agree with you and have long been of opinion that they ought to extend their efforts, and endeavour to act upon the public mind of England, by an uniform impulse, & upon a system devised by judicious persons — but I fear the opportunity has been missed of cultivating such a connection between them and the English Catholics, as would lead them and perfectly fix them to so desireable an object.

You may rely, Sir, upon my giving every circulation in my power to the excellent suggestions contained in your letters, and I trust that thereby a pretty large proportion of the thinking Catholics will be better enabled to appreciate the favour you have conferred upon us, and so benefit by the councils [sic] you have offered. Allow me at the same time to express my sense of the honour and advantage I derive from those communications — and to request a continuance of them. I wish very much to know what has been done towards influencing the press, and what publications are particularly to be favoured: for thus far at least we may cooperate.

Lord Shrewsbury left us yesterday for Killarney, to return here on the 24th.   [*Source*: Throckmorton Papers]

[1]Nos. 169, 170 and 173.
[2]The Cisalpine Club's account book in the Westminster Diocesan Archives shows that Scully paid a subscription of two guineas on 4 June 1808.

175   *To Catherine Eyre, Farm, near Sheffield*

Dublin, 20 July [1808]

Your letter, dear Miss Eyre, has laid me under the greatest obligation to you. Nothing can promise greater happiness to our union than the candour and feeling you have shewn — and it shall be my study to justify your confidence in me. If you feel, as I do, that, this first step being over we are now become allied in heart to each other, and in fact plighted in affection, permit me to hope for a continuance of your pleasing correspondence — until we meet — to say from time to time, at least, that you continue in the same sentiments, and any thing further, that you might consent to add, for our being more acquainted & more nearly known to each other. I would not desire this favour from you (however much I wish it) if I did not consider it to be perfectly correct & natural in our present situation — & likely to promote our mutual happiness & confidence in each other. I would ask more, but for a sense of the timidity of your nature, & of the novelty of your situation to a Lady hitherto free & unattached — and particularly I would entreat that you will not oppose an early day for the happiness I aspire to, but for this time I venture only to request, most earnestly & respectfully, that you will continue your kindness to me, your perfect reliance upon my attachment & esteem, & treat me with favour and indulgence, until there are opportunities of a nearer acquaintance.

I am not so presumptuous as to attribute the kind sentiments expressed in your excellent letter to any impression but that which you mention to have been made by the advice of your mother & friends — be assured it shall be my principal & most pleasing study, when I have the opportunity, to give you reason to be pleased with that advice. The candour & openness, which you are pleased to observe in my conduct, do in truth belong to my character. I am perfectly unreserved & sincere — and disposed to place unlimited confidence in a Lady so deserving as you appear to be — & I think you will find this a substitute for a long acquaintance — having nothing to withhold from you respecting my situation or feelings, & being wholly unattached, until I saw you.

I wish much to remove from your thoughts the awe naturally annexed to the idea of matrimony, change of life etc. The reality in fact is far less formidable than the name. It is no more in this instance, I think, than your agreeing to visit Dublin for one or 2 years in the company of a person constantly interested about you, nearly & intimately attached to you, & bound by inclination & duty to promote your comfort & happiness — with free liberty for your returning to visit your friends in different places, & back again to your House & establishment here, as often as you please. I have already mentioned to you in confidence, some other circumstances, to shew you that you are not taking final leave of your friends, or settling perhaps entirely here[1] — and I think your good sense and justness of reflection will satisfy you as to the rest.

However your sentiments may be upon it (and I shall never attempt to controul them by my own) I shall long very much for an opportunity of conversing with you on this & other subjects, & particularly of expressing my warm & lasting gratitude for the indulgent & honourable part you have acted towards me, which has attached me to you beyond expression.

I regret the tedious interval during the Law Circuit, which will bring about the end of August before I shall have the happiness of waiting upon you. Believe me to be in hope of a line from you with constant regard & esteem Dear Miss Eyre, Your very affectionate & obliged Serv't,

Denys Scully

[P.S.] I shall have the pleasure of writing in a few days to your mother, whom I beg to thank for her letter — & to present my best regards to her & the family.   [*Source*: Scully Papers]

[1]See No. 388, where he again speaks of spending more time in England: he seems to have had hopes of sitting in parliament.

176   *From Charles Butler to Dublin*

Lincolns Inn, 20 July 1808

Dear Sir,

I was duly favord. with your letter.[1] I am greatly concerned to find that no systematic plan for securing your success in the next sessions[2] is yet adopted. It must be an important sessions and may decide the fate of the Roman Catholics. That we gained much by the last debate[3] is beyond a doubt. The effect of a debate when the Ministers make it a party Question is very seldom seen by the immediate division upon it. The old Lord Chatham[4] mentioned to a person who repeated it to me that he believed no one speech he had made gained him six votes on the night but the general effect of his speeches on the house and the general effect of them out of it and the reaction of these on one another produced the repeated changes of measures and men, which were the triumph of his character. Much of this kind is already discernible in the effects of the late debate. Almost the whole body of the Old Pittites express themselves kindly in our regard and even the King is said to speak with less determination than formerly. Sir Francis Burdett has explained himself favorably and professes that his absence on some of the divisions proceeded merely from a wish, that the opposition who in his view of things neglected us in the day of their strength should not avail themselves of us in the day of their weakness. Almost all the newspapers are in our favor and I am not apprised of any publication against us, of any degree of consequence. Under these circumstances we shall be strangely wanting to ourselves if we do not exert ourselves to the utmost in our own cause. Our friends in Part. depended upon our exertions when they stood forth so nobly as our champions. Lord Fingal, yourself and many other Gentlemen know that the English Catholics are anxious that the Irish Catholics should co-operate with them or rather take the lead in the present moment. Of the mode of doing it you must be the best judges. It strikes me that it may be done with effect and advantage if you establish a board on your side of the water similar to ours. But you must take the lead and we can duly be primers to you. I have great doubts whether we can reasonably expect a time more favorable to the discussion of our claims than the present. The only objection arises from the supposed scruples of the royal mind.[5] Now the existence of these scruples had long appeared problematical [and] it is observable that a clear assertion of their existence has never been made by any person of Rank in either house. No such person has done more than throw out an ambiguous hint easily to be explained away if it should be pressed upon him at a future time. Still less has any such person argued for the justice or propriety of these scruples. This they have left to their Pamphleteers. Besides, the discussion which the subject has received has abundantly shewn that no argument even of a plausible kind can be produced by which the scruples can be supported. From all these circumstances I have long looked on the supposed royal opposition on conscientious motives as a fable. I believe the scruple is not really entertained by his Majesty but imputed to him by those whose interest it is that he should entertain it. After all, the present time is allways [sic] the best. Who will assure us that in the succeeding reign there will be fewer difficulties in our way than there are at present. The first year of that reign will pass away in ceremonial and compliment and what may be the state or strength of parties in the second or third years human prudence cannot now discover.

If we look into the history of the bills that have passed in your favor we find them uniformly attended with three circumstances. The first, that no measure for your relief was ever accomplished which had not failed in the first instance. The [second], that when any bill for your relief was passed it gave you more than in the onset of the business you had asked for. The third, that nothing was ever granted to you till the spirit of the time made it impossible to refuse it. Surely our late discomfiture should not make you lose courage. Over and over again you have proclaimed yourselves an aggrieved and degraded race of men. If you do not now avail yourselves of the golden moment which presents itself, it will be concluded either that you wanted sincerity in mentioning your grievances or that you want spirit for procuring their removal. You are not called upon to walk up to the mouth of the cannon or to plunge in to the imminent deadly breach. Yet those who are doing this have not stronger motives for their exertions than you have. All that is wanted of you is to state your wrongs, claim your rights and sign your demands of them with your names. Surely the objects you have in view are worth this little trouble.   [*Source*: Scully Papers]

[1]No. 174.
[2]Of 1809 — when parliament reopened on 18 January.
[3]On the Irish Catholic petition — on 25 May 1808 in the House of Commons and two days later in the House of Lords.
[4]The 1st Earl, William Pitt the elder (1708–1778).
[5]In regard to his coronation oath.

177   *From Charles Butler to Dublin*

                                              Lincolns Inn, 28 July 1808
Dear Sir,
    I fear you will think me a troublesome correspondent.
    You will remember that in the debates in the Houses of Parliament on the Roman Catholic question, it was explicitly stated, that the Irish Roman Catholic Bishops had offered through Doctor Milner, that the King should have a negative on the appointment of Bishops.[1] We were afterwards informed that this offer had not given satisfaction to all the Irish prelates,[2] and that it was to be understood with some qualifications and we were told that a meeting of the Irish Prelates on the subject, was to take place at Maynooth College on the 29th of last month.[3]
    It is extremely desirable, that the result of their deliberations should be known, particularly as the speeches in both houses are to appear in a few days,[4] and it would serve us most essentially that it should be known that Mr Milner's offer had been formally acquiesced in. I have written on the subject to Doctor Troy, but I have had no answer from him. Now I shall be

particularly obliged to you to procure exact information upon this subject and to send it me as soon as possible. It will be a very unfortunate thing for us, if there should be a material difference between the offer made by Doctor Milner, & the actual resolution of the Irish prelates upon it.

[*Source*: Scully Papers]

[1] In the debate on 25 May (see No. 168 n.3) Grattan said that he was authorised by the Catholics, and Ponsonby that he was authorised by Dr Milner, to put forward the proposition of a negative power for the crown, but there was no offer on the part of the Irish Prelates. There had been no time to consult them and Dr Milner had merely expressed his own belief that they would "cheerfully subscribe" to the plan traced out by him (see Ward, *Eve of Catholic Emancipation* I, p. 59).
[2] The campaign against what now became described as the Veto had begun with the publication in the *Evening Herald* of 4 July of the first of a series of articles by "Sarsfield", the pseudonym of Revd James Keelan.
[3] Dr Troy explained to Sir John Newport in a letter of 27 September 1808 that the Maynooth trustees had refused a request to discuss the matter at their meeting in June because they had no authority to act for their absent brethren: a general meeting had therefore been proposed for 24 September (*Dropmore Papers* IX).
[4] The publication seems to have been delayed until the autumn of 1809 (see No. 184 n.1).

178   *From Lord Fingall*

Killeen Castle [Co. Meath] 29 July 1808

Dear Sir,

I have the pleasure to receive your letter enclosing one from Mr Addis.[1] There cannot be a doubt that he is well entitled to a proper remuneration for his trouble and fifty guineas is a very reasonable one indeed. I requested Mr Addis to write to me and shall as soon as I can go to Dublin try to set something on foot to collect the small sum which I think the public at large have more right to be called on for than those who gave their own trouble etc. also. I am sorry Mr Addis' letter did not arrive sooner as now everybody has left town and it will be some time before they return. It is but justice to say Mr Addis was extremely useful to me and I am sure I cannot judge how any persons who may be commissioned by the Catholics to do their best for the public cause can go on in England without some real assistance.

Our brethren in England have lately established a very excellent system as to subscriptions for different purposes connected with their interests and the forwarding their question an example very well worthy of imitation.

[*Source*: Scully Papers]

[1] See No. 97.

179   *To Catherine Eyre, Farm, near Sheffield*

Kilfeacle, Cashell [Co. Tipperary] 6 August 1808

I am still more & more obliged to my dear Miss Eyre, and shall ever highly value the two admirable Letters I have received.

Absence, which I regretted as a misfortune — tho' unavoidable, has yet unfolded to me the sooner those accomplishments & perfections of mind which your Letters announce. I could not blame the discretion, which kept me in suspence for some time — I admire the good sense, that set proper limits to that suspence — and I love the good feeling which hastened a candid avowal, as well as the elegant and modest language & sentiments which you have chosen throughout the entire transaction. Let me entreat a continuance of your very charming correspondence — it affords me, thro' your goodness, the most pleasing substitute for your conversation. It is impossible for me not to feel how valuable would be the possession of such a Heart as yours. I own it is my highest ambition to gain it, & deserve it — to receive with your fair hand, not merely the assent of your reason but also the treasure of your full affections is the greatest happiness I can aspire to — and it would be a very particular good fortune to us both, what happens but seldom, that our acquaintance & union, founded upon mutual esteem & regard, should ripen into the sincerest & closest mutual affection.

I have much pleasure in confirming to you, what I mentioned at Sheffield, that my father & mother are quite pleased & gratified by the circumstances that have taken place — and they are fully prepared to treat you with that kindness and affection that I could wish. My father has also agreed to settle upon me another small Estate of about £160 a year[1] in addition to what was mentioned to Mrs Eyre. This he says is in testimony of the regard he has already conceived for you & his respect for your family.

On the whole, I am truly happy in saying that I see no obstacle to our union, now that you & your mother have been so good as to assent to it.[2]

I do with every pleasure give full credit to you for not permitting any inconvenient delay, and I shall leave those matters entirely, whatever my wishes may naturally be, to the result of your good sense & indulgence. I have full reason to place implicit confidence in you & you shall find that principle of confidence, as well as of esteem and affection towards you personally, pervading every action of mine. Indeed to have such a friend to confide in is no small ingredient in the happiness which I promise to myself in your society.

I hold your letters as too precious to permit myself to lose the opportunity of having one, and shall be exceedingly gratified if I find one from you at Dublin upon my return there about the 20th or until the 23d — and also a line at the Post Office, Buxton,[3] about the 28th.

If you think me asking too much, it is the fault of your writing such excellent Letters — and, if you refuse me one or both of those letters, I hope at least you will pardon my asking them & attribute my request to your own superior merit & excellence, rather than to unreasonable presumption on my part, or any other feeling than those of the sincerest regard & esteem with which you have inspired me. Believe me to be ever, my dear Miss Eyre,

with perfect affection & respect

Your most devoted & faithful servant

Denys Scully

[P.S.] If you write any time until the 16th or 17th it will be in time at Dublin.

[*Source*: Scully Papers]

[1]Probably Knockroe, on the south side of the Golden-Cashel road, which James Scully (Diary 2 March 1908) bought at the same time as Mantlehill (see No. 228 n.2).
[2]Her father had died in 1801.
[3]The Derbyshire spa, some eighteen miles from Sheffield.

180   *To Richard Huddleston*

Dublin, 25 August 1808

Dr Rich'd,

I wrote some time since in answer to your Letter about money matters.

A report has reached me within these few days, that some treaty is on foot respecting Jane's[1] marriage with Mr Canning[2] — & it occurs to me that possibly those Bonds of mine[3] may stand in the way or embarrass the mode of securing an early payment of her fortune. If so, I shall be very willing, upon any application for the purpose, to execute any Deed giving her a priority, & shall be happy, if I can facilitate in that or any other manner an arrangement advantageous or pleasing to the family. I remember her dear sister,[4] who had such excellent judgment, often saying that she thought Mr C would be a very desirable match for Jane, & regretting that it did not proceed.

I suppose you have seen Mr Gibbons.[5] Our Catholic Bishops are to hold a great meeting here on the 12 Septem'r, on the subject of the proposal, that the King should have a Veto in the future appointments to vacant Sees. I hear that many oppose it, & I fear much disunion. Dr Milner is to attend.[6] He & Mr T. Weld Junr. of Dorsetshire landed at Waterford last week, & go on a Tour thence to Cork, Killarney, Limerick & so round to Dublin.[7]

I am about going to England for a month, but fear I cannot see you in Cambridgeshire. In fact, I ought to apprize you (& would have done so some months ago, but for the uncertainty of the matter) that in consequence of the request & importunities of my father & mother etc. upon the subject, & not without much reluctance arising from the great loss I have already sustained, I consented to turn my mind towards again entering upon a married life. I mentioned it to Mrs Bostock, when last in London & she was pleased to receive it with a kindness that has still more encreased my respect for her heart & head — & the person in question, being a connection of Mrs Bostock's family,[8] makes a favourable circumstance. She is a Miss Catherine Eyre, sister of Mr Vincent Eyre — whom probably you know. Some persons, whose acquaintance with her is much longer than mine, have given me the most satisfactory account of her disposition & virtues — &, from what I have seen, I think her sensible, innocent, gentle & good tempered. The affair indeed is drawn almost to a conclusion. There are the usual consents on both sides & my father settles at present £1500 a year, in consequence of her fortune being about £12,000 or more.[9] It is a satisfaction to me to think that considering these circumstances, the good sense & kindness which I have always observed in your family, as well as the sentiments expressed to me upon this subject within these twelvemonths by your late Father,[10] there is nothing in this affair that is likely in any manner to interrupt or even to damp the mutual regard & cordiality subsisting between me & every member of your family. Were it otherwise, it would be a very great misfortune in my mind, & sufficient to incline me to abandon the affair altogether — but I hope it will have the effect of rather confirming the present friendship, & afford me opportunities, by being oftener in England of course, for keeping up occasionally an intercourse that might otherwise be impaired by Time & Distance.

Ld Fingall is said to be very ill at Killeen. I do not know any other particular worth mentioning. Believe me to be, with best regards to such of the family as may happen to be at Sawston.

[P.S.] I saw Frank[11] yesterday — he is very well.

[*Source*: Huddleston Papers C3/S5]

[1]Jane Huddleston.

[2]Francis Canning.

[3]See No. 46.

[4]His deceased wife, Mary Huddleston.

[5]Probably a P. Gibbons who had been a friend of Richard's when he was in Dublin in 1799 (Huddleston Papers C3/G3). They had mutual friends in Sackville Street.

[6]In the event Dr Milner was not admitted to the synod, although he was staying in Dublin. The resolution inviting him to continue acting as agent of the Irish clergy (see No. 185 n.7) mentions that an account of his conduct was received through a friend.

[7]Dr Milner's *Second Tour* published soon after his return to England as an additional letter in a new edition of his *Inquiry into certain vulgar opinions*, otherwise known as *Letters from Ireland* or *First Tour*, published after his first visit in 1807. Thomas Weld (1773–1837), of Lulworth, was the future Cardinal (see *DNB*).

[8]The Huddlestons of Sawston Hall, of whom Mrs Bostock was one, were descended

from Sir William Huddleston, who married an Eyre, but Scully was probably alluding to the marriage of Catherine Eyre's great-grandfather, Vincent Eyre, with a daughter of Nathaniel Bostock of Wroxall.

[9]Against the date 1 March 1810 Scully entered at the back of a notebook (MS.27, 493 ii) an account of his wife's "portion and property". From Consols and Exchequer Bills sold in September 1808, a credit at her bank of nearly £1000, bank notes and the £250 which he estimated as the value of her dresses and other articles before marriage he calculated that she brought him £11,991 English or £13,130 Irish. He added that on 5 June 1811 he received £1097 from his mother-in-law and on 3 February 1816 another £945 from her.

[10]Ferdinand Huddleston had died on 6 April 1808.

[11]Richard's cousin, Francis Huddleston.

181   *To Charles Butler*

Dublin, 25 August 1808

[Copy]

Dear Sir,

I owe you many apologies for having delayed to answer your very interesting and valuable letters[1] upon the Catholic subject. In fact they reached me whilst on the Leinster Circuit, whence I am but just returned, & for the first time at sufficient leisure. Your views of the subject perfectly agree with mine, & with those of every person I know but your clear and impressive manner of unfolding them surpasses any thing of the kind that I am acquainted with. I have taken every opportunity of giving circulation & due weight to your sentiments amongst the Catholics, and indeed have felt it my duty to the Catholic body & to my country to take that liberty with your letters as to afford a perusal of them to very many Catholics, all of whom I found impressed by them as I myself was, & full of respect & esteem for the writer.[2] Now to the subject of them. We have got no Catholic Board for Ireland generally tho' it is generally wished for and the principle much approved of, but in practice we find it would be very difficult. The Catholics here are too numerous & there are too many who are entitled (or conceive themselves to be entitled) to distinguished situations of respect, precedence etc to permit the desired facilities for selecting & constituting a Catholic Board for Ireland generally; such I mean as would be generally acknowledged and could by their situation and conduct insure assent to their measures, & silence jealousies, opposition, censure, & the usual results of personal feelings offended. Besides, the different cities and counties would each claim a right of election — those elected should again agree upon a central place of meeting. Many in the country dislike Dublin on account of the little parties amongst the merchants & orators here — these again would object to the country, and in short the business is not likely to be soon adopted in Dublin.

Under these circumstances I have thought fit to consult some Catholic gentlemen, who from experience, good sense and influence are entitled to great respect, & with their concurrence I resolved to make a beginning in the County of Tipperary, where my family connections & property principally lie. It is the 5th county in extent, the 4th in population, & the first (excepting Cork) in wealth in Ireland. It contains 300,000 persons, of whom 19 in 20 are Catholics — and it bears a marked character for industry, independence & intelligence. We held a Catholic meeting at the Clonmell Assizes[3] for that county, resolved upon a petition, formed a board of 60 Catholic gentlemen of the county, commenced a subscription, as you will see by the circular letter. I understand that Waterford, Cork, Kilkenny, Galway & Limerick will soon follow this example, & thus you will see instead of the national board, the more practicable measure of 32 county boards, who may in time elect from amongst themselves one general board. I am quite clear that there will and must be petitions, and probably early in the session. The Catholics here laugh at the idea of its being indecorous, precipitate etc to come again so soon — & they see no danger in fresh and repeated discussions.

With respect to the meeting of the Bishops, I find it is to take place here about the 10th of Sept'r. Dr Milner arrived last week at Waterford with Mr Weld Jun'r of Lulworth, & they have [sic] proceeding to Cork, where a meeting of the 7 Bishops of the province of Cashell is now holding[4] — and I learn that they come here to attend the general meeting afterwards. Certainly the proposed Veto is not relished by several clergy here — but the laity do not seem much to interest themselves about it — they would rather wish it (if the clergy can agree upon the subject) or any arrangement that would accelerate and secure their favourite object of emancipation. Not being versed in theological matters, I am quite unqualified to form any judgment upon the point likely to be disputed — but I think I can see that the opposition to this veto is not so much of a religious or solid nature in its causes, as of a political one — proceeding from the past very anti-Catholic conduct of Government, the dread & distrust of the future, the aversion felt towards several persons high in offices, and even one personage in particular[5] who has been unfortunately advised to proclaim hostility against a people otherwise inclined to love and revere him. In a word, Sir (& I have no difficulty in making the communication confidentially to you) the personage I allude to is personally unpopular in Ireland — and this feeling of alienation has sunk deeply into the hearts of the people. His health is now omitted at table, his name never mentioned, or only so with expressions very different from those of respect or affection. I could say more on this subject, but you now see enough to guess a cause, why neither the Veto nor any other amicable arrangement with the present Government will be much relished or coveted here. Let the Government retrace its steps, alter its system, repeal the odious code, prove its sincerity towards Ireland, & repair the mischiefs occasioned by past breaches of faith, and they will then acquire confidence here — not otherwise. What can more strongly mark the bad effect of their past impolicy than this, that at this moment, though England rings with noise about these transactions in Spain, & though the Irish sympathise with the patriots there, yet they will not stir or offer the least assistance because that would be for the interest of England. In like manner the enlisting & recruiting services are almost at a stand here,[6] tho' the country advances rapidly in population & wealth. I have already made this letter too long for your patience — when anything particular occurs on the Catholic subject I shall let you know, & hope you will favor me with a continuance of your valuable communications. Are the Board still active? Have they collected much? What publications are actually engaged in its interest? Do they send any circular letters? and would it be too much to send me one, to be communicated to a few Catholic friends here. I am going to Derbyshire for about a month but l[ette]rs addressed to Bagot Street will be regularly forwarded to me.   [*Source*: Throckmorton Papers]

[1]Nos. 176 and 177.
[2]One of the Catholics to whom Scully showed Butler's letters was Counsellor Finn (see No. 183 n.1).
[3]On 16 August, Count Dalton in the chair (Plowden, *History* III, p. 717).
[4]The Catholic Committee of Cork gave a dinner, attended by over 200 people. Among the thirty toasts there was one to Dr Milner "the able advocate of the Catholic cause", with others to the supporters of the cause in parliament (*DEP*, 1 September 1808).
[5] King George III.
[6]Sir Henry McAnally, *The Irish Militia*, p. 228 draws a different picture. Recruiting was going through a bad patch as men who had enlisted in 1803 became due for discharge. Nevertheless by the spring of 1808, 9000 men had been recruited to replace 8400 who had left; and despite a successful volunteering from the militia into the line which began in August the total strength of the militia stood at a higher figure on 1 February 1809 than at any period during the previous two years.

182   *From Patrick Byrne[1] to Baggot Street, Dublin*

Kilkenny, 1 September 1808

Sir,
    The Catholic Committee of this Co[unt]y and City havg. met here on business the 24th of last month, I beg leave, as Secy. of that Respectable Body, to inform you that you were then, Sir, unanimously Elected a member of said Committee and that in consequence of their requesting their

Chairman, Major Bryan, to call a Genl. meeting of the Catholics of this County & City to consider the Expediency of Petitioning the King and both Houses of Parliamt. for a total repeal of the Penal Laws etc. he has appointed the 24th of this month for holding sd. Meeting at the Tholsel in this City. The Committee have likewise appointed the seventh of this month to meet at sd place to prepare the heads of sd. Petitions etc. so as to have matters ready to submit to the considn. etc. of the Genl. Meeting on 24th Inst.

[*Source*: Scully Papers]

[1]Of Walkin Street, Kilkenny.

183   *From Patrick Byrne*

[Kilkenny] 12 September 1808

Dr. Sir,

By desire at Coun. Finn[1] I return you this,[2] & from the want of a frank take this opportunity of letting you know, *Our*[3] Catholic Committee are to meet at the Tholsel here next Sunday the 18th inst. for the purpose of preparing the form of Petitions they intend sendg. to the King & both houses of Parliamt. next Sessns., to be ready to lay before the Genl. meetg. to be on 24th inst.[4] and as you are a member of our Committee, Major Bryan & the rest of the members thereof will be much obliged to you for yr. assistance on that occasion. If inconvent. to you to attend phaps you'd be good enough to send some precedent[5] for them.   [*Source*: Scully Papers]

[1]William F. Finn.
[2]Charles Butler's letter No. 176, on the back of which the present letter was written.
[3]The underlining of the word implies the existence of another Catholic Committee, probably one of Catholics supporting the Prelates who were prepared to endorse Dr Milner's veto formula at the synod due to meet on 14 September in Dublin. For the clash between the two parties at Kilkenny after the synod see Plowden, *History* III, p. 698.
[4]Adjourned to 15 October (*DEP*, 29 September 1808).
[5]No doubt the text of another county's petition.

184   *From Charles Butler*

Lincolns Inn, 16 September 1808

Dear Sir,

I send you the letter I mentioned to you, and as much of the debates as is printed off.[1] I am very sorry your short stay in London prevents our having the pleasure of seeing you.   [*Source*: Scully Papers]

[1]As Parliament had been prorogued on 8 July the debates referred to are probably those on the petition of the Irish Catholics presented in May (see No. 177 n.4).

185   *From Dr John Milner to c/o Vin Eyre, Sheffield, England*

Hotel, 95 Capel Street, Dublin, 17 September [1808]

Dr Sir,

I congratulate with yr.self & Mrs Scully on yr. happy union,[1] & pray the giver of all good gifts to bestow his blessing upon it. Amidst the violent persecutions which I am doomed to suffer in this country one has been from the young Ladies who complain of my having slighted them, in the recommendation which I am understood to have given of a fair country-woman of my own.[2] I have reminded them, however of Lady Shrewsbury's country[3] & have told them that Mrs Scully has brothers unmarried.[4] I am infinitely obliged to you for yr. long, & interesting Memoire which I took up in Bagot St. Be assured it shall never be seen by any other eye but my own & never shall be mentioned or alluded to by me.

The ferment amongst Irish Caths. was never greater than at present. I am held up, in the *Evening Herald*, as the traitor of my religion & am threatened with being burnt in effigie. The writer of this threat is understood to be the pious Mr Comerford.[5] On the other hand, I have much favour among the gentry, Nobility etc. God forbid, however, that I shd. have gained this by any the least sacrifice of my religion. But the violent men of the day do not & will not understand the temperament which I propose. The Prelates, as you will suppose, have been intimidated.[6] They have resolved that "it is inexpedient to make any change — that they will present none but men of unimpeachable loyalty — that Dr Milner be thanked & requested to resume his agency." These resolutions[7] have worked up the nobility, gentry etc. to a degree of fury. They are about holding meetings, making protests etc. — So you see what a scene you are about to enter upon. It is now fixed that we[8] are to sail on Sunday night the 25th inst; so that if you arrive on the 24th, as Mrs Whelan[9] leads me to expect, I shall still have an opportunity of paying my Compts. to you & Mrs S.[10] I write in the greatest hurry etc. etc.

[*Source*: Scully Papers]

[1]Scully married Catherine Eyre on 8 September 1808 at Sheffield. Shortly afterwards he took her to a family dinner with Mrs Bostock, who found in her a likeness to her niece (Scully's first wife), although she was not so genteel or accomplished and was awkward in company despite a good education at New Hall (Huddleston Papers C3/MH28).
[2]If Dr Milner found Scully his wife he did not have to look far: Catherine Eyre's aunt, Mrs Wheble, was a boarder in the house where he himself resided (Husenbeth, *Life*, p. 117).
[3]She had been Elizabeth Hoey, daughter of a Dublin printer.

[4]She had three elder and two younger brothers. The eldest, Vincent Henry, also married in 1808. Of the others one died unmarried and two were unmarried at the time of this letter.

[5]Identified by Dr Milner in No. 198 as the author of a series of articles in the *Evening Herald* who signed himself Laicus. He was probably Richard Esmonde Comerford, son of Adam Comerford, Waterford, educated at St Paul's College, Louvain, and called to the Irish bar in 1803. By the time of this letter two articles had appeared. The first, of 2 September, argued that as a Prelate himself Dr Milner could not be looked upon as a mere agent of the Irish Bishops. The second, of 12 September, commented on the attempt of the Dublin diocesan authorities to restrict the circulation of Dr Milner's *Letter to a parish priest*, which urged the Irish Bishops to adhere to their own resolution of 1799 allowing a negative power to the Crown. This *Letter*, dated 1 August 1808, was published by "Sarsfield" in the *Evening Herald* of 21 and 28 September.

[6]In a letter of 2 June Dr Troy had assured him that his negotiations with Grattan and Ponsonby would be sanctioned by all the Irish Prelates (Westminster Diocesan Archives). On 4 July the campaign against the "veto" had begun (see No. 177 n.2).

[7]Adopted at a synod sitting on 14 and 15 September (copy kept by Scully MS 27524), The Prelates found it "inexpedient to introduce any alteration in the canonical mode hitherto observed in the nomination of the Irish Roman Catholic Bishops"; pledged themselves to the rule hitherto followed and recommend to the Pope only persons of unimpeachable loyalty; and requested Dr Milner to continue acting as their agent at the seat of government.

[8]Himself and Mr Weld junior (see No. 181).

[9]Probably Scully's housekeeper.

[10]The meeting took place (see No. 456).

186   *From Charles Addis to Bagot Street, Dublin*

[13 N]ew Boswell Court, Lincolns Inn, 31 October 1808

Dear Sir,

I hope you will excuse my giving you so much trouble on the subject of what may be due to me for my attendance etc. etc. on the Catholic Deputies in the year 1805.[1] I would not so soon apply to you, after what passed between us when I had the pleasure of seeing you in London, but from some pecuniary arrangements I have lately entered into, what may appear a very trifling sum, is really a matter of moment to me. As to the amount, I will leave that entirely to yourself. If you will therefore have the kindness to make me a Remittance, I will immediately acknowledge the Receipt of it, and the different Noblemen and Gentlemen who composed the Deputation will, no doubt, on your application to them immediately reimburse you their proportions of what you may advance me. There is no other Method, that I know of, that is likely to bring this matter to a Settlement, and I am convinced it would be the most satisfactory way to the Member of the

Deputation, at least, I can answer for the Lords Fingall, Kenmare & Trimlestown. Pray favor me with an answer.   [*Source*: Scully Papers]

[1]See No. 178.

187   *To his wife Catherine*[1]

Bagot Street [Dublin] Thursday afternoon [October 1808]
My dear Catherine,

I write sooner than you expected, but I heard you say you like receiving Letters, tho' not answering them. The first day brought me to Maryborough,[2] and the next morning the Day Coach from Limerick took me up there,[3] & I reached this about 5 in the afternoon. You may suppose I am busy enough. There is already a set of very handsome brass harness put in hands for you, and will be finished by the first of November. There is also a fourpost mahogany bedstead, & 2 small ones; and I get persons to buy other things. I have also looked at Carriage horses, and think I shall get a pair soon.

Mr Burne[4] will probably give me the House in Merrion Square about the middle of next week; and, as soon as I have put a person in possession, I shall leave town — it will probably be about next Thursday — but I shall write again first. Will you find a leisure half hour to write me a Letter, and another to Julia,[5] for I should wish you to keep up your correspondence with her. Believe me to be ever, my dearest Catherine, your sincerely affect'e husband,

Denys Scully

[*Source*: Scully Papers]

[1]He had probably left her at Kilfeacle with his parents. In October James Scully recorded in his diary: "Dennis & his wife got here Friday the 14th — she seems to me to be a prudent sensible fine made young woman and will make him happy if they had a family as is very likely they will soon, she will probably be very soon made a mother". Her first son, James Vincent, was born on 13 September 1809.
[2]Now Port Laoise, in Co. Offaly, at the junction of the Cork–Cashel and Limerick roads.
[3]He means that the Limerick coach picked him up at Port Laoise.
[4]Probably the barrister John Burne.
[5]His wife's sister, Julia Eyre.

188   *From Thomas Wright & Co. to Merrion Square, Dublin*

London, 10 December 1808

Sir,

We take the liberty of mentioning that we have received a Letter from Lord Stourton of which the following is a Copy.

"I desire you would cause to be remitted Five Guineas to Mr Scully's Bank[1] in Tipperary for the use of the Catholic Board of that County."[2]

As we have no means of remitting you so small a sum we shall be obliged by your informing us in what way you would wish to have this sum disposed of, in case you have any Correspondent in London we could pay the amount to him on your furnishing us with directions to that effect.

£5.5.0   [*Source*: Scully Papers]

[1]James Scully and Son (see No. 47 n.2).
[2]For the formation of the Tipperary Board see No. 181. A brief report from Dublin Castle to the Home Office dated 23 November 1808 mentions a petition being in preparation, and a committee of fifty or sixty members with a quorum of five (HO 100/149, f.155).

189   *From Charles Butler to Merrion Square*

Lincolns Inn, 12 December 1808

Dear Sir,

I am duly favored with your last letter,[1] and I am greatly obliged to you for it. The Paper, which the Board here have secured is the *Oracle*; and Mr Perry, the Editor of the *Morning Chronicle*, has most obligingly assured us, that, on all occasions, his Paper is at our service. This he has done in so handsome a manner, that we owe it to him to encourage his Paper as much as possible.

I dined yesterday with some of our friends in Parliament, and I am authorised to say, that they intend making the most strenuous exertions in your favor. The Bishops' dissavowal of Dr Milner's offer of the Veto[2] is a wayward circumstance. There is no doubt our enemies will reproach us with it. In fact it amounts to nothing: but it is always unfortunate to stand in need of an explanation.

The circumstances of the times are certainly favorable to your application. You may be assured that the dissasters in Spain are complete.[3] The number of the Spaniards in arms, and the general zeal of the country in the cause of the Patriots were from the first, immoderately exaggerated. This was known to many but the popular feeling was so great, that it was idle to call in question the general assertion that Spain was a Nation of armed men, heroically zealous and active in the cause. The real fact is, that the Spaniards have never had 80,000 men in arms; and that the antigallican spirit was not, in any sense, so general or so strong among them as it was represented. The strange circumstances attending the expedition to Lisbon are now fully before the public eye.[4] It appears that three generals were sent in a manner obviously calculated to create jealousies among them; that our cavalry was sent to one place, our infantry to another, and our ammunition to a third. The worst part of this eventful story is that, great as our miscarriage has been we do not suffer so much by the disasters consequent to it, as by the ridicule, with which our silly proceedings have covered us in the eyes of all Europe.

You remember the celebrated simile of Junius,[5] — "the Feather which adorns the Royal Bird, supports him in his flight; strip him of his plumage, you fix him to the ground." How beautifully does this express that eternal truth in politics, that the Glory of a Nation is an essential part of her strength! But how much of her Glory has England lost, by the last measures of Administration? Now, *that* Administration which is so hostile to your cause, is the very administration, under which these disasters have happened. It is impossible that this should not lower the Ministerial Phalanx and all their Plans and Projects in the opinion of the Nation: — *"and yet a little while"*,[6] and the wonderful Man, who has shaken all Nations from the Seine to the Volga, will be at Ferrol,[7] at Lisbon, in every other place from which the waves can roll the dreadful visitations with which he threatens us. Will not this stun the anticatholic Divan into a recognition of the good sense and wisdom of acknowledging your claim? We know the loyalty of the Irish — like Milo you will say of your English Friends *Sint felices, sint incolumes, sint beati! Stet haec urbs praeclara, quo cunque modo de me merita sit*[8] — and every good man will encourage these honorable, these magnanimous feelings. But will it be thought wise or prudent or generous to calculate on their eternal permanency? If the Nation were involved to the highest power of exertion to which human nature can be raised, it would scarcely be of sufficient force to resist the attack with which it is threatened. Will it not then be staring madness to oppose to it a single negative to lower its powers? Believe me, these observations now occur more or less to every one. Changes are talked of; — changes probably will take place; and, if there be truth in professions, the opposition will not come into Office, without the promise of your complete, unequivocal, and unqualified emancipation. They avow a determined resolution to bring forward and to advocate your cause. But how much must their exertions be paralysed if you are inactive, if you don't petition, if you don't address, don't remonstrate, don't use every other constitutional and loyal mode of conveying your sentiments, to the Legislature or the Throne. Pray, and it will be granted; — when it is wrong to refuse the prayer, a Petition of favor becomes a Petition of right. Let me hear from you soon.   [*Source*: Scully Papers]

[1]No. 181.
[2]See No. 185 n.7.
[3]News had reached London of the defeat of the army of Castanos, as well as reports from Paris that the French had entered Madrid (*The Times*, 12 December 1808).
[4]Despite Wellesley's victory at Vimeiro outside Lisbon on 21 August a convention had been signed at Cintra on 31 August whereby the French were not only allowed to leave Portugal but conveyed to La Rochelle in British ships. There had been an outcry in England and a court of enquiry had been set up on 28 October (Aspinall; *Later Correspondence of George III*, Vol. IV, pp. 119, 143).
[5]*Letters of Junius*, No. 42 of 30 November 1771.
[6]Seemingly an echo of *John* 16.17.
[7]The port of El Ferrol at the north-west tip of the Iberian peninsula.
[8]A modified citation from Cicero, *Pro Milone* 34, 93: "Let them be prosperous and safe, let them be happy. Let this glorious city stand firm, however she may have treated me".

190   *To his wife Catherine at Kilfeacle*

[Bagot Street] Dublin, Tuesday night [December 1808]
I have been out all day upon business of one kind or other, and upon returning I receive my sweet Catherine's most agreeable Letter, but it is too late to send an answer by this day's post. You may believe it is my chief employment to hasten the hour of our meeting again — but I date still from Bagot Street. Mr Burne[1] has met with delays, and cannot lease his House till Saturday next. However I am throwing as much Furniture into it as I can find useful — and also removing my Books & your Clothes — or at least so much as will leave but little for the servants to remove after I leave this, which will be on Friday next. Will you send Will'm[2] to meet me with the Bay horse at Mr Will'm Murphy's *in Cashell* on *Saturday next at 12 at noon* — and I shall be there from Durrow[3] —or any other conveyance will answer.

The Servants are to leave this House for Mr Burne's next Monday. I am truly gratified that my beloved Catherine is so comfortable at Kilfeacle, and am certain you possess, as you deserve, the esteem and affection of all my family. Whatever pleases you, must certainly make me happy and it shall always be my wish and study to lessen as much as possible your natural regret at leaving your friends and home for my sake. Believe me to be, my ever dearest Catherine, your sincerely affectionate husband,

                                                        D. Scully
[P.S.] No letter for you.   [*Source*: Scully Papers]

[1]See No. 187 n.4.
[2]William Fitzpatrick, his coachman.
[3]Near Tullamore, in Offaly.

191   *From Charles Butler to Merrion Square, Dublin*

Lincoln's Inn, 23 December 1808

Dear Sir,

I hope you have received my letter of the 12th instant. I am anxious to hear what is doing in the business to which it relates. I now mean to trouble you on a very different subject.

By an order made by Lord Redesdale on the 17th June 1806[1] no lands are to be put up to sale by any Master of the Court, till the title is approved of by Counsel, and until the title Deeds, and other documents necessary to make out such title, shall have been deposited with the Master. . . . It is very evident that the Deeds cannot be sent over from England to Ireland without danger. . . . With great deference to Lord Redesdale, I should have thought attested copies should have sufficed in all cases, as it is a strong thing to make Mortgagees part with their Deeds. This would be doubly hard in the case of English Mortgagees, for the reasons I have suggested. I have the honour to be known to Lord Manners,[2] and if you please you may mention to him that the suggestion originates with me.   [*Source*: Scully Papers]

[1]Butler must have made a mistake about the date as one of the first acts of the incoming Grenville administration was to dismiss Lord Redesdale from the Chancellorship and he sat in court for the last time on 4 March 1806 (*DEP*, 6 March 1806).
[2]The Lord Chancellor, who had replaced George Ponsonby on the resignation of the Grenville administration in March 1807.

192   *To his wife Catherine*

Kilfeacle [Co. Tipperary] Wednesday morning 4 January [1809]

My dearest Catherine,

I wrote to you on Monday, and only write now for the pleasure of doing so, as indeed I have nothing particular to say. Since I came here, I ride every day four or five hours, and also walk some time, and already the benefit of the Country air & exercise makes some compensation for the trouble of the journey, and (if possible) for the pain of this separation from my beloved Catherine. I was yesterday in Tipperary & saw Mrs James[1] — she is very large & expects her *accouchement* soon. Mrs Mun[2] is also in a family way. In short they all seem well, & more or less promising. We expect by this morning's post to hear of Jer's having been married on Monday[3] — and all the particulars. It is said he & his wife are to be down here in a week. I hope it may be before I leave this, which I intend to do about Thursday the 11th Inst.[4] Believe me ever my dearest love, very sincerely

Your most affectionate husband, D. Scully

[P.S.] Since writing, the Post is come in, and *no Letter*. I expected one from my Catherine, and her silence at least promises me that she had no *bad news* to write — adieu.   [*Source*: Scully Papers]

[1]Wife of his brother James — a son, Roger William, was born on 10 January.
[2]Wife of his brother Edmund — a daughter born on 15 January died on 5 December.
[3]His brother Jeremiah, who married Alicia, daughter of Francis Arthur — according to his father's diary on Wednesday 4 January.
[4]Scully's prolonged stay at Kilfeacle was probably connected with a meeting of some four hundred Catholics in Tipperary town on 7 January. This approved of a petition to parliament for which five hundred signatures had already been obtained (Francis Magan to Lord Grenville 11 January 1809: *Dropmore Papers* IX).

193   *To his wife Catherine at No. 2 Merrion Square, South, Dublin*

Kilfeacle, Thursday [5 January 1809] [postmarked 10 January 1809] I have just received my beloved Catherine's excellent Letter, and am highly satisfied with your account of what is going on in the House. As to Sheridan,[1] I believe you had better drop him, & call in your Carriage upon McCreery[2] & also upon Norton in High Street,[3] & pick out the handsomest you can. If not there, take one from Briscoe[4] or from Richardson[5] in Grafton Street, though a little dearer — and whatever you buy, will be sure to please me. As to the Fan light, the man's name is Poole,[6] he lives at No. 12 or 13 Great Strand Street. Now, if you have not yet seen him, will you either send for him or call upon him, and, if he has the work actually in hands, bid him go on & finish it — but, if he has *done nothing* to the fanlight part, then tell him to wait till I return — for I mean to look out for a better workman. But, my love, I beg of all things you will not hurry yourself — there is plenty of time for what we have to do — and I would not on any account that you should run the least risk. I hope your sore throat is better. Nitre Lozenges are the best you can take, one at a time to melt in your mouth — they are sold at Callwell's, 41 College Green,[7] & at Ball's, No. 79 Dame Street,[8] in little boxes, & I am sure will cure you.

I am glad you dine today at Mr Maher's.[9] It will be some variety to you, and yet quiet enough I believe. You will let me know what you hear about Jer's marriage[10] & the Company etc. Also when they expect to come down to this Country. I am glad you were not to go to Arthur's[11] Evening party — and this for many reasons — About this day week I mean to leave this, & to be on Friday with you. You will write on *Monday* next to me, & by that time you will know something more about how *Mrs C. Eyre*[12] *is* — for I long to know every particular about a Lady I like so much, & so good & deserving. *Don't write after Monday.* Your ever true & affectionate husband D. Scully [P.S.] Saturday morning — I am made quite unhappy by Peggy's[13] Letter, just rec'd — and long to be with you — to nurse and take every care of you. It was my intention to go next Thursday — but now I shall go next Monday, so as to be with you on Tuesday Evening. I would go this day, but my father had settled to go with me half way & cannot go at the very soonest before Monday. It is on a matter of very great Importance — but, if I were permitted, I would not let any business whatever stand against my flying to my dearest wife — my beloved Catherine, my heart & thoughts are with you and my alarms bind me more to you than ever, for I now feel how dear you are to me. It will be ages till I see you on Tuesday — Your ever affectionate D.S.

[P.P.S.] My Mother & Mrs Mahon[14] have just given me a little comfort for they say a Bowel Complaint is quite common to Ladies in a family way & not at all dangerous — it always prevents a miscarriage, & goes off in a few days. This is what they say, but it does not satisfy me, tho' Mrs Mahon says she had it often herself upon similar occasions. Adieu.   [*Source*: Scully Papers]

[1]Probably Sheridan & Son, Carpet Warehouse, 12 Capel Street.

[2]Possibly Mary McCreery, Carpet and Blanket Draper.

[3]John Norton, Sheriff's Peer and Woollen Draper, described in the 1809 directory as "in the country", previously at 3 High Street.

[4]Probably James Briscoe, Wholesale Woollen Draper, 3 Upper Bridge Street.

[5]Richardson, Nolan & Co., Woollen Drapers, 108 Grafton Street.

[6]Possibly Samuel Poole, Painter and Glazier, although at 98 Bride Street in the 1809 directory.

[7]Callwell's of 35 College Green, stationers and agent for the lottery, also advertised themselves as vendors of "genuine patent medicines", among which were pectoral lozenges (*DEP*, 22 September 1808).

[8]Unidentified.

[9]Probably his first cousin once removed, Nicholas Maher.

[10]The marriage of his brother Jeremiah (see No. 192).

[11]Probably Francis Arthur, father of Jeremiah's bride. He was arrested in 1798 and although the charge against him was dismissed as false he found it advisable to retire to England. He died there in 1824 (NLI MS.5006; John Begley, *The Diocese of Limerick*, Dublin, 1906).

[12]Catherine Eyre, his mother-in-law.

[13]Probably a housekeeper.

[14]His sister Anne or Nancy.

194   *From Bishop Milner to 2 Merrion Square South,*
                                Dublin

Wolverhampton, 15 January 1809

Dr Sir,

If you give me credit for being an honest man, do believe me when I tell you that till the present I have never found a vacant half hour since the rect. of yrs. of the 26th of Oct. to acknowledge the rect. of it. My time has been totally taken up with travelling & writing for the press, with the exception of my religious duties, some little care of my body & the answering of a few letters which I cd. not avoid answering. The picture you draw of yr. domestic happiness is highly pleasing to Mrs Wheble as well as myself, & I earnestly pray God that it may long continue. The advice you gave me by letter in Septr. was certainly good advice, in my own regard: but foresaw that if I declared myself a *mere agent*, which, however, was *strictly the truth*, the bishops & some of them in particular wd. have suffered all that obloquy which is now heaped upon me.[1] One of my correspondents, a bookseller writes that the "people are changed from adoring love to cursing hatred" in my regard: and yet never was a people more completely deceived than they are. — I long ago foresaw that this business in some shape or other wd. come on; & I prepared myself to oppose it with all my might. I believe few modern divines are more entitled to the character of a High Church man than I am. The business, however, was to know how yr. Prelates were disposed, I consulted them when at Maynooth in 1807.[2] The [y] said they cd. not yield a positive power, but wd. agree, not to choose any person obnoxious to government. Accordingly, when interrogated last May by our friends in London, I answered that *I had reason to believe* the Bps. were disposed in this manner. — I took care however, to throw in check upon check[3] to prevent this negative from being abused, & wrote earnestly to the Bps. to convince them of the necessity of them. This part of the business is all that belongs to me. — The Prelates decided, & I have neither by action, word, thought or even by my looks found fault with their decision. — But our Parliamentary friends were accused by the Ministers with telling a downright lie about their conferences with me, & the latter ignorantly cited my words against allowing the King any power over our Church, in proof of the accusation. — Justice required that I shd. state that there had been conferences. — But my chief Political friends had nearly if not quite quarrelled with me,[4] because they thought me punctillious & vexatious with my checks: again many of the Caths. were convinced that I had really surrendered our Church up to the Regal Supremacy; while many great folks of both communions stifly & publicly maintained (as Dr Ryan does in his

Strictures[5] on my Tour lately published) that I was the person who determined the Bps. to reject the *Veto*[6] & that I went over to Ireland for that purpose. — This jumble of things cd. only be set to rights by an explanation to the English public. I was repeatedly called upon to do it. My Letter in the *Morning Chronicle*[7] has completely answered all those purposes, & has moreover mitigated the indignation of our Parliamentary friends,[8] who threatened vengeance against the Bps. & intreated me not to unite my cause with theirs. So matters stand here: but the Irish fancying that my Explanations upon the Veto can have no other object than to recommend its adoption are incensed to "cursing hatred" against me.[9] To be brief, I have found it necessary to draw up an *Appeal to the Caths. of Ireland*,[10] the copy of which I have sent to Mr Fitzpatrick with directs. to send a printed copy to you. — If you found no objection in calling upon him & making any verbal alterations you might think proper, without retarding the publication you will confer a favour upon me. — I am in the greatest hurry of preparation for a journey to London, where my address till about Feb. 10 will be at Keatings, 38 Duke Street, Grosvr. Square. I hope that yr. discernment & experience will be able to throw some light on this cloudy business, particularly after you shall have seen my pamphlet. I trust it will give satisfaction to every one except to the anonymous writers in the *Herald*, one of the most abusive of whom under the name of *Detector*[11] is said to be a distinguished clergyman of my acquaintance. Is he a Superior of Maynooth, or is he Prelate? Mrs Wheble presents her kind love, as I do my best Compts. to Mrs Scully. I shall thank you to send the few lines underneath to Mr Fitzpatrick. They may be sent in an anonymous letter if you do not choose to make yrself known. [Note to Fitzpatrick cut off.]

[*Source*: Scully Papers]

[1] For authorising Grattan, Ponsonby and Grenville to propose the negative veto in May 1808 (see No. 168 n.3).

[2] At the end of June in that year — reported in his *First Tour*.

[3] Whatever he may have said orally there is no mention of checks in anything he put in writing at the time. The memorandum which he sent to Ponsonby the day before the debate in the House of Commons was read out by the latter two years later (*Hansard* XVII, 217) and Dr Milner, replying in *The Statesman* of 2 June 1810, did not deny its authenticity. On the morning of the debate in the House of Lords he saw Lord Grenville and gave him a similar memorandum in which he repeated his formula with the addition only of the words "to a reasonable number of times" (*Dropmore Papers* IX). While he expressed concern over the inferences that had been drawn from the statements in the House of Commons he wrote a note on the day after the debate in the House of Lords saying that Lord Grenville had given a very accurate account of his ideas (Ward, *Eve of Catholic Emancipation* I, p. 64).

[4] The grievance of Dr Milner's political friends was not so much his qualifying what he had said as his unwillingness to confirm publicly and unequivocally that he had ever said it, to the extent even of seeming to disavow it. In a letter to his Irish publisher Coyne which found its way into Waterford and Cork newspapers and was reprinted

by the *Morning Chronicle* of 17 October 1808 he said he would sooner lose the last drop of his blood than be instrument to a non-Catholic king's obtaining *any* power or influence over any part of the Church. Ponsonby, who read the letter when he was in Ireland, told Sir John Newport: "it becomes impossible for me to preserve any measure with him, for I cannot allow him to represent me as uttering deliberate falsehoods in the House of Commons (Newport to Lord Grenville 20 October 1808: *Dropmore Papers* IX). When Dr Milner called at Stowe on 9 November the Marquis of Buckingham found him "very heartily sorry for the publication . . . of that very improper letter . . ." (ibid., 10 November 1808).

[5]*Strictures on Dr Milner's tour, and on Mr Clinch's Enquiry*. . . . by Edward Ryan DD, Dublin 1809.

[6]In his *Appeal* (see n.10) he points out that the word Veto had never occurred in his communications with his parliamentary friends or the Bishops; while he did not consider his own proposal as having constituted a veto he would follow his adversaries in adopting the expression.

[7]It occupied nearly a whole page in the *Morning Chronicle* of 19 November 1808: text given by Ward, *Eve of Catholic Emancipation* I, Appendix B.

[8]While expressing some qualifications in regard to the background Dr Milner had at last confirmed what he said in May 1808 and showed that "our Parliamentary friends were warranted in the declarations which they made".

[9]According to the coadjutor Bishop of Ferns, a letter from whom postmarked 17 December 1808 is reproduced by Bishop Ward (*Eve* I, p. 244), Dr Troy and Dr Moylan gave an assurance at the synod in September that Dr Milner would not in future either write or speak in public in favour of the veto. His letter in the *Morning Chronicle* was regarded as reopening the question because, despite cautionary phrases, it had gone on to restate the proposal for a negative power in a way that seemed to allow the rejection of six candidates, and to emphasise that the word "inexpedient" in the resolutions of the Irish Bishops applied only to existing circumstances.

[10]Published by Fitzpatrick, Dublin, and dated 9 January 1809, with two postscripts dealing with five pamphlets recently received by him. He gives a list of his literary foes and protests at their use of pseudonyms; while still defending the negative veto he points to his opposition over twenty years to any encroachment of the civil power and claims that up to the sitting of the synod he made it his business "to enforce . . . the necessity of those checks or restraints upon the regal interference"; he confesses to his egregious error in failing to understand that the Irish would regard the veto as undermining "the only undestroyed monument of your national grandeur"; defends his letter in the *Morning Chronicle* which had not been regarded in England as a perseverance in a measure which had been decided against; and concludes by affirming that if the Prelates find the measure inexpedient he, Dr Milner, finds it inexpedient.

[11]Identified in No. 198 as Clinch.

195   *From Charles Butler to Merrion Square*

Lincolns Inn, 26 January 1809

Dear Sir,

I am always sorry when a long time passes without my hearing from you, especially as it leads me to think nothing is going on in the catholic concerns. That not to advance is to recede is a truth applicable to all business, it is particularly applicable to the momentous object in which the Irish Roman Catholics are now engaged. Your opponents are active; they have identified their political existence with your bondage, they know that your depression and their pomp and pride must have the same term, and that, when the Roman Catholic rises to a level with his fellow subjects, they must cease to govern, and must fall into the common mass. How jealous must they therefore be of your exertions to emancipate yourselves, especially in the present awful moment, when the dissastrous issue of all their measures[1] affects so greatly the public mind, and leaves them no resource against the indignation either of their master or of their fellow subjects but the Incantation of "No Popery". It is not, however, *their* strength, but *your* want of exertion that will continue your servitude. It is generally understood that a measure is in contemplation to exchange the two militias.[2] Thus do we imitate Buonaparte whom we so much revile! He sent the Spaniards to the extreme north of Germany, and pushed his own troops into Spain, before he began his final operation for the annihilation of the Spaniards. Is this to pass without petition, without remonstrance, without an urgent application for a most explicit enactment that your countrymen when they arrive in this country are to be allowed the full exercise of their religion, etc. that those laws which subject them to military floggins and even to be shot for hearing mass contrary to orders, should be repealed. I was in hopes the summer would not have passed without some regular communications being opened between the Irish and English Catholics; and some regular plan's being devised, for bringing your claims again and again before the public. We are all anxious to see your application again on foot. Pray — for your prayers *must* be heard.

[Source: Scully Papers]

[1]He may have had particularly in mind the retreat of the British army from Spain, which had culminated in the death of Sir John Moore at Corunna on 16 January.
[2]The interchange of the militias was regarded as a natural consequence of the Union and had been favoured by Sir Arthur Wellesley in 1807 when he was Chief Secretary, but it was unpopular with many English officers and the King was prejudiced against it (McAnally, *The Irish Militia*, p. 242). It was not carried into effect until 1811 (see No. 316 n.6).

196   *From Charles Butler to Merrion Square*

Lincolns Inn, 4 February 1809

Dear Sir,

I believe you will think me a very troublesome correspondent. I am now induced to write to you; in consequence of a letter I have this moment received from Ireland[1] intimating that a considerable portion of the Roman Catholics there, are averse from a communication with the English Catholics, on account of former overtures for that purpose having been disregarded or at least received with coolness.

I was much surprised at receiving this information, as I can confidently assure you, that there never has been the least disinclination on the part of the English Catholics to co-operate with the Irish Catholics, or to exert themselves in their cause, by every means in their power. Individually I can say that nothing would give me greater pleasure than being instrumental in promoting their emancipation by any means within my slender powers. I have frequently intimated to you and others my wish for cooperation and mutual communication, and I am very sure that all the Roman Catholics of this country feel on the subject as I do.

At the same time, the Roman Catholics here are fearful of acting without knowing it to be the wish of the Irish Catholics. It is obvious that the strength of your cause lies in the great majority of your members. You know, that the wretched answer given to this by the ministerial Pamphletteers is, that the proportion must be referred to the whole body of the united empire, as it is called, and not to your nation. It has been thought by some, that the English Catholics, by coacervating with you, might give colour to the argument. In my own opinion there is not the least ground of apprehension on this account. At all events I can repeat my strongest assurances both for myself and for every Roman Catholic with whom I am acquainted, that it is their most earnest wish to further the object of your application. They wish this to be generally known and I have no objection to be cited for it. Again I must repeat my individual ardent wishes of being instrumental in furthering your object, and I can also say that nothing but my uncertainty of its being agreeable to the Irish Catholics and my doubt of the exact ground they wish to be taken, has prevented my appearing in print upon the subject.

With respect to the Veto, I beg leave to assure you the English Catholics took no part in it, and I believe that one and all of them were ignorant of it till it was mentioned in parliament. I never heard of it till it was proposed in the house of Lords by Lord Grenville.[2] It is an unlucky business, but only so far unlucky, as it wants more explanation than persons in general are willing to listen to. It was a most silly thing to propose it without a certainty that it would be acquiesced in. After all, the short state of the fact is, that this wonderful veto was proposed without the consent of the body, that the body when they heard of it disclaimed it, and thus, (to use one of Dr Johnson's expressions) there's the end on't. It seems to have given as much offence to the English as to the Irish Catholics.

I am sorry no petition is yet come over; but I hope it will soon come.[3] Lord Henry Petty appears to me to be rising to great popularity; and I know Lord Ormonde to be decided and warm for your emancipation.

Would it not be prudent [about two words missing, paper torn] formal intercourse with them upon [paper torn]

May I beg of you to acquaint me which Irish newspaper or monthly publication contains most Roman Catholic information; and if it can be done to direct the proprietor of it to send it me regularly, and let me know how I am to pay him for it.[4]   [*Source*: Scully Papers]

[1]Probably from James Boyle, a visitor to Dublin, to whom Butler had written on 20 and 24 January asking him to ascertain who the acting men were among the Catholics and urging petitioning (Letter Book: Add. MSS.25, 127).
[2]On 27 May 1808 (see No. 168 n.3).
[3]An informal meeting of some thirty leading Catholics was held at the Cock Tavern in Henrietta Street on 4 February, but the people were reported to be hostile to petitioning and no decision was reached (*DEP*, 9 & 14 February 1809).
[4]In Butler's Letter Book the last paragraph of this letter is in Butler's own hand.

197   *From Joseph Shee to Merion [sic] Square South, Dublin*

London, 10 February 1809

My dear Scully,

After perusing the accompanying Papers[1] I am sure you will excuse the Informality of the mode in which I ask your professional Assistance, & to the Information which they afford I have only one fact to add, viz. that my brother & myself[2] are jointly & severally empowered in the fullest manner to act for Mrs Manuela Gaytè alias Merry, the widow & Executrix of the late Mr Joseph Merry of Seville who was Brother & residuary Legatee of the late Mrs Power of Waterford.[3]

The Difficulty of our Situation is that our Determination to be neither parties nor Instruments to enforce a Law enacted or to assist a suit commenced *in odium fidei*, may expose us to a future attack as unfaithful Agents to the Party whose Powers we hold, & in whose way I think no such Scruples would stand as Impediments to the acquisition of so much Property. I know that this Difficulty might be got rid of by laying the Case before the Person interested, & relinquishing any further interference leaving her to transfer her Powers to other hands, but to this there are some objections.

In the first place the Case appears to press & there is not time for a Letter to go to Spain & an answer to return & indeed no certainty that a Letter would find its way there at all, & in the next how inaccurate soever Mr McCausland's[4] construction may be of the Laws on which he relies, the Probability is that her Powers would come to Persons who would be inclined to act on his advice & thus expose her if unsuccessful to the Expences of a Suit certainly never commenced with a view to her advantage.

Now I do not apply to you thro' the medium of a Sollicitor because I do not know any one that would look upon the matter with your Eyes or mine, & I know not how to give him Instructions without either imposing more restraint than perhaps I could hereafter answer, or allowing more latitude than I think would be prudent at present. What I therefore request of you is to consider the matter & have such Instructions as you think proper given to a Sollicitor, by whom a brief or Case may be formally laid before you. Mr Henry Nixon, No. 11 Leeson Street is the Law Agent we employ — & I leave it to your discretion to avail either of his Services or those of any other you may deem more eligible.

You'll observe that our object is on the one hand to avoid being the Instruments of impugning the bequests of the testatrix for the reason I have already given, & on the other hand if the residuary Legatee has any legal rights not to forfeit them thro' our noninterference thus called upon, but leave her the Opportunity to avail of them if she chuses.

You will best judge how far the mode pointed out by Dr Power may atchieve these objects,[5] but besides the risk of having collusion hereafter imputed to us if we act in Concert with the exors, I think it might embarrass them very much as Trustees to be yoked with Mrs Merry or any of her sons, she totally unlettered & untaught & they not much superior to her, & if intended to preserve their rights, they perhaps would conceive them but imperfectly protected, if when they should find themselves some ten years hence perhaps entitled by law to call for the Money with accumulated Interest, they are offer'd the House which the will order'd to be built, in part payment thereof.

I am sure I run no risk in confiding Dr Power's Sentiments to your discretion; I send him a Copy of this Letter, & I need not assure him that you will pay all due attention to any Communication from him.[6]

I was very sorry to be out of the way when you last called on me & I take this Opportunity to offer my late but sincere Congratulations on the Event[7] which I suppose you came to announce & to request you will present Compliments from me & mine to Mrs Scully, whom I hope we shall have the Pleasure of seeing whèn you & she visit London.

I was at Brighton when Heffernan[8] deliver'd your Letter & for a month afterwards so that I never saw him & if I had seen could have been of little or no Service to him, tho' I should have had much pleasure in helping any one recommended by you or your father to whom I beg to be kindly remembered.[9]

[P.S.] The Papers which accompany this are —
Copies of: Mrs Power's Will; Mr McCausland's Letter to me dated 17 December 1808; my answer dated 21 December 1808; Mr McCausland's 2nd Letter dated 30 January 1809; my answer dated 9 February 1809; Dr Power's Letter to me dated 27 December 1808.   [*Source*: Scully Papers]

[1]Listed in the postcript. From them and from the summary of *Attorney-General v. Power* in *Reports of Cases in the High Court of Chancery* by Thomas Ball and Francis Beatty, Dublin, 1821, it appears that Mary Merry, widow of Robert Power, a Waterford merchant, died after making a will dated 25 May 1804 in which she appointed her brother Joseph as residuary legatee (or his children if he was not living). Her main bequest was a sum of £9332 in trust to the Archbishop of Cashel and the Bishop of Waterford and their successors for ever, to be spent on (1) clothing for poor children at the (Presentation) nunnery school in Hennessy's Road; (2) the purchase of a building to accommodate twelve reduced gentlewomen; and (3) the support and education of poor boys to be nominated by the trustees. On 14 May the Commissioners of Charitable Donations and Bequests challenged the legality of some of these provisions and after an exchange of correspondence with Dr Power, the Bishop of Waterford, there was a preliminary hearing in the Court of Chancery on 23 November 1808. The solicitor to the Board then asked Joseph Shee for the names and addresses of the residuary legatees and an exchange of letters closed with one of 9 February 1809 in which Shee said he was putting the matter in the hands of his solicitor in Dublin.

[2]Joseph and Thomas Shee, merchants of 3 Laurence Pountney Hill, London, came from Thomastown, Co. Kilkenny. Joseph's son, Sir William Shee, became the first Catholic judge in England since James II.

[3]Joseph Merry settled in Seville about 1770 and his wife, Manuela, was a daughter of a Seville merchant. He died in 1804, leaving seven children, of whom Joseph Xavier Merry was the eldest son (see "The Waterford Merrys" in the *Journal of the Waterford . . . Archaeological Society* XVI, 1913, p. 311.

[4]William James McCausland, son of John McCausland of Letterkenny and through his sister brother-in-law of W. C. Plunket, was Law Agent to the Commissioners.

[5]Dr Power had suggested that Mrs Merry might leave the adminstration ad interim to the trustees while reserving to herself or her assigns the right of legal investigation.

[6]On 21 April 1809 the Lord Chancellor delivered an opinion: Scully kept a copy (MS.27, 526) and it was printed by Ball and Beatty. He ruled that as the law of Ireland did not recognise any corporate character in Roman Catholic Bishops the trust would devolve on the court on the death of either of the trustees; that the bequest for clothing was an endowment and therefore illegal; that the purchase of a building would be void under English law but as there was no mortmain statute in Ireland he would have further enquiries made; and that the court would have to intervene if there were any religious discrimination in the education of the poor boys. In due course the residuary legatee intervened to have the will set aside on the ground that it was "unduly obtained and had for its object the disposal of a large property to papists for superstitious uses". When *Merry v. Power* came before Curran as Master of the Rolls he gave judgment against the plaintiff, arguing that the law should be interpreted in the spirit of circumstances that had changed since penal times (Curran, *Speeches* 4th edition, p. 477), but his judgment was set aside by the Court of Chancery on 15 June 1811 (*DEP*, 20 June 1811). See No. 470A for a ruling by the Lord Chancellor in 1813, to the effect that the endowment of a school would be lawful if Protestants were admitted. Whatever the eventual outcome a Ladies' Asylum on Convent Hill came into existence as a charity under the control of the Commissioners but managed by the local Superior of the Christian Brothers (*Waterford Journal* XVI).

[7]Scully's second marriage, on 8 September 1808.

[8]Perhaps delivered soon after the marriage — Burke *IFR* 1976 places Will Heffernan's death in 1808.

[9]James Scully's diary shows that Shee was at Kilfeacle in October 1809.

198   *From Bishop John Milner to 2 Merrion Square, Dublin*

Wolverhampton, 6 April 1809

My Dear Sir,

I was honoured with yr. letter of Jan. 20 whilst I was in London. Ever since my return home I have been taken up with acquitting myself of different literary engagements, & am now, for the first time since my return from Ireland a free man in this respect. My last controversy has been with some obstinate French Schismatics, (who have a strong party in England & some favourers in Ireland, as I judge by the anonymous letters I receive from your side of the water) men who being indignant at the Pope's political conduct have resolved to quarrel with him on the score of religion.[1] — With respect to my numerous Irish antagonists, they are so precipitate, so violent, & so ill-bred that I am forced to give up the contest with them & leave them the entire victory, in their own way & to whatever extent they are pleased to claim it. I have seen Mr *Laicus* Comerford's fourth Letter[2] addressed to me from the Irish Press as likewise Mr *Detector* Clinches Letters, reprinted in London, together with Bishop Coppinger's *Royal Veto*, book.[3] When I compare the private letters & conversation of the two latter persons with their printed assertions & their perseverance in publishing & republishing them with my late *Appeal*[4] before their eyes I am lost in amazement & am unable to decide whether I ought to complain of their heads or of their hearts. I am told that they have some particular object in view in thus forcing their publications upon an English public, which certainly is of itself very indifferent about them, but I am unable so much as to form a guess what this object can be. — I am so completely disgusted with the conduct of these men, & more particularly of Dr Coppinger that I have not only taken my leave of my Irish Catholic enemies, in the *Appeal*; but also of my Irish Protestant Antagonists, the Drs Ryan,[5] Elrington[6] & Ledwich[7] & Sir Rd. Musgrave,[8] each of whom has published one or more Pamphlets against the first edition of my Letters. This farewell is contained in the second edition, copies of which, I suppose are now on their way to Ireland. — I beg pardon for saying so much about myself, & I now proceed to other subjects.

You are informed, Sir, that the English Caths. are to meet on the 10th inst.[9] to form a Committee or board & to deliberate about petitioning Pt. I have been consulted on the latter subject & I have answered that it wd. be madness to talk of petitioning without the concurrence of the Irish Caths., &

that the latter (as I understand) do not mean to petition: an awful circumstance to government, as it ought to appear in my opinion![10] I have within this day or two been consulted as to the propriety of petitioning for those privileges which you enjoy & we are destitute of.[11] — I have answered that the obstacle stands against the thing itself, not against the quantum of the thing. In short *No Popery* would just as soon consent that Caths. shd. be eligible to the Chancellorship or Commandry of the Army as to their being Kings Counsellors or Aid[e]s de Camp. I fancy all our Parliamentary friends will tell the English Caths. this, & that the matter will come to nothing at present. I must not forget, however, that having been consulted about a fortnight ago by Mr Edwd. Jerningham, Secretary of the Cathc. meeting (a gentleman in manners as well as by birth, in short a very different sort of a man from his predecessor Mr Charles Butler) as to the steps proper to be taken, in order to procure the concurrence etc. of the Irish Caths., I took the liberty of referring him to you, Sir, as a person every way qualified & proper to be the correspondent & agent of the English Catholics, if you yrself. have no objection to the office; & I suppose he will recommend you to it.[12]

I take it for granted, Dr. Sir, that yr revision of my *Appeal* only extended to some certain sheets of it as there are many gross *errata* some of which Mr Comerford takes advantage of, in different parts of it. Mrs Wheble joins me in all that is kind & respectful to yrself & Mrs Scully. I hope the latter received the *Laity's Directory*[13] which I sent to her by Mr Coyne. Mrs Vinct. Eyre & her sister[14] have been here on a visit on their way to Bath. Mr Vin is now in London & I suppose will accompany his wife to Sheffield. I have the honor etc. etc.

P.S. I find that Mr Chs. Butler has published something anonymous in Ireland,[15] but whether as a pamphlet or an essay in a News paper I know not. It relates to petitioning Pt., speaks of the Veto & of myself, but not in favorable manner. I believe I can reckon up more than a dozen Pamphlets (independent of Newspaper essays) which have been printed & published against me chiefly in Ireland by Caths. or Protestants since the beginning of the present year without so much as a printed line in my defense from any pen but my own. It is time for me to withdraw. But if the Comerfords & Keelans[16] & Clinches & Coppingers boast of their victories over me, the Elringtons & Ledwiches (no contemptible adversaries) the avowed foes of Catholicity & Ireland make no such boast. They will be still further from it when they see my Second Edition.[17]   [*Source*: Scully Papers]

[1]The Abbé Blanchard and his followers (see No. 296 n.12).
[2]For the earlier letters of Laicus see No. 185 n.5. According to the *Evening Herald* of 3 March 1809 his fourth one had just been published separately by Tyrell.
[3]The book in question was *Royal Veto . . . considered in reply to the Right Reverend Dr Milner's letter to a parish priest, by an Irish Catholic clergyman, to which are added two letters on the same subject by Detector*, London, 1809. Detector (see No. 194) is

now identified as J. B. Clinch. Dr William Coppinger (1753–1830) was Bishop of Cloyne and Ross.

[4]See No. 194 n.10.

[5]Dr Edward Ryan, Prebendary of St Patrick's until his death in 1819; author of the *Strictures* referred to in No. 194 n.5.

[6]Dr Thomas Elrington (1760–1835), Professors of Divinity at Trinity College, Dublin, and its Provost from 1811 to 1820 (*DNB*).

[7]Dr Edward Ledwich (1758–1823), author of the *Antiquities of Ireland* (see DNB). Dr Milner had attacked him vigorously in his *Letters from Ireland* because his theory that Christianity reached Ireland direct from the orient tended to weaken the connexion with Rome.

[8]Whom Dr Milner identified from internal evidence as the author of *Remarks occasioned by some passages in Dr Milner's tour of Ireland*.

[9]The Board decided that it was too late to present a petition in the current session, but that one should be got ready in the autumn for 1810 (Ward, *Eve of Catholic Emancipation* I, p. 105).

[10]As it might imply resorting to unconstitutional measures.

[11]The privileges enjoyed by the Irish but denied to the English Catholics were listed by Earl Grey when he introduced the latter's petition on 22 February 1810. English Catholics could not become magistrates, take degrees at universities, vote in parliamentary elections or serve as officers in the forces, the privates of which could be compelled to attend non-Catholic religious services. The petition itself drew attention to another disability: the non-recognition of marriages performed by Catholic priests in England (*Hansard* XV, 504).

[12]See No. 204 for the decision that the correspondence should be between the secretaries of the two bodies.

[13] The *Catholic Directory*, published annually.

[14]Either the Ann Wright of No. 349 or her sister Lucy.

[15]Probably the work advertised by Coyne in the *Evening Herald* of 22 February 1809: "*An Address to the Irish Roman Catholics* by an English Roman Catholic — the editor has no hesitation in saying that the author of this address is, in point of talent, legal knowledge and political consideration, the first Catholic in England".

[16]Father James Keelan, author of the "Sarsfield" letters which started the veto controversy (see No. 185 n.5).

[17]The second edition of the *Appeal*, mentioned above as being on its way to Ireland.

199   *From Charles Addis, Lincoln's Inn, to Dublin,*
7 April 1809

A reminder of his claim[1] for services rendered to the Catholic deputies in 1805, with a suggestion that Scully should send him a bill of exchange for what he thinks reasonable and recover their shares from the other deputies.

[*Source*: Scully Papers]

[1]See No. 186.

200   *From Charles Addis to Dublin*

New Boswell Court, Lincolns Inn, 5 May 1809
Dear Sir,
I was duly favoured with your letter[1] and have spoken to Lord Kenmare on the subject of a remuneration for my services to the Catholic Deputies in the year 1805, and he thinks the Sum you have mentioned a proper compensation, and with which I beg leave to express myself perfectly satisfied. His Lordship has not, however, taken upon himself to be my paymaster, but has desired me to apply to each Individual of the Deputation for their respective proportions of the before mentioned Sum, which being divided by nine, the Number of the Deputies,[2] makes the Share of each £5.16.8 Perhaps you will have the kindness to call upon Lord French, who I understand resides in Dublin & explain this matter to him, or any other of the Deputies who may happen to be in Dublin. The favor of your answer with a remittance will oblige.[3]   [*Source*: Scully Papers]

[1] Of 23 April, missing.
[2] See No. 85 n.2. In addition to the five nominated deputies four peers had "acceded" to the deputation.
[3] Scully replied on 10 May and there being no further correspondence on the subject it is probable that Addis' account was settled.

201   *To Richard Huddleston from Dublin, 16 May 1809*

He has received £600 through Messrs. T. Wright & Co, which he has acknowledged by letter and by indorsemnt upon the two bonds.[1]

[*Source*: Huddleston Papers C3/S14]

[1] Issued in lieu of a down payment of his first wife's dowry (see No. 46).

202   *From Charles Butler to Merrion Square*

Lincolns Inn, 19 May 1809[1]
Dear Sir,
We are delighted to see you have called a meeting to consider of the propriety of petitioning.[2] I sent you, some time ago, a short address to the Roman Catholics signed Hwyls; I now send you another, and, if you approve of them, I shall be much obliged to you to have them inserted in the Dublin papers and as many provincial papers as you conveniently can.[3] I hope there

is no doubt of your petitioning. And, if you resolve on it, I hope it will be an universal petition, presented for signature to every human being; from the Lord Lieutenant to his lowest footman, and that the names of those who refuse and the reasons assigned by them for their refusal will be taken down on a separate paper. It is contrary to the standing order of the house of Commons, that one person should sign for another but those who can't write may set down their marks; and their names may be written on each side of their mark. If it be universally signed in the manner I have mentioned its effect must be irresistible. I submit that it should be first circulated where the proportion of Catholics is greatest and that, when their names are obtained, it should be moved on to the other counties. You know my opinion of the Veto. I certainly consider it as one of the most unfortunate events which have occurred to the roman catholics, within my memory. At the same time I think that it will have no more consequence than you yourselves are pleased to assign to it. I think it is desireable that it should not be mentioned in the debates on the petition. It will be time enough to think of it, when the petition is presented. I have a letter from one of your respectable prelates,[4] in which he mentions that some pledge might be given for the loyalty of the person nominated bishop. It may be desireable that something of the kind should be deviced [sic] if it were only from respect to those who expressed themselves as they did in parliament concerning the Veto but so far as respects the ensuing debate, I am sure it is prudent that the Veto should not even be ment[ione]d.

A meeting of the English board is to be held on Sunday to consider of the propriety of framing a petition. If the motion be carried, I shall move to have two bills drawn; one, to repeal the remaining laws, by one general enactment, the other, to repeal them separately, by separate enactments. This is the way in which we proceeded in 1791, and we found it of incalculable service, to have these two bills ready. I therefore beg leave to suggest the same measure to you. I shall be very much obliged to you to send me, as soon as you conveniently can, an account of what passes at the meeting,[5] and two or three copies of the first account of it which appears in any of the public papers. I need not add that you may always command me. P.S. As males may marry at 14 and females at 12, and [sic] all of that age or upwards, and as to females whether married or not, should in my humble opinion be called upon to sign the petition.   [Source: Scully Papers]

[1]Butler's Letter Book (Add. MSS.25, 127) shows that letters similar to this one were addressed to Edward Hay and M. Lynch. He had evidently received no news of the Irish Catholics since Scully replied on 26 February to No. 196, for on 6 March he asked Hay for full and speedy information, and wrote again the next day saying: "I have repeatedly written my sentiments . . . to Mr Scully. I wish you would ask him to show you my letters". On 8 April he asked John Keogh: "What occasions the present inertness of the Roman Catholics?"

[2]Following a preliminary meeting held at Dignam's Tavern in Henrietta Street on 10 May (*DEP*, 11 May 1809) fifty-seven Catholics, of whom Scully was one, had placed an announcement in the press (*DEP*, 13 May 1809) calling a meeting for 24 May, time and place being left unspecified.

[3]The letter intended for Scully was sent to Hay by mistake, the letter to whom in the DDA (390/1, XII, 3) asks him to insert the Hywlls articles in a Tipperary newspaper. Butler had received no news of their publication when he wrote to Scully on 9 October (see No. 212).

[4]Dr Moylan, the Bishop of Cork, to whom Butler had written on 1 April asking whether there was any prospect of the veto's being accepted, either in the form offered by Dr Milner or with modifications which would still allow the King a substantial power of interference. He had evidently received a reply allowing of the possibility of some pledge of loyalty, for in writing to the Bishop again on 19 May he asked him to send further particulars "when this has matured" (Letter Book, ibid.).

[5]See No. 203 n.1.

203   *From Charles Butler to Merrion Square*

Lincolns Inn, 1 June 1809

Dear Sir,

I have received this morning a full account of the Irish debate,[1] and am extremely happy to find a petition is resolved upon. I shall be extremely obliged to you to furnish me with the best documents you can to shew that promises of further benefits were held out to the Catholics at the union.

As I shall have occasion for the immediate use of them,[2] I shall be greatly obliged to you for the further information as soon as you can supply me with it.

[*Source*: Scully Papers]

[1]At an aggregate meeting in the Exhibition Room on 24 May, Lord Fingall in the chair, it was decided to have a petition ready by the first fortnight of the next session of parliament. It was to be handled by a committee consisting of the peers; the survivors of the Catholic delegation of 1793; the Dublin Catholics appointed to prepare an address to the Duke of Bedford in 1806; and members of the committees who managed the petitions of 1805 and 1807. A resolution emphasised that they were not representatives of the Catholic body or any portion thereof (*DEP*, 30 May 1809). Scully became a member as he had been on the 1805 committee and was one of the Dublin Catholics (see No. 146).

[2]Possibly in connexion with the petition of the English Catholics — Butler wrote to Sir Samuel Romilly on 26 June asking him to present it (Letter Book: Add.MSS.25, 127).

204   *From Charles Butler to Merrion Square*

Lincolns Inn, 9 June 1809

Dear Sir,

I return you many thanks for your letter of the 5th instant[1] which I have just received, and I am much obliged to you for the information contained in it, which, I make no doubt, will supply all my wants.

We came to a resolution last Sunday that our Secretary should address your Secretary a Letter expressing our attachment to your cause and offering you our services in any manner you think proper. We also came to a resolution to prepare a petition, to have it ready if it should be determined upon.

Mr Jerningham is, and always has been our Secretary, and we are very fond of him. We are to take our letter into consideration on Sunday, and it will be sent off to you on the following Monday.

I received the *Dublin Evening Post*.[2] I think the General Effect of the Debate will essentially serve you. It has been inserted in the *Oracle*[3] and will be inserted in the *Globe*. I hope my plan of getting the Petition signed by all males above 12 and females above 14 [*sic*] will be adopted.[4] I think the success of such a petition indubitable. But those to whom the circulating of it is entrusted, should have it most strongly impressed on them that one person is not allowed to sign for another; and one such signature, will, in strictness vitiate the whole petition. But any person may sign by a mark, and in that case some person should sign the christian and surname of the party on the sides of the mark. I hope it will be tendered to Protestants as well as Catholics. I see the press in Dublin is wholly in your favour. Here, the preponderance of the press is against you. I think it would be for your interest to act on the press in this country.

I desired my Letter signed Hwylls[5] to be sent to you. I hope that and the second letter meet your approbation. Do put your Shoulder to the business. *Husband well your last stake*.

P.S. I believe I took the liberty to suggest to you the propriety of having two Bills drawn, one repealing the laws against you, by one general enactment; the other, by doing it by several. We have come to this resolution in England. I am preparing the bills.   [*Source*: Scully Papers]

[1]Scully's missing reply of 5 June to No. 203 may have reported on not only the aggregate meeting of 24 May but also Hay's circular of 31 May announcing a meeting for 4 November. This referred to the Convention Act but asserted that it did not affect the undoubted right of petitioning (DDA 54/1, III, 4).

[2]Of 30 May, with the resolutions passed on 24 May.

[3]Butler wrote to Hay on 6 June: "For a sum of money we have purchased a right of inserting what we think proper in the *Oracle*. If we want to circulate anything over England we insert it in that paper and direct 200, 300 or 500 copies more than are usually taken off, to be printed. These are circulated by addressing them to some person or coffee house or Library in some of the principal towns of England" (DDA 390/1, XII, 5).

[4]A slip of Butler's clerk (see postscript to No. 202).

[5]See No. 202 n.3.

205   *From Edward Hay to Merrion Square, Dublin, 13 June 1809*

A printed letter inviting Scully to attend a meeting on 17 June to discuss the implementation of the resolutions of the late meeting.[1]

[*Source*: Scully Papers]

[1]On 24 May (see No. 203, n.1). No report has been found of the discussions of 17 June. On 19 June Hay wrote convening a meeting on 3 July of those entrusted with the petition (Minute Book I): see No. 206.

206   *From Edward Hay, Secretary, to 2 Merrion Square, Dublin,*
          6 July 1809

Transmits the resolutions of a meeting of the General Committee[1] held on 5 July 1809 whereby a Committee of peers and twenty-one gentlemen chosen by ballot[2] was appointed to carry into effect the resolutions of the late aggregate meeting[3] and to report to the General Committee on 2 October, with power in the meantime to call a meeting of the General Committee whenever necessary. Any country gentleman on the General Committee might attend the Sub-Committee. Having been chosen a member of the Sub-Committee Scully is invited to attend a meeting on 11 July to arrange the nature of future proceedings.   [*Source*: Scully Papers]

[1]A preliminary meeting on 3 July had appointed six members, of whom Scully was one, to consider a plan for a subcommittee (Minute Book I).
[2]Names given in the Minute Book.
[3]See No. 203 n.1.

207   *From Edward Hay to 3 [sic] Merrion Square, Dublin*

4 Capel Street [Dublin] 21 July 1809

Dear Sir,

At the meeting of the Subcommittee on the 19th[1] they adjourned to Saturday (tomorrow) the 22 at one o'clock P:M: where your attendance is particularly requested.   [*Source*: Scully Papers]

[1]This had been preceded by a meeting of the General Committee on the 18th, which had filled vacancies in the subcommittee and decided that five members should constitute a quorum (Minute Book I).

208   *To his wife Catherine, 2 Merrion Square South, Dublin*

Clonmell, Tuesday, 1 August [1809]

My dearest Catherine,

Just after I had put my Letter to you into this Post Office last Sunday, I had the great pleasure of receiving your affectionate & very excellent Letter of Saturday, and I cannot delay writing to express my admiration of its goodness, not merely in beautiful penmanship, but also for its good sense & neatness, natural & correct language, and in fine every quality of a good Letter. I hope you will keep yourself in practice by writing to me often, if the trouble does not distress you. With respect to the advice you ask of me how to act, I declare I do not see that you can act more properly than you have acted. No doubt the less of *tete a tetes* is afforded, the more it will *keep up* our friend,[1] and preserve respect and esteem, which are no where more in danger of sinking than just *at this stage* — and I have no wish in the matter but for her credit & benefit. I don't see any objection to your asking the whole family to a little family Dinner, or to tea, making apologies for the Dining room being occupied. This might be done still better, when your Mother comes, provided that be soon. In short, whatever you do in it will I am sure be discreet.

I hope this dry weather is not lost upon the Painters, and that they now advance fast. Is McCausland[2] doing any thing in the yard as to flagging? My Father writes to me that he will be here early on Thursday morning. All are well there. I don't find that I forgot any thing in Town, but I want, when Will'm[3] is coming, to get by him a little set of *Acts of Parliament relating to Timber & Planting*.[4] I lent mine to Lloyd,[5] and he says that he left it out to be returned to me on his leaving Town. Will you send to Mrs Lloyd for it, if she has not already sent it. It is a little Book, covered with sewn Blue Paper, not much broader than the Laity's Directory & not so thick. If on the whole it cannot be found, will you have it bought for me at Grierson's, King's Printer, corner House of Parliament Street & Dame Street, & facing the Exchange. It costs 3 or 4 shillings, & Thomas, the servant, can buy it. I hope you call upon Mrs Moore & your other visiting acquaintance all this week, and that you make it a rule to be at least a couple of hours every day under the open air. Will you write to me on Thursday, tho' ever so short. Again on Saturday directed to Kilkenny[6] — and again by William, who will leave Town early on Tuesday morning, so as to meet me there about noon on Wednesday. I take care to burn your Letters, as you desire, tho' with infinite regret for the loss — but I do it to induce you to write with the greater freedom & confidence to me. Believe me to be my dearest Catherine, most sincerely & tenderly,

Your ever affect'e husband D. Scully

[P.S.] What do you think of Lady and Miss F. upon nearer acquaintance?

[*Source*: Scully Papers]

[1]Perhaps the unidentified Lady F. of the postcript.
[2]Unidentified.
[3]William Fitzpatrick, his coachman.
[4]In a note of 1818 in his Common Place Book Scully records having planted thirty to forty thousand young trees.
[5]The barrister John Lloyd (d. 1835), son of Revd Richard Lloyd of Castle Lloyd, Limerick, and brother of the Rector of Fethard, Co. Tipperary.
[6]Where the last Assizes of the circuit were to start on 7 August.

209   *From Edward Hay to Merrion Square, Dublin,*
September 1809

As instructed by a meeting of the Sub-Committee held on 29 August he earnestly requests Scully's attendance at a meeting on 12 September to report progress and consult on the most effective means of carrying into effect the resolutions of the last meeting of the Catholics of Ireland.[1]

[*Source*: Scully Papers]

[1]In summoning this meeting Hay had drawn attention to the lack of a quorum at previous meetings. A further meeting called for 19 September had also to be abandoned (Minute Book I).

210   *From his brother-in-law Vincent Eyre*

Sheffield, 24 September 1809

Dear Bro'r,

I am only this moment returned from London & hasten to thank you for your letter & to say how sincerely I participate in your joy at the Birth of a son[1] & in the well doing of its mother. My wife has, already, expressed her congratulations in a letter to my mother.

It is awkward to let any contrary sentiment enter into a Letter of congratulation, but, I can not omit this opportunity of saying that having been informed by my sister Mary, through my Brother John, that Juliana[2] was actually married, it was with regret that we learnt (almost the next moment) that some unforeseen Objection or Impediment had interposed to prevent a match which seemed, in all points of view, so desirable.

I have just received a Letter from my Cousin Wheble[3] informing me of the Birth of a 4th Daughter.

It is reported that Miss Jane Huddlestone is to be married to Mr Canning of Foxcote. Believe me, with kind regards to all

Yours sincerely,

Vin. Eyre   [Source: Scully Papers]

[1]James Vincent Scully, born on 13 September.
[2]His sister Julia/Juliana Eyre.
[3]James Wheble.

211   *From Bishop John Milner to 2 Merrion Square, Dublin*

Wingerworth, 2 October 1809

My Dr. Sir,

I am sensible that I need a strong apology for leaving *two* of your kind & instructive letters for a long time unanswered;[1] but I conceive that I offer such an apology when I mention the obvious utility which your letters are of to me, as a sort of public man, by the important information & observations which they always convey to me. I will therefore rest my excuse on this single plea, & will say nothing of the controversies in which I have been engaged & the journeys which I have been forced to make during these six months past. At present I am among Mrs Scully's relations & friends,[2] from whom I learn, with the most lively pleasure, that she is well & that you are blessed with a son.[3] I pray God to have them both in his holy keeping.

I seem to think that the time is at last come when government is seriously disposed to grant the Emancipation:[4] but will your countrymen, in the present circumstances, accept it as a boon? Thus much I take for granted that they will not make the smallest concession to obtain it: much less will they consent to the Prelates yielding the *Veto*. However as matters of politics are of so very uncertain a nature, & as I have already burnt my fingers by meddling with them, I shall have as little to do, even with the Veto, as I possibly can. Most undoubtedly it is for the advantage of that cause to which I am solely attached, the cause of the Church, that we Prelates shd. be as independant [*sic*] of worldly statesmen as possible, & nothing but the positive declarations of some of my leading brethren on yr. side of the water, cd. have induced me to hold out the most distant expectation to our Parliamy. advocates of any concession of this nature being made: so that I am, in fact, the emissary goat[5] in all this business. However, the matter having been settled as it has been by the bishops, with the general concurrence of the laity, I hope it may not be agitated again, on either side of the water, though I greatly fear the contrary. The language of our politicians is that "the Bishops were disposed to yield; but that they were overawed by the laity; & that, therefore, it is best to legislate without consulting either one or the other." But I forsee that this attempt to settle matters will more and more disturb & confound them, & I clearly see that our best informed & best inclined friends, such as Lord Grenville, do not understand either our religious economy or our real dispositions. In one point I am & ever have been determined that our Church in both Islands must be free from political authority & influence: & in this cause I should be happy to yeild [*sic*] my life. Already have I sacrificed the favour of most of my great friends by my adherence to this principle;[6] and it is an undoubted fact that I gave equal displeasure to them by that Letter which I published in the *Morning Chronicle*, on the 23d of last Novr.,[7] as I did to yr. Dublin politicians & to some of yr. more zealous Prelates. Happily, however, that letter, which somehow or another found its way to Rome, was viewed in quite a different light by our Holy Father & his consulting Cardinals. Your partiality towards me leads you to judge that the prejudices of the Irish Caths. against me have subsided: the contrary, however, appears to me to be the case. My publishers in Dublin inform me that the second edition of my *Letters from Ireland*, will not sell there, notwithstanding it contains a much more elaborate, &, as I think, a more able defense of them from their several declared foes, than the former edition, merely on account of one note, which I have since ordered to be suppressed by the booksellers. Nay so far does this spirit of hostility proceed that the sale of one of my Pastorals against the French Schismatics[8] was suppressed in Dublin, merely because the turn of my argument led me to say that "St Gregory the Great gave St Augustine jurisdiction in Ireland, as well as in England." The fact is incontestible, from Bede & other original writers: but the Dublin Theologues most falsely asserted that I mentioned the fact for the purpose of insulting the Catholics of Ireland. If the Booksellers of Dublin, will but comply with my directions in advertising this second edition, the Protestants, from hatred, will buy up the remaining copies of it; which I hope will clear-up my accounts with the booksellers, and I shall then take my leave of the Catholics, as a writer, with wishing them a more zealous & a more disinterested advocate than I have been to them.

The news you communicate of the Presbyterians refusing the *Regium Donum* is surprising to me & must be alarming to government.[9]

With respect to the English Petition, you may be assured I am not partial to it on acct. of its author (Chs. Butler) & I think you will give me credit for not being partial to it on acct. of its argument & composition: still I do not distinctly see how it undervalues the Irish Caths. I have procured the suppression of one word in it, viz *apparent* as united with *sacrifice*: signifying, as it did, that the frequentation of the Protes[tan]t service is not *absolutely contrary to the doctrine & discipline of the Cathc. religion*. Butler grumbled, but cd. not help himself.[10] It is really surprising & incomprehensible that the man who originally delivered up the Catholics of England into the hands of *Lord Redesdale* and who has continued in habits of intimacy with him & his friends ever since that transaction, shd. be trusted & employed by them.[11] The *Report of the Debates in 1808*,[12] has lately appeared, but horribly disfigured. The publishers are understood to be leading men amongst the Caths. They have subjoined an Appendix, containing the *Resolutions of the Irish ABps & Bps in 1799*,[13] as likewise that work of deceit & heterodoxy, the origin of all our dissentions in England, *The Protestation* (falsely) said to be deposited in the British Museum.[14] Both these publications have so bad a tendency, more particularly the former, that I am inclined publicly to protest against them. I do not, indeed, think of printing on the subject, but I am disposed to deposit a written declaration in the shops of some of the English & Irish Booksellers, signifying my sentiments as intimated above. It is a fact that one of the chief causes of offence which I have given to some of our Parliamentary advocates is that I refused to publish or even to mention in my printed Letter of Nov. 23 those Resolutions of 1799.

Shd. the Cathc. question be soon again agitated, I expect that Mr Ponsonby will endeavour to exculpate himself at my expense,[15] but I have already given him to understand that I shall defend myself on that subject with all my force, let the consequence, be what it may. I ordered a copy of my Pastoral against the French Schismatics, called *The Supplement*,[16] to be sent to you: I am sensible, Dr. Sir, of yr. kindness in the repeated invitations you have honoured me with to yr. house in Dublin, & I shd. be happy to avail myself of them (with the greatest privacy & without embarking in any business political or religious) but the necessity I am under of redoubling my industry & labours in visiting my Dis[tric]t in consequence of my former visits to Ireland precludes the possibility of my seeing Dublin for some time to come. I beg my kind & respectful Compts. to Mrs Scully, Mrs Eyre[17] & Mr Ths. Eyre,[18] in which all their & yr. friends in these parts join to yrself & to her.   [*Source*: Scully Papers]

[1]Scully minuted on No. 198 that he wrote on 23 April and 4 September 1809.

[2]Wingerworth, south of Sheffield in Derbyshire, was the seat of Sir Thomas Windsor Hunloke, 5th baronet.

[3]James Vincent Scully, born 13 September 1809.

[4]Perceval had invited Lord Grenville and Earl Grey to discuss with him the formation of an extended administration, which might have been more favourable to the Catholics. Dr Milner would not have heard of their refusal to negotiate, published on the day of his letter (*Morning Chronicle*, 2 October 1809).

[5]A literal translation of the French for scapegoat.

[6]Apparently a reference to his letter to Coyne (see No. 194 n.4).

[7]*Recte* 19 November: the 23rd was the date of its republication in *The Oracle*. If Dr Milner had not succeeded in mitigating the indignation of his parliamentary friends it was perhaps because he had explained the Irish objections to the veto in terms of such cogency as to spoil the effect.

[8]In *The sequel to a pastoral letter . . . censuring late publications in the French language*, dated 7 March 1809, Dr Milner had argued that if St Gregory, through St Augustine, had reorganised the dioceses of the British Isles without paying any attention to the old divisions Pius VII could do the same thing in France.

[9]The *regium donum* was a stipend allotted by the government to the Presbyterian clergy, on the understanding that it would not be withdrawn in any individual case so long as it was continued to the body at large. The Presbyterians were however divided between members of the Synod of Ulster and the Seceding Synod, and when there was a revision of the allocation in 1809 the latter were given a lower rate. In an outburst of indignation they had declared in July that they could not accept the terms offered (J. S. Reid, *History of the Presbyterian Church in Ireland*, 1867, III, p. 419).

[10]In the petition as presented to parliament the relevant passage read: "by the articles of war, if soldiers refuse to attend the religious worship of the established church, they are punishable by fine, imprisonment and death: Thus the English Catholic soldiers are incessantly exposed to the cruel alternative of either making a sacrifice of their religion, or incurring the extremes of legal punishment . . . (*Hansard*, XV, 556).

[11]In his *Letters from Ireland* Dr Milner alleged that Lord Redesdale's object had been to divide the Catholics and set the laity against the clergy when as J. F. Mitford he carried the Relief Act of 1791 in the House of Commons.

[12]Of May 1808 when the negative veto was proposed (see No. 168, n.3).

[13]Text in Ward, *Eve of Catholic Emancipation* I, p. 53. The four Archbishops and six Bishops meeting at Maynooth had agreed, subject to the sanction of the Holy See, to present the names of candidates for vacant sees to the government to give the latter an opportunity of objecting. With the refusal of the King to consider emancipation the negotiation came to nothing and the resolutions remained unknown except to a few until Lord Grenville referred to them on 27 May 1808 (*Hansard* XI, 649, 694).

[14]The "Protestation of abhorrence of doctrines imputed to them" signed by the four Vicars Apostolic and thousands of the English Catholics was deposited by Charles Butler in the British Museum at the end of 1791 (Add.MSS.5416A). Dr Milner's assertion that the deposited document was not authentic was repeated by him over the years (see No. 601 n.6).

[15]Probably by publishing the memorandum Dr Milner had given him outlining his plan of a negative veto (see No. 194 n.3), which he did in May 1810 by reading it out in the House of Commons (*Hansard*, XVII, 217).

[16]In which he described the action of the Irish Bishops who had on 3 July 1809 condemned Abbé Blanchard's works as 'not alone schismatical but dogmatising schism" (Ward, *Eve* I, p. 94).

[17]Probably Scully's mother-in-law.

[18]Scully's brother-in-law. An entry for 29 September in James Scully's diary records that he was then at Kilfeacle negotiating for the purchase from Lord Landaff of properties valued at about £81,000. No deal was struck: "Mr Ayre grew shy of his lordship".

212   *From Charles Butler to Merrion Square*

Lincolns Inn, 9 October 1809

Dear Sir,

It is a great while[1] since I troubled you with a letter. As the time of action now approaches,[2] I have a great wish to hear you are proceeding with energy and activity equal to the importance of the cause. The late dissentions in the cabinet have considerably weakened the strength of your enemies, it has also been weakened by the bad success of our expeditions to Holland and Spain. Some circumstances have led me to a more accurate knowledge than the public in general have of the actual state of his Majesty's councils; and I see nothing that is not favorable to you.[3]

I sent you two letters signed Hwylls,[4] and I hope they met your approbation. I mean to write two more but I wait for the publication of Mr Gifford's life of Mr Pitt as I wish to see his account of his concessions to the Catholics.[5]

I am sorry nothing has been done to produce a regular intercourse between the Irish and the English Catholics, but I hope it will be set on foot at your next meeting which I see is advertized for the 8th of next month.[6] In the meantime I shall be very much obliged to you to let me know what is doing. Our petition is universally approved of, and I believe it has been universally signed.

It is probable that parliament will meet soon,[7] this is an additional motive for immediate exertion.[8]   [*Source*: Scully Papers]

[1]Four months (see No. 204).
[2]With the possible recall of parliament.
[3]On 2 September two pieces of bad news reached London: Lord Chatham, having renounced any hope of advancing to Antwerp, was going to bring his forces home; and Wellington, forced to retreat after his costly victory at Talavera, had returned to Portugal. On 6 September the Duke of Portland resigned and on 13 September the King asked Perceval to investigate the possibility of a remodelled administration. While he was doing so the enmity between Lord Castlereagh and Canning resulted in a duel on 21 September. On 2 October, after the plan of an extended administration had been rejected by Lord Grenville and Earl Grey (see No. 211 n.4) Perceval himself had been commissioned to form a new government. It took him two months to complete his cabinet and Butler had good grounds for hoping that the King would yet have to turn to the Whigs (see Aspinall, *Later Correspondence of George III*, introduction to Vol. V).
[4]See No. 204.
[5]The last chapter of John Gifford's *History of the political life of . . . William Pitt*, 6 volumes, 1809, makes much of the Emmet rising of 1803 and sees the Irish Catholic petition of 1805 as a means of harrassing Pitt: "calculated, though cer-

tainly not intended by some who supported it, to excite an odium against the Crown".

[6]The meeting of 2 October referred to in No. 206 had been adjourned to 8 November (Minute Book I).

[7]Parliament was not in fact recalled before the new session, which opened on 23 January 1810.

[8]In Butler's Letter Book there is an additional paragraph which was crossed out: "If any arrangement could be made for the King's having an interfering power in the election of Bishops it would essentially serve your cause, but that I take for granted is wholly out of the question".

213   *From Francis Plowden to Merrion Square, Dublin*

Dawson Street [Dublin] 1 November 1809

Mr F. Plowden took the liberty of leaving a paper with Mr Scully in hopes that he might be induced to mention the Subject of it to any Gentn. of Confidence & will & ability to promote Mr P's object.[1] He put it the more readily into Mr Scully's hands because he found it to be so much in Unison with the resolution of the County of Tipperary — *That public discussions & enquiries into the actual situation of the Catholics of Ireland appeared to have advanced the hope & improved the prospect of Catholic freedom.*[2] Mr P. flattered himself that Mr Scully might exert his influence in his own County with some of the Numerous Names which appear to constitute that respectable board. Mr P. quits Dublin by the Friday packet & shall hold himself particularly obliged to Mr Scully for the Communication of the interesting Narrative of the interview with Mr Pitt[3] — which he kindly offered to Mr P. & for any other information or document relative to the Catholic Concerns in Irel[an]d within the last 9 years.

[*Source*: Scully Papers]

[1]See No. 220. He was possibly canvassing subscriptions to his *History*.

[2]This is the wording of the 1st resolution adopted by the meeting of Tipperary Catholics at the summer Assizes of 1808 in Clonmel (See No. 181). Plowden gives the text of the resolutions in his *History*, p. 717, where he also dwells on the omission of Catholics from the Grand Jury.

[3]Among the Scully papers (MS.27, 514) there are three little notebooks with (i) the Minutes of the Deputation of 1805 to London; and (ii and iii) Denys Scully's Diary. To (i) is pasted a note in Scully's hand reading: "Mr Plowden is requested (when he has had a copy or extracts taken of this book) to send it to Mrs Bostock, No. 11 Upper Titchfield Street — to be forwarded to Mr Scully — Dublin. 3 November, 1809". The Minutes include an account of the interview of the deputation with Pitt.

214 *From Edward Hay*

4 Crow Street [Dublin] 9 November 1809

Dear Sir,

At the meeting of the general Committee of the Catholics of Ireland held yesterday[1] it was determined that the reports relative to Subscriptions should be received on Monday the 13th inst. and the Several Country Gentlemen that attended were requested to attend on Monday for the purpose.

I was instructed to request of the thirty six Gentlemen Selected by the Catholic Citizens in Dublin who were Considered the Managers in their several Parishes[2] to report the progress they have made towards Carrying into effect the resolutions adopted at the late meeting of the Catholics of Ireland[3] which have been Sanctioned and adopted in most parts of Ireland.

Your attendance is therefore earnestly requested at one o'Clock in the afternoon of Monday the 13th inst.[4] [*Source*: Scully Papers]

[1]Its principal business was to elect a sub-committee of seven, of whom Scully was one, to revise the draft petition prepared by a previous sub-committee (see No. 206) and have it ready for a meeting on 11 November. Members of the General Committee present in Dublin were asked to collect subscriptions (Minute Book I).
[2]See No. 146. Scully was a representative of St Andrew's parish.
[3]Of 24 May 1809 (see No. 203 n.1).
[4]The petition was read paragraph by paragraph (Minute Book I). The *Dublin Evening Post* of 14 November 1809 commented: "They have at length adopted a bold and decided language, no longer adhering to . . . the fulsomeness of unprofitable compliment, they venture . . . to remonstrate, like Freemen, upon terms of equality and claim Emancipation as a right". The Committee also decided to order for the committee room for six months Cobbet's *Political Register*, the *Morning Chronicle*, the *Globe* and all the Dublin papers.

215 *To Mrs Denys Scully at 2 Merion [sic] Square S, Dublin*
From Catherine Scully

Kilfeacle [Co. Tipperary] 13 November 1809

My Dr Mrs Scully,

It made us extreamly happy to find by Den's letter this day that you are now well and able to go abroad. You must be surprised at my long silence in not writting to wish you joy of your recovery and your fine boy[1] but I assure you it was not for want of due affection and great feeling for what you must have suffer'd but for fear you may be tempted to write in answer which

I knew must be very inconveniet and painfull to you but thank God that is now over.

Mr Scully and I are highly gratified by you and Miss Eyre[2] being so kind as to consent to come and spend some time with us next Month. We shall try and make this old place as pleasant to ye as an old couple can. I hope Mrs Eyre and Mr Eyre were well when you heard from them and that they had a good passage which will induce them to come often.

I beg to know how your little boy is geting on. Is he growing fat? As for Den's he seldom mentions him. Has he got a good nurse which is a great treat in Dublin? I hope you have him nurs'd in the house which is the best way to see him done justice to. Mr Scully and Mrs Mahon[3] unite in love to you. Best respects to Miss Eyre with My Dr Mrs Scully — Yours most affect'y Catherine Scully   [*Source*: Scully Papers]

[1]James Vincent, now two months old.
[2]Probably Julia Eyre.
[3]Denys Scully's sister Anne or Nancy.

216   *From Charles Butler to Merrion Square*

Lincolns Inn, 17 November 1809
Dear Sir,

I was extremely obliged by your letter.[1] It appears to me to contain a clear and pointed view of the actual state of Ireland, and comprises, in a few lines, the result of all I have read or heard upon the subject. I was sincerely happy to see your name among those of the Committee appointed at the meeting on the 8th.[2] You know all my thoughts and views and I therefore will not trouble you with a repetition of them.

I shall only add that to my certain knowledge Lord Grenville, Lord Gray, and Lord Holland profess that they will not come into office without the promise of Catholic emancipation.[3]

Lord Welesley is certainly on his journey to England, but his dispositions in respect to administration are quite unknown.[4]   [*Source*: Scully Papers]

[1]Of 25 October, now missing, in reply to No. 212. Sending a copy of it to Edward Jerningham, Butler wrote: "I enclose you a letter I have received from our friend Scully which I think the best and most interesting I have ever received on Irish affairs. It presents a melancholy prospect, but things must have their course and we must wait for the result of the proceedings on the fourth" (Letter Book: Add.MSS. 25, 127).
[2]See No. 214 n.1.
[3]Lord Grey told Lord Grenville on 12 December that he would not take office unless the power of immediately proposing measures for Ireland was conceded but advised him against himself presenting the Irish Catholic petition (*Dropmore Papers*, IX).

[4]Lord Wellesley had gone on a mission to Spain and there had been an understanding that he might follow George Canning into the administration when he returned, but Canning had in the meantime resigned and it was not known whether the Marquis would enter the cabinet without him (Aspinall, *Later Correspondence of George III*, Vol. V).

217   *From Charles Butler to Merrion Square*

Lincolns Inn, 23 November 1809

Dear Sir,

I lose no time in informing you of a very singular circumstance, which is, that the Attorney General has filed an information *ex officio* against Mr Perry the editor of the *Morning Chronicle* for inserting a paragraph in favor of the emancipation of the Catholics.[1] He copied it from a Sunday paper. From what he mentioned, it appeared to me very harmless, but it is impossible not to suppose that the Attorney General would. He will advised [*sic*] in the proceedings. I will send you the paragraph as soon as I get a copy of it.[2]

I am Dear Sir etc.

P.S. Not knowing whether you will certainly be in Dublin when this reaches you, I send a similar Letter to Mr Hayes.[3]

Permit me to mention that my eldest dau[ghte]r is to be married on Monday, to Captain Stonor of the Oxfordshire family of that name: with every recommendation to make us pleased with the match but money.[4]

[*Source*: Scully Papers]

[1]James Perry and his printer were acquitted on 24 February 1810 on a charge of libel for publishing on 2 October 1809 a passage from *The Examiner* reading: "What a crowd of blessings rush upon one's mind that might be bestowed upon the country in the event of a total change of system! Of all monarchs, indeed, since the Revolution the successor of George the third will have the finest opportunity of becoming nobly popular". Perry, who conducted his own defence, did not mention Catholic Emancipation (Howell, *State Trials* XXXI, 335).
[2]Not found. There is a copy in the DDA (390/1, XII, 10) sent under cover of a letter from Butler to Hay dated 7 December, in which Butler comments: "I do not see any immediate reference . . . to the Roman Catholics: but Mr Perry understands it in that sense and I suppose it is so understood by those who prosecute".
[3]*Recte* Hay.
[4]Mary Butler and Captain Charles Stonor of the Spanish service.

218   *To Richard Huddleston*

Dublin, 4 December 1809

Dear Rich'd,

I have this day rec'd your Letter of 28 Nov. and learn with sincere pleasure that you and your mother & sister are very well.

With respect to the subject of your Letter,[1] be assured that, whatever right may in strictness devolve upon me, I shall do nothing to the prejudice of yourself & the family. The uniform kindness & good faith I have experienced from you all has left in my mind every sentiment of regard & every wish to oblige and I hope to evince it upon this & every other occasion. Before I make that final Answer (which I believe will fully meet your expectations) I beg to avail myself of your offer respecting the case & opinion, as before Richards[2] — for I own my conception of it is rather indistinct. If you direct it to be enclosed in a sealed cover, well pressed, addressed to "Mr Will'm McDonnell,[3] care of Surgeon Stewart,[4] Upper Merrion Street, Dublin" —and that Letter again enclosed in a sealed cover for the "Rt. Hon. Sir Edw'd Littlehales, Bart.,[5] Castle, Dublin," it will reach me safely thro' the Post Office — and it is quite unnecessary to superscribe "Ireland" after "Dublin" — for the Post Office people sometimes break open such Letters, as suspecting them to come from France or some hostile country. After receipt of this Paper, I shall lose no time in writing to you.

I fear our Cousin Francis[6] has found his Introductions to the Duke of R unavailing. He dined with us a few days ago, and amused us & some friends, at Lord Shrewsbury's expence, by quoting a saying of his Lordship's, upon Jane's[7] authority, "that he could not get a decent Dinner during his Tour in Ireland."[8] It happened, that in the company present was Mr Lyons[9] of Limerick, who had, upon my Letter of Introduction, given a sumptuous Entertainment to Lord S. and, being skilled in the *savoir vivre* had put himself to great trouble & expence about it. Frank and I felt a little confused at his Lordship's liberal requital having thus accidentally transpired.

Believe me to be, with best regards to your mother & Jane.

[*Source*: Huddleston Papers C3/S6]

[1] Probably about the division of Ferdinand Huddleston's estate.
[2] Richard Richards (1752–1823), later a judge. Henry Huddleston reported consulting him in a letter of 2 October 1810 to his mother. The Huddlestons were reluctant to accept from Scully as a favour something to which they were entitled by law (Huddleston Papers C3/HD6).
[3] Unidentified.
[4] The Surgeon General, George Stewart.
[5] Sir Edward Baker Littlehales, of Ashcomb, Sussex, military Undersecretary

at Dublin Castle 1801–19; married in 1805 a daughter of the 2nd Duke of Leinster.

[6]Francis Huddleston. From a letter that he wrote to Gregory on 12 September 1815 (Peel Papers: Add.MSS.40, 201 f.229) it appears that he was in the Stamp Office in 1809; that at some unspecified later stage the Duke of Richmond, in recognition of his services, promised him a situation which with his half-pay would bring his income up to £240 p.a.; but that for want of a suitable opportunity the Duke's intentions had not been fully carried out.

[7]Richard Huddleston's sister.

[8]In the summer of 1808 (see No. 171).

[9]Probably Scully's cousin, James Denis Lyons.

219   *From Francis Plowden to Merrion Square, Dublin*

Renumbered 280

220   *From Francis Plowden to Merrion Square, Dublin*

Essex Street, London, 25 December 1809

My Dr Sir,

Many untoward circumstances prevented me from writing to you — as soon as I wished — after my return to London. Yr valuable Manst. [Manuscript] I have transcribed & placed the original in the hands of Mrs Bostock as you directed.[1] It recurs to me that you mentioned to me in Dublin something of a letter or copy of a letter to or from Mr Huddleston relating to an Audience which Ld Hardwicke had with the King — w[hic]h (if communicable) I should hold myself highly obliged to you for a copy of as indeed I should be for any document that would enable me to bring before the public — facts which it would be the interest of the Irish Catholics to have handed down to posterity.[2]

In speaking to you of *myself* — I can not disclaim a strong right to mingle with it some *Nationality* — a conspiracy existed I doubt not — between my Printer of the last Work[3] & Mr Egerton the publisher of my large Work.[4] I had ordered a large part of the impression of the last to be sent over to Irel[an]d whilst I was there — which the printer most wickedly prevented, holding them back till the injunction was obtained. The Notoriety of all which brought my Credrs. upon me & on my return to London I found an Execution in my house & sevl. Writs out agst me on which account I have been ever since my return obliged to remain *incog.* & consequently shut out of my profession. On Thursday last the Chancellor construed the injunction, which is a loss to me of £2000 in the whole. To you Sir, I need not mention the irreparable loss to me & my son the sale of my books would be & I shall not be able to put off the sale of them beyond the 15th of next Jany. The preservation of them & of my own personal liberty will be necessary for me to accomplish the plan I have determined upon to write the important history of the last 9 years, for which I already have many valuable documents & am in the train of obtaining more. Any Gentn coupling the Will & the means of enabling me to complete the Work by contributing something towards it at present will I hope feel that they are promoting the Credit & Interest of the Country, as well as bestowing a favor upon a person who will make it the study of his life to do justice to the Irish Nation & thereby express the liveliest Gratitude of

Your devoted & obliged humble Servant
Fra Plowden

[*Source*: Scully Papers]

[1]See No. 213 n.3.
[2]In his *History*, II, p. 502 Plowden says that the Earl of Hardwicke tried to persuade the King to keep the Ministry of the Talents in power after they had yielded on the clause in the Mutiny Bill regarding freedom of worship for Catholic soldiers. The letter to which he refers has not been found but there is a reference to it in a letter which Jane Huddleston wrote on 9 May 1807 to her brother Richard: "Mr Scully is much pleased with the account you gave him of Lord Hardwicke's conversation with the King and is high in his praises of Lord H." (Huddleston Papers C3/HD91).
[3]The printer of the volume of the *History of Ireland* which came out in 1809 was R. Wilks, of 89 Chancery Lane.
[4]*An historical review of the state of Ireland* . . ., printed by C. Roworth, Bell Yard, Fleet Street, For T. Egerton, Military Library, near Whitehall.

221   *From Edward Hay to Merrion Square, Dublin*

4 Crow Street [Dublin] 2 January 1810

Dear Sir,

As it is understood that each Gentleman of the Committee of grievances[1] should deliver in writing his Sentiments relative to the report they have been specially appointed to draw up for publication your Attendance is particularly requested at the Committee rooms No. 4 Crow Street[2] at three o'Clock in the afternoon of Thursday the 4th instant.   [*Source*: Scully Papers]

[1]A sub-committee appointed by the General Committee on 15 November 1809 to list the privations and grievances of the Catholics of Ireland. At its first meeting on 24 November it decided to consider them under the headings of: clergy; peerage; commercial and manufacturing; landed interest; military and naval; and the organisation of the Orange system (Minute Book I).
[2]The decision to rent these premises was taken on 10 October 1809 (ibid.)

222   *From Edward Hay to Merrion Square, Dublin*

4 Crow Street [Dublin] 6 January 1810

Dear Sir,

The General Committee of the Catholics of Ireland have instructed me to Call together the Gentlemen who have been Selected by the Catholic Citizens of Dublin[1] in order to Consult on the best mode of Carrying into effect the resolutions of the last general Meeting[2] in their respective parishes. Your attendance is therefore most earnestly Solicited at one o'Clock in the afternoon of Tuesday the 9th Instant[3] when I shall lay before you the Communications that have been made to me from the different parts of Ireland and Great Britain that will exhibit the progress of the petition which the Committee is bound to have ready by the first day of the Session Commencing the 23rd Instant.   [*Source*: Scully Papers]

[1]Originally elected to prepare an address to the Duke of Bedford (see No. 146 n.1) they were constituent members of the General Committee.
[2]On 5 July 1809 a sub-committee had submitted a report (Minute Book I: Appendix No. 1) on the best way of carrying into effect the resolutions of the aggregate meeting of 24 May 1809 which had decided on another petition to parliament. This had recommended the issue of a circular embodying its various proposals: the adoption of their own petitions by county meetings or at least resolutions supporting the general petition; deputations to local members of parliament; and notification to the Committee in Dublin of the names of the local secretaries. At the General Committee's meeting of 14 December Hay had at last been given authority to issue the circular (text in Minute Book I, f.25) and it had gone out on 19 December (DDA 54/1, V, 34).
[3]The Minute Book records that only a few attended, the day being wet. Scully did not return to Dublin from Kilfeacle until 21 January (see No. 228).

223   *From Edward Hay, Secretary, to 2 Merrion Square, Dublin,*
11 January 1810

A printed letter reminding members of the General Committee that they are bound to have the petition ready by the first day of the next session of parliament and inviting them to meet at the Committee Rooms, 4 Crow Street, on 22 January, when he will lay before them the various communications that have been made to him from the different parts of Ireland and Great Britain.[1]   [*Source*: Scully Papers]

[1]See No. 222 n.2.

224   *From Edward Hay, 4 Crow Street, to Merrion Square,*
12 January 1810

A circular asking Scully as one of the Dublin Catholics to carry into effect
the resolutions of the last General Meeting[1] by helping to obtain signatures
for the petition, a copy of which, with ruled paper, has been sent to his parish
priest.   [*Source*: Scully Papers]

[1]Of 24 May 1809.

225   *From Thomas Finn,[1] Secretary, to Merrion Square, Dublin*

[Printed circular]
Sir,
     Your attendance is requested at a Meeting of the City of Dublin Parochial
Nomination, on Friday the 19 January 1810, at the hour of 7 o'Clock in the
Afternoon, Chaple house, Francis Street.[2]   [*Source*: Scully Papers]

[1]Possibly the currier, of 20 Winetavern Street, mentioned in the Dublin Directory.
[2]This meeting, not otherwise recorded, may have been superseded by the one called
for 17 January (see No. 226). According to his father's diary Scully was at Kilfeacle
until the 19th.

226   *From Thomas Finn, Secretary to the Catholick*
Nomination of Dublin, to Merrion Square

Monday, 15 January 1810
[Printed circular]
Sir,
     In consequence of a requisition to me,[1] to assemble the Gentlemen who
were heretofore chosen by the Catholicks of Dublin, to address the Duke of
Bedford: I do entreat the favor of your attendance at the Chapel House of
Francis-Street, on Wednesday evening next, at the hour of Seven o'Clock,
to take into consideration important matters which will be then laid before
you.[2]   [*Source*: Scully Papers]

[1]It remains unknown who initiated the requisition. In the report that he gave to the
General Committee on 22 January Hay said that he had been asked by the committee
of the Dublin Catholics to attend their meeting (Minute Book I; *DEP*, 23 January
1810).

[2]A report had come into circulation that the English Catholics and their parliamentary friends were ready to accept a bill giving a veto to the King. (Hay told the General Committee on 22 January that he had received from Dr Troy a copy of a proposed printed sketch of regulations, concurrent with a state provision for the clergy). As the new session of Parliament was due to open on 23 January and the General Committee were not to meet until 22 January Hay, on the authorisation of the Dublin Committee, addressed letters to Grenville and Grattan on 18 January enquiring whether any such bill had been prepared or was in contemplation. The texts were read to the meeting on 22 January (Minute Book I; *DEP*, 23 January 1810).

227   *From Charles Butler to Merrion Square*

Lincolns Inn, 22 January 1810

Dear Sir,

Mr Jerningham and I have read, with the greatest surprize and indignation, the paragraphs on the Veto, which have appeared in the Dublin *Herald*.[1] Nothing can be more untrue, than the whole of the representation. I have sent a denial of it, under my old signature, and Mr Jerningham sends a denial of it by himself.

The fact is that Sir John Hippisley Cox drew up the heads of such a bill some time ago and printed a few copies of it and I believe shewed them *in confidence* to some of his friends.[2] In the summer of last year the Roman Catholics got his leave to publish a tract in their favor which he had written several years ago, and printed but not sold.[3] It was subsequently to the printing of this tract, that he printed the heads in question. He sent one to Mr Jerningham, desiring that it might be printed in the other tract. *This Mr Jerningham positively refused to do and on the part of himself and the board disclaimed having any thing to do in the printing or circulating it.* He means to send an account of this circumstance to Ireland immediately.[4] For my own part I never heard of it, till Mr Jerningham mentioned it to me this morning.[5]

[*Source*: Scully Papers]

[1]No Evening Herald of this date has been found. The paragraphs were no doubt on the same lines as one that appeared in the *Dublin Evening Post* of 18 January 1810: "We have received from respectable authority the following particulars. The Catholic body of England having resolved even in opposition to their clergy to make an offer of the Veto to His Majesty are stated to have concerted measures to that purpose with certain members of Parliament, who have hitherto advocated the justice and necessity of an uncondtional Emancipation". It goes on to point to another circumstance, that a Baronet MP had prepared a bill.

[2]Under Hippisley's plan, when a vacancy occurred the names of from four to eight candidates were to be sent up and the government was to make a choice from that list. There might be a *placet* or *exequatur* before any Papal bulls could be put in

execution. In return there would be a state provision for the clergy (Ward, *Eve of Catholic Emancipation* I, p. 107).

[3]The *Substance of additional observations* of 1806, mentioned in No. 125 n.1.

[4]Jerningham wrote to Archbishop Troy on 23 January, informing him at the same time that the meeting of the English Catholics had been postponed to 1 February. Dr Troy replied on 3 February (before he had heard the outcome of the meeting), assuring him that his communication had "effectually removed the alarm excited by the reports of our intended legislative provision concerning the Veto" (Ward: *ibid*. p. 109, quoting from the Westminster Diocesan Archives).

[5]Butler wrote a similar letter to Hay on the same day (DDA 290/1, XII).

228   *To Richard Huddleston*

Dublin, 23 January 1810

Dear Rich'd,

I returned only two days ago from a visit of a month at my father's, and, finding your note & the papers here,[1] I beg to offer this apology for my delay in answering.

It has not been my intention, for a moment, to take to myself the money arising from the share in question — at the same time that the other claimants, Henry, Edward, & Jane, appear to me to be, as you observe, perfectly warrantable in availing themselves of their legal rights, and in not relinquishing any part. My desire has been, only so far to interfere, if at all, as I can conceive your excellent deceased Sister would have dictated. She owed many obligations, & pecuniary ones, to Mrs Bostock, whose circumstances are probably now narrow, but who was liberal to her niece in her wealthier days. I shall not go at large into the family considerations (because I would not appear to intrude upon that subject) which incline me to wish that you would agree to let her have the benefit of this Claim so far as £100, by your note to her at 2 or 3 months for that Sum. I shall willingly execute any Release of all my Claims to you, and do assure you most sincerely, that I am very happy in the opportunity of testifying my regard, & wish to oblige you.

I have engaged myself, some months ago, in a considerable purchase of Land,[2] which, tho' at present of moderate profit, will hereafter prove a valuable property. It obliges me for the present to borrow some money, & with difficulty, at six per cent interest, our legal rate — and therefore, if you could procure me assistance in this way, I should be much obliged to you — it would answer in 2, 3 or 4 months hence.

I am much obliged to Jane for her kind note, and beg to assure her of the pleasure it gave me to find that Lord Shrewsbury had not been quite so severe upon us as we had been informed.[3] I shall read the necessary passages of her note to my Cousin Lyons, who will be in Town next week. I have frequently a task in defending the English to my Irish friends, and the Irish to my English friends, being so much connected with both — but it is always pleasant to reconcile them to each other.

It is probable, tho' not very much so, that we may be somewhere about Harrowgate within 2 or 3 years; and, in that case, should we take the London Road, I shall hold in mind your obliging Invitation to Sawston, & endeavour to make it my way, for the purpose of seeing you, Mrs Huddleston & Jane, tho' but for a few hours.

I beg to be most kindly remembered to them, and to any others of the family, who may happen to be under your Roof.

[P.S.] There are thirteen Catholic Petitions from different parts of Ireland, already prepared — viz. Cork, Waterford, Tipperary, Kerry, Kilkenny, Limerick, Galway, Clare, Donegal, Carlow, Queen's County, Kildare & Dublin.[4] There are also the general Petitions of the Catholic Committee, & also of the English Catholics, on the part of whom I see many letters from their Secretary Edw'd Jerningham to ours, Edw'd Hay — so that the No Popery Cry has not daunted or deterred the Petitioners.

[*Source*: Huddleston Papers C3/S7]

[1]See No. 218.
[2]Probably Mantlehill, a property of 614 acres on the north side of the Golden-Cashel road in Co. Tipperary. In one of his account books (MS.27, 493) Scully records having paid his father £14,450 for it between January and May 1809. James Scully noted in his diary (MS.27, 579) that he was declared purchaser for it on 2 March 1808. An indenture of 1 January 1835 (MS.27, 543) shows that the property was previously held by Henry White on a lease of 1785 from the Earl of Clanwilliam.
[3]See No. 218.
[4]The *Dublin Evening Post* of 1 February listed thirteen petitions, leaving out Co. Kildare but including Galway county as well as Galway city.

229   *From John Byrne to Merrion Square, Dublin*

London, 27 January 1810

Dear Scully,

For God's sake endeavour to have the petitions withdrawn for the present or until we see what is best to be done. It will not be supported by 25 members in the Commons as Montague Mathew has just told me, & I need not explain to *you*, the moral influence *such* a falling off of strength must, hereafter, have on our question. Mr Keogh withdrew the petition in 1806[1] after it had done its business — viz. that of upsetting our friends. Let the bad precedent be now used, for a good purpose. Exert I entreat you, & without delay, your influence in Tipperary, Waterford & Cork. Be assured that if

Grenville comes in — & nothing but our question (urged at present) can prevent him,[2] if, I say, he comes in, his Majesty will certainly retire from the cares of public business, before a year — & the day will be our own — when he (G) can, he will force the measure; with or without the Veto. Grattan will not give any advice unasked; but get public bodies to ask him. He appears greatly downcast.

In a word save us from the man of Mount Jerico.[3] The majority against ministers of last night[4] is their death warrant. Keogh, I have no doubt unless the term for which he sold his soul to Castlereagh is at an end — Keogh to embarrass Grenville & keep him out of ministry will press the petition forward; & win popularity by well affected democratic rage. Call upon Lords Gormanston & Southwell & Netterville,[5] Sir Edw. Bellew & upon all ranks to act with vigor at this most critical conjuncture — you can't get the people — so strongly have they been wrought on to concede the Veto[6] — but get them to withdraw the petition, or we are lost. It is a hard measure: but it forms our best alternative — a judicious chain of Evils is the perfection of wisdom.

[P.S.] I have already written to Mr MacDonnell[7] on this subject.

[*Source*: Scully Papers]

[1]See No. 154 for the meeting of 15 April 1807 at which Keogh moved that the petition should be suspended.
[2]The belief that the Whigs were on the point of coming into power again was graphically illustrated when the *Dublin Evening Post* of 1 February published a list of a new cabinet, headed by Earl Grey, with Lord Grenville as Foreign Secretary.
[3]A facetious allusion to Keogh's place of residence — Mount Jerome.
[4]When the government had been defeated by nine votes on a motion for a committee to investigate the disastrous Scheld expedition (*Hansard* XV, 208).
[5]The 12th Viscount Gormanston (1775–1860); the 3rd Viscount Southwell (1777–1860); the 6th Viscount Netterville (1744–1826).
[6]This seems to be the reading, but he seems to have meant to write "wrought on not to concede".
[7]Randal MacDonnell.

230   *From Edward Hay to 2 Merrion Square, Dublin*

4 Crow Street [Dublin] 29 January 1810

Dr Sir,

Several Members have requested of me to call a Special Meeting of the General Committee previous to my Departure for England in Consequence of the answers I have received from Lord Grenville and Mr Grattan.[1]

Your attendance is accordingly requested at the Committee Rooms in Crow Street at One o'Clock in the afternoon of Tuesday the 30th Instant.

[*Source*: Scully Papers]

[1]Both of them assured Hay in reply to his enquiry of 18 January (see No. 226 n.2) that they knew of no bill in contemplation (Minute Book I). The present letter shows that Hay had not yet heard of Lord Grenville's letter to Lord Fingall, dated 22 January, published in the London papers on 25 January and in the *Dublin Evening Post* on 30 January. In this Lord Grenville not only declined to present the Irish Catholic petition himself but said that the extension of civil rights to the Catholics must be accompanied by "extensive and complicated arrangements", including "an effectual negative for the Crown". After an adjournment to the following day the Dublin meeting decided to persevere with the petition and Hay took it with him to London in the night of 2 February. In the meantime the leaders of the English Catholics had also become alarmed and after two meetings with Lords Grenville and Grey succeeded in persuading them to drop any reference to the future nomination of Vicars Apostolic. A compromise text, drafted by Lord Grenville, was accepted on the spot and passed as their Fifth Resolution by the English Catholics at a meeting in St Alban's Tavern on 1 February. This contained the subsequently controversial passage, interpreted by critics as a pledge, that "any arrangements on this basis of mutual satisfaction and security and extending to them the full enjoyment of the civil constitution of their country will meet with their grateful concurrence" (See Ward, *Eve of Catholic Emancipation* I, pp. 129, 253).

231   *From Thomas Finn, Acting Secretary, to Merrion Square*
16 March 1810

In consequence of Grattan's statement in parliament[1] a meeting of the Catholic Committee held on 15 March has called a meeting for 24 April to take into consideration the propriety of solemnly disavowing any offer having been made by the Irish Catholics to concede the veto or any measure connected with it to the Crown. Early notice is given to secure a good attendance.[2]

[*Source*: Scully Papers]

[1]Introducing the Irish Catholic petition Grattan said he had told the House in 1808 that the Catholics were willing to concede a veto but could not affirm that such were their sentiments now (*DEP*, 6 March 1810).
[2]The meeting of 24 April thanked Grattan and resolved "that the Catholic laity of Ireland never have directly or indirectly authorised any person to offer through our friends in parliament or otherwise the conceding to the Crown of any interference whatsoever with respect to the appointment of Catholic prelates in Ireland" (Minute Book I).

232   *To Richard Huddleston*

Dublin, 20 March 1810

Dear Rich'd,

I am much pleased to find by your letter of last month, that the arrangement I proposed[1] has met with your concurrence. . . .

I have communicated to Mr Gibbons,[2] as you desired, the very agreeable news of Jane's approaching marriage, and I beg you will have the goodness . . . to present to her the earnest wish I feel for her happiness — of which indeed her own merits and Mr C[anning]'s excellent character afford the most agreeable prospects.

[P.S.] We are all rejoiced here at Yorke's defeat,[3] tho' we like his brother, Lord H[ardwicke] very well — I am leaving town for a month on circuit.

[*Source*: Huddleston Papers C3/S8]

[1]See No. 228.
[2]P. Gibbons (see No. 180 n.5).
[3]He had conceded defeat on 14 March (*The Times* 16 March 1810). Being badly off he had accepted a sinecure post from the government and had to submit to re-election for his Cambridgeshire seat, where he was unpopular after playing a prominent role in defending the administration for their handling of the Walcheren expedition (*DNB*).

233   *To Sir John Throgmorton, Curzon Street, Mayfair, London*

Merrion Square, Dublin, 6 April 1810

Sir,

The Catholics of the County of Tipperary, whose late resolutions are annexed,[1] have felt it to be due to your distinguished talents and enlightened exertions in the cause of Religious Liberty, to tender to you this communication of their sentiments and wishes.

Always acting for themselves, they have led the way in the recent petitions to Parliament, and have therefore felt it to be their peculiar duty to facilitate the success, immediate or eventual, of their applications.

It appears to be their universal wish, that their Emancipation, the consequent security of their property and improvement of their country, be not impeded, or even retarded, by any differences, which their clergy can conscientiously surmount, or assist in surmounting — and they expect from their clergy, as a public duty at this crisis, that they will not merely stand upon the defensive, or content themselves with assembling merely to negative this or that proposition, or point out objections and obstacles, but that they will actively promote the general cause, define the means of deliverance, and trace the practicable channel, by which the People can recover their political freedom. This is now ascertained to turn upon a single point of Ecclesiastical Discipline, consequently alterable, and which no Divine has yet ventured distinctly to term *essential*.[2]

[*Source*: Throckmorton Papers]

[1]Scully's letter is written on the back of a printed copy of the resolutions, adopted at Clonmel on 31 March 1810. By these the Tipperary Catholics, who were followed by those of Kildare on 9 May, launched the new proposal of domestic nomination on which Grattan took his stand when he moved to go into committee on the Irish Catholic petition on 18 May (*Hansard* XVII, 17). The meeting thought that apprehensions about foreign influence might be obviated if future elections were substantially domestic, either by the votes of the surviving Prelates or by a chapter of clergy, or by such other proceedings as might be compatible with Catholic doctrine.
[2]At a synod in Dublin on 26 February the Prelates had adopted sixteen resolutions (with a seventeenth thanking Dr Milner), which were conveyed to the Catholic committee on 2 March in the form of an address. They reaffirmed their resolution of 14 September 1808 on the inexpediency of the veto (see No. 185 n.7); disclaimed any desire for financial support other than the voluntary contributions of their own flocks; and, in a much quoted 16th article, said they sought for nothing "beyond the mere integrity and safety of the Roman Catholic religion in its Christian faith and communion, and its essential discipline, subordination and moral code" (Minute Book I; Ward, *Eve of Catholic Emancipation*, Ch. X). Scully appears to be referring to the 15th resolution which referred adversely to domestic nomination (see No. 242 n.9).

234   *To Earl Grey, London*

Merrion Square, 7 April 1810

My Lord,

I have the honour to transmit to your Lordship, on the part of the Catholics of the county of Tipperary, the annexed copy of their resolutions lately adopted at a very numerous meeting.[1]

In pressing for their Emancipation with the earnestness natural to men, who understand the value of equal laws & rights, & admire the British Constitution, they do not however seek it upon unreasonable grounds — but are perfectly willing to assent to & promote every accompanying arrangement, consistent with their faith, that shall appear to be calculated to obviate existing difficulties, and conciliate the cordial goodwill of all their countrymen to their cause. Upon this foundation they presume to hope for your Lordship's support. That county is supposed to contain upwards of 340,000 inhabitants, of whom nineteen twentieths are Catholics, including ten thousand Catholic freeholders qualified to vote at the county election.

Your Lordship will excuse this liberty in a person, who is but little addicted to politics, and whose principal object in Catholic Emancipation would be the security of property in Ireland.[2]   [*Source*: Earl Grey Papers]

[1]See No. 233.

[2]In Chapter X of his *Penal Laws* Scully points to the discrimination against Catholics in taxation; the insecurity of titles liable to be assailed by a packed jury or biassed court; the pitfalls resulting from inadvertent or involuntary failure to take the prescribed oaths; and the "remedial" construction put upon laws so as to wean Catholics from their faith and protect the established church. He also notes that no English capitalist had settled in Ireland since the Union, because of the general insecurity of property there. According to an obituary in the Dublin Chronicle of 8 March 1816 the chief object of his father in supporting the Union had been the security of landed property.

235   *From Edward Hay to Merrion Square, Dublin*

4 Crow Street [Dublin] 11 April 1810

Dr Sir,

I would Esteem it as a particular favor if you could attend the funeral Service of my near relative Miss Byrne of Cabbinteely,[1] which is to be performed at French Street Chapel on Friday the 13th Instant at 11 o'Clock and accompany her remains to the Kill of the Grange near the Black Rock. Your Compliance will much Oblige.   [*Source*: Scully Papers]

[1]Mary Clare Byrne, the eldest of the three daughters of Robert Byrne of Cabinteely, had died in Madeira on 14 March at the age of nineteen. Her entry in R. Ryan's *Biographica Hibernica* of 1821 indicates that she was well known for her linguistic and artistic accomplishments. Edward Hay was related to her through the Devereux of Carrigmannin: one of his aunts had married Thomas Ward of Monkstown and their daughter, Mary Thomassa Ward, married Robert Devereux; these had a son, the well known James (c. 1762–1845), and a daughter, Mary, who in 1790 became the wife of Robert Byrne. Thus Hay was only a first cousin twice removed, but it suited him to stress the relationship not only because of Miss Byrne's fame but because she was through her grandmother, Clare Nugent, a second cousin of the Marchioness of Buckingham — on 11 May 1810 Edward Jerningham told him that he had notified Lady Buckingham of the death of "your common relation" (DDA 390/1, XV, 10). See R. R. Madden, *United Irishmen* IV, p. 520; Burke *LG* 1882: Byrne of Cabinteely; note on James Devereux in *Journal of the Waterford and South East of Ireland Archaeological Society*, Vol. XII, 1909, p. 23.

236   *From Lord Donoughmore to Merrion Square, Dublin*

27 Somerset Street, Portman Square [London] 13 April 1810

Dear Sir,

Accept my best thanks for your letter, & say to the Gentlemen, who composed the Catholic meeting at Clonmell,[1] how grateful it is to me to receive any mark of their confidence. I approve *highly* of the conciliating spirit which seems to have guided their proceedings. Something of that sort was not unseasonable just at this moment, when the old friends of your question were rather left naked of any arguments of such a complexion.[2]

The resolutions of the County of Tyrone,[3] which I have just now got, are a tower of strength to you.

My brother & I equally rejoice at the favorable accounts which you are enabled to give of our worthy friend your father.   [*Source*: Scully Papers]

[1]See No. 233 n.1.

[2]Presenting the Irish Catholic petition in the House of Lords on 6 June Lord Donoughmore cited the Tipperary and Kildare resolutions as evidence of the cordial feelings of the Catholic body (*Hansard* XVII, 371).

[3]The Tyrone meeting, held at Omagh on 4 April, was reported in the *Dublin Evening Post* of 12 April with the Tipperary one. Plowden, who published the resolutions in his *History*, p. 804, took a different view from Lord Donoughmore's. Their true purpose, he thought, was to set Catholics against each other by reviving the veto: for while advocating repeal of the penal laws, they specifically approved of Lord Grenville's letter to Lord Fingall (see No. 230 n.3).

237   *From Montagu Mathew to Merrion Square, Dublin*

Brighton, 17 April 1810

My dear Sir,

I did not until yesterday on my leaving London receive your Letter from Kilkenny of the 4th Inst. & beg you will be so kind as to express my warmest acknowledgements to my friends the Catholics of the County of Tipperary for the High Honor they have done me by approving of my feeble efforts in Parliament in behalf of the Catholic Claims.[1] I also beg personally to thank you for the kind manner in which you have Convey'd their Sentiments to me & trust I shall Continue to merit their further Countenance & approbation. [P.S.] I am glad to hear your Father is so much better. Pray remember me kindly to him.   [*Source*: Scully Papers]

[1]On 6 February 1810 he had presented the Tipperary Catholic petition to the House of Commons, where it was laid on the table (*Hansard* XV, 320).

238   *From Sir John Throckmorton to Merrion Square, Dublin*

Buckland [Berkshire] 20 April 1810

Sir,

I feel myself highly honored by the communication made to me of the resolutions of the Catholics of the County of Tipperary.[1] They are such as must meet with the approbation of every liberal mind, & I have no doubt will have a considerable effect towards removing prejudices on one side, & stiffling clamorous bigotry, or affected religious scruples on the other. To the precise measure of the veto, though I could never see any real religious obstacle, yet in the situation in which Ireland has been placed for so many years, many difficulties may be started on the ground of policy & feeling; nor do I think the manner in which it was proposed well calculated for its ultimate success; till we have a government willing to listen to our petitions, it is better for us to adhere to such general declarations as you have adopted, & as our small body did at our last meeting.[2]

In 1778 when the Catholics of this Kingdom addressed the Crown they declared their dissent from the established religion of the country to be purely religious; the consequence of this has always appeared to me that in every thing which our religion would warrant, we ought to conform to the regulations & practises of our fellow subjects.[3]

I propose going to town next week & shall probably stay till after Ld Donoughmore & Mr Grattan have made their motions in each house. I shall be at my brother's[4] 81 South Audley Street, where I shall be very happy to have any intelligence you can give me; in the meantime I beg you will accept my thanks for the communication of the resolutions of the very respectable body of the Catholics of Tipperary.   [*Source*: Scully Papers]

[1]See No. 233 n.1.
[2]Probably that which adopted the Fifth Resolution (see No. 230 n.1).
[3]Among the Throckmorton Papers there is a copy of the *London Gazette* of 2 May 1778 recording the presentation to the King on 1 May of an address of Catholic peers and commoners of Great Britain. While alluding to exclusion from the constitution it was essentially a declaration of unreserved loyalty.
[4]William Throckmorton.

239   *From Earl Grey to Merrion Square, Dublin*

Woburn Abbey,[1] 24 April 1810

Sir,

I yesterday had the honor of receiving here your letter of the 7th inst. enclosing a copy of the resolutions lately voted at a numerous meeting of the Catholics of the County of Tipperary.[2]

It is with infinite satisfaction that I have received this proof of the disposition of so large & respectable a portion of the Catholics of Ireland, in urging their admission to the full enjoyment of the civil constitution of their Country, to assent to & promote every accompanying arrangement, not inconsistent with their faith, that shall appear to be calculated to obviate existing difficulties.

On this basis of mutual satisfaction [and] security I shall feel myself bound to give every assistance in my power to a Cause, which is supported equally by Policy & by Justice, & which, I am persuaded, would at this moment have had a much fairer prospect of success, if the moderate & conciliating spirit, evinced in the resolutions you have done me the honor of transmitting to me, had prevailed in all the proceedings that have taken place upon it.

[*Source*: Scully Papers]

[1]The seat of the Duke of Bedford, in Bedfordshire.
[2]See No. 234.

240   *From James John Bagot to Merrion Square, Dublin*

Castle Bagot [Rathcoole, Co. Dublin] Wednesday [25 April 1810] My Dear Sir,

I send you a statement of our grievances as published in 1807;[1] John Joseph Dillon's,[2] I cannot find. With respect to the excellent statement[3] which you have in preparation, I can only say, that if I possessed such a work, & might use it at my discretion, I should not hesitate to have it printed on one sheet like a newspaper & presented to every man who voted in the minority on our Question at the last discussion.

I think it would be well also to treat the English public to a share of it every day from this day until the 15th of May.[4] I have no doubt the *Statesman* & *Morning Chronicle* would gladly afford a column for the purpose. Much might be done in fourteen days.

I am Dear Sir, your sincere & obedient Servant, (If you could spare me the *little book** printed at New York,*[5] for a few days, or send the bearer of this note where he can get me one it would oblige me much).

[P.S.] Our cause loses more by its *obscurity* than in any other way.
*Sealed or wafered up in paper.

[1]Possibly a pamphlet entitled *The state of the Catholics of Ireland explained by abstracts from the Irish statutes, showing the privileges granted during the present reign and those remaining to be granted*, by a Member of Parliament, 1807.
[2]*Essay on the history of the coronation oath*, London, 1807.
[3]An early version of his *Penal Laws* (see No. 242 n.1).

[4]When he expected the debate on the Irish Catholic petition to begin: it was in the event opened by Grattan on 18 May (*Hansard* XVII, 17).
[5]William James MacNeven's *Pieces of Irish History*, New York, 1807. In addition to the contributions of T. A. Emmet and MacNeven himself it included an "Introduction to the digest of the Popery Laws" by the Hon. Simon Butler (1749–1797, founder of the Dublin society of United Irishmen).

241   *From Lord Grenville to Merrion Square, Dublin*

Dropmore, Beaconsfield [Bucks] 26 April 1810

Sir,

I have had the honour to receive your letter of the 7th Inst. inclosing the copy of the Resolutions adopted at the meeting of the Roman Catholics of the County of Tipperary[1] and I beg leave to assure you of my unalterable solicitude for the extension of the full enjoyment of every Civil Right to that respectable class of my fellow subjects of which they form so distinguished a part. I have seen with infinite satisfaction the expression of their anxiety to facilitate by temperate and conciliatory arrangements the accomplishment of a measure which I consider as highly conducive to the permanent interests of the Empire.   [*Source*: Scully Papers]

[1]See No. 233 n.1.

242   *To [the Earl of Donoughmore]*

[End of April 1810]

[Fragment of a draft][1]

With respect to the Crown, its[2] concurrence will be but reluctant — The Government, before proceeding far, will clearly perceive, that nothing is to be gained in point of influence, & will find itself embarrassed by being embarked in a negotiation, that will promise no satisfactory result — They must either finish it disadvantageously, or break off abruptly, & perhaps ungraciously.

Having however once entered upon it, they admit the necessity of the arrangement — and thus add strength to the obstacles against Emancipation. They injure the cause of the Catholics, prevent or retard the general reunion of the inhabitants of the Empire, and leave in full vigour a standing argument, which the growing exigencies of the State, or change of circumstances, may yet render it expedient, and even necessary, for themselves to encounter.

To obtain the Pope's sanction would be, under the present circumstances of Europe, a matter of extreme difficulty.

There is no access to him personally, for he is a prisoner at Savona[3] — If he has left any *"locum tenens"* at Rome, he too is probably inaccessible — or may not be inclined to promote, or assent to, any measure of the Irish Catholics, that can strengthen the enemies of France, or lessen their disunion & embarrassment.

In speaking of the Pope's sanction, we must not overlook the peculiar delicacy of his situation — The proposed arrangement would imply a concession on his part — a victory on the part of the Protestant religion. Such would be its spirit — such its understood effect, if to be imposed as the equivalent of Catholic freedom. Now, we know how jealous & weak a declining prince, such as the Pope, naturally is of his power or prerogative — nay even of the appearance of it, however slender or shadowy — how tenacious of every feather of rank — still more, when a churchman is the prince. What is sought from him, no doubt, is not to relinquish any effectual power; for he does not possess that — but it is, to relinquish a mark of pre-eminence & respect — a form and memorial of ancient homage — How difficult it is to obtain such a favour from any prince, even in the most favourable moments, how humiliating to his feelings, may well be imagined — I fear that the negotiation would not be conducted throughout on the part of the Crown, with due moderation and address in this particular — And here is another difficulty.

If he is ever accessible, you must have a deputation sent out to him from the Irish Bishops; and also an accredited envoy from the King, in order to conclude the concordat — There will be difficulty in appointing the proper persons, in sending them out, and still more, in protecting them in any part of the continent during their necessary stay.

Besides, the previous instructions to be framed for the envoy on the part of the Crown, and for the deputies on that of the Bishops, will be a subject of infinite nicety — They will require a long time to adjust respectively — they may not tally together, and an essential variance may only be discussed, when the parties meet in conference abroad.

Many lesser difficulties will necessarily occur. Some may be easily foreseen, but not easily obviated — I shall specify *one*, which stands in the way of the entire proceeding.

By an English statute, enacted in 1561,[4] 13 Elizabeth Ch. 2, it is declared to be high treason to obtain from the Pope, or to publish or use, any manner of paper, writing or instrument, written or printed, containing any thing, matter or cause whatsoever. This statute remains unrepealed at this day — and an attempt now to repeal it would probably be attended with as great exasperation and controversy, as to repeal the entire Code. But whilst the statute exists, any person, procuring the Pope's *written* sanction to a concordat, is liable to be punished as a traitor. It is no answer, that the Crown would connive, as in many other instances, particularly Sir John Cox.

Hippisley's, who at the hazard of being punished upon his return procured the Pope's orders, in 1794 & 1795, for the supply of the Toulon fleet with provisions from the Ecclesiastical States.[5] In a great national treaty, and solemn proceeding, such as this concordat ought to be, no connivance will suffice, no illegality should be attempted. It ought to be a fair, avowed & legalised transaction, in its commencement, as well as in its passing through all its stages.

Here I beg leave to refer to some important anecdotes & observations upon this subject, contained in a book entitled "*Betham's Baronetage*[6] quarto" printed about 5 years ago, in the article of "Sir J. Cox Hippisley".

The present Lord Mountcashell also mentioned to me some interesting conversations (very little known) which he held with the present Pope upon this very subject at Rome, so recently as about 1803 & 1804[7] — As he is now in London your Lordship may easily learn it from the best authority.

Such, then being the difficulties in the way of any arrangement, these questions return, namely

"Ought it to be insisted upon in this unfavourable season?"

Is Catholic Emancipation to be postponed *sine die*, or until the arrangement can be effected?" —

"Ought the Catholics to be now saddled with the blame of the repeal or the inconvenience of the delay, when it appears, that the proper season has been neglected by the Government who now exact this condition, and who could, 15 or 20 years ago, have obtained full satisfaction from the Pope, if they had desired it?" —

"Finally, which is at present the most pressing consideration, in justice and sound policy? — the measure of restoring Catholic freedom unconditionally, which the Legislature are perfectly competent to restore — or the measure of a concordat with the Pope, which the Catholics of Ireland are from peculiar circumstances (however well inclined) not competent to effect?"

Such is my view of this subject — If, however, an arrangement or concordat is deemed absolutely necessary by our friends, and is not on any account to be dispensed with, your Lordship sees the long and crooked road that must be travelled in order to arrive at it.

For my own part, I should not object to any terms of arrangement — and I think the Bishops would be found more reasonable than is imagined — this is evident in the 16th article of the late resolutions[8] — and, however highsounding the other articles are, yet it is certain that they *exclude nothing, affirm nothing, deny nothing* — as will be perceived upon a critical examination, and upon weighing every word, particularly, the loose words "essential", "general", "policy", "our present circumstances" & many others.[9]

They were carefully studied, in order to catch the popular approbation, to attach the lower clergy & Catholics, but to let in every useful explanation hereafter — and in fact, they are throughout (tho' with a good intention) elaborately evasive.

Your Lordship's judgment, therefore, will decide, under all those circumstances, whether, in discussing the subject of the Catholic petitions, you will see it in one of these two points of view, *viz* —

1st as an act of general policy and expediency, to be conceded to the Catholics, only in the event of an arrangement being effected, which shall exclude the possibility of all foreign influence in the appointment of the Catholic bishops in Ireland — or

2[ly] as an act of justice and pressing necessity, which ought to be performed immediately and unconditionally — with this accompanying admission, that the proposed arrangement, tho' not really necessary, may yet be a very desirable measure for the purpose of obviating the apprehensions alledged — but that it should be a substantive independent measure, not to be expected, until the situation of the continent and other concurring circumstances shall afford the necessary facilities for its full and satisfactory accomplishment.

I conclude this letter with the draft of an Act of Parliament,[10] which I have sketched out, for your Lordship's assistance, in case your motion shall be shaped for its immediate introduction into the House.

[*Source*: Scully Papers]

[1]The first part is missing. What remains belongs to the same bundle and is written on the same paper as a document entitled: "Commentaries upon the Code of penal and disabling laws now in force against the Catholics of Ireland" — an early version of the *Statement of the Penal Laws*. The reference to a motion in the last paragraph shows that the lordship addressed was the Earl of Donoughmore, who had presented the Irish Catholic petition on 12 March 1810 with the intention of later moving to go into committee (*Hansard* XVII, 439).

[2]Probably the concurrence of the Holy See, which may have been mentioned in the missing first part.

[3]He had been there since 16 August 1809 (Chotard: *Le Pape Pie VII à Savone*).

[4]*Recte* 1571 (see Chapter X of the *Penal Laws*).

[5]In Ch. X of the *Penal Laws* Scully emphasises that Hippisley's order from the Pope was a written one: he should have been hanged on his return but was instead raised to the baronetage.

[6]Sir William Betham: *The Baronetage of England*, 5 volumes, 1801–5.

[7]According to Ch. X of the *Penal Laws* Lord Mount Cashell was asked by the Pope in 1803 why his king had no envoy at the court of a temporal prince governing territories particularly important to a naval power. Every other prince in Europe — Lutheran, Calvinist, Greek — had diplomatic relations with him: only the King of England with five million Catholic subjects and numerous fleets did not. For Sir John Hippisley's doubts about the accuracy of this report see No. 415 n.7.

[8]Of the Irish Prelates on 26 February 1810 (see No. 233 n.2).

[9]"Essential" occurs in the 16th resolution, "points of faith and general discipline" in the 1st. "Policy" does not appear. "Our present circumstances" appears in the 15th article, saying that in the present circumstances of the Irish Catholics domestic nomination would subject their religion to unseemly disadvantages.
[10]Not found (see No. 340).

243   *From Lord Donoughmore to Merrion Square, Dublin*

27 Somerset Street, Portman Square [London] 2 May 1810

Dear Sir,

My Absence from Town during the recess has deprived me of the opportunity of being aware till now of the great kindness which your letter[1] announces your having been so good to intend for me. Accept my best thanks & be assured that I feel all the force of your observations, & the full value of the aid which your kindness has been so good to have in contemplation towards enabling me to do more perfect justice to the subject which has been committed to my hands. But you will have observed before now that I have given notice of the day on which I intend to bring forward the Question, from which it will be obvious to you, that before I could receive the results of your collections, the time for availing myself of them would have altogether elapsed. Believe me however that I am not the less thankful to you — & think I am — with true regards & respects for my valuable friend your father — in which my brother most cordially joins.

P.S. I leave town again in the Course of this day, not having been at all well.

[*Source*: Scully Papers]

[1]No. 242, the missing part of which may have mentioned the collections referred to here.

244   *From Francis Hely Hutchinson to Merrion Square South*

Belcamp [Co. Dublin] 6 May 1810, Sunday morng

My Dear Sir,

On my return to this place, I found the enclosed letter,[1] with one from Lord Donoughmore to me, by which I find that he declines to accept the assistance of that information you have been so good to offer him, under an impression of unwillingness, as I conceive, to induce you to undertake so difficult & arduous a task, & at a period, when he has already arranged in his own mind, the line he means to pursue in discussing this subject. I am heartily glad, however, that your kind & prompt exertion will have anticipated this feeling, & that the able & effectual consideration you have given this great question in all its bearings, will when taken up afford to him, such a Body of connected intelligence & so much information truly valuable.

[*Source*: Scully Papers]

[1]No. 243, which was not postmarked and evidently sent by Lord Donoughmore under cover to his brother.

245   *From Francis Hely Hutchinson to Merrion Square South*

Thursday Morning, 10 May 1810

My Dear Sir,

Not having been in Town on Monday, though expected, I did not receive your note until late on Tuesday afternoon. I forwarded to Lord Donoughmore the supplement in draft.[1] I am hourly in expectation of a letter from him, when I shall have the pleasure of waiting upon you.

[*Source*: Scully Papers]

[1]Perhaps the statement which Lord Donoughmore returned to Scully through his father (see No. 260) and which was perhaps the Commentaries referred to in No. 242 n.1.

246   *To Sir John Throgmorton, at William Throgmorton[1] Esq.,*
                South Audley Street, London

Merrion Square, 14 May 1810

Sir,

I was glad to find, by your letter,[2] that our County of Tipperary resolutions met with your approbation. The Cath[olic]s of the County of Kildare[3] adopted similar resolutions on the 9th inst., which are advertised — and the idea is spreading. As you were pleased to express a desire for any further communication, that might prove useful upon our subject, I write chiefly to apprise you, that in my opinion the Earl of Donoughmore's speech upon the 21 inst.[4] is likely to be a valuable one, worth reporting very accurately. The Hutchinsons are esteemed a family of superior talents. Lord D's father was Provost of Dublin University, Secretary of State in Ireland, an eminent Parliamentary orator, and the first public man in Ireland who declared for Catholic freedom. Lord D., his eldest son, rarely spoke in Parliament, but his speeches were of the best oratory. He is indolent, but capable of great exertion, when roused, as I have reason to believe he is upon the present occasion. Tho' he has been an Union peer since the Union, yet he has hitherto reserved himself, and not ever attended Parliament until lately. I expect therefore a powerful statement — and have some reason to know,[5] that he is better prepared upon the subject, by intimate knowledge of facts, by local feelings, by earnest & genuine sympathy, and by a full and distinct acquaintance with the grievances which affect the Catholics of Ireland thro' all their minute details & operation, than any other speaker, who has hitherto addressed an English audience. No other Member is so capable of producing, if he pleases, that comprehensive Statement of the existing laws, their extent and prepense, which has been frequently called for by the *Edinburgh Review*, and by many other literary friends to our cause — and which will no longer be a "Desideratum" upon this subject, if Lord D. makes full use of the knowledge he possesses, and if care is taken to have his speeches correctly and fully reported. These observations I have thought it right to submit, for your consideration, and that of the English Catholic Board.

[*Source*: Throckmorton Papers]

[1]Sir John's brother.

[2]No. 238.

[3]See No. 233 n.1. The Tipperary and Kildare resolutions were printed by Keating in a collection entitled *Roman Catholic Petitions etc 1810*.

[4]Postponed until 6 June, when Lord Donoughmore, moving on the Irish Catholic petition for the first time, after the refusal of Lord Grenville to present it (see No. 230 n.1), was defeated by 154 to 68 votes (*Hansard* XVII, 35, 353). Grattan's motion to go into committee had been defeated in the Commons on 1 June by 213 to 104 (ibid. 235).

[5]No doubt because he himself had supplied the information (see No. 242).

247   *From Dr J. T. Troy to 2 Merrion Square South*

11 Blackhall Street, 16 May 1810

Dear Sir,

The friend whom I commissioned to procure further information on the subject of grievances affecting our clergy and religious worship has stated that he could not obtain any; and that they are all comprehended under the general heads communicated in my letter to Mr Hay. I sent you Dr Staunton's letter respecting the full window tax formerly exacted from Carlow College.[1]

In O'Flaherty's *Thoughts on the Veto* just published,[2] I observe several disabilities affecting education etc, copied from Mr Parnell's pamphlet.[3] I am much hurried preparing for a short excursion into the country and have the honour to be, with the best compliments to Mrs Scully, etc.

[*Source*: Callanan Papers]

[1]Dr Henry Staunton was President of Carlow College from its opening in 1793 to his death in 1814. He says in his letter that when the window tax was introduced in 1799 he applied to the (Protestant) Bishop of Leighlin and Ferns for exemption, who could not reconcile it with his conscience to defraud the revenue; and to Cooke at the Castle, who

told him there had been a clerical error in the wording of the act. In 1807 Sir John Newport introduced a clause into a bill empowering magistrates to grant a licence and he got from them what the Bishop's conscience had not allowed him to grant.
[2]No copy has been found and O'Flaherty remains unidentified.
[3]Probably Henry Parnell's *History of the Penal Laws*.

248   *From Edward Hay, Secretary, to Merrion Square, Dublin*

4 Crow Street [Dublin] 31 May 1810

Dear Sir,

As a Member of the General Committee I have been requested to call upon you for your contribution towards defraying the expences of the Petitions presented to Parliament pursuant to the Resolutions of the late General Meeting.[1]

As one of those selected by your Catholic fellow citizens[2] your exertions are particularly requested to assist in collecting subscriptions in your parish and I shall esteem it as a particular favor if you can inform me of the progress you have made on or previous to the next meeting of the General Committee on the 8th of June next[3] where your attendance is particularly requested.   [*Source*: Scully Papers]

[1]The aggregate meeting of 24 May 1809 (see No. 203 n.1).
[2]That is, in his other capacity as one of the Dublin Catholics, representing St Andrew's parish (see No. 146).
[3]Scully was in London on this date (see No. 271 n.2).

249   *From Edward Hay to Merrion Square, Dublin*

4 Crow Street [Dublin] 9 June 1810

Dear Sir,

At a Meeting of the General Committee of the Catholics of Ireland held yesterday I was instructed to request of the Gentlemen who were last Chosen by the Catholic Citizens of Dublin to meet those that had been selected along with you at the Chapel House in Townsend Street at ten o'Clock in the morning of Tuesday next the 12th Instant to adopt the most speedy and Effectual means of Collecting subscriptions in your Parish to defray the Expences of the Catholic Petition.[1]   [*Source*: Scully Papers]

[1]No record has been found of this meeting or of the date on which the 36 Dublin parish representatives were last elected.

250   *From Edward Hay to Merrion Square, Dublin*

4 Crow Street [Dublin] 18 June 1810

Dear Sir,

I was this day[1] specially directed by the General Committee to request your Attendance at the Committee Rooms in Crow Street precisely at three o'Clock in the afternoon of Friday the 22nd Instant to take into consideration the propriety of calling a General Meeting of the Catholics of Ireland.[2]

[*Source*: Scully Papers]

[1]The meeting of 18 June had been adjourned to secure a better attendance of members in and around Dublin. One item on its agenda was the landlord's demand for unpaid rent of the Committee's premises in Crow Street (Minute Book I).
[2]An aggregate meeting was called for 13 July and it was decided that expenditure by the General Committee would cease immediately (ibid.).

251   *To his wife Catherine at Kilfeacle, Co. Tipperary*

Merrion Square [Dublin] Sunday night — Ten o'Clock [24 June 1810]

My dearest Catherine,

I write this, in contemplation of a possible result of the Affair,[1] which is fixed for tomorrow morning. I have been forced into it by a wanton & unprovoked newspaper attack upon my name, without a shadow of foundation in truth or probability — and, according to the Laws of Society (which we must all obey) I must preserve that name pure & untarnished for my family, by repelling the aggression.[2]

I have nothing particular to say to you in the way of business. I believe all my worldly affairs are settled. In the Drawers of my Study table, and in the lower shelf & the middle one of the Closet next the window, you will find all my private Papers — my will — Statement of Property — Debts — etc. also in my Pocket Book. But I have every thing to say to you (if language could express it) of my Love, esteem & regard for you — which you deserve, and I feel, in the highest Degree that any man can for a woman of the most exalted merits — such as I know you to be. Adieu — my excellent and beloved Catherine — believe me to be your ever attached and most affectionate husband D. Scully

[P.S.] I would recommend to you, for your assistance in managing the Property, to consult Messrs Reeves & Ormsby,[3] as Solicitors — and lay before them our marriage settlement and my will for their advice. Also you would find it most prudent to return to Town, without delay, for many reasons.

[*Source*: Scully Papers]

[1]See No. 252.

[2]When he was at Cambridge Scully entered in his Common Place Book an extract from Boswell's *Johnson*: "A man may shoot him that invades his character, as he may shoot the invader of his house"; he added the comment: "The most plausible defence of duelling I have ever met with". Scully was "known to be averse to any hostile proceeding to any person" (*DEP*, 30 June 1810) and his first wife was glad of his being too "sober and domestic" for there to be any need to fear for him (see No. 49), but the pressure of "the laws of society" was particularly strong in the Irish bar (cf. Charles Phillips, *Curran and his contemporaries*, p. 359).

[3]Robert Reeves and W. Ormsby, of 19 Upper Merrion Street.

252　　　　　　　*From George Lidwill to Merrion Square*

Kildare Street, Monday evening, 25 June [1810]

[Copy][1]

My dear Scully,

According to your desire I waited upon Mr Luke Plunkett yesterday, to demand an apology for the introduction of the name of Scully into his late publication in the *Evening Herald*.[2] I found him willing, but imperfectly so, to disavow any allusion to you personally, and I understand he had already tendered some written declaration to that effect. But this not being deemed sufficient, he asked permission to introduce his friend Mr Luke Lawless;[3] who having entered, exacted from Mr Luke Plunkett his previous promise to abide by whatever arrangement he, Mr Lawless, should think proper to adopt. This promise Mr Plunkett most unequivocally gave. Accordingly Mr Lawless and I having conferred upon the matter, he concurred with me upon the necessity of Mr Plunkett's signing & permitting to be published the following apology, which is in the writing of Mr Lawless himself: viz

"I can assure Mr Scully, that I did not mean, in my late publication in the *Evening Herald*, to offer any personal offence or disrespect to him or any person of his family, directly or indirectly".[4]

Upon our return, however, he receded from his promise of signing the apology; and his friend Mr Lawless, with great propriety, instantly declined any further interference on his behalf.

Having for some time urged Mr Plunkett to consider the matter more coolly and to act more justly in it, I felt delicacy to be no longer due after so manifest a violation of faith, pledged to his own friend in my presence.

I found myself therefore at last compelled to require his appointment of as early a time and place, as his situation would permit, for the necessary arrangements.

Accordingly the time was agreed to be four o'clock this morning, and the place Balls Bridge. However, having parted from him before five o'clock yesterday evening, I can say, that I have neither heard nor seen any thing of him since — altho' I understood he was to inform me as soon as he could procure a friend — and altho' I attended on your part at the place and time appointed, and waited there upwards of half an hour.

I find, that so lately as midnight he had not provided himself with a friend or any other requisite for such an occasion. The interference of the civil powers[5] against your attendance (which was not effectual until two o'clock this morning) certainly did not proceed from me or my friend Mr H. D. Grady, to whom alone you made it known — and indeed Mr Grady was not out of my sight during that interval. However, I find that the time and place of the intended meeting had become very public; and we can easily imagine, from other circumstances, how and from what quarter the intelligences transpired to the civil powers.

Yours faithfully
George Ledwill

I confirm Mr Ledwill's statement upon the subject of the above apology.

L. Lawless,
25 June 1810

[Source: Callanan Papers]

[1]The copy is in Scully's hand and endorsed by him: "An article having lately appeared in the *Evening Herald*, under the signature of Mr Luke Plunkett of Portmarnock, in which the name of Scully was introduced without authority or other cause, occasioned the transaction, stated in a letter from George Ledwill Esq., of which the following is a copy".

[2]Only a few numbers of the *Evening Herald* for 1810 are extant, but the article which occasioned Scully's challenge has survived in a cutting preserved in the Dublin Diocesan Archives (29/12, 40) which from internal evidence can be dated 22 June. The article proper consists of a long defence of Dr Milner against an attack made against him in the *Hibernian Journal* of 11 June, but this was preceded by the following paragraph headed "Preliminary Observations":

The writer of the following lines submits them dispassionately to the Protestants in both islands, as being calculated to remove the dead weight of false impressions, inflicted on them, through the medium of our secret, or as commonly called respectable correspondents! who know *just as much* of the religious and political feelings of this country, as they do in Tipperary,* Naas or even Trim! Dr Milner speaks of an Englishman, who *though no where seen is every where felt*, always obtruding his influence on Catholic Councils whenever or wherever held — I speak of an Irishman, who, *though no where seen* or *no where felt* (this last would be impossible) is yet always protruding his ugly, grinning, political Caricatures, or Policies of Assurance! upon good company, at the other side of the water, by an almost telegraphic facility of communication, or rather of misrepresentation. I am also informed that he has (strange as it may appear) actually written himself, by the bulk, into a repute, of being of *some consequence*, by having been represented as a leading Catholic of a county, falsely represented to be a leading one on Catholic politics! I call on Mr Butler (of Lincoln's Inn) *particularly* to take notice of this well-intended and much called-for caution — I CALL ON THE EMPIRE to be guarded against such impolitic, dangerous, evil, nay *blood stirring* conduct.

*Some one or other of the name of *Scully*, is said to have moved or rather given us the *last Tipperary touch*! What two feeling and touching subjects, are the Union and Domestic Nomination!!! Tipperary addressed Government in favour of the former — I dare say Mr Grattan expects it will do the same in favour of the latter.

[3]A barrister, born c. 1780, 2nd son of the Dublin brewer Philip Lawless.

[4]The Tipperary resolutions of 31 March 1810 (see No. 233) to which Luke Plunkett is referring were no doubt drafted by Denys Scully but were actually moved by his uncle William Scully of Dualla and Andrew Ryan.

[5]The *DEP* of 26 June 1810 reported that "the gentlemen of the long robe" had been arrested and held to bail. Two days later it published a corrected account which said that the Court of King's Bench took recognizances in heavy sums not merely for the jurisdiction of the city of Dublin but for the whole United Kingdom.

253   *From Charles Butler to Merrion Square*

Lincolns Inn, 25 June 1810

Dear Sir,

This will be put into your hands by Mr Sharpe,[1] a particular friend of mine. He is one of the most leading members in opposition and has always voted for the Roman Catholics; he is very intimate in our family, and I beg leave to recommend him in a particular manner to your attention. You will find him full of information. I believe he is the person in England whose society is most sought for. It naturally is his wish to obtain as accurate information of the state of Ireland as he can; I know no person from whom he can derive so much information as yourself and I can assure you that he is worthy of every kind of attention and confidence.   [*Source*: Scully Papers]

[1]Richard Sharp (1759–1835), known as "Conversation Sharp", a moderate Whig MP who had made his fortune as a hat manufacturer and numbered among his friends many eminent persons. He supported Catholic relief, parliamentary reform and sinecure reform (*DNB*).

254   *From Charles Butler to Merrion Square*

Lincolns Inn, 4 July 1810

Dear Sir,

I don't know whether I am obliged to you, for a written paper, which I have received this morning from Ireland. I had seen Mr Plunkett's letter.[1] It appeared to me an insane performance, and I hoped you would treat it with the contempt which it evidently deserved. I am very happy the matter is ended. I can assure you that you may laugh at all such attacks.

You have seen, I make no doubt, Doctor Milner's insane attack on me.[2] I can most conscientiously assure you, that the whole of it is either pure invention, absolute falsehood, or gross misrepresentation. I believe his conduct is universally given up even by his warmest friends. I have not the least thoughts of replying to him.

We are in great expectation of the event of the next meeting of the Irish Catholics.[3] That, upon the whole, we have gained ground, is clear: every person now believes, that, if it had not been for Doctor Milner's unfortunately provoking the subject of the Veto,[4] we should now be sailing rapidly into port. I fear there is even a Catholic party, which seeks to divide the Irish and English Catholics. I am sure that by doing it, they consult the interests of neither. But in each of the bodies there is, I trust, a fund of good sense, which will preserve and cement their union.   [*Source*: Scully Papers]

[1]The one in the *Evening Herald* which provoked Scully into challenging him to a duel (see No. 252 n.2).
[2]In his letters to the *The Statesman* (see No. 257 n.8). As well as making Butler generally responsible for all the actions of the English Board Dr Milner insinuated that he had bribed the printers to omit the 17th resolution of the Irish Prelates (see No. 257 n.13) and accused him of being paid by the English Catholics, who should "insist upon my capital enemy's quitting his lurking incognito".
[3]The aggregate meeting summoned for 13 July (see No. 250 n.2).
[4]In May 1808 (see No. 168 n.3).

255   *To Richard Huddleston*

Merrion Square [Dublin] 9 July 1810

Dear Rich'd,

I received with sincere pleasure your kind intimation of Jane's marriage[1] upon which I beg to tender her my most hearty congratulations, and the expression of every wish for her happiness. I understand that she and Mr Canning intend some excursions for the summer whilst his Mansion House undergoes some alterations. It would give me and Mrs Scully very great pleasure to see them in Dublin, if they should incline to pass a few weeks in this quarter. From the great number of English families, and those of rank & fortune, who visit Dublin, in increasing numbers, this summer, an Irish excursion appears to be quite the fashion of the Day — and I am sure we should be particularly happy to receive & accommodate in this House Mr & Mrs Canning during their stay, and to render their visit as agreeable as we can. You also would, I hope, be of the party — and I flatter myself, that you need no assurances of the cordial welcome you would receive here, from other friends as well as myself. Here we have still fine Catholic Ladies, some beauties, & some fortunes too, tho' of a different generation from those you saw in 1799. Your friend Miss Maria O'Connor (since Mrs Blake) fell into that Decline which attached to her family, and she died last month at Penzance in Cornwall, after an experimental voyage. Her father[2] is in great affliction. Mrs Moore now resides chiefly with him. Our cousin Frank[3] has got a villa, & appears quite in spirits & high feather — where the "uncle hoc" lies[4] I cannot divine. [*Source*: Huddleston Papers C3/S9]

[1]At Sawston in June (Huddleston Papers, C1/MH30).
[2]Valentine O'Connor senior.
[3]Francis Huddleston.
[4]The words might also be read "uncle hoe", but "uncle" and "hock" being both associated with pawnbroking fit the context of Francis Huddleston's habitual penury.

256   *From Charles Butler to Merrion Square*

Lincolns Inn, 6 August 1810

Dear Sir,

The Bearer of this, is Mr John Gage the brother of Sir Thomas Gage,[1] who is now on a visit at Lord Kenmare's, his father in law. I beg to recommend him to your notice in a particular manner.

I was duly favoured with your letter;[2] and I mean to write to you on the subject of it at some length. What very wrong headed men doth the world abound with. [*Source*: Scully Papers]

[1]Sir Thomas Gage, 7th Baronet, of Hengrave Hall, Suffolk, had married a daughter of the 1st Earl of Kenmare in 1809. John Gage (1786–1842) was a pupil of Charles Butler at Lincoln's Inn. He was called to the bar in 1818 but never practised and instead achieved distinction as an antiquary. He is entered in the *DNB* under the name of Rokewood, assumed when he succeeded to the estate of his brother Robert in 1838.
[2]Missing — of 18 July in reply to No. 254.

257   *From Bishop John Milner to Merrion Square, Dublin*

Wolverhampton, 31 August 1810

Dear Sir,

Yrs. of the 5 Ulto. arrived here while I was absent from home in the Southern parts of this District. To begin with the most important article mentioned in it, you very rightly suppose that I shall condemn the challenge you gave,[1] & which, as you state it, was only prevented from taking effect by the cowardice of yr. adversary. Happy cowardice for you, and yr. wife &

child & father & mother, no less than for your opponent; for suppose he had been killed & had gone to the bar of divine justice to hear the sentence of everlasting torments instead of you, have you a heart to think of that fate befalling him, because he had written some nonsense concerning a person of the name of Scully, without an agony of grief & horror? It was not by way of sporting a Rhetorical Essay but of expressing my real conviction, that I declared in my *Letters from Ireland*,[2] that the Duellist contracts the guilt of *murder & suicide* at the same time when he gives or accepts of a challenge! O that you had consulted yr. Wife or yr. Mother, the church yard or the Crucifix, instead of the Prott. friends you mention,[3] after reading the Newspaper you mention! To conclude this melancholy subject join with me in thanking the mercy of God for the escape you have had of murdering yrself or murdering yr. neighbour; from the bottom of yr. heart beg pardon of his Divine Majesty for transgressing his most essential laws & the scandal you have given, & never speak of the transaction without expressing sentiments of contrition. Such is the advice of a real & fast friend.

It is not only in the instance above alluded to but in many others, nearer my home, that I feel astonishment at the conduct of Catholics in violating the laws of their religion, whilst they profess themselves to be engaged in its service. What misrepresentations, falsehoods, deceptions, & sacrifices of Religion itself are not the Butlers, Jerninghams & their employers guilty of under pretence of serving religion? It has been proved that they are unable to say a word in defense of their conduct,[4] & yet they pretend to justify it on account of its alledged motive; the relaxation of certain penal laws. They now declare, that they will no longer *follow* the Irish, as they professed to do before the meeting of Feb. 1st,[5] but that they will precede them. This implies a threat of bullying the Irish & myself into the proposed arrangements. The object of these I am well assured is to lay our Church gagged & bound under the feet of an hypocritical Protest. establishment; & I am satisfied that our Parliamentary leaders are pledged to the Prott. Prelates & Universities to this effect by way of buying their consent to a measure now essentially linked with their coming into power. Of one fact I am perfectly assured that whenever the Emancipation can be obtained with the arrangements it will be attainable without them. At all events your Bishops & myself will die on the scaffold sooner than concede them: the question is no longer about giving a fresh security to the state, but of one actually cooperating to the security of an heresy & schism we are bound to destroy.[6]

I presume you have seen my letters in the *Statesman*[7] collected into a pamphlet. These letters have had a better effect than I expected & the heads of the Junta promise me that no such scenes as those which have passed shall take place in future. The letter of T.W.J.[8] added great weight to them, & I am much obliged to the author of it; but Mr Jerningham's Reporter, McDougal,[9] has stated the Duke's speech full as much in my favour as that writer has done. It will appear in Coglans Revised Report of the Debate.[10] Being unable any other way of expressing my gratitude to his Grace I begged his leave to dedicate my treatise now in the press, embellished with plates, *On the Ecclesiastical Architecture of the Middle Ages*, to him, which he has consented to. An abstract of that treatise will appear next month, in Rees's grand *Cyclopedia* under the head of *Gothic Architecture*.

I am sorry that Gilbert & King[11] of Dame Street object to dealing with Keating & ?.[12] The latter are not behind hand in complaining of the Irish Booksellers.

My English Brethren are exceedingly angry with the Irish Prelates for their 17th Resolution,[13] & have expressed themselves accordingly. But certainly it does not become three Vicars Apostc. with two coadjutors after being separately "*jockeyed*" into a measure to find fault with a whole Catholic Hierarchy deciding in solemn synod, because the latter have not agreed with them.

I beg my most respectful Compts. to Dr Bray & Dr Lanigan,[14] when you see them, likewise to Mrs Scully. Mrs Wheble desires me to say all that is kind to her & to you.   [*Source*: Scully Papers]

[1]See No. 252.

[2]p. 46.

[3]George Lidwill and H. D. Grady.

[4]On 29 May 1810 a meeting of Catholic noblemen and gentlemen held in Lord Shrewsbury's house in Stanhope Street had disowned Dr Milner and their resolution had been published in the *British Press* on 31 May. Dr Milner had counterattacked in *The Statesman* of 6 June and when there was no reply had claimed in another letter on 18 June that they were unable to defend themselves.

[5]Edward Jerningham had written to Hay on 16 January that it was the wish of the English Catholics "to adopt no measure but what may be considered auxiliary only to the more effectual exertions of the Catholics of Ireland" (Plowden, *History* III, p. 792).

[6]Although Dr Milner accused Catholic vetoists both of heresy and schism he seems here to be saying that it was the duty of the Catholics to destroy Protestantism.

[7]There were five letters, dated 19 and 30 May, 4, 16 and 20 June, published respectively on 31 May, and 2, 6, 18, 23 June.

[8]*Recte* L.T.J. Animadversions having been made on Dr Milner in the debate of 6 June the letter, dated Shrewsbury 10 June, quoted the Duke of Norfolk as praising Dr Milner's qualities and wishing it had never been said (by George Ponsonby on 25 May) that he was a man not to be believed (*The Statesman*, 12 June 1810).

[9]Unidentified.

[10]In *Hansard* (XVII, 411) it is very much abbreviated.

[11]The 1810 Dublin Directory shows only Gilbert and Hodges, of 27 Dame Street, described as Medical Booksellers although they published other material.

[12]Keating, Brown and Keating, successors to J. P. Coghlan who died in 1800. Catholic Library and Printing Office, 38 Duke Street, Grosvenor Square.

[13]In their 17th resolution of 26 February (see No. 233 n.2) the Irish Prelates had

thanked Dr Milner for "his late apostolical firmness in dissenting from and opposing a vague, general and indefinite Declaration or Resolution, pledging Roman Catholics to an eventual acquiescence in arrangements possibly prejudicial to the integrity and safety of our Church discipline". The other Vicars Apostolic, who had thought that Dr Milner had refused to sign the Fifth Resolution only because of his position as agent of the Irish church and who did not regard the resolution as a pledge, resented the implied rebuke (see Dr Poynter's letter of 12 April 1810 to Dr Troy in Westminster Diocesan Archives).

[14]Dr Thomas Bray, Archbishop of Cashel, and Dr James Lanigan, Bishop of Ossory.

258   *From Charles Butler to Merrion Square*

Lincolns Inn, 20 September 1810

Dear Sir,

With this, you will receive a long letter, on the general subject of the Roman Catholic concerns. Nothing was ever so unfortunate as the Veto; but, I really hope that, if the leading men on your side and our side the Channel, could be brought to a good understanding upon the subject, every thing might be arranged to the complete satisfaction of all parties. With this view I have framed the letter I have the honor of sending you. If it meets your approbation and you think it will sooth the angry minds on your side the water, I wish it circulated in any manner you think proper; either as a pamphlet generally published, or in the newspapers; or as a printed Letter for private circulation. On this subject, I wish to be guided entirely by yourself, but, if it is printed, I should wish that instead of my name's being subscribed to the letter, it should be subscribed with my known Signature, Hwyls. Any expence attending it, I will remit to you with great pleasure.

If it should be printed in any Newspaper, I should wish it to appear in the *Evening Herald*,[1] that being the newspaper which I take in, and it has been uniformly friendly to Catholic Emancipation.   [*Source*: Scully Papers]

[1]No copies of the *Evening Herald* of this time have been found, but it is likely that they refused to publish the article (see No. 266 n.1). Instead it appeared in the *Dublin Evening Post* of 30 October 1810 under the heading of "Letter to an Irish Catholic upon the necessity of another petition to Parliament". It argued that debates had a much greater effect outside the walls of the Houses of parliament than within and that the effects of repetition were irresistible: in the last debate no expression had been used that would have made it unpleasant to dine in the speaker's company next day.

259   *From Lord Donoughmore*

Knocklofty [Co. Tipperary] 7 October 1810
Dear Scully,

In the manner of transmitting to you your very able Memoir[1] on the present state of our Catholic Countrymen, I have ventured to commit a breach of your instructions, which I trust you will not think an unpardonable one, by affording to my worthy friend, your father, the same instruction & gratification, which it has so abundantly afforded to myself.[2] I own I was anxious, now on my return, to have given it another persual, but as you seem anxious to have it & I feared to trespass too much on your experienced kindness, I have denied myself that pleasure.

You are now so very near us, that I hope you will do me the additional kindness of not leaving the Country without paying a visit to my Brother & me. Nothing would give either him or me more satisfaction, than the receiving you here. We can ensure you a well aired bed, & good care of your horses. *Do come to us*. We have no intention of leaving home, & a late attack of the gout does not enable me as yet to dine abroad, so that you cannot come on a wrong day.   [*Source*: Scully Papers]

[1]Probably the early version of Scully's *Penal Laws* entitled "Commentaries . . ." (see No. 242 n.1).
[2]See No. 260.

260   *To James Scully from Lord Donoughmore*

Knocklofty [Co. Tipperary] 7 October 1810
My Dear Sir,

During the Course of the last Session, your son Denys had the goodness to confide to my perusal a memoir of his on the Catholic Question, drawn up with singular ability, & (with kindness towards me not less marked) hurried to its conclusion, with the friendly intention of giving me very valuable information on the important subject which I had undertaken to discuss. Having been permitted by him to retain it in my hands till my return to Ireland, I cannot restrain myself from exceeding the limits of this permission, to gratify the strong desire which I feel, that you should also peruse those pages, from which I will be bold to say, you will receive more real instruction, than from all the numerous dull dissertations & declaratory harrangues on the interesting topic of Existing Catholic disability, with which the public attention has been overlayd.

When you have gratified yourself by the perusal of this additional sample of the talents of your Son, will you have the goodness to put the accompanying statement into his hands.

My Brother Lord Hutchinson (now with me) & I have heard with equal satisfaction how strong you are in health & spirits, & how little you value the pressure of seventy two years of laborious & successful industry.

May the remainder of the Evening of your well spent life continue prosperous, unclouded & serene!   [*Source*: Scully Papers]

261   *From Edward Hay to 2 Merrion Square, Dublin*

4 Capel Street, Dublin, 13 October 1810

Dear Sir,

At a general meeting of the Catholics of Ireland held on the 13th of July[1] last it was resolved "That the meeting be adjourned to the second day of November next and that the present Committee do continue the management of Catholic affairs until that period."

The Committee have since met on the 26th of July[2] and first of August[3] when they adjourned to the 25th of October.

As a member of the Committee your presence is earnestly requested at one o'clock in the afternoon of Thursday the 25th Instant at D'Arcey's Hotel in Earl Street in order to secure an union of sentiment so essential to the Interest of the Catholics of Ireland preparatory to the adjournment of the general meeting to be held on Friday the 2d of November at the farming repository in Stephen's Green.[4]   [*Source*: Scully Papers]

[1] An aggregate meeting that was thrown into confusion by an attack on John Keogh in the *Freeman's Journal* of the same day above the signature of *Catholicus Ipse*. No decision could be reached either on whether to petition again after the recent defeats in parliament or on the election of a new committee (see Plowden, *History* III, p. 876).

[2] When a sub-committee of six, of whom Scully was one, was appointed to prepare a circular to the different counties of Ireland (Minute Book I).

[3] When the sub-committee's circular was approved (Minute Book I; text given by Plowden, *History* III, p. 882). Dated 30 July and signed by O'Connell as Chairman it was sent to every Catholic of consequence. It proclaimed the virtues of "self-agency", urged local meetings and observed that permanent boards, holding communication with the General Committee in Dublin, had been deemed useful in several counties. Dublin Castle transmitted a copy of the circular to the Home Office on 2 August (HO 100/159, f.10).

[4] See No. 263.

262   *From Revd Edmund Marnane[1] to Denys Scully, Barrister,*
Dublin

Tipp'y, 21 October 1810

Dear Sir,

I have perused your learn'd Memoir on the Catholic Question — 'tis a masterpiece — 'tis bold and manly — may you live long to enjoy the honor and credit of such an admirable production.

In the 88th page[2] you plead the cause of the Catholic Priest, "who refuses to disclose the secrets of his Penitent" — you do this in a masterly manner — yet I am aware that Protestant Courts of Justice in this Kingdom consider the Priest *only* bound to secrecy by some mere *Ecclesiastical regulation*, which, they think, should give way in cases of public justice and public necessity. I could therefore wish that the 4 last lines at the bottom of that page should be omitted, and that the Paragraph should run thus viz. "Certainly, it may be affirm'd with perfect confidence that no Catholic Priest in Ireland will be found to yield obedience in this Instance, or to betray the Sacred trust reposed in him — for as he believes the Sacrament of Penance to be of divine Institution, that *Confession* is one of its *essential* Parts, that an *inviolable Secrecy* attaches to *Sacramental Confession* — and that the Confessor is bound to suffer Death rather than reveal or divulge (by word or sign, directly or indirectly) and *sin* or *crime* or any *circumstance* attending the same mentioned by the Penitent in confession — yea that the whole Confession is to be buried in eternal silence," that he must forfeit eternal Salvation by such sacrilegious treachery, and even in this Life expose himself to perpetual degradation according to the Laws of the Catholic Church by being immediately deposed from all his *Priestly functions*, and closely confined in a Monastery — there to do penance during his Life — (see the General Council of Latern [*sic*] under Pope Innocent III in the year 1215 chapter *Omnis utriusque Sexus — de poenitentia . . .* (videlicet) [This is followed by seven lines of Latin quotation][3]

Why then should any Court of Justice require a Catholic Priest to give Evidence against his Penitent — to make Confession a State-Engine — to abuse the Sacrament of Penance, which was instituted by the Saviour of the World for *no other purpose* than to reconcile sinful man to his offended God.

Dear Counsellor if this hint meets y'r approbation you can dress it up, and couch it in y'r own stile. I am fully persuaded when your Memoir meets the public eye it will become the General topic of every Catholic family in Ireland and England — it will remind Parliament to do common justice to four millions of Irish Population.

I feel highly honour'd on this occasion, and beg leave to assure you of my most sincere regards and esteem.   [*Source*: Scully Papers]

[1]Edmund Marnane (1748–1827), parish priest of Tipperary 1780–1827, had been parish priest of Golden and Kilfeacle 1778–1780. He was educated at Louvain and ordained in Brussels 1772. In 1786 he opened a boarding school in Tipperary, for the classics, French, philosophy and mathematics.
[2]The reference shows that the Memoir seen by Father Marnane was the early draft of Scully's *Penal Laws* entitled "Commentaries upon the Code of Penal and Disabling Laws" (see No. 242 n.1), on page 88 of which Scully dealt with the secrecy of confession.
[3]In his *Penal Laws* Scully adopted Father Marnane's draft almost word for word, including the extract from the Lateran Council decree omitted here. The only substantive change was the omission, at the instance of Dr Milner (see No. 299) of the words "and closely confined in a monastery".

263   *From Edward Hay to 2 Merrion Square, 25 October 1810*

Pursuant to a resolution of a meeting of the General Committee held that day at D'Arcy's Hotel he asks Scully to attend a meeting of the same committee on the 31st,[1] preparatory to the general meeting intended for 2 November.[2]   [*Source*: Scully Papers]

[1]No record has been found of this meeting.
[2]At this aggregate meeting the decision was taken to petition early in the forthcoming session of parliament. Several Protestant gentlemen attended, and the *Dublin Evening Post* found "the rank and character of the Catholic body more observable than on former occasions" (*DEP*, 3 November 1810).

264   *To Richard Huddleston*

Merrion Square, 10 November 1810

Dear Rich'd,

[Having no banker in London he takes advantage of the offer made by Richard in a missing letter about adjusting the business between them to ask him to lodge £100 at Thomas Coutts & Co for the account of a Mr Tighe now at Vienna.[1] Referring to a release for another sum he says that Richard already has his letter and "if I die, my wife, (who would be my executrix) is an honest woman, as indeed most women are; and she would be as incapable, as I am, of acting unhandsomely."]

When I wrote to you my sentiments upon the subject, I had previously well considered them, and was thoroughly informed of the value and nature of the subject — but the kindness which I have always borne towards your family, their uniformly upright and correct conduct towards me, the accidents which have nearly trebled my income, and especially the well remembered merits of our beloved deceased friend, left me no room to hesitate about relinquishing that claim — and you may assure yourself, that I do fully adhere to the same principles, which then guided me.

We have an intention of going next summer through Scotland and the north of England. If we happen to find ourselves within 20 miles of Sawston, we shall avail ourselves of your invitation. I heard from Jane some time ago, dated Allerby,[3] then on her way to Scotland, whence I suppose she is now returned and settled at Stratford,[4] which town is, as I recollect upon the great Shrewsbury and Irish road.

Your old acquaintance Mrs Major Blake (formerly Maria O'Connor of Dominick Street) died of a consumption two months ago at Bodmin in Cornwall, leaving 3 children.[5] Mrs Moore and her daughter[6] have emigrated to Cheltenham

[P.S.] Frank[7] is naturalised here — and has posted himself in a handsome villa, near Drumcondra.   [*Source*: Huddleston Papers C3/S10]

[1]Probably Lady Mount Cashell's lover, George William Tighe, to whom she had borne a daughter in 1809. Her biographer does not record the visit to Vienna, but Tighe was at this time very hard up paying his father's debts (McAleer, *The Sensitive Plant*, p. 123).

[2]Jane Huddleston, now Mrs Canning.

[3]In Cumbria, west of the Lake District. They may have chosen this route in order to visit the homeland of the Huddlestons, whose senior branch had been the Huddlestons of Millom. When Richard Huddleston was up there in 1800 his aunt Mrs Bostock expected him to have met a Mr Huddleston of Whitehaven (Huddleston Papers C3/B16).

[4]At Foxcote, near Stratford on Avon in Warwickshire.

[5]See No. 255.

[6]Probably Anne Moore.

[7]Francis Huddleston.

265   *From Dr J. T. Troy, Archbishop of Dublin,*
                      to Merrion Square

Sunday, 11 November [18]10

My dear Sir,

I have read not only the chapter of your argumentative digest of the penal code against Catholics,[1] which you pointed out to me, but some others; and all with great satisfaction. The publication of it must prove highly useful, and acceptable to every enlightened & disspassionate Protestant.

I do not think you have omitted any legal grievance affecting Catholic religious worship or the Catholic clergy.

That you may live to witness the favorable impression which your meritorious industry & labour are calculated to make on the minds of our legislators and rulers is the ardent wish of etc, etc.

[P.S.] Best compts. to Mrs Scully

I am much better than I have been these days past, but still confined to my bed chamber.   [*Source*: Scully Papers]

[1]No doubt the same Commentaries as were read by Father Marnane (see No. 262).

266   *From Charles Butler*

Lincolns Inn, 17 November 1810
Dear Sir,

I am extremely obliged to you for your two letters and for your kind attention in sending me the Evening paper.[1] I have paid the £3.1.0 to Mrs Bostock.[2] I shall be much obliged to you to let one of your clerks direct the Editor of the *Evening Herald* to discontinue sending me that paper in future and to send me the *Dublin Evening Post*.

I understand that a new edition of Mr Alban Butler's *Lives of the Saints* is now printing in numbers in Ireland; I shall be much obliged to you to enquire who is the conductor of it;[3] I hope he is a gentleman of character.

I sincerely congratulate you on the event of the late debate. I have read Mr Finerty's speech, and admire it greatly.[4] I should think it cannot fail in producing a great effect. It is much spoken of in this country.

You know that I am a great advocate for the petition's being *universally* signed; may I recommend your taking this into consideration.

The prevailing opinion amongst us is that there will be Regency. It seems to follow of course that the Prince will be Regent; and I think it probable that the Regency will be conferred on him, without any limitation of his powers. To many persons, and to myself personally, His Royal Highness has expressed a decided conviction of the necessity of emancipating the Catholics without delay.[5] Whether, if he should succeed to the Regency, it will be decorous to urge the *immediate discussion* of your petition deserves consideration. Much must depend on the nature of the Regency. It may be considered as likely to last, but for a short time, or as likely to endure for the whole of the King's life. It even may be absolutely conferred for that period. In this last case, the Regent will, to use the expression of the civil law, be *eadem persona cum patre*; invested with all his rights and obligations, and consequently, as fit and proper to concur in the proposed emancipation as the Royal personage himself. But, if his regency should be limited, I think it will require some consideration, whether while it so continues limited, you should urge the discussion of your Petition. There seems ground to argue, that, common sense indicates that, such a Regency, evidently makes it proper that the Regent should generally confine the exercise of his powers to the ordinary acts of government. I think the public would give you great credit for such a forbearance. This is a delicate topic, and it will be time to consider it, when the event arrives.[6]

May I also recommend to you the preparing of the two acts of parliament, I suggested in my former letters;[7] one, that should repeal all the remaining laws, by a single enactment; the other, that should repeal them, separately, by separate enactments.

It seems a proper time to endeavour at the restoration of perfect good humour and harmony between the Irish and English Catholics. What can have indisposed your prelates against ours,[8] passes my comprehension, unless a mischievous person,[9] whom we all know, has effected it, by ungrounded representations of views, and motives, and influence, which I am sure never had an existence except in his own inflamed imagination. I suppose you have seen his two publications.[10] I can at once, most broadly and most explicitly assert, that, so far as respects Mr Jerningham or myself, the whole, without exception, is either absolute invention, (which includes the greatest part of it), or absolute falsehood or such misrepresentation as amounts to absolute falsehood: and I am sure the same may be predicated of what he says of Dr Poynter. If any of your prelates wish to hear more fully from me on the subject, I would write to them with great pleasure: but I must own myself hurt, that they allow the Libeller, after his printed libells, to style himself, publickly, their agent.

There was an Irish priest of the name of Delany,[11] who studied under my uncle Mr Alban Butler. I understood he settled in the neighborhood of Cashel. I shall be much obliged to you to enquire and let me know what has become of him.

If you see no objection I wish you would have the goodness to communicate to Dr Troy what I mentioned in my last letter[12] and what I mention in the present on restoring harmony between us. I really wish that one of your excellent prelates, or some impartial person by their direction, would honour us with a visit, and examine with his own eyes, the real state of things in this country. I am sure the report would be extremely favourable to us, and give great pleasure to your worthy prelates. It is very desireable that the breach should be healed. It not only paralyses the general efforts for the redress of grievances, but it occasions infinite scandal. Singular as it may be, it is very true, that the lower Irish in this country entertain a notion that our prelates have been declared schismatics by your prelates and therefore think and talk disrespectfully of them. The general mischief is incalculable. I really think you would well discern well [sic] of both Countries by doing any thing to heal this unfortunate breach. I hope you will let me hear from you at your earliest convenience, and am Dear Sir etc.   [*Source*: Scully Papers]

[1]The *Dublin Evening Post* of 30 October with his article (see No. 258 n.1).
[2]His first wife's aunt, with whom he still kept an account (MS.27, 493).
[3]The National Library of Ireland catalogue shows no new Irish edition before Coyne's of 1833. Butler may have meant a reissue of an old one — in 1819 J. J. Nolan advertised a reprint of Dr Carpenter's (*FJ*, 4 March 1819).
[4]At the aggregate meeting of 2 November Peter Finnerty's speech turned the scales in favour of petitioning. Scully found it "almost electrical" (*DEP*, 3 and 27 November 1810).
[5]This assertion is qualified in No. 268.
[6]On 15 November the two Houses of parliament had concurred in the administration's proposal to adjourn for a fortnight (*Hansard* XVIII, 21, 42) and it was not until 17 December that a plan for a limited regency was announced (see No. 279 n.3).
[7]Nos. 169 and 204.
[8]Butler had no doubt heard of, and perhaps seen, the acrimonious correspondence between Dr Poynter and Dr Troy regarding the Fifth Resolution (see No. 230 n.1) and the relationship between the Irish Prelates and Dr Milner (see Ward, *Eve* I, p. 154).
[9]Dr Milner.
[10]Possibly letters or articles in the press — his last published pamphlet of 1810 was his *Elucidation of the veto* in May.
[11]Not identified.
[12]No. 258.

267   *From Edward Hay, Secretary, to Merrion Square,*
19 November 1810

The General Committee on 17 November having appointed a sub-committee[1] to prepare the form of a petition and report on the 24th,[2] Scully is invited as a member of the committee to attend a meeting on the 22nd[3] to consider measures for carrying into effect the resolutions of the general meeting.[4]   [*Source*: Scully Papers]

[1]Of eleven members, of whom Scully was one (Minute Book II).
[2]At a meeting of the General Committee, when the petition was recommitted to another meeting on 29 November and a resolution thanking Lord Donoughmore was passed (see No. 271 n.1).
[3]The meeting did not take place, for lack of a quorum (Minute Book II).
[4]Of 2 November 1810 (see No. 263 n.2).

268   *From Charles Butler to Merrion Square*

Lincolns Inn, 19 November 1810

Dear Sir,

I enclose a letter[1] which I have had by me for some days.

It is now admitted that the King's malady is most serious, and that there is little hope of his recovering from it. *All* the Royal Princes side with the Prince of Wales,[2] & many great interests are supposed to be gone over to him.

Writing to you confidentially, I fear he is not *warmly* disposed towards us; but I am confident that if we act in concert unanimously & with prudence we shall succeed. The *Veto* is a giant in our way; I wish Your Prelates could be brought to a reconciliation with ours. There never was the least wish in our Clergy or Laity to [paper torn] the Veto against their wishes.

P.S. I hope my letter, Hwyls, is liked.[3]   [*Source*: Scully Papers]

[1]Possibly his own, No. 266.
[2]The news became public on 26 November when the Privy Council was summoned for the 28th (*Morning Chronicle*, 27 November 1810). The attitude of the Royal Princes was publicly confirmed four weeks later (ibid. 21 December 1810).
[3]Published in the *Dublin Evening Post* of 30 October (see No. 258 n.1).

269   *From Charles Butler to Merrion Square*

Lincolns Inn, 24 November 1810

Thinking the enclosed[1] may be a treat to you & some of your friends, I have had it copied for You: it is not sold, & the Copies of it are extremely scarce. The immediate return of the King's Health appears to me universally despaired of;[2] & there is a great falling off in the confidence of Lord Wellington's eating up the French.[3] But, (which is the best news I have heard for some time), the System of Terror, now carried on in France is full as great, and the Espionage & Imprisonments, as numerous, as in the worst time of Robespierre. It is generally supposed at Paris, that many who are imprisoned are taken off by poison.   Source: Scully Papers]

[1]A dissertation by Francis Hargrave (c. 1741–1821), legal antiquary and Butler's co-editor of "Coke upon Lyttleton", entitled *Brief Deductions relative to the aid and supply of the executive power, according to the laws of England, in cases of infancy, delirium, and other incapacity of the King*, printed but not published on the occasion of the King's first illness in 1788. It argued against limitation of a regent's powers.

[2]On 29 November the report of the physicians made it clear that the King was at that moment incapable of exercising his functions but held out hopes of a recovery, with the result that parliament adjourned to 13 December (*Hansard* XVIII, 78).

[3]Having defeated the French in a delaying action at Bussaco on 27 September Wellington had retreated to the lines of Torres Vedras outside Lisbon, where the French had arrived on 13 October.

270   *From Revd John Lanigan[1] to Merrion Square*

26 November 1810

Dear Sir,

I am very much obliged to you for the honour you have done me in submitting to my perusal your highly valuable treatise,[2] and for the kind expressions, with which you have been pleased to accompany that favour. Whatever my qualifications may be in other respects, I can safely lay claim to a great love for my country and a steady attachment to the cause, which you so ably advocate. This treatise has afforded me, besides a great store of instruction, more delight than I can express, and I sincerely wish that the publication of it be delayed as little as possible. It will not only be highly creditable to your talents and ability, but will also be more serviceable to the Catholic interest of Ireland and of the Empire than any work, which has appeared for a long time. I would advise the striking off a much greater number of copies than are usually worked off in ordinary publications, as I am certain it will meet with a very extended and rapid sale. Your having anticipated in a most masterly manner almost every thing, that could possibly occur to my mind on reading this tract, has left me little room for making use of the liberty you were so good as to allow me. My suggestions, such as they may be, are the result of as attentive consideration, as the extent of my information relative to the subjects treated of, and the limited leasure [sic] of my time would permit. May the Almighty bless your patriotic and truly religious exertions.

Believe me, Most Sincerely Yours, John Lanigan

[P.S.] The sheet of paper containing my observations is annexed to the MS.[3]   [*Source*: Scully Papers]

[1]1758–1828; born near Cashel; returned to Ireland in 1796 after being Professor of Hebrew, ecclesiastical history and divinity in Pavia; author of *The Ecclesiastical History of Ireland to the beginning of the thirteenth century*, published in four volumes in 1822.

[2]The draft of Scully's *Penal Laws*, no doubt the one seen by Dr Marnane (see No. 262 n.2).

[3]Not found.

271   *From Francis Hely Hutchinson to Merrion Square South*

Henrietta Street [Dublin] Monday Morning [26 November 1810]
My Dear Sir,

I received your note & card on my return home at a late Hour yesterday, & shall forward your communication[1] this day to Lord Donoughmore who will necessarily be highly gratified by the expression of the Catholic Body conveyed to him in so distinguished a manner, & I trust I need not say how truly sensible we must all be of the kind & effectual part you have taken on this occasion.[2]   [*Source*: Scully Papers]

[1]Evidently a private letter in advance of the official communication from Lord Fingall (see No. 272) to inform Lord Donoughmore of a resolution adopted by the General Committee on 24 November thanking him for his services in presenting the Irish Catholic petition (*DEP*, 27 November 1810). Scully was probably aware of Lord Donoughmore's feelings, as expressed in a letter of 6 November to his brother Francis: "if they do not express their acknowledgments for my exertions on the last occasion as they deserve I will never present another petition for them" (Donoughmore Papers, F/10/47).
[2]Scully's role had been to second the vote of thanks but he had earned additional credit by carrying the motion in opposition to John Byrne, who thought the Catholics were too prodigal with their votes of thanks. He praised Lord Donoughmore for having taken the petition on at a difficult moment (i.e. after Lord Grenville's refusal to present it — see No. 230 n.1) and said that having been present at the debate on 6 June he could speak of the happy effects resulting from it (*DEP*, 27 & 29 November 1810).

272   *From Lord Fingall to Merrion Square, Dublin*

Killeen Castle [Co. Meath] 29 November 1810
Private
My Dear Mr Scully,

I am extremely obliged to you for your letter to which I could not return an answer till to day having been yester day from home till a late hour. You will add much to the obligation I owe you for what you suggest in your letter by giving me your ideas of those things, which, can be most rested on in a letter to Lord Donoughmore and what you consider would be most acceptable to him and his family. Strongly as I feel disposed to do all possible justice to the Hutchinson family not less am I sensible that I am very inadequate to the task and you will I trust excuse the liberty I take with you, as the public good is at stake and will I am sure be much benefitted by your kind aid and assistance to me on this occasion.

No delay in transmitting the resolution of thanks to Lord Donoughmore will be occasioned, as I have not got that resolution from Mr Hay. This must be owing to his not having received a letter I wrote to him requesting to have that resolution separately as he sent it to me with *the other proceedings* of last Saturday, which I conceived *superfluous*. I shall write to Mr Hay for the resolution unless I receive it by to-morrow's post.

I have not been able to go since to Dublin being very much hurried with business & anxious to get my journey[1] over at this advanced season.

[*Source*: Scully Papers]

[1]To Edinburgh, where his son, Lord Killeen, was a student at the university (*DEP*, 30 November 1809).

273   *From Lord Fingall, Killeen Castle, to Merrion Square,*
1 December 1810

Private — Owing to another appointment he was not able to wait for the meeting of the committee[1] and see Scully. He has sent off his letter to Lord Donoughmore and hopes it will arrive before he leaves Knocklofty.

[*Source*: Scully Papers]

[1]At which a sub-committee was appointed to examine the grievances of the Catholic soldiery and report on 8 December, Scully being requested to communicate to it his digest of the penal code (Minute Book II).

274   *From Lord Fingall, Killeen Castle, to Merrion Square,*
6 December 1810

Private — As there was no post on Monday and he could not see Scully before Tuesday he sent off the letter with the resolution of thanks to Lord Donoughmore on Sunday. He regrets not having waited for Scully's excellent ideas, so well put. He is glad that the Prince has sent for Lord Hardwicke, who will tell him without disguise what ought to be done for Ireland.   [*Source*: Scully Papers]

275   *To Richard Huddleston from Merrion Square,*
6 December 1810

He has received Richard's letter of 18 November authorising him to draw £500 on him.[1] Although he has heard nothing from Coutts' he presumes that the £100 has been paid to them.[2] He has no objection to Richard's following his attorney's advice in the matter of the release. He is going to the country next week, returning after Christmas.   [*Source*: Scully Papers]

[1]Another instalment of his first wife's dowry (see No. 46).
[2]See No. 264 n.1.

276   *To Daniel O'Connell, Merrion Square, from Merrion Square*
                        18 December 1810

The introduction of his name in the *Freeman's Journal* report of 18 December on O'Connell's speech must prevent his putting into any circulation the compilation that he had prepared.[1] He had personal and private reasons against annexing publicity to his name and was now remanding the manuscript to his private drawer, at least until a more favourable occasion should offer.[2]

> [*Source*: O Connell, *Correspondence of Daniel O'Connell* I, No. 314, taken from the O'Connell Papers (NLI MS.13647)]

[1]The *Freeman's Journal* of 18 December had published a garbled report of a speech by O'Connell at the General Committee on 15 December. After moving for the appointment of a sub-committee to consider the best way of extending communications with the country parts of Ireland he suggested the establishment of a committee of grievances in order to have a statement placed in the hands of every member of the House of Commons. He said he would include in that committee a learned gentleman present and the *Freeman's Journal* added in parentheses: "Mr Scully, we believe, was the gentleman alluded to". Minute Book II shows that the task of "procuring an authentic statement of the penalties and privations under which the Catholics of Ireland labour" was to be entrusted, not to a committee of grievances, but to the sub-committee appointed to examine communications with the country parts.
[2]Scully's caution was justified. When writing to the Prime Minister on 21 December 1811 (see No. 321 n.6) Wellesley Pole said of the *Statement* of which he forwarded copies to the Home Secretary: "This is the first part of the work which was undertaken last year by the Committee of Grievances. Some of the Catholic lawyers (at their head Mr Scully) have been at work on it ever since. But they have kept it so secret that altho' I offered any sum for a perusal of the work as it went on I never could get it".

277   *From P. Finnerty to Merrion Square South, Dublin*
                        Marked "To be Forwarded"

                        [Postmarked 18 & 23 December 1810]
Dear Sir,

I hope you will ascertain what may be in your power with respect to the transaction at Monasterevan[1] & if you can without inconvenience to yourself obtain me any further information I will thank you much. I have had your letters forwarded. Compliments to Mr Scully.[2]

[P.S.] I fear the rumour relative to the Prince's intentions towards you is too true.[3]

The sooner I hear from you respecting the Monasterevan affair the more desirable.   [*Source*: Scully Papers]

[1]Finnerty was in Ireland collecting affidavits for his forthcoming trial for libelling Lord Castlereagh, whom he had accused of being responsible for the cruelties used in suppressing the rebellion of 1798. As his defence took the form of justifying his accusations and making further insinuations it is likely that the transactions at Monasterevan were acts which he considered cast further discredit on Lord Castlereagh: they may have had something to do with the hanging of a curate called Prendergast in 1798 and payments to his parish priest out of secret service money. If so, he failed to obtain the evidence as Monasterevan was not mentioned in the report on his trial (*Hansard* XIX, 284; W. M. J. Fitzpatrick: *Ireland before the Union* p. 219; *Proceedings in the case of the King, at the prosecution of Lord Castlereagh against Peter Finnerty*, London, 1811).

[2]Probably Scully's father. Scully had not met Finnerty before the meeting of 2 November (see No. 266 n.5) and there is no record of any further intimacy between them.

[3]Possibly to the effect that the Prince would defer to the King's known scruples on the Catholic question. At the beginning of December he had let it be known that if he became Regent he would not dismiss his father's ministers (Aspinall, *Correspondence of George Prince of Wales* VII, p.61).

278   *From Bishop John Milner to Merrion Square, Dublin*

Wolverhampton 20 December [1810]

Dr Sir,

I have been so much employed in writing for the press as well in the Antiquarian as in the Controversial line, that I have quite neglected some of my most valuable correspondts. & you Dr. Sir among the rest. However, late as it is, I now acknowledge the rect. of yr. letter, informing me & Mrs Wheble of the encrease in yr. family[1] & of the good health of Mrs S. on both which subjects I most heartily congratulate with you. I presume I am indebted to you for a Newspaper containing an admirable speech made by you in yr. Comtee.[2] & last night I was informed by a letter from Dr Troy that you had exerted yrself in behalf of the most oppressed, if not the most deserving part of the Irish Cathc. body, I mean the poor soldiers.[3] You may have seen different things which I have written on the subject of the persecution to which they are subject in the heart of the Catholic Countries of Sicily, Spain & Portugal.[4] Among other things I lately wrote three letters in the character of an Irish Cathc. dated Bristol & published in the

Statesman.[5] I do not wish, however, to inform Butler & Jernm. of this circumstance.[6] I am so much at a loss for want of information, concerning the state of parties in the Irish Catholic body that I do not even venture to form a settled opinion on the subject. On this account, & still more from a sense of duty, my politics are entirely confined to Religion, which I know & am sure is in the utmost danger from my former friends, the Grenvilles. If you doubt of it, read carefully Dillon's *Two Memoirs*, in which he professes (& I have reason from what I know myself & have heared from the same lips that he speaks the truth) to give you a detail of the arrangements & of the objects which they are intended to influence;[7] Read the degenerate *Schismatical* O'Connor's Two Numbers of *Columbanus*.[8] These breathe the spirit & speak the language of the Head of the Grenvilles, to whom he has sold *himself* together with his Irish Papers.[9] Believe me, Dr. Sir, & believe yr. own unbought Prelates that your religion will not be worth the least part of the trouble which you take about it, if Lord Grenville is allowed to fulfill his contract with the Protestant Bishops & Heads of Oxford when he became Chancellor of the University.[10]

When I advocated the Veto between two & three years ago[11] I honestly thought it meant nothing else but the degrading ceremony of giving a fresh test of civil allegiance: but now I find that it means the shackling & the stifling of our Church, in order to appease the jealousy of bigotted unbelieving parsons & their unfortunate head which has been so long subject to a delirium. I shall send you in the course of a few days in a parcel directed for *Mr Fitzpatrick to the care of Griffiths Owen Book-keeper at Holyhead* a new work of mine[12] which I think will throw a good deal of light on the present state of our Religion. When you have read it I shall be glad of yr. remarks on the subject. Alas! What matters the shell of religion, if we lose the kernel? What will it avail us to gain the Emancipation [? if we] lose our *souls*?

I am perfectly shocked at the dishonourable & unprincipled conduct not only of that *Old Rat of the Cathc. cause*, Chs. B[utler], but also of his too promising ape & secretary, my friend Edwd. Jerningham.[13] I have hitherto spared the latter, though you, if you see all the letters which yr. Comtee. or at least which Mr O'Connel[14] receives know that he never spares me, because I wd. not submit to be "*jockeyed*" by him, as he boasted to me of having served my brethren.[15] I believe I told you that when, on the return of the Post from Dublin, Feb. 8th,[16] he found that his decoy trap had failed of enclosing the wild ducks of Ireland, he complained to me that it was "Hard to be tyrannised over by Protestant Lords, as was the case with the English Catholics" at the same time acknowledging that I had "acted right in refusing to sign the 5th Resolution" & that he "wd. have acted the same part had he been in my situation".[17]

If you shew the Spirit of Irishmen you will get Emancipation on yr. own terms: if you submit to be bullied by Lord Grenville, besides all sort of spiritual mischeif yr. country will infallibly become the scene of a new Religious persecution & of all the evils attendant on it. Mrs Wheble joins in all that is kind to Mrs S. & yrself.

P.S. I need not inform you that all O'Connor's History is foul calumny or misrepresentation. He even praises the vile Hypocrite Ormond for giving up Ireland to the Presbyterian murderers, at the same time he considers this Marquis as the prototype of another Marquis his Patron.[18] As to his theology[19] & that of Dillon[20] it is schismatical & heterodox in every part.

[*Source*: Scully Papers]

[1]Vincent James Scully had been born on 8 September 1810.

[2]Probably his speech on the motion of thanks to Lord Donoughmore (see No. 271 n.2) which Dr Milner might have read in the *Dublin Evening Post* of 29 November.

[3]Scully had been in the chair at the General Committee on 8 December when a sub-committee reported on the transportation for life of a Catholic soldier (*DEP*, 11 December 1810).

[4]There are numerous references in his writings of this year to the grievances of Catholic soldiers forced to attend Protestant services even in Catholic countries and denied the consolations of their religion when dying. See particularly his artice of 13 January in Cobbet's *Political Register*.

[5]In the issues of 25 and 27 October, and 7 November. He carried the impersonation so far as to announce that he had just landed from Ireland. He was replying to a letter of 13 October signed by "an English Catholic" who had declared himself an enemy of the veto but advocated an "arrangement" which would secure the established Church against proselytising by Catholics. A passage in the third letter was seemingly directed against Scully himself. The "English Catholic" having cited the Kildare and Tipperary resolutions (see No. 233 n.2) as assenting to the proposed arrangements, Dr Milner replied: "I will not here enter into a detail of the means by which a very few lawyers, or other individuals, may so convene and pack a public meeting, as to make even a county speak directly the reverse of what it means".

[6]In his *Appeal to the Catholics of Ireland* Dr Milner had boasted of not using pseudonyms: Butler, recently called upon to quit his "lurking incognito" (see No. 254 n.2) might have noted the apparent inconsistency.

[7]John Joseph Dillon had recently published in book form *Two Memoirs upon the Catholic question, with an essay upon the history and effect of the coronation oath, and also an appendix*, Bath, 1810. He held that Catholics could take the Oath of Supremacy if the words "ecclesiastical or spiritual" were interpreted in the right sense and argued that the Imperial Parliament had a right, by virtue of the civil supremacy, to enact any regulations it deemed expedient, without the consent of the Catholics themselves, still less of the Pope.

[8]The first number, dated 16 March 1810, was entitled *Columbanus ad Hibernos or a letter from Columban to his friend in Ireland on the present mode of appointing Catholic bishops in his native country*. The undated second, to which Father O'Conor added his name, was *A letter on the novelty and danger of the new discipline now introduced into the Catholic Church of Ireland*. The two had been reprinted with the

addition of Part I of an historical address on "the calamities occasioned by foreign influence in the nomination of bishops to Irish sees". Father O'Conor condemned the existing method of a self-perpetuating hierarchy as uncanonical. Being opposed to any pretensions of the Pope outside the strictly spiritual sphere he was prepared to accept the intervention of the civil power as successor to the old Irish kings and advocated a more positive role both for the lower clergy and laity.

[9]In the correspondence referred to in No. 318 n.7 Dr Hugh McDermot MD, who knew the facts and deplored them, denied Dr Milner's allegation that Dr O'Conor had sold to the Marquis of Buckingham the papers of their common grandfather, Charles O'Conor of Belanagare.

[10]On 13 December 1809.

[11]In May 1808 (see No. 168 n.3).

[12]Probably his *Instructions addressed to the Catholics of the Midland Counties of England* which, although dated 1811, was in the press in December 1810 (Husenbeth, *Life*, p. 197).

[13]He is probably referring to the Stanhope Street meeting of 29 May 1810 (see No. 257 n.4) and perhaps also to an offensively worded letter from the English Catholic Board to Dr Troy about the authenticity of the Irish Prelates' 17th resolution (see No. 257 n.13) thanking Dr Milner — see Ward, *Eve of Catholic Emancipation* I, p. 144.

[14]The correspondence is referred to in a letter of 28 February 1810 from Edward Jerningham to Sir John Throckmorton: "The frenzy of religious and political fanaticism is now raging in Ireland to a degree I cannot make you fully sensible of without your seeing the *private* correspondence and instructions to Mr Hay. Dr Milner has given vent to this flame, and the mischief he has perhaps done is beyond calculation. I am holding a double correspondence with Mr O'Connell the Acting Secretary in Ireland — the one, official, the other, confidential. The first has assumed a character which must preclude all further communication for the present, between the two bodies; the latter discloses the real grounds of this unfortunate division — Mr O'Connell says 'you cannot form an estimate of this propensity to slander you, but the secret really is to be found in the hereditary hatred which seven centuries of oppression has inspired in the Irish mind. *We all* participate, I will frankly avow, in this feeling, which in vulgar minds confounds all distinctions . . . [words omitted by Jerningham] you will I am sure see at once that I write in the most perfect confidence; I should have my head broken, if it were known that I dared to think aloud with an Englishman'" (Throckmorton Papers, Gate Box folder 11). This is probably the letter of 23 February which, with O'Connell's permission, Jerningham copied to Hay on 8 September 1810 (DDA 390/1, XV, 18).

[15]Dr Milner claimed that after the signature of the fifth Resolution on 1 February 1810 he had been told by Jerningham: "do not be angry with your brethren; they resisted as long as they could but we jockeyed them" (Husenbeth, *Life*, p. 213).

[16]The date on which the Irish delegates then in London received a reply to their letter of 1 February about the Fifth Resolution. Dr Milner accused the English Catholics of tricking the Irish into accepting the veto under another guise by "acting the part of a few tame decoy ducks" (*The Statesman*, 23 June 1810).

[17]i.e. as agent of the Irish clergy — a fuller account of the conversation is given by

Husenbeth, *Life*, p. 214. It was not clear at the time to all the others involved that Dr Milner was also opposed to the Fifth Resolution in principle (Ward, *Eve*, p. 122).

[18]The Marquis of Buckingham. James Butler, 12th Earl of Ormonde, was created a marquis in 1642. Father O'Conor, in *Columbanus* No. 2, had excused his giving Dublin up to the parliament side in the civil war on the ground that the Papal Nuncio was plotting to give the crown of Ireland to a foreign prince.

[19]Father O'Conor was suspended in 1812, but no passage sufficiently definite to be declared heretical had been found in his first two *Letters* (Ward, *Eve* I, p. 148).

[20]In Appendix G to his *Instructions* (n.12 above) Dr Milner analysed Dillon's heterodoxy and declared he was no Catholic.

279   *From Lord Fingall, Edinburgh, to Merrion Square,*
                        27 December 1810

Scully's letter of the tenth has followed him to Edinburgh, whither because of the bad weather they travelled very slowly. He returns the copy of a letter to Lord Donoughmore which Scully sent him.[1] A few days ago he sent to Hay for the committee Lord Donoughmore's reply to his own letter.[2] In London things wear an uncertain appearance. The forces are mustering so much on all sides that not a member of either side remains in Edinburgh. He hopes Ireland will not be forgotten in these momentous proceedings.[3] Lady Fingall joins in best compliments of the season to Scully and Mrs Scully.   [*Source*: Scully Papers]

[1]With Scully's papers, but omitted here. It is described as "Draft merely as to the general heads etc" and it is an effusive expression of thanks with an encomium on the Hely-Hutchinson family.

[2]The exchange of letters was published in the *Dublin Evening Post* of 3 January 1811.

[3]The administration's plan for a limited regency had been published on 17 December and following a serious relapse in the King's health on 21 December all Privy Councillors had been summoned to London (*Morning Chronicle*, 18–27 December 1810).

280   *From Francis Plowden to Merrion Square, Dublin*

                                      Arran Quay [Dublin] Wednesday
My dr Sir,

As you ment[ione]d to me the other day, if I mistake not, that you had by you the *Messenger* or some other paper or papers containing Mr Ryan's letters etc.[1] I will thank you extremely for the loan of them for some few days. Shd you have a Copy of the Catholics' address to the Duke of Bedford[2] I will thank you also for it & return you all with gratitude.

[*Source*: Scully Papers]

[1]A letter from James Ryan describing the origins of the Catholic Committee in 1804 and reproducing his correspondence with Charles James Fox in 1806 was published in the *Freeman's Journal* of 11 August 1810. Plowden made use of it in his *History* II, p. 296.
[2]Plowden ibid. p. 323 reproduces the address of the nobility and gentry of 29 April 1806 (see No. 146 n.1).

281   *From Charles Butler*

Lincolns Inn, 15 January 1811

Dear Sir,

I avail myself of Mr Blake's going to Ireland, to request your acceptance of the contents of this Parcel. I believe him to be a very discrete and sensible man, and I have requested him to procure for us, all the information he can, respecting Catholic affairs in Ireland: In which, if you can serve him, you will oblige us. We suppose the Regent will not be constructed before the 24th of this month.[1] It transpires that the King's Malady is very violent, when he is under the influence of it, — sometime supposing himself to be hunting, & sometimes at the head of his army. But this is between ourselves.

I think the prince has gained ground in public opinion: Opposition are thought to have been injudicious.[2] At your leisure, I shall be obliged to you, for your opinion, on the measures we ought, or are likely to be necessitated to pursue.   [*Source*: Scully Papers]

[1]The Regency bill was introduced in the House of Lords on 23 January.
[2]Butler may have been thinking of a remonstrance which Lord Grenville and Earl Grey addressed to the Prince on 11 January "in a manner highly constitutional, but not withal very conciliatory from two statesmen on the eve of their appointment" (Lord Holland, *Further Memoirs of the Whig Party*, p. 85).

282   *From A. R. Blake to Merrion Square, Dublin*

Merrion Square, Sunday [January 1811] ½ past 10 o'clock forenoon
Mr Blake has been requested by Mr Butler of Lincoln's Inn to deliver a parcel to Mr Scully which is left herewith: Mr Butler also wished him to have some conversation with Mr Scully on the Catholic Question, and to show Mr Scully a letter on the subject; Mr Blake will therefore have the honor of calling again on Mr Scully at half past eleven o'clock as he understands that

Mr Scully is expected at home by that hour, and Mr Blake is rather pressed for time, having only arrived from England last night, and being obliged to leave Dublin this afternoon.   [*Source*: Scully Papers]

283   *From A. R. Blake to Merrion Square, Dublin*

Hollypark, Loughrea (Co. Galway] 27 January 1811

Dear Sir,

As the Regency question is still under discussion,[1] perhaps the Catholic Committee may adjourn on Saturday next without transacting any business of importance. I shall be much obliged if you will inform me whether they are likely to do so for my return to Dublin will be regulated by your ideas on the subject.[2]   [*Source*: Scully Papers]

[1]The Regency Bill, which restricted the Regent's powers for twelve months, so that no action of a long lasting character might be taken to which the King might object if he recovered, received its third reading in the House of Lords on 29 January (*Hansard* XVIII, 1086).
[2]At the General Committee's meeting of 2 February there was a call for another aggregate meeting because the position arising from the King's illness had not been foreseen when the decision to petition was taken on 2 November 1810 (see No. 263 n.2). O'Connell, however, carried a motion that the petition be presented forthwith, pointing out that as it could not be debated before May there was ample time to ascertain the sentiments of the counties and if necessary postpone it for another year (*DEP*, 7, 9 and 14 February 1811).

284   *From Lord Donoughmore to Merrion Square, Dublin*

27 Somerset Street, Portman Square [London] 8 February 1811

Dear Scully,

Knowing how much I am interested in whatever relates to the progress of the Catholic cause, Mr Hay is so good as to communicate to me from time to time the transactions of their General Committee,[1] in which you justly take so forward a part. In my reply to one of his late letters, in which he had mentioned the resolution to address the Prince on his assuming the functions of the Regency, I stated candidly to him, how unadvisable I thought it would be to introduce to his Royal Highness the subject of your just expectations, under the circumstances of the moment, such as I then considered them to be. I urged in support of my opinion the weakness that must necessarily attend the Government of any Regent, when put in contradistinction to that of the Monarch administering for himself — the peculiar disadvantages which belonged to a regency so restricted — the endeavours which had been so unceasingly used to mislead & misrepresent on the subject of your particular question — & the impolicy of committing the fate of the Catholic cause to the sinews of such an administration, emasculated, if I may use the expression, by the successful jealousy of their rivals for power — as their leading measure.[2]

If such were my feelings, when I considered a friendly Prince as presiding at the head of a no less friendly Cabinet, what must they be under the present circumstances,[3] when his Royal Highness has felt it to be his painful duty to continue the administration of his father, already stated to be on his progress towards recovery, in the same hands to which he had himself confided it. I call it a painful duty, because the Prince had selected for his Ministers those men, who were alike the objects of his own confidence & of that of the public; & had obtained their acquiescence, however reluctant, in undertaking the fearful responsibility at this terrible crisis of public affairs. His Royal Highness however could not suffer the imputation to rest upon the mind of any man in existence, in case of the relapse of the King after a change of Ministers, that this act on the part of the son could have tended to delay the recovery of his father. Under this impression the Prince released his real friends—I mean the party with whom I am acting—from the engagement which they had made to accept office at the hands of his Royal Highness with prospects however unpromising — & has undertaken the irksome task of taking up the public business, in the same state, & under the same management to which his father had confided it.

Need I say, after such a statement of this transaction & of the grounds on which it has proceeded, that the Prince of Wales possesses still the affectionate duty & undiminished confidence of that powerful body of men, to whom the Government was to have been confided — that they continue to entertain all their former sentiments with respect to the present ministers, tho' they are now the Ministers of the Prince Regent — & are just as ready as they were at any time to oppose their measures, & to resist the unconciliating spirit, which has so long poisoned the springs from which their miserable policy has never ceased to flow.

I have given you this true picture of the state of our political world at the present moment, that you & our other Catholic friends may see things in their proper light, & be enabled to form a correct judgment for their own guidance — under circumstances of unparalleled difficulty. I never meant, by my letter to Mr Hay, either to dissuade or recommend the measure of addressing the Prince Regent, so far as such address should be confined to the expression of confidence in his general administration of public affairs — & of the just reliance which Ireland in particular placed on the well assured regards of his Royal Highness to her interests. In deciding upon the subject of addressing, the Catholic Committee will act upon the impression of their own genuine feelings — & their decision cannot fail of being what it ought to be.

I cannot conclude without apprising you of a wilful misrepresentation of that part of the proceedings of the Catholic Committee, which relates to the selection of 10 persons from each County as additional managers of their petitions to Parliament. This was strongly enveighed against to me on Wednesday last, at the Privy Council which was open to men of both parties, by a leading person amongst the *King's friends*, as a manifest violation of the Convention Act, & as an attempt to assemble in Dublin, a Catholic Parliament, exceeding in its numbers the House of Commons when we had a Parliament of our own.[4] You may be sure I did not suffer this misrepresentation to pass current, & I only mention the fact to you now to shew you how much you must all be upon your guard, & how much your enemies are on the search for any occasion to pick a hole in all your proceedings, however guarded or free from any just cause of offense. What I allude to of course happened in a private conversation between another Individual & myself, & had no reference to any business on which the Council might have been engaged.

[P.S.] I must tell you in confidence, that many a man — unau[thoris]ed I am thoroughly persuaded — takes upon himself to say, [what the] Catholics will do, & what they will not do — & letters have even been read, in which the writer takes upon himself to answer for the conduct of that important body of men. Such persons have of course their own objects in view, to which they would intend to make a great national question the ladder only by which they would ascend to the gratification of their individual interests.[5]

I this moment find that I am too late for this day's post.

[*Source*: Scully Papers]

[1]Hay's circular of 1 January (see n.4 below) and minutes of meetings from 5 January to 2 February concerning a congratulatory Address to the Prince on his becoming Regent, the composition of a delegation to present it and the adoption of a petition (Minute Book II; *Hansard* xix, 17).

[2]See Aspinall, *Correspondence of George, Prince of Wales* VII, No. 2819 for a copy of Lord Donoughmore's letter of 17 January to Hay, together with an extract from Hay's letter of 12 January. Lord Donoughmore wrote another letter to Hay which he sent under cover of a letter of 14 February to Francis Hely Hutchinson, but fearing that Hay might "smother" it he asked his brother to show it to Scully. The letters to Scully and Hay, as well as another to Lord Fingall, are described by Lord Donoughmore as "ostensible" and meant to be "communicated". He himself made known at least the tenor of the present letter to Carlton House where he was received on the 13th: "The Prince and his friends seem to feel much the kindness etc. etc. of my letter to Scully". He hoped to get from Dublin replies that he could show the Prince, intimating that the Irish Catholics would not press their claims — "Let me have letters from Scully and others". On 24 February he explained to his brother that his object had been to put the Catholics on their guard against the delusion which the Prince appeared to be practising on them, by giving reason to suppose that although Perceval was to be his minister the Catholic question would be conceded (Donough-

more Papers F/10/53–6). Scully minuted this letter as having been answered on 23 and 27 February but the letters are missing.

[3]Before being installed as Regent on 6 February the Prince had announced that he would keep Spencer Perceval and his administration in office.

[4]Hay's circular of 1 January, proposing the appointment of ten managers of petitions in each county, claimed that the Convention Act did not interfere with the subject's right to petition, "nor of course with the only method by which so large a body as the Catholics of Ireland could concur in the forwarding of a petition . . .". Lord Donoughmore's informant, one of over ninety Privy Councillors attending the installation of the Regent, would appear to have heard of the circular before the Chief Secretary did (see No. 285 n.1).

[5]Lord Donoughmore made his meaning clearer in his letter of 9 February to Francis Hely-Hutchinson. The letters which had been read, he said, tried to create the impression that the Catholic Committee was a most manageable body and might be moulded to any shape most agreeable to the Prince. As regards those who had their own objects in view he told his brother that he was referring to the would-be delegates who might accompany Lord Fingall and "are desirous of trying their fortunes on this side of the water (as Lord French did heretofore)", but he could not put in writing what might be insinuated in conversation. He added that "it might not be disagreeable to our friend Scully himself, to take a trip to this side of the water as Chargé d'Affaires" (Donoughmore Papers, F/10/54).

285   *From Charles Butler to Merrion Square*

Lincolns Inn, 7 March 1811

Dear Sir,

I write to communicate to you, a piece of intelligence, which I have just heard from the highest Authority. *Both the Duke of Richmond and Government gave up Wellesley Pole.*[1]

I am no believer in the King's soon reassuming the Reins of Government. In the first place, he is himself very desirous of doing it, a strong proof that the Dogstar still rages; I believe this has already given occasion to a Council extraordinary. In the next place, the discussions which took place on Mr Whitbread's motion,[2] have strongly impressed the public with the conviction of the justice of Lord Thurlow's opinion,[3] that when once Madness has completely settled on any person, it is a long time suspended over him, after it ceases to appear; so that a very long interval must take place, before it can be thought to be wholly removed.

As you expressed a wish to hear from me, occasionally, as the first circumstance I have mentioned, seemed to me important, I have troubled you with these Lines.   [*Source*: Scully Papers]

[1]Having only on 10 February learnt of the circulation of Hay's circular of 1 January (see No. 284 n.4) and being informed that the new Committee augmented by the

county delegates would meet in Dublin on 23 February at the latest, W. W. Pole had on 12 February instructed sheriffs and magistrates to take action under the Convention Act of 1793 against Roman Catholics who "are to be called together, or have been called together, to nominate or appoint persons as representatives, delegates or managers, to act on their behalf as members of an unlawful assembly sitting in Dublin and calling itself 'The Catholic Committee'" (see *Hansard* XIX, 1 for text). On 23 February he had sent police officers to disperse a meeting at Fitzpatrick's in Capel Street, but they had desisted on receiving an assurance from Lord French that it was not a meeting of the Committee. Meetings held on 26 February and 2 March were not interfered with, the administration discerning a change of tone and hoping that once the petition had been got off the Committee would quietly expire (Richmond to Ryder 1 March 1811: HO 100/163, f. 174). The government in London had approved of Pole's circular, while expressing the hope that it might not be necessary to enforce the law (Ryder to Richmond 18 February 1811: State Paper Office: Private and Official Correspondence f. 168). However, the suddenness of Pole's proceedings, taken without prior consultation, had placed the administration at a disadvantage and in the debate on 7 March he was left to make his own defence of the measures he had taken (*Hansard* XIX, 278).

[2]On 25 February Samuel Whitbread had moved for a committee to report on the King's illness in 1804 when, he had alleged, Lord Eldon, the Lord Chancellor had improperly signified the King's assent to certain acts although his mind was more disordered than it was now (*Hansard* XIX, 68).

[3]Whitbread had recalled a case in which Lord Eldon had been associated with Lord Thurlow when the latter was Lord Chancellor. They had succeeded in getting a commission of lunacy superseded for a client whom, after a series of interviews, Lord Thurlow considered to be perfectly well; but who on returning to thank him showed such evident signs of insanity as to make him regret his success.

286   *From Edward Hay to 2 Merrion Square, Dublin*

4 Capel Street [Dublin] 13 March 1811

Dear Sir,

At a meeting of the Catholics of Ireland held on the 8th instant[1] it was resolved that an humble petition be presented to his Royal Highness the Prince Regent — praying that he may order an enquiry to be instituted into the private evidence upon which the late Circular letter signed W. W. Pole[2] has been declared to have been grounded, and when it shall on such Enquiry as it must appear that no such Evidence does Exist that his Royal Highness be graciously pleased to remove Charles Duke of Richmond and the Right Honorable W. W. Pole from their Official Situations with Government of this Country.[3]

It was also resolved that our secretary Mr Hay be directed to call a meeting to appoint five persons to prepare the petition to the prince and that it shall be transmitted by the Delegates who Carry over the address.[4]

Your attendance is accordingly requested at the Committee rooms 4
Capel Street at one o'Clock in the afternoon of Saturday the 16th of March.[5]

[*Source*: Scully Papers]

[1]An aggregate meeting, which endorsed the General Committee's resolution of 2
March that petitions to the two Houses of Parliament be transmitted by Lord Fingall
to Lord Donoughmore and Grattan (*Hansard* XIX, 307).
[2]See No. 285 n.1.
[3]In his speech on 7 March Wellesley Pole noted that at the committee meeting of 2
March Major Bryan had given notice of a motion to pray the Regent to dismiss the
Duke of Richmond, but on being informed that he could not do this in the
committee, which had been appointed for a specific purpose, he had deferred it to an
aggregate meeting. He had a perfect right, observed Pole, to do this at an aggregate
meeting (*Hansard* XIX, 307).
[4]i.e. the "dutiful and loyal address", to adopt which the meeting of 8 March had been
called (DDA 54/1, VI, 61).
[5]An entry for 15 March in his father's diary shows that Scully was then at Mantlehill
planting trees. The sub-committee's draft was rejected on 18 March by one prepared
by Fitzsimon (Minute Book II) — probably Michael Fitsimon, a Catholic barrister.

287   *To Richard Huddleston*

Merrion Square, Dublin, 29 April 1811
Dear Rich'd,

I have been for some weeks absent from Town, partly on Circuit & partly
at my father's which your kindness will accept as an excuse for my tardy
Answer.[1]

Accompanying this, is the Deed of Release to you, duly executed by me,
and relinquishing the claim,[2] of which you honourably apprised me. I made
a slight alteration, not in the essential part, but in the formal recital of the
Consideration, more for the sake of recording the true grounds of this Act,
namely my personal regard for yourself & your family, than for any other
reason.

Whenever you meet Lord Hardwicke, I beg you will tell him from me,
that, as a cordial approver of his Administration in Ireland, I shall willingly
afford him any Information he may require concerning affairs here, as
correctly and as candidly as may be in my power.[3]

You have heard of our new Cousin, Don Francisco's[4] Spouse, *nuper*[5] Miss
White — handsome, young, unportioned & a Protestant, she is probably the
counterpart of Harry's Elect[6] — *Sed de Carthagine melius est silere quam
parva dicere.*[7] Do you never intend to ramble from Sawston? We shall
probably not stir from Dublin this Summer, & should be glad to see you.
You might like to see Dublin after 12 years, & form comparisons.

I believe the *Harp* to be a good paper.[8] The Specimens I have seen do great Honour to its Editors. My father & several of my friends take it — and it is peculiarly a Catholic London newspaper.

I hope your mother is well, and beg to be kindly remembered to her.

[*Source*: Huddleston Papers C3/S12]

[1]During his absence from Dublin Scully attended and probably organised an aggregate meeting of Protestants and Catholics held at Thurles on 15 April, Lord Lismore in the chair. An address to the Prince Regent and a petition to the House of Commons were adopted, after which the Protestant gentlemen withdrew "cheered by the rapturous acclamation of a grateful people". Scully then addressed the Roman Catholics: he favoured annual petitioning but did not think it necessary to present a separate petition on the present occasion. (*DEP*, 18 April 1811). A petition of "freeholders professing various religious persuasions of Tipperary" was laid on the table by General Mathew on 22 May (*Hansard* XX, 271).

[2]Probably one which Scully enjoyed as his first wife's legal heir.

[3]No such reports have been found in Lord Hardwicke's papers.

[4]Francis Huddleston.

[5]"Lately". Her name was not White but Pike (see the entry for a son, Thomas Huddleston, in the *King's Inns Admissions Papers*).

[6]Burke's *History of the Commoners*, 1836, says that Henry Huddleston married Miss Ann Goodchild but does not give a date.

[7]A slightly inaccurate quotation from Sallust's *Bellum Iugurthinum*, 19, 2 "As for Carthage it is better to be silent than to say too little".

[8]Published by Ballintine and Byworth: in Ireland subscriptions were received by Hugh Fitzpatrick, 4 Capel Street, Dublin, and John Reynolds, High Street, Kilkenny. The first number appeared on 2 December 1810 and copies are extant in the National Library of Ireland up to 3 February 1811. Dr Milner, who contributed at least two articles, understood it to be edited by a man banished from Ireland for having joined in the rebellion (Husenbeth, *Life*, p. 211).

288   *From Bishop John Milner to Merrion Square, Dublin*

Wolverhampton, 1 May 1811

Dr. Sir,

I have to beg pardon for not answering yr. letter of March 4 immediately upon rect. of it, as one part of it related to practical business, that concerning the admission of a youth[1] to the Park school but I happened to be then engaged in finishing a new work on the old subject, which, I suppose will soon appear in Dublin.[2] Before this was done the youth arrived & of course, the necessity of a *speedy answer* became less urgent. I did not fail, however, to consult with the President of the school as I do not choose to exert my full authority there. He represented that the House was over flowing, there being 201 boys in it besides masters & servants, & that he dreaded taking a youth who had been on shipboard. Still my interest or my authority wd. have prevailed for the reception of the youth at no great distance of time, which I meant to inform you of, when he actually arrived at the Park. The President was greatly displeased & was disposed to have refused him admission, when I interposed. Since that time the boy has been at the point of death; but is recovered & contrary to all expectations behaves extremely well. I shall be extremely happy to see you & Mrs S. at W[olver]h[ampton] when you come to England in case I shd. be at home at the time. Mrs Francis Canning was in my Dist. in Cambridgeshire, as well as she is in it now[3] & I was better acquainted with her before her marriage than I have been since, owing to the different lines of Religious Politics which her husband & I pursue.[4]

The Duke of Norfolk & myself have become exceedingly intimate, in consequence of what took place in the House of Peers on the night when you were there.[5] I made him the only acknowledgment in my power, by dedicating my late "Treatise on the Ecclesiastical Architecture of England during the Middle ages" to him, with which he was highly pleased, & he has since shewn me great civilities.

As I think that my late pamphlet called *Instructions etc.*[6] will have given you some information relative to the plan of arrangements intended by Lord Grenville etc. for the Catholics, so I flatter myself that my new pamphlet, alluded to above will communicate more to you. I foresee, however, that an acquaintance of yrs. in Lincolns Inn[7] will not be over-much pleased with it. For my own part, Bishop as I am, I wd. rather quit my religion at once than submit to its being made a state tool of, in the manner that Mr Pitt & Lord Grenville had planned the matter; and of all hypocrites, in my opinion, the most contemptible is a Catholic clergyman who professes our religion, & betrays it for interest or favour. Such a man is Dr O'Connor, as you will be convinced by reading my pamphlet, or without that, by reading his pamphlets. He & Dillon[8] are the only two Irishmen of any note who appear to be false both to their country & their religion. The former, I fear is gone mad & is in actual confinement at Edinburgh.

I beg my kind & respectful Compts. to Dr Lanigan[9] & regret exceedingly that I shd. have seen less of that great & good Prelate than of any other Catholic prelate in Ireland. Mrs Wheble desires all that is kind to Mrs Scully & yrself.

P.S. For the health of yr. soul & the credit of yr. family do not mix your unsullied reputation with the degraded character of the Old Rat of the Cathc. cause. He never acted or conversed during the 25 years of my acquaintance with him with the fairness & candour of a good Christian & a gentleman. Those who employ him do not trust him. You will recollect how strongly I cautioned you against him in the year 1808.[10]

With respect to myself, though I am flouted by many of the Cathc. Gentry, yet I have proofs that they inwardly respect me & approve of my conduct: & the public has abundant proof that they cannot meet me in fair argument on the present business. You & yr. family have great weight, & if you will support with vigour the Hutchinsons, Genl. Mathews,[11] the Marquis of Tavistock[12] etc., the Emancipation will be carried, whenever it is practicable at all without any degrading or irreligious compromise. For my part, I solemnly vow that I will rather [?lose] my life than submit to the terms of my old [one word missing] the Grenvilles & Sir Jn. Hippisley.

[*Source*: Scully Papers]

[1]Probably a Francis Smith, for whom in September 1811 Scully paid £39–18–6 to the President of Sedgley Park School on behalf of Lady Mount Cashell; and presumably related to Mary Smith, to whom Scully made a payment of £50 on her order in August (account book MS.27493). Mary Smith was Lady Mount Cashell's maid until 1814 (McAleer, *The Sensitive Plant* p. 124).

[2]*Letters to a Roman Catholic Prelate of Ireland in refutation of Charles Butler's Letter to an Irish Catholic Gentleman, to which is added a postscript containing a review of Dr O'Connor's works, entitled Columbanus ad Hibernos on the liberty of the Irish Church*, 1811. The letters are dated respectively 20 March and 8 April.

[3]Formerly Jane Huddleston of Sawston, now at Foxcote in Warwickshire.

[4]The Minute Book of the Cisalpine Club shows that with his father he was a founder member and regularly attended its dinners, enough in Dr Milner's eyes to mark him as a follower of Charles Butler.

[5]On 6 June 1810, when the Irish Catholic petition was debated (see No. 257 n.9).

[6]See No. 278 n.12.

[7]Charles Butler.

[8]John Joseph Dillon, author of the *Two Memoirs* which Dr Milner had attacked (see No. 278 n.7).

[9]Dr James Lanigan. Bishop of Ossory, founder of the Kilkenny Academy where Scully was at school.

[10]Either when Scully was in England in June 1808 (see No. 163 n.5) or when Dr Milner was in Dublin at the end of September 1808 (see No. 185).

[11]*Recte* General Montagu Mathew.

[12]Son and heir of the 6th Duke of Bedford, recently Lord Lieutenant. He was one of the stewards at a dinner given by Protestant sympathisers for the Irish Catholic delegation in London (*DEP*, 21 May 1811).

288A   *From Thomas Wallace*[1]

[? May 1811]

My Dear Sir,

I have read over the sheets you sent me — and find some difficulty in making up my mind upon it with reference to the object for which you requested me to peruse it. It is certainly, upon the whole, an exaggerated statement of Catholic Grievances tho it contains much truth strongly and well put — and had the writer in certain instances confined himself to stating some of the subjects of complaint as evils which the Catholics are *liable to suffer* from the present state of things rather than as *wrongs actually inflicted* by the Government, the *Protestant Church* or the *Protestants* — the work would have been less exceptionable and more certainly useful. As it stands I think if Government should think it prudent to notice them there are passages in it which would most likely maintain an information *ex officio* ag[ainst] the Publisher as libellous. I have made pencil marks in the margin of those passages.

It certainly is difficult to draw the line within which animadversions on *existing laws* of the land are safe — and beyond which they are libellous. Perhaps no such fixed line can be drawn. But I think it is pretty nearly true generally speaking that when such animadversions on existing laws are conveyed in language tending to excite the feelings of the populace to commotion — or to bring the whole system of Government into disrepute & contempt — *those* animadversions will be considered libellous. I am rather inclined to think that the passages I have adverted to and perhaps some others combined with the general spirit & object of the work may be so construed — and therefore I cannot say that the Publisher of such a work will not incur *some* hazard. It must be observed however that as it would be a very ungracious thing in Government to prosecute for such a work professing as it does to be a *Statement of Catholic complaints* the Publisher derives a great chance of safety from that circumstance — and perhaps, if the objectionable passages cannot now be left out, a Publisher circumstanced as Mr F[itzpatrick] is would be right rather to incur some share of responsibility than keep back from the Public a work which upon the whole contains a mass of very important information on a most important subject — and the sale of which must I think be very extensive.[2]   [*Source*: Scully Papers]

[1]Probably Thomas Wallace (1765–1847), called to the Irish bar in 1798.

[2]Part II of Scully's *Statement of the Penal Laws* did not come out until about April 1812 (see No. 345), long before which time it would have been useless for him to pretend that Wallace did not know he was the author. It was probably therefore only on Part I that he was now commenting and on this supposition the letter is entered here because it was on 11 May 1811 that a sub-committee of the General Committee ordered 500 copies to be printed. According to an informer's report on the meeting which the Chief Secretary sent to the Home Office thirty-two pages had already been printed (HO 100/163, f.344).

289   *From Dr J. T. Troy, Archbishop of Dublin,*
                        to Merrion Square

                                        3 Cavendish Row, 1 August 1811
My dear Sir,
    It is stated in the report of your speech[1] yesterday in the Committee, by
the *Freeman's journal* of this morning, that you represented Mr Secretary
Pole as an adventurer, without any landed property in this country.[2]
    I think it due from my friendship & esteem for you to state, that Mr Pole
has a very considerable estate in the Queen's County, of which he is a
representative in Parliament, and a noble mansion at Ballyfin near
Mountrath, inherited from a Colonel Pole,[3] whose name he was obliged to
assume, and add to that of Wellesley.
    It is for you to consider whether your mistake ought not to be corrected in
the same manner it was published.[4]   [*Source*: Scully Papers]

[1]On 9 July 1811 an aggregate meeting had defied Wellesley Pole's circular to
magistrates of 12 February (see No. 285 n.1) by resolving on the formation of a new
committee for preparing a petition, consisting of peers and their eldest sons,
baronets, Prelates, the survivors of the delegation of 1793, ten persons appointed by
the Catholics in each county and five appointed by each Dublin parish. The
resolution had been immediately implemented and one of the earliest results
published had been for the Townsend Street district, where O'Connell and Scully
were elected (*DEP*, 16 and 23 July 1811). Learning what was going on the Castle had
become alarmed and on 20 July the Lord Lieutenant had written a long despatch to
the Home Secretary comparing the new committee with a parliament and enclosing
the opinion of his law officers that the assembly would be illegal under the
Convention Act in which, they argued, the words "under pretence of petitioning" did
not mean "under false pretence". As it would be impossible to test the case in the
courts before November and the Committee would certainly meet before then the
Lord Lieutenant had asked for authority to disperse it if the Catholics did not desist.
On 29 July he had received the Home Secretary's authority and after a meeting of the
Privy Council a proclamation had been issued on 30 July calling on the magistrates to
act (HO 100/164, ff.40, 127). An extraordinary meeting of the General Committee
having been summoned on 31 July it had fallen to Scully, in the absence on circuit of
O'Connell and other barristers, to advise on the legal position. In his long speech he
argued that the first section of the Convention Act interdicting representative
meetings was qualified by the fourth, which recognised the undoubted right of
petitioning, and claimed that the sole question for a jury was whether an assembly
met for the sole purpose of petitioning or some other purpose. Catholic committees,
he pointed out, had been meeting ever since 1804, their "prudential fitness as an
organ of communications" having been recognised by Pitt and Lord Liverpool 1805
and by every subsequent minister (*DEP*, 1 August 1811).
[2]The *Freeman's Journal*'s report was garbled. The text in the *Dublin Evening Post*

shows that it was the Chancellor, Lord Manners, who was one of those without any landed property. Scully was arguing that whereas any ordinary magistrate was exposed to the last shilling of his property if proceeded against for carrying out arrests and dispersals not sanctioned by law, the persons who had signed the proclamation could escape responsibility either because of their official positions or because they owned no property in Ireland that could be distrained upon.
[3]Colonel William Pole.
[4]He did so, in a letter to the *Freeman's Journal* dated Clonmel, 5 August. This was probably the occasion referred to by R. R. Madden in an unpublished draft memoir on Michael Staunton (Gilbert Collection: MS.270). Staunton, at the age of twenty-one, had recently joined the *Freeman's Journal* and when he published a report of a speech by Scully the latter wrote to P. W. Harvey, the proprietor, complaining of his employing "a beardless youth". Harvey showed the letter to Staunton, together with a reply in which he informed Scully that Staunton possessed his complete confidence.

290   *From Charles Butler to Merrion Square*

Lincolns Inn, 6 August 1811
Dear Sir,

I was sitting down to write to you when I had the pleasure of receiving in the *Dublin Evening Post*, your excellent speech.[1] I think you have chosen a strong ground and defended it with great ability.[2]

I beg leave to mention, that, in Cook Littleton[3] 257 A. note 3, you will find some remarks on the law of petitioning. I remember that Mr Dunning,[4] contended, in the affair of Lord George Gordon, that the 3 [*sic*] Chas. 2d, which confines the number of names to a petition, to 20, was repealed by the Bill of Rights.[5]

The particular circumstance, which made me think of writing to you, was a correspondence I have had within this fortnight, respecting a Chapel proposed to be built in Chelsea, in the neighbourhood both of the Hospital and the Barracks. I made an application respecting it to the Duke of York; in which, after stating that the Catholic soldiers in the Hospital and the adjoining Barracks would be the persons chiefly benefitted by the Chapel, I suggested to him the propriety of government's coming to its assistance. His reply was very civil; but he declined affording any pecuniary aid; on the general ground, that an issue of public money for such a service was not within his resort. Upon this, I made an application to Mr Perceval; and I send you a copy of his answer. It strikes me, that the concluding sentences of his letter, express a decided hostility to us, not so much by their language, as by his going out of his way to make the declaration.

The result of the debate on your Petition[6] was extremely favourable to you; and the effect of the public dinner[7] was still more auspicious. But I am convinced, your adversaries will fight the battle against you inch by inch; so that the exertion of your whole powers will be absolutely necessary to insure your success. We understand that you mean to petition by parishes.[8] You know that I have ever been an advocate for individual petitions and I think, it would produce the greatest effect if you were to poll every person whether Catholic or Protestant in Ireland.

We are full of conjecture and uncertainty on the Prince Regent's intentions, with respect to the present administration. There is a general suspicion that he wishes to retain Perceval; and some persons think that an inclination towards him is discoverable in the Prince's appointment of Lord Melville, to the Privy Seal of Scotland.[9] But the appointment is confessedly temporary, so that no conclusion can be drawn from it.

The King's health is not so bad as the papers represent it.[10] There is a reasonable hope of coming to an amicable settlement with Russia.[11]

We are extremely concerned and surprised at the coolness which seems to be shewn to us by the Irish Roman Catholics. Two grounds appear to be assigned for it:— our supposed advocation of the Veto, and our Fifth Resolution. Now, after the publication of the letter to a Parish Priest,[12] it seems impossible to contend that the Veto originated in England, as it is there distinctly said to have been *voluntarily* offered by the Irish Prelates. I think it equally clear, that after it was recalled by your prelates, not a word was printed or said in its favour in this country.[13] In respect to our Fifth resolution, it was merely a preliminary for negociation, which bound neither of the parties to any thing specific; I am therefore wholly at a loss to discover any cause for the offence, that it seems to have given.

Much pains appear to have been taken, to infuse a suspicion of there being, a considerable party among us, to put the Church under the direction or controul of the state. But all this is a perfect Chimoera. Is it not a pity, that two such respectable bodies, as the Irish and English Catholics should be at variance, and lose by it that portion of strength, which a consolidation of their interests would give them?

I can conceive a possible case, in which, in consequence of an invasion of your country, or of some other event, the government of this country, might be panic struck, and surrender to you at discretion. But, unless something of this kind happens you will stand in need of all your strength, to accomplish your aim. I shall be much obliged to you for a line at your leisure.

P.S. Since writing the above, I fell into company, with a very distinguished member of Opposition; who reprobated strongly the Proclamation:[14] "But" he cried "what can you expect from a person governed by Lord Yarmouth & the Duke of Cumberland". The person by whom this was said convinced me that, at present the Prince Regent & a great part of the Opposition at least are at variance.

                                          CB.

[Enclosure]
From Spencer Perceval to Charles Butler

Downing Street, 2 August 1811

Copy

Sir,

I have had the honour of receiving your letter of the 31st of last month. . . . I entirely concur in opinion with His Royal Highness that there can exist no disinclination to see the proper means of religious worship placed within the reach of every description of His Majesty's subjects; but it certainly has not been hitherto the Policy of this Country to furnish any public aid for the purpose of providing such means, except for the established church; and although I might content myself with saying that there certainly were no funds which the Treasury were authorised to apply to the object in question, yet it would not be fair or candid in me not to add that I should doubt extremely of the propriety of applying to Parliament to furnish funds for that purpose. [*Source*: Scully Papers]

[1] Of 31 July (see No. 289 n.1).

[2] In a letter of 7 August Lord Donoughmore thanked Edward Hay for drawing his attention to "my friend Scully's uncommonly able and effective performance" (DDA 390/1, XI, 16). Thomas Grenville, however, wrote to Lord Grenville on 4 August: "I certainly cannot wonder that if the Ministers resist the Catholic question, they should feel it necessary to prevent the assembly of an Irish Parliament of Catholic delegates, and when it is made illegal to elect delegates, or to hold a meeting of them, Councillor Scullie cannot convince me that after passing that law it is still legal to elect delegates and hold a meeting of them" (*Dropmore Papers* X).

[3] *Recte*: *Coke upon Littleton*. Butler was editor of successive updated editions of the *First Part of the Institutes of the Laws of England or a Commentary upon Littleton by Edward Coke*, Volume III. The edition to which he refers Scully would have been the 16th, published in 1809. In note 3 of section 257 a, Sir William Blackstone is cited as expressly stating that the right to petition declared by the Bill of Rights was under the regulation of 13 Car. 2, but a query added "whether the declaration contained in the bill of rights was not, in this particular, a repeal of the 13 Car. 2".

[4] John Dunning (1731–1783), created Baron Ashburton in 1782.

[5] Butler should have added that when the counsel for Lord George Gordon contended that 13 Car. 2 had been virtually repealed by the Bill of Rights Lord Mansfield, the presiding judge, told the jury that he had never heard this supposed, that the Bill of Rights did not mean to meddle with the matter and that it was in full force (Howell, *State Trials* XXI).

[6] On Grattan's motion in the House of Commons on 31 May 1811, lost by 146 to 83 votes; and on Lord Donoughmore's in the House of Lords on 18 June, lost by 121 to 62 votes (*Hansard* XX, 427, 645).

[7] Given on 8 June by the Friends of Religious Liberty for the Irish delegates visiting London and attended by over four hundred people. Writing from the Irish Office on 20 June Wellesley Pole told the Home Secretary that the dinner had revived the

hopes and elated the minds of the Catholics: "The speeches of Lord Moira, Mr Ponsonby and Mr Sheridan are considered harbingers to the great event — Emancipation, and a kind of assurance that the Regent will not oppose, but even support a Catholic petition whenever his Royal Highness ascends the throne" (HO 100/163, f.398).

[8]No confirmation of such an intention has been found.

[9]Lord Melville had been appointed on 20 July in place of his lately deceased father.

[10]Sir Henry Halford, one of the physicians, told the Regent shortly before 13 August that the King's was "a completely gone case", not so much because of the immediate danger as of the mischief he saw approaching (Aspinall, *Correspondence of George Prince of Wales* VIII, No. 3138).

[11]A letter from Tsar Alexander I had recently been received and the question of preliminaries of peace was under discussion (*ibid.* No. 3142).

[12]The *Letter to a Parish Priest*, printed by Dr Milner for private circulation, had been published by the *Evening Herald* in Dublin in September 1808 (see No. 185 n.5). Early in 1811 it was reprinted as Appendix I to *Six letters on the subject of Dr Milner's explanation relating to the election of Roman Catholic Bishops*, which had originally appeared in the *Morning Post* above the signature "A.B." a pseudonym of Spencer Perceval. The passage to which Butler alludes is one in which Dr Milner urged the Irish Prelates to act consistently with their resolutions of 1799: ". . . will you reject those resolutions (for the purpose of quieting the alarms of the nation, and promoting the emancipation) which you heretofore voluntarily made in order to obtain a privilege for yourselves?"

[13]Although they wrote in England Dr Charles O'Conor and J. J. Dillon were Irishmen. Sir John Throckmorton had been silent since he wrote a pamphlet in 1806 regarded by the Vicar Apostolic in London as subjecting the Catholic body to the will of the government (entry for 15 February 1806 in Dr Douglass' diary, Westminster Diocesan Archives).

[14]Of 30 July (see No. 289 n.1).

291 *From Hugh FitzPatrick to Clonmell*

Dublin, 10 August 1811

My dear Sir,

I had the honor & pleasure of your favor this morning; & I trust you will find at the same time that this will reach you, that I have not been inattentive to the commands you were pleased to confide to me.[1] Your M. Rev. friend[2] is at present out of town — nor will he be at home in less than a fortnight — as soon as he arrives, I shall take care he shall be apprized of your sense of his attention to you.

I sincerely congratulate you & the Co. Tipperary on the high spirit of liberality which animates that county — 'tis by such conduct & such expression of public sentiment that the just & constitutional claims of the Irish Catholics will be upheld in defiance of any illiberal minister or intolerant party.

It affords all your friends here, & I may say that includes every Catholic, the greatest pleasure to find that the Co. Tipperary have borne so honorable a testimony of the services you have rendered the Catholic cause, upon the late as upon many other occasions.[3]

No doubt, ere this reaches you, you will have seen in the *Herald* of last night, what occurred in this city yesterday — the arrest of 5 persons, the 6th (Dr Sheridan)[4] being out of town, surrendered this day — of our parish (St Mary's) for having convened with other parishioners, & resolved to petition next Sessions, & for having selected five persons in whom they placed confidence, to prepare their petition. You may possibly recollect that I told you I was one of those who were requested to select proper persons for that purpose — & I assure you, that nothing more was done; if, therefore, we are to be prosecuted for what occurred in Liffey-Street Chapel, we may indeed exclaim, that we are "denied the liberty of complaining" — a consolation not denied the most wretched slave: but we are confident of the constitutional ground we stand upon & have no doubt of a complete victory over our persecutors. They did not *honor* me by an arrest, tho' I stood in the same rank with those that were arrested.[5] I suppose they reserve me for a more grand exhibition.[6] Pardon me, dear Sir, for thus long inflicting upon you my tedious epistle. I must now conclude as it is just 7 o'clock.

P.S. A few minutes since, Ld Frankfort[7] (one of the prosecution) left a letter for Ld Fingall, directed to No. 4, Capel. I forward it to him by the Post. I shall know its contents[8] on Tuesday as he is to be in town. I shall take care of what you promise me on Monday.   [*Source*: Scully Papers]

[1]Perhaps in connexion with the publication of the *Penal Laws* (see No. 288A).

[2]Dr Troy, whom Scully may have wished to thank for his letter, No. 389.

[3]On 8 August, during the Assizes, the Tipperary Catholics had passed resolutions carefully framed to evade the sanctions of the Convention Act. Three old and seven new members of their committee were "requested" to prepare and conduct a petition "with liberty to confer for that purpose with the general Catholic Committee" (*DEP*, 13 August 1811).

[4]On Chief Justice Downes' warrant of 8 August. The other five were: Dr J. Burke, Dr John Breen, Henry Edmund Taaffe, Gregory Scurlog and Thomas Kirwan (Cobbett, *Political Register*).

[5]The Irish administration could not pick and choose. On the one hand, it had to act quickly to discourage further elections; on the other, the secrecy in which the Dublin elections were conducted made it difficult to procure evidence on which a jury could convict (HO 100/164, f.225 and *passim*).

[6]When a Castle spy reported that Fitzpatrick and others expected to be arrested, and that O'Connell was determined to remain in custody rather than give bail, the Chief Secretary had told the Home Office on 17 February that he would take great care not to disperse the next meeting of the Committee, on 23 February (HO 100/ 163, f.109).

[7]Lodge Evans Morres (1747–1822), Baron Frankfort of Galmoye, Co. Kilkenny, created a Viscount in 1816.

[8]Probably in connexion with the prosecutions just instituted, Lord Fingall having been chairman of the aggregate meeting of 9 July which passed the resolutions for electing delegates.

292   *From Charles Butler to Merrion Square*

Lincolns Inn, 13 August 1811

Dear Sir,

What I have now to mention to you you will please to consider a confidential communication for your private use. I took care to call Sir Samuel Romilly's attention to your speech,[1] and this morning I asked him if he had read it. He spoke of it very handsomely and expressed himself very strongly that the Law was against the arrest.

Permit me to suggest that your speech should be printed in the London news papers, and also to suggest your having a case stated for the opinion of some of the leading Lawyers of this country, as Sir Samuel Romilly, Sir Arthur Piggott, Mr Serjt. Sheppard and Mr Dampier. A joint opinion from them must produce the very greatest effect.   [*Source*: Scully Papers]

[1]Of 31 July (see No. 289 n.1).

293   *From Robert Marshall to Merion Square, Dublin*

[26 August 1811]

My dear Scully,

I am very glad the wine proves to be good. After reserving 4 dozen for Townsend[1] according to my promise to Mrs Townsend, I will send the remainder (about 15 or 16 Dozen) to you. I shall be obliged to attend the Auction in Denzil Street tomorrow morning.[2] If Mrs Scully should wish to buy any of the China at the auction, or before it begins, she will find me at the House, when I shall be very happy to shew her all the things. I do not think, however, that there can be any articles worth her notice except possibly a Plateau with an Epergne upon it & Lustres; Two small side Lustres for the Room, with real bronze Figures & brass stands; a work Table; a nest of little Tables, & the China.

When I have the pleasure of seeing you, we can fix upon the time for your receiving the wine. I fancy 4/7d Irish a bottle will reimburse me for the entire cost of the wine, including the Price of the Bottle. If you should find the wine to be Excellent, I shall have a very great profit in the satisfaction it will afford me.

I beg to offer my best Compts to Mrs Scully & believe me always, my dear Scully,

Yours very sincerely
R. Marshall   [Source: Scully Papers]

[1]No doubt John Sealy Townsend, Middle Temple, called to the Irish bar 1787.
[2]An advertisement, appearing on the day of the sale only, in the *Freeman's Journal* of 27 August 1811 reads: ". . . at 32 Denzil Street. The furniture belonging to Robert Marshall Esq., late of Baggot Street, consisting of a general assortment of fashionable furniture, wines, spirits, books etc. Sale to begin at 12 o'clock".

294   *From Lord Fingall to Merrion Square, Dublin*

5 Earl Street [Dublin] Tuesday morning, 27 August 1811

My Dear Mr Scully,

Mr Donelan[1] has informed me you are in Dublin. If you will be so good to set any time after twelve this morning I will have the pleasure of calling on you.[2]   [Source: Scully Papers]

[1]Malachy Donelan, Lord Fingall's brother-in-law.
[2]Probably to discuss the meeting of the Catholics of Co. Meath that was to take place on 29 August. Lord Fingall, who had been summoned to the Castle on 25 July and given advance warning of the proclamation (see No. 289 n.1) but had nevertheless taken the chair at the meeting of 31 July, was being watched by the administration (HO 100/164, ff.75–221).

295   *From Charles Butler to Dublin*

Cheltenham, 30 August 1811

Dear Sir,

Your Letter[1] reached me at this place; where, unless business takes me to London, I mean to remain. You may be assured, that, your Speech[2] has done you great honour, & your cause, great good; & I am sure, that it is much for the advantage of both that it should be published. I shall take care it shall be done in a manner, that will please you: but, as the Town is now very empty, I shall delay it, till the 1st of November.

The report of the Prince Regent's veering to Perceval was on the increase, when I left London: and report added, that he shewed much good will to Lord Grey: and little of it to Lord Grenville. I never disguise my sentiments to you: I therefore add, unreservedly, that I think an active support from him, cannot be expected, unless some event should frighten him and his counsellors, into kindness to us; and *this event, I think very probable.*[3] Our chancellor gives simptoms [*sic*] of retiring from Office.[4]

I wish there could be a congress, of two or three of your side, & two or three on our side the water; & that some mode was settled of making the English Press, subservient to your cause. I still think, that, with wisdom & energy, we may carry our object; but, upon the whole, I fear, that, since the unfortunate Veto was mentioned, we have lost ground.

I have now to trouble you with a request. The *Dublin Evening Post* was regularly sent me, till about a Month ago, when I recd a Letter reminding me, that I was in debt for half a year, & that it was usual to pay in advance: In answer, I desired the proprietor to inform me, where I could pay it in London; & added, that, if *that* could not be managed, I would contrive to remit it to Ireland. Since that time, I have recd. no paper. May I request the favour to you to settle this little matter for me, & that you would direct the man to send me the paper regularly in future.   [*Source*: Scully Papers]

[1]Of 23 August, not extant.
[2]Of 31 July (see No. 289 n.1).
[3]There were rumours in opposition circles of the impending resignation of the Marquis of Wellesley, which might force the Prince to form a new administration, friendly to the Catholics; and speculation that the campaign in the peninsula might have to be abandoned (Thomas Grenville to Lord Grenville: 21 August; and Earl Grey to Lord Grenville: 1 September 1811, in *Dropmore Papers* X).
[4]He was to remain in office until 1827.

296   *From Bishop John Milner to Merrion Square, Dublin*

W.H. 1 September 1811

Dear Sir,

I am ashamed to think that I have never yet acknowledged the rect. of yr. interesting letter dated May 11 & handed to me by Counsellor Hussey,[1] but the Irish Press, (to say nothing of that in England & of numerous journeys & other professional business) will plead, in my behalf that I have not been idle since that period. The vindication of yourself from the charge of being a party to the subjugation of your native Church proved equally convincing & gratifying to me.[2] I have accordingly made the substance of it known to certain respectable personages who previously entertained doubts on that subject.

My objection to the proposed arrangements was grounded, not in peevishness or pride, but in a perfect conviction that the terms exacted of us by the Grenvilles & Hippisleys[3] were absolutely inconsistent with the safety & even the integrity of our Religion. The Fifth English Resolution, I saw clearly was a snare for Irish Catholics & a pledge for future concessions.[4]

You are witness, Dr. Sir, how much I have been abused for opposing it. At present, however, the more intelligent part of my countrymen see the business in the same light that I did & compliment me with the title of a Prophet. Lord Donoughmore & Lord Moira have both expressed to me their wish for *unconditional* Emancipation, which I am inclined to think will be granted, whenever any kind of Emancipation is practicable. I presume you have seen my answer to Charles Butler.[5] It has answered my expectation with respect to Caths. in general, & greatly exceeded them with respect to the gentleman himself. He now appears to be religious in earnest.[6] You have also seen my hasty review of the late Cathc. Debate in the *Dublin Evening Express*.[7] Since that Debate, however, I am inclined to think that many who insisted upon shackling the clergy, have seen the subject in a different light. Sir John Hippisley's speech in Pt.[8] has opened the eyes of many Caths. & Lord Moira's at the public dinner has had the same effect upon an equal number of our Protest. legislators.[9]

I have now to congratulate with you, Dr. Sir, on the splendid part you have lately acted.[10] You have not indeed surpassed the idea I formed of yr. talents, but you have gone far beyond that which I entertained of yr. courage. After all, courage is very often prudence; I myself have frequently found it to be so, & I believe it is so in the present instance.

Lord Moira assured me that the Prince continued to be the steady friend of the Caths., & I am convinced that his Lordship is in point of honour & honesty an exception from the general character of public men. I mean that he is a man of strict truth. Still he himself is liable to be deceived, & it is possible that Mr Perceval may have circumvented his Royal Highness in the course of the last three weeks.[11]

A more important point than that of the 5th Resolution now agitates the Caths. & particularly their Bishops: on this as on other subjects I have the good fortune to stand along with yr. Prelates in opposition to my English brethren. The short of the case is this; Blanchard a French Priest with many of his countrymen in [?Lon]don, consider the Pope & all the Catholics in [?their] native land as involved in schism. The Church in general communicates with them as with good Caths. All the Prelates of both Islands had censured Blanchard,[12] but of late the London Vic. Apost. has restored faculties to one of his public approvers without any retractation & it is possible that he will be supported in this by several English Caths., & in short that an open rupture may take place.[13]

I am truly sorry that you & Mrs Scully have given up your voyage to this island for the present year;[14] I hope, however, that she & yr. little ones no less than yrself enjoy good health. I beg my kind complts. to Mrs S. in which Mrs Wheble joins. Though I have not yet had the pleasure of seeing Mrs F. Canning, I have the satisfaction to have her on my side, in my religious

controversies. I remain, with great esteem & regard, begging my respects to
Dr Bray & Dr Lanigan.   [*Source*: Scully Papers]

[1]P. B. Hussey, accompanied by Major Bryan and Owen O'Conor, sailed for England
on 11 May. Wellesley Pole, then in London, took an interest in their movements
because they were the three delegates most closely associated with the address (see
No. 286 n.3) calling on the Regent to dismiss him and the Lord Lieutenant (HO 100/
163, f.344).
[2]Scully's letter of 11 May was in reply to Dr Milner's of 1 May, No. 288, the postscript
to which warned Scully against Butler.
[3]By Lord Grenville in his letter of 22 January 1810 to Lord Fingall (see No. 230 n.1);
by Sir J. C. Hippisley in his numerous writings and speeches, but most recently on 31
May 1811 when he had proposed the appointment of a select committee to go into
possible arrangements (*Hansard* XX, 391).
[4]See No. 278 n.16.
[5]See No. 288 n.2.
[6]Dr Milner may have heard of a letter (text in Butler's *Historical Memoirs of the
English Catholics* IV, p. 516) which Butler had written to Dr Poynter and was laid
before the Vicars Apostolic who had met, without Dr Milner, at Durham at the end
of August. In this, defending himself against the accusations of Dr Milner, Butler
had offered to retract, if it was pointed out to him, anything unsound or improper in
his writings (Ward, *Eve of Catholic Emancipation* I, p. 168).
[7]No copy has been found.
[8]On 31 May (see n.3 above).
[9]See No. 290 n.7.
[10]With his speech of 31 July (see No. 289 n.1) and the Tipperary meeting of
8 August (see No. 291 n.3).
[11] A letter of 22 October 1811 to Colonel MacMahon (*Correspondence of George
Prince of Wales* VIII, No. 3222) suggests that Lord Moira was deliberately trying to
counteract "the lamentable persuasion adopted by the Catholics that the Prince has
adopted all the hostility of his Cabinet towards them" — a persuasion which he saw as
having the dangerous consequence of their siding with the French. At the same time
Lord Moira no longer enjoyed the continuous confidence of the Regent and on 12
October complained that he knew nothing of what was going on at Carlton House
(Lord Buckingham to Lord Grenville: 13 October 1811, *Dropmore Papers* X).
[12]The Blanchardist schism followed upon the concordat of 1801 between Pius VII
and Napoleon, and the Pope's subsequent call upon all the French Bishops to resign
their sees. Some of the exiled French clergy living in London felt that the Pope was
exceeding his powers and the more extreme, led by Abbé Blanchard, claimed that all
those who adhered to the concordat, and even the Pope himself, were schismatical.
In London the Vicar Apostolic, who was hampered by the presence of French
Bishops, hoped that the movement would die out of its own accord, but a pastoral by
Dr Milner dated 1 June 1808 provoked replies from Abbé Blanchard and Abbé
Gaschet, both of whom lived in the London district. They were suspended by Dr
Douglass on 19 August 1808 and seven others were suspended in September (Ward,
Eve I, Ch. VI). The censures to which Dr Milner refers were those passed by
seventeen Irish Prelates on 3 July 1809 and the English Vicars Apostolic at Durham

in March 1810 (ibid., pp. 94, 158).

[13]At the instance of the Bishop of Angoulême the Vicar Apostolic in London had in June 1810 restored faculties to Abbé Treveaux, one of the suspended seven, without demanding a public retractation. He had good reasons for his moderation but Dr Milner, also with good reason, felt that some public act was necessary to undo the scandal and doubted into the bargain whether the Abbé's orthodoxy had in fact been established (Ward, *Eve* I, Ch. XI and appendix A).

[14]In the end Scully went to England without his wife (see No. 302).

297   *From Lord Fingall to Merrion Square, Dublin*
per favor Honble. Thos. Barnwall

Killeen Castle [Co. Meath] 3 September 1811

My dear Mr Scully,

I was just sitting down to write a few lines to you by Mr Barnwall,[1] my very particular friend, who is particularly anxious to have the pleasure of your acquaintance when I had that of receiving your letter. Mr B wishes to have some conversation with you on our politics into which he enters very warmly & we are much obliged to him for the decided part he has taken in this County. I am glad you approve of our resolutions[2] and I agree with you that their being now widely circulated is the best way.[3]

I fear I cannot have the pleasure of seeing you before you go to England tho' I will go to Dublin the first day I can. I will call on Mr Mahon[4] and Mr MacDonnel[5] and use my efforts to set the subscription so necessary on foot. Some gentlemen who I met last day I was in Dublin suggested that it ought not to be too publick — rather that it should appear that those who are made victims support themselves.

You can render us great services in England in addition to those you have not ceased to do here, by informing our friends of the real state of our cause which is very much misunderstood, & our conduct being mistaken & misrepresented. I am sorry to say I think at this moment we are losing ground the other side of the water.   [*Source*: Scully Papers]

[1]John Thomas Barnewall, later 15th Baron Trimleston.

[2]Adopted by the Meath Catholics at Navan on 29 August for the appointment of delegates to manage Catholic petitions (*DEP*, 31 August 1811). On 3 September the Chief Secretary told the Home Office that they were thought by the law officers to bring Lord Fingall and those who took part with him within the Convention Act and on 6 September he wrote: "It is is somewhat singular that Lord Fingall, who certainly is the most loyal and most respectable among the Catholic body and the person who was most anxious to prevent the violence of the Committee last year, should have presided at the only Catholic meeting that has openly transgressed the law. All the cunning ones have kept out of the scrape" (HO 100/164, ff.337, 339). It is possible that the wording of the relevant resolution was deliberately provocative, for according to the report of a Castle spy sent to the Home Office on 21 July Lord

Fingall's intention then was to get the legality of the meeting tried in the courts (ibid. f.75). By 12 September a prosecution of Lord Fingall and Barnewall had been decided on (ibid., f.428).
[3]The full text was published in the *Dublin Evening Post* of 6 September.
[4]Nicholas Mahon.
[5]Randal MacDonnell. When on 29 November it was decided that a subscription of five guineas a head should be levied on the county members and paid to MacDonnell it was also directed that the latter should be indemnified for any money already advanced for the defence of those prosecuted (HO 100/163, f.51).

298   *From Charles Butler to Fladongs Hotel. [London]*

Cheltenham, 13 September 1811

Dear Sir,

I am much mortified at my being from London during your stay there; as I should have been happy in the opportunity of conversing with you on the momentous scenes in which we are now engaged.[1] I read with great pleasure the concluding part of your Letter,[2] which expresses your satisfaction in the present conduct of the Roman Catholics in Ireland. Their intention of employing my services in procuring the Opinions in question, I consider most honourable to me, and I shall exert myself in it, in a manner, which, I hope will have their approbation.[3] I have not heard yet from Ireland, on the subject; If it be left to me to chuse the council [*sic*], I shall prefer Mr Holroyd to Mr Dampier, the latter, from family connections having a strong tinge of ministerialism. I have conversed, much, since I have been here, with your Master of the Rolls,[4] &, on the legal question, he is decisively with you. It is, I think, impossible to imagine that the Proclamation was without the Prince Regent's full consent:[5] & since I have been here, It has been mentioned to me by one of the Walters, (whose family are proprietors of the *Times*), that the Prince has said that the Catholics will find he is not to be dragooned into a Measure. Your speech[6] carries conviction; the time for printing it in the papers will be about the 20th of Octr; and I will take care, it shall be done.

[*Source*: Scully Papers]

[1]The election of delegates in Dublin and the counties in defiance of the Irish administration's warnings and the impending prosecutions of Dr Sheridan, Thomas Kirwan and others (see notes to No. 291).
[2]Of 5 September: not extant.
[3]See No. 292. The members of the Irish Catholic Committee functioning *ad interim* since the aggregate meeting of 9 July seem to have met only privately during this period and no record has been found of the decision to enlist Butler's services.
[4]J. P. Curran. He and the Knight of Kerry were the only two opposition members of the Privy Council to attend the meeting summoned on 30 July to issue the Proclamation (see No. 289 n.1) which they refused to sign. According to Wellesley

Pole's report to the Home Office Curran argued that, if the Catholic Committee were allowed to meet, the higher orders would prevent the others from doing any mischief (HO 100/164, f.178).
[5]The Proclamation was issued not only with the Regent's consent but on his recommendation (Charles Ryder to the Duke of Richmond 26 July 1811 — HO 100/164, f.127). Writing to Ryder on 30 July Pole said: "We all retain our opinions that a Proclamation was not necessary — but notwithstanding we very cheerfully give way to yours, and it is certainly wise to issue the Proclamation if it gives us one proselyte" (HO 100/164, f.178).
[6]Of 31 July (see No. 289 n.1).

299   *From Dr J. Milner*

[London, 14 September 1811]

Penal Laws.[1]

    Introduction p. III. . . .

Methinks the author in p. 5 aggravates the danger of a mere statement of existing laws (which as such is entitled to the praise of government because it tends to prevent the infringement of them) & that in p. VI he promises himself "a kind reception", "a general approbation" without establishing sufficient ground (after the preceding complaint) for such an expectation.

    p. VIII. The motives for the present publication are here so fairly & dispassionately stated, that I cannot suppose Duigenan himself, if he called it a misrepresentation, wd care to call it a libel.
...

p. 13. I dislike the term Houses of Worship, for chapels. A house is properly a place of abode, see Johnson, & I suspect that chapel is a law term.

p.14. The testimony of the author to the merits of the clergy is most generous as well as just, especially in our country and age. To abuse the Catholic priesthood is a ready passport to the praise of liberality, superior talents etc: such recommendation is, of itself, a measure of support to the cause of religion & morality.

p. 16. Lord Grenville in his speech of 1805 asserted & afterwards stiffly maintained in private conversation with me the contrary. I am convinced, however, he was under an error.[2]

p. 22. "he wd be confined in a monastery". This cd not & therefore wd not be the case in this country, nor even on the continent at the present time.[3]

p. 50. The author is entitled to special thanks for laying open the bigotry & fraud of the New Corporation act.[4] The Cath[s] themselves do not know how much they are wronged.

p. 117. "notorious Dr Duigenan" [one word illegible] wonder if he exert all his influence to inspire the author.
...

142 etc. This display of tyranny in vestry concerns, though necessary for the completion of the piece, & though calculated to rouse the Caths, will render Protestants still more jealous & unwilling to do justice to Caths. for fear of their church.[5]

...

p. 156. Still more alarming truths for the Prot[t] clergy!

I can do nothing but applaud as I proceed. I expect that the ninth and tenth Heads[6] will be the most interesting ones of all.   [*Source*: Callanan Papers]

[1]The comments on Scully's *Statement of the Penal Laws* are in Dr Milner's hand, roughly jotted down on two small sheets of paper and endorsed by Scully: "Recd. from Dr Milner, 14 Septr 1811, London". Comments on mere typographical errors have been omitted in the transcription.

[2]The passage in Grenville's speech has not been identified. The subject would appear to have been the penalties incurred by Catholic priests for marrying Protestants.

[3]Scully accepted this correction on the punishment which a priest might expect from his own church for violating the secrecy of confession (see No. 262 n.3).

[4]Under an act of 40 George III the Irish parliament set up a body of Commissioners of Charitable Bequests who were empowered to sue legally as a corporation for the purpose of enforcing the application of such bequests to the purposes intended by the donors. In his *Penal Laws* Scully alleged that the statute raised a new barrier to Catholic charities and he likened the corporation to a powerful inquisition "eager in the pursuit of its prey, and armed with every necessary authority for discovering and seizing the funds destined by dying Catholics for the maintenance of the pious and the poor of their own communion". Wellesley Pole seized on this passage when he attacked the *Penal Laws* in the House of Commons in February 1812 (see No. 335 n.3).

[5]He presumably means "for fear of prejudicing the interests of their church". The whole of Chapter VII of the *Penal Laws* is devoted to the iniquities of the vestry's powers.

[6]On the administration of justice; and other penalties and disabilities, with the general injury and humiliation inflicted on the Catholics.

300   *From Charles Butler*

Cheltenham, 15 September 1811

Dear Sir,

I hope you have received a Letter which I wrote to you, from this Place. My clerk writes me word, that you have enquired at my Chambers, if I have recd. the Papers from Ireland.[1] I have not as yet received them. I have made some enquiries respecting the Local Situation of our leading Lawyers.

Sir Samuel Romily is at East Cowes in the Isle of Wight;

Mr Serjeant Shepherd, at Tunbridge Wells;

Mr Serjeant Lens at Little Hockham, Harley in Norfolk;

Mr Holroyd, far in the North, but where, is not known.

It is not, quite a matter of course to get Sir Samuel's opinion; but, I believe it may be procured. It would give me prodigious satisfaction to meet you in London, & converse with you on the subject. May I therefore request a Letter by the return of the post to let me know, what stay you make in London. If I should receive the papers, and they arrive in time for my finding you in London, I will set off instantly. Excuse Paper, & believe me, etc.

[*Source*: Scully Papers]

[1]See No. 298.

301   *From Charles Butler*

Cheltenham, 18 September 1811

Dear Sir,

I am greatly obliged by your Letter:[1] If, by any means, you could contrive to let Mr Miles Macdonald[2] know my willingness to come to town, if I can be of the slightest use in procuring the opinions in question, or serving the cause, in any other respect, I shall esteem it a great personal favour done me.

I am extremely happy to find, by your letter, that you are about to take a Circuit, in which I can have an opportunity of meeting you. I quit this place on Wednesday next for Bristol; where, unless I am called by the business in question to London, I shall remain till November. If therefore, you will let me know, when you reach Bath, it will give me great pleasure to attend you.

[*Source*: Scully Papers]

[1]Of 15 September: not extant.
[2]Called MacDonnell in No. 303.

302   *To his wife Catherine at 2 Merrion Square South, Dublin*

Ferme [nr Sheffield] Tuesday 1 October 1811

My dearest Catherine,

The Letter I wrote you from this on Friday last,[1] was by mistake put in the Post Office without a postscript which I meant to write. Here I have been ever since, but I leave this tomorrow morning for Bath — where I expect to be on Thursday, and shall leave that on Sunday for Dublin, where I hope to arrive about Thursday the 10th Inst.

Julia & Thomas returned on Friday from Doncaster races; they had been there 4 days with Mr & Mrs Vincent,[2] & were much amused. Dr Milner & Mrs Wheble came yesterday, & dined at the Ferme[3] & also your Uncle

Edward.[4] We are all to dine today at Vincent's. All are very well — but they cannot come to Dublin this year — tho' Julia promises for next year. I have pressed them very much, but in vain & shall tell you all about it when we meet. John's father in law, Mr Parker,[5] called yesterday here to see your mother. He is a very tall coarse broadspoken honest looking man, but not like a merchant, as I thought. We don't know how John has managed as to fortune with him. John wrote to your mother, that he expects his wife will soon declare herself a Catholic. Mr & Mrs Gainsford[6] are to visit Dublin again next month. I believe this family will soon visit Charles[7] & John, which I am glad of, for they must expect it. Dr Froth[8] has married an elderly widow, & brought her home — she is somewhat lame, but he gives her out as a £10,000 pounder.

I have your dear Letter of Monday the 23rd for which a thousand thanks and I am quite happy that you & the boys are so well. As to the Coals, I leave that subject to your own good judgement. Do you think you could have enquiry made for the servants we want; so as they could be hired on my return. I believe I must go to Kilfeacle about the 20th October, to return in 10 days, as there is business with my father. Thomas & Julia met, at Doncaster races, General Mathew, Val Maher, George Silvertop, Mr Charles Wolseley etc. Julia's partners at the Balls were Wolseley & Jim Hunloke.[9] Sir W. & Lady Hunloke were there — Lady H. looking most beautiful — but dressed shamefully naked, and very forward, affected, flirting, & all that kind of manner — so as to draw universal remark and reproach. Geo. Silvertop came up to Vincent (whom he has formerly pretended not to recollect) and took him warmly by the hand, saying "what a very charming speech that was of your brother in law's, my friend Scully, that we all read in the newspapers.[10] I declare it was admirable." So he became again quite great & intimate with Vincent, but Vincent has told us all, that he considers himself entirely indebted to me for the condescension of this great Northern Star.

I am glad to see from your Letter that you are prepared to excuse my staying here so long — but, when I found I was to return alone, I had resolved to leave this as yesterday — on consideration, I thought that would look like turning my back upon Dr M. & Mrs Wheble, who were to dine here yesterday — and then Mr & Mrs Vincent might take it ill if I refused their very importunate intreaties for me to stay today to dine with them, & join their party for Dr Milner. But I shall not delay any where else, and you see my reasons for this delay.

If I do not put this Letter into this Post Office I shall put it into the P. Office of some Town I may travel through tomorrow: so you will know by the Postmark, where I am. Will you drop me a line about *Tuesday* next the 8th (or perhaps the day before) directed to me at Spenser's Hotel, Holyhead, *to be left till called for* — for I shall be anxious on my arrival to hear from you, and most impatient to meet you again. Nothing else new — or else I defer it till we meet. Believe me to be, my dearest Catherine, ever most sincerely, your attached and affectionate husband,

                    D. Scully   [*Source*: Scully Papers]

[1]Missing.
[2]Vincent and Thomas Eyre, his wife's brothers; Julia Eyre, her sister.
[3]The Farm, Sheffield Park (see No. 172 n.1). It is not known why the family among themselves called it the Ferme.
[4]Revd Edward Eyre (c. 1749–1834), priest at Hathersedge, Derbyshire.
[5]William Parker of Kingston-upon-Hull, whose daughter Sarah had during 1811 married John Eyre, another brother of his wife's.
[6]Because of the Sheffield connexion possibly Robert William Gainsford and his wife Mary Agnes Robinson whom he married in 1806 (see Burke: LG 1898 — Gainsford of Skendleby).
[7]Charles Eyre, a fourth brother-in-law of Scully's.
[8]Perhaps a facetious misspelling of Frith, a Sheffield name. The *Sheffield General Directory* of 1817 shows a W. G. Frith, surgeon.
[9]James Hunloke and his brother Sir Thomas Windsor Hunloke (1773–1816), 5th Baronet, of Wingerworth, Derbyshire. Lady Hunloke had been Anne Eccleston (1788–1872), of Scarisbrick Hall, Worcestershire.
[10]As arranged by Charles Butler, although somewhat earlier than he had intimated (see No. 298), Scully's speech had been reprinted. It took up the whole of the back page of *The Globe* of 12 September 1811 and may have received wider circulation under the procedure described in No. 204 n.3. On 4 October it was published on the back page of *The Pilot*.

303   *From Charles Butler to Merrion Square*

                              Lincolns Inn, 14 October 1811

Dear Sir,

   I set out for London, the day after we met at Bath, and reached [here] on Sunday evening.[1]

   On Monday morning, I went to Mr MacDonnell[2] and found, that the cases [*sic*] has been sent in the usual way of business, to the council [*sic*] before whom they were directed to be laid. I mentioned to him, the probable difficulty of obtaining Sir Samuel Romilly's opinion, and suggested the propriety of sending some person to him with a liberal fee, and a respectful letter, mentioning the great value which the parties set upon his opinion, and requesting it, as a personal favour on the body. I offered myself to go down to him to the Isle of Wight for this purpose at my own expence.

   Hearing nothing from him, I sent a short note to him this morning requesting to know from him, what opinions had been received. I send you a copy of his answer.

I am extremely concerned the business has taken this turn; and lament that Sir Samuel Romilly's opinion had not been singly applied for, in the first instance.

I have nothing of importance to communicate to you, except that you may be assured, that the difference[s] between Mr Perceval and Lord Wellesley are now so great, as to make it highly probable, if not certain, that the latter will retire from office. I find the ministers are extremely struck with the manner in which the protestant gentry of Ireland have come forward in the Catholic cause, and that they are extremely uneasy for the fate both of Spain and of Sicily and the little appearance they discover of Russia's becoming favourable to us.[3]

If any particular information should fall in my way I shall certainly make you acquainted with it.

[Enclosure]

Mr MacDonnell presents his compliments to Mr Butler, and informs him the opinions of Serjt Best & Serjt Lens have been received agreeing pretty much with that of Serjt Shepherd. Sir A. Piggott's is the only one now to come in.   [*Source*: Scully Papers]

[1] 6 October.
[2] Miles MacDonnell, called MacDonald in No. 301.
[3] In Spain Wellington had been forced to give up the investment of Ciudad Rodrigo; in Sicily the Queen of Naples was reported to be intriguing with Napoleon; the Russians, not yet ready to break with Napoleon, had sent back armaments which the English had tried to deliver in the Baltic during the summer (*Annual Register*).

304   *From Charles Butler to Merrion Square*

Lincolns Inn, 17 October 1811

Dear Sir,

I wrote to you a few days ago. I have now to mention to you, that I know, from unquestionable authority, that the Prince Regent, mentions the Prosecutions,[1] as acts, in which he only concurred from a necessary co-operation with his ministers, under his actual state of limited power and that his sentiments are as favourable to the Roman Catholic body as ever. I don't answer for the very words I send you, but that his Royal Highness has used expressions of this import, I have no doubt.   [*Source*: Scully Papers]

[1] Of Dr Sheridan and others in Dublin (see No. 291, n.4).

305   *Notes for a meeting*[1]

18 October 1811

the form of motion recommended may be:

"that the Petition now read is approved of by this committee, and recommended to the adoption of the Catholics of Ireland".[2]

A notetaker or two, of credit & responsibility, ought to be prepared to take down the questions & answers —

Some Protestant persons of respectability ought to be near the Chair, to observe what passes, corroborate the notetaker, and carefully to take written memorandums of the substance of the conversation, as soon afterwards as convenient.

the aggregate meeting recommended in case of dispersion — also a public dinner —

The service of the notices approved of

Whoever speaks to the question, should confine himself solely to the Petition & its subject matter — without a word about the Proclamation or the conduct of Government etc, etc, etc.

An aggregate meeting, very numerous and respectable, ought to be held within a few days after the dispersion.   [*Source*: Scully Papers MS 27,531]

[1]Rough jottings in Scully's hand and dated 18 October 1811.
[2]The motion carried the next day (see No. 306) read: "That the Committee do adjourn to within a fortnight previous to the meeting of Parliament (for the dispatch of business) that full time may be given to revise, modify and alter the Petition now lying on the table" (DDA 54/1, VII, 10).

306   *To the Earl of Donoughmore*

Dublin, 20 October 1811

(private)

My Lord,

I have had nothing very particular to trouble your Lordship with, since my return[1] — Yesterday the expected meeting of our Committee[2] was held — the four preceding days had been occupied in deliberating upon the previous arrangements, and in the heads of conversation with any Peace Officer who shall be sent to disperse — Upon these subjects 3 or 4 of the Kings Counsel, already retained, were frequently consulted — Thus every step was calculated, and every contingency anticipated — Your Lordship's good advice[3] (in favour of finishing at the meeting if not interrupted) was adopted — In the *D[ublin] Evening Post* of yesterday your Lordship will see the best report of what occurred yesterday — The petition was moved, seconded, read & passed — the Committee adjourned — & the meeting dispersed — all peaceably and most satisfactorily, before the officers presented themselves — All was in fact over — and we could not well recommence proceedings, and have the chair taken anew, merely to accommodate the officers — the fact is (and it is become rather a joke)[4] that they came too late — but they may try their hand at the next meeting — Upwards of 300 members attended — and it was pleasing to see the zeal and spirit evinced by all. Our county of Tippy. made the worst figure — only one delegate, Mr Ryan[5] of Tipperary, attended. I don't know whether any one from Cork attended — (indeed the Cork Catholics have never been of any account here, being now mostly placemen, contractors or bankrupts) but it is ascertained that every other county & city in Ireland had delegates present — The Northern counties sent their full complements — About 50 from Dublin, & from 4 to 10 from Kilkenny, Kerry, Kildare, Meath, Westmeath, Sligo, Clare, Wexford, Longford, Kings & Queens counties etc — The general sentiment of this day amongst the public of all classes is that of satisfaction & joy[6] — Many pretend, that Mr Pole purposely sent the magistrates too late, in order to evade the real question under the first clause of the Convention Act:[7] but this I am rather slow to presume.[8]

I have had no opportunity yet of attempting the objects your Lordship mentioned to me, the necessary parties not being in town — Tomorrow I leave town for my father's, at Kilfeacle, to pass a week there and return here about the 1st November. It will give me great pleasure to be honoured with your Lordship's commands at either.

[P.S.] There are to be, during the ensuing week, several dinners (demi-public) of knots of the Committee, from 15 to 25 each, to project further proceedings — The northerns in particular manifest talent & energy — and I suppose there will occur many busy scenes of a popular nature in Dublin, in the course of the winter — O'Connell, O'Gorman, Hussey, Rice etc had not arrived for the meeting of yesterday.[9]

A letter just recd. by me from Mr Charles Butler of Lincolns Inn, dated 17th inst., contains the following paragraphs, viz:[10] . . .

I give these scraps to your Lordship as I have received them — but not knowing, of course, what degree of weight to attach to them.

[*Source*: Donoughmore Papers D/22/3]

[1]From England.
[2]The new General Committee, or Catholic Convention as the Irish administration called it (see No. 289 n.1).
[3]Communicated through Francis Hely-Hutchinson, to whom Lord Donoughmore said in an undated fragment of a letter: "I have timed my present visit so that it might fall upon the appointed meeting of the Catholic Committee. . . . For the honour of the Catholic body I think their committee should assemble, in great strength, that

their discussions should be few, their petitions promptly agreed upon, and their sittings concluded. . . . Before the commencement of the [law] term, I want that the committee shall be *functus officio* and then I can never doubt the decision of an impartial jury. Communicate these my feelings to those of our Catholic friends with whom I am most in habits, particularly to my friends Lord Fingall, Scully and O'Gorman, and also if you should have an opportunity to O'Connell, whose talents I admire, and to McDonnell, the strength of whose understanding I am so well acquainted with" (Donoughmore Papers, F/10/65).

[4]Wellesley Pole wrote to the Home Secretary the same day: ". . . the opposition papers will . . . find it hard to avert the ridicule that must fall upon the convention for the mode in which they conducted themselves". He thought it could not have happened if the Catholics had not been aware of the illegality of their proceedings (HO 100/165, f.144).

[5]Andrew Ryan.

[6]According to Pole's informant many country members were indignant at having been brought from a great distance to be made fools of.

[7]See Appendix A.

[8]The reports of the peace officers transmitted to London by Pole make it clear that they did not arrive too late on purpose. They came as soon as they had been summoned by a man posted at the door but the proceedings were completed in about ten minutes.

[9]No explanation for their absence has been found. Besides writing to other members of the General Committee on 10 October (DDA 54/1, VII, 9) Hay had written on the same day to O'Connell apprising him of a feeling that if there was no attendance from barristers they would be placing others in a situation they were unwilling to encounter themselves (O'Connell, *Correspondence* I, No. 348).

[10]Scully quotes not only the substantive part of No. 304 but also two passages from No. 303 about Perceval's differences with Lord Wellesley and ministers being struck by the support of the Protestant gentry.

307   *From Charles Butler to Merrion Square*

Lincolns Inn, 24 October 1811

Dear Sir,

I am this moment favoured with your letter of the 19th of this month,[1] and very much lament the circumstance mentioned in it, respecting the opinions; However, I still think that the merits of the cause are so great, and the importance of the persons concerned[2] in it so palpable, as to make it probable that the decision on it, will be what we wish it. I lament that the sea will prevent my attendance at your dinner;[3] no distance, without a sea, would prevent my attending it.

A person of considerable importance in this Country, and much distinguished in Parliament, called on me a few days ago; and strongly recommended that in all your debates, petitions and other public Instruments, you should hold it out for granted that the Prince is pledged to you, and both from conviction and feeling, decided in your favour. No one is better acquainted with the Court and the Land about it than this Gentleman.

Two admirable articles in favour of the Irish Catholics have appeared in the *Edinburgh Review*[4] — the first was printed separately. Few of the Impression have been sold, and I understand it may be purchased for £30. Would it not be attended with the very best effect, if it was purchased and generally circulated in Ireland? And might it not be worth while to print and circulate the other in the same manner?

I should like to see a Copy of the Case and Opinions; but I have not mentioned their having been taken, much less the import of them to any one.   [*Source*: Scully Papers]

[1]Missing: it was written on the day of the "convention" (see No. 306 n.2).
[2]Perhaps Lord Fingall and the Hon. J. T. Barnewall, who also faced prosecution.
[3]It took place on 19 December (see No. 322 n.4).
[4]Butler must have seen the November number with (p. 95) a review of Hardy's *Life of Charlemont* and (p. 149) Revd C. Wyvill's *Papers on toleration*.

308   *From Charles Butler to Merrion Square*

Lincolns Inn, 28 October 1811

Dear Sir,

I have no positive information, but I have *real ground* for believing that the ministers here are extremely dissatisfied with the turn which the Irish business takes, and think of removing the great actor in it.[1] They wish however to concede nothing. But the events of the times most powerfully advocate your cause. Nothing can be worse than the news from Portugal: The number of the sick is much greater than is represented.[2] There is an arrear of the Spanish subsidies. All these circumstances add to your importance. But they will not give you the *Palmam sine Pulvere*:[3] I know that Lord Buckingham has uniformly declared that though your Business should move on as prosperously as possible it will never be decided in your favor without a sharp contest. I have the pleasure to see your cause is generally popular in England, which was not the case till lately, and is only to be attributed to the repeated discussions of it. I have my eye upon everything that passes, and will take care to let you know from time to time.

When I communicated to you in my letter,[4] the advice of my friend, that you should always express yourselves as confident of the concurrence of the Prince Regent, I forgot to add that the mention of any particular facts upon which that confidence is grounded should be avoided to prevent the proving and defending which the mention of any particular facts always make possible.

In my opinion the game is your own, if the petition is universal in the manner I have often represented. You also recollect that I am a great advocate for your praying to be heard by council;[5] for notwithstanding the great exertions of your advocates, the House of Commons have not yet heard your story told from yourselves, and in your own manner.

[*Source*: Scully Papers]

[1]Wellesley Pole, the Chief Secretary.
[2]Following the retreat from Ciudad Rodrigo — the *Morning Chronicle* of 23 October 1811 had reported the number of the sick to be daily decreasing.
[3]"The palm (of victory) without the dust" — cf. Horace, *Epistles*, I, 51: "sine pulvere palmae".
[4]No. 307.
[5]On 2 March 1805 Butler had suggested employing J. P. Curran as counsel to present the Catholic case at the bar of the House of Commons (Diary, MS.27, 581).

309   *From Edward Hay to Merrion Square, Dublin*

4 Capel Street [Dublin] 9 November 1811
Dear Sir,

At a meeting of the committee for managing the case of the arrested Catholic Gentlemen,[1] the Honble. Mr Barnwall in the chair, it was resolved "That the thanks of this committee are justly due and are hereby returned to Counsellor Scully for his unwearied zeal and ability in Catholic affairs and being understood to have declined briefs that he be requested to give his advice and attendance at the consultations as usual."

I feel great pleasure in taking the earliest opportunity of communicating this well deserved testimony.   [*Source*: Scully Papers]

[1]See No. 291 n.4 and No. 297 n.5.

310   *From William Parnell to 2 Merrion Square South, Dublin*

Bushy, near Bray [Co. Wicklow] Sunday [24 November 1811][1]
My dear Sir,

I am tempted to write to you because it is pleasant to write on any subject that is likely to remove any annoyance from an individual & because I have a great reliance on your good sense & good temper. And I am emboldened to write because what I have to say is sanctioned by the opinion of Mr Grattan, though I have not his authority to say so.

As you very early mentioned to me the prosecutions that were to take place against Judge Downes[2] I think it likely you may have much influence with the Delegates, if we may call them so, that have laid their actions against him; & if so I would wish to persuade you to use it, now, to have those actions withdrawn. I say *now* because the moment of triumph should open the heart to generosity & abate the feelings of hostility which in a protracted contest have usually risen too high. Judge Downes is not I believe, a man against whom marked or strong enmity would be easily justified; & the public sympathy which hitherto you have enjoyed would be apt under circumstances not very unlike to be transfer'd to him. If he gave any personal offence might it not be overlook'd or might not an apology be sought for it. Is it policy in the Catholics to attack the Judges? We may use the plural number because the *esprit du Corps* will naturally interest their feelings in the cause of their Brother.

Even if Judge Downes has deserved this attack, yet are there not other enemies against whom your money could be expended with more effect. You do not I believe abound in money; and the experience of all parties shews that their zeal soon cools if you make too frequent demands on their pockets. Therefore what you have should be applied in the most effectual manner; & I leave it to your own discernment to decide if this is not in cultivating your parliamentary interest. One Bigot ejected from a county by your interest would I think have more effect in advancing your cause than punishing Judge Downes for leaning to the ministerial construction of an obscure law.

Written on outside of cover

                                    At 25 Merrion Square North

My dear Sir,

   I called in hopes of finding you at home but as I do not leave town till tomorrow would you let me know if I could see you for five minutes before you go out tomorrow.   [*Source*: Scully Papers]

[1]Scully docketed this letter "Jany. 1812", an imprecision which allows of the possibility that he did so from memory some time later. It is placed here because "the moment of triumph" to which Parnell refers can only have been the acquittal of Dr Sheridan on 23 November 1811 (see No. 311 n.2); because the next letter seems to follow naturally from it; and because the two letters were written from the same temporary address, of Parnell's father-in-law.

[2]On 17 October Edward O'Callaghan had served notice on Chief Justice Downes on behalf of the delegates arrested under his warrant of 8 August (*DEP*, 28 November 1811) — see No. 291 n.4. When Edmund Taafe's suit came up on 12 June 1812 the charge was that Downes had made an assault upon the plaintiff and kept him

in custody without provocation and contrary to the law of the land (*Pilot*, 16 June 1812).

311   *From William Parnell to 2 Merrion Square, South, Dublin*

Bushy Park, near Bray [Co. Wicklow] Wednesday [27 November 1811][1]
My dear Sir,

I hope that the Atty General has been as good as his word[2] and if so that peace may be concluded between the Catholics & Govt; tho' I am attached to the opposition, I am more a friend to the Catholics & should be sorry they lost any honorable opportunity of disarming the hostility of their enemies. I am going to Avondale[3] on Friday but if you think there is any probability of my being of use in Dublin, I would go there; but if Saurin acts as he promised, I think any further difficulties might be settled by writing to him. I said nothing to him about checking the Govt newspapers, by the bye — if the action against Judge Downes[4] should be dropped, could you employ the money[5] in any better way than recompensing the newspapers that have fought for you; & by that means you would secure their support for moderate measures. I am very sensible of your extreme disinterestedness in being ready to advise dropping the prosecutions; but it is not more than I expected from you & if a religious peace is restored to this country now, it shall not be my fault if you do not receive the entire merit of it.   [*Source*: Scully Papers]

[1]Postmarked 28 November.

[2]Dr Edward Sheridan, the first to be tried of the arrested delegates (see No. 291) had been acquitted on 23 November, but the jury's verdict had been based on insufficiency of the evidence. Claiming that the court had unanimously decided that the Catholic Committee was an unlawful assembly the Attorney-General had announced that he would not press on the trial of the other delegates during the remainder of the law term in the expectation that the Committee would abandon their project, making a further trial unnecessary (*DEP*, 26 November 1811). The Castle hoped that this statement would induce respectable Catholics to announce that they would discontinue meeting as a delegated body (HO 100/165, f.227), but the Attorney-General was also making a virtue of necessity: it was agreed between the Chief Secretary and the law officers that they stood better as they were than if they had another verdict against them and that during the present term it was hardly possible to strike a jury that would find against Thomas Kirwan, the next to be prosecuted (ibid. f.217).

[3]His own home, near Rathdrum, Co. Wicklow.

[4]See No. 310 n.2.

[5]The subscriptions for the defence of the delegates.

312   *From Charles Butler to Merrion Square*

Lincolns Inn, 29 November 1811

Dear Sir,

I am very much obliged to you for your letter, and most sincerely congratulate with you on the event of the Tryal.[1] The language of our bar is that it was got up by government very ill indeed.

I immediately took care to have the account in the *Dublin Evening Post* printed in two evening papers, and will exert myself to see that your wishes are complied with in respect to the circulation of the tryal when it appears.

I applied to Mr Perry[2] to print your speech, and I was much surprized to hear him decline it, and, between ourselves, it has been observed that his paper has not been so full of acclamation on the happy event which has taken place as might have been expected from his professions of attachment to the Roman Catholic cause.

Lord Manners[3] must have been particularly mortified at the event, as he repeatedly mentioned, when he was last in England, that he had persuaded the Prince of the legality of the Proclamation.

I hear that the opinion of our Bar is, that the actions lie against the Chief Justice, but it seems not to be understood here what is the precise ground of the actions. I should therefore be much obliged to you if, at your earliest moment of leisure, you would let me know what the grounds of them are. I presume it is that his warrant did not sufficiently state the offence of which the parties were accused.[4]

It will be of consequence that I should receive your printed report of the tryal as soon as possible.

I think it probable, that in some form or other, the point between you and the Chief Justice will be brought before the House of Lords here. Would it not be adviseable for you to give general retainers to Sir Arthur Pigott, Sir Samuel Romilly, Mr Serjt Sheppard, Mr Serjt Best, and Mr Brougham.

I believe you will find I have been right in all the information I have to give you.

The report of the Prince's subjugation by Mr Perceval increases every hour.

P.S. Would it not be adviseable to have a reasoned Opinion of some Special Pleader in the Country on the Action agst. Downes?   [*Source*: Scully Papers]

[1]Of Dr Edward Sheridan, one of the arrested delegates (see No. 311 n.2).
[2]The editor of the *Morning Chronicle*.
[3]Lord Chancellor for Ireland.
[4]See No. 310 n.2. Appearing for Edmund Taaffe on 13 November 1812 O'Connell said the simple question was whether there was a class of magistrates entitled to issue

warrants without an information upon oath and without any crime having been actually committed, and entitled upon such warrants to imprison any of the king's subjects without being liable for damages. He claimed that there was no precedent, that Downes' warrant was illegal, that it was a ministerial rather than a judicial act and that he was liable for damages like any other magistrate (*FJ*, 14 November 1812).

313   *From Lord Holland to 2 Merrion Square, Dublin*

Holland House, 1 December 1811

My Dear Sir,

I cannot resist the pleasure of congratulating you & your countrymen on the victory obtained by the late verdict in Dublin,[1] & expressing my sincere hopes that the Catholics may speedily reap the benefits of it in the complete restoration of *all* their political rights as well as that for which they have so firmly & successfully contended upon this occasion. May I, as a very early & very eager supporter of their cause in Parliament[2] & as one consequently well acquainted with the nature & source of the obstacles which they have had & may still have to encounter in *this* country, be permitted to add that moderation in the use of this victory will be as useful & indeed as necessary to the attainment of their general objects as firmness during the contest was to their late success? Nothing believe me would conciliate well meaning but timid men, nothing above all would disarm their more virulent opponents so effectually as a determination (without departing one tittle from their right) of *not resorting to the measure of a Convention*, of dropping the prosecutions against the Chief Justice, & of proving by their temperate but firm manner of petitioning that they are really anxious to enjoy upon equal terms the benefits of the English Constitution & willing to adopt the line of conduct which by conciliating their fellow countrymen on this side of the water, is best calculated to ensure them success. I may be sanguine but I cannot help thinking that the time is come in which it only depends upon them to obtain their wishes. But I know enough of the temper of many persons *here* to know how essential it is to conciliate them by moderation in the moment of victory. Any disposition to triumph in the present humiliation of the Government, though a very natural & therefore in some degree an excusable propensity, would be eagerly adduced & I fear readily received as evidence of the truth of those imputations of disloyalty which your enemies cannot substantiate by law but which they would gladly infer from the slightest appearance of intemperate conduct.

I am almost ashamed of writing so long a letter on a subject on which you are yourself so much more competent a judge, but as I am sure you will give me credit for being as earnest a supporter of the Catholick claims as if I was a

Catholick myself, I thought you would not be displeased at hearing from me the view taken by the English publick of the late events in Ireland. Confidence and cooperation between the friends of the measure here & the promoters of it in Ireland is necessary to its success & some regard to the opinions of the publick here is equally essential to both. You will fully understand that I have here only expressed my private & individual opinion of the line of conduct which policy would enjoin, that I convey those of no other person further than I have collected them from general observation of the publick mind & that my conviction of the justice of your claims & consequently my duty to support them does not & never will depend upon the manner in which you urge them, though I take the liberty of a friend to point out according to the best of my judgment, that which would be most conciliating to others.   [*Source*: Scully Papers]

[1]The acquittal of Dr Sheridan, on 23 November, had been reported in the London papers of the 27th. See No. 315, in which William Parnell says he urged Lord Holland to write to Scully.
[2]In his *Memoirs of the Whig party* I, p. 160, Lord Holland prided himself on his early support of the Catholics, citing an initiative he had taken when the Union bill was on its way through parliament in 1799.

314   *From William Parnell to 2 Merrion Square, South, Dublin*

Avondale, near Rathdrum [Co. Wicklow] 8 December [1811]
Dear Sir,
Saurin returned me your letter.[1] He says that he could say no more than what he did in court. If he said anything I suppose he spoilt it in the manner. At all events he no longer retains any spirit of conciliation.[2] I am sorry for it, for if possible, I think it would be wise for the Catholics to be on good terms with the Irish Govt, who having nothing of consequence in their power to bestow or deny are not worth contending with; and in municipal matters they can teaze & torment.
As to the plan I hinted to you for collecting the sense of the Catholic body it is a simple & constitutional one; & yet I shall not venture to propose it without a little prefacing. In the first place I suppose you will not persist in the convention, it must end in failure (& it is never wise to run the risk of being baffled) for the very insignificance of the Irish Govt makes it impossible for them to exist with a rival that would overshadow them. The Catholics too by yielding the point in a moment of success would appear to act from moderation rather than necessity. Again, is a convention which absorbs all the interests, sollicitude, exertions, & with them all the energy of the Catholic body by seeming to represent them at all desireable? I should think the event of Mr Pole's experiment which by attacking the convention

brought forward the Catholic body in detail is a proof that it is not. Let us consider for a moment the general principle. When moderate & regular movements are alone required, that is when you want order rather than effort, it is best that the mass should be represented; but when the fault of your system is that the party spirit is feeble and prone to indifference that you want sound, movement, & money, then the mass should be brought out as much as possible in detail. The vanities, feelings & interest of individuals should not be merged in a representative body, but should be called into effort by throwing them on their own exertions; and giving them a multiplied scene of action in smaller and more local parts. A Dictator may then be useful but not a parliament. Consider the instance of Spain. While the provincial Juntas were in action, the nation acted: but when these lost their importance in a central Junta the multitude of spirits who had been warmed by the bustle & honor of local employment sank into apathy & Spain lost all vigor worthy so great a nation. So when Mr Pole's attack upon your Dublin Cortes, threw them upon the support of the County Juntas, did you not see the opposite effect take place; new warmth, new vigor, and a general interest in the common cause unknown before. What then do these facts suggest? When you want to take the sense of the Catholics, to call a meeting of all the counties; & then for your executive no matter how composed to take the sense, the aye or no of every County on that question & let the majority of these county votes decide? Yes; this would be better than a convention; but is there not a still better plan?

County meetings are themselves to exclusive; individuals are not sufficiently interested in them; & there is an indisposition in Ireland to attend to them. They are cumbersome machines. But as Mr Pole has proved them to be better than a convention by bringing the question nearer to men's hearts & interests, why not pursue the idea, and call every nerve & sinew of the Catholic body into action by quarterly meetings of all the *Parishes* throughout Ireland.

The advantages appear so many, that Dublin can scarcely have felt fairly for the nation or some such plan would sooner have been adopted. In the first place how easy (a point of great importance) it would be to procure these meetings at the Chapels. In this case some 5 or 6 men in every parish of superior sense & respectability would take the lead; would acquire controul over the people, would connect the whole Catholic body; you would cease to be afraid of your strength when it was well disciplined; & to give a hint which you will easily pursue, in case of rebellion or invasion, your leading men would then have the power of keeping the lower ranks quiet, and removing all obloquy of being a French faction from the Catholics. I perceive a great many more contingent advantages from this plan but I think that you will perceive them too. I shall only mention one; which is affording you a regular fund of money without being burthensome to anyone.

When Jefferson gave up some very small tax, the only one, paid by the back settlers in America he was very justly blamed as having with it given up a bond of union on a visible chain of connection. And on the same principle, I think, nothing would give more union to the Catholic body than to raise generally & annually a very small voluntary contribution, if only a penny from each laborer, a shilling from each farmer & five from each gentleman.[3] Your parish collectors & your Treasury would be the connecting medium between you & the people; so small a donation could scarcely become an object of great obloquy. It might be raised for the ostensible purpose for paying the law expenses where poor Catholics were oppressed; & for the necessary expenses of your petitions; but your executive in Dublin might be allowed a sum for secret service money accountable to a select committee, for contesting the elections of members inimical to your cause, and for remunerating the newspapers & employing the press. This would remove the necessity of too frequent drafts on the pockets of your aristocracy, for men however rich do not like to be often called on for five guineas & get tired of the cause.

Your executive however chosen, (it must not be elected) may safely be extremely numerous. Every country gentleman's name of respectability should be enrolled in it & this may be done with very little inconvenience for as its sittings should be private & there would be no exhibition, you would find the attendance of this class would always be small, & the direction of affairs would in fact soon rest, where it ought, in the hands of the residents in Dublin who were most zealous in the cause.

In one word instead of a Parliament, I would propose an executive, & the people.

You are now in some degree impelled to persist longer in your convention than is prudent, by the expectation of your body at large who always look upon retracting [as] pusillanimous, but in the measure I propose, you would only appear to take a stronger position; and their vanity would be too much gratified by it, not to make it better relished than the Convention. Another advantage would be that as you would soon begin to have real power by your encreased influence in the house of Commons, you might give up all the language of irritation & invective which is generally the language of angry weakness. Hitherto the Catholics like most public bodies have reversed the old proverb and have acted *suaviter in re fortiter in modo*; they have been loud but have done little but what Govt has forced them into. These actions against Downes alone excepted. Petitioning is certainly indispensible, but if perpetual rejection is only followed by petitioning it will soon produce no effect except it is a ridiculous one. The Catholics relying on a vague feeling of importance from their numbers have wholly neglected encreasing their political power which in these days can only be encreased by weight in the house of Commons. One bigotted Irish Member clearly ejected at an election by a powerful interposition of the Catholics, would disarm many of the rest, would lessen the hostility of all. If the Catholics had only a party in the house of Commons equal to the Saints,[4] that would avoid taking a decided part either with Govt or opposition, their question would be carried. At present they have not a supporter that is not more devoted to a party than to the Catholics & of course can have no weight except as a party man.

Pray excuse this long letter.   [*Source*: Scully Papers]

[1]Scully minuted on William Parnell's letter No. 311 that he answered it on 28 November: it may have been this reply that was shown to Saurin.

[2]The hardening of his attitude may have been due not only to the absence of any public admission from the Catholics that the law was against them but also to the evidence of continued defiance provided by Castle spies. He had learnt that on 27 November there had been a private meeting of some thirty of the most active leaders at Fitzpatrick's where it was decided that there would be a general meeting of the Committee on 23 December; that a petition should be prepared in advance so that it might be passed with the same expedition as before (see No. 306); that the newspapers were to be cautioned not to comment; and that it should be left to the Secretary to decide how members should be convened. At a second secret meeting on the 29th methods of raising money from the counties were discussed and it was agreed to send out 1000 invitations for a dinner to be held on 19 December. Because of their nature and their not being promulgated in the press the Lord Lieutenant did not think it prudent to molest these meetings but on 1 December he wrote to the Home Secretary that if the meeting of the 23rd took place he would disperse it. A reply dated 7 December said that the Prince Regent entirely approved (HO 100/165, ff.227, 242).

[3]In the Peel Papers (ADD.MSS.40,231, f.222) there is a copy of a "Plan suggested for parochial subscriptions" dated 26 October 1813. Under this one person was to be appointed in each parish to ask each householder to contribute ten pence or more towards defraying the expenses of the Catholic petitions. "Refused to contribute ten pence" would be entered against the names of all who refused and the list would be read out in chapel. No sum, however, was expected from any person that he could not afford to give. A report of 16 December 1813 from Cork to the Castle shows that the contribution was being collected there (HO 100/175, f.194). On 17 May 1814, however, Sir J. Hippisley applauded the Catholic clergy for refusing to undertake the task the Board had imposed on them (*Hansard* XXVII, 933).

[4]William Wilberforce and his followers in parliament.

315   *From William Parnell to 2 Merrion Square South, Dublin*

[Avondale, Rathdrum, Co. Wicklow] [Postmarked 8 December 1811] My dear Sir,

I enclose you a note from Ld King[1] which I will thank you not to shew to anyone — but as it is written from Ld Grenville's, you may judge by it that there is not much chance of that party coming in at present & that probably nothing will determine the prince in favor of the Catholics but their firmness & success. You will excuse my urging Ld Holland to write to you,[2] independent of the object I had in view; I wished to revive a good intelligence between the Catholics & opposition & I wished you to be the medium. If you can cultivate an intercourse with Ld Holland without exciting the envy of your Catholic friends; I can get Ld King & Ld Ponsonby to unite Ld Grey & Ld Grenville with Ld Holland & perhaps something might be done to get rid of the difficulty of the Veto. At all events a cordial understanding might be established.

I am very sorry I cannot attend the Catholic dinner;[3] I cannot leave my young wife[4] alone in a wild country & she cannot go to town with me. I wish that the friends of Catholic freedom could be got in force enough to give a dinner in return to the Catholics.

Did you get my project?[5]   [*Source*: Scully Papers]

[1]Not found among the Scully Papers.
[2]See No. 313.
[3]For the Friends of Religious Liberty on 19 December (see No. 322 n.4).
[4]Frances Howard, whom he married during 1811. She must have been very young as her mother was expecting another child in June 1813 (see No. 444).
[5]No. 314.

316   *To Richard Huddleston*

Dublin, 9 December 1811

Dear Richard,

I have waited for some time in expectation of meeting with a conveyance for the Bonds to you — but, finding none, I send them to Lord Hardwicke with this Letter, requesting that he will forward them to you. You will see my receipts for the entire Sums endorsed upon the two Bonds[1] — and, if you require any further form of Discharge for the amount, you have only to let me know.

You have by this time learned the full extent of our cousin Frank's[2] malpractices — but your surprize has been lessened by the previous intimation I gave you upon the subject, when lately at Sawston.[3] I never was more astonished, however, than at hearing him aver publicly his Protestant-ism — and that of some years standing, (*mentally*, he added) but he was seen at Mass within these 2 years to a certainty.[4] As I feared you might have some exaggerated accounts, thro' third persons, I had some of the Dublin newspapers forwarded to you, that you might learn the real facts. I don't know now what he will do with himself — he can scarcely continue his residence in Ireland, being caricatured and lampooned in the Shops, and even in some of the Dublin Magazines, as an Informer etc.[5]

We have two English Militia Regiments stationed here.[6] Major Stoddart of the Enniskillen Dragoons (the 6th) dined with us last week. His Regiment is here. You may have formerly known him, as he had a letter to me from Edward some years ago.[7] He tells me, that there is a Major Cooper of the Nottingham Militia, and a Lieut-Colonel Hulse of the Leicestershire, with whom you have been formerly much acquainted.[8] I wish to know what you think of them, their manners etc. and what their families are in their own Counties — as I should be very glad to pay them any attention here, and to visit them etc., if you recommend them — tho' I did not like the Colonel of the Leicestersh' — the D. of Rutland, when at Trinity College Cambridge.[9]

I beg you will present my best regards to your mother.

Compt's to Mr Tottevin.[10]   [*Source*: Huddleston Papers C3/S13]

[1]In part payment of his first wife's dowry (see No. 46).

[2]Captain Francis Huddleston, first cousin of his first wife.

[3]Before he left for England in September Scully would have seen the charge against the arrested delegates (see No. 291) beginning with the words: "The King at the prosecution of Francis Huddleston".

[4]At the Sheridan trial in November he said he was now a member of the established church (Howell, *State Trials* XXXI, 666).

[5]There is a caricature of him as such in the *Irish Magazine* of December 1811. Whether or not he was one of the spies who had given the Castle advance information about the plans of the Catholic Committee he admitted at the Kirwan trial that he had given the Undersecretary, Sir Charles Saxton, a report on the Catholic Committee from 15 December 1810 to 6 February 1811 (Howell, ibid. 817). He attended meetings as a reporter for the *Hibernian Journal* (*DEP*, 1 December 1810).

[6]English militia regiments had been brought to Ireland following the passing of the Interchange bill on 5 June 1811 (*Hansard* XX, 130). On 23 July the Chief Secretary had urged that no time be lost in sending them and getting rid of some Irish regiments (HO 100/164, f.104).

[7]See No. 51 n.13.

[8]Major Cooper remains unidentified. The other may have been Richard Hulse of the Coldstream Guards, holding local rank of colonel.

[9]John Henry Manners (1778–1857), the 5th Duke. An entry of 3 June 1795 in Scully's Common Place Book (MS.27, 502) notes "D. Rutland" and Parnell senior among others in the second class at Trinity.

[10]Probably one of the five exiled French priests called Tostivin(t), all from the St Malo diocese, listed by D. A. Bellenger, *The French Exiled Clergy*.

317   *To the Earl of Hardwicke*

Merrion Square, 9 December 1811

My Lord,

I have occasion to transmit to Richard Huddleston two bonds, which his father passed to me in 1801, and since discharged, but can make out no direct conveyance.[1]

I am certain he will feel himself obliged by your Lordship having the goodness to receive them for him in the enclosed packet, and, when an opportunity occurs, you may perhaps forward them to him at Sawston without inconvenience.

Tho' I am perhaps amongst the latest, yet I am assuredly amongsst the most earnest, in tendering my cordial congratulations to your Lordship & to Lady Hardwicke upon the marriage of Lady Catherine.[2] No event, relating to the welfare of your house or to your personal happiness, can be indifferent to me: and I rejoice sincerely in an event of such agreeable promise to both. I had not the good fortune to be in Dublin, when Lord and Lady Caledon passed through, and I have therefore had no opportunity of paying my respects to them.

Our local events have followed nearly in the order of succession which your Lordship had calculated[3] — and, tho' some have occasioned pleasure, yet none have excited in me any surprise. It is to be regretted, for the general cause of good government in Ireland, that so naked an exposure of imbecility and blunder should have been forced upon public observation, as now presented. However vigorous the present men may be in intention, yet they now appear utterly feeble in contrivance & conduct, and powerless in execution. Never had Ireland a government so little supported by *any* class — so abandoned by its habitual champions, so assailed by talent and exertion, so ridiculed for its errors and disappointments. I dread to look forward to the eventual mischief, resulting from their disparagement, if some effectual measure be not speedily resorted to for retrieving the character of power, so degraded in the existing instance. Still we are all in the dark as to future proceedings:[4] and, here, we are not able even to divine when the veil of mystery shall be withdrawn.

I hope that Lady Hardwicke & the other amiable members of your Lordship's family are well.

[*Source*: Hardwicke Papers Add.MSS.35, 649, f.339]

[1]See No. 316.
[2]Their 2nd daughter, Catherine, who on 16 October 1811 had married Alexander Du Pre (1777–1839), from 1802 2nd Earl of Caledon, a representative peer from 1804 and Governor of the Cape of Good Hope 1807–11.
[3]Scully may have met Lord Hardwicke on the visit to Sawston mentioned in No. 316.
[4]He may have meant that he was still in the dark as to whether the Attorney-General would bring on another trial (see No. 311 n.2).

318   *From Bishop John Milner to Merrion Square, Dublin*

W.H. 11 December 1811

My Dear Sir,

I am ashamed to say that this is intended to be an answer to a letter of yours dated so far back as the 5th of October. In the first place, then I have to thank you for the information contained in that letter. I make no doubt that my poor brethren signed whatever papers Dr Poynter proposed to them for signature, & I take it for granted that these were drawn up by Mr Charles Butler.[1] One of these, I take it for granted, was a Protest against the interference of the Irish Bishops & of myself with the concerns of the London District.[2] The fact, however, is we do not interfere with any such concern. We do not say to Blanchard's associates: *Bishop Douglas releases you but we bind you.* What we say is to Bishop Douglas himself, namely: *Do you or do you not hold to the terms of Catholic Communion, which require uniformity of doctrine & adherence to the centre of Unity, the Pope? For we are credibly informed that you have lately admitted to the ministry of the Gospel & the Sacraments a man*[3] *who publicly proclaims that the Pope is the author of schism & heresy?*

You informed me by word of mouth[4] that these Prelates had appealed from Dr Troy, the usual organ of the Irish Prelacy, to the ArchBps. of Armagh & Cashel.[5] Their letter is now before me, a wretched specimen of Dr Poynter's & Chs. Butler's logic. The apposite & dignified answers of those Metropolitans is likewise in my possession. It proves that schism is openly countenanced by the restoration of the Blanchardist without retractation & that this is a common concern of all Cathc. Pastors.[6]

I presume you see me from time to time in the *Dublin Evening Post.* You will probably see me there again in answer to Mr McDermot[7] concerning *Columbanus* etc. I am surprised that none of your spirited Patriots shd. expose the hypocrisy & treachery of that base parasite, the hireling tool of the Buckingham party. This party had certainly sold us to the Protestant Bishops in return for their promise of the latters support: but the sale turned out to be that of the bear's skin before the bear was taken. My assertions would be demonstrated cd. we get at a copy of Lord Grenville's Letter to Dr Hodson of Brazen Nose.[8] With a little more patience & perseverance you will gain the Emancipation without any irreligious or degrading compromise. The Emancipation will be an inestimable benefit in Ireland: but I fear it will do full as much harm as good among English Catholics. However they will get it when you get it; if Buonaparte do not come amongst us in the meantime. I was the first man to make them sensible that all their dependence is upon Ireland: still they cannot help occasionally shewing their contempt of Irishmen. They are a poor set, in point of intellect, not excepting Charles Butler who manages them all, clergy as well as laity, one individual excepted; & that individual he dares no more face on any part of his past conduct, than I dare box with Mendoza or Crib.[9] *A propos*, about yr. book, I am anxious for its appearance; first because it will be an inestimable advantage to the Caths.; secondly, because I think it will be greatly for yr. honour & future benefit: Surely the triumph of the Catholics[10] will inspire you with a little courage. In return for the information you gave me, I can tell you from the lips of those who are most intimately acquainted with the Prince & who have had the very best opportunities of knowing him that he is a weak undecided man, & who of course, is quite irresolute, at the present moment, what set of men or what men of any parties to employ. One thing, however, seems certain that he is tired of the Duke of Cumberland.[11] Perhaps the state of affairs in Ireland may determine him to take right measures & employ proper men. But, when I think of it, where are such men to be found? I am sure that the Grenvilles have a large portion of their innate bigotry still lurking in their bosoms. *They* will never give you *complete* Emancipation.

I must not forget to thank you for the intelligence about the Cardinals caps, & I shd. like to know how far you were enabled to trace the story. Who, in particular, is this Dr Cameron of Leghorn,[12] the supposed depository of the Bulls? It is a fact, however, that so much of the story I heared from Italy, nearly two years ago; namely that it was currently reported there that the Pope had created several Cardinals out of Bonaparte's reach, & some of them in Ireland & England.[13]

Many inquiries are made about Capt Huddlestone, the informer:[14] probably you can inform me who he is: but what I wish principally to know is whether you know any thing of a Miss Ann Kelly[15] who is or was in the keeping of one of the Huddlestones, as I have an article of furniture which devolves to her by the death of her aunt to whose executor I am executor.

Mr Wheble[16] has been spending ten days here, where he happened to meet Messrs Vincent & Thos. Eyre who came to look at an estate upon sale in this neighbourhood. Mrs Wheble desires all that is kind to Mrs S. & yrself. I beg also to be respectfully named to that Lady.   [*Source*: Scully Papers]

[1]Probably the then unpublished resolutions (reproduced by Ward, *Eve of Catholic Emancipation* I, Appendix D) adopted by the Vicars Apostolic, other than Dr Milner, at Durham in August 1811. As Scully's letter must have been written from Bath (see No. 303) he probably got his information from Butler when he met him there.

[2]The Vicars Apostolic took particular objection to a declaration of an Irish synod on the Blanchardist schism, feeling that it was not addressed to the Irish Catholics but expressly sent to their agent to be circulated among the English.

[3]Abbe Treveaux (see No. 296 n.13).

[4]No doubt at The Farm, Sheffield, in September (see No. 302).

[5]Before separating at Durham the Vicars Apostolic had invited the Archbishops of Armagh and Cashel to mediate between them and the Irish Bishops in an approach to Dr Troy. They complained that the latter sent their letters on to Dr Milner and did not reply until he had received instructions from him (Ward, *Eve* I, p. 169).

[6]It took the form of six resolutions adopted at an informal meeting of Dr Troy and six other Prelates, asking the other Vicars Apostolic to intercede with Dr Douglass of London (Ward, *Eve* I, p. 170). It asserted that "Schism, though unintentionally on the part of Dr Douglass, is openly countenanced".

[7]The *Dublin Evening Post* of 17 December published a letter from him replying to two written by Dr Hugh MacDermot on 6 August and 19 November defending his brother-in-law, Dr Charles O'Conor.

[8]The letter, dated 2 November 1809 is printed in *Dropmore Papers* IX.

[9]Daniel Mendoza and Tom Cribb, both in the *DNB* as well known pugilists.

[10]With the acquittal of Dr Sheridan (see No. 311 n.2).

[11]A notorious opponent of concessions to the Catholics.

[12]Unidentified.

[13]Pius VII created no new Cardinals between 1804 and 1816 (Schmidlin: *Papstgeschichte* I, p. 350).

[14]Frank Huddleston (see No. 316 n.5).

[15]Not identified.

[16]Mrs Wheble's son, James Wheble.

319   *To Lord Hardwicke*

Merrion Square, 14 December 1811

My Lord,

Tho' I did myself the honour of addressing your Lordship so lately, yet I believe it will not be disagreeable to you to receive an early and full report of Dr Sheridan's trial.[1] It has been just published, and I beg to send a copy under this cover. It is observable, in reading Mr Bushe's concluding speech, that he leaves unanswered the strong arguments exposed by Mr Burrowes, & scarcely touches them. This is noticed here, and deemed of great weight.

It is a fact that Messrs Saurin, Burnes[2] and Bushe revised their own speeches for this publication, and improved them by every grace and afterthought that occurred to them, so that we have here the best efforts of these gentlemen. There are some little inaccuracies & omissions in other parts of this report, but scarcely deserving of notice.

[P.S.] May I beg to trespass upon your Lordship's goodness, in sending also a copy for Mr Charles Butler, of Lincoln's Inn.

[*Source*: Hardwicke Papers, Add. MSS.35, 649, f.341]

[1]See No. 317.

[2]The lists of counsel give by Howell, *State Trials* XXXI, do not include a name with this spelling, but give John Burne, counsel for the defence.

320   *From Lord Hardwicke to Merrion Square*

Wimpole, 20 December 1811

Dear Sir,

as soon as I received your letter of the 9th[1] with the pacquet under Mr Beckett's cover,[2] I informed Huddleston that I would send it to Cambridge by a first opportunity.

I was not in the least surprised at the result of the first trial that was brought forward in consequence of the proceedings on the proclamation.[3] I am sincerely rejoiced at it, for though it has not yet been explicitly so declared, I presume there is no intention of bringing forward any other upon the same grounds — Nothing can be more just than your observation on the effect which these proceedings must have in respect to the lowering of government in the eyes of the publick in Ireland. It is so far undoubtedly very unfortunate & much to be deplored by all good subjects. — I heard from good authority a few days ago that nothing was fixed about a ministry, notwithstanding the assertions of the friends of the present cabinet — At the same time I should not be surprised if no very great change should take place — a very few weeks[4] must develope the whole mystery, and decide whether the Prince of Wales will act upon honourable and consistent principles, or in a manner that will I fear be more likely to produce a troublesome reign.

I return many thanks for your obliging congratulations on my daughter's marriage — We are in hopes that she & Lord Caledon will be in London in the early part of the session, but I presume they will only pass thro' Dublin on their way from the County Tyrone.

[P.S.] I am much obliged to you for a copy of the trial[5] which I found on my table on my arrival in London last Monday, with a copy for Mr Butler, which I forwarded to Lincoln's Inn.   [*Source*: Scully Papers]

[1]No. 317.
[2]John Beckett, Undersecretary at the Home Office.
[3]The proclamation of 30 July 1811 (No. 289 n.1), followed by the prosecution of members of the Catholic Committee (No. 291 n.4) and the acquittal of Dr Sheridan (No. 311 n.2).
[4]When the restrictions on the Regency imposed on 6 February 1811 would expire.
[5]Of Dr Sheridan.

321   *To Lord Holland*

Merrion Square, 24 December 1811

My Lord,

The kind and valuable communication, conveyed by your Lordship's letter of the 1st inst.,[1] has been felt by me, as it might, with deep respect & gratitude. The subject is perhaps too large for my capacity, difficult too of explanation to those even who may thoroughly understand it, and habitually misrepresented — It involves feelings, which admit of no cold language, and yet its delicacy and importance require, for ordinary purposes, expressions so qualified and guarded, that I hazard a serious error in venturing to write upon it.

Permit me to thank your Lordship most sincerely for the sympathy you evince towards us, and for your kind & beneficial advice. As an upright and generous statesman, and as the worthy representative of the illustrious friend of the Catholics & of humanity, you have long possessed the unqualified confidence of the warmhearted though oppressed people, whose interests are discussed in your Lordship's letter.

I can truly say, that the conciliatory principles, so powerfully urged by your Lordship, perfectly accord with my own — and not with mine only, but also (as far as I can judge) with those of the Catholics of Ireland. Of this fact their history, and especially for the last few years, affords many, and strong, proofs. What their future temper may be, I find it difficult to conjecture. The provocation of yesterday[2] was deeply felt — and every engine of exasperation is employed by the present Government (i.e. by the D[uke] of Richmond, Lord Manners, Mr Wellesley Pole, urged by the Attorney & Solicitor General, Messrs Saurin and Bushe) and their numerous dependants, their writers in hired newspapers etc., etc. No other individual has hitherto committed, or even attempted, any violation of our peace & concord in Ireland.

Your Lordship recommends (and, as I observe, in decided terms) two acts of concession: the abandonment of the Catholic Committee, and of the civil actions against Mr Downes[3] — I fear that the Irish people, of every description, are now very ill disposed towards such acts — and will continue so, whilst any one of the five men above named continues in office. These men are become more obnoxious in Ireland, than any others have been within my recollection. Were the Catholics to recede now, they would incur fresh insult & persecution: they would distrust one another, lose the alliance of other Irishmen, and *all confidence even in themselves* — To a kind and sincere friend they can sacrifice much: their interests, their feelings and even their lives. But to an imperious, vulgar, bigoted and ungenerous Junta, they can scarcely be persuaded to crouch. The Protestants, Dissenters, Quakers etc., who have honourably supported the Catholics throughout the perilous autumn, and stood by their sides at every county meeting, would abandon the Catholics with disgust, as faithless & unsteady. The Catholics are fully aware, that the conflict will be dangerous, and perhaps destructive to all: but they feel also, that it is an *honourable* one: that they stand upon good ground: that, in withdrawing from their present position, they might chance to stumble upon a very bad and untenable one: their motives and views are pure & innocent: and I think they are determined to persevere *"ad imum".*[4]

I see no means of terminating this ruinous contest, but by good humour and just conduct, *emanating from your Lordship's side of the water — and speedily.*

As an individual, I must bow my head to the disasters, which misgovernment must accumulate upon these Islands — Yet I cannot see, without regret & indignation, how cruelly the English name & character suffer in Ireland, how fatally every hostile sentiment spreads, and what an aversion to England is inculcated here, by the active virulence of the present Irish Government. Having no personal object in view, no place or title to seek, or promotion to wish for, I have nothing to gain or lose but in common with my country — If my private property is ample enough to place me far above selfish objects, it augments, however, the interest which I feel in the general welfare — and I own I do feel the most intense alarm upon this head — I am attached to your country by education, by many years of residence, by many very precious ties of friendship, and by marriage — My family, to a man, supported the union, we never have been separatists, or looking for a repeal of the union:[5] and my character is, I believe, known to be more partial to England, than is to be found in many Irishmen, of whatever religion: yet I must concur, with the almost universal voice of Ireland, in reprobating the misgovernment of the 5 persons I have named, as surpassing in acrimony, violence & folly, all that has been exhibited by the most desperate & unprincipled of their predecessors in office — In other respects, it is a matter of indifference to me, in whose hands power shall be deposited, provided it be exercised honestly, prudently, impartially and with kindness.

I fear, my Lord, I have trespassed far upon your patience: even to egotism: and have fallen into the error anticipated in commencing this letter — but I have yielded to the temptation of being frank & confidential, in writing to a distinguished statesman, who condescends to avow himself "as earnest a supporter of the cause as if he were a Catholic himself" — and I am the less apprehensive of prejudicing the cause in your Lordship's estimation by any errors of mine, when I see your Lordship's assurance "that your opinion upon the subject never will depend upon the *manner* in which it may be urged" — Would that all our friends had acted on this clear & simple rule of justice.

Permit me, before I pass from the subject, to observe to your Lordship, that the time has been for some time coming, and is perhaps now arrived, when the confidence which the Catholics and the Irish at large have hitherto placed in certain beneficial changes, may be shaken — Opinions already waver — Your Lordship knows, that there is a period during which the public mind balances, before it rejects a fond hope, or a favourite prepossession. I think we are now at that point — Distrust will probably soon follow — and, if so, adieu to the hope of graceful concessions, of fervid gratitude, of enthusiastic attachment — Your Lordship will, I believe, perfectly understand what I allude to — but, in this particular, I offer only my individual surmise, not the sentiments of the Catholics — Much mischief has already been done in this way and this mischief is fast spreading — It is cruel, not merely to withhold just rights, but to inflict new injuries & affronts; these are felt the more bitterly, as being unexpected, & opposite to long cherished hopes, grounded upon broad facts and even upon personal assurances of favour & protection.

I have sent to your Lordship (addressed to the care of J. Ridgeway, bookseller, 170 Piccadilly) a printed "Statement of the Penal Laws which now aggrieve the Catholics of Ireland" — of which I beg to solicit your favourable acceptance[6] — I wrote it for the use of our friends in Parliament, & for the reasons specified in the Introduction: but for certain personal reasons (arising from the state of our society and the temper of our Government) I do not avow myself as the author — but I can vouch to your Lordship for its truth & fidelity, as fully as if I had affixed my name to it — If it shall appear to your Lordship too strong or harsh, I beg that the fault may be laid upon the Penal Code, not upon the author's nature: for my mispleasure is directed against the system, not against its instruments — and after many alterations and attempts to soften it down, I found that I must suppress many truths, and enervate the work & defeat its principal object, were I to expunge every unpleasant passage — As it is, I think it liable to the Attorney General's information (according to our strange law of libel) and therefore I do not allow the printer to advertize it — but I believe it will be circulated notwithstanding.

Once more, I beg to repeat my grateful sense of the high honour conferred upon me by the distinction of your Lordship's estimable letter.

[*Source*: Holland House Papers, Add. MS.51826, f.56]

[1]No. 313.

[2]The dispersal of the meeting of the Irish Catholic Committee adjourned from 19 October (see No. 306). It was reported in the *Dublin Evening Post* on 24 December and on the same day the Lord Lieutenant and the Chief Secretary sent accounts to the Home Office (HO 100/165, ff.295, 299). Although the meeting was not advertised until the day itself the Fishamble Street Theatre was nearly full with county and city members, and some hundreds of Protestants. Since 27 November (see No. 314 n.2) it had evidently been decided not to rush the proceedings through before the arrival of the peace officers, for Lord Fingall did not arrive until half an hour after the advertised

time. Alderman Hare was waiting for him and went through the motion of a formal arrest by placing a hand on his arm. There was then an adjournment to D'Arcy's Crown and Anchor Tavern in Earl Street, where Major Bryan took the chair. Alderman Hare, who had followed, withdrew on being told that those present were there in their individual capacities. It was decided to call an aggregate meeting and in deference to the county members, who wished to get back to their families, this was fixed for 26 December. According to the Chief Secretary's informant, Scully moved that a petition, of which he was the framer, should be entered on and passed, but withdrew the motion on being told by the chair that the meeting was not one of the General Committee. He then put forward a second proposal, which was adopted: the appointment of a committee of twenty-one to prepare an address to the Regent. At the instance of O'Connell this was done at once, the method chosen being for the chairman to nominate one person, that person another, and so on until the number was complete.

[3] See No. 310 n.2.

[4] "To the end".

[5] See No. 31 n.3 for his father's support of the Union.

[6] Prostrated with gout and excusing himself for not attending parliament, Wellesley Pole wrote to the Prime Minister on 21 December and among other things told him that he had sent the Home Secretary twelve copies of *A Statement of the Penal Laws*, which had come out on 19 December, the day of the Catholic dinner: "from just dipping into it I think it will be found to contain enough to draw the most serious attention from the Established Churchmen and, if I may use the expression, the established Statesmen of England" (HO 100/165, f.259). This was Part I of the *Statement*.

322   *From Charles Butler to Merrion Square*

Lincolns Inn, 28 December 1811

Dear Sir,

I am much obliged to you for your letter.[1] I have sent the two guineas to Mrs Bostock. I had spoken to Captain Blake, whom you saw in Ireland,[2] to remit them to you.

I sincerely congratulate with you, on the event of the trial,[3] and that your public dinner[4] went off so well. The papers of this morning inform me, of the late achievement of government.[5] I think it requires little foresight to predict that it will end still more favourably to you than the former.[6]

The day after your letter reached me, I received a packet from Lord Hardwicke.[7] On opening it, I found that it contained, not the account of the trial of Doctor Sheridan, but Mr Finnerty's trial,[8] so that I apprehend there has been some mistake respecting the parcel.

I assure you that nothing can exceed the general wishes of the Roman Catholics of this country, and particularly of those whom I most see, to do every thing that the Irish Catholics wish. In respect to the Press, the board has printed, at their own expence the debates in parliament on each of your petitions; and have spent much money in procuring the insertion in our papers, of such articles as they thought most likely to produce a favourable impression in the public mind, in respect to the common cause. On my own part, I have contributed my mite of exertion; by inserting four long letters in the newspapers,[9] a kind of publication which till this occasion, I uniformly and constantly avoided: and which nothing but the Interest which I take in the concern would have drawn from me. I am sure every cordial and respectful attention was shewn to the Delegates;[10] and they were repeatedly asked by many, and among others, by myself what the English Catholics could do, which would be most acceptable to the Catholics in Ireland.

I myself asked, more than once, to what, we were to attribute some symptoms of coldness, that we heard of. I could get no answer, except a reference to our Fifth Resolution, and an intimation of our being suspected of advocating the Veto.

If any one thing be more certain than another, it is, that the English Catholics have had no concern whatever in the Veto, as it must be admitted by all parties, that it was proposed by your prelates in 1799, and by their Agent in 1809,[11] without the concurrence, and even without the knowledge of any English Catholic and that, since that time no English Catholic, (except the Agent of your prelates in his *Letter to a Parish Priest*[12] and his subsequent Letter in the *Morning Chronicle*),[13] has ever written a word in its defence.[14] I may add, that, in two printed letters,[15] I myself have, strongly and unequivocally spoken of it, as a project totally and absolutely abandoned, and which never ought to be proposed.

As to the Fifth Resolution,[16] it is amazing to me that it has ever been thought to refer to the Veto; but without uttering further on the subject, I put this short question to the feelings of yourself and to every other gentleman in Ireland. When such persons, as Lord Grey and Lord Grenville on the one hand, and Lord Stourton, Sir J. Throckmorton and Mr Jerningham on the other, solemnly and explicitly assure you, not only that the Veto was not referred to, but that there was an anxious wish on all sides to avoid the slightest expression which could be thought to refer to it, or which by any possible construction could at any future occasion be construed to refer to it; — Is it fair, just or congruous to make or persist in the charge?

That you have gained much by your late contest: that you will gain more by your present contest, is, most certain; but, the renewal of the attack clearly shews, that it is the intention of those in whose hands the government of the country is now placed and is likely to continue, to resist your claims to the utmost. That you will overpower them, is my most earnest wish. Petition by the head, and you will do it. Such a petition will speak to our wise ones in thunder, and stun them into reason. The Prince Regent does not avow the late or present acts of his ministers: but it is impossible to suppose they are without his knowledge, and whatever is with his knowledge, will always be suspected of having his tacit approbation.[17]

From the admirable mixture of Firmness and Energy you have shewn and continue to shew every thing great and good may be expected from you. That the new year may be a year of triumph, of perfect, absolute, unqualified and unburthened triumph to you is all our wishes.

P.S. Mr Lidwill's speech[18] is particularly admired by us.

[*Source*: Scully Papers]

[1]Of 14 December, not extant.

[2]In January 1811 (see No. 281).

[3]The acquittal of Dr Sheridan on 23 November.

[4]Held on 19 December at the Rotunda in Dublin for the Friends of Religious Liberty and attended by over eight hundred people (*DEP*, 21 December 1811).

[5]The dispersal of the meeting of 23 December, reported in the *Morning Chronicle* of 27 December (see No. 321 n.2).

[6]The attempted dispersal on 19 October (see N. 306) having been followed by the acquittal of Dr Sheridan, Butler hoped that the dispersal of 23 December would be followed by another acquittal or the government's desisting from further prosecutions. He would not yet have seen the outcome of the aggregate meeting of 26 December. This appointed a new committee under the name of Board, but consisting of some three hundred named individuals, seen by the Castle as identical with the delegates of the dispersed Committee. The Board was to meet once a week, prepare an address to the Regent and meet as the Committee again on 28 February 1812, when the restrictions on the Regency would have ended. On 28 December the law officers told the Chief Secretary that they did not think the Board was an unlawful assembly under the Convention Act, although after it met and acted it might come within its provisions (Pole to Home Secretary 27 December 1811, HO 100/165, ff.304, 341).

[7]See postscript to No. 320.

[8]On 7 March 1811 for a libel on Lord Castlereagh (see No. 273 n.1).

[9]Unidentified. They may have included his Hwyls letters of 1809 and 1810 (see Nos. 202, 212, and 268).

[10]Who presented to the Regent the two addresses mentioned in No. 286 on 26 May 1811 and stayed on for the debates on the petitions in parliament (Aspinall, *Correspondence of George, Prince of Wales* VIII, No. 3060).

[11]*Recte* 1808 (see No. 177 n.1).

[12]See No. 290 n.12.

[13]See No. 194 n.7.

[14]See No. 290 n.13.

[15]One was probably the *Address to the Irish Roman Catholics by an English Roman Catholic* advertised by Coyne as by "the first Catholic in England" (*EH*, 22 February 1809).

[16]See No. 230 n.1.

[17]On 31 December Wellesley Pole sent the Home Secretary a long memorandum urging that the Regent should make up his mind on his attitude to the Catholics and

publicly announce it. As evidence of their increasingly menacing attitude he sent him a long synopsis of the *Penal Laws* and suggested that the Prince should read it (*HO* 100/165, f.344: there is a printed copy in Spencer Walpole, *Life of Perceval*, 1874, p. 248).
[18]At the dinner of 19 December.

323   *From Francis Plowden to 4[sic] Merrion Square, Dublin*

Cork, 21 January 1812

Permit me, my dear Sir, to express my warmest thanks to you for your luminous manly patriotic & resistless exposure of the Protestant Ascendancy.[1] A friend lent it to me yesterday & I devoured it. Never since I bent my mind to Irish Affairs have I met with any publication so useful. You have completely unveiled the idol. I have humbly endeavoured to detail the means by which its wicked Ministers seduce the people to worship it. This brings to my grateful Memory the obligations I owe & which I now beg leave to repeat to you for having furnished me with valuable helps towards accomplishing my undertaking.[2]   [*Source*: Scully Papers]

[1]The *Statement of the Penal Laws*.
[2]For his *History of Ireland* from 1801 to 1810, which had been published in the late summer of 1811 (*Irish Magazine*, September). For Scully's help see Nos. 220 and 280.

324   *From Charles Butler to Merrion Square*

Lincolns Inn, 22 January 1812

Dear Sir,

Sir Arthur Pigot has this moment left me full of the opinions & sentiments which you would wish him to have — particularly respecting Chief Justice Downes' warrant[1] which he considers to be perfectly insupportable either in a legal or constitutional point of view. He wishes much for an exact copy of it, & I shall therefore be much obliged to you to let me have it by the return of the Post; and will be much obliged to you for any other papers respecting either the action against Doctor Sheridan[2] or the action against Chief Justice Downes[3] which you think could be useful to him or his friends in the approaching discussions[4] particularly for your own speech,[5] two or three copies of which he will be much obliged to you for. I have read two thirds of your pamphlet[6] & I think it does you the greatest honor. I am surprised at the proceedings of the court of Aldermen[7] but I hope the Catholics will make it a common cause. I need not add that on that or any other circumstance my services are ever at your command.

In respect to the Prince Regent's dispositions towards you, appearances are certainly [paper torn] favourable, but there are not wanting those who hope the best from him. It is quite certain that the ministers have some doubts of him.[8]   [*Source*: Scully Papers]

[1]See No. 291 n.4.
[2]In addition to the published report of the trial (see No. 322).
[3]See No. 310 n.2.
[4]Lord Fitzwilliam's motion for going into committee on the state of Ireland was to be debated in the House of Lords on 31 January; and a similar motion by Lord Morpeth in the House of Commons on 3 February — *Hansard* XXI, 407, 454.
[5]Of 31 July 1811 (see No. 289 n.1).
[6]Part I of the *Statement of the Penal Laws*.
[7]On 17 January the General Assembly of the Dublin Corporation had passed a resolution (inserted as a front page announcement in the *Dublin Evening Post* of 21 January) protesting against the assertion in the *Penal Laws* that "the Catholic more than doubts of obtaining the same measure of justice, of favour or respect . . . that is attached to his Protestant neighbours".
[8]The approaching end of restrictions on the Regency was encouraging speculation as to the Prince's intentions. On 17 January the Marquis of Wellesley, who differed from Perceval on the Catholic question as well as the conduct of the war in the peninsula, had told the Prince of his desire to resign and it was doubtful whether Perceval could survive without him (see Aspinall, *Correspondence of George, Prince of Wales* VIII, p. 304).

325   *From Lord Fingall to Merrion Square, Dublin*

No. Earl Street [Dublin] 25 January 1812

My Dear Mr Scully,

This morning a notice was sent to me by Mr Kemmis[1] to attend as a witness in the trial of Mr Kirwan on Monday — to prove I suppose the business of the ninth of July.[2] I am to be tried *in fact for* the same[3] & my law agent, Mr Johnston[4] to whom I sent the summons suggested to me the necessity before Monday of having the matter taken into consideration. He will try to get Mr Burrughs,[5] & has given notice to Mr Kirwan's Law Agent[6] that some of the Council will meet at his house at one o'Clock to morrow, as he is ill & confined at home.* If you have no particular engagement at that hour & wd be so good as to call there it would much oblige.
*47 York Street.   [*Source*: Scully Papers]

[1]Thomas and William Kemmis, Crown Solicitors for Dublin and the Leinster circuit, were agents for the prosecution (Howell, *State Trials* XXXI, 543).
[2]When he had taken the chair at the aggregate meeting which resolved on the election of delegates (see No. 289 n.1).
[3]Because he was also in the chair at the Meath meeting (see No. 297 n.2).

[4]James Johnston.
[5]Peter Burrowes, chief counsel for the defence at the Kirwan trial.
[6]Edward O'Callaghan.

326   *From William Parnell to 2 Merrion Square South, Dublin*

Avondale [Co. Wicklow] Sunday [26 January 1812]

My dear Sir,

I am afraid the enclosed[1] has been long delayed as Ld Holland mislaid your address & sent it to Ld King who forwarded it to me and as our post is only three times a week I could not send it before today. I am much obliged to you for your letter & for your book[2] which I have not yet got but Capt Howard[3] will forward it to me by the first opportunity. Ld Meath[4] has sent me the Protestant Petition which is to travel about for signatures, I suppose you have seen it. It is Grattan's composition & contains about six lines.[5] I observed in the newspapers the sensation your book had created in the corporation.[6] How any body of men in Ireland can have the impudence to say that the magistrates are impartial towards the R. Catholics is astonishing. I am urging Ld King to try & persuade Ld Grenville to abandon the Veto. Do you not think some less obnoxious measure of the same kind might be enacted, without a formal bargain with your Hierarchy, such as a testimony to the loyalty by the Assistant Barrister[7] in the several counties previous to investiture of a Cath. Bishop which would be a sufficient pretext to the Prince for granting the emancipation etc. etc.   [*Source*: Scully Papers]

[1]No. 327.
[2]Part I of the *Penal Laws*.
[3]His father-in-law, the Hon. Hugh Howard.
[4]John Chambre Brabazon (1772–1851), the 10th Earl.
[5]See *Hansard* XXII, 481, where it occupies seventeen lines of a column. This petition in favour of the Catholics originated at a big dinner given at the Black Abbey, Kilkenny, in December 1811 on the occasion of the new Duke of Devonshire's visiting his Irish estates (Grattan, *Life and Times* V, p. 466). An advertisement in the *Dublin Evening Post* of 18 January announced that it was open for signatures in Dublin.
[6]See No. 324, n.7.
[7]A salaried inferior judge who sat on the bench with the justices in each county (R. B. McDowell, *The Irish Administration 1801–1914*, p. 113).

327   *From Lord Holland*

[January 1812]

Dear Sir,

I ought long ago to have acknowledged your friendly letter[1] & your very useful & interesting pamphlet in which I have not found exaggeration either in opinion or expression nor do I think that any apology is required for feeling warmly such a subject. Indeed I should not be so eager in your cause though perhaps equally bound in justice to support it if those who were the objects of this disgraceful code were not sensible of the wrongs which it inflicts on them. The more earnestly you contend for your rights the more worthy are you of enjoying them — *Eos demum sentio qui de libertate tam acriter contenderant dignos esse qui Romani fiant.*[2]

When I wrote to you first[3] I imagined things to be in a different state than my letter found them & I not only acquiesce in your reasons for not giving up the Convention but I think your view of the subject proved to be correct by the event.

We are here so convinced of the evil consequences of delay that we are on the point of bringing the state of Ireland before Parliament[4] from a conviction that those among us who would defer it only deceive themselves & that the expectation of benefits which have now been delayed for near twelve years will no longer satisfy the great body of the community in Ireland. It was I think prudent in the Catholicks to defer their measures[5] but I think it equally becoming in us to shew that the time for finally settling the affairs of Ireland is arrived & cannot either with honour or safety be postponed. You will have the grace of trusting to your hopes to the last moment, we the merit of warning the publick against any attempt of deferring that decision beyond it.

[*Source*: Scully Papers]

[1]No. 321, in which Scully said he was sending a copy of his *Penal Laws*.
[2]"I feel that only those who fought so valiantly for freedom are worthy to be Romans" — probably a free rendering of Livy VIII, 21, 9. Peter Burrowes used Lord Holland's version, with one small change, to close his peroration at the trial of Thomas Kirwan on 29 January (see No. 330 n.1).
[3]On 1 December 1811, No. 313.
[4]Lord Fitzwilliam's motion (see No. 324 n.4) was originally fixed for 17 January but was postponed to give the Irish peers more time to reach London (*Hansard* XXI, 72). In anticipation of a change of administration when the Regent's restrictions ended on 17 February the Whigs wished to make it clear where they stood in regard to the Irish question (Aspinall, *Correspondence of George, Prince of Wales* VIII, p. 303).
[5]The resolutions of the aggregate meeting of 26 December 1811 (see No. 322 n.6), one of which was that a petition to the Prince should be presented after the restrictions on his regency had ceased.

328   *From Charles Butler to Merrion Square*

Lincolns Inn, 31 January 1812

Dear Sir,

I was yesterday favoured with your letter. All the papers were received by Sir Arthur Piggott,[1] and I can assure you, that your friends in the upper house,[2] will make the best use of them. I hope you will be satisfied with what you see in the *Morning Chronicle* of today.[3]

Mr Perry[4] has composed, with great care, an abstract of your excellent Pamphlet;[5] and intended to insert it, in his paper of this morning, but the very important matter arrived from Ireland,[6] intervened. A letter has been sent to him for insertion in his paper. It is an answer to your Pamphlet, and he tells me that it discloses no common talent. I conjecture from what he said, that the object of it is to shew, that your Pamphlet is of the most inflamatory nature; but I don't discover, that it controverts any of the facts which you alledge. He has declined inserting it.[7] His best agent will report the debate. In the *Globe*, and the *Press*, a short account will be given, in the first instance, and a more detailed account of it afterwards.

Lord Wellesley has certainly signified his resolution to resign; but has been desired to keep his place, till the 18th,[8] and, it is generally believed that Lord Camden and Lord Bathurst will follow him; and that one or other of them will be succeeded by Lord Castlereagh.

I am disabled, by an accident which I have met with, from attending the house, but I hope to learn the general impression which the debate makes; and will inform you of it. I hear the Prince's stand against your claims, is to be his Filial Piety![9]

The letter, which Mr Perry has received, is one of an intended Series; and will probably be sent to some other paper.[10] I will be much obliged to you to send me any remarks which occur to you upon them. No person feels more than I do, how inconveniently these matters, press on professional employments; but, in your case and in mine, I think they are duties, from which, however unpleasant they may be, it would be very wrong for either of us to shrink. This makes me devour their unpleasantness. I think it would be attended with very great good, if some gentleman in this country, were intrusted by your Committee with a general commission of feeding the newspapers with such paragraphs as might serve your cause, and with the disposition of a certain sum of money upon this service. I don't know any one who would execute this commission so well as Mr Blake, who took a letter from me to you.[11] But how far this suggestion from me should be mentioned, you are best judge. I have had the pleasure of seeing Mr Shiel,[12] several times, and I flatter myself he is pleased with the reception he has met with from me. I strongly recommend that he should be put into the office of a Special pleader. I have seldom seen a youth from College, quite so well informed; and he seems to have a very docile disposition.

[*Source*: Scully Papers]

[1]See No. 324.
[2]In the debate on Lord Fitzwilliam's motion that was to take place that evening (see No. 327 n.4).

[3]Containing a report on the first stage of the Kirwan trial: the defence's challenging of the jury.

[4]The editor of the *Morning Chronicle*.

[5]The *Penal Laws*.

[6]There is no matter from Ireland other than that on the Kirwan trial.

[7]Possibly *A refutation of the Statement of the Penal Laws*, published in Dublin, the preface to which is dated 23 January 1812.

[8]The Marquis of Wellesley had tendered his resignation on 26 January but had been asked to continue in office until 18 February, the first day of the unrestricted regency (Buckingham to Lord Grenville 2 February 1812: *Dropmore Papers* X).

[9]See Lord Grenville's memorandum of 6 February in *Dropmore Papers* X: ". . . the Prince has thought of a new pretence for evading [the Catholic question] by alleging that, although he himself is persuaded of the justice of the claim, he is only administering the government in the name of the king, who, when capable of acting, thought himself restrained on this subject by his oath".

[10]Not found.

[11]In January 1811 (see No. 281).

[12]Richard Lalor Sheil, who had graduated from Dublin University in 1811.

329   *From Charles Butler to Merrion Square*

                                        Lincolns Inn, 1 February 1812
Dear Sir,

I have the greatest satisfaction in informing you, that nothing could go off better than the Debate of yesterday. Every Roman Catholic present, was perfectly satisfied with it! I hope that, after the explicit declarations made by Lord Grey and Lord Grenville of the complete understanding between them and the English Catholics, that neither the Veto nor any thing which it expresses or implies, was in the contemplation of their Lordships, or those who attended them, or was intended to be expressed or intimated, either directly or indirectly, in their Fifth Resolution we shall no more be insulted on that subject.[1]

Lord Wellesley's Speech served us; but it was miserably fenced in with "ifs," and "ands".[2] Over and over again was the Chancellor most pointedly called upon, for his opinion on the legality of the proceedings in Ireland against you: but he preserved an expressive silence, which left us to muse the rest.[3]

Lord Sidmouth was litterally laughed down.[4] Lord Somer's speech had a wonderful effect.[5] Much indeed have [*sic*] been gained.

[P.S.] The part of Lord Somer's Speech, which produced the greatest effect, was that in which he descanted on the Delusions practiced on the Prince of Wales, to make him forego his promises to the Catholics.[6]

                                        [*Source*: Scully Papers]

[1]In the debate on Earl Fitzwilliam's motion (see No. 327 n.4). Lord Grey had denied that either he or Lord Grenville had considered the veto as indispensable; and Lord Grenville had stated "that he never regarded the veto as a *sine qua non* . . . it was an arrangement to which he attached no great importance, and from the moment he learned that the measure, instead of conciliating, had produced irritation, he abandoned it[11] (*Hansard* XXI, 474, 476).

[2]Ibid. 431. Lord Wellesley was at odds with himself: he favoured concessions but supported the enforcement of the Convention Act.

[3]The repeated calls were not recorded by the *Hansard* reporter but Lord Grenville, arguing that the word "pretence" in the Convention Act was not synonymous with "purpose" asked the Lord Chancellor whether he himself had not introduced both words in a similar bill of 1796 (ibid. 476).

[4]He argued that if concessions were a matter of right they ought to be enjoyed by the whole people, not just men of wealth and consequence. In the past Catholic had always been told that the time was not ripe and he did not see why the answer should be different now (ibid. 423).

[5]Lord Somers (1760–1841, 2nd Baron) observed that the Union could not have been carried without the Catholics, who therefore had a strong claim in justice. Where was the danger of a dozen Catholic peers in the Lords or fifty members in a Commons of seven hundred? In official appointments the King was no more likely to appoint Catholics who might overturn the government than similar Protestants. Emancipation might affect only the higher orders, but the lower orders would then be led by men of property and distinction already disposed to venerate the constitution (ibid. 428).

[6]Not included in the *Hansard* report.

330   *From Charles Butler to Merrion Square*

Lincolns Inn, 3 February 1812

Dear Sir,

I am much obliged, by your Letter. I heard last night that Mr Kerwan had been found guilty;[1] for which your former letters and other circumstances, had prepared me: but we must not lose courage.

You hear that Lord Wellesley has resigned;[2] and it is expected that his resignation will be followed, by Lord Bathurst, Lord Camden and Mr Ryder's.

Nothing can be more decisive, than the language of all your friends.

The real fact is, that the opposition refused to come into power, without making stipulations for you, and respecting some other great constitutional measures, to which the Prince Regent would not accede: and they also refused to carry some measures, upon which the Prince had set his heart, and on which Mr Perceval was willing to indulge him. The communications between them broke off, on these grounds; and there is at present, a complete understanding between the Prince, and them, that they will not come into office, on any terms, than those which they signified to him in the course of this treaty:[3] of which your emancipation makes a leading article. The Prince is extremely hurt, and is certainly greatly alarmed, *not to say terrified.*[4]

This is increased by the strange continuance of the riots at Nottingham;[5] and by the discovery of Simon's plot,[6] for arming the french prisoners. The extent, and almost the existence of that tremendous enterprise have been generally kept from the public, but are not the less certain.

The Debate was tolerably well given, in the *Globe* and the *Press*; but justice is not done to Lord Grey's speech, and still less to Lord Grenville's; whose bitter addresses to Lord Liverpool produced a great effect.[7]

The Debate in the Commons will come on tonight.[8]

The opposition have now identified themselves completely with your cause; and it is impossible that they should come into administration without making your cause their own. No one has taken greater pains to make himself master of it than Sir Arthur Piggott and I have no doubt, that he will acquit himself tonight with great ability.[9]

Does not the event of things completely shew the advantages which might be derived by procuring, the individual signatures of the whole Kingdom, to an energetic petition, which I have so often taken the liberty to suggest.

[*Source*: Scully Papers]

[1]Thomas Kirwan, one of those arrested under Chief Justice Downes' warrant of 8 August 1811 (see no. 291 n.4) was found guilty by the jury on 29 January. On 3 February the Attorney-General announced that, enough having been done both to show what the law was and that it could be enforced, he would not proceed with the trials of the other offenders and would drop the prosecution of Lord Fingall. Kirwan was let off with a fine of one mark (two thirds of a pound) (Howell, *State Trials* XXXI, 810). Not all members of the Catholic Board accepted the decision as final (see No. 338 n.5).

[2]See No. 328 n.8.

[3]Butler seems to be referring to an interview which Lord Grenville and Earl Grey had with the Regent early in January (Aspinall, *Correspondence of George, Prince of Wales* VIII, p. 303).

[4]The Regent was equally afraid of the unpopularity he would bring on himself if he abandoned the Whigs, the friends of his early life, and of the Tories being too weak to survive if he kept them in office (ibid., p. 313).

[5]The riots consisted of systematic frame breaking and two more regiments had been sent to Nottingham when they broke out again on 8 January (*Hansard* XXI, 871).

[6]Simon was a French general who had escaped from prison in Hampshire and had been arrested in Camden on 16 January. It was alleged that correspondence had been found concerning a plan for French prisoners to link up with a French landing in Cornwall (*The Times*, 16 and 18 January 1812).

[7]See No. 329 n.1. According to *Hansard* it was 5.30 in the morning when Lord Grenville rose to speak.

[8]On Lord Morpeth's motion on the state of Ireland.
[9]He traced the history of the Convention Act and argued that the word "pretence" in it meant "false pretence". As regards the proclamation of 30 July 1811 (see No. 289 n.1) he doubted the legality of the authority given to magistrates to commit the accused: they had a right to interfere only in cases of treason, felony or breach of the peace, but the offence for which the Catholic Committee were arraigned was in the act itself only a misdemeanour. He thought it at least indecorous that the Lord Chief Justice (Downes) had been applied to for the issue of a warrant when there were eight hundred other magistrates who could have served the purpose as well (*Hansard* XXI, 558).

331   *From Charles Butler to Merrion Square*

Lincolns Inn, 6 February 1812

Dear Sir,

I sincerely congratulate with you to the success of the late Debate. The encrease of numbers is something, as you will see by the enclosed statements;[2] but the general effect in your favour appears to have been much greater from the following circumstance. It is thought that Ministers intended that some of their Favourites should move an amendment to the Motion, by which they should expunge the whole of it, and declare, that any further concessions to the Irish were inexpedient; and could not be reasonably called for. Sir John Nichol's speech, was intended to prepare the house for this amendment;[3] but all he said was so compleately shivered by Mr Canning's reply, as made the Ministers think, the amendment would not be disrelished.[4] Mr Perceval spoke under visible embarrassment; he began very loftily, and acquitted himself very tolerably, so far as respected the point of Law. But, on the general policy of the case, he was much below his usual exertions.[5] A Member, who has a perfect knowledge of the constitution and temper of the house, told me that, if the motion had contained nothing respecting the law,[6] and had been confined to a Resolution for taking the state of Ireland into consideration, with a view to the Catholic question, we should have had between 10 and 20 more votes. He recommends that you take care, not to express any thing which seems to identify the Prince with his present Ministers, or which seems to suppose, that they act with his approbation. He also recommends that your Petition should be uncommonly temperate, and unequivocally disclaim all dissorganizing principles, which your adversaries effect to impute to you. I transmit to you this suggestion, as I receive it, but to that and to all other suggestions of the kind, I always say that, you are on the spot, and the best judges of your own strength, views and means.

[*Source*: Scully Papers]

[1]On Lord Morpeth's motion to go into committee on the state of Ireland, lost after a second day of debate by 229 to 135 (*Hansard* XXI, 669).
[2]Not found.

[3]Sir Samuel Romilly says in his *Memoirs*, II, p. 236, that the plan was to get the House of Commons to adopt some resolution that would seem to put the Catholic question at rest, at least for the time being, but it was frustrated by the large size of the minority.

[4]A lapse of Butler's clerk: "would not be relished".

[5]Perceval said that it was not proper to bring the conduct of the Irish courts under the review of the House of Commons; that if there had been no Convention Act it would have been the duty of the government to introduce a similar measure; and that for himself he "could not conceive a time or any change of circumstance which could render further concessions to the Catholics consistent to the safety of the state" (*Hansard* XXI, 661).

[6]The motion itself made no reference to the law and Lord Morpeth said he would abstain from a discussion of the legality of the Irish government's conduct, but this conduct was questioned by others, particularly Sir Arthur Pigott (see No. 330 n.9).

332   *From Charles Butler to Merrion Square*

Lincolns Inn, 15 February 1812

Dear Sir,

I am much obliged to you for your Letter,[1] which I have this moment received. Lord Holland was kept from the House, by illness, but sent his proxy. Sir S. Romilly is your decided friend. I can give no reason for the absence of the Burdettites. You know they are *Genus per se*.[2]

You may be assured, that, at this moment, there is a complete separation, between Lord Grey and Lord Grenville and the Prince. A Proposal was made by him, to them, (which is considered to have been done merely to save appearances), and was declared by them to be wholly inadmissible. Early in this week the language and acts of the Chancellor[3] intimated his probable removal from Office; but yesterday, both his language and his acts were very different. It is supposed that, the Prince wishes some arrangement which will keep Perceval in a high situation in the administration, and that the Two Lords oppose this, unless Mr Perceval agrees to concur in your Emancipation, and to some other salutary measures.

You must pay no attention whatever, to what you read in the *Morning Chronicle* of today.[4]

I earnestly wish £100 could be impressed, to the person I mentioned in my last letter[5] or some other person, to feed the press with proper articles.

You must look into the *Pilot* of the 7th instant.[6] I will attend to the utmost of my power to all the circumstances you mentioned. [*Source*: Scully Papers]

[1]Of 9 February, not extant.
[2]This paragraph refers to the debates on Lord Fitzwilliam's and Lord Morpeth's motions to go into committee on the state of Ireland.
[3]i.e. the Chancellor of the Exchequer, Perceval.

[4]It contained an editorial report that there had been a communication the previous day between the Regent and Lords Grey and Grenville. Butler evidently disbelieved it, but the *Morning Chronicle* was correct. In the morning of 14 February the Duke of York had read to them a letter which he had received from the Regent in which the latter said how gratified he would be "if some of those persons with whom the early habits of my public life were formed would strengthen my hands and constitute a part of my government" (Aspinall, *Correspondence of George, Prince of Wales* VIII, p. 315).

[5]He must mean the Mr Blake of No. 328.

[6]It contained a letter from Butler under his pseudonym of Hwyls. It was on the "breach of the promises and expectations" held out to the Irish and dealt specifically with the Treaty of Limerick in 1691, the recall of Earl Fitzwilliam in 1795 and the hopes held out at the time of the Union.

333   *From Charles Butler to Merrion Square*

Lincolns Inn, 17 February 1812

Dear Sir,

I believe no public or private abode was ever filled with so much negotiation, as Carleton House has been for these last forty eight Hours. It is certain, that the Prince has sent an express to the Duke of Norfolk;[1] and been closeted during a long time with Mr Sheridan.[2] I know that both Lord Grenville and Lord Grey expressed themselves unequivocally that your Emancipation must be immediate and absolute; and the language which persons very near the Minister, hold seems to shew that they consider it unavoidable that they should surrender to you almost at discretion.

It is understood that a powerful attack is to be made on Mr Perceval tonight for holding himself out as the Prince's decided Minister, at the very time that proposals of the Prince to the leaders of the opposition were laying before them.[3]   [*Source*: Scully Papers]

[1]Apparently informing him, as one of his oldest friends, of the Duke of York's interview with Lords Grenville and Grey and seeking support for the view that the Catholic question had been settled for the moment by the recent votes in parliament (see No. 331 n.3). Norfolk replied on 17 February saying that he concurred with Lords Grey and Grenville, and that another parliament might reach a different conclusion. If the Prince determined otherwise he, Norfolk, must retire from politics (Aspinall, *Letters of George IV*, I, No. 7).

[2]Richard Brinsley Sheridan, like the Duke of Norfolk an old friend of the Regent, was torn between the ties of friendship and faithfulness to the Whig principles the Regent was about to sacrifice.

[3]No such attack was made. Butler was evidently still unaware that Grey and Grenville had told the Duke of York, orally on the 14th and in writing on the 15th, that they could not join a government formed on the lines of the Regent's letter to the Duke (see No. 332 n.4).

334   *From Charles Butler to Merrion Square*

Lincolns Inn, 18 February 1812[1]

Dear Sir,

From a quarter, upon which I can rely, it appears, that the Prince Regent's letter was communicated to the two noble Lords, thro' the Duke of York; and it began by an intimation, that the Catholic Question was decided by the last proceedings of the two houses of Parliament upon it;[2] on that assumption it proceeded, and the offers made to the noble Lords were expressed in very general terms. When they delivered their answers to the Duke of York, his Royal highness observed this circumstance to them; and seemed to think their answer indicated, that they did not feel the extent of the offer.[3] Both the answer which they gave in writing, and the language which they held to the Duke of York, were, that their objection to coming into administration, was not to individuals whom the Prince might wish to be joined with them, but to the measures which seemed to be expected from them; particularly in respect to the Catholic Question, the settlement of which, on the broadest and most liberal terms, admitted of no delay.

I have the pleasure, to ascertain that, with a trifling exception of the underlings of the household, all your friends have behaved nobly. Lord Moira has refused the blue ribbon;[4] and Mr Sheridan, in a long conference with the Prince Regent, pressed your cause upon him with all his Eloquence and address. Lord Yarmouth is certainly the Vizir. The Prince's health and Spirits, are not better than they are represented to be. This information coming to me from an unquestionable source I lose no time in transmitting it to you. The events will now speak for themselves.   [*Source*: Scully Papers]

[1]The first day of the unrestricted regency.
[2]See No. 331 n.3.
[3]Grey and Grenville were under the impression that they were being invited to join an already existing administration. Following an intervention by the Marquis of Wellesley the Duke of York told them on the morning of the 15th that the existing administration would be dissolved, but they refused to reconsider their answer, saying they differed too much from ministers on other matters to be able to act with them (Aspinall, *Correspondence of George, Prince of Wales* VIII, p. 316).
[4]When on 28 February Lord Moira wrote to the Regent remonstrating with him on his change of course he explained that he had refused the Garter because if he accepted it everyone would be convinced "that your aberration was systematic" (Aspinall, *Correspondence of George IV*, I, No. 23).

335   *From Henry Parnell to Merrion Square, Dublin*

London, 21 February 1812

Private

Dear Sir,

I have received your letter of last Monday[1] & am very glad to find I was correct about the Penal Laws. I ought to have told you that the speech of Sir John Seabright[2] rendered it necessary to give an explanation of the nature of the work, independent of Mr Pole's critique upon it.[3] He had declared his intention to have been to vote with Ld Morpeth; but what he had heard respecting this work from Mr Pole, he said, made him feel the conduct of the Catholics so improper & menacing that he would vote against him.

I feel extremely anxious to know the impression which the Prince's conduct has made,[4] & also in what manner that of Lords Grey & Grenville has been received. Not a word is uttered here in praise of the one, or blame of the other except in the most venal of the public papers.

I sincerely hope you will persevere in petitioning Parliament. The speeches of Lords Grey & Grenville in respect to the Veto,[5] & their late answer[6] must place their sincerity beyond all cavil. They will, I know from Lord Grey personally, but I mention it as *private* information, use every exertion in their power to secure the fullest possible attendance in both Houses,[7] & as Perceval's new Govt. will be weaker even than his late one, by the loss of Ld Wellesley; & as Lord Wellesley & Canning will, I understand, vote for the Petition, the division will in all probability be so much in favor of the Catholics as to secure the downfall of Perceval & Emancipation.

Notwithstanding the untoward appearances, I feel the most sanguine hopes, that if the Catholics give their strenuous support to opposition by petitioning, & calling upon *all* their County members to *detach* themselves from Govt. the question will very soon be carried;[8] for it must be remembered that the great power of the Crown in the last reign in resisting popular claims, & leading Parliament, was in a very great degree owing to the personal character & peculiar talents and courage of the King.

Of all things declining to Petition would be that proceeding which would be most agreeable to Government, & in my opinion, most fatal to the Catholics & their friends. If the Petitions were from all the Parishes of Ireland the greatest effect would be produced.

There exist great difficulties in forming the new arrangements. The accession of Lord Sidmouth is held to be indispensable to enable it to go on. But Lord Lowther who has twelve votes in the House of Commons will not support Govt. if he is admitted. There is also a difficulty about the Admiralty. Pole is intended for it but great opposition is made by great men against such an appointment — & even Ld Castlereagh is not yet in office — Not a single individual of opposition has gone over & on the whole, therefore, the new Government will be the weakest that has ever been formed.

As the next discussion will turn very much upon the securities which may be conceived esssential for the establishment, I should feel much obliged to you for information concerning the *practical* influence of the Pope in respect to Bishops etc.[9]   [*Source*: Scully Papers]

[1]17 February.

[2]*Recte* Sebright. In the debate on Lord Morpeth's motion of 3 February he asserted that the Irish Catholics had formed a society dangerous to the existence of any state: "a book had been published, with their concurrence, which was of a most inflammatory tendency" (*Hansard* XXI, 612).

[3]Pole had gone a step further and on the authority of a recent pamphlet claimed that the *Statement of the Penal Laws* was a production of the sub-committee of Grievances. Attacking the credibility of the *Statement*, he argued that the conduct of the Committee had made it impossible for parliament to alter the condition of the Catholics. On the second day of the debate Parnell corrected him. In 1810 a sub-committee had been appointed to examine what laws still operated against the Catholics, but this information had been required only in connexion with the petition of the time and the sub-committee had never made a report: "the pamphlet which gives an account of them is, in point of fact, the work of a most respectable Catholic barrister, who alone is responsible for it" (ibid., 575, 622).

[4]In retaining Perceval as his first minister.

[5]See No. 329 n.1.

[6]To the Duke of York (see No. 334 n.3).

[7]For the debate on the Irish Catholic petition. On 9 March Perceval gave notice that he would move for a call of the House on 13 April so that there should be as large an attendance as possible (ibid., 1239).

[8]That Scully took this advice to heart is shown by a resolution adopted by the Tipperary Catholics on 20 March: "Catholic freeholders are bound by a paramount duty to their families and their country, to withhold their votes and interest from every candidate who shall appear to be a partisan or supporter of an administration avowedly and rootedly hostile to the Catholic population and generally to the best interests of Ireland and the Empire" (*DEP*, 31 March 1812). A similar resolution was adopted by an aggregate meeting in Dublin on 18 June 1812: "That from recent examples of political duplicity, we feel it necessary to recommend most earnestly, to all Catholic freeholders throughout Ireland, steadily to resist the pretensions of any candidates who shall hesitate to pledge themselves publicly to the uniform support of Catholic Emancipation; or who shall have lent, or are likely to lend, their support to any administration founded on intolerance and hostile to the full enjoyment of religious liberty" (*Pilot* 22 June 1812). F. W. Conway told Beckett at the Home Office that Scully was the author of this resolution (Peel Papers, Add.MSS.40, 223 f.195).

[9]Parnell was no doubt speaking to Scully's brief when in the debate on Canning's motion on 22 June he informed the House, on the strength of a document "of the

highest ecclesiastical and legal authority", that the Pope's authority was confined to (1) marriage dispensations; (2) as a dernier resort in disputes between members of the clergy; and (3) the appointment of Bishops, which was entirely nominal in the case of Ireland, where the Bishops themselves filled up the vacancies, consecrated and installed — the final institution by the Pope sometimes not following for two or three years (*Hansard* XXIII, 680).

336   *From Charles Butler to Merrion Square*

Lincolns Inn, 26 February 1812

Dear Sir,

The nature and extent of Mr Perceval's declaration that the business of the Catholics should not be a Cabinet measure is greatly misstated in the papers. All he has said is that he will not object to any persons holding a seat in the Cabinet, or any other office of Trust with him, who votes for Catholic emancipation, but he admits that so far as depends on himself he will exert all the strength of Government to resist it.[1] This is even less than Mr Pitt affected to do for the abolition of Slavery. All the opposition remain according to their Tenets, but some of them dine and visit at Carleton House, which the others disapprove of.   [*Source*: Scully Papers]

[1]Perceval's understanding of the situation was explained in the *Courier* of 24 February 1812. Although the government were of opinion that concessions to the Catholics could not be made at present and "Mr Perceval and many others think that it cannot be right to make them at all", they would not refuse the assistance of any man in office merely because he differed from the government on the question.

337   *To Edward Hay*

[Merrion Square, 28 February 1812]

Dear Sir,

As our friend Mr Magee wishes much to see the Address etc mentioned in my note to you, I beg to say, I entirely dispense with any view of it before it comes to his hands — for I am confident that he will make no use of it, injurious to our interests: and we are all agreed, I believe, that the eminent merit of the *D[ublin] Evening Post* claims from every Catholic every accommodation and every priority of correct intelligence, that our poor opportunities can afford.

You will therefore oblige me by affording this assistance to Mr Magee, and letting him have the Address.[1]

[*Source*: Dublin Diocesan Archives 390/2, I, (5)]

[1]John Magee, proprietor of the *Dublin Evening Post*, passed on to Hay the note which Scully had given him asking Hay "to give Mr Magee the use, for a few hours, of the Address to the Prince etc in my handwriting, contained in the papers which I had the pleasure of handing to you at the Meeting this day". It was dated 28 February. In another file (DDA 54/2, II, 31) there is a draft in Scully's hand, dated 27 February, of the "Address etc". It consists of an address to the Prince Regent and alternative passages for substitution in a petition to the two Houses of parliament. It was probably from this draft that the text was read out to the aggregate meeting — by Scully himself, as Hay said he was not familiar with the writing (*DEP*, 29 February 1812).

338   *From Henry Parnell to Merrion Square, Dublin*

London, 6 March 1812

Dear Sir,

I have sent you by this post a copy of Sir John Newport's population bill.[1] Mr Pole brought in a bill last session on Education — it was printed & postponed. He intends to bring in another with some alterations.[2] I will send you a copy as soon as I can get one.

The enclosed has been sent to me by Mr Smythe,[3] Professor of Modern History at Cambridge with a strong recommendation of Mr Nightingale.[4]

No further arrangements have taken place of the Cabinet.

Your resolutions & address[5] have met with the unqualified approbation of everyone I have heard speak of them. They were eminently well calculated for all the circumstances just now bearing on the question.

[*Source*: Scully Papers]

[1]To ascertain the population of Ireland. He deprecated any distinction being made in regard to religious adherence, which would be "ranging in hostile array those who being kindred in blood and nation differed only in religious creeds" (*Hansard* XXI, 177).
[2]A bill for "the apointment of commissioners for the regulation of the several endowed schools of public and private education in Ireland" — not ordered to be printed until 21 December 1812.
[3]William Smyth (1765–1849), Regius Professor from 1809.
[4]Joseph Nightingale, author of *A Portraiture of the Roman Catholic Religion . . . with an appendix containing a summary of the laws now in force against English and Irish Catholics*. The preface is dated 18 July 1812. The summary is acknowledged as having been principally collected, with the approbation of the respective authors, from an *Historical Account of the laws against the Roman Catholics of England* by Butler *and the Statement of the laws which aggrieve the Catholics of Ireland*.
[5]The resolutions of an aggregate meeting held on 28 February, with an Address to the Regent and petitions to the Houses of parliament. One of the resolutions retreated from the decision taken on 26 December that the delegates should meet

again as the Committee that had been dispersed (see No. 322 n.6). It was now resolved that this Committee should not meet or function "until the question lately raised on the Convention Act be decided" (*DEP*, 29 February 1812). Many Catholics were loath to accept the verdict of the Kirwan trial (see No. 330 n.1) and a remark made by Lord Moira in the House of Lords on 19 March suggests that an appeal to the Lords was in contemplation (*Hansard* XXII, 87). If so, no action was taken and the interim Board set up on 26 December 1811 functioned henceforth on a permanent basis, tolerated by the Irish administration as a non-delegated body.

339   *From William Parnell to 2 Merrion Square South, Dublin*

Bushy Park near Bray [Co. Wicklow] [postmarked 7 March 1812]
My Dear Sir,

Mr Scott[1] signed the protestant petition[2] of this Co. at my request but upon the condition of his approving of the Catholic petition to which it refers & if he does not I have promised to strike out his name. So I would be much obliged to you if you would send me a copy of the Catholic petition that I may forward it to him & if you wish, it shall go no further. I have had very indifferent success in this County not being able to obtain the signature of even one of Ld Fitzwilliam's tenants who engross the greater part of the Co. This will surprise you but his agent Mr Wainwright[3] is a narrow minded illiberal man, & the tenants are more afraid of him than of Ld Fitzwilliam. However I have some of the most respectable independent gentlemen. But I hope to form a committee in Dublin & a subscription to defray the expence of distributing cheap tracts in favor of the Catholics among the protestants, so as to prepare things better next year in case things remain as they are. I wish to print, *Testimonia*, from the speeches & writings of Pitt, Burke etc. etc. in favor of the Catholics; and if you consent a very cheap edition of your admirable work;[4] which I did not get; owing to Capt Howard forgetting to forward it to me till I came here. I scarcely know how to believe that this is the work that the corporation of Dublin[5] & Poole[6] stigmatised; I can imagine them stupid enough to read it without being convinced, but I could not suppose they had ingenuity enough to pervert its meaning to any bad purpose. I suppose you know that Major Stanhope is put off the staff (by which he loses 400 a year) to punish him for his speech at the Catholic Dinner.[7] Here is an instance that shews how much you want funds, for if properly assessed on the whole body of the Catholics they would not feel the burthen of compensating such losses received in their service. Now the Catholics can do nothing material for him but I wish you would use your influence to obtain for him some honorable testimonial of the sympathy of the Catholics for the injury he sustains.[8]

I am glad to perceive your body forced by circumstance into something approaching the plan I sent you[9] & there if the contest continues you must end. You cannot do without money, & people get tired of being asked for 5 or 10 guineas, but ten shillings a piece would not be felt by thousands of your body & would do the business effectually. My brother says they will turn Perceval out, but I rather think Percival [sic] will compromise the matter if he finds the Prince in earnest. [*Source*: Scully Papers]

[1]unidentified.

[2]See No. 326 n.5. The text of the Protestant petition referred to but did not particularise the contents of the Catholic one.

[3]William Wainwright; steward of the Fitzwilliam estates from 1812. Died 1813.

[4]No information has come to light to show whether he carried these intentions into effect.

[5]See No. 324 n.7.

[6]The spelling, as in No. 406, shows how the name was pronounced. He is probably referring to Wellesley Pole's denunciation of Scully's *Penal Laws* in the House of Commons (see No. 335 n.3).

[7]Captain Leicester Stanhope's dismissal had been announced in the *Dublin Evening Post* of 5 March. As he was not only ADC to his father, Lord Harrington, Commander-in-Chief of the forces in Ireland, but held a post in the Quartermaster's Department which made him responsible for collecting and quartering troops in the event of trouble, the Chief Secretary regarded it as inadmissible that he should have attended in uniform an anti-administration demonstration at which the Lord Lieutenant's health had been omitted from the toasts (HO 100/165, ff.259, 271).

[8]The Catholics of Tipperary voted on 20 March to present him with a sword and a hundred guineas; and on 2 April the Board in Dublin voted him a silver cup (*DEP*, 24 March 1812, 4 April 1812).

[9]See No. 314. The aggregate meeting of 28 February had recommended that members of the Board should raise subscriptions in their areas (*DEP*, 29 March 1812).

340   *From Charles Butler to Merrion Square*

Lincolns Inn, 10 March 1812

Dear Sir,

I was duly favoured with your letter,[1] and I saw Lord Grey on Sunday.[2] He recommends that your petition should be presented as soon as possible. I believe our friends have some apprehensions that the cry of the church being in danger, and of no popery will be renewed. I do not think it will take.

At present the state of the house in our regard, is very nearly what it was in the last division.[3] Mr Canning and his friends seem to be with us, but on the other hand some, but not many of the Prince's friends will side against us. We have a flying report that Lord Lowther is gone over to opposition.

Lord Grey spoke of your Pamphlet[4] in very handsome terms. Why is it not printed in this country [?] If you do not mean to publish it here, I wish you would send me over half a dozen copies, as I would put them in hands where they would be very useful.

Lord Grey has desired me to prepare an act of Parliament for repealing all the laws in force against the Irish Catholics, (but I beg of you not to mention this circumstance, least it should expose his Lordship to animadversion in this country).[5] I recollect to have heared [sic], that you have prepared a bill of this kind for Lord Donoughmore.[6] If this is the fact, I should be much obliged to you to let me know it as soon as possible; and that you would favour Lord Grey with a copy of it. The Prince Regent is certainly very ill in body, and in great agitation of mind. I have only to add that they have prevailed upon Lord Donoughmore not to anticipate Mr Grattan's motion,[7] by a motion in the house of Lords. For they recollect, that the last time, the Catholic business, came on, during Mr Pitt's administration, the first motion respecting it were [sic] made in the Lords and negatived. Mr Pitt availed himself with much success and effect of this circumstance to persuade the house of Commons not to go into a committee, on the ground, that, after a decided negative in the house of Lords, a committee could produce no good.[8] Upon the whole I cannot say that the general posture of affairs looks favourable: but we must hope the best and not relax in our efforts.

[*Source*: Scully Papers]

[1]Of 2 March, not extant.
[2]8 March.
[3]On Lord Morpeth's motion, lost on 4 February by 229–135 (see No. 331 n.1).
[4]Part I of the *Penal Laws*.
[5]In his letter of 22 March 1813 to Hay (Appendix B) Butler says that he asked Scully for his opinion of a sketch of an act of parliament and that Scully returned it, declining "any particular consideration of it" but writing some short heads for Butler's observation. To these Butler attended and made some alterations. In this state the sketch remained until he received a letter from Grattan asking him to prepare a general act (*DEP*, 29 June 1813). For Grattan's approach see No. 360 n.5.
[6]See No. 242 n.10. Scully's draft has not been found.
[7]Postponed, on the day of Butler's letter, to 14 April.
[8]They failed to prevail, since Lord Donoughmore, having already given notice, was unable to change his date. Earl Grey thought the division in the House of Lords would be better than in the Commons (see his letters of 6 and 7 March in *Dropmore Papers* X). In the event the debate in the Lords took place on 20 April and that in the Commons was opened on 23 April.

340A   *From Edward Hay*

12 March 1812[1]

Dear Sir,

I cannot describe the alarm excited by the passage contained in the address and petitions "we are ready to give every further pledge that can be requested in this respect" as several of the Board have expressed their determination not to sign the address or petitions if these words are not omitted in those that are to be presented — they declare that most members have the same objection.[2] I think it but right to communicate this circumstance to you as I used every argument I could to banish those scruples but without effect
believe me with sincerity yours most faithully

[*Source*: Dublin Diocesan Archives 390/2, V, 11.]

[1]This letter and No. 340B, which is a reply to it, are written on the same sheet of paper. The reply is dated 11 March.
[2]Having been adopted by the aggregate meeting of 28 February the address was sent out by Hay for signatures under cover of a circular dated 8 March (*DEP*, 14 March 1812). The passage to which Hay refers reads in full: "We have publickly & solemnly taken every oath of fidelity and allegiance to the crown, which the jealous caution of the Legislature has from time to time imposed as tests of our political and moral principles. We are ready to give every further pledge in this respect . . ." (DDA 54/2, II, 31).

340B   *To Edward Hay*

11 March 1812[1]

Dr. Sir,

The Catholics are always ready to give any further pledge that can be required, touching the purity and excellence of their *moral and political* principles — such is the passage: and nothing further.

People in power use every engine to obstruct our petition, and to disunite the Catholics. Ready instruments are always found in the Catholic Body — the objection you mention is drawn from this source — I ascertained this fact a week ago.[2] It is too silly to be noticed — The same passage is in the petition of 1805 (which Dr Troy and the other Prelates certified to Lord Grenville in 1805 — that they subscribed to and approved).[3] It relates merely to *moral & political* principles.

Trace these objections & you will find the source to be venal, bigotted, crafty and AntiCatholic — To attempt to reason with such Catholics is to sanction their venality.[4]

Yours etc.

DS.

[*Source*: Dublin Diocesan Archives 390/2, V, 11.]

[1]See No. 340A n.1.
[2]4 March was the day on which 21 delegates were chosen by ballot to go to London with the address to the Prince Regent and the petitions to the two Houses of Parliament (*DEP*, 5 March 1812). No clue has been found as to the nature of Scully's information.
[3]The passage in the House of Lords petition of 1805 reads: "Your petitioners . . . can with perfect truth affirm, that the political and moral principles which are thereby [in the test oaths] asserted, are not only comfortable to their opinions and habits, but are expressly inculcated by the religion which they profess". There is no mention of a pledge, a word that had become associated in the minds of many Irish Catholics with the Veto ever since the English Catholics had used the expression "will meet with their grateful concurrence" in the Fifth Resolution of 1 February 1810 (see No. 230 n.1).
[4]Scully was nevertheless overruled. At a meeting of the Board on 26 March it was decided that the clause regarding a pledge to the crown was ambiguous and should be deleted (DDA 54/2, I, 30), and it does not appear in the text presented by Lord Donoughmore in the House of Lords on 20 April 1812 (*Hansard* XXII, 453).

341   *From Charles Butler to Merrion Square*

Lincolns Inn, 18 March 1812

Dear Sir,

You will see by the papers that Lord Ormond has accepted the place of Lord of the Bed Chamber, to the Prince Regent.[1] His friends say that this is no dereliction of party, as he always professed himself attached to the Prince, and only so far attached to the opposition, as the opposition was attached to his Royal Highness. I believe that I can confidently assure you, that, on the Catholic Question his Lordship will always vote for the Catholics.[2]

[*Source*: Scully Papers]

[1]His appointment as Groom of the Bed Chamber was announced in the *DEP* of 21 March 1812.
[2]He was prevented from voting by illness and Lord Donoughmore presented on his behalf a petition from the county and city of Kilkenny (*Hansard* XXII, 459).

342   *To his wife Catherine*

Kilkenny, Thursday morning, 26 March [1812]

My dearest Catherine,

I congratulate you most sincerely upon your happy "accouchement"—and upon the appearance of another son,[1] who will live, I trust, to encrease your happiness and to be of use to his family and Country. Pray, my Love, take the greatest care as to keeping off the cold. My fears on this subject are continual — but I trust that, with good care of all about you, all danger will soon be over. I left Clonmell yesterday morning, and Peggy's Letter (which should have been directed to this town) was sent after me this morning from Clonmell. You will have a letter from me (by Mr W. Parker, 22 South Cumberland Street)[2] tomorrow morning. I shall write to Julia[3] and to my Mother etc. and hope to see you on next Monday or Tuesday. I think the name may remain, as we agreed, to be *Henry Rodolphus*, unless you would choose to substitute *Thomas*, or some other name, in the place of Henry. If you should I shall be perfectly well pleased, and even obliged to you, for using your own Discretion and I shall be equally fond of him. I hope little James & Vincent go on well. The weather here is fine and sunny, but yet cold. We have a report here, that O'Connell has been engaged in some Duel upon his Circuit,[4] and that Mrs O'Connell left Dublin yesterday to join him. Don't mention it, for fear it may give alarm, & perhaps it may not be true — but you could get Peggy to enquire privately.[5] I hope for a line by Saturday's Post — and I shall receive it here on Sunday morning — and to tell me how you go on. Adieu, my Love, ever most affectionately, your attached husband, Denys Scully   [*Source*: Scully Papers]

[1]Born on 22 March. Scully was at Kilkenny for the Assizes.
[2]The barrister William Parker, born 1776, third son of Anthony Parker of Castlelough, near Nenagh.
[3]His wife's sister, Julia Eyre.
[4]The report was based on a row that O'Connell was supposed to have had with H. D. Grady during the Limerick Assizes (see O'Connell, *Correspondence* I, No. 372).
[5]Peggy seems to have been a housekeeper. Scully no doubt meant that she should enquire from the staff at O'Connell's house in Merrion Square.

343   *From William Tighe to Merrion Square, Dublin*

London, 4 April 1812

Dear Sir,

I have received your letter[1] & am indebted to you for the information it contains. The refusal of bail by magistrates should be noticed — in the house of Commons at least. I wish for all the *facts* to this effect that can be obtained & also for all circumstances relative to the conduct of petty juries with regard to Catholics.[2]   [*Source*: Scully Papers]

[1]Missing.
[2]The information was required in connexion with a proposal to ask for juries to be

composed as to half of Catholics when Catholics were being tried (see No. 355). Tighe wrote to Edward Hay on the same day telling him that Scully approved of a bill relative to petty juries and asking him to provide facts about the conduct of Orange juries in Wexford or elsewhere, or as to the conduct of magistrates in refusing bail (DDA 390/1, VII, 7).

344   *Peter Bodkin Hussey to Merrion Square, Dublin*

London, 8 April 1812

My dear Scully,

I arrived here this morning after being up three nights.[1] The address is not to be presented untill the 16th.[2] Indeed Hay will not be in Town untill some time [to]morrow. Our friends here are very angry at the postponement,[3] but I am satisfied it will be attended with advantage, as twenty four members had agreed to tye & go to Newmarket, which would lessen our Minority.

I saw Mr Grattan this day, & he says he will positively give notice for Tuesday the 21st in which case Lord Donoughmore told me he would fix the discussion in the Lords for Friday the 17th Inst. as it could on no account be postponed longer.[4] The English Catholics present an address to morrow to the Prince & also present a petition to Parliament alltho' they have greatly divided on the Subject amongst themselves.[5]

Every engine is used to raise a cry against us. Pamphlets are publishing every day. I saw [one] this day posted up in St James's Street, in which the Question of (whether the naturalisation of the Jews, or the Emancipation of the Catholics should be most injurious to the Empire!!) was fixed as a subject for Debate this Evening in one of the Established Forums of this City.[6]

The Prince refused giving the Duke of Bedford any ansr. when he had an audience with him, on the subject of the promises he held out to the Catholics, pursuant to the written instructions of the prince.[7]

The Dukes of Clarence & Kent will not vote at all. The Dukes of York & Cumberland will vote against us & the Duke of Sussex for us.

I am quite fatigued or should write you at great length. Poor Sheridan who will then probably want his dinner intends speaking on our Question & then resigning his Seat & the place he holds under the prince — but I am told, Jerningham, Clifford[8] & some others intend returning him for Stafford.[9]

I am sorry to conclude by expressing the general opinion that nothing is to be expected from the prince but ———

Rem[embe]r me to all friends.   [*Source*: Scully Papers]

[1]Hussey was one of the 21 delegates appointed on 4 March to carry the address to the Prince Regent and the petitions to parliament: see No. 340B, n.2; and No. 346 n.2 for Scully's declining to be one of them.

[2]It was presented on that date, as confirmed by Hussey at the aggregate meeting on 18 June (see No. 359 n.3).

[3]The postponement in presenting the petitions. Lord Donoughmore had fixed his motion in the House of Lords for 10 April and Grattan his in the House of Commons for 11 April (Earl Grey to Lord Grenville 7 April 1812 — *Dropmore Papers* X). The delay was due to the decision taken on 26 March to revise the text read at the aggregate meeting on 28 February (see No. 340B n.4).

[4]In the end Lord Donoughmore's motion was debated in the Lords on 21 April and lost by 174 – 72 votes; and Grattan's on 23 April in the Commons, where it was defeated by 310 – 215 votes (*Hansard* XXII, 1039).

[5]The petition of the English Catholics was introduced by William Elliot in the House of Commons on 20 April (ibid., 478).

[6]Since Jews born in Great Britain and Ireland became British subjects by birth, naturalisation could only be a real issue when there was a large influx of refugees. When in 1753 an act was passed for the naturalisation of foreign born Jews there was such an agitation against it that it had to be repealed in 1754 (See M. C. N. Salbstein: *The Emancipation of the Jews in Britain 1828–1860*, 1982). The organisers of the meeting were probably comparing Catholic Emancipation with that event.

[7]See Aspinall, *Letters of George IV*, I, No. 6 for a long and strongly worded remonstrance addressed to the Prince Regent by the Duke of Bedford in February. When he was Lord Lieutenant of Ireland, he said, the Prince had authorised him to assure the leading Catholics of Ireland that he acknowledged the full justice of their claims and would not fail to redress their grievances whenever he felt authorised to do so. On 23 April George Ponsonby, who had been Chancellor in Ireland at the time, confirmed in the House of Commons that this assurance had been received and acted upon (*Hansard* XXII, 1011).

[8]Probably the lawyer Henry Clifford (1768–1813) of Tixall, Staffordshire, a founder member of the Cisalpine Club.

[9]He did not resign his seat or give up his post as Receiver of the Duchy of Cornwall. Since November 1811 he had been canvassing in his old constituency of Stafford, where he came bottom of the poll at the general election in the autumn of 1812 (Aspinall, *George IV*, I, p. 82).

345   *From William Tighe to Merrion Square, Dublin*

London, 15 April 1812

Dear Sir,

I am much obliged for the part of the Pamphlet which I duly received.[1] You mention in a note the case of a man called Barry having been convicted & hung at Kilkenny in 1810 though his innocence appeared *before the execution*.[2] What documents or proof are there of this? Or that the government were informed of it, or convinced of it in time?

Neither Mr Grattan nor Mr G. Ponsonby seem to approve of my idea of a motion to bring in a bill relative to Juries — the latter thinks it would

displease many of those protestants who are favorable to the Catholic
Cause.[3]   [*Source*: Scully Papers]

[1]The earlier chapters of Part II of the *Penal Laws*: in the postscript to No. 355 Tighe
asks to see the conclusion.

[2]The note that led to the prosecution and conviction for libel of Hugh Fitzpatrick the
printer. Scully gave all his references in the margin and in the whole work there are
only three notes at the foot of the page. This one, taking up about a third of the page,
was bound to catch the eye of the most cursory reader. It illustrates a point in section
V of Chapter IX dealing with the disadvantages suffered by Catholic as opposed to
Protestant prisoners. In the 1st edition it read:

> "At the summer Assizes of Kilkenny, 1810, one Barry was convicted of a capital
> offence, for which he was afterwards executed — This man's case was truly
> tragical. — He was wholly innocent — was a respectable Catholic farmer in the
> county of Waterford; in good circumstances. — His innocence was clearly
> established, in the interval between his conviction and execution — yet he was
> hanged; publicly avowing his innocence!!! — There were some shocking
> circumstances, attending this case — which the Duke of Richmond's Administra-
> tion may yet be invited to explain to Parliament".

[3]See No. 355 n.3.

346   *From John Lalor to Merrion Square, Dublin*

St James Hotel, Cleveland Row [London] 20 April 1812
My Dear Scully,

I would have written to you before (had not Hussey told me that he would
inform you of all our proceedings)[1] to return you many thanks for a letter I
have seen in the *Evening Post* signed *Scurge*.[2]

You have seen in the papers we presented our petition, *passed in review*
before the Prince, had the Honor of kising [*sic*] his hand;[3] Lord Kenmare
came to Town the day before the presentation of our petition with his
son-in-law Sir Thos. Gage, who came to Levee to apologise for his
Lordship's not attending there being prevented he said by indisposition. The
day following there was a meeting of the Delegates at Lord Fingall's; Lord
Kenmare was there. It was all our opinion that both the Lords should require
a private audience of the Prince. Lord Fingall agreed to do so, but Lord
Kenmare declined it saying he should leave town.[4] I do not think the
Catholics have a greater enemy than he is, I am sure he is intrigueing. I have
given public notice (in B. Coyle's expression) that I will denounce him to the
Board on my return to Ireland. There was a meeting here yesterday to
consider the propriety of Lord Fingall's writing to Mr Rider[5] to require an
answer from the Prince to our Petition. It was agreed upon that he should do
so; Lord Fingall has just left this; he says he sent the letter this morning but

has not received an answer. Genl. Mathew neglected presenting our Petition[6] on Thursday last, he came to town the day following, he visited me yesterday, said he was delaid in Cheltham, that he would present our County Petition on Thursday next at Levee or on the Thursday following which ever I chose, I declaired [sic] I would have nothing to do with it, and that he was responsible for neglecting to present it on Thursday last.

All the Delegates except Sir Francis Goold, Hussey, & Baggot,[7] dined yesterday with Mr McDonald[8] at his Country House at Hamstead. I never saw a more elegant entertainment than he gave us, the best of wines of every discription and what I admired most with the greatest Irish hospitality, Lord Donoughmore and Mr Grattan are to dine with us on Sunday next. I proposed to Lord Kenmare and the rest of the Delegates that we should entertain all the Opposition of both Houses but they declined doing so.

[*Source*: Scully Papers]

[1]See No. 344. If Hussey wrote other letters they are missing.
[2]Scourge's letter, dated Cahir 4 April, appeared in the *Dublin Evening Post* of 7 April. It was a blistering attack on a certain Buddough and his brother Davy for criticising Lalor's conduct. An entry in James Scully's diary for 12 April identifies Buddough as Dennis Maher of Kilmoylę.
[3]At the Regent's levee on 16 April.
[4]At the aggregate meeting of 18 June (see No. 359 n.3) Hussey reported that Lord Fingall had also declined: although entitled to an audience as a peer he preferred to act in common with his fellow delegates.
[5]Richard Ryder, the Home Secretary.
[6]An address adopted by the Tipperary Catholics on 20 March (*DEP*, 24 March 1812) which General Mathew had evidently undertaken to present at the Regent's weekly levee on the 16th.
[7]James John Bagot.
[8]Miles MacDonald or MacDonnell.

347   *From Henry Parnell to Merrion Square, Dublin*

Stratford Place, London, 7 May 1812

My Dear Sir,

I write these few lines to suggest to you, that in consequence of Mr Canning's notice for the 28th,[1] it is very important that some immediate steps should be taken by the Catholics to prevent some of the Irish members from voting as they did on Mr Grattan's motion.[2] It appears to me that if the Catholics of the Counties of Longford, Wexford & King's Co. etc. were to remonstrate with their members as they ought to do, several votes would at least be lost to the Minister, if not gained over to your cause. I hope the Catholics will observe the list of the minority on Mr Bankes's Sinecure Bill.[3]

Their success so obviously now depends upon the ministerial existence of Mr Perceval, that no man can have the smallest claim to their favour who gives him a vote on any occasion.

I feel the more anxious that what I here suggest should be attended to, because the state of politicks is just at this moment such, that a very good division on Mr Canning's motion might be productive of a change even in this session.

I should have written to you after the late debate,[4] but that there was nothing to be communicated, which was not in the public papers. I gave your observations on the Veto etc. to Lords Grey & Holland.[5] The nature of Mr Canning's notice will give us an opportunity of referring to the matter of them, I hope, in the advantage to the question.   [*Source*: Scully Papers]

[1] On 6 May Canning had given notice that he would move on 28 May for an address to be presented the Prince Regent praying that during the parliamentary recess he would take into consideration the condition of the Roman Catholics "with the view of ascertaining the nature and extent of such securities as might be necessary to fence the Established Church, in case any further concessions to them should be deemed advisable and expedient" (*Hansard* XXIII, 55).

[2] For a committee to enquire into the state of the penal laws as they affected the Catholics of Ireland: presented on 23 April and defeated on the following day by 300 − 215 votes (*Hansard* XXII, 1039).

[3] The administration were defeated on this by 134 − 123 votes on 4 May. None of the six county members referred to by Parnell is recorded as having voted on either side (*Hansard* XXII, 1180).

[4] On Grattan's motion.

[5] Not found among the Earl Grey and Holland House papers.

348   *From Henry Parnell to Merrion Square, Dublin*

London, 8 May 1812

Private

My Dr Sir,

Mr Hay called on me this morning & informed me that your friends here[1] were apprehensive that Mr Canning's notice[2] would lead to the appointing of an aggregate meeting & subsequent proceedings injurious to the cause. I have, in consequence of this communication, seen Mr Canning & received from him what appears to me to be a very satisfactory explanation of the object of his motion. It is simply to require from those, who say securities are necessary, to prove the danger to be guarded against; & to state the plan of security which they conceive best suited to their view of the subject, & it is not either to bind himself or any one who votes with him, against making the concession to the Catholics without qualification, if no danger can be made out by those who at present apprehend one. His motion is in fact intended to remove a great deal of the difficulty belonging to the question of securities by getting it more investigated & better understood. In truth, I believe, that he is no further a friend to the plan, than as one which might contribute to allay prejudices & expedite the completion of the wishes of the Catholics.

I hope, therefore, the apprehensions of Mr Hay etc. will prove groundless & that the Catholics will not feel it necessary for them to express any opinion concerning the Securities, as it is a matter that belongs, must obviously for many excellent reasons, to be propounded, if thought right, by the Executive Govt.

I find many calculate on Mr Canning having a majority.

Some say that the Regent is not averse to the motion. I think you ought to be glad at its coming forward.   [*Source*: Scully Papers]

[1] Among the twenty-one Irish Catholic delegates (see No. 344 n.1).
[2] Of 6 May (see No. 347 n.1).

349   *Catherine Eyre to her daughter Mrs Denys Scully*
              No. 2 Merrion Square, South, Dublin

Ferme [Sheffield] 12 May 1812

My Dearest Catherine,

I have just received your letter, as we don't send to the post every day, I fear, it may have been there some days. I am sorry to find you make yourself so unhappy about the children. I fear it may hurt your milk, & be injurious to poor little Henry.[1] You know these are complaints all children are liable to, tho' we certainly could have wished it defered till they were a little older, but it could not have happen'd at a better time of the year as the approaching warm wheather will make it of short duration; You seem to have given them every chance of getting well over it, by useing those means, the best calculated to remove the complaint. Putting the feet every two or three days into luke warm water is a good thing, also to keep the body open by now and then taking eather a little rhubarb or stewed senna & pruanes; if the disorder is very voilent a blister is more efficacious, then a pitch plaster. Be carefull they dont get cold as that will much aggravate the disorder: if the cough makes them sick it will be of great use, otherwise a few grains of emetic in hyssop or penny royal tea sweetened, & to take a little every hour till it operates. Their diet to be of easy digestion, light pudding, chicken broth etc. Change of air is always strongly recomended. I expect Mrs Gainsford[2] here this afternoon & will not close my letter till I hear if she has anything to recommend. I think her a pretty good doctoress.

I hope there is no danger of Henry taking it, if the cow pox can be called a disorder, it will surely prevent his taking any other complaint at the same time.

Julia[3] desires her best love & will write to you soon. James Weld is to marry the late Lord Petre's second daughter, it is expected to take place soon.[4] Mr Sutton is to be married next week to Miss Roberts,[5] it has been defered on account of her health. I think she is not likely for long life, but she will leave him a large fortune.

The riots in Sheffield[6] were very much exaggerated in the papers. The town is full of soldiers in consequence, which will help to make provisions more scarce instead of cheaper. I have lately received a letter from James Wheble with an invitation to spend some time at Woodley[7] this summer which we mean to decline. He informs me his wife is again in the family way, & he hopes now out of all danger. I hope he wont be again disapointed of this long expected son & heir. John[8] was to get into his house last week, it is a very good one, tho' not exactly what a person wou'd build now, eighty acres of Land for six thousand seven hundred pd. He does not yet understand much of farming but he will have some employment & I hope amusement from it. Mrs Vin[9] is expecting every day, when she gets abroad again, Ann Wright[10] goes to London, I suppose preparatory to her Wedding. Thos.[11] & Julia join me in kind regards to Mr Scully. We have all received letters from the tax office amongst the rest one for you, on arrears of duties on dividends. Yours is £6.12.3 I don't mean to take any notice of it. If Mr Scully thinks it necessary he may write to Wrights,[12] as they managed your stock. I hope my Dear Catherine you will soon be able to give us a more favorable account of the children, which is the sincere wish of your affect'e Mother, C. Eyre.
[P.S.] Mrs G. says oatmeal & treacle poultice will be of use to your Breast. Any salves only keep it soft from healing. She has given me a receipt of Doctor Pitcarns which has been of great use in the hooping cough.

Dr Pitcairn's Receipt
¼ Grain of Emetic tartar for a child 6 years old
⅕ Grain of Emetic tartar for a child of 1 or 2 years old to be taken when going to bed in a little warm water or Water Gruel — Every night.

For the Hooping Cough — Dr Pitcairn
¼ ounce of spirits of Hartshorn ⎤
⎟ mix'd together
½ oz of Amber Oil ⎦
and therewith rub the Patient's back bone with the hand morning and evening.   [*Source*: Scully Papers]

[1]Seven weeks old.
[2]See No. 302 n.6.
[3]Her daughter Julia Eyre.

[4]J. Weld of Cowfield House, Wiltshire, married Julia Petre in July.

[5]Unidentified. Mr Sutton may have been Revd Thomas Sutton, Vicar of Sheffield.

[6]On 14 April a body of poor labourers started a riot in the potato market and joined by others broke into the arms depot of the Sheffield Militia. A party of the 15th Light Dragoons from the barracks restored order and four of the ringleaders were sent to York for trial (*Annual Register; Cobbet's Political Register*).

[7]Woodley Lodge, Berkshire.

[8]Her son John Eyre, who married Sarah Parker in 1811.

[9]Her daughter-in-law, wife of Vincent Eyre.

[10]Her daughter-in-law's sister, who married Charles Wolseley as his second wife on 23 May 1812.

[11]Her son Thomas Eyre.

[12]At this time called Wright, Selby and Robinson, of 5 Henrietta Street, London.

350   *From Henry Parnell to Merrion Square, Dublin*

London, 23 May 1812

My Dr Sir,

I have called several times at Ridgways[1] about your work but have not been able to see him. I find about 70 are sold & his people promise to use every exertion to sell the 2d part if you send it to them. Budd[2] says he never received any copies.

I feel I may safely wish you joy of the certainty of your question being soon carried. Tho' I can give you no authentic intelligence relative to the new arrangements, it may be regarded as settled that the ministry will be composed of the Wellesley & Opposition parties, & from all that has passed we may confidently look forward to a sincere & liberal conduct on their part.

It is reported that Lords Grey & Grenville will not take office but give all their support to the new administration.[3]

I feel very anxious to know what were the proceedings of the Board on Tuesday.[4] I trust that Mr Perceval's death prevented any measure relating to the very unfounded rumour that he had commenced a negotiation with the English Bishops.[5] For I am quite sure any such proceeding would contribute very much to embarrass the measures & exertions of those who sincerely desire to make the concession without any contingent securities. I feel quite sure that much of the language of Mr Canning & others on this point which appears to favour the claim of ministers, is made use of to avoid alarming wavering[?] minds, & to lead by degrees to the most liberal concession that circumstance will admit of.   [*Source*: Scully Papers]

[1]James Ridgway, Bookseller, 170 Piccadilly.

[2]J. Budd, Bookseller, 100 Pall Mall.

[3]Spencer Perceval having been assassinated on 11 May the Marquis of Wellesley had been commissioned to take soundings for a new administration. He had seen Earl Grey and Lord Grenville on 23 May, when they refused to take office under him (*Hansard* XXIII, Appendix).

[4]19 May. No record has been found of the meeting.

[5]Probably a slip of the pen. The current rumour in the opposition was that Perceval had been negotiating with the Irish Bishops in regard to securities (cf. Thomas Grenville's letter of 3 May 1812 to Lord Grenville in *Dropmore Papers* X). O'Connell had already been told by Dr Troy that no such proposition had been made by Perceval (O'Connell, *Correspondence* I, No. 376; DDA 54/2, II, 23).

351   *To [William Tighe]*

Dublin, 28 May 1812

[Draft]

Dear Sir,

I have been in daily expectation of being enabled to send you an authentic statement[1] of the facts relative to Barry, who was executed at Kilkenny in 1810, but his Counsel, Mr Burrowes Campbell, who promised it to me, has been delayed by one obstacle or other, and I now fear I cannot obtain it before the summer vacation. The outline of it, as I have frequently heard him relate it in the presence of many of the Bar, was nearly as follows[2] —

Barry was a very small farmer[3] of the county of Waterford. In the spring of 1810 he was imprisoned in Clonmell gaol. At the Summer Assizes, 1810, for Clonmell, he was ordered to be transmitted to Kilkenny gaol to take his trial for a highway robbery.[4] On Friday he reached Kilkenny. On Sunday, for the first time, he received a written notice from the Crown Solicitor, that his trial should take place on the following day, Monday. On that Monday morning, Lord Norbury opened the commission at Kilkenny. The indictment against Barry was found, immediately, & his trial was called on. His Counsel, Mr Campbell, moved to have his trial postponed till the ensuing Assizes. Upon the affidavit of Barry, stating that it was only on the preceding day that he had the first intimation, from any quarter, of the nature or particulars of the charges against him, that he was innocent of the charges — and could clearly establish his alibi if allowed time to procure his witnesses, credible neighbours, who could testify that he was in the county of Waterford where the witnesses resided, at a place 36 miles distant from the place of the robbery, at the time of the robbery committed. His affidavid contained all the usual ingredients necessary in such cases. When this was read, Lord Norbury observed, that he considered the whole to be a fabrication, and (as a mark of his superior penetration) he considered the very correctness of the affidavit, its fullness as to facts, and sufficiency in form, as incontestible proofs of the artifice & contrivance used in framing it. He at length consented, however but with difficulty, to allow the trial to stand over for the following day, Tuesday — but solely on the ground, that he had business enough to occupy him in court for that day, without entering upon Barry's trial.

On Tuesday morning Barry's trial was called on. His Counsel, Mr Campbell, renewed his motion of the preceding day, for a postponement of the trial. It was peremptorily refused. Mr Campbell then said, that he could not properly defend a prisoner, whose trial was thus precipitated, and that Barry's blood should not rest on *his* head. He threw in his brief, & took up his hat, about to leave court — Lord Norbury commanded him to stay in court and defend his client. Mr Campbell replied "you have no authority to impose such a command, and I will not obey it". He then left the court. The trial then proceeded. The prosecutor proved the necessary facts, and swore positively (tho' in mistake as appeared afterwards)[5] to the identity of Barry — who was thereupon convicted, sentenced, and left for execution on that day fortnight. The circuit ended at Kilkenny. The judges, Bar etc returned to Dublin.

In 3 or 4 days, Mr Campbell was called upon, in Dublin, by two respectable farmers, well recommended, who had come up from the county of Waterford, upon learning what had passed at Kilkenny: they stated a positive alibi, and a good character for Barry. Mr Campbell sent them to make affidavits of these facts before the Lord Mayor. After they had left him, 2 other credible persons of that county called upon Mr Campbell, corroborated the innocence of Barry, and were sent to make similar affidavits before the Lord Mayor.[6] Mr Campbell then took these affidavits and delivered them to Lord Norbury.[7] But, suspecting that they would not be delivered, he went personally to Mr Saurin, the Atty. General, related the entire transaction to him, & pledged his professional character (which is highly respectable) for the truth of his statement.[8] The Attorney General, upon this statement, felt as any body else must, that Barry was innocent & cruelly wronged. He promised instant and effectual interference. The whole was thus laid fully before the Duke of Richmond's administration.[9] There were yet some days to elapse, during which Mr Campbell received no message, desire of further information or intimation of any kind. Finally, Barry was executed, solemnly protesting his innocence. Waters, the Subsheriff, told me that he attended his execution, that he appeared to be a very decent man, firmly conscious of his innocence, and earnestly asserting it — that his body was sent on a car towards Carrickonsuir — and that before it had proceeded 4 miles on the road from Kilkenny, it was met by several very respectable farmers of the county of Waterford, who came thus far to pay this mark of respect to his good character and conduct.

The event excited sensations of great horror & regret amongst all classes, and generally in the Four Courts, which have not yet subsided. Had he been a gentleman etc. I expect a much more full & detailed account from Mr Campbell himself, which I shall have great pleasure in forwarding to you.

Altho' facts are numerous upon this subject, and the consequences are felt very generally & grievously, yet it is difficult (unless the individuals were actually summoned & examined upon oath before the House of Commons) to obtain them in that detailed form that can originate a statement.[10] In this country, private persons are timid, interested, shrinking from publicity, dependent upon power in one way or other — and they submit, having no hope of benefit from complaint. A man injured in this way, is little obliged to another who complains of his individual case, or states names or facts — tho' he will exult in the accusation generally made. In fact, this country has descended to a very degraded & slavish policy in this & many other respects.

[*Source*: Callanan Papers]

[1]Asked for by Tighe in No. 345.

[2]Among the Callanan Papers there are what seems to be a draft letter dated 16 June and a series of incomplete rough notes, showing that Scully's account underwent several revisions. These and the evidence given at the trial of Hugh Fitzpatrick (Howell, *State Trials* XXXI) reveal a number of mistakes or omissions in the present letter.

[3]Later demoted to "a labourer", but with respectable connexions.

[4]In both cases the year was 1809. Barry was in prison at Clonmel after being convicted and sentenced to transportation for two offences committed on the Tipperary side of the county border. There was a third offence committed on the Kilkenny side.

[5]Scully later dropped this claim. The question of Barry's identity was not raised at the Fitzpatrick trial.

[6]Barry's employer, Rogers, and three others swore affidavits in Waterford. Rogers alone saw Campbell.

[7]He sent them under cover of a letter.

[8]Campbell did not go to the Attorney General but sent him a letter. In one of his revised accounts Scully says Rogers took this to the Attorney General's house at Blackrock, where he was given a packet to take to Sir Charles Saxton at Dublin Castle.

[9]At the Fitzpatrick trial the Attorney General produced Campbell's letter dated 18 August, which he said was the first he had heard of the affair, and Lord Norbury's reply dated six o'clock the same day, containing his implied refusal to reconsider the sentence.

[10]In his *Memoirs* II, p. 311 Sir Samuel Romilly says that when he was considering bringing the Barry case before parliament he got Ponsonby and Plunket to make enquiries: "The result . . . is, that although the man's trial was very improperly hurried on by Lord Norbury . . . and that on that ground alone the application to the Lord Lieutenant for mercy ought to have been attended to, yet I do not find that there is any sufficient reason for doubting that the man was guilty".

352   *From William Parnell to 2 Merrion Square South, Dublin*

Avondale [Co. Wicklow] Friday [29 May 1812]

My dear Sir,

I am very much obliged to you for remembering me & will thank you to have the *Statement*[1] left for me to the care of Capt Howard at the Stamp Office.[2] I am glad that no deceitful prospect of immediate success tempts you to remit your labours & I wish the united exertions of your whole body only produced as much effect as your single exertions but they seem to me employed in words & forms. However perhaps it is better it should be so; in these times events are impelled forward with such precipitancy that a considerable degree of *vis inertia* may be of use at the first movement. But surely you might manage without such unwieldly machines as aggregate meetings of which you neither can calculate the power or effect; which in general do little but hazard much. You have no established forms to embarrass you & why should you not adopt the plan universally allowed to be desireable at elections, & poll the sense of your body in parishes; if County mobs are found so inconvenient how much worse are aggregate meetings where neither numbers or ranks are defined; and the influence of individuals by which they are to be controul'd is exposed to the attacks of every ambitious individual. Their only use is that they gratify the self complacency of your body at large but the other plan would do that more effectually. Your own good sense, I know would wish for less sound & more effect, & I should not say all this but I know every one takes a stronger part when he is conscious that his opinions are fortified by those of his friends — & I hope you will esteem me one of yours.   [*Source*: Scully Papers]

[1]Part II of Scully's *Penal Laws*.
[2]Of which his father-in-law, the Right Hon. Hugh Howard was joint chairman.

353   *From Henry Parnell to Merrion Square, Dublin*

London, 30 May 1812

My dear Sir,

Though your letter was Private on the subject of Mr Canning's motion[1] I felt that under the circumstance of its being an answer to mine[2] containing his explanation of the motion he had given notice of on the Catholic Question, that I might communicate it to him as a private letter without incurring your displeasure. I received the enclosed from him in reply.

There is nothing finally settled about the Administration. We expect Mr Wortley will give notice tonight of another address on Monday.[3]

[Enclosure]
Gloucester Lodge, Thursd. 28 May 1812

Dear Sir,

I return you the letter which you have been so good as to send me with many thanks for the communication of it. I will not deny that it is highly gratifying for me to find my motions and intentions justly and favourably understood in Ireland. And if you shall think fit to mention to Mr S. your having shewn me his letter, I hope you will not think it improper to add that I am fully aware of the weight & value of his testimony on such a subject, as well as of his individual good opinion.   [*Source*: Scully Papers]

[1]Originally tabled for 28 May but postponed after the assassination of the Prime Minister and did not come on until 22 June (*Hansard* XXIII, 633).
[2]No. 348.
[3]On 21 May Stuart Wortley had carried an address asking the Regent to form an efficient administration and the government headed by Lord Liverpool had tendered their resignation. When the House met on 1 June he was forestalled by an announcement that the Marquis of Wellesley had formally been invited to form an administration (*Hansard* XXIII, 313).

354   *From Charles Butler to Merrion Square*

Lincolns Inn, 4 June 1812

Dear Sir,

It is a long time since I have written to you.[1] The *Morning Chronicle* and the *Times* have contained very accurate information of the various attempts which have been made for effecting a Coalition ministry.

All these attempts have now proved abortive;[2] and it remains to be settled, whether the old Liverpool party, with or without Mr Canning, (but certainly without the Marquis), or the old opposition with or without the Marquis or Mr Canning, will compose the new administration. I think another trial will be made to introduce the former, and that it will not succeed.[3]

The Catholic question will be immediately agitated,[4] and will be the signal of war. To use the expression of the Abbé Siese [*recte* Sieyès], when he voted for the death of Lewis XVI, *La Mort et sans Phrases*; the question for the House to decide upon will be Catholic Emancipation without phrase, that is, without Circumlocution, qualification guards or pledges. I think the motion will be carried. You know how near a majority they were on the last division.[5]

You may depend on this information, and best know what measures should be taken on your side of the water to cooperate with the exertions of your Friends.

While Mr Perceval lived, Mr Canning's intended motion was excellent, as it was to have been framed in such a manner as to gain the votes of all, who did not wish the actual disabilities of the Catholics to be eternal: but Mr Perceval's death makes the motion good for nothing.

The general insurrection of the public opinion against the No-popery administration, the firmness shewn by Lord Grey and Lord Grenville and the increase of the nations dislike to the Prince have added prodigiously to the strength of the Catholic phalanx: *Ca ira.*

[*Source*: Scully Papers]

[1] Not since No. 341 of 18 March 1812.
[2] See No. 353 n.3. The Marquis of Wellesley gave up his attempt on 3 June and on the following day the Regent commissioned Lord Moira to form an administration. On 6 June his negotiations with Grey and Grenville broke down on the issue of changes in the Regent's household and when other difficulties frustrated a plan for an all party administration without them the Regent turned to Lord Liverpool again on 9 June (*Hansard* XXIII, Appendix).
[3] Lord Liverpool was to remain in power until 1828.
[4] On Canning's motion, 22 June.
[5] Grattan's motion on the Irish Catholic petition, defeated on 23 April by 300 to 215 votes (*Hansard* XXIII, 728).

355   *From William Tighe to Merrion Square, Dublin*

London, 8 June 1812

Dear Sir,

I have just received your letter respecting the case of Barry[1] — which I think as well as that of Hall,[2] must be noticed by the House of Commons. I wish that the affidavits sworn before the Lord Mayor could be procured — or the copy of any memorial (if any exists) presented to Government on the subject.

I by no means consider the idea of a bill for trials *de medietate*[3] as relinquished, but while Mr Canning's notice[4] is depending it might not be prudent to interfere in the Catholic cause. In the present state of things there is a probability of the Catholic claims either being fully allowed or at least greatly advanced — & it is better to suffer this to be done with the greatest possible support & union of parties — the rejection of the Catholic claims, would call for every subsidiary motion or measure as far as it could assist the cause — but one must be careful not to injure the cause in its present state.

I have not heard how the affair of Silk, guard of the mail-coach, who shot the chairman ended? or if he was tried, or found guilty?[5]

[P.S.] I shall be very happy to see the conclusion of your work on the penal laws[6] — & be very grateful to you for sending it.

[*Source*: Scully Papers]

[1] No. 351.
[2] Walter Hall, who had shot dead a young Irish Catholic (see No. 357).

[3]Or *per medietatem* as Scully puts it in Chapter IX of his *Penal Laws*: the meaning is "half and half". Its scope is defined in one of the resolutions adopted by an aggregate meeting of 9 June 1813: "to take into consideration the form of a petition to Parliament praying that the Catholics of Ireland may, during further continuance of the penal and disabling laws, obtain the benefit of that principle of the constitution which gives to aliens a jury of one half foreigners", that is, by having half the jury Catholic at the trial of a Catholic. Scully revived the proposal again at a meeting of the Board on 5 February 1814 (DDA 54/1, X, 7) but nothing ever came of it.

[4]See No. 353 n.1.

[5]Not found.

[6]The last chapters of part II of the *Penal Laws* (see No. 345 n.1).

356   *From Henry Parnell to Merrion Square, Dublin*

                                                    [9 June 1812] 6. o'clock

My Dr Sir,

Since I wrote this morning[1] I have learnt that Ld Liverpool at a meeting this morning declared that Mr Canning's motion was not to be opposed by Govt.[2] I am told this by a person present.

It is said this is the price of Ld Moira's support.[3] But such a transaction must only contribute to express the character & weight of both parties.

                                                    [*Source*: Scully Papers]

[1]Missing from the collection, in which the next letter from Parnell is that of 1 March 1813, No. 411.

[2]On 9 June the Earl of Liverpool held a meeting of the friends of the new ministry in both Houses and read the minutes of the correspondence that had taken place between himself, the Marquis of Wellesley and Lord Moira. "We understand", said the *Morning Chronicle* of 10 June 1812, "the noble Earl intimated that members, the friends of the Government, would be pleased to exercise their own free judgment in voting upon this [the Catholic] question, when it should again come on".

[3]When Lord Liverpool had informed the House of Lords on 8 June that he had been entrusted with the formation of a government Lord Moira had announced that under the present circumstances of the country he would support the new administration so far as was consistent with the public principles which he had so often avowed (*Hansard* XXIII, 359).

357   *From William Tighe to Merrion Square, Dublin*

                                    St James's Place, London, 13 June 181?

Dear Sir,

I have just moved for the papers relative to the pardon given to *Walte*

Hall.[1] I wish to know if you can obtain any further information as to his case — your letter states that he is *at liberty*, Mr Pole says[2] that he is certainly *in confinement* — if so, upon *what committal* or *warrant* is he confined? Or upon what *order* of court, or under *what* verdict? Can you procure any minutes of the trial?

You ought, for your own sake, not to have published the note relative to Barry;[3] unless you can justify it, by complete evidence — to say "a man was wholly innocent" — & that "yet he was hanged," — will certainly be noticed as a libel on the government of Ireland — you should be prepared to justify it completely — or else suppress the publication of it, for your own sake, if it is not too late.[4]

[*Source*: Scully Papers]

[1]The papers asked for by Tighe (*Hansard* XXIII, 467) are probably those contained in the Home Office file HO 100/167, f.360. These show that after being sentenced to death in February 1812 Walter Hall was twice reprieved before being pardoned. The minutes of evidence taken by a judge and a memorandum by a friend of Hall's do not give the date of the murder, but show that it took place at about nine in the evening in Aungier Street, when Hall, who was in the dress of a yeoman, shot a man called Byrne. It was explained that because he had been a boy in Co. Wexford during the rebellion he had developed an obsession about rebels over which he was liable to lose control when under the influence of alcohol.

[2]No doubt in the conversation behind the Speaker's chair mentioned in No. 358. On 7 July Pole revealed that Hall was on his way to Botany Bay (*Hansard* XXIII, 936).

[3]See Nos. 345 and 351.

[4]For Henry Parnell's taking a different view from Tighe's about the footnote see Hay's letters to O'Connell of 12 and 13 June (O'Connell, *Correspondence* I, Nos. 385, 386). It was already too late to act: on 15 June a sub-committee of the Catholic Board was formed to distribute 300 copies of the *Penal Laws* (DDA 54/2, II, 29) and by 30 June the London bookseller Ridgway had received a supply (see No. 361). The footnote was retained, only slightly modified, in the second edition.

358   *From William Tighe to Merrion Square, Dublin*

London, 20 June 1812

Dear Sir,

I have this moment received your letter[1] & lose no time to inform that the whole conversation that took place between me & Mr Pole, was of about two minutes duration & behind the Speaker's chair in the house. As soon as I had mentioned the case of Hall,[2] Mr Pole told me that he should be glad to have it enquired into, that the D. of Richmond was very cautious in such affairs, that he acted by the recommendation of the two judges who tried the cause & that such a recommendation was never refused & that he would send me all the papers in his office relative to it. I told him I should be obliged to him, if he would send them to me to peruse (which he did the next day) — & I said "that I thought it right at the same time to tell him, that another case had occurred in the county of Kilkenny,[3] which I might think it right to enquire into, if the circumstances turned out to be as they had been represented to me, that it was the case of one Barry, who had been hung at Kilkenny two years ago." He said, he had no recollection of it — I replied, that, "Barry was hung in 1810, for a robbery, & that he was, [a] farmer from the county of Waterford". Mr P. then said "that he remembered a Waterford farmer having suffered for a most aggravated & *atrocious* robbery, but he had no papers upon the subject, but he would write to Ireland to enquire if any existed in the office there & then he took down in pencil a note of the *name of Barry & the date* — there was no question of you — & Mr P. naturally supposed that my information came from the County of Kilkenny[4] — & this was the whole of our conversation — to the best of my recollection. Mr P. was in a hurry all the time to return to the debate in the house.

I never shewed your letters to any person — I read part of them to Mr Hay,[5] & we conversed about the case of Barry, & we agreed that the publication of it would probably be noticed by the Irish government, & that you had better not have published it, unless you had full documents to prove your statement. Mr Hay will himself inform you that he then suggested first the idea of your suppressing if possible, & asked if he should write to you. I told him it was unnecessary, as I was going to write to you the next day & would mention it, but I believed it was too late. I accordingly wrote to you on the next day. I told Mr Hay that I was sure Mr Pole had then never seen the printed statement in the note — & I do not believe any member of the Irish government here has seen it yet. Nothing more has been said or done by me as to the case of Barry. I will write again to you relative to it, when I have read Mr Campbell's statement.[6]

I am happy that the Aggregate Meeting[7] are likely to approve of the conduct of Lords Grey & Grenville. I believe Lord Grey will entirely agree with them in the rejection of the *veto*, or its *substitutes*. I think no dissatisfaction ought to be expressed with Lord Moira[8] — he is a determined friend of the Catholics & refuses to go to Ireland as Ld Lieutenant, unless their claims are fully[?] granted.[9]   [*Source*: Scully Papers]

[1]Of 16 June, missing.
[2]See No. 357 n.1.
[3]See No. 351.
[4]Tighe lived at Woodstock, sixteen miles from Kilkenny. During Pole's absence in London the Castle had discovered for themselves the Barry footnote. An entry for 16 June in the Calendar of Official Papers (276) reads: "Catholic Board: Scully to be prosecuted for libel"; and on 20 June the Lord Lieutenant, in sending the Home Secretary Part II of the *Penal Laws*, drew attention to the footnote on p. 219, which he thought should be submitted to the law officers (HO 100/167, f.188).

[5]In London with the Irish Catholic delegation (see No. 348).

[6]Promised by Scully in the penultimate paragraph of No. 351.

[7]Of 18 June: the conduct of the two lords was duly approved (*DEP*, 19 June 1812).

[8]Apart from announcing his conditional support of Lord Liverpool's government (see No. 356 n.3) Lord Moira had incurred the displeasure of the opposition for refusing to discuss with the two lords the question of changes in the Regent's household, thus frustrating the possibility of an alternative administration being formed (see the exchange of correspondence in the appendix to *Hansard* XXIII). The aggregate meeting passed no resolution condemning him, but he was criticised in speeches.

[9]Lord Moira wrote to Colonel MacMahon on 31 August 1812 that he might have gone to Ireland as Lord Lieutenant if Lord Wellesley's motion (see No. 362 n.3) had not been defeated on 1 July, but that he regarded the settlement of tithes as more important than Catholic emancipation (Aspinall, *Correspondence of George IV*, I, No. 140).

359   *From William Parnell to 2 Merrion Square South, Dublin*

Avondale [Co. Wicklow] 26 June 1812

My dear Sir,

I have just finished reading your book[1] which I think quite perfect. You have left nothing undone & have done everything well; when the Catholic question is settled it will remain as a valuable description of the precise effects of penal statutes; if any Government should hereafter be tempted to revive any code of a similar nature. I congratulate you on the result of the late debate;[2] and at this distance can sympathise in the joy which must pervade all ranks of Catholics in Dublin where these things are felt more speedily & with more warmth than in the Country. Still I am a little afraid of the Catholics that they should not meet this triumph with a noble & generous spirit. You know as well as I do that these penal laws sometimes shew that they live in a contracted & even ungenerous mode of thinking among the Catholics. Sometimes too timid in adversity, sometimes too overbearing in prosperity. I make no apology in saying I expect you will exert yourself that the concessions of ministers may not now be made a source of humiliation to them but that they may be met on the part of the Catholics with at least good humour. No one I think feels more angry or less inclined to a truce than I do when in battle, but when the battle is won I had rather concede the points I was most tenacious of than appear ungenerous. But a triumph of pure reason which this is, is so rare & valuable it is a pity it should be disgraced in the conduct of it — and yet these aggregate meetings! You know how much public events depend on personal feelings & I quite tremble for the Catholic cause when I see how unnecessarily the Prince is attacked.[3] Surely there ought now to be an end of all this; and even Pole & Castlereagh as far as the

Catholics are concerned, may be considered as carrion & no longer worth hunting.

[P.S.] We should be very glad if you and Mrs Scully could pay us a visit here as soon as your business in town will let you.   [*Source*: Scully Papers]

[1]Part II of the *Penal Laws*.

[2]The second edition of the *Dublin Evening Post* of 25 June had announced the carrying of Canning's motion of 22 June (see No. 347 n.1).

[3]He is referring to the "witchery resolutions" of the aggregate meeting of 18 June, the fourth of which complained of "the fatal witchery of an unworthy secret influence" that had prevented the promised boon of Catholic freedom (*DEP*, 18 June 1812). They echoed the parliamentary opposition's insinuations about the influence of Lady Hertford and more particularly a passage of Lord Donoughmore's speech on the Irish Catholic petition in which he referred to "the allurements of Calypso's court" and "the charms of that matured enchantress" (*Hansard* XXII, 524). The manner of their insertion, at the last minute and without the Chairman's having seen them, gave rise to controversy and speculation, and in 1819 O'Connell, refuting allegations against the Ponsonby family, denied that either he or Scully had had confidential communication with the opposition (*DEP*, 10 August 1819). A letter of Lord Donoughmore's written on 23 June 1812 and thanking his brother, Francis Hely Hutchinson, for "the effectual execution of all my wishes on the subject of the late Catholic meeting" (*Donoughmore Papers*, F/10/76), confirms Thomas Wyse's statement (*History of the late Catholic Association*, p. 152) that Lord Donoughmore himself was the instigator. How the text came into being was explained by O'Connell to an aggregate meeting on 1 July 1819: drafts, he said, had been prepared by Dr Dromgoole and Counsellor Finn but when the Board assembled on the morning of the meeting to arrange details "a learned gentleman produced resolutions, bearing the same import and tendency, but infinitely better in point of diction, upon which Dromgoole and Finn tore up their drafts" (*DEP*, 3 July 1819). The learned gentleman was generally reputed to be Scully — see Wyse ibid. and R. L. Sheil: *Political Sketches* p. 172.

360   *From Charles Butler to Merrion Square*

Lincolns Inn, 27 June 1812

Dear Sir,

I was favoured with your letter[1] this morning; and I will take care to see that your books[2] are properly distributed.

I only withheld from writing to you, on account of my having nothing of importance to communicate.

The general opinion was, at first, very much against Lord Grey and Lord Grenville;[3] it is now more favourable to them. In my own opinion, they have acted perfectly right: but I incline to think, that, with some contrivance, they might have put their adversaries more in the wrong, in Public opinion, than they did.

Mr Canning's motion[4] has served us much. It compels the Ministry to make specific averments of the particular reasons, for which they object to emancipate us. This alone is greatly in our favour; but the great advantage, which we have derived from the success of his motion, is, the effect which it has had on the mind of the public. The opinion, that there is no solid reason for continuing the Laws in force against us; that the repeal of them will be attended with little public sensation, and that in fact they are even now virtually repealed, now gain ground most rapidly.

If I should learn, what limitations or guards are intended to be introduced, I will apprise you of them. I have heared, (but from no authority), that it is intended to provide, that no person of Irish extraction, shall be returnable for any place in England, and that the number of Roman Catholic Members is to be limited.

On a sudden, I was desired to draw an act of Parliament for the Emancipation of the Catholics; and I drew the Act, of which I send you a Copy.[5] As the Irish and English Catholics have sworn to the Act of Settlement, I think that Act, and the Act respecting Royal Marriages should remain sacred. With that exception, the Act I send you places the Roman Catholics exactly on the same footing as his Majesty's Protestant Subjects. For this we should contend; and *if we act wisely we shall certainly obtain it*. I must express my wonder, that there is such apparent backwardness on the part of our Irish brethren, to co-operate with us. It has been proved beyond doubt that two letters,[6] officially written by Mr Jerningham to Mr Hay, strongly expressing the wish of the English Roman Catholics to cooperate with you, were not communicated to the Irish Roman Catholics.

I had the pleasure of seeing many of your Delegates, and I was the proposer of the motion for giving them a public dinner,[7] Mr Jerningham holding the official situation of Secretary, I make it a point to keep myself in the back ground, but you are sensible of my zeal in the cause and my willingness to promote it by every exertion in my power.

The Act I send you is very short, and might be shortened. Of course, in adverting to particular Laws, I had, in view, the English Statute book more than the Irish. I wish you would make such additions and alterations in it as you think proper: In every sense of the word, it is an hasty Sketch.

[*Source*: Scully Papers]

[1]Of 23 June, not extant.
[2]Part II of the *Penal Laws*.
[3]In rejecting the overtures from the Marquis of Wellesley and the Earl of Moira (see No. 354 n.2).
[4]Of 22 June (see No. 359 n.2).
[5]Not found among the Scully Papers. Butler already had a sketch in readiness — see No. 340 n.5. On the evidence of a letter from Lord Clifford dated 18 February 1813 Bishop Ward says (*Eve of Catholic Emancipation* II, p. 28) that in consequence of the

vote on Canning's motion (on 22 June 1812) Grattan felt so confident of success that he formed a small committee, consisting of himself, Ponsonby and Elliot, and that this committee commissioned Butler to draft a bill.

[6]Not identified.

[7]On 30 April 1812 at the Thatched House. Sir George Jerningham wrote to Lady Bedingfeld the next day: "It went off extremely well and I trust all animosity is now done away with between the two bodies" (*Jerningham Letters*).

361   *From James Ridgway*

Piccadilly, 30 June 1812

Sir,

   Your letter arrived yesterday, and the box[1] today: all you request shall be Executed by tomorrow Evening. I am very sorry my friends feel a want of attention in replies to letters. I must own that on the subject of the first Part of the Penal Laws, I did receive one letter requesting an answer to a letter which I had answered a fortnight before. I am very sorry I do not feel warranted in puting [*sic*] the Volume to Press immediately — you will perhaps think it Extraordinary — but there is not that feeling on the Catholic question in this country which there is in Ireland — and the best proof of it is, that Neither Pains nor Expense has Procured anything like a tollerable sale to any one Publication on the Subject. I think However 25 or 50 of the Second Part ought to be sent Here. I see there are about 20 of the first Part on hand so that Mr Fitzpatrick[2] will know How the Matter stands.

   I am of opinion the *Present men intend nothing good* to the Catholic Cause.

   Pray Excuse this scrawl as I write on the Counter to save the Post under constant interruptions.   [*Source*: Scully Papers]

[1]Probably containing presentation copies of Part II of the *Penal Laws*.
[2]Hugh Fitzpatrick, publisher of the *Penal Laws*.

362   *From Lord Holland*

Holland House, 3 July [1812]

Dear Sir,

   allow me to express very inadequately but very sincerely my thanks as a publick man for the manner in which you have promoted a great publick cause by a clear, useful & manly exposition of the present state of the Laws effecting the Roman Catholicks & at the same time for the obligation you have conferred upon me by sending me the work[1] *from the Author*, a testimony of your regard which I assure you I value as I ought.

It is with real satisfaction that I have to add that notwithstanding the many untoward & unexpected events which have occurred to damp the hopes entertained by the friends of religious & civil liberty, the progress in the great work of conciliation both in Parliament & in the English publick has been very great indeed in the course of this Session. The vote of the House of Commons[2] & the large minority in the House of Lords[3] are considered by every rational man here as certain prognosticks not only of the ultimate but of the speedy success of the measure. Would to God that it had been accomplished *now* — the languid tone of the Opposition made to the measure is indeed in my judgment an earnest of its success next year but I am sure it is a proof of the facility with which it might have been carried this if it had received the active & cordial support of the executive Government.[4]

[*Source*: Scully Papers]

[1]Part II of the *Penal Laws*.
[2]On Canning's motion, carried on 22 June by 235 to 106 votes (*Hansard* XXIII, 710).
[3]The Marquis of Wellesley's similar motion in the House of Lords on 1 July, lost by only one vote: 126 to 125 (ibid., 868).
[4]Lord Liverpool voted against Lord Wellesley's motion.

363   *To Earl Grey*

Merrion Square, Dublin 5 July 1812
My Lord,

I trust that you will readily pardon the liberty I take in apprizing your Lordship (as I think it right and necessary to do), that the Irish Government, for obvious purposes, is about to recommence a religious persecution — and they time it, as last year, for the rising of Parliament.[1] They are now instituting a criminal prosecution against Mr Hugh Fitzpatrick, printer, for having printed the second part of the "*Statement of the Penal Laws in force against the Catholics*."[2] Your Lordship has probably received a copy of this work, lately forwarded to you through Jas. Ridgeway of Piccadilly, bookseller. Tho' the Irish Government employs many mercenary pens, yet no person has questioned the fidelity of the references, or the fairness of the conclusions, contained in this *Statement*. It stands, uncontradicted in law and in fact. They intend to put it down by *force* disguised under the name of Law — and, with a biassed court and a packed jury (consisting of the Dublin Corporation, placemen etc) the Crown here is as certain of a verdict against a Printer *in any case*, as the Dey of Algiers is of the implicit obedience of his slaves.

Now, my Lord, this prosecution can only exasperate the Irish people even beyond former acts. It excludes all discussion: it affords no test of truth or of falsehood. Though every syllable of this book be true, yet the traverser is not allowed to prove its truth in his defence — for truth (such are our legal doctrines) is not receivable as a justification in any criminal proceedings. The Catholics invite inquiry — they are urged to particularise their grievances — they do so, perhaps warmly — prosecution is the reply. So much for the candour and manliness of the legal *Junta* who now govern Ireland.

It was understood by us, that, in the recent debate upon Mr Canning's motion, the Ministers (or at least Lord Castlereagh[3] etc) did promise to employ this summer in efforts to promote kindness & conciliation, yet this is the mode of the performance. The Catholics have universally read & adopted this *Statement*. They have, at the late Aggregate Meeting,[4] voted their unanimous thanks to the author. The clergy, in particular, hold it in estimation. Yet the Irish Government stigmatize it as a false and seditious libel[5] — and wantonly enter upon a new conflict with the Irish people. They thus heap insult upon injury — and will affect wonder, when the Catholics shall vent their indignation and discontent.

Our Chancellor, Lord Manners, is the slave of the merest bigotry — and is as averse to freedom as any other member of the house of Rutland.

Our Chief Justice Downes is a man of the same stamp — and has risen as a mere partizan — he is moreover full of resentment at the actions brought against him by the arrested delegates, in which his plea in defence is likely to be overruled.[6]

Our Attorney General Saurin, & Solicitor General Bushe (both crafty and intriguing men) naturally seek to divert public attention from a scrutiny of their own practices. They have been receiving, from the public funds, for the last few years, several thousand pounds, under the pretence of revenue fees — altho' we have a regular establishment of revenue counsel, at a heavy expense — (see the recent report of the Commissioners of Irish Enquiry into Fees — No. 8, 9, 10 etc and the supplement thereto).[7] Their object is to embroil the country in fresh agitation, to open a field for new professional exhibitions, to renovate their fading importance, and to earn a set off against the public claim of overhauling these large sums thus received by them, *without any value*.

Such is our legal *Junta* now misgoverning Ireland (for I do not find, that Mr Wellesley Pole is active at present)[8] and thus are they instigated to mischief. The consequence may be general ruin, if not checked by a seasonable and effectual exertion in Parliament.

It would greatly disappoint the *Junta*, and impose lasting obligations upon the Irish people, if this subject were again brought before Parliament, and in both Houses, *previously to the rising* — It would be noble and wise to make another effort for our salvation, to rescue us from this miserable condition. Your Lordship, and the noble and honourable friends who have concurred with you in supporting us, possess our full confidence, as the recent resolutions, as well as the universal feeling, sufficiently testify — and I need not suggest any proceedings for this purpose.

Mr Tighe some time ago talked of moving for a committee to inquire into the state of the administration of justice in Ireland — and he is possessed of some strong facts to support such a notion — I wish he had executed this intention — but it is not yet too late.

Your Lordship will perceive, from the enclosed copy of the summons served upon Fitzpatrick,[9] how novel and arbitrary a summons is resorted to by the Attorney General. His object can only be to sift for evidence and to entrap an unwary printer. For, no notice is necessary. He may go into the court of the King's Bench (according to present practice) with his Ex Officio information in his hand, and put it upon the file of the court. He assumes more, however, in this instance — He claims to hold a previous court of inquisition in *his own dwelling house*, — tho' not authorized to do so, or even administer an oath to any person — I hope this will be severely noticed. Your Lordship is aware, no doubt, that a similar assumption by Empson and Dudley formed one of the articles of impeachment, for which they were adjudged to death.[10]

Your Lordship now has all the materials of this case — and, in your hands, and those of your public spirited friends, we leave it with confidence — we know, that our recent avowal of gratitude to you and them has whetted the hostility of the Irish Government, but we are prepared for all hazards, *& for every event*. I shall only add, that this prosecution is not the only symptom of this revived hostility — as will shortly appear.[11]

[Enclosure]

(Private)

Perhaps your Lordship would also cause the subject to be spoken to in the
  upper House by Lords Holland (to whom I write), Lansdowne, Erskine, Donoughmore —
  in the lower House by Messrs G. Ponsonby, Whitbread, Tierney, Sir
  A. Piggott, Sir S. Romilly, H. Parnell, W. Tighe.

[*Source*: Earl Grey Papers]

[1]Parliament was prorogued on 30 July (*Hansard* XXIII, 1288).

[2]In a communication dated 3 July Fitzpatrick had been required by the Crown Solicitor to appear at the Attorney General's house in Stephen's Green on or before 8 July to show cause why a criminal information should not be filed against him for publishing a seditious libel entitled *A Statement of the Penal Laws* — in two parts, Part II (letter from "A barrister" in *DEP* of 7 July 1812).

[3]Although the Prime Minister, Lord Liverpool, voted in the House of Lords against an enquiry into Catholic claims several members of the cabinet had voted for it, including Lord Castlereagh in the House of Commons (*Hansard* XXIII, 693).

[4]On 2 July (see *DEP* of 4 July 1812).

[5]After Tighe's warning (see No. 357) Scully must have realised that the Attorney General would base the prosecution on the Barry case, but at the time of this letter the charge against Fitzpatrick had not been particularised.

[6]See No. 310 n.2. On 8 February 1812, in the Court of Common Pleas, the defendant's counsel asked for further delay and it was reported in the *DEP* of 13 February that no trial at the bar was likely before November.

[7]On 7 February 1812 parliament had ordered to be printed the 12th in the series of reports of "the Commissioners appointed to enquire into the fees, gratuities, perquisites and emoluments . . . received in certain public offices in Ireland" (1812(33) V.191).

[8]Wellesley Pope was about to be replaced as Chief Secretary by Robert Peel. On Canning's motion of 22 June he spoke in favour of concessions to the Catholics. Because of his official situation, he explained, he had hitherto abstained from discussing the question, but he now regarded himself as having retired from it (*Hansard* XXIII, 670).

[9]Not found.

[10]King Henry VII's ministers, Sir Richard Empson and William Dudley, who were executed in 1510. In the brief report on their trial the only charge which seems to have any relevance to Scully's statement was one of usurping the jurisdiction of other courts (Howell, *State Trials* I, 283).

[11]On 4 July the Irish Catholic Board had passed resolutions as a result of which the Secretary was instructed to issue a circular regarding the Board's serious fears of a renewed religious persecution. Transmitting a copy of the resolutions in his despatch of 10 July to the Home Secretary (HO 100/167, f.298) the Lord Lieutenant suggested two possible reasons for their fears: (1) a call by one of the governors of County Sligo, dated 26 June, for the county's representatives in parliament to safeguard the existing constitutional security of the Protestant establishment, which the Board feared might be followed by similar proceedings in other counties; and (2) advertisements which had appeared in Sligo and Antrim for Orange meetings to be held on 12 July — the Lord Lieutenant observes that the Catholic resolutions were "well fitted to exasperate the resentments and alarms that unhappily too often revived with the anniversary of the battle of Aughrim."

364   *From Earl Grey*

Portman Square, 14 July 1812

[Draft]

Sir,

I had the honour of receiving your letter of the 5th inst. on Saturday [11th] evening on my return from the country, after an absence from London of a few days.

I have read with emotions of regret rather than surprise your account of the proceedings of the Irish government; as I certainly had not before entertained any very sanguine hope that the great work of national conciliation wd. be undertaken by the present Ministers in the spirit which can alone ensure its success.

In consequence of the desire so strongly expressed by you for another discussion in the House I should not have hesitated at another period of the session to bring that most important subject again under the consideration of Parlt. But so many of our friends here have left London (amongst others Mr Grattan, Mr Ponsonby & Lord Donoughmore) & there would be so little hope of procuring a good attendance in either House that I am persuaded no advantage would be derived from bringing forward this question under the present circumstances.

I took occasion however on a notice given yesterday by Lord Holland respecting two bills now depending in the House of Lords on the subject of *ex officio* informations (the further progress of which the necessity I am under of immediately returning to Northumberland, will prevent my attending) to draw the attention of the House & of the public to the recent proceedings of the Irish Attorney General on the information filed against the printer Fitzpatrick.[1] This I believe will have as much effect as anything I could do in the way of a more formal proceeding at the present period of the session, & I can only regret my inability to serve your cause more successfully.

I cannot conclude without expressing my obligation to you for the communication you have been so good as to make to me, & the gratification I have derived from the confidence you are pleased to repose in me.

I shall always be happy to hear from you when any occasion presents itself in which I may be useful in a cause which I have so sincerely at heart.

[*Source*: Earl Grey Papers]

[1]Lord Holland having announced postponement of the second reading on his two bills (one to prevent delays in filing and acting on informations *ex officio*, the other in regard to holding to bail under such informations), Earl Grey had referred to the Irish Attorney-General's prosecution of a printer, who had been summoned to attend him at his own house, and said that he had consulted several of his friends, who had all declared that such a thing was utterly unknown to them (*Hansard* XXIII, 995).

365   *From William Tighe to Merrion Square, Dublin*

London, 14 July 1812

My dear Sir,

I have received your letter[1] with much gratitude but I only write this day to say that I perceive the Government have published a statement of their own of the conversation in the house between me & Mr Pole on the subject of

Hall. I deprecated a discussion untill all the documents were before the house, but I replied to all Mr Pole's assertions as fully as the occasion required, & most of that reply is suppressed. And besides, some observations are published in *the Correspondent of the 11th inst.*[2] prejudging the question, & taking for granted unfairly that the question was brought on, when only papers were moved for — & vindicating the government. Some answer should be given to this. I had wished the question to come on the day first fixed — but on reading the papers with Mr Ponsonby it was suggested that as the principal blame lay with the judges, time should be given for a full consideration & in a fuller house. Sir John Newport had gone out of town, at that time, & also Mr M. Fitzgerald or I should have had their assistance, but no debating on that subject was expected on that day, for which reason Mr Ponsonby was not in the house — but Mr Pole has endeavoured by his intemperate speeches & his account of the debate to prejudge the question & to prejudice the public.[3]

[P.S.] I suppose I have to thank you for the late *Dublin Evening Posts* — they are highly interesting & material. I have not taken that paper since they chose to publish a malicious libel against me & my relations & then refused to publish the answer — or to do what they promised — & give a true account of the trial of Kilkenny[4] — & I have known them behave in the same infamous manner in other cases.

You will see that Lord Grey & Mr Sheridan were in possession of Saurin's notice[5] before your copies could reach them from me. I am very glad to hear of the civil action,[6] that being the only way of having the truth elicited.

[*Source*: Scully Papers]

[1]Probably with reference to his letters Nos. 357 and 358.

[2]In a leading article it announced that expresses had arrived in town the day before for the purpose of putting "the Treasury prints" in possession of all that Pole had said about Hall. It went on to say that as public opinion had been misled it had become peculiarly necessary to set it right and in words which implied that it accepted the fact of Hall's insanity it criticised Pole for letting the suspicion gain ground in the first place.

[3]In addition to the reasons given here for postponing a debate another arose when Tighe found that despite his request for all the papers to be laid before the House these did not include a respite order which he had not specifically asked for. In consequence he had to make another motion for this to be provided. This meant waiting until the next session of parliament and Pole said that he could not leave until then a reply to the "misrepresentations of a most flagitious nature" that had already gone abroad, including the insinuation that a free pardon had been given on the ground of the offender being an Orangeman (*Hansard* XXIII, 934).

[4]Neither the article nor a report on the trial has been found.

[5]Summoning Hugh Fitzpatrick to his house: Earl Grey received his copy direct from Scully (see No. 363 n.9).

[6]See No. 366 n.6.

366   *To Daniel O'Connell at Limerick*

Kilfeacle [Co.] Tipperary, 17 July 1812

My dear O'Connell,

The enclosed letter from William Tighe[1] shows how keenly he hunts the case of Hall the murderer. It is full of matter: his queries appear most justly pointed and we must support Tighe *totis viribus*. I know you need not be urged. I take it that your public exposure[2] of this case has pushed it upon the notice of Tighe and of Parliament, and most justly. Observe Tighe's concluding remarks[3] and consider with him whether this case does not open the door to ample inquiry concerning the state of criminal justice in Ireland. It is a *lever* by which the enormous mass of wrong may be raised to the notice and reprobation of mankind and a *point d'appuy* for our future statements. Try to sound Baron Smith[4] upon this subject. I am told his recommendation to mercy has been, in more instances than one, slighted and that he feels sore about it. This may put him in the right humour for disclosing the secrets of the prison house, and speaching against the Castle.

What would you think of writing to Tighe himself? I know he would be delighted to hear from you. Give him all the information you can for the present, and write in detail hereafter at your leisure. His address is No. 18 St James's Place, London.

I wish you would keep a copy of the enclosed letter for regulating your inquiries and send me the original enclosed (under cover to the *Bank, Tipperary*)[5] by any of the Tipperary attornies or clients, coming from Limerick assizes. I go to Clonmel on Tuesday and thence to Kilkenny to return here about the 2nd August and to Dublin about the 15th.

[P.S.] How do you like Saurin's appearance in the *Dublin Evening Post* of last Tuesday, the 14th?[6]   [*Source*: O'Connell Papers, MS.13647]

[1]No. 365.

[2]At the aggregate meeting of 18 June 1812 (*DEP*, 20 June 1812).

[3]i.e. in the House of Commons. Tighe had pointed out that in a case similar to Hall's the height of political animosity had been such that the jury would not find the prisoner guilty — a state of affairs that called for enquiry (*Hansard* XXIII, 934).

[4]Sir William Cusack Smith, 2nd Baronet, who after being Solicitor-General in 1800 had been appointed Baron of Exchequer in 1801.

[5]The bank of James Scully and Son.

[6]The paper reported that an act for defamation had been instituted by Fitzpatrick against the Attorney-General.

367   *From Lord Holland to Merrion Square, Dublin*

Hd. House [London] 20 July 1812

Dear Sir,

In consequence of your obliging letter[1] & in obedience to your commands I consulted with Ld Grey and others on the propriety of some parliamentary notice of the proceedings to which you had called our attention and which, as you observe, are strong indications of the prosecuting spirit of the Law advisers of your government though very equivocal proofs either of their learning in their profession or of their ability to carry their designs into Execution. The Session is so far advanced that all hopes of attendance on the part of opposition would be hopeless and this consideration even if there were no other objections to *making a motion* on the subject seemed to us to render such a measure quite unadvisable. A Division on any subject connected with the Catholicks in which the relative force of Ministers would be greater than on late occasions, would be construed by the publick as a real loss of strength & very materially diminish the effect produced by the late large divisions on the main question.[2] We have however contrived to draw the publick attention to Mr Saurin's proceedings[3] & to express our own opinions upon them. Ld Grey did so before he left town[4] & I did not fail on my motion on *Ex Officio* Informations to dwell on the folly of Mr Saurin's summons to Mr Fitzpatrick if meant as a mere offer of conversing on the subject with him & on the dangerous consequences of such a pretension to the liberty of the subject if by being submitted to, it were to become an usage & then be construed into a legal proceeding.[5] Eldon said nothing & Ellenborough[6] though he ridiculed the possibility of its doing harm, said not a word in defence of the practice. I had occasion to notice another proceeding of your Attorney General, as mentioned in a Dublin paper of last December, in the case of Mr Cox[7] & the only justification alledged for him was that the conduct described was so bad that it could not be true. This practice of filing informations is I understand new in Ireland but Mr Saurin seems disposed to claim the arrears which his predecessors have neglected. If you could procure me a list of the Informations filed *ex officio* for two or three years you would add to the many obligations you have conferred upon me, among which I do not reckon the least important, that publication which has entitled you to the thanks of your countrymen & the enmity & persecution of the Law faction you describe.[8]

Your enemies are busy here as well as in Ireland & I sincerely wish that there was some organised system for the purpose of counteracting the vulgar publications which are reviving the exploded horrors of bloody Q. Mary, the Pope & what not. Temperate exposures of the injustice of such imputations on Catholicks of this day, statements of the advantage to the state & the army in particular, in admitting Catholicks to Commissions & office fortified by the authorities of Burke, my uncle,[9] Ld Cornwallis & all English Viceroys in Ireland (Ld Westmoreland[10] excepted) are the topicks best calculated to soften & remove prejudices *here* & I am very well convinced that if urged with temper & disseminated with proper zeal & address they will be sufficient to counteract the designs of the wicked & the bigotry of the foolish which at this moment are more active than we could wish.

[*Source*: Scully Papers]

[1]In the Callanan Papers there is a much damaged draft dated 4 July, addressed to a lord. Its tenor is similar to that of No. 363.

[2]On Canning's motion of 22 June and Lord Wellesley's of 1 July (see No. 362 notes 2 and 3).

[3]Against Hugh Fitzpatrick (see No. 363).

[4]See No. 364.

[5]See *Hansard* XXIII, 1069. The Chief Secretary pointed out in reply that, no penalty having been attached, Fitzpatrick had been under no compulsion to attend at the Attorney General's house; and Fitzpatrick having replied that he had nothing to say the Attorney General had not seen him. He went on to inform the House that the ground for prosecution was the Barry case and read out part of the offending footnote in the *Penal Laws* (see No. 345 n.2).

[6]While attributing to the Attorney General the best of motives Lord Ellenborough, who was Lord Chief Justice, criticised his inviting Fitzpatrick to his house "as allowing room for those misconstructions which had already taken place on the subject" (ibid., 1087).

[7]Walter or Watty Cox, in prison for a libel called "The Painter Cut" in his *Irish Magazine*. What would he or the public think, asked the Chief Secretary, if Fitzpatrick were not prosecuted? (ibid., 1115).

[8]In paragraphs 5 and 6 of No. 363.

[9]Charles James Fox.

[10]The 10th Earl (1759–1841), Lord Lieutenant 1790–5.

368   *From Thaddeus R. Ryan,[1] Scarteen, Limerick,*
to Kilfeakle 27 July 1824

As Chairman of a Catholic meeting of the county and city of Limerick held on 24 July he transmits a resolution thanking the author of the *Penal Laws* for "his honest and feeling digest of our grievances" and conveys his personal regards "for the person who by his writings and exertions . . . has so signalized himself".

[*Source*: Scully Papers]

[1]1760–1843, of Scarteen, Knocklong, Co. Limerick.

369   *From James Lawlor,[1] Killarney, to Clonmel,*
                          4 August 1812

Transmits a resolution adopted by an aggregate meeting of the Catholics of Co. Kerry on 1 August, affirming that the thanks of the Catholics of Ireland are due to the author of the *Statement of the Penal Laws*, a work which "forcibly discloses the grievances and oppressions necessarily consequent on a code of intolerance".
                                                    [*Source*: Scully Papers]

[1]James Justin Lawlor of Killarney; died 27 May 1836.

370   *From Bishop Milner to Merrion Square, Dublin*

                                    Wolverhampton, 5 August 1812

Dear Sir,
     If suspicion were not the appendage of a character that I do not wish to be considered as possessing, I should suspect that I had unwittingly given you some offense or that my numerous enemies on this side of the water had misrepresented me to you. In fact you have not only left my letter[1] unanswered, & the rect. of my last pamphlet (an Unpublished Explanation with the Rt. Rev Dr Poynter,[2] of which you are one of the only three laymen in Ireland to whom I sent copies) unacknowledged, but also you have omitted to send me the Second Part of your celebrated work, in which I have a certain interest, having used all my influence with you to publish it, & having predicted the fame which it wd. acquire for you. But as I am not of a suspicious temper, & as my conscience tells me that I have done nothing to forfeit yr. friendship, I have no doubt but you will briefly explain the circumstances here stated.
     The only consequence I dread from this publication is that it may be detrimental to Mr Fitzpatrick, though I remember yr. telling me last autumn, that he gloried in the prospect of suffering in the cause of his religion & country. So you are fairly committed with our *Ministre de Culte*,[3] that would be. He was irritated at the freedom of yr. remarks to him last autumn;[4] but I hear he is quite outragious at what you have said of him in your Second Part.[5] I can readily believe this when I witnessed his transports at the publication of my *Instructions to the Caths.*[6] On that occasion he declared to me that he wd. have laid down 5,000 Guineas to have prevented the appearance of that work, & he has since complained of having spent £60,000 in the Cathc. cause. However it is now evident that he had his own ends to answer in all that he has spent in this cause, as he incessantly labours to prove the necessity of erecting a new Office to inspect & regulate the

interior concerns of the Caths., in order that he himself may be promoted to fill it: heretofore his ambition was to be appointed English Ambassador to the Court of Rome. However his conduct is excusable:[7] not so that of the base & traiterous Dr Charles O'Conor who has sold his principles, religious as well as political to a Protestant nobleman[8] for the honour of sitting at the bottom of his table & becoming the but of all his family & company.

I fail not to follow you in the Irish News papers through all yr. progresses, & I have just now been reading yr. speech at the Tipperary Meeting[9] & the high compts. paid you by Gen. Mathew.[10] The time will soon come when you will look down upon Mr Saurin, the Orange Hugenot.

But what after all is fame & wealth & dignity! As the cause in which you are engaged is in itself divine, so have God before your eyes, & by an act of pure intention offer up the course of yr. life & every act of it to the Great Master, every morning when you say: *Sanctificetur nomen tuum*. As you have lost your sage & holy monitor, Dr Lanigan,[11] you will not be displeased with my putting myself for a minute, in his place. I ought to preach a sermon of humility to Mrs Scully no less than to yr.self as she must be equally with you exposed to frequent temptations of vanity. Good Mrs Wheble joins with me in all that is kind & respectful to her as well as to yr.self.

P.S. I was once involved in difficulties similar to those of Mr Fitzpatrick, namely of impeaching the verdict of a jury, where an innocent man suffered death. What saved me was the consciousness of my prosecutors that I could prove my charge & that the defectiveness of the evidence wd. come out, if the affair came into court.[12] Can not you make yr. enemies sensible that the same will be the consequence of their prosecuting yr. printer?

Aug. 9. This letter has been detained some days in expectation of Dr Moylan's conveying it, but as His Ldp. is detained some time longer in England, Dr Milner commits it to the Post.   [*Source*: Scully Papers]

[1]No. 318 of 11 December 1811.

[2]Dated 25 March 1812, printed and circulated but not published. It went over all the old ground of his disagreement with the other Vicars Apostolic, repeated his once retracted assertion that Butler composed Dr Poynter's letters to the Irish Bishops and bracketed him with Dr O'Conor and the Blanchardists as a heretic (Ward, *Eve of Catholic Emancipation* I, p. 175).

[3]Sir John Coxe Hippisley.

[4]As Hippisley lived at Ston Easton near Bath Scully may have met him when he visited Bath in October 1811 (see Nos. 303).

[5]Not mentioned by name in the *Penal Laws* but referred to as "an Englishman, Clerk to the Neapolitan Embassy".

[6]See No. 278 n.12.

[7]Because he was not a Roman Catholic.

[8]The Marquis of Buckingham, to whom he was librarian at Stowe.

[9]On 23 July, attended also by Protestants (*DEP*, 30 July 1812). He adverted to the great progress made since 1805 and said the question now seemed to turn on a single

point: "the theoretical danger of setting us free". Every "arrangement" was impracticable — the consent of the Pope would be necessary, there would have to be many synods, meetings etc which would arouse controversy, years would be needed and anything might happen in the interval. A reference to the obstacle of an Elizabethan statute still in force suggests that he was drawing on his letter of April 1810 to Lord Donoughmore (No. 242).

[10]In an address concluding the meeting General Mathew had said: "Look at the publication of the Penal Laws, a work which shows you, that it is not only from a Fingall and a French, that Ireland is to look for support . . . when I mention the name of Counsellor Scully, I name a man allowed by his country as one of the most useful, the most active and able of the Irish community".

[11]Dr James Lanigan, Bishop of Ossory, who had died on 11 February 1812.

[12]At Winchester in 1788 Dr Milner attended on a ratcatcher before his execution. After making enquiries he wrote three letters to the local papers proving his innocence. His biographers says it was afterwards fully admitted (Husenbeth, *Life*, p. 16).

371   *From Hon. Francis A. Prittie to Kilfeacle, Co. Tipperary*

Killboy [Nenagh, Co. Tipperary] 8 August 1812

Dear Scully,

I received yours yesterday in Nenagh where I have been doing the needful, (registering Freeholders).[1] I enclose you Mr Hussey's[2] certificate of Registry.

I fear the attendance[3] from this side will be very small indeed, the instance, of this busy period of the Harvest furnishes many with excuses for not going & some say their attendance at the Catholick meeting during the Assizes has carried their good wishes.

If you could send me directed to Corville[4] a copy of the resolutions as quickly as possible, it might be of use.   [*Source*: Scully Papers]

[1]In preparation for the next elections.
[2]Unidentified.
[3]At an aggregate meeting of Catholics and Protestants due to be held at Clonmel on 17 August. This meeting appointed a committee to draw up a petition, of which Lord Llandaff, Viscount Lismore and George Lidwill were the most important Protestants, while Denys Scully, John Lalor and Andrew Ryan were among the Catholics. When the Protestants withdrew Scully's father took the chair at the ensuing Catholic meeting (*DEP*, 20 and 22 August 1812).
[4]Prittie's home, near Roscrea, Co. Tipperary.

372   *From Henry Bathurst, Bishop of Norwich to Merrion Square*

Morants Hotel,[1] Dublin, 24 August 1812

Dear Sir,

Accept my grateful acknowledgments for your very kind Letter: the favourable opinion which you are so good as to entertain of me, is sufficient to excite an emotion of vanity, even in the breast of an aged bishop; but when I recollect the respectable source from which this approbation flows, it gratifies a far nobler passion; it gratifies that love of honest fame, which is one of the purest motives of action, which can influence the conduct of so imperfect a being as man.

Should any thing bring you to England, I shall be happy to have an opportunity of assuring you, in person, that I am, with great truth,

Yours etc

Henry Norwich [*Source*: Scully Papers]

[1]*Recte* Moran's Hotel. The Bishop, well known as a supporter of the Catholic claims since his speech in the House of Lords in May 1808, had been the guest of honour at a dinner organised by the Catholic Board on 20 August. There is a guest list in DDA 54/2, I, (1).

373   *From Bishop John Milner to Dennis Scully*
            at Mrs Eyre's, Ferme, Sheffield

Oscot nr. Birm. 11 September 1812

My Dear Sir,

At the time when your letter[1] arrived at Wolverhampton I was engaged in an expedition into the North of England by my friend Dr Moylan, the cheif [*sic*] object of which was to unite my brethren the VVA assembled at Durham[2] to concur with the Irish Prelates & myself in *publicly* declaring 1st that "we will not concur in any changes in the established mode of appointing Cc. B.ps., & VVA without the authority of the Holy See. 2d that we will not grant spiritual powers to any Priest who refuses to acknowledge that the Pope, Pius 7, is not a heretic or schismc., nor the author or abettor of heresy or schism".[3] We failed in this pacific negociation, as I foretold we should; not because my brethren are heterodox, but because (from want of experience) they have permitted themselves to be overreached & hampered in engagements by two different parties who are not so orthodox & good as themselves. Upon my return home a week ago, I found two intimate friends from Winchester waiting for my arrival the attendance upon whom at home & in different excursions into the country has not left me time to read & much less to answer the letters which have been addressed to me during the last six weeks.

I am happy to learn that your business & Mrs Scully's health permit you to visit England this season & I am extremely anxious to have the pleasure, as, I know, Mrs Wheble is also, of seeing you both before your return to Ireland. I shall think myself honoured, no less than I shall be gratified in case you can put up with the humble accommodations of my house at Wolverhampton; in which case the gentlemen of this college depend on the honour of a visit from you & Mrs S.

It is true that I have a number of missionary journeys to make, &, among them, a pretty long one into Lincolnshire: nevertheless, when I know your plan, I will endeavour, as far as possible, to make mine tally with it. In case you can be in Staffordshire at the end of the month, as I understand you to intimate you can, I will take care not to go far from home before that time. Shd. it be impracticable for you to come this way at all, when I learn your route, I will see if it be not practicable for me to catch you somewhere in the course of it. In my way to Durham I spent three days at York, where I saw our common friend, who joined with me in hailing your rising fame & in wishing to enjoy your company; but Charles[4] is not so comfortably situated as he wishes to be for the sake of his friends, being in lodgings, while his house in the country is under repairs & augmentation.

I have not leisure nor space in this paper for politics of any kind foreign or domestic: besides I hope to discuss them with greater advantage when I have the pleasure of meeting you. I beg my kind compts. to Mrs S., also to Mrs Eyre, Mr & Mrs Vincent Eyre, & Miss Juliana. I ought to add Mr Wm. Eyre,[5] who left Ushaw College the very day I enquired after him there, in order to form an acquaintance with him & to present him with his aunts regard.

P.S. I expect to return to WHampton tonight.   [*Source*: Scully Papers]

[1]Of 23 August (not extant) in reply to No. 370.
[2]Dr Francis Moylan, Bishop of Cork, and his coadjutor, Dr MacCarthy, had taken advantage of a visit to England to try and restore peace between the English Vicars Apostolic and the Irish Bishops. With Dr Milner they attended three conferences at Durham from 21 to 23 August. The two resolutions mentioned by Dr Milner were rejected by the other Vicars Apostolic who, although they agreed with their substance, felt that by signing them they would seem to assent to the charges brought against them (Ward, *Eve of Catholic Emancipation* II, pp. 9–17).
[3]For the Blanchardist schism see No. 296 n.12.
[4]Scully's brother-in-law, Charles Eyre.
[5]William Eyre (1792–1855), Scully's youngest brother-in-law; a nephew of Mrs Wheble.

374   *From Edward O'Callaghan to Merrion Square, Dublin*

                              Culloville, Carrickmacross, 12 September 1812
Dear Sir,

The Catholics of this county (Armagh) have fixed to meet on the 29th inst. The enclosed resolutions, with the exception of the 5th[1] are merely an echo of those adopted in other parts of Ireland & I suppose would meet no opposition, but I find some here averse to any direct allusion to an attempt now making (under pretence of petitioning parliament in the event of any relaxation of the penal code to provide safeguards for the present church establishment) to rouse the orange feeling & revive the spirit of persecution which has already been productive of such dreadful effects in this county, a measure which comes forward under the auspices of the Primate & Dr Duigenan who are using every exertion to procure signatures.[2]

The petition is very cautiously worded[3] & the arguments against noticing the proceeding are perhaps natural enough to men whose spirit has been depressed by the system acted on here for the last twenty years & the total absence of confidence in the protection of the laws administered as they are with very few exceptions by the persecutors themselves; there may be something in the apprehension of inciting the *lower orders* of orangemen to acts of violence against their neighbours particularly as even *these* are watchful of political movements, forming themselves into small clubs & taking the newspapers, but for my own part I do not think that anything of the kind is to be dreaded at present, even the affair of the 12th July last[4] which was noticed in the public prints to near observers shewed symptoms of declining strength in the party & the subsequent disbandment of the Armagh Yeomanry consisting of a Corps of 500 men (whose fine appearance & state of discipline would have done credit to a better cause) for refusing obedience to one of their officers merely because he had signed the petition in our favour has tended very much to dishearten them.[5]

However I am unwilling to press this measure simply on my own opinion of its expediency, & would gladly have your advice upon the subject; if you think a resolution of the nature proposed would be productive of any advantage to the cause & will have the kindness to prepare & send me such I think my brother[6] who resides here would have influence to procure it to be adopted. If on the other hand you esteem the measure immaterial in itself or of doubtful efficacy I shall feel obliged by an intimation of your opinion.[7]

I hope the motive of this intrusion will excuse the liberty I take.

[*Source*: Scully Papers]

[1]The first four resolutions are omitted. The 5th and last reads: "that our warmest thanks are due to our liberal fellow countrymen of all religions who recently petitioned parliament on our behalf, & that the puny efforts now making by an ascendancy junta in this country to perpetuate the disabilities under which we labour in opposition to the declared voice of the nation & the sense of parliament is such an instance of inveterate prejudice & impotent malignity as eludes indignation by its folly & leaves upon our minds but a mixed impression of scorn & pity for the measure & the men".
[2]Dr Patrick Duigenan represented the city of Armagh in parliament.
[3]He is thinking of the statement in parentheses in the first paragraph of this letter.
[4]When a party of Orangemen provoked the Catholics by decorating an ancient

cross with a canvas of King William, coloured in orange and purple (*DEP*, 18 July 1812).

[5]The incident occurred on 4 June 1812. The corps was disbanded in August by order of the Lord Lieutenant (*FJ*, 21 August 1812, taken from the *Belfast Chronicle*).

[6]Probably Hugh O'Callaghan, of Culloville, Carrickmacross.

[7]Scully did not mark this letter as having been answered and as Edward O'Callaghan normally lived in Dublin they may have settled the matter between them there. No record has however been found of a meeting of the Armagh Catholics on 29 September: perhaps because news of the elections left no space in the press or it was postponed on account of the elections, news of a probable dissolution having reached Dublin before it was due (*FJ*, 28 September 1812).

375   *From Bishop John Milner to Dennis Scully at*
                        Mrs Eyre's, Ferme, Sheffield

W[olver]h[ampton] 28 September [1812]

Dr Sir,

I have been waiting with the utmost impatience for the last fortnight to hear from you, in order to fix certain stations of a Mission which I have promised to make this autumn in Lincolnshire etc. Towards the end of last month a letter arrived here from you, while I was absent from home, saying that you would be [in] England about 1st inst. giving me hopes that you wd. honour my humble dwelling & fare with yr. & Mrs S.'s company & telling me to address you at the Farm. Accordingly I wrote a letter to you there from Oscot Friday was a fortnight[1] requesting a line in answer respecting yr. movements, in order to regulate my own. Not receiving any answer & not hearing by any chance that you are in England I begin to doubt whether yr. voyage took place. I shall conclude that some accident prevented it, shd. I not hear from you by the 1st Of Octr. Shd. the contrary be the case, & yr. stay in England shd. be protracted, as my Mission need not of necessity be of longer continuance than a fortnight, I might perhaps have the pleasure of seeing you at W.H. after my return from the Mission. Shd. you decide that it is impossible for you to come thus far South, & you shd. stop a day at Buxton or anywhere within 40 miles distance from W.H. I wd. still endeavour to see. But all is conjecture & speculation without my hearing from you. Shd. I remain deprived of that satisfaction on the first of next month, I shall think it necessary to write letters fixing my first station on Sunday 11th, & my second on Sunday 18th. Mrs Wheble joins me in kind compts. to Mrs S., yrself, Mrs Eyre, Mr & Mrs Vint. etc. etc.

P.S. Clinches book[2] wd. do honour to a sound Canonist in a learned age, but it is a prodigy coming from an English lawyer in a superficial age.

[*Source*: Scully Papers]

[1]Of 11 September (see No. 373).

[2]J. B. Clinch had published *Letters of Church Government* (Dublin, 1812), a work of 722 pages in refutation of Dr Charles O'Conor's interpretation of church history, beginning with the Council of Nicea. Clinch was an Irishman and a member of the Irish bar: Dr Milner may have meant that he was writing in English rather than Latin.

376   *From Bishop John Milner to Denys Scully to the care of*
              Mr James Ridgeway, Bookseller, Piccadilly, London

WHampton, 3 October 1812

My dear Sir,

I have been duly honoured with your letters from York[1] & Sheffield.[2] In consequence of the former I fixed the first station of my intended progress for Sunday the 18th inst. which will leave me at leisure to enjoy yr. company till Saturday the 17th.

Yr. second letter informs me that, you expect to be here on or before Monday the 12th. When you have absolutely fixed on the day of your leaving London & the coach by which you mean to travel I shall be glad to be informed of the particulars, as I wish to meet you at Birmm. & to convey you in my humble gig to Oscot & after spending a day there to bring you on to Wolverhampton, if this plan is agreeable to you. Oscot is six post miles to the N.N. East of Birm. & twelve miles from this town. Dr Potts[3] the celebrated classical master of it wishes much for the pleasure of being acquainted with you, & I wish to shew you my little [?] Seminary. If you do not like the gig, I will be at Oscot or at W Hampton to receive you at any time you may choose.

Last Sunday Mahon[4] dined with me, & I thought him deserving of the character which Mr Southworth[5] gives him, that of a good & well behaved youth. I am sorry, however, to learn that he has not yet been put to the study either of Latin or French. Mr Southworth says that this is not done unless the friends of the children desire it. When you come you will look into this matter.

As you will doubtless hear among the Caths. of London, concerning the late meeting of Dr Moylan & three of the Vicars Apostc. at Durham, & infallibly with an accompaniment of falsehoods as I happened to be one of them, I think it right to tell you in short, that Dr Moylan & myself proposed the following plan of pacification:— a general oblivion of all past differences, together with a joint & public Resolution not to consent to any changes without the Pope's authority, & not to allow faculties to any Priest who does or shall refuse to acquit the Pope of the charge of heresy, schism or of being the author or abettor of heresy or schism, or to declare himself in communion with those whom the Pope acknowledges to be in his Communion. These terms were rejected by my Brethren, who declared they wd. sign nothing except this Article: "Having met together we have found that we are all of one faith & Communion."[6] Dr Poynter [went] so far as to require the Irish Prelates & myself to make an *amande honorable* to him.[7]

So Lord Liverpool & Ld Castlereagh have given you the slip by dissolving the House of Commons that was pledged to you.[8] What will be the effect of all this in Ireland? Which is the wiser our present or our late Regent? But these matters I hope we shall have time to talk over by word of mouth, & therefore request you will prolong yr. stay in these parts as long as possible.

Presuming that you are well acquainted with Mr Ridgeway[9] to whose care this letter will be consigned, I shd. be obliged to you to sound him how his engagements & dispositions respecting our Cathc. affairs, in the way of his business, [are] The fact is, Messrs Keating & Co. are overawed by our leading Caths. & dare not publish for me as they used to do, & therefore I must look out for some independant publisher. Is Mr Ridgeway such a one? I mean wd. he be such a one in my regard? Mrs Wheble joins me in Compts. to you.   [*Source*: Scully Papers]

[1]Where Charles Eyre lived (see No. 373 n.4).
[2]Where he left his wife and two sons at The Farm, Sheffield Park.
[3]Thomas Potts, President of the Oscott seminary.
[4]John Mahon, second son of Scully's widowed sister, Anne; at Stonyhurst from October 1812 to July 1813.
[5]Revd Thomas Southworth, headmaster of Sedgley Park school.
[6]See No. 373.
[7]As part of the reconciliation attempted at Durham Dr Milner had made a carefully phrased apology, confined to regretting offensive terms and ending: "Whereas my brother [Dr Poynter] and other brethren have treated me in my view of things very disrespectfully . . . I hereby acquit them of all obligation of retracting these assertions or insinuations" (Ward, *Eve of Catholic Emancipation* II, p. 14).
[8]Pledged by Canning's motion of 22 June to go into the Catholic question during the then expected recess (see No. 359 n.2). As the existing parliament had nineteen months to run others besides Dr Milner suspected that opponents of the measure took this means of defeating it (*Annual Register*, 1812, p. 135).
[9]James Ridgway, of Piccadilly, bookseller.

377   *From William Tighe to Fladong's Hotel, Oxford Street,*
London

Mt. Ephraim, Tunbridge Wells, 6 October 1812
Dear Sir,
I have no thoughts of leaving this place immediately & should be very happy to see you, if you think it worth your while to take the trouble of the journey before your return to Ireland.   [*Source*: Scully Papers]

378   *From Charles Butler to Fladong's Hotel [London]*

6 October 1812

Dear Sir,
    The Enclosed will speak for itself. I will attend you, whenever you please.

[Enclosure]
From John [?] Dagford to Charles Butler
Kensington Palace, Tuesday 6 October

Sir,
    His Royal Highness the Duke of Sussex who is so much indisposed with rheumatism as to be unable to write himself, has desired me to acquaint you, that he will be very happy to see you with Mr Scully between 12 & 1 o'clock, either tomorrow, Wednesday, or Thursday morning as may best suit you.

[*Source*: Scully Papers]

379   *From Charles Butler*

Lincolns Inn, 10 October 1812

Dear Sir,
    As soon as I received your Letter I wrote to the Duke of Sussex, informing him that on account of your being obliged to go out of Town, we could not wait on him at the time he mentioned, but that with his Royal Highness's leave we would wait on him this day. I have heard nothing from him, and I think without hearing from him, it would be most adviseable not to go.
    I shall see Lord Sidmouth this morning, and if any thing particular occurs I will let you know.[1]   [*Source*: Scully Papers]

[1]Butler's Letter Book in the British Library (Add.MSS.25, 128) shows that Lord Sidmouth sent for him in response to a letter that Butler had written to him on 3 October about an Irish soldier who had been shot at in Bristol without any reward having been offered for the discovery of the perpetrator. Lord Sidmouth observed that it was not the custom in such cases to offer a public reward and mentioned two cases of Protestant sentries having been shot at without a reward being offered.

380   *To his wife Catherine at Mrs Eyre's, Ferme, Sheffield*

London, Sunday 11 October [1812] Noon, Just leaving town

My dearest Catherine,
    I wrote to you on Monday last — dined that day with Mr C. Butler — we had only Miss Cormack,[1] Mr Stoner senior,[2] & Mr Blake.[3] The Ladies had just gone to Brighton a few days before, where they have got a House at 8

Guin's per week. Mr Stoner, the son in law,[4] is in declining health. We had a pleasant Evening, but mostly of politics. Miss Cormack said repeatedly (on the part of Mrs B. & Mrs Stoner) how happy they would be to see you in town, & be much acquainted with you. I was not able to dine on Tuesday at Lord Holland's, but postponed it to Friday,[5] on account of City Business. Wednesday I went to Tunbridge Wells, which I reached that night at Eleven. Thursday I breakfasted & dined with Mr Tighe. They are a pleasing family — Mrs T. is a lively & beautiful woman, about 36 years old — was a Miss Gahan[6] of the County Tipperary & a great fortune. She has one daughter about 15 years old; who sat at table, & resembles her mother. The 2 sons are at School. My business with him is nearly settled. Friday I returned to town — was engaged in the City till 4 — then went to dine at Ld Holland's beyond Kensington. We had only 6 in company[7] — but every thing very superb — dined on silver — You have heard Lady Holland's history — but she has no beauty after all — tho' very clever & agreeable. The House is a noble one — and they use the Library as a sitting room — it is one of the largest & most splendid private Libraries I have seen. The party was very agreeable — and she was particularly affable — enquired much after you — and offered (if you pleased) to make you acquainted with the young Marchioness of Lansdowne[8] & with Lady Grey[9] when you come to town — but she makes it a point to become acquainted with you at any rate one day. There were 8 Servants attending, in 3 different Liveries — 2 little Pages in bright purple & silver stood behind her Chair, to whom she always gave orders in French, which she speaks well. She is very large & corpulent, & has a voice like Mrs Jordan's [10] — and is certainly a very remarkable woman in her appearance & talents, tho' far from being so captivating to men as one would suppose from the great noise her story made, whilst she was Lady Webster.[11] Their Cookery was all French, & excellent *maigre*.[12] I wished you to be there. You might understand it for me. Saturday I dined with Lady Mount Cashell, who is just returned from Paris, in good health & spirits. She has lately seen the Pope,[13] the Bonaparte family[14] etc. etc., and is exceedingly entertaining, but it is all too long & too various to repeat in a Letter. You shall see her in Dublin.

Mr Stoner Sen'r of Oxfordshire[15] lodges at this Hotel. He seems a respectable man & was kind enough to come up to me, and say that we are connected together, as he is a cousin of Mrs V. Eyre thro' the Biddulphs[16] and I have the honour to be married to you — so we have become much acquainted. He is cousin to C. Butler's son in law. I have also made acquaintance with a Mr Mich'l Jones (lodging here) who seems to know every Catholic in England, male & female, old & young. I understand he is related somehow to the D. of Norfolk, has some stewardship under him, and is a widower.[17] I thought he was rather *pumping* me to know what fortunes your sisters[18] have — but I drew off, and only said they were a vast deal beyond the common opinion. Mrs Bostock was much pleased with the extracts I gave her from the Eyre Pedigree, and has copied them out.[19]

I forgot to say, that Chas. Butler on Wednesday last sent me a Letter he had from the Duke of Sussex[20] (which I keep for you) desiring to have me introduced personally to him at Kensington palace on Wednesday or Thursday last. As I do not like the Princes, and dread the name of running after any of those titled folks, I made answer, that it was for that time wholly out of my power, as I was going upon important private business to Tunbridge Wells, but that I should be happy in the Honour at some future time, when I should again visit London.

I have heard here, that Mr Withy[21] (whom we saw at Harrowgate) has not the good fortune to be reckoned amonst the most reputable or upright of the London attornies.

Thus far, I have given you some Chitchat but it has been a most busy week with me — and I write so very fast that I fear you cannot read all this.

No further news from Dublin. I shall keep this open till I get to Birmingham.

Give my love to all friends at the Ferme, and believe me, my dearest Catherine, always very sincerely your attached and affectionate husband — D. Scully

[P.S.] *Monday noon.* Just arrived at Birmingham, and on getting out of the Coach found Dr Milner waiting for me. He says that your aunt[22] is very well. I am now going with him to dine & sleep at Oscot, 6 miles off — tomorrow I go on to Wolverhampton — and expect to sail from Holyhead on Thursday evening. On my landing I shall write to you by the first post. Adieu my dearest Catherine — D.S. You will mention particularly to me, in what health etc. you and the boys[23] continue to be.   [*Source*: Scully Papers]

[1]Unidentified.

[2]Thomas Stonor (1766–1831) of Stonor Park, married to Catherine Blundell.

[3]Probably A. R. Blake, who called on Scully in Dublin (see No. 282).

[4]Captain Charles Stonor, a cousin of Thomas Stonor.

[5]A letter from Lord Donoughmore dated "Thursday night" and addressed to Fladong's Hotel suggests that the invitation was sent through him: another engagement prevented him from attending.

[6]Marianne, daughter of Daniel Gahan, of Coolquill, Co. Tipperary.

[7]The Holland House dinner book (Add.MSS.51, 923) shows that the three other guests were Mr and Mrs Smith and Miss Vernon. The last would have been Elizabeth Vernon (d. 1830), who lived at Little Holland House and was a daughter of Richard Vernon, "father of the turf", who was the second husband of the widow of Lord Holland's maternal uncle, the Earl of Upper Ossory. Mrs Smith was probably her sister Caroline Maria Vernon (1762–1833), who married in 1797 Robert Percy (Bobus) Smith, an elder brother of Sydney Smith — he had returned from India in 1810.

[8]Louisa Emma, 5th daughter of the 2nd Earl of Ilchester by his first wife Mary Theresa, a daughter of Standish O'Grady.

[9]Mary Elizabeth Ponsonby, a daughter of William Brabazon, 1st Baron Ponsonby, and niece of George Ponsonby.

[10]The actress, Dorothea Jordan (in *DNB*).

[11]Her first husband, from whom she was divorced, was Sir Geoffrey Webster. She may not have been looking at her best, having recently been ill after giving birth to a still-born daughter in the summer (Sydney Smith, *Letters*, No. 224).

[12]The day of the dinner being Friday.

[13]Pius VII had been in confinement at Fontainebleau since 19 June, after having been removed from Savona on 9 June (Schmidlin: Papstgeschichte). She had known him in Rome (McAleer, *Sensitive Plant*, p. 101).

[14]When she and her husband were in Paris in 1802 they dined with Napoleon himself: her biographer says nothing about her knowing other Bonapartes.

[15]The Thomas Stonor mentioned above.

[16]His grandmother, Mary Biddulph, had a sister, Anne, who married Anthony Wright of Wealside, Essex. Their daughter, Mary Wright, married Vincent Eyre, Scully's brother-in-law.

[17] Michael Jones was the second son of Michael Jones of Caton, near Lancaster; he died c. 1851. He was a collector not only of ancient manuscripts but also of pedigrees of English Catholic families. There is no record at Arundel Castle of a stewardship but he was connected with the Dukes of Norfolk in that his family would inherit the ancient barony of Scrope on the death without issue of the 11th Duke — Gillow gives the details in his *Biographical Dictionary*.

[18]Mary and Julia Eyre.

[19]Perhaps because it showed the Eyre connexion with the Bostocks and the Huddlestons (see No. 180 n.8).

[20]No. 378.

[21]Robert Withy, of 18 Buckingham Street, Strand.

[22]Mrs Wheble.

[23]James, aged three, and Vincent, aged two.

381   *From Bishop Milner to Merrion Square, Dublin*

WHampton, 12 November 1812

Dr Sir,

Being now returned from my Lincolnshire Visitation, & presuming that you also are returned home from yr. Tipperary triumphs[1] I acquit myself of the agreeable task you imposed upon me of writing to you about the present time. I learn from Mr O'Connel's speech[2] that the elections have been generally favourable to the Cathc. interest in Ireland, but the reverse appears to be the case in England: but what can the few independent men in Pt. do, if they were as numerous as they possibly can be against the overwhelming majority of those who are & who must be dependent? The *Dutch paracide*,[3] as I think you once called him, instead of enfranchising the Constitution has actually enslaved it; & we have now a supreme governor, whose base & selfish habits will strain corruption to its utmost extent for his own narrow minded & selfish purposes. I often think of yr. prophecy uttered 14 months ago[4] that in the course of three months from that time, the boasted Prince wd. be the most unpopular man living, in Ireland.

I have mentioned yr. two proposals to my brethren in Ireland, & they will confer with you on those subjects.[5] They alledge that they never refused to sign petitions, & they say that they never promoted a soldier's life as the best way to heaven; but that poverty, drunkenness etc., always has & always will drive many into it.

In case you ever read Theology & Canon Law, I hope you will cast an eye over Bernd. Clinch's Answer to O'Conor:[6] it will convince you that of all literary impostors this sanctimonious Doctor is the most impudent. I am satisfied from many circumstances that his collation of MSS. is a mere pretext for his mission to Ireland, & that the real object of it is to divide the Catholics.

To be brief I am confirmed in my original opinion that nothing short of some great national calamity, such as our expulsion from the Peninsula will bring about the Emancipation & that thus it will come, suddenly indeed, but still a day too late.[7]

It is time for you now to determine whether we shall have the pleasure of seeing you & Mrs Scully & yr. children. I understood you that the continuance of yr. family in England was not to extend beyond the present month. Shd. you afford us that pleasure my poor accommodations will be much at yr. service: we have two beds to spare, such as they are, but we have plenty of beef & mutton. I go from home tomorrow into Worcestershire; but with God's blessing I shall be home again in ten or twelve days. I can not conclude without again congratulating with you on your honours at all the principal Cathc. Meetings: I fancy myself also to participate in those honours as I hold myself instrumental in engaging you to write & afterwards to publish yr. immortal work. Mrs Wheble joins me in all that is kind.

[*Source*: Scully Papers]

[1]In the elections (see No. 384).

[2]At a meeting of Dublin Catholics on 5 November O'Connell reviewed the results by constituencies and claimed that if there were a Protestant parliament in Ireland there would be emancipation (*FJ*, 6 November 1812).

[3]No record has been found of Scully's calling William of Orange a parricide. In 1803 he called him a "Dutch invader" (see No. 56 n.2).

[4]In late September 1811 when Scully met Dr Milner with the Eyres (see No. 302).

[5]In a letter of 1 November to Dr Troy, Dr Milner had written: "Mr Scully, whose merit towards the clergy and church in fairly stating their grievances and in abstaining from profane sallies which most lawyers indulge in, is very great, requested me during his late visit here to use my influence with the Prelates to . . . aid the cause of Emancipation two ways: one by lending their names to the intended petitions for this

purpose; the other the discouragement of the enlistment of soldiers, through the means of their respective clergy. I told him that I thought they would not refuse to concur in the former measure, but that I could answer nothing about the second" (DDA, Green File 5, 29/12, 49).

[6]Referred to in the postscript to No. 375. Clinch's general contention was that "the Historical Addresses of Columbanus have no drift, no meaning unless ancillary to a conspiracy against the Irish Catholics".

[7]Possibly for Scully and his contemporaries to benefit from it (see No. 388 n.4).

382   *To his wife Catherine at Mrs Eyre's, Ferme, Sheffield*

Merrion Square [Dublin] Friday, 13 November 1812

My dearest Catherine,

Upon my return here last night, I received your affectionate Letter of 4th Inst. and am happy to find that you and all friends with you were well. By this time you have had the two last Letters I wrote you from Clonmell[1] — one franked by Thos. Bernard[2] — the second by George Ponsonby Senr.[3] The Election was spun out to a far greater length than I had expected.[4] The accounts of it in the *Dublin Evening Post* were all very correct and amusing. I rode over with Peter[5] to Kilfeacle to dinner on Sunday last — rode back alone on Monday morning — returned to Kilfeacle on Tuesday night — left Kilfeacle for Cashell on Wednesday afternoon after Dinner in my Father's covered Gig (the rain pouring heavily) stepped into the Mail Coach at Cashell about midnight, and was conveyed safely here last night — after an absence of 25 days[6] — and, fortunately, without broken bones, or a shot, or a cough, or any other maladventure, for which I may probably thank the prayers of so pious a wife as I am blessed with. Little Henry is getting his teeth still — his mouth continues running — and he has at times a dry cough, which they say is owing to the teeth coming. He looks fat and strong, but pale coloured: he is quiet & goodhumoured, & any little matter will make him laugh. His mouth is becoming large, like James's — his nose is rather small and stumpy — his skin very white, soft, & smooth — eyes large, black & intelligent. I cannot think as yet whom he resembles — but he has some general look like his brother James. I did not see many of our County of Tipperary friends at Kilfeacle. James & Mun attended at the Election. So did Jerry & James Mahon[7] for 3 or 4 days. Mun has got much credit by his intrepidity & coolness throughout his Duel.[8] My father seems in good health — my mother visibly broken, & declined in hearing & memory. My father told me, that Mrs James is going fast — & cannot outlive a year[9] — Mrs Mun & Jer are both well, but I saw none of these Ladies — Mrs Sadleir[10] has had a son, Clement. Mrs Keating[11] a daughter, Lucinda.

Jerry's Lease of Mountwilliam has just expired, by the fall of the surviving life in the old Lease. He is now treating for renewing the Lease, or purchasing it up.

The Timber & Bark, sold at Mantlehill[12] during my absence since August, produced about £200. My Election Fee was very genteel. I expected but £400 from my two honourable Clients — but, as the contest was unreasonably tedious, and the labour arduous beyond precedent, Lord Lismore proposed to Lord Llandaff & Lord Dunally (who were to pay all expenses for the 2 Candidates, their brothers)[13] that they should advance my compensation in proportion — to which they acceded in the promptest and handsomest manner — and accordingly, when I was leaving [?for] Town, they both addressed me with much compliment, expressions of gratitude, & engagement to send me in future all their professional business — added, that what they were going to offer me, was far below the real value they attached to my Services — and they then handed me *five hundred Guineas* in five Bank of Ireland notes.[14] This was very pleasing — and, in addition, I received about forty Guineas more, from Attornies, in odd fees upon Opinions etc. whilst in Clonmell. So, you see I come home, after making a tolerable harvest. Peter rides my bay horse up to town — as I want some riding & country air after all my fatigues at Clonmell.

I now take up your Letter, to see what may require my answers. In the first place, my passage to Dublin was not unpleasant. We landed at Bray only because we were becalmed there, & would not wait for the turn of the tide (6 hours) to bring us down into the Bay. Besides it was breakfast hour — we were hungry — & we knew there were excellent Chaises & Hotel there.

Next, we have had no snow in this Country — but much rain. Bread & potatoes are still very dear. Tell Vincent[15] that I am much indebted to him for the use of his Manuscript Books, but shall not detain them from him a day longer than he pleases to let me have them.

I do not know what to think of John's[16] project of studying the Law; he would do well to form an acquaintance with Mr Thelwall[17] of Bloomsbury or some other eminent teacher of public speaking, read and declaim often before him, pay him well for his advice & opinion and be governed very much by his judgment upon his probable success in Elocution. If John is qualified to become a good distinct impressive public speaker, his speculation may prove a very prudent one. If not, it is time & money thrown away. But, of this, my degree of acquaintance with him has not authorized [me] to form any kind of opinion.

If Julia will not accompany you over here, will you invite Mary[18] — and I hope she will have the courage to venture. I should like to have both, or at least one.

You ask, what they say at Kilfeacle of your staying in England. I do not know: but I hear nothing — and I have said, that I expect you early in

December. However, do not suppose that I would ask you to take the journey. I shall not attempt to influence you either way — and so you will do what will most please yourself. Certainly, if you stay away the whole time until May next the time will appear very long — but this we knew already; and, if it will add to your happiness, you have my full consent to do so. You allude somewhat to the state you suppose yourself to be in — and, perhaps this state may be such, as at all events to prevent your undertaking any long journey. Will you explain this to me more fully — and let me know in what month you might expect to be confined, as far as you can guess — for I thought you reckoned upon May next.

I take every care you can wish about the child,[19] socks, dresses, mending, clothes etc. etc.

Do you remember my wishing to have a copy made out of the large sheet of your family Pedigree. The Book is in Thomas's room. It is the first large page in it — containing a handsome Map of all the different Branches from the beginning. If your mother or Thomas,[20] can hire Barberry[21] or some neat writer to copy or paint it out for me handsomely, I shall cheerfully pay the expence — but first make the bargain at a fixed price, and to have it an *exact* Copy. Do not omit this little job for me.

Mr Yeomans[22] of Sheffield, the scissars maker, was again one of my fellow passengers in the Packet this time. I am trying to make him out now — or some other Sheffield man who might take you over some little parcel. If you should hear of any such being now in Dublin, let me know his Address here, and I shall make him out.

I find Dublin pretty full now — the Lawyers & Country visitors all come to town — & the Streets tolerably gay. They talk of expelling John Lalor & Andrew Ryan etc. etc. from the Catholic Board for having voted for Government Candidates at the recent Elections. A motion to that effect is to be made today, but I doubt whether it will pass. Certainly, they have fallen into heavy public odium and disgrace all over Ireland.[23]

I find no House in the Square on sale, except Sir Jonah Barrington's.[24] The House is daily growing worse — the title is not a safe one — and £3400 has been refused for it. However, I shall keep a good look out for any on Sale. There is a very large one on Sale, No. 12 Upper Merrion Street. It is exactly facing *Waller's*,[25] and 2 doors higher up than Prendergasts,[26] which you may remember on Sale here. I was in to view it this morning. It is certainly spacious — has 2 staircases — 3 rooms upon each floor — and a large grass garden in the rear, with abundant room in Coach house, Stables etc. The House was built and inhabited by the Earl of Mayo[27] — who sold it 10 years ago to Mr Davis,[28] the attorney, brother to Colonel Davis of Harrowgate. Davis is now insolvent — and the House on Sale. It is built about 36 years — has been much neglected in Davis's time — wants new painting and papering all over — and would require about £300 (besides other furniture) to put it in neat order — but is certainly a grand lofty House with fine spacious Hall etc. The Rent is £140. The fine is £3000. The Taxes about £80. Let me know your inclination — and it shall wholly govern me in the purchase, or the refusal of it.

I have had letters from Lord & Lady Mount Cashell — and believe that they will soon be able to execute the Articles of Separation, which both so much desire. He is to allow her £800 yearly for separate maintenance — and the only difference now remaining is, whether he shall clear off her Debts (necessarily contracted in France) about £2200 or a part, or no part.[29]

The foregoing items comprize all the news that I am able, in my present fatigue & hurry to collect for my dear Catherine. If my next shall be short, do not blame my inclination — but my want of time or the barrenness of materials.

Remember me kindly to your mother, Mary, Julia, Thomas & all enquiring friends and believe me to be, my dearest Catherine, Ever most sincerely, your attached and affectionate husband, Denys Scully

[P.S.] I should add, that the House in Merrion Street has about 6 or 7 steps to the Hall door — the Door very large & lofty — 2 windows on one side and one on the other — which one is in the Hall and under the grand stair case. The Drawingroom floor contains 4 windows in front, and the same in rear — the Bed Chambers on the upper 2 floors are many and there is one too, a well sized one, upon the Drawing room floor, looking into the Garden. The House is larger than any House on *this* side of the Square but it certainly looks in bad condition, & will take 6 months to be well dressed up.

[*Source*: Scully Papers]

[1]Missing.
[2]MP for King's County; brother-in-law of Lord Dunalley and the Hon. F. A. Prittie.
[3]The former Lord Chancellor for Ireland, as distinguished from his nephew, the Hon. George Ponsonby, MP for Cork County until he lost his seat.
[4]It started in the middle of October and it was not until 7 November that the *DEP* reported it all but finished.
[5]A groom.
[6]He would have left Dublin on 19 October, having returned from England on the 16th (see postscript to No. 380).
[7]James, Edmund and Jeremiah Scully, his brothers; James Mahon his nephew.
[8]Some animadversions on the misconduct of the polling deputies having led to words passing between Edmund Scully and Nicholas Sadleir, one of John Bagwell's agents, the former called the latter out and there was a meeting at Two Mile Bridge. After they had fired from a distance of ten paces a friend of Sadleir's came forward and made them shake hands. The numerous assemblage of spectators cheered Edmund Scully as he left the scene (*DEP*, 27 October 1812).
[9]She had been taken to Clifton, near Bristol, in the autumn of 1811, when Scully's father reckoned her chance of recovery "but very little", and she was still there. But she survived until 1848.

[10]His sister Joanna, wife of Clement Sadleir of Shronehill.

[11]His sister Lucinda or Lucy, wife of Robert Keating of Garranlea.

[12]His estate near Golden, Co. Tipperary.

[13]General Montagu Mathew and the Hon. F. A. Prittie.

[14]According to the *Freeman's Journal* of 9 December 1812 Scully's fee was the highest ever received by a barrister in Ireland.

[15]His brother-in-law, Vincent Eyre.

[16]His brother-in-law, John Eyre.

[17]John Thelwall, a noted elocutionist of the times (in *DNB*).

[18]His unmarried sisters-in-law, Julia and Mary Eyre.

[19]The baby, Henry.

[20]His brother-in-law, Thomas Eyre.

[21]Unidentified.

[22]John Yeomans, scissors manufacturer, of Fargate, Sheffield.

[23]Scully evidently finished his letter on the 14th, the day the Board met. He mentions John Lalor and Andrew Ryan because his wife would have known them, but there were others who had voted for government candidates although urged not to do so in the 11th resolution passed at the aggregate meeting of 18 June 1812, and feeling ran high against them. The meeting was a stormy one and had to be adjourned for a fortnight. On the 28th Lalor made an effective defence of his conduct in sticking to a promise he had given in 1811 and a resolution was passed declaring to have lost the confidence of the Board only those members who had pledged themselves to government candidates after the resolution of 18 June. The case of Andrew Ryan does not appear to have been discussed at all (*FJ*, 16 & 30 November 1812). F. W. Conway, who was probably the author of the vivid descriptions of the meetings in the *Freeman's Journal*, wrote privately about them to John Beckett, of the Home Office, on 5 and 6 December (Peel Papers, Add.MSS.40, 223, ff.195, 199) putting the blame for alleged intimidation on Scully. The leaders in the agitation against the offending members, he said, belonged to a city faction, two of whom were William Murphy and Silvester Costigan. The third, he went on, was Mr Scully, "the only lawyer who supported the resolutions, not by his vote or speech, for he is too wary to commit himself, but by his influence and intrigue . . . who at all costs, is linked to the opposition and to whose artifice it has been principally owing that the Catholic cause has been so far and so unfortunately identified with the opposition".

[24]8 Merrion Square.

[25]Unidentified.

[26]Samuel Prendergast, Crown Solicitor for the Munster circuit, 10 Upper Merrion Street.

[27]John Bourke (1766–1849), the 4th Earl.

[28]James Davis, 12 Merrion Street.

[29]Scully probably succeeded in getting at least part of her debts paid off, since her biographer notes that she and George William Tighe started discharging their debts in 1812 (McAleer, *The Sensitive Plant*, p. 123).

383   *From Charles Butler to Merrion Square*

Lincolns Inn, 17 November 1812

Dear Sir,

Owing to the absence both of Mr Williams[1] and myself from London, it was not, till now, in my power to answer your enquiries respecting the sales of the lots in question of Lord Ormonde's estates. Lot I. has been sold for 24 years purchase; and Mr Williams sees no reason to be satisfied with a much less price for any of the other lots.[2]

It is generally supposed that ministers have not gained as much as they expected, by the change of Parliament. You see that there has been a petition against Roman Catholic Emancipation both by the County and the University of Oxford;[3] in each case the petition was strenuously opposed; and I believe there will be a very respectable counter Petition from the county. The University of Cambridge meet today on the subject of a Petition, and it is thought to be doubtful whether it will be carried.[4]

You naturally suppose that much is said and thought in this country, on it's appearing, that the Irish Elections are so much less favourable to the Catholics than they were generally expected.[5]

[*Source*: Scully Papers]

[1] Agent to Lord Ormonde's trustees.

[2] Among the Scully papers (MS.27,485, 3) there are letters from William Barron of Carrickbarron, tenant of the farm of Donoskeigh belonging to the Ormonde estate, showing that he invited Scully to join with him in bidding for four lots put up for sale. Scully made an offer which was not considered enough and Barron bought the lot with Donoskeigh separately. On 29 October he had written to inform Scully of this and referred to an overture which had been made by Williams to Scully's father.

[3] Lord Grenville, Chancellor of the University of Oxford, presented it in the House of Lords on 1 December 1812 but expressed disagreement with its contents (*Hansard* XXIV, 115).

[4] Presented by the Duke of Gloucester on the same date: it was strongly challenged by Lord Hardwicke on the ground that it had been rushed through without adequate notice (ibid., 111).

[5] Out of the hundred Irish seats only 27 had been contested, of which 20 belonged to ten counties (B. M. Walker, *Parliamentary Election Results in Ireland*). The losses, which Scully accounts for in his letter No. 384 to Lord Holland, were therefore conspicuous, and J. P. Curran's poor showing at Newry was also a disappointment.

384   *To Lord Holland*

Merrion Square, 19 November 1812

My dear Lord,

I have been continually obliged, since my return to Ireland, to defer offering my thanks to your Lordship for your politeness to me when in England:[1] but I have not the less gratitude, or the less admiration of that noble feature of character which extends the distinction of your notice to a person oppressed by unjust laws — I have felt too, that these laws and their operation have formed my sole recommendation to your liberal nature — and that the same accident, of an hereditary creed, which subjects me to unmerited exclusion in my native country, has opened my admission to the society of generous Englishmen, exciting in my behalf a sympathy, which would almost compensate for civil privations — From the instant of my return, about five weeks since, I became occupied with our great County of Tipperary election, as sole counsel for the popular candidates, Mathew & Prittie — It was an arduous & turbulent contest — The Government candidates have had, throughout Ireland, and especially in Tipperary, Carlow, Cork County & City, the advantage of earlier preparation and perfect discipline of their forces — In Tipperary we had to resist a powerful & well organised attack upon the independence of the county[2] — and, after a struggle of 26 days, we finally triumphed — owing to the good sense, public spirit and freedom from venality which distinguish the lower class of freeholders in that great county[3] — The details of this memorable election have latterly occupied our newspapers — and especially the *Dublin Evening Post* — and therefore I shall not trouble your Lordship upon the subject — but, it is believed, that, as the Government had entertained sanguine expectations of throwing out Prittie and had even placarded Bagwell's temporary majority over him for some days about the streets of Dublin,[4] so their defeat in this instance was probably the sorest and most galling of any that they have met with.

In the county of Carlow Mr Bagnell[5] lost his seat to Mr Bruen[6] — but Mr Bagnell has not been seen in that county for about 30 years — and, tho' his ancestors had great property there, and he had hereditary claims, as they are termed, yet these claims are not nowadays of much weight here — Besides, his finances are narrow, & he did not appear at the election — On the other hand, Mr Bruen is young, resident, very wealthy (being the eldest son of the famous Colonel Bruen, the American Commissary under General Clinton) & lavish of his money — It is true that Bagnell has always voted for the Catholics & with opposition, & ought to have been returned — and so he would (by the exertions of the spirited Catholics) but that his brother in law

Mr Newton,[7] who has 200 votes, threw in all his second votes to Mr Bruen — This was resented by the Catholics, as wantonly injuring Mr Latouche,[8] the other popular candidate, and therefore to disappoint Newton (who speculated upon one day succeeding Bagnell) they were resolved to bring in Latouche at all events — Thus, Bagnell lost his election.

In the County & City of Cork, Ponsonby[9] & Hutchinson[10] lost their seats, thro' the earlier preparation of their opponents, some accidental errors, and, principally, too great security — They have learned, by their experience, the truth of the witch in Macbeth[11] — that security

Is mortal's chiefest enemy.

However, it is satisfactory to know, that, neither in Carlow, nor in the City or County of Cork, have the popular candidates failed, thro' want of intrinsic strength, or of popular zeal, or of earnest good feeling in the country — but merely thro' the neglect or mismanagement of the Candidates or of their friends — Were there new elections tomorrow, the result, for these 3 places, would be directly opposite —

I should not omit another cause — The young Duke of Devonshire,[12] who has developed a noble and munificent disposition here, as well as a warm spirit in Election affairs, fell into an unlucky error, tho' a natural one. He attempted to contest the Borough of Youghall with Lord Shannon, tho' quite unprepared.[13] This was the error of some of those advisers, rather precipitate, into whose hands such a young man is generally apt to fall — The Shannon interest is as yet too powerful in Youghall to be shaken — the attempt failed, and Keane[14] was returned. But, from resentment, Lord Shannon's interest in the County and City of Cork (which is considerable) became violently hostile to Ponsonby & Hutchinson — & this unforeseen circumstance also influenced the Elections — However, the Duke has not been deterred — & he is right — He is persevering actively in extending his interest, making freeholders & registering them — If he continues steady, there is no doubt that he and his friends (of the liberal interest) in the County of Cork will return both the members, to the exclusion of Lords Shannon, Bernard[15] etc — and that he will also return both the members for the County of Waterford, to the exclusion of the Marquis of Waterford[16] etc, etc. But then he must have the interest properly nursed and be served by faithful and liberal land agents etc — As for the City of Cork, I am pretty well informed, that, from the arrangements now forming and soon to be executed, the Hutchinsons, & Catholics etc, will return both members at any future Elections.

In the other elections of Ireland,[17] the Catholics have generally succeeded — either by expelling bad members, or by forcing them to change their principles (or rather their vote).

The Irish Government are straining every nerve to procure anti Catholic petitions, resolutions etc from the venal and bigoted part of the Protestants — and, tho' a vast majority of the Protestants are decidedly in our favour, yet many too must yield to the influence of a hostile government — It is scarcely in human nature, that such an effect should not be produced, to a certain extent —

Our Catholic bishops have just closed a session of 14 days duration — The proceedings[18] are not yet divulged — but I understand they are to appear in a printed form in a few days — and, if of any interest, I shall send a copy to your Lordship.

I beg of you to present my best regards to Lady Holland.

[P.S.] We are putting forward our Catholic petitions actively — but probably shall not have them presented until next February. It is said here, that the present Ministry are also preparing bills for our emancipation[19] — but the event appears to be most effectually forwarded, at present, by Generals Soult, Suchet etc.[20]

[*Source*: Holland House Papers, Add.MSS.51, 826 f.168]

[1]See No. 380.

[2]What Scully meant by this independence is shown in another light by the correspondence which the government candidate and his son conducted with the Chief Secretary (Peel Papers, Add.MSS.40, 222). On 14 October John Bagwell complained of the government's "immediate and most dependent servants . . . subverting that very source from which they derive their consequence". On 22 October he reported that Lord Donoughmore had turned against him "altho" his family hold several of the most lucrative offices under the Crown". He asked particularly that pressure should be exerted on Holmes of the Stamp Office, who was connected with Prittie.

[3]The Bagwells did not see it in the same light. On 28 October William Bagwell told Peel that General Mathew was continuing to harangue the mob from the top of a carriage, that he had induced the priests to come forward on his behalf and that violence was being exercised against freeholders coming to poll for his father.

[4]Bagwell's agent reported on 20 October that his election was almost certain. In the end he polled 2616, against 3813 for Mathew and 3175 for Prittie (*DEP*, 14 November 1812).

[5]Walter Bagenal (c. 1762–1814); MP for Co. Carlow since 1802.

[6]Henry Bruen (c. 1789-1852), son of Colonel Henry Bruen (d. 1797).

[7]Philip Newton (d. 1833), of Dunleckney, Bagenalstown; married Sarah Bagenal in 1785.

[8]Colonel David Latouche (c. 1769–1816).

[9]Hon. George Ponsonby, a brother of Lord Ponsonby.

[10]Christopher Hely Hutchinson.

[11]IV iii.

[12]From 29 July 1811 the 6th Duke.

[13]Henry Boyle, 3rd Earl of Shannon; his candidate was the Hon. William Francis Spencer Ponsonby, a son of Lord Ponsonby.

[14]Sir John Keane (c. 1757–1829), of Belmont, Co. Waterford, MP for Youghal 1801–6, 1808–18.

[15]James, Viscount Bernard, from 1830 2nd Earl of Bandon.

[16]Henry de la Poer Beresford (1772–1826), the 2nd Marquis.
[17]See No. 383 n.5.
[18]See No. 390 n.3.
[19]The *Dublin Evening Post* of 21 November claimed to have heard from a highly respectable authority that the English law officers had been instructed by ministers to prepare the draft of a bill for the beginning of the next session. The authority for this baseless report may have been H. A. Dillon (see No. 390 n.5).
[20]Wellington had been forced to raise the siege of Burgos on 27 October and the French entered Madrid on 1 November. Napoleon was in Moscow until 18 October (*Annual Register*).

385   *From Charles Butler to Merrion Square*

Lincolns Inn, 21 November 1812

Dear Sir,

   I had the pleasure of writing to you some days ago. I now write to you with the leave of Mr Eyre of Sheffield[1] from whom I believe you have already heard on the subject.

   It is to request the favor of you to send me his Two volumes of opinions and other documents respecting the Roman Catholic concerns which he tells me he lent you some years ago, and with the loan of which he has now promised to favor me on account of an investigation in which I am now concerned for the Newburgh Family.[2] The late Mr Eyre[3] did me the favor to lend me these volumes, and I recollect that, under real or fictious [*sic*] names, they contain some cases and opinions respecting the concerns of that family.

   One opinion, if it is found among them, will be of incalculable use.

   May I request the favour of you to let your clerk call on Mr Codd[4] a Bookseller in Dublin & mention that I have received no answer to a letter which I wrote to him last August respecting a translation he had published respecting the works of Thomas a Kempis.   [*Source*: Scully Papers]

[1]Scully's brother-in-law Vincent Eyre, to whom Butler had written on 10 October asking for a loan of the two volumes, explaining that he had been asked by Lord Newburgh to frame an application to parliament for an increase in his annuity from Greenwich Hospital (Letter Book, Add.MSS.25, 128, f.133).
[2]For the relationship of the Eyres of Hassop, Derbyshire, to the Newburghs see Rosamund Meredith: "The Eyres of Hassop", *Recusant History* Vol. 9, No. 6, 1968. On the death of Lord Newburgh, the 5th Earl, without issue in 1814, Francis Eyre of Hassop assumed the title.
[3]Scully's father-in-law, Vincent Eyre, who died in 1801.
[4]Thomas Codd, of 59 Great Britain Street.

386   *From M[argaret, Countess of Mount Cashell]*
                             to Merrion Square[1]

[Postmark] 28 November [1812]
....

This is all I have been able to discover in the first part,[2] except the motto,[3] which I don't like, being of no authority & lacking the dignity of classical quotation. Could you not find something in Tacitus, Sallust, Livy or Cicero to substitute for this french sentence? I make no apology for my presumption — the highest genius may learn something from the lowest[4] & if I suggest but one alteration that you approve I shall be extremely gratified. Were it not for the wretched state of my eyes I should have finished the entire — however I shall soon read it. I am more and more pleased with it on better acquaintance. I am not well by any means but hope to recover when I get out of this town. You I am sure will prevent delays. Adieu for the present — ever most truly and affectionately,

Your obliged friend M.

Saturday (I believe) 18th Novr.

[P.S.] Pray tell me when you write how soon all will be finished.[5] I don't like to leave town till then & yet it is a dreary time of year to make a habitation in the country.   [*Source*: Scully Papers]

[1]This and No. 387 can be identified as Lady Mount Cashell's by the writing, which is like that of No. 149.

[2]Of Scully's *Penal Laws*. Her note follows after twenty-three comments or queries covering the first 137 pages, which are here omitted.

[3]In French, from an obscure French author, to the effect that the true worth of a people in chains cannot be judged.

[4]Lady Mount Cashell was a writer herself, having under the name of Mrs Mason contributed to William Godwin's juvenile series a number of stories which were published in book form at the end of 1807 as *Stories of Old Daniel* (McAleer, *The Sensitive Plant*, p. 121).

[5]Probably in connexion with her separation arrangements (see No. 382).

387   *From the Countess of Mount Cashell*[1]

[1812]
....

This is all I have been able to discover[2] with the greatest attention & you see they are in general merely trivial remarks about words — but when the *fourth* edition[3] is coming out I will again search diligently for what may possibly have escaped me this time — take care of the typographic errors which you have corrected with the pen in Mrs Bostock's copy as they are (some at least) important. I am delighted with the book and want to have it read by every one who has a tolerable head — the next edition ought to be advertised in some of the principal London papers. Pray let me see a handsome clasical quotation in the title page — if I had eyes at present I would search the Latin historians for something suitable, but I dare not undertake it & you will probably recollect *where* to look better than I should. Though I plagued you yesterday with a long stupid letter[4] I will not defer sending this and remember it is quite a secret that I have eyes to write even to you — one of these days I shall explain *entirely* the reason of sheltering myself under my eyes.[5]

[*Source*: Scully Papers]

[1]See No. 386 n.1.

[2]Twenty-eight points in Part II of the *Penal Laws*, from pages 141 to 366, on which she makes comments or queries which are omitted here. A few of her observations have an interest that goes beyond the immediate context. She does not like the word *influential*, but if it is in Johnson it must be right. *Absurd enough* she believes to be an Hibernianism. She twice condemns *favouritism*, as savouring a little of the burlesque and not sufficiently dignified for a serious subject. She asks if there is good authority for *advocacy*, and *impliedly*, a word that she does not like. She asks if *inequitable* is a right word. She does not like *engaging* when Scully speaks of "an engaging situation". That Scully acted on her suggestions is shown by a note in his hand "corrected to this" after page 288.

[3]A third edition of the *Penal Law* was advertised at the time of Fitzpatrick's trial (*DEP*, 11 February 1813). In an undated memorandum in a notebook (MS.27,513, ii) Scully refers to a "new 3rd edition" for which he was to collect further material and take the motto from *Genesis* or *Exodus* about the Egyptians persecuting the Jews before their departure from Egypt.

[4]Probably one of her matrimonial affairs, which would have gone into Scully's professional file, No. 386 not being long, even with the queries.

[5]Her reasons remain unknown.

388   *To Catherine Scully at Mrs Eyre's, Ferme, Sheffield, Yorks.*

Merrion Square [Dublin] 30 November 1812, Monday
   I thought my dear Catherine's Letter long in coming, & felt even hurt at so long a silence — but have, at length, the pleasure to receive your Letter of the 25th and to learn that you were all well.
   I find you had two Letters from me from Clonmell, and afterwards my Letter of 13th from Dublin,[1] and did not sit down to write to me till the 25th and I have had almost a mind to leave your Letter at least as long unanswered. The only visible mark of affection that one absent friend can give to another is by Letter — and, frequently, both affection & remem-

brance are observed to decline with a decline of correspondence — so I shall at least avoid that tendency.

I cannot answer your question whether Henry is better looking than either of his brothers — but I do not know of any advantage on either side in that respect. It would be necessary to see them all together — and I cannot say that I now recollect (after 2 months) the little faces of his brothers sufficiently to form a judgment.

I leave to yourself the time of your return — and I take for granted that Thomas[2] will escort you. It seems, you will not be able to come over before July, at the soonest, if you are to wait the *accouchement* — and you would therefore choose December, January or April. The passages are generally excellent in January. What would you think of fixing to leave the Ferme some day between the 6th and 12th of January — rest a couple of days at Wolverhampton[3] — come on to Holyhead — and sail or delay there, as you like the weather. The wind is generally about Easterly until the 25th of that month. For these last four days the weather here has been most delightful — the wind East, & South — and passages to Dublin between 7 and 10 hours. I wish you may have the like. You will then have been absent about 5 months. You say it will probably be many years before you make this journey again — but depend upon it, the great probability, and almost certainty, is, that you will yet have *full enough* of England, and that we shall pass much time there, when it will be *more convenient* in every respect than at present.[4]

My father & mother both appear very much broken — and his letter of Saturday to me was rather melancholy.

I shall not think any more of the House in Merrion Street[5] for the present. Barrington's House is just sold to a Mr Knox,[6] Lady Mary Knox's son, for about £3500 & £100 Guins. Rent. It will take £300 to put it in order. I think we might have bought it, if you had been here. What would you think of Nugent's[7] (No. 9 on *this side*) — between Judge Boyd's[8] & Lord Allen's.[9] It is large — but will sell very high — and it has been *whispered* to me that he would sell it. It goes the entire depth, as far back as Gordon's[10] or Burne's,[11] and as wide in front. Probably £4000 would be asked.

I saw a bill on Houghton's[12] in Bagot Street, my old House. He & she are going to live near Bath & of course he retires from the Bar. If you bring over the Sheet of Pedigree,[13] I can copy it and return it but do not, unless it be *perfectly* agreeable to all our friends with you.

You will use your own Discretion as to invitations etc. I shall be happy to see any of the family here — as you know already.

I hope you have bought oats for the Horses. It is good for them — but *half feeds* will be sufficient at present from what you mention. I hope William[14] takes them out daily to air. He would rather keep them in, to save the trouble of the cleaning, wisping etc.

Peter[15] goes on tolerably well, honest & civil, but rather stupid.

I dine out often — yesterday at Judge Fletcher's in town — a party of 14 — and, amongst others, the Burtons[16] — Miss B looks well — but I hear no more of her match with Bushe.[17] The Dinner, wines etc. all rich & elegant — and the Company agreeable. Mr & Mrs Wyse[18] are in Town. I met them at Dinner at Edw'd Moore's where Mrs Moore is now staying. She sails next week for Liverpool, where she resides until Summer with her son Walter who is become a merchant there. He has commenced a partnership with a Mr. —— (I forget his name, but he is an English Catholic — I recollect since it is Selby of Northumberland, nearly related to the Wrights)[19] and the O'Connors[20] here are to support them as Moore & Selby in credit & business.

Von Feinagle[21] has been here some time — & doing pretty well. He has got 70 Subscribers for his first course of 15 days, at 5 Guineas for each subscriber. I hear him well spoken of — and (on account of Charles & John[22] having desired it) I assist now & then in sounding his praises, and putting him in fashion. There is no doubt that he will succeed in his object here — namely that of getting much money.

There is to be a grand Ball and Masquerade on Wednesday next at Thomastown, given by Lord & Lady Llandaff, as well to celebrate the late Election as to open their newly finished House. About 400 cards have been issued — and many, of both sexes, are going down to it from Dublin.

A piece of best nankeen sells in the top Linendrapers Shops, from 18/– to 20/– and 7¼ yards to a piece.

There is a very handsome Barouche now to be sold here for 220 Guineas — newly from London — & has only made the one journey. Some services of China too, the property of a titled Lady, for private sale at Keene's in Dame Street[23] but I do not meddle with these Articles in your absence.

We are to have the usual leave for flesh meat here next Lent — and several intended marriages are buzzed about — but not of any near friends of ours.

Little Henry is becoming great company for me — he now knows me very well — is wonderfully good humoured and smiling — makes good efforts to mimick the cries of "bogwood", "cloaths" etc. outside. When they tell him in the kitchen that they are going to take him up to *Dada*, he begins to bounce & shake his little legs and hands, in great glee. The colour of his hair is now a light brown — and, without his cap, he resembles James far more than Vincent but his mouth a little smaller, and his eyes softer & less piercing. He has just got another tooth & gets them with ease. He now has 5 teeth. He never wants medicine & has but a slight running from his mouth and nose. These are all the particulars I can give you. He is quite the better, & the hardier, for not wearing shoes or stockings and the soles of his feet are become hard & firm. We dip him every morning in cold water up to his shoulders — and he likes it very well — never cries or grumbles, but seems quite merry.

I ride out every other day or thereabouts — mostly in the Park — but of late our Roads are pretty dry & clean every where. My plans of staying in Town or leaving it for Kilfeacle, will depend upon your next letter — and, for goodness sake, do not make so long a business of it again. The Distance is little more than 2 days quick journey — and yet we write as if it was from Madrid to Dublin.

I repeat, that I leave entirely to yourself the choice of time & manner of your returning; & mean always to do so, as to your visits to England or elsewhere — it being my chief wish that you should be pleased & happy, as far as lies in my power.

Give my love to your mother, Julia, Thomas and all friends & believe me to be, my dear Catherine, your sincerely affectionate husband, D.S.

[P.S.] I omit, or forget, a quantity of little news, anecdotes etc. etc. too many and too long for any Letter.

If you can get a Box Coat to your mind for 5 Guineas, or even 6 Guin's — buy it but be satisfied of its being quite fashionable etc. etc.

Tuesday Even'g, 1 Dece'r. I have just now enquired of Stamper.[24] The price of an excellent drab coachman's coat, with sufficient capes, is about 5 Guineas. He has just finished a very superior Box Coat for a nobleman — of best Cloth — many capes, all real cloth, lined with handsome shalloon & very complete: it came to £7.10/– Irish: about £7 English.

[*Source*: Scully Papers]

[1]No. 382. The Clonmel letters are missing.

[2]Her brother Thomas Eyre.

[3]With Dr Milner (see No. 381).

[4]See No. 175 in which Scully told his wife to be that she might not be living entirely in Ireland and Dr Milner's remark in No. 381 about emancipation coming a day too late. The inference that he was hoping to sit in parliament is supported by a letter of 6 December 1812 in which F. W. Conway told John Beckett of the Home Office that he understood Scully to have pretensions to the representation of Co. Tipperary (Peel Papers, Add.MSS.40, 223, f.199).

[5]No. 12 Upper Merrion Street (see No. 382).

[6]The Rt. Hon. George Knox, called to the Irish bar 1788, MP for TCD 1802–6.

[7]Joseph Nugent, an attorney.

[8]Robert Boyd, a former judge of the King's Bench, who died in 1814.

[9]Joshua, 5th Viscount Allen (1728–1816).

[10]Unidentified.

[11]John Burne KC, according to the directory at 20 Merrion Square.

[12]Henry George Houghton (b. 1779), of 34 Baggot Street, called to the Irish bar 1802.

[13]Which he had asked to be copied (see No. 382).

[14]William Fitzpatrick, Scully's coachman.

[15]A groom.

[16]Charles Burton KC.

[17]Unidentified — the name could also be read as Burke. Eliza Felicia Burton, an only child, married the barrister John Beatty West in 1819.

[18]Thomas Wyse senior, of the Manor of St John, Waterford, whose sister Margaret was married to Scully's brother James, and his wife Frances Bagge.

[19]Thomas Wright and Nicholas Selby of Biddleston, Northumberland, were brothers-in-law and partners in the bank of Wright, Selby and Robinson, Henrietta Street, London. Moore's partner, Robert Selby, was a nephew of Nicholas.

[20]Valentine O'Connor's firm, of which Edward Moore was a partner.

[21]*Recte* Gregor von Feinaigle — the mnemonist (in *DNB*).

[22]His brothers-in-law Charles and John Eyre.

[23]The directory shows John Keene, goldsmith and jeweller, of No. 67; and Jane Keene, goldsmith, of No. 73 Dame Street.

[24]John Stamper, tailor and woollen draper, 4 Church Lane.

389   *From Lord Holland to Merrion Square, Dublin*

St James's Square [London] 12 December 1812

My Dear Sir,

I am really ashamed of having deferred so long my thanks for your very kind & interesting letter[1] which gave me more insight into the elections & general state of Ireland than all the speeches & publications I had read on the subject. The result will I hope be more favourable than was at first apprehended & even where the Catholicks have not been so firm as you & I could have wished them, the very fault which we lament furnishes an answer to their enemies, as it proves that the ordinary relations of life sway them as much as other motives [?] & that they are capable of voting for their Protestant Landlord against the wishes of their brethren & their priests & even the interests of the body to which they belong. Why then is it to be supposed that a Catholick Lawyer or a Catholick Member of Parliament will be insensible to those party connections & those motives of honourable ambition which have weight with other men & that his conduct & his vote will never be activated by any other consideration of patriotism, party interest or vanity or by any other sense of duty but that of devotion to the Pope?

But though the result of the elections is by no means bad in England & Ireland I cannot disguise from you that the state of the publick mind *here* is not so favorable to our cause (I call it *our* for I am sure no Catholick is more sincerely eager about it than I am) as it was last year. This is in part to be attributed to the more avowed *hostility* of Carlton House,[2] to the activity of the Church, the cooperation of the Methodists[3] & the prodigious & *purchased* activity of the press. Against the latter there is no combined effort whatever & calumnies, libels, misrepresentations & fanatical invectives are handed about gratis against the Catholicks without answer or remark while the *premature* jealousy expressed of any veto, security or guard by your Irish Prelates tends to confirm the prejudices of the foolish & to furnish a handle to the designing & an excuse to the wavering & timeserving. Believe me, My Dear Sir, there is no method so likely to defeat our object as premature discussion of its details. A large body of men are pledged to the principle of Catholick concession & by their means & their exertions we must strive to get Parliament pledged to it also. That once effected, your rights cannot long be withheld — but if you take pains to apprize your false friends & artful enemies beforehand what are the points in detail which you cannot concede they will spare no endeavour to persuade the good people of this country that that is the precise measure which in return for the concession (as they term it) it will be prudent & even necessary to exact. In urging this point to you, do not suspect me of any very strong predilection or wish for any security. I consider them all as useless & absurd & some I even think to a degree objectionable but I have always held this language to friends & enemies on the subject. I cannot *exact any security* from the Catholicks as the price of a right which I think they are in justice entitled to & which I am convinced they can enjoy without danger to Church or state, but on the other hand, I am ready to acquiesce in any accompanying measure which, without excluding so large a portion of my fellow-countrymen from their rights, allays the apprehensions & reconciles the prejudices of protestants in England & Scotland. I am well persuaded that if we can get the principle of concession established by parliament, & if on your side of the water you can contrive to allay any feverish apprehension of improper securities being exacted from you & *not to reject the offers before they are made*, nothing of an inadmissible kind will be offered you, but on the other hand if you get the Clergy of the two persuasions previously engaged in the endless controversy of the respective authorities & constitutions of the two Churches we shall find as much difficulty & require as much time in adjusting the details as we have in establishing the principle of the measure. In short, every Protestant who *now* talks of the securities he will exact is in my mind if not an intentional a very formidable enemy to the Cause & every Catholick who *now* explains what are the securities he will agree to & what are those he will reject is perhaps equally unintentionally but not less effectually an enemy of the rights of his brethren.

For the purpose of making any impression in England the press should work the following topicks — 1st, the number & above all the *increasing wealth* of the Irish Catholicks; 2ndly, the support their claims have received from *Irish Protestants*, 3rdly, the Protestant authorities in favour of their concession — Burke, Pitt, Windham, Mr Fox; 4thly, the present helpless state of the Pope; 5thly, the fact of the Pope in 1695 being a Member of the Protestant league, the resistance made by the Popes to the two, most orthodox as you would say, bigotted as we Protestants call them, of powerful

Sovereigns — Philip 2nd & Lewis 14; 6thly, the gross inconsistency of the laws & the fact of the good conduct of Catholick soldiers & sailors on whose minds, if on any, the interference of foreign jurisdiction through the priesthood would have an effect.   [*Source*: Scully Papers]

[1]No. 384.
[2]Residence of the Prince Regent.
[3]Lord Holland may have been thinking of the formation by Methodists and other dissenters of the Protestant Society early in 1812 in order to procure the repeal of the Conventicle Act. They had been well received by Perceval, the Prime Minister, whose object, it was suspected by the opposition, was to range the dissenters on his side and crush other demands for religious liberty (Wyvill to Whitbread 2 and 11 January 1812: Calendar of Whitbread Papers, Nos. 4326, 4329).

390   *From Bishop John Milner to Merrion Square, Dublin*

W.Hmpton. 16 December 1812

My Dear Sir,

I was duly honoured with your letter of the 18th Ult., and learnt from it that I had more reason to congratulate with you on the success of the Tipperary Election than I was before aware of. But Mrs Wheble pointed out to me a passage about pistols in the *Dublin Evening*,[1] relating to that election & I still meet with other passages of the same nature in that News paper which fill me with fears & also with shame for my fellow Catholics. For my part if I were one of those *Animalia popularis aurae*[2] as Tertullian calls the ancient philosophers, & if God has blessed me with a head & a tongue equal to those of the persons I allude to I should disdain to appeal to the brutal contest of fighting, in order to prove that I was right in any cause: but being a Catholic Christian I would try to get rid of my religious belief, if ever I had made up my mind to kill or to be killed.

You have now seen in print the cheif matter of the Irish Prelates' late deliberation.[3] Their Resolutions support my opinion & conduct in every particular, especially in the cheif contest now going on between me & my vacillating brethren concerning the Blanchardist schism & a certain Abbé Trevaux. When you informed me more than a year ago that my brethren had appealed at Durham from Dr Troy to Drs O'Reilly & Bray[4] I remarked to you that they had *jumped out of the frying pan into the fire* & so the event proved. I can assure you on the testimony of some of them that no annual million, or other money has been offered to them, & that they have not had any communication of late with Ministry or other Statesmen. Indeed I think you must be convinced that the whole of the Hon. Aug. Dillon's information to you was grounded in mistake.[5] Lord Liverpool's declaration in Pt.[6] admits of no question, as to the meaning & determination of Ministry.

But Ministry itself will be turned out, if we lose the Peninsula, or any other great public misfortune happen. It appears to me that few of yr. great Orators read books of information which are every where open before them; were it otherwise I am convinced that they wd. pass a much severer censure upon Chs. O'Conor as an Irishman, than the Bishops have passed upon him as a Catholic: so flagrant & base is his Apostacy from the cause of his country; so anxiously intent is he to vilify everything that is Irish & Catholic & to exalt every thing that is English & Protest.; so notoriously is he sold to betray every thing that yet remains free in Ireland to his pay-masters & its oppressors. There is but one voice in this country as well as in Ireland relative to the merits of *The Statement of the Penal Laws*. Hence I cannot but wish that it may be as generally known & read as possible: to which Mr Saurin and his No-Popery crew will most effectively contribute by their prosecution of Mr Fitzpatrick.[7] Nevertheless I must confess my incompetency to pronounce on the several points relative to a future edition or editions of that work which you propose to me. Some of them are entirely within the department of the Booksellers. I am still more unqualified to point out faults in a book which I so much admire. Nevertheless if I must find some fault or other, I think your own experience will disprove one assertion in yr. *Introduction*, p. IV that "No praise or gratitude awaits" the author of a work like yours. Again I think that the term which occurs at p. 13 of the work & elsewhere of *Houses of Worship*, for *Chapels* is neither usual nor appropriate. Johnson describes "a *house*" to be a place for a man to *live in*, *a human habitation*. A more important point appears to be yr. not taking sufficient notice of the hardships which half a million of Irish who, from circumstances are obliged, in the course of a few years are forced to come over to England, endure. Women & children accompany their husbands & parents to Portsmouth, for example & then are seperated from them, & obliged to crawl back to Holyhead without support, lashed by the beadle at every town or village, the women hunted like wild beasts from Parish to Parish when at the point of childbirth.[8] Add to this that the Irish Caths. who constitute the mass of population in many Districts of London & elsewhere, naturally marry & are obliged by their religion to be married by the Priest — which marriages are invalid. Hence how many destitute women & children?[9] I speak of miseries which I have often witnessed. Mrs Wheble desires her kind compts. to you & will be equally happy with myself to see Mrs Scully with the children, at Wolverhampton on her return to Ireland, as likewise yrself shd you conduct her thither. I only hope that I may not be upon one of my journeys when she arrives here. Dr Potts & the other Gentn. of Oscot are grateful to me for bringing them acquainted with Mr Scully & expressly charged me the other day when I wrote to him to present their best compts.

P.S. I have heared great personages express a doubt whether a Cathc. marriage performed in Ireland, was valid for beneficial effects in England.

P.S. I open my letter to explain one passage in it. I sd. yr. Prelates had no offer of money etc. I alluded precisely to the time of the Meeting,[10] for early in the summer my Ven. friend & fellow traveller,[11] as he mentioned to several persons in England, was waited upon by the Protest. Bishop of his see[12] (whom he describes as a man acquainted with all the secrets of the Castle) & told by him that it was the wish & intention of Government to settle £1,000 an. on each Bp. & £1200 on each A.B. To this my friend made answer: Be assured, My Lord, that the Prelates will never touch a shilling till the Emancipation be granted.[13] *O Magnifica Vox & fulgaris instar* as St Jerome calls that of St Peter: *Pecunia tua tecum sit in perditione.*[14] I forgot to say that the Bps tell me they *always have signed* the Petitions; that they dislike the recruiting, but that they must prepare for the gallows were they to be found actively opposing it.[15]   [*Source*: Scully Papers]

[1]Of 27 October 1812, with reports on Edmund Scully's duel with Nicholas Sadleir (see No. 382 n.8) and an averted duel between Bagwell and Prittie, two of the candidates.

[2]"Creatures of popular favour". *Aura popularis*, "breath of popular favour" was an expression used by Cicero — in his speech of 31 July 1811 Scully disclaimed seeking it. Tertullian's editor, J. S. Waszink, lists no other use of *animal* than in *De Anima* 1, 2, where the expression is *philosophus gloriae animal* but quotes St Jerome (*Letters* 66, 8, 3): *philosophus, gloriae animal et popularis aurae*".

[3]The *Dublin Evening Post* of 1 December published the resolutions, dated 18 November, of a synod that sat in Dublin for two weeks. The Prelates confirmed their resolutions of 26 February 1810 (see No. 233 n.1); commended Irish Catholics for their willingness to forgo civil advantages rather than compromise their religion; announced that as they were cut off from communication with the Pope they could not propose or agree to any change in the long established mode of appointing Irish Bishops; expressed their conviction that no pledges or securities could be devised more effectual than those they had already given; condemned the latest publications of the Blanchardists; and warmly thanked J. B. Clinch for refuting the errors of *Columbanus ad Hibernos* (see No. 375 n.2).

[4]The Archbishops of Armagh and Cashel, from whom the other Vicars Apostolic had sought help in healing their breach with Dr Troy (see No. 318 n.5).

[5]The rest of the information may have included what Scully said about two alleged government bills in the postscript to No. 384, written the day before he wrote to Dr Milner.

[6]Probably his speech of 1 July 1812 on Wellesley's motion (see No. 362 n.4).

[7]See No. 363 n.2.

[8]The problem arose from the lenity of the military authorities in letting families accompany militiamen to England when there was no provision for repatriating them if husbands volunteered for the line and went overseas (Sir H. McAnally, *The Irish Militia*, p. 245).

[9]Because, not being legally married, they had no redress if abandoned.

[10]The synod of November see No. 3 above.

[11]Dr Francis Moylan, Bishop of Cork, whom Dr Milner had accompanied to

Durham in August (see No. 373 n.2).

[12]The Hon. Thomas St Lawrence, Bishop of Cork and Ross 1807–1831.

[13]Eneas McDonnell told an aggregate meeting on 16 February 1815 that he had heard the same thing from Dr Moylan before his death but expatiated on the corrupting influence of clerical salaries in any circumstances (*DEP*, 21 February 1815).

[14]"Oh magnificent voice like unto a thunderclap" and (from *Acts* 8, 20) "May you and your money come to a bad end" — as St Peter said to Simon when offered money for the laying on of hands.

[15]See No. 381 n.5.

391   *To Lord Holland*

Merrion Square, 19 December 1812

My Lord,

   I am highly gratified by your favourable reception of my letter[1] — and much indebted for the precise observations contained in your Lordship's obliging favour. We could scarcely have expected from our opponents a more candid or generous warfare than was consistent with their narrow principles — and therefore I wonder not at their renewed attempt to rouse the dormant bigotry of Britain — It also serves as a diversion from the pursuit of reform and peace. We in Ireland are, I fear, too distant from the scene to produce any effect — Our writings would be outwritten by a hired tribe of trading pamphleteers, and by expectant clergy, lawyers etc — And our purses (were we disposed to send money to London) would be outweighed by those of the pluralist, the Bishops, Deans, placemen etc — In this predicament we can perhaps only work by perseverance, importunity, & unanimity, taking chance for events — The recruiting service is pretty well stopped in Ireland[2] — and many of our people are now in the French army:[3] these two dispositions operate with daily encrease, and may yet be *taken into consideration*.

   The arguments in our Common Pleas court upon the Demurrer in the case between Mr Taaffe, a Catholic delegate, and the Chief Justice Downes have been lately closed;[4] and the cause now stands for judgment, which may be expected early in the next term, about the 24th Jan'y. I have some recollection of an observation made by your Lordship to me, that "There is probably no instance of the arrest of any person for a mere misdemeanour before indictment or information, and that such seemed to be the opinion of Sir Arthur Pigot". I know not whether your Lordship may have opportunities, or may feel disposed (for the promotion of our common object in defending the delegates against the Irish Government) to put a few queries to him, in conversation, upon this subject: it may possibly (thro' some channels in my power) produce a beneficial and deciding influence upon the impending judgment — and, at all events, would be of great value upon the argument on appeal to the 12 judges in the Court of Error. Two of these 4 judges[5] are courtiers; one is a staunch patriot (Fletcher, the only law judge appointed by the Bedford administration) and the 4th Fox is doubting (this is *private*) — If you should be pleased to give us this aid, you will find the queries in the paper, which I take the liberty of enclosing:[6] and, if you should not think proper to interfere, I beg you will consider this application, as if it had not been made — We wish to have it done thro' an authentic channel & confidentially — but no other person is apprized that I mention the subject to your Lordship — I think that the authority of Sir A. Pigot would be of the highest value in this stage — but that of any other experienced King's Bench lawyer would be also desirable — The first King's Bench lawyer in England is Lord Erskine: he has had the greatest share of practice: and I dare say these queries would appear easy of solution to him — The answers will be in time, on any day to about the 18th of January.

As time now presses I beg leave to reserve for a future letter some observations which I propose to submit to your Lordship respecting the points so ably and liberally suggested by your letter.

[P.S.] I need not observe, how useful it may prove to the friends of liberty in Parliament and to the Catholics in Ireland, if we can succeed in fixing an illegal act (or at least a very questionable one) upon the Irish Government, thro' their Attorney General, Saurin, who was Downes' adviser & prompter in issuing the warrant[7] — particularly as it grows out of Lord Morpeth's motion of Janu'y or Febru'y last.[8]

[*Source*: Holland House Papers, Add.MSS.51, 826 f.172.]

[1]No. 384.

[2]A falling off of enthusiasm for recruiting and enlistment had become noticeable in 1812 and on 26 February 1813 a circular was issued authorising the levying of fines on parishes for deficiencies in numbers (H. McAnally: *The Irish Militia* p. 250). No figures are available for direct enlistment into regiments of the line, but if there was a shortfall of recruits from Ireland it did not seriously affect the overall picture. In the debate on the army estimates on 8 March 1813 the Secretary for War said that between the end of 1811 and the end of 1812 there had been an increase of 10,200 in the effective strength of the forces. The majority of these were foreigners, but the British alone accounted for 2000 (*Hansard* XXIV, 1168).

[3]There were at this time three battalions in the French service, under the command of Colonel Lawless (*Memoirs of Miles Byrne* II, p. 221).

[4]When the charge against Chief Justice Downes (see No. 310 n.2) had come up in the Court of Common Pleas on 12 June 1812 the defence had entered pleas, on the one hand justifying Downes' warrant for the arrest of the Catholic delegates on the ground that an oath had been sworn by Francis Huddleston; on the other hand claiming that even if the facts alleged by the plaintiff were true the Chief Justice could, by the patent of his office, arrest any person he chose and hold him to bail in

any capacity, whether judicial or ministerial, without being accountable to any tribunal but the King in parliament. This latter was the demurrer to which Scully refers. After hearings on 13, 20 and 24 November judgement had been postponed until the next term (*FJ*, 14 November 1812, 7 December 1812). On 4 February 1813 three of the four judges gave their opinion on the demurrer against the plaintiff (*DEP*, 4 February 1813) and on 22 May 1813 the Board advised the delegates to drop their actions (*DDA* 54/2, III, 56).

[5]He means the four Justices of the Common Pleas. Fletcher, who had dissented from the others on the demurrer, was the only judge who owed his appointment to the opposition. Luke Fox (c. 1757–1819) became mentally deranged in 1815.

[6]Not found.

[7]This charge is confirmed by Wellesley Pole's letter of 6 August 1811 to the Home Secretary: "The Attorney General thought it would be more impressive to act through the Chief Justice's warrants than by those of the other magistrates, and by a trying the parties in the King's Bench during term instead of at the Commission we shall have I am told a better jury and the benefits of the Chief Justice's authority". On 9 August he wrote again: "The Chief Justice is very decided upon the practice of committing before a bill of indictment is found. He can produce forty instances of this from the best English judges" (HO 100/164, ff.250, 252).

[8]See No. 331 n.1.

392　　　　*From Jane Canning to Merrion Square, Dublin*

Foxcote, 1 January [post marked 1813]

My Dear Mr Scully,

I am extremely obliged to you for your kind wish to comply with my desire. I most sensibly feel your expressions of regard & am happy in having made a request that has occasioned your addressing so affectionate a letter to me.

I enter entirely into your motives for not making an application to Lord Moira[1] & feel even a wish you should not speak to Lord Mount Cashel,[2] as doing so might be considered as an indirect one at least to Lord M.

I was unfortunately never acquainted with Lady Charlotte Rawdon,[3] a circumstance to be regretted upon every account & I have always heard she is very amiable.

I am sorry you think I have a disinclination towards Ireland. I dislike nothing, I assure you but the sea that divides us. I certainly have still my *old* principles, yet Mr Canning cannot feel more interested than I do for the success of your cause or more indignant at the unworthy manner it appears lately to be treated with by our wise governors.

It would give me the greatest pleasure to visit Ireland & I do not think it improbable that we may one day do so. I am extremely sorry that Mrs Scully is to return home so soon & that it must be so long before I can hope to see her at Foxcote. I shall really be mortified if you pass our road without coming to us. I am sure it would give Mr Canning the greatest pleasure to see you here.

I heard lately of my Aunt.[4] She was looking tolerably well. I fear however the cold weather is a great trial to her constitution. Mr Canning unites with me in every thing kind & believe me my dear Mr Scully

Yours ever most sincerely

Jane Canning   [*Source*: Scully Papers]

[1]Lord Moira's appointment to the governorship of Bengal had been announced early in November 1812 (*FJ*, 7 November 1812) and Mrs Canning may have been looking for a situation for a relative or friend. There is no evidence that Scully knew Lord Moira, despite his friendship with his mother and his visit to Donington in 1799 (see No. 31 n.9].

[2]Through his mother the 2nd Earl of Mount Cashell was a step-nephew of Lord Moira.

[3]Lord Moira's sister.

[4]Mrs Bostock.

393   *From Lord Holland to Merrion Square, Dublin*

12 January 1813

Dear Sir,

I have deferred writing[1] in hopes of being able to send you some detailed & decisive opinions but this is an idle season & our leading Lawyers seem averse either from scruple or indolence to giving any written opinion in other than a professional way. From what I have collected from conversation with Sir Arthur Piggott in particular this is of the less importance because Sir Vicary Gibbs's iniquitous act of 1808[2] gives a Judge distinctly the right of holding to bail for any offence which can be proceeded against by information or indictment, on information only. Consequently you must travel round to the same point as before namely whether your Meeting[3] was an indictable offence or misdemeanour under the Convention Act. On some motion, I think of Ld Stanhope's upon Mr W. Pole's letter in 1811,[4] I contended that no one could be held to bail for a misdemeanour which was not a breach of the peace. I was furnished with a decision of Ld Camden's in Wilkes' case[5] & entered a protest which you will find in the debates[6] & which the Chancellor could not deny to be Law but the bill which had passed a few years before distinctly gives an Attorney General on *Ex Officio* information and a Judge on any information the right to hold to bail for any indictable misdemeanour. So much so that on the principle of *Exceptio probuit regulum* that very act of Parliament was quoted in defence of my position. I have neither the Statutes nor the debates with me in town or would refer you to both with more precision.

Sir Arthur Piggott as you know in the Hse of Commons[7] & Ld Erskine in the Lds[8] argued most directly against Wellesley Pole's & the Chief Justice's construction of the Convention Act.

We are doing what we can to stem the torrent of publications & petitions[9] which are pouring out to overwhelm your cause. I own I have less hopes of success this year than I had but if I am to confess the whole truth to you I do not think it is entirely tho' chiefly owing to servility or prejudice on this side of the water, & must attribute some part of our failure to a want of discretion on yours. You know, My Dear Sir, that *I* personally neither require nor value any guards or securities but why should your Bishops[10] at a period when many persons hitherto your enemies shew a disposition to concede the principle, unnecessarily put forward & squabble with them about the details before the principle is completely & finally conceded.

I have written in hurry & am now interrupted — pray excuse my scrawl.

[*Source*: Scully Papers]

[1] In reply to No. 391.

[2] Probably 48 Geo. III Cap. 58: "An Act for amending the law . . . on Indictments and Informations in the court of King's Bench. . . ." The opposition maintained that under guise of strengthening the hands of the revenue officers new powers covering all informations had been conferred on the Attorney-General without parliament's realising what had happened (*Hansard* XIX, 558). Sir V. Gibbs was Attorney-General 1807–12.

[3] The meeting in St Mary's parish for the election of five delegates in August 1811 (see No. 291).

[4] His circular of 12 February 1811 (see No. 285 n.1).

[5] The 1st Earl. As Chief Justice Pratt he had ruled in 1763 that general warrants were illegal (see Howell, *State Trials* IX, 998).

[6] In his *Further Memoirs of the Whig Party*, p. 98 Lord Holland says that his protest was not printed in the Registers, but it was approved of by Sir Arthur Piggott and Lord Eldon had acknowledged to him in private that the law of Secretary Pole's letter was indefensible.

[7] See No. 330 n.9.

[8] In the debate on Lord Fitzwilliam's motion of 31 January 1812 (*Hansard* XXI, 462).

[9] The great Majority of the petitions were not presented until after the Christmas recess, but the newspapers were full of reports on meetings held to prepare them, charges by the clergy to their flocks etc. They were analysed by Sir Henry Parnell on 2 March and shown to be less impressive than they seemed (*Hansard* XXIV, 1017).

[10] See No. 390 n.3.

394   *From Charles Butler to Merrion Square*

Lincolns Inn, 15 January 1812 [*recte* 1813][1]

Dear Sir,

I received to-day the two volumes; and have found, in one of them an opinion of the very utmost consequence, to Lord Newburgh. I mean to write to you, towards the end of the month, at some length on the subject of R.C. affairs. My hopes are strong. I know for certain, 1st that a person of unquestionable character (an Irishman), called on Lord Limerick and entreated him to wait on Ministers, and inform them, that their raising up the protestant petitions[2] had put the whole kingdom into an alarming flame, & that the Catholic question must now, be finally disposed of; 2dly That Buonaparte's naval preparations, alarm Ministers greatly; 3dly That they are quite satisfied of Lord Castlereagh's inefficiency; & 4thly, much may be expected from Lord Moira.[3]

We are determined to petition early in the Session.

P.S. I suppose you have seen the Accounts given of your Work in the Reviews.[4] It had done more good, (than any work yet published), to your cause.

[Source: Scully Papers]

[1]The two volumes mentioned in the first line were asked for by Butler in No. 385.
[2]For the English petitions see No. 393 n.9. For Ireland see No. 363 n.11 and No. 384, where Scully told Lord Holland that the Irish government were straining every nerve to procure such petitions. In their speeches on Grattan's motion on 1 March 1813 both Wellesley Pole and his successor Peel interpreted the outbreak of Irish Protestant petitions as a natural reaction to the success of the Catholics reflected in Canning's motion of 22 June 1812 (Hansard XXIV, 892, 904).
[3]See enclosure C in No. 397 for Butler's expectations of Lord Moira at the end of December. Lord Moira was in the throes of preparation for his departure for India but was giving out assurances of his continued support of the Catholic cause. The Statesman of 26 January reported his having told Lord Liverpool "that if the Catholic question was brought forward before he left England he would exert himself more than he had ever done before in its support".
[4]No notices have been found in the leading reviews.

395   *From Dr Edward Sheridan to 2 Merrion Square, South*

Dominick Street [Dublin] 19 January 1813

My Dear Sir,

I have been from home, or I should have immediately communicated to you all I know about our anonymous Correspondent.[1] The poetical packet which was left with me I had only time to look over in a very cursory manner, when Doctor Dromgoole called for it. I shall send for it this evening, and forward it to you tomorrow with my tribute of applause to that patriotic spirit which animates you. The author writes I believe with the best intentions: the wrongs of Ireland are his theme in a dialogue between the Rose and the Shamrock; and all this seems to be but a preface to a larger work to which he would seem to wish to conciliate the patronage of the

Gentlemen whom he addresses. As far as I can see by the slight glance which I have taken of it, the poetry is not above mediocrity. But you shall judge of it yourself, if I can procure it: and you will not wonder that I have not dipped deeper into it, when I assure you that I have as yet given but one reading to your masterly *Statement of the Penal Laws*. My first reading of any work is slight and cursory. If the Work is indifferent, I never read it a second time but if of superior excellence I give it a Second and Sometimes a third reading; and these readings I perform with my utmost attention. When I have time to do that Justice to your book I shall take the liberty of addressing you my plaudits; for I am confident they will be the only remarks I can offer.   [*Source*: Scully Papers]

[1]Unidentified.

396   *From Lord Donoughmore to Merrion Square, Dublin*

Knocklofty [Co. Tipperary] 21 January 1813

Dear Scully,

I was in constant expectation of seeing you here, from the hopes which I thought you had given me, when I saw you in Merrion Square. On receiving a letter from Lord Grenville[1] I wrote to Kilfeacle, thinking I might have just caught you there before your departure for Dublin. But you had left Kilfeacle, & my letter was returned to me. My object in writing was, to have prevailed upon you to have come hither, that we might have discussed Ld Grenville's communication; or to have let me call upon you for the same purpose.

Ld Grenville's object is immediate discussion — or rather the presentation of both petitions to the Lords & Commons — on the first possible days after the next meeting,[2] & the *prompt* discussion in the *Commons*, suppose after an interval of 10 days or a fortnight, waiting a little longer for the discussion in the Lords.

Ld Grenville also makes use of this expression, viz — *The Bill* — as if the intended made *now* has to be, the introduction of a Bill.[3] This reminds me of a hint which you gave me of something, which you conceived to have been then in contemplation & which did not appear to meet with your concurrence much more than it did with my own.[4]

Ld Grenville mentions also his having written to Mr Grattan, to the same effect as he was then doing to me. You must therefore, of course, have been apprized of that Communication. But do you conceive it to have been a letter from Ld Grenville in the first instance, or an answer from him to a letter from Mr Grattan, or some other person on the Catholic subject to him?[5]

You will oblige me by giving me a prompt & confidential account of whatever may have taken place, & of which the decisions or feelings of the Catholic Board are — whether they have decided upon the immediate introduction of a Bill & what Bill.[6]

Let me know also, when the petitions can be prepared, & signed so as to be prepared for presentation to Parliament.

For my own part I more than doubt the prudence of pressing on the discussion of these petitions so much & whether there will be as full an attendance procured of the Irish members before the Circuits as after them. I also continue to hold all those objections to the proceeding by Bill in which you seemed to agree in our late conversation upon the subject.

What have you done with the petitions from this County, which Prendergast,[7] the Sheriff, has told me more than once he was ready to sign as Sheriff if they were presented to him for that purpose. This would be a great object — to counteract the counter petition now in progress.[8] Write to me with as little delay as possible.[9]   [*Source*: Scully Papers]

[1]Not among the Donoughmore Papers.

[2]That is, when parliament met again after the Christmas recess.

[3]He evidently understood Lord Grenville to mean that Grattan was going to introduce a bill immediately.

[4]According to Grattan, *Life and Times* V, p. 487 Grattan summoned W. C. Plunket, Peter Burrowes, Charles Burton and Thomas Wallace in December 1812 to his home in Co. Wicklow for the purpose of preparing a bill. This is described as simple, short and without clauses, and probably therefore did not follow the draft that Butler had been asked to prepare — see No. 360 and Butler's letter of 22 March 1813 in Appendix B. In a speech on 13 June 1813 O'Connell indicated that he had heard of the meeting and complained that the bill prepared by three gentlemen of the bar had been considered too important a secret to be confided to any Catholic (O'Connell, *Life* I, p. 412).

[5]A letter of 1 November 1812 from Earl Grey to Lord Grenville suggests that the latter wrote to Grattan on his own initiative. Grey wished to move an amendment on the address if the Catholic question was not mentioned in it, provided Lord Donoughmore and Grattan could attend (*Dropmore Papers* X).

[6]The Board met on 23 and 30 January when the composition of a delegation to go to London with a petition was settled (DDA 54/2, III, 13, 19). No evidence has been found of their having discussed a bill.

[7]Unidentified.

[8]At a meeting in Limerick on 5 January George Lidwill said that on the ground of its being improper for a sheriff to convene only one sect he had got the sheriff of Tipperary to convene a meeting of both Catholic and Protestant freeholders (*Pilot* 11 January 1813). When Colonel William Bagwell presented the Protestant petition on 24 February General Mathew, who followed with the Protestant-Catholic one from Co. Tipperary, denied that the first could be called a petition from the Protestant freeholders, no meeting having been convened by the sheriff or two or more

magistrates. In the House of Lords on 19 March Lord Donoughmore said that his petition, being signed by the High Sheriff on behalf of a county meeting, could only be received as the petition of the sheriff (*Hansard* XXIV, 727).
[9]Lord Donoughmore replied to Lord Grenville on 1 February. While expressing the doubts mentioned in the present letter he told him that those who were supposed to direct the Catholic Board were in agreement with him, Lord Grenville (Dropmore Papers: Add.MSS.58, 963).

397   *From Charles Butler to Merrion Square*

Lincolns Inn, 25 January 1813

Dear Sir,

I send you three Letters: the first[1] which is crossed over, was designed for yourself; but hoping I should have something of more consequence to communicate to you, I delayed sending it. The second[2] contains a long account of a conversation between Lord Castlereagh and myself. I left his Lordship with a conviction on my mind, that for *some reason or other*, he was a friend to Roman Catholic Emancipation to a certain extent. The third letter[3] is to Sir John Hippesley. Several Paragraphs have appeared in our paper intimating that he has abandoned us: I believe he is indignant at the conduct of the Irish Bishops and Doctor Milner on the business of the Veto: But I believe he will always be our friend. He certainly intends publishing a pamphlet in the form of a Letter addressed to Lord Fingall;[4] but what the tenor of it is to be I don't know. On the eighth we shall have a meeting of some of the English Catholics.[5] I have already mentioned to you that I have great hopes of our success, But I almost stand single; as the general opinion is against us. I send you a Worcester Paper, in which you will find an excellent letter from Mr Hornyold.[6]

I wish you would send a copy of your excellent *Statement* to every Member of both houses of Parliament: it would be of incalculable service to the cause. Your funds cannot be better employed than on this measure. I have shewn our petition to the speaker, to ascertain that the reference in it to our former petition and to the Resolution for taking our affairs into consideration[7] were conformable to the rules of the house. I was glad to hear from him that they were. I am with great respect etc.

P.S. I have to request a further favor from you: Which is that you would procure me authentic information on the three following points. 1st What were the arrear of causes when Lord Clare resigned the Chancellorship. 2nd What was the arrear when Lord Redesdale resigned. 3rd And what is the present arrear.[8]

P.S. I have just seen the insertion in the *Morning Post*.[9] At present I think it sho'd be answered, formally, on both sides the water.

[Enclosure A]

Charles Butler to Denys Scully

Lincolns Inn, 28 December 1812

Copy

Dear Sir,

I was duly favoured with your last Letter respecting the two Law books and I am much obliged to you for it.

The English Roman Catholics are determined to Petition this year and that the House shall determine upon it.[10]

I have great hopes of its success. I think the cause has been hurt by the conduct of your bishops[11] and by some intemperate speeches on your side of the water: still I have greater hopes than ever of our success. I hope to receive the two volumes of opinions as I am in great want of them.

I send you a copy of a Letter written by me to Mr Grattan and also a copy of a letter written by me to Sir John Hippisley.

[Enclosure B]

Charles Butler to the Rt Hon. H. Grattan

[December 1812]

Copy

Sir,

Last Saturday[12] I had a long conversation with Lord Castlereagh, in consequence of a message from his Lordship.

He began it, by saying, that, as he knew I had paid much attention to the Roman Catholic concerns, he wished to hear from me, what occurred to me on the subject.

I told his Lordship, that there was no communication between the Irish and English Catholics; and that they stood on very different grounds. He mentioned, (but without much harshness), the intemperance, of some of the speeches at the Irish meetings. He observed, that Lord Fingal presided at those meetings, from which, it was fair to infer, that Lord Fingal and his friends did not dislike the general turn of them. He spoke much in favor of the English Catholics; and seemed to intimate, that there would be no objection in raising them to the level of Irish Catholics. I told his Lordship, that, I did not undertake to speak the sentiments of the body; but that, as far as my opinion went, I thought this would not be a boon, acceptable to the English Catholics. This appeared to me to give him some surprise; but I distinctly repeated it.

I observed to him, that the Catholics complained that Government never explained to them what was the extent of relief, to which Government would go. His Lordship said this seemed unnecessary, as the Irish insisted upon having every thing, without any qualification whatsoever. I observed, that, this had never been explicitly announced to Government by the body, or by any persons appointed by them to represent them: and that in all events, the expression must be understood, even by those, who used it, with some limitation: for, as to the act of Settlement, I believe, there was not a Catholic, in the united Kingdom, who would petition for any relief, which trenched upon that act. I pressed him, (as far as was becoming), to inform me, what was the plan of Government in our respect. He persisted in repeating, that, it was in vain to propose any thing, as the Irish had explicitly declared, that they would be satisfied with nothing short of every thing. He observed, that You, were in Ireland, and probably communicated with the leading Roman Catholics; and that Government would therefore wait to see, what plan You would suggest, on Your return to this Country.[13]

On my mentioning to him, that I had drawn a sketch of a bill, for the repeal of all the Laws against the Roman Catholics,[14] he expressed, (with something like earnestness), a wish to see it. I promised to send it to him and he begged me to send with [it], any suggestions which might occur to me.

His Lordship mentioned the communications between him and the Irish Prelates;[15] he assured me, that, in obtaining their resolutions, there has not been any intimidation used by him, or any other persons in or near Government, and that he had told the Prelates, that, in framing their Resolutions, he wished them to consult, not only their principles, but their feelings. He said the business had gone so far, that the amount of the salaries, and even, the fund, out of which they were to come, had been settled, with the full concurrence of the Prelates. I understood from him, that he had explained to them, that he had made them nothing of a promise, respecting Catholic Emancipation: He denied the existence of any such promise to others; and he expressed himself on this, in terms so explicit, as surprised me a good deal. He stated this very extraordinary fact, that, when he was requested to take part in Lord Sidmouth's administration,[16] he required as a preliminary, that his promise, respecting salarizing the Catholic Clergy should be performed; and that it was agreed to; and he understood that the King did not object to it. On some future occasion, he understood from the Irish bishops, that it would appear to the Irish public, ungracious in them to accept a boon for themselves, if nothing was done for the body at large; and that, on this account, they declined the promised boon. He seemed to think that this proceeding did them great honor.[17]

Tho' I don't think these particulars of much importance I thought it might be agreeable to you to be informed of them.

[Enclosure C]

Charles Butler to Sir John Hippisley

Lincolns Inn, 28 December 1812

Copy

Dear Sir,

I was duly favoured with your Packet; and I hope it is now safely returned into your hands, as I have paid particular attention that your directions respecting it, should be observed.

There is no doubt that the Author of the Supplement[18] intended it to pass, as a real Continuation of the Statement, and I think it well calculated for the purpose. For, tho' every person of moderate discernment, will soon perceive the imposture, numbers will be deceived by it. This was noticed by the *Dublin Evening Herald*, but I think the circumstance should be frequently repeated; and in my next letter to Ireland, I shall suggest its being done.

I suppose you have seen the Resolutions of the Irish Prelates.[19] There are two ways of considering them; — as guarding their flocks, against the schismatical tendency of the doctrines of the french priests; and as a rejection, by anticipation, of all arrangements respecting the Irish Hierarchy. For the first, there was not the least necessity, no one here pays the slightest attention to the french priests, or reads their writings. I dare say, that there are not ten englishmen protestant or catholic, who altogether have read ten pages of the writings of Blanchard, or any of his brethren. With respect to the second, the resolution was very improper. It was not called for; and, as it disgusts our friends, and furnishes arms to our enemies it must be considered as an unwise measure. I am sorry for the unqualified approbation, which the Prelates have expressed, of Mr Clinche's work; as it contains some very unguarded expressions, and some, which it is not easy to distinguish from formal heresy.[20]

I send you a copy of a letter which I have received from Mr Grattan; and of a letter, I have written to him, giving him an account of a conversation I have had with Lord Castlereagh, on the subject of Roman Catholic affairs. I left his Lordship, with an impression on my mind, that, for some reason or other, his Lordship is a real well wisher to Catholic Emancipation, to a great extent.

It is impossible for an Englishman not to rejoice on the success of the Russians.[21] In one point of view, it is very great: as five years will not enable Buonaparte, to collect such an army, either in numbers and discipline, or such a material,[22] (to use his own expression), as he has left between the Dwina and the Volga. On the other hand, a disposable force of 300,000 men at least, remains to him. What may he not do with these in the Peninsula? And his establishing himself there, will bring him very near us. Reasoning in this manner, it is fair to ask, whether it was not better for England, that he should be employed on his gigantic efforts in Asia, than, on more contracted, but more practical operations in Europe. I strongly incline to suspect, that, it would have been better for us, if the ruin of his army had not been so compleat: A partial defeat, might have induced him to continue his expense of blood and of treasure, on the Russian sands and snows. Would it not have been worse for France, and better for us, if the surrender of Saratoga had happened in the first year of the American war. This appears to me a proper view of things, supposing events proceeded regularly. But how much fuel is there, in every part of the continent, for Volcanoes? And, if a single Volcano bursts forth, it may produce a general conflagration, in which the scourge of the world may be consumed.

Leaving the speculation to itself, the question for *our* consideration, (as you are pleased to make yourself one of us), is how the catholic affair stands. After much consideration, and some waivering, my present opinion, is, that it stands very well. I believe some speeches in Ireland, have disgusted our friends, and afforded arms to our enemies; and that the divisions among the Catholics themselves, and their want of active and energetical leaders, are great impediments of our success. I am also convinced, that the Ministers entertain no *immediate* apprehension of the Irish Catholics. On the other hand, they know that the momentum of 3/5ths of the Irish population must be irresistible; and that the accidents, which may call it into action are numerous: they also feel, that its negative effect, even in a state of quiescence, is very great. We must also take into account, the undeniable promises of the Prince; the possibility of Lord Moira's being driven into a situation, in which he must bully his Royal Highness;[23] and his Royal Highness's great unfitness for such an assault: and above all, the falling off of the Recruiting service in Ireland, which mere whisky will not adequately supply.[24] When, in addition to all this, we find that of the 100 Irish members, 80 at least, are decidedly favourable to Emancipation,[25] and that besides these Mr Canning has 30 votes; the ministerial strugglers, headed by Lord Castlereagh, our friends among the dissenters, and our tried friends of the true Whig school; and when we also reflect that while we have Grattan, Ponsonby, Canning etc. the whole opposite array does not furnish a single speaker, the result evidently leads to a favourable conclusion.

I think, the English Catholics, should for this once, lead the way.[26] It is the fashion for the Ministerial Phalanx, to praise their conduct. Now, if the Petition of the Irish Catholics, (with some of whom they profess to find fault), produced a resolution in the House of Commons, for taking the Catholic concern into consideration,[27] the Petition of the English Catholics ought, under existing circumstances, to produce an equal effect. This argument will have its weight; and it may also tell much in our favour, that the situation of the English Catholics, is much worse than that of the Irish

Catholics. On this head, I have only to add, that it seems adviseable for us, that our Petition should be brought forward as soon as possible. But it is the decided resolution of the English Catholics to accept of no boon, which does not equally advance the Irish Catholics, in their view of Emancipation.

It seems to be admitted that Lord Castlereagh is little attended to, in the house of Commons; and that the inadequacy of Mr Vansittart to his present situation,[28] so far as it unavoidedly obliges him to appear a prominent figure in the House of Commons, is every day felt more and more. The turn of affairs in America,[29] is by no means favourable to Ministers: and the distractions in Carlton House, and its appendances, are visibly on the encrease.

It is supposed that there will not [be a] Vice-Chancellor. The plan is not much relished by the Bar.   [*Source*: Scully Papers]

[1]Marked below as Enclosure A.

[2]Enclosure B.

[3]Enclosure C.

[4]Sir J. C. Hippisley's *Letters to the Earl of Fingall on the subject of the Catholic claims* had been published by the end of February. His main point was that when he was revising his tract of 1805 (see No. 125 n.1) and sought corrections from Dr Troy and Dr Milner they scarcely corrected a dozen lines, of which none affected the principle of his proposed regulations. Dr Milner's letter, he said, was still in his possession.

[5]See No. 403 n.5.

[6]Thomas Hornyold, of Blackmore Park, Worcestershire. No Worcester paper of this date has been preserved at the Newspaper Library, Colindale.

[7]The resolution on Canning's motion of 22 June 1812 (see No. 359 n.2). Butler's doubt arose from the convention that no parliament could bind its successor.

[8]Butler may have wanted the information in connexion with Lord Redesdale's bill for the creation of a new post of Vice-Chancellor in order to clear the back-log of cases in the Court of Chancery and prevent future delays. When the bill received its second reading on 11 February (*Hansard* XXIV, 459) Lord Castlereagh pointed out that in Ireland business was so arranged that the Master of the Rolls afforded the same assistance to the Lord Chancellor as was proposed in the bill to be given by the Vice-Chancellor.

[9]The *Morning Post* of 20 January had reported on an anti-Catholic meeting in Flint. After the Earl of Grosvenor had urged the meeting to separate for the present and not fetter the hands of Parliament Lord Kenyon carried the day against him by dwelling on the Pope's coronation of the "sanguinary usurper", Napoleon; the punishment by the Irish and English Bishops of two French priests for refusing to abandon the old independence of the French church; the recent declaration of the Irish Bishops that they would do nothing without the Pope's authority; and the shameful interference of the popish priests in the late elections.

[10]In previous years the petitions of the English Catholics were only ordered to be laid on the table.

[11]See No. 390 n.3.

[12]Enclosure B starts on the same sheet of paper as Enclosure A and was probably of

the same date, which is also the date of Enclosure C. If so the interview with Castlereagh, on a strict reading, took place on 26 December; but Butler may have drafted his letters during the week preceding Christmas and 19 December is a more probable date.

[13]Grattan was at his home in Co. Wicklow preparing the bill (see No. 396 n.4).

[14]See No. 340.

[15]In January 1799, when the four Archbishops and five Bishops adopted a resolution accepting state provision for the clergy and a measure of government interference in the appointment of prelates to vacant sees: for the text see Ward, *Eve of Catholic Emancipation* I, p. 33. Details of the settlement to which Castlereagh refers are in Home Office file 100/99 at the Public Record Office.

[16]On 12 July 1802.

[17]On 28 February 1821 Lord Castlereagh confirmed in the House of Commons that he had made the offer and received the reply as here described by Butler (*Hansard* NS IV, 1029).

[18]A pamphlet published anonymously under the title of *The third part of the Statement of the Penal Laws*. Its author was the barrister Edmund Swift, described by Jonah Barrington (*Personal Sketches* I, p. 405) as "as fanatical an ultra-royalist as the king's dominions afforded". He sent a copy to Peel under cover of a letter dated 27 October 1812 (Peel Papers, Add.MSS.40, 222, f.274), in which he interpreted the first two parts of the *Statement* as showing that the Catholics claimed not only equal or superior but exclusive occupancy of Church and State and said that he had endeavoured "according to their own stile and own arrangement, to say for them what they do not yet dare say for themselves". A notice of the work appeared in the *Evening Herald* of 6 December, which described it as a well executed hoax.

[19]Of 18 November 1812 (see No. 390 n.3).

[20]See No. 375 n.2. Clinch was thanked in the 7th resolution for "the ability, learning and zeal which he has successfully displayed in his refutation of the errors and slanders published under the title of *Columbanus ad Hibernos*".

[21]Reports in the London press of 24 December suggested that Napoleon had been cut off in his retreat to Minsk.

[22]Butler no doubt intended his clerk to write *matériel*.

[23]See No. 394 n.3.

[24]See No. 391 n.2.

[25]According to the division list of 3 March (*Hansard* XXIV, 1074) 21 Irish members voted against Grattan's motion out of the 74 who voted.

[26]In the event the English Catholic petition was presented before the Irish one but on the same day and not separately debated (ibid., 742).

[27]On Canning's motion of 22 June 1812 (see No. 359 n.2).

[28]As Chancellor of the Exchequer.

[29]The United States had been at war with England since 18 June 1812. Butler may have been thinking of American naval successes and the rejection by President Monroe on 27 October of a proposal for an armistice (S. E. Morison: *History of the United States* I, p. 291).

398   *From Charles Butler to Merrion Square*

Private   Lincolns Inn, 28 January 1813

Dear Sir,

I suppose you have received my large packet. I find that Your Petition is considered, by many of our friends in Parliament, as likely to prove highly detrimental to your cause. I, yesterday, met several of our friends, some of them persons of the most liberal and enlarged minds, and they all agreed in expressing this opinion of it. For my own part, I can truly say, that I have always been sensible, that you are the best judges of your own strength and bearings; and I, therefore, think that the great probability, in all these cases, is, that you are in the right. The attempts that are making in this country to prejudice the public mind against us, are very great, but I am not alarmed at any thing I have yet seen. The circumstance that alarms me most, is, that there are about fifty members in the House who may be gained or lost by good or bad management; and (*between ourselves*), I think we shall lose a great proportion of them by the tone of your Petition. I should therefore be very much obliged to you to favour me with a few lines upon the subject. This is between ourselves; but you may confidently assure your friends, from me, that the English catholics will never seek or accept any boon from Government, unless the same favor is shewn to the Irish.

[*Source*: Scully Papers]

399   *From Charles Butler to Merrion Square*

                                     Lincolns Inn, 2 February 1813

Dear Sir,

I learn from the *Dublin Evening Herald*, that the prosecution against Fitzpatrick goes on.[1] I understood it had been given up. Of course the circulation, which I recommended of it,[2] should be suspended. I need not add, that, if I can be of any use to you in this business, you may command me. Members are now pouring rapidly into town, and I am sorry to say that I find all our friends extremely dejected. A very remarkable event has lately taken place. The protestant students of our Inns of Court had come to a resolution to petition Parliament in favor of the Irish Catholics, but they have now dropped their plan, and the reason alledged is the intemperance of some of the speeches and some of the resolutions in Ireland. This is too common a discourse among our friends, and I wish a letter was written to some person of distinction, in this country, to be generally shewn. It might soothe the unfortunate irritation upon the subject.

There seems to be a strong wish among the English Catholics for a separate discussion on their bill; and it was once the general opinion, that it should come on before yours; but if your leading friends think this would be prejudicial to your cause, it certainly will not be done.

[P.S.] The Hunts are to be brought up for Judgment tomorrow.[3] Burdet, it is supposed, will start the Princesses game immediately.[4] It is contrary to the wishes of the opposition.   [*Source*: Scully Papers]

[1]See No. 363 n.2. Following the summons of 3 July 1812 to appear at the Attorney-General's house and the subsequent filing of an *ex officio* information against him Fitzpatrick had been indicted on 6 November in the court of King's Bench for libelling the Lord Lieutenant. On 28 January the court had appointed 6 February for the trial (*DEP*, 30 January 1813).

[2]The *Statement of the Penal Laws*, which Butler in No. 397 wished to be sent to every member of both Houses of parliament.

[3]James Leigh Hunt and his brother John had been convicted in 1812 for a libel on the Prince Regent. Each was sentenced to two years imprisonment and a fine of £500 (*DNB*).

[4]It was common knowledge in London at the beginning of February that the Prince Regent had returned unopened a letter from his wife, Princess Caroline, about his treatment of their daughter, Princess Charlotte. Burdett had just given notice of a motion (which he introduced on 23 February — *Hansard* XXIV, 706) to provide against any interruption in the exercise of the royal authority in the event of the death of the Regent; and as Princess Charlotte was next in the line of succession this could be seen as a step in the campaign, just beginning, to bring the wrongs of the two princesses to public notice.

400   *To Charles Butler, Lincoln's Inn, London*

Merrion Square [Dublin] 3 February 1813

Copy — Private

Dear Sir,

I have had the Honor of receiving your letter of the 28th Jan'y marked Private — also your letter of the 25th Jan'y and your two Packets of the 26th January under franked Covers, which contained in two large sheets, the Copies of 3 Letters, dated the 28 Decemb'r last, & written by you — one of which 3 letters appears to have been intended to be addressed to me, but not before forwarded; another addressed to Mr Grattan respecting an important Interview between Lord Castlereagh & yourself upon Catholic affairs, and the third addressed to Sir J. Hippesley upon the same subject.[1]

These last two Letters appear to be in form of a Circular communication; and, being of serious moment coming at this crisis, from a Gentleman of your rank & respected Character, demanded my utmost consideration and respect. In this busy Term, I am unable to devote as much time as I could wish to these subjects; but I have deposited these Copies of your Two Letters, to Mr Grattan and Sir J. Hippesley in the hands of Mr O'Connell and his friends at the Board, for their earnest consideration.

For the present, I am unable to make any satisfactory communication to you upon the subject of those Letters — but, from the general sentiment here, I own I could wish, for the sake of those cordial feelings which you wish to promote and from personal regard towards yourself, that the Petition to which you allude[2] should not be presented or proceeded upon until you can see Lord Fingall & his Co-Delegates[3] (who will probably arrive in London about the 14th inst.) and that you may find it right to suspend any further Interviews with any of the ministers upon the affairs of the Irish Catholics until you have conferred and fully debated the matter with these Delegates. There is a great, and *unanimous* jealousy of feeling at the Board, upon these subjects — and I fear much any incident, which may excite a misunderstanding. The passage in Mr Ed. Jerningham's late Letter to the Board (in which he desires not to be *again misunderstood* by the Irish Catholics), has been ill received.[4] Could not that Letter have been conceived and worded without such a retrospective wound? Or why unnecessarily lay yourselves open to the necessity of a further explanation?

The Article in the *Morning Post*,[5] to which you refer me, is not within my reach. That Paper is not taken in here by any Society or Individual that I can hear of — neither is the *M. Herald*.

You observe, that some of our friends object to the *tone* of our Petition. Do they actually know what its tone or Language is? Or are they aware, that it is nearly a transcript of the short and rational Petition presented to Parliament last year by the united three Dissenting Bodies of London, praying for *universal* religious freedom.[6]

It varies from that Petition merely in *softening* a certain Passage, declaratory of an abstract right of free worship. And is this the violent tone? But surely you will always find persons ready to find fault. The Irish Catholics, be assured, were never so strong (because never *so unanimous*, so earnest, and so determined) as at this moment. This is a good answer to all objections, and should acquit them of intemperance on the one hand, and of want of energy on the other.

I have the Honour to be, Dear Sir with great respect,

Your most Obedient Servant,

D.S.

[P.S.] Perhaps you are not apprized, that Sir J. Hippesley is of no weight or consideration in Ireland: and is rather doubted by many Catholics.

[*Source*: Scully Papers]

[1] See No. 397 and enclosures.

[2] In Enclosure A of No. 397.

[3] On 30 January Randal MacDonnell, Owen O'Conor, Lord Kenmare, Sir Francis Goold and P. B. Hussey had been chosen by the Board to accompany Lord Fingall (DDA 54/2, III, 39).

[4] On 2 February a letter from Edward Jerningham was read at the Board saying that the English Catholic Board felt they should try to have a separate discussion in parliament of the English Catholic petition. The Secretary was directed to reply that the Irish Board had nothing to say on the subject (ibid., 40). The misunderstanding referred to by Jerningham was in regard to the events leading up to the Fifth Resolution of 1 February 1810 (see No. 230 n.1).

[5] See No. 397 n.9.

[6] A petition for liberty of conscience from "several dissenting ministers in and about the city of London and Westminster" was presented by William Smith on 23 April 1812 (*Hansard* XXII, 727). On 1 July 1812 this had been read at the meeting of the Irish Catholic Board which then adopted its own petition based on it [DDA 54/2, III, 9).

401 *From Bishop John Milner to Merrion Square, Dublin*

W.Hmpton, 3 February [1813]

My Dear Sir,

I found myself honoured, (on my return from the North of Staffordshire, where I had been consecrating a chapel) with your kind & interesting Letter of the 13th Ult. I regret that I did not know in time of yr. intention of meeting Mrs S. at Chester,[1] as, in that case, I shd. have made an effort to meet you both there & to pass two or three hours in yr. company.

In case the Resolutions of yr. Prelates[2] are approved of in Ireland, it is not so in England, or at least in London. Indeed I observe that some of yr. orators, not without a plausible pretext, now distinguish between a *London Catholic* & *a Roman Catholic*. Our self appointed board are to meet next Monday to form *a Petition*, *an Address*, & certain *Conciliatory Resolutions*; all ready manufactured by that inflated nerveless writer Chs. Butler. (His person is emblematic of his style). It will be well if the Resolutions do not bring on a fresh quarrel between the English & Irish politicians as well as Divines.[3] For my part I shall certainly side with my countrymen, when I find that they have the advantage of good sense, genius & Religion on their side: but this has not been the case hitherto & I almost despair of its ever being so. Jos. Berington has published an Octavo of 464 pages, with the imposing title of *The Faith of Caths. confirmed by Scripture, the Fathers etc.*[4] It is a most clumsy, inaccurate, or rather erroneous symbol of belief; & I fear it may give rise to much dispute. I despair of producing any further effect on yr. Prelates than I have produced: I am confident though they much disapprove of enlisting, they wd. not venture to oppose it on a *settled organised plan*.[5] Does not the Universal *No-Popery* cry appal your Irish Politician: those in England are in Despair; & several of them have descended to ask for the feeble aid of my pen. My answer is that they discarded me when they voted that no Priest or Bishop shd. be admitted as a member of their *controversial society*[6] (for such was the professed & real nature of our *Board* at its first foundation) & again when they published in the Newspapers that they were "not implicated in the political writings etc. of Dr M": for it is obvious that I never was concerned in any *politics*, except in furthering the Emancipation.[7] When a *single soul* is in *danger of perversion* from the pamphlets, then, I say, I will do my best to refute them.

I must, with the utmost sincerity & the purest friendship, declare my utter incompetency to advise you on the subject of yr. book.[8] I recommend it on every occasion, as a prodigy in its kind: but I am sure the person who cd. write it, is better able to judge of the several matters, relative to it, which you propose to me, than any other person is; at all events, better than I am. Mrs Wheble joins me in all that is kind to Mrs S & regrets having missed seeing her, when she was in England.   [*Source*: Scully Papers]

[1]See No. 388. Scully had been hoping that she would be escorted by her brother.
[2]See No. 390 n.3.
[3]See No. 403 n.5. for the outcome.
[4]Joseph Berington (1745–1827) had been leader of the "Staffordshire Clergy" in 1791 and a supporter of Butler's Catholic Committee; he was twice suspended by his Bishop but made a retractation in 1801; now chaplain to Sir John Throckmorton. His book was written in collaboration with Father John Kirk. A dedication explains that the greater part of its propositions were taken from a work of the time of Charles II called *Roman Catholic Principles*.
[5]See No. 381 n.5.
[6]Bishop Ward states that the new Board formed in 1808 invited all the Vicars Apostolic and the clergy generally to join (*Eve of Catholic Emancipation* II, p. 99).
[7]See No. 257 n.4.
[8]The *Statement of the Penal Laws*.

402   *From Jane Canning to Merrion Square, Dublin*

Foxcote, 12 February [postmarked 1813]
My Dear Mr Scully,

I have just received a letter from Mr Canning in which he tells me you are coming to England & he desires me to write to you immediately to beg of you to take Foxcote in your way to London.[1] He wishes most particularly to see you. He returns from town where he has been upon the petition business, tomorrow.

He has enquired in vain in London for the *Statement of the Penal Laws*. He would be much obliged to you to procure him a copy in Dublin if possible.

I have just finished reading the trial for the libel[2] & feel most happy that as far as appears the statement of the fact *however* deemed *libellous* seems perfectly accurate & I think you could hardly do better to give authenticity to the whole statement than by making the trial an addition to it.

[*Source*: Scully Papers]

[1]It appears from Dr Milner's letter of 3 February, No. 401, that Scully had already met his wife at Chester and returned to Dublin.

[2]The trial of Hugh Fitzpatrick (see No. 404 n.1). On this same day Gregory wrote to Peel from Dublin Castle saying that he proposed to get the trial published, with the addition of full statements of all the particulars respecting Barry. On 30 March he dropped the idea, as the Attorney-General thought it would look like an appeal from the government to the public and subject them to answers and animadversions (Peel Papers, Add. MSS.40, 195).

403   *From Charles Butler to Merrion Square*

Lincolns Inn, 13 February 1813

Dear Sir,

I am favoured with your letter of the 3d of this month.[1] Nothing could be more contrary to my intentions or wishes, than that the letters, of which I sent you copies,[2] should, in any manner, become generally public: and I really am surprised to find you thought they were intended for a circular communication. It appears to me that on the very face of them, they bespoke a confidential communication. I am much mortified therefore, at what you mention, respecting them: and I should be extremely obliged to you to let me know what degree of publicity, I may consider them to have obtained:[3] and to stop it as much as in your power.[4]

We have had two days meeting. The first was a day of missunderstanding. The second a day of the most perfect harmony. I hope you will like our resolutions and petition.[5] The time and mode of bringing on the latter, was left, by unanimous consent, to be settled by Mr Grattan and Mr Eliot.

I hope you have seen my letter in the *Morning Chronicle*.[6] I shall be happy to hear that it is approved of by you and your friends. If there be any one of the delegates with whom you particularly wish me to confer on our affairs, or to whom you wish me to shew particular civilities, I shall be happy to attend to your suggestions.[7]

[*Source*: Scully Papers]

[1]No. 400.
[2]Enclosures B and C in No. 397.

[3]The letters were read at the Board on 2 February and were referred to again on 13 February when a resolution was passed that there should be no communication with government without the express and public authority of the Catholic body (DDA 54/2, III, 40, 43). O'Connell protested against "the gratuitous interference of a gentleman in England, and a Catholic too" (O'Connell, *Life and Speeches* I, p. 280).
[4]Although the letters were not published until 26 June their substance seems to have soon become widely known. Grattan had heard of their receipt by 23 February, when, through Edward Hay, he asked for a copy of Butler's letter to himself so that he could compare it with the original (O'Connell, *Correspondence* I, No. 408). On the same day the *Kilkenny Chronicle* published an article, which was reprinted as a leaflet (copy in Throckmorton Papers) rebuking Butler for his interview with Lord Castlereagh.
[5]The formula agreed upon was: "Your petitioners also humbly conceive that further securities cannot reasonably be required from them; but this, with a perfect spirit of conciliation, they leave to the wisdom and decision of the legislature, feeling confident that the legislature will never undo or render nugatory its own work by accompanying the relief with any clause or clauses to which your petitioners cannot conscientiously assent" (Ward, *Eve of Catholic Emancipation* II, p. 23).
[6]The so-called letter, in the *Morning Chronicle* of 6 February, was a long "Address to the Protestants of Great Britain and Ireland". It gave a list of the penal laws still in force against the English Catholics, argued that their general effect was to depress every member of the Catholic body below his legitimate level in society, and answered in detail the numerous allegations made against Catholics as to their tenets. Butler reprinted the address in his *Historical Memoirs* IV, pp. 197–227.
[7]Scully endorsed Butler's letter as having been replied to on 16 February. With that reply the correspondence between them seems to have ceased, there being no known letters of a later date.

404   *To Lord Holland, St James' Square, London*

Merrion Square, 16 February 1813

My Lord,

I have taken the liberty to send you a few of our recent Dublin papers occasionally — as an intimation of the events of this country — You have read of the trial of Mr Fitzpatrick[1] — It has caused uncommon interest here — and it is intended to bring before Parliament the conduct of Lord Norbury[2] and of the Irish administration respecting the maladministration [of] justice — A petition to the purpose is in contemplation.[3]

We have rumours in circulation, favourable to the result of our Catholic petitions, at least to a certain extent — but these rumours are scarcely credited, so often have we been deceived and disappointed.

[P.S.] Many thanks for your admirable victory in Wiltshire[4] — Would that the like energy were displayed by the talent & integrity of the other shires.

[*Source*: Holland House Papers Add. MS.51826 f.187]

[1]If he had not read about it in an Irish paper Lord Holland would have seen reports in the opposition press. The trial, an account of which is given in Howell, *State Trials* XXXI, 1170ff., had taken place on 6 February before Chief Justice Downes in the King's Bench and the jury had found Fitzpatrick guilty of having libelled the Duke of Richmond in the footnote on page 229 of the *Statement of the Penal Laws*, Part II (see No. 345 n.2). On 11 February O'Connell, one of the counsel for the defence, had moved for the verdict to be set aside, but as it was the last day of term the hearing had been postponed and Fitzpatrick admitted to bail. Scully attended the trial and when towards the conclusion of his opening speech the Attorney-General denounced the anonymous author of the *Penal Laws* he interrupted him to say that he would tell who the author was if the Attorney-General would consent to have the truth of the *Statement* tried in any fair mode of investigation where the truth could legally be received in evidence (*FJ*, 9 December 1813). The Attorney-General, hinting that he well knew who the author was, complained of having been drawn before parliament for having served a notice on the defendant before filing an information against him (see No. 363 n.2) and traced the questioning of the acts of government to the principles of Jacobinism. He was there, he said, to prosecute a libel and he would not stoop to defend the government on the arraignment of the libellous author of the "Statement of the Penal Code". Reporting to Peel on 8 February Gregory said that Scully fully felt the blows inflicted; but the Solicitor-General, he complained, had gone out of his way, courting popularity, to pour balm into the deep wounds by bestowing an encomium on the work: "Scully's vanity has been soothed, tho' with honest men his character has been stigmatized" (Peel Papers, Add.MSS.40, 195, f.87) On 28 May 1813 the court upheld the jury's verdict and Fitzpatrick was sentenced to eighteen months imprisonment, with a fine of £200 (*FJ*, 29 May 1813).

[2]In his speech for the defence Peter Burrowes argued that the footnote charged with being libellous was directed, not against the Lord Lieutenant, but against the judge, Lord Norbury, "whose conduct was so revolting". A judge being answerable only to parliament the object of the prosecution, Burrowes alleged, was to anticipate and influence an enquiry by parliament.

[3]It did not materialise. Sir Samuel Romilly, who had satisfied himself of Barry's guilt (see No. 351 n.10), writes in his *Memoirs* (II p. 312): "I have therefore abandoned my intention of bringing the subject before the House of Commons. However culpable the judge and the Government may have been, it is certain that the House will not think them so, if the prisoner were really guilty".

[4]A county meeting had been convened at Devizes on 27 January for the purpose of opposing the Catholic claims but it had terminated in a petition to the legislature in their favour (*FJ*, 5 February 1813). In *Further Memoirs of the Whig Party*, p. 169, Lord Holland attributed his success to the cooperation of the Methodists, to whom he had been of service in 1811.

405   *From Peter Bodkin Hussey to Merrion Square, Dublin*

Steevens Hotel, New Bond Street, London, 23 February 1813
Private

My dear Scully,

On my arrival here, I went to Boswell Court in search of Addis & Norris.[1] They have quitted that place & dissolved the partnership. It was only yesterday I found out where Addis lives. He has removed to Threadneedle Street in the City. We have a meeting this day, but I will call on Addis tomorrow. I am very sorry to tell you we won't succeed this time; tho' the opposition are using every exertion, the entire influence of the Crown will be used against us. I understand the docile Castlereagh will even oppose going into a Committee.[2] *You may rely on it* that the Prince is more *violent & prejudiced* against us than even his Father was. They blame our proceedings — it is easy for them to find excuses. Hay is here acting as we predicted; he insists he is one of the Delegates as also Secretary etc. He seems inclined to quarrel, I am sadly afraid to say no worse, he will cover us with ridicule — which we can't well afford in the present State of our cause. The Question certainly comes on the 25th. Lord Donoughmore is not yet come to town. Of course no time is fixed for the debate in the Lords.

You will hear I dread some violent attempt against the Princess of Wales — the ministers, good conscientious men will support the Prince *in all his wishes*.[3] When I have any thing to communicate I will write you.

[P.S.] We have written to Sidmouth, to know when & *how* the Prince will receive the address.[4] We have press'd for an audience, but have not as yet got an answer. Grattan would not on any acct. put off the debate. John Burke[5] is not yet come nor is Lord Kenmare[6] in town. He has written that he will be here to morrow.   [*Source:* Scully Papers]

[1]Charles Addis and Thomas Norris, attornies.
[2]In the event Castlereagh spoke in favour of Grattan's motion for a committee on the claims of the Roman Catholics, but his name does not appear in the division lists (*Hansard* XXIV, 1018, 1074).
[3]See No. 399 n.4: the Princess of Wales' letter to the Prince Regent had been published in the *Morning Chronicle* of 10 February and she had been informed by Lord Liverpool on 14 February that Princess Charlotte's visit to her should not take place. On 19 February senior Privy Councillors had been shown the documents and they recommended on 23 February that the intercourse between Princess Charlotte and her mother should continue to be subject to restraint (*Hansard* XXIV, notes to 1107–1127).
[4]Lord Fingall was told on the 23rd that the Prince would receive the Irish Catholics' address at his levee on the 25th but owing to a misunderstanding their reception was postponed for a week (Fingall Papers).

[5]John Ignatius Burke of Glynsk (1784–1845); succeeded a cousin in 1814 as 10th Baronet.
[6]Valentine Browne, since October 1812 the 2nd Earl of Kenmare.

406   *From William Tighe to Merrion Square, Dublin*

London, 24 February 1813

My dear Sir,

I have to thank you for your two last letters[1] & several newspapers — the *Evening Post* which I received this day contains Barry's case[2] — it is well that it has been investigated & that Lord Norbury's [conduct] appears to justify any censure that can be published against it. I doubt however if the prosecution of Fitzpatrick originated with Mr Poole [Pole] and had any thing in the least to say with my conversation with him or motion about Hall[3] — the only conversation I had with him, was to tell him that I intended to move for papers about Hall, & to know if [he] had them in his office & was ready to produce them. He said he was to produce them & to send them to my house, which he did. At the same time I mentioned that I had some idea of moving also for papers relating to the case of one Barry hanged at Kilkenny some time ago. He said he had no such papers & had no recollection of the case. I never mentioned having seen the fact in print, nor any thing more about it, nor could he suppose that I had any other knowledge than a gentleman of the County of Kilkenny might naturally have had of such a fact. It never was afterwards even alluded to, in what was said in the house relative to Hall.

If such petitions as you mention[4] were to be presented to Parliament, arraigning the conduct of the Irish government, in the cases you mention, you may be sure that I should give them every support in my power, for I fully concur to your opinion as to the heinousness of the facts & think that with a free parliament & just government they ought to be fully investigated — but the petitioners are the best judges whether they would be likely to receive in the present state of things either due support or cordial inquiry — & whether if such a petition was signed principally by Catholics it might injure *their cause*.

I have been very unwell lately & though I shall certainly attend the house during the debate of tomorrow,[5] & untill it concludes, & shall be ready to bear my testimony in your favour should it be called for by circumstances, however little or ineffectual what I can say may be — yet I feel too unwell to use any exertion or to express any of that indignation which I conceive of the conduct of those here & principally of the English Clergy, who are daily pouring from the press & the pulpit all the old calumnies against Irish Catholics so constantly repeated, though a hundred & a hundred times refused.   [*Source*: Scully Papers]

[1]Not found.

[2]The trial of Hugh Fitzpatrick (see No. 404 n.1).

[3]Walter Hall (see No. 358, of which the remainder of this paragraph is a repetition).

[4]One of them no doubt about the Barry case (see No. 404 n.3).

[5]On Grattan's motion for a committee on the claims of the Roman Catholics (*Hansard* XXIV, 747). His name is included in the list of the majority in the division of 3 March (ibid., 1076).

407 *From Dr Edward Sheridan, Dominick Street to Merrion Square, 24 February 1813*

He is so pleased with the *Statement of the Penal Laws* that he cannot forbear communicating his impressions. "It traces those laws to their true origin, a malignant spirit, and it shows that these laws in their turn keep that spirit alive, a spirit which when deprived of some of its instruments is naturally impelled to give a new edge and more energy to the remainder."

[*Source*: Scully Papers]

408 *From Lord Donoughmore to Merrion Square South, Dublin*

Cheek Point,[1] 26 February 1813

Dear Scully,

It is certainly time that I should acknowledge your kind & valuable communications,[2] in which you are always prompt, & ever satisfactory. Indeed, having been entirely the seeker for Information, there was nothing to be done on my part, but to have expressed my thanks for the friendly & effectual manner in [which] you have afforded it to me.

To my brother Francis, who will be the bearer of this, I must refer you for my intentions as to our Question, as well as for an explanation, why I did not think my earlier appearance in the field, on the part of my Catholic friends, necessary.[3] If I had thought it so, I am sure it will not be necessary for me to say a word, that nothing would have detained me a moment from their service.

I ought to have returned Ld Holland's letter[4] long since but it had slipped amongst some papers to which it had no reference & it therefore had escaped me but I made a general review of them just before my coming home.

What is to be done respecting the inclosed communication from the late Sheriff of the Co. of Tipperary[5] — not having taken any part in that meeting, I did not feel myself as entitled to say any thing. But something ought to be done, if nothing has been done yet.[6]

[P.S.] My brother, Ld Hutchinson, is at my side & desires to be remembered most kindly to you. Direct to me in London to 4 Bulstrode Street, Manchester Square.   [*Source*: Scully Papers]

[1]The embarkation point in the port of Waterford for the packet to England.
[2]Not among the Donoughmore Papers.
[3]The reason was probably that which he gave when presenting the Irish Catholic petition on 19 March (*Hansard* XXV, 201) and elaborated in an open letter to Lord Fingall, published in *The Pilot* of 4 June: it would have been to risk the failure of the question by bringing it on prematurely in the House of Lords, where it had never succeeded, while discussion was in progress in the Commons in the most encouraging circumstances.
[4]Probably No. 389.
[5]Probably the unidentified Prendergast mentioned in No. 396.
[6]See No. 396 n.8 for the two meetings — one Protestant, the other Protestant-Catholic. What the point at issue was remains obscure.

409   *To his wife Catherine at 2 Merrion Square South, Dublin*

Enniscorthy [Co. Wexford] [27 February 1813]
Saturday night [postmarked 3 March 1813]

My dearest Catherine,

When you see Enniscorthy above, you will perhaps be puzzled, and have recourse to your map—but, to prevent suspence, it is 60 miles from Dublin & 12 from Wexford, where I mean to breakfast & hear mass tomorrow—and I write now, as I shall probably not have time to write again until next Tuesday night, after I receive your letter and parcel of Monday's Post.

I came 38 Miles yesterday, with rather wet weather until noon, but very fine afterwards — breakfasted at Blessington — dined & slept at Tullow, a good Town, and very civil comfortable Inn. The Landlady spoke much of Marshall,[1] whose Estate lies near, and said he was the best and most generous man they ever knew there, & that his absence is universally regretted. I dined and slept there. She had excellent salmon for me. This morning I heard Mass at the large new Chapel.[2] It is very large, far beyond any in Dublin, built of white hewn stone, on an eminence, over a fine river and commanding a beautiful prospect. There is attached a Convent of 12 nuns,[3] with a neat ornamented garden, the whole looks exceedingly well, and was built under the inspection of the Catholic Bishop of Kildare, Dr Delany, who has a handsome villa[4] within half a mile, and in sight of the Chapel of Tullow.

These matters so detained me, that I have come only 20 miles today — the weather and country beautiful, through the Counties of Carlow and Wexford, and the roads dry and well made. There are pretty Seats & Cottages, and a fine river, the Slaney, all along.

Our business[5] in Wexford begins on Monday at noon & will finish on Wednesday. I leave Wexford on Thursday morning, and expect to sleep in Waterford that night — and I mean to leave Waterford for Clonmell on Monday Evening or Tuesday morning following.

Will you write to me at Waterford on Friday next — and at Clonmell on Monday or Tuesday following — and you may direct in my own name.

Will you tell Peggy[6] to see particularly whether there is enough of *Oats and Straw* to last till my return.

If not of Oats, she will call in my name upon my friend Michael Dwyer at Messrs Fox Dwyer and Co., Batchelor's Walk (No. 7 or 10 — I think) and request him to send in 5 or 6 Barrels of good oats to me.

If Straw be wanting, you must send Peter[7] to the Market at Smithfield for one or 2 loads on a Wednesday or Saturday. The General Price is from 7/– to 10/– per load.

Let me know if any written or verbal Messages, or other calls for me — or if any from Fitzpatrick.[8] Of course you will send me any printed Sheets (or proofs, as they are called) that come from Fitzpatrick. I hope the children will continue well — and that you will cure James of his stammering: this would be a great matter. Excuse this scrawl — with the bad pen of the waiter — & believe me to be your ever affectionate husband D.S.

[P.S.] Will you let me know how many of the Notes for *One pound five* each I left with you on Thursday night. And, if you can conveniently, send me one or two notes of Five pounds each in your letter *to Waterford*. Adieu.

Take no notice of the above. I wrote it in consequence of having missed some notes, which I have since found safe hidden in my pocket book. Ever yours.

Sunday morning.

[*Source*: Scully Papers]

[1]Robert Marshall. The estate may have been one left to him by Anne Echlin, a Dublin spinster, under the terms of a will dated 28 December 1804 (index of Wills, Public Record Office of Ireland).

[2]Completed in 1805 (M. Comerford, *Collections of the Diocese of Kildare and Leighlin*, Dublin, 1886, I p. 89).

[3]Of the congregation of the Sisters of St Brigid. The convent was founded in 1807 (ibid., III, p. 414).

[4]Agars House.

[5]The Assizes.

[6]Seemingly the housekeeper.

[7]A groom.

[8]Hugh Fitzpatrick, convicted for libel but not yet sentenced (see No. 404 n.1).

410   *From Peter Bodkin Hussey*

Steeven's Hotel, New Bond Street, London, 1 March 1813

My dear Scully,

After calling on Addis in Threadneedle Street,[1] I find he has only an office there. I have however left the papers there and Mr McDonnell,[2] who lives near it, will send me the opinions[3] when they are received, which I shall take care to publish if favorable.

Our Question has been twice debated.[4] It comes on this night again; the knowing ones say it will certainly go into Committee. I have no doubt if any thing was offered respecting domestic nomination,[5] the Question was carried but of course we could give no opinion on the subject. Castlereagh will speak for us this night. You read I suppose Plunkett's speech; I believe he regrets much having stated there was a disaffected party in Ireland.[6] He says it escaped from him in the heat of debate. His speech actually it is said brought over almost the entire of what is call'd the floating party in the house. Wm. Fitzgerald[7] delivered a splendid speech. Lord Liverpool is very angry with him. He assailed most pointedly the hypocrisy of Bankes, York[8] & Sir John Stuart.[9] Hay as usual tiring all our friends with his tedious & tiresome visits. The English Catholics have kept clear of us. I met Lord Holland in the house of Commons, whose person I did not know, & Lord Lansdowne. They were very inquisitive about Ireland; I can assure you I gave them a true history of Fitzpatrick's trial[10] & the persecutions of the Duke of Richmond.[11] It would be of *the most decisive advantage* if the 3rd part of the *Statement*, the printing, circulating, or publishing of it, could be traced to the Duke of Richmond; his ministers have disowned all knowledge of it.[12] It has done us great service here; the attempt at forgery has damned all their protestant petitions; they consider the cause rotten that requires it.

[P.S.] Lord D[onoughmore] not yet arrived.   [*Source*: Scully Papers]

[1]See No. 405.
[2]Probably Miles MacDonnell, of M. I. Macdonnell and J. Bushell, merchants, of 4 Broad Street Court.
[3]Although the word is in the plural only one opinion is further heard of — that of Serjeant Shepherd in the Fitzpatrick case (see No. 451).
[4]On 25 and 26 February (*Hansard* XXIV, 742, 849).
[5]This solution, once favoured by Scully and proposed by Grattan when presenting the Irish Catholic petition on 18 May 1810 (see No. 233 n.1) had been ruled out by the Irish Prelates, most recently on 18 February 1812 (see No. 390 n.3).
[6]*Hansard* XXIV, 818.
[7]William Vesey Fitzgerald, who as Chancellor of the Exchequer for Ireland was a member of Lord Liverpool's government, had said that the vote he would give was one which he would give whether in or out of office (ibid., 869).

[8]Philip Yorke.

[9]Sir John Stewart (?1785–1825), of Ballygawley Park, Co. Tyrone, MP for County Tyrone 1802–6 and 1812–25.

[10]See No. 404 n.1.

[11]See No. 363 n.11.

[12]When a petition from Anglesea was presented on 11 February Sir Henry Parnell pointed out that it was filled with quotations from the *Third Part of the Penal Laws* taken from the *Anti-Jacobin Review*; and Grattan read out an Irish Catholic Board resolution of 6 February denouncing the forgery as "originating in a venal branch of the Dublin press". Peel intervened to say that he had heard for the first time that night from what press the pamphlet had issued and that he had only learnt of the publication from having received a copy from the anonymous author. On 24 February he again defended the Irish administration from taking any part in the publication (*Hansard* XXIV, 453, 456, 734). There is nothing in the author's letter to Peel (see No. 397 n.18) suggestive of prior knowledge on the part of the administration and Gregory assured Peel on 1 March that he had had no communication with the author (Peel Papers, Add.MSS.40, 195).

411   *From Sir Henry Parnell[1] to Merrion Square, Dublin*

Stratford Place [London] 1 March 1813

Private

My Dear Sir,

I have not leisure to reply further to your letter than to thank you for it & to say I will pay due attention to what you desire. I rather am induced to write these few lines to tell you that there is every prospect of a majority tonight on Mr Grattan's motion. Mr Plunkett's speech[2] has produced a greater effect than ever was known to be made by any other at any [word illegible] period.

I also feel anxious to convey to you a hope that if we do succeed your body will feel it to become an essential duty to themselves, under all the circumstances of the case, at least, to meet the victory with strong conciliatory language, even if they may still adhere to the strict letter of their declarations in respect to conditions. Such a course would, I think, not only carry the question soon & ultimately in a manner perfectly satisfactory to them, but lead to a general change in the system of Government.

[*Source*: Scully Papers]

[1]On the death of his elder brother Parnell had succeeded to the baronetcy on 30 July 1812. This is his first extant letter to Scully since No. 356 of 9 June 1812.

[2]*Hansard* XXIV, 795–820.

412   *From Sir Henry Parnell*

London, 3 March 1813

Private

My Dear Sir,

I sincerely congratulate you on the triumph of your cause, for I cannot help considering the vote of last night,[1] carried as it was against the most powerful exertions that ever a court made to defeat a measure in Parliament, as conclusive in regard to your final emancipation.

But your body should take great care clearly to understand the true state of opinion here before they appear in public under the new circumstances of their situation. To me it seems to be quite certain that the Bill will not pass without an arrangement relative to foreign influence, & that this arrangement will in effect be quite different from any that has hitherto been suggested, provided the decision of last night is received in Ireland with grateful & conciliatory language. The truth is people's feelings are hurt in this Country, more, however, by the false character that has been industriously given to the Catholic Debates & resolutns. than by these proceedings themselves, & it is but a sacrifice that good policy requires to be made to do these trifling things, which in all such cases are alone sufficient to soothe & reconcile.

The only point which the opponents to the motion urged with the least effect during the debate consisted in this charge of violent & menacing language & I am quite sure that if your Body was to repel it in an effectual manner that you would carry your cause almost without another struggle.

In the present state of the business more is not called for than conciliatory professions, as we are sure of passing th[r]o' the Committee & laying the foundation of the Principle of the Bill. But before the time arrives for going into the Committee on the Bill, your body should go as far as they really can go, consistent with their religion, & a fair jealousy of the influence of the Crown, in respect to the conditions to form the projected securities of the Prot. Establishment. I still think the whole matter a gross absurdity — but it will be very difficulty [*sic*], almost impossible with an adverse Court to get people here to think the same.

I know there are great obstacles in the way of reconciling the Catholics to any conditions, & of providing any way by which they could express them, if agreed upon, before the Legislature makes its own venture; but some mode might be devised by which their friends here might be made acquainted with their real sentiments prior to our going into the Committee on the Bill, so that they might at least be able to anticipate in Debate in what manner any particular kind of securities would or would not be acceptable to them.

My speech is very badly reported. Dr Duigenan walked out of the House in the middle of it, tho' I quoted the conviction of his book of a libel to prove the same end ought to belong to the Charge of Dr Tomline.[2] I also applied this conviction to do away Peel's charge against the *Statement*.[3]

I shall take some steps for having a better report come before the public.

[*Source*: Scully Papers]

[1]At 4 a.m. on Wednesday 3 March the House of Commons had by 264 to 224 votes resolved to go into committee to consider the laws affecting the Roman Catholics "with a view to such a conciliatory and final adjustment as may be conducive to the peace and strength of the United Kingdom, to the stability of the Protestant establishment, and to the general satisfaction and concord of all classes of his Majesty's subjects" (*Hansard* XXIV, 763, 1074).
[2]Dr George Tomline, Bishop of Lincoln, had published a pastoral charge of 1812 in which he had called the rebellion of 1798 a Catholic rebellion. If this accusation had been made against an individual, Parnell maintained, the Bishop might have been liable to conviction for libel, for a Mr [Patrick] Lattin had been awarded damages of £500 for a similar charge made by Dr Duigenan in a pamphlet of 1800 (ibid., 986).
[3]This passage of Parnell's speech was not reproduced by *Hansard*. In a debate of 11 February he had told Dr Duigenan that he had no doubts about the accuracy of the *Statement of the Penal Laws*, upon which Peel had informed the House that its printer had a few days ago been convicted of a libel "charging the Lord Lieutenant with deliberate murder" (ibid., 453, 457).

413　　　*From Sir Henry Parnell to Merrion Square, Dublin*

London, 10 March 1813

Private

My Dear Sir,

I sincerely congratulate you on the vote of last night,[1] which may fairly be considered, as a vote of Catholic Emancipation.

Not being desirous to speak myself, I gave Sir John Newport the *Evg. Post* containing Mr Lawless' proposed Resolution, which was received with great applause & completely silenced the clamour about your former proceedings.[2] The effect it produced is quite decisive of the great power that is now in your hands of forcing forward the question in its other stages, in defiance of all the efforts of the Court. As, however, nothing more will be done till after Easter, there is no occasion for any immediate declaration of the sentiments of your body in regard to details; perhaps it will be better to say nothing concerning them, till every opportunity is afforded to those who claim securities, to understand the question better, & go the full length of concession on their part. What will be asked of you cannot be precisely known till the bill is in committee, &, therefore if you were now to come to any decision it would necessarily be formal without sufficient information. You should always bear in mind that almost all that has been urged by leading men concerning securities, has had for its object, the getting votes, & carrying the general Principle of Emancipation. That being now attained & every one's attention called to the single point of foreign influence, the probable result will be a very great change in opinion as to the policy of securities, certainly as to the conditions of them. I have great hopes the whole difficulty will vanish, & that the bill will yet be easily framed so as to satisfy all parties.

I shall be glad to hear from you what impression has been made in Ireland.

[*Source*: Scully Papers]

[1]When the House of Commons went into committee and passed by 186 to 119 votes a resolution proposed by Grattan that ". . . it is highly advisable to provide for the removal of the civil and military disqualifications under which his Majesty's Roman Catholic subjects now labour, with such exceptions and such regulations as may be found necessary for preserving, unalterably, the Protestant succession to the crown . . . and for maintaining inviolate the Protestant episcopal church of England and Ireland" (*Hansard* XXIV, 1203, 1247).

[2]Sir John Newport read out a resolution proposed by John Lawless at the Catholic Board on 6 March congratulating the Catholics' fellow subjects on the recent success in the House of Commons and looking forward to a harmony among men of all denominations that would obliterate the memory of past injuries. The motion was duly carried at the next meeting on 13 March (DDA 54/2, III, 48). Lawless (1773–1837) was later editor of the *Ulster Register* and *The Irishman*.

414   *From Sir Henry Parnell to Merrion Square, Dublin*

House of Commons, 5 o'clock, 11 March 1813

Private

My Dear Sir,

I have this moment learnt that there exists a misapprehension, concerning the manner in which Mr Grattan means to conduct his bill, which may probably lead to mischief; & I write this second letter to you to tell you exactly what he means to do. He will not bring in the bill till after Easter. If he finds that he can carry it through the House of Commons he will press it on; but if there is no probability of his being able to secure a Majority, he will let it lie over till the next Session. This is the course of proceeding which he has just told me he will adopt.[1] His reason for not bringing the bill in immediately is founded on the great probability that those who are now the loudest in demanding securities will relax considerably in their claims in the interval that will take place before the subject is again discussed, & his reason for not pressing the bill in this session with a certainty of being outvoted, is the certainty that a victory gained in this way by our opponents would very much contribute to throw back the question & revive the struggle.

I have not time to say more. [*Source*: Scully Papers]

[1]George Ponsonby wrote to Lord Fingall on 24 March saying that it had been settled the night before between him, Grattan and Canning that the bill should not be brought in until after the Easter recess (Fingall Papers).

415   *From Bishop John Milner to Merrion Square, Dublin*

W.H. 13 March [1813]

My Dr. Sir,

I herewith send you a Pamphlet[1] I have published. You have seen my *Memorandum*[2] in the Newspapers, it was intended as a Peace offering to our Grandees including Butler, with whom I have made peace upon *proper terms*,[3] and likewise as a diversion for our Statesmen from Sir John Hip[pis]ley's Veto & proposed new office of a *Ministre de Culte*, to be filled by himself.[4]

You have seen how he has abused yr. incomparable work.[5] In return, I enjoin you, not from resentment, but in order to defeat that most dangerous enemy of the Church in this crisis, to unmask him in some public speech or Newspaper Essay. I know nothing about his Clerkship to the Neap. Embassy,[6] but I know that he was originally a Woolen draper [?in] Bristol & afterwards studied the law. His passion long was to be Ambassador from this court to Rome[7] (in the neighbourhood of which he has a sister married)[8] & with a view to this he prevailed on good Pius VI to send Mr Erskine[9] to the English Court. His alledged facts are many of them lies but supposing them to be true, & that such & such are the practices of arbitrary Courts abroad, what is that to us who choose to have a free Church & religion while we give security to the state? He knows that yr. countrymen are angry with him, but he says, in one of his speeches, that if he cannot *get yr. praises he will deserve them*. I told you how he *damned* them in my presence threatening to *pacify them as the English always have pacified them* with fire & sword. His plan of the Veto which he has five or six times over published[10] is an unrestricted one in every respect, except that the Minister may, *if he pleases*, mention the ground of his exercising it. My respectful Compts. to Mrs S.   [*Source*: Scully Papers]

[1]Probably the first of three charges entitled "Pastoral on the jurisdiction of the Roman Catholic Church" (Husenbeth, *Life* p. 573).

[2]Published in *The Statesman* of 1 March it attempted to show why emancipation was desirable in the interest of all and answered objections. It contained a reference to Scully's *Penal Laws*.

[3]On 19 February, but the peace did not last long (see Ward, *Eve of Catholic Emancipation* II, p. 27).

[4]See No. 370.

[5]In the Commons on 9 March, when he questioned whether parliament would place confidence in the *Penal Laws*, where the text of the laws was overwhelmed by the commentary and its acrimony of controversy (*Hansard* XXIV, 1216).

[6]Without naming him Scully had in part II of his work referred to Hippisley as a "clerk to the Neapolitan Embassy", for reasons which he did not disclose.

[7]In his speech of 9 March Hippisley insisted that it was not the practice of the Holy See to accept accredited envoys from non-Catholic sovereigns, although there were agents for commercial purposes or communication with the Datary. Dr Milner may have been thinking in terms of a special mission.

[8]His first wife's sister, Elizabeth Stuart, married to Cavaliere Antonio Cicciaporci.

[9]Charles Erskine (1739–1811), a Roman of Scottish descent, who was a Monsignor in 1793 when Pius VI, on Hippisley's recommendation, chose him for a mission to London (see Ward, *Dawn of the Catholic Revival* II). He was made a Cardinal after his return.

[10]The veto proposals in his tract of 1805 (see No. 125 n.1) had been republished in various later pamphlets. They provided for a list to be submitted to the government before an election took place: the government was to have the option of stating its objection or simply replying that the election of so-and-so would not be expedient.

416   *From Sir Henry Parnell to Merrion Square, Dublin*

London, 25 March 1813

Private

My Dear Sir,

I have received your letters, for which I feel extremely obliged to you, as they contain a great deal of the most valuable information, & will greatly assist me in forming my opinion on the Catholic Bill. The first persons appointed to prepare it were fixed on without any previous consideration. Some days afterwards Mr Whitbread & the Knight of Kerry were added on the motion of Mr Grattan, & last Friday Sir S. Romilly, Sir A. Pigott & myself were appointed on the motion of Mr Plunket. I have not, however, been summoned to any meeting on the subject, & am quite ignorant of what has as yet been done. I suppose that this strange way of going on is not intended to be persevered in, & must be owing to Mr Grattan's habit of deferring his own opinion on minor points to others & Mr Ponsonby's excessive negligence in all matters belonging to his situation.[1]

I shall watch very closely all temporising & half stipulations. Tho' I cannot bring myself to think that there will be any occasion for it so far as the opposition Leaders are concerned, except indeed from a wish to secure the assistance of Castlereagh & Wilberforce.

Sir John Hippisley you may rest assured has not & will not be consulted. Nor do I think the opinion of the English Catholics is much attended to.

Your letter about the Grand Canal I shall attend to, & shall always be happy to contribute in any way to promote the wishes of your friend Judge Fletcher.[2]

[*Source*: Scully Papers]

[1]As leader of the opposition.

[2]Parnell was a member of the committee appointed on 11 March to consider the affairs of the Grand Canal (*Journal of the House of Commons*).

417 *From Peter Bodkin Hussey to Killfeacle, Golden, Tipperary*

16 Gloucester Street, Dublin, 31 March 1813

Dear Scully,

I left London before yours of the 21st arrived but it followed me here. We are now more critically situated than ever.[1] I am very anxious to see you to communicate what occurr'd in London, as I fear our expectations will not be realized. I understand it is finally determined[2] not to present our Bill untill after the recess. Fingall is expected every day — the cause is entirely taken out of our hands — nor have our wishes been complied with — Lords Donoughmore & Hutchinson I found truly steady — Byrne the Marplot of our Body was near doing us mischief last Saturday.[3] As it was he did us no good — I shall explain fully to you when you come to town — what occurred — don't take the report from the *Evening Post*, which only copied it from a morning paper.

Let me know when you come to town. The Duke of Richmond is become quite furious which I assure you I did not fail impressing strongly on the minds of many of the leading men in England. The yeomanry are in a state of constant exercise, the Canal Bridges are guarded with Centinels as in '98 — & the Protestants are every hour receiving *confidential* assurances that nothing effectual will be done for the Catholics. I have written[4] over an acct. of these vicious acts in order that some Questions may be asked in Parliament.

[*Source*: Scully Papers]

[1]Hussey's fears reflect the situation described in No. 416 by Sir Henry Parnell, who was also in the dark as to what was going on.

[2]The final decision had been taken on 23 March (see No. 414 n.1).

[3]John Byrne had proposed a vote of thanks to W. C. Plunket, whose speech on Grattan's motion (see No. 411 n.2) had been widely acclaimed but was open to the objection that it left the door open for "arrangements". At the meeting of the Board on 28 March Byrne had offered to postpone the motion, as there was doubt whether Plunket would be gratified by a compliment confined to himself, but the question had

been decided by Randal McDonnell giving notice of a motion to appoint a committee which would prepare a suitable address of thanks to all the friends of religious freedom. Such are the main facts in the *Dublin Evening Post*'s report of 30 March: it is not clear why Hussey was dissatisfied with it.

[4]No doubt to a member of the Irish Catholic delegation still in London.

418   *Proposal in case of Catholic Emancipation by a Catholic of Co. Tipperary*[1]

[April 1813]

That in gratitude for our full Emancipation, the Catholic Noblemen & Gentlemen of Ireland, shall at their own expence raise & cloath five regiments of 1000 men each to be named "The Duke of Sussex's[2] Legion or Emancipation Guards" — conditioned to serve the King in any part of the United [Kingdom] & defend the Crown, under which they enjoy freedom.

The officers of those regiments to be recommended by the following personages, vizt —

Earl of Fingall	Rt. Hon. Geo. Ponsonby
Earl of Donoughmore	Rt. Hon. H. Grattan
Lord Glenthworth	Geo. Lidwill Esq.
General M. Mathew	
Mr Prittie	Rt. Hon. C. Plunkett[3]

and the Catholic Board to nominate 10 officers — of the rank of Captains.

No officer to be appointed who shall not have a freehold estate of at least £200 yearly in possession — or have served at least three years in a regiment of the line. The proposer offers — as his proportion of the general subscription — to pay one hundred pounds for every & each of such five regiments raised, towards defraying the expences — and that the subscriptions be received by the undermentioned banks, and by them paid over to a Committee to be named by the Catholic Board within one month, from such receipts

Dublin	Messrs Latouche	Galway county	Ffrench
Cork	Roches	Kilkenny	Loughnan
Limerick	Bruen-Roche	Wexford	Redmond
Waterford	Newport	Tipperary	Scully
Galway town	Joyce		

[*Source*: Callanan Papers]

[1]This document, written in an unknown hand, is docketed in Scully's writing: "April 1813. Intended proposal of James Scully Esq. of Kilfeacle in the event of the success of the bill for Catholic emancipation now pending in Parliament". No evidence has

been found of it's being published and with the defeat of the bill in committee on 24 May the occasion for the offer disappeared. Nor has any record of its communication to the Irish administration been found in the files of the Home Office or in the Peel Papers. It is unlikely that it would have appealed to the government. On the one hand, the proposal for nominating officers involved handing over patronage to members of the opposition and the Catholic Board; on the other, the real constraint on the government's war effort was not shortage of men but shortage of foreign exchange resulting from the deteriorating trade balance (see the debate of 12 March 1813 on the army estimates — *Hansard* XXV, 73). It must remain a matter for conjecture whether the present proposal for raising one thousand men was the one that O'Connell had in mind when he revealed sixteen years later that before the battle of Leipzig Scully had made an offer of 100,000 men to Peel through D'Arcy Mahon (O'Connell, *Correspondence* IV, No. 1545), but Peel's long report on his interview with the latter on 4 October (twelve days before the battle), which is reproduced in Appendix C. makes no mention of any offer to raise forces.
[2]The Duke of Sussex, brother of the Prince Regent, had been a steady advocate of Catholic claims.
[3]William Conyngham Plunket.

419   *From Lord Donoughmore to Kilfeacle, Cashell or Tipperary, by Waterford*[1]

4 Bulstrode Street, Manchester Square [London] 3 April 1813

Private

Dear Scully,

I have written by this post, a letter to my Brother[2] of a very confidential nature, on the subject of the pending state of Catholic matters, & inclosing a suggestion of my own, to be delivered by him to a Revered Person, of great authority in your Communion.[3] I sincerely wish that you were in Town. The time presses very much, as Grattan has given the House reason to expect his Bill immediately after the recess.

I have empowered my brother to talk freely to yourself, & O'Connell, & Hussey, & to Ld Fingall.

If you happen to be at Kilfeacle, to which place I shall address this letter, assure your worthy father of my persevering regards & esteem.

[*Source*: Scully Papers]

[1]Where the letter might have caught Scully at the Assizes.
[2]Francis Hely-Hutchinson (see No. 423).
[3]Dr Troy. This would have been the letter from a noble lord dated 2 April to which Dr Troy referred in a letter of 4 June 1813 to O'Connell (O'Connell, *Life* I, p. 356). It communicated the manuscript heads of Canning's clauses, which at this stage provided for commissions of five lay persons in England and Ireland to certify the loyalty of new Bishops — for the later stages see No. 427 n.5. A letter of 13 April

from Lord Donoughmore to his brother suggests that an officer of the government, such as the Secretary of State, should be added, for the sole purpose of inspecting the nature of correspondence with the Holy See (Donoughmore Papers, F/10/87).

420   *From Sir Henry Parnell to Merrion Square, Dublin*

London, 3 April 1813

Private

My Dear Sir,

I shall be very much obliged to you if you will let me know whether I am correct in my opinion that an act of Parliament which shall generally repeal all disabilities under which the Catholics labor, will still leave them subject to the effects of those statutes & clauses of statutes which shall not be specifically repealed.

I conceive that the Catholic Bill to be perfect as a complete repeal should not only declare eligibility to Parliament & to office but refer to & repeal each of those particular statutes & parts of statutes which make the Catholics as Catholics subject to Penalties.

A Delay has arisen in the progress of the bill owing to Mr Canning not having yet declared his sentiments upon it. I find this is the reason why the Committee has not been assembled. I do not believe that there will be any thing in it, but those matters which Mr Grattan stated to be his intention to put into it in his last speech.[1]

I feel great satisfaction in having so copious & accurate an explanation of the sentiments of your body, as that which you have written to me, to assist me, in taking my share in assisting to frame the bill. I still continue to think that the best policy for you to adopt is to maintain a perfect silence till the terms which the House, when in Committee shall require, are exactly known.   [*Source*: Scully Papers]

[1]See No. 413 n.1.

421   *From Peter Bodkin Hussey to Kilfeacle, Tipperary*

Dublin, 8 April 1813

Dear Scully,

I have only this day received yours of the 4th.[1] The delay is surprizing.

Tho' I am sure a little recreation must be of great use to your health after the labors of a long winter, and Spring, I yet hope you will come to town on receipt of this, and sacrifice your present comfort to that Question which already stands so deeply your debtor.

I would not send for you on a trifling occasion but our affairs *are in a most critical state*. I received a letter this day from Lord Donoughmore,[2] which he desired me shew you. Hely Hutchinson[3] is anxious you should come — but all this, *is in the strictest confidence* the way I received it —hoping soon to see you.

[P.S.] I have received Sergeant Shepherd's Opinion.[4] I will keep it untill you come to town, unless you otherwise direct.[4]   [*Source*: Scully Papers]

[1]In reply to No. 417.
[2]See No. 419.
[3]Francis Hely Hutchinson.
[4]In the Fitzpatrick case (see No. 410 n.3).

422   *From Earl of Mount Cashell to Kilfeacle, Golden,*
Co. Tipperary

Moore Park [Co. Cork] 10 April 1813
My dear Sir,
    I received yours and have paid the money you desired to Margaret Griffen,[1] who was very thankful to Lady Mount Cashell for this remittance. I feel much obliged for your kind congratulations on my Daughter's[2] marriage, and hope that her union with Mr Robinson,[3] a young man of most excellent character, will be attended with much happiness. Should business, or any other circumstance ever induce you to visit the County Cork, it would afford me much satisfaction to have the pleasure of seeing you here. Being always with great truth my dear Sir,
                Very Faithfully yours,
                    Mount Cashell   [*Source*: Scully Papers]

[1]Unidentified.
[2]The Hon. Helena Eleanor Moore.
[3]Richard Robinson, of Rokeby Hall, Co. Louth, who succeeded his father as 2nd Baronet in 1832.

423   *To [Francis Hely Hutchinson[1]]*

Kilfeacle, 12 April 1813
My dear Sir,
    I have just received a letter from Lord D[onoughmore] referring to a letter written by him to you.[2]
    I wish merely to say, for the present, that I expect to reach Merrion Square on Thursday afternoon next[3] — and shall feel myself much obliged by

receiving a note there from you upon my arrival, appointing any time and place most convenient to you.   [*Source*: Donoughmore Papers D/22/8]

[1]Scully's letter is minuted by the recipient: "F.H.H. to Dr Troy April 9 1813"; and on the reverse of it there is a draft/copy of the letter to Dr Troy in which Francis Hely-Hutchinson sums up his understanding of what Dr Troy said at a meeting that day about the composition of the Board of commissioners proposed in the Canning clauses (see No. 419 n.3).
[2]Probably No. 419.
[3]15 April.

424   *From Peter Bodkin Hussey to Merrion Square*

                    No. 16 Gloucester Street [Dublin] Thursday [15 April 1813]
Dear Scully,

   I this moment received your letter of the 12th. I suppose it is uncertain what time you may be here this day, therefore I would be glad to see you here, *at any time* convenient to you in the morning. I shall wait within for you. I would call on you but as we may go to Mr Hutchinson, this is near his house.[1]   [*Source*: Scully Papers]

[1]Francis Hely-Hutchinson lived in Henrietta Street.

425   *From Hon. Francis A. Prittie to Merrion Square, Dublin*

                                                          26 April [1813]
Dear Scully,

   I enclose you the list,[1] return it to me, I much approve of the plan you mention and as you have the pen of a ready writer, shall be much obliged by your giving me a line in London to remind me of it when on the spot at least with Tighe.   [*Source*: Scully Papers]

[1]Probably for the Tipperary contribution to the *Dublin Evening Post*'s "Temple of Fame" series, putting before the public the names of the signatories of the Protestant anti-Catholic petitions. It had started on 23 March with the Dublin petition which had been presented at the bar of the House of Commons on 23 February 1813 (*Hansard* XXIV, 698). The Tipperary petition was presented by Colonel William Bagwell on 24 February (*ibid.* 726). There is a sheaf of notes among the Scully Papers (MS.27, 537) showing that Scully worked hard compiling a list of the signatories and the "Temple of Fame" published the first of four lists on 9 November 1813.

426   *From Sir Henry Parnell to Merrion Square, Dublin*

London, 29 April 1813

Private

My Dear Sir,

I trouble you with another letter in consequence of Dr Milner's letter which appeared last night in the *Statesman*.[1]

As the whole of his reasoning is founded on a misconception of Mr Canning's Clauses,[2] I hope it will not do all the mischief it seems calculated to do. The commissioners are not to have any of those powers which are complained of by him as so obnoxious. So far as they are to have any thing to say to the appointment of Bishops, their whole power is to be confined to certifying the loyalty of the Person nominated. The nomination is to remain as it now takes place. It is not, I believe, finally settled whether the Commissioners are to be lay or clerical or partly one & partly the other.

In regard to the Clause relating to the correspondence between the Catholics & the Pope, that is not yet determined upon.

I mention these things to shew how premature Dr Milner's letter is, & how cautious your body should be in suffering themselves to be influenced by it. I cannot help strongly suspecting that Dr Milner's plan is to do all in his power to obstruct Emancipation, as a measure inconsistent with the security of the Catholic Religion. For no man wishing well to the cause could calmly sit down, & write such a letter under all the circumstances of popular irritation in Ireland, & of difficulty in managing the prejudices of the people of this Country.

This publication induces me to be still more anxious to see an efficient committee appointed to consider Mr Canning's Clauses. If this mode of proceeding shall be adopted, let what will be the result, however adverse to his Plan, it will be well received here, & will take away all ground for new reproaches against the Catholics.

Dr Milner's character here is viewed in such a light, in consequence of his former conduct respecting the Veto,[3] that nothing can be more injurious to us, than any thing that shall shew he possesses any influence in Ireland. My own decided opinion is, that if your body submits to be governed by him, & if the question is lost this session, there would not [?be] thirty members to be found in the next session to vote for your claims.

P.S. Since writing the above I have seen Mr Canning. His present intention is to bring up his Clauses tomorrow when Mr Grattan brings in his bill, so that they may be printed & known together.   [*Source*: Scully Papers]

[1]Dr Milner, whose letter was dated Wolverhampton 23 April, said that among other rumours he had heard of a project "for appointing a Board of Lay Catholic

Commissioners under the Crown, for regulating the appointment of Catholic Bishops, and their intercourse with foreign Catholics, under pretence of securing their loyalty. . . . What is this but the Veto in disguise?" He went on to ask whether lay Catholics, looking up for the good things that the crown had to offer, would be less obseequious than Protestants, and raised the question of how a Catholic was to be defined. The Catholic Church, he pointed out, "denounced excommunication" against those who did not receive the sacraments at Easter: "To whom now are your Royal Catholic Commissioners to present their Easter billets . . . to Ministry, or to their own clergy? . . . . do you mean, in giving the laymen a power of Veto over the appointment of Bishops, to deprive the Bishops of their power of Veto over the Catholicity of laymen?"

[2]See No. 427 n.5.

[3]In 1808 (see No. 194 n.3 and n.4).

427   *From Sir Henry Parnell to Merrion Square, Dublin*

London, 1 May 1813

Private

My Dear Sir,

I feel very much flattered by your approbation of my speech; & particularly glad that that part of it which relates to your *Statement of the Penal Laws*, is so correct.[1] I had intended to send Mr Magee[2] a copy & to ask him to publish the latter part of it, as a refutation of Mr Weber's attack on the speech I made at Maryborough,[3] but forgot to do so. Your kindness will, by this time, have carried my wishes into effect.

The Bill was presented yesterday,[4] & it was agreed to have Mr Canning's clauses[5] printed & circulated with it. Having met him in the morning I asked him if he would consent to make any alterations in them, if your body should advance any reasonable & well grounded objections to them; he answered he certainly would consent to alter them. I also spoke to Mr Wilberforce[6] respecting the clause that relates to the correspondence, & found him very ready to listen to information, & to be influenced by it.

The conclusion I draw from their disposition to listen to & take advantage of what may be said against their plan is that they are very sincere in wishing to carry the Bill; & that your body have the fairest opportunity of getting rid of any serious objection, so far as they are concerned.

It should allways be remembered that this plan of Mr Canning's, has been framed in concurrence with Mr Wilberforce, & with the view of securing his support to the bill, & which is of vital importance to its success.

I have not heard what Ld Castlereagh thinks of Mr Canning's clauses. Very much of what is to happen, will depend upon the line he takes.

It is not supposed that Sir J. C. Hippisley's motion[7] will do us any harm.

There will be a very full attendance on our part to secure a majority against him.

As I have not been able to have the bill as perfect as it ought to be, as a repealing bill, I should be obliged to you if you could consider of the practicability of securing the object of it more effectually by some emendment to be moved in the committee.[8] I have looked into the Bill of 1795 & feel very much inclined to move the Clauses relating to arms, schools, & soldiers.[9]

I shall be very anxious to hear how you receive Mr Canning's plan.

P.S. I shall not forget to set Mr Bankes right on the first opportunity.[10]

[*Source*: Scully Papers]

[1]No doubt a fuller and corrected text of his speech of 3 March (see No. 412).

[2]John Magee, proprietor of the *Dublin Evening Post*.

[3]Parnell had made a speech in the Catholic chapel at Maryborough (*FJ*, 27 November 1812). At an anti-Catholic meeting held in Sligo on 7 January 1813 Daniel Webber had attacked it and impugned Parnell's character (*DEP*, 9 January 1813).

[4]By Henry Grattan, who gave notice for a second reading on 11 May: for the text see *Hansard* XXV, 1108. Its general principle was to avoid repealing individual laws, which would only stir up animosity, and concentrate on abolishing the test oaths (see No. 432 n.7). There was to be a new and more stringent oath which it was thought all Catholics could conscientiously take. The clergy were to swear not to concur in or consent to the appointment of any Bishop, Vicar Apostolic or Dean not of unimpeachable loyalty, and to have no correspondence with the Holy See on "any matter or thing not purely spiritual or ecclesiastical". No foreign priest nor any priest who had not resided within the United Kingdom for the preceding five years was to be raised to the episcopate. There was no provision however for a Veto or *exequatur*.

[5]Canning's clauses, which were longer than Grattan's whole bill, had been altered from the draft that Dr Troy had seen (see No. 419 n.3). To gain the support of Lord Castlereagh, high officers of state had been added to the proposed commissions — in Ireland the Lord Chancellor and the Chief Secretary. As a concession to Dr Troy, who had objected to being subjected to Catholic laymen, the Roman Catholic Archbishops of Armagh and Dublin had been added (in England the Vicar Apostolic of the London district). The main functions of the commissions were to furnish certificates of loyalty and peaceable conduct for nominees to the episcopate, in default of which they would not be allowed to exercise their functions and might be expelled from the country, and to examine communications with Rome unless it was certified on oath that they concerned only spiritual matters (text in *Hansard* XXVI, 88).

[6]William Wilberforce.

[7]Sir J. C. Hippisley had named 11 May as the date when he would bring up his motion for a select committee, thus getting in the way of the debate on Grattan's bill (*Hansard* XXV, 1087).

[8]Scully tried to get his criticisms of the bill put to the committee through Lord Donoughmore. Asking his brother Francis in a letter of 8 May to thank Scully for his "acute observations" Lord Donoughmore said that while a comprehensive bill

completely extinguishing every grievance would be more consonant with his own feelings as well as Scully's, it would have been scouted out of the House: "Being aware of the value of our friend's communication, I would gladly give it currency through the Bill Committee, as I did with respect to Dr Troy's letter to me. . . . But on considering the form and structure of his observations — that they offer no facilities but contain a general reprobation of the whole measure . . . and of every part, I did not think the communication would be attended with any practical result" (Donoughmore Papers, F/10/88).

[9]Grattan's abortive relief bill presented in the Irish House of Commons on 24 April 1795 provided (clause 1) for Catholics to bear arms on the same terms as Protestants; (clauses 5–7) for the repeal of penal statutes in regard to Catholic education; and (clause 10) for the freedom of Catholics in the services to attend Mass (*A report on the debate in the House of Commons on the Bill . . . for the further relief of his Majesty's Roman Catholic subjects*, (Dublin, 1795), p. 132).

[10]Henry Bankes, having voted in favour of Canning's motion in 1812, had announced his change of mind. Referring to the Irish Catholic Board's resolutions of 4 July 1812 about the beginning of a new persecution (see No. 363 n.12) he had argued that the Irish Protestants had turned against concessions (*Hansard* XXIV, 789).

428   *From Francis Canning to Merrion Square, Dublin*

No. 3 Hanover Square, London, 4 May 1813

My Dear Sir,

Give me leave to return you my best thanks for your kind Letter. I take the Liberty of writing to you again[1] to request your opinion upon the proposed Catholic Bill and particularly upon Mr Canning's clauses.[2] We have a meeting of Catholics on the 13th Inst. which will probably be pretty numerously attended.[3] I should be extremely glad to know before that time how the Bill is relished in Ireland. Some notice will probably be taken of it at the meeting and I am extremely anxious that nothing should be done but what would be in perfect unison with the feelings of the Irish. I am not aware that it is intended to propose any public Resolution respecting the Bill, but should any such Resolution be proposed I should much wish to state if necessary what the Sentiments of the Irish are as I think it of very great importance that no difference of opinion should appear to the publick to exist between the Irish and English Catholics. I foresee considerable objections may be made to the appointment of the Commissioners, altho' if it be necessary to give any greater security than that of an oath, I think this as little objectionable as any that could be devised. What a misfortune it is that Parliament will not act at once with Liberality. I much fear our *Quondam* friend Sir J. Hippesley will prove our most dangerous Ennemy, many of the Lukewarm friends and all the Ennemies of the cause will join with him in trying to delay the decision. Milner also does harm, his last Letter in the

Statesman is I think quite unjustifiable.[4] You have probably seen one which he has since written, but not published, in answer to a publication of a Statement of what passed at a conference at Lord Clifford's: whether the Statement be correct or not I do not know not having been there; but that Dr Milner and Mr Butler shook hands in token of reconciliation and went away together apparent Friends is certain.[5] I hope you will excuse my troubling you with this hasty scrawl. I shall be very much obliged to you for an answer directed as above. I shall of course mention no name nor make use of any information you may be so good as to give me beyond what you may [autho]rise me to do.

I sincerely hope the next time you visit England we shall have the pleasure of seeing you and Mrs Scully at Foxcote.   [*Source*: Scully Papers]

[1]There is no other letter from Francis Canning in the collection.
[2]See No. 427 n.4 and n.5.
[3]No record of this meeting has been found.
[4]See No. 426 n.1.
[5]See No. 415 n.3. After the meeting of 19 February Lord Clifford and Thomas Stonor published details of it in a *Statement of the Conference*. Dr Milner took offence and reopened all the old controversies in a *Restatement of the Conference* dated 22 April (reprinted in the *Freeman's Journal* 10 June 1813: see Ward, *Eve of Catholic Emancipation* II, p. 27).

429   *From Sir Henry Parnell to Merrion Square, Dublin*

London, 5 May 1813
Private
My Dear Sir,

I have received your letter of the 28th. Your intelligence was most welcome in respect to the determination not to give any public opinion on the Bill till you are in possession of Mr Canning's Clauses.[1]

Sir J. Hippisley's motion connected with the determination of the Anticatholics to make use of it to attempt to stop the bill for this session places our prospects here in considerable doubt. Tho' it is generally supposed he will be defeated, I have great apprehensions that the plausible plea of obtaining information will carry many weak members, who give the question a sort of neutral support, along with it. If we succeed we shall endeavour to carry the second reading without much debate.

I understand the Leading Catholics of this Country have held a meeting & declared their approbation of Mr Canning's clauses.[2] I believe, there is no doubt of the fact.

I am glad to find Dr Troy's opinion has so much weight. I hope he will give it without any deference to Dr Milner.

I saw Mr Finlay[3] yesterday, & told him, generally, what my thoughts were as to future proceedings, the same I have communicated to you.

If a new delegation comes over it would be of the greatest advantage to your cause if you and Mr O'Connel were to belong to it.[4] I am sure your opinions would have great weight with your leading friends here.

[*Source*: Scully Papers]

[1]It was arranged for the meeting of 1 May to be held behind closed doors so that "nothing should emanate from the board that could possibly, by verbal inaccuracy, be perverted by an adversary, or mistaken by a friend", but the editor of the *Dublin Evening Post* obtained a summary of the proceedings which he published on 4 May. While it was conceded that "the imperfections of the bill might yet be removed if any opportunity should remain" criticisms were listed under fifteen heads and the general tone was hostile. Speaking against Sir J. C. Hippisley's motion on 11 May (*Hansard* XXVI, 40) Grattan was forced to explain the report away as representing only the opinions of individuals. At a meeting of the Board on 24 May both O'Connell and Scully confirmed its accuracy, and O'Connell said: "We had seen the draft of the bill that morning. Our professional pursuits and habits gave to us, of course, a greater facility than others possessed, to form a judgment of it" (O'Connell, *Life and Speeches* I, p. 295).
[2]No record has been found of this meeting.
[3]The barrister John Finlay (1780–1856), who had recently drafted a relief bill which O'Connell commended at a meeting on 8 May (ibid. p. 285).
[4]At the meeting on 1 May it had been resolved not only that the delegates appointed at the end of January (see No. 396 n.6) should return to London but that four additional delegates should join them — Sir E. Bellew, Major Bryan, Bagot and Scully. Scully immediately declined the honour, giving his reasons (*DEP*, 4 May 1813). These were probably those he gave when the composition of the original delegation was discussed. He then said that he was on the whole inclined to favour a large deputation, as it would make more Catholics turn their mind to the subject and their zeal would spread to their families. It would give the English a wider opportunity to see the Irish and find that they were as capable of appreciating the value of the constitution as Protestants. Otherwise there was no use for one. If there were to be no negotiations they might as well send their petition by post (*DEP, 26 January 1813*). In the event none of the additional delegates went.

430   *From Viscount Forbes to Merrion Square*

Friday [7 May] 1813

My dear Sir — Lord Kinnaird[1] and myself are very anxious to be present tomorrow at the debate of the Catholic Board. I am not aware whether I am asking what it is improper to grant if so I beg you will accept my apologies — should the meeting be publick perhaps you would allow us to accompany you there.[2]

[*Source*: Scully Papers]

[1] Charles Kinnaird (1780–1826), 8th Lord Kinnaird of Inchture, Scotland.
[2] The meeting of the Board on 8 May was attended not only by Lord Forbes and Lord Kinnaird, but also by the latter's brothers-in-law the Duke of Leinster and Lord William Fizgerald. Reporting to Peel on the same day Gregory regretted that the Duke had lent his countenance to the proceedings, in which O'Connell had been violent in the extreme and had moved that if the Dublin Corporation refused to do justice to the Princess of Wales the Catholics should set the example. He also mentioned that a letter from Dr Milner had been read in which Dr Troy heartily joined (Peel Papers, Add.MSS.40, 196, f.149).

431 *From Bishop John Milner to Merrion Square, Dublin*

[Postmarked 8 May 1813]

My Dear Sir,

I am ashamed to look back to the date of yr. last kind favour,[1] which like all your other writings, carries the double light of useful information & sound reflection along with it. But you will excuse me when I inform you that I have printed half a dozen things, long or short since that period. As I always speak of yr. *Statement* in public & in private, as I think of it, & as every body else speaks of it except the disappointed Baronet,[2] I am not sure whether you call for one of my numerous Newspaper Essays[3] or for my *Pastoral Charge on the Jurisdiction of the Ch.*[4] At any rate I will send you the latter in a parcel I am making up for Dr Troy to be addressed to Coyne.

I hope you have seen my letter in the *Statesman* of the 28 ult.[5] It has exasperated those of our English Caths. who were in Cannings secret, as I can prove Chs. Butler & his select friends were. You will see by this printed letter how he has outwitted me, & I remit you to a letter[6] which I write by this Post to Mr Fitzpatrick to be communicated to yr. board, not knowing who is the Vice-Secretary of it, concerning the various tricks, which, in my opinion, have been played upon the Irish Catholics. I wish no further notice to be taken of it or its writer than barely to understand, through yrself or Dr Troy that I have given no offense. I am impatient to learn how Grattan & Canning's Bill will go down in Ireland & am sorry that I gave up the *Evening Post* on acct of the badness of the Print etc. I have, however, requested Coyne to send me a weekly Paper if there be one of good principles & decently printed. Sir Jn.[7] is preparing a grand attack upon me, in which you may perhaps come in for a blow; he has two or three times made a display against you.

It mortifies me that I cannot find among my Chaos of papers the Census you want;[8] but it will be easily seen in any Magazine, Annual Register or Newspaper of the times.

I am much obliged [to] you for the interesting extract from Lady Mt. Cls [Mount Cashell] letter.[9] I perfectly agree with her Ladyship in all her observations except as to the inference she draws from the Empr. Francis's processions.[10]

I beg my kind Compts. to Mrs Scully & hope God has protected her in her trial. Mrs Wheble begs all that is kind to her & to yrself.

P.S. I wrote to yr. friend Gen. Mathew requesting he wd. oppose Sir John's motion for a *Secret Committee*.[11] I shd. not like his deeds of darkness, nor his Report of them afterwards. The Genl. answered me kindly & has acted as I wished him. It wd. give me great pleasure to steal over to Ireland & spend a fortnight there incog: but the thing is this year impracticable.

[*Source*: Scully Papers]

[1]According to the endorsement on No. 401 Scully's last letter to Dr Milner was dated 27 March and sent on 3 April.

[2]Sir J. C. Hippisley.

[3]Including attacks in *The Statesman* of 11 March on J. J. Dillon and the Bishop of Meath (Dr L. O'Beirne) "who has preferred a carriage and sinecure of £6000 per annum to walking on foot through the murky cottages of Ireland".

[4]See No. 415 n.1. It may have been the pastoral from which Hippisley read extracts when introducing his motion for a select committee on 11 May and which he said was dated 24 March (*Hansard* XXVI, 14). The learned Prelate, said Hippisley, had done him the honour of giving his conduct near twenty pages in this pastoral charge.

[5]See No. 426 n.1.

[6]Probably the one read at the Irish Catholic Board's meeting of 8 May (see No. 430 n.1).

[7]Hippisley. He did not go out of his way to attack Dr Milner when introducing his motion, but his plan for a Veto and *exequatur* involved challenging Dr Milner's views. He did not again mention the *Statement of the Penal Laws* but perhaps damned it by omission: "we shall have the assistance of many highly useful compilations . . . those of a profound lawyer, Mr Butler, Sir Henry Parnell and others will direct us to the statutes themselves" (*Hansard* XXVI, 29).

[8]Possibly the census of England, Scotland and Wales published in January 1812 (see No. 338 n.1).

[9]Not found.

[10]Francis reigned at Vienna 1792–1835. Whatever Lady Mount Cashell may have said Dr Milner perhaps regarded appearances as deceptive. Outwardly a pious Catholic, the autocratic Francis treated the Church as an instrument of the state (see Viktor Bibl, *Kaiser Franz*, 1938, p. 283).

[11]He used the same facetious expression in his letter to *The Statesman*.

432   *From Sir Henry Parnell to Merrion Square, Dublin*

London, 8 May 1813

Private

My Dear Sir,

I have received two letters from you today of the 2d & 4th.[1] I am very much obliged to you for your information & advice respecting Dr Milner. As he possesses so much weight his good opinion should undoubtedly be cultivated by all who wish to carry the Bill. I fear Mr Canning's employing Mr Butler to draw his clauses,[2] has proved another piece of mismanagement in addition to that of other leading persons.

Upon receiving the *Evg. Post*[3] this morning I called on Grattan, & succeeded in getting him to consent to a free & full communication with your Delegates immediately upon their arrival. Some of the objections to the bill will be found either unfounded or to be removed with the insertion of a few words. Others will be provided for by new clauses & the remainder will be got rid of by a new bill to remove all sorts of lesser grievances that will exist if the present bill shall pass.

I am very sorry that you do not come over.[4] The Anti-catholics are making great exertions to gain a majority for Sir John Hippisley's motion. The issue is very doubtful. If we beat him I think we shall get through with the second reading of the bill.

If your Bishops cannot agree to the clauses about securities, I hope Mr Canning will not press them to a discussion in the House without a communication with them. I could not go over, being upon the Galway Election committee which renews its sittings on next Friday.[5]

I can give you no information as to the Authorship of the Bill.[6] It was settled before I saw it, & I found that it was useless to press objections with a view of obtaining any alteration, &, therefore, I merely mentioned them. I stated all the arguments you sent me in respecting [*sic*] to the principles which ought to govern a repealing law & generally mentioned the number of matters that were omitted but it was visible that there was no inclination to depart from what had been determined on.[7]

If you will let me know how & what the Bishops think respecting Mr Canning's Clauses I will communicate with him, privately, & endeavour to reconcile him to any objections they may entertain. The great difficu[lty], however, will be to get the House to be satisfied with any thing short of what he has proposed.

[*Source*: Scully Papers]

[1]The former no doubt giving Scully's own account of the meeting of 1 May, the latter perhaps commenting on the *Dublin Evening Post*'s report of 4 May (see No. 429 n.1). [2]Scully may already have heard of the authorship of the clauses from Dr Troy, to

whom Butler had sent a copy of them on 3 May, assuring him that none of them were imagined by him: the only part he took was, when safeguards were required, to work day and night to draft such as would be acceptable to both Catholics and parliament (DDA 30/1 153). In 1828 Butler repeated that he had been consulted only in his professional capacity and to the best of his knowledge he was the only English Catholic who saw anything of the clauses before they were read in the House of Commons (Ward, *Eve of Catholic Emancipation* II, p. 38).

[3]Evidently that of 4 May, giving the names of the additional delegates.

[4]See No. 429 n.4.

[5]Valentine Blake had petitioned against the irregular election of the Hon. Frederick Ponsonby for Galway city: he was awarded the seat in June (B. M. Walker, *Parliamentary election results in Ireland*).

[6]In a speech of 5 June O'Connell said he had heard that the bill drafted by Grattan's three lawyer friends (see No. 396 n.4) had been abandoned and a new bill got up by some worthy English gentleman who had not consulted the Irish delegates although they were in London (O'Connell, *Life and Speeches* I, p. 368). The gentleman was perhaps Sir Arthur Pigott (see No. 586 n.6).

[7]In the debate on Hippisley's motion on 11 May Grattan replied to crticisms of this sort by explaining that the repeal of the penal laws was subsidiary to the repeal of the oaths which prevented the incorporation of Catholics into the general body of the empire: once the oaths were gone the rest would naturally follow. To pursue a different course would have been to bring forward matter of a very irritable description. Alluding to Hippisley's opposition to a book "which enumerated a considerable number of the penal laws still in existence" (see No. 415 n.5) he criticised Hippisley for asking a committee "themselves to furnish those topics for animosity by holding forth to the public as Acts in force, those which were in fact and in practice obsolete" (*Hansard* XXVI, 58, 63). Hippisley's motion was for a report on the penal laws; the state of the Roman Catholic clergy and their intercourse with Rome; the situation in the colonies; and the practice of foreign states in regard to nomination of Bishops and intercourse with Rome (*Hansard* XXV, 1087).

433   *From Sir Henry Parnell*

London, 21 May 1813

Private

My Dear Sir,

I send you by this post the Catholic Bill as emended on Wednesday.[1] Tho' it will probably pass the House of Commons its fate in the House of Lords will entirely depend upon what may be the declared sense of your body in respect to it. Of this, no doubt is entertained by those who are the best acquainted with the sentiments of the Peers. If the arrangements about your Bishops & the correspondence with the See of Rome are not inconsistent with the principles of the Catholic religion; & assuming that unqualified emancipation is the object to be attained, the real question to be determined upon is, whether or not the passing of the bill, in its present form, will contribute to promote or defeat that object.

The way in which I bring my mind to any thing like what seems to me to be a correct judgment upon it, is by examining the sentiments of Parliament & of the people, as they now exist, & as they are likely to be affected by the fate of the Bill; & having done so, I feel very confident that the shortest way to gain the object, is to carry the Bill with all its imperfections.[2] Such a proceeding presents no obstacle whatever to the course that those may pursue who may hereafter attempt to emend the Bill; on the other hand, the false apprehensions of the influence of the Pope are sure to subside, & the Catholic members will form a most powerful aid to the assistance of those who will never relax in their exertions to get rid of every religious & grievous obstruction.

I am able to collect from the enquiries I have made among the English members that, notwithstanding the silence of the people, there prevails a universal dislike of the concessions to you, & that nothing preserves the quiet state of things but the expectation of what they call effectual securities. Many members who allow the absurdity of them, give their votes for them to keep well with their constituents; & thus it is, that no bill could now be carried without them. I believe that if the Opposition were in office they could not carry Mr Grattan's Bill without the clauses of Mr Canning. If the Bill is thrown out by the conduct of your Body it will add to the difficulty of removing these prejudices. Whereas if it is carried the practical effect will demonstrate how unfounded they are, & make a complete opening for carrying new Bills to establish the most perfect final adjustment.

I believe that some of the most obnoxious parts of the arrangement of the Board of Commissioners will be altered.

As I have great doubts respecting the sense of your body concerning the Bill, I shall be glad to hear from you all that can be said to prove it to be against it, before I form any decision on a point which is of such great importance, just at this particular moment.[3]   [*Source*: Scully Papers]

---

[1]Text in *Hansard* XXVI, 296. Sir J. Hippisley's motion for a select committee had been defeated on 11 May by 235 to 187; the second reading of Grattan's bill had been carried on 13 May by 245 to 203 votes; on 17 May the House had gone into committee to examine the new clauses; and on Wednesday the 19th the committee had agreed that the whole bill, incorporating the new clauses, should be printed in time for a debate on 24 May (ibid. 88, 171, 219, 249).

[2]On 26 May Gregory sent Peel a report by an informer: "The new bill gives general discontent to the Catholics and Plunket, through the agency of that active citizen Peter Burrowes, is trying to quiet or rather silence O'Connell and Scully by endeavouring to persuade them that they ought to let the bill pass as it is, and that then they may again recommence their complaints". In another letter of the same day he reported that the determinations of the Bishops at their meeting were being

kept secret; that O'Connell was said to have had an interview with them: and that he and Scully had expressed an opinion that the laity wished the Bishops to reject the bill (Peel Papers, Add.MSS.40, 196, ff.238, 232).
[3]Scully endorsed this letter as having been answered on 25 May, thus showing he had received it while the Prelates were still sitting in Dublin.

434   *From Bishop John Milner to Merrion Square, Dublin*

12 Great Tichfield Street, Cavendish Square, London, 21 May 1813
Dr Sir,

I send you exclusively of all laymen, a squib of mine[1] to retard Mr C. Butler's & Ld Castlereagh's manoeuvres[2] till the decision of yr. Prelates (which if decided will be decisive) arrives here in town.[3] Do, my Dr friend, by return of Post tell me how matters stand in Dublin & in Ireland with the laity & with the Bishops & Clergy. Speak out clearly & impartially. I am prepared & accustomed to hear every thing disagreeable. I have been here these three days, after conducting good Mrs Wheble to Woodley Lodge. I think it is almost worth yr. while coming to England in order to enjoy the honours & the comforts you will meet with at Woodley Lodge.

I have discontinued the *Dublin Evening Post*, so that I have known nothing of what has passed in Ireland for this month Past. Kind compts. to Mrs Scully etc. etc.   [*Source*: Scully Papers]

[1]His letter is written on the back of the squib itself, which is entitled *A brief memorial on the Catholic bill* and also dated 21 May. It was an uncompromising repudiation of Grattan's bill and was regarded by the leading English Catholics as having tilted the balance against it (see No. 440 n.3). Dr Milner reprinted it in his *Supplementary Memoirs* but omitted a postscript reading: "Such measures never could have been countenanced by any member of the legislature, had they not been suggested by certain false brethren of the Catholic body". To this Scully added in square brackets on his copy "C. Butler and *some* delegates from Ireland".
[2]Castlereagh had cooperated with Canning in revising the latter's clauses (*Hansard* XXV, 247). For Butler's role see No. 432 n.2.
[3]In the event the whole issue was decided before the Prelates even met. When the House met in committee on 24 May the Speaker, Charles Abbot, no longer in the chair, moved that the words "to sit and vote in either House of parliament" be left out of the bill. This was carried by 251–247 votes and the bill was abandoned. *Hansard* XXVI, 322.361. The news was published in Dublin on 29 May.

435   *From Dr Edward Sheridan to Merrion Square, Dublin*

Friday, 28 May [1813]
My Dear Sir,

I shall be very happy in waiting on your tomorrow, and in meeting those venerable Prelates, whose conduct you so justly estimate and applaud; as I believe one of that R.R. body, Doctor Plunkett, Bishop of Meath,[1] who has done me the honour of taking a bed in my house will leave town tomorrow. If he does not, you will be good enough to excuse my waiting on you.[2]

[*Source*: Scully Papers]

[1]Dr Patrick J. Plunkett (1738–1827), Catholic Bishop of Meath from 1779 — in Dublin for the meeting of the Prelates that began on 25 May.
[2]Reporting on the meeting of the Board on 29 May the *Dublin Evening Post* of 5 June 1813 mentioned that Scully and Sheridan were obliged to leave it at 7 p.m. "upon an appointment with the Bishops".

436   *From Dr Daniel Murray to Merrion Square, Dublin*

Cumberland Street [Dublin] 28 May [1813]
My dear Sir,

I most sincerely congratulate you on the happy event which has taken place in your Family, and I will have great pleasure in baptizing your little girl[1] at ¼ past five tomorrow.

I am instructed by the Prelates now in Dublin to transmit to the Cath. Board the enclosed paper.[2] Would it be too much trouble to request you to execute that commission for me?[3] You would oblige me also, if you think it right, by sending it afterwards to Fitzpatrick to be printed in the same manner as on former occasions. You are also, of course, at liberty to give it any kind of publicity which you may deem expedient. It probably might be useful to soften down a little the harshness of the other Resolutions.[4]

I remain with much esteem, My dear Sir,
Very sincerely Y'rs,
D. Murray   [*Source*: Scully Papers]

[1]Scully's first daughter, Catherine Julianna Maria, born on 26 May, the only child of his baptised by a Bishop.
[2]The Irish Prelates had ended their meeting on 27 May with a series of resolutions, the most important of which condemned the ecclesiastical clauses in Grattan's bill as utterly incompatible with the discipline of the Church. These were accompanied by a *Pastoral Address* to the clergy and people which in conciliatory language gave a fuller explanation of the Prelates' reasons and included an assurance that "should any other oath, not adverse to our religious principles, be yet devised, which could remove the unfounded apprehensions of any part of our countrymen, we would willingly take it" (*DEP*, 29 May 1813).
[3]O'Connell read the *Address* to the Board on 29 May and said that Dr Murray had been prevented from presenting it himself "by avocations connected with the discharge of his sacred functions, too urgent to afford him leisure or admit of delay" (O'Connell, *Life and Speeches* I, p. 327).
[4]Those in the *Address*.

437   *From John Joseph Dillon to Dublin*

2 Abercromby Place, Edinburgh, 28 May 1813

My Dear Sir,
    When we met in London[1] I communicated to you my views and plans in regard to Scotland. They have more than succeeded.
    I not only contributed to keep this country quiet during all the agitation which pervaded England last winter but have the satisfaction of informing you that the General Assembly (the most grave and important body after parliament) *yesterday* rejected an anticatholic petition and voted one favourable to our claims[2] upon the motion of the Solicitor General[3] to whom I trust the thanks of the Irish Catholics will instantly be voted.
    The petition was brought up for signature this day, when we received news of our discomfiture in the house of Commons,[4] it was nevertheless confirmed by the venerable assembly, and thus we have a *national declaration* favorable to our claims *following* our defeat in the house of Commons and therefore the more important.
    [P.S.] Remember me to Mr O'Connell whom I unfortunately have not the pleasure of knowing personally.   [*Source*: Scully Papers]

[1]The occasion is unknown.
[2]From a pamphlet published by J. J. Dillon in Glasgow, on *The Claims of the Irish Catholics considered*, it would appear that an adjournment was secured to secure a better attendance and that the pamphlet was written to influence the result. The petition was presented by Lord Castlereagh on 1 June (*Hansard* XXV, 485).
[3]Alexander Maconochie (1777–1861), appointed Solicitor-General for Scotland in February 1813 (in *DNB*).
[4]See No. 434 n.3.

438   *From Dr Daniel Murray to Merrion Square, Dublin*

Cumberland Street [Dublin] 29 May [1813]

My dear Sir,
    I find that in the Second Resolution contained in the address, a copy of which I sent you last night,[1] I have written *exposing ourselves* to etc. whereas, by referring to the original, I find that it should be *incurring* etc.[2] Have the goodness to correct this mistake. Pardon all this trouble and believe me most truly.[3]

Your obliged & faithful serv't

D. Murray

[P.S.] Have the goodness also to add to the signatures (By Proxy) John Flynn.[4]   [*Source*: Scully Papers]

[1]See No. 436 n.2.

[2]The published text reads "without incurring the heavy guilt of schism".

[3]There was opposition to the intervention of the Prelates, which might have been stronger had not the news arrived of the dropping of Grattan's bill. When O'Connell moved a vote of thanks "for their communication to us this day, and for their ever vigilant and zealous attention to the interests of the Catholic church in Ireland", Counsellor Hussey, seconded by James Bolger, and strongly supported by Sir Edward and William Bellew, moved that all the words following "communication" should be left out. This was defeated by 61 to 20 votes — Scully did not vote (*DEP*, 1 June 1813). An anonymous Castle informant reported that the "respectable members" of the Board were indignant with O'Connell and Scully: however, "the measures suggested by Scully but put forward by O'Connell have been and will be carried. The mob and the Evening Post terrify the very few reasonable men who continue to attend from opposition in public, and when in private they urge the impolicy they are teasingly asked by Scully why they do not state their sentiments at a public meeting". The same source says that O'Connell and Scully were admitted to the recent meeting of the Bishops (Peel Papers, Add. MSS.40, 227, f.209).

[4]The name was added but without the words "by proxy".

439   *From Francis Hely Hutchinson to Merrion Square Sth.*

Henrietta Street [Dublin] Friday Evening, 4 June 1813
My Dear Sir,

In the hurried conversation I had with you to day, I may perhaps have misunderstood something of what you mentioned to me. I understand you to have said that there is an intention in some quarter, to draw into public discussion the results of a private conversation which took place at Carlton House between the Prince Regent & Lord Donoughmore.[1] In my brother's absence, & on the view I have taken of such a proceeding, I think myself called upon, strongly to protest against any such introduction of the name of Lord Donoughmore as greatly disrespectful to him & in every point of view in which it can be considered, highly indecorous & unwarrantable.

The regards by which we have been long personally bound to you, will I am persuaded sufficiently excuse me, in your mind, for giving you my feelings upon this occasion, and in earnestly suggesting to you, to exert your influence to prevent so great an offense, & to interpose between Lord Donoughmore & so marked an insult, to arise out of a communication made by his Lordship to yourself.
                                                          Source: Scully Papers]

[1]The subject was probably the pledges alleged to have been given to the Catholics by the Prince of Wales before he became Regent. O'Connell brought the matter up at the Board's meeting of 5 June, when it was decided to ask Lord Fingall to confirm in writing what he had said orally about a pledge (DDA 54/2, III, 58).

440   *From Bishop John Milner to Merrion Square, Dublin*

London, 4 June 1813

My Dear Sir,

Yr. letter of the 17th of May arrived at W.H. after I had left it, & was recd. by me here subsequent to the receptn. of yours of the 26th,[1] both of which, like the rest of the letters, which you honour me with are full of information & just observation, independently of the proofs they furnish of yr. friendship for me. The English Newspapers, especially the *Statesman*, on one side, & the *Press*[2] on the other, will have furnished you with evidence of the busy scenes I have been engaged in. The latter, under the direction of Butler & Co. ascribes to me the *defeat of the Bill*, in consequence of which, the General Board has expelled me from their *Private Meetings* with circumstances of peculiar acrimony & indignity.[3] This is not otherwise displeasing to me (for my conscience was really aggrieved at the fear of partaking in several of their measures) than as it affords me a melancholy proof how light the Religion of their ancestors sits upon them. On the other hand I read at their Meeting & printed in the *Statesman* a *Protest* against their proceedings which anticipates my answer to several of yr. questions which I afterwards read in yours of May 17th. A sort of Appendix to my Protest will appear in the *Statesman* of this day.[4] I am greatly obliged to you for the two numbers of the *Dublin Evening*.

Shd. my name, per chance, occur in the sd. paper between the 1st & the 15th Inst. I shall be greatly obliged to you to send me a copy of it directed to *Dr Milner, at Mrs McDonells,*[5] *Peter Street, Winchester*, & subsequently to me, at *Wolverhampton*. I wd. not wish for more than one or at most two of the *Dublin Evenings*, previously to my taking measures in concert with Mrs Wheble for being regularly served with some Irish Paper. She justly complains that the *Dublin Evening* is so ill printed as to be illegible to aged eyes.

With respect to your Irish Deputies here[6] I am acquainted with none of them except Ld Fingall, who appears very low & complains of the impossibility of pleasing every body. I have however, heared from very good authority that the Hon. Augustus Dillon declared that one of these Deputies (previously to the rejection of the Bill) had been intriguing to get appointed a Commissioner under it, on the speculation that *if he cd. make a Bishop that Bp wd. be able to make him a Pt. man.*[7]

London is certainly the most infectious of all places, & our English Caths. of rank are up to every art of deceit & corruption. Hence your deputies hither ought to be strengthened with the grace of the three children in the fiery furnace. I must mention what just occurs to me, that one of these

Gentn. two days ago was employed in running to the Presses of all the Newspapers in order to *correct* Mr Canning's speech uttered the day before; just as he & Butler corrected Lord Grey's speech about the 5th Resolution. What Canning really said was this or to this effect: *that the English Caths. by their Resolutions on the 29th against me* (& this after hearing the substance of yr. Bps. Resolution) *had extricated themselves from the trammels of the Priesthood, & that he trusted the Irish Caths. wd. follow their example.*[8]

Two days ago I waited on the Duke of Norfolk, (who of his own accord spoke of you in the highest terms). When His Grace informed me that two of our Great Caths. had just been with him & had asked his opinion about the scene of the 29th,[9] & that he had answered them: "You have just done what I wished you to do & applaud you for having done, you have followed my example: but certainly Dr Milner is defending the *Old Cathc. Religion.*"[10] Two things I wish yr. countrymen clearly to understand, & I call upon your talents & patriotism to assist in making them understand in order to prevent a recurrence of the present evils: 1st that Mr Charles Butler has *settled* with Mr Canning, Ld Castlereagh etc., the whole plan & clauses of the late Bill (just as he tells the public he settled with Ld Grenville & Grey the 5th Resolution the day before it was voted, & as the Blue Books prove he settled the schismatical oath etc. of 1791) with little or no communication with the Irish Bishops or laity & that he encouraged them to drive it, whip & spur thro Pt. to prevent any effectual opposition. His constant visits to the above named & their visits to him were as notorious during the last four months as the levees at Carlton House.[11]

The other point which I hope the Irish will be sensible of is that our English secret Cabinet counsel consisting of Ld Stourton, Ld Clifford, Sir Jn. Throck[morto]n, George Silvertop & Edwd. Jerningham; in addition to Butler, were *privy & consenting* to the plan & clauses in all the several stages of the Bill.[12] I hope you will take care that such a negociator (who may serve a bad cause, but must spoil a good one, because he is not an honest man) shall not transact the business of Cathc. Ireland in future, & that the above named little contemptible Junta shall not agree to terms on her part, while she possesses so many men of real talents as well as virtue both civil & religious. I have written a hasty letter to Mr O'Connel & when I get a little time at Winchester I may probably address another to Mr Magee.[13]

1. Our Board is a self appointed Committee having one Scotsman, Mr Menzies, among them; they call themself the C. Board of Gt. Britain. Chs. Butler & George Silvertop founded it (precisely when Ld Grenville was turned out) as a literary club to write pamphlets. Paragraphs 3, 4, 5. They have acquired credit with the public, which I hope the Irish will destroy, & my poor three weak confreres (Dr Poynter having taken money collected by them to a large amount) have, in fact, submitted entirely to their power, still they are dreaded & hated (being the remnant of the Old Cc. Committee) by

the great body of the Caths. who rejoice at the rejection of the Bill, & henceforward they will be hated more. 6. My friends are more numerous than theirs, but the latter are more active & ostensible. 7. The same men who supported the 5th Resolution[14] support the board & the bill, among these is a majority of the London clergy & opulent *English* tradesmen, but the Clergy of England at large & the Irish merchts. are mostly on my side. 8. The Cathc. Religion is more deeply implanted in Irish than English breasts.

Mrs Bostock will write to you soon to congratulate with you on the failure of the Bill. I conducted Mrs Wheble to Woodley a fortnight ago. She is to join me ten days hence at Winchester: thence we return to W-Hampton. My respectful compts. to Mrs Scully etc. etc.   [*Source*: Scully Papers]

[1]Replying respectively to Nos. 431 and 434 — not extant.

[2]The *British Press*.

[3]His expulsion was reported in the *Freeman's Journal* of 6 June. For a full account see Ward. *Eve of Catholic Emancipation* II, p. 50. At a meeting of English Catholics in Stanhope Street on 29 May resolutions were passed condemning the *Brief Memorial* (see No. 434 n.1) and renewing the resolution of 1810 in which they dissociated themselves from Dr Milner's political writings (see No. 257 n.4). Dr Milner was then asked whom he meant by "false brethren" in the *Memorial* and when he replied that he alluded to Charles Butler two more resolutions were passed — one thanking Butler for his exertions, the other deeming it inexpedient that Dr Milner should remain a member of the Private Board, appointed by the General Board on 11 May 1813.

[4]This claimed that the English Board had thought better of their action since they had not published their resolutions, and they had now seen the resolutions of the Irish Prelates. He indulged the hope that they had become ashamed of their negotiator, Charles Butler, whom he now publicly accused of being a false brother.

[5]Unidentified. Dr Milner had been in charge of the mission at Winchester from 1779 to 1803.

[6]When the Friends of Religious Liberty gave a dinner for the delegates on 10 June the only ones reported as attending, apart from Edward Hay their Secretary and two Irish residents of London, were Lords Fingall and Kenmare, Sir Francis Goold, Owen O'Conor, John Bourke and J. Howley (O'Connell, *Life* I, p. 376).

[7]Each of the commissions envisaged by Canning (see No. 427 n.5) was to have five Catholic peers or rich commoners. According to Butler (Ward, *Eve* II, p. 35) the persons thought of for the Irish commission were Lords Fingall, Kenmare, Gormanston, Trimleston and Southwell. Only Sir Edward Bellew and Sir Francis Goold among the delegates could have aspired to membership.

[8]When the petition from the General Assembly of Scotland was presented on 1 June (see No. 437) Canning took the opportunity "to state the great satisfaction he felt at the stand that had been made within these few days, by the lay Catholics of England, against the efforts of an insulting and domineering priesthood. . . . He hoped that their example would have due effect with the lay Catholics of Ireland" (*Hansard* XXVI, 486).

[9]At the meeting of the English Catholic Board (see n.3 above).
[10]The *Dublin Evening Post* of 10 June published "a private letter just received", no doubt from Dr Milner, giving a fuller account of the meeting with the Duke of Norfolk.
[11]These allegations remain unverifiable.
[12]Butler expressly denied that any English Catholics besides himself had any knowledge of the Canning Clauses before they were presented in the House of Commons (see No. 432 n.2).
[13]Proprietor of the *Dublin Evening Post*. The next paragraph seems to be an outline of what he intended to write.
[14]Of 1 February 1810 (see No. 230 n.1).

441 *From Dr J. T. Troy, Archbishop of Dublin, to Merrion Square*

3 Cavendish Row, 6 June 1813

My dear Sir,
    You will oblige exceedingly by procuring for me the copies of Mr Charles Butler's letters to Mr Grattan & Sir John Cox Hippisley, which were read at the Board about three months ago.[1] I shall return them safely with thanks.

[*Source*: Scully Papers]

[1]Enclosures B and C in No. 397 which had been read at the Board on 13 February (see No. 403 n.3).

442 *From Dr J. T. Troy, Archbishop of Dublin*

Cavendish Row, 8 June 1813

My dear Sir,
    As from your *private* communication of Mr Butler's letters,[1] I cannot make that use of them which I intended, I return them to you with my thanks for it.
    There was no *settlement* with Lord Castlereagh about salaries for the bishops and clergy; & altho' he made no explicit or formal promise of emancipation, he distinctly said the Union would facilitate it.[2] I shall go to Maynooth tomorrow for the ordinations, & remain there during the week. I am very indifferent about the thanks of the Board valuable as I know they are, to myself. But I am very desirous they should be given to Dr Milner at the present time.[3] He well deserves them. You will see the thanks of our Prelates to him in the *D[ublin] E[vening] Post* of this day.
P.S. Dr Milner has left London.   [*Source*: Scully Papers]

[1]See No. 441.
[2]See the seventh paragraph in enclosure B in No. 397.

[3]He probably had in mind the aggregate meeting due to be held on 15 June (see No. 445 n.9).

443   *From Francis Hely Hutchinson to Merrion Square South*

Two o'Clock Thursday 10 June 1813

Private

My Dear Sir,

The business will not be effectually done unless we can prevent a war of Paragraphs upon this subject. Let me hope for your kind interference upon this Point — with the *Dublin Evening*;[1] my wish is that there should not be any animadversions.   [*Source*: Scully Papers]

[1]He is probably referring to articles criticising "the veto bill" and denigrating the Irish vetoists, which would have been distasteful to the Catholics' friends in parliament who had supported Grattan's bill.

444   *From William Parnell to 2 Merrion Square South, Dublin*

Avondale [Co. Wicklow] 13 June 1813

My dear Sir,

Your American friend did not come here but put your letter into the post office at N[ewtown] M[ount] Kennedy. I suppose the County of Wicklow would not appear very striking to an American particularly if he had seen Niagara, which every American ought to do before he leaves his own country. I should have been very glad to see Mr Parkman[1] or any friend of yours but I had rather see you yourself if you and Mrs Scully could come here. Mrs Howard[2] is going to lye in which will take us away on the 16th but I hope to return here early in August & be stationary; and any time after that you would be sure to find us at home.

I have two topics I should like to talk with you about — Ly Mountcashel & the old subject. Could it not be brought about by their mutual friends; that Ly Mountcashel should at least live in a house of his Lordship's in London — it need not be an expensive one and his name being on the door, though a trifling circumstance would do much towards saving her from the irretrievable false step she appears to me to be taking.[3]

I am very melancholy about your affairs; you have no luck, and let wise people say what they will, luck goes for much in all public affairs. Your business ought long ago to have been accomplished if it had depended on wisdom.   [*Source*: Scully Papers]

[1]Perhaps a member of the well-to-do and cultivated Boston family to which the historian Francis Parkman belonged (see *Dictionary of American Biography*).

[2]His mother-in-law, Catherine, wife of the Hon. Hugh Howard of Bushy Park, Co. Wicklow.

[3]She may have been on the point of openly living with George William Tighe, to whom she had borne a daughter in 1809. On 19 August 1814, calling herself Mrs Mason, she left with Tighe for Pisa and remained in Italy until her death (McAleer, *The Sensitive Plant*).

445 *From Bishop Milner*

Wolverhampton, 17 June 1813

My Dear Sir,

Late last night I returned home from London, having taken Winchester & Woodley[1] in my way. I fancy I have regularly received all the letters with which you have honoured me, as likewise the Newspapers with which you have favoured me. The *Dublin Evening* of the 8th[2] reached me at Winchester, that of the 10th,[3] I found upon my arrival here. They have afforded me equal pleasure & information, & I propose writing in some detail to Mr Magee, after seeing the number which is to give an acct. of the debate at the Aggregate Meeting.[4]

How shall I, my dear friend, express the extent of my obligations to you at this critical time, or my sense of the honour conferred upon me by Catholic Ireland! I know that I ought to be dead to all interested feelings, & to grieve & rejoice at events solely as they affect the honour of God & the salvation of souls; & yet I must confess to you that I do not barely feel but that I deeply feel the super-abundant recompense which the Catholics of Ireland have made to me for the affronts put upon me by my half-Catholic brethren of this Island.[5] Certainly I never looked for the high compliment paid to me by the Venerable Bishops & still less for that of the Catholic laity: but I did expect & I predicted what I sincerely hope for the Religion of both Islands that Ireland may take that lead in any future negociation for Emancipation, to which on every account she is entitled, & that the terms of the next Bill may not be left to the religion & the talents of Charles Butler, Lord Stourton, Sir John Throckmorton, George Silvertop & Edward Jerningham, who are the efficient Directory of the Stanhope Street Junta.[6]

I wrote to the Gentleman,[7] whom you named to me; but not so fully or carefully as I wished to have done, being then overwhelmed with business & anxiety. I also ordered copies of my Letters in the *Statesman*[8] to be sent to him.

To conclude this article: I little expected from the Report of yr. Board's debate on Saturday, as given in the *Freeman's Journal*, which Dr Troy sent to me, such an issue of Mr O'Connel's motion, as you inform me has taken place.[9]

It is time, Sir, that I shd. congratulate with you on the birth, spiritual as well as carnal of Cathe. Juliana;[10] in these congratulations the family at Woodley & my friend, Mrs Wheble, sincerely join. The pleasure which the latter experiences on the subject of yr. letter, to return for an instant to that subject, can only be compared with that of Mrs Scully at the compliments paid to her on the publication of the *Statement of the Penal Laws*.[11] With respect to Woodley Lodge, I can assure you that your visit there, when you next cross the water will be esteemed an honour as well as a favour; so just a sense does Mr Wheble entertain of the merits & talents of the author of the above mentioned work. My friend here joins with me in kind compts to & sincere prayers for Mrs Scully & her family. I have the honour to remain etc. etc.

P.S. Will you excuse my troubling you to send the following note to Mr Magee. [Rest of page cut off here]

I waited on Mrs Bostock.[12] She was going to write to you to congratulate with you on the defeat of the Bill. I hope the irreligious youths from Oscot are not any of the *New Regime* during the last five years.[13] Mr Wheble begs to thank you for a copy of the *Dublin Evening* though he regularly takes that paper.   [*Source*: Scully Papers]

[1]Woodley Lodge, Berkshire, the home of James Wheble.

[2]With a report on the Board's meeting of 5 June, at which O'Connell had given notice of a motion for thanking Dr Milner.

[3]With an article on the vote of thanks to Dr Milner and the "private letter" about the interview with the Duke of Norfolk (see No. 440 n.10).

[4]of 15 June.

[5]Who expelled him from the Private Board of the English Catholics (see No. 440 n.3).

[6]The meeting at which Dr Milner had been expelled was held in Lord Shrewsbury's house in Stanhope Street.

[7]Unidentified.

[8]No doubt including those of 28 April (see No. 426 n.1) and 4 June (with his comments on the Stanhope Street meeting).

[9]The *Freeman's Journal* sent by Dr Troy would have been that of 14 June, containing a long report on the Board's meeting of 12 June, on the agenda of which was a vote of thanks to Dr Milner to be proposed by O'Connell. This was opposed, most strongly by Counsellor Hussey, who argued that thanking Dr Milner would be an insult to their parliamentary friends. O'Connell withdrew his motion, saying that it would be better to follow a mode of proceeding that would not cause a division (in reality, insinuated Hussey, to wait until the country gentlemen had returned home). This outcome was regarded as a victory for the moderates. However, before the aggregate meeting took place on 15 June twenty-four members of the Board met to consider its agenda and by a majority of three a compromise was carried (*FJ*, 16 June 1813): Dr Milner was to be thanked solely for joining with the Irish Bishops (i.e. not for his own intervention with the *Brief Memorial* — see No. 434 n.1). This would have been the news that Scully conveyed to Dr Milner in his letter of 14 June.

[10] See No. 436 n.1.

[11] During her stay with her family at Sheffield in the autumn and winter of 1812.

[12] When Dr Milner visited London at this period he lodged with Mrs Ireland, of 12 Great Titchfield Street, and would have been close to Upper Titchfield Street, where Mrs Bostock lived.

[13] Dr Milner had taken over responsibility for the college in 1808 (Husenbeth, *Life* p. 157). The List of Lay and Divinity students published in the centenary number of *The Oscotian* contains the names of twenty boys who can be identified as Irish and attended the school up to the time of this letter. Among those who left by 1809 were two Blakes (one from Ballyglunin), two Donelans (probably nephews of Lady Fingall), Thomas Nolan, Daniel O'Farrell, Nicholas and Patrick Power of Waterford and five Ryans of Inch. George Bryan of Jenkinstown, probably a son of Captain George Bryan, left in 1813.

446   *From Dr J. T. Troy, Archbishop of Dublin,*
                      to Merrion Square

Cavendish Row, 18 June 1813

My dear Sir,

If I had entertained a doubt or suspicion of your aiding or assisting Mr C. Butler in his theological pursuits the perusal of the enclosed would effectually remove either.[1]

I return it with thanks.   [*Source*: Scully Papers]

[1] Both Dr Troy and Scully were no doubt aware that Edward Hay was going to give notice the next day for Scully's correspondence with Butler to be brought before the Board on 26 June (see No. 448 n.6). The enclosure mentioned by Dr Troy is not attached to his letter. It was perhaps the draft of an article on the English Catholics (NLI MS.10, 971) which from internal evidence can be dated to soon after the defeat of Grattan's bill on 24 May. In this Scully took Dr Milner's line about the English Board being unrepresentative of the English Catholics and belittled Butler as a lawyer. He did not go into the latter's theological writings but in asking rhetorically whether Butler or Dr Milner was to direct the consciences of the English Catholics he touched on the point that Dr Troy probably had in mind.

447   *From William Tighe to Merrion Square, Dublin*

Woodstock, Inistiogue [Co. Kilkenny] 3 July 1813

My dear Sir,

I have this moment received your letter & should be very happy to return you the papers you mention but as they are safely locked up in London it is not possible for me to get at them at present & probably there is nothing in them that you were not perfectly acquainted with.   [*Source*: Scully Papers]

448   *From Bishop John Milner to Merrion Square, Dublin*

W.H.mptn, 19 July [1813]

My Dear Sir,

I ought to be master of your energetic diction, combined with your classical taste, in order to express properly my sense of the services you have rendered me, or rather the great Everlasting cause in which I am enlisted, during the busy scenes of the two last, or, to speak more correctly, of the six last months.[1] I can only say with the simplicity & sincerity of your honest beggars, when relieved: *May God be your reward*: conformably to his own Divine promise, made to the father of the faithful: *Ego ero merces tua, magna nimis*.[2] I must add that your relatives on this side of the water, including the Squire of Woodley, who always greatly admired you, now greatly love you for your conscientious support of Religion & its Ministers. I hope that Cathc. Ireland has taught a lesson to our Protestantising Lordlings & Baronets which will be for their good: and I trust that the able men with whom you associate & of whom you are *Pars magna*, will verify my prediction, by taking effectual care that the Old Rat of the Catholic cause,[3] shall not again undermine it by his numberless arts of seduction & disguise. He is of all lawyers living the best to manage a desperate bad cause; because such a one can only succeed by trick & deceit; but it is impossible that a good & hopeful one should succeed in his hands who never acts or speaks like an honest Christian or a Gentleman. I am exceedingly anxious to learn how our Protestant advocates, especially Mr Grattan, will look & talk on your side of the water, since the seasonable rebuke you have given them:[4] but Grattan himself never made a speech so replete with argument & so beautifully composed in every particular, as my friend of Merrion Square delivered at the late Meeting.[5] I presume I am indebted to the author of it for the printed copy of it in the *Freeman's Journal* which I recd. the other day. By the bye, I am surprised that the *Freemans Journal* seems to be taken up & the *Dublin Evening Post* discarded by the Caths. This much is certain that the latter has not been forwarded to me (though I ordered it a month ago) nor to several other subscribers of my friends since the news of Ireland has become so peculiarily interesting & that the *Freemans Journal* has been often sent hither by some one or other of my Irish friends. Is it not possible for me to procure copies of Mr Chs. Butler's interesting letters to Sir John Hippisley & Mr Grattan from the copies of them which I know were read at your public board? I presume the latter are now become the property of the *Catholics of Ireland*, & therefore I who am agent to the Prelates of Ireland may hope to become acquainted with their contents.[6] Sir John Hippisley threatens another attempt to get me before his Secret Committee.[7] This may arise from my writing to him repeatedly in answer to his bullying requisitions that "I will tell him *upon my oath* whether or no he is the MP who in my hearing *damned the Irish & threatened to pacify them, as heretofore, with fire & sword*, if they refused the Veto,[8] whenever he can procure his select Committee!" I hold [hi]m so cheap that I have not yet thought it worth my while to answer the crowded columns he has inserted in the *Globe* paper[9] against me. Shd. I think otherwise I think I can let him down some pegs lower than he is at present. Mrs Wheble joins me in all that is kind to Mrs Scully & yr.self: she was delighted at the number & quality of yr. guests at the initiation of Catherine Juliana into the congregation of the faithful.[10] I hesitate whether to expose the leaders of our mock Board, in their proper persons to the opinion of the public: if I thought they were not low enough already I shd. think it right to do so, but as I bear them no ill-will I do not wish to exceed the *Moderamen justae tutelae*[11] allowed by the theologians. Their names are C. Butler, Lord Stourton, Sir J. Throckmorton, Sir Hen. Englefield,[12] & Mr Silvertop a *novus homo*, who is called in the higher circles *Mr Copper-bottom*; a dull pragmatical upstart, who alone of all mankind thinks that he has talents to shine in Pt. All the rest are precisely the rump, that is, all that is left alive of the old *Protesting Dissenting Blue Book Committee*.[13]

P.S. May yr. friends ask what is to befall you that you will not be able to enlighten the public again for some time to come?[14]   [*Source*: Scully Papers]

[1]One of them being the vote of thanks secured for him on 15 June (see No. 445 n.9).

[2]"I shall be thy exceeding great reward" — a perversion of *Genesis* 15.1 where God says to Abraham (the father of the faithful) in the Vulgate version: *ego protector tuus sum et merces magna nimis*. As the following verses make clear, Abraham's reward was to be his numerous progeny.

[3]Charles Butler.

[4]When the aggregate meeting of 15 June supported the Irish Prelates in opposing Grattan's bill.

[5]Published in the *Dublin Evening Post* of 1 July 1813. It was delivered at the aggregate meeting of 29 June and was one of Scully's few set piece orations. Advocating a further petition to parliament, he reviewed the progress of the last nine years and claimed that consequent upon petitioning the difference between advocates and opponents had been narrowed to a very fine point. With Grattan's bill the discussion on securities had given a clearness and decision which could not otherwise have been attained. The bill had been framed to satisfy all who looked for securities and it was therefore fair to argue the question upon propositions laid down in it. No correspondence with the Holy See except on spiritual affairs — the Prelates had already agreed to this. Loyalty of Bishops — the Prelates had offered their oaths. On these oaths the framers of the bill had said they believed them perfectly — but as with a contract between merchants of unimpeachable honour, there must be a guarantor. "The whole machinery of Boards etc", he said, "comes to nothing more than this: the purpose, therefore, as far as an honest regard for the constitutional

fidelity of the Bishops is concerned, is a mere nullity; and, indeed, except for the object of patronage, I do not know of one thing for which the proposed Board can be desirable".

[6]In accordance with notice given on 19 June Edward Hay moved on 26 June that the letters read at the Board on 13 February (see No. 403 n.3) together with Scully's reply (No. 400) should be laid on the table: he said that doubts had been voiced about their authenticity and Butler wished to deny allegations that he had been disrespectful to Lord Fingall. Scully, while admitting a difference of feeling, acquitted Butler of any sinister intentions. A letter of 22 March from Butler to Hay was then read, in which Butler defended his own conduct and described the nature of his correspondence with Scully — see extracts in Appendix B. Copies of the letters to Grattan and Hippisley taken out of a sealed packet were found to be identical with the originals in Scully's possession and released to the press for publication (*FJ*, 28 June 1813; *DEP*, 29 June 1813).

[7]Dr Milner's facetious name for Hippisley's Select Committee.

[8]See No. 415.

[9]No copies for this period are held at the British Library Newspaper Library.

[10]At the christening of 29 May (see No. 436 n.1).

[11]Cf. Chapter XVIII of the old *Corpus Juris Canonici* (Richter, 2nd Leipzig edition 1881) which allows force to be used "*cum moderamine inculpatae tutelae*" — within the bounds of innocent self defence.

[12]1752–1822, 7th Baronet; antiquary and scientific writer (*DNB*).

[13]The expression "Protesting Catholic Dissenters" was coined in connexion with the English Catholic relief bill of 1791. It was dropped as a result of opposition from the Vicars Apostolic and Dr Milner, and the new term "Roman Catholic" substituted for it, but Charles Butler and the Catholic Committee had defended the original wording (see Ward, *Dawn of the Catholic Revival* I, p. 155).

[14]Scully had begun his speech of 29 June by saying that it was perhaps his last opportunity for a long time to address his countrymen.

449   *From Canon Laurence Reynolds to Clonmell[1]*

Thomastown [Co. Kilkenny] 6 August 1813

My Dr Sir,

I have just received a Note from my brother[2] the Printer in Kilkenny, in which he earnestly begs of me to apply to you for the Copy of the Speech you delivered in the Black Abbey.[3] Unable to refuse him, I take the liberty of making the application. I am informed that you had no intention of speaking there; & consequently that at present you can give but a faint sketch of it, & that from memory. But even so, if your avocations will at all permit you to do so, I will consider it a great favour if you send him direct to Kilkenny such passages of it as you can bring to recollection.

I can assure you, it has been so much admired, that I am very sorry, I had not the pleasure of hearing you deliver it. I shall only add, that no one shall ever know you conferred on me this favour, should I be so fortunate as to obtain it from you. The hurry in which the Bearer is, will be an apology for the Errors etc of this scroll.[4]   [*Source*: Scully Papers]

[1]Where the Assizes were being held.

[2]John Reynolds, printer and publisher of the *Kilkenny Chronicle*.

[3]At the aggregate meeting on 4 August, which adopted the resolutions that led to the second prosecution for libel of John Magee, proprietor of the *Dublin Evening Post*, where they were published on 7 August. No copy of the *Kilkenny Chronicle* is available to show whether Scully complied with the request.

[4]On 14 August Peel sent the Home Secretary the text of the Kilkenny resolutions in a cutting from a newspaper, on which he sidelined the most objectionable passages. In his covering letter (HO 100/171, f.254) Peel wrote: ". . . we think that the more numerous & respectable the meeting was at which the resolutions were adopted, the more dangerous will be their effect, & the more incumbent it is upon us to notice them. There is an insinuation in one of them in reference to the late trial of Mr Magee, that the judge who presided was partial, the jury corrupt, & the law officer who directed the prosecution venal. This is sent forth to the Catholic population of this country in a manner more calculated to impress them with a conviction of its truth than is generally resorted to in the daily attempts which are made to create dissatisfaction amongst them. . . ." He added that the Attorney-General was of opinion that the resolutions were libellous in the eyes of the law; that he proposed to proceed against the authors and those principally concerned; and, if he could not succeed against these, the publishers.

450   *From William Parnell to 2 Merrion Square East [sic] Dublin*

Avondale [Co. Wicklow] 8 August 1813

My dear Sir,

I spoke to Lord Roden at Powerscourt about Fitzpatrick;[1] he said it was certain it would be in vain to apply to the Duke & he did not like to ask a favor with a certainty of being refused. I had not much hopes when I applied to Lord Roden[2] but I did not know any one else more likely to succeed. After all, I think it much the wisest way for Fitzpatrick to make up his mind to the imprisonment & endure rather than crouch. It is what all people must do who wish to be consistent.[3] I think it is the vice of this age to try & reconcile the principles of Zeno with the habits of Epicurus; I do not mean that Fitzpatrick has either the one or the other — his was merely a speculation & he is unwilling to abide by the contingencies that attended it.[4]

I hope when you return from Circuit you will pay us a visit & bring Mrs Scully with you.   [*Source*: Scully Papers]

[1]Hugh Fitzpatrick, in prison since 28 May (see No. 404 n.1).

[2]The 2nd Earl of Roden (1756–1820) was one of several people approached (see No. 472 n.5) before the Duke of Richmond left Ireland on 26 August. On 12 June Gregory at the Castle received "a most impudent approach" from John Byrne, who told him that it would be an act of humanity to release Fitzpatrick "as it was notorious that Scully, not he, was the author of the libel". Gregory replied that if it were left to his decision Fitzpatrick would remain in prison (Peel Papers Add.MSS.40, 197, f.14).

[3]See No. 370 in which Dr Milner mentions having been told by Scully that Fitzpatrick "gloried in the prospect of suffering in the cause of his religion and country".

[4]Among the Callanan Papers there is a draft in Scully's hand about "this old man's case", written after Fitzpatrick had been nearly twelve months in prison. In this it is stated that Fitzpatrick undertook to print the *Statement of the Penal Laws* partly from an earnest zeal for the cause, partly for his emolument in his trade; that he obtained the copyright from the author, as a gift, but was cautioned by him and others against any *indiscriminate* sale. "He was inclined however, to hazard the consequences: and finally, after having taken the written opinion of his own counsel (a Protestant barrister) and balancing the risks, he undertook the publication and sale for his own sole emolument, at his own sole risk, and upon his single responsibility. He looked to no indemnity, but in the goodness of his cause". A later paragraph adds that the heaviness of the punishment was never for a moment expected.

451   *From Charles Addis to Dublin*

39 Threadneedle Street, London, 27 August 1813

Dear Sir,

I feel particularly obliged by your having mentioned my name to Mr Hussey and take the liberty of inclosing you my Bill[1] for taking Mr Serjeant Shepherd's opinion upon the information filed against Mr Fitzpatrick.

[*Source*: Scully Papers]

[1]For £11–3–6, the principal item being £6–8–1 to Sergeant Shepherd and clerk.

452   *From Dan O'Brien[1] to 4 [sic] Merrion Square, Dublin*

Clonmell, 27 September 1813

Dear Sir,

As I know it will give you pleasure to hear of the Unanimity which prevails here amongst our friends in this town, I will give you a sketch of it and as you will be hereafter call'd upon to espouse our honorable cause, if any attack is made, I now inform you we have opened a book for receiving Subscriptions to defray the expence of any attack made upon any one of our Society for Customs, & are getting large sums for that purpose the year ends 29th of this month which they have paid, and after they intend to a man to refuse paying any Custom & to resist to the last. I set the good example for them & have succeeded by getting free this year, & tho' Bagwell sent several people to me I refused any terms from him. There will be money enough to defend any attack he may make and we will to a man be firm. I have the pleasure to add that all our good friends say Jephson,[2] Donoughmore, Dunally, Lismore, Mathew & Prittie etc. will stand by us & will rise & fall with us.

I have made out some papers which expect will be of use enclos'd[3] I send you a Copy of one of them, and hereafter will send more. It will shew you that Bagwell himself was a leading member to oppose the Corporation in Lord Mount Cashell's time,[4] & we are now only following his plan. If you approve of it, I would like to give it this paper publicity in the *Dublin Evening Post*. This is a true copy of the proceedings of the meeting in 1782 & if now published it would shew the publick that we are following his plan. It need not be known who got it done.

From the conversation I had with you on the subject of a discount office in Clonmell (the necessity of which is very apparent from many causes) I called on Mr Gorman[5] to know if you wrote to him. He replied not and remark'd Should your House[6] decide upon such, he would undertake same. I have only then to add, that such an Office in this town is greatly wanted and would be sanction'd by many, particularly at this period. I expect you'll write Mr Gorman on this subject soon as convt. & the sooner the better.

[P.S.] I beg the favor of a line on this subject.   [*Source*: Scully Papers]

[1]He described himself as a shopkeeper of Clonmel when his second son, Daniel, entered the King's Inns in 1830. In 1804 he was given a contract by the Clonmel Corporation for lighting lamps (W. P. Burke, *History of Clonmel*, p. 180).

[2]Possibly Colonel William Jephson (d. 1816), of Mallow Castle, who had succeeded to the property on the death of his cousin, Denham Jephson, on 9 May 1813.

[3]The enclosures are copies of (1) two resolutions signed by 125 persons at a meeting on 23 June 1782, appointing a committee and thanking John Bagwell of Marlfield; and (2) a series of resolutions adopted by the committee. The complaint was that the freedom and immunities to which a large number of traders and artisans claimed they were entitled by birthright, were being withheld from them by the Corporation. There is no reference to a refusal to pay customs, but one resolution alleged that tolls collected by the Corporation were oppressive and unwarranted by the borough's charter.

[4]During the forty years of the Moore family's supremacy which ended when John Bagwell of Marlfield took the borough over by arrangement in 1800 (*History of Clonmel*, pp. 119, 174).

[5]Unidentified.

[6]The Tipperary bank of James Scully and Son (see No. 47 n.2).

453 *From William Bayly to Tipperary*

Dungarvan [Co. Waterford] 2 October 1813

My Dear Sir,

I have recommended the parishioners of this place to put themselves under your professional guidance in sketching of the Draft of a Deed of Conveyance, or Lease as to you may appear under the Existing penal Statutes most Safe & Salutary for the future Interests of the parish.

They are about building a Chapel, & the Ground or Site, they are to get from the Duke of Devonshire[1] as a gift. The Lessees or Grantees, as the Case may be, will be Selected by the Parish Committee, as Trustees for the parish, though Trustees for Such purposes may not be recognised by Law;[2] we must purchase the Interest of an undertenant of the Duke; *quere* who are to be the purchasers on Behalf of the parish?

You will have the goodness to frame the Draft with your usual talent & Care & give us Such general Instructions as you may deem necessary. The Draft must of Course be Sent to the Duke; & by him laid before his Counsel.

[*Source*: Scully Papers]

[1]Since 29 July 1811 the 6th Duke. Controversy over the building of an imposing new Catholic church had been dragging on since 1803, when the Catholics had asked the 5th Duke for the plot of land on a prominent elevated site where the present church stands. There had been strong opposition from the Protestants, who feared that their own established church would be eclipsed, and from the Duke's Irish agents, who argued that the site could be better used for building a terrace of houses (from information kindly supplied by Mr William Fraher of Dungarvan).
[2]Scully explains the difficulty in Chapter 1 of his *Penal Laws*. Since the law did not recognise a Catholic Bishop or priest and his successors as a body corporate there existed no Catholic corporation, civil or religious, legally competent to take donated lands on trust.

454 *From Dr J. T. Troy, Archbishop of Dublin,*
to 4 Capel Street

3 Cavendish Row, 18 October 1813

My dear Sir,

As Dr Plunkett[1] Vicar Capitular of Elphin is alluded to in the *Freeman's Journal* of this day, in its report of proceedings at the Catholic Board on last Saturday, I think it proper to enclose a letter from him on the Catholic petition,[2] which I pray you to return when convenient, and am in haste etc.

[*Source*: Scully Papers]

[1]Dr George Plunkett (d. 1827), elected Bishop of Elphin 5 October 1814.

[2]A petition drafted by Charles Phillips had been adopted at the aggregate meeting of 29 June (*DEP*, 29 June 1813). Because of certain expressions in it regarded as bordering on Socinianism and Deism Dr Troy had intimated that he and the clergy of the Dublin province would not be able to sign it. At the meeting of the Board on Saturday 16 October a proposal to refer the petition to the Committee of Accounts (as the only committee likely to meet soon) for "verbal alterations" had been opposed by James Kennedy, who did not think that such an important matter could be thus "huddled off" and asserted that the orthodoxy of the petition had been defended at a county meeting by "a most respectable Catholic Divine". This must have been Dr Plunkett, who is not mentioned by name in any part of the *Freeman's Journal*'s report.

455   *From Richard McGrath to Tipperary*

Dungarvan [Co. Waterford] 19 October 1813

Sir,

I have a Case to lay before you for your Advice and also to draw a Deed therefrom relative to a Piece of Land given here by the Duke of Devonshire for the purpose of building a new Chapel thereon.[1]

I would therefore be much obliged to you if you had the kindness to say by return of Post on what day it would be Convenient to you to receive the Messenger I mean to send with the papers and when I would send him to be good enough to give him as little Delay as possible.   [*Source*: Scully Papers]

[1]See No. 453.

456   *From Bishop John Milner to Merrion Square, Dublin*

WHmpton, 19 October 1813

My Dear Sir,

I was duly honoured with yours of Sept. 28th & am greatly obliged to you for the interesting intelligence it contains. You will have seen by my letters in the *Dublin Evening Post*, that I am duly sensible of the generosity of the Irish Catholics in supporting me, under the persecution I have been suffering from a powerful party of my countrymen, but still more of their orthodox firmness which in supporting their own religion, prevents the downfall of it amongst us English. Our leading men, particularly Sir John Throckmorton & Chs. Butler would not be satisfied with their own complete Emancipation, if it were not accompanied with the subjugation of their clergy. I guess that they are by this time employed in fabricating a new Bill for this purpose. My brethren, the three Vicars Apostc. with, perhaps one or two of the same order from Scotland, having taken their lesson from certain persons of the Stanhope Street Junta[1] are now deliberating at Durham what concessions they can make, in order to form a groundwork for the intended Bill.[2] You may be sure that I was not invited to this *Conciliabulum*. I am termed by the men to whom my brethren are subject an *hibernized English Vicar*. You cannot conceive the pains which some of the Junta, who are the best disposed & with whom I was best acquainted took, last winter to induce me to resign my commission as agent to the Irish Prelates & to break off all communication with Ireland: but, first & last I have openly maintained two points, that Cathc. Bishops ought to act in concert throughout the whole Church, & that the English Caths. never will get any substantial benefits from the legislature, but through the weight & efforts of those of Ireland. Still it is possible that the English Caths. may ask for & obtain those privileges which the Irish actually enjoy.[3]

I can perceive that Grattan & all his party are horribly out of humour with the Irish Caths. & myself; & I shall not be surprised if they realize what, I understand, they threaten, namely to bring in a Bill similar to the late one,[4] & to leave those Caths. to take advantage of it who will. This wd. instantly produce a real & terrible schism among us. We have a truly *Orthodox Journal*[5] published by noble spirited Cathc., a Mr Andrews of Fenwick Court, Holborn every month, in most numbers of which I have hitherto written. The next number will contain some remarks of mine upon the late Bill, which I think will place its horrors in a stronger light than it has yet been exhibited in to the public; I will contrive to get a copy of it very early in the month for the *Dublin Evening Post*, & hope it may be deemed worthy of insertion, for the information of the Caths. of Ireland: I say information for the letter contains anecdotes relating to the subject matter yet unknown to any one but myself & the other parties concerned in them.

You will perceive by my letter already printed in the *Dublin Evening Post* that I have seen Mr Charles Butler's communications with Sir Jn. Hippisley, Grattan etc.,[6] & that I am not disposed to treat him so politely as you have done in yr. acct. of those communications. I dare say you will remember the warmth with which I spoke to you against [him] when first I gained the honour of yr. acquaintance in Dublin:[7] the fact is I have long & intimately known him, & I have always found him to be the most dangerous enemy of the religion he professes & the most destitute of candour & truth of all men whom I ever met with. I presume you perused the anecdote of his interview with Coyne, the Printer, in my *Restatement of the Conference* in Portman Square.[8] What individual, calling himself a Cathc. Gentleman but himself could demean himself in the manner he did on that occasion!

I rejoice that the difficulties are gotten over respecting the petition. I was about to write to you concerning the expression of *Christ* being the *type of* our adoration, when Dr Troy sent to you on the subject. Had that Socinian term continued in the Petition I am confident the Prelates, at their ensuing meeting wd. have resolved not to sign it. Corrected as it is, I have no doubt but they will cheerfully add their names.[9] There is another point which I wished to submit to yr. consideration. Yr. petition has been often printed; now I understand it is a rule of Pt. not to receive any petition which has been printed. However, the alterations you have made in the text, though ve[ry] slight will I hope obviate the objection, by enabling you to say that it is a new petition. But I am here instructing you on points which you must understand better than I do.[10]

I heartily wish prosperity to the Dominicans & Jesuits Colleges on yr. side of the water, & in particular that they may implant sentiments of religion deeper in the minds of their youth than you say Oscot does.[11] I am sure no pains are omitted by good Mr Walsh, Mr Quick[12] etc. for the purpose in question: but there never has been found out a means of securing youth in piety & morality. As to nationality, I am sure there is not & never has been, since I knew Oscot, any the least prejudice either among the superiors or the students against Irish men. In proof of this I may mention that more than one copy of the *Dublin Evening* is regularly sent thither & eagerly perused by every one.

I am glad to hear so favourable an acct. of yr. young family & wish it were in my power to recommend a Tutor for yr. eldest son. Mrs Wheble joins me in kind Compts. to Mrs Scully.

Since I wrote to you last I have laboured hard, & at one time with a prospect of success to bring about a second link of Union between two families in this Island between which you Dr. Sir, are the only bond at present.[13]

[*Source*: Scully Papers]

[1]The English Catholics who had expelled him from their Private Board (see No. 440 n.3).

[2]At the end of June the English Catholic Board, in anticipation of a relief bill's being brought in during 1814, had suggested that the Vicars Apostolic should agree among themselves as to what might be conscientiously admitted or submitted to in regard to the nomination of Bishops, their correspondence with Rome and other matters. After delays a meeting had been fixed to take place at Durham on 25 October. Dr Milner had not been invited for a number of reasons but primarily because it was feared that if an approach to Rome was decided upon he would get in first with a misstatement (Ward, *Eve of Catholic Emancipation* II, pp. 57–60).

[3]Two of the chief ones being eligibility for commissions in the armed forces up to the rank of colonel and the recognition of marriages performed by Catholic priests. (see No. 198 n.11).

[4]Grattan's bill (see No. 427 n.4).

[5]The first number of the *Orthodox Journal* had come out in July 1813. It was founded by William Eusebius Andrews "to aid the cause of the Catholic Church, and to caution my Catholic brethren against a Party, who have entailed more disgrace upon

the Catholic name by their casuistical policy than all the calumnies raised against it by our enemies since the Reformation" (Ward, *Eve* II, p. 174).

[6] See No. 441 n.1.

[7] On 24 September 1808 (see No. 185).

[8] See No. 428 n.5. The anecdote as told in the *Restatement* revolved around an allegation by Coyne that in 1809 Butler had asked him to reprint the Blue Books of 1791 and Butler's assertion that he could have done no such thing, as he still had a hundred copies in his possession.

[9] See No. 454 n.1. A comparison between the text in the *Dublin Evening Post* of 29 June 1813 and that of *Hansard* XXVII, 1016 shows that the difficulty was got over by omitting the words "like the great type of our salvation"; and substituting for "a Gospel which excludes all distinctions" the phrase "a Gospel which breathes charity towards all".

[10] Scully had been aware of this in 1805 (see No. 106A). Parliament, however, would appear to have turned a blind eye until the multiplication of Reform petitions forced a change in 1817 (see No. 566 n.3).

[11] See No. 445 n.13.

[12] Revd Thomas Walsh; Vice-President; and Revd Francis Quick (1778–1818) who had been at Oscott since 1808.

[13] He presumably hoped to arrange a match between Richard Huddleston, brother of Scully's first wife, and one of the unmarried sisters of his second wife.

---

457   *From Hon. F. A. Prittie to Merrion Square, Dublin*

Corville, Roscrea [Co. Tipperary] 24 October 1813

Dear Scully,

Well knowing your hand writing, & fearing that Llandaff may have left town I enclose to you the Lists you sent me.[1] In this immediate quarter I find nearly all the signatures which have been procured, were at the instigation of the *Revd Mr Hamilton*.[2] On looking over the lists and seeing some of my labourers & yeomen subscribed I sent for them, when they told me that after Parade Mr Hamilton sent for them, that they went to his House, were shewn into his parlour & then asked to sign, which they did; others told me whose names are not down that they were sent to by him but did not go, & one whose name is down will prove he did not sign it, tho sent to by Mr Hamilton, quere "Whether a Magistrate applying to Yeomen under arms is *strictly constitutional*."

If you procure me the list of Roscrea names I will ascertain any thing connected with it.   [*Source*: Scully Papers]

[1] Of the signatories of the Tipperary Protestant petition (see No. 425).

[2] Revd John Hamilton, who in a pamphlet of 1816 described Prittie as his mortal enemy.

458   *From the Earl of Llandaff to Merrion Square, Dublin*

[undated]

Private

Dr. Scully,

I this morning recd. the enclosed from Prittie. You see Mr Hamilton has been at work — return me the enclosed.[1]   [*Source*: Scully Papers]

[1]Evidently a letter from Prittie similiar to No. 457.

459   *From Canon Laurence Reynolds to Merrion Square, Dublin*

Thomastown [Co. Kilkenny] 26 October 1813

My Dr Sir,

I understand that my friend Mr Scot,[1] Kilkenny, (Atty) has this day sent you for your opinion the particulars of a Case, by which it appears that a young man of the name of Walsh[2] is unjustly prevented from getting possession of a certain property. I will consider it a singular favour if you do everything in your power for Walsh, it being the Will of the deceased, as well as the unalterable resolution of Walsh to apply this property, (if obtained), to the upholding of a Religious House in Kilkenny.[3] A principal object of this pious Institute is the Education of poor boys. If the Members have the means of support, they will do incalculable good — if the property in question is withheld from them, I fear the Institution will fall, never to rise. I shall say no more, as I am certain that the above is sufficient to excite your best wishes and call forth your best Exertions for the success of poor Walsh.

The Catholics of our County & City are to meet on Thursday next.[4] I believe their proceedings will be published in Saturday's Paper; if so, it shall be sent you by my Brother. It has been hinted to me, that Kennedy is to be *Bulgerised*,[5] as they term it. Whether any specific Resolution to this effect will be adopted or not, I cannot say.[6] But it appears certain that he is completely *dis*possessed of the Confidence of the Catholics here. Being in a hurry as usual I shall only add, that by presenting my best Respects to Mrs Scully you will much oblige.   [*Source*: Scully Papers]

[1]Probably Barnaby Scott.
[2]Unidentified.
[3]Possibly one of the two free schools in Chapel Lane, controlled by a committee of the Charity School Society, to which Laurence Reynolds and Barnaby Scott were subscribers (Revd Peter Birch: "Some Early Schools of Kilkenny" in *Old Kilkenny Review* No. 12, 1960).
[4]28 October.

[5]After James Bolger (presumably pronounced Bulger), a landowner of Bally-
barney, Ross, Co. Kilkenny, who forfeited the confidence of the Kilkenny Catholics for opposing the intervention of the Prelates on 29 May (*FJ*, 4 June 1813):
see No. 438 n.3.
[6]See No. 461.

460   *From Lord Llandaff to Merrion Square, Dublin*

Thomastown [Co. Tipperary] 27 October 1813

Dr Scully,
    The enclosed I rd: this morning from Prittie.[1] I am sorry he sent you the
lists as I want them to make some enquiries in this neighbourhood. Have
the goodness to send them down to me. Has Johnston[2] passed before you
the papers etc. respecting Mr Creaths[3] business?   [*Source*: Scully Papers]

[1]See No. 457.
[2]Unidentified.
[3]Unidentified. The name can also be read McCreath, a variant of McCraith, both of
which are attested in Co. Tipperary (Ambrose Leet, *Directory*, 1814; *DEP*, 3 April
1819).

461   *From John P. Ryan[1] to Dublin*

Kilkenny, 29 October 1813

Dear Scully,
    After a very hard fought battle we succeeded in putting Kenedy off the
Board yesterday[2] — no electioneering candidate ever used greater exertions in canvasing than his father[3] & brother[4] did, they even went to
manufactories etc. He had Lee,[5] Finn[6] etc. "all the talents" on his side but
in vain.
    The long threatened informations were filed against the Printers of the
two Papers here[7] and they were serv'd with notices this day. They say
Bryan[8] is to be served also; I have not heard if my Father [is] getting any
trouble about them.[9]

[*Source*: Scully Papers]

[1]Of King Street, Kilkenny; died c. 1845. See n.9 below.
[2]At an aggregate meeting in the Black Abbey, Kilkenny. On 30 October, however,
Kennedy argued that his membership of the Dublin Board did not rest on
delegation from the Catholics of Kilkenny but on his election to it by a Dublin
aggregate meeting (see No. 312 n.6). He was nevertheless voted off the Board on 6
December (*FJ*, 1 and 8 November 1813).

[3]Edmund Kennedy, called merchant of Kilkenny in *King's Inns Admission Papers*, a shoemaker by the *Irish Magazine* of May 1814.

[4]Unidentified.

[5]Probably Nicholas H. Lee, of Springmount, Callan.

[6]Counsellor W. F. Finn.

[7]D. Kearney was printer of the *Leinster Journal* and John Reynolds of the *Kilkenny Chronicle*. At the Dublin Board on 30 October Kennedy announced that he too had been served with a notice of prosecution for resolutions at Kilkenny "of which he believed some gentleman in the corner (alluding to Mr Scully) might be able to give some account" (*FJ*, 1 November 1813).

[8]As chairman of the meeting of 4 August which had passed the Kilkenny resolutions. On 2 February, the day after John Magee was sentenced to a further six months in prison for publishing them in the *Dublin Evening Post*, Peel wrote to Charles Abbot that the object of prosecuting him was to make Bryan as chairman and Scully as author avow themselves or "commit them with the press" (Parker, *Sir Robert Peel from his private correspondence*).

[9]This statement contradicts the genealogy given by Revd William Carrigan in his *History and Antiquities of the Diocese of Ossory* (Dublin 1905), IV, p. 42 where John Peter is shown as a younger brother of Peter Ryan of Danganmore but their father John Ryan as having died in 1806 aged 83. As Peter Ryan not only proposed the vote of thanks at the meeting but carried a resolution for giving a public dinner for the chairman he would seem to have been the father in question.

462 *From Canon Laurence Reynolds to Merrion Square, Dublin*

Private   Thomastown [Co. Kilkenny] 2 November 1813

My Dear Sir,

I have just received your kind Letter.[1] It must be to a press of business that Mr Scot's delay in sending up the Case is attributable.[2] I have no doubt, that you will be so good as to pay due attention to it.

You may rest assured, that long before your disapprobation of his Conduct was known, the people of Kilkennny had deeply lamented that Mr K[ennedy] was a Member of the Board.[3] Immediately at his return from England (I believe in August 1812) he incurred general odium for having at a public Meeting censured the Resolution of the Board relative to My Lord Moira.[4] I was present at that Meeting & can assert that his conduct was very reprehensible. However, in a very short time after, at an Aggregate Meeting, he so explained & so apologized that to my utter astonishment, he was voted possession of their Confidence by the very people who had so lately & so deservedly censured him. He then got a share in the *Chronicle* & was Editor of it. For some time the paper was conducted on liberal & popular principles;[5] when on a sudden he fills its Columns again with the praises of Lord Moira. The people got so disgusted at this, that though he was dangerously ill at the time, instead of feeling pity for him, it was imprecations they were pouring on him. He was not content with publishing these sentiments in the *Chronicle*. No, but he drew up a string of Resolutions on his sick bed for an Aggregate Meeting that was held about this time 12 month, one of which went to censure the General Board for their conduct to his favourite L. Moira. This attempt of his was publicly known, and excited such indignation, that very few persons at least when sick ever left Ireland more unpitied & more unpopular than he left it for Lisbon. All this would perhaps have been forgiven, were it not that his first public act on his return from Lisbon was to plant a thorn in the breast of L[ord] Ormonde & to give great uneasiness to the whole Company, at the dinner given by the Catholics to the Noble Earl.[6] Having perceived that the Citizens were much displeased at his language & conduct on that occasion, instead of apologizing, he was heard after to declare that "the politics of the Catholics of Kilkenny were not his Politics" — "that their sentiments were widely different, and in many essential cases diametrically opposite". This happened in July last, when to my knowledge the desire of expelling him was (at least morally speaking) general. Indeed so openly did the Catholics speak then, that I was much surprized, when I heard he was not expelled at the Aggregate Meeting in August.[7] For the simplest men amongst them reasoned thus: "Mr K. declares 'that his Politics are not our Politics', 'that his sentiments are opposite to ours'. Surely then we cannot expect that he will speak our sentiments at the Board & of course, we ought to withdraw confidence from him." If to all this is added, the indignation they felt at the Caricature description he gave of Captain Bryan's Dinner,[8] you will be convinced, and so will every dispassionate man be convinced that his Expulsion had been resolved on before you & he came any way in contact — or rather before he manifested his desire of getting into notice by his impertinence to you. I admit at the same time, that some of the young Orators at the B[lack] Abbey Meeting Thursday last,[9] did say as I am informed, that his impertinence to you[10] would be sufficient ground for his Expulsion but Counsellor Finne [*sic*] I understand made some sensible (and indeed to you friendly) remarks on that point. I was not at this last mentioned Meeting for which absence I am sincerely [sorry]. There was much confusion there, which is to be deeply lamented. As on all occasions of the kind, the conduct of persons on both sides was censurable. But I have [heard?] from undoubted authority that Mr K. was to blame for all. It appears that he wrote several Letters to his friends to exert themselves in his behalf. Some of these were Schoolfellows;[11] & two were priests. During the Debate there was much interruption, much clamour. His Correspondents shewed much zeal in collecting their forces. To augment the number they were heard often to say to the people: "Will you desert your Priests?" "Which of the two will you vote for: God or Peter Ryan?" These unwarrantable expressions called forth similar ones from the others — such as "Will you vote for *Luther*" (a name they have given to Mr. K).[12] At length notwithstanding every effort made by Mr K's adherents, to prevent it, they divided, and there were 3 to 1 against him. 190 against, 63 for him. My Brother's Reporter[13] could not take Notes. I shall lose no time in urging one of the Delegates to go down for the purpose you mention.[14]

[*Source*: Scully Papers]

[1]Missing:(it was dated 1 November by when Scully would have been able to report the outcome of the Board's meeting of 30 October (see No. 461 n.2).

[2]See No. 459.

[3]The *Freeman's Journal* of 29 October had made Scully responsible for the move to get Kennedy off the Kilkenny Board. On 3 November it published a letter from him denying that he was "the beginning, middle and end of all concerns relating to Kilkenny".

[4]At the end of June 1813 Kennedy had argued at the Board against letting the Catholic cause be a party matter and said he was convinced that had it not been for the (witchery) resolutions of 18 June 1812 (see No. 359 n.3) Lord Moira would be now Lord Lieutenant of Ireland (*FJ*, 29 June 1813).

[5]For instance, when it criticised Charles Butler for his interview with Lord Castlereagh (see No. 403 n.4).

[6]Kennedy was one of the Vice-Presidents at the dinner given in July and made a speech praising the Marquis of Ormonde for having made his choice between the court and the Catholics (*DEP*, 17 July 1813 from the *Kilkenny Chronicle*). The Marquis had in fact resigned his post as Groom of the Bed Chamber because he had been refused the nomination of the sheriff of Co. Kilkenny (Gregory to Peel 5 June 1813: Add.MSS.40, 196, f.307).

[7]Of 4 August, when the resolutions leading to the second prosecution of Magee were adopted (see No. 449 n.3).

[8]Kennedy's account, presumably published in the *Kilkenny Chronicle*, is not available. The dinner was given on 13 September in honour of Captain Bryan, with Peter Ryan in the chair, and some two hundred people attended. Among the numerous toasts was one to Scully, "the eloquent exposer of the pretexts of our oppressors", which was cheered by many but drunk in silence by some (*FJ*, 16 September 1813).

[9]On 28 October. The *Irish Magazine* of November says that this meeting solemnly disclaimed Kennedy and "for the present the Kilkenny people have preserved the objects of their solicitude [Scully and O'Connell] from legal assassination".

[10]For instance, at the Board's meeting of 16 October (see No. 454 n.2) Kennedy had taken exception to Scully's manner and said it was not to be endured that a member could not speak out his free opinion without encountering "the monopolising spirit and dictating tone of the learned gentleman" (*FJ*, 18 October 1813).

[11]He had been sent to the lay college of Maynooth by the "veto priest" Patrick McGrath (*Irish Magazine*, January 1814).

[12]He was called "the young Luther" by Lord Norbury, to whom he had revealed the secrets of Maynooth (*Irish Magazine* ibid.).

[13]i.e. the reporter of the *Kilkenny Chronicle*.

[14]This may have had to do with a document in Scully's handwriting which would have exposed him to prosecution as the author of the Kilkenny resolutions of 4 August (see No. 449 n.4). Articles in the *Irish Magazine* for May and August 1814, written after Kennedy's death, allege that Kennedy had offered to prove that Scully was the author of the resolutions and was in a position to do so, as he had been present when the resolutions were written down for insertion in the *Kilkenny Chronicle*. The June number of the magazine says that an offer of £500 a year was made to John Reynolds, the printer, through a priest. According to a letter of 4 April 1814 from Mary O'Connell to Daniel O'Connell (O'Connell, *Correspondence* I, No. 469) a newspaper proprietor was offered £500 a year to give the framer of the resolutions up. The former, she says, had offered to suffer imprisonment if the expenses of the trial were paid by the author of the resolutions but Scully was unwilling to pay them, thinking that the resolutions in his handwriting had been destroyed, which was not the case. As Kennedy had been part owner of the Kilkenny Chronicle he was probably the proprietor to whom she was referring. Mrs O'Connell goes on to say that the Attorney-General, having heard what she had heard, had sent a person express to Kilkenny in the previous week. It was probably to this that the Lord Lieutenant was referring when he wrote to Peel on 14 April: "The mention of Scully's name reminds me of the fair prospect there is of obtaining the important document we have so often talked of" (Peel Papers, Add.MSS.40, 187, f.258).

463   *From Lord Donoughmore to Merrion Square, Dublin*

Knocklofty [Co. Tipperary] 3 November 1813

Dear Scully,

In the anatomy of the Protestants, or rather the Anti-Catholic Petition of this County,[1] which your letter exhibits, you have sufficiently shewn the contemptible folly of endeavouring to marshall the enforced names of a small packed minority, against the declared sense & feeling of the great body of the people. So far as the narrow circle goes, within which I am enabled to judge, I can assist a little in taking off the mask, & shewing the nothingness which is thus left behind.

The List, which you have given me of the Subscribers to this Petition at Ardfinnan — my little miserable village — consists of 7 names only. Of these, one name — that of *Thomas Guthrie* — is a palpable duplicate — this name being twice repeated & there being — to my knowledge only one Thos. Gutrie [sic] to be found there — & he is the parish Clerk & Schoolmaster & who had not got his licence till he had his name to that notable petition.

John Hickey — John Cowan — (for *J. Conn* must be an error in the writing) *— & Edmund Prendergast —* are subconstables, all appointed by myself, & creatures under my sole & absolute controll: who would no more have thought of signing any paper, that could be disagreeable to me, as of eating it.

Richard Page stands with respect to me just in the same way — & he is besides an absolute pauper, receiving at times a part of the Sunday's Collection at the Church. All these men, with the exception of J. Hickey, who is poverty itself, live in houses of mine, which they hold, with a garden annexed to each, at a rent not a third of the value.

Such are the materials of the Reverend Gabriel Stokes's[2] ragged regiment of Protesters. With respect to himself, he is a little retailer of tythes, who came into the parish by a clerical swap, for the purpose of grinding hard, & making a good thing of the Exchange. The people however did not like to be rode so hard, & they kicked a little — & frightened his Reverance — or at least they gave him colour to say that he was afraid to reside in his parish — & to his Bishop to permit him to live 6 miles from his duty in Clonmell.

Worrall[3] — of whom I know almost nothing — tho' I pay him £15 a year — by my great uncle's will — as the Dissenting Minister of Clonmell — is a reserved, distant man — who mixes very little in society — & whom I have never met any where. He has the character of being a scholar — & a man of an Independent mind. What the secret history may be of the shabby part which he has taken on the late occasion, I have no means of finding out.

Stokes must have known the *Carte du pays* perfectly well — & that he was humbugging — & perhaps greatly injuring those miserable blackguards of mine — by thus penning them — blindfolded as they were — agst. their best friend & patron — & they knew not for what — & so acting, this Reverend Gentleman was a much greater blackguard than themselves.

[*Source*: Scully Papers]

[1]See No. 425 n.1.

[2]Probably the later Vicar-General of Killala and Achonry, aged seventeen when he entered Trinity College, Dublin, in 1779, died 1834.

[3]Revd James Worrall. W. P. Burke, *History of Clonmel*, p. 295 says that for a considerable period he was concurrently postmaster.

464   *From Lord Donoughmore to Merrion Square, Dublin*

Knocklofty [Co. Tipperary] 3 November 1813

Dear Scully,

After I had written my reply[1] to your late letter on public matters, which circumstances have forced me to delay longer than I could have wished, your conversation respecting my place at Palmerston[2] came to my recollection; &, on tumbling over my papers, I have found the two which I inclose, & which were prepared to be transmitted to you, as you will see from the endorsement on one of them, so long ago as last September. I thought I could not put you more fully into possession of my ideas upon that subject, than by communicating to you, what I had actually written to my Brother, as the result of my fullest consideration, of an offer made for my Interest there in May or June last. In the second paper I have turned those conceptions of mine into pounds, shillings & pence.

I have thus given you my notions of the value of what I have to dispose of. If they should not agree with your own, or with those of the person for whom you were inclined to treat, I beg you may feel no delicacy in mentioning whatever may be your conceptions or his.[3]

[*Source*: Scully Papers]

[1]No. 463.

[2]Now called Palmerstown: the site of Stewart's Hospital, about five miles from the centre of Dublin on the road to Lucan. Lord Donoughmore held it on a lease from the Viscounts Palmerston going back at least as far as 1793. In June 1814 he declined an offer of £13,000 from Colonel Grogan and he was still trying to dispose of it in 1821, when the Catholic Archbishop of Dublin showed an interest but was unable to find the money (Donoughmore Papers: F/10/96; D/48/225).

[3]This is the last letter from Lord Donoughmore in the collection and with Scully's missing reply of 12 November the correspondence between them seems to have ceased. At a meeting of the Catholic Board on 6 November an attempt began to make Lord Donoughmore and Grattan consult the Catholics on the form of a relief bill, and both of them objected to being dictated to. On 21 December Lord Donoughmore wrote to Francis Hely Hutchinson about a communication from him to "that ill omened Catholic Board", the leaders of which "seemed to have lost sight of common sense and discretion", and went on: "I gave Denis Scully at the last Assizes some cautionary advice, to litle purpose as it should seem, when I bid him beware of offering *his* bill to the parliamentary advocates of his cause" (Donoughmore Papers, F/10 f.92). On 26 January 1814, apparently suspecting Scully of intriguing against him, he wrote to Hay: "The Jesuit is always one and can never know the use of any arms but a stiletto" (DDA 390/1, XI, 22).

465 *From Dr J. T. Troy, Archbishop of Dublin, to 4 Capel Street*

Cavendish Row, Saturday, 13 November 1813

My dear Sir,

The Prelates here assembled[1] unanimously think, that any cognisance or investigation of the difference between Revd Mr O Mullan & his Bishop[2] by the Board would establish a most dangerous precedent, & therefore request that Mr O'Connell & you will endeavour to prevent it. In haste.

[*Source*: Scully Papers]

[1]For this synod, which assembled on 11 November, see Ward, *Eve of Catholic Emancipation* II, p. 75. A long document was drawn up, going over the old

ground of the veto controversy and the restoration of faculties to the Abbé Treveaux.
[2]See No. 468.

466   *From Richard McGrath, Secretary to Intended New Chapel,*
            Dungarvan, to Merrion Square South, Dublin

Dungarvan [Co. Waterford] 15 November 1813

Sir,
   Mr Greene[1] of this Town will hand you the Package containing the Deeds, Papers and Case necessary for your Perusal relative to our intended new Chapel.[2] Mr Wm. Bayly has also taken the trouble together with our Chairman, Mr Kennedy[3] to write to you on the Subject. I enclose you 7 Guineas as your fee, the smallness of which the low state of our Funds will I hope excuse.
   The Case with your opinion and the Draft of the Deed you'll have the goodness to send me as soon as possible by return of the Post, as we are in a great hurry about them, and the Remainder of the Deeds and Papers you'll have the kindness to hand back to Mr Greene carefully sealed up.

[*Source*: Scully Papers]

[1]Rodolphus Greene, an attorney.
[2]See No. 453.
[3]Unidentified.

467   *From William Bayly, Dungarvan, to Merrion Square,*
            16 November 1813

   The documents connected with the purchase of a ground for the Dungarvan chapel mentioned in his letter of 2 October[1] have now been sent. Scully has been selected as their guardian because he conducted the Townsend Street parishioners through their difficulties.[2] Hubbart, the Duke of Devonshire's undertenant, has not been able to give a title because he had executed a deed conveying the property to his two daughters, who are not of age. Scully is asked for his advice as to how the purchase money of £150 can be secured until the daughters are old enough to join in a conveyance. The parish want in the meantime to raise building stones from a quarry. His partner Mr Maxwell[3] is sending a packet via Waterford and the coach.

[*Source*: Scully Papers]

[1]See No. 453.
[2]Scully was a trustee of the Townsend Street chapel in Dublin (see No. 67).
[3]Unidentified.

468   *To Counsellors Scully and O'Connell at the Catholic Board*
From Revd Cornelius O'Mullan

Dublin, 20 November 1813

My Dear friends,

You see by the inclosed that his Lordship[1] wishes to sacrifice me to gratify the Orangemen of Derry[2] — he ea [paper torn] the other motive for his conduct [hole in paper] — now [paper torn] catholic children of Derry are without a guardian — they are truly orphans — they are now the real victims of his Lordship's *Vengeance*. I am willing to withstand all the storms of adversity, and educate them in the religion of their fathers, if countenanced by my catholic fellow suffers [*sic*] in Ireland and in a few years, *Deo adjuvante*, will catholocise, at present, *anti-catholic Derry*. Believe me with every sentiment of gratitude and esteem yours affectionately,

[Enclosures]

Copy
An answer to the Rt. Rev Dr O'D[onnell]'s proposal of the Parish of Urney to the Revd C. O'Mullan. Dublin 19 November 1813.

My Lord, I return you many thanks for your kind offer of the Parish of Urney, which I accept of provided your Lordship will undertake the responsibility which I owe to the Architect Mr Stewart,[3] who has built the C[atholic] Poor School house of Derry on the *faith* of my word.[4] It would appear very inconsistent in me to accept of any situation, whilst I am so circumstanced — your L'Ship deprived me of the situation that would enable me to defray the expenses incurred; this your L'p did for reasons known only to yourself and as you have done so I trust your Lordship will hold me no longer responsible — were your L'ship to constitute me the Parish Priest of Urney I then became responsible to God for my duty towards the Pari'h'rs which I am willing to do, if you unburthen me of the former obligation.

To the Rt Revd Dr O'Donnell,
Belton Street Dublin,
favoured per Mr McSheffry.[5]

Copy
From Dr Charles O'Donnell to Revd C. O'Mullan, 11 Gloucester Street, Dublin.

Revd Sir,

I told you more than once this day that I would not become responsible in any respect to the Architect of the poor school of Derry. I now tell you the same.   [*Source*: Scully Papers]

[1]Dr Charles O'Donnell, Roman Catholic Bishop of Derry.

[2]By transferring him to another parish and refusing to accept responsibility for the poor school. Father O'Mullan had been suspended before 18 October 1813, when Dr O'Donnell announced that he had withdrawn jurisdiction from him only in the parish of Templemore (*FJ*, 11 December 1813). The action would appear to have been taken because Father O'Mullan had made himself obnoxious to the Derry Protestants and had been prosecuted for marrying a Catholic to a woman who was not a Catholic (ibid.).

[3]Unidentified.

[4]Father O'Mullan came to Dublin in October (*DEP*, 7 October 1813) and distributed a leaflet (DDA 54/1, IX, 54) seeking subscriptions and donations for his poor school, which was attached to the chapel at Derry. He said it had been founded to obviate the danger from the Charter Schools, work had already begun and the Catholics of Derry necessarily looked principally to the Catholics of Dublin for assistance.

[5]See No. 469 n.2.

469   *From Revd Cornelius O'Mullan to 2 Merrion Square, Dublin*

11 Glo'ster street [Dublin] 29 November 1813

My Dear friend,

The Colerain [*sic*] Resolutions would have received the sanction of the Board last saturday[1] were it not for Doctor Drumgoole who opposed their reading. He spoke a long time against them. He shew'd that they were the Resolutions of a few discontented persons who had been expelled the confidence of the City and County Catholics at two aggregate meetings held in the City Chapel and in the first town in the County.[2] The Dr also said that some of these fellows had sworn examinations against the Chairman and several of the most respectable persons who attended the late meeting in Derry[3] and that the Board by receiving these Colerain Resolutions would assist these *moderees*[4] in laying a basis for calling all county meetings in future *riotous* meetings because there might be still members found in every county base enough to undertake such proceedings. My Dear friend, if you and my friend O'Connell suffer them to be sanctioned by the Board they will militate very strongly against me. It will assist Sir George in his prosecution[5] against me and the other gentlemen whom Rich'd O'Dogherty swore against. Mr Lalor[6] said the Board should not receive them and he ventured to say they were spurious. Mr McGuckin[7] of Belfast said that he knew Mr Begly[8] who acted as chairman and that he was a respectable character tho' he held the situation of Barrackmaster in Colerain under Mr Ray[9] the high sheriff. Mr Hay was then ordered to write to the two secretaries[10] and have their answers before next day of meeting. Now it is well known that the two sheriffs of Derry are my determined enemies. It is also known that these men who forwarded these latter Resolutions are under the influence of Sir George and the sheriffs of Derry and that they could not ensure their situations in a more effectual manner than by giving me all the opposition possible.[11] It is also a well known fact and which is to be seen upon the face of Mr Hay's books[12] that Mr McSheffry[13] and the other gentlemen have remitted money to the Board and that none of this faction ever gave a shilling to forward our interest. Mr Drummond[14] received a considerable deal of money to be sent to the Board and because Richard O'Dogherty was not received by the Catholics into confidence he would not nor did not forward it. This fact Doctor O'Donnell[15] himself stated I believe to C'r O'Connell and I am sure to Mr Hay. He also wrote last year a letter to Mr Hay concurring in their expulsion. He himself attended the meeting that expelled them which was the only meeting he ever attended. Mr O'Connell knows they brought an action against Mr McSheffry who acted as Chairman to the meeting that expelled them.

Pardon me for taking up so much of your precious time. I thought to have a few minutes conversation with you in the Hall[16] but seeing you so much engaged with other gentlemen I was delicate to obtrude myself. My friends say that I cannot in justice to myself and also on account of what happened between his Lordship[17] and me but give to the public a true statement of the entire and particularly my final determination of superintending the school. This will be more trouble to *my friend*.[18] Ever truly yours, C. O'Mullan

[*Source*: Scully Papers]

[1]The holding of the meeting was briefly reported in the *Freeman's Journal* of 29 November but the proceedings in regard to the Derry and Coleraine resolutions were not mentioned.

[2]The first was probably that of 21 December 1812, when the Derry Catholics adopted resolutions, signed by Daniel McSheffrey as chairman and John McSheffrey as secretary, withdrawing their confidence from Richard O'Dogherty and James McElevey. The second was that of 4 November 1813 which confirmed the expulsions and included Father O'Mullan in a revised list. The resolutions of this meeting and the new list had been published by the *Dublin Evening Post* on 9 November; and on the same page there had appeared a requisition for a meeting to be held at Coleraine on the 11th, signed by twenty Derry Catholics who claimed that the sense of the respectable Catholics was against the measures adopted on the 4th. The Coleraine meeting duly took place but according to a statement made to the Board in Dublin only seven persons attended (*DEP*, 4 December 1813).

[3]i.e. that charges had been laid not only against creators of disturbance but also against respectable people merely for being present.

[4]In an editorial of 11 June 1813 the *Freeman's Journal* had divided the Board into "moderees or conciliators" and "vigorees . . . or non-conciliators". Gregory used the expression when he wrote to Peel on 14 June 1813 (Add.MSS.40, 197, f.14).

[5]The case against Father O'Mullan had been formally brought by Richard O'Dogherty, a writing clerk of Derry and described in 1815 as a coroner of Donegal.

He and Father O'Mullan had been prominent among the supporters of General William Ponsonby in the 1812 elections and attended the victory dinner given for him. A friendly toast to the Catholics given by Sir George Hill was interpreted by Father O'Mullan in a letter to the press as a pledge of support for emancipation; Hill denied that this had been his meaning; and O'Dogherty published a letter supporting him. When Father O'Mullan called a meeting at which this letter was declared a fabrication O'Dogherty was forcibly ejected and laid information for a riot. Father O'Mullan, defended by N. P. O'Gorman, was tried and found guilty in January — see O'Gorman's report to the Board in the *Freeman's Journal* of 24 January 1814; the case of *James Magee v N. P. O'Gorman* before the King's Bench on 3 July 1815 (published in six instalments in the *DEP*); and further retrospective references in the *DEP* of 16 December 1815 and the *Dublin Chronicle* of 15 April 1816.

[6]James Lalor of the Kilkenny committee (*FJ*, 2 December 1813). One of the 1811 delegates, whose address then was Mountbrilliant, Co. Kilkenny.

[7]James McGuckin, who had a practice in Dublin.

[8]Listed as Alexander Begley of Coleraine in the 1811 Londonderry list.

[9]Unidentified.

[10]John McSheffry of the Derry and R. O'Dogherty of the Coleraine faction.

[11]Sir George Hill's reports to the Castle referred to riots on 11th and 18th as well as 4 November. He told Peel on 1 January 1814 that the 9000 Derry Catholics were chiefly of the lower order and had "under the ribbon system and the guidance of priest O'Mullan, and thro' the influence of the Board, become lately turbulent and ill disposed". Peel thought that the turbulence of the lower orders might have beneficial consequences "for thus shall the eyes of the blind be opened" (HO 100/176, ff.123, 238).

[12]The Board's accounts, kept by Edward Hay.

[13]Either Daniel or his son John.

[14]Lewis Drummond of Coleraine, one of those who called the Coleraine meeting.

[15]Dr Charles O'Donnell, Roman Catholic Bishop of Derry.

[16]Of the Four Courts.

[17]His Bishop.

[18]The Board voted unanimously to receive only the Derry resolutions. Scully was one of the speakers and launched an attack on the notion of "respectability". When all Catholics were slaves how could "respectable Catholics" be distinguished from "the people"? (*FJ*, 2 December 1813).

470   *From Bishop John Milner to Merrion Square, Dublin*

W.H. 29 November [1813]

My Dr. Sir,

Having issued the present Circular[1] I think it incumbent on me to send you a copy of it, because your partiality towards me makes you wish to see every publication from my pen, & because the subject of it is not uninteresting to the Cathc. politics of Ireland.

From this letter you will gather the result of that Meeting of British Prelates, (namely three English V.V.A, two Scotch & two Coadjutors) which has been mentioned in the Newspapers, & from which I was excluded. This *Conciliabutum* as we Canonists call a packed synod was got together by Dr Poynter under the directions of the Stanhope Street Junta.[2] It satisfies neither party, not my friends, because it indirectly affronts me & renews the 5th Resolution, & not the other party because it does not lay down any positive groundwork for a fresh security Bill. I have no doubt but Chs. Butler & his adherents mean now to bring in a separate Bill to obtain yr. franchises & that they will purposely get *securities* as they are ludicrously called, hooked into it, as a foundation for a general Emancipation Bill, which they expect thus to force upon you.

I lately sent to Secretary Hay a *List of the English Board*,[3] so called, printed by themselves & which they are sure to distribute among the leading Members of Pt. etc. for the purpose of representing themselves as possessing all the great Cathc. names in yr. Island as well as in ours. In fact all your Peers are there put down as Members of this English Board. I beg pardon they call it British because Sir James Gordon & Mrs Menzies have given their names & Lord Traquair, I understand, has refused to do so.[4] Now I did not nor do I wish to be mentioned by yr. Board on such an occasion as this: still I think the circumstances itself of the puny *English Board*, so called, dressing itself in the gawdiest colours of yr. Committee is deserving the attention of the latter, especially as the two parties are pursuing different lines of politics.

I admire & pity Mr Magee[5] but I am angry with his Clerk who will not send me an acct. of what I am indebted to him for the *D.E. Post* during the interrupted periods of my taking it. When I call on Taylor & Newton[6] in London as I have done twice I find they know nothing of the matter: no not so much as the amt. of the annual subscription.

Mrs Wheble joins me in all that is kind to Mrs S.   [*Source*: Scully Papers]

[1] An *Encyclical Letter to the Midland Catholics*, dated 22 November 1813 — his reply to a joint pastoral adopted by the other Vicars Apostolic at Durham at the end of October (see No. 456 n.2).

[2] Those who had expelled Dr Milner from the Private Board (see No. 440 n.3).

[3] His letter was read at the Board on 6 November (*FJ*, 8 November 1813). A copy of the enclosure in the Throckmorton Papers is headed "List of the General Board of British Catholics" and dated 1 August 1813. The first page displays in large capital letters the names of the Vicars Apostolic, peers, sons of peers and baronets. Against the laity of England and Scotland an initial letters indicates the ecclesiastical district to which they belonged. Two columns on the opposite side show their first and second subscriptions. No Irish baronets or sons of peers are included but among the peers are inserted, in order of rank, the Earls of Fingall and Kenmare, Viscounts Gormanston, Netterville and Southwell, Barons Trimleston and French, without any indication of district or amount of subscription.

[4] Sir James Gordon of Letterfourie, 7th Baronet; John Menzies of Pitfodels; and

Charles Stewart, 7th Earl of Traquair. Dr Milner omits two other subscribers in Scotland: M. Constable Maxwell of Everingham and James Maxwell of Kirkconnell.
[5]John Magee, in prison for libelling the Duke of Richmond.
[6]Taylor and Newton, General Advertising Office, Warwick Square, London.

470A   *To Revd P. Kenny SJ*

19 December 1813

Dear Sir,

In the following observations, I shall endeavour to comprize the legal topics which appear to me likely to assist you and the other gentlemen, interested in the security of the title to the Estate,[1] lately purchased by you.

The capacity to acquire and hold lands, and the legality of the purpose for which the purchase is intended, are distinct subjects of consideration in the case. With respect to the former, it is beyond all doubt, that *you* are by law as capable of purchasing, as any Catholic layman, who has taken the oath and subscribed the Declaration prescribed to Catholics by the Statute of 33 George 3 Chap. 21 (1793). There never did exist any law in Ireland rendering a Catholic clergyman, of whatever rank or order, less qualified to acquire or dispose of property than Catholic laymen. The Statutes, which incapacitated Catholics in this respect, affected the entire Catholic community, without distinction: and of course all the classes of that community have equally participated in the relief secured by the later Statutes of 1778–1782, and 1793 — you should, however, obtain from the officer, and carefully preserve, a certificate of your qualification.

The *legality of the purpose*, for which this purchase has been made, is in fact the only subject for reasonable apprehension. The grounds of this apprehension have been already detailed at large, in the "Statement of the Penal Laws, page 44 to 48". Opposite opinions have been pronounced by the present Chancellor, Manners, in 1809 — and in 1813 — and in the same cause. In 1809 he declared the endowment of a Catholic school in Ireland to be unlawful, upon the authority of the illadvised preamble to the Statute of 1795, for founding Maynooth College:[2] and, in 1813,[3] he declared a similar endowment to be lawful, provided that it received or would receive Protestant pupils. Under these conflicting authorities, therefore, the safest course for you appears to be that of admitting, or expressing a willingness to admit, any Protestant pupils who may seek admission. And this is not now prohibited by any law: for the Statute of the 21 and 22 Geo. 3, which disabled Catholic schoolmasters from receiving Protestant scholars, is substantially repealed in this respect by the Statute of the 33 Geo. 3 Ch. 21, the first section of which removes all existing disabilities and incapacities, save such as are expressly reserved by the subsequent sections, and this disability has not been so reserved.[4] By this rule, the proposed establishment will, in my opinion, be the better enabled to steer its course thro' the perplexities of legal doctrine upon this subject.

I should advise, that the Memorial of the conveyance from General Browne[5] to Mr Kenny, be executed by the General and registered immediately: and that Mr Kenny should afterwards assign the premises to a Trustee to the use of himself and of four or five other persons (whether clergy or laity) in whom a confidence can be reposed. The latter deed need not be registered: the consideration recited in it should be only 10/– and thereby the stamp duty will be saved: and the expence will be trifling, as no recitals or covenants will be necessary. Two or three parts of it may be executed: and deposited in different hands. The conveyance should be to the use of those 5 or 6 persons, and the survivors and survivor of them and his heirs. I should prefer the larger number to that of 2 or 3 only: for it will become the less necessary to execute new conveyances. When the number becomes, by deaths, reduced to two, the survivors may fill up the vacancies, and execute a new conveyance in like manner: but this intention should be expressed, if at all, upon a separate Memorandum or recommendatory paper, not in the conveyance itself.

I should decidedly recommend the substitution to be made by a deed "inter vivos", to be executed by the 2 or 3 survivors, rather than by the will of the longest liver, for its advantages of greater facility, privacy, and security.

A will of lands requires to be executed with peculiar formalities — in the presence of 3 subscribing witnesses, who must attest it in the testator's presence. It may relate to the testator's other property, and so be multifarious in its objects. It is generally deposited in the Ecclesiastical Courts, and is open for inspection and investigation by persons of hostile feelings. It cannot be produced in proof, when necessary, without a considerable expence — and it is often liable to be disputed by the heir at law. But a deed is sufficiently attested by one subscribing witness. It may be concise, private, confined to the single object, deposited in the hands of a trustee or friend — always forthcoming without expence — and not subject to the hourly scrutiny of the Commissioners of Charitable Donations, or of their agent, or of an heir at law etc.

Allow me to conclude by the expression of my cordial wishes for the success and permanency of your intended establishment — and the hope, that, whatever fluctuations we may be destined to witness in the temporal condition of our aggrieved countrymen, their religious duties will be long enforced, and their religious feelings derive augmented strength, under the influence of the undertaking, which you have in hand, and which is expected by the Catholic community with general satisfaction.

[*Source*: Jesuit Archives, Dublin]

[1]Castle Browne, Clane, Co. Kildare. The purchase money of £16,000 had been deposited by September 1813; legal possession was secured on 4 March 1814 and Father Kenney took up residence on 5 April (*Clongowes Record*, pp. 42, 45).

[2]See No. 197 n.6. In his opinion of 1809 the Lord Chancellor cited a passage in the preamble to 35 Geo. III Cap. 21 declaring that it was unlawful to endow any college or seminary for the education exclusively of Catholics — before going on to make an exception in the case of Maynooth.

[3]The occasion has not been identified.

[4]For a contrary opinion by senior counsel see *Clongowes Record*, p. 45.

[5]Lieutenant General Michael Wogan Browne (d. 1824) was at this time in the service of the King of Saxony and was a Catholic. He had succeeded to the property in 1812 on the death of his brother Thomas Wogan Browne, who had conformed to the established church.

471 *From Richard McGrath to Merrion Square South, Dublin*

Dungarvan, 12 February 1814

Sir,

Your very kind Letter of the 21st Jany. I have laid before the Committee. They feel grateful for this Mark of your Generosity and Attention to their Business[1] and requested I would Express to you their warmest Acknowledgments for the Same. They have according to your desire Enrolled your Name as one of their Benefactors. As the Hurry of term will prevent your drawing the Deeds immediately, they will wait your Leisure until after term and must apologize for giving you the trouble of Drawing the Entire yourself, as giving Instructions to any other Person to draft them would be only attended with additional Delay, which they are very anxious to avoid as Mr Hubbart[2] is a very old man (near 80) and Every Moment's Delay is attended with very great Risque.

When you have completed those Deeds you will have the Kindness to send them by the Mail Coach to Waterford directed to me to the Care of Mr Martin Boggan, Coach Office, Waterford and to favour me with a Line by Post Enclosing the 7 Guineas you were Kind Enough to say you would return.[3]

[*Source*: Scully Papers]

[1]The conveyance of the land donated by the Duke of Devonshire (see No. 466).

[2]The undertenant whose interest had to be purchased (see No. 467).

[3]On 15 February Scully minuted on the cover: "I sent a 7 guinea B.I. bill — his favour not accepted". The return of the deeds by Scully did not lead to an early completion of the transaction for on 12 April 1815 Rodolphus Greene (see No. 466) was paid a fee for drawing a grant of the ground and another on 23 October 1815 for preparing a lease of ground to the Bishop (Estate ledgers of William S. Cavendish for Cork and Waterford: NLI MS.6915, 6923). It was not until 27 March 1828 that the new church, "a plain but commodious edifice", was opened (Patrick Power, *Waterford*

and Lismore: a compendious history of the united dioceses, Cork University Press 1937).

471A   *To Revd P. Kenney SJ*

Merrion Square, 27 February 1814

Dear Sir,

I return Mr O'Brien's[1] letter enclosed. It shows his research and discernment — *Clon* must mean "churchland", but, as to "*Gos*" or "*Gose*", I think that he has not hit upon the original meaning, for the Irish language would not have designated the place by a word signifying a stream, where no stream existed.

As to "Clongowes Castle", my only repugnance is to the word "Castle" — and it seemed to me a bad part of the present name. It is becoming vulgar in Ireland, and almost ludicrous, by the indiscriminate assumption of it — and even where no Castle, or trace of a Castle, appears.

What would you think of *Clongos Vale*, if the locality of the ground corresponds to the name of *Vale*? — or, if not, *Clongos wood*, your own original intent, if there be sufficient wood to justify the name — or, perhaps best of all, *Clongos College*.

For my part, I lean towards *Clongos vale* (if there is a vale, or *Clongos College* — but I have no reason to presume upon my own taste, and shall find greater pleasure in a name of your own selection than in any fancy of mine.

[*Source*: Congowes College Archives]

[1]Unidentified.

471B   *To Revd Peter Kenney SJ*

Kilkenny, 22 March 1814

My dear Sir,

I have this moment received your letter.[1] On receipt of this I recommend your going directly to the Kildare Street Hotel, and enquire there for General Montagu Mathew, who left Clonmell on Saturday last for Dublin on his way to London. If you can catch him in Dublin, you may freely explain all matters to him, & fully confide in him. Use my name, and it will be enough.

I write also to Sir Henry Parnell, who is at Maryborough and will soon be in Dublin. You will hear of him at Fitzpatrick's, and at Leech's hotel, Kildare Street — Have him watched, and see him before he sails. Mr George Ponsonby, if not gone, is at Newlands[2] on the Rathcoole Road, 3 miles from

Dublin. See him also, and state the facts fully to him. You may freely use my name to those persons.

I think you ought to enclose a printed prospectus to Lords Holland, Lansdowne, Grenville, Grey, the Duke of Norfolk — and Earl Donoughmore — also to Messrs Grattan, Canning, Whitbread, Tierney, Sir James MacIntosh, the Bishop of Norwich & other Members — adding a few lines of apology, on account of Sir J. H[ippisley]'s threatened motion;[3] and claiming the protection due to freedom of education, and free enjoyment of private property.[4] The Address of each Peer is "House of Lords" London. That of each Commoner is "House of Commons London".

I like your prospectus much — but by all means endeavour to have the [?] words "Blenkinsop Printer etc etc" expunged. They are unsightly,

I write in haste of Assizes business — but I shall write again in 2 or 3 days when I can add more.   [*Source*: Clongowes College Archives]

[1]Missing.
[2]The seat of the Wolfe family.
[3]Hippisley had first voiced suspicions about the remission of Jesuit funds to Ireland when he spoke on 11 May 1813 (*Hansard* XXVI, 15). The threatened motion came up on 17 May 1814 (see No. 480 n.1).
[4]On 24 February Father Kenney had had an interview with Peel. He told him that the purchase funds were exclusively his own and refused to reveal where they came from in the first place. He said that although he was a Jesuit the school had no connexion with his order, that it was for the education of laymen, and that it was open to Protestants as well as Catholics (Peel to the Home Secretary: HO 100/177, f.122).

472   *To Lord Holland*

                    Merrion Square, 24 March 1814
My Lord,

I am persuaded that your Lordship will lend a favourable attention to this letter, when you find that it regards the exercise of those humane & benevolent feelings, for which your character stands fully distinguished.

Without preface, I wish to interest your Lordship for poor Fitzpatrick the printer, and through your powerful influence to soften the resentment of his Grace the Duke of Richmond (your Lordship's relative)[1] to which his imprisonment is attributed — You are apprized of the entire history of this affair — of the publication of the "Statement of the Penal Laws which aggrieve the Catholics" — the prosecution instituted against Fitzpatrick — the heavy punishment of £200 — and 18 months imprisonment.[2]

We trust, that the time has arrived, when the offence may be considered as expiated by suffering, and anger may have subsided — Twelve of these 18 months will have elapsed on the 28th of April.[3] The man is aged, infirm, inoffensive, & never intended any offence to the Duke. To continue his imprisonment during the remaining six months, would be severe indeed — It would expose him to the gaol fevers which arise from the heats of the summer — and debar him from the opportunity, which the long days would afford, of reestablishing his broken health by country air and exercise. His wife is sickly — his children unprotected — his trade impaired. Surely enough has been inflicted.

A line from his Grace to Lord Whitworth,[4] signifying his wish for the enlargement of the sufferer, would do more honour to his character than fifty victories over printers. It would be attended to directly — for Lord Whitworth is already well disposed — and his good feelings are only checked by a reluctance to interfere in a matter, that is supposed to relate personally to his Grace the Duke of Richmond.

I have always heard that his Grace before he fell into the hands of the managers (or rather Mamelukes) of Dublin Castle, was deemed to be a humane, benevolent, kindhearted man — He is now freed from this bad influence — his feelings have had time to cool — and I trust he will now show himself in his proper character.

Previous to his departure, our R. Catholic Archbishop of Dublin, Doctor Troy, and others,[5] had waited upon his Grace, and entreated some mercy for the printer, who is really an esteemed and popular man. The application was fruitless — probably owing to the then influence of our Irish Attorney General (Saurin) and his unrelenting coadjutors at the [one word illegible] Castle.

Such, however, is the warm interest taken by the public in this case, that several distinguished persons propose a subscription for this man, as you will see by the enclosed copy of the prospectus.[6]

I have thought it best, for the sake of the Duke and of human nature, that the good deed should be anticipated by the voluntary interference of his Grace — and the occasion now offers for an exertion, honourable to the goodness of his heart.

If a personal delicacy towards his Grace may have restrained the public expression of your Lordship's sentiments upon the general mischiefs of his Irish administration, we can easily understand and make allowance for the natural operation of private feeling in such a case. But the forbearance, dictated by such delicacy, appears to entitle your Lordship's interference, in the present instance, to augmented weight and authority: and I flatter myself that it will prove successful now.

At present it has been so contrived by the insidious friends of his Grace in Dublin, that the entire odium (and it is not light) of the severity exercised upon poor Fitzpatrick should lie upon his Grace's shoulders alone — To him is attributed its origin — to him its prolongation — to him also the death of this man (if it shall ensue) will assuredly be ascribed: and the Irish public, whilst they commemorate the martyr, will never forget his supposed persecutor — I firmly believe all this to be wrongful — and that his Grace has been rather the instrument of wicked men, who abuse his name and degrade his character for venal purposes of their own — May we hope, that his Grace, by one worthy and magnanimous act, will dissipate the error, assert his real nature, and restore a worthy & respectable family to peace & freedom.

I think I know your Lordship's kind and noble nature too well to offer another apology for this application — you will feel it to be a case worthy of your humane efforts — and you best know the surest channel of success. Every hour is important to the health of this enfeebled prisoner — I shall anxiously await the honour of a line from your Lordship.

[P.S.] I have not had, till now, anything particular to write, since I was honoured by a letter from your Lordship about twelve months ago[7] — Our Catholic affairs have been of a gloomy & bad aspect — since the Prince[8] & Lord Moira[9] deserted us — and Mr Grattan's Relief Bill[10] was a most unfortunate blunder throughout.

I need scarcely apprise your Lordship, that my name, if mentioned in this affair, might be rather prejudicial than otherwise.

[*Source*: Holland House Papers, Add.MS.51827 f.89]

[1]Through his grandmother, Lady Georgiana Lennox, Lord Holland was a first cousin once removed.

[2]See No. 404 n.1.

[3]The *Freeman's Journal* of 29 May 1813 says that Fitzpatrick was committed to prison on 28 May: perhaps he had served a month before the sentence was passed.

[4]The 1st Viscount Whitworth, since 26 August 1813 Lord Lieutenant.

[5]In a letter to Peel of 16 July 1813 the Duke said that Dr Troy had brought a memorial, that he had told him he thought Fitzpatrick richly deserved his punishment and that Dr Troy said "he was so much pressed to bring the memorial that he could not avoid it" (Peel Papers: Add.MSS.40, 186, f.150). For the other interventions see No. 450 n.2.

[6]While this emphasised that Fitzpatrick had undertaken the publication of the *Penal Laws* on his sole responsibility, it said the people of Ireland owed a debt of gratitude to the accredited printer of their clergy and laity and proposed the creation of a fund not merely to compensate his losses but mark his services by remuneration.

[7]Lord Holland's last letter in the collection is No. 393 of 12 January 1813.

[8]By continuing the No Popery administration in office after the restrictions on the regency expired (see No. 334 n.4).

[9]Perhaps by giving loyalty to the Regent first place and finally by his "flight from the Catholic question to the banks of the Ganges" (Thomas Grenville to Lord Grenville 1 November 1812 in *Dropmore Papers* X).

[10]Defeated on 24 May 1813 (see No. 434 n.3).

473   *From Sir Henry Parnell to Merrion Square South, Dublin*

Emo Park [Queen's Co.] 31 March 1814

My Dear Sir,

I have received your letter of the 25th & shall be very happy in assisting Mr Kenny in any way in my power, as I am sure his undertaking[1] must be attended with the most useful consequences in the general improvement [in] our country.   [*Source*: Scully Papers]

[1]See No. 471B.

474   *To Lord Holland, St James' Square, London*

Merrion Square, 8 April 1814

My Lord,

I troubled your Lordship some time ago with an application on behalf of Hugh Fitzpatrick, the old printer — I have this day obtained from him the enclosed copy of a letter, which he lately wrote to the Duke of Richmond upon the same subject:[1] and I take the liberty of sending it, because it will put your Lordship more fully in possession of his case & his feelings — The letter, it is true, is not that of a Regulus or a Cato — it evinces no great fortitude — but, tho' it may not inspire respect for magnanimity, yet I think it must awaken compassion by its penitent & sorrowful tone — It is a further proof of what I have observed in my last, that he is not a fit object for the hostility or resentment of the Duke or of any elevated character — and that, to persecute him, is only to trample on a worm.[2]

Your Lordship will extend your indulgence to this trouble also.

[*Source*: Holland House Papers, Add. MS.51827 f.95]

[1]A copy of Hugh Fitzpatrick's memorial of 28 March 1814 to the Duke of Richmond, the key passage of which read: "In this work [the *Penal Laws*] a short note of six lines was unfortunately inserted, of which at that time I was wholly unconscious but which I do most contritely confess contained a libel on your Grace". He said he was encouraged by what Dr Troy had told him about his interview with the Duke to hope that a period would arrive when he would be considered to have done sufficient atonement.

[2]On 17 May 1814 the Duke of Richmond told Peel that Fitzpatrick's letter of 28 March had reached him only on the previous day, by a roundabout way, and sent him a copy of his reply. In this he told Fitzpatrick that he must have misunderstood his conversation with Dr Troy. He had told the latter that while as an individual he held the attack on him cheap, as the head of the government he thought it necessary to

take notice of it. The licentiousness of the press had increased so much that it was his duty to correct it as far as the laws allowed, and he conceived the sentence of the court to be a perfectly fair one. If Lord Whitworth saw anything in Fitzpatrick's case to make him remit part of the sentence he (the Duke) had not a word to say against it, but he declined taking any further part than to transmit Fitzpatrick's letter to the Castle (Add.MSS.40, 186, f.233).

475   *From Bishop John Milner to Merrion Square, Dublin*

W[olver]Hmptn 14 April [1814]

My Dear Sir,

I was last night honoured with yours of the 9th inst. enclosing a copy of Mr Fitzpatrick's petition,[1] which latter I send off by the present post to his Grace of Norfolk, with an apology for the liberty I take in doing this without knowing on what footing he stands with his neighbour at Goodwood.[2] As they are men of every different characters I think it not unlikely that they may not be on friendly terms with each other. If the Duke of Norfolk can do any good in the business, I am confident he will do it: hence if no good is done through him I shall take it for granted, as I have told him it is because he can do none. With respect to the Cathc. nobility I am out of favour with them all, & therefore have no interest with any of them, the natural consequence of the part I have taken with the Catholics & the cause of Ireland. Much pains have been taken to detach me from them, but my conscience has bound me fast to them. In case you see the *Orthodox Journal*[3] as it comes out every month, you cannot but be acquainted with my sentiments & resolutions on the points alluded to. Charles Butler has adopted the course which I predicted.[4] Having failed in raising an interest in Ireland, he has induced his brother board-men, to use every means in their power to get their petition discussed separately from that of Ireland, & to accept of any Emancipation & upon any terms that a Protest. or rather Deistical Pt. may choose to dictate. Any restrictions which may be imposed upon us will serve as a precedent for the terms of yr. pretended relief. It is as true as it is strange that our supposed friends are, in the direct ration, our most unrelenting oppressors, as far as they have it in their power, witness Henry Grattan & Sir Jn. Hip[pis]ley. Nothing proves more clearly the truth of the Statements in your Book than the vile & tyrannical persecution exercised against the printer of it.[5] True is the saying in your country: *There is no justice for a Catholic in Ireland*. Still the book has done an immense deal of good. I have heared, but I forget from whom, that King Wilberforce[6] who heretofore always voted against the Caths. has said that he will now always vote for them till the *Statement of the Penal Laws* is answered.

I shd. find great pleasure in stealing over to Ireland & passing a week incog. under yr. roof, according to yr. kind invitation; but I am oppressed with professional business & expect to be still further loaded with it when the Pope is at liberty to look into our affairs.[7] I am pleased with yr. brother-in-law Francis Canning, who almost *alone* was found *just* at the Stanhope Street Meeting of March 3.[8] I passed a very agreeable day at Sawston,[9] where as well as at Woodley[10] I know yr. company wd. be deemed an honour. I have not seen the Eyres of late, but they are always found on the right side of the question. When you write about my long silence you seem to forget that you were too [*sic*] long letters in my debt at the date of yr. last to me.

Mrs Wheble who is a good deal reduced by a long continued cold joins me in compts. to yourself & Mrs Scully.

P.S. How happens it that yr. Board permits the Stanhope Street Junta to put down the names of all yr. Irish Peers as belonging to them? I send you a list of their *pretended* associates.[11]   [*Source*: Scully Papers]

[1]See No. 474 n.1.

[2]The Duke of Richmond's residence in Sussex, not far from the Duke of Norfolk's castle at Arundel.

[3]In the January number there was a letter from him on Catholic Affairs, going over the old ground of his controversies with Butler. In February he continued a newspaper controversy with Robert Clifford, now revealed, he said, as the author of the pamphlet *Origin and purpose of the veto*, first published in the summer of 1813. In March he wrote on the English Catholic Board and its petition.

[4]See No. 470.

[5]Hugh Fitzpatrick.

[6]William Wilberforce.

[7]Having been sent back to Savona and released on 17 March Pope Pius VII was waiting for his cardinals to assemble before returning to Rome (where he made his entry on 24 May). Bishop Ward (*Eve of Catholic Emancipation* II, p. 87) cites a letter of 20 March in which Dr Milner informed Dr Troy of his intention to go to Rome. On 2 May he crossed the Channel in an open boat and reached Rome a few days after the Pope (Husenbeth, *Life*, p. 272).

[8]See No. 440 n.3. Bishop Ward (*Eve* II, p.53) gives the names of only two persons who showed their displeasure by following Dr Milner out of the room and Francis Canning was not one of them. He may have been one of the small minority who voted against his expulsion.

[9]Sawston Hall, Cambridgeshire, the home of Scully's first wife.

[10]Woodley Lodge, Berkshire, the home of Mrs Wheble's son, James Wheble.

[11]See No. 470 n.4. The list to which he alludes is missing.

476   *From Lord Holland to Merrion Square, Dublin*

Holland House, 21 April [postmarked 20] 1814

Dear Sir,

I should have had very great pleasure in interceding for Mr Fitzpatrick with the Duke of Richmond as he seems in every respect a hard used man & as I should be much gratified in shewing my readiness to obey any commands of yours,[1] but the fact is that though I have the honour of being nearly related to the Duke of Richmond[2] I hardly know him to bow to, & have no sort of pretension to ask a favor of him especially on a subject connected with his political conduct or sentiments. I will, however, try through other channels[3] to have the case represented to the D. of Richmond whom I believe to be a very humane, good-hearted man & whose conduct in Ireland is I believe to be ascribed in some measure to the causes you mention & in some to the hasty & I thought unnecessary personal attack made upon him by the motion for his recall.[4]

With respect to the Catholick business I am sorry to say that the prospect of a repeal of the disqualifying statutes grows daily less. Had the Catholicks in Ireland placed unlimited confidence in their friends here & not been too eager & anxious to express their disapprobation of measures before they were completed I am thoroughly convinced that they would by this time or at least before the end of this year have had their grievances redressed in a manner that none of them could have objected to. A disposition to conciliate Protestant prejudices as well as individual opinions would have secured the recent converts to our cause & procured us more; as it is, I must confess that the new converts are lost & the zeal even of those who still support the principle of Religious Liberty materially abated. The circumstances of Europe[5] make the discontent of any portion of our people less formidable to Government than it was & I am sorry to say that the language held on your side of the water makes many well meaning people here more fearful of Catholick pretensions than they have been for many years. I need not I hope say that nothing that has occurred or that can occur has shaken or can shake my opinion of the propriety of repealing all disabilities on account of religion or my conviction that other securities, than the oath which you now take, are nugatory or unnecessary, but I am at the same time convinced that nothing is so calculated to defeat the whole measure or to clog it with vexatious regulations & conditions, as strong & premature objections to such securities as are talked of, from the Catholicks themselves. If Catholicks had expressed no apprehensions of the securities few I am convinced would have been required by law & none exacted in practice. By regarding them with jealousy they give them importance & their unwillingness to acquiesce in them is a motive with many for withholding a boon which but for their resistance to such provisions, would in all probability have been granted without them.

With many apologies for this hurried scrawl.

P.S. Lady H. begs her best compts & we hope you will not visit England without giving us an opportunity of seeing you at Holland House.

[*Source*: Scully Papers]

[1]See Nos. 472 and 474.
[2]As a first cousin once removed (see No. 472 n.1).
[3]See No. 488 n.3.
[4]At the aggregate meeting of 8 March 1811 (see No. 286).
[5]On 17 April a convention for the suspension of hostilities had been signed and on 20 April Napoleon left Fontainebleau for his exile in Elba (*Annual Register*).

477   *To Lord Holland*

Merrion Square, 1 May 1814

My Lord,

I feel every sentiment of gratitude for your kindness & condescension in obliging me in the affair of Mr Fitzpatrick: and, tho' I find that you are not able personally to represent his case to the Duke of R[ichmond], yet I trust that the object may be attained thro' some of the channels to which your letter alludes — Sir Henry Parnell was kind enough to promise me, on his way to London last month, that he would interest himself to procure, if possible, this man's liberation: and I am certain that he will be perfectly ready to take such proceedings for that purpose, as your Lordship may suggest to him.

Indeed, in every point of view, the continuance of political animosity in Ireland must appear to be very illsuited to the present posture of affairs — and no instance could be more unprofitable to any good purpose, public or private, than that of Mr Fitzpatrick. The sacrifice of his health, or of his life, may ensue: but, as he never was an obnoxious man, politically or otherwise, the example (if any example were necessary) would only serve to shew, that the most inoffensive conduct and character are not available for a case of mitigation. To show the comparative severity of his punishment, allow me to advert to a contemporaneous case in London —

Mr White, the Editor of the *Independent Whig*, was convicted last year at Westminster, before Lord Ellenborough, of a libel upon the Duke of Cumberland — imputing to him pretty plainly the murder of one D. Sellis.[1] White was already an obnoxious man, conducting a newspaper offensive to Government — he was tried by a jury of his own city, and of his own religion

— he had libelled a Royal Duke — the crime imputed was actual and direct murder, of the most atrocious nature. Fitzpatrick was an inoffensive character, privately esteemed even by members of the Irish Government, never connected with a newspaper — he was tried by a jury and a bench of a different religion, and of alienated feelings — the crime imputed by his publication, when read coolly and considerately, was at most the mere neglect of duty in the Duke's administration (that is, the Attory General), whereby an unfortunate man, illegally convicted, was suffered to be executed, tho' innocent — It was so difficult to construe the words into a libel, that two of the 4 judges, who tried him, expressed their strong doubts upon the subject at the time of the trial, and all the Treasurers counsel without exception (men eminent in their profession) concurred in advising the motion for arresting the judgment, argued it solemnly for several days, and, tho' the court finally overruled the motion, the Bar generally disapprove of their decision.

Yet after all, the sentences upon White & Fitzpatrick were precisely alike — 18 months imprisonment, and £200 fine upon each. And yet Lord Ellenborough's court is not reported to be a mild or lenient tribunal — This comparison may show at once, how hardly and oppressively Mr Fitzpatrick has been dealt with — and what a disparity subsists between the subjects of these two Islands in the administration of justice.

Allow me again to express a hope, that your Lordship will have the goodness to procure, thro' some channel, an abridgment of this man's imprisonment — If you can, I am sure that you will have saved his life also — His 12 months expired on the 28th of April.

With respect to the Catholic petitions, the view taken by your Lordship is most just and clear — what, indeed, can be expected from the deliberations of 4 or 5 millions of people crowded together in this remote Island, heated by suffering and wrong, insulted daily by the ruling powers, and purposely disunited and defamed by those who ought to conciliate and cherish them? Yet, their most crying sin has been their steadfast & sanguine adherence (in a trying moment) to the Grey & Grenville interest, when severed from the Prince & Lord Moira[2] — Had the Catholics selfishly taken the opposite course, and clung to the Carleton House politics, how different would have been their treatment? The best protection, however, in all vicissitudes, rests upon the clear and unerring principle, which your Lorship has laid down, namely "to decide upon the Catholic petitions upon public & general grounds, not according to the good or ill conduct, the servility or the intemperance, of the Catholics themselves, or of any part of their body". They who, with your Lordship, act upon this pure and enlightened principle, will ever preserve the path of consistency, and avoid the fluctuations of conduct, which minor considerations and feelings so often produce in the many. They also are, ultimately, the most sincerely respected and confided in by the Catholic body — and, I believe, by the public at large — And indeed, were I to desire for our friends in Parliament any particular line of conduct peculiarly calculated to promote our just claims, and preserve us from disunion whilst it should constantly command our respect and esteem, it would be precisely that line which I have, with perfect satisfaction, observed your Lordship adhering to invariably, from your entrance into life. [P.S.] May I be allowed to offer my respectful thanks to Lady Holland, & hope that she is well — I shall not fail to pay my respects personally at Holland House, in case I shall visit London — and, indeed, I shall be ungrateful if I could omit to do so.

[*Source*: Holland House Papers, Add.MS.51827 f.97]

[1]Sellis was the Duke of Cumberland's valet and although he escaped conviction because he committed suicide it was generally accepted that he had tried to murder his master. First reports, however, had had it that it was the Duke who tried to murder him (see under Ernest Augustus, Duke of Cumberland in *DNB*). Henry White's trial took place a month after that of Fitzpatrick — he was found guilty of a libel on 5 March 1813 (*The Pilot* 6 March 1813).
[2]Scully may have had particularly in mind the "witchery resolutions" of 18 June 1812 which had echoed the opposition's criticisms of the Prince Regent's advisers (see No. 359 n.3).

478   *From Bishop Dan Delany to No. 2 South Side,*
Merrion Square, Dublin

Tullow [Co. Carlow] 1 May 1814

Most Worthy Good Sir,

To whom should one labouring under the pressure of a *Catholic grievance* look for relief, but the distinguished, permit me to say, & truly Patriotic Character whom I have the Honour to address? To Counsellor Scully, surely, must every Individual thro' the Land *in that Predicament*, naturally stand in the relation of a *client*. Without further preface, I beg Leave to submit the following case to his consideration. I am, by the Blessing of Divine Providence possessed of a considerable Sum, (*nine thousand Pounds sterling) which it is my Determination to dedicate wholly to religious & charitable Purposes; as I have, indeed, already appropriated for some years, may I be allowed to say, a large Portion of the Interest to such uses. It is needless to express here my Solicitude to place this, [as] far as possible, out of the reach of Penal Laws still existing against Popish Donations, & to rescue it from the accur[s]ed Gripe, on a future Day, of a D-n or S-n.[1] I must also ingenuously confess, that I am not at all prepossessed in favour of the certain operation & eventual Efficacy in all Instances of Last Wills & Testaments, of Probates, and Executorships, & Trusteeships, & Guardianships etc. etc. in securing inviolably the faithful, rigid application of pious Bequests, agreeably to Testators original real Intentions. I should therefore anxiously wish, if by any means practicable, to be my own Executor & Trustee in the Execution of this Business. My objects are as follow[s], 1st — The partial Endowment *in perpetuum* of two poor Female & two male religious Communities which I have established in the Towns of Tullow & Mountrath,[2] who are by the nature of their Institute, to combine the double Functions of Martha & Mary in the Exercise alike of an active & contemplative Life, for their own & neighbours Sanctification. 2nd — a Fund for the support, or at least in aid towards it, of an additional officiating Clergyman in each Town. 3rd — An annual Sum for the relief, *exclusively*,[3] of the poor distressed *Catholic* Inhabitants of both Places. 4th — a Fund for the Purchase of Books to be annually distributed among the Children & adults of both Sexes who attend the Catechistical & other Schools for pious Instruction held on Sundays & Festivals of obligation in the Parochial Chapels by the members of the above religious Institutions. 5th — D[itt]o for the rent, Improvement & Decoration of the P. Chapels. Lastly, a competent sum to keep a Lamp, to be suspended before the Blessed Sacrament in each Sanctuary, perpetually burning in Honour of that adorable mystery.

Now, how put such Matters into a Will or abstracting from the paramount consideration of Discovery confide their strict Execution even to a Trustee, whose Son or Successor in the Trust, however Orthodox the Father in Principle, might nevertheless, perhaps, become as staunch a Protestant as Jack Giffard. They would I suppose be pronounced of a most obnoxious & illegal nature & the money left for those Ends be applied to objects the very Antipodes to the Purposes for wh. it was designed. It occurred to me strongly some Time back, that my best way would be to deliver myself whilst yet in the Land of the Living[4] & above Ground, the Debentures with my own hand, to the Persons for whom They were intended & bid Them look Themselves to the Preservation & Safety of articles in which They were so essentially interested. I was, however, dissuaded from the adoption of this measure by Mr Gibbons,[5] Public Notary in Dame Street, with whom I had some Transactions, & whom a respectable Friend of mine in Town advised me to consult on the Subject. To this Gentleman, who is I presume very intelligent & whom I found at least very obliging, I did not hesitate to make a candid explicit Exposure[?] in a great Degree of my views & apprehensions; but He disapproved of the Procedure, and suggested another mode of acting in their regard, which appeared to me very specious & eligible. He asked me if there were any of the Persons in Question on whom I could place a perfect reliance. I replied in the affirmative, but that I would not trust any of their relatives for sixpence. Are you also willing to divest yourself of your Property during your Life? On the Spot, answered I — well then, said He, to obviate all your difficulties respecting Discoveries[6] & wills, I recommend it to you to select 3, 4, or more of the Persons in Question, in whom you can most confide & deposit the Debentures in the Bank, *in their names*, as *their common Property collectively*, without any partition; in which case no Particular among them can have any legal claim to any Dividend of the Principal, or Portion of the Interest without the Joint Concurrence of the rest, who will take care not to give it away to their own prejudice. Moreover, when an Individual dies, there will be no need for a Will, as their part of the Property devolves, *ipso Facto*, to the Survivors; who will not fail for their own sakes, to fill up the vacancy by the nomination of another proper Partner wh. can be done at a trifling expence. Thus will the powerful Motive of Self Interest added to that of conscientious Principle operate as a twofold check & prove an infallible safeguard against the Evils you dread. I instantly followed this counsel & accordingly deposited £7000 in 5 per cent Govt. Debs. & have wherewith actually to purchase another £1000 besides 10 Gr: Canal ones, all destined for the same End. I have now to request, Sir, you be so good to give me your opinion respecting this Transaction; whether it is a prudent safe scheme or any way precarious & exposed to risk & what further Steps or Precaution (besides a receipt for the Deposit made at different Times wh. I have got), should be taken to render it, supposing the arrangement itself meets your approbation, perfectly secured. When I speak of risk I do not allude to any on the Part of the Persons whose names I have entered, 4 Members of the Female religious Communitys in whom I am fully persuaded I can repose the most unbounded Confidence. In them have I vested the whole Property trusting to their incorruptible Integrity for a faithful Discharge of the various obligations above specified. I ask a Thousand Pardons for this interminable ill digested Epistle which the sudden Departure of the Gentleman who will hand it to you obliged me to write in the midst of much Pace[?], Hurry & Embarassment. I *felt* indeed, *extremely unhappy* (no common place assertion this be assured, on the present occasion) not to have had the good Fortune to meet you when you were pleased to Honour me with a call last year on your way to Wexford.[7] I wrote to Doctor Troy, at the approach of the late assizes of that Place soliciting him, earnestly to conjure you on my Part, adding his Grace's own preponderating Influence in the Scale, to favour me with your Presence here for a Day in passing thro' Tullow thither. But I was unhappily disappointed in this Expectation. Indeed, few Things could afford me more Gratification than the Pleasure of an Interview with Counsellor Scully, should any propitious Gale waft Him on a future Day to these Parts.

*Private   [*Source*: Scully Papers]

[1]Patrick Duigenan, who as judge of the Consistorial Court dealt with the probate of wills; and William Saurin, who as Attorney General would be consulted by the

Commissioners of Charitable Donations and Bequests when there was a *prima facie* case for their intervention.

[2]The nuns were the Sisters of St Brigid. Three nuns from the Tullow convent (see No. 409 n.3) founded the Mountrath convent in 1809 (Comerford; *Diocese of Kildare and Leighlin* III, p. 415). The male communities were of the Institute of St Patrick. The Tullow house was founded in 1808 for the religious and literary education of youth and the instruction of the faithful. The Mountrath one followed in 1810 (ibid., p. 412).

[3]The Bishop underlined the word because of the doubtful legality of a charity confined to papists.

[4]He may have realised that he had only a few months to live — for his death see No. 487.

[5]Probably E. H. Gibbons of 38 Dame Street.

[6]In Chapter X of his *Penal Laws* Scully explains that if a Catholic failed to take the oaths of 1773 and 1793 any Protestant could file a bill of discovery against him and sue for possession of his property.

[7]See No. 409, where however Scully does not mention calling on the Bishop.

478A *To Hon. Colonel Gore,*[1] *Dublin Castle, from Merrion Square, 9 May 1814*

Private. Hugh Fitzpatrick, the printer, has completed twelve of the eighteen months of his imprisonment, his health is wasting and he will assuredly be commemorated as a martyr if he dies. The Lord Lieutenant could do nothing more conciliatory to public feeling than to remit the residue of the sentence. He has marked his letter Private as he is aware that his name makes him a bad intermediary: "the colour of party tinges every action".

[*Source*: Whitworth Papers, U.269/0225/5]

[1]William John Gore (1767–1836), 2nd son of the 2nd Earl of Arran, a retired Colonel of the 9th Foot who became Master of the Horse to the Lord Lieutenant.

479   *From Sir Henry Parnell to Merrion Square, Dublin*

7 Mount Street, London, 11 May 1814

My Dear Sir,

The Duke of Richmond has not been in town since I arrived here. I shall take the first opportunity of seeing him.

In regard to any claim I may have upon him, your opinion I think, must be founded on some mistake as to what occurred at the Queen's Co. Grand Jury on the subject of addressing him.[1] An address was read containing no sort of comment on any public matter but merely complimentary to him for his social & personal qualities. In explaining to the jury the course I should take, I said that the address containing nothing but was quite true, I could not give a negative to it; but in abstaining from so doing, I desired it to be understood, that no construction should be put on my conduct, as in any degree approving of any one of the public measures of the Duke's administration. I said I wished this to be distinctly understood, because the mere circumstance of addressing would in all probability be considered as doing more, than the words of the address conveyed to be the meaning of the jury, if alone considered. I did not even sign the address.

Having said so much concerning the address I must add one word more about the Duke; to say, that until he fell into the hands of Mr Saurin he was very impartial in his conduct towards the Catholics. In my own application to him, he gave such immediate & particular orders to the genl. of the district that 18 of the Mountrath yeomanry were lodged in jail for a party attack on a Catholic House: & my own opinion is that he would always have acted in the same way if his inclination to act impartially had been more cultivated by the conduct of your body.   [*Source*: Scully Papers]

[1]On the termination of his appointment as Lord Lieutenant.

479A   *From Dr Charles Lindsay, Bishop of Kildare,*
                        to Merrion Square

Printed copy   13 May 1814
    Your letter was left by the Revd Kenney . . . I do not know how exactly the Law stands regarding Licences. . . . It is the province of the Consistorial court to grant such Licences, and I should suppose it to be quite a matter of course . . . for Mr Kenney to apply to and receive from Dr Mitford,[1] through the medium of the Revd Rawdon Greene, Registrar of the Diocese of Kildare, such a paper . . .

            [*Source*: *The Clongowes Record* p. 54, from the now missing original]

[1]Dr Bertram Mitford LL.D., Vicar-General of the Consistorial Court of the diocese; a barrister of the Inner Temple.

479B   *To Revd Peter Kenny SJ*

                                    Merrion Square, 13 May 1814
Dear Sir,
    Enclosed is the letter,[1] which I have just received from the Bishop of Kildare, under his Episcopal Seal. You will find it as courteous and liberal as we could wish. He never means less of kindness than he utters. I think it only

remains for you, to have application made to the Reverend Rawden Greene at No. 5 St Andrew Street — and he will have the licence made out.

With respect to the law of these licences, you can apprize him that Catholic schools do *not*, by law, stand in need of any licence — For, in 1792, it was enacted by the Irish Parliament as follows: "that it shall not in future be necessary that the licence of the Ordinary shall be obtained, in order to authorize any person of the R. Catholic religion to keep or teach school — provided that such person has taken the qualifying oaths prescribed to R. Catholics by the Statute of 1773". This Statute was of 32 George 3d, Chapter 21, Section 15 — And it was entitled "An Act to remove certain restraints and disabilities from his Majesty's Roman Catholic subjects". The only use of a licence at present to a R. Catholic schoolmaster is, therefore, (as the Bishop observes) merely fiscal, and for bringing the school, by courtesy within the exemptions from the window tax.

I need not observe, to you, that Mr Greene, like all Registrars, is most easily to be enlightened and accelerated by an intimation, that his fees of office shall not be forgotten by you.

If you choose, I can lend you the Act, in case it should be necessary to produce it to the Bishop or to his Registrar.

Your letter of the 11th reached me. Mr Maher[2] was not canvassed by me. He came of his own accord, to enquire after your College, and I referred him to No. 3 George's hill. He is a cousin of mine, who made a large fortune in America, a very worthy, sensible, well conducted man, whom you will like to know. I know nothing of his objections to Maynooth, or why he leaves it. Many others have made enquiries from me, as to the time of opening the College and other particulars — Not having had any more copies of the prospectus, I thought it best to refer them to you.

But I think you will anticipate some applications, and diffuse a useful knowledge of your system, if you will take the trouble to forward by the post copies of the prospectus to the persons named in the enclosed list, accompanied by a manuscript line or two, specifying the probable time of commencement, and any other particulars that may occur to you. I name them to you as Catholics of property and respectability, who have sons, for whom I believe they are seeking, or will soon seek, a seminary of this description.

As for the gentlemen of Stonyhurst, I do not apprehend that their apprehensions will infect you, for their condition is widely different from yours, for reasons I have mentioned.

P.S. It will be right to specify to the public what is the regular daily Post town of Clongoweswood — Naas or Clane etc, etc.

[Enclosure]

Mathias Maher Esq., Ballymullen, Abbeyleix.

Thomas Lenigan Esq., Castlefogarty, Thurles.[3]
James Scully Esq. Jnr., Banker, Tipperary.
Edmd. Scully Esq., Mountbruis, Tipperary.
Leonard Keating Esq, Garranlea [paper torn].[4]
Richard Sause Esq., Banker [paper torn].[5]
Mrs Lyons — Cr[oom].[6]
Roger Scully Esq., Elmpark, Lim[erick].[7]
Daniel Callaghan,[8] Stephen Roche, James Roche,[9] Denis Moylan[10]
Esquires, Cork.

I am well acquainted with Dr Mitford,[11] to whom the Bishop alludes — he
will give us every facility (tho' he *is* Ld Redesdale's nephew) — for he prefers
a bottle of good wine to the whole Church ascendancy.

[*Source*: Jesuit Archives, Dublin]

[1]The preceding letter.
[2]Identified below as Mathias Maher (died 1824). Through Mary, daughter of Gilbert
Maher, who married Roger Scully of Cashel, he was a first cousin of Scully's father.
His elder son, John of Ballinkeele, was born in 1801.
[3]Castle ffogarty in Burke: *LGI* 1912. Thomas was the son of Elizabeth Lenigan, who
acquired the property on the death of her unmarried brother James ffogarty in 1788.
He had two sons, born in 1797 and 1798.
[4]Husband of Scully's sister Lucinda, whose son Robert was born in 1802.
[5]By his second marriage Richard Sause had at least four sons, the eldest of whom was
born c. 1798.
[6]According to *LGI* 1912 there were no married Lyons men at this date and she must
have been the widow of Denis Lyons, who died in 1809 — but her youngest son is
recorded as having been born in 1795.
[7]Roger (1770–1860) was the eldest son of Jeremiah (Derby) Scully of Silverfort and a
first cousin of Denys Scully. He married Ellen, daughter of Denis Lyons of Croom, in
1802 and had five sons, of whom the eldest was born in 1804.
[8]Either Daniel Callaghan (1760–1824), a wealthy provision merchant of the South
Mall, Cork; or his second son Daniel (1786–1849), MP for Cork City 1830–1849.
[9]First and third sons of Stephen Roche of Limerick (1724–1804) by his second wife.
[10]Probably a brother of the Bishop of Cork, who in 1811 performed the marriage of
his daughter to James Darby Scully of Tullamaine, Scully's first cousin.
[11]He was the fourth son of Lord Redesdale's elder brother, William Mitford of
Exbury. His mother was Frances Molloy of Dublin and in 1806 he married Frances
Vernon of Clontarf Castle.

480   *From Revd Peter Kenney SJ to 2 Merrion Square, South*

Clongowes Wood [Co. Kildare] 29 May 1814
Dear Sir,

I had just determined on the *manner* of throwing a few thoughts together
on the subject of Sir [J.] Hippisley;[1] I had resolved to address a letter to him,

defending myself on the broad grounds of equity & common justice, avoiding all controversy with him about the Jesuits, denying his false allegations without entering into any explanation that would give him more knowledge than he had yet acquired. This I say I had settled in my mind, when I received a letter of which the enclosed is nearly an entire copy. I send you all, that Mr Stone[2] has written on the affair & will say no more before I hear your opinion of the propriety of his communication meant for his Parliamentary friends. Whether I ought to change my proposed mode of defence, whether I ought not to write to Sir H. Parnell[3] & Sir J. Newport,[4] as much as Mr Stone sends to Lord Clifford?

I feel very much the difficulty of asking you in this busy time to send me a few lines but I cannot think of answering the letter or of taking any other step in the business before I see what you think of Mr Stone's statement which is in *short* the history of that *source* which I have so studiously kept out of view.[5]

I have got it copied by a legible hand, that in such a document you might not be puzzled by my scrawl. So many things press on me here, that I fear to be a day absent. The letters too at this important crisis have been sent to Dublin & back again on account of my late absence.

With best wishes to Mrs Scully I remain, Yours etc.

Peter Kenney

[Enclosure]

I yesterday sent off to Mr Tristram[6] in London two comments on the speech of Sir John Cox Hippesley last year,[7] in which he endeavoured to excite the alarms of Parliament against this establishment, & Jesuits in England & Ireland. I have desired Mr Tristram to communicate these comments to Lord Clifford with as little delay as possible, & to request his Lordship to engage Mr Canning, Whitbread & others of his friends & acquaintances to counteract Sir John's mischievous designs. I think it proper you should be acqainted with what is said respecting the Irish Jesuits, & your affairs in the comment, I sent up & therefore lose no time to inform you of it. After commenting on the particulars of Sir John's speech of last year, we have added: "Since writing the above observations on Sir John Hippesley's speech of the year 1813, we find from the public papers, he has again introduced the subject of seizure of Jesuit property at the period of the dissolution of the order in Catholic Countries & likewise has insisted much on the conduct of the government of this country in Canada. He has also called for documents containing their instructions to the administration of that Colony on that subject.[8] Perhaps his view in this may be to induce the house to adopt some resolution relative to the supposed property of Jesuits in Ireland. But how totally do the cases differ. In Catholic Countries the Jesuits were a corporate body of men acknowledged by the State, possessing considerable real estates, with which they had been endowed for certain public uses; education instruction etc. etc. In this manner, they must be considered as holding their large establishments in the different cities of Europe, as a sort of trusts for the public advantage; & when they no longer existed to perform the duties of the trusts, other persons were appointed to take their establishments & fulfill the trusts. This was their situation in Canada. But how widely different was their situation in this country & in Ireland, particularly in the latter, in neither recognised by the state to have any existence as a body. In Ireland particularly, they consisted of a few scattered individuals who had received their education in different & distant establishments of the body, & were not even acknowledged by it as a portion under the denomination of a province. The little property they possessed, was all personal & at the suppression of the body it was not supposed to exceed six or seven thousand pounds, & then became the individual property of each. If in the 40 years since the body was dissolved, the property has been encreased, it is owing to the frugality & management of each individual, who possessed a share of it, with full power to dispose of it by will as his private property, which some may have done in favor of their relations, but mostly in succession to each other. The property originally was never received either from the state, or from the public, was no trust from either, but accumulations & savings of the private individuals & as much at their disposal as the private property of any other British subject whatever.[9] After these individuals had qualified themselves by the oath of allegiance, in which they positively disclaim all power & authority in the Pope or his Agents to meddle or interfere in temporal concerns, can it be supposed that any obedience would ever be paid or thought due to any mandate of the *Sacred Congregation de propaganda* issued on such matters, & affecting the temporal rights of individuals? And is it not surprising that a British Senator, who would know how so well to defend his own property protected by British law, can view without indignation any such attempt or interference from Rome with regard to others, his fellow subjects, much less that he should lean on such authority in support of his arguments to induce Parliament to interfere with the property of an individual.[10] A marked distinction also exists between the authority of a Government over distant & conquered Colonies & the Constitutional rights of a British born subject at home, who in conformity to the law, has duly qualified himself by his oath of allegiance to receive the full benefit of the laws already passed in favor of Catholics."   [*Source*: Scully Papers]

[1]On 17 May Sir John Hippisley had moved for the printing of instructions given to the Governor of Lower Canada on 22 October 1811 about the attitude he should adopt towards the religious orders there. He mentioned in his speech that £30,000 had been sent to Ireland, out of which £16,000 had been spent on a "seminary" at Castle Browne. Peel said that he had warned Mr Kenney that "the British Government had

manifested so much jealousy of the Society of the Jesuits that their property in Canada had formerly been confiscated" (*Hansard* XXVII, 934, 938).

[2]Father Marmaduke Stone, Rector of Stonyhurst College and Provincial of the English Jesuits.

[3]He had intervened in the debate and cited a precedent of 1806 or 1807 showing there was nothing in the statute book to prevent Mr Kenney keeping a school (ibid., 937).

[4]He too had spoken, questioning the accuracy of Peel's statement about confiscation.

[5]See No. 471B n.4.

[6]Father Joseph Tristram SJ, at this time resident in London.

[7]On 11 May 1813 (see No. 471B n.1).

[8]See n.1 above. On 24 May he asked for further papers.

[9]After the suppression of their order the fifteen surviving Jesuits agreed in 1775 to keep their capital intact and in 1793 the remaining five survivors agreed that if the order should not have been restored the last three survivors should consult with the Irish Bishops on how the money should be used. In 1803 Father Richard O'Callaghan was admitted to the informally restored English province and when he died in 1807 all the money passed under his will to Father Marmaduke Stone. Augmented by gifts and bequests the sum credited to the future Irish mission was £30,000 (see R. Burke Savage SJ in *The Clongownian*, 1981).

[10]In 1807 and 1808 the Archbishop of Dublin had corresponded with Propaganda Fide in Rome about what he considered the misappropriation of the money and Father Charles Plowden at Stonyhurst had asked whether he wished to invoke the spiritual power to invalidate the will of a British subject (ibid. p. 9). Sir J. Hippisley may have heard of this, but it is not clear where or when he made the point that alarmed Father Stone. In the debate on 17 May he was reported as saying that money had been sent from Rome to Ireland but he corrected this on the 24th to read "from hence to Ireland" (*Hansard* XXVII, 1018).

481   *From Revd Peter Kenney SJ to 2 Merrion Square South,*
                      Dublin

                                    Clongowes Wood [Co. Kildare] 3 June 1814
Dear Sir,

Before the arrival of your late favor I wrote to Mr Stone expressing my surprize, that he should make such an avowal as is contained in his instructions or comments on Sir J. C. H's speech.[1] The cause might have been defended without telling friends & enemies, that the Irish Ex Jesuits possessed at the suppression six or seven thousand pounds; & without admitting, that it has since been amassed & bequeathed from one to another. This, I feared would be taken as a proof, that the property in question is the property of Ex Jesuits secreted & amassed for some superstitious purpose. I was I confess alarmed at this, for it was publickly telling what I have refused to acknowledge & what I did not communicate to those members, who have so kindly spoken for me. You were perfectly correct in supposing that Mr Stone had no right to dictate to or to answer for me; but as he was on the spot and about to reply for himself he thought that the affair did not allow of any delay. I approve his zeal for the common cause: all my apprehension was about the manner in which he defended me.

I will remain here all next week & shall feel very great pleasure in receiving your kind visit. Though I am far from that state of order & finish necessary to entertain you according to my wish & your desert, I must protest against your returning on the same day. I have just got into some state of cleanliness a room for some dignified stranger, who may honor us with a visit. It is here called *the bishops room*. I shall be much obliged to you to make it yours, as long, as you could favor me with your company.

Yours sincerely,
P. Kenney   [Source: Scully Papers]

[1]See enclosure in No. 480.

482   *From William Parnell to 2 Merrion Square South, Dublin*

Bushy [near Bray Co. Wicklow] 6 June [1814]

My dear Sir,

I send you without *reserve* my opinions on your affairs[1] relying that as I once submitted with thankfulness to your criticisms you will not take any offence at mine. I will thank you not to mention me in what I now tell you. James Ryan fortified with a letter from Ld Holland, I believe is preparing some sort of an attack on you & the board on the next aggregate meeting and probably though he will be outnumber'd he will be able to gather against you a large body of respectable men.[2] I wish you would anticipate him & by a communication with Ld Fingall etc. put an end to all hazard of feuds.[3] I own I am provoked to see Ryan the confident of the opposition. This was the place you & O'Connell ought to have held; & I know that if you had not got, the Lord knows how, into a kind of squabble with them,[4] it was their intention on getting into power to have placed you both in official law situations as a proof of proper impartiality[5] — & for this you at least owe them your gratitude. I wish you could any how get the aggregate meeting postponed till the heat & anger arising from the proclamation is over.[6] At least keep yourself out of Kilmainham[7] this summer as I expect to see you & Mrs Scully at Avondale.

[P.S.] Pray direct to me at Avondale, Rathdrum. As I wrote what I send you in a hurry I will thank you if you make any use of it — and make what you please — to send me a copy of it.   [Source: Scully Papers]

[1]See No. 483. The occasion was the issue of a proclamation on 3 June declaring the Catholic Board to be an illegal body. News of it reached Parnell and Scully while they

were talking together on 4 June and Scully was saying that if the Board knew how to regulate their meetings so as not make them offensive to the government they would do so. Although Scully said that if they made any overtures it would now look like yielding to intimidation Parnell went on to see Gregory, who had just started a letter to Peel reporting on the first reactions to the proclamation. Telling him what Scully had said he asked whether it was not possible to withhold the proclamation, but Gregory said that it was too late and that in any case he would not have delayed the publication one hour "in consequence of the desire of an individual or any Body not recognised" (Peel Papers: Add.MSS.40, 198, f.312).

[2]At the aggregate meeting of 19 May 1814 Ryan had come forward in an attempt to secure an adjournment but found no seconder (*Orthodox Journal* 1814, p. 194). Nothing has come to light to account for Parnell's warning: if there was any attack at the aggregate meeting of 9 June it was not reported.

[3]He is referring to the so-called seceders. Lord Fingall took the chair at the Board for the last time on 1 May 1813, Randal MacDonnell on 24 July (DDA 54/1, VIII, 9).

[4]No record of a personal squabble has been found. Parnell may have been thinking of the embarrassment caused to the Whig ministry in 1806–7 by the persistence of some of the Irish Catholics in petitioning (see No. 153 n.1).

[5]No other reference to this intention has come to light. There may be an echo of it in a letter which Lord Whitworth wrote to Peel on 14 April 1814 (Add.MSS.40, 187, f.258). Matthew Lynch having recently revived his dormant claim to the post of Assistant Barrister for Co. Galway the Lord Lieutenant commented: ". . . by all accounts he is no more fitted for that office than Mr O'Connell or Mr Scully".

[6]The meeting took place. Resolutions were passed asserting that the Board, which was not elected, did not contravene the Convention Act; expressing a determination to persevere by "all warrantable means"; and deciding on a continuance of petitioning. It then adjourned to 24 June. For the clandestine formation of an Association to succeed the Board see No. 486 n.6.

[7]Kilmainham Gaol, outside Dublin.

483   *From William Parnell to 2 Merrion Square South, Dublin*

Dear Sir,   [6 June 1814]

As you are kind enough to think that my opinion may have some influence in the present crisis of your affairs, I am tempted to express it, although I have hitherto studiously avoided any interference of this kind, content with giving such little assistance to your good cause as circumstances placed in my power.

I must first bespeak your indulgence, if what I have to say should appear to wear a tone of censure, it must necessarily do so, for to praise would be superfluous. Your Body has displayed the good qualities, which every assembly of Irishmen always does display; courage, candour, the indignation of virtuous feeling, and eloquence, that native eloquence which is its proper organ. I should not even now mention them, but that from their misapplication, what I take the liberty to call the errors of your conduct appear to me to have flowed. Allow me to make one distinction, and I think that this will not be doubtful.

The Catholic Committee, and Board, the aggregate meetings or by whatever other body your affairs have been conducted, were possess'd of a twofold capacity. They were parties concern'd, they acted in their own cause, but they were also agents & trustees for a far more numerous portion of their fellow sufferers & countrymen. In the first capacity as acting for themselves alone they were at liberty to sacrifice their public interests to their private feelings of injury, to their personal habits of candour & openess, or to their tenaciousness of an uncompromising spirit of right, but in their second capacity as agents for & trustees of the interests of many milions, it was a clear and unexcusable breach of trust to risk the cause of their clients by yielding to any private feelings however natural or intrinsically honorable, that hazarded the success of this cause.

What advocate would be excused who in pleading his client's case should from an impulse of private feeling, even the most natural or honorable, run the risk of exciting any adverse feelings in the breast of the judge, or awaken any dormant prejudices, or party animosities in the minds of the Jury. Is not an advocate bound not only to suppress every private feeling that can injure, but even to make use of every device and legal stratagem, not inconsistent with moral honesty, to promote the cause of his client?

Unfortunately this distinction though just, and scarcely controvertible was not likely to occur and the very magnitude of their wrongs & of their resentments has led every constituted body of the Catholics to consider themselves, and to act only as parties concern'd; whereas let their numbers have been what they will, take even the multitudinous aggregate meetings of Dublin and what are they compared with the remainder of their fellow sufferers whose interests all depend upon their conduct? Surely their personal concern in the cause should sink to nothing before the overwhelming responsibility they contract when advocating the cause of five millions of their countrymen?

Had they acted as trustees, had they at every step decided only by this consideration, "will or will not, this measure advance the emancipation of the Catholics"; had every speech that has been made and every resolution that has pass'd, been temper'd and regulated by this unostentatious but really honest principle, I cannot think the Catholic affairs would have worn their present ominous aspect — at war with the local government of your Country, bickering with your best friends, and divided against yourselves.

All this has aris'n, if I may again repeat it, from the difficulty of bodies of men feeling the superior duty of the trust, where they also feel an interest as parties concern'd.

Had the aggregate meeting[1] which took place in Dublin when the court of the Regency first seem'd to recede from the Catholic cause, been sensible only to the magnitude of its trust, would it with an unbridled indignation, which was fit only for private wrongs, have proceeded to cut off all chance of compromise and reconciliation; would they have alienated the Regent by an interference in his private conduct which no private individual would patiently submit to? However alive as Irishmen to the supposed wrongs of a woman, a foreigner & a Princess, as advocates for their Catholic Brethren, her injuries could not be included in their brief except by some construction most strain'd and foreign to the purpose.[2] As advocates for the Catholic cause (for, still this function must supercede every other) how have the several bodies of Catholics been justified in their resolutions reflecting attacks on the Duke of Richmond, the Chief Justice and the Attorney General?[3] I do not question but as individuals the Catholics were moved by the most honorable resentment; but how was the common cause of emancipation forwarded by engaging against it the local Government of Ireland, the *esprit de corps* of the Bench, and animating the activity of the Attorney General.

If the Catholic Board had been influenced *only* by considerations how to forward the emancipation of the Catholics, would it have been so prone to embarrass itself, with the interests of the Catholic clergy, which might have been safely left to their own good sense & discretion. Or if the members of the Board had quite subdued & put under the subjection of this consideration, all private feelings as Catholics or all peculiar feelings as men, would they have spoken of Mr Grattan's bill[4] which was simply an ideal concession to remove ideal objections and conciliate wavering opponents, would they have spoken of this obviously inefficient measure, this friendly stratagem, with such monstrous exaggeration, representing it as the most malignant & fatal blow the bitterest enemy could have devised. You will perhaps be inclined to defend some of these measures, & perhaps there is more to be said for them than I am aware of, but I am not particularly hostile to any of them, but only wish you to try the conduct of your board etc. etc. by this test, whether they have *prudently*, fulfilled their duty as agents, trustees & advocates of the Catholic cause, not only avoiding all encounters that might retard it but using every fair & honest means of conciliation to forward it.

The doubt of this is the extent of my censure. You have now a right to ask me what better plan I propose to substitute. Relying on the disinterestedness of my motives rather than my capacity for the task, I will venture to leave the following hints to your partial consideration.

1st. Whatever men have the conduct of your affairs, whether they are entrusted to boards, aggregate meetings or private persons, it should be understood that their functions are strictly a trust; that their feelings as individuals or Catholics should be made entirely subservient to the single object of obtaining the emancipation of the Catholics. That this should be the test of every measure propos'd, and that any not having plainly this tendency should be consider'd as foreign to the purpose & irrelevant.

Your affairs appear to me to have suffer'd by being conducted by a public and a debating body. Every body that is to act is of the nature of an executive particularly where great & important interests are entrusted to its charge, and it seems contrary to every received principle that an executive trust can be well conducted by a public & debating body. Has not every kind of inconvenience arisen from it in your case? Too much impulse from a sanguine and angry audience, too great a desire of their approbation, opinions delivered in the haste & heat of declamation, sometimes erroneous yet maintained from the fear of publickly appearing inconsistent. Every personal dispute & difference exposed to the scandal of your friends & gratification of your enemies. No regular system or plan of conduct, but everything left to the impulse of circumstance & the varying tide of public opinion. Your enemies have compared you to a parliament,[5] but with very little accuracy. There the discredit thrown upon one party, encreases the reputation of another, and the estimation of the whole is perhaps not diminished; but you are surveyed through a medium of suspicion & dislike; all that redounds to your credit is suppress'd or forgotten; all that occurs to your discredit is magnified and recorded. The greatest discretion, therefore, is required in whatever body has the management of your affairs. But this can only be had by their conduct being private or obnoxious only to the scrutiny of such censors as you yourselves may appoint.

Let your affairs then be no longer conducted by a body meeting & debating in public. As you are debarr'd from representation, the most convenient form in which you can collect the sentiments of your body at large on the few occasions where it may be required, may probably be best done by meetings of the principal inhabitants of your parishes, the questions being proposed to them by the body conducting your affairs, and the sense being taken from the majority of parishes. Probably by this means though you would have less of sound you would have more of movement. Your business would proceed without being embarrassed, with perpetual conflicts that are of very little advantage to the main purpose, without exciting unnecessary alarm and odium and without the present perpetual collision with personal feelings & interests.

As to the line of conduct to be pursued. If your affairs cease to be carried on by a debating body, where everything was overdone, from the necessity of having something to do, it seems to be very short & simple. If you are guided by the rule of abstaining from everything that may retard the emancipation of the Catholics, much that has been contested with so much heat, will cease to occupy your attention. If you confine your views only to those means which are likely to effect the emancipation of the Catholics, I think they may be stated very shortly.

With contest or intimidation you have nothing to do; your means must be to influence, to conciliate, & to convince. The influence which the Catholics can legitimately exert is by operating on the election of the Irish members of parliament. This constitutes the permanent weight they have in the house of Commons and to their exertions to encrease this no one can object, not by sordid or dishonest means but simply by employing a careful agent in each county to provide for the registring of votes. The neglect of this lost several friends of the Catholics their seats at the last election.[6]

The means of conciliation are many & obvious; one or two need only be instanced. And first, if the Catholics honestly sacrifice their personal feelings to the interest of the body, they ought to loose [sic] no time in endeavouring to recover the good will of the Regent. He is a man of sense and totally averse to the bigotry and the shallow pretences by which the enemies of the Catholics justify their hostility. However irritated his resentments may be, his conviction must be still with you, and though success in this quarter may be improbable the case is not desperate.

In the next place all contest with the Irish administration should be avoided; it is a conflict where no advantage flows from victory but much loss from defeat. Constituted as the Irish administration is, without any sympathy with the great mass of the nation, with little of the dignity & none of the popularity which gives respect to Governments, it cannot but be conscious of insignificance and consequently captious & impatient of any thing like rivalry or competition. A Catholic board or committee might exist in London without exciting the jealousy of the English government. They would never dream of comparing it to a Parliament etc. etc. but in Dublin where it absorbs all the sympathy & attention of the public mind, and almost throws the administration into shade, it was not to be expected that it could be tolerated. The point should at once be given up and no attempt made to constitute a regularly debating body of the Catholics. Not only this but every step that can give the least offence to the Irish government should be avoided with the greatest discretion. They are in fact mere lookers on, whose influence can have little to say to the favorable termination of the question, but whose report is of some consequence & measures should be taken, that it may be at least as little unfavorable as possible. Many other effectual means of conciliation might be devised such as a deputation of your principal gentlemen to reside in London for the purpose of personal applications in your favor; but these will readily occur to the persons who have the direction of your affairs, when their attention is no longer taken off by discussions, though interesting at the moment, very foreign to the object in view.

The last means proposed is by acting on the conviction of the public mind.

This must principally be done by an active use of the press, not employed in wanton personal abuse, but in a serious, honest & steady effort to promulgate & enforce the great maxims of truth, policy and justice on which your question rests. This means I consider has been much, very much, neglected by the Catholics. What has been done has principally been done by volunteers, & of course the exertion has been remitting, fluctuating & irregular. Look to the exertions of any of the English Bible & Missionary Societies and you must be sensible how inferior the efforts of the Catholics have been.

To conclude, all questions that may embarrass or retard the event of your emancipation should be avoided. As an instance I shall only mention that of the regulation of your Clergy. Formerly it was an established principle among you all, not to blend the interests of the Clergy & the laity, and surely it will be well to return to it. You would not relish an interference on the part of the Clergy in your affairs. Why should you meddle with theirs? Why not fairly trust them to their own acknowledged purity, good sense & discretion.

Though what I have proposed to you may not appear very efficient, at least I have made use of no *charlatanerie*. The principles are sound and honest and though they may not work immediate wonders, their effect may be expected to be steady, uniform & progressive. At least I know you will do me the justice to attribute them to a sincere & sole anxiety to forward the great & good work of Catholic emancipation.   [*Source*: Scully Papers]

[1]That of 18 June 1812 which adopted the "witchery resolutions" (see No. 359 n. 3).
[2]The reference is to an address to the Princess of Wales adopted at an aggregate meeting of 15 June 1813, when O'Connell said: "Yes, let this address injure our cause, yet I would recommend it to your adoption on that account; because, thus you would have some sacrifice to offer upon the altar of justice and of persecuted innocence" (O'Connell, *Life and Speeches* I, p.403).
[3]For instance in the Kilkenny resolution of 4 August 1813 (see No. 449 n.3) and the Board's resolution of 25 February 1814 (DDA 54/1, X, 12) supporting Magee after his conviction for libelling the Duke of Richmond, as well as the petition demanding the recall both of the Duke and Wellesley Pole (see No. 286). The actions against Chief Justice Downes (see No. 310 n.2) had been brought by the arrested delegates as individuals but at the instigation of the Catholic Committee (see for instance John Burke's letter in the *Dublin Evening Post* of 21 November 1816).
[4]See particularly Sir Henry Parnell's letter of 21 May 1813, No. 433.
[5]See No. 289 n.1.
[6]See No. 384.

484   *From Revd Peter Kenney SJ to 2 Merrion Square, Dublin*

Clongowes Wood [Co. Kildare] 19 June 1814

Dear Sir,
    I take the liberty of enclosing for your perusal the better part of a letter

lately received from Mr Tristram & which contains his entire account of the papers printed in consequence of Hippesley's motion.[1] You are the better judge of what bearing they can have on my affair.

Mr Peel read to me[2] from a paper, which seemed printed, the only part that seemed to threaten me; but he did not read the latter part, which *inhibits* not only Jesuit missioners but every other Romish eclesiastick to speak against the Protestant religion in their sermons and orders all missioners amongst the Indians to be withdrawn & Protestant missioners established in their stead! Such an instance of ministerial bigotry would appear incredible if we were not indebted to themselves for the information. I send you the lines, because it may possibly happen that you have not seen this private document. I find that the mention *of property etc*. which we so much disliked in the Instructions sent to London[3] has been an oversight or mistake rather than any premeditated disclosure. Since I expressed my disapprobation of it letters have been sent to London to recall that part & prevent it from being seen in public. Graydons Steward[4] has made the assignment you sketched for me. I have received a letter from Mr Green[5] saying that the license cannot be granted in consequence of the parson's refusal to recommend me. A Letter from Sir H. Parnell politely acknowledges the receipt of letter of thanks, assures me that no one will read Hippesley printed papers and another written by Sir J. Newport to a friend of mine in answer to his enquiries about me says "that he considers an investigation of my title at least on *public grounds* as an impossibility. Says that he cannot guess at Hippesley's ulterior views, that nothing is too absurd to appear to him incredible when it relates to Jesuits who like phantoms haunt him by day & night."[6]

I am much indebted to you & Mrs Scully for your wonted kindness to me & beg of you to make her the assurances of best regard,

[P.S.] You will preserve the enclosed for me.   [*Source*: Scully Papers]

---

[1]See No. 480 n.1. The enclosure consists mainly of a long extract from the parliamentary paper. Father Tristram observes that the principal instruction to the Governor of Lower Canada was a renewal of one issued in Quebec in 1763 whereby no new members were to be admitted to religious orders and the Society of Jesus was to be suppressed, its property being vested in the King. Catholic missionaries among the Indians were to be gradually replaced by Protestants, Catholic ecclesiastics were not to influence Wills and priests were not to inveigh against the religion of the Church of England in their sermons.

[2]See No. 480 n.1.

[3]The enclosure in No. 480.

[4]Unidentified.

[5]The Registrar of the Kildare diocese (see No. 479B).

[6]"The Jesuit at Castlebrowne is likely to do more mischief than a rebel army on the Curragh" (Gregory to Peel 24 June 1814, transmitting a report by an informer called "Q": Add.MSS.40, 199, f.100).

485   *From William Parnell to 2 Merrion Square South, Dublin*

Avondale, near Rathdrum [Co. Wicklow] 21 June 1814

My dear Sir,

I was very much obliged to you for your letter[1] which I should have answered sooner but that I felt that I had a great deal to say to you. However, I will defer it rather than be silent so long, as I am very much afraid of appearing to interfere, and even when I have made up my mind hesitate to write. I shall certainly be here the time you mention & hope to see you & Mrs Scully or sooner than that if it is convenient to you as I have no intention of going to Dublin. I gave you full credit for your feelings on the point I mentioned to you — nor should I have mentioned it only to disarm any hostility you might have felt to the opposition in case any existed.[2] If it had not been for the very flattering manner in which you speak of me, I should have been tempted to have asked your leave to have communicated your letter.[3] But I will write again to you shortly, if I can think of any thing likely to carry the great point. I cannot think it so very difficult where the object is so important and now allow'd on all sides to be desireable & the obstacles *comparatively* so very insignificant.   [*Source*: Scully Papers]

[1]Probably Scully's missing reply to his review of 6 June, No. 483.
[2]See No. 482.
[3]Probably to Lord Holland.

486   *From Sir Henry Parnell to Merrion Square, Dublin*

Brighton, 29 June 1814

Private

My Dear Sir,

I have not been able to get any opportunity of speaking to the Duke of Richmond concerning Mr Fitzpatrick.[1]

I called several times upon him in London, & since I have been here, tho' he has the command of the district,[2] he has been absent, except for a few days last week.

I called upon him on Monday last, & was shewn in, but the servant came back to me, evidently after having seen him, & told me he had gone out. The next day he went to his seat at Goodwood.

I feel, however, I could have done no good. I once heard him give his opinion about the note in the *Penal Laws* & the feelings he expressed were so strong & of such a nature, that any liberality of conduct on his part must be hopeless.[3]

I was determined to have tried what a frank statement of the cruelty of the case would have done, & should have made it had I succeeded in obtaining an interview.

I think some effect has been produced on Lord Whitworth by what I said on presenting the Orange Petitions.[4] Peel's declaration respecting them when he moved for leave to bring in his new Police Bill, was quite different from what he had expressed to me on the subject in private, &, therefore, I conclude Lord Whitworth feels as he ought to do.[5] I should have made a distinct motion upon them if I could have obtained the support of Lord Grenville etc. Without it I should have been in a minority to a certainty & I should have given the Orange societies an appearance of being protected by Parliament.

I hope you will form some sort of committee[6] to carry on correspondence & communications concerning the Catholic Bill. I am quite certain you have lost nothing by the silence of this session.[7] But every thing should be done to secure the earliest discussion of a Bill in the next.   [*Source*: Scully Papers]

[1]See No. 479, first paragraph.

[2]He had been promoted to full General on 4 June and was Colonel of the Sussex Regiment of Foot.

[3]The Duke had already replied to Fitzpatrick (see No. 474 n.2).

[4]He means the ten petitions which he presented on 8 June against the Orange societies, claiming that they disturbed the peace, were illegal in England because of their secret oath and ought to be suppressed in Ireland. The government having just suppressed the Catholic Board as an illegal association their conduct on the Orange subject, he said, ought to be carefully watched (*Hansard* XXVIII, 34).

[5]Introducing his Preservation of the Peace bill on 23 June Peel had claimed that "there was indisputable evidence to show the lower orders of Catholics were satisfied, that government were determined to treat all offenders against the public peace, whatever religious creed they might profess, most impartially". However, when Parnell again drew attention to the Orange societies on 14 July Peel stoutly defended them, their only fault, he said, being an exuberance of loyalty. The petitions against them, he asserted, were the work of the Catholic Board and Parnell was its agent (ibid. 170, 739).

[6]On 8 June a meeting was held in O'Connell's house to consider what should be done following the proclamation of 3 June (see No. 482 n.1). Gregory, whose informer was present, informed Peel on the same day that the Board was extinguished, but he wrote again on 14 June: "I have this morning had a communication from McG that the club or association which was proposed a few days since at O'Connell's house and not then agreed to, has been carried into effect, and O'Connell is elected secretary. I have desired Mr McG to be a subscriber, the association will probably not be numerous, as the subscription is to be five guineas, but the members will be choice spirits" (Peel Papers: Add.MSS.40, 198, f.332; 40, 199, f.73). It is unknown whether the association met before it was openly constituted by the 7th resolution of an aggregate meeting on 24 January 1815 (*FJ*, 25 January 1815). In the meantime the idea of meeting again as a Board in order to get the question tried before a jury had not been totally abandoned (*DEP*, 18 June 1814). but *The Sentinel* of 4 July

announced that the Board would not reassemble until after the long vacation as the
question could not be tried before a jury until November.
[7]Grattan had presented the Irish Catholic petition in the House of Commons on 21
April but said he would not move for a discussion of it because of the end of the war
and the new situation created by the liberation of the Pope (*Hansard* XXVII, 459,
1027).

487   *From James Nowlan[1] to Merrion Square*
                    forwarded to Post Office, Kilkenny

                                            Tullow, 12 July 1814
My Dear Sir,
    With the greatest sensation of Grief & regret, I communicate the mournfull
Intelligence of the Death of our *much Respected & Revered Bishop*.[2] He
departed this life at half after two O'Clock on Saturday morning last, & was
Interr'd in the Chapel of Tullow yesterday at three O'Clock, at which Hour
there was a most numerous attendance of his clergy, & laity, who displayed
that Excessive Grief that I do believe was never before witnessed on any
similar occation [*sic*]. We had the Honour of Doctor Troy's presence, & He
poor Gentleman had the happiness & consolation to Receive all the spiritual
comforts he cou'd administer him on Friday last before he Died. May he rest in
peace *Amen*. This day His Will has been opened in the Presence of Doctor
Troy, Miss Browne,[3] some Rev'd Gentlemen etc. when we find Miss Browne
sole Executrix & Legatee. Therefore at her Request, I write you this Letter, to
Inform you that she will go to the Revd Mr Cullen's,[4] Leighlin Bridge, & that
she begs you'll be so good to come down one day earlier than you intended for
the assizes of Kilkenny, in order to Wait on her at Mr Cullen's, when Mr
Cullen & she will be very happy to see you. She will take all the necessary
papers with her, for your Perusal; and if you find it necessary to bring an
Attorney down with you, she requests you'll do so, as it will be right, & I think
approved of by your opinion, that she must make her will & confirm all other
writings that your judgment may direct, in order that the Poor Bishops good
intentions may be put fully into Effect. Our Late Revered Friend had every
confidence in your zealous attachment to Catholic affairs & in protecting
property left for such Laudable purposes from the Claws of Our Enemies.[5]
We have all the same good Opinion of you, therefore hope you'll not by any
means neglect paying the necessary attention to this important subject. You'll
have the goodness to inform me by Return of post, the day you'll be in Leighlin
Bridge, & I will have the pleasure of meeting you there, where your Fees, the
Atty's Expenses etc. will be paid with pleasure. I remain Dear Sir, most truly,
                    Your obliged hum. Serv't, Jas. Nowlan

                                    [*Source*: Scully Papers]

[1]Unidentified.

[2]Daniel Delany (see No. 478).

[3]Judith Wogan Browne (1750–1848), sister of Thomas Wogan Browne, of Castle Browne, Co. Kildare. She had settled at Tullow in 1780 to be close to her spiritual adviser, Father Delany, then parish priest, and assisted him when, as Bishop, he founded the Brigidine congregations.

[4]Revd William Cullen, parish priest of Leighlin, who became Dean of the diocese on the death of Revd Henry Staunton on 1 September and was perhaps already acting Dean.

[5]See No. 478 n.1.

488   *From Nicholas Mahon*

                                    Merchants Quay [Dublin] 16 September 1814
My dear Sir,

I handed the Money you gave me namely three hundred pounds to our mutual friend Mr Fitzpatrick[1] and communicated to him your farther intentions. He expressed himself in the strongest terms of thankfull gratitude and appears most anxious that you shou'd understand he feels those sentiments. He will adopt your idea as to makeing the previous arrangements[2] so as that no delay may happen in his enlargement when the period of his imprisonment expires but as to any farther application for a remission of one or lessening the other I consider it quite fruitless as Mr F. showed me a letter from Lord Ossory[3] dated late in Aug'st to Mr Dowling[4] of London wherein his Lordship declares he applied without effect to Lord Whitworth for a mitigation but cou'd make no impression w'ch he imputes to the party spirit w'ch at present prevails in this unfortunate Country and to w'ch in his Lordship's words the Lord Lt is obliged to submit without any wish of his own.

Mr Fitzp. is in good health and spirits and will no doubt communicate with you himself.[5]

                                                        [*Source*: Scully Papers]

[1]Among the Callanan Papers there is a list in Scully's hand of subscribers to a collection which was probably for Fitzpatrick. Initials N.M. for Nicholas Mahon and D.S. for Denys Scully indicate by which of them donations were received. It is headed by Lord Fingall, with Dr Troy next. At £22–15–0 Scully's contribution was the largest and he put his three boys down for £5–3–9 each.

[2]No doubt for paying his fine of £200.

[3]As the Earl of Upper Ossory (1745–1818) was Lord Holland's maternal uncle this would have been the approach promised in No. 476.

[4]Probably either Vincent Dowling (1756–1825), who had been a bookseller in London and was connected with *The Times*, or one of his two sons, Vincent George and James (both in the *DNB*). Vincent Dowling and Sons had been commissioned by Edward Hay, through Edward Jerningham, to publish the 1810 debates on the Catholic question (DDA 390/1, XVI, 7).

[5]The *Dublin Chronicle* of 29 January 1816 published a letter from Fitzpatrick saying that while he was owed £552 for expenses incurred on behalf of the Catholic Board, Association etc., nothing was due to him for the *Penal Laws*. He had undertaken this work, he said, at his sole risk and against the advice of the author had continued the sale up to the date of prosecution; ample support and compensation had flowed in upon him, and the defence costs had voluntarily been paid by the Catholic Board.

489   *From Thomas Cloney to Merrion Square, Dublin*

Graig [Co. Kilkenny] 10 January 1815

My dear Sir,

When I take up my pen to address you on the subject of our enslaved and insulted state, I am certain of meeting that attention which the true Patriot is ever ready to give the humblest labourer in his Country's cause, if he only considers him to have a reasonable claim to principle and integrity alone. Little as you know of me I flatter myself you will give me credit so far. I feel then a confidence that you will believe me when I tell you that at this moment of political vacillation and abject and pussillanimous [*sic*] despondency, more of the independent part of the Catholic Body than you can be aware of, look to you for some fixed standard or principle to be ruled by in seeking Redress of their daily multiplying grievances. Your uniformly bold opposition to servile measures has ensured you much publick Confidence as any Irishman should be proud of. You will then I am persuaded feel the call on you to come forward imperative.

To the proceedings of the 24th inst.[1] the people look with a lively interest, it is expected that you & other independent men may be able to stem the torrent of Corruption that seems to sweep all remains of publick spirit before it. The Vetoists are all in motion congratulating one another on their certain prospects of success, before this cursed Veto must vanish the last remnant of Irish freedom. It will (if carried) at no distant day reduce unfortunate Ireland to the state of a closely besieged fortress, called on from without to surrender at discretion or meet immediate annihilation, so the last remnant of liberty and religion go together, to ensure this, there is only wanting a Clerical apostate, inquisitorial Police within. Here will be the unnatural union of a nominal Catholic Church with Protestant ascendancy. What an anomaly in Religion & Politicks. Should not then every honest citizen stand to his post and resign his last breath in the breach rather than surrender the only proud privilege we possess. I am sure there is no Irishman more alive to this feeling than you are, and it is to be hoped that you and other independent men will be able to defeat the schemes of the time serving part of our Body, so appropriately called, by Barney,[2] Orange Catholics.[3] You have the people at your back and you can do much to rouse the press from its lethargy. It is now evident that from our firmness and perseverance alone we may expect any thing, as to Parliamentary friends I don't conceive we have one. The Whigs are rotten to the heart's core. They have too long made tools of us to advance their own interests, and it is full time that the Peoples' eyes should be opened to this. Again allow me to tell you that from you much is expected. If you only speak out you will be heard with respectful attention through the Country, and any independent measures you propose will I expect be well supported. For my part I can not pretend to do much, but this I will say I am free from the influence *of Party*, *faction* or *individual* amongst either Protestants or Catholics, and my humble support shall be ever given to the most independent measures proposed to relieve my unfortunate Country from thraldom and degradation, provided they have the appearance of Practicability. I will not from my state of Health be able to attend the aggregate meeting which I regret much, altho' I could add but little with consequence, yet by meeting friends I might the better know how to act in the Country, but any communication made to me in this way shall be always made use of with discretion.   [*Source*: Scully Papers]

[1]When an aggregate meeting was to be held (see No. 490 n.3). An attempt to reunite the Catholic body had begun with a circular letter of 16 November 1814 signed by O'Connell. Lord Fingall and most of the seceders stayed away from a meeting convened for 26 November, but on 3 December Lord Fingall agreed to sit with a committee of thirty-one which would prepare a new petition. Scully declined to join this, arguing that no new petition should be adopted until it was ascertained that the 1814 petition, still lying on the table, could not be presented (*DEP*, 17 & 29 November 1814; 6 December 1814). On 10 January a sub-committee of five was appointed to consider drafts submitted by R. L. Sheil and Lord Fingall (*Sentinel*, 11 January 1815).
[2]Possibly Bernard Coile, the Barney Coile of some verses in the *Irish Magazine* of April 1812 containing the refrain "Barney, Barney, buck or doe". When Cloney was transferred to Kilmainham Gaol in 1804 he moved into Coile's room there (*Personal Narrative*, p. 166).
[3]According to James Ryan (*FJ*, 11 August 1810) John Keogh described Weldon of Dame Street as an Orange Catholic as early as 1804.

490   *To Thomas Cloney, Graig, Co. Kilkenny*[1]

Merrion Square, 13 January 1815
Private
Dear Sir,
    I feel very sensibly the kind and flattering sentiments expressed by your Letter, and can assure you I know the full value of such approbation as yours, coming, as it does, from equal integrity and intelligence.

You judge me rightly in attributing to me fair & upright views respecting our common Interests. Indeed, I cannot lay claim to any merit for purity of motive — being placed, by accidents, beyond the reach of allurement or temptation: and indisposed, by my education & the constitution of my mind, towards sordid or unworthy actions.

I own to you, that the present juncture of our affairs appears to me perplexed & embarrassing. It is also new, at least to persons of my standing, who have not known the subject, otherwise than as affected, and very much so, by a state of War between G. Britain and France. The Peace,[2] you must see, has greatly changed the posture of our case. It has crushed, for the present, that revolutionary sentiment, which served us so much, collaterally, as an auxiliary in past years. It has releived Monarchs from apprehensions: and has enabled Intolerance to become more insolent and more regardless of justice & policy. You must daily perceive the consequences — our Enemies, tho' not more strong, are less placable than before — Our friends, so called, are dropping off one after another: and very recently, some splendid instances of base & shameless apostacy have been exhibited. From private knowledge I am sorry to say, that we shall soon be deserted by other *friends*, whose names will surprise you, but who never advocated our Cause, but upon interested speculation. In fact, we shall scarcely have a Protestant friend left, at least openly so, except Judge Fletcher, George Lidwill and half a dozen more. For this desertion the Catholic Board is assigned as the cause, especially by the apostates themselves. But the real cause is the fall of Bonaparte, the Peace, and the total change of speculating prospects. The conduct of the Board had no more to do with it than that of a Debating society.

In this state of things, I do not see well what wiser course the upright part of the Catholic Body (Happily, an immense majority) can take, than to stand firmly to their position, to concede nothing, to retract nothing, to qualify nothing — but to watch events as they may occur and interfere, only when necessary. Another change may arrive, perhaps within a short time, which may restore to them that influence, which is due to their population and importance, but which has been curtailed by the late Peace.

For the present, therefore, I should wish to see the opportunity taken of strengthening ourselves at home, supporting each other by preferences in private life, by *confining dealings to each other*, by marking & avoiding those trading or professional Protest[ant]s who have acted hostilely towards us, and by preserving our own stations and industry, as well as we can, for a more favourable occasion than the present. Moreover, our Enemies will be the more reduced & humbled by such conduct — the Peace must put thousands of them out of employment, in the Military, yeomanry & civil departments. They & their families must speedily choose between indigence and emigration: and at all events we and the Country will get rid of them. In this way, the Peace will probably work for our advantage — but not immediately.

I am unable to anticipate the proceedings of the intended meeting of the 24th[3] but I have no apprehension of mischief from it, or indeed from any other public & open meeting of Catholics. Upon this subject, however, I cannot speak from actual knowledge, being only just returned to town after an absence of 3 weeks in the Country.

You may be assured, that I am at all times willing to come forward whenever I can be useful but never, for mere notoriety, or for the passing honours of the day. I have not been in the least checked or discouraged by any of our domestic events — nor even by the wretched compound of vices and follies, which I have seen in the Catholic Gentry of the County & City of Kilkenny (with scarcely three exceptions) since our meeting of the 4 August 1813.[4] I know that all the middling and lower Classes are sound and faithful — they do not cherish any envy towards Catholic wealth, talent or virtue — nor would they betray their benefactors, nor abandon their Printers,[5] nor involve themselves in the general contempt & odium, which now cover several of the Gentry, the placehunters, and money dealers.

It is for the sake of our people at large, and from a sense of original duty towards our country, that an honest & reflecting man would at any time undertake any share in these affairs — or apply to such subjects his mind or his leisure, which might otherwise be more profitably employed for his private advantage or that of his family.

I am, Dear Sir, with sincere sentiments of gratitude for your good opinion & for the trouble you have had the goodness to take in the present instance.

[*Source*: Scully Papers]

[1]This letter is not a copy but the original, possibly never sent, there being no postmark or other indication of delivery.

[2]The suspension of hostilities was announced in parliament on 27 April 1814 (*Hansard* XXVII, 559).

[3]At a meeting of the committee of thirty-one (see No. 489 n.1) on 17 January the attempt to re-unite the Catholic body ended in failure, the majority refusing to delete the word "unqualified" before "Emancipation". On 19 January a form of petition drafted by Eneas McDonnell was adopted and a proposal to entrust its presentation to other hands than those of Lord Donoughmore and Grattan was only dropped after an intervention by George Lidwill. When the aggregate meeting assembled on 24 January Lord Fingall refused to take the chair and walked out when a motion for "unqualified Emancipation" was put (*Sentinel*, 20 & 25 January 1815).

[4]When Scully's Kilkenny resolutions were adopted (see No. 449 n.1).

[5]On 22 March 1814 the Kilkenny Catholics had resolved to "proceed forthwith to take such measures as will secure to Mr Magee a full indemnification of the amount of the pecuniary losses incurred by this gentleman, for his steady and persevering fidelity to the Catholic cause" but when on 30 December 1815 Magee complained

to the chairman of the meeting that nothing had been done he was told that there was indeed no settled plan for reimbursing him (*DEP*, 10 February 1816).

491   *From William Parnell*

Avondale [Co. Wicklow] 25 January [1815]

Sir:

I am infinitely obliged to you for your valuable remarks; your praises are of course very agreeable to me, & your strictures are so very just, that I acquiesce in them without any reluctance and am happy in the improvement my pamphlet[1] will derive from them.

I plead guilty to the deficiencies in point of information with which you charge me, and have nothing more to say on that head, but to return you my thanks for setting me right. But when you attack my general principles, I do not feel prepared to yield with so good a grace. I own I am warmly attached to them, it may be perhaps because though of little value in themselves they have cost me much labour & thought, like the partiality of a Parent to a sickly child. You object to my municipal plan, and I really am sorry for it; for after agreeing with you on so many points I am impatient that we should differ on one where I foresee you cannot convince me. I must therefore try to make a convert of you.

Are you certain that you have addressed the *real* reason why the Catholics disapprove this municipal plan? Is it not because they think it would be a partial alleviation of their present grievances, which might have the effect of defrauding them of their full right? Is it not because they are averse to allow that any measure can be good which leaves Catholic emancipation out of the question? If this is the case, I think the Catholics impolitic. Every measure that encreases the liberty of the nation, opens a better prospect to their's. Little would be gained, it is true, compared with the great measure of Catholic Emancipation; but the more we possess the greater facility we have of acquiring, and even a well contrived attempt is pregnant with improvement.

But I maintain that a municipal representation would lead at once to Catholic Emancipation, and that without it Catholic emancipation would produce no very real benefit. You do not give sufficient importance to the plan of *annual* elections. If sheriffs, if grand jurors, if magistrates etc. had salaries & were annually elected, would not more Catholics be appointed to these offices, nay would they not be almost entirely filled by Catholics? Need I point out the consequence.

You seem yourself to allow the *emancipating* effect of county representation when you say that "it is by the influence of the county members alone that the Catholics are appointed magistrates and grand jurors. That is, the elective right possessed by the Catholics makes the county representatives in a certain degree dependant on them. So far, so good. I wish therefore to *extend* this principle and to make more protestants dependant on the Catholics and by the same means, representation. County members learn now to sacrifice their prejudices to their interests, so would Protestant magistrates & Jurors, if they found themselves dependant on their Catholic neighbours, but most particularly if these offices had salaries; as I think they ought.

We know that the laws which granted priviledges to the Catholics have had little effect, & this little only proceeded from their elective right. We may justly conclude that a compleat grant of priviledges will also have a very limited effect the elective right remaining the same. The object then is to extend the elective right which can only be done by a municipal plan of Government. This would carry the effect of emancipation through every vein & fibre of the Catholic body; without it, the mere power of sitting in Parliament will only give consequence & decoration to the upper ranks.

But I consider this municipal plan in a more important point of view than as it regards the Catholics; I consider it as a principle essential to the liberties of the nation, of mankind. What I have already said will I think suggest to you the reasoning I should use to enforce the utility of a municipal plan as a general measure applicable to all counties. For local interest there must be a local administration. To make this administration efficient, accountable, & congenial to liberty it ought to be paid, and it must be elected annually. The collateral benefits arising from it are encreased respectability thrown upon the electors & elected; a common interest generated between the higher & lower orders; habits of assembling & discussion without turbulence, & great subordination without any sense of oppression. Constitutional meetings are the support of free government; at these men of abilities acquire their proper ascendancy, and the many (as they ought) are accustomed to be led. Why did the English Revolution & American succeed? Because the people from the habit of constitutional meetings knew each other & knew whom to trust & follow? Why did the French revolution fail? Because from the want of constitutional meetings there was no previous subordination, and leaders chosen at the moment of phrenzy were sure to be frantic.

You say my instance of the Grand Jurors is unfortunate. I do not think so. It is an *a fortiori* instance. If Grand Jurors constituted as they are, make better cross roads than are made in the world beside, what might we not expect if they were made active by being paid and if they were made honest by being annually elected? It is true they make bad jobs, but they make good roads. Whereas in other countries you have bad jobs and bad roads too.

Did you ever take the trouble of enquiring into the present municipal system in France imperfect as it is, it is the only good that has been left from the wreck of the French revolution. Almost every book of travels bears testimony in favor of the French Justices of peace, (I was under great obligations to them) they are paid & are elected but I believe not so directly by the people as they ought to be. [Source: Scully Papers]

[1]No pamphlet published in 1815 under his name has been found.

492   *From Dr Edward Sheridan to Merrion Square, Dublin*

Gr. Dominick Street, 9 February 1815

My Dear Sir,

At this moment so critical to the fate of our religion, I feel a strong impulse to lay open my mind to you, in hopes that you may get some measure adopted in time, which may secure from impending ruin in this country, that which all true Catholics so highly value. The base artifices, the low cunning, the deep laid intrigues, the secret and mysterious communications, the various and contradictory reports, which have for some time prevailed, and still prevail, leave me scarce a doubt but something is meditated on one side, and not absolutely rejected on the other, which is highly disgusting, and most justly so, to the Catholic people of Ireland. My fears on this subject were greatly increased a few days ago by the judicious remarks of a friend. He observed that it is possible, perhaps not improbable that the Court of Rome and the Court of St James might come to a compromise on the business of the *Veto* without the acquiescence, or even the knowledge of the Catholics of Ireland.[1] This might seem strictly and justly authorised by the power which his Holiness has for some time exercised of nominating to Irish Sees. You know, Sir, that it is not long since his Holiness assumed that power, and you also know that the consequences of such a compromise would not be the less pernicious by that power giving to it, a legal form.[2] Quarantotti's Rescript proves to a demonstration that there are many learned divines in Rome very obsequious to the Court of St James, and very ignorant of the state of this country.[3] My friend further remarked that domestic nomination would be an effectual, and the only effectual barrier against this dreaded evil; and he doubted not but the unanimous call of the Catholic clergy and laity of Ireland for that ancient and canonical right would obtain it. He suggested the propriety of a deputation from the Laity waiting on our Prelates and proposing the measure to them. I applauded all his observations, but said, I feared the attempt would be fruitless, for that I believed the Prelates would reject it. He answered, if so, and if religion fell the Laity would then have the satisfaction to reflect that they had done their duty.

I recollect well when the *Veto* first came under public discussion, that mention was made of domestic nomination.[4] I did not then relish it, because I could not entertain the most distant suspicion that we had any thing to fear from Rome; I thought the only power we had to contend with was our own intolerant Ministry, and that entertaining any other question at the time would distract and weaken us. But from late appearances I infer that it is our only resource, and I wish we could avail ourselves of it as speedily as possible. It is a great misfortune that there should be a difference between us Catholics on a subject so important. I am sure there is no man respects our Venerable Prelates more than I do. Yet I must be open with you, Sir, and declare my sentiments. I wonder at it, yet from my observations I am led to believe that some of our Good Shepherds are less jealous, and less fearful of the ravenous Wolves that are attempting to break into the fold, than of the faithful dogs that are barking against them. Yet History does not furnish, I believe, a single instance of bad consequences following from the second order of the clergy, or the Laity exerting themselves in defence of religion, whereas mischief has invariably ensued, whenever religion became subject to Court intrigues.

I have thus, Sir, taken the liberty of addressing to you a hasty, a very hasty sketch indeed of my ideas on a subject which appears to me, to be of the last importance. If I am happy enough to arrest your attention on it, I make no doubt but you will bring my crude ideas to maturity; *verbum sapienti*, and cause them to produce substantial fruits. In expectation of such fortunate results I remain, My Dear Sir, with unfeigned respect and esteem.

[*Source*: Scully Papers]

[1] At the meeting in Lord Fingall's house on 17 January (see No. 490 n.3) R. L. Sheil had pointed out: "The points to be settled are not between cabinet and Ireland but between the cabinet and Rome" (*Sentinel*, 20 January 1815).

[2] A right of nomination to Irish sees had been conceded by the Holy See to the later Stuarts but this lapsed after the death of the Old Pretender in 1766 and Dr Sheridan may have had in mind the resumption by the Pope of his powers on that occasion (see Cathaldus Giblin OFM: *Irish exiles in Catholic Europe*, Dublin, 1971, p. 47).

[3] As a result of the English Catholic Board's request that the Vicars Apostolic should agree among themselves on the attitude to be taken if Grattan's bill was reintroduced in 1814 (see No. 456 n.2) Dr Poynter had approached the Congregation of Propaganda Fide and this had resulted in a rescript signed by Monsignor Quarantotti, dated 14 February and received in London on 27 April 1814. This conceded that "Catholics may with satisfaction and gratitude accept and embrace the bill which was last year presented for their emancipation", subject to a modification in the oath to be administered to priests. As a result of lobbying by Dr Milner the rescript was virtually revoked on 25 June 1814 but nothing was put in its place until the so-called Genoese Letter of 26 April 1815, which however remained unpublished until December 1815 — see No. 529 n.5 (Ward, *Eve of Catholic Emancipation* II, pp. 82, 101, 149).

[4] In May 1810 (see Nos. 233 n.1; 242 n.9 and 390 n.3).

493   *From Peter Kenney SJ to Merrion Square South, Dublin*

Clongowes Wood [Co. Kildare] 12 February 1815

Dr Sir,

The bad weather & many troublesome affairs united to prevent the accomplishment of my promise to call a second time to your house. May I beg the favor of a line to say how you, Mrs Scully & youngest daughter[1] do.

For the satisfaction for having you informed of every thing, which concerns a cause in which you have already laboured much, I in confidence add an extract hastily taken from a letter just received from a very intelligent gentleman at the other side of the water.

"It seems to be beyond a doubt, that there is an agreement between Ministry & our Cathol'c enemies. It is now said that ministers themselves will move the C. question. We know that the 3 Bps[2] have pledged themselves to the full extent of the *5 resolution* & it seems to me, that ministry has promised to exterminate Jesuitism. Either Hippesley or some other of their agents fill the papers every day with extravagant rants against Jes'ts, & this is done to prepare the public for the intended *Bill*.[3] I have expressly advised Mr Stone to take the best legal advice for the security of our property. I presume you watch the approaching storm."

So much for the fears of our freinds [*sic*] on the other side. Though, there is no chain of dependance or ostensible connexion between us, yet if a storm come, I fear, that we shall be all involved in it. I am uneasy about this house & I beg that you will give a leisure moment to think, if there yet remain any legal move of putting it out of grasp.[4] Yous sincerely, P. Kenney

[*Source*: Scully Papers]

[1]Marianne, born on 18 January 1815.
[2]The Vicars Apostolic, other than Dr Milner, who had reaffirmed their adherence to the English Catholics' Fifth Resolution of 1 February 1810 when they met at Durham on 25 October 1813 (see No. 456 n.2). The qualification "to the full extent" is an *ex parte* interpretation by Father Kenney's informant.
[3]He evidently believed that the bill would contain anti-Jesuit clauses, but no evidence has been found of any intention by the government to introduce one.
[4]Of the government (see No. 480 n.1).

494   *From Thomas Cloney to Merrion Square South, Dublin*

Graig [Co. Kilkenny] 17 April 1815

Dear Sir,

You will see by the *Evg. Post* of tomorrow that a Catholic meeting is to take place in Wexford on the 24th.[1] May I beg of you to draw up &

transmit me before Saturday next such resolutions as you think will answer Wexford. However firm & decided so they do not savour of intemperance there can be no doubt but they will pass. I would be very glad to have an explicit and decided one against any Ecclesiastical arrangements,[2] and would you think it wise to demand of Mr Carew[3] to whose care the Petition to the Commons has been hitherto entrusted a promise that he will oppose any such arrangments before he gets the Petition. It might certainly hobble us to have any difference with him, but is it not ridiculous to resolve on taking nothing less than unqualified Emancipation & yet entrust Petitions to members who will not vote for this. You will not I am certain be less anxious than I am that my application to you should not be mentioned. I have many reasons for it which I'll mention when I have the pleasure of seeing you.

P.S. Immediately after returning from Wexford I'll apply to some acquaintances in this County to urge a meeting. I think if we pass a string of bold & manly resolutions in Wexford it will help very much to spirit up other Counties. I know Sir T. Esmonde will be all for moderation, he objected to a meeting but reluctantly submits to the People.   [*Source*: Scully Papers]

[1]No such announcement has been found but the meeting on 24 April took place (DDA 390/2, VI, 40) and a petition from Co. Wexford, described as identical with that of the Roman Catholics of Ireland, was presented on 30 May 1815 (*House of Commons Journal*, p. 336).

[2]In regard to the nomination of Bishops, communications with the Holy See etc.

[3]Robert Shapland Carew (1787–1856), later 1st Baron Carew, MP for Wexford county.

495   *From Sir Henry Parnell to Merrion Square South, Dublin*

Holyhead, 4 May 1815

My Dear Sir,

I shall be much obliged to you if you will send me a dozen of the printed Bills[1] as soon as convenient.

If you send them to Mr Kemmis[2] he will get a Castle frank for them. You may tell him I asked you to do so.   [*Source*: Scully Papers]

[1]The Catholic Association's own relief bill, published in the *Freeman's Journal* on 19 May. An aggregate meeting of 23 February having resolved to entrust their petition to a member other than Grattan, and the Knight of Kerry having declined the charge (O'Connell, *Correspondence* II, 543), a deputation had waited upon Parnell who, in the words of the *Freeman's Journal* of 26 April, "entirely concurred . . . on the propriety of bringing on the petition immediately" and stated that "to suggestions or instructions he had no sort of objection".

[2]Either Thomas Kemmis or his son William, who were Crown Solicitors.

496   *From Sir Henry Parnell to Merrion Square South, Dublin*

23 Bury Street, London, 9 May 1815

Private & confidential

My Dear Sir,

The House is but ill disposed to the discussion of your Petition; & an opinion prevailing generally that there will be a great majority against you.

I shall present the petition on Thursday & fix the Monday senight[1] following for moving to refer it to a Committee of the whole House. The Speaker is of opinion that this step must be taken before a Bill can be brought in.[2]

I shall only propose to have the laws affecting his Majesty's Roman Catholic subjects taken into consideration, leaving out the latter part of Mr Grattan's motion[3] — "with a view to a final adjustment etc."

Tomorrow I am to see Lord Castlereagh, & I shall endeavour to speak to all the principal public men, who have before taken a part in the discussion, previous to making my motion. The more communication of this kind takes place, & the longer the final decision of the House is postponed, the better will be the chance of success, as most of the difficulty that presses is occasional, & capable of being got over by explanation. The resolutions of the Catholic Board in 1813 form the principle obstacle.[4]

[P.S.] Sir J. C. Hippisley will not move for a Committee.[5]

[Source: Scully Papers]

[1] 22 May, but subsequently postponed to 30 May.

[2] On 6 June 1816, at Peel's request, the standing order was read "by whch it was declared, that no bill which went to make an alteration in the religion of the country, should be discussed . . . until the proposition had been first considered by a committee, or agreed to by the House". The Speaker then went on to say that it was the practice to begin with a committee of the whole House; he did not know that a member was precluded from moving abstract resolutions, but certainly no bill could be introduced without the sanction of a committee (*Hansard* XXXIV, 1012).

[3] Of 3 March 1813 (see No. 412 n.1).

[4] He probably means in particular the Board's approbation of the Prelates' condemnation of Grattan's bill (see No. 438 n.3).

[5] i.e. a select committee, which he had moved for when Grattan's bill was being introduced in 1813 (see No. 427 n.7).

497   *From Sir Henry Parnell, London, to Merrion Square,*
1 o'clock 10 May 1815

Private. It will not be expedient for him to make any observations on
presenting the petition, as they may arouse unfavourable sentiments which
cannot be soothed before the debate. The success of his motion so entirely
depends on private efforts to make friends of the cause give it zealous
support that he will name a long day, tomorrow fortnight, for bringing it
on.
                                                          [*Source*: Scully Papers]

498   *From Sir H. Parnell, London, to Merrion Square,*
11 May 1815

Private & Confidential. He has this moment presented the petition and
given notice of a motion for 25 May[1] to go into committee. As the necessity
for going into committee prevents him from bringing the Catholics' bill
itself before the House[2] he has also given notice that in a week's time he
will submit resolutions embodying each clause of the bill and containing a
full exposition of what the Catholics desired from the House — not for the
purpose of discussion but in the hope of getting them printed.[3] If this
should not be allowed he would like to have them privately printed. When
[W. C.] Plunket came into the House after the petition had been ordered
to be laid on the table he told Parnell that if he had been present he would
have contradicted his statement that the petition spoke the sentiments of
the Catholic body at large.   [*Source*: Scully Papers]

[1]Later postponed to 30 May (*Hansard* XXXI, 451).
[2]See No. 496 n.2.
[3]They were printed with the speech with which he presented them — according to
Henry Bankes "through a sort of private consent between gentlemen on both sides
of the question" (*Hansard* XXXI, 258, 263).

499   *From Sir Henry Parnell addressed to Mr C. Mahon*
13 Merrion Square Sth, Dublin

23 Bury Street [London] 12 May 1815

My Dear Sir,
    I think it right to acquaint you, as well as I am able, with the opinions
entertained by the several parties in the House of Commons upon your

claims. The opposition Whig party, which may consist of about sixty or seventy members, is the only one that will vote for unqualified emancipation.

That part of the Government party which is in favour of qualified emancipation, together with Mr Canning's & Mr Wilberforce's friends form a numerous body; but just at the present moment, I think they feel inclined not to give another vote for you, until your body shews itself disposed to accede to some ecclesiastical arrangements.

Lord Grenville's immediate friends, who are about twenty in number, I apprehend will vote against you or stay away on the ground of this not being a proper time to discuss the question.[1]

Sir William Scott, Sir John Nichol, Mr Yorke & those who voted with them in 1813 will again vote against all concessions.

If this is in any degree a correct view of the present state of parties, it is obvious that there is no chance of carrying my motion, unless your body shall take some step previous to the discussion of it to shew in what way the Government party, who are friendly, can see a prospect of obtaining some ecclesiastical arrangements with the approbation at least of your Clergy. This I suppose is a proceeding that is not at all likely to take place.

If upon a reconsideration of the question of arrangements, an aggregate meeting would go so far as to say they would leave them to be resisted or acceded to by the Clergy, according to their opinion of their expediency, when any shall be proposed to them for their consideration,[2] I think that such a declaration would secure a majority for going into a committee, & the success of the relief Bill, tho' not perhaps in this session.

It may possibly be proposed by some of the leading members, who are advocates for arrangements, to agree to vote for the committee & to allow me to propose my resolutions, with an understanding that they would propose other resolutions containing their plan of arrangements; & that both sets should be printed & all further proceedings postponed till the next session. If this shall happen, I shall act, as the Catholics would wish me to do. At present, I think it would be prudent to accept the offer & that by doing so considerable progress will be made toward the carrying of the Bill.

[*Source*: Scully Papers]

[1]Scully crossed this paragraph out on the receipt of No. 500.
[2]See No. 505 n.2.

500 *From Sir H. Parnell, London, (to Mr Mahon), Merrion Square,*
                              13 May 1815

He asks Scully to run his pen through the third paragraph of his letter of 12
May.   [*Source*: Scully Papers]

501   *From Sir Henry Parnell to Merrion Square Sth., Dublin*

                                              London, 16 May 1815
Private & Confidential
My Dear Sir,
     I received your enclosures[1] yesterday. I have framed my resolutions by
omitting those parts & those expressions which immediately belong to the
form of a Bill. If they were to pass the Committee, a Bill ordered to be
brought in upon them would be your Bill.
     I wish to know whether the Catholic Body would approve of taking any
thing less than the whole of what is asked by the Bill.
     If it should appear certain, that there would be a considerable majority
against my motion for going into a committee, on the ground of asking for a
repeal of all disqualification, it would be very desireable to protect your
cause from an event which would injure it considerably.
     This might be done by postponing the application for seats in Parliament
& for high official situation till next session; & confining the resolutions
when moved in the committee to all those other objects to which they relate.
I would not, however, recommend such a course unless the previous consent
of Government could be obtained to the whole of them. The admissions of
the Speaker, Mr Bankes, Sir Wm. Scott & others in the last debates[2]
naturally lead one to suppose there would be no great difficulty in securing
the consent of Government. Such a proceeding I think would contribute
very much to the reconciliation of all parties, & thereby lead to the more
easy attaining of the great objects of all in the next session. The lateness of
the session would be a fair reason for postponing these contested points. The
deliberations which are said to be still pending on the part of the Cardinals[3]
on the ecclesiastical arrangements would be another, tho' perhaps not a
palatable argument to some persons.
     I am induced to throw out these topics of consideration from a wish to turn
the effort of this session to some good account, & to disappoint the
speculations of those who foretell that the discussion will do injury. From
what I know of Parliamentary impressions, & management, it is certainly a
most essential object to avoid a division which shall be very unfavourable in

point of numbers. The opinion of the House is very much governed by effect & very little by just reasoning. The people out of doors too, might be induced again to fight the Battle of petitioning if they conceived any change had taken place in the sentiments of the House.

I saw Lord Donoghmore this morning, & told him you had sent a copy of the Bill to him.[4]

P.S. I directed my two last as you desired.[5]   [*Source*: Scully Papers]

[1]Probably the copies of the printed bill asked for in No. 495.
[2]Probably of 1813, as the Irish Catholic petition was not debated in 1814. The Speaker's amendment in committee on 24 May 1813 implied that everything in Grattan's bill would be conceded short of seats in parliament (see No. 434 n.3).
[3]See No. 492 n.3.
[4]It was sent through Lord Hardwicke, who wrote to Lord Donoughmore on 24 May enclosing not only the bill but Scully's covering letter to him, now missing. Lord Hardwicke expressed misgivings about showing it, as it spoke of Lord Donoughmore's loss of popularity among the Irish Catholics, and asked Lord Donoughmore not to let it make any difference in his manner to Scully (Donoughmore Papers, D/22/13).
[5]By addressing them to Mr Mahon, as on Nos. 499, 500 and other covers. Although the initial when given looks like C the Mahon in question was probably Scully's nephew John (James being at this time at Kilfeacle acting as secretary to James Scully, his grandfather) — Scully's J could sometimes be taken for a C.

502   *From Sir Henry Parnell to Merrion Square St., Dublin*

London, 19 May 1815
Private
My Dear Sir,

I have this moment received your letter in which you ask me whether I have any objection to my letter of the 12th[1] being read to the Association. The use you made of it, of shewing it to the Gentlemen you mention, is exactly that which I had in contemplation when I wrote it & I think it will answer every good purpose if it is confined to that extent of publication. I therefore, am very glad you did not agree to it being read at the association.

You will see by the papers that I have had a full opportunity of explaining everything to the House & also that the Speaker, Mr Yorke & Mr Bankes did every thing in their power to stop me.[2] All the reasonable members approved very much of the course I took.

In regard to the resolutions, I think you will find no material word omitted. I transferred the 2d Clause of the Bill to the last resolution in order to bring all the minor objects together, & prevent the reader, by coming too soon upon the greater, from being discouraged to give due attention to those points which come last in the form of the Bill.[3]

If ever we get into a committee, the original framing may be restored.

Dr Milner called on me a few days ago, & told me a negotiation was still going on with the Pope on the subject of arrangements.

If so, the Government must be somewhat inclined to your cause.[4]

P.S. I made the penalty £100 instead of £50 for Priests marrying Protestants, as the following clause gave that Penalty against Officers etc.

[*Source*: Scully Papers]

[1]No. 499.

[2]Parnell had presented his resolutions to the House on the previous day. There is no mention of an intervention by the Speaker in the *Hansard* report except when he briefly confirmed that it was a standing order of the House for a question respecting religion to be considered by a committee of the whole House. Yorke objected that Parnell's observations would be irregular unless he intended to conclude with a motion, whereupon Parnell said he would move the first resolution in order to conform to order. Bankes said that as the first resolution was one of a string of resolutions he would have to vote against it and Parnell's object would thus be defeated. Parnell acquiesced in this view and withdrew his motion, explaining that his only object had been to explain what would satisfy the Catholics of Ireland (*Hansard* XXXI, 257). The first resolution dealt with property rights.

[3]The second clause of the bill dealt with entitlement to office, the franchise etc. Parnell amalgamated this with the 3rd clause in the bill, regarding sitting and voting in parliament, and combined the two in his 8th and last resolution.

[4]Parnell evidently understood Dr Milner to be referring, not to the representations of the Vicars Apostolic (see No. 492 n.3) but to talks that had taken place in Rome when Edward Cooke, Undersecretary at the Foreign Office, was there before Easter, and Lord Castlereagh's talks with Cardinal Consalvi at Vienna (Ward, *Eve* II, p. 127 ff.).

503   *From Sir Henry Parnell to Merrion Square Sth., Dublin*

23 Bury Street, London, 22 May 1815

My Dear Sir,

I have received your letters to the 19th which prove very useful to me, in my communications with Lord Castlereagh & others.

By letters received yesterday from Italy, I think it not improbable that some plan of arrangements will soon appear with the concurrence of the Pope. Dr Poynter is expected daily.[1] I shall confine my conduct to a steady resistance to any thing of the kind.[2] At the same time, I should be glad an opportunity was given to the advocates of them to propose them.

No adverse observations have yet appeared in the Public Papers. No fault has yet been mentioned to me in the resolutions.[3] I am sure the making the public familiar with the details will have the best effect.

The conduct of the Irish Govt. & the writings of the Irish Press are never thought of here.[4] I wish they were treated with the same contempt in Ireland, as they give an improper direction to the range of Catholic opinion.

I cannot as yet at all guess at the number that will divide with me. At present I should say very few.

As I conceive discussion is your great object & not merely to know how many would divide for unqualified emancipation, I shall secure the one, but carry my motion for going into a Committee, if possible, without compromising my opposition to arrangements.   [*Source*: Scully Papers]

[1]He did not get back to London until 13 June (Ward, *Eve* II, p. 134).
[2]Presumably any tacking of "arrangements" on to his bill.
[3]See No. 502 n.2. They were published as part of the speech with which he had introduced them on 18 May.
[4]Parnell amplified this point in a letter that he wrote to O'Connell on the same day and O'Connell told him in reply that he treated too lightly the government and its hired press (O'Connell, *Correspondence* II, Nos. 551 and 551A).

504   *From Sir Henry Parnell, London, to Merrion Square,*
26 May 1815

Private. He has received Scully's letter of the 20th. The questions put in his last letters to Scully have been with a view of collecting information for use in possible contingencies, not because a necessity has occurred of forming decisions on their subject matter. The public mind is so wholly occupied with the war that the Catholic question has been little thought of.[1] As every day contributes to wear off adverse feeling he would have no objection to postponing the debate for another week, but cannot. The press has continued silent, but conversation in the House is hostile, from a general idea that the Catholics are unreasonable. He trusts the discussion will make it practicable to carry the bill next session. A new attempt should begin with an address to the Regent[2] and an effort to get the support of government. The Regent's opposition two years ago[3] was to prevent his political opponents from attaching the Catholics to their support. Conversations with persons intimate with him suggest he will be placable and perhaps flattered by a direct application. Such a measure might be so conducted as to lead to a union with Lord Fingall etc[4] and finally to a more liberal settlement than obtainable by a mere petition to parliament. He hopes abuse received in the debate will not lead to recrimination, for many use violent language in order to provoke angry discussion from the Catholics and keep alive a useful argument for resisting their claims.   [*Source*: Scully Papers]

[1]The campaign which ended at Waterloo on 18 June was about to begin. Between 18 May, when Parnell introduced his resolutions, and 30 May, when the debate on the

Irish Catholic petition came on, over 175 columns of *Hansard* were given to various aspects of the war.

[2]This recommendation was reported in *The Sentinel* of 14 June.

[3]On Grattan's bill (see No. 427 n.3).

[4]The seceders (see No. 490 n.3).

505   *From Sir Henry Parnell addressed to Mr Mahon*
                13 Merrion Square South, Dublin

London, 28 May 1815

Private

My Dear Sir,

I never felt so much gratified, as I did this morning, on receiving your letter from Avondale,[1] as the spirit of it, when there is an opportunity to bring it into action will inevitably carry your question. As the debate must come on tomorrow, & as the prepossession against my motion is very general, there is not time now to turn it to any effectual account. For this reason, I have shewn it only to Lord Castlereagh, & with the strongest injunctions to secrecy, & I do not intend to shew it or mention it *to any one* else, as I very well know the necessity of its being kept wholly secret. Lord Castlereagh observed, that it was very surprising how little it seemed to be understood in Ireland, what the difficulty was of carrying a Bill; that it would require the most active & public cooperation of the Catholics to enable their Parliamentary friends to overcome the obstacles that were now in its way. I told him it was to be attributed to your having no communication with Grattan, & that I was sure that he would find the system on which I acted would go a great way to establish a better understanding & to approximate feelings. He read the letter with very great attention & I am sure was much pleased with its contents.[2] For the present we must be contented with the benefit discussion will do which I feel will be considerable but a course of operations should be immediately commenced to prepare for next session. The abstinence of the Catholic Association from expressing any public opinion on the failure of this effort will alone be of use. Your private communications with your own friends will be of great utility. But the most effectual means will be a well formed plan of a deputation with an address to the Regent. This should take place before the meeting of Parliament.

I am to present a Petition tomorrow from 6000 English Catholics.[3] I shall give notice of a motion to be made in case I am defeated tomorrow, as I shall certainly be, for the purpose of placing them on a footing with you, & in this way something more may be obtained for both. I am sure this wd be of use toward carrying the remainder. I shall confine my observations to shew that no ground has been laid for the claim of securities & make but a short speech assuming the principle of relief to be carried, & that the old arguments may be passed by.

Lord Castlereagh said the great mistake the Catholics fell into was that you were always making war, when you ought to be making love. This will explain his sentiments fully.   [*Source*: Scully Papers]

[1]William Parnell's home in Co. Wicklow.
[2]These remain unknown but may be reflected in a letter of Daniel O'Connell to Parnell postmarked 31 May, saying that if the Irish people were treated to a free emancipation bill they would cheerfully leave the government and the Bishops to make any arrangement they pleased (O'Connell, *Correspondence* II, No. 551A).
[3]For unqualified emancipation (see *Hansard* XXI, 474). The motion of which Parnell speaks is not recorded.

506   *From Sir Henry Parnell addressed to Mr Mahon*
                    13 Merrion Square South, Dublin

                    23 Bury Street, London, 30 May 1815 — 4 o'clock
Private
My Dear Sir,

I received your letters & enclosures[1] this morning. I think of reading the Cork Paper[2] to the House to shew the absolute necessity of at least passing one resolution. From all I can collect the division will be above 250 against my motion, & not more than 170 for it. Lord Castlereagh has had a meeting this morning at the foreign office of all the members who voted with him in 1813,[3] to endeavour to carry them with him to-night. I called on Mr Huskisson who is the representative of Mr Canning[4] with his party, & urged him, with sucess, to keep them with us. Mr Wilberforce will I believe vote with me — in fact we have votes enough to carry the question if we could bring them all to attend. We shall be beat [*sic*] by the members, who are friendly to the measure who will stay away.   [*Source*: Scully Papers]

[1]Perhaps press cuttings, used by Parnell in his speech to describe the reactions of Irish Protestants to his resolutions (*Hansard* XXXI, 479).
[2]It was a notice posted on a Cork church about a soldier in the Cork militia who had been forced to attend a service at the established church (ibid., 481).
[3]On Grattan's bill.
[4]Absent as Ambassador in Portugal.

507   *From Sir Henry Parnell addressed to Mr Mahon*
13 Merrion Square South, Dublin

London, 31 May 1815

My Dear Sir,

I am happy to be able to tell you the debate went off uncommonly well, & quite to the decided advantage of your cause. An impression is allowed to be established of its being a matter, *now*, of no difficulty (as far as the sentiments of this Country or of the House are in question) to carry a Bill, if any sort of adjustment can be made of the ecclesiastical part of the subject. Besides the 149 members who voted, 34 paired off & 10 were shut out, so that 193 actually appeared, under all the unfavourable circumstances, in favour of the motion.[1]

The whole force of the opposition, in argument, was rested on the assumption, that the Catholics were determined *not to be conciliated*!! I think it would be adviseable to answer it by some public resolution, in general terms, provided such a matter could be effected, without any warmth of language in discussion, or rather without the publication of any discussion the Association might have on the subject. All the good, (which has been very considerable), has been done, which public discussion on your part can do & it evidently is not by any means a fit course for managing the intricate details of a measure, which is at present a measure wholly of feeling. Any sort of conciliatory expression of your feelings, just now, while the public opinion here is alive to the question, would be of great use, preparatory to the next effort. But the most useful proceeding of all, will be an address to the Regent, containing a full & temperate refutation of all the arguments & assertions, which have been urged in the debate of last night.

Mr Peel's speech was so triumphantly answered by Mr Whitbread, that I hope it will be left where it is & not suffered to do the mischief it is so well calculated to do, by its intemperate attack on the member of the Association.[2]

None of the Papers give a very accurate report of my speech. I have therefore corrected the best I have met with, & I send it you, requesting you will give it to the *Freeman's Journal* or *Evening Post*, as its arrival may suit their time of publication.

[P.S.] Mr Peel's attempt to make the publication of the Bill a matter of serious complaint, was so immediately scouted by the gestures & cheering of Mr Whitbread & others, that he was obliged to desist from it. All Lord Grenville's friends & the whole opposition in London voted with me, or paired off.

[P.S.] [Written on separate sheet of paper] Be so good as to send me the Paper that contains my speech. You will observe I made free use of your reading on the Bill.[3] Grattan expressed himself very strongly to me in approbation of it.[4]   [*Source*: Scully Papers]

[1] According to *Hansard* XXX, 524 only 147 voted for the motion, with 228 against.
[2] Peel tried to prove that there was no disposition towards conciliation by quoting the most intemperate utterances of O'Conell. He claimed that O'Connell had drawn up the resolutions and the bill, which to save parliament the trouble of legislating had been previously circulated and presented as the only measure the Catholics would have. Whitbread observed that O'Connell's conduct was the same as that of Peel, who by all kinds of exaggeration endeavoured to aggravate the Protestants just as O'Connell inflamed the Catholics (ibid., 505, 516).
[3] Having explained that his resolutions had been modelled on the Irish Act of 1793 Parnell went on to give a summary of them and in the course of his exposition drew attention to some of the laws they were intended to repeal (ibid., 479).
[4] While voting for the motion Grattan nevertheless said in his speech that he could not vote for some of the resolutions and condemned the application for unqualified emancipation (ibid., 522).

508   *From Sir Henry Parnell addressed to Mr C. Mahon*
                        13 Merrion Square South, Dublin

                                        Bury Street, [London] 2 June 1815
Private
My Dear Sir,
    I called on Lord Liverpool today & asked him if he would support a Bill for giving some of the minor concessions. He expressed himself against the proceeding at first, but on my telling him it would be well received by the Catholics, & contribute to conciliation he said he would consider the business & give me an answer at some other time.[1]
    I explained to him that you were anxious to stand well with the Regent's Government; & that I could take it upon myself to say, that if he would make concessions to you, he would find your leading men willing to promote any reasonable arrangement Government might require about the appointment of Bishops etc. I mentioned no names, & requested, that he would consider this communication as quite confidential. He appeared to hear what I said with considerable satisfaction, & although he told me he differed with Lord Castlereagh, he allowed it would be desireable to put an end to the discussion & irritation necessarily belonging to the state of things under the existence of the present laws.   [*Source*: Scully Papers]

[1] See No. 510.

509   *From Sir Henry Parnell addressed to Mr C. Mahon*
13 Merrion Square South, Dublin

Very Private   [7 June 1815]

I met Sir —— Holmes[1] to day who is the active assistant of the Regent in the House of Commons & takes a principal share in opposing the Catholic question, & had a long conversation with him, which I know will go to the Regent. I told him I hoped you would address him next year & shew him you are willing to deserve his countenance. He replied, that he was sure this course would go a great way to secure it.

[this note was not signed]
[*Source*: Scully Papers]

[1]Parnell must have confused him with Sir Leonard Thomas Worstley Holmes, but he is obviously Mr William Holmes (1779–1851), the member for Tregony, who acquired a reputation for calculating party strengths and became in 1818 Treasury whip (Thorne, *House of Commons*).

510   *From Sir Henry Parnell addressed to Mr C. Mahon*
13 Merrion Square South, Dublin

Private   [London] 9 June 1815
My Dear Sir,

I called some days ago on Ld Liverpool to urge him to support the minor concessions relative to Worship, Charities[1] etc. & the main question now being settled,[2] I today wrote to him to press him still more, & to ask his answer to my previous application.[3]

Mr Wilberforce met me some days ago & took great pains to impress on me, that nothing but very severe indisposition prevented him from voting with me. I have heard similar excuses made by Sir James McIntosh & several others, all which looks exceedingly well for the next attempt.

[*Source*: Scully Papers]

[1]The Catholic Association's draft relief bill contained a clause, embodied in one of the resolutions which Parnell presented on 18 May (see No. 502), providing that charitable bequests for Catholics should be on the same footing as for dissenters. On 3 July 1823 Parnell and Sir John Newport were given leave to bring in a bill on the subject (*House of Commons Journal*, p. 451), but it never materialised, perhaps because of Scully's failure to recover from his stroke (see No. 612). It was not until 1844 that the law was changed: on the second reading of the bill of that year Peel

defended himself against criticism for not having consulted the Irish Catholics by showing that he had read the *Penal Laws*, "written by a great lawyer, a man indisputably of high reputation" (*Hansard* LXXVI, 1511).
[2]By the House of Lords having negatived on the previous day, by 86 to 60 votes, Lord Donoughmore's motion to go into committee.
[3]Not found among Lord Liverpool's papers in the British Library.

511   *From Sir Henry Parnell addressed to Mr C. Mahon*
13 Merrion Square South, Dublin

London, 10 June 1815

Private
My Dear Sir,
   I am much obliged to you for your attention to my wishes relative to my speech,[1] & feel very much gratified by the reception it has met with.
   Though it is impossible to be surprised at the general sentiment of indignation which you describe to prevail, I am sure you do not estimate the effect of the debate here correctly, where all the personal matter is a good deal overlooked & opinions are formed upon voting more than when speaking. I have no doubt whatsoever that a Bill will pass next session if you only take the several opportunities you will have of exciting an interest in your favour.
   The more I reflect upon the expediency of addressing the Regent, the more convinced I am of its indispensable necessity. Your object should be to prevail on Lord Liverpool to advise him to recommend your measure to Parliament in the next speech from the Throne & though appearances may be very much against the success of the attempt, a variety of things may happen before November[2] to lead him to take up the question.
   The list of the minority was published in the *Chronicle*[3] last Monday & will of course have been republished before you receive this.
   I have delivered your note to Ridgway.[4]
   What you say in regard to your letter from Avondale[5] I shall attend to.

[*Source*: Scully Papers]

[1]See postscript to No. 507.
[2]When parliament might be recalled or the business for the next session settled.
[3]The London *Morning Chronicle* of 5 June. The list appeared in *The Sentinel* of 7 June.
[4]James Ridgway, bookseller, 170 Piccadilly.
[5]Acknowledged in No. 505.

512   *Conduct of the Irish members of Parliament on*
Sir Henry Parnell's motion[1]

[June 1815]

We promised some time since to keep a watchful eye upon the conduct of the Irish members, when the Catholic petitions should be brought under discussion. It is well that the people of Ireland should be rightfully informed upon this subject: and enabled to record, *for the proper season*, the fidelity of some, the hostility of others, and the neglect or desertion of more — The London prints are, as usual, deficient of the necessary information. They give a list of the minority only, but a list of the majority, who voted against Sir Henry Parnell's motion, remains a *"desideratum"*. Probably, some interference has been used to suppress the names of those who so voted: or perhaps the voters are ashamed of their conduct. Be this as it may, we have endeavoured by diligent scrutiny to supply the deficiency, from private sources of information, as nearly as the distance of place admits. We give separate lists of those Irish members

1. who voted for Sir Henry's motion
2. who have publickly absented themselves
3. who are known to have opposed it
4. who either opposed it, or absented themselves (but not yet known, which course they pursued).

1. The following Irish members voted for Sir Henry Parnell's motion [37 names follow]
2. That class of members who have absented themselves wilfully from this opportunity of healing the wounds of Ireland, is not very numerous.
   At their head stands a member of the Irish Bar.
   1. Wm. Conyngham Plunkett Esq. Dublin University
   2. Denis Bowes Daly Esq — Galway County.
   3. Honble General Mathew, Tipperary County
   4. James Daly, Galway County.

Mr Plunkett's conduct is already before the public[2] — They will judge him.

Mr Bowes Daly undertook to present the County of Galway petition — He brought it to Dublin, loitered here very agreeably, finally declined to attend his duty in Parliament, but very politely handed over the petition to his colleague, Mr James Daly, who barely presented it, and afterwards voted against Sir Henry Parnell's motion for taking it into consideration.[3] So much for the knights of the shire for the county of Galway.

As for General Mathew, he has been rambling about Italy during the last 16 months: and has deserted his station as an independent county member. His colleague, Mr Prittie, has voted faithfully, and indeed has never disappointed his constitutents.

We have not yet learned the names of the other defaulters.

3. The next class consists of those Irish members who are known to have voted stiffly against Sir Henry's motion — [22 names follow]
4. The fourth & last class consists of those Irish members, who neither voted for Sir Henry's motion nor are known to have opposed it.

It remains yet to be discovered whether these gentlemen voted against the Catholics, or absented themselves altogether, or were accidentally shut out.

This much is certain, that they did not vote *for* the motion — [39 names follow, one crossed out]   [*Source*: Scully Papers MS 27,539]

[1]This is evidently the draft of an article intended for publication. If published it has not been found.

[2]Plunket had stayed long enough to support the government in the debate of 25 May on the peace treaties but had left London immediately afterwards, thus missing the debate on Sir H. Parnell's motion (*Statesman* 7 June 1813).

[3]James Daly of Dunsandle (1782–1847), married to a niece of Denis Bowes Daly, presented the Galway petition the day after Parnell's motion, when he explained that he had been shut out of the division and expressed his entire concurrence with the honourable baronet (*Hansard* XXXI, 524).

513   *From Revd Peter Gandolphy to No. 13 Mahon [sic] Square, Dublin*

Spanish Place, London, 10 June 1815

Dr Sir,

As I know your sentiments on our common affairs, & I believe you are partly acquainted with mine[1] I take the liberty, at the end of our catholic campaign, of communicating with you — and as you have resided at a distance from the scene of action, it may not be unacceptable to have the sentiments of one, who has been occupied in coolly looking on.

I must tell you, that I have been in dailly [sic] intercourse with Sir Hen. Parnell — have had interviews with Lords Donnoughmore [sic], Grey etc. & have exerted myself in every way I could, to serve the common cause — and I must now express to you my opinion of the man, whom you have chosen to advocate & present your Petition in the House of Commons. It is with extreme pleasure then, that I throw into the common sentiment expressed by Ireland in her choice of Sir Hen. Parnell, the mite of my approbation, & I declare to you, I do not think that you could name an other member of either house so proper as he is. I can assure you he has proved himself in my eyes a man of merit — a man that has undergone no little persecution on your account — a man eminently entitled to the confidence & thanks of the Catholics of both countries. Both Catholics & Protestants in this country of all parties have endeavoured to run him down, & undervalue his exertions — some have blamed him because he would not follow the counsel of those who have no intention of serving us — others have censured him because he would be directed by the wishes of the catholics.[2] In these trying circumstances, Sir, I have observed him uniformly steady, & without wishing to appear victorious, by right & by left endeavouring to gain his object. I was in great hopes that he would have partially succeeded — but we are already at the end of the session, & it is too late to urge the resolutions *separately* as he intended.[3] He thought it best therefore to take a civil hint of those *in power*, & to appear to acquiesce in their wish to allow the subject to stand over the summer. In the divisions of both Houses, I think we have a very encouraging prospect.

Having written so much in commendation of Sir H. Parnell, I shall now freely express to you an other sentiment arising out of all I know & have witnessed, which is, that the Catholics of Ireland must place no dependence upon any but themselves. All else will be found to be very hollow — all else will be false. Your tepid friends & enimies [*sic*] have complained of your pretending to dictate[4] — believe me they only complain because you have put an end to their *fun*, & you have made them play the serious game of *pay or win*. I praise you much for what you have done & think you have done it in the style of *good controversy*. You know how we are situated in England — we can't do much, yet we might prove good seconds. Sir Hen. strongly recommends the catholics of England to address the Regent — and I should wish to put something forward before our Board stir in it.[5] Yet I only wish to see the English follow in the wake of the Irish — that we may have no cause for disunion. If you would send me over an address, I would endeavour to get it adopted. Sir H. recommends, that it be formed on the resolution on the journals of the House of Commons. I shall now conclude this letter, by saying, that I think the catholics are at the top of the Hill & completely overlook their enemies — and that it is only necessary for them, the catholics, to be steady, & to pay a little court to power.

Dr Poynter is not yet arrived — he is the bearer of three copies of a Brief — one for himself — another for Dr Troy — and an other for Dr Milner. It is a definitive act, & principally arranges everything regarding the election of Bishops.[6]

[*Source*: Scully Papers]

[1]Father Peter Gandolphy (1779–1821 — in *DNB*) had been censured by his Vicar Apostolic in London for two publications of 1812 and 1813 but had been supported by Dr Milner, who let them circulate in his district. In December 1815 he set off for Rome to appeal against the decision (Ward, *Eve of Catholic Emancipation* II, Ch. 18).

[2]In the debate on 30 May most speakers regretted the Catholics having forsaken Grattan and Parnell was taunted by Peel for letting himself be the agent of the Catholic Association.

[3]See No. 502 n.2.

[4]By drawing up their own relief bill (see No. 495).

[5]Peter Gandolphy was a member of the Board, to which he subscribed £1 in 1813.

[6]Dr Poynter reached London on 13 June, bringing with him the brief, addressed to him and signed by Cardinal Litta, known as the Genoese Letter. Drafted by a special Congregation of Cardinals it had been revised by the Pope himself and was dated 26

April. There were copies for Dr Troy and Dr Milner, which Dr Poynter immediately posted to them. The brief declared inadmissible any *exequatur* or *placet* but allowed the submission to the King's ministers of a list of candidates for a bishopric so that anyone who was obnoxious might be expunged. When emancipation was granted the Pope would issue another brief giving Catholics formal permission to accept it under conditions which had already been made known to the British government (Ward, ibid., p. 133).

514   *From Sir Henry Parnell addressed to Mr C. Mahon*
13 Merrion Square South, Dublin

London, 13 June 1815

My Dear Sir,

I have received your several letters to the 7th & the Cork & Belfast Papers. I have sent the former to the Office of the *Statesman*.[1] I could not get Ridgway[2] to publish the Bill but the Edr. of the *Pamphleteer*, a periodical work of considerable circulation, has promised to print it with the reading on it.[3]

I think it would be very well done to get the *Evg. Post* to publish Mr Grattan's Bill of 1795,[4] to shew what a House of Commons will do when directed by a minister.

One of the most intelligent & independent members of the House came up to me yesterday & said he was quite astonished at the progress your question had made, that the late debates had proved the opposition to it to be nearly worn out, & that he thought a Bill must pass next session. I mention this circumstance to you, as affording the strongest possible demonstration of the impression which has been made here, & also of the want of foundation for that which seems to have been made in Ireland. So far from anything that has passed being a just cause for despair or even disappointment, every thing leads to an inference of exactly opposite character.

Among those who are accustomed to hear frivolous excuses for bad votes, all that fell in the debate about agitators, securities etc. goes for nothing. Much of it is advanced on the calculation of irritating the Catholics, & leading them into acts of intemperance, in order to obtain new food for inaction & opposition. If you would always look forward, & never care about anything past, you would take the most effectual course of really annoying your enemies, & speedily accomplishing your measure. Feeling must give way to policy to fight the battle with every possible advantage. I have prepared the heads of what I think ought to be the subject of an address to the Regent, which I will send you in a day or two.[5].

[*Source*: Scully Papers]

[1]Not found in *The Statesman*.
[2]James Ridgway, bookseller, 170 Piccadilly.
[3]Not found in any number of *The Pamphleteer* in 1815.
[4]When in February 1795 Grattan applied for leave to bring in his bill only two members of the Irish House of Commons opposed him (Lecky, *History* III p. 287). Parnell evidently believed that it would have been carried without difficulty if Earl Fitzwilliam had not been recalled and policy in regard to the Catholics changed.
[5]Not found. In No. 530 Scully says it was sent in July.

515   *From Sir Henry Parnell addressed to Mr C. Mahon*
            13 Merrion Square South, Dublin

London, 17 June 1815

My Dear Sir,

I have received your letter enclosing one to me & shall attend to your wishes concerning it.

As I find no Paper has given with any thing like common fairness to the public the debate that took place last night on the Irish Budget, I think it right to let you know that Lord Castlereagh declared himself more explicitly & more earnestly desirous of *burying in oblivion all religious animosities* (his own words) than he ever did on any former occasion. In the last sentence of his speech he said, that he looked forward to the next session as likely to confer measures of great advantage on the British Empire by the more complete consumation of the Union of these Countries (meaning the consolidation of the Treasuries) & *not to the exclusion of that measure which had been alluded to by the Rt. Hon. Bart.* (Sir John Newport — the Catholic question). The words underlined are his own.[1] This is only one of many circumstances that daily occur to shew that you are much nearer gaining your end than your imagine.

Peel made a most liberal speech on education.[2]   [*Source*: Scully Papers[3]]

[1]The report on Lord Castlereagh's speech in *Hansard* XXXI, 880 makes no mention of either of the two passages underlined by Parnell.
[2]In the course of his speech (ibid., 878) Peel said he was convinced that "the only rational plan of education in Ireland, was one which should be extended impartially to children of all religious persuasions — one which did not profess to make converts — one which, while it imparted general religious instruction, left those who were its objects to obtain their particular religious discipline elsewhere".
[3]The next letter from Sir Henry Parnell in the Scully collection is that of 15 April 1816. As the original of No. 529, dated 19 December, is missing there may be others missing.

516   *From Revd John England[1] to Merrion Square, Dublin*

St Mary's College, Cork, 20 June 1815

My Dr Sir,

I was too much flattered by your kind letter & your opinion that my effusions have in any way contributed to do good at so critical a moment as the present has amply compensated as well as encouraged me.

My conviction of the necessity of having some paper open to truth for the public guidance & my knowledge of the mischievous principles of the generality of Editors, as well as the little interest which they or their employers feel, have led me to run great risks & take very great trouble. I am driven to be the registered proprietor of the *Chronicle*,[2] & since the departure of my friend McDonnell[3] I am Editor because I know of no one who is sufficiently honest & intelligent whom I might employ, & because the enmity of our false brethren & of our open foes have succeeded in crippling the establishment to such a degree as to make me hesitate before I would engage to pay such a one, could I find him, what he ought reasonably to expect, but what I might not be able easily to procure. For all this am I exposed to much calumny & vituperation from persons of every description & degree. I am imprudent, I am a politician, I am going quite out of my way as a clergyman etc., I am doing incalculable mischief. It is more fitting my character to instruct the people from the altar on Religious subjects, (which by the bye I do, at least twice on every Sunday) etc. etc. Under these circumstances since the departure of my friend Eneas, I have not one to assist me with a line for the *Chronicle* or the *Repertory*[4] & I am by my duty in this house to provide for the heads & bellies of 23 students besides attending to the Confessional & the pulpit. You would therefore do me an incalculable piece of service by furnishing me sometimes with the facts & I would add the arguments if you had not leisure to do so yourself & thus the *Chronicle* would sometimes have the appearance of "good controversy," for I am *determined* to hold to it in support of the Association, let the consequences be what they may.

But, Sir, with respect to the pamphlet, judge you, from my statement, of the great leisure which I have, I assure you I am not idle by day, nor do I dream by night. Yet if it could & ought to be done I would attempt it. You think it ought. In your next you will tell me if it could & your answer will determine me. In the first place then if I write I intend to put *my name* to the production for a variety of reasons, & principally, because I think any thing with *my name* will attract more attention. It is less subject to the attacks, particularly of anonymous scribblers, & facts which may be stated upon the mere authority of the writer will be better upheld. I have however no ambition to appear as an author if those reasons have no weight, & I see the consequences which I am to expect from jealousy, & malevolence, & from even well disposed but weak friends who will accuse me of pride, arrogance etc. etc. and who in conjunction with the enemies of my principles will attribute to me a thousand motives, not one of which I ever had. In the next place, though I do not stand in need of my Bishop's[5] leave, still I would wish his sanction. I believe he is at present in Dublin. Again, Pamphlets published in a Provincial town never circulate for the printers of the Metropolis prevent their circulation. I have *paid* for this knowledge. Then the only way would be, as I want no profit, to find a printer who would do it *on his own acct.* in Dublin, & engage to give suppose 500 copies, *not to be sold*, & not more than *20* to be given gratis *in Ireland* except to Members of Parliament, the copies thus obtained to be distributed where they may be deemed most serviceable in England. The little work itself to be an address to the Irish Catholics on the present posture of their affairs. Moderate in its manner, well founded in its facts, correct in its principles, calculated to shew the Protestant that he has nothing to apprehend & the Catholic that he has nothing to sacrifice, soothing him without relinquishing a particle of right, & as decently written in a plain style as my pen would allow.[6]

I see much for & against but if you think anything in that way can be done in the manner that I have suggested, I shall begin to send manuscript before this day week, & finish from 80 to 100 octavo pages of good moderate size type in less than three weeks.

I would be better pleased the task was committed to a more able person, but I know it could not be entrusted to one more honest.

We have regularly sent those papers which could interest Sir H. Parnell, to him, to others who may be pleased or *vexed* at reading them.

[P.S.] Your letter to the *Chron.* office will reach me six hours sooner than to the College. I feel much obliged for your kindness in forwarding my letter to Mr O'Connell.[7]   [*Source*: Scully Papers]

[1]1786–1842. President of St Mary's College, Cork 1812–17; parish priest of Bandon 1817–20; Bishop of Charleston, South Carolina, 1820–42.

[2]The *Cork Mercantile Chronicle*, of which he had taken over the trusteeship in 1813 (Peter Guilday; *Life and Times of John England*, New York 1927).

[3]To be editor and proprietor of the *Dublin Chronicle*, the first number of which came out on 26 June 1815.

[4]The *Religious Repertory*, which he himself had founded in Cork to diffuse a spirit of piety (M. Comerford, *Diocese of Kildare and Leighlin* I, p. 174).

[5]Dr John Murphy.

[6]Not found. On 16 October 1815 the Protestant Dean of Cork sent the Home Secretary a tract which he said was generally believed to be by "a friar in this city, of the name of England". It had not, he said, been openly published but was to be had without difficulty. There had been a temporary suspension occasioned by the desire to get legal advice from O'Connell. The Protestant Bishop had remonstrated with Dr

Murphy "who fully agreed in the mischievousness of its dissemination and said he had done all in his power to prevent publication, but in vain" (HO 100/187, f.125).
[7]Not in O'Connell, *Correspondence*.

517   *From a notebook*

Wednesday, 28 June 1815

This day I have agreed with Mr Rich. Newton Bennett of Harcourt Street — barrister — for the sale to him of my dwelling house, offices, stables & premises in No. 2 Merrion Square, South, as follows

"Lease about 150 years from 1788 —
   Rent £60 —
   Fine £1772 — payable in 3 years — and interest in meantime
          half yearly."

"The articles upon the premises to go with the house (except only the two mirror glasses pier table & side lustre in the drawing room — & the hanging bookshelf in the study —

I am to be entitled to repurchase the premises & furniture aforesd. (for myself or for any of Mrs Scully's family) at any time after 3 years and before 6 years at the same upon giving six months notice

D.S.

Rent from the 1st July,
Taxes to be paid up.[1]   [*Source*: Scully Papers]

[1]By the middle of May Scully had been giving 13 Merrion Square as his new address (see No. 499).

518   *From Bishop John Milner to Post Office, Golden,*
                            Co. Tipperary

Alfreton, Derbyshire, 3 August 1815

My Dear Sir,

It is a fact that I have been very little at home since I returned from the continent.[1] I was absent when your letter arrived at Wolverhampton & I am now engaged in visiting the Northern parts of my District. These circumstances will account for my not acknowledging the honour of yours sooner. I can give little account of my pilgrimage to Rome except that from the first of my arrival there I found that Quarantotti's rescript was disapproved of & its author was in disgrace.[2] This & other business connected with it was not done in that explicit handsome manner that we wished & expected during my residence in that capital, owing to the dilatoriness of the Sovereigns &

their ministers at Vienna. Still the Rescript, is in a general way & this authentically rejected, whether any other plan may be adopted in its place is more than I can say.[3]

I have made every inquiry in my power after a tutor for yr. children,[4] such as you describe, but have been unable to find one whom I could recommend. The young as you say are giddy & the old (who are unemployed) mostly vicious.

I have ceased for this year & a half to have anything to do with the *Dublin Evening Post*. It was Mrs Wheble who took it in & paid for it during all that period. Latterly she became disgusted with it & ordered it to be discontinued. At the same time hearing a good account of a Weekly Irish Paper called *The Sentinel*,[5] in which you were supposed occasionally to write, she got a friend to order it to be sent to her. She had not, however, received a single number of it when I saw her last which mortified her much. She thinks that in addition to *the English Papers* which she takes in, a *Weekly Irish Paper* will be sufficient for her purpose. For my part, as I have been mostly absent from home of late, so I expect to be absent for a long time to come.

I presume you have been informed of Mr Wheble's second marriage[6] & that the object of his choice was an Irish Lady, or at least the daughter of an Irish Gentleman, the late worthy Major O'Brien. I have long known her & her merit. This at present is known to & acknowledged by a great proportion of the English Cathc. Gentry.

I applaud the perseverance of the Irish in asserting their claims, but cd. wish they would confine themselves to the proper objects of them. As an Irish deputy I was called to a severe account by the leading Cardls. at Rome, in consequence of your interfering in the dispute between the Prince & the Princess.[7] I saw yr. friend Genl Mathews[8] both before & after his expedition to Naples. Of course you formed part of [?our] conversation on both occasions.

I beg my kind compts. to Mrs Scully . . .   [*Source*: Scully Papers]

[1]By the middle of May (see No. 502).

[2]Although the rescript was set aside Monsignor Quarantotti continued to be Secretary of Propaganda and was made a Cardinal in 1816 (Ward, *Eve of Catholic Emancipation* II, pp. 101, 109).

[3]More than he cared to tell Scully. He had received the Genoese Letter which replaced the rescript and had written to Dr Troy about it on 31 July (Ward, ibid. p. 138).

[4]The eldest of whom was nearly six.

[5]*The Sentinel and Herald Evening Post*, the first number of which appeared on 22 June 1814. It was not a weekly, being published on Mondays, Wednesdays and Fridays.

[6]His first wife having died in July 1814 at the age of thirty-four, leaving him with five infant daughters, James Wheble had on 21 June 1815 married Mary, eldest daughter of the late Major Timothy O'Brien.

[7]On 15 June 1813 (see N. 483 n.2).

[8]General Montagu Mathew, according to Scully (No. 512) rambling about Italy.

519   *From a notebook*

[6] September 1815

Travelling — Memorandum — 1815
Sept. 5 & 6.
My two black horses, aged 11 years, performed the following journey —
    Sept. 5 Tuesday — They drew the carriage and 7 persons (Mrs S[cully]
and Bridget[1] — & W[m][2] & 4 children) and 5 trunks — besides bundles and
parcels —
                    from Kilfeacle to Maryborough —
    44 miles Irish = 56 English — in 3 stages only — from 5¼ in morning to 7
O'clock in evening — including 2¾ hours rest —
    that is 56 miles English in 11 hours = 5 miles per hour.
    Sept. Wednesday — They drew the same, from Maryborough to Merrion
Square —
    40 miles Irish = 51 English — In 3 stages from 6 in morning to 6 in evening
— including 2½ hours rest
    that is, 51 miles English in 9½ hours = 5⅓ miles per hour.

[*Source*: Scully Papers]

[1]Bridget Motleigh, a nursery maid.
[2]William Fitzpatrick, the coachman.

520   *From a notebook*

7 September 1815

Coals etc at Rathmacan[1]
Recd. two letters from Nich[s] Lalor — as follows — announcing discovery of
culm pit on top of Rathmacan hill
    Seam 20 inches thick — depth of 12 feet from surface.
    Also another pit, seam 36 inches — depth 13 feet from surface.
    Also another at the but of the hill near Widow Maher's house — seam 24
inches — depth 11 feet
Sept. 3 Mr Nicholas Fanning — Grand Canal Director — wrote upon this
            subject for me to Mr. Ross — the Grand Canal Engineer — at
            Domane colliery — to go, and inspect; & examine mine.

[*Source*: Scully Papers]

[1]In the parish of Tullaroan, Co. Kilkenny. It was one of Scully's properties and left in
his will to his son Thomas.

521   *From Richard Newton Bennett*

Newberry [Co. Kildare] 8 September 1815

Private

My dear Scully,

I have your letter of yesterday for which I thank you, not having recd any answer to my letter & concluding it had missed you, I went to town to pay my note, & left the money in the hands of Laughton[1] the day it came due to pay it when called for, but if I am obliged to go to a distance on a sudden mission I may perhaps avail myself of your kind offer, unless some funds I expect arrive before my departure, but at all events it shall be taken up within the time I mentioned.[2]

From the manner in which you mention recent occurrences in Dublin you seem to be unacquainted with the part I have had in them. I was in town at the commencement of the business,[3] but the first step was taken an hour or two before I was consulted. I would have acted quite differently & in a way that I am convinced would have put an end to the matter in an amicable manner. The affair proceeded & Saxton bungled so egregiously that he gave his enemy the advantage, got nothing for his friend. No publication took place for a day after the transaction appeared to close, & things appearing quiet I left town. Then comes the publication,[4] & O'Connell's impudent letter giving *fresh* offences without which P[eel] must have remained in the mire where his friend had flung him,[5] & without which if he had sent a message, his doing so would have been condemnation out of his own mouth of his former step, but this letter overthrew all my calculations & gave opening which was immediately taken advantage of. I was one day here when an express arrived here about 3. o'clock on Tuesday morning from O'C[onnell] requiring me to go out with him. I was in town at 9 o'c. & found him in the custody of the Sheriff!! You must have heard what caused this unfortunate occurrence, & how suspicious a circumstance it is.[6] I was deputed to meet P's friend, feeling as I did the impression of the town & of P[eel] agt O'C[onnell] & G[eorge] L[idwill] I knew nothing remained for me to do in order to redeem what was in danger but to make demonstrations of great promptness as if indignant at the disappointment. It took well, the impression was removed & at the second or third interview I recd the acknowledgements of our opponents for the manner in which the affair was conducted. O'C then demands the delay of a week or 10 days — no time will be given — I entered into a contract in writing fully empowered by him to do so — I urge the necessity of acting quickly & decisively — he pleads his wife — Imagine my situation — I am reduced to the necessity of special pleading on the terms of the contract to cover his retreat while he takes his wife to the country. I am in the most extreme anxiety lest he will be unpunctual, if so all is ruin — if he is disgraced you can have no conception what injury it will do your affairs. The thing has been but poorly managed up to this time but now I promise you that the termination will be creditable holding him with the check[7] I have over him if I can get him away from his *wife* in time. No man will do better if led up as he ought but he has so much kindness & softness of heart that he requires to be held by a firm hand, who has more real regard for him than he has for himself. How unfortunate that you were not in town one day sooner![8] What wd I give to see you for half an hour? I would go to you but I am watched here; I wrote a letter to you (which I have destroyed) under my first impression on receiving yours begging of you to take a ride down here on Sunday, but I saw that was unreasonable, tho' I did not request it on my own account, but could I see you I have much to say on these subjects that I cannot write. I beg of you to write to him not to lose a moment in meeting me.[9]   [*Source*: Scully Papers]

[1]There is no such spelling in the directory: possibly Leslie Lawton, law agent, of 20 South Anne Street.

[2]Probably in connexion with his purchase of Scully's house (see No. 517).

[3]The arrangements for the duel between O'Connell and Peel, starting from Sir Charles Saxton's call on O'Connell on 31 August to ask him to explain a passage in a speech of 29 August accusing Peel of saying in parliament what he dared not utter about O'Connell elsewhere. The details given in the present letter cannot be fully understood without reference to the Peel Papers (Add.MSS.40, 201) but the main facts are given by Fagan, *Life and times of Daniel O'Connell* I, p. 163 ff.

[4]In the *Dublin Chronicle* of 4 September.

[5]Gregory, in a letter of 3 September to the Lord Lieutenant (Add.MSS.40, 201, f.213) said: "I never could assist to raise him [O'Connell] out of the mire in which he now flounders . . .".

[6]At the instance of his wife O'Connell had been arrested by the sheriff: Bennett evidently feared that this would be regarded by the Castle as a trick, to evade the encounter with Peel.

[7]The contract mentioned above, signed by Bennett and Colonel Samuel Browne, who now represented Peel. The parties were to make all convenient speed to Ostend, but if either found it necessary to delay the journey he could exercise the option by informing the other.

[8]Bennett left Dublin for Edenderry sometime after 2 p.m. on 6 September. Scully presumably arrived later the same day although he did not travel with his family in the same coach (see No. 519).

[9]Scully's role seems to have been to maintain liaison between O'Connell's friends and probably deal with the press. He may also have used his old friend Robert Marshall to keep the Castle informed (Gregory to Peel 8 September 1815. Add.MSS.40, 201, f.222).

522   *From Richard Newton Bennett to 13 Merrion Square South,*
Dublin

8 September [1815]

Private

My dear Scully,

Inclosed you have a letter to yourself & others which after reading you will have the goodness to have put in the post. You will judge by my letter to O'C how I feel & what I think *necessary* to state to *him*. I expected to have been able to have sent you the papers signed & letters between Brown[1] & me but time would not allow. My family have no idea how I stand, & how to deceive them I know not but I cannot leave our friend to chance & *too friendly* advisers. Let me have a line by the post. I send this by the boat,[2] having got my letters too late for the post. & insure their delivery in time I tax you 10d[3] — adieu.   [*Source*: Scully Papers]

[1]See No. 521 n.7.
[2]His home, Newberry Hall, Carbury, near Edenderry, Co. Kildare, was about two miles from the Grand Canal.
[3]He wrote on the cover: "Give the bearer 10 Pence if this letter is delivered before halfpast 12 o'clock tomorrow".

523   *From Daniel O'Connell, Waterford, to Merrion Square,*
13 September 1815

He is disappointed at not meeting Bennett. He asks Scully to get McDonnell[1] and Sugrue[2] to send a horse express for him and urge him to be at Waterford as soon as possible. They will sail in the evening packet and have decided not to travel under feigned names.

[*Source*: O'Connell, *Correspondence* II No. 584, taken
from the now missing original in the Scully Papers]

[1]Probably Eneas MacDonell.
[2]James Sugrue, an unidentified financial agent of O'Connell (O'Connell, *Correspondence* I, No. 323).

524   *From Daniel O'Connell, Cheltenham, 16 September 1815*

On arrival at Milford their names had been carefully taken down. Bennett had reached them at Waterford. They would reach London tomorrow, procure passports on Monday, reach Dover on Tuesday, Calais on Wednesday. On Thursday their affair would be over. Bennett bids him say that the enemy had not the least advantage in the time consumed.[1]

[*Source*: O'Connell, *Correspondence* II, No. 585, taken from the now missing original in the Scully Papers]

[1]Peel's arrival at Dover on the 13th and at Ostend on the 15th were reported in the press (Fagan, *O'Connell* I, p. 192).

525   *From Daniel O'Connell to Merrion Square,*
                 20 September 1815

What a glorious opportunity had they not deprived him of, living or dying! The Chief Magistrate at Bow Street[1] had intimated to him that any fatal consequence would now be followed up by a rigorous prosecution and a certain execution in case of conviction. A hundred constables on the coast had been awaiting their arrival, but their adversaries had been allowed to go on unimpeded. The scoundrels could now safely calumniate them.

[*Source*: O'Connell, *Correspondence* II No. 588, taken from the now missing original in the Scully Papers]

[1]Having obtained passports for France and Holland O'Connell had been arrested in London on 19 September as he was setting off for Dover and conducted to Bow Street (Fagan, *O'Connell* I, p. 194).

526   *From Revd F. J. L'Estrange, Clarendon Street,*
                 to Merrion Square, 22 September 1815

Scully is asked for his advice about two gold watches in the writer's possession. They had been illicitly acquired but had been accepted by a certain Horish,[1] who died in December 1811, in lieu of rent. Horish had been persuaded to give them up but a person claiming to be acting for his son was now demanding them.   [*Source*: Scully Papers]

[1]Probably Wiliam Horish of Pye Corner, of whom there is an obituary in the January 1812 number of the *Irish Magazine*, where he is described as an opulent chimney-sweeper and a man of upright character. The March issue adds that he was flogged on 29 May 1798 after the outbreak of the rebellion.

527   *From Bishop John Milner to Merrion Square, Dublin*

Woodley Lodge, 9 October 1815

My Dear Sir,

For a variety of reasons, which it would take too much time & paper to state, I was particularly obliged to you for your late letter.[1] I found that letter on one of those short flying visits which I have been in the habit of paying my home since my return from Italy, & I could not find a leisure minute to acknowledge the rect. of it till I arrived at this pleasant & hospitable place where I now am for the third time since the above mentioned period for the purpose of reconducting Mrs Wheble Senr. to Wolverhampton. Mr Wheble does not consider it as an extraordinary circumstance that you shd. not have heared of his marriage[2] from his aunt or cousins[3] [?as] he considers them as very irregular correspondents. He charges me as does his Lady also (who has the rare fortune of pleasing & being commended by all mankind) with his kind compts. He again requests me to tell you what he desired me to tell you, two or three years ago, that he will be exceedingly happy to see you & Mrs Scully at Woodley whenever you visit England.

The Duke of Norfolk has twice called upon me of late, but never mentioned the business of Mr Fitzpatrick on which I wrote to him,[4] as you desired: probably he keeps up no acquaintance with the Duke of Richmond. The latter has now had his revenge, & the printer is, I trust not the worse for it: while the *State. of the Penal Laws* lives in every creditable library, & will continue to enlighten liberal statesmen till it produces its proper effect in the abrogation of those laws. By what I learn from the Prelates of Ireland, two of whom spent a day with me about a month ago on their way to Rome,[5] Mr O'Connel's hasty sortie upon me[6] has not injured me more, than His Grace of Richmond's malice now injures Mr Fitzpatrick: I should bear him no malice, had he actually hurt me, as I am & I trust, ever have been guided by a steady conscientious principle of zeal for the independency of one of the fairest portions of the Catholic Church & not by a contemptible lust of fame in whatever I have done or written respecting it. You have seen my letter to the Editor of the *Dublin Chronicle*[7] on the business, which letter expresses my genuine sentiments concerning it. I fear the grand deceiver,[8] (I mean the man who betrayed your Prelates into the Resolutions of 1799 & your laity into a consent to the Legislative Union) has, in part, deceived Cardl. Consalvi, on the subject now under discussion: to this unconsecrated[9] Secretary of State & not to the High Church Bishop, Card. Litta, the late letter from Genoa is to be ascribed. As matters have turned out, I am sorry I did not accept of the latter's invitation to stay with the Papal court till he could reconduct me in his own carriage to Rome:[10] but really when I set off

for England, there was every prospect of Murat's conquering the whole of
Italy, including Genoa, & the only question among the Cardinals was
whether to fly to Sardinia or to Spain.[11]

I again repeat the compts. of Mr & Mrs Wheble to you & Mrs Scully to
which I must add those of Mrs Wheble, Senr. I beg mine to your good
Lady . . .

P.S. Mrs Wheble says she was well acquainted with Mrs Scully at the York
Barr.[12]

I presume you give up all expectation of justice from government, saving
from what commotions may grow out of the general discontent of Europe.

[*Source*: Scully Papers]

[1]Dated 16 September, a missing reply to No. 518.
[2]See No. 518 n.6.
[3]Mrs Wheble senior, and the brothers and sisters of Scully's wife.
[4]See No. 475.
[5]Dr Murray, coadjutor Archbishop of Dublin, and Dr Murphy, the new Bishop of
Cork, had been deputed by a synod held on 23 and 24 August to go to Rome to
protest against the Genoese Letter (Ward, *Eve of Catholic Emancipation* II, p. 146).
[6]At an aggregate meeting on 29 August O'Connell accused Dr Milner of having
written to the Irish Bishops asking them to accede to the veto plan of the Genoese
Letter (*DEP*, 30 August 1815).
[7]The *Dublin Chronicle* is not available but the correspondence is reprinted in the
September number of the *Orthodox Journal*.
[8]Lord Castlereagh.
[9]Cardinal Consalvi was not an ordained priest.
[10]He says in his *Supplementary Memoirs*, p. 335 that the Pope wished to keep him
until the Congress of Vienna and the Italian troubles were ended.
[11]After the escape of Napoleon from Elba Joachim Murat, King of Naples since
1808, had advanced north and occupied Rome.
[12]Dr Milner misunderstood. Scully's wife was at the Barr convent until she went to
New Hall, but James Wheble's wife, Mary O'Brien, was only at New Hall.

From a notebook

9 November 1815

Gave to Mr Thomas Warren 42 Prussia Street (recommended by Mr
Hatchell)[1] the first part, a thick one, of my father's old journal[2] commencing
in 1773 — to be copied out fair at two pence per sheet of 72 words (also my
MS Precedents, Volume 7 to write in).[3]   [*Source*: Scully Papers]

[1]Probably the John Patrick Hatchell, son of a Dublin merchant, who was called to the
bar in 1809 and published the report on the trial of Dr Edward Sheridan referred to in
No. 319.

[2]A fragment of the original survives, in a very fragile condition, along with the manuscript copy and a typescript copy made by Denys Scully's grandson, Vincent Scully (NLI MSS.27,479, 27,571, 27,579).
[3]An entry of 14 July 1816 in Scully's account book (MS 27,493) shows that Warren had then received £15–0–1 for copying the journal from 1774 to 1813; and that a further 2/6 had been spent on binding.

529   *From Sir Henry Parnell*

Copy/draft   19 December 1815
My dear Sr,

As I see by the *Chronicle*[1] that it is intended to submit to the Association a communication from me, I feel anxious that such a communication should be strictly confined to the subject of the proposed Address to the Regent, the other subjects of conversation at your house being discussed, as I conceive, incidentally & without any idea of being made public.

In order to avoid any misunderstanding in respect to my opinion of the expediency of addressing the Regent, I take this opportunity of restating the grounds on which I have recommended it.

I think that when a body of the people forming so large a part of the power and population of these kingdoms seek from the legislature the redress of a grievance of such magnitude as the exclusion from the enjoyment of the most essential rights of the constitution they ought to submit their case to each of the three branches of it.

If they do not address the executive they do not give it the opportunity of originating in the most effectual manner those proper measures of relief, secured by a government measure, which it is your interest to obtain.

If the Address should contain a request to the Regent to recommend the situation of the Catholics to the consideration of Parliament the Ministers will necessarily lay such an address before the Cabinet for their advice to the Regent in respect to the answer to be given to it & in this way that portion of the Cabinet which is favourable to the Catholics will have an opportunity of exerting their influence in the manner the most likely to prove of the greatest service to their interests. The Catholic question will thus become a Cabinet question, all the various considerations which at this moment point out the expediency of a final settlement of it, in the utter absence of any one reason for further postponement of it, must give great weight to the opinion of those members of the Cabinet who have already supported it, & may possibly induce the minister himself to think the time is arrived, when according to his own voluntary acknowledgment,[2] he can himself abandon all further opposition to it, & give his aid to render the measure of redress as satisfactory as practicable to those who are to be benefitted by it.

Again if the Address shall contain as it no doubt will a spirited but respectful appeal to the Regent, it may induce him to reconsider what has been the conduct of the Catholics during the period he has discharged the duties of the Executive, & thereby to learn that they have done nothing which ought to deprive them of that protection which he was disposed to give them when forming a new administration to succeed that of Mr Perceval.

If also on the subject of securities the address shall explain that the opposition which the Catholics have made to them has not originated in any perverse or prejudged view of the question, or in any disinclination to conciliate & to satisfye adverse opinions, but that it has been the result of an apprehension that securities as set forth to them were calcu[lated] to be so framed as to shake the Catholic religion, & to give the crown an influence which would be inconsistent with the constitutional rights & liberties of the subject, this explanation would place the question on such grounds, as would remove much of the repugnance that prevails & serve to give the general question at this time a calm & dispassionate hearing. There could be no objection to the accompanying such an explanation with a declaration that the Catholic Body can never consent to any conditions which shall in any way injure their religion or compromise their liberties.

To give to the proposed address its fullest effect in attaining its legitimate object, namely the favourable reception of the Catholic Petition by Parliament, it is necessary that it should be presented by delegates capable of giving to ministers & to the leading parliamentary friends of the Catholics the most satisfactory explanations of the extent of what is required to be conceded & of the best method of framing a bill of relief. It will be most essential to secure the service of Lord Fingal.[3] Such explanations would remove almost all the difficulties in the way of a legislative measure as these have arisen for the most part either from the misrepresentations of that class of opponents who practise any artifice to defeat the objects of the Catholics, or from the misapprehensions of those who have had no opportunity of perfectly comprehending the circumstances as they really are under which the Catholics of Ireland present themselves as claimants on the justice of the legislature.

Having said so much in compliance with the request which has been made of me to communicate my sentiments to the Association on the manner proper to be adopted in respect to a new application to Parliament, I also take the liberty of offering a few remarks on an advertisement I have read today,[4] of a special meeting of the Association to take into its consideration a communication from Rome. As this refers to the letter of Cardinal Litta[5] I conclude the discussion which it is intended to have upon it will be in point of fact a new discussion of the question of securities. If that is the case I do not hesitate to express great regret that it should apear adviseable to stir again that question in any way whatever until it shall be regularly & duly brought forward, if it ever shall be, either by Government or by some vote of Parliament, because in the first place such discussion must inevitably counteract in a great degree the tendency of addressing the Regent to improve the state of public opinion; & secondly, because after all that has been so often set forth in repeated resolutions there can be no necessity whatever for any further exposition of the sentiments of the Catholic body. As in point of fact the question of Emancipation has been conceded by the House of Commons in principle it appears to me the benefit of public discussion has been completely obtained — & that what remains to be done is more properly the business of private & amicable communication between the heads of the Catholics & their leading Parliamentary friends — The whole of their efforts conducted in the most cautious & able manner are wanting to secure complete success, & therefore, it is more than probable that every step which is taken of a different character will create some new difficulty. I give this opinion very freely & very decidedly because the opportunity I have had of weighing all the circumstances with great deliberation & of communication with the best friends of the cause has fully convinced me of its correctness.

The more I have the means of judging of the probable impression which will be produced by simply confining the measures of the Association to recommending application to be made to each branch of the Legislature, to be supported by the assistance of a well supported deputation, the more I am satisfied that such a course will at the same [time] the most effectually put down the efforts which are making to defeat its objects, & most powerfully contribute to induce all the friends of emancipation to make a great exertion to carry that measure in the ensuing session. It is to this conviction I have to refer you for my apology in so warmly pressing my opinion & so strongly opposing that of others — which appears not to coincide with it.

[*Source*: Congleton Papers]

[1]Not extant, but probably followed by the *Orthodox Journal* which in its December number p. 474 reported that at the meeting of the Catholic Association on 25 November a sub-committee had been appointed to confer with Sir Henry Parnell, who was then in Dublin. This no doubt met in Scully's house.
[2]In his speech in the House of Lords on 8 June (*Hansard* XXXI, 681) Lord Liverpool had spoken of the possibility of some change in the Catholic Church or in the opinion of the Irish Catholics but "for the present he was of the opinion that no concession which the legislature might prudently grant would meet a graceful reception from the Catholics".
[3]For the last attempt at a reconciliation with Lord Fingall and the seceders see No. 489 n.1.
[4]The advertisement has not been found.
[5]The so-called Genoese Letter of 26 April allowing the crown a form of veto (see No. 513 n.6). Having been suppressed by its three recipients, Dr Poynter, Dr Milner and

Dr Troy, it was now to be made public for the first time as a result of the Pope's having given a copy to Revd R. Hayes. It was read at the Association on 22 December and published in the *Freeman's Journal* of 26 December (the text in the *Orthodox Journal* was taken from the *Dublin Chronicle*).

530   *To Sir Henry Parnell*

Merrion Square, 20 December [1815]

private

My dear Sir,

Your very valuable and important letter of the 19th[1] has just reached me. It is a fresh proof of your solicitude & sincerity in the good cause. It comes critically, and, I trust, fortunately, for the prevention of error & mischief.

I write, first, to thank you cordially — next, to ask, whether it is not your wish, or (in other words) whether you do not think it useful, to have this letter read to the Association on Friday?[2] — and, if so, to drop me a line by the return of the post.

Next, I wish to relieve your mind from any apprehension of indiscreet or too familiar a use of your name in the intended communication, announced in the *D[ublin] Chronicle*[3] — Like you, I felt rather startled at first, when I read the Notice — I lost not a moment in applying to the proper quarters, and making it a point peremptorily, that your name shall not be bandied about, or loose conversation quoted, or the remotest mention made of any meeting at my house. This was acceded to, and the arrangement is simply this — "that the Address to the Regent shall be urged and hastened, that for this purpose the authority of your name shall be adduced *generally*, as warmly recommending it, and as deeming it to be a most useful measure". It is quite agreed, that, in the Address to the R., not a word shall be said of securities, one way or the other — he is merely to be prayed "to recommend to his Houses of Parlt. the favourable consideration of our case — It is also agreed, that the Address shall consist of the excellent topics, so judiciously recommended by you in July last.[4] So far, I trust you will feel no alarm. This is the course I expect to be taken. If it be deviated from, it shall not be my fault. Latterly I have not attended at the meetings of the Association — in order that our pecuniary engagements may be discharged — & to shame individuals into the necessary measures for raising a fund.

Permit me now to offer a few words respecting the matter of your letter. In every sentiment & word of it, I heartily concur. It is only with reference to the publication or (what is the same thing) the public reading of it at the Association,[5] that I would beg leave to suggest the alteration of one or two passages, upon prudential grounds. I make no apology, as I am sure you will not impute to me any but fair & upright motives.

First, then, I would omit the second sentence — as it refers to a private conversation at my house. This may excite jealousies against me, tho' no doubt it would reflect honour etc etc upon me: but my views are never personal, upon this question. It may do you some harm also — and your main object & the meaning, may stand as well without this sentence.[6]

Secondly — the excellent suggestions — respecting the effect of an Address upon our friends in the Cabinet — may not these passages (in page 3 etc) lay open our proceedings too much to the enemy — or is it quite discreet to give them this vein? Upon this topic, I merely doubt.[7]

Thirdly, your proposed mode of introducing the mention of securities is so very eligible & excellent, that it subdues my aversion to the introduction of the subject.

Fourthly — In page 6, you say — "It will be most essential to secure the services of Lord Fingall." I greatly fear, that this may tend to divisions, to strengthen the Seceders, Grattanites etc; and bolster up a man who, tho' a good private character, is (*entre nous*) very dangerous to our real independence. He has been the instrument of much mischief, during the last 2 years — Could we not expunge this sentence?[8]

Fifthly — I perfectly concur in your objections to any further discussions about Rome, the veto etc — and I hope the proceedings of Friday will not extend beyond the mere reading of the documents.

I am persuaded that your letter, coming at this juncture, will have a decisive influence upon the Catholic Body. I know it will be scanned & scrutinized minutely, by friends & enemies, and it is therefore that I wish it to be above all exception. At the same time I freely admit, that I am not at all confident in the validity of my objections — I merely submit them to you in order to be favoured with your decision by the post of Friday morning.

It is my earnest wish, that this great & happy work of our Emancipation may be effected next session — and that it may be effected thro' you, and by your means. It is but common sense & common justice, that you should be armed by us with every aid in our power — & that to you the Regent & his Ministers may ascribe the merit of taming our intemperance, reclaiming our waywardness and guiding us by gentleness & good humour to the fold of freedom — I think it will be done now — tho' my sanguine expectations have been so often & so grievously disappointed.

I have some intention of troubling you in a post or two upon another branch of this subject — but this need not delay your favouring me with an answer upon the pressing topics.[9]   [*Source*: Congleton Papers]

[1]No. 529.
[2]22 December.
[3]See No. 529, 1st paragraph.
[4]See No. 514 n.5.
[5]A revised version of the letter was read out to the meeting on 22 December and

published in the *Freeman's Journal* of 26 December. Its date was changed to 20 December.

[6]The difficulty was got over by omitting the whole of the first paragraph.

[7]The passage was left in and duly noted by Peel, who in a letter of 9 February 1816 from the Irish Office paraphrased it for Lord Sidmouth as stating that the members of the Cabinet friendly to the Catholics "would probably overpower their colleagues who are adverse" (HO 100/189, f.92).

[8]The sentence was omitted.

[9]Sir Henry Parnell's reply is missing — the next letter from him is that of 15 April 1816, No. 536.

531   *From Bernard Wright*

Clonmel, 30 December 1815

Dear Sir,

I expect you'll pardon the freedom I make in hastily writing these few lines without a frank. Lord D.[1] was not here today. The faction unmask[ed][2] is bandied about as a complete piece of oratory. I just now perused it, & wrote the following:

> *Here* impotent faction with pen of detraction
> Assail some great Catholic Leaders
> But Framers of lies are all Knaves in disguise
> Vile orange men — cowardly Seceders.
> *Arrangements* are made with the Church it is said
> The *prince* our high priest has bought over
> By Government pension (how much we can't mention)
> Our Clergy will *now* live in Clover
> Oh strange reformation in this happy Nation
> We now must yield *foreign* obedience
> The *pope* & the *King* will both settle the thing
> And dispense with our Oath of Allegiance.

Again Dr Sir I ask pardon for this intrusion, but nothing of *this sort* would get admission in the papers here & I feel for the subject, & I thought you should be acquainted with the pulse of the *Literati* in our quarter who are so highly delighted with the production of Young Gr-t-n[3] as tis called. Should you allow me the favour of addressing y[ou?] I shall make some observations on a *Sermon* lately published here for the benefit of the Widows & orphans caused by the Battle of Waterloo, at present I shall only mention that the *Revd* preacher said that "popery is not yet subdued."

[*Source*: Scully Papers]

[1]Donoughmore, who had been behind the attack on John Bagwell in the *Clonmell*

Gazette which cost Wright his post as editor when Bagwell was awarded damages for libel in July 1804. Scully assisted Curran in this case as one of the junior counsel for the defence (W. P. Burke, *History of Clonmel*, p. 349; *DEP*, 1 August 1804).

[2]*Faction Unmasked — A letter to the Roman Catholics of Ireland on the conduct of certain men who compose the Catholic Junta*, 1815. It had come out by the beginning of December, when O'Connell threatened the publisher with prosecution (*FJ*, 9 December 1815). In a long catalogue of the sins and follies of the Catholic leadership it picked particularly on O'Connell and Scully.

[3]The attribution to Henry Grattan's son remains conjectural.

532   *From Bernard Wright to Merrion Square, Dublin*

Clonmel, 4 January 1816

Franked by Lord Donoughmore

Dear Sir,

I mentioned in the letter[1] I wrote in haste that I should wait yr permission to address you but I met Lord D. just now, and as you must *entre nous*, know *everything*, he asked me as he was writing the address how I would have it *directed*. Merion Square — Won't *Ireland* do? — he is such a great man he may be offended? — I hope my Lord (wishing to *pun* a little) Ireland will do after all — yes after all the abuse I got, but you must not tell Skully a word of *this* or there would be a paragraph as long as my arm in the next *Chronicle*. — My Lord, I heard Mr Sk. speak of yr L. Sh'p in terms of great respect. Oh Skully is a great man, & so are O'G ——n & O'C———l & who is the other?[2] — I am not able to *stenograph* the rest — nor to mention what wd be of more importance now. I shall only state that our *Clonmel press* refused the following *Epigram* "*quorum pars magna fui*" tho' it was innocent. It might give *offence*.

> "Come where your wise *forefathers* went,
> Forsake the Pope, old Mass & Lent,
> Said *Martin* to his cousin *Peter*
> (Names of renown in prose & metre)
> Peter rejoined farewell — adieu,
> For I can never go with you,
> And much I fear to leave you in the lurch,
> Should you require an explanation,
> Tis this — that since the Reformation,
> *Three of my Fathers* only went to Church."
> Should you wish to know anything of the *Revd*
> Gentleman of whom I gave a hint, it shall be at yr service.

[*Source*: Scully Papers]

[1]No. 531.

[2]For the beginning of Lord Donoughmore's dissatisfaction with the Catholic leaders see No. 464 n.3. On 30 December 1815 he was speaking to Edward Hay of "your shabby agitators". As for Scully, he was on 30 January 1815 "that little Jewish conspirator who puts others forward to satisfy his own malignity" (DDA 390/1, XI, 29). Lord Donoughmore suspected him of being the author or instigator of attacks on him in the *Dublin Evening Post* (Donoughmore Papers, F/10/109) and until 5 March 1817, when he again became "that noble lord who has always been true to our cause" he was regularly abused and ridiculed in the *Dublin Chronicle*.

533   *From Bishop John Milner to Merrion Square, Dublin*

Wolverhampton, 1 February 1816

My Dear Sir,

For the last three weeks or more Mrs Wheble & myself have been very uneasy concerning the health of Mrs Scully, as we had heared that Mrs Eyre with Juliana etc. had left Arundel[1] in haste to attend her in Dublin but two days ago we were relieved from our anxiety by a letter from Miss Mary Eyre to Mrs Wheble, stating that your good lady had got over the worst part of her illness.

I felt myself greatly indebted to you for the part you took in my behalf when I was publicly attacked as a traitor to the Caths. of Ireland four months ago,[2] & as I take it for granted that I am now or shall be very soon misrepresented throughout your Island on much the same ground I take the liberty of putting the whole of my case in your hands: not that I wish any speech or publication to be made by you or any one else on my account, but barely to enable you in conversation with your respectable friends to defend me, as I am sure you wish to do, when my cause admits of a defense.

To be brief: the following paragraph of a letter written by the Rev. Richard Hayes[3] from Rome has been sent to me from the Northern & the Southern parts of England & therefore can hardly be supposed not to have found its way into Ireland. "English calumny has perhaps a greater influence in the Court of Rome than even at St James's. The most infamous paragraphs of Irish & English Anti-Catholic Newspapers are constantly forwarded hither by English Catholics (a) You will be sorry to find that Dr Milner, after all his opposition, *demanded* the Veto at Genoa (b) & *advocated* it at Rome, (c) He had *joined with Dr Poynter*[4] (d) & the English Vetoists (e) & *both* have written & inclosed scraps of News papers to Cl. Litta *to the prejudice of our Remonstrance.*"[5] (1st) I shall first lay down my principles, next acquaint you with certain facts, & lastly answer the accusations against me as I have marked them with alphabetical characters.

In the first place, then, I have invariably, since the year 1808, adhered to the decision of your Prelates that *it is not expedient to alter the discipline of the Cathc. Church of Ireland as to the appointment of its Bishops & have been* persuaded that the interference of the Crown in this business would be injurious to the cause of our Holy Religion in Ireland.[6] I am of the same persuasion at the present moment. 2nd I am convinced that the alteration, in this point, proposed in the late Bill[7] & consented to by many English Catholics, not being sanctioned by any competent Ecclesiastical authority involved the guilt of Schism, with respect to its adherents as I asserted before the Pope & his Cardls. But 3rd I know that the Supreme Head of the Church has power to alter the discipline of any particular church, & whatever power the ordinary Prelates of such Church have to remonstrate on such an occasion I am conscientiously persuaded that, it is my duty as his Vicar Apostolic to obey him in this case, however mortifying it may be to my feelings.

Now then as to facts: I singly opposed the alteration, *in limine*, at the beginning of 1810, at the St Albans Tavern.[8] I singly opposed it, (I mean among English Caths) when it had nearly passed the H. of Commons in May 1813.[9] I went to Rome in May 1814 to oppose Mgr. Quarantotti's Rescript & Dr Murray has on various occasions acknowledged that I had completely defeated it before he came to my assistance.[10] I strained every nerve in my power *during the whole time of my stay beyond* the Alps to *prevent the Holy See's* consenting to *any concession at all*, in this important business, but when I clearly saw, (what Dr Murray must have apprehended from the Pope's answer to him in my presence) that concessions were inevitable, & that the plan of them was arranged then, I own on a particular occasion I expressed by letter, my submission, at the same time endeavouring to restrain it within the narrowest bounds possible & retain as much liberty as possible: but neither then nor at any other time did I act as agent for the Irish Prelates: on the contrary I first & last protested that the Caths. of Ireland wd. relish no concession. On the first proposal of the plan to me, I urged various objections to it in writing as well as by word of mouth. This brought upon me such reproaches as at once alarmed my conscience & overwhelmed me with grief: Napoleon in the zenith of his power cd. not thus have terrified me. I then retired & wrote my submission, as I have intimated, still endeavouring to restrain the plan. On presenting my paper, I found that the arguments contained in my former paper had produced a powerful effect on the party alluded to & I really began to flatter myself that no concession at all wd. be made. Soon after this the Pope fled from Rome & put himself under the protection of England at Genoa. I followed him requesting a letter which had been promised me for the Irish Prelates. It was refused to me: but a fortnight after was given to Dr Poynter.[11]

I now answer Mr Hayes (a) What he here says may be to a certain degree true, for any thing I know: all that I have occasion to say is that the man who complains so bitterly of calumny in others, *ought to have been careful not to commit it himself*. (b) It is a downright falsehood that I *demanded* or otherwise promoted the Veto *at Genoa* (c) & equally false that I *advocated* it at *Rome*: on the contrary I did everything in my power to avert it at both places, & barely on one single occasion at the latter place signified my submission to what I cd. not hinder, on which very occasion, as I have explained, I was in hopes, I had averted it. (d) It is false that I have joined Dr Poynter. We never saw one another at Rome except to give & receive a single visit of ceremony. I have never seen him since my return to England & have never corresponded with him directly or indirectly except about certain money matters.[12] (e) It is another calumny that I have *joined the English Vetoists*. I have indeed received overtures from some of them, but I have kept myself clear of any connexions with them. (f) The most unaccountable of all Mr Hayes's calumnies is that I as well as Dr P. have written & *sent scraps of* Newspapers to Cl. Litta to the prejudice of the *Remonstrance*. I never sent a piece of a News paper or any other printed paper[13] to any person at Rome, & the few letters which I have written thither since my return have all been in the plaintive & prophetic style with respect to the decision on our affairs & the consequences to be expected from it. I have now to apologise, My Dr. Sir, for troubling you with so long & so frightful a scrawl. In case, you can decypher it, your prudence will suggest the best use that can be made of it, without quoting it in a speech or printing it in a Newspaper. I wish, however, it may be read to Mr Hayes at his return,[14] in order to see what he can say in opposition to it. His Grace, Dr Troy, is already in possession of a great part of what is here stated.[15]

Mrs Wheble joins me in kind & respectful Compts. to Mrs Scully, Mrs Eyre, Miss Juliana & Mr Thomas.[16]   [*Source*: Scully Papers]

[1]The seat of the Dukes of Norfolk. They were probably visiting the new 12th Duke, a Catholic, who had succeeded his apostate third cousin on 16 December 1815.

[2]When he was denounced by O'Connell (see No. 527 n.6).

[3]An aggregate meeting of 29 August 1815 had appointed three delegates to take to Rome a remonstrance against the Quarantotti rescript (see No. 492 n.3), of whom only Father Richard Hayes OF had agreed to go. He arrived in Rome on 25 October 1815, two days after Doctors Murray and Murphy, who were presenting a remonstrance from the Irish Prelates (Ward, *Eve of Catholic Emancipation* II, p. 149).

[4]Dr Poynter arrived in Rome on 14 January 1815 to answer in person Dr Milner's charges against him and he was called on by a number of English Catholics, some of whom would have been regarded by Father Hayes as vetoists (see Ward, ibid., p. 121).

[5]See n.3 above.

[6]A paraphrase of the resolution of September 1808 (see No. 185 n.7).

[7]Grattan's bill, with the Canning clauses, defeated in committee on 24 May 1813 (see No. 434 n.3).

[8]Where the English Catholics adopted the Fifth Resolution (see Nos. 230 n.1 and 257 n.13).

[9]Dr Milner later said that Grattan's bill was about to come up for its third reading, but it was only in the committee stage and one of the reasons why Dr Poynter did not

share Dr Milner's sense of urgency was that he hoped to secure satisfactory amendments (Ward, ibid., pp. 43, 47).

[10]The letter revoking the rescript had been signed on 25 June 1814, a few days before Dr Murray's arrival in Rome (see No. 492 n.3).

[11]See No. 513 n.6.

[12]Possibly in respect of compensation received by Dr Poynter for the English colleges on the continent occupied during the war. While in Rome Dr Milner accused Dr Poynter of withholding the share due to him: the latter so successfully refuted the charge that Cardinal Litta's confidence in Dr Milner was shaken (ibid., p. 123).

[13]Cardinal Litta had however carefully studied Dr Milner's pamphlets (ibid., p. 103).

[14]Father Hayes did not return as expected: no reply being given to his remonstrance he remained until he was expelled in July 1817 (ibid., p. 153).

[15]At an aggregate meeting on 5 March 1816 O'Connell apologised for his attack on Dr Milner (see No. 527 n.6) and read an extract from a letter from Father Hayes so much at variance with the paragraph here quoted by Dr Milner as to suggest that Father Hayes had either been misrepresented or had been prevailed upon in the meantime to eat his words (see Ward, *Eve* II, p.150).

[16]Thomas Eyre, Scully's brother-in-law.

534   *From his brother James Scully*

Kilfeacle, 19 February 1816

I wrote to William Murphy this day to pay Walsh the gravedigger, also to have a stone erected[1] and to consult him on the best mode of distributing the fifteen pounds legacy amongst the poor of Cashell parish, & also of applying the legacy left to poor paternal & maternal relations, and sent him a copy of the clause in the Will for that purpose.[2]

[*Source*: Scully Papers]

[1]James Scully senior had died at Kilfeacle on 11 February. A short obituary in the *Dublin Chronicle* of 14 February remarked that during the last few years he had been disabled by age and growing infirmities from attending assizes and other meetings. A longer one on 8 March included some points of current relevance: his loyalty to George III; his support of the Union, at the time of which "certain persons, of rank and office, actually pledged themselves to Mr Scully for the relief from the Penal Code and the Tithes system"; and his offer to raise a regiment at his own expense in 1803 (see No. 53).

[2]The executors and main beneficiaries of the will were Denys and James Scully junior. They were given probate on 26 June, but before the end of the year their mother filed a bill against them to assert her rights under her marriage settlement and litigation followed which only ended in June 1825 when the House of Lords upheld the Irish Court of Chancery's ruling of 8 December 1821 in favour of the plaintiff (see No. 617 n.3).

535   *Revd F. J. L'Estrange to 13 Merrion Square, Dublin*

Clarendon Street [Dublin] Friday [12 April 1816]

My dear Sir,

Not having an opportunity of answering your note at the time I recd. it this morning I now beg leave to acknowledge the receipt of it. Since you spoke to me concerning the Address[1] I was on the watch for you each day. I have however now left it in the Lodge where you may see it when convenient. If you could influence some Gentlemen to attend on Sunday many signatures I am sure may be procured. At present there are scarce any to the Address.

I had the pleasure of hearing the Most Revd. Doctor Murray this morning condemn in most pointed terms the conduct of the "Mischievous Catholicks" as we may now call the Lords & Gentlemen both on his & Earl Stanhope's authority.[2] The *Chronicle* of this night will contain some of the most pointed remarks.[3] I see now no reason why we should despair if we be but firm and united. I am happy to inform you likewise that in the late Provincial Synod,[4] (of which we entertained some well founded apprehensions, from the well known character of some & the doubtful hue of others of the members who composed it,) the spirit of Antivetoism ran as high as we could wish. The best hopes may be therefore entertained of the result of the National Synod to Assemble on the 24th at Kilkenny.[5]

I am extremely sorry that a most particular and long standing engagement will prevent me the pleasure of availing myself of your kind favor on Sunday next.   [*Source*: Scully Papers]

[1]The address to the Prince Regent, recommended by Sir H. Parnell and adopted at an aggregate meeting on 5 March 1816 (*DC*, 8 March 1816).

[2]Speaking after Lord Liverpool, who had repeated his view that securities were of no avail, Lord Stanhope (1735–1816, 3rd Earl) had said in a debate on 2 April: "The fact was, that this question of the veto was first forced upon them by mistaken or mischievous Catholics". He went on to say that he had first heard of the veto from Fox (*Hansard* XXXIII, 820).

[3]The significance of the sermon was that it was preached from the pulpit on Good Friday. Under the heading "Condemnation of the Vetoists" the *Dublin Chronicle* attributed to him the words "those mischievous Catholics who would endeavour to bind the mystic body of the Church by pernicious restrictions", but on the 15th it published a letter from Dr Murray who, quoting from the text of his sermon, said that he had referred to "our mistaken brethren" failing to realise that the conciliation they sought would imply the degradation of the Sacred Ministry. On the 22nd it published the correspondence between the seceders and Dr Troy, who admitted that Catholics could sign the seceders' petition without breaking the law of the Church or incurring his personal displeasure.

[4]Of the Dublin province, held on 27 March (*DC*, 25 March 1816).

[5]The synod, attended by fourteen Prelates, resolved to send another remonstrance to Rome and to petition both Houses of parliament through Lord Donoughmore and Sir Henry Parnell (*DC*, 29 April 1816).

536 *From Sir Henry Parnell to Merrion Square Sth. Dublin*

Emo Park [Queen's Co.] 15 April 1816

My Dear Sir,

I shall be in Dublin this evening on my way to London. I wish to be able to present the Petition[1] before Sir John Newport's motion[2] & therefore I hope it will be ready for me at farthest by Wednesday.   [*Source*: Scully Papers]

[1]The one he presented on 26 April (*Hansard* XXXIV, 9). Being subsidiary to the address to the Regent it aroused little interest in Dublin. Gregory wrote to Peel on 14 February that after two Saturdays had passed without a quorum the petition expressing the wishes of millions of Catholics had been adopted on 10 February at a meeting of five persons (Add.MSS.40, 202, f.3). One of them was his own informer, McG.

[3]On the state of Ireland — tabled to be debated on 26 April.

537 *From Sir Henry Parnell to Merrion Square South, Dublin*

Carlton Club, St James' Street, [London] 29 April 1816

Private

My Dear Sir,

I find a great improvement in the disposition of the House of Commons. The soreness felt by several last year has disappeared & there is every prospect of an excellent division. I am anxious to receive the letter from the Association to Lord Liverpool[1] as everything stands still waiting its arrival. When I get his answer to it, it will be known whether the Govt. will do any thing for you. If they will not then I shall name a day for taking the Petition into consideration.

It would be better for the division if Grattan should take the lead again on the occasion of having the other Petition to present.[2]

No one here seems at all to enter into the feelings of mutual animosity which prevails in Dublin in consequence of this second Petition, which is a favourable circumstance, as the Govt. are trying to find an apology for not coming forward in the divisions which they say exist in the Catholic Body. I have endeavoured to counteract the success of their attempt by what I said on presenting the Petition, though at some risk of incurring the displeasure of those who are so angry with the Seceders.[3]

The Debate on Sir John Newport's motion[4] fell very far short of what it should have been; both Plunket & Grattan speaking prevented me from taking a part, as both the subject & the House were too much exhausted to have afforded a fair opportunity of transgressing the rules of moderation which they laid down.

I expect we shall have another general debate, upon the Statement the Regent is to send us[5] when I shall tell all I know of the system of political influence which is practiced in every way by the Irish Government. I mean to-night to take the opportunity of a motion which is to be made for a committee on the Grand Jury Laws[6] to give some details & make the abuses which flow from them fully understood by the House. Incessant discussion, on all these matters, now that the House is disposed to listen & attend to them, will necessarily lead to many emendments.   [*Source*: Scully Papers]

[1]To accompany the address to the Regent (see No. 535 n.1).

[2]The seceders had taken advantage of the absence of Lord Fingall, who opposed an open schism in the Catholic body, to meet in Lord Trimleston's house on 13 February and adopt a petition of their own, which Grattan was invited to present in the House of Commons and Lord Donoughmore in the House of Lords (*DEP*, 17 February 1816; Peel Papers: Add.MSS.40,242, f.28). Peel told Lord Sidmouth on 17 February: "I think you will find the mob and the Priesthood and the Prelacy will adhere to the *Leaders*" (HO 100/189, f.125).

[3]By saying that it was unfair to accuse the seceders of sacrificing religion for personal advantage, and perhaps also by assuring the House that the persons whose petition he presented were not so exceedingly unreasonable as to do away altogether with measures of temperate and proper regulation. It being the intention of the Catholic body to put their case in the hands of ministers he would not, he said, give notice of any motion (*Hansard* XXXIV, 10).

[4]Calling for an enquiry into the state of Ireland and defeated by 187 to 103 votes (ibid., 12).

[5]No record of such a statement has been found: Parnell may have hoped for one as a result of the Association's approach to Lord Liverpool.

[6]Not reported in *Hansard*. *The House of Commons Journal* shows that Parnell was made a member of the committee.

538   *From Sir Henry Parnell, London, to Merrion Square,*
2 May 1816

Notice was given by Sir J. Hippisley last night of a motion for a select committee.[1] It was received with a general laugh but he will probably get it and the entertaining of the question even in this shape will contribute very much to the success of the general measure. Parnell will divide the House and thus test its opinion on the subject of arrangements. He hopes the Catholics will not express any opinion until the House has taken some step of a decisive nature, as the granting of a committee does not imply positive consent to Hippisley's views. He is going to-day to Lord Liverpool with the address.   [*Source*: Scully Papers]

[1]See No. 550.

539   *From Sir Henry Parnell, London, to Merrion Square,*
3 May 1816

Yesterday he handed the Association's letter and Address to Lord Liverpool,[1] who said that official forms required that he should pass it to the Home Secretary but that this would not cause any delay.[2] He promised a written answer within a few days. Parnell explained that the address had been sent to him to convey in the strongest possible manner the wishes of the Catholics to place their cause in the hands of government and referred to the direct communication between the Irish Catholic delegates and Pitt. Parnell will move for copies of the Address, the letter and the reply to be laid on the table in the House of Commons, and he has got Finerty to undertake to print them immediately in the *Morning Chronicle*.[3]   [*Source*: Scully Papers]

[1]See No. 535 n.1. A letter signed by Nicholas Mahon as chairman, a copy of the address and the minutes of the meeting of 5 March at which it had been adopted are among the Liverpool Papers (Add. MSS. 38,379, f.189), together with a short letter from Parnell.
[2]On 1 May Lord Shrewsbury had gone direct to the Home Secretary with addresses of the seceders and the English Catholics to the Regent (*Orthodox Journal*, May).
[3]The *Morning Chronicle* did not publish them (see No. 541).

540   *From Sir Henry Parnell to Merrion Square Sth., Dublin*

London, 4 May 1816

My Dear Sir,

I have sent Mr Mahon[1] today a letter from Ld Liverpool in which he wholly avoids meeting the application made to him. Ld Sidmouth may yet be more communicative. But if he is not I shall take an early opportunity, when your Catholic Petition is presented to ask Ld Castlereagh what the intention is of Government on the question.[2]

No public mention I think ought yet to be made of Lord Liverpool's answer as the proceeding is as yet not complete.[3]

There is a general expectation of a majority in favour of the Catholics if nothing unforeseen occurs to make a change in the opinions of the Members.

[*Source*: Scully Papers]

[1]Nicholas Mahon.
[2]He did so on 15 May (see No. 543 n.1).

³The *Dublin Chronicle* published it on 15 May. It merely stated that the papers had been sent to Lord Sidmouth at the Home Office.

541   *From Sir Henry Parnell to Merrion Square Sth., Dublin*

St James's Hotel, 1 James's Street [London] 10 May 1816

Private

My Dear Sir,

I have not yet named any day for a discussion of the Petition, as I wish to see the other Petition brought up which Mr Grattan has to present,¹ & also to allow sufficient time for the Petition of the Bishops² to come over.

Sir John Hippisley's motion³ will not go to require any opinion to be given by the Committee on the question of securities but only to report the facts of such securities existing in foreign countries. It will give rise to a good deal of discussion, & so far contribute to be of use.

I have not been able to get the letter of the Association to Lord Liverpool published in any other paper than the *British Press*.⁴   [*Source*: Scully Papers]

¹See No. 537 n.2.
²See No. 535 n.5.
³At this time due to come up on 16 May.
⁴Very few copies of the *British Press* are extant. Extracts taken from it by the *Orthodox Journal* at this period show that it gave coverage to Catholic affairs.

542   *From Sir Henry Parnell to Merrion Square Sth., Dublin*

St James's Hotel [London] 14 May 1816

My Dear Sir,

Mr Eliot is to present the English Catholics' Petition¹ & Mr Grattan Ld Trimbleston's on Wednesday.² They will both speak at large on the occasion. I expect Mr Grattan will name a day for a general discussion of the question either on Wednesday, or on Thursday after the debate on Sir J. C. Hippisley's motion. If he does not I shall do so. It would have been very ill received by the House, & injured the division very much if I had not waited for his bringing up the Petition of the Seceders & also for his having his own way in disposing of it as he thought proper. As the question of arrangements will be disposed of on Thursday by sending it to a Select Committee,³ the general discussion will necessarily be entirely on the merits of the civil concessions. Sir J. Hippisley will certainly carry his motion, as Lord Castlereagh will support it. I saw the terms of his motion with Lord Castlereagh's emendments. It will, I expect, occasion a full discussion of the

Veto. I shall take care the House divides, that the sense of it on the question may be fully known.[4]

In respect to the popular feeling against the seceders & the charges which are made against them, they are so very unfair & unjust, & as I think so very unnecessary, & so much the result of personal & partial feelings, that I think it does a great deal of harm to give them any countenance. I know the mischief here would be incalculable, if it was not for the total ignorance which prevails of any thing passing in Ireland. The little I said[5] disarmed a good deal of hostile feeling & will contribute very much to improve our division.

I shall do all I can to obtain a succession of debates during the remainder of the session. The repetition of the discussion will produce a great deal more impression than one or two general debates. If Sir J. Hippisley gets his committee I think it would be well done to move our attention to it, to examine & report upon the laws now in force against the Catholics.

On the whole it now seems almost certain that the question will be carried in some shape or other in the course of next session but to secure this it is absolutely necessary that it should be focused on immediately after Parliament meets. The address to the Regent should be repeated & a deputation sent with it, a considerable time before Parliament assembles. I shall ask Ld Castlereagh in the House for an answer to the address of this year.

[*Source*: Scully Papers]

[1]Presented on 21 May by William Elliot but not debated (*Hansard* XXXIV, 649).
[2]15 May, when Grattan gave notice that he would move for a committee of the whole house on 21 May (ibid., 512).
[3]He must mean Sir J. Hippisley's select committee, whose terms of reference indirectly concerned arrangements (see No. 550 n.1).
[4]His plan was frustrated when Hippisley postponed his motion to 28 May.
[5]When presenting his own petition on 26 April (see No. 537 n.3). There would have been time for him to hear from Scully that his remarks had not been well taken by the popular party in Dublin.

543   *From Sir Henry Parnell, London, to Merrion Square,*
16 May 1816

Private

As he expected, ministers have refused to advise the Regent to accede to the prayer of the Address,[1] but it has done much to appease the hostile feelings that prevailed last year. Grattan presented his petition yesterday. He had determined not to make any motion on it but as his declining to do so would have made a difference of at least fifty votes and left no chance of a majority Parnell prevailed on him to change his mind. He took this course because it was clearly in the interest of the cause to obtain the best possible division by letting Grattan take the lead. The debate on Hippisley's motion, postponed to the 28th, will give him the opportunity to set forth and support the wishes of the Catholic body at large. In contrast with last year, every effort will be made to obtain a full attendance. Letters are to be written today to all friends of the measure who are out of town and notes sent to those in London. Lord Duncannon,[2] who is in the habit of assisting on these occasions, is anxious to get everyone to divide who has before divided on the question. There are 250 members who have at one time or another voted for it and the greater part of them are now in London. Unless the Regent exerts himself personally, these may make a majority. He has been told that the Regent's language is much softened. Parnell feels confident that a bill will pass in the next session. He adds in a postscript that he has learnt ministers were particularly annoyed by Grattan's notice as they thought he had abandoned all idea of moving on the subject in the current session.

[*Source*: Scully Papers]

[1]After Grattan had given notice of his intended motion Sir H. Parnell asked Lord Castlereagh whether the address of the Irish Roman Catholics had been presented to the Prince Regent and whether ministers intended to advise His Royal Highness to recommend their situation to the attention of parliament. Lord Castlereagh replied that the address had been presented but he was not prepared to say that ministers intended to advise him to make any recommendation (*Hansard* XXXIV, 513).
[2]John William Ponsonby, Viscount Duncannon, later 4th Earl of Bessborough.

544   *From Sir Henry Parnell to Merrion Square Sth., Dublin*

St James's Hotel, St James's Street [London] 18 May 1816
My Dear Sir,

I have heard nothing since I have been here of any intention to interfere with the Jesuits or their establishments. Nothing will certainly be done this session & I cannot conceive that any measure will ever be adopted which will have a retrospective effect. There is no illiberal feeling here amongst any class of society except the small Irish Anticatholic party who have no weight. I, therefore, think Mr Kenny's alarms have no good foundation & that he need not torment himself by giving way to them.[1] Sir John Hippisley will probably speak harshly on the subject but it is so much the fashion to ridicule his views, that his efforts will go for nothing.

I believe Mr Grattan will only move that the situation of the Catholics shall be taken into consideration early next session. If that is the case, & if I find I can get any support, I shall move an emendment to go now into a Committee upon the Penal Laws. I fear very few will approve of my doing so, particularly as it is supposed the session will be over in a few weeks. He will in all probability carry his motion by taking this course, & if he does, it will have a better effect, than being beaten on a motion for a committee.

I am anxious to know what interpretation is to be put on the proposed Domestic Nomination[2] by the Catholic Bishops. I fear their petition[3] will not arrive before the Debate. It will, however, be more applicable to that which will take place on Sir John Hippisley's motion. [*Source*: Scully Papers]

[1]Sir H. Parnell may have heard from Scully that news of Sir J. C. Hippisley's intended motion had rekindled Father Kenney's fears, last mentioned in No. 484, of 19 June 1814.
[2]The plan put forward by Father Hayes in Rome provided for the parish priests of the diocese putting forward three names, to which the Bishops would add their comments but no fresh names, and the Congregation of Propaganda Fide's instituting one of the three. In the case of coadjutors the Bishop himself was to nominate and his candidate be accepted or rejected by the parish priests. It was not until 16 May 1817 that the Congregation reached a decision, which was unfavourable to the proposal (Ward, *Eve of Catholic Emancipation* II, p. 152).
[3]See No. 535 n.5.

545   *From Sir Henry Parnell to Merrion Square South, Dublin*

St James's Hotel, St James's Street [London] 20 May 1816
My Dear Sir,
I send you the enclosed to shew you that every exertion is making to secure a good division to-morrow.

I do not find that the Regent is making any exertions to oppose us, but on the contrary, I hear his opinions are very much changed.

[Enclosure]

19 May 1816
The favour of your attendance in the House of Commons is *earnestly requested* on Tuesday next on the *Catholic question* when a division will certainly take place.   [*Source*: Scully Papers]

546   *From Sir Henry Parnell to Merrion Square South, Dublin*

St James's Hotel [London] 21 May 1816
My Dear Sir,
I have not been able to get any members to approve of attempting to emend Mr Grattan's motion, so, therefore, I shall merely express my disapprobation of it.[1]

There is every appearance of an excellent division. No efforts have been made by the Regent's friends to secure a majority, & I know it is the opinion of those who are best capable of judging correctly, that we shall have the majority on our side.

The further discussion on Sir J. Hippisley's motion, & even his getting a committee will contribute to assist the progress of the question.

[*Source*: Scully Papers]

[1]Speaking after Grattan on his motion that the House should take the laws affecting the Roman Catholics into consideration next session Parnell cited the amendment which he had contemplated but would not put forward because of the lateness in the present session. So far from confining himself to this expression of disapproval, however, he went on to second Grattan's motion (*Hansard* XXXIV, 662). His reasons for so acting are explained in No. 551.

547   *From Sir Henry Parnell, London, to Merrion Square,*
             22 May 1816

The debate last night was wholly in favour of the early success of the measure. Until the House was counted it was thought on both sides that the majority would be for the motion.[1] Above twenty of the friends of the measure arrived too late, thinking the division would not take place until a late hour. From what fell from Lord Castlereagh[2] he cannot help thinking that the government will take the question up next session, his understanding of his speech being that the report to be made by Hippisley's committee will bring over public opinion in England and enable the government to act if the Catholics display no great hostility. The accession of Canning to the cabinet[3] will materially change the state of the Regent's counsels, especially if some of its members most hostile to the Catholics retire. There will be another debate on Sir J. Hippisley's question and he is thinking of moving for leave to bring in a bill to grant everything except sitting in parliament and the high offices of state. In a separate note marked *Private* he says that he has sent corrected copies of his speech to the *Chronicle* and *Evening Post* and observes that 149 members divided with him last year — he thinks the division would have been better if Grattan had moved to go into committee of the whole House. Several of the Prince's friends were absent from the division.   [*Source*: Scully Papers]

[1]The motion was defeated by 172 to 141 votes.
[2]*Hansard* XXXIV, 669.
[3]See No. 552 n.3.

548 *From Sir Henry Parnell to Merrion Square South, Dublin*

London, 23 May 1816

My Dear Sir,

It has been ascertained beyond any doubt that there were sufficient members in town to have carried Mr Grattan's motion with a considerable majority, if they had attended. As the Government acknowledge this to have been the case, nearly the same influence will be produced by the discussion & division upon it, as if we had actually the majority.

I took care to get lists made very accurately both of the minority & majority; they are in the *Morning Chronicle* of this morning.[1]

If I find I can secure any support I shall give notice of a motion for leave to bring in a Bill of relief for some day next week.   [*Source*: Scully Papers]

[1] An article in the *Dublin Chronicle* of 10 June 1816 analysed the voting of the Irish members. Out of 97 members (three seats being vacant) 38 voted for the motion, 28 against, and 31 did not attend. Its comments are similar in tone to those expressed by Scully in his review of the 1815 voting (see No. 512).

549 *From Sir Henry Parnell to Merrion Square South, Dublin*

St James's Hotel [London] 27 May 1816

My Dear Sir,

I have been able to ascertain beyond all doubt that the opponents to Mr Grattan's motion had determined not to divide the House, under the conviction of their being in a minority; & that this intention was not abandoned till within a short time before the division took place.

The discussion has had this good effect at least, of proving that the obstacles in the way of the measure are not any longer those arising from Ecclesiastical arrangements or the supposed violent conduct of individuals but altogether confined to the personal opinions of the Prince Regent. To judge from the late opposition to the question, & particularly from the silence of those who used formerly to be forward, it is reasonable to infer that their opinions are very much changed. From all I hear I believe this to be the case.

The course I adopted in suffering Mr Grattan to lead the discussion, has had the effect of reconciling a great deal of adverse & angry feeling & can alone account for our being so near succeeding. I think, another year, I shall find no jealousy on the part of the Opposition leaders. But I really believe that you will not stand in need of any advocate here, in consequence of the question being taken up by Government.

I send you by this post the report of the Committee on the Grand Jury Laws.[1] The regulations were carried with great difficulty, & are considered as greatly encroaching on the power of Grand Juries. [*Source*: Scully Papers]

[1]See No. 537 n.6. When the report came up on 6 June notice was given for a motion in a future session to consolidate all the acts relating to the raising of money by Grand Jury presentments in Ireland, but the Irish members urged immediate action to place the taxes under control and Sir Henry Parnell carried an amendment whereby a bill was to be brought in solely to amend the existing acts (*Hansard* XXXIV, 1007).

550   *From Sir Henry Parnell, London, to Merrion Square,*
               29 May 1816

Sir John Hippisley having worded his motion so as to confine the functions of his committee merely to make an abstract of the papers from time to time laid before parliament,[1] and the whole House being so much in favour of the committee, not more than two or three would have voted with him if he had pressed a division. The motion passing unanimously, on the other hand, will produce a very favourable impression on the public. On the 6th Parnell will move for an instruction to the committee to take into consideration the penal laws, thus turning it to a useful purpose.[2] The Bishops' petition has not yet arrived. A reference to it last night by Peel[3] gave him the opportunity of making some observations.[4] He hopes he is correct in his conjecture that the question of securities will be left with the Bishops. There is an indescribable prejudice in parliament against its being introduced at popular meetings.

[*Source*: Scully Papers]

[1]The terms of reference of the committee provided that it should report on "the nature and substance of the Laws and Ordinances existing in foreign States, respecting the regulation of their Roman Catholic subjects in ecclesiastical matters, and their intercourse with the see of Rome, or any other foreign jurisdiction". Twenty-one members were appointed to it, of whom Sir H. Parnell was one. By 18 June six more had been added. Five were to constitute a quorum and the committee could sit even when the House was adjourned (*Journal of the House of Commons* 28 May 1816, p. 408).
[2]This intention was abandoned, perhaps because of instructions received to press for a debate on the petition itself (see No. 551).
[3]Peel, while not opposing Hippisley's motion, suggested that any motion grounded on securities would not meet the general approval of the Catholic body (*Hansard* XXXIV, 874). As proof he mentioned the recent resolutions of the Irish Bishopes, i.e. those adopted at Kilkenny on 28 April (*DC*, 29 April 1816).
[4]Having accused Sir J. Hippisley of ascribing to the petitioners opinions which they had not expressed, Sir H. Parnell had gone on to say: "In the part of the petition to which he appeared to refer, they spoke of civil liberties. On this point he was certain,

for he had made inquiries amongst those who were best acquainted with the subject: by them he was told, that this point of the petition related to civil rights, and that, with respect to spiritual matters, their clergy would be left to decide. This he believed to be the case; and they would in consequence find that subjects of Church discipline would not in future be agitated in popular assemblies, but would be left, where they now rested, with the Roman Catholic clergy" (*Hansard* xxxiv, 875).

551   *From Sir Henry Parnell to Merrion Square South, Dublin*

London, 30 May 1816

My Dear Sir,

As the Edr. of the Dublin *Chronicle* has thought proper to attribute a very unfounded & unfair motive to my conduct in supporting Mr Grattan's motion, I have written to him to retract it.[1]

I find all the opinions which prevail in Dublin so different to what they would be, if there was a full opportunity of knowing all the various circumstances which occur here, that must necessarily have some influence on the mode of conducting so difficult a question as that arising from the Catholic Petition, that I shall not undertake to present another unless a deputation is appointed to assist me.

The Petition of the Prelates not coming over,[2] absolutely deprived me of a proper opportunity of calling upon the House to consider of the Petition of the aggregate meeting[3] till this moment & the real cause of my seconding Mr Grattan's motion was merely that of getting an opportunity to speak, before the House became too impatient for a division, to allow me to say anything. Any one who knows any thing of the House, is aware that when an exhausted question comes on very late, & that members come down at eleven or twelve o'clock merely to vote, unless one takes the first opportunity that presents itself, it frequently happens, that even the best speakers on the most popular subjects cannot get a hearing — in point of fact they are too prudent to attempt it. By seconding a motion one has a right of precedence & must be called on by the Chair.[4]

I shall present the Prelates' petition to-night & give notice of a motion to take the other Petition into consideration this day se'night tho' I fear it will be rejected with a very great majority & make things appear worse than they now do. I shall state my principal object to be to secure the minor concessions this session but shall move in case the committee is granted the whole of the resolutions which I brought forward last year. The forms of the House preclude a motion for leave to bring in a Bill.[5]

Should the Catholics think proper again to ask me to present their petition, you must expect to receive an answer from me expressing the difficulties I have felt this year from the want of personal communication with persons authorised to act for them, & requiring such assistance in future.

[*Source*: Scully Papers]

[1] In introducing the motion which Parnell had seconded (see No. 546 n.1) Grattan had cited the Genoese Letter (see No. 513 n.6) and a reported statement by the Pope as endorsing the terms on which the House was prepared to grant Emancipation. Reporting the debate under the headline "Defeat of the Veto" the *Dublin Chronicle* of 27 May had printed Parnell's "excellent speech" but added a paragraph reading: "Sir Henry Parnell seconded the motion — we regret that he did so — however we are satisfied that it was a mere lapse of thought on his part. There is an unsuspecting good nature about Sir Henry, that with all his good sense, and all his unquestionable honesty, renders him sometimes a prey to the delusion of the Whig or Grattan party . . . notwithstanding his direct disavowal of the veto — his coming forward to second Mr Grattan will be represented by his enemies, to imply an assent to that abominable persecution". No retractation has been found but an article of 14 June put his behaviour in another perspective (see No. 558 n.4).
[2] See No. 535 n.5.
[3] Of 4 July 1815. So described by Parnell to distinguish it from the petition of the seceders presented by Grattan.
[4] His procedural difficulties are more clearly set out in No. 572.
[5] See No. 496 n.2.

552   *From Sir Henry Parnell to Merrion Square South, Dublin*

St James's Hotel, 31 May 1816

My Dear Sir,

I presented the Petition of the Bishops & Clergy yesterday. You will see by the Papers what an unworthy attempt was made to prevent its being received. The admissions of Mr L. Foster & Sir J. Nichol deprived me of the opportunity of entering into the statutes which were referred to.[1] I am very sorry the Bishops thought it necessary to present this petition & also to observe the renewal of so much hostility against Securities. For tho' I think them unnecessary & very objectionable, I fear the question will be again lost for a period of some years, as the prevailing opinion here in favour of these securities is just as fixed as the opposite opinion is in Ireland. After so much pain has been taken here to impress on the English public the danger of emancipation unless securities are connected with it, no minister, if ever so well disposed to take the part of the Catholics, would be able to succeed in conducting an unconditional measure through Parliament. We are, therefore, placed in this alternative, either to wait till public opinion shall change in either England or Ireland, or to have the question carried by force of numbers in Parliament in a way repugnant to Catholic feeling.

All the present difficulty I attribute to the manner in which Ld Trimbleston's Petition was received, & attacked by the Dublin *Chronicle*.[2] If it had been left alone it would have been perfectly harmless. For my own part I consider the course of writing which has appeared in the *Chronicle* as completely counteracting every effort I have been able to make, or that any other friend of the Catholics has made, to promote their objects, & I shall consider it quite useless to continue them, if every thing that occurs contributes only to make matters go backward instead of forward. If the efforts of the *Chronicle* & the great talents that are connected with it, were all applied to conciliate animosities, & to appease passions, & to place the question on its true merits, as a plain matter of just & political expediency, all obstacles would soon disappear. But so long as a contrary course is taken a satisfactory end to the labours of the friends of the Catholics is not to be expected.

I gave notice yesterday that I should submit a motion to the House next Thursday to take the Petitions into consideration, in order fully to meet the wishes of the Petitioners. The only course the form of the House will allow me to take is to move for its resolving itself into a committee to take them into consideration, but after the decision on Mr Grattan's motion I cannot expect to carry it. I do not believe that there will be an attendance of members, &, I am sure but twenty or thirty will divide with me, unless the English Catholics should make some exertions to try to secure the subordinate concessions, & thus get Lord Castlereagh to vote with me. As it is so manifest that the right of sitting in Parliament & the High Offices of the State will not now be conceded, I must place the motion very much on the justice & utility of making these concessions.

Mr Canning is appointed to a seat in the Cabinet.[3] This is a most important matter for your cause & I have no doubt would secure a general measure next session, if it is not defeated by what may occur in Ireland. You ought to have another address to the Regent & a deputation in London before the 1st of August. What has occurred this session fully shews how much is lost by being too late.

[P.S.] The *Globe* contains an accurate report of what I said on presenting the Petition of the Bishops. [*Source*: Scully Papers]

[1]Sir J. C. Hippisley had concurred with Colonel Barry in doubting whether the House could receive petitions from persons who called themselves Bishops instead of titular Bishops in Ireland and referred to the Irish Act of 21 & 22 George III prohibiting Popish ecclesiastics from assuming any ecclesiastical title within the realm. Leslie Foster, supported by Sir John Nichol, however, had argued that the House should consider, not their titles as stated at the beginning of the petition, but how they affixed their signatures — which were those of their Christian and sur-names (*Hansard* XXXIV, 976).

[2]The petition of the seceders was published by the *Dublin Chronicle* on 19 February, interspersed with a running commentary of derogatory or sarcastic remarks in

brackets. Throughout February, March and April it devoted more space to discrediting and ridiculing the seceders than to any other subject.

[3]His appointment as President of the Board of Control (or India Board) had been formally announced on 30 May (*Morning Chronicle*, 31 May 1816).

553   *From Sir Henry Parnell to Merrion Square South, Dublin*

London, 3 June 1816

My Dear Sir,

I find my bringing forward again the discussion of your question so much disapproved of, that I fear you will be extremely disappointed in the result. Was I to place it on the simple grounds of unqualified emancipation, I am sure I should not have ten members to vote with me. In order to have any chance of a tolerable good division I must press chiefly the subordinate concessions, not however leaving out the greater ones. There was so great an indisposition even to debate Mr Grattan's motion, that I even calculate upon none at all on mine, & that I shall be defeated by a motion for the previous question. But this apparent neglect of the House ought to be considered as a good omen, as a similar state of things has always immediately preceeded [*sic*] the final success of some of the most important & long pending questions.

If Mr Canning has acted with any consistency whatever, he must have made terms for the Cabinet bringing forward a general measure next session; if you will look at the correspondence between him & Ld Liverpool in 1812, at the end of Cobbet's Debates of that year[1] you will see how fully committed he stands, not to take office without having secured the sanction of Govt. to the question.

With the view of turning the approaching discussion to some account, I shall move nearly the same resolutions I brought on last year.[2] I shall propose the least objectionable the first & end with that for seats in Parliament & high offices. The resolutions on this head I have framed out of Mr Grattan's Bill of 1795[3] making two distinct classes, one containing the offices of political power, the other the offices which the Speaker admitted ought to be granted.[4]

It would have been much better to have remained satisfied with the discussion of Mr Grattan's motion for this session, & to have brought on a discussion on the general Petition, that I have presented, early in the next but as I found so general an opinion in favour of a distinct discussion on this Petition, I have not hesitated to undertake it, as my notion of the duty of a member of Parliament, on all such occasions is to be governed by what he sees is clearly the wish of the Petitioners, without suffering himself to be influenced, even by the conviction which he may

feel, that their way of thinking may be inconsistent with their own
interests.   [*Source*: Scully Papers]

[1]In the appendix to volume 23 of *Hansard*. Canning wrote to Lord Liverpool on 18
May 1812: "To become a part of your administration with the previous knowledge of
your unaltered opinions as to the policy of resisting all consideration of the state of
the laws affecting his Majesty's Roman Catholic subjects would, it is felt, be to lend
myself to the defeating of my own declared opinions on that most important
question". In defence of his subsequent conduct in joining the administration
Canning argued in 1819 that the formation of any ministry united on the Catholic
question had shown itself to be impossible and that its settlement would have to be
left until public opinion had come round to it (*Hansard* XL, 537).
[2]See No. 502 n.2.
[3]Defeated in the Irish House of Commons on 4 May 1795 (Lecky, *History* III, p.
315).
[4]By implication on 24 May 1813 (see No. 434 n.3).

554   *From Sir Henry Parnell, London, to Merrion Square,*
                          5 June 1816

   The close of the session being expected in three weeks and it being so soon
after the division on Grattan's motion he feels he would injure the cause if he
were to force another division on a general proposition. He will however
give notice in tomorrow's debate that he will fix a day in the first week after
the new parliament meets next year, for a discussion of the petitions. In the
meantime he will move resolutions for conceding subordinate objects, thus
making the House better acquainted with the question. He suggests that
Scully's friends should back this course by sending over a deputation and an
address to the Regent this summer. If Scully and O'Connell were in London
to give explanations themselves and make ministers understand the real
sentiments of the Catholic body they would completely set aside Lord
Trimleston's party.   [*Source*: Scully Papers]

555   *From Sir Henry Parnell, London, to Merrion Square,*
                          7 June 1816

   The result of his complying with the wishes of those who gave him their
petitions has been exactly as he foretold. Although he brought the question
on in a new form there was no attendance and he was glad to get an excuse
for withdrawing his motion.[1] If there are any new petitions the same sort of
contempt of the Catholic body may be shown as exhibited last night unless

the Catholics make their cause of all the importance it admits of. To produce a proper impression both on government and opposition petitions should be obtained from every parish and considerable town in Ireland, to be ready for presentation in February. On the whole, he thinks, the discussions which have taken place this session (which he attributes to his not yielding to the decision of the opposition leaders) have placed the question on better grounds than it ever stood before, there now existing not a single declared obstacle in the way of its success. But this will not be brought about until government takes it up and another address should be presented to the Regent, with weight being attached to the manner of carrying it to him. It would be most valuable if Scully, O'Connell and some others could devote a month of the summer to visit London as a deputation and call on Liverpool, Canning, Castlereagh etc. He has received Scully's letter and one from Mr McDonald[2] and will think nothing further about the latter's observations on him. Lord Donoughmore has arrived and will present his petition on Tuesday.[3] Parnell expects more from the House of Lords than the Commons, where all feeling is divided between Peel's views and those of Grattan. [*Source*: Scully Papers]

[1]Having announced that on the first day of the next session he would give notice of a motion for complete emancipation he had urged that subordinate concessions would do a great deal towards appeasing the agitation in Ireland, which was greater than ever before known, and proceeded to re-submit the resolutions which he had put forward in 1815 (see No. 498 n.3). After the Speaker in response to an intervention by Peel had read the standing order requiring any alteration in the religion of the country first to be discussed in committee, and Lord Castlereagh had expressed the hope that he would not persevere with his imprudent motion, Parnell had withdrawn it (*Hansard* XXXIV, 1007).

[2]Probably Eneas McDonnell, editor and proprietor of the *Dublin Chronicle* of whom Parnell had complained in No. 551. For a similar interchange in the case of Miles McDonnell/Macdonald see Nos. 301 and 303.

[3]Giving notice on 11 June Lord Donoughmore explained that he was presenting several petitions. That known as Lord Trimleston's expressed a readiness to submit to any regulations not incompatible with the petitioners' religion. That of the Irish Bishops and clergy put a decided negative on the veto, but offered domestic nomination. The others were from three counties and from "the general body, denominated at all times the petition of the Catholics of Ireland" (*Hansard* XXXIV, 1049).

556 *From Sir Henry Parnell*

[London] 8 June [1816]

Confidential
My Dear Sir,
    The very extensive mischief which has been the result of the attacks made

by the *Chronicle* on Mr Grattan & the Opposition, & also on Mr Fitzgerald[1] & others, have induced me to write the accompanying letter,[2] which I do with great reluctance, and not without feeling there exists a great degree of justification for all that has been said.

The *Chronicle* might be turned to the greatest possible use by its having gained so much circulation, if the question was continuously set forth with all the advantages of argument which might so easily be brought forward in favour of it.

I sincerely hope this line of conduct will be adopted.

[P.S.] I have put *private* on my letter as only to be communicated privately to friends.   [*Source*: Scully Papers]

[1]The *Dublin Chronicle* of 31 May had described Grattan as wholly impotent to conduct the Catholic cause. Its criticism of Vesey Fitzgerald may have been in its next issue, of 3 June, which is missing.
[2]No. 557.

557   *From Sir Henry Parnell to Merrion Square South, Dublin*

London, 8 June 1816

Private

My Dear Sir,

I wish you to know the absence of the members of opposition from the House on my motion[1] is wholly to be attributed to the observations which they read in the *Chronicle* at Brooke's upon them & the conduct of Mr Grattan.

Had it not been for these reproaches I could, from my own influence with many members, have secured a tolerable support to my motion. If instead of fault having been found with them, their exertions & attendance on Mr Grattan's motion had been spoken of, as it deserved, with proper acknowledgement of their advantage to the Catholic cause, I feel sure, they would have omitted no opportunity of supporting it, even on the most liberal principles.

It is really impossible for me to think I can be of any service in bringing on any new discussion, if it is deemed expedient to persevere in giving offence to the Opposition party. I am quite ready to say, I do not think Mr Grattan & that party have done all the justice to the question which it deserved. But still they have effected a vast deal for it, & they form the only large body of the English Community that is sincerely friendly to the Catholics.

With a view of succeeding in carrying emancipation, I should advise that for the future a different course should be pursued. I think, at least, it would be prudent to abstain from personal attacks on Mr Grattan & other individuals who have voted for the question, & also from general censure of the

Opposition and I also think it would be better to leave the question of Veto at rest until Parliament or Government actually propose it.

If this course is taken I shall always feel exceedingly happy in devoting my exertions, & facing all difficulties in attempting to meet the wishes of the Catholics; but you must not be surprised if I should decline presenting any more petitions, or making the motion I have given notice of for next session, should I find myself not supported, but opposed by the Catholics themselves.

[*Source*: Scully Papers]

[1] The one he withdrew on 6 June (see No. 555 n.1). According to the *Dublin Chronicle* of 14 June only twenty-four members of the opposition attended, as against sixty-one on the ministerial side.

558   *From Sir Henry Parnell to Merrion Square Sth. Dublin*

London, 17 June 1816

Private

My Dear Sir,

Though it may seem to be a very hopeless undertaking, I cannot help throwing out the idea of the great utility which could arise from a coalition of the two parties, into which the Catholics are now divided.[1] If such an event could by any possibility be brought about, it would, I feel quite sure, make sure of a satisfactory settlement of the question in the next session. The grounds on which it might be, I think, arranged would be by adopting a preliminary condition, that no mention should be made in any new petition to be presented next year of the ecclesiastical securities; & that the prayer of it should be for the repeal of Penal disabilities, or perhaps the better way would be to have only an address to the Regent in the first place & that *immediately*, leaving the propriety of petitioning Parliament to be determined by the results attending the presenting of the address by a deputation composed of persons of both parties.

The effect of such an address brought over by a deputation consisting of Lords Kenmare, Fingal & Trimbleston, you, Mr O'Connell, Mr O'Connor & Mr Mahon,[2] would be most striking & salutary at this particular crisis just as Mr Canning is coming into an active share in public affairs.

The opportunity you would have to see & converse with the Ministers, Lords Wellesley, Grey etc. would lead to a better understanding of the question, & to much more liberal terms both in respect to civil concession, & ecclesiastical arrangement than can be expected without an active & impressive interference on your part.

You should not feel at all discouraged by any thing that has happened in the House of Commons as that is all to be attributed to the delay & not to the indisposition of Government to adopt the question.

The dissatisfaction of Lord Trimbleston's party at the overstatement of the intent of their petition leads me to suppose they would be glad of an opportunity of coming back to the views at least of the moderate part of the popular side.

[P.S.][3] *Confidential*

Lord Donoughmore shewed me a letter he wrote to Mr Hay expressive of great surprise & regret at the publication of the letter he lately wrote to him & said every thing he could to induce me to feel assured that he had no idea of making any public commentary on my conduct.[4]   [*Source*: Scully Papers]

[1]For the failure of the last attempt to re-unite the two parties see No. 490 n.3.
[2]Owen O'Conor and Nicholas Mahon.
[3]This postscript is on a separate sheet of paper.
[4]Lord Donoughmore had probably just seen the *Dublin Chronicle* of 14 June, with an article lampooning him for a letter he had written to Hay speaking of the "miserable" failures in the House of Commons and Sir H. Parnell's incapacity. The article admitted that Parnell "was no doubt misinstructed" but was at a loss to imagine "why Lord Donoughmore should claim any preeminence over that steady, disinterested and truly consistent Senator".

559   *From Sir Henry Parnell, London, to Merrion Square,*
                              18 June 1816

Private. Sir J. Hippisley will make his report on 24 June. From what Parnell can collect some plan very different from that of 1799[1] or of Canning's clauses[2] will be proposed,[3] so there may be no foundation for the opposition that continues to be set forth on the supposition that these will be persevered in. Hippisley thinks that it would be objectionable to exercise a veto after an election by Dean and Chapter had taken place and suggests that they should choose from lists of persons unobjectionable to the state. Details might be arranged to guard against the Crown's injuring the Catholic religion or the constitution. Parnell will remain in London all next month and if a deputation should come over the foundations might be laid for a measure next session.   [*Source*: Scully Papers]

[1]When ten Irish Prelates had agreed to allow the crown a negative in the appointment of Bishops (see No. 211 n.13).
[2]Of 1813 (see No. 427 n.5).
[3]Presumably by ministers: the Select Committee had not been asked to submit proposals.

560   *From Sir Henry Parnell, London, to Merrion Square,*
19 June 1816

He is glad to find by Scully's letter of the 16th that the writings of the
Chronicle may be considered as belonging to the Editor and are disapproved
of by all right thinking people.[1] He is also happy to observe that Scully
calculates on a restoration of unanimity in the Catholic body. This will have
the best possible effect if it is soon brought about and an immediate
application is made to the Regent, particularly before Canning has time to
find an excuse for being less forward than formerly in the Catholics' favour.
The Regent by his own act has already abolished all religious distinctions in
Hanover.[2] As Hippisley's committee will be revived next session to examine
how Catholic Bishops are appointed in other countries some of the Irish
Bishops will probably be examined and there will thus be no sound reason
for the laity to mention securities in any new address or petition. Should the
parties agree to unite, proceeding by address[3] would get over the difficulty of
selecting parliamentary advocates. Should petitions be deemed necessary it
might be better to select new advocates in order to avoid a difference of
opinion.   [*Source*: Scully Papers]

[1]Scully's papers thrown no light on his connexion with the *Dublin Chronicle* except
for four entries in one of his notebooks (MS.27, 493). He made three payments of
£50 to Eneas McDonnell — on 27 January, 10 February and 2 May 1816, the last
being the date on which McDonnell was convicted got s libel (*DC*, 3 May 1816); and
on 10 October 1816 he lent him £140 for his fine.
[2]Of which he was the Elector. Lord Castlereagh made a passing reference to this in
his speech of 21 May (*Hansard* XXXIV, 669).
[3]i.e. to the Prince Regent.

561   *From Sir Henry Parnell, London, to Merrion Square,*
25 June 1816

The division in the House of Lords[1] has produced a general impression
that the question will be carried next session and confirms Parnell's opinion
that all that remains to be done is to follow up the advantages gained by an
address to the Regent and an effective deputation. The Regent's immediate
friends did not vote and Lord Liverpool's silence is an omen of some change
on his part. Lord Wellesley thinks that concessions and arrangements should
be made the subject of two separate bills. He seems to enter more warmly
into the Catholics' feelings than any other friend they have. Parnell got the
address to the Regent published in the *British Press* on the morning of the

debate and it has been referred to constantly as proof of a change in the temper and conduct of the Catholics. Even if a deputation did not come now Scully could do a vast deal in London by giving explanations to leading men.

[*Source*: Scully Papers]

[1]Lord Donoughmore's motion that the disabling statutes should be taken into consideration in the next session was defeated by 73 to 69 votes, of which 64 were given by proxy (*Hansard* XXXIV, 1254).

562   *From Sir Henry Parnell to Merrion Square Sth., Dublin*

London, 26 June 1816

My Dear Sir,
    You will see by the *Globe* I took advantage of Sir J. Hippisley's bringing up his report[1] to explain more fully the proposal made by the Bishops of Domestic Nomination. The letter I quoted, I received from Dr Milner, with his permission to publish it.[2]
    The speech of Mr Canning[3] has produced a great impression in favour of the expectation of a measure next session. It appears, however, that he has joined the present Cabinet without making any terms in favour of the question with Lord Liverpool, for when Mr Horner said that this inference was to be drawn from his Declarations, both he & Ld Castlereagh shook their heads, denying it.[4] I have no doubt, however, that if you pressed Lord Liverpool you would bring him over. There has been some communication between the Regent & Ld Hutchinson, promoted by the former, which looks very well.   [*Source*: Scully Papers]

[1]Not published until early 1817 (*Orthodox Journal*, January 1817). It dealt with the appointment of Bishops; "rescripts and mandatory missives from the see of Rome, or any other foreign jurisdiction"; and other matters (*Hansard* XXXIV, 1254).
[2]According to *Hansard* (ibid. 1258) the communication was from "the Catholic prelates of Ireland", who had proposed of their own accord that Bishops should be elected by the dean and chapter.
[3]He argued that without the settlement of the Catholic question no other evil could be radically cured (ibid. 1256).
[4]Ibid. 1259. Francis Horner (in *DNB*) was MP for St Mawes.

563   *From Sir Henry Parnell to Merrion Square Sth., Dublin*

London, 1 July 1816

My Dear Sir,
    I forget whether I told you that Lord Castlereagh told me he wished Sir J. Hippisley's Committee to be revived next sessions to make a report upon the existing Penal Laws in the United Kingdom. If this plan goes on as it no

doubt will, it would be of great utility to have a new edition of your work upon the subject.[1] If you was to give a short History of the proceedings of the Catholics since 1813, shewing how their proceedings have been misunderstood & misrepresented, I am sure some thousand copies would be sold & that the greatest benefits would be conferred on the cause. You would, I know from Sir J. Hippisley be examined, & probably, whatever you state would be adopted by the Committee, if prepared for the purpose, free from observation & classed under the proper Heads. This would bring you in the way of communication with the framers of the bill & give you an opportunity of being of great service, not only in the drawing of it but the general management of the question.

I can easily conceive that the pestering of Grattan etc make everything a great deal worse than it ought to be & almost make it impracticable to bring about a reconciliation. I still think, however, some effort ought to be made, when matters cool a little.

In order to prevent Sir J. Hippisley's report from having too great an influence in favour of the Veto, I sent an abstract of it to the *Globe* with a note in favour of Domestic Nomination.[2]

There are various reports of change in the Ministry but no appearance of any foundation for them. [*Source*: Scully Papers]

[1] The *Statement of the Penal Laws*, probably out of print since the prosecution of Fitzpatrick (see No. 488 n.5).
[2] *The Globe* of this date is not available.

564   *From Bishop John Milner to Merrion Square, Dublin*

Wolverhampton, 24 July 1816

My Dear Sir,

A few days ago I was honoured with your letter of the 11th inst. & recd. together with it from some neighbouring town yr. present of O'Halloran's *Ancient History of Ireland*,[1] superbly bound, for which I return you my best thanks. Having been in possession of the 4th Edition of that work for some time past, I am enabled to place one of the copies of it in the library of my growing seminary at Oscot. I perceive that yr. female prodigy, the Ursuline nun of Cork,[2] has borrowed copiously from the work in question. For my own part, I am glad that I am not obliged to admit, as articles of faith, all the wonderful things contained in this primaeval History: I may add that one particular which struck me, when I first perused it I utterly disbelieve, namely that the Irish were converted to Christianity by Asiatic Christians. This the author,[3] after Dr Ledwich endeavours to prove by a supposed conformity between the Irish & the Asiatic Churches with respect to the time of keeping Easter; whereas I have proved, in my *Tour* that no such conformity existed at *any time*, & that in the reign of the Emperor Constantine our British Churches observed that festival as Alexandria, Rome, Antioch & the Church in general did.[4]

I was disappointed at finding that yr. letter said nothing about the grand attempt of the disciples of Pitt, Castlereagh & Canning, to subjugate the Clergy & the Religion of Ireland.[5] Hippisley is no more than the tool of the former; though should the infamous scheme succeed I dare say he will be rewarded with his darling office of *Ministre du Culte Catholique*. Nothing, in my opinion, can save yr. Church & ours, next sessions, but a demonstration of the continued hatred of the detestable yoke, on the part of yr. people & particularly of yr. Prelates & Clergy.

You have seen a little pamphlet, called *The Inquisition*,[6] which I published, when I was last in town, & I am only waiting for a sight of the boasted Report of the sour old Inquisitor (which is to teach us Bishops theology & Canon Law) to put forth a more copious work on the subject, shd. no other sound Cathc. attempt the task, which I earnestly hope may be the case. The worst part of the business is that Castlereagh enthralled Card. Consalvi at Vienna, & keep[s] him enthralled by all sorts of temporal considerations, [with] which Consalvi rules all at Rome. Still if Cathc. Ireland continues firm, she will continue free. You will readily conceive that my motives for dreading the yoke are cheifly of a religious nature; for I know how numerous & how fatal to religion will be the restraints laid upon it & its ministers if Pitt's plan is carried.

I must mention, *en passant* that Dr Poynter with his friends, has entirely broken off from his friend & counsellor, the invisible agent in all Cathc. movements, Chs. Butler. The former now says that Dr Milner has faithfully depicted the character of the latter.[7] Mrs Wheble who is tolerably well desires me to say all that is affectionate to her niece Mrs S. & respectful to yourself. We have not yet heared of Mrs Eyre's reaching Highfield.[8] I expect to be in the neighbourhood of it shortly.   [*Source*: Scully Papers]

[1]*In introduction to the study of the history and antiquities of Ireland* by Sylvester O'Halloran, London, 1772.

[2]Mother Ursula Young, who had written *A compendious history of the United Kingdom of Great Britain and Ireland*, which was on sale in Dublin in December 1815 (*FJ*, 11 December 1815).

[3]O'Halloran.

[4]Having made out a case for a connexion between Ireland and Egypt in Druidic times O'Halloran goes on (p. 59) to show that it did not cease on the reception of Christianity. He draws attention to the form of tonsure; the time of celebrating easter; and the anchorite towers still standing in Ireland. He does not mention Dr Edward Ledwich, whose similar views had been censured by Dr Milner in 1809 (see No. 198 n.7).

[5]In the debate on Sir J. C. Hippisley's report on 25 June Lord Castlereagh had rejected domestic nomination as a matter in which parliament could not meddle and

added that he "could not consider such a mode of election as a substitute for the security proposed to be taken". Canning had concluded his speech by saying that "with the conditions which it might be thought advisable to annex to the boon, the final settlement of the question ought not to be delayed" (*Hansard* XXXIV, 1258).

[6]"*The Inquisition. A letter addressed to the Hon. Sir John Cox Hippisley . . . by a Catholic Christian*" was a skit in which Sir J. C. Hippisley was imagined as a Grand Inquisitor taking depositions from various Catholics, including Dr Milner himself (Husenbeth, *Life*, p. 315).

[7]Whether or not Dr Poynter actually used such words elsewhere, Dr Milner is clearly referring to a passage in the evidence he gave on 17 June 1816 to the Select Committee appointed to inquire into the Education of the lower orders of the metropolis (*Third Report*—1816 (495) IV 165 p.299). He was being examined on the awkward question of the use of the bible in schools and complained that Butler, who had suggested his being summoned by the committee without consulting him, wished to force him to give a public answer to questions which for prudential reasons he had declined answering in private to him.

[8]In Derbyshire, the home of her son Vincent Eyre, Scully's brother-in-law.

565   *From Sir Henry Parnell to Merrion Square, Dublin*

18 Bury Street, London, 5 October 1816

My Dear Sir,

Having been travelling through several parts of France since the beginning of July I did not receive your letter of the 21st of that month till a long time afterwards.

If Mr McDonald[1] should still be in want of the assistance of a Member's name, I shall be very ready to allow him to make use of mine. I must, however, make it a condition that he will do every thing in his power, whenever we have another division on the Catholic question to secure votes, without much minding what has hitherto been the conduct of the individuals on former occasions. This I am now more anxious about than ever, because I think the question is brought to be one of name polling, & that it will rest just where it is, until by some means or other a majority can be got to force it forward.

It is now quite clear the Cabinet will not originate it & that the Regent will not propose it to Parliament. But though they take this unfavourable course, they will, I understand, take no active part in opposing any motion which may be brought forward in Parliament & if it should be carried, they will make the opinion of Parliament the grounds of abandoning all future opposition, & giving the measure their support.

A Government man in the Regent's Household told me a few days ago that Lord Castlereagh had been taking the greatest pains to persuade him to vote for you, & had held out [to] him the great probability of success in the next session. Mr Canning's accession to the Cabinet, & his being in the way to assist in Debate with all his influence & talents will contribute most essentially to a good division. These circumstances together with the very favourable impression that was established by the Debates of last session of the improvement in the temper & tone of the Catholics all contribute to shew that the question will stand next session under much more favourable circumstances than it has done since 1813. But it must be brought forward early. I feel disposed to move an emendment to the address on the first day of the session so as to force a debate at once, & a division if the body of opposition will support me. I am sure a similar proceeding in the House of Lords would be attended with the best effect. If you petition Parliament you should make a point of having the Petitions to both houses ready before the opening of the session, & you should require of those you employ to present them, to secure a Debate upon them in the course of the first month of the session. For no measure can be carried through all its stages on so extensive a subject, if the groundwork of it is not settled before the Easter recess.

On the question of securities I hope nothing more will be said.[2] It cannot stand better than it does with the proposal of the Bishops of Domestic Nomination on one side & Sir J. Hippisley's report on the other. My own opinion is the whole will end in nothing but some clauses of regulation of no kind of effect one way or the other.   [*Source*: Scully Papers]

[1]Probably Eneas McDonnell (see No. 555 n.2).
[2]By the Irish Catholics.

566   *From Sir H. Parnell, Emo Park, Queen's Co., to Merrion Square, 9 February 1817*

Private and confidential — Sir J. Hippisley having declined to do so and knowing that Lord Castlereagh is in favour[1] he himself proposes to move for a Select Committee on the Penal Laws immediately after presenting the petition.[2] To achieve success two or three preliminary discussions and much private communication will be necessary. He will go at some length into the question on presenting the petition and the motion for a select committee will give the opportunity of going into details that are not much attended to in a set debate. To such a course he is the more inclined because the House will for some time be occupied with the reformers[3] and finance. If he cannot fix a date before the Easter recess for the petition, one soon after it will give time for a legislative measure if the sense of the House is for one. He hopes to hear from Scully as he will be glad to follow the wishes of the petitioners. He will go over the first moment he can, but must return for the assizes in the middle of March.   [*Source*: Scully Papers]

[1]See No. 563.
[2]See No. 567 n.2.
[3]On 12 March there were 527 petitions before the house, 468 of them printed and the great majority for reform of parliament. Lord Castlereagh spoke of "the systematic trade of framing petitions" and the House decided not to receive printed petitions (*Hansard* XXXV, 991).

567 *From Sir Henry Parnell to Merrion Square, Dublin*

Cooper Hill,[1] [Carlow] 18 February 1817

Private
My Dear Sir,
    I wrote last Tuesday to Mr Brougham[2] to give notice for me that I would move for a Select Committee to inquire into the Penal Laws on Tuesday the 11th of March. This will start the question, & secure the attention of Parliament & be a good preparation for subsequent motions. It will also give me a fair opportunity for writing to the leading friends of emancipation.[3] I must not, however, hurry it on, but postpone the motion to the end of the month in order to get as much support as possible. Should I succeed in getting the committee I would have a report ready to be presented to the House the first week after the Easter recess & thus take care not to delay the discussion of the general question.
    I am very glad to find so much doing towards uniting all the Catholics & I hope the effort will prove successful.[4] As I think my presenting the Petition may form a great obstacle, I wish very much to have it understood that I think the wisest step that could be taken would be to give it to Mr Grattan. I should have no objection to write such a letter to Sir Thos. Esmonde, as would open the way to the rescinding of the resolution,[5] by which I was called upon to present it. This resolution sufficiently marks the kindness & confidence of the body in again selecting me & I could have no other feeling than that of the perfect satisfaction upon a new decision being made, by which Mr Grattan should be able to tell the House of Commons that all divisions were at an end.
    I shall be glad to hear from you — my address will be Athy until Friday & then at Emo Park.

[*Source*: Scully Papers]

[1]The residence of William Cooper.
[2]Henry Brougham gave notice on 24 February for a motion on the penal laws, explaining that it was not intended to urge the general question until a time that might be convenient for the Irish members (*FJ*, 4 March 1817).
[3]He had already written to Grattan on 14 February (Grattan, *Life and Times* V, p. 537).
[4]The activity had started on 12 December 1816 with a decision of the Committee of

the Catholic Association, endorsed by an aggregate meeting on 17 December, to adopt for 1817 the text of the 1812 petition (drafted by Scully — see No. 337 n.1), as expressing Catholic feeling before the withdrawal of the seceders (*DC*, 13 & 20 December 1816). On 4 February 1817 O'Connell and other members of the Committee had gatecrashed a meeting called by the seceders but failed to carry a motion for a joint conciliation committee (*DC*, 5 February 1817). On 8 February fifty-four Catholics (including Scully) had published a requisition for a meeting on 14 February "of all such Catholic gentlemen as are desirous to put an end to all dissensions in the Catholic body, and to devise means to make a combined and unanimous effort for obtaining legislative relief in the present session of Parliament" (*DC*, 12 February 1816). As a result of discussions initiated at that meeting a sub-committee of five had been appointed on 17 February to promote conciliation (*DC*, 17 February 1817; DDA 60/2, IV, 5).
[5]Of the aggregate meeting of 17 December 1816.

568   *To Sir Henry Parnell, Emo Park*

private   Merrion Square, 21 February 1817
My dear Sir,

I recd. your letter of the 18th, and am very glad you have decided to give notice of your motion — as people begin latterly to enquire what are we doing? As for what has been done here lately, it has had the effect of shaming the Seceders, and even bringing back some of them to the people, but there is no expectation of reclaiming their principals,[1] who shape their conduct wholly according to their ideas of what will please the Government — & indeed a chief effect of the late meetings here has been that of putting the obstinate Seceders still more in the wrong, in the eyes of the public.

As far as I can observe or learn, there is no probability, that the Catholic Body will consent to admit Mr Grattan to any share of their confidence or to employ him in the management of their Petition, in any stage. Indeed their affections seem to be completely alienated from him. When some allusion of this kind was thrown out by Mr O'Connell in the warmth of his eagerness for conciliation, at the late meeting in Townsend Street,[2] it was greatly disrelished — a general murmur was heard, & there has since been a commotion about town, under the apprehension, lest it might be in contemplation to reinstate Mr Grattan as our advocate. Our clergy, high or low, distrust & dislike him — and all the middle & lower classes view him as a Trimmer: and, reviewing all the instances of his acquiescence with a Government, hostile to the people, during the last 10 or 12 years, they draw from them the most unfavourable inferences. So far therefore as regards such a step towards conciliation, it does not appear to be at all a probable event — Your offer to write a letter to Sir Thos. Esmond, for opening the way to a substitution of Mr Grattan for yourself, is only a fresh instance of that sincere feeling and unaffected zeal for the general good which has uniformly marked your public conduct, but I do not think it would be attended with the good effects you would have a right to expect; and possibly it might be misconstrued: for those, who feel a repugnance towards Mr Grattan, and they are very numerous, might become jealous of any particular leaning towards him on your part. I own, that I am not anxious to see him taking *any* part in our question. I have often thought, that, if he had not been in Parlt., we should not have met with so many divisions amongst our Parliamentary friends, so much ill treatment & invective in their speeches, or so many little contemptible squabbles amongst ourselves. Our Seceders etc have been principally created, and are still abetted, by the Grattan party & followers, who appear to have no public or enlarged objects in view, or to labour any other point, but how to keep up their idol, & thrust him forward as our grand leader & manager, in every proceeding, so as that no Resolution should be carried, nor even a meeting be held, unless under the previous sanction & private advice of this oracle. Of all this puffing & pitiful system, we have long been heartily sick & tired. It was, after a painful effort, shaken off about 3 years ago,[3] by the Body at large — and they feel very much disinclined to resume the burthen.

I had a visit a few days ago from Dr Everard, one of the 2 Archbishops (Dr Murray is the other) deputed by the Irish Prelates[4] to attend the Debates upon our petition. It was wished by many of the Prelates that they should proceed directly to London — but they judge it better not to go over, until about the expected time of the discussion, that is about the middle of April. Of course, they will wait upon you, and as they are both men of prepossessing manners & good information, it occurs to me that you might with advantage procure them an introduction to Mr Wilberforce, Mr Stuart Wortley, or any other men of weight & independent minds, whom it might be useful to canvass. Dr Everard in particular is highly calculated to serve us in this way, being a man of the world, has resided many years in England, & formed many respectable acquaintances there. He was a favourite too of Mr Edmund Burke. His rank here is that of Co Adjutor Archbishop of Cashell — I hope you will allow me to see you in town for a few minutes in your way to London.   [*Source*: Congleton Papers]

[1]Viscount Southwell, Sir Edward Bellew and William Bellew. Lord Trimleston is not recorded as having played any part in this year's proceedings and Lord Fingall remained quiescent.

[2]On 14 February, when a discussion had taken place on the desirability of making a further effort to secure unanimity in the Catholic body. The details were not published (*DC*, 17 February 1817).

[3]Two years ago (see No. 495 n.1).

[4]Probably at their synod of 23/24 January, the proceedings of which however were not published.

569   *From Sir Henry Parnell to Merrion Square Sth., Dublin*

Emo Park [Queen's Co.] 23 February 1817

Private

My Dear Sir,

I made my arrangements for going to London this week & wrote to Mr Brougham to name the 11th of March[1] as the first open day as far as I could judge from the notices I observed to be given by other Members. I intended to present the petition some days before.

My plan was to bring forward the Question on four distinct occasions. The first on presenting the Petition by entering upon the circumstances of the question distinct from the general merits of it, as they relate to the conduct of the leading members of Government & opposition. The second, by going into the grievances in detail on the motion for a Select Committee on the Penal Laws. The third, by moving to have Sir John Hippisley's report[2] taken into consideration in a committee of the whole House with the view of shewing from it that Domestic Nomination was the true practice of the Church. And the fourth, by moving upon the general question of emancipation.

Mr Grattan having undertaken the last motion,[3] & the endeavours to produce a union not being yet closed,[4] I am obliged to reconsider what I had determined upon, & for the present to postpone any immediate proposition to the House of Commons.

From what occurred last session you must be well aware that Mr Grattan has such an influence in the House, as to deprive me of the power of obtaining a general discussion & any support upon a motion to take the Petition into consideration. I persevered last year[5] against the opinion of every one in London in making the attempt, merely to shew the true state of the case & after what happened I hope it will not be expected of me to do the same again. The use I am capable of turning my exertions to, is that of securing a discussion every session, so long as it is requisite to do so & of obtaining repeated debates; & also of canvassing for support & obtaining information for you. But whenever Mr Grattan chooses to bring the question forward, the House will only attend to him, & come to a fair vote upon his motion. It is not correct to think that every one who supports him, supports the particular petition which he last presented.[6] The Petition itself cannot be the subject matter of Debate, but the broad question of Emancipation. To act upon the principle, that he ought to be opposed, because this Petition is objectionable, would be to carry the divisions which prevail into the House, & defeat all efforts of succeeding.

If the Petition, remains in my hands, contrary to my opinion of the policy of witholding it from Mr Grattan, I should be glad before I go over, to know exactly what it is desired I should do & I shall have the opportunity of talking the matter over when in Dublin.

I am exceedingly glad to find that Doctor Murray & Doctor Everard are going to London. I think the sooner they go the better. I would give them letters of introduction to Mr Wilberforce,[7] & to any other Members or Peers you name to me. I should be glad to have an exact description of the purpose they have in view & of their proper titles. I am sure their communications with the leading friends of the question will be of the greatest service. Their going to London will introduce it into general discussion, & the information they will convey will remove many misconceptions.

If I really thought my going over immediately would in the smallest degree benefit the cause I should not hesitate to do so, but under all the circumstances under which the business at present rests, there can be no general debate till after the Easter recess. The difficulty of obtaining the attendance of freeholders at the sessions for registering votes, leaves me near two hundred still to have brought forward & was I not to be on the spot myself this force would be wholly lost for another year. This circumstance together with the necessity of attending my assizes induces me to wish very much to postpone going over till the end of the month when I shall make emends by constantly bringing up the question for my present omissions.

[*Source*: Scully Papers]

[1]See No. 567 n.2.
[2]On the practice in other countries regarding the appointment of Bishops and their intercourse with the Holy See (see No. 562 n.1).
[3]On 5 February Lord Southwell had invited Grattan to ground a motion based on a resolution adopted by the seceders at their meeting of 4 February and on 7 February he had replied agreeing to do so (*DC* 10 February 1817).
[4]On 18 February the sub-committee of five (see No. 567 n.4) had addressed a circular letter to all those who had signed the Trimleston petition of 1816 (see No. 537 n.2). It was pointed out to them that they had the clergy and the great mass of the people against them and they were urged to reunite on the basis of domestic nomination (*DC*, 21 February 1817).
[5]See No. 555 n.1.
[6]That of 1816, which Grattan had been asked by the seceders to bring up again.
[7]For William Wilberforce's entertaining the two "infectious doctors" to breakfast in May see R. and I. Wilberforce, *Life of William Wilberforce* IV, p. 322.

570   *To Sir Henry Parnell*

Dublin, 27 February 1817

My dear Sir,

I am favoured with your letter, and perceive clearly, that it will be proper, on every account, to postpone your departure until Easter. The permanency of your seat in Parliament[1] is too valuable an object to the Catholics and the country, to be endangered for the sake of having our Petition discussed 2 or 3 weeks earlier or later — and the utility of registering your freeholders without delay necessarily dispenses with your engagements respecting the Petition for the present. These are also the sentiments of Messrs O'Connell & N. Mahon — to whom I have taken the liberty of showing your letter in confidence: for, tho' it is marked *private*, yet I am persuaded you have no objection to put them in possession of your general views of the subject, and the letter appears to be too valuable to be confined to myself alone. I take care, however, that the Dublin newspapers do not catch hold of it — especially as they are now, generally, in very bad hands.

Your chief difficulty seems to rest in the bringing on of the motion upon the general question of Emancipation — for, as to the three other opportunities of discussion which you have selected, I do not apprehend that you feel the same repugnance to them. I own that, feeling as you do & with the experience you must now possess of the character & bearing of the House and the sort of monopoly that Mr G[rattan] has contrived to attain, your repugnance to this fourth motion does not seem extraordinary — and certainly, it cannot be expected or wished, that you should undertake it contrary to your own feelings and judgment. I rather think the best course will be, to act according to the circumstances, guided by your own discretion. There exists, as I have said, an insurmountable objection to the reinstatement of Mr G — committed as he stands by his declarations upon Ecclesiastical restrictions, and the unfortunate part he took upon the Bill of 1813[2] — and he is too tenacious to follow the example of Lord Grenville in giving a manly retractation.[3] Yet, it is from himself alone, as far as I can judge, that any solution of the difficulty can now be expected to come — and this is perhaps suggested by the present state of the question. Might he not now seize upon the late offer of Domestic Nomination for the purpose — and say, without inconsistency, that here is a sufficient security, to answer the purposes he has had in view, and that he can now, upon this basis, close with the Catholic clergy & people, and concur fully in their objects? I think he may take this course successfully, if he has the inclination to do so, and may effect the purpose of a useful discussion, without abandoning the general principles he has professed — I merely throw out this observation, as you may probably find some opportunity of communicating with him, which may effect a satisfactory arrangement of the discussion, so as to relieve you from what you may feel to be an invidious situation, and ensure the main object, a good debate and division. It will only remain with Mr G. to lend his hand cordially, and take the opportunity of doing good.

I believe that the object of the 2 Archbishops in going to London will be merely that of being in the way, to give every explanation, to soften opposition, meet objections and promote the general object by every means in their power. No specific directions have been given to them. This was mentioned to me yesterday by Dr Murray, who refers to Dr Everard, as the principal & chief manager of the Deputation, under whose directions he considers himself bound to act. As I propose to see Dr Everard in a few days, in the Co. Tipperary, I may be able to learn something more particular. If you should not think it too troublesome, nothing could be more useful to them than your general suggestions of the proper course & measures to be adopted by them, when in London, for assisting the great object of a beneficial discussion. They would add to the many services you have rendered to the Catholic cause, and would, I am sure, be observed with scrupulous attention — I mean, a statement of such proceedings as you think they ought to take for promoting the object of the Petition & clearing away doubts & difficulties, especially upon the ecclesiastical questions — with names of such leading persons — in & out of Parlt. — as they ought to visit and canvass. Their Titles in the Church are these — Dr Everard is Archbishop of Hierapolis in Phrygia — and Dr Murray is Archbishop of Mitylene in Crete — these are called sees *in partibus infidelium*. They act, however, by Vicarial powers, as Coadjutor Archbishops in Ireland: the former for Cashell, and the latter for Dublin — *cum jure successionis*. Their ordinary address in this country does not name their sees,[4] but merely entitles them "Most Reverend Dr Everard etc." — you will find them very pleasing and intelligent men. Dr Everard has resided many years in England, and has already a very respectable & extensive acquaintance there. Dr Murray is very popular in Dublin & an eminent preacher. Both are very adverse to a Veto.

I mean to leave town about Tuesday next — after which I shall be at Kilfeacle near Tipperary until April.

[P.S.] There are Catholic meetings held daily at Fitzpatrick's, & pretty well attended — for the purpose of bringing about a reunion & recalling the Seceders.

I had lent your last letter to Mr O'Connell, for his deliberate reading and consideration — and its existence having somehow transpired,[5] he was called upon to produce it yesterday: and, always being ready to yield to solicitations and first impulses, he produced it yesterday under a sense of its high value, & read to the meeting some extracts of a general nature, which I find have been reported this morning[6] — and, tho' he tells me the effect was not injurious to your name or the general cause, yet I am sorry he took that liberty without permission, and have told him so. At these meetings Mr G's name is frequently introduced, and in terms of severity and disapprobation.

I was told by Mr P. Burrows, who is a confidential friend of Mr G's upon Catholic subjects, that the security of Domestic Nomination meets all Mr G's ideas upon the subject of security, and that he would now willingly bring forward a general motion upon this principle.[7] You can make use of this fact in arranging any future cooperation with him upon the motion. It is said too, that Lord Castlereagh has an Emancipation Bill ready drawn by him.

[*Source*: Congleton Papers]

[1]The existing parliament having sat since 1812 there was much intermittent speculation about a dissolution.

[2]Grattan's own bill, with the Canning clauses (see No. 427 n.4).

[3]See N. 329 n.1.

[4]It being illegal under the penal laws (see No. 552 n.1).

[5]Scully would appear not yet to have read the *Dublin Chronicle* of the previous day, which reported that on 25 February Nicholas Mahon had told the committee: "a learned gentleman had shown him a very important communication from Sir H. Parnell — so important that he thought the learned gentleman should be requested to produce it to the committee". The meeting was adjourned to the following day in order to take the letter into consideration.

[6]In the *Freeman's Journal* of 27 February, which reproduced the first five paragraphs of No. 569.

[7]He had already done so in 1810, referring to resolutions adopted by the Catholics of Tipperary and Kildare (see No. 233 n.1). He had good reason to believe that the seceders would accept the formula for William Bellew had written to him on 1 February: ". . . if domestic nomination should be deemed satisfactory to the legislature, it will derive value in our eyes, from appearing to be the measure most agreeable to the Bishops and others of our religious communion" (Grattan, *Life and Times* V, p. 53).

571   *From William Parnell addressed to Mr Fitzpatrick's, Bookseller, Capel Street, Dublin*

Avondale near Rathdrum [Co. Wicklow] 28 February 1817

My dear Sir,

I do not wish to interfere often, but where any one appears to be treated unjustly and that by a misconception one can rectify, one ought not to be silent. It was not long ago that Mr Grattan told me that the dearest wish he now had left was to see the Catholic question carried, that if it was he thought one Catholic member ought to be returned for Dublin and that he would resign his seat to make room for one. It appeared to me that this was a very striking proof of disinterestedness, and that Mr Grattan scarcely had justice done to him and I have since been anxious that my brother[1] should exert himself to produce a better understanding between Mr Grattan and the great body of the Catholics. I know that Mr Grattan has no farther attachment to the Veto than as the only probable means of having the question carried, and I do not see what great obstacle there can be to Mr

Grattan's presenting the petition for I suppose that all personal ones or extraneously political ones such as aversion to Mr Grattan's war measures,[2] would be sacrificed to the general interest of the Catholic cause. There can [be] no doubt that Mr Grattan is the most efficient, and I should think sincere friend to the Catholic cause; a little too deferential perhaps to Mr Canning and the house of Commons; perhaps too anxious to carry the question by compromise but still most anxious to carry it. Pray excuse my writing in haste as our post is most inconvenient.

[P.S.] I direct this to Fitzpatrick's as I know you have left your old house in Merrion Square.[3]   [*Source*: Scully Papers]

[1]Sir Henry Parnell.

[2]Grattan had been a firm supporter of the government's war policy, but Parnell may have been thinking rather of internal measures taken as a result of the war. Grattan's support of the Insurrection Act of 1807 cost him much of his popularity in Ireland.

[3]The contents of this letter are equally applicable to the circumstances of February 1815, about the time when Scully was moving from 8 to 13 Merrion Square (see No. 517 n.1), but the date given on the letter is supported by the postmark on the cover, which is addressed "at Mr Fitzpatrick's". Scully resided at 13 Merrion Square from May 1815 until his death.

571A   *From Thomas Mahon*[1]

4 Bishop Street, 2 March 1817

Dear Uncle,

Mr Mahon[2] is in treaty for the purchase of an estate in the Co. Waterford and for which he has the money ready, which makes it necessary for him to know the particulars of the security you would give for the £2500 you want, so that he might be able to get the money on the security if he required it to make good his purchase. If you send me the particulars per penny post tomorrow directed 26 Merchants Quay I shall call on you [:] on Sunday morning my being obliged to go out of town a short distance in the morning will prevent me waiting on you at the hour you mentioned.[3] I shall return about twelve o'clock tomorrow.   [*Source*: Scully Papers]

[1]Fourth and youngest son of Scully's sister Anne (Nancy).
[2]Nicholas Mahon of 26 Merchants Quay.
[3]There is no punctuation. Although dated 2 March, a Sunday, the letter was perhaps written the day before.

572   *From Sir Henry Parnell to Merrion Square, Dublin*

Emo Park [Queen's Co.] Sunday Eve. 2 March 1817

Private

My Dear Sir,

I have only this moment received your two letters & that of Sir Thos. Esmonde — too late to be able to answer it this Evg. I shall send an answer to-morrow.[1]

From what had occurred between us on former occasions I expected & even wished you should shew my letter to Mr O'Connell & Mr Mahon but I was, certainly, surprised to see any part of it in the public papers, more particularly so as no communication had been made to me, requiring any public notice. All that was going on was a much fitter subject of conversation amongst a few Catholics of influence, as preparatory to public discussion at meetings, than for extended debate. As, hearing the extracts were well selected, I am not on the whole sorry at what has happened & it will get the subject into the circles of political parties, & thus serve to make some progress towards a full discussion & a successful decision.

The difficulty I have to contend against arises from the practice of the House never admitting of two identical discussions upon one & the same motion. If it is known Mr Grattan means to bring on the general question, the members will say I ought not to attempt to forestall it & if I did, they would not attend. If Mr Grattan begins, then they will say the House has given its opinion & settled the question for the session. As it is impossible now to have the general debate sooner than the middle of next month, it would be, I think, adviseable, to come to no fixed plan, until after some further consideration of the business.

I shall forward your letters.   [*Source*: Scully Papers]

[1] After Sir Henry Parnell's letter had been read at the meeting of 26 February (see No. 570 n.5) Sir Thomas Esmonde, as the chairman, had addressed him a letter, drafted by a sub-committee, saying that no reason was seen why he should depart from his original intention of moving on the general question. With it was enclosed a copy of a letter from Sir Thomas Esmonde to Grattan which, on the one hand, asked Grattan to support the petition to be presented by Sir Henry Parnell and, on the other, told him that "if it is impossible to alter our condition without a veto, we should be more satisfied at being left as we are" (texts in *Orthodox Journal*, March 1817).

573   *To Sir Henry Parnell, Emo Park, readdressed to Maryboro*

Dublin, 4 March 1817

My dear Sir,

I had the pleasure of receiving your letter of Sunday, and was sorry, indeed vexed, to see that any extract from your former letter had found its way into the papers. I told Mr O'C[onnell] so, but the fact is, he had the use of your letter for a whole day, for the purpose, as was understood, merely of enabling him to communicate, discreetly and sparingly, the substance of certain parts of it to the meeting. However, such is the facility of his nature, when assailed by the many headed monster, a mob, and such the voracity of that monster for any article in the shape of a letter, when once scented, that he had much ado, he says, to protect himself from yielding up the whole letter, as was loudly demanded. He compromised, by giving certain selections; and Mr Hay, who knows neither discretion nor delicacy, could not resist the temptation of giving copies to his associate, one Staunton,[1] the editor of the *Freeman's Journal*. However, this will close any such communication in future, on my part. It is some consolation, that this indiscretion, tho' unwarr[ant]able, may prove beneficial in some respects. It will impress upon the Catholic body, by the authority of your avowed recommendation, the wisdom & necessity of the course you suggest, and render them more willing to submit to an application to Mr G[rattan] — It will also tend to disarm any personal jealousies, that Mr G. & his friends may have conceived towards you on account of the preferences of the Catholic body — and dispose him & them to cooperate with you effectually and *de bonne foi*. Perhaps some other advantages may flow from this circumstance, when the discussion comes on in the House — I see that Lord Grey, in a late speech upon Lord Sidmouth's Bill,[2] made a kind and happy use of the admission "that Ireland is now tranquil", by [?] expressing the present season as a proper time for Catholic Emancipation.

From your letter, I presume that your answer to Sir Thos. Esmonde will arrive this morning. There is an anxious interest excited for its reception.[3] Mr Grattan's is also expected, but I have heard nothing further.[4]

I leave town tomorrow night.   [*Source*: Congleton Papers]

[1]Michael Staunton. No light can be thrown on the nature of Hay's association with him.
[2]On the second reading of the Habeas Corpus Suspension Bill on 24 February Lord Sidmouth had said there was no need to extend it to Ireland, where the disaffected of England did not appear to have made a single convert (see *Hansard* XXXV, 558, 581).
[3]In his reply dated 3 March Parnell said he would continue his efforts (*Orthodox Journal*, March 1817, p. 112).

[4]Grattan replied on 2 March that he would always be ready to hold communication with Parnell and support the application for Emancipation but must "decline the function of being the advocate of any opinion which would import my concurrence in the idea that a perpetual exclusion from the constitution is preferable to liberty with the veto" (ibid.).

574   *From Sir Henry Parnell to Merrion Square Sth., Dublin*

                    32 Duke Street, St James's [London] 29 April 1817
Private
My Dear Sir,

I am glad to be able to tell you that every thing is going on very favourably. The Archbishops[1] have been very well received, & the question has become again popular & in favour with all its old advocates.

The Petition was very well received.[2] Not so, the attempt to do away its effect by one of the members.[3]

A Bill is preparing on the probability of Mr Grattan's motion being carried; those who know the House very well are of opinion we shall succeed. I gave Mr Grattan a copy of your Bill[4] & he observed it contained a great deal of valuable matter.

As the departure of the Post suits the Saturday's publication of the *Evening Post*, & would be too late for the *Chronicle* I have sent a *Morning Chronicle* to the Editor, as containing the most accurate report of what I said on presenting the Petition.

[P.S.] I have found Lord Grey & Lord Holland particularly anxious about the question, & quite ready to assist in carrying it on the most liberal feelings. Should Mr Grattan not succeed, I shall then move for the Select Committee on the Penal Laws.   [*Source*: Scully Papers]

[1]Doctors Everard and Murray (see No. 570).

[2]Presented on the previous day and ordered to be laid on the table. It was the 1812 petition (drafted by Scully — see No. 567 n.4) with the insertion of a new passage on domestic nomination. Having drawn attention to this Sir Henry Parnell added: "he was enabled further to say, that should the general outline of this plan of domestic nomination be approved of, but should it be thought that it might be rendered more efficient by additional regulations, the Catholics would have no objection to accede to any propositions which might be thought necessary to the security of the Protestant institutions, and which would not endanger their own" (*Hansard* XXXVI, 3).

[3]Daniel Webb Webber, MP for Armagh city since the death of Dr Duigenan, warned that concessions would effect "nothing short of an incipient revolution in the protestant church of Ireland" (ibid., 8).

[4]The Irish Catholics' own bill of 1815 (see No. 495 n.1).

575   *From Sir Henry Parnell, London, to Merrion Square,*
9 May 1817

Private. The prevalent opinion is that Grattan's motion[1] will be carried. The leaders of both parties have shown greater interest in promoting success than ever before and no hostile measures are believed to have been taken at Carlton House. It will be a great object to prevent the debate from being adjourned, so that the bill can be brought in at once in the event of success. Parnell will therefore not take up time that might be better occupied by other speakers, but he might speak on domestic nomination or reply to any unfair or incorrect statements. Grattan has told him again[2] that he will make use of a good deal of "your bill" if he has to bring one in.

[*Source*: Scully Papers]

[1]To be debated that evening, when Grattan called for the seceders' petition of 1816 (see No. 542) to be read and moved that the House should resolve itself into a committee: *Hansard* XXXVI, 301.
[2]See No. 574.

576   *From Sir Henry Parnell to Merrion Square Sth., Dublin*

32 Duke Street, St James's [London] 10 May 1817

Private & Confidential
My Dear Sir,

The division left us in a minority of twenty four, 245 to 221.[1] I did not think the majority would have been so great but the other side, I really believe, expected to have been beat.

The debate was nearly quite free from reproaches. Mr York's speech & vote[2] was quite unexpected, but it produced no following. It will, however, have influence in the Country. Lord Castlereagh[3] made a very good speech.

I think it may still be possible to obtain the minor concessions; Mr Canning said he had changed his opinion on & was in favour of giving them.[4] If I find I can get any support, I will give notice of a motion for a committee of the whole House to consider of the repeal of those laws which relate to them. I am endeavouring to get the English Catholics to exert themselves in favour of this proceeding.

The Pope's Bull relative to the Bible societies in Poland[5] lost us several votes. The probability of a general election may also have had some influence.

I shall write again to you more fully.   [*Source*: Scully Papers]

[1]*Hansard* XXXVI, 438. There was a better attendance of Irish members than in 1815 (see No. 512): 47 voted for and 32 against the motion.
[2]A stout opponent of Catholic claims when in office. His speech appeared to support going into committee but he ended by voting against the motion (ibid. 339).
[3]Ibid. 396. It was conciliatory and optimistic in tone, but after referring to the document signed by the Irish Bishops in 1799 and expressing his belief that there was no serious repugnance to what parliament might decide he went on to say that if the Catholics should not be sensible of the benefit "he would act in this case as he had acted at the Union — he would adopt a measure, the advantage of which time would demonstrate."
[4]Ibid., 426.
[5]See Ward, *Eve of Catholic Emancipation* II, p. 196. London papers of April had published a translation of a Papal brief of 29 June 1816 commending the Polish Primate on frustrating an attempt to form a Polish bible society. Leslie Foster and Daniel Webber cited passages in which the Pope spoke of "this pestilence . . . this defilement of the faith" (*Hansard* XXXVI, 324, 352).

577   *From Sir Henry Parnell to Merrion Square, Dublin*

32 Duke Street, St James's [London] 13 May 1817
Private & Confidential
My Dear Sir,

I am quite sure that all the minor concessions,[1] that is everything short of Parliament & the High Offices of State, might be obtained if I could get the opposition party to support me. I have been endeavouring to persuade them to do so, but have met with considerable opposition & if I am not sure of certain individuals not getting up & opposing me, there would be no chance of succeeding & no use in the attempt. As the concessions would be of great positive value to the Catholics & as the making of them would very much help to establish a good temper in Ireland I think that it would be of great use to have a Petition from an aggregate meeting to ask Parliament to give what the Speaker etc. are willing to give.[2] There would still be time enough to pass a Bill, if no delay took place in holding the meeting.[3]

I am almost sure that the question will never be carried in the whole, & that if we had got a majority this year, or if we get one next, it will end in the Government giving the minor concessions & postponing the others, so that it is quite essential towards securing all to get in the first place the lesser objects.

In my opinion it was very fortunate that we lost the question, for the plan of proceeding if we had carried it, was to have passed resolutions in the committee containing Lord Castlereagh's plan of securities,[4] & to have put off all further proceedings to next session. If this course had been adopted, it is very probable that meetings would have [been] held in Ireland to object to his securities, & no doubt, meetings would have been held throughout all England for presenting Petitions & reviving the cry of No Popery.

A short Petition signed by a few hundreds would be sufficient for me to act upon; in the mean time I shall do what I can to induce the English Catholics to stir[5] & to reconcile the opposition leaders to the measure.[6]

[*Source*: Scully Papers]

[1]For his failure to secure these in 1816 see No. 555 n.1.

[2]That is, everything short of seats in parliament (see No. 434 n.3).

[3]The next aggregate meeting, of 3 July, adopted a resolution in favour of unqualified emancipation (*FJ*, 4 July 1817).

[4]On 9 May, speaking on Grattan's motion, Lord Castlereagh had mentioned "an interference on the part of the Crown in the nomination of Catholic Bishops" and "an examination of the correspondence between the see of Rome and the Roman Catholic Church". It may have been tacitly understood that stipends would be offered to the clergy, for Lord Donoughmore assured the House of Lords on 16 May that the clergy were desirous of no other stipend but what they received from their religious labours (*Hansard* XXXVI, 396, 607).

[5]Copies of their minutes in the Dublin Diocesan Archives (60/2, IV, 13) show that the British Board voted on 29 May not to apply for partial relief. On 2 June O'Connell, on a visit to London, addressed them and denied that the Irish had asked for partial redress (*FJ*, 7 June 1817).

[6]On 10 July the royal assent was given to a measure of partial relief which was of particular importance to the English Catholics: an Act 57 Geo. III Ch. 92 "to regulate the administration of certain oaths to officers of the army and navy". This allowed Catholic officers to make the declaration against transubstantiation after instead of before they received their commissions and consequently to benefit from the annual indemnity act if they failed to make it at all. For the first time English Catholics could become officers, while Irish officers could now rise above the rank of colonel. See Ward, *Eve of Catholic Emancipation* II, p. 246.

578   *From Sir Henry Parnell to Merrion Square Sth., Dublin*

32 Duke Street [London] 17 May 1817

Private

My Dear Sir,

The Debate went off very favourably in the House of Lords & the members who voted for the question are considered as shewing an encreasing strength.[1]

The point which presses most against you is the dictum that "Allegiance to the Pope must interfere with Allegiance to the King". This has weight from a supposition that the Pope is a person continually directing Irish ecclesiastical affairs.[2] In any new petition, I think it would be well done to confine it merely to a refutation *raisonné* of this doctrine. Another topic which would be well to explain more fully is that the Pope's right to give institution cannot be injurious, because the discipline of the Irish Church affords a complete security against any possible attempt that might be made to fill the sees with individuals hostile to the State.

I have got Mr Ponsonby to call a meeting today to consider of the expediency of passing a measure for partial relief.[3] I shall propose that an amendment should be moved to the address to the Regent at the opening of the next sessions, & also that a committee should now be moved for to report upon the Penal Laws.[4]

I enclose you a copy of a note I took of what Ld Liverpool said last night[5] on the subject of partial relief & upon the Veto.

"I will not refuse anything that can be asked to afford partial relief provided the Government remains essentially protestant."

"If concession is to be made it ought to be made without legislative interference with the Catholic Church."

"I will give nothing for a veto or Domestic Nomination. I renounce all imputation against the Clergy & the manner of appointing them. The Bishops are as respectable a Body of individuals as are likely to be chosen in any other way."

"If you are to make concessions do not embarass them with painful conditions, the more simple the measure is made the better."

"The report upon foreign regulations is not applicable to this Country, because the right of interference with the appointment of the Catholic Bishops is alone founded in their Possessing temporalities & establishments."

These are very nearly the exact words made use of by Lord Liverpool. I read them over to Dr Everard immediately after making the notes of them. P.S. Would it not be of use for the Association to meet & give publicity to Lord Liverpool's opinions in order to lessen the clamour for the Veto. A few resolutions embodying them, with thanks for his liberality & statesmanlike sentiments, & published in the *London papers* would have a considerable effect.

If a resolution was added testifying gratitude for the discussion & attention that has been given to the question, & also for the liberal behaviour & reception towards the Archbishops[6] it would go a great way to serve the cause in another session.   [*Source*: Scully Papers]

[1]Lord Donoughmore's motion to go into committee to consider the Catholic petitions was defeated on 16 May by 142 to 90 votes, 96 of the total being given by proxy. The petitions were two left over from 1816: Lord Trimleston's (see No. 569 n.3) and that of the Irish clergy (see No. 552); and two new ones: the general petition of the Catholics of Ireland and one from Waterford (*Hansard* XXXVI, 270, 442, 600, 678).

[2]Lord Liverpool himself said that the source of his scruples and apprehensions was that, however nominated, Catholic bishops were necessarily subject to foreign influence (ibid. 648).

[3]For the outcome see No. 579.

[4]No more is heard of these two proposals.

[5]The excerpts come from that part of Lord Liverpool's speech covered by columns 646–648 of the *Hansard* report, in which the points noted by Sir Henry Parnell do not stand out with the same clarity.

[6]Dr Everard and Dr Murray (see No. 570).

579   *From Sir Henry Parnell to Merrion Square Sth., Dublin*

[London] 17 May 1817, 4 o'clock

Private & Confidential

My Dear Sir,

The leading members of opposition[1] are all against partial relief & would not support me if I was to propose it. It would, therefore, answer no good purpose to do so, unless I could do it at the instance of the Catholics themselves. I do not think the measure would weaken the question for Parliament & high offices but on the contrary I think it would help it because I think the public opinion here would lean in favour of concessions to the Catholic aristocracy.

In case any public notice should be taken of Ld Liverpool's opinions upon the Veto,[2] great care should be had to keep back any fresh opinion of the Catholics on the subject, & to confine the matter of the resolutions wholly to a justification of the fitness of the existing system of appointing the Bishops. I should not wish my note of his opinion to be published as coming from me.

[*Source*: Scully Papers]

[1]At the meeting called by Ponsonby (see No. 578). It was probably to this meeting that Edward Hay referred when he wrote to Lord Donoughmore on 6 June 1817: "I rejoice in the defeat of the petition for minor objects. Miserable must be the policy of urging such a proceeding. I dare to say Sir Henry Parnell was made to believe that he was to secure the good wishes of the Catholics of Ireland by the introduction of his intended bill, and if he is not already undeceived by the person who boasts that he has them in his pocket [Scully], he will find his mistake the more egregiously erroneous" (Donoughmore Papers, T/3549/D/16).

[2]See No. 578.

580   *From Sir Henry Parnell to Merrion Square, Dublin*

32 Duke Street [London] 30 May 1817

Private & Confidential

My Dear Sir,

I write these few lines to say, there is now a newspaper that will publish anything I send on the Catholic question. It is set up by the opposition, the *Guardian.*[1] The Bishop of Ossory,[2] Mr Foster[3] & Mr Webber[4] having printed their speeches, some notice in the way of short replies should be taken of them. There was an answer to Mr Peel's speech[5] in it a few days ago. The cause suffers very much by leaving the press at liberty to circulate misstatements without any observation in refutation.[6] [*Source*: Scully Papers]

[1]No trace of this newspaper has been discovered. It is not to be confused with a weekly of the same name but supporting the government, the first number of which came out on 19 December 1819.

[2]Dr Robert Fowler (*Hansard* XXXVI, 625).

[3]Leslie Foster (ibid., 304).

[4]D. W. Webber (ibid., 352).

[5]Ibid., 404.

[6]Sir Henry Parnell made an opportunity to reply to some of the misstatements himself on 7 July, by calling for papers on the course of education pursued at Maynooth since the last return of April 1813. He denied Foster's allegation that a "transalpine doctrine" in regard to the powers of the Pope was taught at Maynooth or upheld by the Irish clergy; and produced statistics of the sale of the bible and pious literature to refute the assertion that the Irish clergy were opposed to the education of the lower orders (*ibid.*, 1306).

581   *From William Parnell to Merrion Square, Dublin*

Avondale [Co. Wicklow] 5 July 1817

My dear Sir,

When I went to England I left the letters of my Brother[1] etc. etc. you lent me with Mr Robert Daly[2] to forward to you and I find he neglected to do so. I have written to him to leave them at your house. I wish I could get you to interest yourself in the education of the lower orders.[3] Our Clergy are not sufficient for the task and yours as more engaged still less so, and unless the laity on both sides exert themselves actively it will never be done.[4]

[*Source*: Scully Papers]

[1]Sir Henry Parnell.

[2]Probably Revd Robert Daly (1783–1872), Rector of Powerscourt until he became Bishop of Cashel and Waterford in 1843 (*DNB*).

[3]He is probably referring to his activities in connexion with the Society for the Education of the Poor in Ireland, otherwise known as the Kildare Place Society. For his success in securing the assent of Dr Troy to the publication by the Society of an interdenominational New Testament selection for use in schools see *Catholicon*, 1813, pp. 275, 337.

[4]This is William Parnell's last letter in the collection. On 12 August 1817 he was elected to the Co. Wicklow seat in parliament vacated by the death of George Ponsonby, the leader of the Whig opposition (B. M. Walker, *Parliamentary election results in Ireland*).

582   *To the Hon'ble Richard H. FitzGibbon, Mount Shannon,*
Castle Connell, Co. Limerick

Merrion Square [Dublin] 30 August 1817

Copy

Dear Sir,

I have had the Honour of your Letter upon the subject of the ensuing Election[1] for the County of Limerick, and am sorry that I am prevented for the present, by very particular circumstances, from making any positive promise upon the subject — and particularly as, from a private regard towards the Chief Baron[2] and an acquaintance of several years, I should feel unwilling to do any act that may clash with his feelings or Interests.

At the same time, I am bound to say, that, from every report of your character and many excellent qualities, I should be happy to see you placed in Parliament, and should consider you as a most valuable acquisition to that body. I cannot but feel much gratified and honoured by your recognition of the friendly footing which subsisted between my late father and your noble parent, and I have frequently heard my father acknowledge with pleasure the attachment & gratitude which he uniformly felt towards the late Earl of Clare for his just and upright conduct towards him.[3] Upon my private account, I should be happy to be ranked amongst your wellwishers — but I need scarcely suggest to a Gentleman of your rank and information (and I trust you will excuse the liberty I am taking) that strong claims of a *public* nature would prove material in carrying a County, in which a large portion of the freeholders are, like myself, excluded from their civil rights and compelled for several years past to make earnest annual applications to Parliament for redress — and the more so, as they are called upon to displace one or both of the present Members,[4] who can at least plead the merit of having uniformly and faithfully supported *in person* the applications to which I allude, altho' their general public conduct in other respects must be admitted to be wholly destitute of any claim to the support of independent freeholders. Their past conduct upon *this* subject may perhaps dispense with any declaration of their principles upon the present occasion: but it may be thought otherwise of a young candidate, yet unassayed in public life. You will further indulge me, I hope (for my motives are purely of a friendly nature) when I observe that much might be done in furtherance of your canvass, even before an Election can take place, if your noble Relative,[5] who has a Seat and a voice in the upper House, and whose sentiments upon the subject I allude to are, as I understand, corresponding with his mental endowments and liberal Education, were to cast the weight of his high name and distinguished abilities into the Scale of his Country's Interests in the discussions of the next Session, and were to advocate the sufferings of his petitioning Countrymen with those powers which he is generally reputed to possess.

I would beg leave to urge this the more, because I know that the absence of his Lordship's support hitherto, even by proxy, is a subject of regret amongst many freeholders of your County — and because another noble Peer, of your acquaintance and Interest, possessing a large property in the City of Limerick, thought proper to vote decidedly *against us* upon the late Division.[6] All this may, however, be set to rights before a General Election can call upon the freeholders to come to any determination.

Requesting your excuse for these observations, I beg to assure you how much I am, Dear Sir,

Your very obedient & faithful humble Servant

Denys Scully   [*Source*: Scully Papers]

[1]The next general election — see below. This did not take place until 1818 but rumours of a dissolution had been taken seriously enough for the *Dublin Chronicle* of 31 March to devote an article to the subject.

[2]Standish O'Grady senior.

[3]No information has been found as to the nature of their relationship. As James Scully and his family frequently went to Castleconnell for their summer holidays the acquaintanceship may have been formed there.

[4]The Hon. W. Quin and William Odell. They had voted for Grattan's motion (see No. 576) but on every other matter they supported the administration.

[5]Presumably his brother, the 2nd Earl of Clare.

[6]The Earl of Limerick, whose family gave its name to the part of the city known as Newton Pery, was one of the three Irish peers who voted against Lord Donoughmore's motion on 8 May (see No. 578 n.1).

583   *From S. O'Grady to Merrion Square, Dublin*

M[ount] P[rospect] Bruff [Co. Limerick] 5 September 1817

My dear Sir,

I have been very much engaged or I should have made an earlier reply to your very kind communication; I enclose you Mr FitzGibbon's Letter and return you my best thanks for having answered it in a manner so favorable to me. As we have nothing to apprehend so much as a junction between the Government Candidates[1] it is of the utmost importance that our Friends should withhold their second voices; we have been on the alert & since my return from Circuit, Standish[2] has registered near four hundred *new* Freeholders which must make some sensation in his favour. He has written to Lord Cloncurry for his support & perhaps it may come in your way to put in a good word for him. His Lordship's friends are very well disposed but neither Party would wish to do any thing that did not meet his Lordship's concurrence.   [*Source*: Scully Papers]

[1]The two sitting members (see No. 582 n.4).
[2]His son, Standish Darby O'Grady, who came bottom of the poll in the 1818 election.

584   *From Bishop John Milner to Merrion Square, Dublin*

Wolverhampton, 8 September 1817
Dear Sir,
    I am honoured with yr. letter of the 2d Inst. & though a considerable time has elapsed since I had the honour of writing to you last, yet I believe that the balance of correspondence is in my favour. Upon inquiring of the Rev Mr Birch,[1] Head Master of Sedgeley Park school (Mr Kirk[2] has nothing to do with the school, nor Mr Roe[3] further than as executor to the late Mr Southworth)[4] I found that Mrs Mahon[5] had paid her debt amounting to about £38, on being applied to by Mr Birch in consequence of a friendly letter signed *Fidelis* which he had recd. from Ireland.
    I am in daily expectation of seeing Mr Hayes here on his return to Ireland. If he has not been a successful he has been at least a faithful envoy.[6] While Consalvi is in power nothing is to be expected from Rome in favour of religion in these Islands. I did, indeed hope that the voluminous Parliamentary Report which Mr Walsh,[7] the Jesuit carried with him to Rome would have roused that Court: but it seems to have been insensible (at least Consalvi was insensible) even to this. I presume you saw two pamphlets *The Inquisition*,[8] & the *Remonstrance on The Report to The House of Commons* (The Irish Edition of the latter is sadly mutilated)[9] which Sir Jn. Hippisley attributes to me.[10] They have been applauded at Rome, but have not produced any effect there that I can hear of.
    I am in hopes still that my brethren in Ireland will be able to stop the threatened subjugation of our Churches, but of late I have heared nothing from any of them.[11] I presume you see the *Orthodox Journal*; this will give you an insight into the Catholic politics of England: sometimes I am charged with writing letters in it which are by no means relished in Lincolns Inn.[12]

Finding that the Cathc. Bible Societies & the *Charte Blanche* respecting the *Veto* etc. have had so little effect the Gentn. who as you once expressed it are so good as *to think & act for the Body*, of their own accord, now promise to have nothing more to do with either, & they will keep their promise till Castlereagh, Canning or Grey orders them to act otherwise.[13]

Mrs Eyre & family[14] are now at Leamington near Warwick, & seem anxious to find a fixed residence before the Winter sets in. Mrs Wheble joins me in proper compts. to Mrs Scully & yrself.

P.S. It is a fact that, since yr. first application to me, to look out for a domestic tutor for yr. sons I have never met with one, whom, on the whole I cd. recommend to you.   [*Source*: Scully Papers]

[1]Revd Joseph Birch (c. 1776–1821), of Staffordshire; at Sedgley Park since about 1802, succeeded Thomas Southworth as headmaster 1816.

[2]Revd John Kirk had been headmaster for a short time in 1793.

[3]Revd John Roe (1757–1838) had been at Sedgley Park for two short periods after his ordination in 1784.

[4]Thomas Southworth, headmaster before Joseph Birch.

[5]Scully's widowed sister Nancy, whose son John had been at Sedgley Park before he went to Stonyhurst in 1812 (see No. 376 n.4).

[6]On 16 May 1817 the congregation of Propaganda Fide had rejected the Irish Prelates' proposals for domestic nomination (see No. 544 n.2), saying it would give rise to local jealousies, create room for undue interference by the laity and bring about the very mischief it was desired to prevent by giving the government an excuse for the veto (Ward, *Eve of Catholic Emancipation* II, p. 152).

[7]Edward Walsh (1739–1822), a Jesuit before the suppression of the order, now a secular priest at Durham, went to Rome early in 1817 at the request of the Stonyhurst Jesuits in connexion with the restoration of the Jesuits in England (Ward, *Eve* III p. 28). The parliamentary report would have included the papers printed for Sir J. C. Hippisley (see No. 480 n.1).

[8]Probably the second edition, with emendations and additions, of the pamphlet referred to by Dr Milner in No. 564 (Husenbeth, *Life* p. 315).

[9]By "A Native Roman Catholic Prelate", first published in 1816. It argued that the practice of foreign states in the nomination of Bishops was not relevant, being either an abuse of canon law or not applying in conditions of constitutional monarchy. In 1817 it had been reprinted in Dublin, with many alterations and omissions unauthorised by Dr Milner (Husenbeth, *Life* p. 313).

[10]He said that Dr Milner's "solemn address" had coarsely accused him of the wilful statement of an untruth and represented him as a candidate for office, either on an embassy to Rome or as Ministre de Culte (*Hansard* XXXVI, 1316).

[11]Doctors Everard and Murray having been deputed to represent the Irish hierarchy (see No. 568 n.4) Dr Milner was no longer the agent of the Irish church. According to Sir J. C. Hippisley the two Prelates strenuously denied that he was when they were in London (*Hansard* XXXVI, 1315).

[12]By Charles Butler.

[13]After the publication in London on 17 April 1817 of the papal brief condemning the

Polish Bible Society the English Catholic Bible Society had thought it prudent to drop its name (Ward, *Eve of Catholic Emancipation* II, p. 197). The *Carte Blanche* was probably the discretion allegedly given by the British Catholic Board to their friends in parliament in regard to securities: no evidence has been found which would throw further light on Dr Milner's statement.

[14]Presumably Scully's mother-in-law and her two unmarried daughters.

585   *From Sir Henry Parnell to Clonmel,*[1] *Co. Tipperary*

Emo Park [Queen's Co.] 6 July 1818

My Dear Sir,

Sir Charles Coote[2] having retired from the contest,[3] I write to you among my first friends, to thank you for the exertion you made in my behalf. You will I am sure be glad to hear that the Catholic Clergy were incessant in their endeavours in every possible direction to contribute to my success & that the Catholic freeholders gave me the most decided proof of a real determination to return me. Had it been necessary, I feel sure that I could have polled the whole Catholic tenantry of the County, but the course [of] the election rendered it unnecessary to require more from them than the natural support of their land-lords.   [*Source*: Scully Papers]

[1]Scully, whose account book (MS.27, 493) shows that he had been to Limerick for the elections on the 6th and 7th, was in Clonmel for the Co. Tipperary elections, in which he was once again counsel for Prittie and General Mathew. Replying to an allegation that he was behind an "unnatural combination" between Mathew and Lord Caher to oust the honest Prittie, he told the *Dublin Evening Post* in a letter published on 14 July that he had in fact polled for Mathew and Prittie on the 9th, going on to observe however that all three candidates were supporters of Catholic Emancipation. When Lord Caher succeeded in ousting Prittie the *Dublin Evening Post* of 28 July 1818 alleged that although Denys Scully did not vote for Lord Caher himself he caused all his family interest to vote for him, despite the fact that he was a partisan of Pitt's principles and supported the present government.

[2]From 1802 the 9th Baronet, of Ballyfin House, Queen's County.

[3]The first contested election in Queen's County since 1790 (*FJ*, 9 June 1818). Sir Henry Parnell had been declared elected on the day of his letter, having polled 2400 votes as against Wellesley Pole's 2453 (B. M. Walker, *Parliamentary election results in Ireland*).

586   *From Sir Henry Parnell to Merrion Square Sth. Dublin*

Avondale[1] [Rathdrum, Co. Wicklow] 13 December 1818

Private & Confidential

My Dear Sir,

Mr Grattan is anxious to get a copy of the Bill of 1813[2] & I should be much obliged to you if you could procure one for me. He admits that many alterations are wanting. I should be glad to know all the objections that were made to it at the time[3] & what could be done to render it satisfactory to your body.

Mr Grattan is certainly very anxious to have such a bill ready as shall meet the wishes & secure the support of the Catholics.[4]

I also beg you will let me have a copy of your bill.[5] The Bill of 1813 was drawn by Sir Thos. Pigott[6] & I am sure it will not be difficult to get him to alter it in any way you could wish.

I shall return to Dublin on Thursday.   [*Source*: Scully Papers]

[1]The address of his brother, William Parnell.
[2]Grattan's own bill (see No. 427 n.4).
[3]See No. 429 n.1.
[4]O'Connell's letter of 21 December 1818 to Owen O'Conor (O'Connell, *Correspondence* No. 754) shows that the Catholic leadership had as yet made no arrangements for petitioning in 1819. There had been no petition in 1818. At a meeting held on 29 April, before the dissolution of parliament had been announced, the Board had accepted Lord Donoughmore's advice that the circumstances were too unpropitious to make it worth while presenting one (*FJ*, 30 April 1818).
[5]Probably that of 1815 (see No. 495 n.1).
[6]*Recte* Sir Arthur Pigott.

587   *From Sir Henry Parnell to Merrion Square Sth., Dublin*

2 Lower Grosvenor Place, London, 15 February 1819
Private & Confidential
My Dear Sir,

I received a letter last week from Mr Grattan, asking me to give notice of his intention to bring forward the Catholic question, but without naming any particular day. Upon consulting with Mr Tierney, I thought it better to postpone giving the notice, until I could hear from Mr Grattan in answer to a letter I wrote to him, requesting him to allow me to say when he would bring the Question forward. I expect he will name some day in the first week of March.

You will derive very essential advantage from the arrangement which has placed Mr Tierney at the head of the opposition.[1] I have had several conversations with him, & find him very earnest & anxious to serve you. In point of fact, the management which formerly interfered so much, on this side, with your best interests, has ceased altogether; & I have great hopes, that every thing will be left to Mr Tierney & me, in making the minor arrangements, in respect to the motion to be brought forward & the proper times of discussing them. He has had interviews already with Lord

Castlereagh & Mr Canning on the subject, & has been able to collect from them, that there is no foundation for the rumours that Government would themselves propose some measure of relief. Mr Butler saw Lord Liverpool last week & is impressed with the same opinion. There appears, however, to be a disposition to concede very extensively if the Government can contrive to do so by indirect & quiet means.[2] Lord Liverpool has shewn considerable leaning in favour of some alteration in the Oath of Supremacy, to confine it to a denial of the Temporal power of Foreign Princes, & if Mr Grattan's motion was for a Select Committee in the first instance, to state in a short report what oaths affect the Catholics, &, afterwards, for a Bill to alter the Oaths, there is every probability that such a course of proceeding would be successful. In this way Catholics would be enabled to sit in Parliament & this object once obtained the others would soon be secured.

The English Catholics are particularly anxious to have this plan adopted & everyone I have spoken to prefers it to a motion for a general emancipation. It is by no means certain that the new House of Commons is more favourable than the last. The Anti-Catholics say they have gained twenty seven votes. But, even if we succeeded in carrying a Bill for general emancipation through the House of Commons, there is no chance of having a majority in the House of Lords, so that we might rather injure, than advance the question by endeavouring to gain all; whereas by limiting the effort to seats in Parliament, though we should fail, the information which would be obtained, & the discussion of the particular absurdities of the Oath of Supremacy & the Declarations against Popery would essentially contribute to better success in another session.

There is a general wish among the English Catholics & the Opposition to avoid doing any thing which the Irish Catholics would not approve of, & I have been applied to by many to give them my opinion in that respect. I have given for answers that the conduct of the Irish Government had deprived you of any way of expressing an opinion by any plan of delegation;[3] & that as there was no Catholic Board,[4] it would not be possible to know what would be approved of in Ireland, except by communication with those who may be supposed to be best acquainted with Catholic feelings.

As an aggregate meeting would be a very unfit place to discuss the details & manner of managing the question, I hope that you & a few more, who have opportunities of judging of the wishes & expectations of the body, would have no objection to state, what you think in respect to the plan of confining the effort of this session to the alteration of the Oath of Supremacy & the repeal of the Declarations.[5] That you have done so need not appear to the public, but be made use of only to assist us here in determining upon the course to be adopted.

If Doctors Murray & Everard would come over accompanied by you & Mr O'Connell you would be essentially useful. For as the English Catholics & the opposition are very anxious to cooperate with you, some kind of deputation is quite necessary. But if this cannot take place, some few should associate together in Dublin, to correspond with us here.

[*Source*: Scully Papers]

[1]George Tierney had succeeded George Ponsonby as leader of the opposition in 1817 but as the Catholic question had not been brought up in 1818 this was the first time the opportunity for collaboration with him arose. For Parnell's disillusionment with him see No. 590.
[2]Such as allowing army and navy officers to postpone the oath against transubstantiation until after receiving their commissions (see No. 577 n.6).
[3]As a result of the proclamation of 30 July 1811 and the dispersal of the committee of delegates on 23 December 1811 (see Nos. 289 n.1 and 321 n.2).
[4]The most recent meeting of the revived Board which superseded the Association in July 1817 seems to have been that of 29 April 1818 (see No. 586 n.4). In a letter of 21 December 1818 O'Connell described it as defunct (O'Connell, *Correspondence* II, No. 754).
[5]Forming part of the oaths.

588   *From Sir H. Parnell, London, to Merrion Square,*
9 March 1819

Very private and confidential — Although he gave Parnell the strongest assurance last December[1] that he would bring the Catholic question forward in February, and authorised him to tell the Catholics so, Grattan could not be prevailed upon to name a day earlier than 22 April and does not appear to have a plan or bill ready to propose. At so late a date it will be impossible to get more than one night's debate, when many of upwards of two hundred new members, who could be won over by delay, might be led into a premature vote against the question. In the circumstances he thinks it would be better to have no debate this year but make a great effort to secure one early in the next session, supported by petitions from every parish in Ireland. If Grattan could be persuaded to give up a debate on the general question Lord Nugent would move for a Select Committee on the Oaths, thus making quiet progress in clearing away obstacles.

The Pope having made known a wish that some explanation should be given of Mr Hayes' conduct in Rome[2] an article criticising this conduct had appeared in the *Literary Journal*.[3] Mr Hayes has sued the editor for libel and as the author of the article is a person of considerable rank and weight, and a strenuous friend of the Catholics, the prosecution will greatly injure the general cause. Parnell asks if there is any way of bringing about an abandonment of the suit and feels that he cannot place this delicate business in better hands than Scully's.   [*Source*: Scully Papers]

[1]No doubt on the occasion referred to in No. 586.

[2]While waiting for a reply to the Irish laity's remonstrance (see No. 533 n. 3). He had caused great offence and been expelled from the Papal States on 16 July 1817 (Ward, *Eve* II, p. 152).

[3]On p. 482 of its issue for 24 October 1818 the *Literary Journal and General Miscellany* had printed a document dated Rome, 10 May 1818, given to its unnamed source by Cardinal Consalvi and describing Father Hayes' rudeness to the Pope. On 12 December a short note on p. 604 recorded receipt of a complaint and offered space for a reply. The offer was not taken up and on 1 May the periodical reported that six actions had been instituted against "the publisher etc". With this issue the *Journal* ceased publication (see Alvin Sullivan, *British Literary Magazines 1789–1830*).

589   *From Sir Henry Parnell to Merrion Square, Dublin*

Tuesday, 4 May 1819

Private

My Dear Sir,

There will, no doubt, be some disappointment, at the Debate having concluded without more discussion.[1] But the impression is most decidedly favourable to the question, that has been made by our being so near carrying the question. Had we devided in the regular way[2] we should have been in a minority of forty or fifty. It is likewise a matter of great importance that Mr Peel did not speak.[3] The speeches were so excellent on the side of the Catholics, that they must produce a good effect on public opinion here. Mr Grattan's speech was equal to any of his former ones.

I shall now try to get some effort made to carry some point or other this session. I think of giving notice for a repeal of the laws concerning Property, Religious Worship, Education etc. for I am sure we might get everything very soon by beginning at the bottom & persevering.

I hope Mr Hayes's business[4] will be dropped. His adversary will spare no expence in the defense, & is of a disposition to do the general cause a vast deal of mischief.

I think steps ought to be taken, even now, to secure an early discussion of the Catholic question next session. An association of Catholics & Protestants in London to correspond with a similar one in Dublin & to collect subscriptions for keeping the English London & Provincial Press constantly employed in combating the charges which are brought against the Catholics, would prove particularly useful. Could such an association be arranged in Dublin?   [*Source*: Scully Papers]

[1]On 3 May Grattan had presented eight Roman Catholic and five Protestant petitions, and moved that a committee of the whole House should "consider the state

of the laws by which oaths or declarations are required to be taken or made as qualification for the enjoyment of offices, and the exercise of civil functions, so far as the same affect his Majesty's Roman Catholic subjects, and whether it would be expedient in any or what manner to alter or modify the same, and subject to what provisions or regulations". He was seconded by John Wilson Croker, Secretary to the Admiralty, and Leslie Foster made the main speech on the other side. Only five other members had spoken when there was a general cry of "question" and the Speaker having ruled that the Noes had it the House proceeded to a division, in which 241 voted for the motion and 243 against (*Hansard* XL, 6).
[2]He probably means that more of the opponents than supporters of the motion missed the division as a consequence of premature closure of the debate.
[3]Peel, as also Lord Castlereagh, had intended to speak but had been unable to do so when the Speaker closed the debate (ibid., 79).
[4]See No. 588 n.3.

590   *From Sir Henry Parnell to Merrion Square, Dublin*

London, 29 May 1819

My Dear Sir,

I sent you the Tythe Bill[1] by last night's post. If anything appears to be wrong in it, be so good as to write to me. I shall get the further proceeding with it postponed.

The impression made by the late Debates & discourses upon the Catholic Question is most favourable. It is admitted by all that it must be very soon carried. Ld Grey's new motion[2] will be of the greatest use. I do not see how you can get out of the difficulties which are produced by the mismanagement of your present leaders in Parliament[3] except by leaving the question next session to the English Catholics. They are quite ready to undertake it. This latter point I mention to you quite confidentially. Had we begun the session with the same divisions, we should have been able to do something in the course of it. After the manner in which I was deceived this winter I shall place no more confidence in any new promise to bring the Question on early in the next.

[P.S.] The principle of Parish Petitioning[4] must be persevered in. Nothing did so much good as the numbers presented this session & the short debates upon them.   [*Source*: Scully Papers]

[1]Leslie Foster's bill, ordered to be printed on 20 May, "for the better collection of Church rates, and for the amendment of the laws regarding proceedings before magistrates for the recovery of tithes in Ireland" (*Journal of the House of Commons*, p. 467).
[2]For "abrogating so much of the Acts of the 25th and 30th Charles 2nd, as prescribed to all officers, Civil and Military, and to Member of both Houses of Parliament, a declaration against the doctrine of Transubstantiation, and the Invocation of saints" — presented on 24 May and defeated on 10 June by 141 to 82 votes (*Hansard* XL, 748, 1057).

[3]Presumably Grattan and his friends among the Whig opposition.

[4]Entries under 29 and 30 April, and 3 May in the *Journal of the House of Commons*, pp. 364, 367, 387 reproduce the prayers of at least forty parish petitions. A printed circular of 23 February, signed by William Parnell from the committee room of the Friends of Civil and Religious Liberty, indicated how petitioning might be effected. Recipients of the circular were to collect Catholic signatures without delay, preferably at chapel on Sundays so as to save time and avoid special meetings; the petitions were then to be passed on to friends who would collect more signatures; and they were finally to be sent to W. S. Hart, Fownes Street (DDA 60/2, VII, 5). In Dublin at least there were some special meetings (*FJ*, 25 February and 4 March 1819).

591   *From Revd Walter Blount to Merrion Square, Dublin*

W.hampton, 12 June 1819

Dear Sir,

Will you permit me to introduce a brother of mine[1] on his first visit to your interesting country, to the honor of your acquaintance? He has lately established a very extensive Repository in the Fancy Iron Trade, at Liverpool the nature of which he will best explain to you himself. I believe his prospects in that place are very flattering, but he is of opinion it would contribute much to his advantage could he form a few good connexions in Ireland. I have no other acquaintance to whom I can give him any recommendation, & I know not how to apologise for taking so great a liberty with you, but my kind friend & father Bishop Milner encouraged me by saying that he would add a few lines to support my request, which is, that you would have the goodness to introduce my brother to any of your acquaintance you may deem likely to patronise his undertaking. With kind respects to Mrs Scully & family. . . .   [*Source*: Scully Papers]

[1]George Blount (see No. 592).

592   *From Bishop John Milner to Merrion Square, Dublin*

Wolverhampton, 13 June 1819

Dr. Sir,

It is a long, a very long time since any direct communication has taken place between us:[1] & yet on my part I have endeavoured to convince you that I am still in existence & mindful of your civilities to me, especially by sending you, through Keating, the second edition of a work which I published last autumn, called *The End of Cont[roverse]y*[2] etc. which had been much applauded on this side of the water. I shd. have been particular[ly] happy to have heared something from you on the Religious politics of yr. Island, for such a sudden cooling of a violent heat, as that which appears to have taken place there respecting your second subjugation, I mean that of your Religion to the hypocritical system of this Island, I never witnessed in my life.[3] Are the Irish & Mr O'Connel among others really indifferent on this point? Or do they only appear to be so? I cd. forgive them on this score, if they had not witnessed the infamous Bill which Chs. Butler & George Canning, with the help of Castlereagh endeavoured to palm upon them in 1813;[4] but there being moral evidence that the success of Mr Grattan's last motion[5] wd. have been instantly followed by a Bill of the same nature would lead a plain man to suppose that yr. people were on a sudden become insensible not only to their religious but also their civil rights. One thing above all others surprises me in the conduct of the Irish laity as well as clergy that they should abandon the management of their concerns both civil & religious to Charles Butler & half a dozen leaders of what is called *The British Board*, acting under his directions![6] Yet this is & almost always has been the case for these 16 years past. But where, you may say, shall we find agents or even one agent, to reside in London of sufficient integrity & talents to cope with the bribing, cajoling & feasting enemies, Cathc. & Protestt. of Ireland & Catholicism? I own the choice wd. be difficult but I hope not impossible.

The letter on the opposite leaf[7] of yr. acquaintance & my chaplain, the Revd Walter Blount expresses my wish that you wd. serve his brother George, if it be in yr. power in the line of his business. In consequence of yr. recommending Mr Callaghen,[8] as a solicitor, he has been employed in the affairs of Oscot College connected with Ireland.

Mrs Wheble joins me in begging to be remembered to Mrs Scully in the kindest way.

[*Source*: Scully Papers]

[1] Dr Milner's letter of 8 September 1817, No. 584, was not marked by Scully as having been answered.

[2] *The End of Religious Controversy*.

[3] To all appearances the leaders of the Irish Catholics had left the running to their Irish Protestant supporters and the English Catholics, with Grattan in undisputed control of measures in the House of Commons (see Nos. 587 n.4 and 590 n.4).

[4] The bill which Dr Milner had helped to frustrate with his *Brief Memorial* (see No. 434 n.1).

[5] On 3 May 1819 (see No. 589 n.1).

[6] On 19 June the British Catholic Board resolved not to petition parliament for a while, on the ground that it would injure the cause if petitioning came to be looked upon as routine (Ward, *Eve* II, p. 252).

[7] No. 591.

[8] A document in the Oscott archives indicates that Edward O'Callaghan, attorney, procured from the Court of King's Bench a certificate of judgment dated 20 March 1820 showing that in the Hilary term of that year Dr Milner, the Rev Thomas Potts and the Revd Thomas Walsh obtained a judgment for £286–5s–4d against Dominick

Daly of the town of Galway. The action would have been initiated before the death of Mr Potts on 5 December 1819.

593   *From Sir Henry Parnell to Merrion Square, Dublin*

London, 16 June 1819

My Dear Sir,

I received your observations on the Church Rates Bill[1] the day before the 3d Reading of it & though I told Mr Foster I intended to oppose it & take the sense of the House upon it, he took advantage of my absence from the House to have the Bill read & passed.[2] I was stopped on my way down to the House by a severe fall of rain, & arrived there at 20 minutes before five o'clock.

I have given your notes to Lord Donoughmore & I have spoken to Lord Lauderdale[3] & several other Peers to do all in their power to stop the Bill. Lord Limerick is very violent against it & he perhaps will influence Lord Liverpool to postpone it.

Several emendments were made in the Commons to the Bill.

I shall send you back your notes.   [*Source*: Scully Papers]

[1]Five pages of detailed criticism and suggestions for amendments if it was determined that a bill should be carried "by the weight of Church influence and numbers".

[2]At the report stage on 7 June Sir H. Parnell said he had received a communication from Ireland and forwarded a copy of the bill to Dublin, but no answer having arrived he hoped time would be given to examine it on its merits (*Dublin Weekly Register*, 12 May 1819). On 10 June, however, it had been read a third time and passed up to the Lords (*Journal of the House of Commons*, p. 517).

[3]James Maitland (1759–1839), the 8th Earl, who had been Keeper of the Great Seal of Scotland in the Grenville administration.

594   *From Sir Henry Parnell to Merrion Square, Dublin*

London, 25 June 1819

My Dear Sir,

I am happy to be able to inform you that I have completely succeeded in my exertions to oppose Mr Foster's Bill in the House of Lords. So many peers were present to speak & vote against it that the Bishop of Limerick,[1] contrary to his repeated assurances proposed himself to postpone it.

I am sorry to see that it has been thought necessary to have an Aggregate Meeting in Dublin.[2] There exists here, even amongst the best friends of liberal principles so great prejudice against the name even of an aggregate meeting, that I am always afraid of something happening to interrupt the silent though certain progress the question is making in public opinion in England.   [*Source*: Scully Papers]

[1] Dr Charles Mongan Warburton, Bishop of Limerick, introduced the bill in the House of Lords on 14 June, when the Earl of Limerick supported Lord Donoughmore in asking for more time for consideration. When he moved the second reading on 25 June Dr Warburton offered at once to postpone it till the next session, but this did not prevent Lord Donoughmore from stating his detailed objections, which were no doubt based on Scully's notes: see No. 593 (*Dublin Weekly Register*, 19 June and 3 July 1819).

[2] Announced for 1 July in the *Dublin Weekly Register* of 26 June.

595   *From Sir Henry Parnell to Merrion Square, Dublin*

[London] 5 July, 1819

My Dear Sir,

I have opened this cover[1] to say how happy I feel at the meeting on the 1st going off so well.[2] The resolution for Parish Petitions is I think, the best thing that could have happened.   [*Source*: Scully Papers]

[1] Enclosing Scully's notes on the Church Rates Bill.

[2] The meeting, reported as "most crowded", seemed to mark a revival of enthusiasm for the cause; and while there had been expressions of disappointment or resentment over the outcome of the last motion in parliament the resolutions adopted were temperate and constructive. The Catholics of Ireland were urged to renew their petitions which "can be most advantageously communicated to Parliament by separate petitions from every County, City, Town and Parish in Ireland" (*FJ*, 2 July 1819).

596   *From Sir Henry Parnell to Merrion Square, Dublin*

London, 17 July 1819

My Dr Sir,

I sent you yesterday — House of Lords Copy of the Grand Jury Bill — at [*sic*] the Lords did not, nor could not, make any emendments it is equally correct as the Act itself will be.[1]   [*Source*: Scully Papers]

[1] An "act to amend the laws for making, repairing and improving the roads and other public works in Ireland by Grand Jury presentments. . . ." was passed on 6 July (*Journal of the House of Lords*, p. 847).

597   *From Eneas MacDonnell to 13 Merrion Square South, Dublin*

15 Duke Street, Adelphi, London, 24 December 1819

Dr Scully,

As I make no doubt that O'Connell has mentioned to you the substance of my letters to him,[1] it is not necessary I should repeat their contents. Suffice it to say that every Protestant friend with the exception of Mr Plunkett to whom I have spoken urges our early application to the Legislature, and untill I had seen Mr Plunkett[2] I was led by Jerningham and Butler to suppose that he concurred with this general opinion. All the Catholics here wish for an early discussion and some of the English wish for a separate discussion on their claims. Of this opinion is the Duke of Norfolk as I observe by a letter received from him by Jerningham which he read to me yesterday. This notion confirms our grounds for urgency, and also must make us feel more sensibly that there is a danger our Question will be made the secondary one on account of the delays in Ireland.[3] I was glad to learn yesterday from Jerningham that the Security Bill of 1813[4] has been abandoned on all sides. In any interviews I have had I have pointedly avoided the slightest reference to the Subject.

Taking a general view of our condition and prospects I am perfectly satisfied that all depends on ourselves. If we evince anxiety we may attain some success, but if we should not, I do not hesitate in making this assertion that the arts and intrigues and hostilities of open and disguised enemies and of self-interested and self-actuated friends will prevail against us.

I am this moment returned from the City, where I had an interview with Alderman Wood.[5] I had gone, in pursuance of the wish of one of my brothers[6] to speak with him relative to his Partnership Bill lately intro-duced,[7] and I availed myself of the occasion to thank him for the part he had taken in our affairs. His answer was prompt and decisive. He declared energetically, that he would support us even at the forfeiture of his Seat were he even sure that such would be the consequence of his giving us his aid. I told him of Smyth[8] the Loyal Charity Plunderer and of his being a leading loyalist in the Dublin Corporation. I mentioned his former plunders in Chapels and Churches, and the circumstance of his being the leading supporter of Giffard and the seconder of his resolutions in the last year against the Catholics, his own brother[9] and Alderman McKenny.[10] He was very anxious to know whether these circumstances had been mentioned in any Dublin Paper. I could not say they had. He appears *extremely anxious* that those facts should be put in a train of publication or of authenticated statement to which he could refer, as he would refer to them to shew the value of the Corporation Loyalty of Dublin. He observed that when a general vote of thanks to him was proposed in the Dublin Corporation at the time he obtained the liberation of the four poor Irishmen, the Loyal men of the Corporation objected to the generality of the vote on account of his Politicks but agreed in a vote thanking him for the single act.[11] I expressed my confident belief that it would be found in reference to the discussions of the Dublin Corporation at that time that this same Smyth was one of his opponents. He was also anxious to ascertain how that fact stood — M[ay] I beg you to take the trouble of looking to this but I think it would not be prudent to introduce into any *public* statement a reference to Smith's [*sic*] conduct respecting Wood himself as it might make him feel delicate in referring to the publication lest his doing so might be attributed to personal vindictiveness. I own it strikes me that it would be a favorable combination of circumstances, to have the conduct of a Dublin Corporation Loyalist exposed and that, too, by the most popular Member of the London Corporation.

I beg you will let me hear from you, as soon as convenient; and should any thing be published on this matter or otherwise affecting our case that you will be so good as to have the paper containing such forwarded to me, as I am disposed to make myself as useful as I can while here. I have not had one word from O'Connell, although I am exceedingly anxious to know whether any thing and what has been done in consequence of my communications to him. This determined silence on O'C's part appears to me unaccountable.

I learn here that Grattan is so alarmingly ill as not to be likely to come over at all. God Bless you all and guard against Donoughmore's making our question a family property.[12] It would be the greatest curse that could befall us. *Verbum Sat.*

[*Source*: Scully Papers]

[1]Missing.

[2]W. C. Plunket.

[3]A petition, in substance the same as that of 1818, had been adopted at an aggregate meeting on 6 November (*DEP*, 6 November 1819), but as late as 26 February 1820, when an address to the King was under discussion, it had failed to get an adequate number of signatures (*Orthodox Journal*, 1820, p. 202).

[4]Grattan's bill with the Canning clauses (see No. 427 n.4).

[5]Matthew Wood (1768–1843), Lord Mayor of London in 1816 and again in 1817; MP for London City 1817–43; a vigorous member of the opposition (in *DNB*).

[6]Unidentified. He had three brothers, one of whom was called Randle and another James.

[7]On 8 May 1819 Alderman Wood had been given leave to bring in a bill "to promote the employment of persons in the Fisheries, Trade and Manufactures of Ireland, by regulating and encouraging partnership in that part of the United Kingdom" (*Hansard* XL, 124).

[8]Richard Smyth, a haberdasher of 16 Dame Street, Lord Mayor of Dublin 1823–4.

[9]According to the *Dublin Evening Post* of 20 January 1818 when John Giffard moved

his anti-Catholic petition at the Quarter Assembly he was seconded by William Smith, described as late chairman of the parochial deputies.

[10]Thomas McKenny (1770–1849), Alderman of the Dublin Corporation from 1811, Lord Mayor in 1819.

[11]The resolution was adopted on 18 October 1816 (Lady Gilbert. *Calendar of ancient records of the city of Dublin* XVII, p. 156). Three (not four) poor Irishmen had been falsely accused of coining and saved by Matthew Wood's intervention. A fund was raised for them to which the Lord Lieutenant contributed (Sir Samuel Romilly, *Memoirs* III, p. 264; *DEP*, 12 October 1816).

[12]By entrusting the Catholic cause to Christopher Hely-Hutchinson in the House of Commons. In 1815, when the possibility of taking it away from Grattan was being canvassed, Scully had given his opinion that no one would have been so well fitted if he had not lost his seat (*Sentinel* 22 February 1815). On 27 May 1820 Francis Hely Hutchinson reported to Lord Donoughmore a suggestion by O'Connell that Christopher might be invited to take charge of the petition (Donoughmore Papers, D/48/161).

598   *From Bishop John Milner to Merrion Square, Dublin*

St Mary's College, Oscot, 13 January 1820

My Dear Sir,

The honour of yr. letter of Nov. 26 has not been received so long as to stand in need of an apology for not answering it sooner. It gave me as well as Mrs Wheble, & her son & amiable daughter, heretofore, Miss O'Brien,[1] sincere pleasure to learn that yourself, Mrs Scully & your family enjoy good health. I mention the Woodley family because they were in this part of the country when yr. letter arrived here. I am mortified that Keating[2] did not take care that my orders shd. be fulfilled with respect to a copy of the *End of Controv.*,[3] especially as my only pay for the work was a few copies of it for my friends. If you inquire of Nolan,[4] I trust the copy may yet be procured. My *Summary of the Holy Scriptures*,[5] published [?after] the Book of Controversy & given by me to Andrews,[6] does not se[?em] to take so well in Ireland as the latter, though calculated by me cheifly for that country. It seems that Rome is now ala[?rmed] at the insidious attempts making both in yr. country & in [?mine] to seduce Irish children: it is the business of us Pastors [?to] counteract such efforts. You tell me, Dr. Sir, that the minds of your clergy & people, with respect to the independency of the former are not changed since 1813:[7] I pray this may be the case; but if it is so, would it tend to agitate the public mind, just to hint in yr. petitions, that you trust, whenever Emancipation is granted, that it will be granted without inju[ry] or degradation of our Religion? I have got petitions to this effect sent up to the House of Pt. as riders to Chs. Butler's petitions both in 1818 & 1819,[8] for doing which he & his associates are very angry with me & try to disarm me by affiliated Societies of the Board in the different counties: but I laugh at their puny efforts & have given notice to my people to sign similar petitons next spring, in case the Board continue indifferent to the one thing necessary in my late Pastoral,[9] printed in all yr. Newspapers as well as in ours.

Shd. Mr O'Connel & the rest of your leaders be found really indifferent on this grand point, I shall be tempted to consider it as a reflection on the character of Irishmen. In consequence of yr. suggestions concerning the *Orthodox Journal*, its editor has exerted himself to get it introduced in Dublin. I fear, however, it will not stand long in consequence of the turn & the violence of his politics.[10] This event I shd. bewail, as I consider it, in other respects, as a useful vehicle of information. You will suspect that there are more articles from the pen of yr. friend in it than appear with his name.

I believe that our Board are altogether by the ears on the reform question; the Prince[11] is said to be violently incensed against the Duke of N., Lord Stourton & his brothers, Lord Arundell & several other leading Caths. for the public expression of their sentiments on the above mentioned topic[12] & that the Business of Emancipn. in England is given up as a lost cause; perhaps the unexpected tranquility of Ireland may more than overbalance that irritation.

Mr Blount,[13] to my knowledge has made many inquiries after a tutor & a governess for your young family. The former he despairs of finding qualified as you expect him to be: the latter he thinks easy to be found. The L.H., Lucy Hendren,[14] who advertised from Birmingham has changed her plan & set up a school. I think he knows or has heard of another, who he thinks might suit you. Mr Walsh[15] who is now President of this college (Mr Potts being no more), has mentioned to me a Miss Darw [hole in paper] who has educated young Ladies of the first distinction, & who, [in] addition to her other qualifications can teach the Piano & the Harp: but her terms are very high: she asks 100 guineas per an. I beg my respectful Compts. to Mrs Scully. . . .

P.S. The wandering trio,[16] I believe, are still in London, unable to find a place to rest in. What a misfortune it is sometimes to have too much money! Mrs Eyre has been dangerously ill but is now recovered. Mrs W. & myself will be happy to see you at yr. intend. journey into this country: so, I have no doubt, will the Esqr. of Woodley.[17] He has lately taken into his estate a great part of Bull-march heath, made great lakes etc.   [*Source*: Scully Papers]

[1]Wife of James Wheble, of Woodley Lodge, Berkshire.
[2]Of Keating and Brown, booksellers, 38 Duke Street, Grosvenor Square.
[3]See No. 592 n.2.
[4]James Joseph Nolan, printer, of 3 Suffolk Street, Dublin.
[5]*A brief summary of the history and doctrine of the Holy Scriptures*, reviewed in the *Orthodox Journal* for November 1819. Drawn up at the request of some of the Irish Bishops for use in schools, it was intended to supersede the use of heterodox

abridgments and unfaithful translations in schools and families (Husenbeth, *Life*, p. 413).

[6]Eusebius Andrews, editor of the *Orthodox Journal*, who printed the work.

[7]When the Irish Prelacy and laity condemned Grattan's bill (see No. 438 n.3).

[8]The *Journal of the House of Commons* records no petitions in 1818. Entries under 29 April 1819 include a petition from Liverpool praying for "total and unqualified repeal"; and another from Birmingham, Walsall, Wolverhampton and Newcastle-under-Lyme which pointed out that previous relief measures had never entailed government interference.

[9]Published in the *Dublin Evening Post* of 28 October 1819. It warned his flock against growing radicalism and infidelity, and impressed on them their duty to be faithful subjects of the legitimate government to which they had pledged their allegiance by solemn oaths. A postscript warned against signing any resolution, petition or address in which the interests of religion were concerned "without a saving clause for its integrity and safety" (Husenbeth, *Life*, p. 412).

[10]Having annoyed Dr Milner by publishing articles defending John Lingard and Charles Butler against his attacks, Eusebius Andrews, on publishing his pastoral, had asked "when these officious intermeddlings of the clergy are to cease" (*Orthodox Journal*, p. 406).

[11]Still Regent: George III died on 29 January.

[12]The aftermath of the so-called "Peterloo massacre" at the Manchester reform meeting of 16 August 1816. For criticising the conduct of the yeomanry Earl Fitzwilliam was dismissed from his post as Lord Lieutenant of the West Riding of Yorkshire and the Stourtons had played a prominent part at a meeting at Wakefield held in November to demonstrate support for him. The Duke of Norfolk, unable to attend, had sent a letter which was read out by Lord Petre's son. Lord Arundel is not mentioned in the report in the *British Press* of 23 November but a letter from him dated 25 October is reproduced in the *Orthodox Journal* for November, p. 404, in connexion with an earlier county meeting at York. Dr Milner himself was present at Wakefield.

[13]Revd Walter Blount, his chaplain.

[14]Perhaps related to the Francis Hendren of Birmingham who subscribed to the Catholic Board in 1809.

[15]Revd Thomas Walsh, in succession to Revd Thomas Potts, who had died on 5 December 1819.

[16]Probably Scully's widowed mother-in-law and her two unmarried daughters.

[17]James Wheble, whose address when his sons went to Oscott was Bulmershe Court.

598A   *To Dr Marum, Bishop of Ossory, 20 January 1820*

(Abstract)

Scully's opinion on the case of Revd Michael Fitzgerald, seemingly a Waterford friar, who had read Catholic prayers in a churchyard outside Waterford and had been threatened with prosecution by the Protestant Bishop of Ossory.[1]   [*Source*: Carrigan MSS. 3G]

[1]Dr Kyran Marum, previously President of the Kilkenny Academy, had been Bishop of Ossory since 1814. The Protestant Bishop was Dr Robert Fowler (see No. 580). Scully's opinion, in the diocesan archives, has not been found. The question at issue was probably whether a Catholic priest, debarred by the penal code from officiating at a cemetery, might nevertheless say a few prayers — see the *Freeman's Journal* of 11 December 1818 and the *Cork Advertiser* of the following day for an incident at St Finbar's parish, Cork.

599   *From Daniel O'Connell*

(Private)   Thursday [? 24 February 1820][1]
My dear Scully,

I enclose you Power's[2] letter to me. I wish you could go into this business with Daniel[3] *this day*. I am quite impatient to know what Bennett's[4] claims are on me.

With respect to Hickson,[5] who is the holder of the bill, I wish to inform you that he is a man stubborn and proud with the pride of wealth, the most unpracticable of all pride. If he imagined it was believed that I could control him or that *any man* could control him he would instantly run riot and fling off everything of that kind. He is in a high state of irritation against Bennett and I have I fear no chance whatever of managing him. I will however try.   [*Source*: NLI MS.13, 647: typescript taken from
                                the now missing original in Scully Papers]

[1]So dated because of the apparent connexion with No. 600.
[2]Unidentified.
[3]George Robert Daniel, born 1772, called to the Irish bar 1795.
[4]Richard Newton Bennett.
[5]John C. Hickson, woollen draper of 26 College Green, who was also a discounter of bills.

600   *From Daniel O'Connell*

                                       Merrion Square, 27 February 1820
My dear Scully,

I enclose you the account between us signed. Send me a counterpart signed by you. Many, many thanks my very kind and good friend.

I also enclose you the papers on the B——— controversy.[1] The charge was given me yesterday by Daniel. I return it with my reply. Poor B———. How sincerely I feel for his *exposure*. In truth there is as little talent as good feeling in this composition. It is after all the remote holding out of an uncertain pistol in order to extort money.

[*Source*: *Correspondence of Daniel O'Connell* II, No. 812, taken from the now missing original in the Scully Papers]

[1]Among the Fitz-Simon Papers there is an undated letter from Richard Newton Bennett which shows that at the time of writing he was in prison as a result of Viscount Harberton's having foreclosed on a security. In a postscript he says that Scully will speak to O'Connell on the subject and it seems likely therefore that the exposure of "poor B." refers to the same affair, Hickson being involved as discounter of a bill (see No. 599).

601   *From Bishop John Milner to Merrion Square, Dublin*

Wolverhampton, 22 July 1820

Dear Sir,

I am greatly obliged to you for the honour of yr. letter of the 5th ult. & the draft of an Emancipn. Bill[1] which accompanied it. I waited to make this acknowledgement, till I could send with it a copy of the work, which I promised you & which has but just made its appearance. It remains to be seen whether Mr C.B. will fulfill his promise of annexing my remarks on his *Memoirs* to his next edition of them. I fancy, that, at all events, he will omit the *Dissertation on the Protestation in the Museum*.[2]

I think it right, as you observe that a draft of an unexceptionable Bill shd. be in readiness for any sudden emergency: but what will this avail if your agents in Parliament & the Pope's Secretary at Rome[3] & the acting Vic. Ap. Dr Poynter[4] are leagued together to deliver yr. virgin-church gagged & bound to the Ministerial ravishers? Nothing short of a miracle can save you & us: I expect to see the fatal day; but I hope in God, that among my sins, I shall not have to answer for any share in the foul guilt alluded to. I rejoice that Mr O'Connel who is himself a host has proved staunch to his cause in spight [*sic*] of clamour & every interested motive.

About the middle of August (indeed on the festival of the Assumption) I have given notice that I shall administer Confirmn. at Wingerworth: I know not, however, whether I shall meet yr. Lady & her relatives in that neighbourhood or not.[5] Should I meet them & you at that period, it will be a complete alleviation of my Pastoral labours.

I take the liberty of troubling you with letters & copies of my new work,[6] for Dr Troy & Dr Curtis[7] & have the honour to remain. . . .

P.S. Mrs Wheble & Mr Blount returned last night from Woodley Lodge, where the former has been spending six weeks; they both desire to be kindly remembered to you.   [*Source*: Scully Papers]

[1]Probably the Irish Catholics' one of 1815 (see No. 495 n.1). Grattan having died on

4 June the 1820 petition had been presented by W. C. Plunket on 17 July, but he had refrained from making a motion on it so as not to distract parliament from the "momentous question" of the divorce proceedings against the Queen (*Hansard* NS II, 496).

[2] Butler had published his *Historical Memoirs* at the end of January 1819 and in response to Dr Milner's objections had agreed to insert observations by him in a later edition provided he repeated his acknowledgment of 1813 that his charges against Butler were untrue (Ward, *Eve* II, p. 294).

[3] Cardinal Consalvi.

[4] Possibly a playful allusion to the no doubt accidental omission of Dr Poynter's appointment as Vicar Apostolic in Butler's list of bishops.

[5] Wingerworth was the seat of the Hunloke family. Scully had left Dublin on 21 May to take his wife and two girls to her brother Vincent's home at Highfield in Derbyshire. He was back in Dublin by 1 June (MS.27, 493).

[6] His *Supplementary Memoirs of the English Catholics*, where he repeated his allegation that the copy of the Protestation deposited by Butler in the British Museum was spurious (see No. 211 n.14). On 1 June 1820 he had himself presented to the Museum "eighteen papers printed and manuscript relating to the Protestation" (Add.MSS.5416B).

[7] Dr Patrick Curtis, recently Rector of the Irish College at Salamanca, who had been appointed Archbishop of Armagh in 1819 (see *DNB*). He had been strongly recommended for the position by the Duke of Wellington, who was asked by the Lord Lieutenant to approach him about a suitable successor to Dr Everard at Cashel in 1821 (HO 100/200, f.227).

602   *From Sir Henry Parnell addressed to J. D. Scully[1] &*
            forwarded to Post Office, Clonmell

London, 19 March 1821

My Dear Sir,

The committee on the Catholic Bills[2] will be postponed this evening to Wednesday as some important alteration will be made in it in compliance with the wishes of Doctors Poynter & Collingridge.[3]

There prevails a great degree of confidence of their passing. The King has not taken any part against them. Lord Keith[4] one of his greatest friends, has given his Proxy to Ld Hutchinson in favour of the Bills.

[P.S.] The silence of Ireland on the Bills has been attended with the best effects. Mr Peel endeavoured on Friday to excite an expectation that what took place in 1813 wd be resumed — but failed.   [*Source*: Scully Papers]

[1] James Derby Scully of Tullamaine, Co. Tipperary, a first cousin of Scully.

[2] On 28 February W. C. Plunket had carried by 227 to 221 votes a motion to go into committee and on 16 March the second reading had been carried by 254 to 243. On 19 March the House, again in committee, had begun its examination clause by clause.

At this stage there were two separate bills, which were later combined into one. The first, for civil emancipation, attached to the Oath of Supremacy a declaration interpreting its meaning in a sense thought to be acceptable to Roman Catholics: those taking the new oath would be eligible for parliament and, with stated exceptions, all offices, civil and military. The second bore on the clergy, all of whom were to be required to take the new Oath of Supremacy, while Boards of Commissioners sitting in London and Dublin were to examine correspondence with Rome and, in regard to new appointments, certify the loyalty of Bishops and Deans. Should a report be adverse the King would be free to exercise a veto (*Hansard* NS IV, 951–1313; Ward, *Eve* III, Ch. XXXVII).

3Dr Peter Bernardine Collingridge (1757–1829), a Franciscan, had been coadjutor in the Western District since 1807. His objections were no doubt the same as those of Dr Poynter, who had put them in writing on 5 March. The principal ones were met: the Oath of Supremacy was revised and the explanatory clause was incorporated in it (Ward. ibid., p. 62).

4George Elphinstone, 1st Viscount Keith.

603   *From Bishop John Milner to Merrion Square, Dublin*

W.Hmpton, 26 March [1821]

My Dear Sir,

I hope you recd. through Mr G. Blount of Liverpool my answer to Dr Poynter's *Apologetic Letter*, edited by Chs. Butler,[1] the conclusion of which[2] exactly predicts what is now going forward in the Cathc. body & in Pt. & explains the meaning of the Oath & Declaration contained in the *Petition* of *The Civil Sword*, as it is called, which I saw was a prelude to the proposal of our taking the Oath of Supremacy. You have seen in the *Dublin Herald*, *The Theological Judgment* of my Divines & myself on the two Bills,[3] with which our Petition to the Houses of Parliament is in perfect unison. I have now the honour of sending you a document,[4] which vindicates the Petition from the cavils of Lord Nugent[5] & other members of the lower house, who are for the most part personal enemies to me, no less than they are to *a true & real Emancipation*. I have read with a raptured delight Mr O'Connel's truly Catholic, as well as argumentative & eloquent letters in the *Herald*, as far as they have appeared, & I have engaged Keating to give a fresh edition of them in London.[6] I have, however, taken the liberty of adding a note in the margin, to that passage where the author says that *the authority which propounds an Oath is competent to explain its meaning.*[7] This I grant as to *all matters within its sphere of competency.* But if the Civil power, for example rushing out of this sphere, undertakes to pronounce what are the respective *ecclesiastical & spiritual rights of the Pope & Church* on one hand & of the *King & his Courts*, on the other, I maintain that it belongs to the former & not to the latter to pronounce on propositions of this nature. I then deny that Parliament has explained the Oath of Supremacy (in the proposed Act) in an orthodox sense, on which head I make use of the arguments contained in the Theological Judgment & in the present paper. Certain it is that Charles Butler & Co. want to reduce the power of the Pope & the Church to *a mere internal belief*, which indeed they equivalently express in the Bill, to the utter exclusion of all external discipline & laws. Nor would the Church be allowed or have it in her power to pronounce even on articles of Faith, *in this land of Religious liberty*! if all decisions & decrees, even of this nature were made subject to the *Licet* of a Protestant Secretary of State. I shall be obliged to you, Dr Sir, to communicate the substance of this note, with my respectful & most grateful compliments to the Catholic champion.

I am impatient to learn the result of the Clerical Meeting in Dublin which is advertized for today,[8] & not less so of the lay Meeting which is announced for the end of the week.[9]

I have received by the present post an anonymous letter postmarked Crosskeges or Croskell, Meath, the writer of which[10] abuses me for "getting up a petition against the Bills," threatens that "the Priests in his neighbourhood who take part with me shall be deprived of their support & boasts of the efforts he is making both in England & in Ireland to oppose me. I suspect who the ungentlemanlike & dishonest writer is, who can write me a letter he is ashamed to put his name to & can rob me of one shilling & seven pence English to abuse me. I am confirmed in my opinion by the speech of an Irish Gentleman in the Debate of last Friday,[11] who says he has *letters from a Catholic of distinction in* Ireland who has presided at some of the Meetings, in which he begs that the Members of Pt. will not attend to my representations, or those of certain Lawyers in Ireland who he says are brewing mischeif against the Bills. Mr Talbot of Castle Talbot, Co. Wicklow,[12] now on his way to France, writes to me in the opposite style to the anonymous. His letter is truly consoling to me. I have tried in vain to rouse my English brethren to co-operate with me in saving our common Religion. Dr Poynter sways the others, & he keeps back to see the issue of the contest, depending on the support of Lord Castlereagh's friend, Cardl Consalvi. I shall hope to be honoured with a letter from you, on the important business at issue, as soon as yr. leisure will permit.

Mrs Wheble sends her love to her niece & your children. She begs also to be kindly remembered to you.

[*Source*: Scully Papers]

[1]When he was in Rome in 1815 Dr Poynter had given the Pope a long document in Latin defending himself against Dr Milner's charges (see No. 533 n.4). Charles Butler had obtained a copy of it and had published it about November 1820 with an English translation entitled "An Apologetical Epistle". After some hesitation Dr Milner had taken notice of it by adding twenty pages of Additional Notes to his

Supplementary Memoirs of the English Catholics (Husenbeth, *Life*, p. 432; Ward, *Eve* II, p. 298).

[2]i.e. the Additional Notes referred to above, in which he explained his refusal to sign the English Catholic petition of the previous year (presented to the King at a levee on 7 June). The assurance that "in his Majesty alone they recognised the power of the civil sword within the realm of England" involved, he claimed, recognising the validity of numerous unlawful marriages (Husenbeth, *Life*, p. 425). Charles Butler observes in his *Memoirs* IV, p. 287 that Dr Milner had nevertheless allowed the clergy and laity of his district to sign the petition.

[3]His two divines were his Archpriest and chaplain, Revd Walter Blount, and his Secretary, Revd William Benson. The pamphlet, dated 13 March and entitled *The Theological Judgment of the Catholic Divines of the Midland District*, denied that Catholics could take the proposed Oath of Supremacy (see No. 602 n.2) and censured the arrangements for submitting correspondence with Rome to the boards of commissioners (Husenbeth, *Life*, p. 439).

[4]The present letter was written in the margins of this document, a leaflet entitled *Letter of thanks from the R.R. Dr Milner to Wm. Wilberforce Esq., MP*. It thanked Wilberforce for having presented (on 16 March) a petition, signed by Dr Milner himself and the clergy and laity of Staffordshire and Warwickshire, expressing dismay at the bills before parliament; went into objections in some detail; and in a postscript criticised the amended oath. An uninformed reader of the leaflet would have thought that Wilberforce supported the petition, but Wilberforce (who supported Plunket's bill through all its stages) had expressly said when he presented it on 16 March that he did not concur in the prayer of it (*Hansard* NS IV, 1266).

[5]Lord Nugent had presented the English Catholic petition on 28 February.

[6]Not found.

[7]In an "Address to the Irish People" dated 17 March O'Connell had accepted the first of Plunket's bills on the understanding "that the doctrine of our Church respecting oaths is that the oath is to be taken according to the meaning given to the words by the propounder" (Ward, *Eve* III, p. 70).

[8]It was a meeting of the Prelates of the Province of Leinster and the clergy of the Archdiocese of Dublin. When it closed on 28 March resolutions expressed "unmingled satisfaction in regard to the first bill (in its amended form — see No. 602 n.2) and in regard to the second voiced concern which fell short of outright rejection (*DEP*, 29 March 1821).

[9]An aggregate meeting had been expected but it failed to materialise (*DEP*, 7 April 1821).

[10]The postmark which Dr Milner could not read was probably that of Crossakeel, in the parish of Kilskeer, Co. Meath.

[11]16 March. No such speech by an Irish member was reported by *Hansard* or in the *Dublin Evening Post*.

[12]Unidentified. Castle Talbot was in Co. Wexford.

604   *From Sir Henry Parnell to Kilfeacle, Co. Tipperary*

London, 27 March 1821

My Dear Sir,

I am very happy in being able to tell you that we had a majority of eleven last night on the question of Parliament.[1]

There is every prospect of the Bill passing both Houses. The opponents have been calculating, with great anxiety, upon some stir on the part of the Catholics against the Intercourse Bill.[2]   [*Source*: Scully Papers]

[1]An amendment proposed by Bankes and supported by the Speaker (who was not in the chair) to maintain the exclusion of Catholics from both Houses of Parliament was according to *Hansard* (NS IV, 1468) defeated by 223 to 211 votes.

[2]The second bill, regulating the intercourse of the clergy with Rome (see No. 602 n.2). Like Dr Milner, the opponents were no doubt waiting to hear the outcome of the meeting of the clergy in Dublin (see No. 603 n.8).

605   *From Sir Henry Parnell forwarded to Kilfeacle,*
Co. Tipperary

London, 2 April 1821

My Dear Sir,

Lord Grenville is to take the charge of the Catholic Bill in the House of Lords.[1] His opinion about securities is said to be materially changed, & there is every prospect of those modifications being adopted which are required by the Dublin Resolutions.[2] It is expected that we shall have a majority tonight exceeding twenty,[3] but it is by no means certain that the 2d Reading of the Bill will be carried in the House of Lords.

Numerous letters have been received by the Irish Members from Catholic Gentlemen from all parts of Ireland stating their approval of the Bill & on the whole the adverse opinions make very little impression.

[*Source*: Scully Papers]

[1]As Sir Henry Parnell was writing Lord Donoughmore was determined to relinquish his advocacy of a measure that he regarded as "encumbered with so much objectionable matter". When, however, the opposition peers met at Lansdowne House on 3 April he failed, as he put it, to excite in any of them feelings similar to his own. Yielding to the persuasions of Lord Grenville he agreed to accept charge of the bill on the understanding that it would be altered, if it reached the committee stage, by the omission of the clause imposing the Oath of Supremacy on all the clergy and by confining the Commissioners (see No. 602 n.2) to a single board sitting in London

(Lord Donoughmore to Archbishop Troy 4 April 1821: Donoughmore Papers, D/18/3).
[2]See No. 603 n.8. The concluding resolution had urged Lord Donoughmore and W. C. Plunket to use their influence "to obtain from the justice and magnanimity of Parliament such modification of the aforesaid Bill, as shall not allow it to aggrieve the consciences of his Majesty's Roman Catholic subjects".
[3]The third reading was carried that night by 216 to 197 votes (*Hansard* NS IV, 1548).

606   *From Sir H. Parnell, London, to Merrion Square, Dublin*
19 April 1821

Private and Confidential. The lists of peers who voted on the Catholic bill[1] show the King was favourable to it, a circumstance all the more important because of the part taken by the Duke of York, with whom the King cannot feel pleased for assuming a sort of authority founded on his heirship to the crown.[2] It will be of the greatest advantage to the cause if the Catholics take advantage of the opportunity they now have[3] of gratifying the feelings of the King and he suggests numerous addresses alluding delicately to his supposed favourable sentiments. The Queen's business is now so entirely forgotten[4] that no improper construction would be put on them. Such addresses would produce a great sensation as they would be inserted in the *Gazette*. Little or nothing should be said about claims or disabilities, as this would exclude them from the Gazette.   [*Source*: Scully Papers]

[1]Deafeated on its second reading in the House of Lords on 17 April by 158 to 120 votes, 48 of the minority and 69 of the majority being given by proxy. Out of 27 Prelates 25 voted against the bill (*Hansard* NS V, 355).
[2]The Duke said his opposition was based on principles which he hoped he would cherish to the last day of his life (ibid., 281).
[3]The King's projected visit to Ireland.
[4]The attempt to carry a divorce bill in the House of Lords had been abandoned in November 1820. Sir Henry Parnell probably means that Catholic support for the Queen had been forgotten.

607   *From Sir Henry Parnell, London, to Merrion Square, Dublin*
20 April 1821

The only way of accounting for the King's not taking an open part for the bill is the consequence it would have of breaking up the cabinet and placing him in the hands of the opposition. If the Catholics persevere in petitioning the question will force itself on the cabinet, where the opposite views of Lord Londonderry[1] and Lord Eldon[2] must before long lead to a rupture. He hopes that an early meeting will decide to present petitions very early next session. The less said about the second bill the better. He thinks the right course would be for the bill to be brought forward in the House of Lords next year, where it would be free of all securities.[3] Their majority in the House of Commons should not be risked while it was doubtful what the Lords would do.

[*Source*: Scully Papers]

[1]Viscount Castlereagh had succeeded his father as 2nd Marquis of Londonderry on 6 April 1821.
[2]The Lord Chancellor, who had made the principal speech against the Catholic bill.
[3]The second bill contained the securities (see No. 602 n.2). The implication seems to be that while the House of Commons had committed itself to the two bills by passing them, a fresh start could be made in the House of Lords.

608   *From Bishop John Milner to Merrion Square, Dublin*

Wolverhampton, 5 May 1821

My Dear Sir,

I deferred acknowledging the honour of your letter till I could visit Oscot College in order that the worthy President of it, The Rev. Mr Walsh, might subjoin to my answer the particulars you inquire about, relative to his charge, most of which are unknown to me. Accordingly I paid my visit and left my letter to be filled up by the above named gentleman & transmitted to you: but by today's Post I learn that by some accident or blunder the sheet of paper was defaced & rendered unfit to be sent to you. I therefore write to acquaint you with these particulars, that I may not appear neglectful of yr. commission or indifferent to your important information & remarks. In the course of a few days you may expect to hear from Mr Walsh, who I know, will be happy to receive one or both of yr. sons[1] at St Mary's College, as I shall be [able] to afford you the hospitality of my poor house, in case I shd. receive sufficient notice of the time of your arriving in this time [*sic*] that I may arrange my different visitations, so as not to be then absent from home. At present, I am going to pay my first visit at Winchester & in London, having business of importance in both those cities.

We have just passed through a fiery ordeal, & thanks be to God, your Prelates, Clergy & People have, as heretofore shewn themselves to be the legitimate children of the Glorious St Patrick.[2] At the beginning of the trial, I own, I trembled for the safety of some of my former friends: but, thank God, the danger has passed away without much mischeif, & I hope we shall, all of us, have gained some wisdom by our experience. I rejoice to see that the illustrious O'Connel has detected the *old rat*[3] at the bottom of the Catholic cause, on the late occasion, as he was, when Mr Grattan's Bill[4] & every other irreligious project was on the tapis for these five & thirty years past. I have never ceased to reproach my brethren, your Venerable Prelates with their supineness in leaving it to that wrong-principled lawyer to frame religious symbols & oaths for themselves, as well as their flocks to subscribe & swear to; nor can I excuse yourself & Mr O'Connel for permitting that egregious blunderer to draw up restrictions in Lincolns Inn for enslaving Catholic Ireland. I hope that this may never be permitted in future, & that if another Bill is drawn, it may be prepared & approved of in your Island, before it reaches this.

I beg my best compliments to Mrs Scully & hope that the sprightly fairies[5] she brought hither with her are both well. Mrs Wheble sends her love to them all three & her compts. to you.   [*Source*: Scully Papers]

[1]James Vincent aged 11 and Vincent James aged 10. According to the Oscott school list the younger went in May 1824, the elder in August 1825, both of them leaving in 1828.

[2]See No. 603 n.8 for the failure of the Archdiocese of Dublin to speak out firmly against the arrangements proposed for the clergy. On 12 April a meeting of Prelates in Dublin had agreed to a petition to the House of Lords expressing opposition to the bill in more forcible terms and putting forward an amended oath. According to Francis Hely-Hutchinson Dr Troy was overruled by the southern Bishops, principally by Dr Murphy of Cork (Donoughmore Papers, D/48/193).

[3]Charles Butler. Although Dr Poynter had written to Edward Jerningham on 5 April that the Vicars Apostolic, having no authority themselves to approve of the ecclesiastical clauses in the relief bill before the Lords, could give no authority to Roman Catholics to approve of them, the English Board had adopted an unqualified vote of thanks to the government proposed by the Duke of Norfolk and seconded by Lord Arundell (Ward, *Eve of Catholic Emancipation* III, p. 71).

[4]Of 1813.

[5]Scully's two daughters who had accompanied their mother to England in 1820 (see No. 601 n.5).

609   *From Bishop John Milner to Dublin*

Wolverhampton, 29 September 1821

My Dear Sir,

It has long been my intention to write to you for the purpose of thanking you for your hospitality & civilities to me during my late abode in Dublin,[1] but more particularly for your bringing me acquainted with the great & good O'Connel, whose amiable qualities I could not have associated, in my mind, with his well known great qualities, had not I seen & conversed with him. This intention, however, has been delayed till the present time, by reason of the several long journeys throughout England & some parts of Scotland, which I have undertaken, on the same motive which conducted me into Ireland. I mean that my object was to unite the Catholic Prelates of England

& Scotland with their brethren on yr. side of the channel, in preparing & offering to the Legislature certain forms of oath (when our Question comes next to be debated) which may express full allegiance, without injury, real or apparent to the purity of our Faith, & which might afford adequate security to the Establishments in Church & State, without degradation or oppression of the ancient Religion.[2] The performance of this duty, on the part of my brethren would prevent Mr Charles Butler with such counsellors as Mr George Silvertop & Mr Edward Blount from dictating religious tests to bind the consciences of 37 Bishops, 3000 Priests & five millions of other Catholics, in the manner they have been accustomed to do, in former Bills, as well as in that of the present year. That the Oath of Supremacy in this last Bill was framed by the above named Edward Blount of Bellamore is expressly declared by Mr C. Butler in a letter under his own name to Mr Rayment of York & dated Aug. 2d in the present year, which letter now lies before me.[3] Now, My Dr Sir, if Mr Butler, or any of his friends are left to draw up a test oath for the Catholics (as they are those English Caths., of whom Lord Melvill declared in Parliamt.[4] that "they differed essentially from the Caths. of Ireland & would be *sorry to accept of Emancipation, destitute of the proposed restraints on the Priesthood*") the consequence, I am perfectly sure will be, that an incurable schism among the Caths. of both Islands will follow the passing of an Act for our civil Emancipation. I am very far from pressing the acceptance of the oaths which accompany this letter:[5] let any other forms be drawn up & offered on the part of yr. Bishops, or let the one inserted in yr. Bill of May 1815,[6] be substituted for them: all that I contend for is, that the oaths should be framed, or at least approved of by the Prelates.

But why, My Dear Sir, should not the Bills themselves, together with the Oaths be framed in Ireland, by Irish Catholics! You are the Catholics of the Empire. You form the weight of Catholics in the national scale; you possess the wealth as well as the numbers of the Catholic body. You command our Parliamentary interest in the Legislature. Are you then inferior in abilities to the miserable junta of Lincolns Inn? Is O'Connell beneath Charles Butler in the scale of beings? Or is Scully unable to cope with Silvertop or Jerningham? In the name then of commonsense, for the honour of Catholic Ireland, &, what is of most consequence, for the sake of moral honesty & the Catholic Religion, let our friend O'Connel (I presume to call him my friend) exert the talents which God has given him for the benefit of others as well as for his own, &, with the encreased influence which he has acquired within these few months, let him say that the final struggle for Emancipation shall originate in Catholic Ireland, where the interest of our H. Religion is concentrated. In a word let him, with yr. assistance & that of his other Irish friends frame such a Bill, as he & they, after they have made suitable inquiries, find *can be carried*. Let him & they canvass their Parliamentary friends & appoint their leaders, & let the Parish Priests be solicited to make collections for defraying the expenses of trusty agents in London & for the other necessary expenses of the Bill.[7] I, for my own part, offer fifty pounds, in aid of the good work. I suppose, all along that your Prelates are called upon to furnish the proper Oaths. When this is done, let Lincolns Inn join you, if it will.

All this, I trust you will communicate to Mr O'Connel, with my respectful compts. & congratulations.

I beg to be kindly remembered to Mrs Scully. Her brother Vincent is returned for a short time, from Brussels; I met him last week at Oscot. He will return & bring Mrs Eyre back with him about Christmas. On my way to Scotland I called at York, & saw Mrs Charles Eyre,[8] Mr Eyre & Miss Eyre were then on the Continent but must, by this time, be returned. Mrs Wheble is pretty well & begs her affectionate regards to her niece.

[*Source*: Scully Papers]

[1]Dr Milner left Wolverhampton on 21 June and was back there on 16 July, having visited Cork as well as Dublin (Husenbeth, *Life*, p. 443).

[2]Dr Milner had drawn forms of two oaths in readiness for the next Catholic application to parliament. At a meeting at Maynooth these were provisionally accepted and then printed. On his return he set off again and secured the approval of the other Vicars Apostolic, with the exception of Dr Poynter, who was to be approached by Dr Curtis, Archbishop of Armagh (Ward, *Eve of Catholic Emancipation* III, p. 79).

[3]Edward Blount was to become Secretary of the English Catholic Board on the death of Edward Jerningham in 1822. Revd Charles Rayment was a priest at York. Denying Dr Milner's accusation that he had framed the Oath of Supremacy in the recent bill Butler had told Father Rayment that "Mr Edward Blount of Bellamore would inform him that it was framed by himself, another gentleman and Mr Plunkett. . . ." (Ward, ibid., p. 81).

[4]Lord Melville's speeches on the Catholic question in *Hansard* read as if they were much abbreviated: the reference has not been found.

[5]The printed texts mentioned in note 2 above, with some small corrections in Dr Milner's hand.

[6]See No. 495 n.1.

[7]For the last attempt to raise parish subscriptions see No. 314 n.3.

[8]Formerly Mary Slaughter Pyke. Charles Eyre was one of Scully's brothers-in-law: the York directory of 1823 gives his address as Micklegate.

610   *From Bishop John Milner to Merrion Square, Dublin*

WHmptn, 14 December 1821

My Dear Sir,

From the importance of the subject, on which I wrote to you last, namely the great propriety & probable advantages of the next Emancipation Bill's originating in the clear air of Merrion Square, rather than in the murky cellar of Stone Buildings, Lincolns Inn, I did promise myself the honour & the advantage of hearing your & Mr O'Connel's opinions concerning it.[1] Having expressed the same sentiments to Dr Troy, which I communicated to you, His Grace answered me that he would consult with you both on the matter when an opportunity presented itself. I do not take upon myself to decide whether it is right to petition & prepare a Bill, or not. All that I contend for is that if there is to be a Bill it ought, for all the reasons I assigned in my last to you, to be prepared in Ireland rather than in England. I have avowed to you the motive of my solicitude in this business, namely the orthodoxy of the oath or oaths to be contained in any new Bill, & the security of the Cathc. discipline, in the securities that will be required of us in favour of the Established Church.

The sketches of Oaths for these purposes, a second copy of which I here enclose,[2] have been approved of by most of the Cathc. Prelates in Ireland, England & Scotland during my visits to them, in the course of the Summer: still I am no way attached to these precise forms, but will cheerfully subscribe to any other which may be preferred by yr. Prelates.

As I am now closely engaged with yr. quibbling & at the same time swaggering countryman, Mr Grier,[3] I beg leave to conclude with requesting you will present my respectful compts. to Mrs Scully & the O'Connel of Ireland, & with conveying Mrs Wheble's affectionate regard to her niece.

[*Source*: Scully Papers]

[1]Dr Milner's letter of 29 September, No. 609, was not marked by Scully as having been answered.
[2]For the first copy see No. 609 n.5.
[3]Revd Richard Grier (c. 1774–1829), Vicar of Templebodane (Cloyne) 1817–1829; Chaplain to Lords Lieutenant Earl Talbot and Marquis of Wellesley. He had just published a work of 416 pages entitled *A reply to the End of Religious Controversy* (Husenbeth, *Life*, p. 460).

611   *From Bishop John Milner to Merrion Square, Dublin*

WHmptn, 18 February 1822

My Dear Sir,

I was duly honoured with your letter & felt the truth of your observations, as to the wish of a certain great man[1] to be popular without incurring the displeasure & opposition of the stronger party. Indeed this I have learnt of his character from those who have been for several years the most intimate with him, that however rightly he thinks & feels on different subjects, he is an errant coward & always sides with the stronger party. Hence I do not expect that any thing more than a little spouting will take place in our favour this year: still as I plainly percieve that the religious sentiments of our English Caths. become more & more languid, & the manoeuvres of Butler, Jerningham etc. more artful & diversified, I think it my duty, to warn my own flock at least against the danger to which I foresee they will sooner or later be exposed. This is the object of the present pastoral,[2] which I sent you, & to the other gentlemen whose names appear on the enclosed papers. I have to apologise for troubling you with the direction & conveyance of them: but I depend upon your kindness & friendship. I have sent other copies of the Pastoral to Dr Troy, Dr Murray & other Prelates in a parcel which Keating & Co. have addressed to good Mrs Akenhead.[3] I beg that in presenting the papers addressed to Mr O'Connel you will express to him not barely my approbation of his conduct in our Cathc. affairs of late years, but also my admiration of it, under the difficulties he has had to encounter & my gratitude for it. He has proved himself to be the *Magnum decus columenque rerum*.[4] Had he not proved himself to be that zealous & edifying Catholic which you, Sir, represented him to be in my presence, I should try to get a statue erected in his honour, but believing him to be such a Catholic, I judge that he prefers my poor prayers & mementos which are constantly offered up for him & his family, as well as your own, to the worldly honours that I have mentioned.

You will find a blank paper containing our young Oscotians Address to the Lord Lieutenant,[5] & which he humbly begs you will get, by some means or another presented to his Excellency.

The Papers for Mr Sheehan[6] & Father Hayes, require nothing but to be wafered & properly directed to be conveyed by the Post.

Mrs Wheble begs her compts. to you & her love to her niece.[7] Her son & daughter[8] are not on a visit to the Trio at Bath.[9] Julia is not well; the mother & brother are in good health. Begging to be kindly remembered to Mrs Scully. . . .   [*Source*: Scully Papers]

[1]Probably W. C. Plunket, who on 15 January had taken office, for the second time, as Attorney-General in Ireland.

[2]His Lenten Pastoral of 2 February 1822 had condemned the Oath of Supremacy in all its disguises, claimed that by full and undivided allegiance Lord Liverpool meant entire submission to the Crown in spirituals as well as temporals, and argued that the oath that passed the House of Commons in 1821 was the same as the one condemned by the Bishops and the Holy See in 1789 and 1791 (Husenbeth, *Life*, p. 446).

[3]Mary Aikenhead (1787–1858), founder of the Irish Sisters of Charity (in *DNB*).

[4]After Horace's ode (II, 17) to his patron Macaenas: "great glory and support of affairs". The *Dublin Evening Post* of 29 March 1821 had used the same line in praise of O'Connell.

[5]The school magazine, *The Oscotian*, was not published in 1822, and the Address has not been found.

[6]Probably Revd John Sheehan, parish priest of St Patrick's, Waterford, from 1828 until his death in 1854.

[7]Scully's wife.

[8]He means daughter-in-law, Mrs James Wheble.

[9]Scully's sister-in-law and mother-in-law, visiting his brother-in-law, Thomas Eyre of Bath.

Correspondence on personal matters

1823–1830

612   *To his wife Catherine at Kilfeacle, Co. Tipperary*

Dublin, Thursday, 28 May 1823

Dear Catherine,

I send you a paper which I have cut from Saunder's paper.[1] It gives an account of our horse[2]. . . . I have been confined to my bed for two days by an accident, a fall from my horse, but I shall be quite well again tomorrow.[3] I hope William[4] will get down safe.

Yours affect. Den. Scully

[*Source*: Scully Papers]

[1]Thursday was the 29th, when the letter was probably written.
[2]*Saunder's News Letter* of 28 and 29 May advertises horses for sale, with longer or shorter descriptions.
[3]In a letter to his wife dated 29 May O'Connell reported that Scully had come down on the crown of his head, whether because of a fault of the horse or a fit he did not know. When he went to see him Scully was vomiting and a little deranged. He added the next day that the incident had turned out to be a mere nothing but he remained convinced that it was near apoplexy (O'Connell, *Correspondence* II, No. 1025). The present letter, which is barely legible, suggests that Scully had lost the use of the hand he normally wrote with. There may have been a temporary recovery, but the last entry in his own hand in his account book is 12 June and that in his Tipperary Bank account 30 June. He seems to have started on the Leinster Circuit in July but his expenses were entered by another hand and no finishing date was given (MS.27, 493 ii).
[4]Unidentified.

613   *To Daniel O'Connell, Merrion Square*

Merrion Square, 23 November 1823

Dear O'Connell,

I am sorry to be troublesome to you but I am extremely in want of the thousand pounds which you promised to pay me in December last, and I shall be exceedingly obliged to you if you will endeavour to collect this money for me and pay it to me in the course of a week. I don't know what I shall do if you disappoint me now, for I have contracted very heavy engagements which I am wholly unable to discharge without the help of this money. The two notes of a thousand pounds are dated upwards of eight years ago,[1] and you promised faithfully to have them paid in the summer following that date, yet they are still unpaid though I confidently expected the contrary. Try and stir yourself and endeavour to get rid of this engagement without delay. I expect your speedy compliance with this my desire, and I am, yours very faithfully, D. Scully.

[*Source*: O'Connell Papers, NLI MS.13647]

[1]A list of O'Connell's debts drawn up by his brother James O'Connell on 1 March 1817 shows that Scully was then owed £2274 on money lent by him in December 1815 — no doubt £2000 plus the interest to that date (O'Connell, *Correspondence* II, No. 683).

614   *From Daniel O'Connell*

Merrion Square, 26 November 1823

My dear Scully,

I am excessively pressed this being the last week of the law term, but I will certainly see you on the subject of your letter on Monday at ten o'clock in the morning. I trust I shall then be able to satisfy you.[1]

You may judge how my time is *consumed* when I have not been able even to ask you how your health is.[2] But I will see you and give you the best satisfaction I can on Monday morning.

[*Source*: Typed copy in NLI MS.24, 922 taken from the now missing original in the Scully Papers]

[1]Apart from Nos. 616 and 618 below the remaining correspondence about the debt is omitted, having already been published in volume III of O'Connell's *Correspondence* (see therein Nos. 1062, 1068, 1086, 1098, 1100, 1111 and 1122 taken from the now missing originals in the Scully Papers, and No. 1123 from the Fitzsimon Papers).

[2]On 6 November it was bad enough for Father Peter Kenney to be unwilling to trouble "good Mrs Scully" with an inquiry (O'Connell, *Correspondence* II, No. 1054).

615   *To Richard Huddleston, Sawston Hall*

Merrion Square, 8 February 1824

[He thanks him for his letter of the third and for the trouble he has taken about the purchase of Ballyneale[1] from the Corporation of Yarmouth].

It can be no object to the Corporation to retain this estate, when the fair value is bid for it. I will bid liberally, and even temptingly for it. No other person besides myself will buy this estate, and I only buy it because I do not like the trouble of paying the rent annually, and because it is a convenience to me. Such are the tenants, that, if you distrain them for rent it is a great chance, that the cattle are rescued, & the keepers killed or desperately maimed. The tenants immediately under me have under-let the lands at high rents far above the value to the present occupying tenants, who are terribly oppressed by them, but I cannot help it. £2000 is four years purchase above the market price of such estates in this country. I will pay them that sum, or any other sum, that you or your friend may think the value. . . . Let your friend write another letter to Sir E. Leacon[2] pressing him strongly upon the subject of the bargain and I give you full power to conclude it for me upon any terms you may think proper; always taking care to keep my name out of view, as it must not be mentioned on any account. It will be proper to write also to Mr Sam'l Tolver, the Town Clerk of Yarmouth. He receives my rent and has great influence with the Corporation in the management of this estate. It may be right to offer him £50 or £100 for his services and to gain his goodwill upon this occasion[3]. . . .   [*Source*: Huddleston Papers C3 S15]

[1]A property of a thousand acres near Clonmel held under a thousand year lease from the Corporation of Yarmouth granted in 1714. A memorandum ED 206 in the Norfolk Record Office shows that the Corporation was awarded the property, one of the confiscated estates, in return for having contributed to the funds raised by parliament for suppressing the Irish rebellion of 1641. It was left to Scully by his father, half of it in trust for his third son.
[2]Probably Sir Edmund Knowles Lacon, MP for Great Yarmouth.
[3]Scully did not succeed: the Norfolk Record Office file shows that the Corporation surrendered the freehold to the Irish Land Commission in 1925.

616   *From Daniel O'Connell*

[Spring, 1824][1]

My dear Scully,

....

I send a voucher showing that only £1,000 remains due. If you refuse to sign it without the interest on the bond, tell my clerk so and you shall have that interest immediately.

I do not see any possibility of obtaining a compromise of your cause *on your terms*.[2] I really think it idle to make the offer you suggest but I will do as you desire the first possible opportunity.

[*Source*: As for No. 614]

[1]It was at about this time that O'Connell had reduced his debt to £1000 (see O'Connell, *Correspondence* III, No. 1122).
[2]Probably in the *Scully-v-Scully* lawsuit. A letter written by Denys Scully's brother and co-executor after 1830 refers to an offer made "some years ago". It was to the effect that the legacies and annuities mentioned in the body's of their father's will should be halved — the codicil having reduced them by one quarter and their mother's suit having deprived the executors of one third of the means to pay them (Scully Papers, MS. 27, 485, f.30).

617   *From William & Robert Magee[1] to c/o James Scully*
                  Banker Tipperary forwarded to Merrion Square

                                                    Dublin, 29 October 1825
Sir,
     Annexed you have copy of a letter we recd. a few days ago from Monsr.
J. B. Pasquet ainé of Bordeaux[2] in consequence of which we called at your
house in Merrion Square, where we were informed you were in the country
and would not return to town till after Christmas. We request your answer to
this letter to us No. 31 Mecklenburgh Street, this [gentleman] was introduced
to us by our particular friends, Messrs Walter & David Johnston of Bordeaux.
     We hear the suit this gentleman alludes to in his letter was decided in the
Lords in May or June last,[3] we therefore request you will be particular in what
answer you give us, what the amount of the Legacys are & what vouchers you
will require to be given on their being paid, that I may acquaint Monsr.
Pasquet ainé thereof.   [*Source*: Scully Papers]

[1]Merchants, of 31 Mecklinburgh Street.
[2]J. B. Pasquet senior was Scully's brother in law, having in 1793 married his elder sister
Frances, who died in 1795. There was a son who was a beneficiary under the wills both
of his grandfather and grandmother, James and Catherine Scully, and his father's
letter, which is in French and dated 9 October, gives particulars of his claims.
[3]Ten days having elapsed since the full hearing, the House of Lords gave judgment
against the appellants on 23 June (*House of Lords Journal*, p. 1108).

618   *From Daniel O'Connell*

                                              Merrion Square, 2 November 1825
My dear Scully,
     I enclose your own account.[1] You will find it, I believe, perfectly correct.
My wish is to close it. I propose by a cash payment of £206.3.11½ to reduce it to
£375 and for that sum to give you five notes payable with interest on the 10th of
every month after this, to begin, say 10th of December and so on till the five
are discharged, getting up of course my mortgage and other securities. The
sum in each note to be £75 principal which would make exactly the £375. I
hope this will meet your concurrence. You can negotiate my notes for this
latter sum as they will be paid punctually as they fall due.[2]

                                              [*Source*: As for No. 614]

[1]Now missing. Not very legible entries in Scully's hand suggested that O'Connell's
debt was liquidated on 10 November 1825 (O'Connell, *Correspondence* III, No. 1259

n.1). This is confirmed by a deed of conveyance dated 10 November 1825 between Leonard Doherty of Cashel, Denys Scully and Daniel O'Connell, whereby a mortgage of £2000 on 30 Merrion Square, held by Doherty in trust for Scully, was given up (Archives Department, University College, Dublin, P12/5/121).
[2]In a short letter written in his own shaky hand Scully replied that O'Connel's plan would answer very well (O'Connell Papers, MS.13647).

619   *From Charles Addis to Kilfeacle near Tipperary*

10 Great Queen Street, Westminster, 5 January 1826

Dear Sir,

Every paper mentioned in your letter (except the case with Dr Radcliffe's[1] opinion thereon) has been long since given up by me. The most important of the documents were put into a packing case and delivered by myself to Mr James Scully on the 28 June last, and on the 16 July last I forwarded to Mr Beere a deal box filled with several other papers.[2] I do not think I have a single document that can be useful, but such as I have I will forward without delay. As it may be satisfactory I furnish you below with lists of the papers delivered up by me.

My best regards to Mrs Scully.   [*Source*: Scully Papers]

[1]Probably Dr John Radcliffe, Judge of the Prerogative Court in Ireland. He was made a Privy Councillor in 1818.
[2]Perhaps the attorney William Beere, admitted to the King's Inns in 1789.

620   *From John Evans[1] to Kilfeacle*

Shelbourne House, Stephen's Green, 25 November 1826

Dear Sir,

In reply to your letter I mean that you should instead of 5 per cent interest receive 7½ per cent thus suppose you were now to pay off the £4000 Bonds of 1828 I should take about £3900 besides the interest from January last to this time.

As to Cooleen[2] I think it is probable that it will be disposed of before the 10th December, together with Aillahill which adjoins it. If you had been in Dublin as you are a prompt man of business I think I could have given you a very good thing.

My best regards to Mrs Scully.   [*Source*: Scully Papers]

[1]Unidentified.
[2]In the barony of Ida, Co. Kilkenny.

621   *To Daniel O'Connell, Merrion Square*

Dawson Street,[1] 4 March 1827

Dear O'Connell,

I enclose you the 2 bills for £2,100 and £900 which are so completely filled up that you need only put your name to them. They are so arranged as to rates and terms that they will *certainly* be paid on the days when they become due and you will not have the trouble of applying for a renewal of either of them. Get the bill of £2,100 discounted for me at any rate. I am very much obliged to you for the accommodation to me on the present occasion and will be very glad to do the like again for you whenever it may be necessary.   [*Source*: Fitz-Simon Papers (as printed in O'Connell, *Correspondence* III, No. 1369]

[1]No explanation has come to light for Scully's use of this address.

622   *From Daniel O'Connell to Kilfeacle, Tipperary*

Derrynane, 3 September 1827

My dear Scully,

When I saw you at Dublin some time ago you told me you would require some extension of the period for the payment of the bills I got discounted for you at the Hibernian Bank. Let me know precisely which and how many of those bills it will be your convenience to get *extended*, that is, send me a list of them by dates and precise sums. We must for these things make our arrangements beforehand.

The way I can arrange for you is this, by your sending me a new note or notes for similar sum or sums. I say a note if you want to have but one extended in point of time, notes if you want more than one.

According as you happen to require this accommodation, shape your notes. Enclose them to me here. Date them the first of September and make them if you choose payable one in three and the other in four months, or at any rate four and five months. But let me have them now that it may not appear at the bank to be the same but rather a distinct transaction. Fill them for the sum or sums you want to have renewed and the amount of the discount from the day the original bill will become due until the second one, I mean the substituted one, is payable. I will then be prepared to take up your first bills and you *must* be prepared to take up the substituted ones. Do not postpone making these arrangements whilst we have time to preclude the possibility of disappointments. I need not say that it would be much preferable not to want this species of accommodation but, although I say *that*, I am perfectly willing to procure it for you if you desire.   [*Source*: As for No. 614]

623   *From Daniel O'Connell*

Derrynane, 19 September 1827

My dear Scully,

I have received your letter which is perfectly satisfactory. We can settle for the December bill when you come to town. The fact candidly is that your own conversation made me apprehensive that it would not be your convenience to be so punctual. I ought however to have recollected that you very wealthy gentlemen are in the habit of affecting to want money.

[*Source*: O'Connell, *Correspondence* III, No. 1412, taken from the now missing original in the Scully papers]

624   *From Daniel O'Connell*

6 December 1827

My dear Scully,

I have a bond of yours amongst my papers. I will send it to you cancelled the moment I get it as you do not owe me one shilling of any kind.

[*Source*: As for No. 614.]

625   *From Charles King[1] to Kilfeacle, Tipperary*

30 Dorset Street, Dublin, 14 June 1828

Sir,

I received yours of 8th inst. Upon looking into the pleadings in the Cause of *Scully-v-Scully* I find that the third part which Mr Jeremiah Scully recovered was that which was left to your Mother & belonging to her and that it has nothing whatever to do with the annuity of £75 bequeathed by the will of James Scully to Miss Mary Scully[2] and as I find that there is not any chance of succeeding for her by fair means, and as her circumstances at present require some immediate steps to be taken to recover her rights & having laid all the facts of her claim before Eminent Counsel who is now instructed to prepare a bill against you & her Brother, unless by *return of* post the arrear of her annuity is either remitted to me or Mr Magee.[3] I understand a bill was sometime since filed by one of the annuitants[4] to which you immediately yielded & paid all the Costs. Mr Magee with whom I have conferred since receipt of your Letter, states to me that he has several Letters of yours promising payment which he has promised to hand over to me.

I have paid the postage of this Letter least you might hereafter plead want of notice of my intentions, as I shall not put myself again to the trouble or expence of addressing you.   [*Source*: Scully Papers]

[1]Charles Croker King, attorney, admitted to King's Inns in 1805.
[2]The will may have been badly drafted. In contrast with the bequests to Catherine Mahon's three daughters which were charged on the lands of Ballinacurra Weston (*i.e.* property covered by James Scully's marriage settlement) the immediately preceding ones, to Mary Scully and Lucinda Keating and her daughters, had been followed merely by the words "the same shall be payable by my executors".
[3]Of the firm of William and Robert Magee (see No. 617).
[4]Unidentified.

626   *From B. Pasquet Senior to 13 Marion Square South*

Bordeaux, 16 July 1829

Dear Sir and Parent,[1]
   I remember to your obliging me the letter you had the kindness to write to me last July 1828, I was then in Dublin, and by which agreed with your brother James, both you and he summed me up £20 together £40,[2] my receipt was of July 9th 1828. You told me in the letter that every year, you would sum me up the same sum to assit [*sic*] your sister Maria[3] to be an annuity to her of £75, laid in your deceased father's will and which has not been paid to her since March 25th 1826. Consequently of this I am just sending my receipt of that sum of £20, it will be presented to you, have the goodness to clear it if already it is not. By the same opportunity I write my friend Richard Simpson Esq.[4] to give it you again. Your sister's situation is the sadest, my fortune don't permit me to help her in her most urgent wants, in spite she received little help of gentlemen I[r]landais. Justice would be to pay her her annuity of £75 since the years it is owed to her, and for years to come be so kind in clearing my receipt of £20 to let know my friend R. Simpson of your willing in it, and to recknon [*sic*] to him by his receipt all the sum you will pass in an account to Maria by yourself or jointly with your brother James.

   I am waiting for the legacy of £500 laid in your deceased father's will which is owed since 1816[5] pray inform me in your answer if every difficulties to receive are removed with your brother Jeremie,[6] and make me the favour to direct your letter like those you will write me for time to come to R. Simpson Esq. who will send them to me in France, I will have to you the greatest obligation.   [*Source*: Scully Papers]

[1]From the French, in the sense of "relative", Scully being Pasquet's brother-in-law. The letter is not in Pasquet's hand.

[2]The £40 which the two executors had agreed to pay between them would have been arrived at by reducing the £75 by a quarter in accordance with the codicil to the will and then deducting a further third for the loss of a third of the assets as a result of the law suit (see No. 616 n.2).

[3]Scully's sister Mary, born in 1761, had settled in Bordeaux, where she died in 1831. She too was entitled to an annuity under her father's will.

[4]Probably Richard Annesley Simpson, attorney, of 2 Lower Gloucester Street, Dublin, educated at Stonyhurst.

[5]The legacy due to Pasquet's son was £750 in the body of the will, reduced to £564 by the codicil. The deduction of a further third would have left it at £376. The £500 might have been this sum plus interest.

[6]It was perhaps hoped that he would accept responsibility for the third which Denys and James Scully would not pay; or the Bordeaux relatives may have had claims under Catherine Scully's will, of which her son Jeremiah was the executor.

627   *From Richard Scott[1] to Kilfeacle*

Dublin, 28 December 1829

Sir,

Your brother Mr Wm. Scully has directed me as his Solicitor, to apply to you for payment of his annuity of £225 under his father's will, which is now in arrears for several years, and in case same is not settled that I should take proceedings for recovery thereof.[2] I beg to know whether I shall be driven to the necessity of doing so, or not.   [*Source*: Scully Papers]

[1]An attorney admitted to the King's Inns in 1805; in partnership with William Cullen, 25 North Cumberland Street.

[2]Dr William Scully's claim against the executors of his father's will was not finally settled until 10 November 1834; in 1837 he made a separate settlement with his brother Jeremiah (NLI MSS.27,547; 27,543).

628   *From Edmund Slattery to 13 Merrion Square*

Kilfeacle, 24 March 1830

Sir,

Pat Lahy desired me to mention to you that Mr Walsh's son in Mantlehill[1] ploughd up six acres of pasture land last week, called the lime kiln field. Walsh sayes that he is not bound down by Mr White[2] in any writing not to break any part of his land in Mantlehill. He says let Mr White be at the loss of any cost. Also Michl. Hogan[3] of Golden collected men and horses on Tuesday last 23 inst and ploughed up and dug up from 2 to 3 acres of the bullockfield in Mantlehill. Pat Lahy gave Mr White notice of it on the same day.

Michl. Dalton of Ballynaclough[4] was here with me on Saturday last. He told me to mention to you what the Quinlans[5] intend doing about Springmount, if you serve them with ejectments they will on the very day after cut down all the timber on the land and sell it. Also they will pull down the house and sell off all the slates roof doors and windowes and everything there. Can they have people to buy all those things they have a counsellors opinion on the case they say they can do so as they have a lease forever. You can eject them when one years rent is due, but if one year and a half rent was due they could not do anything. You could seize all for the one half year after serving them with ejectments. So Michl. Dalton says and desired me to mention it all in this way to you. Michl. has it from the Quinlans so Dalton desired to keep it private and not to make mention of his name I should write as he desired. . . .   [*Source*: Scully Papers]

[1]Mantlehill was acquired by Scully after his second marriage. The house was built on the northern outskirts of Golden; the lands of Great and Little Mantlehill extended eastward. No Walsh is listed in the surviving 1834 Tithe Applotment Book for Athassel at the Irish Public Record Office.
[2]Part of Great Mantle Hill was known as White's Lot and it was a Henry White to whom, according to a Scully indenture of 1835, Mantlehill was demised by the Earl of Clanwilliam in a lease of 1785. An entry in James Scully's diary shows that a Mr White gave up Mantlehill from May 1812. The 1834 Tithe Applotment Book of 1834 lists a well-to-do Henry White of Golden Lands.
[3]Listed as a small tenant in Murphy's Lot of Great Mantlehill.
[4]Listed as a well-to-do tenant. Ballynaclough was left by Scully to his son William.
[5]Of Knockatoor (see No. 635). Knockatoor is just west of Springmount, which adjoins Great Mantlehill.

629   *From Daniel O'Connell 5/4/30 continued*

Merrion Square, 5 April 1830

My dear Scully,
    I got so little encouragement in your answer to my last communication respecting my poor friend Bennett[1] that perhaps you will deem it an obtrusion that I should write to you again. You indeed doubted my veracity when you suggested that I could get for you better terms than those which I offered as being to my knowledge the utmost he could do for you. It is therefore nearly in despair that I write to you again. Neither should I do so if

I could not assure you, whether you believe me or not, that it is in your interest to accede to the terms that Bennett now offers. You can easily drive him to insolvency and ruin, total ruin, but you will thereby only make yourself be placed in a worse situation than you would be by accepting his offer. At all events nothing shall induce me to trouble you again on this subject and shall conclude by saying that I am quite convinced you ought not in any point of view drive him to desperation.

I pray of you to excuse me for thus again interfering and believe me etc.

[*Source*: As for No. 614]

[1] Richard Newton Bennett. O'Connell's earlier letter is missing.

630   *To Daniel O'Connell, Merrion Square South*

Merrion Square South, 7 April 1830

My dear O'Connell,

You do not mention Bennett's mortgage for £500 of 200 acres of land in the Queen's County & the house in Hume Street which his friend Mr Browne[1] the sollicitor offered to me a few days ago. It is imposing on you and me to pretend that he can offer no more when he has this mortgage to give & he ought to give it to me who am his only creditor. As for his bond of £500 payable in 4 years you do not say it is payable with interest but I suppose it is so although you do not mention it the bond of £500 of his collateral security I suppose is payable now by the terms of your letter it will be tangible security shortly & no mention is made of any installments.[2] But I must insist upon my attorney Mr Cahill[3] being paid on settlement with for his costs both at law & equity, which I compute at about £60. Upon these terms only will I accept Mr Bennett's proposal. I am letting him off very gently. Let him set about the work immediately the interest upon the securities must be calculated from 31st Decr. last 1829 being the date of your first letter to me offering interest on his part.   [*Source*: O'Connell Papers (NLI MS.13, 648)]

[1] Unidentified.
[2] Scully signed this letter but evidently did not check the punctuation of his amanuensis.
[2] Unidentified.

631   *From Edmund Slattery to 13 Merrion Square South*

Kilfeacle, 7 April 1830

Sir,

I received your letter on Sunday last I was at the fair of Tipperary on Monday we sold two cows and a heiffer for you for £21.5.0 it was Mr James

your brother that bought them. . . . On Tuesday I went to Cashell to see Mr
Thos. Pennefather[1] according as you mention. He was not at home that day.
I went this morning again to Cashell and I see Mr Pennefather. He told me
that he did not hear from you nor from Mr Gordon[2] about anything of the
kind and that he got no instructions about it at all but when he will he will do
it with pleasure, it is time enough for the Quinlans do not intend doing the
House or trees any damage tho they gave out that they would [There follow
particulars of rent collection and distraint for non payment of stock placed in
Cappa and Golden pounds].

On the night of the 26th of March last there was an ash tree cut at the end
of the lawn here, in the morning we tracked it along through Horney's
meadow and through John Mullany's land and we found it in John Mullany's
yard in a house had no roof on it and we brought it to Kilfeacle house. It was
in two pieces, we left the long piece in the yard about 16 feet long the but
about ten feet long, I put it into my office. On the night of the 28th some
people came over the walls and took away the long piece and put it over the
wall at the end of the stabel. The night of the 2nd inst. some people got in
over the walls and came to my office doors and broke open the lock of it and
took away £ – 8–6 in silver I had convenient to hand and other small things.
Mr James desired me to mention all this to you about the tree. Now if there is
anything to be done about the tree [?] Toby [?] Bourke can do it for I will not
have anything to do in the case.   [*Source*: Scully Papers]

[1]Probably Thomas Pennefather of Maryville, Cashel, 2nd son of Thomas Pennefather of Marlow.
[2]Unidentified.

632   *From Edmund Marum, Kilkenny, to 13 Merrion Square,*
                              8 April 1830

Transmits an order for £170, about £90 from the Kilkenny and £80 from
the Tipperary estates. Thos who have paid have been entered in the book at
Kilfeacle. He gives a list of those who have not paid: he will send Lynch and
Lahy with assistants to drive their stock to pound.   [*Source*: Scully Papers]

633   *From Edmund Slattery to 13 Merrion Square South*

                              Kilfeacle, 19 April 1830

Sir,
      I received your letter of the 17th inst. I was in Cashel on Friday last with
Mr Penefather[1] and I got the affidavit and the notice for Springm[oun]t done

by him I brought them and the Act of Parliament to Mr Richard Creagh[2] & Son, Mr Richd signed them for me. I was with Mr Creagh before and he told me that he could not prevent the Quinlans of doing damage if they had a mind to do so but if you will write him a letter and say that you will secure him in anything that may come across him hereafter, if you do he says that he and his son will keep them down if they attempt doing any damage to the house or place. The notices were servd. before the ejectments upon the Quinlans and others and posted upon the door of the house in Spring Mt I think I lost no time. Mr Penefather told me the affidavit and the notice was enough but if the least damage was done after this to let Pat Lahy and me go to Cashell to himself and that he would draw information for us and that untill then [? words omitted], we are going on with the garden wall here since Easter Tuesday they are going on well. All the money that Mr Lynch will bring in to me this day I will send it on Tuesday or Wednesday next to Clonmell. I got but £3– from John Ryan of Donoskeigh, I find that Pat Lahy gave eight days more time to the Donoskeigh tenants to see if they would do some good before the cant. Mr Lynch is this day I think canting in Pallas. After this remittance any money that I will get I will lodge it in Tipperary with Mr Henston[3] as you desired and it is the best way. I told Toby Bourk to go to Mr Creagh about John Mullany and the ash tree. I suppose he will. . . .

[*Source*: Scully Papers]

[1]Thomas Pennefather (see No. 631 n.1).
[2]Of Castle Park, Golden.
[3]Perhaps Robert Henston, mentioned in the enclosures in No. 619 as receiving a payment from Scully's mother in 1816.

634   *From John Connors to Mrs Scully 13 Merrion Square*

Golden [Co. Tipperary] 26 April 1830

Madam,

I hope you will excuse my presumtion at troubling you with a few lines as I did not wish to trouble Mr Scully hearing he was angry with me for the turning up of about one acre and one rood of part of Mantlehill last year. Mr White I understand proved I turned it up but it was not, it was the widow of the late John Bourke it being her part of the land, as her husband and I was joined in a proposal to the late Edmd. Murphy Esq. for about four acres of that part of Mantlehill that part that was broke by her last year she grazed but Mr White deprived her of the little cow she had to support her six orphans canted her and took her to himself, and left them and her orphans for the neighbours to support them, then the widow turned up that part, but Mr White has turned all on me and brought an attachment agt. me, has bailiffs this month watching to arrest me and made quit house and home, but I will leave it all in the hands of God who knows all. Then has differerent people of respectability applied to Mr White about to have forgiven me, and that my ugly carcass was of no use in gaol but his answer was, it was Mr Scully had the doing of all; if so Madam in honour of the great great God, have the goodness to interfere with Mr Scully in my behalf and keep Mr White from putting me to gaol from an unhealthy wife and five children and myself as unhealthy as her and with lifted hands me and my little family will pray to the God of mercy during our lives to grant you and family a long and happy life in this world and eternal happiness in the next.

[P.S.] I heard Mr White proved I was the first broke any of that field in Mantlehill but Patk. Ryan had five acres broke five years before and Patk. Bourke in my bounds nearly five acres.   [*Source*: Scully Papers]

635   *From Richard Jordan[1] to Merrion Square*

6 May 1830

Dear Sir,

May I beg to know the amount of the rent due to you from the Quinlans, of Knockatoore, as a professional gentleman of the name of White[2] called upon me for the purpose as he says of paying it.

I have had no letter from the Revd M. Pennefather[3] since I wrote to him that you refused paying his rent until renewals were executed. I dare say he is not well pleased, and should not be surprized if he issued an ejectment by some other law agent.

P.S. I called at your house this day and yesterday, but you had gone out.

[*Source*: Scully Papers]

[1]An attorney of this name was admitted to the King's Inns in 1802.
[2]Unidentified.
[3]Burke *LGI* 1958 shows only a Reverend John Pennefather, Rector of Burrosolit-tleton.

636   *From Edmund Slattery to Merrion Square South*

Kilfeacle, 9 May 1830

Sir,

I recd. your letter of 24 April last also your letter by Wiliam Naill with the two notices for Mr Sadleir.[1] I will send them to Clonmell on Tuesday next and if Mr Sadleir is not in Clonmell they will be sent by post from Clonmell. Also I will send what money I have to Clonmell on that day I would write sooner but expecting to get more money day by day from Thos. Lynch and Pat Lahy they can't get money at all. As for canting they say they will not cant any until the fair day of Golden, after that day they will cant all they can whatever the stock will sell for. Thos. Lynch says that he and Pat Lahy has all the stock of the backward tenants under seizure to be canted the day after the fair of Golden. . . .

As for John Mullany and the ash tree I consulted Mr Jams. Scully about it. He told me that he would not do anything about it until you would come home but let me write to you about it. And so I did and at the same time I told Toby Bourk to go to Mr Creagh as you mention to me I do not know whether he did or did not for Toby Bourk and me are no friends. I suffered a good deal about this business and but for Mr James in Tipperary I could not do much here. The Kilfeacle tenants are not whitewashing their houses yet for I had no lime fresh . . . we will all be at it next week. We are building the garden wall it is now about 6 feet high . . . I will be at paving the coach house tomorrow. I agreed with a man in Tipperary for it at 2^d per yard. . . .

[*Source*: Scully Papers]

[1]Probably Scully's brother-in-law, Clement Sadleir of Shronehill.

637   *From Edmund Marum to 13 Merrion Square*

Rathpatrick [Co. Kilkenny] 30 May 1830

Dear Sir,

Annexed I send you a letter of credit for two hundred and forty six pounds ten shillings stg. . . . I had four days delay at Ballyneal.[1] I had to distrain Tobin's and Kenedy's stock. Tobin rescued his cattle from my man in my absence, but his brother came into town afterwards, and gave bail to the pound keeper, that the rent should be paid in fifteen days. I distrained Kielly's stock also, & he promised to send and sell them. Henry Daniel & Richd. O'Donovan have not a pig cow or anything I could distrain — but they have very fine crops growing. We must let them alone until October next, when we shall seize on their crops & make them pay to the last farthing. . . . Butter is bringing in a good price at present — if it continues so I shall be able to send you a large remittance from your Co. Kilny. tenantry in about three weeks. The season has been very moist. The lands in the neighbourhood are naturally wet and cold, & it is but just now they are beginning to do something. Patt. [?]Feehan of Gortnagap has been with me several times about his money — which he expects he will get immediately — & complains of the bad treatment he received.

I have recd. your letter, with two notices, for registering freeholders, which has been attended to, according to directions.[2] [*Source*: Scully Papers]

[1]See No. 615 for Scully's difficulties with this property.
[2]The general elections of 1830 took place in August. The 40 shilling freeholders having been deprived of the franchise by the Irish Parliamentary Act of 1829 only 1871 votes were cast in Co. Tipperary as against 4869 in 1826. There was no contest in Co. Kilkenny (B. M. Walker, *Parliamentary election results in Ireland*).

638   *From Edmund Marum to Kilfeacle*

Rathpatrick, 27 August 1830

Dear Sir,

....

I forgot to get an acknowledgment for the £70 Kilkenny entry and the £14–5 Tipperary. I shall be up on the 15th Sept. next to see what corn each tenant has & to make them begin to thresh.[1]   [*Source*: Scully Papers]

[1]Scully made a will on 3 August 1830, perhaps as a result of a change for the worse in his health. On 10 October, a fortnight before his death, O'Connell wrote to R. Newton Bennett: "I cannot do anything with the Scullys. It is vain to attempt to soften the great brute of brutes in his present state" (O'Connell, *Correspondence* IV, No. 1714).

Undated Letters

639, 640   *From Lord Moira and Lady Ailesbury to*
15 Featherstone Buildings, Gray's Inn, Sunday 25 March

Short notes asking Scully to take letters and a parcel to Dublin.[1]

[1]25 March fell on a Sunday in 1798 and 1804. The latter year is the more probable, Scully perhaps using the address of his brother-in-law, Henry Huddleston.

641   *From Henry Grattan*

Tinnehinch, Bray, 2 July

Sir,

I have seen some very intelligent sensible observations of yours on the subject of the charges of the clergy in your part of the country — you would much oblige me if you could inform me with certainty what the highest ratage is in your part of the country ever paid for potatoes, wheat etc. I know very well that the [1 word illegible] is apt to overstate these payments & therefore I rely on you that you will send me only such as you are sure to be accurate.

642–5   *From Lord Ponsonby to Bagot Street/? March 1807/*

Four notes thanking Scully for information and arranging meeting.

646–7   *From Lord Ponsonby to 11 Upper Titchfield Street/*
?October 1807/

Two notes about his impending arrival and hope of seeing Scully before he leaves London.

648   *From Francis Hely Hutchinson to Merrion Square South*
Thursday night [1810]

He has not received Scully's papers[1] from Lord Donoughmore, who was for a long time detained in England by the gout, but he will write to remind him.

[1]Probably the memoir referred to in No. 259.

649   *From Francis Hely Hutchinson to Merrion Square South,*
                                Friday morning

Scully's note[1] not having reached him until late the preceding day he
proposes to call on Scully in the afternoon.

[1]Probably Scully's letter of 12 April 1813, No. 423.

650   *From William Fletcher*

                                                                Sunday
Dear Scully,
   I have just seen Grattan. I want to speak with you if you can come to me
for a few minutes *now*. I would go to you but cannot conveniently.

651   *From William Fletcher*

Dr. Scully,
   I found my notes on the Arguments before the judges. I know not whether
you can read them — do not give them in my handwriting to Dixon[1] but take
what you will from them, I will call on you for them in the morning as I go to
court.[2]

[1]Unidentified.
[2]Some abbreviated and not easily intelligible notes in Scully's hand are scribbled on
the back of the letter. They begin with a heading "the law of heirs".

The Convention Act of 1793
(33 Geo. III Ch. XXIX)

Whereas the election or appointment of assemblies purporting to represent the people of this realm, under pretence of preparing or presenting petitions, complaints, remonstrances and declarations, and other addresses to the King, or to both or either houses of parliament, for alteration of matters established by law, or redress of alleged grievances in church and state, may be made use of to serve the ends of factious and seditious persons, to the violation of the public peace, and the great and manifest encouragement of riot, tumult and disorder, be it declared . . .

[I] That all assemblies, committees or other bodies of persons elected, or in any other manner constituted or elected to represent, or assuming or exercising a right or authority to represent the people of this realm, or any number or description of the same, or the people of any province, county, city, town or other district within the same, under pretence of petitioning for, or in any other manner procuring an alteration of matters established by law in church and state, save and except the knights, citizens and burgesses elected to serve in the parliament thereof, and save and except the house of Convocation duly summoned by the King's writ, are unlawful assemblies; and it shall and may be lawful for any mayor, sheriff, justice of the peace, or other peace officer, and they are hereby respectively authorised and required . . . to disperse all such unlawful assemblies, and if resisted to enter into the same and to apprehend all persons attending in that behalf.

[II] And be it further eneacted, That if any persons shall give or publish, or cause or procure to be given, any written or other notice of election to be holden, or of any manner of appointment of any person or persons to be the representative or representatives, delegate or delegates, or to act by any other name or description whatsoever, as representative or representatives, delegate or delegates, of the inhabitants, or of any description of the inhabitants of any province, county, city, town or other district within this kingdom, at any such assembly; or if any persons shall attend and vote at such election or appointment, or by other means vote or act in the choice or appointment of such representatives or delegates, or other persons to act as such, every person who shall be guilty of any of the said offences respectively, being convicted thereof by due course of law, shall be deemded guilty of an high misdemeanour.

[III] Provided always, That nothing herein contained shall extend or be construed to extend to or affect elections to be made by bodies corporate, according to the charters and usage of such bodies respectively.

[IV] Provided also, That nothing herein contained shall be construed in any manner to prevent or impede the undoubted right of his Majesty's subjects of this realm to petition his Majesty, or either house of parliament, for redress of any public or private grievance.

[*Source*: *Statutes passed in the parliaments held in Ireland*, Dublin, 1799 Vol. IX]

Extracts from Charles Butler's letter of 22 March 1813 to Edward Hay

(as reported in the *Dublin Evening Post* of 29 June 1813)

. . . . I have been in frequent and intimate correspondence with Mr Scully, during many years, communicating to him everything respecting the Roman Catholics, which came to my knowledge, or fell under my observation and which I thought would be agreeable or useful for him to know. In his answers to me, he has expressed himself pleased with these communications, and desirous of their continuance. In conformity to this general practice, I sent him a copy of a letter to Mr Grattan: . . . The occasion of my sending it to Mr Grattan was as follows: about a year and a half ago one of our most ready and active friends in parliament, desired me to prepare a sketch of an act of parliament for the repeal of every law in force against his Majesty's Roman Catholic subjects in every part of the United Kingdom. . . . I had very little time allowed me for the doing it, and it was intended only to serve as the groundwork of an act to be prepared at a future time when there should be more leisure for it. . . . I sent to [Mr Scully] a copy of a sketch and desired him to favour me with his opinion of it, and to make any additions or alterations in it he thought proper. He returned it with a letter in which he declined any particular consideration of it, but wrote at the end of it some short heads for my observation. To these, of course, I attended, and I afterwards made some alterations in the sketch. In this state it remained, until I received a letter from Mr Grattan, desiring me to prepare a general act . . . ; upon which I sent him the sketch in question, accompanied with some observations. A short time after, the conversation between Lord Castlereagh and me took place; as Mr Grattan's attention appeared to be then employed on our concerns, I sent him an account of this conversation. I have only further to observe that the effect of the act, as it was sketched by me, was to repeal every act against the Catholics of Great Britain and Ireland, without any qualification or restriction whatsoever; and to abolish every oath, except the common oath of allegiance; and that it did not give the slightest right to government to interfere in our ecclesiastical concerns in any form or manner whatsoever. . . .

I shall only add that I was the more unreserved in my communication with Mr Scully, as from his letters, *and his conversations with me* in this country, I considered that his sentiments and mine, on all that relates to Roman Catholic concerns, were the same.

The Right Honourable Robert Peel
to Viscount Sidmouth

Private & Confidential

Phoenix Park [Dublin] 7 October 1813

Dear Lord Sidmouth,

Though I cannot say I attach much importance to the communication to which the inclosed memorandum refers I have thought it right to transmit it to your Lordship.

You will perceive that the gentleman with whom it was held expressly stated that he waited upon me with authority from Mr Scully. Your Lordship is aware I have no doubt of the character of Mr Scully. He is a Catholic barrister of great eminence & the admitted author of a work which has attracted very considerable notice "The Statement of the Penal Laws". Mr Scully is supposed to influence Mr O'Connell and the whole of his faction. O'Connell is better known & more talked of than Scully because he is a better speaker in public, & possibly because he is not so deep and designing a character — There is no doubt that Scully is a man of considerable talent & powers as a writer, and I believe them to be fully equalled by his desire to do mischief & to escape the consequences —

I dare say Mr Mahon, who holds a considerable office in the Stamp Department, & was confidentially employed I believe both by Lord Castlereagh and Mr Abbot, had the interview with Mr Scully which he states himself to have had, but I can hardly think that the Party to which Mr Scully belongs or even Mr Scully himself would have chosen Mr Mahon as the channel of such a communication to the government as that with which Mr Mahon professed himself to be charged.

I know that Mr Scully & his friends are most anxious to procure the release of Mr Fitzpatrick (who published Scully's book & is in jail for the libel it contained on the Duke of Richmond) & of Mr Magee the Editor of the Dublin Evening Post who shares the fate of Fitzpatrick for the same offence, they might hope that the Government could be induced to release these persons in the hope of conciliating the faction to which they belonged, & nothing could be more easy to disavow hereafter the *pacific overture* as Mr Mahon was pleased to term his communication to me —

I hope you will think that whatever the object might be I said nothing of what any advantage can be taken.

P.S. I beg to add that I gave *positive assurances* that Mr Scully's name should not be disclosed on any account whatever.

[Enclosure]

Most Secret
Memorandum

Mr D'Arcy Mahon a gentleman holding a situation in the Stamp Department called twice on Sunday the 3rd of Oct. at my house in the Phoenix park, and left a note informing me that he had something to communicate which deserved immediate consideration, and left a message that he should call at the Castle the next day.

I saw him on the following day (Sunday Oct. 4) and received from him the following communication.

He said that he had long been in the habit of intimacy with Mr Scully, & that a few days since he had some conversation with Mr Scully on the present state of Catholic affairs, that he had expressed to Mr Scully his regret that there had been so much violence on the part of the Catholics, and his opinion that it had been of material disservice to the cause. Mr Scully replied that the prosecutions instituted by the government some time past commencing with the circular letter of Mr Pole had created dissatisfaction among the Catholics, and had caused that irritation and intemperance which had been laid at their charge. Mr Mahon said that he observed to Mr Scully that the appointment of a new viceroy opened the way for mutual conciliation between the government and the Catholics. Mr Scully admitted that it did and said that the Catholics would gladly avail themselves of it, and if any disposition was shown on the part of government to conciliation it would be amply returned by the Catholic body at large.

I here asked Mr Mahon whether he waited upon me by permission of Mr Scully, he said he did, and I inferred (though he did not state it in express terms) at the desire of Mr Scully.

Mr Scully observed to Mr Mahon, that there was a disposition on the part of the Catholics to give such securities in return for the concessions which they required, as would satisfy any reasonable person. I remarked that this was a subject for the consideration of parliament, Mr Mahon replied that he was aware of that, but observed that there might also be a spirit of conciliation existing between the Catholic body and the Irish government, that Mr Scully had assured him that the Catholics had every disposition to be on good terms with Lord Whitworth, and that he (Mr Scully) was satisfied that Lord Whitworth might by commencing his administration by some act which might be considered by the Catholics as an act of favour toward them, give very great satisfaction and promote the disposition which already existed on the part of the Catholics toward conciliation.

I asked Mr Mahon what he meant by an act of favour, he replied that the remission of the punishment to which Fitzpatrick and Magee had been, or probably would be sentenced would be considered as such. Mr Scully assured him that such an act on the part of Lord Whitworth would very much gratify the Catholics & was certain though he did not give a positive pledge that the Catholic body at large would vote an address to Lord Whitworth to acknowledge it. Mr Mahon said that he had *distinct authority* from Mr Scully to wait upon me and wished to know in what light I considered the communication and to have my opinion upon the overture, as he termed it which had been made. He added that he supposed the Govt. in England would be apprised of it.

I told him that it was impossible for me to return any answer or to authorise any communication to Mr Scully whom I could recognise in no other capacity than as an individual, possessing indeed as I had been informed considerable influence over part of the Catholics of this country, that I believed I understood fully the purport of the communication which he had made to me, but I must content myself with hearing whatever he might say, without giving him any opinion upon the effect which it might produce.

[*Source*: HO 100/173 f.85]

Biographical Notes

The following entries are confined to persons mentioned more than once in the letters or accompanying notes. Those whose names are marked with an asterisk are in the Dictionary of National Biography, *which however is not necessarily the only source drawn upon.*

ABBOT*, Charles (1757–1829), from 1816 1st Baron Colchester   MP 1795; Irish Chief Secretary 1801; Speaker of the House of Commons 1802–16.

ADDIS, Charles   An attorney, probably Catholic, introduced to Denys Scully by Henry Huddleston; for a time in partnership with Thomas Norris.

ANDREWS*, William Eusebius   (1773–1837) Publisher of the *Orthodox Magazine* and other periodicals.

ARUNDELL, Lord   James Everard Arundell (1785–1834), from 1817 the 10th Baron; married in 1811 the only daughter of the Marquis of Buckingham.

BAGOT, James John, of Belcamp, Coolock, Co. Dublin   2nd son of John Bagot of Castle Bagot; educated by Jesuits at Liège; King's Inns 1802; still living in 1858 when he was JP and DL.

BAGWELL, John (c.1752 — 21 December 1816), of Marlfield, Co. Tipperary   MP for Co. Tipperary 1792–1806; changed sides twice over Union, which he ended by supporting; was refused a title but before 1807 elections obtained post of Mustermaster General for his son; Colonel of Tipperary Militia until 1805.

BAGWELL, William, (c. 1776–1826) son of the preceding   MP for Clonmel 1798–1819, for Co. Tipperary 1819–26; active opponent of the Grenville administration and appointed Joint Mustermaster General after its fall; Trustee of the Linen Board 1808; Irish Privy Councillor 1810. Gave the "No Popery" administration general support but voted for Catholic claims from 1813. Colonel of the Tipperary Militia from 1805.

BANKES*, Henry (1757–1834)   A crossbencher MP, whose main interest was control of government expenditure; at the height of his influence c. 1812.

BARNEWALL, Hon. John Thomas (1773–1839), from 16 April 1813 15th Baron Trimleston   Brought up in France and spoke with a French accent.

BARRINGTON*, (Sir) Jonah (1760–1834) Barrister; MP in Irish House of Commons; judge of Admiralty Court 1798–1830. Knighted 1807.

BATHURST*, Henry (1744–1837) Bishop of Norwich from 1805.

BATHURST*, Lord Henry Bathurst (1762–1834), 3rd Earl; President of the Board of Trade from March 1807 and Secretary for War from November 1812.

BAYLY, William, of Abbey Lodge, Dungarvan, Co. Waterford
Started as a clerk to the agent of the Duke of Devonshire's estates and later did much of the Devonshire business, acting also as election agent.

BEDFORD*, Duke of John Russell (1766–1839), from 1802 6th Duke, in succession to his brother. Appointed Lord Lieutenant by Lord Grenville: landed in Dublin 28 March 1806 and left 21 April 1807.

BELLEW, Sir Edward (c. 1760–1827), 6th Baronet, of Barmeath, Co. Louth.

BELLEW, William (c. 1762–1835), brother of the preceding Lincoln's Inn 1782; called to the Irish bar 1792. For his services in preventing a Catholic declaration against the Union he was promised a chairmanship of Quarter Sessions in Co. Louth but on the local Protestant gentry objecting he was awarded a pension instead.

BENNETT, Richard Newton (1769–1836) Called to the Irish bar 1796; Chief Justice of Tobago 1832.

BERWICK*, Revd Edward (1750–c. 1817) Rector of Clongish and chaplain to the Moira family. Consulted by Sir Walter Scott for his edition of Swift's works.

BEST*, William Draper (1767–1845) Serjeant-at-law from 1799; later Chief Justice of Common Pleas and a peer.

BLAKE, Anthony Richard (1786–1849), a younger son of Martin Blake of Hollypark, Co. Galway A pupil of Charles Butler (who proposed him for the Cisalpine Club in 1813); solicitor in London; appointed Chief Remembrancer by Marquis of Wellesley in 1823.

BLANCHARD, Abbé Pierre Louis Born in Normandy 1758; fled to England c. 1791; refused to accept Concordat of 1801; went back to France 1814 but returned on Napoleon's escape from Elba and may have died in England; still living in 1826.

BLOUNT, Revd Walter 5th son of James Blount of Cleobury Forge
Douai; St Gregory's College, Paris, until the revolution; then at Ware; priest at Wolverhampton from 1804; President of Sedgley Park school 1821.

BOSTOCK, Mrs Mary Huddleston (c. 1738–1817), sister of Ferdinand Huddleston and from 1803 widow of Henry Bostock, whose business partnership with Ferdinand's brother Thomas was ruined by the French war.

BRAY*, Dr Thomas (1759–1820) Archbishop of Cashel from 1792.

BROUGHAM*, Henry (1778–1868) Called to the English bar 1808; entered parliament 1810; best known in the following decade as the champion of the Princess of Wales.

BROWNE, Colonel Samuel A Major in the Yorkshire Light Infantry with local rank of Colonel; Deputy Quartermaster-General of the forces in Ireland.

BRYAN, Captain/Major George (1770–1843), of Jenkinstown, Co. Kilkenny and Henrietta Street, Dublin Spent much of his youth on continent and was imprisoned by Robespierre; in 1797 bought a commission in the 1st Foot but lost it in 1803 because he was a Catholic; inherited Jenkinstown from an uncle and settled there in 1804; 1806–8 a Major in the county militia.

BUCKINGHAM*, Lord George Grenville (1753–1813), of Stowe, Buckinghamshire, 1st Marquis from 1784; Lord Lieutenant of Ireland 1782–3 (as Lord Temple) and 1787–89. His Catholic wife, Mary Elizabeth Nugent, was created Baroness Nugent in 1800.

BURDETT*, Sir Francis (1770–1844), 5th Baronet MP from 1796, representing Westminster 1807–37; imprisoned on political charges 1810 and 1820.

BURKE*, Edmund (1729–1797), statesman.

BURNE, John KC (c. 1760–c. 1827) Son of Edward Burne, a Dublin merchant; called to the Irish bar 1784.

BURROWES*, Peter (1753–1841), son of Thomas Burrowes of Portarlington Middle Temple; called to the Irish bar 1785; sat for Enniscorthy in the Irish parliament; a United Irishman and vigorous opponent of the Union; a friend of Henry Grattan.

BURTON, Charles (1760–1847) A London attorney from Aynho, Northamptonshire, who was invited to Ireland by J. P. Curran and called to the Irish bar in 1792; KC 1806; Judge of King's Bench 1820.

BUSHE*, Charles Kendal (1767–1843) Called to Irish bar 1790; sat for Callan and Donegal in Irish parliament; opposed the Union; Solicitor-General for Ireland 26 October 1805 to 1822, when he became Chief Justice of the King's Bench.

BUTLER*, Charles (1750–1832), of Lincoln's Inn Descended from the Butlers of Appletree, a nephew of Alban Butler, his mother French. Educated at Douai; Lincoln' Inn; took up conveyancing; called to the bar after 1791 Relief Act; Secretary to the Catholic Committee 1782–91; moving spirit in foundation of Cisalpine Club. Married Mary Eyston of East Hendred, who died in 1814.

BYRNE, John, of Merrion Square and Mullinahack, Co. Dublin Son and heir of the rich Dublin merchant Edward Byrne (died December 1804), who employed him in his overseas business.

CAMDEN*, Lord Sir John Jeffreys Pratt (1759–1840), 2nd Earl and from 1812 1st Marquis Camden. Lord Lieutenant of Ireland 1795–8; Secretary for War and President of the Council under Pitt 1804–6; President of Council again 1807–12.

CAMPBELL, Burrowes Burke   Son of Alexander Campbell and Jane Burrowes. Trinity College Dublin and Lincoln's Inn; called to the Irish bar 1792.

CANNING, Francis (1772–1831)   Head of the senior branch of the family established at Foxcote, Warwickshire, since the 15th century; educated at Douai; with his father a founder member of the Cisalpine Club; Lieutenant Colonel of the Warwickshire Militia 1808; stood surety for Cartwright after "Peterloo" in 1819. Married Jane Huddleston 1810, died without issue.

CANNING*, George (1770–1827)   Belonged to a junior branch of the Foxcote family which settled in Ireland. Held office under Pitt 1796–1801 and 1804–6; Foreign Secretary under Portland March 1807 to October 1809; on an embassy to Portugal October 1814 to June 1815. President of Board of Control under Lord Liverpool from March 1816 but resigned 1820 as a supporter of Queen Caroline. Foreign Secretary September 1822; Prime Minister 1827.

CASTLEREAGH*, Lord   Robert Stewart (1769–1822), from 6 April 1821 2nd Marquis of Londonderry. Irish Chief Secretary 1798–1801; joined Addington's ministry 12 July 1802 and continued under Pitt 1804–6. Secretary for War under Portland 1807; resigned after Walcheren disaster and duel with Canning September 1809; Foreign Secretary from 4 March 1812 to his death. As the Prime Minister and Home Secretary were in the House of Lords he spoke for the government on Catholic affairs in the House of Commons.

CHARLOTTE, Lady   See Rawdon, Lady Charlotte.

CLARE*, Lord   John Fitzgibbon (1749–1802), 1st Earl; Lord Chancellor of Ireland 1789–1802.

CLIFFORD, Lord   Charles Clifford (1759–1831), 6th Baron, of Chudleigh. Educated at Douai, St Omer, Bruges and Liège.

CLINCH, James Bernard (1770–1836)   5th son of a Dublin merchant; educated in Rome; professor at Maynooth 1795–1802; entered Middle Temple 1805; Bachelor of Law 1807; author of an influential pamphlet against the veto in 1808.

CLONCURRY*, Lord   Valentine Browne Lawless (1773–1853), 2nd Baron, of Lyons, Co. Kildare. United Irishman and twice imprisoned 1799–1801; in Paris and Rome 1802–5.

CLONEY, Thomas (1774–1850)   Born near Enniscorthy, Co. Wexford, later of Graig, Co. Kilkenny; popularly called General for his part in the rebellion; a death sentence quashed by Cornwallis in 1799, but he was advised to reside in England; returned February 1802; arrested after the

Emmet rising; released October 1804; published his *Personal Narrative of 1798* in 1832.

COILE, Bernard (Barney)   A manufacturer of muslins at Lurgan, Co. Antrim, until arrested on a false charge in January 1796; set up as a linen merchant in Dublin after his release; taken into custody after the Emmet rising.

CONSALVI, Cardinal Ercole (1757–1824)   A Cardinal Deacon; Secretary of State to Pius VII 1800–6 and again from 1814; arrived in London on an unofficial visit 30 May 1814 and was received by Prince Regent; left in July for Congress of Vienna.

CONWAY, Frederick William (1779–1864)   Son of a Protestant newspaper owner of Loughrea. Joined *Freeman's Journal* c. 1805 and became its editor until 1812 (he claimed that its political leading articles were the first of their kind in the British press); applied in vain in 1812 for a post in the Customs and corresponded with John Beckett in the Home Office on Irish Catholic affairs; from February to May 1813 published his unsuccessful *Dublin Political Journal*; worked as a journalist in London 1814–15 and wrote four plays; joined the *Dublin Evening Post* and became its editor in 1820.

CONYNGHAM*, Lord   Henry Burton Conyngham (1766–1832), 1st Earl from 1797, Marquis from 1816. Brigadier General 11 February 1804. His wife was the well known favourite of George IV.

CORNWALLIS*, Lord   Charles Cornwallis (1738–1805), 2nd Earl and 1st Marquis. In American war and capitulated at Yorktown 1781; in India 1786–93; arrived in Dublin as Lord Lieutenant and Commander-in-Chief 20 June 1798; left 25 May 1801; negotiated Peace of Amiens 1802; died in India.

COYNE, Richard   A Dublin printer and bookseller active between 1808 and 1846. Settled at 16 Parliament Street c. 1813; on death of Hugh Fitzpatrick in 1818 took over his premises at 4 Capel Street. An only son was called to the bar in 1826.

CUMBERLAND*, Duke of   Ernest Augustus (1771–1851), 5th son of George III, King of Hanover from 1837. Chancellor of Trinity College, Dublin, 1805; Grandmaster of the Irish Orange Order.

CURRAN*, John Philpot (1750–1817)   Called to the Irish bar in 1775; sat in the Irish House of Commons, where he supported Catholic claims and parliamentary reform; defended leaders of the United Irishmen; appointed Master of the Rolls by the Grenville government in 1806, with a seat in the Irish Privy Council; resigned 1816.

DALY, Denis Bowes (c. 1745–1821), of Daly's Town, Co. Galway   Married a sister of George Ponsonby 1780; MP for King's County until 1802, then for Galway city and (1805–18) county; Joint Mustermaster of the forces in Ireland 1806–7.

DAMPIER, (Sir) Henry (1758–1816)   A barrister of the Middle Temple who was made a Judge of the King's Bench in 1813 and knighted.

DELANY, Dr Daniel (1747 — 9 July 1814) Bishop of Kildare and Leighlin from 1787. Son of a wealthy farmer near Mountrath; sent to St Omer at age of sixteen; returned to Ireland 1777.

DEVONSHIRE*, Duke of William George Spencer Cavendish (1790–1858), 6th Duke from 29 July 1811.

DILLON*, Henry Augustus (1777–1832), from 1813 13th Viscount; assumed additional surname of Lee Colonel of the Irish Brigade 1794; MP for Harwich 1799, for Co. Mayo 1802–13; raised 101st Regiment from Mayo 1806; published pamphlets in 1801 and 1805 supporting Catholic claims.

DILLON, (Sir) John Joseph (died 1837), of Lincoln's Inn and later of Hatch House, Wiltshire Younger son of William Mervyn Dillon, of Proudstown, Co. Meath. Called to the English bar 1801; an adviser to the Duke of Sussex on his matrimonial affairs and on the Catholic question; wrote under the pseudonym Hibern Anglus; had been knighted by 1829 when he published a memorial claiming for his brother the Grand Chamberlainship of all England.

DONOUGHMORE*, Lord Richard Hely-Hutchinson (1756–1825), of Knocklofty, Co. Tipperary, son of Provost John Hely-Hutchinson; succeeded his mother as 2nd Baron 1788; created Viscount 1797 and Earl 1800; a representative peer. Called to the Irish bar 1777 and sat in Irish House of Commons until 1788; commanded Cork legion in the rebellion; actively supported the Union. Commissioner of Accounts 1801–6; of Revenue 1785–1801; Chief Commissioner 1801–6; Joint Postmaster General for Ireland 1806–7.

DOUGLASS*, Dr John (1743–1812) Vicar Apostolic of the London District from 1790; given a coadjutor in 1803.

DOWNES, (Sir) William (1752–1826), son of Robert Downes of Donnybrook and grandson of Bishop Downes of Cork Justice of King's Bench 1792, Chief Justice and knighted 1803. Already troubled by deafness in 1812 but did not retire until 1822, when he was made a Baron.

DRENNAN*, Dr William MD (1754–1820) Drafted first prospectus of United Irishmen 1791; tried for sedition 1794 but acquitted; founder of the *Belfast Magazine*.

DROMGOOLE*, Dr Thomas MD (c. 1750 — c. 1826), of Dawson Street, Dublin Trained at Edinburgh. Occasionally Acting Secretary of the Irish Catholic committee. Censured for a speech on 8 December 1812 in which he said Catholics were bound by their religion to subvert the established church; thereafter dropped into the background and ended his days in Rome.

DUIGENAN*, Dr Patrick LLD (1735–1816) Son of a Dublin parish clerk; baptised a Catholic but brought up by a Protestant clergyman who sent him to Trinity College; his first wife a Catholic. Judge of the Prerogative and Consistorial Court; MP for Armagh City 1801–16; Irish Privy Councillor May 1808. Grand Secretary of the Orange Order 1801.

DUNALLEY, Lord   Henry Sadleir Prittie (1775–1854), from 1802 2nd Baron, of Kilboy, Nenagh. His brother's attachment to the opposition prevented his becoming a representative peer and he took a seat for Okehampton in 1814, sitting on the opposite side of the House from F. A. Prittie.

ELDON*, Lord   John Scott (1751–1838), created Baron 1799, Earl 1821. Lord Chancellor of England 1801–6 and 1807–27.

ELLENBOROUGH*, Lord   Edward Law (1750–1818), created Baron in 1802 when he became Lord Chief Justice; Speaker of the House of Lords 1805; a member of Lord Grenville's cabinet 1806–7.

ELLIOT, William (1766–1818)   Sat in the Irish House of Commons; MP for Portarlington 1801–2 and Peterborough 1802–18. Private Secretary to Thomas Pelham in 1786; Undersecretary in the Military Department at Dublin Castle 1796–1801; Chief Secretary for Ireland 1806–7.

EMMET, Maryanne (1773–1804)   Sister of Thomas Addis and Robert Emmet. A contributor to *The Press* and reputed author of two anti-Union pamphlets. Married Robert Holmes about September 1799 and lived with him at Casino, her parents' home.

EMMET*, Robert (1778–1803)   In hiding during the rebellion and again after 3 April 1799 when a warrant was issued for his arrest; returned from France in November 1802 and organised the rising that broke out on 23 July 1803; arrested 20 August and executed 20 September 1803.

EMMET*, Thomas Addis (1764–1827)   Married Jane Patten 1791. A principal leader of the United Irishmen; arrested 12 March 1798; on 25 July, with W. J. MacNeven and Arthur O'Connor, made a compact with the government to spare further bloodshed; deported to Fort George in Scotland March 1799; went to Paris after his release in 1802 but, failing to get support from the French government, emigrated to New York, where he was called to the bar in 1804.

ERSKINE*, Lord   Thomas Erskine (1750–1823), from 1806 1st Baron. A specialist on the law of libel who greatly influenced the 1792 act under which juries and not judges were to decide whether the facts constituted a libel. MP from 1783. A close friend of the Prince of Wales and Fox. Lord Chancellor 1806–7.

ESMONDE, Sir Thomas (1786–1868)   Son of Dr John Esmonde who was hanged for treason in the rebellion; in 1803 succeeded his uncle as 9th Baronet, of Ballynastragh, Co. Wexford.

EVERARD, Dr Patrick (1751–1821)   Born at Fethard, Co. Tipperary; President of Maynooth 1810–13, retired to Ulverston in Cumbria where he had opened a school in 1793; returned as coadjutor to Dr Bray 1815 and succeeded him as Archbishop of Cashel 1820.

EYRE, Mrs   Catherine Eyre (1757–1820); daughter of William Parker, of Rainhill, Prescot, Lancashire; widow of Vincent Eyre (1744–1801).

EYRE, Catherine (1784–1843)   Daughter of the preceding; educated at the Bar Convent, York (1795) and New Hall, Essex (1799–1801); married Denys Scully as his second wife 8 September 1808.

EYRE, Charles   A brother of the preceding who lived at York.

EYRE, Julia/Juliana   A sister of the preceding who died unmarried in 1873.

EYRE, Mary   An unmarried elder sister of the preceding.

EYRE, Thomas, of Bath   A brother of the preceding who died in 1866.

EYRE, Vincent (1744–1801), of 17 Far Gate, Sheffield, and later of The Farm, Sheffield Park   Son of Nathanial Eyre of Glossop; educated at Douai; Lincoln's Inn; assistant to a lawyer who looked after the Duke of Norfolk's affairs and on his death in 1776 took over the management of the Duke's Sheffield and Worksop estates.

EYRE, Vincent (1774–1851), of The Farm, Sheffield Park, and Highfield, Derbyshire   Eldest son of the preceding, whom he succeeded as agent for the Duke of Norfolk's estate but resigned c. 1813. In 1808 married Mary, daughter of Anthony Wright, of Wealside, Essex.

FINGALL, Lord   Arthur James Plunkett (1759–1836), of Killeen Castle, Co. Meath, 8th Earl; 15th in the list of precedence of Irish peers and senior Catholic peer; married Frances Donelan (1766–1835). An original member of the Cisalpine Club in London. With his yeomanry helped defeat rebels at Tara Hill in 1798; supported the Union; secured a pension for his brother-in-law, Malachy Donelan; his application for a commission as JP in 1803 led to a correspondence with Lord Redesdale, which was leaked to the press, about the latter's contention that Catholics could not make good subjects.

FINN, William F. (1784–1862), of Tullaroan, Co. Kilkenny   3rd son of the owner of the *Leinster Journal*; called to Irish bar 1805; married Daniel O'Connell's sister Alicia 1812; MP for Co. Kilkenny 1832–7.

FINNERTY*, Peter (c. 1766–1822)   Publisher in 1797 of Arthur O'Connor's *The Press*; convicted of seditious libel and punished in the pillory; subsequently a journalist in London; accompanied the Walcheren expedition 1809 as correspondent for the *Morning Chronicle*; sent home for indiscretion and attacked Lord Castlereagh in the *Chronicle*; convicted of libel 7 February 1811 and sentenced to eighteen months in Lincoln gaol.

FITZGERALD*, Maurice (1774–1849)   18th Knight of Kerry; married to a daughter of David Latouche. MP for Kerry 1794–1831; a Commissioner for Customs 1799–1801 and Lord of the Treasury (Ireland) 1801–7, with a seat in the Privy Council.

FITZGERALD, Major Thomas (1735–1812), of Snowhaven, Co. Kilkenny   Spent eighteen years with the East India Company and distinguished himself in the first Mysore war; returned from India in 1771; married Jane Frances Lattin 1786; supported the Union; died at Adelphi Terrace, Cork.

FITZGERALD, Thomas   Only son of the preceding; died before 1839.

FITZGERALD*, (Sir) Thomas Judkin (d. 1810)   High Sheriff for Co. Tipperary during the rebellion and notorious for his severity in the suppression of it.

FITZGERALD*, William Vesey (1783–1843)   Son of Prime Serjeant James Fitzgerald who was dismissed for opposing Union; 2nd Baron from 1832. Chancellor of the Irish Exchequer 1812–16.

FITZPATRICK, Hugh (1754 – 23 October 1818)   Printer and publisher, whose premises at 4 Capel Street provided a meeting place for Irish Catholics and for many years housed their committee room.

FITZWILLIAM*, Lord   William Wentworth-Fitzwilliam (1748–1833), 2nd Earl. Lord Lieutenant of Ireland from December 1794 to March 1795; President of the Council in the Grenville ministry 1806–7.

FLETCHER, William (1750–1823), of 26 Merrion Square, Dublin, son of a doctor   A follower of Grattan; made a KC by Earl Fitzwilliam 1795; briefly MP for Tralee; with Curran represented Lord Edward Fitzgerald in 1798; appointed a Justice of the Common Pleas by the Grenville government in 1806.

FORBES, Lord   George John Forbes (1785–1836), styled Viscount; eldest son of Earl of Granard. Pursued an army career and became a Major General in 1825. MP for Co. Longford from 1806; ADC in Prince Regent's household; regarded in 1813 as being in opposition but gradually became a supporter of the government.

FOSTER*, John (1740–1828)   The last Speaker of the Irish House of Commons; MP for Co. Louth 1769–1821; Chancellor of the Exchequer for Ireland 12 July 1804 to 24 February 1806, and from 3 April 1807 to June 1811. Created Baron Oriel 1821.

FOSTER*, John Leslie (1781–1842), eldest son of Bishop of Clogher   MP from 1807 to 1830 when he was made a Baron of the Exchequer.

FOX*, Charles James (1749–13 September 1806)   After seven years of retirement he resumed political life at the beginning of 1804. Foreign Secretary and leader of the House of Commons in the Ministry of All the Talents.

FRENCH/FFRENCH, Sir Thomas/Lord (c. 1765–1814), of Castle French, Co. Galway   From 8 December 1805 2nd Baron in succession to his Protestant mother who, in recognition of his services in influencing Catholic opinion, had been created a Baroness in 1799, the King refusing to bestow a direct honour on a Catholic. Established a bank at Tuam c. 1804; a branch opened at 23 Lower Dominick Street, Dublin, in 1807. In May 1814 the bank stopped payment and he committed suicide on 9 December.

GAGE, Sir Thomas (d. 1820), 7th Baronet, of Hengrave Hall, Bury St Edmund's   Married Lady Mary-Anne Browne, daughter of Lord Kenmare, in 1809.

GEORGE III* (1738–1820) King from 1760. Attacked by mental illness 1765, 1788, and 1801; permanently deranged from 1811.

GEORGE IV See Prince of Wales/Prince Regent.

GIBBONS, Patrick A son of Ricard Gibbons of Minola, Co. Mayo.

GIFFARD, John (1745–May 1819), of Dromartin Castle, near Dublin Son of John Giffard of Wotton and Great Torrington, England, who had been disinherited by his father, and of Dorcas Murphy of Oulartleigh, Co. Wexford, widow of Francis Robinson of Dublin; through his fourth son grandfather of 1st Earl of Halsbury. Began life as an apothecary; editor of the *Dublin Journal* 1788 and its proprietor 1793–1816; a member of the Dublin Corporation and High Sheriff 1794; Accountant General of the Customs. According to Jonah Barrington he originated the term "Protestant Ascendancy".

GLENTWORTH, Lord Henry Hartstonge Pery (1789–1834), styled Viscount, eldest son of Earl of Limerick. Married Annabella Edwards 11 May 1808.

GOOLD, Sir Francis (d. 20 August 1818), 2nd son of George Goold of Old Court, Co. Cork Made a Baronet in 1801 in discharge of one of Cornwallis' Union engagements.

GORMANSTON, Lord Jenico Preston (1775–1860), 12th Viscount.

GOULDSBURY, Revd Ponsonby Rector of Multyfarnan, Co. Westmeath, from 1799; of Raddonstown 1803–30.

GRADY, Henry Deane (c. 1764–1847), 2nd son of Standish O'Grady of Lodge, Co. Tipperary Called to Irish bar 1787; MP for Limerick city until 1802, when he was appointed Second Counsel of Revenue Board. Was refused a baronetcy in 1810 for attacking Baron O'Grady in a pamphlet; supported the opposition. A noted duellist.

GRANARD, Lord George Forbes (1760–1837), 6th Earl. Owner of boroughs of Mullingar and St Johnstown in Irish parliament. Colonel of the Royal Longford Militia. Created Baron in the English peerage and Clerk of the Hanaper 1806–7; followed the Prince of Wales and his reappointment to the Hanaper in 1815 marked his abandonment of opposition.

GRANARD, Lady Selina Frances Rawdon (1759–1827), wife of the preceding, daughter of 1st Earl of Moira by his 3rd wife. Apart from two children who died young she had four sons (George, Francis, Hastings and Angoulême) and three daughters (Elizabeth, Adelaide and Caroline).

GRATTAN*, Henry (1746–4 June 1820) In retirement after opposing Union in Irish Parliament, he was brought in by Fox for Malton in time to support the Irish Catholic petition in 1805; sat for Dublin City 1806–20; refused office in Grenville ministry 1806; supported the Insurrection Act of July 1807; introduced Irish Catholic petitions from 1808.

GREGORY*, William (1766–1840) Trinity College Cambridge 1787 and Inner Temple; sat for Portarlington 1798–1800; Undersecretary in the Civil Department at Dublin Castle 1812–31.

GRENVILLE*, Lord   William Wyndham Grenville (1759–1834), 1st Baron, of Dropmore, Buckinghamshire, and Camelford House, London; a younger brother of the Marquis of Buckingham. Chief Secretary for Ireland 1782–3; Foreign Secretary under Pitt 1791–1801; Prime Minister February 1806 to March 1807.

GREY*, Mr/Lord   Charles Grey (1764–1845), styled Viscount Howick from 11 April 1806, 2nd Earl Grey from 27 November 1807; married to a niece of George Ponsonby. Opposed the Union. First Lord of Admiralty and after death of Fox Foreign Secretary in the Grenville ministry; Prime Minister 1831; carried Reform Bill 1834.

HAMILTON, Revd John   Curate of Roscrea, Co. Tipperary and a very active magistrate until August 1816 when he was dismissed for setting up a dummy of himself to provoke an attack.

HARDWICKE*, Lord   Philip Yorke (1757–1834), 3rd Earl, of Wimpole Hall, Cambridgeshire. Colonel of the Cambridgeshire Militia which he raised in 1793 and took to Dublin in 1799. Appointed Lord Lieutenant of Ireland by Addington 17 March 1801; arrived in Dublin on 25 May and left in April 1806; joined the opposition on his return to England and became a supporter of Catholic claims. Married Elizabeth Lindsay, a daughter of 5th Earl of Balcarres.

HARDY*, Francis (1751–1812)   MP for Lord Granard's seat of Mullingar from 1792 to the Union, which he opposed. Induced by Grattan to write Life of Lord Charlemont, published 1810. Lady Granard obtained a place for him as a Commissioner of Appeal in 1807.

HARNEY, Charles   The anglicised form of the surname being Hartney, he was probably the son of John Hartney of Somerville (Summerville), Co. Limerick, who signed the 1805 petition.

HAY*, Edward (c. 1761–1826), eldest but disinherited son of Harvey Hay of Ballinkeele, Co. Wexford   Educated in France and Germany; represented Wexford in Catholic Committee 1791; one of the delegates who petitioned the King 1795; under suspicion during the rebellion, when his brother John was hanged and he himself for a time under sentence of death; his History of the Insurrection of the County of Wexford published March 1803; from early 1807 Secretary to the Irish Catholic body and re- elected as such at successive general meetings; in 1818 imprisoned for debts which he claimed were incurred on behalf of the Catholics.

HAYES, Revd Richard OFM (d. 1824), of the Franciscan College, Wexford   As delegate of the Irish Catholic laity he was in Rome from 25 October 1815 to 16 July 1817, when he was expelled.

HEFFERNAN, Will, of Derk, Pallasgreen, Co. Limerick   A friend of the Scullys of Kilfeacle. On his death in 1808 his estate passed to his nephew

Heffernan Considine.

HELY-HUTCHINSON*, Christopher (1767–1826), 5th son of Provost John Hely-Hutchinson A Lieutenant Colonel in the Volunteer army, who accompanied his brother John to Helder 1799 and Egypt 1801, and was with Russian army at Eylau and Friedland 1807. Unlike the rest of his family he opposed the Union. MP for Cork City 1802–12 and 1818–26.

HELY-HUTCHINSON, Francis (1759–1827), of Henrietta Street, Dublin, and Belcamp, Co. Dublin, 3rd son of Provost Hely-Hutchinson Called to Irish bar 1782; MP for Naas in Irish House of Commons; from 1800 Collector of Customs for port of Dublin. Looked after the family interests and was Lord Donoughmore's link with the Irish Catholics, lay and ecclesiastical.

HELY-HUTCHINSON*, John (1724–1794) Born Hely, assumed additional surname 1751; Provost of Trinity College Dublin from 1774; a notorious pluralist and refused a peerage in 1785 rather than give up offices, but obtained one for his wife, who became Baroness Donoughmore.

HILL, Sir George Fitzgerald (1763–1839), 2nd Baronet Recorder of Derry and MP.

HIPPISLEY*, Sir John Coxe (1749–1825) Oxford University, Inner Temple. Went to Rome in 1779 where he married Margaret Stuart (d. 1799); in the East India Company 1786–9; MP for Sudbury 1790–6; in Rome again 1792–6, when he acted as semi-official agent of the British government; negotiated marriage of Princess Royal 1796 and made a Baronet; married the widow Mrs Hippisley Cox in 1801 and moved to her house at Ston Easton, near Bath; MP again for Sudbury 1802–19.

HOLLAND*, Lady Elizabeth Vassall (1770–1845), daughter of Richard Vassall of Jamaica. Divorced from Sir Godfrey Webster and married 3rd Baron Holland 1797.

HOLLAND*, Lord Henry Richard Vassall Fox (1773–1840), 3rd Baron. Active in the House of Lords from 1798 and after the death of his uncle, C. J. Fox, Lord Privy Seal in the Grenville administration, but frequently absent on the continent.

HOLROYD*, (Sir) George Sowley (1758–1831) A barrister of Gray's Inn. Appeared for Burdett against the Speaker 1811; Judge on King's Bench 1816–28.

HOWARD, Captain Hon. Hugh Howard (1761–1840), a younger son of 1st Viscount Wicklow; sat for St Johnstown in Irish parliament; Commissioner and then Joint Chairman of the Stamp Office. In 1792 married Catherine Bligh, daughter of the Dean of Elphin and niece of 1st Earl of Darnley.

HUDDLESTON, Edward (1774–1852), 3rd son of Ferdinand Huddleston In Cambridgeshire Militia 1793–8; Cornet in Enniskillen Dragoons 17 May 1799 but sold his commission about March 1800. Succeeded his brother Richard at Sawston Hall in 1847.

HUDDLESTON, Ferdinand (1737–1808), of Sawston Hall, Cambridge-shire   Studied law before he succeeded to the estate in 1860. Married Mary Lucas by whom he had five children — Richard, Henry, Edward, Mary and Jane.

HUDDLESTON, Frances (Fanny)   A daughter of Thomas Huddleston of Milton, Cambridgeshire, who died in 1779, and niece of Ferdinand Huddleston. Married John English, a solicitor, in 1810.

HUDDLESTON, Captain Francis (Frank)   Brother of the preceding. Volunteered from the militia (probably the Cambridgeshire) and appointed Captain in 46th Foot 26 November 1799; at Limerick with his regiment 1800; on half pay 1802; in prison in Dublin for debt 1805; employed in Stamp Office about 1809; by 1810 a reporter for *Hibernian Journal*; Catholic delegates arrested on his deposition 1811; in same year married sister of William Patrickson Pike, an attorney; conformed to established church; in 1817 living in Paradise Row with "numerous progeny"; still living in 1837 and described as a landing waiter on admission of his second son to King's Inns.

HUDDLESTON, Henry (b. 1772), 2nd son of Ferdinand Huddleston   A barrister of Gray's Inn.

HUDDLESTON, Jane (b. 1771), younger daughter of Ferdinand Hud-dleston   Accompanied her brother Richard to Dublin 1799 and was befrien-ded by Lady Moira; dined with Hardwickes at Wimpole March 1800; consid-ered herself in 1801 to have been jilted by Edward Jerningham; married Francis Canning 1810.

HUDDLESTON, Mrs   Mary (d. 1823), daughter of Timothy Lucas of Marlborough and wife of Ferdinand Huddleston.

HUDDLESTON, Mary (1769–17 April 1806), elder daughter of Fer-dinand Huddleston   Married Denys Scully 26 November 1801.

HUDDLESTON, Major Richard (1768–1847), "the bachelor squire", eldest son of Ferdinand Huddleston   Educated at Brussels and once thought of becoming a Dominican; in January 1793 given a commission in Cam-bridgeshire Militia by Lord Hardwicke; in Dublin as Second Major in 1799; shown kindness by Lady Moira, who gave him a portrait of Cardinal Pole.

HUSKISSON*, William (1770–1830)   Secretary to the Treasury under Pitt and Duke of Portland; Minister for Woods and Forests under Lord Liverpool; later at Board of Trade and Colonial Secretary.

HUSSEY, Peter Bodkin (1778–1838), of 16 Gloucester Street, Dublin   Son of John Hussey of Dingle, Co. Kerry and Helen Bodkin of Annagh, Co. Galway; Gray's Inn; called to Irish bar 1803. In 1804 married Mary Hickson of Farrinakilla, Co. Kerry, who was a Protestant; under the marriage settlement the children were brought up in established church.

HUTCHINSON*, Lord   John Hely-Hutchinson (1757–1832), 1st Baron, of Alexandria and Knocklofty from 1801; 2nd son of Provost Hely-Hutch-inson. In command in Connaught when French landed in 1798; succeeded

Abercromby in Egypt and captured Cairo and Alexandria 1801; on a mission to Prussia and Russia 1806–7; promoted General 1813; succeeded as 2nd Earl of Donoughmore 1825.

JERNINGHAM, Edward (1774–1822), 3rd son of Sir William Jerningham of Costessey, Norfolk   A barrister of Lincoln's Inn; Secretary of the English Catholic Board 1808–22. Married Mary Middleton, a convert to Catholicism, in 1804. An ardent supporter of the exiled French royal family.

KEATING*, George (1762–1842)   Catholic printer and bookseller, in partnership with his father Patrick Keating until latter's death in 1816. On the death in 1800 of J. P. Coghlan, the leading Catholic publisher of the day, the Keatings amalgamated with his firm under the name of Keating, Brown and Keating, the second partner, Richard Brown, being a nephew of Coghlan; changed to Keating, Brown & Co. after 1816.

KEATING, Mrs   Lucinda Scully (1767–1843), a sister of Denys Scully, who married Leonard Keating of Garranlea, Co. Tipperary, in 1800.

KEELAN, Revd James (d. 1824)   Author of the "Sarsfield" letters in the *Evening Herald* which started the Veto controversy in 1808. Graduated at Louvain 1793; founded an academy at Drogheda which closed in 1807; moved to Dublin in 1808 and ran a small school in Aungier Street; moved to another school near Ballinakill which closed in 1820.

KEMMIS, Thomas and William   Father and son, of Kildare Street, Dublin. Crown Solicitors for Dublin City and the Leinster Circuit.

KENMARE, Lord   Valentine Browne (1754–3 October 1812), Viscount, promoted Earl in 1800 for supporting the Union. Owner of 130,000 acres in Co. Kerry. Married 1777 a daughter of 11th Viscount Dillon, who died leaving an only daughter, Charlotte; in 1785 married Mary Aylmer, of Lyons, Co. Kildare. Succeeded by his son Valentine (1788–1853).

KENNEDY, James (d. 1814)   Son of Edmond Kennedy, merchant of Kilkenny, and Catherine Glennan. Educated at lay college Maynooth; admitted King's Inns June 1808 but not called to the bar; for some months a journalist in London; part owner for a time of *Kilkenny Chronicle*; editor of the Kilkenny *Moderator* which first appeared on 1 January 1814, but he left Kilkenny on 20 February following and died before May, when an obituary appeared in the *Irish Magazine*.

KENNEY*, Revd Peter James SJ (1779–1841)   Carlow College; novitiate at Hodder, near Stonyhurst; ordained at Palermo 1808; while in Sicily was involved in negotiations between local British commanders and the Pope; attempted to act as chaplain to British forces in Sicily and Malta; returned to Dublin 1 September 1811; Vice-President of Maynooth 1812–13; founder of Clongowes Wood College and its Rector 1814–17, 1821–30.

KEOGH*, John (1740–13 November 1817), of Mount Jerome, Co. Dublin   His visits to London in 1791 and 1792 prepared the way for the 1793 Relief Act. Arrested 1796 because of his connexions with United Irishmen and went to England after his release, thus being absent during the rebellion; his house searched in 1803 after the Emmet rising; thereafter in poor health but from 1806 to 1810 established himself as leader of the Dublin Catholics and a popular party.

KING*, Lord   Peter King (1776–1833), 7th Baron. Trinity College Cambridge 1792. In the summer of 1804 he proposed raising the Catholic question in parliament but on Fox urging that the Irish Catholics should make the first move he consulted William Parnell of Avondale, who persuaded James Ryan to form a committee.

KIRK*, Revd John (1760–1851)   Parish priest at Lichfield from 1801; author of a biographical work on English Catholics in the 18th century.

KIRWAN, Thomas   A merchant of Fleet Street and 92 Upper Abbey Street, Dublin.

LAKE*, Gerard (1744–1808), Baron 1804, Viscount 1807   As commander in Ulster carried out the disarming of the north in 1797; commander-in-chief during the rebellion from April to June 1798.

LALOR, John (d. 7 September 1828)   Of Crannagh, Templemore, Co. Tipperary.

LANIGAN, Dr James (c. 1747–1812)   Ordained 1771 and taught mathematics at Nantes; co-founder of the Kilkenny Academy, of which he was Rector until 1791; Bishp of Ossory from 1789.

LANSDOWNE, Lord   See Petty, Lord Henry.

LENS*, John (1756–1825)   Barrister of Lincoln's Inn; appointed King's Serjeant 1806.

L'ESTRANGE, Revd Francis Joseph (d. 1833)   Born in Dublin as William L'Estrange. Provincial of Irish Carmelites.

LIDWILL, George (d. 1839)   Landowner of Dromard, Templemore, Co. Tipperary; High Sheriff in 1807.

LIMERICK*, Lord   Edmund Henry Pery (1758–1845), 2nd Baron Glentworth, created Earl of Limerick 1803; a representative peer.

LINDSAY, Dr Charles Dalrymple (d. 1846)   A son of 5th Earl of Balcarres and brother-in-law of Lord Hardwicke, who brought him to Dublin as his private secretary. Bishop of Killaloe 1803 and of Kildare 1804–46, with residence at Glasnevin.

LISMORE, Lord   Cornelius O'Callaghan (1775–1857), from 1797 2nd Baron and from 1806 1st Viscount. Entered Trinity College Cambridge 1793.

LITTA, Cardinal Lorenzo (1756–1820)   Prefect of the Index 1801 and of Propaganda Fide after Pope's return to Rome in 1814.

LIVERPOOL*, Lord   Robert Banks Jenkinson (1770–1828), created Baron Hawkesbury 1803, 2nd Earl of Liverpool from 1808. As Home Secretary under Pitt and Duke of Portland dealt with Catholic question in House of Commons. Secretary for War 1809–12; Prime Minister 1812–27.

LLANDAFF, Lord   Francis James Mathew (1768–1833), of Thomastown, Golden, Co. Tipperary; styled Viscount 1797 to 1806 when he succeeded as 2nd Earl; married a daughter of John Latouche 1797; sat for Co. Tipperary in Irish parliament and 1801–6.

LOWTHER*, Lord   William Lowther (1787–1872), styled Viscount; from 1844 3rd Earl of Lonsdale. MP from 1808; junior Lord of the Admiralty 1809; on Treasury Board 1813–26.

LYONS, James Denis (1785–1853)   3rd son and successor of Denis Lyons of Croom House, near Limerick; first cousin of Denys Scully.

"M", "M.G.", "McG."   An informer who reported to William Gregory at Dublin Castle: probably James McGucken.

McDERMOT, Dr Hugh MD (1756–1824), of Coolavin, Co. Sligo; married in 1793 Elizabeth O'Conor, sister of Owen O'Conor of Belanagare.

McDONNELL, Eneas (1783–1858), 4th son of Charles McDonnell of Clonagh, Westport, Co. Mayo   Lay college, Maynooth; called to Irish bar 1810; editor of *Cork Mercantile Chronicle* until 1815 when he became proprietor and first editor of the new *Dublin Chronicle*; fined and imprisoned in February 1814 for an anonymous article written by Denys Scully; from 1824 agent of the Irish Catholics in London.

MacDONNELL/MacDONALD, Miles   A partner in the firm of M. I. MacDonnell and J. Bushell, merchants, of 4 Broad Street Court, London.

McDONNELL, Randal (d. 1821), of Allen's Court, Mullinahack, Co. Dublin, and Kilmore and Brackney, Co. Antrim   In partnership with Edard Byrne and after his death in 1804 the leading Catholic merchant of Dublin: estimated in 1806 to be worth over £100,000; one of the few Catholics invited to join public bodies; treasurer to lay college of Maynooth; a Conservator of the Peace after the Emmet rising; on the Committee of the Commercial Buildings Company etc.

McGRATH, Richard   A tavern owner of Dungarvan, Co. Waterford, who acted as an election agent for the Duke of Devonshire.

McGUCKEN, James   A Belfast attorney who practised in Dublin, at 131 Capel Street. As a law agent of the United Irishmen he was entrusted with the defence of Antrim prisoners in the rebellion, but is recorded as in receipt of secret service money at least from 1798 to February 1804. He played an active part in the Catholic Committee at Belfast and in 1811 was elected as one of the Antrim delegates to the General Committee in Dublin.

McKENNA*, Theobald (1765–1808)   Son of a Carrick-on-Suir merchant and married to an aunt of the Countess of Shrewsbury. Secretary of the old Catholic Committee and mouthpiece of the seceders in 1791; published an influential pamphlet supporting the Union, which he expected to be followed by emancipation; on being rewarded with a pension he lost the confidence of the Catholic body. Published anonymously in 1802 a pamphlet on the expediency of providing an establishment for the Roman Catholic clergy.

MacINTOSH*, Sir James (1765–1832)   A barrister of Lincoln's Inn who had written on the law of nations and served as a judge in Bombay before entering parliament for Nairn in 1813.

McMAHON, Colonel John (c. 1754–1817), brother of Sir William McMahon, the Irish barrister and judge. MP for Aldeburgh 1802–12. Acted as private secretary to the Prince of Wales, to whom he had been introduced by Lord Moira.

MacNEVIN*, William James (1763–1841)   A medical practitioner who joined the United Irishmen in 1797 and suffered the same fate as T. A. Emmet, like whom he settled in the United States.

MAGEE*, John   Editor and proprietor of the *Dublin Evening Post*, in succession to his father. When he was imprisoned for libel legal ownership of the paper was taken over by his younger brother James.

MAHER, Nicholas   of Thurles, Co. Tipperary; son of John Maher (Meagher) whose sister married Roger Scully of Cashel, Denys Scully's grandfather.

MAHON, Mrs   Anne (Nancy) Scully (1766–1841), sister of Denys Scully and wife of Thomas Mahon, a Dublin businessman who stopped payment in 1802 and seems to have died soon after.

MAHON, James   Eldest son of the preceding. Acted as secretary to his grandfather, James Scully, and was employed in the Scully bank in Tipperary town.

MAHON, Nicholas (c. 1746–1841)   Of 26 Merchants Quay, Dublin, son of Murtagh Mahon of Ennis; married in 1791 his first cousin, Margaret Mahon; his niece Susanna married N. P. O'Gorman. A rich woollen merchant and one of the few Catholics in lists of public bodies. A Conservator of the Peace for St Patrick's district after the Emmet rising. One of the delegates to the Catholic Convention in 1792.

MANNERS*, Lord   Thomas Manners-Sutton (1756–1842), created Baron 1807; younger brother of the Archbishop of Canterbury. Lord Chancellor of Ireland 1 May 1807 to 1827.

MARSHALL, Robert   A protégé of Thomas Pelham, Irish Chief Secretary 1795–8; treasurer of Maynooth until 1799, when he was appointed Inspector General of Exports and Imports; employed by Castlereagh as private secretary in promoting the Union and acting as go-between with the Catholics; in April 1804 he gave evidence to a House of Commons committee on the Irish currency; retired with a pension in 1811.

MATHEW, General Montagu (1773–1819), brother of 2nd Earl Llandaff   Colonel in the 114th (Llandaff's) Regiment of Foot 1800; one of four Irish landowners invited in 1804 to raise a battalion of infantry, with himself as Colonel; promoted Major-General 20 April 1808, Lieutenant-General 4

August 1813. MP for Co. Tipperary 1806–19.

MELVILLE*, Lord   Henry Dundas (1742 — 29 May 1811), created Viscount 1802. As Home Secretary received the Irish Catholic delegation in 1792; at the War Office 1794–1801; Privy Seal of Scotland 1800. First Lord of Admiralty 1804 but had to resign in 1805 when impeached for malversation of funds; restored to Privy Council 1807.

MELVILLE*, Lord   Robert Saunders-Dundas (1771–1851), 2nd Viscount. President of Board of Control 1807–9; nominally Irish Chief Secretary 13 April 1809 to fall of Portland government in October. First Lord of the Admiralty 1812–27.

MENZIES*, John (1756–1834), of Pitfodels, Aberdeenshire   Founder of Blair College.

MILNER*, Dr John (1752–1826)   Son of a tailor who became mentally deranged; after a year at Sedgley Park went to Douai 1766 and was ordained there 1777; appointed to Winchester 1779; from October 1789 involved in first controversies with English Catholic Committee over Catholic oath and nomination of Bishops; consecrated titular Bishop of Castalba and Vicar Apostolic of the Midland district 1 March 1803; moved from Longbirch to Giffard House, Wolverhampton, 1804; in 1806, after being appointed agent of the Irish clergy, tried in vain to change places with Dr Poynter in London; in Ireland June to August 1807 (*First Tour*) and August–September 1808 (*Second Tour*); from 2 May 1814 to May 1815 absent on journey to Rome; third visit to Ireland June–July 1821; given a coadjutor 1 May 1825.

MOIRA, Lady   Elizabeth Hastings (1731–11 April 1808), third wife of 1st Earl of Moira (d. 1793), daughter of 9th Earl of Huntingdon and Selena Shirley (1707–1791) of the Calvinist Methodist sect known as "Lady Huntingdon's Connexion". On the death in 1789 of her brother, the 10th Earl of Huntingdon, his titles transmissible in the female line devolved on her, the principal being the barony of Hastings. She had eleven children, of whom five died young. Hostess at Moira House in its heyday as the social centre of the Irish Whigs. Her hobby was genealogy.

MOIRA*, Lord   Francis Rawdon-Hastings (1754–1826), son of the preceding, from 1793 2nd Earl of Moira; created Baron Rawdon in English peerage 1783; as heir to 10th Earl of Huntingdon assumed additional surname of Hastings 1791. Distinguished himself in American war; introduced 1791 Catholic relief bill in House of Lords; commanded expedition to Brittany 1793; in Flanders 1794; an intimate friend of Prince of Wales; opposed Irish administration's policies before the rebellion; godfather to Wolfe Tone's fourth child; opposed the Union; Commander-in-Chief Scotland 1803; married Flora Countess of Loudoun 1804; Master of the Ordnance 1806–7; thereafter gave his first loyalty to the Prince; sailed April 1813 to become Governor-General of Bengal; created Marquis of Hastings 1817.

MOORE, Mrs Anne, daughter of Denis Byrne of Co. Wicklow; married 1776 James Moore, son of Edward Moore of Mount Browne, a brewer; left a widow c. 1785 with two sons, Edward and Walter, and a daughter, Anne, who married William Charles Jerningham in 1816.

MOORE, Edward   Son of the preceding; in partnership with Valentine O'Connor, who was married to his aunt, Maria Moore.

MOORE, George (1773–1840)   Son of George Moore of Moore Hall, Co. Mayo, and younger brother of the John Moore who was installed by the French as President of Connaught in 1798. A barrister of Lincoln's Inn; supported the Union; attached to the Prince of Wales.

MOORE, Hon. William (1775–1810)   Of Stephen's Green, Dublin, and Sapperton, Tallow; 3rd son of 1st Viscount Mount Cashell. Represented the family borough of Clonmel until the Union.

MORPETH*, Lord   George Howard (1773–1848), styled Viscount; from 1825 6th Earl of Carlisle. MP for Cumberland 1806–20.

MOUNT CASHELL, Lady   Hon Margaret King (1773–1835), eldest daughter of 2nd Earl of Kingston; married in 1791 the 2nd Earl of Mount Cashell, by whom she had eight children. Influenced by Mary Wollstone-craft, governess in her family 1787–8; of republican sympathies and by 1800 a friend of William Godwin; in Paris and Rome 1802–5; did not return with her husband but went to Germany; was back in London in 1807 when she contributed short stories to Godwin's juvenile publications; in 1809 gave birth to her first daughter by George William Tighe, whom she had met in Rome; under the name of Mason left with him for Pisa in 1814 and married him in 1826; friend of Shelley and his circle; supposed to be the lady in his poem *The Sensitive Plant*.

MOUNT CASHELL, Lord   Stephen Moore (1770–1822), of Moore Park, Kilworth, Co. Cork, 2nd Earl. His mother, Hon. Helena Rawdon, was a daughter of the 1st Earl of Moira by his 1st wife, Helena Perceval, and through her he was a second cousin of Spencer Perceval. Elected a representative peer in March 1815.

MOYLAN*, Dr Francis (1735–10 February 1815)   Catholic Bishop of Cork from 1786.

MURPHY, Dr John (1772–1847)   Successor to the preceding as Bishop of Cork, having previously been Archdeacon and Vicar-General of the diocese. Educated at Lisbon. A collector of Irish manuscripts.

MURPHY, Revd John (c. 1770–1847)   Son of Revd Samuel Murphy MusD; at Trinity College Dublin 1786–1793; chaplain of Magdalen Church, Dublin, but found this closed against him when he returned from ac-companying Lady Pamela Fitzgerald to England in 1798. Married a Miss St Leger of Dublin, by whom he had three children, one of them called Selina and another Hastings (after his godmother, Lady Moira). Seems to have lived at Moira House until after the death of Lady Moira in 1808. Appointed

Rector of Kilflyn 1813, of Kiltallagh 1817.

MURPHY, William   2nd son of Edmund Murphy of Ballinamona, near Cashel, and Margaret Scully (1743–1800), aunt of Denys Scully.

MURRAY*, Dr Daniel (1768–1852)   Educated at Salamanca; in 1809 appointed coadjutor to Dr Troy, whom he succeeded as Archbishop of Dublin 1823. President of Maynooth 1812–13.

MUSGRAVE*, Sir Richard (c. 1757–1818)   MP for Lismore in Irish parliament. Author of a history of the rebellion and numerous anti-Catholic pamphlets.

NEPEAN*, Sir Evan (1751–1822)   As Undersecretary of the Home Office was involved in discussions with the Irish delegation leading to Relief Act of 1793; Secretary to the Admiralty 1795; MP 1796–1812; made a Baronet 1802; arrived in Dublin as Chief Secretary 1 February 1804; when he left for London at the end of the year the Lord Lieutenant broke off relations with him for dealing with the Catholics behind his back and he did not return; Governor of Bombay 1812–19.

NEWPORT*, Sir John (1756–1843)   A banker of Waterford and MP for the city 1802–32. Chancellor of the Exchequer for Ireland in the Grenville administration 1806–7.

NICHOLL*, Sir John (1759–1838)   MP 1802–32; Dean of the Arches and Judge of Prerogative Court of Canterbury 1809–34.

NORBURY*, Lord   John Toler (1745–1831); made a Baron and Chief Justice of the Common Pleas 1800; retired in 1827 and made an Earl.

NORFOLK*, Duke of   Bernard Edward Howard (1765–1842), of Glossop, 12th Duke from 16 December 1815 in succession to his third cousin. Educated at Douai.

NORFOLK*, Duke of   Charles Howard (1746 — 16 December 1815), 11th Duke. Educated at Douai but conformed to the established church in 1780 to contest an election at Carlisle. Lord of the Treasury in 1783 but in 1784 followed Fox into opposition. A friend of the Prince of Wales.

NORRIS, Thomas   An attorney of 12 King's Road, Bedford Row, London; a subscriber to the English Catholic Board.

NUGENT*, (Sir) George (1757–1849), of the 84th Foot, Major-General from 1796   MP for Buckinghamshire 1790–1800; Lieutenant-Governor of Jamaica 1801–6; Commander-in-Chief India 1811–13.

NUGENT*, Lord   George Nugent Grenville (1788–1850), younger son of 1st Marquis of Buckingham; succeeded his mother 1813 as 2nd Baron Nugent in Irish Peerage; MP for Aylesbury 1812–32.

O'BEIRNE*, Dr Thomas Lewis (c. 1748–1823)   Educated for Roman Catholic priesthood at St Omer but was refused ordination; conformed to established church; chaplain in the navy; chaplain to Duke of Portland and Earl Fitzwilliam when they were in Ireland; Bishop of Ossory 1795, of Meath 1798. Married 1783 a grand-daughter of 6th Earl of Moray. Had a brother who was a Catholic priest.

O'BRIEN, Mary   Daughter of Major Timothy O'Brien and 2nd wife of James Wheble; educated at New Hall, Essex.

O'BRIEN, Mary Anne   Daughter of Carberry O'Brien of Nenagh, Co. Tipperary; married Edmund Scully 6 January 1806.

O'CALLAGHAN, Edward, of 19 Lower Ormond Quay, Dublin   4th son of Owen O'Callaghan of Culloville, Carrickmacross; an attorney from 1809.

O'CONNELL*, Daniel (1775–1847)   Educated at St Omer and Douai; called to Irish bar 1798; a member of Lawyers Corps but retired to Kerry during the rebellion; made his first public speech 13 January 1800 when he urged Catholics as a body to oppose the Union; attended Catholic Committee at end of 1804 and over the next ten years established his ascendancy; took up Repeal of the Union 1810 and parliamentary reform 1813; elected MP for Clare July 1828.

O'CONNOR*, Arthur (1763–1852)   Born as Arthur Conner at Mitchelstown, Co. Cork; MP for Philipstown 1790, High Sheriff for Co. Cork 1791; joined United Irishmen 1796; arrested at Margate 28 February 1798 and re-arrested after acquittal; joined other leaders in compact with Irish administration at the end of July; sent to Fort George 18 March 1799; released in 1802 and spent rest of his life in France.

O'CONNOR, Maria (d. 1810)   Daughter of Valentine O'Connor senior; married 4 August 1803 Maurice Blake of Towerhill, Co. Galway, a Major in the North Mayo Militia.

O'CONNOR, Valentine senior (c. 1744–1814), of 6 Dominick Street, Dublin   Married to Mary (d. 1813), eldest daughter of the brewer Edward Moore of Mount Browne. A prominent Dublin businessman and senior partner in the firm of Valentine O'Connor, Hugh O'Connor, Hugh O'Connor and Edward Moore with which Denys Scully kept an account. Testified against Thomas Reynolds at trial of Oliver Bond 1798. His son, Valentine junior, was an importer, who moved his office in 1809 from 37 Granary Row to 9 Dorset Street.

O'CONOR*, Dr Charles (1764–1828), younger brother of Owen O'Conor   In 1792 made parish priest of Castlerea, a living in the gift of the O'Conor Don; in 1799 went to Stowe as chaplain to the Marchioness of Buckingham and librarian; translated Irish annals into Latin; wrote on Catholic question under name of Columbanus; went senile before he died.

O'CONOR, Owen (1763–1831)   Of Belanagare and Clonalis, Co. Roscommon; styled O'Conor Don after the death of his distant kinsman Alexander O'Conor in 1820; married Jane Moore of Mount Browne 1792. A Volunteer in 1792 and a delegate to the Catholic Convention 1793; continued active in Catholic affairs; returned unopposed for Co. Roscommon in the election following emancipation.

O'DONNELL, Dr Charles (1749–1824)   Catholic Bishop of Derry from 1797.

O'GORMAN, Nicholas Purcell (1778–1857)   2nd son of James O'Gorman of Ennis; married to a niece of Nicholas Mahon. Trinity College, Dublin, and Gray's Inn; called to the Irish bar 1803; Secretary of the Catholic Association of 1823.

O'GRADY*, Standish (1766–1840), from 1831 1st Viscount Guillemore   Attorney-General for Ireland 1803–5; Chief Baron of the Exchequer 1805–31.

O'MULLAN, Revd Cornelius   Parish priest of Templemore, Derry, until 1813; accompanied Devereux to Venezuela in 1820 and died there late 1821.

ORMONDE, Lord   Walter Butler (1770–1820), 18th Earl and from January 1816 1st Marquis of Ormonde. Made a Groom of the Bedchamber in 1812 but resigned in June 1813 on being refused nomination of the sheriff of County Kilkenny.

PARNELL*, Sir Henry Brooke (1776–1842)   Succeeded his brother as 4th Baronet 30 July 1812; created Baron Congleton 1841. Trinity College Cambridge; MP for Maryborough in Irish parliament, briefly for Portarlington 1802, for Queen's County from 1806. In July 1804 made an offer, not accepted, to raise a regiment in Queen's County; Commissioner for Treasury in Ireland 1806–7; not in office again until 1831. Author of works mainly on economic matters; a short *History of the Penal Laws* published in 1808.

PARNELL*, William (1780–1821)   Younger brother of the preceding and grandfather of Charles Stewart Parnell; assumed additional surname of Hayes in honour of the previous owner of his estate at Avondale, Rathdrum, Co. Wicklow. Trinity College Cambridge. Involved in formation of Irish Catholic Committee 1804; published pamphlets sympathetic to Catholics in 1805 and 1807; one of the founders of the Friends of Civil and Religious Liberty 1813; after several applications to Earl Fitzwilliam became MP for Co. Wicklow on 12 August 1817 on death of George Ponsonby. On 1 October 1811 married Frances, daughter of Hon. Hugh Howard of Bushy Park.

PASQUET, Jean B., of Bordeaux   Husband of Denys Scully's sister Frances, who died 1795, leaving an only son.

PEEL*, (Sir) Robert (1788–1850), from 1830 2nd Baronet   Entered parliament for Cashel 1809; Undersecretary for War 1810–12; appointed Chief Secretary for Ireland 4 August 1812; arrived Dublin 1 September 1812, left 3 August 1818; Home Secretary 1822 but resigned in opposition to emancipation 1827; as Home Secretary under Wellington carried emancipation 1829; Prime Minister 1834–5 and 1841–6.

PERCEVAL*, Spencer (1762–1812)   2nd son of 2nd Earl of Egmont.

Solicitor-General 1802, Attorney-General 1804–6; Chancellor of the Exchequer under Duke of Portland 1807 and succeeded him as Prime Minister 4 October 1809; assassinated 11 May 1812. His sister married Lord Redesdale, Chancellor for Ireland, 1803.

PERRY*, James (1756–1821)   Proprietor and editor of the *Morning Chronicle* from 1789; several times prosecuted for his radical opinions.

PETTY*, Lord Henry (1780–1863), from 1818 Petty-Fitzmaurice   3rd Marquis of Lansdowne from 15 March 1809; MP from 1802; Chancellor of the Exchequer in Lord Grenville's administration 1806–7; not in office again until 1827. Married in 1808 a daughter of the 2nd Earl of Ilchester by his first wife who was a daughter of Standish O'Grady of Capercullen.

PIGOTT*, Sir Arthur Leary (1752–1819)   A barrister of the Middle Temple who had once been Attorney-General at Grenada; MP 1806 and Attorney-General under Lord Grenville 1806–7.

PITT*, William (1759–23 January 1806)   Prime Minister 1783 to end of January 1801, when he resigned after King's refusal to countenance his cabinet's proposals of 25 January for measures of Catholic relief; during the King's illness in February–March, however, he conveyed an assurance that he would not again raise the Catholic question during the King's lifetime; formed his second administration in May 1804.

PIUS VII   Barnaba Chiaramonti (1742–1823), elected Pope 14 March 1800. Concordat with Napoleon 1801; broke with him 1806; forcibly removed from Rome 10 July 1809 and held prisoner at Savona; removed to Fontainebleau June 1812; returned to Rome 24 May 1814.

PLOWDEN*, Francis Peter (1749–1829)   Brother of two Jesuits and himself in Jesuit novitiate until the dissolution of the order. Assisted Vicars Apostolic on Relief Act of 1791 but then sided with Catholic Committee against them; called to the bar 1797 and became a conveyancer; pamphlets against Pitt; his *Historical Review of the State of Ireland* published in 1803 and brought up to date with a *History* published in 1811; in 1813 prosecuted for using secret material and fled to France to escape £5000 damages.

PLUNKET*, William Conyngham (1764–1854)   Solicitor-General for Ireland 8 November 1803 and Attorney-General 24 October 1805 but resigned in May 1807; MP for Dublin University from 1812; Attorney-General again 13 January 1822; Chief Justice of the Common Pleas and Baron 1827; Lord Chancellor of Ireland 1830–41.

PLUNKETT, Luke (born c. 1778)   Son of Thomas Plunkett of Portmarnock; lived in Paradise Row, Drumcondra. Trinity College Dublin; Gray's Inn; called to the Irish bar 1805; editor of *The Irishman* 1816.

POLE   See Wellesley-Pole.

PONSONBY*, George (1755–1817)   Trinity College Cambridge. Seceded from Irish parliament in 1797 but returned to oppose the Union; Chancellor for Ireland in the Grenville administration; arrived Dublin 25

March 1806, resigned April 1807; leader of the opposition after the elevation of Grey to the House of Lords in 1808. He was uncle of Lady Grey.

PONSONBY*, Lord   John Ponsonby (c. 1770–1855), of Bishopscourt, Co. Kildare, from 5 November 1806 2nd Baron; married a daughter of 4th Earl of Jersey; his sister was the wife of 2nd Earl Grey. From 1826 a diplomatist.

PORTLAND*, Duke of   William Henry Cavendish Bentinck (1738–1809), 3rd Duke. Lord Lieutenant of Ireland April to September 1882; Home Secretary 1794–1801; President of the Council 1801–6; Prime Minister March 1807 to September 1809.

POTTS, Revd Thomas (1754–1819)   Went to Douai 1765, ordained at Arras 1778. Vice-President at Oscott 1796, President 1808; suffered a stroke in 1815 which left him only nominally in charge.

POWER, Dr John (c. 1765–1816)   Bishop of Waterford and Lismore from 1804. A native of Waterford; in business before he went to Louvain to study for the priesthood. His funeral was attended by the Protestant Bishop and his clergy.

POYNTER*, Dr William (1762–1827)   Prefect of studies at Douai; imprisoned by French revolutionaries; President of St Edmund's College, Ware, 1801; coadjutor Bishop of London district 1803; succeeded as Vicar Apostolic 1812.

PRINCE OF WALES/PRINCE REGENT*   George Augustus Frederick (1762–1830), from 29 January 1820 King George IV. Resided at Carlton House. Married Princess Caroline of Brunswick 1795 but separated from her 1796; deprived of care of his daughter 1805; installed as Regent 6 February 1811 under restrictions which ended 17 February 1812.

PRINCESS OF WALES*   Caroline of Brunswick (1768–1821), wife of the preceding. Denied access to her daughter 1812; allowed to travel abroad 1813; returned on death of George III; a divorce bill initiated in House of Lords in July 1820 was dropped in November; excluded from the coronation 29 July 1821.

PRITTIE, Francis Aldborough (1779–1853)   Of Corville, Roscrea, Co. Tipperary; younger brother of 2nd Baron Dunalley; married to George Ponsonby's daughter Martha. MP for Carlow Borough 1801 and for Co. Tipperary 1806; lost this seat in 1818 but regained it in a by-election April 1819 and held it until 1831.

QUARANTOTTI, Monsignor Giovanni Battista   Made a Cardinal in 1816 when he was over eighty. Secretary of Propaganda Fide from 1807 and stayed on when its Cardinal Prefect left Rome with the Pope in 1809.

RANCLIFFE, Lord   Augustus Henry Anne Parkyns (1785–1850), from 1800 2nd Baron; married eldest daughter of Lord Granard 15 October 1807.

RAWDON, Lady Charlotte (1769–1834)   Youngest surviving child of Lady Moira; married Hamilton Fitzgerald in 1814.

REDESDALE*, Lord   John Freeman Mitford (1748–1830), 1st Baron from 1802. Carried 1791 relief act through House of Commons; Solicitor-General 1793; Attorney-General 1799; Speaker 1801; Lord Chancellor of Ireland 1802; married a sister of Spencer Perceval 1803; early in 1804 his letters to Lord Fingall questioning whether Catholics could be good subjects found their way into the press; dismissed by the Grenville ministry in 1806.

REYNOLDS, John   Printer, stationer and bookseller of The Parade, Kilkenny; printer and publisher of the *Kilkenny Chronicle*. Educated at the Kilkenny Academy, where he was in the 1790 prize list.

REYNOLDS, Canon Laurence (c. 1763–1817), brother of the preceding. Irish College, Paris; curate of St Mary's, Kilkenny, 1795–1800: professor of classics at Maynooth 1801–2; at St Mary's again 1802 to 1810, when he was appointed parish priest at Thomastown, Co. Kilkenny, and made a canon.

RICE, Dominick (b. 13 June 1762), 3rd son of Thomas Rice, of Dingle, Co. Kerry   Middle Temple; called to Irish bar 1794; a member of Dublin Society of United Irishmen; when he signed 1805 petition his address was Dawson Street.

RICHMOND*, Duke of   Charles Lennox (1764–1819), from 1806 4th Duke. A soldier; Lieutenant-General 1805; on appointment as Lord Lieutenant arrived Dublin 19 April 1807; handed over to Lord Whitworth 26 August 1813; promoted General 1814; present at Waterloo 1815; Governor of British North America 1813–19.

RIDGWAY, James   Printer and bookseller of 1 York Street, St James, until he moved to 170 Piccadilly c. 1805. Fined in 1793 for publishing three libels, one of them being Paine's *Rights of Man*.

ROMILLY*, Sir Samuel (1757–1818)   A barrister of Gray's Inn brought into parliament in 1806 to be Solicitor-General in the Grenville ministry. His main interest was the reform of the criminal law.

RYAN, Andrew, of Bansha Castle, Co. Tipperary   One of the few Catholics on the Co. Tipperary Grand Jury; married to Mary, daughter of Edmund Scully of Cashel, an uncle of Denys Scully.

RYAN, James   Of Marlborough Street, Dublin, and probably from Ballinakill, Co. Kildare. Apprenticed to Randal McDonnell and prospered in business. Secretary of the public meeting of 13 January 1800 calling on Catholics to oppose the Union; following an approach by William Parnell he organised the Catholic meetings of the autumn of 1804 which resulted in the formation of the Catholic Committee. As a member of the 1805 deputation to London he became acquainted with Fox and applied to him in 1806 for an appointment involving the handling of government funds in Dublin. On this becoming known he lost all credit with the Irish Catholics.

RYAN, Jeremiah   A younger brother of Peter Ryan; wine merchant of Bayley's New Street, Waterford.

RYAN, Peter (c. 1749–1828), of Danganmore, Co. Kilkenny   Son of

John Ryan who fought in the Irish Brigade at Fontenoy and died in 1806. Married in 1773 Mary Wall of Waterford, by whom he had an only daughter.

RYDER*, Richard (1766–1832)   Son of 1st Baron Harrowby, barrister and MP for Tiverton 1795–1830; refused Irish Chief Secretaryship 1804; Home Secretary 1808–12.

SADLEIR, Clement   A tenant farmer of Shronehill, Co. Tipperary, husband of Denys Scully's sister Joanna. He was a Protestant but his four sons were brought up as Catholics and educated at Clongowes, one of them being the notorious politician and swindler, John Sadleir*.

SAURIN*, William (c. 1757–1839)   A barrister of Huguenot descent; in command of the Lawyers Corps; a violent opponent of the Union. Appointed Attorney-General 15 May 1807; dismissed by Lord Wellesley in 1822, when he resumed his practice at the Chancery bar.

SAUSE, Richard   Son of James Sause, of Annsborough, Co. Kilkenny; a banker of Carrick-on-Suir, Co. Tipperary. His 1st wife was Denys Scully's sister Catherine, who died in 1789 leaving an only child, Mary. His 2nd, Jane Duffy, bore him several sons, one of whom became Chief Justice in Bombay. He spent his last years at Toulouse and assumed the name of de la Saussaye, under which his heir received a grant of arms in 1866.

SAXTON, Sir Charles (1773–1838), 2nd Baronet, of Circourt, Berkshire   Undersecretary in the Civil Department at Dublin Castle 1808–12, having previously been a Commissioner of Inquiry. MP for Cashel 1812–18.

SCOTT, Barnaby   An attorney of High Street, Kilkenny, son of Barnaby Scott, a merchant. Educated at Kilkenny Academy, where he was in the prize lists 1788 to 1792; graduated from King's Inns 1803.

SCOTT*, Sir William (1745–1836), brother of Lord Eldon. Judge of the Consistory Court of London 1788–1821; MP for Oxford University 1801–1821.

SCULLY, Catherine (1739–1818), daughter of Denis Lyons of Croom, Co. Limerick and mother of Denys Scully.

SCULLY, Catherine   See Eyre, Catherine.

SCULLY, Edmund (1739–1806) of Cashel, younger brother of James Scully of Kilfeacle and a well-to-do grazier   Married Dora Ryan of Kilcloan, by whom he had a son and six daughters, one of whom married Andrew Ryan and another Michael Lidwill, nephew of George Lidwill.

SCULLY, Edmund (Mun) (1779–1839)   5th son of James Scully of Kilfeacle; married Mary Anne O'Brien 6 January 1806. Made a JP in 1815 on an application through Lord Donoughmore.

SCULLY, James (1737–1816), son of Roger Scully and Mary Meagher. Settled at Kilfeacle in 1780 when his father moved from there to Cashel. Farmed from the age of fifteen; married Catherine Lyons of Croom 1778 and had twelve children by her in sixteen years; took oath of allegiance in 1778 as prescribed by the act of that year allowing Catholics to hold leases of up to

999 years; increased his holdings; on his own farms raised cattle and sheep; by 1797 had over £15,000 in Grand Canal and other stock; c. 1804 opened a bank in Tipperary town in partnership with his third son, James; appointed a magistrate on passage of 1793 Relief Act; visited England 1797; deplored the rebellion; supported the Union; kept a journal from 1772–1814; credited with a thorough knowledge of the Irish language.

SCULLY, James (1777–1846), of Shanballymore and Dublin   3rd son of the preceding and his partner in the Bank of James Scully & Son. Married Margaret Wyse of the Manor of St John, Waterford, 17 January 1806; co-executor with Denys Scully of their father's will.

SCULLY, James Vincent (1809–1842), eldest son of Denys Scully.

SCULLY, Jeremiah (Derby) of Silverfort (1741–1807)   A younger brother of James Scully of Kilfeacle; married Barbara Hourigan of Limerick, had twelve children and left £60,000.

SCULLY, Jeremiah (1782–1840), of Middle Gardiner Street, Dublin, and Dorset Square, London; 6th son of James Scully of Kilfeacle   After whose death in 1816 he instigated his mother to contest the will, thus initiating the *Scully v. Scully* lawsuit which went up to the House of Lords in 1825.

SCULLY, Joanna (1776–1858), youngest daughter of James Scully of Kilfeacle, wife of Clement Sadleir.

SCULLY, Vincent James (1810–1871), 2nd son of Denys Scully   Barrister and MP. Built Scully's Cross on the Rock of Cashel.

SCULLY, William Timothy (Thady) MD (1778–1842), 4th son of James Scully of Kilfeacle   Was cut off in 1798 with £50 a year for making an imprudent marriage and after training in Edinburgh became a doctor, first at Totnes, then at Torquay.

SHEIL*, Richard Lalor (1791–1851), eldest son of Edward Sheil of Spring House, Co. Tipperary   Educated at Stonyhurst and Trinity College Dublin; a playwright from 1813; called to the English bar 1814; MP for Co. Tipperary after emancipation.

SHEPHERD*, (Sir) Samuel (1760–1840)   King's Serjeant from 1796; Solicitor-General 1813; Attorney-General 1817; Chief Baron of Scottish Exchequer 1819–30.

SHERIDAN, Dr Edward, of 46 Dominick Street, Dublin   A physician trained at Rheims.

SHERIDAN*, Richard Brinsley (1751–1816), the dramatist, parliamentary orator and friend of Prince of Wales.

SHREWSBURY, Lord   Charles Talbot (1753–1827), 15th Earl of Shrewsbury; Earl of Waterford and Wexford in Irish peerage. A mathematician with an interest in mechanics; entertained lavishly at his house in Stanhope Street, London. His wife, Elizabeth Hoey (c. 1771–1847), was the eldest daughter of a Dublin printer.

SIDMOUTH*, Lord Henry Addington (1757–1844), from 12 January 1805 1st Viscount Sidmouth. Speaker of the House of Commons 1789–1801; Prime Minister February 1801 to 26 April 1804; joined Pitt's second ministry in January 1805 but resigned in July; Lord Privy Seal and after the death of Fox President of the Council in the Grenville government 1806–7; joined Perceval's cabinet as President of the Council in April 1812; Home Secretary under Lord Liverpool June 1812 to January 1822.

SILVERTOP, George (1775–1849), of Minster Acres, Northumberland. At Douai 1784–92.

SLATTERY, Edmund Described in Denys Scully's will as "steward, Kilfeacle".

SLIGO, Lord John Denis Browne (1756–1809), of Westport House, Co. Mayo, 3rd Earl of Altamont, created Marquis of Sligo 1800 for his support of the Union; a representative peer, but chagrined at not obtaining an English peerage until he was created Baron Monteagle in February 1806. Reported frequently to Dublin Castle.

SOUTHWELL, Lord Thomas Anthony Southwell (1777–1860), 3rd Viscount, of Castle Mattress, Rathkeale, Co. Limerick.

SOUTHWORTH, Revd Thomas (1749–1816) Ordained at Douai and sent as assistant to Sedgley Park school, of which, with a gap of some five years, he was headmaster from 1781 until his death. One of the "Staffordshire clergy" of the period 1790–2; made a retractation 1803.

STONE, Revd Marmaduke SJ (1748–1834) President and Rector of Stonyhurst College 1794–1808; English Provincial 1803–17.

STONOR, Captain/Lieutenant-Colonel Charles (1782–1834) Son of Henry Stonor of San Lucar de Barrameda and 1st cousin of Thomas Stonor (1766–1831) of Stonor Park.

STOURTON, Lord Charles Philip Stourton (1752–29 April 1816), 17th Baron, of Allerton Park, Yorkshire. Succeeded by his son William Joseph Stourton.

STRANGFORD, Lord Lionel Smythe (1753–1801), 5th Viscount. Took holy orders on retiring from the army in 1784; Rector of Kilbrew, Co. Meath, and Prebendary of St Patrick's, Dublin.

SUSSEX*, Duke of Augustus Frederick (1773–1843), 6th son of George III. Until 1806 lived mostly on the continent and when in Rome in 1791 frequently met the Pope; active in many causes, including Catholic emancipation; made an enemy of the Prince Regent by siding with his daughter, Princess Charlotte.

TAAFFE, Henry Edmund, of Terenure and Dominick Street, Dublin A partner in the bank of Lord ffrench & Co.

THROCKMORTON, Sir John Courtenay (1753–1819), 5th Baronet, of Buckland, Berkshire From 1782 active in the London Catholic Committee; published pamphlets taking an anti-papal position and arguing for domestic nomination of Bishops; his last publication, of 1806, suggested that nomination by the King could be conceded if asked for; a member of the new English Catholic Board from 1808. Chairman of the Society of Friends of the People.

TIERNEY*, George (1761–1830) Treasurer of the Navy 1802–4; President of Board of Control in the Grenville ministry after the death of Fox; after the death of George Ponsonby leader of the opposition 1817–21.

TIGHE, George William (1776–1837), son of Edward Tighe and first cousin of William Tighe MP Met Lady Mount Cashell in Rome 1803, subsequently became her lover and was father of daughters born in 1809 and 1815. Calling themselves Mr and Mrs Mason, they settled at Pisa in 1814 and were married at Leghorn in 1826.

TIGHE, William MP (c. 1766–1816) Of Woodstock, Inistiogue, Co. Kilkenny; married in 1793 Marianne Gahan of Coolquill, Co. Tipperary, whose mother was Hannah Bunbury of Kilfeacle. A steadfast opponent of the Union but received £30,000 for the disenfranchisement of his two boroughs, Wicklow and Inistiogue; MP for Co. Wicklow 1806–16. Author of a *Survey of Kilkenny* 1800.

TREVEAUX, Abbé Jérôme de (1732–1815) A French priest of the Paris diocese living in exile in London.

TRIMLESTON, Lord Nicholas Barnewall (1726–16 April 1813), 14th Baron. Lived much of his life in pre-revolutionary France.

TRISTRAM Revd Joseph SJ (1766–1843) Educated at Liège; entered restored Society of Jesus 1803; in London 1813–17; Rector of Stonyhurst 1819–27.

TROY, Dr John Thomas (1739–1823) Joined the Dominican order in Rome 1756; Rector of St Clement's there; Bishop of Ossory 1776; Archbishop of Dublin 1784; given a coadjutor in 1809. His interventions at Dublin Castle on behalf of a nephew, John James Troy, whom he got made a revenue officer at Baltimore, Co. Cork, lost him some respect.

WALSH, Revd Thomas (1776–1849) At Oscott from 1808 and President of the college 1818 to 1825, when he was appointed coadjutor to Dr Milner and succeeded him as Vicar Apostolic in 1826.

WEBBER, Daniel Webb (c. 1757–1847), of Leekfield, Co. Sligo An Assistant Barrister, made KC in 1814, who succeeded Dr Duigenan as MP for Armagh City in May 1816 but did not contest the seat in 1818.

WELLESLEY*, Lord Richard Colley Wellesley (1760–1842), created Marquis in the Irish peerage 1799; elder brother of William Wellesley-Pole and Duke of Wellington. Governor-General in India 1797–1805; on a special mission to Spain 1809; Foreign Secretary in the Perceval ministry 1809–12; Lord Lieutenant of Ireland 1821–8.

WELLESLEY-POLE*, William (1763–1845), brother of the preceding. Took additional surname of Pole on succeeding to a cousin's estate in 1778.

Secretary to the Admiralty under Portland 1807; Chief Secretary for Ireland October 1809 to August 1812; Master of the Mint 1814–23.

WELLINGTON*, Lord/Duke of Arthur Wellesley (1769–1852), created Viscount 4 September 1809, Duke 1814. Chief Secretary for Ireland from March 1807 to April 1809, during which period he also commanded the army in Portugal and won the battle of Vimeiro 21 August 1808.

WHEBLE, Mrs Jane Eyre (d. 1839), widow of James Wheble, a tallow chandler of London who died 9 June 1801 leaving £200,000. She was an aunt of Denys Scully's second wife and had three brothers who were priests.

WHEBLE, James (d. 1840) Of Woodley Lodge and Bulmershe Court, Berkshire, only son of the preceding. Educated at Oscott 1795–1800; in 1802 married Maria Talbot, a niece of the Earl of Shrewsbury, who died in 1814 leaving him with six girls; on 21 June 1815 he married Mary O'Brien and had five sons who went to Oscott, the last of them named Daniel O'Connell Wheble.

WHITBREAD*, Samuel (1758–1815) Son of a brewer; at school with 2nd Earl Grey and married his sister 1789; MP from 1790; split the Whigs with his peace policy 1809; took up cause of Princess of Wales 1812.

WHITWORTH*, Lord Charles Whitworth (1752–1825), created Baron 1800, Viscount 1813, Earl 1815; married widowed Duchess of Dorset 1801. A diplomatist; Ambassador in Paris 1802–3; in Ireland as Lord Lieutenant from 26 August 1813 to 9 October 1817.

WILBERFORCE*, William (1759–1833) From 1787 parliamentary leader of the campaign for the abolition of slavery: a bill carried by House of Commons in 1804 but rejected by the Lords; carried by both Houses 1807.

WINDHAM*, William (1750–1810), of Felbrigg, Norfolk Chief Secretary for Ireland in 1783; Secretary for War under Pitt 1794–1801 and again under Lord Grenville 1806–7.

WOLSELEY, (Sir) Charles (1769–1846), of Staffordshire From 1817 7th Baronet. Converted to Catholicism in 1837; supported parliamentary reform.

WORTLEY*, Mr James Archibald Stuart-Wortley Mackenzie (1775–1845), created Baron Wharncliffe 1826. MP from 1797.

WRIGHT, Bernard Grandson of John Wright of Cloneen, son of John Wright who with his brother Abbé Wright was disinherited for becoming a Catholic; a second cousin of Robert Shaw, MP for Dublin City. Trained for the priesthood in France but was driven out by the revolution; gained a livelihood by teaching French; a letter in French being found on him he was flogged in 1798. In 1800 appointed editor of the *Clonmel Gazette*, which was bankrupted in August 1804 when John Bagwell (1752–1816) sued it for libel. Attended Co. Tipperary Catholic meetings and was Secretary of one at Clonmel in 1819.

WYSE, Thomas (1770–1835), of the Manor of St John, Waterford, father of Sir Thomas Wyse   His wife was Frances Bagge (d. 1845) and his youngest sister Margaret was the wife of James Scully junior. Headed the Waterford list of supporters of the Union. Spent much of his life on the continent and died in Bath.

YARMOUTH*, Lord   Francis Charles Seymour-Conway (1777–1842). Styled Earl of Yarmouth as son of 2nd Marquis of Hertford, whose wife enjoyed Prince Regent's favour. In House of Commons from 1797.

YORK*, Duke of   Frederick Augustus (1763–1827), 2nd son of George III. Commander-in-Chief 1798 to 1809 when he resigned on account of a scandal; reinstated 1811.

YORKE*, Charles Philip (1764–1834)   Half brother of Lord Hardwicke, on whom he was financially dependent until Perceval gave him a Tellership of the Exchequer in 1810. Secretary for War 1801; Home Secretary from 17 August 1803 to February 1804; First Lord of the Admiralty 1810–11.

Select Bibliography

This bibliography, arranged in short title order, lists the main sources used in the preparation of this edition.

UNPUBLISHED

BRAY PAPERS   Papers of Dr Thomas Bray, Archbishop of Cashel, at Archbishop's House, Thurles: citations are from the calendar.

BUTLER: LETTER BOOKS   Letter Books of Charles Butler in the British Library, Add.MSS 25,127–9: (1) April 1808 to November 1809; (2) April to November 1812; (3) March 1817 to May 1818.

CALLANAN PAPERS   Papers of Dr Martin Callanan, National Library of Ireland MSS 11,421–2.

CARRIGAN MSS   Papers of Canon William Carrigan at St Kieran's College, Kilkenny.

CLONGOWES COLLEGE ARCHIVES   At Clongowes Wood College, Clane, Co. Kildare.

COMMON PLACE BOOK   Of Denys Scully, MS 27,502 of the Scully Papers.

CONGLETON PAPERS   Parnell family papers in the possession of the 8th Baron Congleton, West End Farm, Ebbesbourne Wake, Wiltshire.

DIARY OF DENYS SCULLY   In two notebooks covering the period 26 February to 27 March 1805: MS 27,514 of the Scully Papers.

DIARY OF JAMES SCULLY   Covering the period 1772–1814: MS 27,571 and MS 27,579 (typescript) of the Scully Papers.

DONOUGHMORE PAPERS   Correspondence and papers of the Hely-Hutchinson family, Earls of Donoughmore, at Trinity College, Dublin.

DROPMORE PAPERS   The papers of the 1st Baron Grenville, formerly in the possession of J. B. Fortescue Esq., now at the British Library, Add.MSS 58,855–59,478.

DUBLIN DIOCESAN ARCHIVES   At Archbishop's House, Drumcondra, Dublin.

EARL GREY PAPERS   Correspondence of the 2nd Earl Grey, Department of Palaeography and Diplomatic, University of Durham.

FINGALL PAPERS   Letters and papers of the Plunket family, National Library of Ireland MS 11,294.

HARDWICKE PAPERS   Correspondence and other papers of Philip Yorke, 3rd Earl of Hardwicke, British Library Add.MSS 51,520–51,978.

HOLLAND HOUSE PAPERS   Correspondence and other papers of Henry Richard Vassal Fox, 3rd Baron Holland, British Library Add.MSS 51,520–51,978.

HOME OFFICE   Papers relating to Ireland in the series HO 100 at the Public Record Office, Richmond, Surrey.

HUDDLESTON PAPERS   Papers of the Huddleston family of Sawston Hall, at the Cambridgeshire Record Office, Cambridge.

JESUIT ARCHIVES   Archives of the Irish province of the Society of Jesus, Leeson Street, Dublin.

LIVERPOOL PAPERS   Correspondence of Robert Banks Jenkinson, 1st Baron Hawkesbury and 2nd Earl of Liverpool, British Library Add. MSS 51,520–51,978.

LOUDOUN PAPERS   A collection sold in 1939 by Edith Countess of Loudoun, to the 4th Marquis of Bute, Mount Stuart House, Rothesay, Isle of Bute.

MINUTE BOOKS   Minute Books of the Irish Catholic Committee (I) May 1809 to August 1810; (II) August 1810 to June 1811, National Library of Ireland MSS 4321–2.

NORMANTON PAPERS   Papers of Charles Agar, 1st Earl of Normanton, Archbishop of Cashel, at the Hampshire Record Office, Winchester.

PEEL PAPERS   Official and private correspondence and papers of Sir Robert Peel, British Library Add. MSS 49,173–49,176.

PERCEVAL PAPERS   Official and personal correspondence and papers of Spencer Perceval, British Library Add. MSS 49,173–49,176.

REDESDALE PAPERS   Papers of John Freeman Mitford, 1st Baron Redesdale, at the Gloucester Record Office: citations are from the Historical Manuscript Commission's calendar, No. 17,639.

RICHMOND PAPERS   Correspondence etc., of Charles Lennox, 4th Duke of Richmond, National Library of Ireland MSS 58–75A.

SCULLY PAPERS   Papers of the Scully family of Kilfeacle and Mantlehill, Co. Tipperary, National Library of Ireland MSS 27,478–27,599 (List No. 378).

STATE PAPER OFFICE   Official and Private correspondence in the State Paper Office at Dublin Castle.

THROCKMORTON PAPERS   Papers of Sir John Courtenay Throckmorton, 5th Baronet, at the Warwick County Record Office, Warwick.

WESTMINSTER DIOCESAN ARCHIVES   At Archbishop's House, Ambrosden Avenue, London.

WHITWORTH PAPERS   Whitworth Papers in the Sackville MSS, Kent Archives Office, Maidstone.

PUBLISHED

ASPINALL, Arthur, *The Later Correspondence of George III*, Cambridge, 1962.

ASPINALL, Arthur, *The Correspondence of George Prince of Wales 1770–1812*, London, 1963.

ASPINALL, Arthur, *Letters of George IV, King of England, 1812–1830*, Cambridge, 1938.

BURKE, Revd W. P., *History of Clonmel*, Waterford, 1907.

BUTLER: HISTORICAL MEMOIRS *Historical Memoirs respecting the English, Irish and Scottish Catholics, from the reformation to the present time*, by Charles Butler, in 4 volumes, London, 1819.

CLONCURRY, Lord, *Personal Recollections*, Dublin, 1849.

CLONEY, Thomas, *A personal narrative of those transactions in the County of Wexford in which the author was engaged, during the period of 1798*, Dublin, 1832.

Clongowes Record 1814–1932, Dublin, 1932.

DRENNAN LETTERS . . . *a selection from the correspondence of William* Drennan . . . during the years 1776–1819, edited by D. A. Chart, Belfast, 1931.

DROPMORE PAPERS The manuscripts of J. B. Fortescue Esq., preserved at Dropmore [now in the British Library], Historical Manuscripts Commission, 13th Report, Appendix, part III, in ten volumes.

FAGAN: O'CONNELL *The Life and Times of Daniel O'Connell*, by William Fagan, Cork, 1847–8.

GILLOW, Joseph, *A Literary and Biographical Dictionary of the English Catholics*, London, 1885–1902.

GRATTAN: LIFE AND TIMES Memoirs of the Life and Times of the Rt. Hon. H. G. Grattan, by his son, 5 volumes, London, 1839–46.

HANSARD *The Parliamentary Debates from the year 1803 published under the superintence of T. C. Hansard.*

HANSARD NS A new series starting on 21 April 1820 after the death of George III.

HOLLAND, Lord, *Memoirs of the Whig Party . . . 1807–1821*, London, 1852–4.

HOLLAND, Lord, *Further Memoirs of the Whig Party 1807–1821*, London, 1905.

HOWELL: STATE TRIALS *A Complete Collection of State Trials . . . compiled by T. B. and T. J. Howell 1163–1820*, London, 1809–26.

HUSENBETH: LIFE *The Life of John Milner, Bishop of Castalba*, by Frederick Husenbeth, Dublin, 1862.

Irish Ecclesiastical Record, Dublin, 1817, 1818.

JERNINGHAM LETTERS *The Jerningham Letters 1780–1843: Excerpts from the correspondence and diaries of Lady Jerningham and her daughter Lady Bedingfeld*, edited by Egerton Castle, 1896.

King's Inns Admission Papers, edited by Edward Keane, P. B. Phair and T. U. Sadleir, Irish Manuscripts Commission, 1982.

LECKY: HISTORY *A History of Ireland in the eighteenth century* by W. E. H. Lecky, cabinet edition, 1902, 5 volumes.

LEET, Ambrose, A *Directory to the Market Towns and Villages, Gentlemen's seats and other places in Ireland*, Dublin 1814.

McALEER, E. C., *The Sensitive Plant: Life of Lady Mount Cashell*, Chapel Hill, North Carolina, 1958.

MADDEN, R. R., *The United Irishmen, their lives and times*, in 3 series, London, 1842–6.

MADDEN, R. R., *History of Irish Periodical Literature*, London 1867.

MILNER: FIRST TOUR/LETTERS FROM IRELAND   Both these short titles are widely used for the pamphlet *An Inquiry into certain vulgar opinions concerning . . . the Catholic inhabitants of Ireland*, by Dr John Milner, London, 1808.

MILNER: SECOND TOUR   An additional letter from Ireland included in a second augmented edition of the abovementioned *Inquiry* published in 1809.

O'CONNELL: CORRESPONDENCE   *The Correspondence of Daniel O'Connell*, edited by Maurice R. O'Connell, 8 volumes, Dublin, 1972–80.

O'CONNELL: LIFE AND SPEECHES   The Life and Speeches of Daniel O'Connell, edited by his son John O'Connell MP, 2 volumes, Dublin and London, 1846.

PARNELL, Henry Brooke, *History of the penal laws against the Catholics from the Treaty of Limerick to the Union*, Fitzpatrick, Dublin, 1808.

PLOWDEN: HISTORY   *A History of Ireland from its Union with Great Britain, 1801–10*, by Francis Plowden, 3 volumes, London, 1811.

ROMILLY: MEMOIRS   *Memoirs of the life of Sir Samuel Romilly, written by himself*, London, 1840.

SCHMIDLIN: PAPSTGESCHICHTE   *Papstgeschichte der neuesten Zeit 1800–1839*, by Joseph Schmidlin, Munich, 1933–9.

SCULLY: PENAL LAWS   *A Statement of the Penal Laws which aggrieve the Catholics of Ireland, with commentaries*, in two parts, Dublin, 1811–2.

SHEIL, Richard Lalor, *Sketches, Legal and Political* (reprinted from the *New Monthly Magazine*), London, 1855.

THORNE: HOUSE OF COMMONS   *The History of Parliament: The House of Commons 1790–1820*, edited by R. G. Thorne, London, 1986.

WALKER, B. M., *Parliamentary Election Results in Ireland*.

WARD: EVE   *The Eve of Catholic Emancipation*, by Monsignor Bernard Ward, in 3 volumes, London, 1812 (reprinted 1970).

WYSE, Thomas, *Historical Sketch of the late Catholic Association of Ireland*, London, 1829.

Index of Persons

References are to letter numbers

Index of Subjects and Places

(References are to letter numbers)